P9-AEY-986

Northeast Lakeview College
33784 0001 2684 7

2nd Edition

Financial Accounting

An Integrated Statements Approach

Jonathan E. Duchac
Wake Forest University

James M. Reeve
University of Tennessee, Knoxville

Carl S. Warren
Professor Emeritus of Accounting
University of Georgia, Athens

Australia · Canada · Mexico · Singapore · Spain · United Kingdom · United States

Financial Accounting: An Integrated Statements Approach, Second Edition
Jonathan E. Duchac, James M. Reeve, Carl S. Warren

VP/Editorial Director:
Jack W. Calhoun

Publisher:
Rob Dewey

Executive Editor:
Sharon Oblinger

Associate Developmental Editor:
Allison Haden Rolfes

Marketing Manager:
Robin Farrar

Production Project Manager:
Heather Mann

Manager of Technology, Editorial:
Vicky True

Technology Project Editor:
Sally Nieman

Web Coordinator:
Scott Cook

Sr. Manufacturing Coordinator:
Doug Wilke

Project Manager:
LEAP Publishing Services, Inc.

Compositor:
GGS Book Services, Inc.

Printer:
Quebecor World
Dubuque, Iowa

Art Director:
Bethany Casey

Internal Designer:
Stratton Design

Cover Designer:
Stratton Design

Cover Photo:
Veer, Inc. Digital Vision photography collection

Photography Manager:
John W. Hill

Photo Researcher:
Rose Alcorn

Printed in the United States of America
1 2 3 4 5 08 07 06 05

Student Edition: ISBN 0-324-31211-3
Instructor's Edition: ISBN 0-324-37460-7

Library of Congress Control Number: 2005936759

For more information about our products, contact us at:
Thomson Learning Academic Resource Center
1-800-423-0563

Thomson Higher Education
5191 Natorp Boulevard
Mason, OH 45040
USA

Brief Contents

Contents

Preface

AN INNOVATIVE APPROACH

Financial Accounting: An Integrated Statements Approach is an innovative text that uses a unique pedagogical approach to enhance student learning of financial accounting. Designed for a one-term financial accounting course, the text is written for either undergraduate students at two- or four-year colleges and universities or by first-year MBA (Masters of Business Administration) students with no prior accounting background. The text combines a thorough understanding of accounting concepts, principles, and reporting with applications to actual business settings. The text emphasizes the "why" rather than just "how" generally accepted accounting principles are applied.

Using a unique *Integrated Financial Statements (IFS) Approach*, the text describes and illustrates the integrated nature of the financial statements, how transactions affect the statements, and the importance of using all the financial statements in analyzing and interpreting a company's performance and financial condition. The *IFS approach* is composed of IFS exhibits, IFS spreadsheets, and IFS margin notations.

The text uses a simple to complex approach that first allows students to better grasp basic financial accounting concepts before advancing to more complex topics. For example, *Financial Accounting* does not introduce debits and credits until students have a solid understanding of how to prepare financial statements, how to analyze transactions, how to record transactions, and how to interpret the integrated nature of transactions.

By carefully structuring its illustrations, *Financial Accounting* also explains and illustrates why the accrual basis of accounting is required by generally accepted accounting principles. Rather than covering the statement of cash flows late in the text, *Financial Accounting* integrates the statement of cash flows and its importance throughout the text. The early coverage of the statement of cash flows is enhanced by the *IFS Approach*, which reduces its complexity. The authors describe and illustrate each of the preceding characteristics of *Financial Accounting* next.

THE INTEGRATED FINANCIAL STATEMENTS APPROACH

The *Integrated Financial Statements (IFS) Approach* focuses on enhancing student understanding of the integrated nature of the financial statements and how transactions affect the statements. The *IFS Approach* is composed of IFS exhibits, IFS spreadsheets, and IFS margin notations.

IFS Exhibits

The *IFS Approach* is first introduced in Chapter 1 in Exhibit 8 as shown at the top of the following page.

Exhibit 8

Integrated Financial Statements

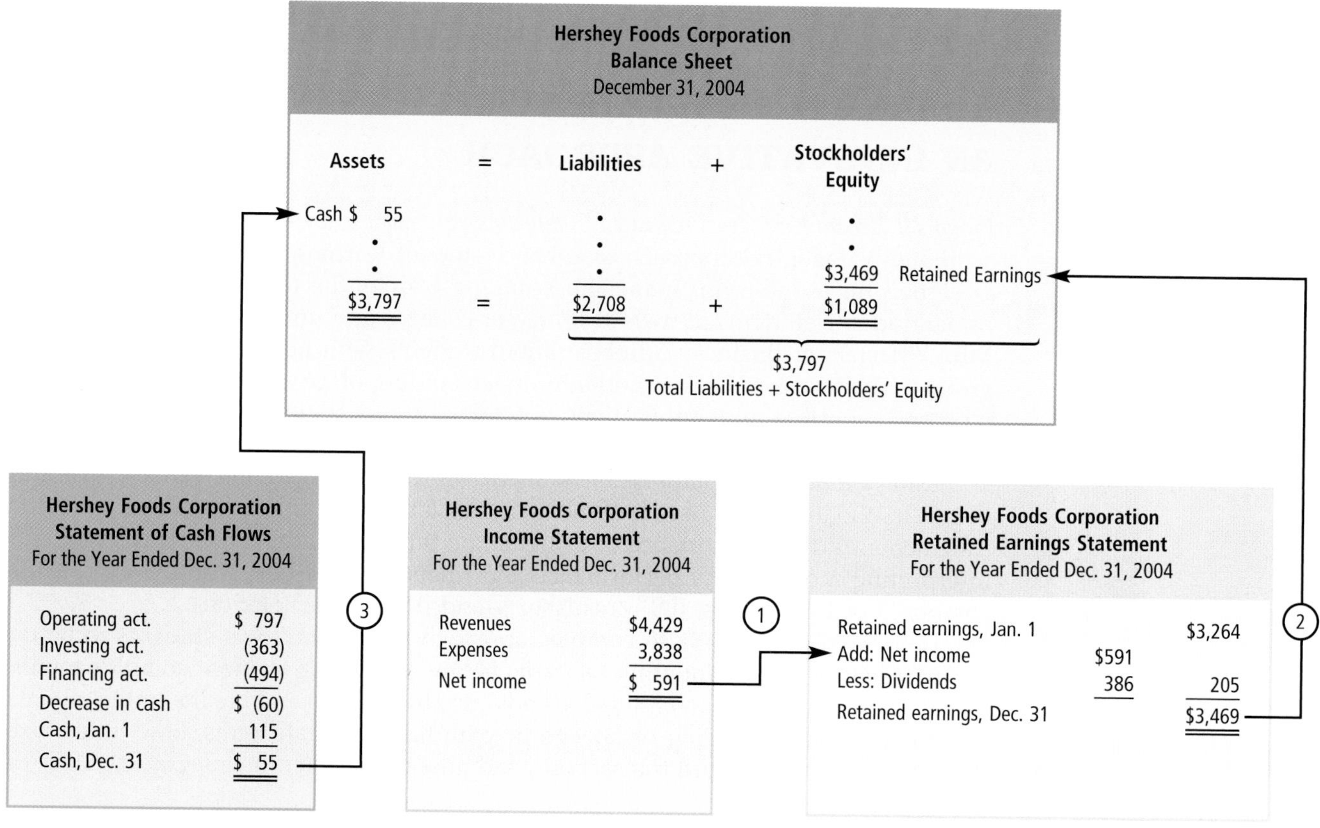

FROM PAGE 20

The preceding exhibit illustrates how the financial statements are integrated (or linked) together. Specifically, the exhibit illustrates how the statement of cash flows is linked to the balance sheet by the amount of cash at the end of the period. The income statement and retained earnings statement are linked by the net income (or net loss) for the period. In turn, the retained earnings statement and balance sheet are linked by the amount of retained earnings at the end of the period.

To reinforce the importance of the integrated nature of the financial statements, the authors include IFS exhibits similar to that shown above each time financial statements are prepared or illustrated. Such IFS exhibits appear in Chapters 1, 2, 3, 4, and 5.

IFS Spreadsheets

Financial Accounting uses a specially designed IFS spreadsheet to record transactions before the introduction of debits and credits. An example of the IFS spreadsheet is shown at the top of the next page.

Since each transaction affects at least two elements of the balance sheet, the balance sheet in an accounting equation format appears in the top center of the IFS spreadsheet. A statement of cash flows column is shown below the cash account column of the balance sheet. Each transaction affecting cash is shown as an increase or decrease in the balance sheet cash account as well as an increase or decrease in operating, investing, or financing cash flows in the statement of cash flows column. The effect of the transaction on the two statements is shown with a connecting colored arrow.

An income statement column is shown below the retained earnings account column of the balance sheet. Each income statement transaction is shown affecting the

Statement of Cash Flows	Cash	+	Land	=	Notes Payable	+	Capital Stock	+	Retained Earnings	Income Statement
	Balance Sheet									
	Assets			=	**Liabilities**	+	**Stockholders' Equity**			
Balances	4,000		12,000		10,000		6,000			
d. Fees earned	5,500								5,500	d.
Balances	9,500		12,000		10,000		6,000		5,500	

Statement of Cash Flows

d. Operating	5,500

Income Statement

d. 5,500 Fees earned

FROM PAGE 59

balance sheet retained earnings account as well as a revenue or expense account in the income statement column.

The IFS spreadsheet highlights the integrated nature of how transactions affect the financial statements. In addition, the IFS spreadsheet provides an effective tool for summarizing transactions and facilitating student preparation of the financial statements. An example of an IFS summary spreadsheet is shown below.

The financial statements can easily be prepared from the IFS summary spreadsheet. The balance sheet is prepared from the last row of ending balances for the period.

Exhibit 6

Family Health Care Summary of Transactions for October

Statement of Cash Flows	Cash	+	Land	=	Notes Payable	+	Capital Stock	+	Retained Earnings	Income Statement
	Balance Sheet									
	Assets			=	**Liabilities**	+	**Stockholders' Equity**			
Balances, Oct. 1	5,100		12,000		10,000		6,000		1,100	
a. Fees earned	6,400								6,400	a.
b. Paid expenses	−3,180								−3,180	b.
c. Paid dividends	−1,000								−1,000	
Balances, Oct. 31	7,320		12,000		10,000		6,000		3,320	

Statement of Cash Flows

a. Operating	6,400
b. Operating	−3,180
c. Financing	−1,000
Increase in cash	2,220

INTEGRATED FINANCIAL STATEMENT FRAMEWORK

Income Statement

a.	6,400	Fees earned
b.	−1,370	Wages expense
	−950	Rent expense
	−540	Utilities expense
	−100	Interest expense
	−220	Misc. expense
	3,220	Net income

FROM PAGE 67

The income statement is prepared from the income statement column, and the statement of cash flows is prepared from the statement of cash flows column.

The IFS summary spreadsheet also illustrates the dynamic nature of the balance sheet as it changes over time with the recording of transactions. Specifically, as transactions occur and are recorded, the beginning balances change until the end of the period. While the balance sheet is prepared as a point-in-time statement, the IFS summary spreadsheet illustrates its dynamic nature.

IFS Margin Notations

Financial Accounting uses IFS spreadsheets to record transactions before the introduction of debits and credits. Accounting systems including the rules of debits and credits are described and illustrated in Chapter 4. With the introduction of debits and credits, journal entries and ledger (T) accounts are used to record transactions. In order to emphasize the integrated nature of the effects of transactions on the financial statements, a specially designed IFS margin notation accompanies each journal entry throughout the text. An example of an IFS margin notation is shown below.

SCF	BS	IS	Date	Account	Debit	Credit
I↓	A↑↓	—	Nov. 5	Land	20,000	
				Cash		20,000
—	A↑ L↑	—	10	Supplies	1,350	
				Accounts Payable		1,350
O↑	A↑ SE↑	R↑	18	Cash	7,500	
				Fees Earned		7,500
O↓	A↓ SE↓	E↑	30	Wages Expense	2,125	
				Rent Expense	800	
				Utilities Expense	450	
				Miscellaneous Expense	275	
				Cash		3,650
O↓	A↓ L↓	—	30	Accounts Payable	950	
				Cash		950
F↓	A↓ SE↓	—	30	Dividends	2,000	
				Cash		2,000

FROM PAGE 159

The IFS margin notation illustrates with arrows what elements of the statement of cash flows, balance sheet, and income statement are affected by a transaction. Upward pointing arrows indicate increases in the element, and downward pointing arrows indicate decreases. In addition, the columns of the IFS margin notation are shown in colors corresponding to the colors of the statements on the IFS spreadsheet and the formal statements.

The combined effect of the IFS exhibits, IFS spreadsheets, and IFS margin notations is that students will have a better understanding of the integrated nature of the financial statements and effects of transactions on the financial statements. In turn, this understanding will enhance the student's ability to analyze and interpret financial statements.

THE STRUCTURING OF TRANSACTIONS AND EXAMPLES

Financial Accounting uses a simple to complex pedagogy that allows students to better grasp basic financial accounting concepts before advancing to more complex topics. The result is that students find it easier to learn and understand financial accounting. Examples of this pedagogy taken from the first four chapters of *Financial Accounting* are described below.

Chapter 1

The objective of Chapter 1, "The Role of Accounting in Business," is to introduce students to the nature of business and the role of accounting in business. The financial statements of Hershey Foods Corporation are illustrated in a simplified form by adapting Hershey's statements filed with the Securities and Exchange Commission. The authors illustrate the integrated nature of Hershey's statements by using the IFS exhibit shown previously. The authors also begin laying the foundation for recording transactions and interpreting the financial statements by describing eight basic accounting concepts.

Chapter 2

After exposing students to financial statements, Chapter 2 introduces the recording of transactions using the IFS spreadsheet. The Family Health Care illustrations in Chapter 2 are carefully structured so that only cash transactions occur. This is done for the following reasons:

1. Students often have difficulty determining whether an event (transaction) should be recorded. By using only cash transactions in Chapter 2, students don't have this difficulty. That is, if cash is received or paid, then the transaction must be recorded.
2. Students understand cash transactions since they have checking accounts and enter into cash transactions daily.
3. By using only cash transactions in Chapter 2, no adjustments are necessary for preparing the financial statements. Thus, the discussion of adjustments is delayed until the students have a solid foundation of recording transactions using the IFS spreadsheet and preparing financial statements.
4. By using only cash transactions in Chapter 2, the statement of cash flows can be easily prepared. This is important since the statement of cash flows is an integral financial statement.
5. By using only cash transactions in Chapter 2, net cash flows from operations on the statement of cash flows equals net income. Thus, the integration of the statement of cash flows, the retained earnings statement, and the income statement can easily be shown in an IFS exhibit. This facilitates explaining in Chapter 3 why net cash flows from operations is normally *not* equal to net income.

Chapter 3

After exposing students to recording and preparing financial statements for only cash transactions, Chapter 3 introduces accrual accounting concepts. At this point, students have a solid foundation of how to use the IFS spreadsheet to record transactions and how to prepare financial statements from the IFS summary spreadsheets. Continuing with the Family Health Care illustration, accrual accounting transactions are described, illustrated, and recorded in IFS spreadsheets. After recording transactions for November, the necessity of making adjustments is described and illustrated. One of the learning outcomes from Chapters 2 and 3 is that students understand that adjustments (adjusting entries) are required only under the accrual basis of accounting. This is a learning outcome that is missed by students using the traditional pedagogical approaches that begin with accrual accounting transactions.

Chapter 3 contains an IFS exhibit illustrating the integration of the financial statements under the accrual basis of accounting. The difference between the cash and accrual bases of accounting is discussed. As exemplified in the next section, one of the important learning outcomes from this discussion is that students learn why the accrual basis of accounting is required by generally accepted accounting principles.

Chapter 4

Chapter 4 introduces debits and credits, journal entries, and ledger accounts. At this point, students have a solid understanding of the following:

1. How to record transactions using the IFS spreadsheet.
2. How to record adjustments using the IFS spreadsheet.
3. How to prepare financial statements from IFS summary spreadsheets.
4. Why the accrual basis of accounting is required by generally accepted accounting principles (see the next section for how this is done).

The only new material that is added in Chapter 4 is the description of the double-entry accounting system using debits and credits, journal entries, and ledger accounts. The double-entry accounting is described and illustrated using the hypothetical company Online Solutions. The Online Solutions illustration is designed so that the concepts discussed in Chapters 1 through 3 are reviewed and reinforced.

The IFS margin notation is also introduced in Chapter 4 to aid the student's transition from recording transactions using IFS spreadsheets to double-entry accounting with journal entries and accounts. The IFS margin notation accompanies each journal entry throughout the remainder of text.

WHY IS ACCRUAL ACCOUNTING REQUIRED BY GAAP?

An understanding of why the accrual basis of accounting is required by generally accepted accounting principles (GAAP) is an important learning outcome for students using *Financial Accounting: An Integrated Statements Approach*. Traditional pedagogical approaches simply begin with accrual accounting without ever explaining or illustrating why accrual accounting is required by GAAP.

Financial Accounting explains and illustrates why accrual accounting is required by GAAP by carefully structuring the illustration of Family Health Care in Chapters 2 and 3. Specifically, Chapter 2 illustrates the recording of transactions and the preparation of financial statements for September and October using only cash transactions. As a result, net cash flows from operations equals net income for September and October. Chapter 3 illustrates the recording of transactions and the preparation of financial statements for November using accrual transactions. At the end of Chapter 3, the following table is presented:

	Net Cash Flow from Operations	Net Income
September	$ 2,600	$2,600
October	3,220	3,220
November	(1,690)	6,390

FROM PAGE 118

This chart clearly shows students that if the cash basis had been used for all three months, a net loss of $(1,690) would have been reported in November. Students can see that, if cash basis had been used, the financial statements might misrepresent the financial performance of Family Health Care, which is actually a successful, rapidly expanding business. This is illustrated by the net income under the accrual basis of accounting of $6,390 for November. In other words, students learn that the accrual basis of accounting is a better indicator of the financial performance of a business than is cash flows; this is why the accrual basis of accounting is required by GAAP.

While illustrating and explaining why the accrual basis of accounting is required by GAAP, the authors also emphasize the importance of the statement of cash flows and net cash flows from operations. For example, a business cannot survive in the long-term without positive cash flows from operations.

STATEMENT OF CASH FLOWS

The statement of cash flows is described and illustrated throughout Chapters 1–5. In addition, end-of-chapter exercises and problems allow instructors the choice of assigning homework that requires students to prepare the statement of cash flows.

The importance of communicating the effects of financing, investing, and operating business activities through the statement of cash flows is described in Chapter 1. In addition, Chapter 1 includes exercises and problems that require the preparation of the statement of cash flows from summary data.

Chapter 2 uses only cash transactions to illustrate the recording of transactions using IFS spreadsheets. As noted earlier, the statement of cash flows can easily be prepared from the IFS summary spreadsheets.

Although Chapter 3 introduces the accrual basis of accounting, the statement of cash flows can easily be prepared from the IFS summary spreadsheets. An appendix at the end of Chapter 3 gives instructors the option of covering the reconciliation of net cash flows from operations with net income under the accrual basis.

Chapters 4 and 5 also provide additional chapter illustrations of the statement of cash flows. In addition, both chapters provide appendices that illustrate how the statement of cash flows is prepared by analyzing the cash account under a double-entry accounting system. These chapter appendices allow instructors to continue their coverage and discussion of the statement of cash flows. Both chapters contain appendix exercises and problems for instructors who want to assign statement of cash flows homework.

Chapters 6 through 12 contain boxed statement of cash flows items that further explain how more complex accounting topics impact the statement of cash flows. Chapter 13 is a traditional statement of cash flows chapter, illustrating the indirect and direct methods of cash flows from operating activities. However, instructors who cover the statement of cash flows in earlier chapters may choose to omit Chapter 13 or cover it in an overview manner. Instructors who choose to cover Chapter 13 in depth will find that students will have an easier time grasping and understanding the statement of cash flows.

SARBANES-OXLEY

Because of the importance of the Sarbanes-Oxley Act, Chapter 7, "Sarbanes-Oxley, Internal Control, Cash," has been revised to include a discussion of Sarbanes-Oxley and its importance for business. The coverage of Sarbanes-Oxley naturally leads into the discussion of internal controls. Chapter 7 concludes with a discussion of how internal controls are applied to cash.

NEW TO THIS EDITION

- **New Co-Author** Dr. Jonathan Duchac of Wake Forest University. Dr. Duchac brings a fresh perspective to the accounting profession with his teaching awards and professional involvements. His contributions to every chapter in the second edition have given the text effective pedagogy and real world relevance.
- **Unique Approach!** The second edition utilizes the Integrated Financial Statement Framework to clearly show the impact of transactions on the balance sheet, income statement, and the statement of cash flows, while showing the interrelationship among these financial statements. This approach provides students with a sound understanding of how the financial statements work together to provide a picture of a company's financial performance, while at the same time teaching students the impact of transactions on the financial statements. This helps students get to the "ah-ha" moment in accounting sooner by focusing on how the financial statements come together *before* introducing debits and credits.
- **Basic accounting concepts are introduced in Chapter 2** using only cash transactions and the integrated financial statements framework. Accrual accounting concepts and transactions are introduced in Chapter 3 using the integrated financial statement framework. Debits and credits are not introduced until Chapter 4, when students have a firm understanding of basic and accrual accounting concepts. The authors gradually move first to cash, and then to accrual, making it easier for students to first pick up the basic framework of accounting, and then move on to the more complicated material of accrual accounting.
- **Added coverage of Sarbanes-Oxley and Responsible Reporting** to enhance students' understanding of how the information in this course can be applied in the real world, with real regulations and real consequences. Chapter 1 has a new section on "Responsible Reporting" analyzing how individual character, firm culture, and laws and enforcement contribute to accounting fraud. A new chart summarizes "Accounting Fraud in the 2000's," illustrating how 11 companies violated accounting concepts and highlighting the result of their fraudulent actions. Chapter 7, "Sarbanes-Oxley, Internal Control, and Cash," has been revised and begins with a discussion of Sarbanes-Oxley.
- **Emphasis on Ethics** Featured in the "Integrity, Objectivity, and Ethics in Business" boxed items throughout the chapters. The ethics boxed feature emphasizes the

INTEGRITY, OBJECTIVITY, AND ETHICS IN BUSINESS

Integrity and Honesty Make a Difference

Herb Kelleher, chairman and former chief executive of Southwest Airlines, is known for his honesty and integrity among Southwest employees. In the mid-1990s, Kelleher negotiated a 10-year union contract with Southwest pilots in which the pilots agreed to freeze their wages for the first five years of the contract. A primary reason Kelleher was able to successfully negotiate the contract was that he constantly worked at building trust among his employees. When he was negotiating the contract, he told the pilots he would freeze his own pay for the same five years. The pilots' union believed him, knowing that Kelleher wouldn't ask them to do something he wouldn't do. Jackie Freiberg, co-author of the book, *Nuts! Southwest Airlines' Crazy Recipe for Business and Personal Success*, says: "Kelleher is a man of his word. He thinks straight and talks straight, so people respect and trust him."

Source: Steve Watkins, "Leaders and Success," *Investor's Business Daily*, November 5, 2004.

FROM PAGE 153

importance of not only knowing how to apply accounting concepts learned in the course, but also how to apply those concepts ethically, with integrity and objectivity.

- **New Chapter Openers** Each chapter opens with a unique company scenario revised to speak directly to student interests and experiences. The chapter openers tie directly to the chapter topics providing students with the invaluable experience of seeing how theory translates into real practice. The revised opening scenarios are written to relate to students, using real-life examples, such as playing football, receiving birthday money, subscribing to magazines, and organizing music on an MP3 player.
- **"How Businesses Make Money" boxed feature** Formerly called "Strategy in Business," this feature emphasizes practical ways in which businesses generate profits and make money. The boxes help generate student interest in business and accounting.

HOW BUSINESSES MAKE MONEY

Under One Roof at JCPenney

Most businesses cannot be all things to all people. Businesses must seek a position in the marketplace to serve a unique customer need. Companies that are unable to do this can be squeezed out of the marketplace. The mall-based department store has been under pressure from both ends of the retail spectrum. At the discount store end of the market, **Wal-Mart** has been a formidable competitor. At the high end, specialty retailers have established a strong presence in identifiable niches, such as electronics and apparel. Over a decade ago, **JCPenney** abandoned its "hard goods," such as electronics and sporting goods, in favor of providing "soft goods" because of the emerging strength of specialty retailers in the hard goods segments. JCPenney is positioning itself against these forces by *"exceeding the fashion, quality, selection, and service components of the discounter, equaling the merchandise intensity of the specialty store, and providing the selection and 'under one roof' shopping convenience of the department store."* JCPenney merchandise emphasis is focused toward customers it terms the "modern spender" and "starting outs." It views these segments as most likely to value its higher-end merchandise offered under the convenience of "one roof."

FROM PAGE 213

- **New Chapter Organization** Chapter 2 is now "Basic Accounting Concepts." Chapter 3 has been renamed "Accrual Accounting Concepts." Chapter 6 is now "Inventories" (formerly Chapter 8). Chapter 7 (formerly Chapter 6) has been renamed "Sarbanes-Oxley, Internal Control, and Cash" to reflect the new emphasis on Sarbanes-Oxley. Chapter 8 is "Receivables" (formerly Chapter 7). The chapters have been reorganized and renamed to facilitate an improved learning progression.
- **New charts, tables, and illustrations** Numerous summary charts and tables have been added, along with new illustrative diagrams and infographics. Margin notations reflective of the "Integrated Financial Statement Framework" are included for each journal entry. The new charts, tables, and illustrations effectively summarize important material for students to assist with visualizing accounting processes and concepts. The "Integrated Financial Statement Framework" margin notations facilitate student understanding of the impact of each transaction on the financial statements. This reinforces the integrated financial statement emphasis in the early chapters of the text.

SCF	BS	IS	Date	Account	Debit	Credit
—	A↓ SE↓	E↑	Dec. 31	Supplies Expense	2,040	
				Supplies		2,040
—	A↓ SE↓	E↑	31	Insurance Expense	100	
				Prepaid Insurance		100
—	L↓ SE↑	R↑	31	Unearned Rent	120	
				Rent Revenue		120
—	L↑ SE↓	E↑	31	Wages Expense	250	
				Wages Payable		250
—	A↑ SE↑	R↑	31	Accounts Receivable	500	
				Fees Earned		500
—	A↓ SE↓	E↑	31	Depreciation Expense	50	
				Accumulated Depreciation—Office Equipment		50

FROM PAGE 165

- In Chapter 8, "Receivables," the discussion of the direct write-off method now precedes the discussion of the allowance method. Both methods have been significantly revised and expanded to include more examples, summary charts, and two new end-of-chapter exercises comparing the methods. This is a more student-friendly presentation, moving from simple to complex. Method comparisons also help students to discern the advantages and disadvantages of each method.

RETAINED FEATURES

- **International Coverage!** An "International" margin item is included where appropriate to describe global issues related to business and accounting, exposing students to the considerations and complexities of international concepts as they relate to accounting today. Accounting does not function in a vacuum—everything that happens in a company's accounting department is connected with every other

International Perspective

department. As businesses become increasingly global, students need to understand how accounting practices affect the global economy. The international icons encourage students to think about how accounting actions play out globally.

- **Analytical Focus!** An "Analysis" section is included in each chapter, generally at the end of each section of discrete topical material. This feature helps develop students' analytical thinking skills. By including an "Analysis" section at the end of each chapter, the student is challenged to utilize concepts learned within the chapter to answer difficult business questions.

ILLUSTRATIVE ACCOUNTING APPLICATION PROBLEM

Q. IBM's balance sheet as of December 31, 2004, reported assets of $109,183 million and liabilities of $79,436 million. What is IBM's stockholders' equity as of December 31, 2004?

A. *$29,747 million ($109,183 million – $79,436 million)*

- **"Illustrative Accounting Application Problem"** This feature has been retained for the second edition. Each "Illustrative Application Problem" is patterned after an end-of-chapter problem and assists students in reviewing chapter content and preparing them for end-of-chapter homework assignments.
- **Check for Understanding!** A "Question and Answer" is included in the margins at appropriate points within each chapter to ensure that students grasp the concepts as they proceed through the chapter. The questions are designed as a checkpoint and serve to reinforce accounting concepts within the chapter.
- **Cash Flow Connection!** A "Focus on Cash Flow" box is included in Chapters 6–12 as a vehicle for students to make the connection between cash flows and the specific chapter topic. The Cash Flow Connection reinforces the concept of cash flow and how it affects accounting activities and components.

FOCUS ON CASH FLOW

Inventories and Cash Flows

If a company increases its inventory balances from period to period, then the amount of cash invested in inventory is increasing. In contrast, if the inventory balances are decreasing, cash is being returned to the business. This is why companies use inventory reduction strategies, such as quick response, in order to capture one-time cash benefits from reducing inventory. On the other hand, if management grows inventory in anticipation of sales that do not materialize, then cash will be used.

The impact of changes in inventory balances is shown in the operating activities section of the statement of cash flows. For example, **Best Buy** reported the following (in millions):

Net income	$ 984
Inventory, February 28, 2004	2,611
Inventory, February 26, 2005	2,851

The operating section of the statement of cash flows is reproduced for Best Buy below, with the shaded area showing the impact of inventory changes.

(in millions) For the Fiscal Year Ended	Feb. 26, 2005
Operating activities:	
Net income	$ 984
Depreciation	459
Other adjustments to net income	(33)
Changes in operating assets and liabilities:	
Receivables	(30)
Merchandise inventories	(240)
Liabilities	891
Other operating activities	(190)
Total cash provided by operating activities	$1,841

As you can see, the increase in inventory from $2,611 to $2,851 is reflected as a use of $240 cash on the statement of cash flows. Best Buy is a growing business; thus, using cash to increase inventories would be expected.

FROM PAGE 283

- Chapter Review for Students! A Chapter Review section includes a Summary of Learning Goals, a Glossary, an Illustrative Accounting Application Problem, Self-Study Questions (five per chapter), and Discussion Questions. The review summarizes the learning goals and key achievement benchmarks presented throughout the chapter. It provides the student with an opportunity to reinforce key concepts through self-study questions and questions for discussion.
- Skills-Based End-of-Chapter Material! The end-of-chapter materials include:
  - Summary of Learning Goals
  - Glossary
  - Illustrative Accounting Application Problem
  - Self-Study Questions and Answers
  - Discussion Questions
  - Exercises
  - Accounting Application Problems
  - Alternate Accounting Application Problems,
  - Financial Analysis and Reporting Cases
  - Business Activities and Responsibility Issues

  The end-of-chapter materials provide the student with the opportunity to review key material in a variety of ways, including exercises, problems, cases, group activities, general ledger, and Excel spreadsheet activities.

SPREADSHEET GENERAL LEDGER GROUP ACTIVITY

INNOVATIVE TECHNOLOGY!

Your Course. Your Time. Your Way.

Thomson NOW!

Introducing ThomsonNOW for Duchac/Reeve/Warren: *Financial Accounting: An Integrated Statements Approach.* This powerful and fully integrated on-line teaching and learning system provides you with flexibility and control, saves valuable time, and improves outcomes. Your students benefit by having choices in the way they learn through our unique personalized learning path. All this is made possible by ThomsonNOW!

- Homework
- Integrated eBook
- Personalized Learning Path
- Interactive Course Assignments
- Assessment Options
- Test Delivery
- Course Management Tools, including Grade Book
- WebCT & Blackboard Integration

General Ledger Network Disks **(0-324-37443-7).** This network resource helps students understand the use of general ledger software in an accounting environment. Selected assignments, identified by icons in the text, may be completed using the general ledger software.

General Ledger Software **(0-324-37442-9).** This resource helps students understand the use of general ledger software in an accounting environment. Selected assignments, identified by icons in the text, may be completed using the general ledger software.

WebTutor® Toolbox on WebCT® or Blackboard® **(0-534-27488-9 and 0-534-27489-7).** Available on both platforms, this course management product is a specially designed extension of the classroom experience that enlivens the course by leveraging the power of the Internet. Instructors or students can use these resources along with those on the Product Web Site to supplement the classroom experience. Use this effective resource as an integrated solution for your distance learning or web-enhanced course! Contact your local sales representative for details! http://webtutor.swlearning.com.

Text Web Site

http://duchac.swlearning.com. The web site for the text offers an array of teaching and learning resources for instructors and students. Among the many elements available, without charge, to **students**, are:

- Quizzes with feedback
- Check figures for selected assignments
- Enhanced Excel® Templates

For **instructors**, in addition to full access to the student resources listed above, a password-protected section of the web site contains a number of resource files, including:

- Online quizzing
- Supplemental material including:
  - Instructor's Solutions Manual
  - Instructor's Manual
  - PowerPoint® slides
  - Enhanced Excel® Templates and Solutions

All instructor material is password-protected.

OTHER HELPFUL SUPPORT MATERIALS

For Students

Enhanced Excel® Templates **(0-324-37450-X).** These templates are provided for selected long or complicated end of chapter exercises and problems, and provide assistance to the student as they set up and work the problem. Certain cells are coded to display a red asterisk when an incorrect answer is enter, which helps students stay on track. Selected problems that can be solved using these templates are designated by an icon.

Working Papers **(0-324-37438-0).** The Working Papers contain forms for preparing solutions for end-of-chapter materials. This handy book provides all the forms students will need when manually preparing the homework assignments from the text.

For Instructors

Instructor's Solutions Manual **(0-324-37445-3).** Prepared by the text authors, the Instructor's Solutions Manual provides solutions for all end-of-chapter material. The Instructor's Solutions Manual will also be available on the Instructor's Resource CD-ROM and text website.

Instructor's Manual **(0-324-37447-X).** Written by Dr. Jonathan Duchac, the printed Instructor's Manual features a chapter overview, teaching opportunities, and end-of-chapter activities grouped by learning goal. The second edition of the Instructor's

Manual also features a comprehensive outline, including page numbers, for each chapter, as well as hints and tips for teaching the Integrated Financial Statement Framework approach. The Instructor's Manual is also available on the IRCD and web site.

Inspector CD **(0-324-37563-8).** The Inspector CD, available on the Instructor's Resource CD, benefits instructors by allowing them to check students' work in General Ledger.

Test Bank **(0-324-37457-7).** The printed test bank features a variety of question formats such as multiple-choice, true/false, essay, problems, and cases. In addition, questions are correlated to the individual chapter's learning objectives, as well as ranked by difficulty based on a clearly described categorization. The second edition test bank also classifies each question according to its related AACSB and AICPA standard. Through this helpful output, making a test that is comprehensive and well-balanced is a snap!

Algorithmic Test Bank **(0-324-37775-4).** For each quantitative learning objective, this additional test bank provides several algorithmic formats drawn from the textbook's end of chapter material and printed test bank. Each algorithmic structure can create hundreds of variations for each exercise, effectively providing a limitless bank of questions for instructor use when creating quizzes or exam materials.

ExamView® **(0-324-42090-0).** This electronic testing software makes it easy to edit questions and customize exams. Containing the same questions as the printed Test Bank, the questions are correlated to the individual chapter's learning objectives and ranked by difficulty. This correlation is reflected in the general information for the question, so it's easy to sort by learning objective or level of difficulty through ExamView®. This software requires PC compatibility.

Enhanced Excel® Templates **(0-324-37449-6).** The Instructor Spreadsheet Templates, available on the web site and IRCD, provide solutions to Excel exercises for students. Excel templates with validations are provided on the web site for solving selected end-of-chapter exercises and problems that are identified in the text with a spreadsheet icon.

PowerPoint® slides **(0-324-37458-5).** The PowerPoint® slides provide an interesting and visually stimulating outline of each chapter in the text. They are designed to use both as instructor lecture tools and student study templates.

Instructor's Resource CD-ROM **(0-324-37444-5).** Contains electronic files for all the resources an instructor needs to teach from this text. It includes the computerized test bank in ExamView® format and the ExamView® testing software, as well as the Microsoft Word files for the Instructor's Manual, printed Test Bank, and Solutions Manual. Finally, this handy reference contains the Instructor PowerPoint Presentations and Excel® Template Solutions.

Solutions Transparencies **(0-324-42091-9).** The solutions transparencies provide the majority of material found in the Instructor's Solutions Manual and give instructors a platform for classroom lecture.

Innovate and Motivate (0-324-37776-2). JoinIn on Turning Point is interactive PowerPoint®, simply the best classroom response system available today! JoinIn allows lectures to be transformed into powerful, two-way experiences. This lecture tool makes full use of the Instructor's PowerPoint® presentation but moves it to the next level with interactive questions that provide immediate feedback on the students' understanding of the topic at hand. Visit http://turningpoint.thomsonlearningconnections.com/index.html to find out more!

ADDITIONAL FINANCIAL ACCOUNTING RESOURCES

Acquire, Assess, and Apply!

Financial Statement Analysis: Blue Company—An Interactive Approach **(0-324-37764-9).** Prepared by Larry Rankin and Dan Wiegand (Miami University), this powerful hands-on tool allows students to interact directly with financial statement elements. At the conslusion of the financial statement analysis exercises, students are asked to complete an Annual Report Project. Students receive a printed booklet with instructions for setup, and exercises that demonstrate vertical, horizontal, and ratio analysis as well as financial modeling.

A grading CD-ROM for instructors (0-324-37867-X) allows for automatic batch grading of each student's Annual Report Project.

Drive Real-World Experience Into the Classroom via the Business & Company Resource Center. Put a complete business library at your fingertips with The Business & Company Resource Center. The BCRC is a premiere online business research tool that allows seamless searches of thousands of periodicals, journals, references, financial information, industry reports, company histories, and much more. For more information, visit http://bcrc.swlearning.com.

Acknowledgments

The authors wish to thank the following individuals who reviewed manuscript, participated in focus groups, and provided helpful comments and suggestions.

Focus Group Participants

Cynthia Bolt, The Citadel School of Business
Mark Camma, Atlantic Cape Community College
Sean Chen, Loyola Marymount University
Scott R. Colvin, Naugatuck Valley Community College
Margaret Costello-Lambert, Oakland Community College
Helen Davis, Johnson & Wales University
Robert Derstine, Villanova University
James M. Emig, Villanova University
Sheri L. Erickson, Minnesota State University Moorhead
Anthony Fortini, Camden County College
Lucille S. Genduso, Nova Southeastern University
Catherine Jeppson, California State University, Northridge
David Juriga, St. Louis Community College
Sudha Krishnan, Loyola Marymount University
Laurie Larson, Valencia Community College
Patricia Lopez, Valencia Community College
Cynthia Miglietti, Bowling Green State University Firelands
Florence McGovern, Bergen Community College
R.L.C. Miller, California State University, Fullerton
David Mona, Champlain College
J. Lowell Mooney, Georgia Southern University
Charles T. Moores, University of Nevada, Las Vegas
Blanca R. Ortega, Miami-Dade College—Kendall Campus
Ginger Parker, Miami-Dade College—Kendall Campus
Jan Pitera, Broome Community College
Kevin Poirier, Johnson & Wales University
Donald Raux, Siena College
John D. Rossi, III, Moravian College
Richard Sarkisian, Camden County College
Joann Segovia, Minnesota State University Moorhead
Kathleen Sevigny, Bridgewater State College
S. Murray Simons, Northeastern University
Michael Tyler, Barry University
Shafi Ullah, Broward Community College
James E. Williamson, San Diego State University
Ping Zhou, Baruch College—City University of New York

Reviewers

Noel Addy, Mississippi State University
Richard Aldridge, Western Kentucky University
Progyan Basu, The University of Georgia
Robert Bloom, John Carroll University
Cynthia Bolt, The Citadel School of Business
Mark Bradshaw, Harvard Business School
Janet Caruso, Nassau Community College
Janet Cassagio, Nassau Community College
Betty Chavis, California State University, Fullerton
Sean Chen, Loyola Marymount University
Allison Collins, University of Memphis
Scott R. Colvin, Naugatuck Valley Community College
Teresa Conover, University of North Texas
Sue Counte, St. Louis Community College & St. Louis University
Marcia A. Croteau, University of Maryland, Baltimore County
Helen Davis, Johnson & Wales University
Araya Debessay, University of Delaware, Newark
D. Kemerer Edwards, Bryant University
James M. Emig, Villanova University
Denise M. English, Boise State University
Tom English, Boise State University
Christopher Gilbert, Glendale Community College
Alice Goodyear, University of Denver
Barbara Gregorio, Nassau Community College
Terri Gutierrez, University of Northern Colorado

James Hurley, Winona State University
Frederic W. Ihrke, Winona State University
Bikki Jaggi, Rutgers The State University of New Jersey
Sanford R. Kahn, University of Cincinnati
Jocelyn Kauffunger, University of Pittsburgh
Neung Kim, California State University, Los Angeles
Rita Kingery, University of Delaware
Evelyn A. Koonce, Craven Community College
Joan Lacher, Nassau Community College
Teresa Lang, Columbus State University
Dan Law, Gonzaga University
Oliver Zhen Li, University of Notre Dame
James Lukawitz, University of Memphis
Lynn Mazzola, Nassau Community College
Florence McGovern, Bergen Community College
Noel McKeon, Florida Community College
Yaw M. Mensah, Rutgers The State University of New Jersey
R.L.C. Miller, California State University, Fullerton
Charles T. Moores, University of Nevada, Las Vegas
Andrew Morgret, University of Memphis
Garth Novack, Utah State University
Adel M. Novin, Clayton State University
William R. Pasewark, Texas Tech University
Glenn Pate, Palm Beach Community College
Franklin J. Plewa, Idaho State University
Roderick B. Posey, University of Southern Mississippi
Mary Anne Prater, Clemson University
K.K. Raman, University of North Texas
Donald Raux, Siena College
Marianne M. Rexer, Wilkes University
Luther Ross, Central Piedmont Community College
Robert Rouse, College of Charleston
Lynn Saubert, Radford University
Albert Schepanski, University of Iowa
Kathleen Sevigny, Bridgewater State College
Cindy Siepel, New Mexico State University
W.R. Singleton, Western Washington University
Gerald Smith, University of Northern Iowa
Jill M. Smith, Idaho State University
Talitha Smith, Auburn University
Tracy Smith, The University of Memphis
Joanie Sompayrac, The University of Tennessee at Chattanooga
Ronald Strittmater, North Hennepin Community College
Frank R. Urbancic, University of South Alabama
Andrea Weickgenannt, Northern Kentucky University
James E. Williamson, San Diego State University
Louis D. Wolff, Pepperdine University
Gail Wright, Bryant University
Ping Zhou, Baruch College—City University of New York

Supplement Reviewers

Janet Caruso, Nassau Community College
Janet Cassagio, Nassau Community College
Sue Counte, St. Louis Community College & St. Louis University
Barbara Gregorio, Nassau Community College
Frederic W. Ihrke, Winona State University
Evelyn A. Koonce, Craven Community College
Joan Lacher, Nassau Community College
Teresa Lang, Columbus State University
Lynn Mazzola, Nassau Community College
Florence McGovern, Bergen Community College
Noel McKeon, Florida Community College
Charles T. Moores, University of Nevada, Las Vegas
W.R. Singleton, Western Washington University
Gerald Smith, University of Northern Iowa
Talitha Smith, Auburn University
Joanie Sompayrac, The University of Tennessee at Chattanooga

Diary Keepers

Janet Cassagio, Nassau Community College
Adel M. Novin, Clayton State University
Ping Zhou, Baruch College—City University of New York

SPECIAL THANKS TO THE FOLLOWING SUPPLEMENT PREPARERS AND VERIFIERS:

Mark D. Beck, Beck Publishing Services
David M. Cottrell, Brigham Young University
Robert Derstine, Villanova University
James M. Emig, Villanova University
Linda Fischler, Nassau Community College
Barbara Gregorio, Nassau Community College
Christine A. Jonick, Gainesville State College
Ann E. Martel, Marquette University
Ken Martin, Martinique Development Services
Jane Y. Stoneback, Central Connecticut State University
Janice A. Stoudemire, Midlands Technical College
Gail B. Wright, Bryant University

2nd Edition

Financial Accounting

An Integrated Statements Approach

About the Authors

Jonathan E. Duchac

Jonathan Duchac is the Merrill Lynch and Co. Associate Professor of Accounting Policy and Director of the Program in Enterprise Risk Management at Wake Forest University. He earned his Ph.D. in accounting from the University of Georgia, and currently teaches introductory and advanced courses in financial accounting. Dr. Duchac has received a number of awards during his career, including the Wake Forest Graduate Accounting Student Teaching Award, the T.B. Rose award for Instructional Innovation, and the University of Georgia Outstanding Teaching Assistant Award.

In addition to his teaching responsibilities, Dr. Duchac serves as Accounting Advisor to Merrill Lynch Equity Research, where he works with research analysts in reviewing and evaluating the financial reporting practices of public companies. He has testified before the U.S. House of Representatives, the Financial Accounting Standards Board, and the Securities and Exchange Commission; and has worked with a number of major public companies on financial reporting and accounting policy issues.

In addition to his professional interests, Dr. Duchac is the Treasurer and Director of the Finance Committee for *The Special Children's School of Winston-Salem*; a private, nonprofit developmental day school located in Winston-Salem, North Carolina, serving children with and without special needs.

Dr. Duchac is an avid long-distance runner, mountain biker, and snow skier. His recent events include the Grandfather Mountain Marathon, the Black Mountain Marathon, the Shut-In Ridge Trail run, and NO MAAM (Nocturnal Overnight Mountain Bike Assault on Mount Mitchell).

James M. Reeve

Dr. James M. Reeve is the William and Sara Clark Professor of Accounting and Business at the University of Tennessee. Professor Reeve has been on the accounting faculty since 1980, after graduating with a Ph.D. from Oklahoma State University.

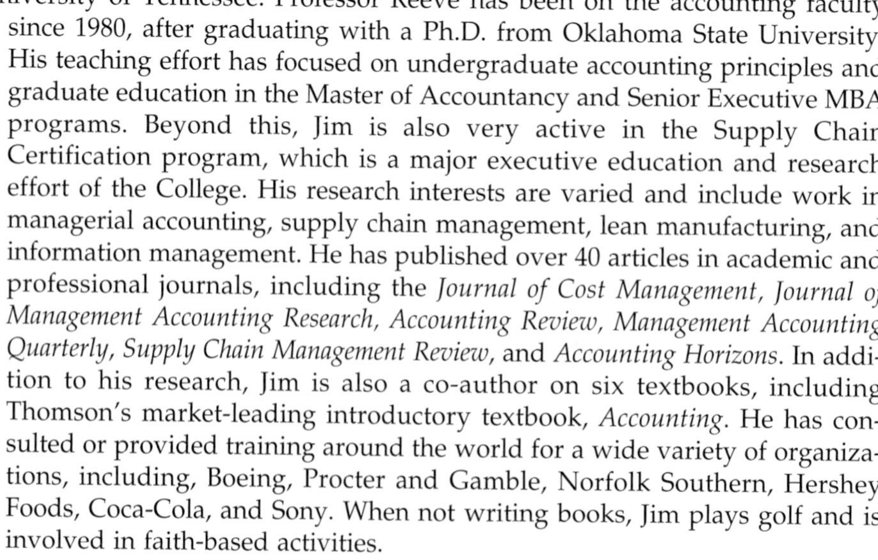

His teaching effort has focused on undergraduate accounting principles and graduate education in the Master of Accountancy and Senior Executive MBA programs. Beyond this, Jim is also very active in the Supply Chain Certification program, which is a major executive education and research effort of the College. His research interests are varied and include work in managerial accounting, supply chain management, lean manufacturing, and information management. He has published over 40 articles in academic and professional journals, including the *Journal of Cost Management*, *Journal of Management Accounting Research*, *Accounting Review*, *Management Accounting Quarterly*, *Supply Chain Management Review*, and *Accounting Horizons*. In addition to his research, Jim is also a co-author on six textbooks, including Thomson's market-leading introductory textbook, *Accounting*. He has consulted or provided training around the world for a wide variety of organizations, including, Boeing, Procter and Gamble, Norfolk Southern, Hershey Foods, Coca-Cola, and Sony. When not writing books, Jim plays golf and is involved in faith-based activities.

Carl S. Warren

Dr. Carl S. Warren is Professor Emeritus of Accounting at the University of Georgia, Athens. For over twenty-five years, Professor Warren taught all levels of accounting classes. In recent years, Professor Warren focused his teaching efforts on principles of accounting and auditing courses. Professor Warren has taught classes at the University of Iowa, Michigan State University University of Chicago, and the University of Georgia. Professor Warren received his doctorate degree (Ph.D.) from Michigan State University and his undergraduate (B.B.A) and masters (M.A.) degrees from the University of Iowa. During his career, Professor Warren published numerous articles in professional journals, including *The Accounting Review, Journal of Accounting Research, Journal of Accountancy, The CPA Journal, and Auditing: A Journal of Practice & Theory.* Professor Warren's outside interests include writing short stories and novels, oil painting, handball, golf, skiing, backpacking, and fly-fishing.

1 The Role of Accounting in Business

Learning Goals

1. Describe the types and forms of businesses, how businesses make money, and business stakeholders.
2. Describe the three business activities of financing, investing, and operating.
3. Define accounting and describe its role in business.
4. Describe and illustrate the basic financial statements and
5. Describe eight accounting concepts underlying financial reporting.
6. Describe and illustrate how horizontal analysis can be used to analyze and evaluate a company's performance.

Hershey Foods Corporation

© BERIT MYREKROK/DIGITAL VISION/GETTY IMAGES

When two teams pair up for a game of football, there is often a lot of noise. The band plays, the fans cheer, and fireworks light up the scoreboard. Obviously, the fans are committed and care about the outcome of the game. Just like fans at a football game, the owners of a business want their business to "win" against their competitors in the marketplace. While having our football team win can be a source of pride, winning in the marketplace goes beyond pride and has many tangible benefits. Companies that are winners are better able to serve customers, provide good jobs for employees, and make more money for the owners.

An example of such a successful company is the Hershey Foods Corporation, founded by Milton Hershey in the early 1900s. Hershey Foods Corporation is America's leading chocolate manufacturer, producing more than a billion pounds of chocolate products each year. In addition to Hershey chocolate bars, the company sells candy under such brands as Reese's, Twizzlers®, York®, Almond Joy®, and Kit Kat®.

The success of Hershey Foods brought wealth to the Hershey family. So what did Milton and his wife do with their wealth? First, they built a model town that included comfortable homes and an inexpensive public transportation system for their employees. Although Milton and his wife, Catherine, had no children of their own, they established a school for orphan boys. Following Catherine's premature death in 1918, Milton endowed the school with his stock in the Hershey Chocolate Company. Today, the 10,000-acre school nurtures over 1,300 financially needy boys and girls in grades K-12. Through the Hershey Trust Company, the school controls 78% of the voting shares of Hershey Foods Corporation. Thus, when Hershey Foods wins, so does the Hershey School.

As we begin our study of accounting in this chapter, we will first discuss the nature, types, and activities of businesses, such as Hershey's. In doing so, we describe business stakeholders, such as the owners, customers, and employees. We conclude the chapter by discussing the role of accounting in business, including financial statements, basic accounting concepts, and how to use financial statements to evaluate a business's performance.

Describe the types and forms of businesses, how businesses make money, and business stakeholders.

THE NATURE OF BUSINESS

You are familiar with many large companies, such as General Motors, Barnes & Noble, and AT&T. You are also familiar with many local businesses, such as gas stations, grocery stores, and restaurants. You may work for one of these businesses. But what do they have in common that identifies them as businesses?

In general, a **business** is an organization in which basic resources (inputs), such as materials and labor, are assembled and processed to provide goods or services (outputs) to customers.[1] Businesses come in all sizes, from a local coffee house to General Motors, which sells several billion dollars worth of cars and trucks each year. The customers of a business are individuals or other businesses who purchase goods or services in exchange for money or other items of value. In contrast, a church is not a business because those who receive its services are not obligated to pay for them.

The objective of most businesses is to maximize profits by providing goods or services that meet customer needs. Profit is the difference between the amount received from customers for goods or services provided and the amount paid for the inputs used to provide the goods or services. Some businesses operate with an objective other than to maximize profits. The objective of such not-for-profit businesses is to provide some benefit to society, such as medical research or conservation of natural resources. In other cases, governmental units such as cities operate water works or sewage treatment plants on a not-for-profit basis. Our focus in this text will be on businesses operated to earn a profit. However, many of the concepts and principles also apply to not-for-profit businesses.

Types of Businesses

There are three different types of businesses that are operated for profit: manufacturing, merchandising, and service businesses. Each type of business has unique characteristics.

Manufacturing businesses change basic inputs into products that are sold to individual customers. Examples of manufacturing businesses and some of their products are shown below.

Manufacturing Business	Product
General Motors	Automobiles, trucks, vans
General Mills	Breakfast cereals
Boeing	Jet aircraft
Nike	Athletic shoes
Coca-Cola	Beverages
Sony	Stereos, televisions, radios

Merchandising businesses also sell products to customers. However, they do not make the products but purchase them from other businesses (such as manufacturers). In this sense, merchandisers bring products and customers together. Examples of merchandising businesses and some of the products they sell are shown below.

Merchandising Business	Product
Wal-Mart	General merchandise
Toys"R"Us	Toys
Barnes & Noble	Books
Best Buy	Consumer electronics
Amazon.com	Books

1 A glossary of terms appears at the end of each chapter in the text.

Service businesses provide services rather than products to customers. Examples of service businesses and the types of services they offer are shown below.

Service Business	Service
Disney	Entertainment
Delta Air Lines	Transportation
Marriott	Hospitality and lodging
Merrill Lynch	Financial
Google	Internet search

Forms of Business

A business is normally organized as one of three different forms: proprietorship, partnership, corporation, or limited liability company. A **proprietorship** is owned by one individual. More than 70% of the businesses in the United States are organized as proprietorships. The popularity of this form is due to the ease and low cost of organizing. The primary disadvantage of proprietorships is that the financial resources available to the business are limited to the individual owner's resources. Small local businesses such as hardware stores, repair shops, laundries, restaurants, and maid services are often organized as proprietorships.

As a business grows and requires more financial and managerial resources, it may become a partnership. A **partnership** is owned by two or more individuals. Like proprietorships, small local businesses such as automotive repair shops, music stores, beauty shops, and men's and women's clothing stores may be organized as partnerships. Currently, about 10% of the businesses in the United States are organized as partnerships.

Like proprietorships, a partnership may outgrow its ability to finance its operations. As a result, it may become a corporation. A **corporation** is organized under state or federal statutes as a separate legal entity. The ownership of a corporation is divided into shares of stock. A corporation issues the stock to individuals or other businesses, who then become owners or stockholders of the corporation.

A primary advantage of the corporate form is the ability to obtain large amounts of resources by issuing shares of stock, which are ownership rights in the corporation. For this reason, most companies that require large investments in equipment and facilities are organized as corporations. For example, Toys"R"Us has raised over $800 million by issuing shares of common stock to finance its operations. Other examples of corporations include Yahoo!, Ford, Apple Computer, Coca-Cola, and Starbucks.

About 20% of the businesses in the United States are organized as corporations. However, since most large companies are organized as corporations, over 90% of the total dollars of business receipts are received by corporations. Thus, corporations have a major influence on the economy.

A **limited liability company (LLC)** combines attributes of a partnership and a corporation in that it is organized as a corporation, but it can elect to be taxed as a partnership. In addition, its owners' (or members') liability is limited to their investment in the business.

In addition to the ease of formation and ability to raise large amounts of capital, the legal liability, taxes, and limitation on life are important considerations in choosing a form of business organization. For sole proprietorships and partnerships, the owners have unlimited liability to creditors and for other debts of the company. For corporations and limited liability companies, the owner's liability is limited to the amount invested in the company. Corporations are taxed as separate legal entities, while the income of sole proprietorships, partnerships, and limited liability companies is passed through to the owners and taxed on the owners' tax returns. As separate legal entities, corporations also continue on, regardless of the lives of the individual owners. In contrast, sole proprietorships, partnerships, and limited liability companies may terminate their existence with the death of an individual owner.

The characteristics of sole proprietorships, partnerships, corporations, and limited liability companies discussed in this section are summarized below.

Organizational Form	Ease of Formation	Legal Liability	Taxation	Limitation on Life of Entity	Access to Capital
Proprietorship	Simple	No limitation	Nontaxable (pass-through) entity	Yes	Limited
Partnership	Simple	No limitation	Nontaxable (pass-through) entity	Yes	Average
Corporation	Complex	Limited liability	Taxable entity	No	Extensive
Limited Liability Company	Moderate	Limited liability	Nontaxable (pass-through) entity by election	Yes	Average

The three types of businesses we discussed earlier—manufacturing, merchandising, and service—may be either proprietorships, partnerships, corporations, or limited liability companies. However, businesses that require a large amount of resources, such as many manufacturing businesses, are corporations. Likewise, most large retailers such as Wal-Mart, Sears, and JCPenney are corporations. Because most large businesses are corporations, they tend to dominate the economic activity in the United States. For this reason, we focus our attention in this text on the corporate form of organization. However, many of the concepts and principles that we discuss also apply to proprietorships and partnerships.

How Do Businesses Make Money?

The goal of a business is to make money by providing goods or services to customers. How does it decide which products or services to offer its customers? For example, should Best Buy offer warranty and repair services to its customers? Many factors influence this decision. Ultimately, however, the decision is based on how the business plans to gain an advantage over its competitors, and in doing so, make money and maximize its profits. *Profits* are the excess of revenues from selling services or products over the cost of providing those services or products as illustrated below.

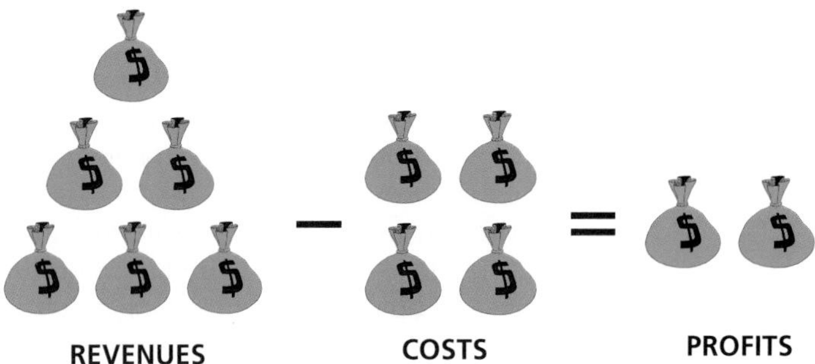

Businesses try to maximize their profits by generating high revenues, low costs, and thus high profits. However, a business's competitors are also trying to do the same and, thus, a business can only maximize its profits by gaining an advantage over its competitors. So, how can a business accomplish this?

INTEGRITY, OBJECTIVITY, AND ETHICS IN BUSINESS

A Good Corporate Citizen

Many argue that it is good business for a company to be a good corporate citizen and contribute to the welfare of the society and the local communities in which it operates. **Hershey Foods** has a long history of such involvement that includes the establishment and operation of the Milton Hershey School for disadvantaged children. The school is funded by an endowment of over $5 billion of Hershey Foods' stock. In addition, Hershey gives nonprofit, charitable organizations cash awards of $200 for each employee that can document 100 hours of volunteer work for the organization. Hershey also recently donated $500,000 over five years to scholarships for minority students in south-central Pennsylvania. The money will be used to fund scholarships of $5,000 a year for 20 students living within the region.

Sources: Bill Sutton, "Donations to Aid Minority Students," *The Patriot-News*, November 12, 2004, and "Hershey Throws Greenline a Kiss," *The Commercial Appeal*, September 26, 2004.

Generally, businesses gain an advantage over their competitors by using either a low-cost or a premium-price emphasis. Under a *low-cost emphasis*, a business designs and produces products or services at a lower cost than its competitors. Wal-Mart and Southwest Airlines are examples of businesses with a low-cost emphasis. Such businesses sell no-frills, standardized products and services.

Under a *premium-price emphasis*, a business tries to design and produce products or services that serve unique market needs, allowing it to charge premium prices. For example, customers may perceive a product or service as unique based upon quality, reliability, image, or design. John Deere, Tommy Hilfiger, and BMW are examples of businesses that charge premium prices for their products. To illustrate, John Deere emphasizes the reliability of its lawn equipment, Tommy Hilfiger emphasizes the unique image of its clothing, and BMW emphasizes the unique driving style and prestige of its automobiles.

Since businesses are highly competitive, it is difficult for them to sustain a competitive advantage over time. For example, a primary concern of a business using a low-cost emphasis is that a competitor may copy its low-cost methods or develop technological advances that enable it to achieve even lower costs. A primary concern of a business using a premium-price emphasis is that a competitor may develop products with characteristics perceived as more desirable by customers.

Examples of how businesses use the low-cost and premium-price emphases to try to gain advantages over one another include the following:

- Local pharmacies try to develop personalized relationships with their customers. By doing so, they are able to charge premium (higher) prices. In contrast, Wal-Mart's pharmacies use the low-cost emphasis and compete on cost.
- Grocery stores such as Kroger and Safeway also try to develop personalized relationships with their customers. One way they do this is by issuing magnetic cards to preferred customers to establish brand loyalty. The cards also allow the stores to track consumer preferences and buying habits for use in purchasing and advertising campaigns. In doing so, Kroger and Safeway hope to compete on a premium-price basis against Wal-Mart Supercenters which use a low-cost emphasis.
- Honda advertises the reliability and quality ratings of its automobiles and is thus able to charge premium prices. Similarly, Volvo's premium-price emphasis uses safety as the unique characteristic of its automobiles. In contrast, Hyundai and Kia use a low-cost emphasis.
- Harley-Davidson emphasizes that its motorcycles are "Made in America" and promotes its "rebel" image in implementing a premium-price emphasis. This allows Harley-Davidson to charge higher prices for its motorcycles than does Honda, Yamaha, or Suzuki.

Some well-known businesses struggle to find their competitive advantages. For example, JCPenney and Sears have difficulty competing on low costs against Wal-Mart, Goody's Family Clothing, Kohl's, T.J. Maxx, and Target. At the same time, JCPenney and Sears have difficulty charging premium prices for their merchandise against competitors such as The Gap, Old Navy, Eddie Bauer, and Talbot's. Likewise, Delta and United Airlines have difficulty competing against low-cost airlines such as Southwest and JetBlue. At the same time, Delta and United don't offer any unique services for which their passengers are willing to pay a premium price.

Exhibit 1 summarizes the characteristics of the low-cost and premium-price emphases. Common examples of businesses that employ each emphasis are also listed.

Exhibit 1

Business Emphasis and Industries

	Industry					
Business Emphasis	**Airline**	**Freight**	**Automotive**	**Retail**	**Financial Services**	**Hotel**
Low cost	Southwest	Union Pacific	Saturn	Sam's Clubs	Ameritrade	Super 8
Premium price	Virgin Atlantic	Federal Express	BMW	Talbot's	Morgan Stanley	Ritz-Carlton

Business Stakeholders

A company's business emphasis, often termed a strategy, directly affects its economic performance. For example, Kmart was unsuccessful in implementing a business emphasis that would allow it to compete effectively against Wal-Mart. The result was that Kmart filed for bankruptcy protection in early 2002, and Kmart stakeholders, including employees, creditors, and stockholders, suffered.

A **business stakeholder** is a person or entity that has an interest in the economic performance and well-being of a business. For example, stockholders, suppliers, customers, and employees are all stakeholders in a corporation. Business stakeholders can be classified into one of the four categories illustrated in Exhibit 2 and the top of page 10.

Capital market stakeholders provide the major financing for a business in order for it to begin and continue its operations. Banks and other long-term creditors have an economic interest in recovering the amount they loaned the business plus interest.

HOW BUSINESSES MAKE MONEY

Where's Rudolph?

In future years, holiday shoppers won't find as many seasonal products as they have in the past. For example, **Hershey Foods** has decided not to rely as heavily on seasonal products such as Christmas-colored candies. Hershey and other retailers don't want to be stuck with excess seasonal, time-limited products that they might have to discount heavily in after-holiday sales. Instead, retailers are using "limited edition" items during the year that don't have natural time boundaries.

Customers are often willing to pay premium prices for such limited editions, which also increases demand for the original brands and showcases innovative products. For example, Hershey's sales rose last year with the aid of limited edition white chocolate Reese's and inside-out Reese's.

Source: Pallavi Gogoi, "Avoiding Retail's Post-Holiday Blues," *BusinessWeek Online*, November 23, 2004.

Exhibit 2
Business Stakeholders

Business Stakeholder	Interest in the Business	Examples
Capital market stakeholders	Providers of major financing for the business	Banks, owners, stockholders
Product or service market stakeholders	Buyers of products or services and vendors to the business	Customers and suppliers
Government stakeholders	Collect taxes and fees from the business and its employees	Federal, state, and city governments
Internal stakeholders	Individuals employed by the business	Employees and managers

Owners and stockholders want to maximize the economic value of their investments. Capital market stakeholders expect to receive a return on their investments proportionate to the degree of risk they are taking. Since banks and long-term creditors have first preference to the assets in case the business fails, their risk is less than that of the owners, thus, their overall return is lower.

Product or service market stakeholders include customers who purchase the business's products or services as well as the vendors who supply inputs to the business. Customers have an economic interest in the continued success of the business. For example, in the early 2000s, customers of the Internet provider @home.com were initially unable to retrieve their e-mail or connect with the Internet when @home.com declared bankruptcy. Customers who purchase advance tickets on Delta Air Lines have an economic interest in whether Delta will continue in business. Similarly, suppliers are stakeholders in the continued success of their customers. Suppliers may invest in technology or other capital equipment to meet a customer's buying and manufacturing specifications. If a customer fails or cuts back on purchases during downturns, suppliers may see their business decline also. This has been the case for Delphi, a major supplier to General Motors, during GM's downturn in 2005.

Various governments have an interest in the economic performance of businesses. As a result, city and state governments often provide incentives for businesses to locate within their jurisdictions. City, county, state, and federal governments collect taxes from businesses within their jurisdictions. The better a business does, the more taxes the government can collect. In addition, workers are taxed on their wages. In contrast, workers who are laid off and unemployed can file claims for unemployment compensation, which results in a financial burden for the government.

Internal stakeholders include individuals employed by the business. The managers are those individuals who the owners have authorized to operate the business. Managers are primarily evaluated on the economic performance of the business. The managers of businesses that perform poorly are often fired by the owners. Thus, managers have an incentive to maximize the economic value of the business. Owners may offer managers salary contracts that are tied directly to how well the business performs. For example, a manager might receive a percent of the profits or a percent of the increase in profits.

Employees provide services to the company they work for in exchange for pay. Thus, employees have an interest in the economic performance of the business because their jobs depend upon it. During business downturns, it is not unusual for a business to lay off workers for extended periods of time. In the extreme, a business may fail and the employees may lose their jobs permanently. Employee labor unions often use the good economic performance of a business to argue for wage increases. In contrast, businesses often use poor economic performance to argue for employee concessions such as wage decreases.

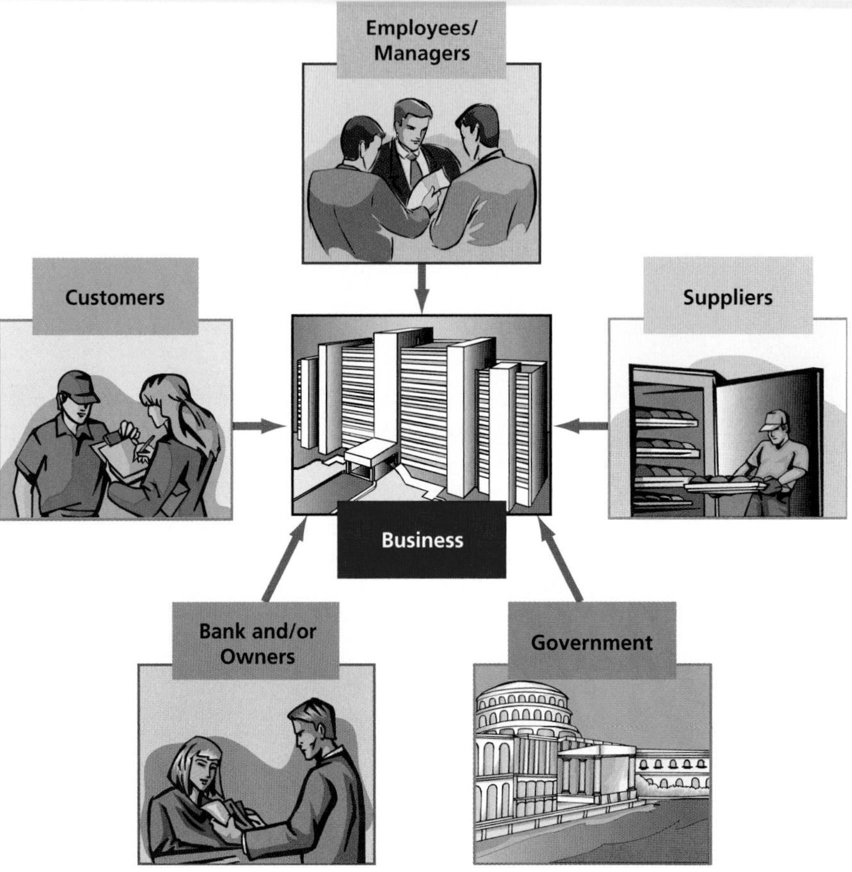

Describe the three business activities of financing, investing, and operating.

BUSINESS ACTIVITIES

Regardless of whether the company is Microsoft or General Electric, all businesses are engaged in the activities of financing, investing, and operating, as shown at the top of page 11. First, a business must obtain the necessary funds to finance the costs to organize, pay legal fees, and pay other startup costs. Next, a business must invest funds in the necessary assets such as buildings and equipment to begin operations. For example, Milton Hershey invested in the German chocolate-making machinery he saw at the Chicago International Exposition. Finally, a business must utilize its assets and resources to implement its business emphasis. Milton Hershey's business emphasis was to mass-produce chocolate candies at an affordable cost.

As we will discuss later in this chapter, a major role of accounting is to provide stakeholders with information on the financing, investing, and operating activities of businesses. Financial statements are one source of such information.

International Perspective While Hershey's main market is in the United States, the company also exports chocolates to over 90 countries around the globe.

Financing Activities

Financing activities involve obtaining funds to begin and operate a business. Businesses seek financing through the use of capital markets. This financing may take the form of borrowing or issuing shares of ownership. Most major businesses use both means of financing.

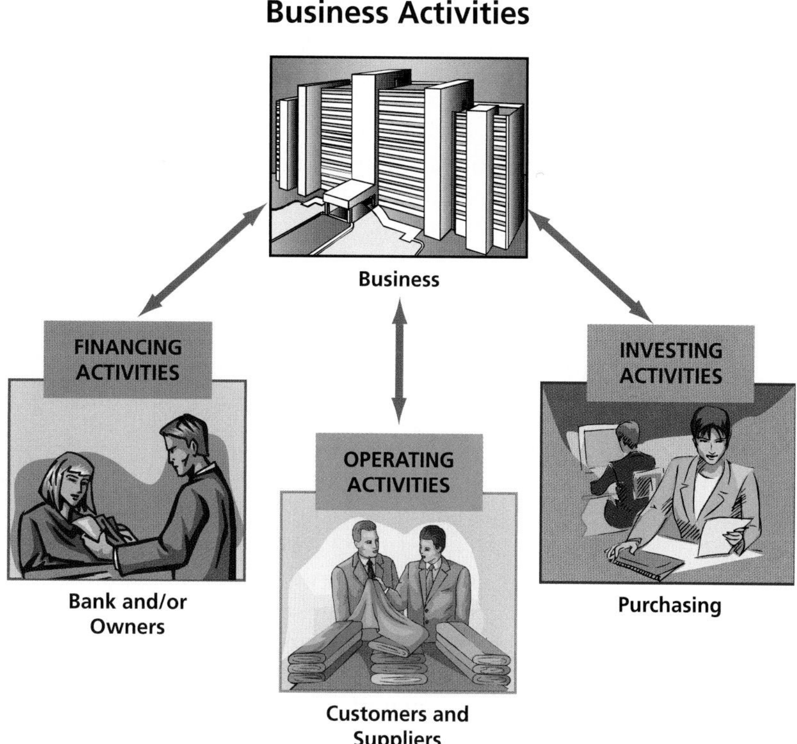

When a business borrows money, it incurs a liability. A **liability** is a legal obligation to repay the amount borrowed according to the terms of the borrowing agreement. For example, when you use your credit card, you incur an obligation to pay the issuer (bank). When a business borrows from a vendor or supplier, the liability is called an **account payable**. In such cases, the business is buying on credit and promising to pay according to the terms set forth by the vendor or supplier. Most vendors and suppliers require payment within a relatively short time, such as 30 days. As of December 31, 2004, Hershey Foods Corporation reported approximately $472 million of accounts payable.

A business may borrow money by issuing bonds. *Bonds* are sold to investors and normally require repayment with interest at a specific time in the future. Bonds are a type of long-term financing, with a face amount that is normally due after several years have passed. In contrast, the interest on bonds is normally paid semiannually. Bond obligations are reported as **bonds payable**, and any interest that is due is reported as **interest payable**. Examples of well-known companies that have bonds outstanding include American Telephone and Telegraph (AT&T), John Deere, and Xerox.

Most large corporations also borrow money by issuing a note payable. A **note payable** requires payment of the amount borrowed plus interest. Notes payable may be issued either on a short-term or a long-term basis.

A business may finance its operations by issuing shares of ownership. For a corporation, shares of ownership are issued in the form of shares of stock. Although corporations may issue a variety of different types of stock, the basic type of stock issued to owners is called **common stock**. For our purposes, we will use the term **capital stock** to include all the types of stock a corporation may issue.[2] Investors who purchase the stock are referred to as **stockholders**.

2 Types of stock are discussed in Chapter 11, "Stockholders' Equity: Capital Stock and Dividends."

The claims of creditors and stockholders on the corporation's resources are different. The resources owned by a business (corporation) are called its **assets**. In case of a corporation's liquidation or bankruptcy, creditors have first claim on its assets. Only after the creditors' claims are satisfied can the stockholders obtain corporate assets. In addition, while creditors expect to receive timely payments of their claims, which may include interest, stockholders are not entitled to regular payments. However, many corporations distribute earnings to stockholders on a regular basis as long as the claims of creditors are being satisfied. These distributions of earnings to stockholders are called **dividends**.

Investing Activities

Once financing has been obtained, a business uses **investing activities** to obtain the necessary assets to start and operate the business. Depending upon the nature of the business, a variety of different assets must be purchased. For example, Milton Hershey purchased the German chocolate-making machinery and later constructed a building to house the Hershey operations. In addition to machinery and buildings, other assets could include computers, office furnishings, trucks, and automobiles. Although most assets have physical characteristics, such as equipment, some assets are intangible in nature. For example, a business may purchase patent rights for use in a manufacturing process or product.

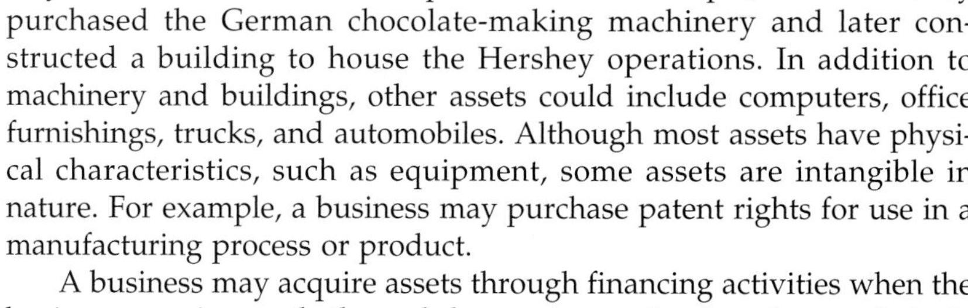

© JANIS CHRISTIE/PHOTODISC/GETTY IMAGES

A business may acquire assets through financing activities when the business acquires cash through borrowing or issuing shares of stock. Cash is used to purchase assets through investing activities, such as in the preceding paragraph. Finally, assets may be acquired through operating activities, as we will describe in the next section.

Assets may take a variety of different forms. For example, tangible assets include cash, land, property, plant, and equipment. Assets may also include intangible items, such as rights to patents and rights to payments from customers. Rights to payments from customers are called **accounts receivable**. Other intangible assets, such as goodwill, copyrights, or patents, are often grouped together and reported as **intangible assets**. A business may also prepay for items such as insurance or rent. Such items, which are assets until they are consumed, are normally reported as **prepaid expenses**.

Operating Activities

Once resources have been acquired, a business uses **operating activities** to implement its business emphasis. **Hershey's** emphasis was to mass-produce and distribute chocolate candies at affordable prices. When Hershey sold its chocolates, it received revenue from its customers. **Revenue** is the increase in assets from selling products or services. Revenues are often identified according to their source. For example, revenues received from selling products are called *sales*. Revenues received from providing services are called *fees*.

To earn revenue, a business incurs costs, such as wages of employees, salaries of managers, rent, insurance, advertising, freight, and utilities. Costs used to earn revenue are called **expenses**. Depending upon the nature of the cost, expenses may be identified in a variety of ways. For example, the cost of products sold is often referred to as the *cost of merchandise sold*, *cost of sales*, or *cost of goods sold*. Other expenses are often classified as either *selling expenses* or *administrative expenses*. Selling expenses include those costs directly related to the selling of a product or service. For example, selling expenses include such costs as sales salaries, sales commissions, freight, and advertising costs. Administrative expenses include other costs not directly related to the selling, such as officer salaries and other costs of the corporate office.

As we will discuss later in this chapter, by comparing the revenues for a period with the related expenses, you can determine whether the business earned net income or incurred a net loss. A **net income** results when revenues exceed expenses. A **net loss** results when expenses exceed revenues.

Define accounting and describe its role in business.

WHAT IS ACCOUNTING AND ITS ROLE IN BUSINESS?

How do stakeholders get information about the financing, investing, and operating activities of a business? This is the role of accounting. Accounting provides information for managers to use in operating the business. In addition, accounting provides information to other stakeholders to use in assessing the economic performance and condition of the business.

In a general sense, **accounting** can be defined as an information system that provides reports to stakeholders about the economic activities and condition of a business. We will focus our discussions in this text on accounting and its role in business. However, many of the concepts in this text also apply to individuals, governments, and other types of organizations. For example, individuals must account for activities such as hours worked, checks written, and bills due. Stakeholders for individuals include creditors, dependents, and the government. A main interest of the government is making sure that individuals pay the proper taxes.

Accounting is sometimes called the "language of business." This is because accounting is the means by which business information is communicated to the stakeholders. For example, accounting reports summarizing the profitability of a new product help Coca-Cola's management decide whether to continue offering the new product for sale. Likewise, financial analysts use accounting reports in deciding whether to recommend the purchase of Coca-Cola's stock. Banks use accounting reports in deciding the amount of credit to extend to Coca-Cola. Suppliers use accounting reports in deciding whether to offer credit for Coca-Cola's purchases of supplies and raw materials. State and federal governments use accounting reports as a basis for assessing taxes on Coca-Cola.

As we described above, accounting serves many purposes for business. A primary purpose is to summarize the financial performance of the firm for external users, such as banks and governmental agencies. The branch of accounting that is associated with preparing reports for users external to the business is termed *financial accounting*. Accounting also can be used to guide management in making decisions about the business. This branch of accounting is called *managerial accounting*. Financial and managerial accounting overlap in many areas. For example, financial reports for external users are often used by managers in considering the impact of their decisions.

In this text, we focus on financial accounting. The two major objectives of financial accounting are:

1. To report the financial condition of a business at a point in time.
2. To report changes in the financial condition of a business over a period of time.

The relationship between the two financial accounting objectives is shown in Exhibit 3. You may think of the first objective as a still photograph (snapshot) of the business and

Exhibit 3

Objectives of Financial Accounting

Financial Condition at January 1, 2007

Change in Financial Condition for Year Ending December 31, 2007

Financial Condition at December 31, 2007

the second objective as a moving picture (video) of the business. The first objective measures the financial status of a business. This measure is used by stakeholders to evaluate the business's financial health at a point in time. The second objective measures the change in the financial condition of a business for a period of time. This measure is used by stakeholders to predict how a business may perform in the future.

The objectives of accounting are satisfied by (1) recording the economic events affecting a business and then (2) summarizing the impact of these events on the business in financial reports, called **financial statements**. We will describe and illustrate the basic financial statements next.

Describe and illustrate the basic financial statements and how they interrelate.

FINANCIAL STATEMENTS

Financial statements report the financial condition of a business at a point in time and changes in the financial condition over a period of time. The four basic financial statements and their relationship to the two objectives of financial accounting are listed below.[3]

Financial Statement	Financial Accounting Objective
Income statement	Reports change in financial condition
Retained earnings statement	Reports change in financial condition
Balance sheet	Reports financial condition
Statement of cash flows	Reports change in financial condition

The income statement is normally prepared first, followed by the retained earnings statement, the balance sheet, and the statement of cash flows. The nature of each statement is described below.

- **Income statement**—A summary of the revenue and the expenses for a specific period of time, such as a month or a year.

3 Instead of the retained earnings statement, companies often prepare a statement of stockholders' equity. This statement reports changes in retained earnings as well as changes in other stockholders' equity items. We describe and illustrate the statement of stockholders' equity in a later chapter, after we have discussed stockholders' equity in more detail.

- **Retained earnings statement**—A summary of the changes in the earnings retained in the corporation for a specific period of time, such as a month or a year.
- **Balance sheet**—A list of the assets, liabilities, and stockholders' equity as of a specific date, usually at the close of the last day of a month or a year.
- **Statement of cash flows**—A summary of the cash receipts and cash payments for a specific period of time, such as a month or a year.

In the next section, we describe and illustrate the preceding four financial statements for Hershey Foods Corporation. Our objective in this section is to introduce you to the financial statements that we will be studying throughout this text. In later chapters, we will expand upon these concepts and terminology. The four financial statements are illustrated in Exhibits 4–7. The data for the statements were adapted from the annual report of Hershey Foods Corporation.[4]

Income Statement

The income statement reports the change in financial condition due to the operations of a business. The time period covered by the income statement may vary depending upon the needs of the stakeholders. Public corporations are required to file quarterly and annual income statements with the Securities and Exchange Commission. The income statement shown in Exhibit 4 for Hershey Foods Corporation is for the year ended December 31, 2004.

Since the focus of business operations is to generate revenues, the income statement begins by listing the revenues for the period. During 2004, Hershey Foods Corporation generated sales of over $4.4 billion. These sales are listed under the revenue caption. You should note that the numbers shown in Exhibit 4 are expressed in millions of dollars. It is common for large corporations to express their financial statements in thousands or millions of dollars.

Following the revenues, the expenses that were used in generating the revenues are listed. For Hershey Foods, these expenses include cost of sales, selling and administrative, interest, and income taxes. By reporting the expenses and the related revenues for a period, the expenses are said to be matched against the revenues. This is known in accounting as the *matching concept*. We will further discuss this concept later in this chapter.

When revenues exceed expenses for a period, the business has *net income*. If expenses exceed revenues, the business has a *net loss*. Reporting net income means that the business increased its net assets through its operations. That is, the assets created

Exhibit 4

Income Statement: Hershey Foods Corporation

Hershey Foods Corporation
Income Statement
For the Year Ended December 31, 2004 (in millions)

Revenues:		
Sales		$4,429
Expenses:		
Cost of sales	$2,679	
Selling and administrative	847	
Interest	67	
Income taxes	245	3,838
Net income		$ 591

4 The financial statements for Hershey Foods Corporation can be found at http://www.hersheys.com by clicking on "Investor Relations."

Q. For 2004, General Motors reported net sales of $193,517 million and net income of $2,805 million. What were General Motors' total expenses for 2004?

A. *$190,712 million ($193,517 million − $2,805 million)*

by the revenues coming into the business exceeded the assets used in generating the revenues. The objective of most businesses is to maximize net income or profit. A net loss means that the business decreased its net assets through its operations. While a business might survive in the short run by reporting net losses, in the long run a business must report net income to survive.

During 2004, Hershey Foods earned net income of almost $600 million dollars. Is this good or bad? Certainly, net income is better than a net loss. However, the stakeholders must assess the economic performance of the corporation according to their own standards. For example, a creditor might be satisfied that the net income is sufficient to assure that it will be repaid. On the other hand, a stockholder might not be satisfied if the corporation's profitability is less than its competitors' profitability. Throughout this text, we describe various methods of assessing corporate performance.

Retained Earnings Statement

The retained earnings statement reports changes in financial condition due to changes in retained earnings during a period. **Retained earnings** is the portion of a corporation's net income that is retained in the business. A corporation may retain all of its net income for use in expanding operations, or it may pay a portion or all of its net income to stockholders as dividends. For example, high-growth companies like Google Inc. and Sirius Satellite Radio do not distribute dividends to stockholders; instead, they retain profits for future expansion. In contrast, more mature corporations like Coca-Cola or General Electric routinely pay their stockholders a regular dividend. Thus, investors such as retirees who desire the comfort of a routine dividend payment might invest in Coca-Cola or General Electric. In contrast, younger and more aggressive growth-oriented investors might invest in Google or Sirius.

Q. Apple Computer Corporation's retained earnings were $2,670 million and $2,394 million as of September 26, 2004 and 2003, respectively. If Apple earned a net income of $276 million during 2004, did Apple pay any dividends during 2004?

A. *No. The increase in retained earnings of $276 million is due entirely to the net income of $276 million.*

Since retained earnings depend upon net income, the time period covered by the retained earnings statement is the same period as the income statement. Thus, the retained earnings statement for Hershey Foods Corporation shown in Exhibit 5 is for the year ended December 31, 2004.

You should note that dividends are reported in Hershey's retained earnings statement rather than in the income statement. This is because dividends are not an expense, but are a distribution of net income to stockholders. During 2004, Hershey distributed (declared) dividends of $386 million and retained $205 million of its net income in the business. Thus, Hershey's retained earnings increased from $3,264 million to $3,469 million during 2004.

Balance Sheet

The balance sheet reports the financial condition as of a point in time. This is in contrast to the income statement, the retained earnings statement, and the statement of cash flows that report changes in financial condition. The financial condition of a business as

Exhibit 5

Retained Earnings Statement: Hershey Foods Corporation

Hershey Foods Corporation
Retained Earnings Statement
For the Year Ended December 31, 2004 (in millions)

Retained earnings, January 1, 2004		$3,264
Add net income	$591	
Less dividends	386	
Increase in retained earnings		205
Retained earnings, December 31, 2004		$3,469

Q. IBM's balance sheet as of December 31, 2004, reported assets of $109,183 million and liabilities of $79,436 million. What is IBM's stockholders' equity as of December 31, 2004?

A. *$29,747 million ($109,183 million − $79,436 million)*

of a point in time is measured by its total assets and claims or rights to those assets. Thus, the financial condition of a business can be represented as follows:

Assets = Claims (Rights to the Assets)

The claims on a business's assets consist of rights of creditors who have loaned money or extended credit to the business and the rights of stockholders who have invested in the business. As we discussed earlier, the rights of creditors are liabilities. The rights of stockholders are referred to as **stockholders' equity**, which is sometimes referred to as **owners' equity**. Thus, the assets and the claims on those assets can be presented in equation form as follows:

Assets = Liabilities + Stockholders' Equity

This equation is called the **accounting equation**. As we shall discover in later chapters, accounting information systems are developed using this equation as their foundation.

The balance sheet, sometimes called the statement of financial condition, is prepared using the framework of the accounting equation. That is, assets are listed first and added to arrive at total assets. Liabilities are then listed and added to arrive at total liabilities. Stockholders' equity items are listed next and added to arrive at total stockholders' equity. Finally, the total assets must equal the combined total liabilities and stockholders' equity. In other words, the accounting equation must balance; hence, the name *balance sheet*. The balance sheet for Hershey Foods Corporation as of December 31, 2004, is shown in Exhibit 6.

Exhibit 6

Balance Sheet: Hershey Foods Corporation

Hershey Foods Corporation
Balance Sheet
December 31, 2004 (in millions)

Assets	
Cash	$ 55
Accounts receivable	409
Inventories	557
Prepaid expenses	161
Property, plant, and equipment	1,683
Intangibles	589
Other assets	343
Total assets	$ 3,797
Liabilities	
Accounts payable	$ 149
Accrued liabilities	472
Notes and other debt	1,716
Income taxes	371
Total liabilities	$ 2,708
Stockholders' Equity	
Capital stock	$ 388
Retained earnings	3,469
Repurchased stock and other equity items	(2,768)
Total stockholders' equity	$ 1,089
Total liabilities and stockholders' equity	$ 3,797

As of December 31, 2004, Hershey had total assets of $3.8 billion, of which creditors had claims of $2.7 billion and stockholders had claims of $1.1 billion. One use of the balance sheet by creditors is to determine whether the corporation's assets are sufficient to ensure that they will be paid their claims. In Hershey's case, as of December 31, 2004, the assets of the corporation exceed the creditors' claims by $1.1 billion. Therefore, the creditors are reasonably assured that their claims will be repaid.

Statement of Cash Flows

The statement of cash flows reports the change in financial condition due to the changes in cash during a period. During 2004, **Hershey**'s net cash decreased by $60 million, as shown in Exhibit 7.

Earlier in this chapter, we discussed the three business activities of financing, investing, and operating. Any changes in cash must be related to one of these three activities. Thus, the statement of cash flows is organized by reporting the changes in each of these three activities, as shown in Exhibit 7.

In the statement of cash flows, the net cash flows from operating activities is reported first, because cash flows from operating activities are a primary analysis focus for most business stakeholders. For example, creditors are interested in determining whether the company's operating activities are generating enough positive cash flow to repay their debts. Likewise, stockholders are interested in the company's ability to pay dividends. A business cannot survive in the long term unless it generates positive cash flows from operating activities. Thus, employees, managers, and other stakeholders interested in the long-term viability of the business also focus upon the cash flows from operating activities. During 2004, Hershey's operations generated a positive net cash flow of $797 million.

Because of the impact investing activities have on the operations of a business, the cash flows from investing activities are presented following the cash flows from operating activities section. Any cash receipts from selling property, plant, and equipment would be reported in this section. Likewise, any purchases of property, plant, and equipment would be reported as cash payments. Companies that are expanding rapidly, such

Exhibit 7

Statement of Cash Flows: Hershey Foods Corporation

Hershey Foods Corporation
Statement of Cash Flows
For the Year Ended December 31, 2004 (in millions)

Net cash flows from operating activities	$ 797
Cash flows from investing activities:	
Investments in property, plant, and equipment	$(363)
Net cash flows used in investing activities	$(363)
Cash flows from financing activities:	
Cash receipts from financing activities, including debt	$ 411
Dividends paid to stockholders	(205)
Repurchase of stock	(617)
Other, including repayment of debt	(83)
Net cash flows used in financing activities	$(494)
Net decrease in cash during 2004	$ (60)
Cash as of January 1, 2004	115
Cash as of December 31, 2004	$ 55

as startup companies, will normally report negative net cash flows from investing activities. In contrast, companies that are downsizing or selling segments of the business may report positive net cash flows from investing activities.

As shown in Exhibit 7, Hershey reported negative net cash flows from investing activities of $363 million. This negative net cash flow was from the purchase of property, plant, and equipment. Thus, it appears that Hershey is expanding operations.

Cash flows from financing activities are reported next. Any cash receipts from issuing debt or stock would be reported in this section as cash receipts. Likewise, paying debt or dividends would be reported as cash payments. Business stakeholders can analyze cash flows from financing activities to determine whether a business is changing its financing policies.

Hershey paid dividends of $205 million and repaid debt of $83 million. Cash of $411 million was received from financing activities that included additional borrowing from creditors. Finally, Hershey purchased its own stock at a cost of $617 million. A company may purchase its own stock if the corporate management believes its stock is undervalued or for providing stock to employees or managers as part of an incentive (stock option) plan.[5]

The statement of cash flows is completed by determining the increase or decrease in cash flows for the period by adding the net cash flows from operating, investing, and financing activities. Hershey reported a net decrease in cash of $60 million. This increase or decrease is added to or subtracted from the cash at the beginning of the period to determine the cash as of the end of the period. Thus, Hershey began the year with $115 million in cash and ended the year with $55 million in cash.

So what does the statement of cash flows reveal about Hershey Foods Corporation during 2004? The statement reveals that Hershey generated over $797 million in cash flows from its operations while using cash to expand its operations and pay dividends to stockholders. Overall, Hershey appears to be in a strong operating position to generate cash and pay its creditors.

Q. **Hershey Foods Corporation**'s balance sheet in Exhibit 6 reports cash of $55 million and retained earnings of $3,469 million. In what other Hershey exhibits do these numbers also appear?

A. *Cash of $55 million also appears in Exhibit 7, Statement of Cash Flows; retained earnings of $3,469 million also appears in Exhibit 5, Retained Earnings Statement.*

Integrated Financial Statements

As we mentioned earlier, financial statements are prepared in the order of the income statement, retained earnings statement, balance sheet, and statement of cash flows. Preparing them in this order is important because the financial statements are integrated. Based upon **Hershey Foods Corporation**'s financial statements in Exhibits 4–7, this integration is shown in Exhibit 8 as follows:[6]

1. The income and retained earnings statements are integrated. The net income or net loss appearing on the income statement also appears on the retained earnings statement as either an addition (net income) to or deduction (net loss) from the beginning retained earnings. To illustrate, Hershey's net income of $591 million is also reported on the retained earnings statement as an addition to the beginning retained earnings.
2. The retained earnings statement and the balance sheet are integrated. The retained earnings at the end of the period on the retained earnings statement also appears on the balance sheet as a part of stockholders' equity. To illustrate, Hershey's retained earnings of $3,469 million as of December 31, 2004, is also reported on the balance sheet.

---

5 We will discuss the accounting for a company's purchase of its own stock in a later chapter.

6 Depending upon the method of preparing cash flows from operating activities, net income may also appear on the statement of cash flows. This link and the method of preparing the statement of cash flows, called "the indirect method," is illustrated in a later chapter. In addition, as we will illustrate in Chapter 2, cash flows from operating activities may equal net income.

Exhibit 8

Integrated Financial Statements

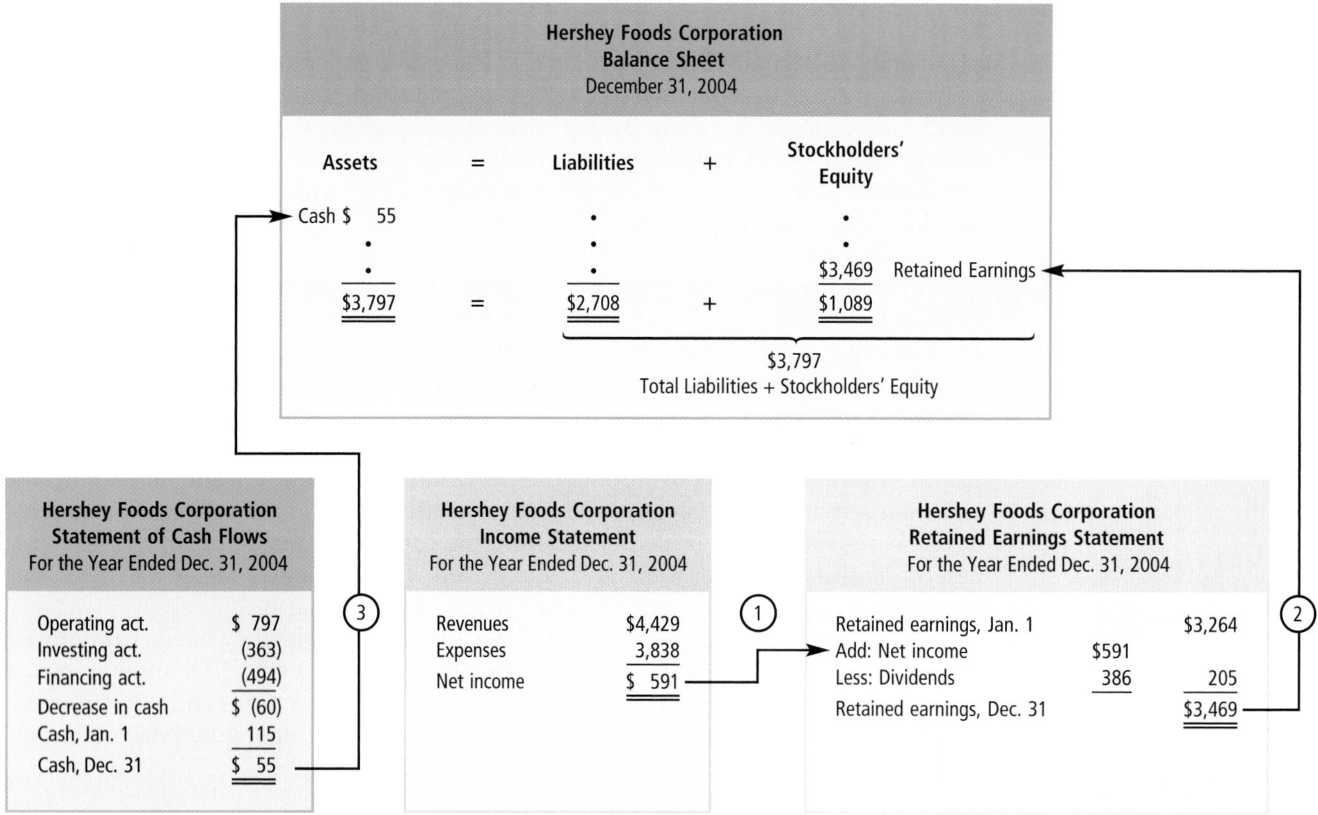

Hershey Foods Corporation
Balance Sheet
December 31, 2004

Assets	=	Liabilities	+	Stockholders' Equity	
Cash $ 55		•		•	
•		•		•	
•		•		$3,469	Retained Earnings
$3,797	=	$2,708	+	$1,089	

$3,797
Total Liabilities + Stockholders' Equity

Hershey Foods Corporation
Statement of Cash Flows
For the Year Ended Dec. 31, 2004

Operating act.	$ 797
Investing act.	(363)
Financing act.	(494)
Decrease in cash	$ (60)
Cash, Jan. 1	115
Cash, Dec. 31	$ 55

Hershey Foods Corporation
Income Statement
For the Year Ended Dec. 31, 2004

Revenues	$4,429
Expenses	3,838
Net income	$ 591

Hershey Foods Corporation
Retained Earnings Statement
For the Year Ended Dec. 31, 2004

Retained earnings, Jan. 1		$3,264
Add: Net income	$591	
Less: Dividends	386	205
Retained earnings, Dec. 31		$3,469

3. The balance sheet and statement of cash flows are integrated. The cash on the balance sheet also appears as the end-of-the-period cash on the statement of cash flows. To illustrate, the cash of $55 million reported on Hershey's balance sheet is also reported as the end-of-the-period cash on the statement of cash flows.

The preceding integration is important in analyzing financial statements and the possible impact of economic events or transactions on a business. In addition, this integration serves as a check on whether the financial statements have been prepared correctly. For example, if the ending cash on the statement of cash flows doesn't agree with the balance sheet cash, then an error exists.

Describe eight accounting concepts underlying financial reporting.

ACCOUNTING CONCEPTS

In the preceding section, we described and illustrated the four basic corporate financial statements. Just as the rules of football determine the proper manner of scoring touchdowns, accounting "rules," called **generally accepted accounting principles (GAAP)**, determine the proper content of financial statements. GAAP are necessary so that stakeholders can compare the financial condition and operating results across companies and across time. If the management of a company could prepare financial statements as they saw fit, the comparability between companies and across time periods would be difficult, if not impossible. In other words, this would be like allowing a football team to determine the point-count for a touchdown every time it scored.

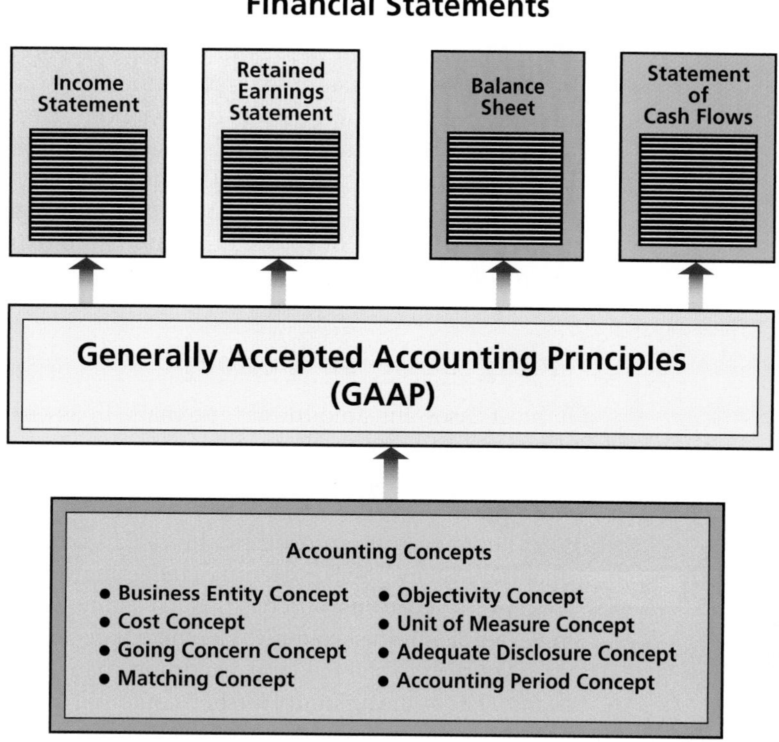

As shown above, GAAP supports and determines the content of the financial statements. GAAP are established in the United States by the **Financial Accounting Standards Board (FASB)**.[7] In establishing GAAP, the FASB publishes *Statements of Financial Accounting Standards*. The FASB establishes GAAP by relying on eight supporting accounting concepts.

Understanding these concepts that support the FASB pronouncements is essential for analyzing and interpreting financial statements. We discuss these concepts next. We conclude this section by describing recent financial reporting frauds, the accounting concepts that were violated, and underlying contributing factors.

Business Entity Concept

A business entity could be an individual, a not-for-profit organization such as a church, or a for-profit company such as a real estate agency. The **business entity concept** applies accounting to a specific entity for which stakeholders need economic data. Once the entity is identified, the accountant can determine which economic data and activities should be analyzed, recorded, and summarized in the financial statements for stakeholders.

The accounting for Hershey Foods Corporation, a for-profit corporation, is separated from the accounting for other entities. For example, the accounting for transactions and events of individual stockholders, creditors, or other Hershey stakeholders are not included in Hershey Foods Corporation's financial statements. Only the transactions and events of the corporation as a separate entity are included in Hershey's financial statements.

---

7 The Securities and Exchange Commission also has authority to set accounting principles for publicly held corporations. In almost all cases, the SEC adopts the principles established by the FASB.

Cost Concept

The **cost concept** determines the amount initially entered into the accounting records for purchases. For example, assume that Hershey purchased land for $2 million as a site for a future plant. The cost of the land to Hershey is the amount that would be entered into the accounting records. The seller may have been asking $2.3 million for the land up to the time of the sale. The land may have been assessed for property tax purposes at $1.5 million. A month after purchasing the land, Hershey may have received an offer of $2.4 million for the land. The only amount that affects the accounting records and the financial statements is the $2 million purchase price.

Going Concern Concept

In most cases, the amount of time that a business will be able to continue in operation is not known, so an assumption must be made. A business normally expects to continue operating for an indefinite period of time. This is called the **going concern concept**.

The going concern concept affects the recording of transactions and thus affects the financial statements. For example, the going concern concept justifies the use of the cost concept for recording purchases, such as the land purchased by Hershey in the preceding example. In this example, Hershey plans to build a plant on the land. Since Hershey does not plan to sell the land, reporting changes in the market value of the land is irrelevant. That is, the amount Hershey could sell the land for if it discontinued operations or went out of business is not important because Hershey plans to continue its operations.

If, however, there is strong evidence that a business is planning to discontinue its operations, then the accounting records should show the values expected to be received. For example, the assets and liabilities of businesses in receivership or bankruptcy are valued from a quitting concern or liquidation point of view, rather than from the going concern point of view.

Matching Concept

In accounting, revenues for a period are matched with the expenses incurred in generating the revenues. Under this **matching concept**, revenues are normally recorded at the time of the sale of the product or service. This recording of revenues is often referred to as *revenue recognition*. At the point of sale, the sale price has been agreed upon, the buyer acquires ownership of the product or acquires the service, and the seller has a legal claim against the buyer for payment.

The following excerpt from the notes to Hershey's annual report describes when Hershey records sales:

> *. . . The Corporation records sales when . . . a . . . customer order with a fixed price has been received . . . the product has been shipped . . . there is no further obligation to assist in the resale of the product, and collectibility (of the account receivable) is reasonably assured.*

Objectivity Concept

The **objectivity concept** requires that entries in the accounting records and the data reported on financial statements be based on objective evidence. If this concept is ignored, the confidence of users of the financial statements cannot be maintained. For example, evidence such as invoices and vouchers for purchases, bank statements for the amount of cash in the bank, and physical counts of supplies on hand support the accounting records. Such evidence is objective and verifiable. In some cases, judgments, estimates, and other subjective factors may have to be used in preparing financial statements. In such situations, the most objective evidence available should be used.

Unit of Measure Concept

In the United States, the **unit of measure concept** requires that all economic data be recorded in dollars. Other relevant, nonfinancial information may also be recorded, such as terms of contracts. However, it is only through using dollar amounts that the various transactions and activities of a business can be measured, summarized, reported, and compared. Money is common to all business transactions and thus is the unit of measurement for reporting.

Adequate Disclosure Concept

Financial statements, including related footnotes and other disclosures, should contain all relevant data a reader needs to understand the financial condition and performance of a business. This is called the **adequate disclosure concept**. Nonessential data should be excluded in order to avoid clutter. For example, the balance of each cash account is usually not reported separately. Instead, the balances are grouped together and reported as one total.

Accounting Period Concept

The process in which accounting data are recorded and summarized in financial statements is a period process. Data are recorded, and the income statement, retained earnings statement, and statement of cash flows are prepared for a period of time such as a month or a year. The balance sheet is then prepared as of the end of the period. After the accounting process is completed for one period, a new period begins and the accounting process is repeated for the new period. This process is based on the **accounting period concept**. Hershey's financial statements shown in Exhibits 4–7 illustrate the accounting period concept for the year ending December 31, 2004.

The financial history of a business may be shown by a series of balance sheets and income statements. If the life of a business is expressed by a line moving from left to right, this series of financial statements may be graphed as follows:

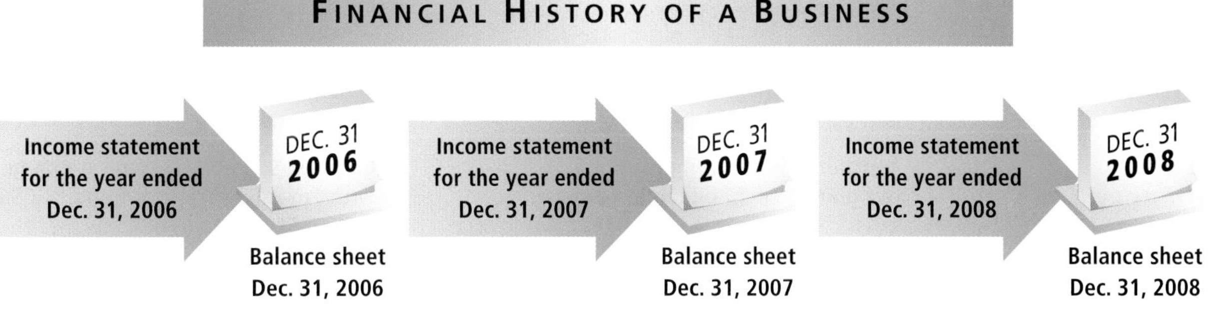

Responsible Reporting

The reliability of the financial reporting system is important to the economy and for the ability of businesses to raise money from investors. That is, stockholders and creditors require accurate financial reporting before they will invest their money. Scandals and financial reporting frauds in the early 2000s threatened the confidence of U.S. investors. Exhibit 9 is a partial list of some of the financial reporting frauds and abuses.

The companies listed in Exhibit 9 were caught in the midst of ethical lapses that lead to fines, firings, and criminal or civil prosecution. The second column of Exhibit 9 identifies the accounting concept that was violated in committing these unethical business practices. For example, the WorldCom fraud involved reporting various expense items as though they were assets. This is a violation of the matching concept and resulted in overstating income and assets. The third column of the table identifies some of the results of these events. In most cases, senior and mid-level executives lost their jobs and were sued by upset investors. In some cases, the executives also were criminally prosecuted and are serving prison terms.

Exhibit 9

Accounting Fraud in the 2000s

Company	Concept Violated	Result
Adelphia	*Business Entity Concept:* Rigas family treated the company assets as their own.	Bankruptcy, Rigas family members convicted of fraud and lost their investment in the company.
AIG	*Business Entity Concept:* Compensation transactions with an off-shore company that should have been disclosed on AIG's books.	CEO (Chief Executive Officer) resigned. AIG paid $126 million in fines.
AOL and PurchasePro	*Matching Concept:* Back-dated contracts to inflate revenues.	Civil charges filed against senior executives of both companies. $500 million fine.
Computer Associates	*Matching Concept:* Fraudulently inflating revenues.	CEO and senior executives indicted. Five executives pled guilty. $225 million fine.
Enron	*Business Entity Concept:* Treated transactions as revenue, when they should have been treated as debt.	Bankruptcy. Criminal charges against senior executives, over $60 billion in stock market losses.
Fannie Mae	*Accounting Period Concept:* Managing earnings by shifting expenses between periods.	CEO and CFO fired. $9 billion in restated earnings.
HealthSouth	*Matching Concept:* $4 billion in false entries to overstate revenues.	Senior executives face regulatory *and* civil charges.
Qwest	*Matching Concept:* Improper recognition of $3 billion in revenue.	CEO and six other executives charged with "massive financial fraud." $250 million SEC fine.
Tyco	*Adequate Disclosure Concept:* Failure to disclose secret loans to executives that were subsequently forgiven.	CEO forced to resign and was convicted in criminal proceedings.
WorldCom	*Matching Concept:* Improperly treated expenses as assets.	Bankruptcy. Criminal conviction of CEO and CFO. Over $100 billion in stock market losses. Directors fined $18 million.
Xerox	*Matching Concept:* Recognized $3 billion in revenue in periods earlier than should have been recognized.	$10 million fine to SEC. Six executives fined $22 million.

What went wrong for these companies and executives? The answer to this question involves the following three factors:

1. Individual character
2. Firm culture
3. Laws and enforcement

Individual Character. Executives often face pressures from senior managers to meet company and analysts' expectations. In many of the cases in Exhibit 9, executives initially justified small violations to avoid such pressures. However, these small lies became big lies as the hole was dug deeper and deeper. By the time the abuses were discovered, the misstatements became sufficient to wreck lives and ruin businesses. For example, David Myers, the former controller of WorldCom, in testifying about his recording of improper transactions, stated the following:

"I didn't think that it was the right thing to do, but I had been asked by Scott (Sullivan, the VP of Finance) to do it . . ."[8]

Individual character is important. It embraces honesty, integrity, and fairness in the face of pressure to hide the truth.

Firm Culture. By their behavior and attitude, senior managers of a company set the firm culture. As explained by one author, when the leader of a company is put on a pedestal, "they begin to believe they and their organizations are one-of-a-kind, that they're changing the face of the industry. They desire entitlements beyond any other C.E.O.'s (chief executive officers)."[9] In most of the firms shown in Exhibit 9, the senior managers created a culture of greed and indifference to the truth. This culture flowed down to lower-level managers creating an environment of short-cuts, greed, and lies that ultimately resulted in financial fraud.

Laws and Enforcement. Many blamed the lack of laws and enforcement for contributing to the financial reporting abuses described in Exhibit 9. For example, Elliott Spitzer, attorney general of New York, stated the following:

". . . a key lesson from the recent scandals is that the checks on the system simply have not worked. The honor code among CEOs didn't work. Board oversight didn't work. Self-regulation was a complete failure."[10]

As a result, Congress enacted new laws, and enforcement efforts have increased since the early 2000s. For example, the Sarbanes-Oxley Act of 2002 (SOX) was enacted. SOX established a new oversight body for the accounting profession, called the Public Company Accounting Oversight Board (PCAOB). In addition, SOX established standards for independence, corporate responsibility, enhanced financial disclosures, and corporate accountability.

---

8 Susan Pulliam, "Crossing the Line: At Center of Fraud, WorldCom Official Sees Life Unravel," *The Wall Street Journal*, March 24, 2005, p. A1.

9 Tim Race, "New Economy Executives are Smitten, and Undone by Their Own Images," *New York Times*, July 7, 2002. Quote attributed to Professor Jay A. Conger.

10 Eliot Spitzer, "Strong Law Enforcement Is Good for the Economy," *The Wall Street Journal*, April 5, 2005, p. A18.

Describe and illustrate how horizontal analysis can be used to analyze and evaluate a company's performance.

HORIZONTAL ANALYSIS

The basic financial statements illustrated in this chapter are a primary source of information that financial analysts use in evaluating a company's performance. One method of analyzing financial performance is to compute percentage increases and decreases in related items in comparative financial statements. This type of analysis, called **horizontal analysis**, compares each item on the most recent financial statement with the related item on one or more earlier statements. The amount of the increase or decrease in each item is shown along with the percent increase or decrease.

To illustrate, income statements for Hershey Foods Corporation will be used for the years ending December 31, 2004 and 2003. For analysis purposes, the income statements have been condensed and adapted to emphasize the operating aspects of Hershey's performance. For example, other expenses, interest expense, and income taxes have been omitted from the income statements. This allows us to focus on the basic operating aspects of Hershey's business without being distracted by unusual items, such as other expenses related to asset impairments. The exclusion of income taxes helps simplify the analysis and also recognizes that the amount of income taxes is largely beyond the operating control of the business. Interest expense is omitted, since it deals more with the financing rather than the operating aspects of the business. The resulting comparative income statements are shown in Exhibit 10.

International Perspective International Accounting Standards (IASs) are the accounting rules that determine the content of certain international financial statements. Beginning in 2005, publicly listed companies in the European Union are required to use IASs in preparing their financial statements.

The income statements shown in Exhibit 10 report **gross profit** as sales less the cost of sales. Gross profit represents the amount that Hershey marked up the cost of its products in selling them to its customers. Gross profit is a useful performance measure in analyzing the profitability of the company's products from one period to the next.

Did Hershey improve its operations during the year ending December 31, 2004? Exhibit 10 indicates that Hershey was able to increase its sales by 6.1%, while the cost of sales increased by a lesser amount, 5.3%. This combination of sales increasing faster than cost of sales caused gross profit to increase by 7.5%. Selling and administrative expenses increased only 1.9%, which is probably related to headquarter's efficiency efforts. The overall impact on operating income before taxes is an increase of 13.3%. This would generally be considered a favorable change in operating performance. However, before arriving at a final conclusion on Hershey's operating results for 2004,

Exhibit 10

Comparative Income Statements Using Horizontal Analysis: Hershey Foods Corporation

Hershey Foods Corporation
Income Statements
For the Years Ended December 31, 2004 and 2003 (in millions)

			Increase (Decrease)	
	2004	**2003**	**Amount**	**Percent**
Sales	$4,429	$4,173	$256	6.1%
Cost of sales	2,679	2,545	134	5.3
Gross profit	$1,750	$1,628	$122	7.5
Selling and administrative expenses	847	831	16	1.9
Operating income before taxes	$ 903	$ 797	$106	13.3

additional analyses as well as comparisons with the operating results of competitors should be performed, as discussed at the end of Chapter 14.[11]

11 Additional financial statement analyses will be discussed and illustrated throughout the remainder of this text.

SUMMARY OF LEARNING GOALS

1 Describe the types and forms of businesses, how businesses make money, and business stakeholders. The three types of businesses operated for profit include manufacturing, merchandising, and service businesses. Such businesses may be organized as proprietorships, partnerships, corporations, and limited liability companies. A business may make money (profits) by gaining an advantage over its competitors using a low-cost or a premium-price emphasis. Under a *low-cost emphasis*, a business designs and produces products or services at a lower cost than its competitors. Under a *premium-price emphasis*, a business tries to design products or services that possess unique attributes or characteristics for which customers are willing to pay more. A business's economic performance is of interest to its stakeholders. Business stakeholders include four categories: capital market stakeholders, product or service market stakeholders, government stakeholders, and internal stakeholders.

2 Describe the three business activities of financing, investing, and operating. All businesses engage in financing, investing, and operating activities. Financing activities involve obtaining funds to begin and operate a business. Investing activities involve obtaining the necessary resources to start and operate the business. Operating activities involve using the business's resources according to its business emphasis.

3 Define accounting and describe its role in business. Accounting is an information system that provides reports to stakeholders about the economic activities and condition of a business. Accounting is the "language of business."

4 Describe and illustrate the basic financial statements and how they interrelate. The principal financial statements of a corporation are the income statement, the retained earnings statement, the balance sheet, and the statement of cash flows. The income statement reports a period's net income or net loss, which also appears on the retained earnings statement. The ending retained earnings reported on the retained earnings statement is also reported on the balance sheet. The ending cash balance is reported on the balance sheet and the statement of cash flows.

5 Describe eight accounting concepts underlying financial reporting. The eight accounting concepts discussed in this chapter include the business entity, cost, going concern, matching, objectivity, unit of measure, adequate disclosure, and accounting period concepts.

6 Describe and illustrate how horizontal analysis can be used to analyze and evaluate a company's performance. One method of analyzing financial performance is to compute percentage increases and decreases in related items in comparative financial statements. This type of analysis, called horizontal analysis, compares each item on the most recent financial statement with the related item on one or more earlier statements.

GLOSSARY

Account payable The liability created when a business borrows from a vendor or supplier.

Accounting An information system that provides reports to stakeholders about the economic activities and condition of a business.

Accounting equation Assets = Liabilities + Stockholders' Equity.

Accounting period concept A concept of accounting in which accounting data are recorded and summarized in a periodic process.

Accounts receivable Rights to payments from customers.

Adequate disclosure concept A concept of accounting that requires that the financial statements include all relevant data a reader needs to understand the financial condition and performance of a business.

Assets The resources owned by a business.

Balance sheet A list of the assets, liabilities, and stockholders' equity *as of a specific date*, usually at the close of the last day of a month, a quarter, or a year.

Bonds payable A type of long-term debt financing with a face amount that is due in the future with interest that is normally paid semiannually.

Business An organization in which basic resources (inputs), such as materials and labor, are assembled and processed to provide goods or services (outputs) to customers.

Business entity concept A concept of accounting that limits the economic data in the accounting system to data related directly to the activities of a specific business or entity.

Business stakeholder A person or entity who has an interest in the economic performance of a business.

Capital stock Types of stock a corporation may issue.

Common stock The basic type of stock issued to stockholders of a corporation.

Corporation A business organized under state or federal statutes as a separate legal entity.

Cost concept A concept of accounting that determines the amount initially entered into the accounting records for purchases.

Dividends Distributions of earnings of a corporation to stockholders.

Expenses Costs used to earn revenues.

Financial Accounting Standards Board (FASB) The authoritative body that has the primary responsibility for developing accounting principles.

Financial statements Financial reports that summarize the effects of events on a business.

Financing activities Business activities that involve obtaining funds to begin and operate a business.

Generally accepted accounting principles (GAAP) Rules for how financial statements should be prepared.

Going concern concept A concept of accounting that assumes a business will continue operating for an indefinite period of time.

Gross profit Sales less the cost of sales.

Horizontal analysis A method of analyzing financial performance that computes percentage increases and decreases in related items in comparative financial statements.

Income statement A summary of the revenue and expenses *for a specific period of time*, such as a month or a year.

Intangible assets Assets that are rights to future benefits such as patent or copyright rights.

Interest payable A liability to pay interest on a due date.

Investing activities Business activities that involve obtaining the necessary resources to start and operate the business.

Liabilities The rights of creditors that represent a legal obligation to repay an amount borrowed according to terms of the borrowing agreement.

Limited liability company (LLC) A business form consisting of one or more persons or entities filing an operating agreement with a state to conduct business with limited liability to the owners, yet treated as a partnership for tax purposes.

Manufacturing A type of business that changes basic inputs into products that are sold to individual customers.

Matching concept A concept of accounting in which expenses are matched with the revenue generated during a period by those expenses.

Merchandising A type of business that purchases products from other businesses and sells them to customers.

Net income The excess of revenues over expenses.

Net loss The excess of expenses over revenues.

Note payable A type of short- or long-term financing that requires payment of the amount borrowed plus interest.

Objectivity concept A concept of accounting that requires accounting records and the data reported in financial statements to be based on objective evidence.

Operating activities Business activities that involve using the business's resources to implement its business emphasis.

Owners' equity The rights of the owners of a company.

Partnership A business owned by two or more individuals.

Prepaid expenses An asset resulting from the prepayment of a future expense such as insurance or rent.

Proprietorship A business owned by one individual.

Retained earnings Net income retained in a corporation.

Retained earnings statement A summary of the changes in the retained earnings in a corporation *for a specific period of time*, such as a month or a year.

Revenue The increase in assets from selling products or services to customers.

Service A type of business that provides services rather than products to customers.

Statement of cash flows A summary of the cash receipts and cash payments *for a specific period of time*, such as a month or a year.

Stockholders Investors who purchase stock in a corporation.

Stockholders' equity The rights of the owners of a corporation.

Unit of measure concept A concept of accounting requiring that economic data be recorded in dollars.

ILLUSTRATIVE ACCOUNTING APPLICATION PROBLEM

The financial statements at the end of Spratlin Consulting's first month of operations are shown below.

Spratlin Consulting
Income Statement
For the Month Ended June 30, 2007

Fees earned		$36,000
Operating expenses:		
Wages expense	$12,000	
Rent expense	7,640	
Utilities expense	(a)	
Miscellaneous expense	1,320	
Total operating expenses		23,120
Net income		$ (b)

Spratlin Consulting
Retained Earnings Statement
For the Month Ended June 30, 2007

Net income for June	$ (c)
Less dividends	(d)
Retained earnings, June 30, 2007	$ (e)

Spratlin Consulting
Balance Sheet
June 30, 2007

Assets	
Cash	$ 5,600
Land	50,000
Total assets	$ (f)
Liabilities	
Accounts payable	$ 1,920
Stockholders' Equity	
Capital stock	(g)
Retained earnings	(h)
Total stockholders' equity	$ (i)
Total liabilities and stockholders' equity	$ j

Spratlin Consulting
Statement of Cash Flows
For the Month Ended June 30, 2007

Cash flows from operating activities:		
Cash received from customers	$36,000	
Deduct cash payments for operating expenses	(k)	
Net cash flows from operating activities		$14,800
Cash flows from investing activities:		
Cash payments for acquisition of land		(l)
Cash flows from financing activities:		
Cash received from issuing capital stock	$48,000	
Deduct dividends	7,200	
Net cash flows from financing activities		(m)
Net cash flow and June 30, 2007, cash balance		$ (n)

Instructions

By analyzing how the four financial statements are integrated, determine the proper amounts for (a) through (n).

Solution

a. Utilities expense, $2,160 ($23,120 − $12,000 − $7,640 − $1,320)
b. Net income, $12,880 ($36,000 − $23,120)
c. Net income, $12,880 (same as b)
d. Dividends, $7,200 (from statement of cash flows)
e. Retained earnings, $5,680 ($12,880 − $7,200)
f. Total assets, $55,600 ($5,600 + $50,000)
g. Capital stock, $48,000 (from the statement of cash flows)
h. Retained earnings, $5,680 (same as e)
i. Total stockholders' equity, $53,680 ($48,000 + $5,680)
j. Total liabilities and stockholders' equity, $55,600 ($1,920 + $53,680) (same as f)
k. Cash payments for operating expenses, $21,200 ($36,000 − $14,800)
l. Cash payments for acquisition of land, $50,000 (from balance sheet)
m. Net cash flows from financing activities, $40,800 ($48,000 − $7,200)
n. Net cash flow and June 30, 2007, cash balance, $5,600 ($14,800 − $50,000 + $40,800)

SELF-STUDY QUESTIONS

Answers at end of chapter

1. A profit-making business operating as a separate legal entity and in which ownership is divided into shares of stock is known as a:
   A. proprietorship.
   B. service business.
   C. partnership.
   D. corporation.

2. The resources owned by a business are called:
   A. assets.
   B. liabilities.
   C. the accounting equation.
   D. stockholders' equity.

3. A listing of a business entity's assets, liabilities, and stockholders' equity as of a specific date is:
   A. a balance sheet.
   B. an income statement.
   C. the retained earnings statement.
   D. a statement of cash flows.

4. If total assets are $20,000 and total liabilities are $12,000, the amount of stockholders' equity is:
   A. $32,000.
   B. ($32,000).
   C. ($8,000).
   D. $8,000.

5. If revenue was $45,000, expenses were $37,500, and dividends were $10,000, the amount of net income or net loss would be:
   A. $45,000 net income.
   B. $7,500 net income.
   C. $37,500 net loss.
   D. $2,500 net loss.

DISCUSSION QUESTIONS

1. What is the objective of most businesses?
2. What is the difference between a manufacturing business and a merchandising business? Give an example of each type of business.
3. What is the difference between a manufacturing business and a service business? Is a restaurant a manufacturing business, a service business, or both?
4. Why are most large companies like Microsoft, Pepsi, Caterpillar, and AutoZone organized as corporations?
5. Both KIA and Porsche produce and sell automobiles. Describe and contrast the business emphasis of KIA and Porsche.
6. Assume that a friend of yours operates a family-owned pharmacy. A Super Wal-Mart is scheduled to open in the next several months that will also offer pharmacy services. What business emphasis would your friend use to compete with the Super Wal-Mart pharmacy?
7. What services does eBay offer to its customers?
8. A business's stakeholders can be classified into capital market, product or service market, government, and internal stakeholders. Will the interests of all the stakeholders within a classification be the same? Use bankers and stockholders of the capital market as an example in answering this question.
9. The three business activities are financing, investing, and operating. Using United Airlines, give an example of a financing, investing, and operating activity.
10. What is the role of accounting in business?
11. Briefly describe the nature of the information provided by each of the following financial statements: the income statement, the retained earnings statement, the balance sheet, and the statement of cash flows. In your descriptions, indicate whether each of the financial statements covers a period of time or is for a specific date.
12. For the year ending January 31, 2004, The Limited Inc. had revenues of $8,934 million and total expenses of $8,217 million. Did The Limited (a) incur a net loss or (b) realize net income?
13. What particular item of financial or operating data appears on both the income statement and the retained earnings statement? What item appears on both the balance sheet and the retained earnings statement? What item appears on both the balance sheet and statement of cash flows?
14. Deana Moran is the owner of First Delivery Service. Recently, Deana paid interest of $3,600 on a personal loan of $60,000 that she used to begin the business. Should First Delivery Service record the interest payment? Explain.
15. On July 10, Elrod Repair Service extended an offer of $100,000 for land that had been priced for sale at $120,000. On July 25, Elrod Repair Service accepted the seller's counteroffer of $112,000. Describe how Elrod Repair Service should record the land.
16. Land with an assessed value of $300,000 for property tax purposes is acquired by a business for $500,000. Seven years later, the plot of land has an assessed value of $400,000 and the business receives an offer of $600,000 for it. Should the monetary amount assigned to the land in the business records now be increased?

EXERCISES

Exercise 1-1

Types of businesses

Goal 1

Indicate whether each of the following companies is primarily a service, merchandise, or manufacturing business. If you are unfamiliar with the company, you may use the Internet to locate the company's home page or use the finance Web site of Yahoo.com.

1. Alcoa
2. AT&T
3. Boeing
4. Caterpillar
5. Citigroup
6. CVS
7. Dow Chemical
8. FedEx
9. First Republic Bank
10. Ford Motor

11. The Gap
12. Hilton Hotels
13. H&R Block Inc.
14. Procter & Gamble
15. Sears Roebuck

Exercise 1-2

Business emphasis

Goal 1

Identify the primary business emphasis of each of the following companies as (a) a low-cost emphasis or (b) a premium-price emphasis. If you are unfamiliar with the company, you may use the Internet to locate the company's home page or use the finance Web site of Yahoo.com.

1. BMW
2. Charles Schwab
3. Circuit City Stores
4. Coca-Cola
5. Dollar General
6. Goldman Sachs Group
7. Home Depot
8. Maytag
9. Nike
10. Office Depot
11. Sara Lee
12. Southwest Airlines

Exercise 1-3

Accounting equation

Goal 4

Coca-Cola, $15,935

The total assets and total liabilities of Coca-Cola and PepsiCo are shown below.

	Coca-Cola (in millions)	PepsiCo (in millions)
Assets	$31,327	$27,987
Liabilities	15,392	14,464

Determine the stockholders' equity of each company.

Exercise 1-4

Accounting equation

Goal 4

Toys"R"Us, $4,222

The total assets and total liabilities of Toys"R"Us Inc. and Estée Lauder Inc. are shown below.

	Toys"R"Us (in millions)	Estée Lauder Inc. (in millions)
Assets	$10,218	$3,708
Liabilities	5,996	1,974

Determine the stockholders' equity of each company.

Exercise 1-5

Accounting equation

Goal 4

a. $96,500

Determine the missing amount for each of the following:

	Assets	=	Liabilities	+	Stockholders' Equity
a.	X	=	$25,000	+	$71,500
b.	$82,750	=	X	+	$15,000
c.	$37,000	=	$17,500	+	X

Exercise 1-6

Accounting equation

Goal 4

a. $2,607

Determine the missing amounts (in millions) for the balance sheets (summarized below) for The Limited Inc., FedEx Corporation, and Ford Motor Co.

	The Limited	FedEx Corporation	Ford Motor Co.
Assets	$7,873	$ (b)	$292,654
Liabilities	(a)	6,727	276,609
Stockholders' equity	5,266	5,478	(c)

Exercise 1-7

Net income and dividends

Goal 4

The income statement of a corporation for the month of January indicates a net income of $112,750. During the same period, $128,000 in cash dividends were paid.

Would it be correct to say that the business incurred a net loss of $15,250 during the month? Discuss.

Exercise 1-8

Net income and stockholders' equity for four businesses

Goal 4

Company O: Net loss, ($50,000)

Four different proprietorships, M, N, O, and P, show the same balance sheet data at the beginning and end of a year. These data, exclusive of the amount of owners' equity, are summarized as follows:

	Total Assets	Total Liabilities
Beginning of the year	$ 750,000	$300,000
End of the year	1,200,000	650,000

On the basis of the above data and the following additional information for the year, determine the net income (or loss) of each company for the year. (*Hint:* First determine the amount of increase or decrease in stockholders' equity during the year.)

Company M: No additional capital stock was issued, and no dividends were paid.
Company N: No additional capital stock was issued, but dividends of $60,000 were paid.
Company O: Capital stock of $150,000 was issued, but no dividends were paid.
Company P: Capital stock of $150,000 was issued, and dividends of $60,000 were paid.

Exercise 1-9

Accounting equation and income statement

Goal 4

1. $2,956,252

Staples, Inc., is a leading office products distributor, with retail stores in the United States, Canada, Asia, Europe, and South America. The following financial statement data were taken from Staples' financial statements as of January 29, 2005 and 2004:

	2005 (in thousands)	2004 (in thousands)
Total assets	$ 7,071,448	$6,503,046
Total liabilities	(1)	2,840,146
Total stockholders' equity	4,115,196	(2)
Retained earnings	2,818,163	2,209,302
Sales	$14,448,378	
Cost of goods sold	10,343,643	
Operating and other expenses	2,989,163	
Income tax expense	407,184	

a. Determine the missing data indicated for (1) and (2).
b. Using the income statement data for 2005, determine the amount of net income or loss.
c. Did Staples pay any dividends to stockholders during 2005? [*Hint:* Compare the change in retained earnings to your answer for (b).]

Exercise 1-10

Balance sheet items

Goal 4

From the following list of selected items taken from the records of Ishmael Appliance Service as of a specific date, identify those that would appear on the balance sheet.

1. Supplies
2. Wages Expense
3. Cash
4. Land
5. Utilities Expense
6. Fees Earned
7. Supplies Expense
8. Accounts Payable
9. Capital Stock
10. Wages Payable

Exercise 1-11

Income statement items

Goal 4

Based on the data presented in Exercise 1-10, identify those items that would appear on the income statement.

Exercise 1-12

Financial statement items

Goal 4

Identify each of the following items as (a) an asset, (b) a liability, (c) revenue, (d) an expense, or (e) a dividend:

1. Amounts due from customers
2. Amounts owed vendors
3. Cash on hand
4. Cash paid to stockholders
5. Cash sales
6. Equipment
7. Note payable owed to the bank
8. Rent paid for the month
9. Sales commissions paid to salespersons
10. Wages paid to employees

Exercise 1-13

Retained earnings statement

Goal 4

Retained earnings, April 30, 2006: $358,200

SPREADSHEET

Financial information related to Madras Company for the month ended April 30, 2006, is as follows:

Net income for April	$ 73,000
Dividends during April	12,000
Retained earnings, April 1, 2006	297,200

Prepare a retained earnings statement for the month ended April 30, 2006.

Exercise 1-14

Income statement

Goal 4

Net income: $89,320

SPREADSHEET

Hercules Services was organized on November 1, 2006. A summary of the revenue and expense transactions for November follows:

Fees earned	$232,120
Wages expense	100,100
Miscellaneous expense	3,150
Rent expense	35,000
Supplies expense	4,550

Prepare an income statement for the month ended November 30.

Exercise 1-15

Missing amounts from balance sheet and income statement data

Goal 4

(a) $156,300

One item is omitted in each of the following summaries of balance sheet and income statement data for four different corporations, A, B, C, and D.

	A	B	C	D
Beginning of the year:				
Assets	$720,000	$125,000	$160,000	$ (d)
Liabilities	432,000	65,000	121,600	150,000
End of the year:				
Assets	894,000	175,000	144,000	310,000
Liabilities	390,000	55,000	128,000	170,000
During the year:				
Additional issue of capital stock	(a)	25,000	16,000	50,000
Dividends	48,000	8,000	(c)	75,000
Revenue	237,300	(b)	184,000	140,000
Expenses	129,600	32,000	196,000	160,000

Determine the missing amounts, identifying them by letter. [*Hint:* First determine the amount of increase or decrease in owners' (stockholders') equity during the year.]

Exercise 1-16

Balance sheets, net income

Goal **4**

b. $36,340

SPREADSHEET

Financial information related to Derby Interiors for October and November 2006 is as follows:

	October 31, 2006	November 30, 2006
Accounts payable	$12,320	$13,280
Accounts receivable	27,200	31,300
Capital stock	15,000	15,000
Retained earnings	?	?
Cash	48,000	81,600
Supplies	2,400	2,000

a. Prepare balance sheets for Derby Interiors as of October 31 and as of November 30, 2006.
b. Determine the amount of net income for November, assuming that no additional capital stock was issued and no dividends were paid during the month.
c. Determine the amount of net income for November, assuming that no additional capital stock was issued but dividends of $10,000 were paid during the month.

Exercise 1-17

Financial statements

Goal **4**

Each of the following items is shown in the financial statements of ExxonMobil Corporation. Identify the financial statement (balance sheet or income statement) in which each item would appear.

a. Accounts payable
b. Cash equivalents
c. Crude oil inventory
d. Equipment
e. Exploration expenses
f. Income taxes payable
g. Investments
h. Long-term debt
i. Marketable securities
j. Notes and loans payable
k. Operating expenses
l. Prepaid taxes
m. Retained earnings
n. Sales
o. Selling expenses

Exercise 1-18

Statement of cash flows

Goal **4**

Indicate whether each of the following cash activities would be reported on the statement of cash flows as (a) an operating activity, (b) an investing activity, or (c) a financing activity.

1. Sold excess office equipment
2. Paid rent
3. Paid for office equipment
4. Issued capital stock
5. Sold services
6. Paid for advertising
7. Paid officers' salaries
8. Issued a note payable
9. Paid rent
10. Paid dividends

Exercise 1-19

Statement of cash flows

Goal **3**

Indicate whether each of the following activities would be reported on the statement of cash flows as (a) an operating activity, (b) an investing activity, or (c) a financing activity.

1. Cash received from fees earned
2. Cash paid for land
3. Cash received from investment by stockholders
4. Cash paid for expenses

Exercise 1-20

Statement of cash flows

Goal **4**

Net cash flows from operating activities, $24,240

SPREADSHEET

Hoist Inc. was organized on March 1, 2007. A summary of cash flows for March is shown below.

Cash receipts:	
Cash received from customers	$ 37,600
Cash received for capital stock	144,000
Cash received from note payable	16,000
Cash payments:	
Cash paid out for expenses	$ 13,360
Cash paid out for purchase of equipment	120,000
Cash paid as dividends	8,000

Prepare a statement of cash flows for the month ended March 31, 2007.

Exercise 1-21

Using financial statements

Goal **4**

A company's stakeholders often differ in their financial statement focus. For example, some stakeholders focus primarily on the income statement, while others may focus primarily on the statement of cash flows or the balance sheet. For each of the following situations, indicate which financial statement would be the likely focus for the stakeholder. Choose either the income statement, balance sheet, or the statement of cash flows and justify your choice.

Situation One: Assume that you are considering investing in eBay (capital market stakeholder).

Situation Two: Assume that you are considering purchasing a personal computer from Dell.

Situation Three: Assume that you are a banker for Citigroup (capital market stakeholder), considering whether to grant a major credit line (loan) to Wal-Mart. The credit line will allow Wal-Mart to borrow up to $400 million for a five-year period at the market rate of interest.

Situation Four: Assume that you are employed by Sara Lee Corporation (product market stakeholder) and are considering whether to extend credit for a 60-day period to a new grocery store chain that has recently opened throughout the Midwest.

Situation Five: Assume that you are considering taking a job (internal stakeholder) with either Sears or JCPenney.

Exercise 1-22

Financial statement items

Goal **4**

Starbucks Corporation purchases and roasts high-quality whole bean coffees and sells them, along with fresh, rich-brewed coffees and a variety of other complementary items, primarily through company-operated retail stores.

The following items were adapted from the annual report of Starbucks Corporation for the period ending October 3, 2004:

	In thousands
1. Accounts payable	$ 199,346
2. Accounts receivable	140,226
3. Accrued expenses payable	356,317
4. Additions to property, plant, and equipment	412,537
5. Inventories	422,663
6. Cost of sales	2,191,440
7. General and administrative expenses	304,293
8. Income tax expense	231,754
9. Net cash provided by operating activities	826,209
10. Net sales	5,294,247
11. Other income (loss)	74,797
12. Other operating expenses	460,830
13. Property, plant, and equipment	1,551,416
14. Retained earnings (October 3, 2004)	1,448,899
15. Store operating expenses	1,790,168

Using the following notations, indicate on which financial statement you would find each of the above items. (*Note*: An item may appear on more than one statement.)

IS	Income statement
RE	Retained earnings statement
BS	Balance sheet
SCF	Statement of cash flows

Exercise 1-23

Income statement

Goal **4**

Net income, $390,559

Based on the Starbucks Corporation financial statement data shown in Exercise 1-22, prepare an income statement for the year ending October 3, 2004.

Exercise 1-24

Retained earnings statement

Goal **4**

Based on the Starbucks Corporation financial statement data shown in Exercise 1-22, prepare a retained earnings statement for the year ending October 3, 2004. The retained earnings as of October 4, 2003, was $1,058,340, and Starbucks paid no dividends during the year.

Exercise 1-25

Financial statement items

Goal **4**

Though the McDonald's menu of hamburgers, cheeseburgers, the Big Mac®, Quarter Pounder®, the Filet-O-Fish®, and Chicken McNuggets® is easily recognized, McDonald's financial statements may not be as familiar. The following items were adapted from a recent annual report of McDonald's Corporation:

1. Accounts payable
2. Accrued interest payable
3. Capital stock outstanding
4. Cash
5. Cash provided by operations
6. Food and packaging costs used in operations
7. Income tax expense
8. Interest expense
9. Inventories
10. Long-term debt payable
11. Net income
12. Net increase in cash
13. Notes payable
14. Notes receivable
15. Occupancy and rent expense
16. Payroll expense
17. Prepaid expenses not yet used in operations
18. Property and equipment
19. Retained earnings
20. Sales

Identify the financial statement on which each of the preceding items would appear. An item may appear on more than one statement. Use the following notations:

IS	Income statement
RE	Retained earnings statement
BS	Balance sheet
SCF	Statement of cash flows

Exercise 1-26

Financial statements

Goal **4**

Correct amount of total assets is $48,750

Americana Realty, organized October 1, 2007, is owned and operated by Marlene Laney. How many errors can you find in the following financial statements for Americana Realty, prepared after its first month of operations? Assume that the cash balance on October 31, 2007, is $11,650 and that cash flows from operating is reported correctly.

Americana Realty
Income Statement
October 31, 2007

Sales commissions		$77,100
Operating expenses:		
Office salaries expense	$43,150	
Rent expense	7,800	
Miscellaneous expense	550	
Automobile expense	1,975	
Total operating expenses		53,475
Net income		$33,625

Marlene Laney
Retained Earnings Statement
October 31, 2006

Retained earnings, October 1, 2007	$ 4,450
Less dividends during October	3,000
	$ 1,450
Net income for the month	33,625
Retained earnings, October 31, 2007	$35,075

Balance Sheet
For the Month Ended October 31, 2007

Assets		
Cash		$11,650
Accounts payable		3,125
Land		15,000
Total assets		$29,775
Liabilities		
Accounts receivable		$20,300
Prepaid expenses		1,800
Stockholders' Equity		
Capital stock	$25,000	
Retained earnings	35,075	60,075
Total liabilities and stockholders' equity		$82,175

Statement of Cash Flows
October 31, 2007

Cash flows from operating activities:		
Cash received from customers	$56,800	
Cash paid for operating expenses	52,150	
Net cash flow from operating activities		$ 4,650
Cash flows from financing activities:		
Cash received from issuance of capital stock	$25,000	
Dividends paid to stockholders	(3,000)	
Net cash flow from financing activities		22,000
Net cash flow and cash balance as of October 31, 2007		$26,650

Exercise 1-27

Accounting concepts

Goal **4**

Match each of the following statements with the appropriate accounting concept. Some concepts may be used more than once, while others may not be used at all. Use the notations below to indicate the appropriate accounting concept.

Accounting Concept	Notation
Accounting period concept	P
Adequate disclosure concept	D
Business entity concept	B
Cost concept	C
Going concern concept	G
Matching concept	M
Objectivity concept	O
Unit of measure concept	U

Statements

1. This concept justifies recording only transactions that are expressed in dollars.
2. Material litigation involving the corporation is described in a footnote.
3. If this concept was ignored, the confidence of users in the financial statements could not be maintained.
4. Personal transactions of owners are kept separate from the business.
5. Changes in the use of accounting methods from one period to the next are described in the notes to the financial statements.
6. This concept supports relying on an independent actuary (statistician), rather than the chief operating officer of the corporation, to estimate a pension liability.
7. July utilities costs are reported as expenses along with the July revenues.
8. The changes in financial condition are reported for November.
9. Land worth $800,000 is reported at its original purchase price of $220,000.
10. Assume that a business will continue forever.

Exercise 1-28

Business entity concept

Goal **5**

Bechler Sports sells hunting and fishing equipment and provides guided hunting and fishing trips. Bechler Sports is owned and operated by Lefty Wisman, a well-known sports enthusiast and hunter. Lefty's wife, Betsy, owns and operates Eagle Boutique, a women's clothing store. Lefty and Betsy have established a trust fund to finance their children's college education. The trust fund is maintained by First Montana Bank in the name of the children, Jeff and Steph.

For each of the following transactions, identify which of the entities listed should record the transaction in its records.

Entities	
B	Bechler Sports
F	First Montana Bank
E	Eagle Boutique
X	None of the above

1. Lefty paid a local doctor for his annual physical, which was required by the workmen's compensation insurance policy carried by Bechler Sports.
2. Lefty received a cash advance from customers for a guided hunting trip.
3. Betsy purchased two dozen spring dresses from a Billings (MT) designer for a special spring sale.
4. Betsy deposited a $2,000 personal check in the trust fund at First Montana Bank.
5. Lefty paid for an advertisement in a hunters' magazine.
6. Betsy purchased mutual fund shares as an investment for the children's trust.
7. Lefty paid for dinner and a movie to celebrate their twentieth wedding anniversary.

8. Betsy donated several dresses from inventory for a local charity auction for the benefit of a women's abuse shelter.
9. Betsy paid her dues to the YWCA.
10. Lefty paid a breeder's fee for an English springer spaniel to be used as a hunting guide dog.

ACCOUNTING APPLICATION PROBLEMS

Problem 1-1A

Income statement, retained earnings statement, and balance sheet

Goal 4

Net income: $55,550

SPREADSHEET

The amounts of the assets and liabilities of Chickadee Travel Service at April 30, 2006, the end of the current year, and its revenue and expenses for the year are listed below. The retained earnings were $35,000, and the capital stock was $15,000 at May 1, 2005, the beginning of the current year. Dividends of $30,000 were paid during the current year.

Accounts payable	$ 12,200
Accounts receivable	31,350
Cash	53,050
Fees earned	263,200
Miscellaneous expense	2,950
Rent expense	37,800
Supplies	3,350
Supplies expense	7,100
Taxes expense	5,600
Utilities expense	22,500
Wages expense	131,700

Instructions

1. Prepare an income statement for the current year ended April 30, 2006.
2. Prepare a retained earnings statement for the current year ended April 30, 2006.
3. Prepare a balance sheet as of April 30, 2006.

Problem 1-2A

Missing amounts from financial statements

Goal 4

j. $40,440

SPREADSHEET

The financial statements at the end of Ameba Realty's first month of operations are shown below.

Ameba Realty
Income Statement
For the Month Ended June 30, 2006

Fees earned		$18,800
Operating expenses:		
Wages expense	$ (a)	
Rent expense	1,920	
Supplies expense	1,600	
Utilities expense	1,080	
Miscellaneous expenses	660	
Total operating expenses		9,560
Net income		$ (b)

Ameba Realty
Retained Earnings Statement
For the Month Ended June 30, 2006

Net income for June	$ (c)	
Less dividends	(d)	
Retained earnings, June 30, 2006		$ (e)

Ameba Realty
Balance Sheet
June 30, 2006

Assets		
Cash		$11,800
Supplies		800
Land		(f)
Total assets		$ (g)
Liabilities		
Accounts payable		$ 960
Stockholders' Equity		
Capital stock	$ (h)	
Retained earnings	(i)	(j)
Total liabilities and stockholders' equity		$ (k)

Ameba Realty
Statement of Cash Flows
For the Month Ended June 30, 2006

Cash flows from operating activities:		
Cash received from customers	$ (l)	
Deduct cash payments for expenses and payments to creditors	9,400	
Net cash flows from operating activities		$ (m)
Cash flows from investing activities:		
Cash payments for acquisition of land		28,800
Cash flows from financing activities:		
Cash received from issuing capital stock	$36,000	
Deduct dividends	4,800	
Net cash flows from financing activities		(n)
Net cash flow and June 30, 2006, cash balance		$ (o)

Instructions

1. Would you classify a realty business like Ameba Realty as a manufacturing, merchandising, or service business?
2. By analyzing the interrelationships between the financial statements, determine the proper amounts for (a) through (o).

Problem 1-3A

Income statement, retained earnings statement, and balance sheet

Goal 4

Net income, $705

SPREADSHEET

The following financial data were adapted from the annual report of Best Buy Inc. for the period ending February 28, 2004:

	In millions
Accounts payable	$ 2,535
Accrued liabilities	1,598
Capital stock	954
Cash	2,600
Cost of goods sold	18,350
Income taxes	496
Interest expense and other items	103
Inventories	2,607
Goodwill and other intangible assets	514
Other assets	344
Other liabilities	1,097
Property, plant, and equipment	2,244
Receivables	343
Sales	24,547
Selling, general, and administrative expenses	4,893

Instructions

1. Prepare Best Buy's income statement for the year ending February 28, 2004.
2. Prepare Best Buy's retained earnings statement for the year ending February 28, 2004. (*Note*: The retained earnings at February 28, 2003, was $1,893. During the year, Best Buy paid dividends of $130.)
3. Prepare a balance sheet as of February 28, 2004, for Best Buy.

Problem 1-4A

Statement of cash flows

Goal 4

Net decrease in cash, $427

SPREADSHEET

The following cash data were adapted from the annual report of Apple Computer Inc. for the period ended September 25, 2004. The cash balance as of September 26, 2003, was $3,396 (in millions).

	In millions
Receipts from issuing capital stock	$ 427
Payments for property, plant, and equipment	176
Payments for purchase of other investments	1,312
Payments for long-term debt	300
Net cash flows from operating activities	934

Instructions

Prepare Apple's statement of cash flows for the year ended September 25, 2004.

Problem 1-5A

Financial statements, including statement of cash flows

Goal 4

1. Net income, $315,000

SPREADSHEET

Conwell Corporation began operations on January 1, 2007, as an online retailer of computer software and hardware. The following financial statement data were taken from Conwell's records at the end of its first year of operations, December 31, 2007.

Accounts payable	$ 42,000
Accounts receivable	67,200
Capital stock	350,000
Cash	?
Cash payments for operating activities	980,000
Cash receipts from operating activities	1,171,800
Cost of sales	560,000
Dividends	35,000
Income tax expense	196,000
Income taxes payable	28,000
Interest expense	21,000

Inventories	$ 126,000
Note payable (due in 2015)	140,000
Property, plant, and equipment	529,200
Retained earnings	?
Sales	1,239,000
Selling and administrative expense	147,000

Instructions

1. Prepare an income statement for the year ended December 31, 2007.
2. Prepare a retained earnings statement for the year ended December 31, 2007.
3. Prepare a balance sheet as of December 31, 2007.
4. Prepare a statement of cash flows for the year ended December 31, 2007.

ALTERNATE ACCOUNTING APPLICATION PROBLEMS

Alternate Problem 1-1B

Financial statements

Goal 4

Net income: $71,400

SPREADSHEET

Following are the amounts of the assets and liabilities of Greco Travel Agency at December 31, 2006, the end of the current year, and its revenue and expenses for the year. The retained earnings were $8,700, and the capital stock was $7,500 on January 1, 2006, the beginning of the current year. During the current year, dividends of $47,000 were paid.

Accounts payable	$ 5,120	Rent expense	$36,000
Accounts receivable	31,200	Supplies	3,000
Cash	11,520	Supplies expense	4,500
Fees earned	188,000	Utilities expense	16,500
Miscellaneous expense	2,800	Wages expense	56,800

Instructions

1. Prepare an income statement for the current year ended December 31, 2006.
2. Prepare a retained earnings statement for the current year ended December 31, 2006.
3. Prepare a balance sheet as of December 31, 2006.

Alternate Problem 1-2B

Missing amounts from financial statements

Goal 4

j. $30,000

SPREADSHEET

The financial statements at the end of Zeppelin Realty's first month of operations are shown below and on the next page.

Zeppelin Realty
Income Statement
For the Month Ended November 30, 2006

Fees earned		$ (a)
Operating expenses:		
Wages expense	$8,500	
Rent expense	3,200	
Supplies expense	(b)	
Utilities expense	1,800	
Miscellaneous expense	1,100	
Total operating expenses		17,600
Net income		$12,400

Zeppelin Realty
Retained Earnings Statement
For the Month Ended November 30, 2006

Net income for November	$ (c)	
Less dividends	6,000	
Retained earnings, November 30, 2006		$ (d)

Zeppelin Realty
Balance Sheet
November 30, 2006

Assets		
Cash		$ 5,800
Supplies		2,200
Land		40,000
Total assets		$ (e)
Liabilities		
Accounts payable		$ 1,600
Stockholders' Equity		
Capital stock	$ (f)	
Retained earnings	(g)	(h)
Total liabilities and stockholders' equity		$ (i)

Zeppelin Realty
Statement of Cash Flows
For the Month Ended November 30, 2006

Cash flows from operating activities:		
Cash received from customers	$ (j)	
Deduct cash payments for expenses and payments to creditors	18,200	
Net cash flows from operating activities		$ (k)
Cash flows from investing activities:		
Cash payments for acquisition of land		(l)
Cash flows from financing activities:		
Cash received from issuing capital stock	$ (m)	
Deduct cash dividends	(n)	
Net cash flows from financing activities		(o)
Net cash flow and November 30, 2006, cash balance		$ (p)

Instructions

1. Would you classify a realty business like Zeppelin Realty as a manufacturing, merchandising, or service business?
2. By analyzing the interrelationships among the four financial statements, determine the proper amounts for (a) through (p).

Alternate Problem 1-3B

Income statement, retained earnings statement, and balance sheet

Goal **4**

1. Net income, $4,304

SPREADSHEET

The following financial data were adapted from the annual report of Home Depot for the period ended February 1, 2004.

	In millions
Accounts payable	$ 7,764
Accounts receivable	1,097
Capital stock	2,727
Cash	2,826
Cost of goods sold	44,236
Dividends	595
Income taxes	2,539
Interest expense	62
Inventories	9,076
Long-term debt	2,332
Other assets	1,375
Other expense	27
Other liabilities	1,934
Property, plant, and equipment	20,063
Sales	64,816
Selling, general, and administrative expenses	13,648

Instructions

1. Prepare Home Depot's income statement for the year ended February 1, 2004.
2. Prepare Home Depot's retained earnings statement for the year ended February 1, 2004. (*Note*: The retained earnings at February 2, 2003, was $15,971.)
3. Prepare a balance sheet as of February 1, 2004, for Home Depot.

Alternate Problem 1-4B

Statement of cash flows

Goal **4**

Net decrease in cash, $54,170

SPREADSHEET

The following cash data were adapted from the annual report of Harley-Davidson, Inc., for the period ended December 31, 2004. The cash balance as of January 1, 2004, was $329,329 (in thousands).

	In thousands
Cash receipts from issuing debt	$ 305,047
Cash payments for capital stock repurchases	501,961
Cash payments for dividends	119,232
Cash from investing activities	1,189
Cash payments for investments	495,389
Cash payments for property, plant, and equipment	213,550
Net cash flows from operating activities	969,726

Instructions

Prepare Harley-Davidson's statement of cash flows for the year ended December 31, 2004.

Alternate Problem 1-5B

Financial statements, including statement of cash flows

Goal 4

1. Net income, $243,000

SPREADSHEET

Shiver Corporation began operations on September 1, 2006, as an online retailer of camping and outdoor recreational equipment. The following financial statement data were taken from Shiver's records at the end of its first year of operations, August 31, 2007:

Accounts payable	$ 32,400
Accounts receivable	51,840
Cash	?
Cash receipts from operating activities	903,960
Cash payments for operating activities	756,000
Capital stock	270,000
Cost of sales	432,000
Dividends	27,000
Income tax expense	151,200
Income taxes payable	21,600
Interest expense	16,200
Inventories	97,200
Note payable (due in 2015)	108,000
Property, plant, and equipment	408,240
Retained earnings	?
Sales	955,800
Selling and administrative expense	113,400

Instructions

1. Prepare an income statement for the year ended August 31, 2007.
2. Prepare a retained earnings statement for the year ended August 31, 2007.
3. Prepare a balance sheet as of August 31, 2007.
4. Prepare a statement of cash flows for the year ended August 31, 2007.

FINANCIAL ANALYSIS AND REPORTING

Case 1-1

Hershey's annual report

The financial statements of Hershey Foods Corporation are shown in Exhibits 4 through 7 of this chapter. Based upon these statements, answer the following questions.

1. What are Hershey's sales (in millions)?
2. What is Hershey's cost of sales (in millions)?
3. What is Hershey's net income (in millions)?
4. What is Hershey's percent of the cost of sales to sales? Round to one decimal place.
5. The percent that a company adds to its cost of sales to determine the selling price is called a markup. What is Hershey's markup percent? Round to one decimal place.
6. What is the percentage of net income to sales for Hershey? Round to one decimal place.

Case 1-2

Income statement analysis

The following data (in thousands of dollars) were adapted from the December 31, 2004, financial statements of Tootsie Roll Industries Inc.:

Sales	$420,110
Cost of goods sold	244,501
Net income	64,174

1. What is Tootsie Roll's percent of the cost of sales to sales? Round to one decimal place.
2. The percent a company adds to its cost of sales to determine selling price is called a markup. What is Tootsie Roll's markup percent? Round to one decimal place.

3. What is the percentage of net income to sales for Tootsie Roll? Round to one decimal place.
4. Compare your answers to (2) and (3) with those of Hershey Foods Corporation in Case 1-1. What are your conclusions?

Case 1-3

Horizontal analysis

The following data (in millions of dollars) were adapted from the January 29, 2005 and 2004 financial statements of The GAP Inc.:

For year ending	2005	2004
Sales	$16,267	$15,854
Cost of sales	9,886	9,885
Operating expenses	4,296	4,068

1. Prepare a horizontal analysis income statement for GAP that includes gross profit and operating income before taxes. Round to one decimal place.
2. Comment on the results of your horizontal analysis of GAP.

Case 1-4

Horizontal analysis

SPREADSHEET

The telecommunications industry suffered a severe business downturn during the early part of this decade. Lucent Technologies Inc. is one of the major equipment providers to this industry. Below are the comparative income statements for Lucent Technologies for the fiscal years ended September 30, 2004 and 2003.

Lucent Technologies Inc.
Consolidated Statements of Income
For the Years Ended September 30, 2004 and 2003

	In millions	
	2004	2003
Revenues	$ 9,045	$ 8,470
Costs of revenues	5,266	5,818
Gross profit	$ 3,779	$ 2,652
Operating expenses:		
Selling, general, and administrative	$ 1,296	$ 1,509
Research and development	1,270	1,488
Total operating expenses	$ 2,566	$ 2,997
Operating income (loss)	$ 1,213	$ (345)
Other income (expense)—net	246	(305)
Interest expense	(396)	(353)
Income (loss) from continuing operations before income tax (expense) benefit	$ 1,063	$ (1,003)
Income tax (expense) benefit	939	233
Income (loss) from continuing operations	$ 2,002	$ (770)

1. Prepare a horizontal analysis income statement for Lucent Technologies.
2. Interpret your analysis.

Case 1-5

Financial analysis of Enron Corporation

Enron Corporation, headquartered in Houston, Texas, provides products and services for natural gas, electricity, and communications to wholesale and retail customers. Enron's operations are conducted through a variety of subsidiaries and affiliates that involve transporting gas through pipelines, transmitting electricity, and managing energy commodities. The following data were taken from Enron's December 31, 2000, financial statements.

	In millions
Total revenues	$100,789
Total costs and expenses	98,836
Operating income	1,953
Net income	979
Total assets	65,503
Total liabilities	54,033
Total stockholders' equity	11,470
Net cash flows from operating activities	4,779
Net cash flows from investing activities	(4,264)
Net cash flows from financing activities	571
Net increase in cash	1,086

At the end of 2000, the market price of Enron's stock was approximately $83 per share. As of April 17, 2005, Enron's stock was selling for $0.03 per share.

Review the preceding financial statement data and search the Internet for articles on Enron Corporation. Briefly explain why Enron's stock dropped so dramatically in such a short time.

Case 1-6

Horizontal revenue analysis

United Parcel Service provides parcel delivery services around the world. The following table shows the various revenue sources for the comparative years ended December 31, 2004 and 2003:

	2004	2003
Revenue (in millions):		
U.S. domestic package:		
Next Day Air	$ 6,040	$ 5,580
Two-to-Three Day Air	3,161	2,982
Ground	17,409	16,460
Total U.S. domestic package	$26,610	$25,022
International package:		
Domestic	$ 1,346	$ 1,134
Export	4,944	4,001
Cargo	472	426
Total international package	$ 6,762	$ 5,561
Non-package:		
UPS Supply Chain Solutions (consulting services)	$ 2,346	$ 2,126
Other	864	776
Total non-package	$ 3,210	$ 2,902
Total	$36,582	$33,485

1. Provide a horizontal analysis of UPS revenues.
2. Why is the total percentage change not equal to the sum of the percentage changes for each of the major subcategories (U.S. domestic, international, and non-package)?
3. Interpret the horizontal analysis.

BUSINESS ACTIVITIES AND RESPONSIBILITY ISSUES

Activity 1-1

Integrity, objectivity, and ethics at Hershey Foods

The management of Hershey Foods has asked union workers in two of their highest cost Pennsylvania plants to accept higher health insurance premiums and take a wage cut. The worker's portion of the insurance cost would double from 6% of the premium to 12%. In addition, workers hired after January 2000 would have their hourly wages cut by $4, which would be partially offset by a 2% annual raise. Management says that the plants need to be more cost competitive. The management has indicated that if the workers accept the proposal that the company would invest $30 million to modernize the plants and move future projects to the plants. Management, however, has refused to guarantee more work at the plants if the workers approve the proposal. If the workers reject the proposal, management implies that they would move future projects to other plants and that layoffs might be forthcoming. Do you consider management's actions ethical?

Source: Susan Govzdas, "Hershey to Cut Jobs or Wages," *Central Penn Business Journal*, September 24, 2004.

Activity 1-2

Ethics and professional conduct in business

GROUP ACTIVITY

Sue Alejandro, president of Tobago Enterprises, applied for a $300,000 loan from First National Bank. The bank requested financial statements from Tobago Enterprises as a basis for granting the loan. Sue has told her accountant to provide the bank with a balance sheet. Sue has decided to omit the other financial statements because there was a net loss during the past year.

In groups of three or four, discuss the following questions:

1. Is Sue behaving in a professional manner by omitting some of the financial statements?
2. a. What types of information about their businesses would owners be willing to provide bankers? What types of information would owners not be willing to provide?
   b. What types of information about a business would bankers want before extending a loan?
   c. What common interests are shared by bankers and business owners?

Activity 1-3

How businesses make money

GROUP ACTIVITY

Assume that you are the chief executive officer for Gold Kist Inc., a national poultry producer. The company's operations include hatching chickens through the use of breeder stock and feeding, raising, and processing the mature chicks into finished products. The finished products include breaded chicken nuggets and patties and deboned, skinless, and marinated chicken. Gold Kist sells its products to schools, military services, fast food chains, and grocery stores.

In groups of four or five, discuss the following business emphasis and risk issues:

1. In a commodity business like poultry production, what do you think is the dominant business emphasis? What are the implications in this dominant emphasis for how you would run Gold Kist?
2. Identify at least two major business risks for operating Gold Kist.
3. How could Gold Kist try to differentiate its products?

Activity 1-4

Net income vs. cash flow

On January 3, 2007, Dr. Rosa Smith established First Opinion, a medical practice organized as a professional corporation. The following conversation occurred the following August between Dr. Smith and a former medical school classmate, Dr. Brett Wommack, at an American Medical Association convention in Nassau.

Dr. Wommack: Rosa, good to see you again. Why didn't you call when you were in Las Vegas? We could have had dinner together.

Dr. Smith: Actually, I never made it to Las Vegas this year. My husband and kids went up to our Lake Tahoe condo twice, but I got stuck in New York. I opened a new consulting practice this January and haven't had any time for myself since.

Dr. Wommack: I heard about it . . . First . . . something . . . right?

Dr. Smith: Yes, First Opinion. My husband chose the name.

Dr. Wommack: I've thought about doing something like that. Are you making any money? I mean, is it worth your time?

Dr. Smith: You wouldn't believe it. I started by opening a bank account with $60,000, and my July bank statement has a balance of $240,000. Not bad for seven months—all pure profit.

Dr. Wommack: Maybe I'll try it in Las Vegas. Let's have breakfast together tomorrow and you can fill me in on the details.

Comment on Dr. Smith's statement that the difference between the opening bank balance ($60,000) and the July statement balance ($240,000) is pure profit.

Activity 1-5

The accounting equation

Obtain the annual reports for three well-known companies, such as Ford Motor Co., General Motors, IBM, Microsoft, or Amazon.com. These annual reports can be obtained from a library or the company's 10-K filing with the Securities and Exchange Commission at http://www.sec.gov/edgar.shtml.

To obtain annual report information, click on "Search for Company Filings." Next, click on "Search EDGAR Historical Archives." Key in the company name. EDGAR will list the reports available for the company. Click on the 10-K (or 10-K405) report for the year you want to download. If you wish, you can save the whole 10-K report to a file and then open it with your word processor.

Examine the balance sheet for each company and determine the total assets, liabilities, and stockholders' equity. Verify that total assets equal the total of the liabilities plus stockholders' equity.

Activity 1-6

Certification requirements for accountants

By satisfying certain specific requirements, accountants may become certified as public accountants (CPAs), management accountants (CMAs), or internal auditors (CIAs). Find the certification requirements for one of these accounting groups by accessing the appropriate Internet site listed below.

Site	Description
http://www.ais-cpa.com	This site lists the address and/or Internet link for each state's board of accountancy. Find your state's requirements.
http://www.imanet.org	This site lists the requirements for becoming a CMA.
http://www.theiia.org	This site lists the requirements for becoming a CIA.

ANSWERS TO SELF-STUDY QUESTIONS

1. **D** A corporation, organized in accordance with state or federal statutes, is a separate legal entity in which ownership is divided into shares of stock (answer D). A proprietorship (answer A) is an unincorporated business owned by one individual. A service business (answer B) provides services to its customers. It can be organized as a proprietorship, partnership, or corporation. A partnership (answer C) is an unincorporated business owned by two or more individuals.

2. **A** The resources owned by a business are called assets (answer A). The debts of the business are called liabilities (answer B), and the equity of the owners is called stockholders' equity (answer D). The relationship between assets, liabilities, and stockholders' equity is expressed as the accounting equation (answer C).

3. **A** The balance sheet is a listing of the assets, liabilities, and stockholders' equity of a business at a specific date (answer A). The income statement (answer B) is a summary of the revenue and expenses of a business for a specific period of time. The retained earnings statement (answer C) summarizes the changes in retained earnings during a specific period of time. The statement of cash flows (answer D) summarizes the cash receipts and cash payments for a specific period of time.

4. **D** The accounting equation is:

Assets = Liabilities + Stockholders' Equity

Therefore, if assets are $20,000 and liabilities are $12,000, stockholders' equity is $8,000 (answer D), as indicated in the following computation:

Assets	= Liabilities + Stockholders' Equity
+$20,000	= +$12,000 + Stockholders' Equity
+$20,000 − $12,000	= Stockholders' Equity
+$8,000	= Stockholders' Equity

5. **B** Net income is the excess of revenue over expenses, or $7,500 (answer B). If expenses exceed revenue, the difference is a net loss. Dividends are the opposite of the stockholders investing in the business and do not affect the amount of net income or net loss.

2 Basic Accounting Concepts

Learning Goals

1. Describe the basic elements of a financial accounting system.
2. Analyze, record, and summarize transactions for a corporation's first period of operations.
3. Prepare financial statements for a corporation's first period of operations.
4. Analyze, record, and summarize transactions for a corporation's second period of operations.
5. Prepare financial statements for a corporation's second period of operations.
6. Describe and illustrate how vertical analysis can be used to analyze and evaluate a company's performance.

Wm. Wrigley Jr. Company

Suppose you were to receive $100 as a result of some event. Would it make a difference what the event was? Yes it would! If you received $100 for your birthday, it's a gift. If you received $100 as a result of working part time for a week, then it's the result of your effort. If you received $100 as a loan, then it's money that you would have to pay back in the future. If you received $100 as a result of selling your stereo, then it's the result of giving up something tangible. Thus, we see that the $100 received can be associated with different types of events, and that these events have different meanings to you. You'd much rather receive a $100 gift than a $100 loan, given the choice. Likewise, a company would also view events such as these differently.

For example, Wm. Wrigley Jr. Company receives money in return for providing a very simple, but widely used product: chewing gum. So, what's the attraction of gum?

Scientific studies have shown that chewing gum relaxes nerves and muscles, eases tension, facilitates concentration, helps keep one alert, helps keep teeth clean, and freshens breath. Even ancient civilizations recognized the benefits of gum. For example, the populace of early Greek civilizations chewed gum made from the bark of the mastic tree.

In addition to its gum, Wrigley is famous for its corporate headquarters building on North Michigan Avenue, along the north bank of the Chicago River. The Wrigley Building is a symbol of Chicago and has appeared in numerous articles, books, movies, and television programs, including *ER*, *My Best Friend's Wedding*, and *While You Were Sleeping*.

Wm. Wrigley Jr. Company's history is part of the lore of Chicago. As the company moves forward, its stakeholders are interested in its future financial condition and success. As we discussed in Chapter 1, the financial condition and changes in financial condition of a business are assessed through analyzing financial statements.

COURTESY WM. WRIGLEY JR. COMPANY

In this chapter, we continue our discussion of financial statements. We begin by describing the basic elements of a financial accounting system that will enable the preparation of financial statements. We then distinguish types of accounting systems and illustrate the simplest form of an accounting system based upon a cash basis. In doing so, this chapter will serve as foundation for our later discussions of modern day accounting systems and financial reporting.

Describe the basic elements of a financial accounting system.

ELEMENTS OF AN ACCOUNTING SYSTEM

A financial accounting system is designed to produce financial statements. You should recall from Chapter 1 that the basic financial statements are the income statement, retained earnings statement, balance sheet, and statement of cash flows. So what are the basic elements of an accounting system that will enable the preparation of these statements?

The basic elements of a **financial accounting system** include (1) a set of rules for determining what, when, and the amount that should be recorded for economic events, (2) a framework for preparing financial statements, and (3) one or more controls to determine whether errors may have arisen in the recording process. These basic elements are found in all financial accounting systems—from a local retailer or hardware store to Microsoft, Sony, Boeing, and Wrigley.

Q. The receipt of cash for capital stock affects what elements of the accounting equation?

A. *Total assets (cash) increases, and stockholders' equity (capital stock) increases.*

Rules

A set of rules for determining what, when, and the amount that should be recorded for an entity's economic events are derived from the eight concepts we discussed in Chapter 1. These concepts form the foundation for generally accepted accounting principles. Throughout this text, we describe and illustrate generally accepted accounting principles based upon these eight concepts.

A **transaction** is an economic event that under generally accepted accounting principles affects an element of the financial statements and, therefore, must be recorded. A transaction may affect one, two, or more elements of the financial statements. For example, equipment purchased for cash affects only assets. That is, one asset (equipment) increases while another asset (cash) decreases. If, on the other hand, the equipment is purchased on credit, both assets (equipment) and liabilities (accounts or notes payable) increase.

Framework

In order to prepare financial statements, transactions must be analyzed, recorded, and summarized using a framework. The accounting equation provides a starting point for designing such a framework. You should recall from Chapter 1 that the accounting equation is expressed as follows:

$$\text{Assets} = \text{Liabilities} + \text{Stockholders' Equity}$$

We use an *integrated financial statement approach* for analyzing, recording, and summarizing transactions by expanding the accounting equation as shown in Exhibit 1. We do this by including columns for the statement of cash flows, balance sheet, and income statement.

The left-hand column in Exhibit 1 shows the effects of transactions on the statement of cash flows. Each cash transaction is recorded and classified into operating, investing, and financing activities as a basis for preparing the statement of cash flows. The cash amount at the beginning of the period plus or minus the cash flows from operating, investing, and financing activities equals the end of the period cash. This end of the period cash amount is reported as an asset on the balance sheet. Thus, the statement of cash flows is integrated with the balance sheet.

The far right-hand column in Exhibit 1 records and summarizes revenue and expense transactions as a basis for preparing the income statement. Recall, net income, which is revenue less expenses, affects retained earnings. Thus, revenue and expense

Exhibit 1

Integrated Financial Statement Framework

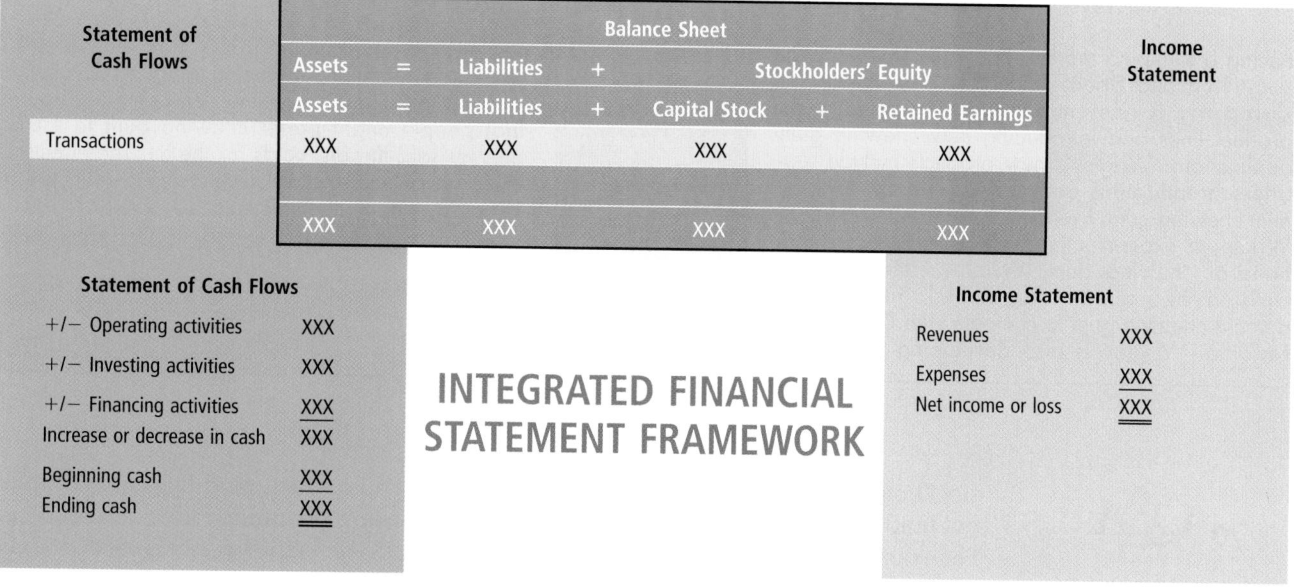

transactions are also recorded under the retained earnings column of the balance sheet. By doing so, the balance sheet is integrated with the income statement.

Exhibit 1 also illustrates the importance of the balance sheet as the connecting link between the statement of cash flows and the income statement.[1] Later in this chapter, we illustrate the use of this integrated financial statement approach for analyzing, recording, and summarizing transactions.

You will find the integrated financial statement approach, shown in Exhibit 1, an invaluable aid in analyzing the financial condition and changes in financial condition of a company. This is because, without understanding how a company's financial statements are prepared and integrated, you may miss important trends or events. To illustrate, assume a company reports net income (profits) on its income statement. This might lead you to mistakenly conclude that the company's operations are doing well and no major changes are necessary. In fact, if the company has negative net cash flows from operations, it may be headed toward bankruptcy. This is why it is essential to analyze all the financial statements and why we emphasize the integrated financial statement approach throughout this text.

Controls

The integrated financial statement approach shown in Exhibit 1 has built-in controls that transactions are analyzed, recorded, and summarized correctly. Specifically, the accounting equation ensures that total assets must equal total liabilities plus total

1 In Chapter 3, we describe and illustrate how balance sheet elements can be used to reconcile net cash flows from operating activities with net income.

HOW BUSINESSES MAKE MONEY

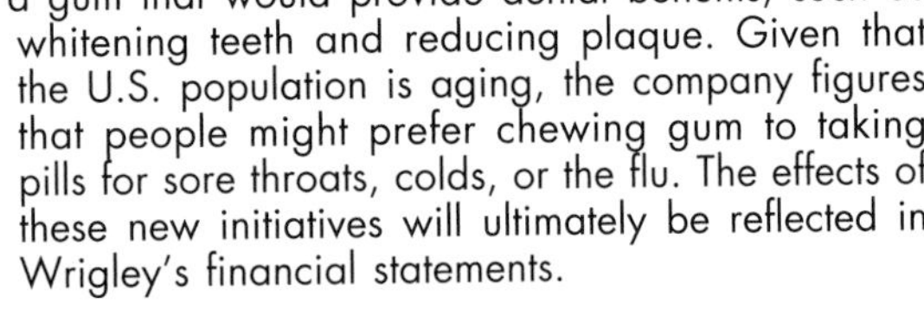

Got the Flu? Why Not Chew Some Gum?

Facing a slumping market for sugared chewing gum, such as Juicy Fruit and Doublemint, **Wm. Wrigley Jr. Company** is reinventing itself by expanding its product lines and introducing new chewing gum applications. Wrigley's new products include sugarless breath mints and more powerful flavored mint chewing gum, like Extra Polar Ice. In addition, Wrigley is experimenting with health-care applications of chewing gum. Wrigley's Health Care Division has already developed Surpass, an antacid chewing gum to compete with Rolaids and Mylanta. Wrigley is also developing a cold-relief chewing gum and a gum that would provide dental benefits, such as whitening teeth and reducing plaque. Given that the U.S. population is aging, the company figures that people might prefer chewing gum to taking pills for sore throats, colds, or the flu. The effects of these new initiatives will ultimately be reflected in Wrigley's financial statements.

Source: Adapted from "A Young Heir Has New Plans at Old Company," by David Barboza, *The New York Times*, August 28, 2001.

Q. When $3,000 of cash was received for fees earned, it was erroneously recorded as an increase in cash of $300 and an increase in retained earnings (fees earned) of $3,000. Will the accounting equation balance?

A. *No. Total assets will be less than total liabilities plus stockholders' equity by $2,700.*

stockholders' equity on the balance sheet. If at the end of the period this equality does not hold, then an error has occurred in either recording or summarizing transactions. For example, if a $10,000 purchase of equipment for cash is incorrectly recorded as an increase in both equipment and cash, the total assets will exceed the total liabilities and stockholders' equity by $20,000 at the end of the period. Likewise, if equipment was increased by $10,000, but cash was not decreased by $10,000, the total assets will exceed total liabilities and stockholders' equity by $10,000 at the end of the period. In both cases, the inequality of the equation will indicate that an error has occurred in the recording process.

The equality of the equation at the end of the period doesn't necessarily mean that no errors have occurred. For example, assume that a business purchased $10,000 of equipment on credit and recorded the transaction as an increase in equipment of $10,000. However, instead of increasing the liabilities by $10,000, the transaction was recorded as a $10,000 decrease in cash. In this case, the accounting equation still balances, even though cash and liabilities are understated by $10,000.

The integrated financial statement approach provides two additional controls. First, the ending cash amount shown in the statement of cash flows column must agree with the end of the period cash amount shown under assets in the balance sheet column. Second, the net income or loss from the income statement column must agree with the net effects of revenues and expenses on retained earnings.[2]

Analyze, record, and summarize transactions for a corporation's first period of operations.

RECORDING A CORPORATION'S FIRST PERIOD OF OPERATIONS

Using the integrated financial statement framework shown in Exhibit 1, we will illustrate the recording of transactions for a corporation's first period of operations. We will assume that on September 1, 2007, Lee Landry, M.D., organizes a professional corporation to practice general medicine. The business is to be known as Family Health Care, P.C, where P.C. refers to professional corporation. We describe each

2 We discuss additional accounting controls in Chapter 7.

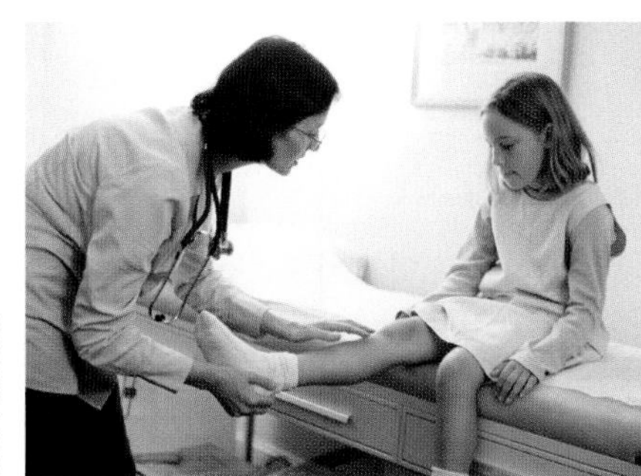

transaction or group of similar transactions during September, the first month of operations. We then illustrate how Exhibit 1 can be used to analyze, record, and summarize the effects of these transactions on the financial statements. We begin with Dr. Landry's investment to establish the business.

Transaction a. Dr. Landry deposits $6,000 in a bank account in the name of Family Health Care, P.C., in return for shares of stock in the corporation. We refer to stock issued to owners (stockholders) such as Lee Landry as capital stock. The effect of this transaction is to increase cash from financing activities by $6,000 under the statement of cash flows column. Increases are recorded as positive numbers, while decreases are recorded as negative numbers. In addition, the transaction increases assets (cash) in the left side of the accounting equation under the balance sheet column by $6,000. To balance the equation, the stockholders' equity (capital stock) on the right side of the equation is increased by the same amount. Since no revenues or expenses are affected, there are no entries under the income statement column. The effect of this transaction on Family Health Care's financial statements is shown below:

Statement of Cash Flows	Balance Sheet					Income Statement
	Assets	=	Liabilities	+	Stockholders' Equity	
	Cash	=		+	Capital Stock	
a. Investment by Dr. Landry	6,000				6,000	

Statement of Cash Flows	
a. Financing	6,000

Note that the equation relates only to the business, Family Health Care, P.C. Lee Landry's personal assets (such as a home or a personal bank account) and personal liabilities are excluded from the equation. The business is treated as a separate entity, with cash of $6,000 and stockholders' equity of $6,000.

Transaction b. Family Health Care's next transaction is to borrow $10,000 from First National Bank to finance its operations. To borrow the $10,000, Lee Landry signed a note payable in the name of Family Health Care. The note payable is a liability or a claim on assets that Family Health Care must satisfy (pay) in the future. In addition, the note payable requires the payment of interest of $100 per month until the note is due in full on September 30, 2012. At the end of September, we will record the payment of $100 of interest.

The effect of this transaction is to increase cash from financing activities by $10,000 under the statement of cash flows column. In addition, cash is increased and liabilities (notes payable) are increased under the balance sheet columns. Observe how this transaction changed the mix of assets and liabilities on the balance sheet but did not change Family Health Care's stockholders' equity. That is, assets minus liabilities still equals stockholders' equity of $6,000 on the balance sheet. Since no revenues or expenses are affected, no entries are made under the income statement column. The effect of this transaction on Family Health Care's financial statements follows.

Statement of Cash Flows	Balance Sheet					Income Statement
	Assets	=	Liabilities	+	Stockholders' Equity	
	Cash	=	Notes Payable	+	Capital Stock	
Balances	6,000				6,000	
b. Loan from bank	10,000		10,000			
Balances	16,000		10,000		6,000	

Statement of Cash Flows	
b. Financing	10,000

Transaction c. Next, Family Health Care buys land for $12,000 cash. The land is located near a new suburban hospital that is under construction. Lee Landry plans to rent office space and equipment for several months. When the hospital is completed, Family Health Care will build on the land.

The effect of this transaction is an outflow of cash as an investing activity. Thus, a negative $12,000 is entered in the statement of cash flows column as an investing activity. On the balance sheet, the purchase of the land changes the makeup of the assets, but it does not change the total assets. That is, cash is decreased and land is increased by $12,000. The effect of this transaction on Family Health Care's financial statements is shown below:

Statement of Cash Flows	Balance Sheet							Income Statement
	Assets			=	Liabilities	+	Stockholders' Equity	
	Cash	+	Land	=	Notes Payable	+	Capital Stock	
Balances	16,000				10,000		6,000	
c. Purchase of land	−12,000		12,000					
Balances	4,000		12,000		10,000		6,000	

Statement of Cash Flows	
c. Investing	−12,000

INTEGRITY, OBJECTIVITY, AND ETHICS IN BUSINESS

A History of Ethical Conduct

The Wrigley Company has a long history of integrity, objectivity, and ethical conduct. When pressured to become part of a cartel, known as the Chewing Gum Trust, the company founder, William Wrigley Jr., said, "We prefer to do business by fair and square methods or we prefer not to do business at all." In 1932, Phillip K. Wrigley, called "PK" by his friends, became president of the Wrigley Company after his father, William Wrigley Jr., died. PK also was president of the Chicago Cubs, which played in Wrigley Field. He was financially generous to his players and frequently gave them advice on and off the field. However, as a man of integrity and high ethical standards, PK docked (reduced) his salary as president of the Wrigley Company for the time he spent working on Cubs related activities and business.

Source: *St. Louis Post-Dispatch, "Sports—Backpages," January 26, 2003.*

Transactions (b) and (c) have not improved the stockholders' equity of Family Health Care. They have simply changed the mix of assets and increased the liability, notes payable. However, the objective of businesses is to improve stockholders' equity through operations.

Transaction d. During the first month of operations, Family Health Care earns patient fees of $5,500, receiving the amount in cash. The effect of this transaction is an inflow of cash flows from operating activities of $5,500. Thus, a positive $5,500 is entered in the statement of cash flows column as an operating activity. Since cash has been received, cash is increased by $5,500 under the balance sheet column for assets. Fees earned of $5,500 is a revenue item that is entered in the income statement column as a positive amount. Since net income retained in the business increases stockholders' equity (retained earnings) and since revenues contribute to net income, $5,500 is also entered as an increase in retained earnings in the stockholders' equity column of the balance sheet. Entering the increases of $5,500 for cash and retained earnings in the balance sheet columns retains the equality of the accounting equation. The effect of this transaction on Family Health Care's financial statements is summarized below:

Statement of Cash Flows	Balance Sheet									Income Statement
	Assets			=	Liabilities	+	Stockholders' Equity			
	Cash	+	Land	=	Notes Payable	+	Capital Stock	+	Retained Earnings	
Balances	4,000		12,000		10,000		6,000			
d. Fees earned	5,500								5,500	d.
Balances	9,500		12,000		10,000		6,000		5,500	

Statement of Cash Flows	
d. Operating	5,500

Income Statement
d. 5,500 Fees earned

Transaction e. For Family Health Care, the expenses paid during the month were as follows: wages, $1,125; rent, $950; utilities, $450; interest, $100; and miscellaneous, $275. Miscellaneous expenses include small amounts paid for such items as postage due and newspaper and magazine purchases.

The effect of this transaction is an outflow of cash of $2,900 for operating activities. Thus, a negative $2,900 is entered in the statement of cash flows column as an operating activity. Expenses have the opposite effect as revenues on net income and retained earnings. As a result, each of the expenses is listed as a negative amount in the income statement column. Finally, a negative $2,900 is also entered in the cash and retained earnings columns of the balance sheet. The effect of this transaction on Family Health Care's financial statements is summarized on the next page.

Transaction f. At the end of the month, Family Health Care pays $1,500 to stockholders (Dr. Lee Landry) as dividends. Dividends are distributions of business earnings to stockholders.

Statement of Cash Flows	Balance Sheet					Income Statement
	Assets		= Liabilities	+ Stockholders' Equity		
	Cash	+ Land	= Notes Payable	+ Capital Stock	+ Retained Earnings	
Balances	9,500	12,000	10,000	6,000	5,500	
e. Paid expenses	−2,900				−2,900	e.
Balances	6,600	12,000	10,000	6,000	2,600	

Statement of Cash Flows	
e. Operating	−2,900

Income Statement	
e. −1,125	Wages expense
−950	Rent expense
−450	Utilities expense
−100	Interest expense
−275	Misc. expense

The effect of this transaction is an outflow of cash of $1,500 for financing activities. Thus, a negative $1,500 is entered in the statement of cash flows column as a financing activity. In addition, the cash and retained earnings are decreased under the balance sheet column, by $1,500. The effect of this transaction on Family Health Care's financial statements is summarized below.

Statement of Cash Flows	Balance Sheet					Income Statement
	Assets		= Liabilities	+ Stockholders' Equity		
	Cash	+ Land	= Notes Payable	+ Capital Stock	+ Retained Earnings	
Balances	6,600	12,000	10,000	6,000	2,600	
f. Paid dividends	−1,500				−1,500	f.
Balances	5,100	12,000	10,000	6,000	1,100	

Statement of Cash Flows	
f. Financing	−1,500

You should be careful not to confuse dividends with expenses. Dividends do not represent assets consumed or services used in the process of earning revenues. The decrease in stockholders' equity from dividends is listed in the equation under "Retained Earnings." This is because dividends are considered a distribution of earnings to the owners.

The transactions of Family Health Care are summarized in Exhibit 2. The transactions are identified by letter, and the balances are shown as of the end of September. You should note that under the balance sheet columns the accounting equation balances. That is, total assets of $17,100 ($5,100 + $12,000) equals total liabilities plus stockholders' equity of $17,100 ($10,000 + $6,000 + $1,100).

International Perspective
International Accounting Standards (IASs) require the same four general financial statements that are required under U.S. GAAP. However, IAS only requires one year of historical financial information, while public companies in the United States are required to present three years of comparative financial information (two years for balance sheet information).

In reviewing the preceding illustration and Exhibit 2, you should note the following, which apply to all types of businesses:

1. The balance sheet reflects the accounting equation (assets = liabilities + stockholders' equity).
2. The two sides of the balance sheet (accounting equation) are always equal.
3. Every transaction affects (increases or decreases) one or more of the balance sheet elements—assets, liabilities, or stockholders' equity.
4. A transaction may or may not affect (increase or decrease) an element of the statement of cash flows or the income statement. Some transactions affect elements of both statements, some transactions affect only one statement and not the other, and some transactions affect neither statement.
5. The effect of every *cash* transaction increases or decreases the asset cash on the balance sheet. Every cash transaction also increases or decreases an operating, investing, or financing activity on the statement of cash flows.
6. The net increase or decrease in cash for the period shown in the statement of cash flows ($5,100 in Exhibit 2) agrees with the ending cash balance shown on the balance sheet. In this illustration, this resulted because it was the entity's first period of operations. In future periods, the net increase (decrease) in cash will be

Exhibit 2

Family Health Care Summary of Transactions for September

Statement of Cash Flows	Balance Sheet									Income Statement
	Assets			=	Liabilities	+	Stockholders' Equity			
	Cash	+	Land	=	Notes Payable	+	Capital Stock	+	Retained Earnings	
a. Investment by Dr. Landry	6,000						6,000			
b. Loan from bank	10,000				10,000					
c. Purchase of land	−12,000		12,000							
d. Fees earned	5,500								5,500	d.
e. Paid expenses	−2,900								−2,900	e.
f. Paid dividends	−1,500								−1,500	
Balances, Sept. 30	5,100		12,000		10,000		6,000		1,100	

Statement of Cash Flows

a. Financing	6,000
b. Financing	10,000
c. Investing	−12,000
d. Operating	5,500
e. Operating	−2,900
f. Financing	−1,500
Increase in cash and Sept. 30 cash	5,100

INTEGRATED FINANCIAL STATEMENT FRAMEWORK

Income Statement

d. +5,500	Fees earned
e. −1,125	Wages expense
−950	Rent expense
−450	Utilities expense
−100	Interest expense
−275	Misc. expense
2,600	Net income

added to (subtracted from) the beginning cash balance to equal the ending cash balance. This ending cash balance will appear in both the statement of cash flows and balance sheet.

7. The stockholders' equity is increased by amounts invested by stockholders (capital stock).
8. Revenues increase stockholders' equity (retained earnings) and expenses decrease stockholders' equity (retained earnings). The effects of revenue and expense transactions are also shown in the income statement column.
9. Stockholders' equity (retained earnings) is decreased by dividends distributed to stockholders.
10. The change in retained earnings for the period is the net income minus dividends. For a net loss, the change in retained earnings is the net loss plus dividends.
11. The statement of cash flows is linked to the balance sheet through cash (an asset).
12. The income statement is linked to the balance sheet through revenues and expenses (net income or loss), which affects retained earnings.

Exhibit 3 summarizes the effects of the various transactions affecting stockholders' equity.

Exhibit 3

Effects of Transactions on Stockholders' Equity

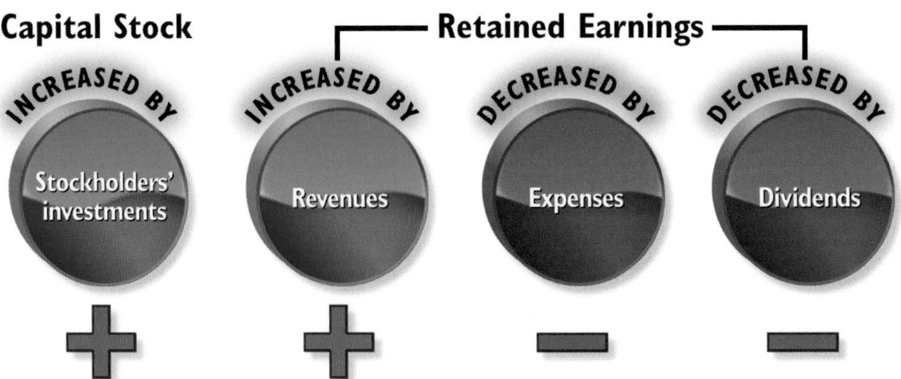

Prepare financial statements for a corporation's first period of operations.

FINANCIAL STATEMENTS FOR A CORPORATION'S FIRST PERIOD OF OPERATIONS

In Exhibit 2, the September transactions for Family Health Care are listed in the order that they occurred. This exhibit, however, is not very user-friendly in that it does not group and summarize like transactions together. As we described and illustrated in Chapter 1, the accounting reports that provide this summarized information are financial statements. Such financial statements can easily be prepared from the integrated financial statement framework shown in Exhibit 2.

The September financial statements for Family Health Care are illustrated in Exhibit 4. The data for the statements were taken from Exhibit 2.

Exhibit 4

Family Health Care Financial Statements for September

Family Health Care, P.C.
Income Statement
For the Month Ended September 30, 2007

Fees earned		$5,500
Operating expenses:		
Wages expense	$1,125	
Rent expense	950	
Utilities expense	450	
Interest expense	100	
Miscellaneous expenses	275	
Total operating expenses		2,900
Net income		$2,600

Family Health Care, P.C.
Retained Earnings Statement
For the Month Ended September 30, 2007

Net income for September	$2,600
Less dividends	1,500
Retained earnings, September 30, 2007	$1,100

Family Health Care, P.C.
Balance Sheet
September 30, 2007

Assets		
Cash		$ 5,100
Land		12,000
Total assets		$17,100
Liabilities		
Notes payable		$10,000
Stockholders' Equity		
Capital stock	$6,000	
Retained earnings	1,100	7,100
Total liabilities and stockholders' equity		$17,100

Exhibit 4
Concluded

Family Health Care, P.C.
Statement of Cash Flows
For the Month Ended September 30, 2007

Cash flows from operating activities:			
Cash received from customers	$ 5,500		
Deduct cash payments for expenses			2,900
Net cash flow from operating activities			$ 2,600
Cash flows from investing activities:			
Cash payments for acquisition of land			(12,000)
Cash flows from financing activities:			
Cash received from sale of capital stock	$ 6,000		
Cash received from notes payable	10,000	$16,000	
Deduct cash dividends		1,500	
Net cash flow from financing activities			14,500
Net increase in cash			$ 5,100
September 1, 2007, cash balance			0
September 30, 2007, cash balance			$ 5,100

The income statement is normally prepared first using the income statement column of Exhibit 2. The income statement is prepared first because the net income or loss is needed to prepare the retained earnings statement. The retained earnings statement is prepared next because the ending balance of retained earnings is needed for preparing the balance sheet. The retained earnings statement is prepared using the income statement and the amount recorded for dividends for the period. The balance sheet is prepared next using the balances as of September 30 shown in Exhibit 2. The statement of cash flows is normally prepared last using the statement of cash flows column of Exhibit 2. You should note that each financial statement is identified by the name of the business, the title of the statement, and the date or period of time.

Income Statement

As shown in Exhibit 4, the income statement for Family Health Care reports fees earned of $5,500, total operating expenses of $2,900, and net income of $2,600. The $5,500 of fees earned was taken from the income statement column of Exhibit 2. Likewise, the expenses were summarized from the income statement column of Exhibit 2 and reported under the heading "Operating expenses." The expenses were listed in order of size, beginning with the largest expense. Miscellaneous expense is usually shown as the last item, regardless of the amount. The total operating expenses were then subtracted from the fees earned to arrive at the net income of $2,600. The effect of this net income will be to increase retained earnings and stockholders' equity.

Retained Earnings Statement

Since Family Health Care has been in operation for only one month, it has no retained earnings at the beginning of September. The ending September balance is the change in retained earnings that results from net income and dividends. This change, $1,100, will be the beginning retained earnings balance for October.

Balance Sheet

The amounts of Family Health Care's assets, liabilities, and stockholders' equity as of September 30 appear on the last line of the balance sheet columns of Exhibit 2. The balance sheet is prepared as shown in Exhibit 4.

In the liabilities section of Family Health Care's balance sheet, notes payable is the only liability. When there are two or more categories of liabilities, each should be listed and the total amount of liabilities reported. Liabilities should be presented in the order that they will be paid in cash. Thus, the notes payable due in 2012 will be listed after the obligations that are due in shorter time periods.

For Family Health Care, the September 30, 2007, stockholders' equity consists of $6,000 of capital stock and retained earnings of $1,100. The retained earnings amount is also reported on the retained earnings statement.

Q. At January 1, 2007, total assets and total liabilities were $600,000 and $380,000, respectively. At December 31, 2007, total assets and total liabilities were $950,000 and $580,000, respectively. If dividends of $75,000 were paid in 2007, what was the net income or loss?

A. *$225,000 [($950,000 – $580,000) – ($600,000 – $380,000) + $75,000]*

Statement of Cash Flows

Family Health Care's statement of cash flows for September is prepared from the statement of cash flows column of Exhibit 2. Cash increased from a zero balance at the beginning of the month to $5,100 at the end of the month. This $5,100 increase in cash was a result of cash flows from operating activities of $2,600.

In addition to cash inflows of $2,600 from operating activities, Family Health Care spent $12,000 of cash for investing activities involving the purchase of land. This cash outflow related to investing activities was financed by an increased investment of $6,000 by Dr. Landry and $10,000 borrowed through a note payable at First National Bank. Family Health Care also distributed $1,500 in cash dividends during September.

Integration of Financial Statements

Exhibit 5 shows the integration of Family Health Care's financial statements for September. The ending cash balance of $5,100 on the balance sheet equals the ending cash balance reported on the statement of cash flows. The net income of $2,600 is reported on the income statement and the retained earnings statement. The ending retained earnings of $1,100 is reported in the retained earnings statement and the balance sheet. The cash flows from operating activities of $2,600 reported on the statement of cash flows equals the net income on the income statement. However, as we illustrate and explain in the next chapter, while cash flows from operating activities and net income are related they are normally not equal.

Analyze, record, and summarize the transactions for a corporation's second period of operations.

RECORDING A CORPORATION'S SECOND PERIOD OF OPERATIONS

To reinforce your understanding of recording transactions and preparing financial statements, we continue with Family Health Care's October transactions. During October, Family Health Care entered into the following transactions:

a. Received fees of $6,400 in cash.

b. Paid expenses in cash, as follows: wages, $1,370; rent, $950; utilities, $540; interest, $100; and miscellaneous, $220.

c. Paid dividends of $1,000 in cash.

Exhibit 5

Family Health Care Integrated Financial Statements for September

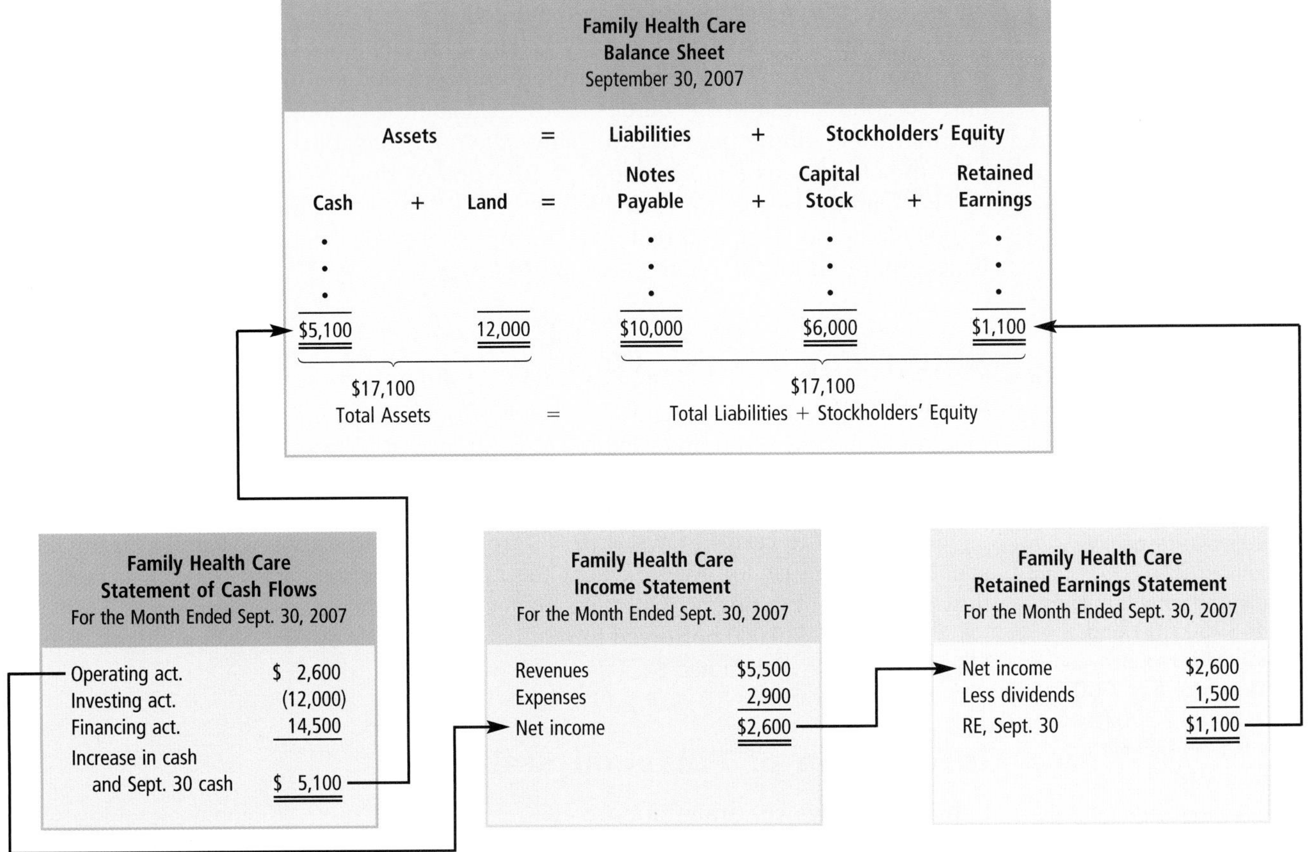

The preceding October transactions have been analyzed and entered into a summary of transactions for October, as shown in Exhibit 6. You should note that the balance sheet columns of Exhibit 6 begin with the ending balances as of September 30, 2006. This is because the balance sheet reports the cumulative total of the entity's assets, liabilities, and stockholders' equity since its inception. In other words, as of October 1, Family Health Care has cash of $5,100, land of $12,000, notes payable of $10,000, capital stock of $6,000, and retained earnings of $1,100. In contrast, the statement of cash flows and the income statement report only transactions for the period.

Prepare financial statements for a corporation's second period of operations.

FINANCIAL STATEMENTS FOR A CORPORATION'S SECOND PERIOD OF OPERATIONS

Family Health Care's financial statements for October are shown in Exhibit 7. These statements were prepared from the integrated financial statement framework shown in Exhibit 6.

The income statement for October reports net income of $3,220. This is an increase of $620, or 23.8% ($620/$2,600), from September's net income of $2,600. This increase in net income was due to fees increasing from $5,500 to $6,400, a $900, or 16.4% ($900/$5,500), increase from September. At the same time, total operating expenses

Exhibit 6

Family Health Care Summary of Transactions for October

Statement of Cash Flows	Cash	+	Land	=	Notes Payable	+	Capital Stock	+	Retained Earnings	Income Statement
	Balance Sheet									
	Assets			=	**Liabilities**	+	**Stockholders' Equity**			
Balances, Oct. 1	5,100		12,000		10,000		6,000		1,100	
a. Fees earned	6,400								6,400	a.
b. Paid expenses	−3,180								−3,180	b.
c. Paid dividends	−1,000								−1,000	
Balances, Oct. 31	7,320		12,000		10,000		6,000		3,320	

Statement of Cash Flows

a. Operating	6,400
b. Operating	−3,180
c. Financing	−1,000
Increase in cash	2,220

INTEGRATED FINANCIAL STATEMENT FRAMEWORK

Income Statement

a.	6,400	Fees earned
b.	−1,370	Wages expense
	−950	Rent expense
	−540	Utilities expense
	−100	Interest expense
	−220	Misc. expense
	3,220	Net income

increased only $280, or 9.7% ($280/$2,900). This suggests that Family Health Care's operations are profitable and expanding.

The retained earnings statement reports an increase in retained earnings of $2,220. This increase is the result of net income ($3,220) less the dividends ($1,000) paid to Dr. Landry.

The balance sheet shows that total assets increased from $17,100 on September 30, 2007, to $19,320 on October 31. This increase of $2,220 was due to an increase in cash from operations of $3,220 less the dividends of $1,000 that were paid to Dr. Landry.

Exhibit 7

Family Health Care Financial Statements for October

Family Health Care, P.C.
Income Statement
For the Month Ended October 31, 2007

Fees earned		$6,400
Operating expenses:		
Wages expense	$1,370	
Rent expense	950	
Utilities expense	540	
Interest expense	100	
Miscellaneous expenses	220	
Total operating expenses		3,180
Net income		$3,220

Exhibit 7
Concluded

Family Health Care, P.C.
Retained Earnings Statement
For the Month Ended October 31, 2007

Retained earnings, October 1, 2007		$1,100
Net income for October	$3,220	
Less dividends	1,000	2,220
Retained earnings, October 31, 2007		$3,320

Family Health Care, P.C.
Balance Sheet
October 31, 2007

Assets		
Cash		$ 7,320
Land		12,000
Total assets		$19,320
Liabilities		
Notes payable		$10,000
Stockholders' Equity		
Capital stock	$6,000	
Retained earnings	3,320	9,320
Total liabilities and stockholders' equity		$19,320

Family Health Care, P.C.
Statement of Cash Flows
For the Month Ended October 31, 2007

Cash flows from operating activities:	
Cash received from customers	$ 6,400
Deduct cash payments for expenses	3,180
Net cash flow from operating activities	$ 3,220
Cash flows from investing activities	0
Cash flows from financing activities:	
Deduct cash dividends	(1,000)
Net increase in cash	$ 2,220
October 1, 2007, cash balance	5,100
October 31, 2007, cash balance	$ 7,320

Total liabilities remained the same, but retained earnings and stockholders' equity increased by $2,220.

The statement of cash flows shows net cash receipts from operations of $3,220 and a cash payment for dividends of $1,000. The ending cash balance of $7,320 also appears on the October 31 balance sheet. The integration of these statements is shown in Exhibit 8.

Exhibit 8

Family Health Care Integrated Financial Statements for October

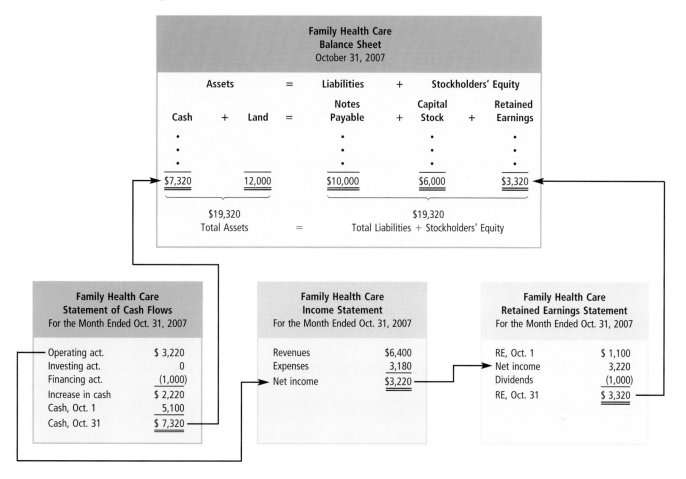

Family Health Care
Balance Sheet
October 31, 2007

Assets			=	Liabilities	+	Stockholders' Equity		
Cash	+	Land	=	Notes Payable	+	Capital Stock	+	Retained Earnings
$7,320		12,000		$10,000		$6,000		$3,320

$19,320 Total Assets = $19,320 Total Liabilities + Stockholders' Equity

Family Health Care
Statement of Cash Flows
For the Month Ended Oct. 31, 2007

Operating act.	$ 3,220
Investing act.	0
Financing act.	(1,000)
Increase in cash	$ 2,220
Cash, Oct. 1	5,100
Cash, Oct. 31	$ 7,320

Family Health Care
Income Statement
For the Month Ended Oct. 31, 2007

Revenues	$6,400
Expenses	3,180
Net income	$3,220

Family Health Care
Retained Earnings Statement
For the Month Ended Oct. 31, 2007

RE, Oct. 1	$ 1,100
Net income	3,220
Dividends	(1,000)
RE, Oct. 31	$ 3,320

VERTICAL ANALYSIS

6 Describe and illustrate how vertical analysis can be used to analyze and evaluate a company's performance.

The basic financial statements illustrated in this and the preceding chapter are primary sources of information that financial analysts and other stakeholders use in evaluating a company's performance. In Chapter 1, we illustrated horizontal analysis as one method of analyzing financial performance. Another method of analyzing comparative financial statements is to compute percentages of each item within a statement to a total within the statement. These percentages can then be compared across years. This type of analysis is called **vertical analysis**.

© TIM BOYLE/GETTY IMAGES

In vertical analysis of the balance sheet, each asset item is stated as a percent of the total assets. Each liability and stockholders' equity item is stated as a percent of total liabilities and stockholders' equity. To illustrate, Exhibit 9 shows comparative balance sheets for Wm. Wrigley Jr. Company, using vertical analysis.[3]

3 These financial statements have been adapted, based upon Securities and Exchange Commission filings.

Exhibit 9

Comparative Balance Sheets Using Vertical Analysis: Wm. Wrigley Jr. Company

	December 31, 2004		December 31, 2003	
	Amount (millions)	Percent	Amount (millions)	Percent
Assets:				
Cash and cash equivalents	$ 629	19.9%	$ 505	20.0%
Short-term investments	23	0.7	23	0.9
Accounts receivable	356	11.2	329	13.0
Inventories	398	12.6	350	13.9
Property, plant, and equipment	1,143	36.1	956	37.8
Other assets	618	19.5	365	14.4
TOTAL ASSETS	$3,167	100.0%	$2,528	100.0%
Liabilities:				
Current liabilities	$ 718	22.7%	$ 472	18.7%
Long-term liabilities	270	8.5	235	9.3
Total liabilities	$ 988	31.2%	$ 707	28.0%
Stockholders' equity:				
Total stockholders' equity	$2,179	68.8%	$1,821	72.0%
TOTAL LIABILITIES AND STOCKHOLDERS' EQUITY	$3,167	100.0%	$2,528	100.0%

To simplify, the current liabilities and stockholders' equity are shown as a single amount. A review of Exhibit 9 reveals the liabilities as a percent of total liabilities and stockholders' equity increased by 3.2 (31.2% − 28.0%) percentage points, while the stockholders' equity decreased by 3.2 (72.0% − 68.8%) percentage points between the comparative years. Other than this minor change, no major changes occurred in the makeup of Wrigley's December 31 balance sheets for 2004 and 2003.

In vertical analysis of the income statement, each item is stated as a percent of sales. To illustrate, Exhibit 10 shows comparative income statements of Wm. Wrigley Jr. Company, using vertical analysis.

Exhibit 10 reveals a slight decline in overall net income as a percent of sales from 14.6% to 13.6% between the two years. Gross profit as a percent of sales declined over a full percentage point from 57.1% to 55.9%. In addition, selling and administrative expenses increased slightly as a percent of sales from 35.9% to 36.1%. As a result,

Exhibit 10

Comparative Income Statements Using Vertical Analysis: Wm. Wrigley Jr. Company for Years Ending December 31, 2003 and 2004

	2004		2003	
	Amount (millions)	Percent	Amount (millions)	Percent
Net sales	$3,649	100.0%	$3,069	100.0%
Cost of sales	1,610	44.1	1,317	42.9
Gross profit	$2,039	55.9%	$1,752	57.1%
Selling and administrative expenses	1,319	36.1	1,102	35.9
Operating income	$ 720	19.8%	$ 650	21.2%
Other income (expense)	—	0.0	2	0.1
Income before income taxes	$ 720	19.8%	$ 652	21.3%
Income taxes	227	6.2	206	6.7
Net income	$ 493	13.6%	$ 446	14.6%

operating income decreased from 21.2% to 19.8% of sales. Other income and expense remained approximately the same, while income taxes decreased from 6.7% to 6.2% of sales. Overall, operating costs increased as a percent of sales with a slight offset in taxes, causing net income as a percent of sales to decline.

SUMMARY OF LEARNING GOALS

1 **Describe the basic elements of a financial accounting system.** The basic elements of a financial accounting system include (1) a set of rules for determining what, when, and the amount that should be recorded for economic events, (2) a framework for facilitating preparation of financial statements, and (3) one or more controls to determine whether errors may have arisen in the recording process.

2 **Analyze, record, and summarize transactions for a corporation's first period of operations.** Using the integrated financial statement framework, September transactions for Family Health Care are recorded and summarized in Exhibit 2.

3 **Prepare financial statements for a corporation's first period of operations.** The financial statements for Family Health Care for September, its first period of operations, are shown in Exhibit 4.

4 **Analyze, record, and summarize transactions for a corporation's second period of operations.** Using the accounting equation as a basic framework, October transactions for Family Health Care are recorded and summarized in Exhibit 6. The financial statements for Family Health Care for October, its second period of operations, are shown in Exhibit 7.

5 **Prepare financial statements for a corporation's second period of operations.** The financial statements for Family Health Care for October, its second period of operations, are shown in Exhibit 7.

6 **Describe and illustrate how vertical analysis can be used to analyze and evaluate a company's performance.** Vertical analysis is a method of analyzing comparative financial statements in which percentages are computed for each item within a statement to a total within the statement. In vertical analysis of the balance sheet, each asset item is stated as a percent of the total assets. Each liability and stockholders' equity item is stated as a percent of total liabilities and stockholders' equity. In vertical analysis of the income statement, each item is stated as a percent of sales.

GLOSSARY

Financial accounting system A system that includes (1) a set of rules for determining what, when, and the amount that should be recorded for economic events, (2) a framework for facilitating preparation of financial statements, and (3) one or more controls to determine whether errors may have arisen in the recording process.

Transaction An economic event that under generally accepted accounting principles affects an element of the accounting equation and, therefore, must be recorded.

Vertical analysis A method of analyzing comparative financial statements in which percentages are computed for each item within a statement to a total within the statement.

ILLUSTRATIVE ACCOUNTING APPLICATION PROBLEM

Beth Sumner established an insurance agency on April 1, 2007, and completed the following transactions during April:

a. Opened a business bank account in the name of Sumner Insurance, Inc., with a deposit of $15,000 in exchange for capital stock.
b. Borrowed $8,000 by issuing a note payable.
c. Received cash from fees earned, $11,500.
d. Paid rent on office and equipment for the month, $3,500.
e. Paid automobile expenses for month, $650, and miscellaneous expenses, $300.

f. Paid office salaries, $1,400.
g. Paid interest on the note payable, $60.
h. Purchased land as a future building site, $20,000.
i. Paid dividends, $1,000.

Instructions

1. Indicate the effect of each transaction and the balances after each transaction, using the integrated financial statement framework.
2. Prepare an income statement and retained earnings statement for April.
3. Prepare a balance sheet as of April 30, 2007.
4. Prepare a statement of cash flows for April.

Solution

(1)

Statement of Cash Flows	Balance Sheet					Income Statement
	Assets		= Liabilities +	Stockholders' Equity		
	Cash +	Land =	Notes Payable +	Capital Stock +	Retained Earnings	
a. Investment	15,000			15,000		
b. Issued note payable	8,000		8,000			
Balances	23,000		8,000	15,000		
c. Fees earned	11,500				11,500	c.
Balances	34,500		8,000	15,000	11,500	
d. Rent expense	−3,500				−3,500	d.
Balances	31,000		8,000	15,000	8,000	
e. Paid expenses	−950				−950	e.
Balances	30,050		8,000	15,000	7,050	
f. Paid salary expense	−1,400				−1,400	f.
Balances	28,650		8,000	15,000	5,650	
g. Paid interest expense	−60				−60	g.
Balances	28,590		8,000	15,000	5,590	
h. Purchased land	−20,000	20,000				
Balances	8,590	20,000	8,000	15,000	5,590	
i. Paid dividends	−1,000				−1,000	
Balances, April 30	7,590	20,000	8,000	15,000	4,590	

Statement of Cash Flows

a. Financing	15,000
b. Financing	8,000
c. Operating	11,500
d. Operating	−3,500
e. Operating	−950
f. Operating	−1,400
g. Operating	−60
h. Investing	−20,000
i. Financing	−1,000
Increase in cash and April 30 cash	7,590

INTEGRATED FINANCIAL STATEMENT FRAMEWORK

Income Statement

c.	11,500	Fees earned
d.	−3,500	Rent expense
e.	−650	Auto expense
e.	−300	Misc. expense
f.	−1,400	Salary expense
g.	−60	Interest expense
	5,590	Net income

(2)

Sumner Insurance, Inc.
Income Statement
For the Month Ending April 30, 2007

Revenues:		
Fees earned		$11,500
Expenses:		
Rent expense	$3,500	
Salaries expense	1,400	
Automotive expense	650	
Interest expense	60	
Miscellaneous expense	300	
Total expenses		5,910
Net income		$ 5,590

Sumner Insurance, Inc.
Retained Earnings Statement
For the Month Ending April 30, 2007

Net income	$5,590
Less dividends	1,000
Retained earnings, April 30, 2007	$4,590

(3)

Sumner Insurance, Inc.
Balance Sheet
April 30, 2007

Assets		
Cash		$ 7,590
Land		20,000
Total assets		$27,590
Liabilities		
Note payable		$ 8,000
Stockholders' Equity		
Capital stock	$15,000	
Retained earnings	4,590	
Total stockholders' equity		19,590
Total liabilities and stockholders' equity		$27,590

(4)

Sumner Insurance, Inc.
Statement of Cash Flows
For the Month Ending April 30, 2007

Cash flows from operating activities:		
Cash receipts from operating activities		$ 11,500
Cash payments for operating activities		5,910
Net cash flows from operating activities		$ 5,590
Cash flows from investing activities:		
Cash payments for land		(20,000)
Cash flows from financing activities:		
Cash receipts from issuing capital stock	$15,000	
Cash receipts from note payable	8,000	
Cash payments for dividends	(1,000)	
Net cash flows used in financing activities		22,000
Net increase in cash during April		$ 7,590
Cash as of April 1, 2007		0
Cash as of April 30, 2007		$ 7,590

SELF-STUDY QUESTIONS

Answers at end of chapter

1. The purchase of land for $50,000 cash was incorrectly recorded as an increase in land and an increase in notes payable. Which of the following statements is correct?
   A. The accounting equation will not balance because cash is overstated by $50,000.
   B. The accounting equation will not balance because notes payable are overstated by $50,000.
   C. The accounting equation will not balance because assets will exceed liabilities by $50,000.
   D. Even though a recording error has been made, the accounting equation will balance.

2. The receipt of $8,000 of cash for fees earned was recorded by Langley Consulting as an increase in cash of $8,000 and a decrease in retained earnings (revenues) of $8,000. What is the effect of this error on the accounting equation?
   A. Total assets will exceed total liabilities and stockholders' equity by $8,000.
   B. Total assets will be less than total liabilities and stockholders' equity by $8,000.
   C. Total assets will exceed total liabilities and stockholders' equity by $16,000.
   D. The error will not affect the accounting equation.

3. If total assets increased $20,000 during a period and total liabilities increased $12,000 during the same period, the amount and direction (increase or decrease) of the change in stockholders' equity for that period is:
   A. a $32,000 increase.
   B. a $32,000 decrease.
   C. an $8,000 increase.
   D. an $8,000 decrease.

4. If revenue was $45,000, expenses were $37,500, and dividends were $10,000, the amount of net income or net loss would be:
   A. $45,000 net income.
   B. $7,500 net income.
   C. $37,500 net loss.
   D. $2,500 net loss.

5. Which of the following transactions changes only the mix of assets and does not affect liabilities or stockholders' equity?
   A. Borrowed $40,000 from First National Bank
   B. Purchased land for cash
   C. Received $3,800 for fees earned
   D. Paid $4,000 for office salaries

DISCUSSION QUESTIONS

1. What are the basic elements of a financial accounting system? Do these elements apply to all businesses from a local restaurant to General Motors? Explain.
2. Provide an example of a transaction that affects (a) only one element of the accounting equation, (b) two elements of the accounting equation, (c) three elements of the accounting equation.
3. Indicate whether the following error would cause the accounting equation to be out of balance and, if so, indicate how it would be out of balance. The payment of wages of $6,750 was recorded as a decrease in cash of $6,750 and a decrease in retained earnings (wages expense) of $6,570.
4. For each of the following errors, indicate whether the error would cause the accounting equation to be out of balance, and if so, indicate how it would be out of balance. (a) The purchase of land for $50,000 cash was recorded as an increase in land of $50,000 and a decrease in cash of $5,000. (b) The receipt of $7,500 for fees earned was recorded as an increase in cash of $7,500 and an increase in liabilities of $7,500.
5. What is a primary control for determining the accuracy of a business's record keeping?
6. Fathom Consulting Services acquired land three years ago for $25,000. Fathom recently signed an agreement to sell the land for $80,000. In accordance with the sales agreement, the buyer transferred $80,000 to Fathom's bank account on October 6. How would elements of the accounting equation be affected by the sale?
7. (a) How does the payment of dividends of $30,000 affect the three elements of the accounting equation? (b) Is net income affected by the payment of dividends? Explain.
8. Assume that Donahue Consulting erroneously recorded the payment of $11,500 of dividends as salary expense. (a) How would this error affect the equality of the accounting equation? (b) How would this error affect the income statement, retained earnings statement, balance sheet, and statement of cash flows?
9. Assume that Kilgore Realty, Inc., borrowed $80,000 from First City Bank and Trust. In recording the transaction, Kilgore erroneously recorded the receipt of $80,000 as an increase in cash, $80,000, and an increase in fees earned, $80,000. (a) How would this error affect the equality of the accounting equation? (b) How would this error affect the income statement, retained earnings statement, balance sheet, and statement of cash flows?
10. Assume that as of January 1, 2007, Milliken Consulting has total assets of $562,500 and total liabilities of $350,000. As of December 31, 2007, Milliken has total liabilities of $375,000 and total stockholders' equity of $281,250. (a) What was Milliken's stockholders' equity as of December 31, 2006? (b) Assume that Milliken did not pay any dividends during 2007. What was the amount of net income for 2007?
11. Using the January 1 and December 31, 2007, data given in Question 10, answer the following question. If Milliken paid $22,500 of dividends during 2007, what was the amount of net income for 2007?
12. In Chapter 1, we described and illustrated horizontal analysis. (a) What is the difference between horizontal and vertical analysis? (b) Can horizontal and vertical analysis be used together in analyzing a company?

EXERCISES

Exercise 2-1

Accounting equation

Goal **1**

a. $193,000

Determine the missing amount for each of the following:

	Assets	=	Liabilities	+	Stockholders' Equity
a.	X	=	$50,000	+	$143,000
b.	$165,500	=	X	+	$30,000
c.	$74,000	=	$35,000	+	X

Exercise 2-2

Accounting equation

Goal **1**

a. $23,791

The Walt Disney Company had the following assets and liabilities (in millions) as of September 30, 2003.

Assets	$49,988
Liabilities	26,197

a. Determine the stockholders' equity of Walt Disney as of September 30, 2003.
b. If assets increased by $3,914 and stockholders' equity increased by $2,290, what was the increase or decrease in liabilities for the year ending September 30, 2004?
c. What were the total assets, liabilities, and stockholders' equity as of September 30, 2004?
d. Based upon your answer to (c), does the accounting equation balance?

Exercise 2-3

Accounting equation

Goal 1

a. $387

Campbell Soup Co. had the following assets and liabilities (in millions) as of August 3, 2003.

Assets	$6,205
Liabilities	5,818

a. Determine the stockholders' equity of Campbell Soup as of August 3, 2003.
b. If assets increased by $470 and liabilities decreased by $17, what was the increase or decrease in stockholders' equity for the year ending August 1, 2004?
c. What were the total assets, liabilities, and stockholders' equity as of August 1, 2004?
d. Based upon your answer to (c), does the accounting equation balance?

Exercise 2-4

Accounting equation

Goal 1

a. $423,239

One item is omitted in each of the following summaries of balance sheet and income statement data (in millions) for General Motors and Coca-Cola as of December 31, 2004 and 2003.

	General Motors	Coca-Cola
December 31, 2003:		
Assets	$448,507	(e)
Liabilities	(a)	(f)
Stockholders' equity	(b)	$14,090
Increase (Decrease) in assets, liabilities, and stockholders' equity during 2004:		
Assets	$ 31,096	(g)
Liabilities	28,638	$ 2,140
Stockholders' equity	2,458	(h)
December 31, 2004:		
Assets	(c)	$31,327
Liabilities	$451,877	(i)
Stockholders' equity	(d)	15,935

Determine the amounts of the missing items (a) through (i).

Exercise 2-5

Accounting equation

Goal 1

b. $310,000

Chris Lund is the sole stockholder and operator of Saluki, a motivational consulting business. At the end of its accounting period, December 31, 2005, Saluki has assets of $475,000 and liabilities of $200,000. Using the accounting equation and considering each case independently, determine the following amounts:

a. Stockholders' equity, as of December 31, 2005.
b. Stockholders' equity, as of December 31, 2006, assuming that assets increased by $75,000 and liabilities increased by $40,000 during 2006.
c. Stockholders' equity, as of December 31, 2006, assuming that assets decreased by $15,000 and liabilities increased by $27,000 during 2006.

d. Stockholders' equity, as of December 31, 2006, assuming that assets increased by $125,000 and liabilities decreased by $65,000 during 2006.
e. Net income (or net loss) during 2006, assuming that as of December 31, 2006, assets were $425,000, liabilities were $105,000, and there were no dividends and no additional capital stock was issued.

Exercise 2-6

Effect of transactions on stockholders' equity

Goals **2, 4**

For Kroger Co., indicate whether the following transactions would (1) increase, (2) decrease, or (3) have no effect on stockholders' equity.

a. Purchased store equipment.
b. Paid dividends.
c. Paid store rent.
d. Borrowed money from the bank.
e. Paid creditors.
f. Made cash sales to customers.
g. Paid interest expense.
h. Sold store equipment at a loss.
i. Received interest income.
j. Paid taxes.

Exercise 2-7

Effect of transactions on accounting equation

Goals **1, 3, 4, 5**

Describe how the following business transactions affect the three elements of the accounting equation.

a. Received cash for services performed.
b. Borrowed cash at local bank.
c. Paid for utilities used in the business.
d. Issued capital stock for cash.
e. Purchased land for cash.

Exercise 2-8

Effect of transactions on accounting equation

Goals **1, 2, 4**

(1) Assets increase $50,000

A vacant lot acquired for $50,000, on which there is a balance owed of $30,000, is sold for $130,000 in cash. The seller pays the $30,000 owed. What is the effect of these transactions on the total amount of the seller's (1) assets, (2) liabilities, and (3) stockholders' equity?

Exercise 2-9

Effect of transactions on stockholders' equity

Goals **2, 4**

Indicate whether each of the following types of transactions will (a) increase stockholders' equity or (b) decrease stockholders' equity.

1. Paid cash for rent expense.
2. Paid cash dividends.
3. Received cash for fees earned.
4. Issued capital stock for cash.
5. Paid cash for utilities expense.

Exercise 2-10

Transactions

Goals **1, 2, 4**

Salvo Delivery Service had the following selected transactions during February:

1. Received cash from issuance of capital stock, $35,000.
2. Received cash for providing delivery services, $15,000.
3. Paid creditors, $1,800.
4. Billed customers for delivery services, $11,250.
5. Paid advertising expense, $750.
6. Purchased supplies for cash, $800.
7. Paid rent for February, $2,000.
8. Received cash from customers on account, $6,740.
9. Determined that the cost of supplies on hand was $135; therefore, $665 of supplies had been used during the month.
10. Paid dividends, $1,000.

Indicate the effect of each transaction on the accounting equation by listing the numbers identifying the transactions, (1) through (10), in a vertical column, and inserting at the right of each number the appropriate letter from the following list:

a. Increase in an asset, decrease in another asset.
b. Increase in an asset, increase in a liability.
c. Increase in an asset, increase in stockholders' equity.
d. Decrease in an asset, decrease in a liability.
e. Decrease in an asset, decrease in stockholders' equity.

Exercise 2-11

Nature of transactions

Goals **1, 2, 4**

b. $4,000

Mike Renner operates his own catering service. Summary financial data for March are presented in equation form as follows. Each line designated by a number indicates the effect of a transaction on the balance sheet. Each increase and decrease in owners' equity, except transaction (4), affects net income.

	Cash	+	Land	=	Liabilities	+	Capital Stock	+	Retained Earnings
Bal.	18,000		54,000		5,000		10,000		57,000
1.	+25,000								+25,000
2.	−10,000		+10,000						
3.	−16,000								−16,000
4.	−3,000								−3,000
Bal.	14,000		64,000		5,000		10,000		63,000

a. Describe each transaction.
b. What is the amount of net decrease in cash during the month?
c. What is the amount of net increase in retained earnings during the month?
d. What is the amount of the net income for the month?
e. How much of the net income for the month was retained in the business?
f. What is the amount of net cash flows from operating activities?
g. What is the amount of net cash flows from investing activities?
h. What is the amount of net cash flows from financing activities?

Exercise 2-12

Net income and dividends

Goals **3, 5**

The income statement of a corporation for the month of October indicates a net income of $158,250. During the same period, $180,000 in cash dividends were paid.

Would it be correct to say that the business incurred a net loss of $21,750 during the month? Discuss.

Exercise 2-13

Net income and stockholders' equity for four businesses

Goals **1, 3, 5**

Company G: Net income, $132,000

Four different corporations, E, F, G, and H, show the same balance sheet data at the beginning and end of a year. These data, exclusive of the amount of stockholders' equity, are summarized as follows:

	Total Assets	Total Liabilities
Beginning of the year	$420,000	$176,000
End of the year	776,000	340,000

On the basis of the above data and the following additional information for the year, determine the net income (or loss) of each company for the year. (*Suggestion:* First determine the amount of increase or decrease in stockholders' equity during the year.)

Company E: No additional capital stock was issued, and no dividends were paid.
Company F: No additional capital stock was issued, but dividends of $40,000 were paid.

Company G: Capital stock of $60,000 was issued, but no dividends were paid.
Company H: Capital stock of $60,000 was issued, and dividends of $40,000 were paid.

Exercise 2-14

Missing amounts from balance sheet and income statement data

Goals **1, 3, 5**

a. $172,500

One item is omitted from each of the following summaries of balance sheet and income statement data for four different corporations, O, P, Q, and R.

	O	P	Q	R
Beginning of the year:				
Assets	$300,000	$190,000	$100,000	(d)
Liabilities	195,000	90,000	80,000	$450,000
End of the year:				
Assets	$675,000	$250,000	$120,000	$930,000
Liabilities	375,000	70,000	105,000	510,000
During the year:				
Additional issue of capital stock	(a)	$ 44,000	$ 10,000	$150,000
Dividends	$ 30,000	16,000	(c)	225,000
Revenue	187,500	(b)	175,000	420,000
Expenses	135,000	104,000	177,000	480,000

Determine the amounts of the missing items, identifying them by letter. (*Suggestion:* First determine the amount of increase or decrease in stockholders' equity during the year.)

Exercise 2-15

Net income, retained earnings, and dividends

Goals **3, 5**

a. $388 increase

Use the following data (in millions) for Campbell Soup Co. for the year ending August 1, 2004, to answer the following questions.

Retained earnings August 3, 2003	$5,254
Retained earnings August 1, 2004	5,642
Net cash from operating activities	1,106
Net decrease in cash	3

a. Determine the net increase or decrease in retained earnings during 2004.
b. If dividends in 2004 are $259, what was the net income or loss for Campbell Soup for the year ending August 1, 2004?

Exercise 2-16

Balance sheet, net income, and cash flows

Goals **3, 5**

b. $33,000

SPREADSHEET

Financial information related to Thorstad Interiors for June and July of 2007 is as follows:

	June 30, 2007	July 31, 2007
Notes payable	$30,000	$45,000
Land	51,000	75,000
Capital stock	18,000	27,000
Retained earnings	?	?
Cash	54,000	81,000

a. Prepare balance sheets for Thorstad Interiors as of June 30 and July 31, 2007.
b. Determine the amount of net income for July, assuming that dividends of $6,000 were paid.
c. Determine the net cash flows from operating activities.
d. Determine the net cash flows from investing activities.

(continued)

e. Determine the net cash flows from financing activities.
f. Determine the net increase or decrease in cash.

Exercise 2-17

Income statement

Goals 3, 5

Net income, $22,500

SPREADSHEET

After its first month of operation, the following amounts were taken from the accounting records of Three Rivers Realty, Inc., as of November 30, 2007.

Capital stock	$10,000	Notes payable	$30,000
Cash	21,500	Rent expense	6,000
Dividends	4,000	Retained earnings	0
Interest expense	2,000	Salaries expense	9,000
Land	37,000	Sales commissions	49,500
Miscellaneous expense	2,500	Utilities expense	7,500

Prepare an income statement for the month ending November 30, 2007.

Exercise 2-18

Retained earnings statement

Goals 3, 5

Retained earnings, November 30, 2007, $18,500

SPREADSHEET

Using the financial data shown in Exercise 2-17 for Three Rivers Realty, Inc., prepare a retained earnings statement for the month ending November 30, 2007.

Exercise 2-19

Balance sheet

Goals 3, 5

Total assets, $58,500

SPREADSHEET

Using the financial data shown in Exercise 2-17 for Three Rivers Realty, Inc., prepare a balance sheet as of November 30, 2007.

Exercise 2-20

Statement of cash flows

Goals 3, 5

Net cash flows from operating activities, $22,500

SPREADSHEET

Using the financial data shown in Exercise 2-17 for Three Rivers Realty, Inc., prepare a statement of cash flows for the month ending November 30, 2007.

Exercise 2-21

Effect of transactions on accounting equation

Goals 1, 2, 4

Describe how transactions of Lucent Technologies, Inc., would affect the three elements of the accounting equation.

a. Received cash from issuing stock.
b. Paid off long-term debt.
c. Received proceeds from selling a portion of manufacturing operations for a gain on the sale.
d. Paid dividends.

e. Made cash sales.
f. Received cash from the issuance of long-term debt.
g. Paid research and development expenses for the current year.
h. Paid employee pension expenses for the current year.
i. Paid taxes.
j. Purchased machinery and equipment for cash.
k. Paid officer salaries.
l. Paid selling expenses.

Exercise 2-22

Statement of cash flows

Goals **3, 5**

Based upon the financial transactions for Lucent Technologies, Inc., shown in Exercise 2-21, indicate whether the transaction would be reported in the cash flows from operating, investing, or financing sections of the statement of cash flows.

ACCOUNTING APPLICATION PROBLEMS

Problem 2-1A

Transactions and financial statements

Goals **1, 2, 3**

3. Net income, $4,820

SPREADSHEET

GENERAL LEDGER

Debbie Woodall established an insurance agency on July 1, 2007, and completed the following transactions during July:

a. Opened a business bank account in the name of Woodall Insurance, Inc., with a deposit of $18,000 in exchange for capital stock.
b. Borrowed $10,000 by issuing a note payable.
c. Received cash from fees earned, $9,500.
d. Paid rent on office and equipment for the month, $2,000.
e. Paid automobile expense for month, $1,000, and miscellaneous expense, $400.
f. Paid office salaries, $1,200.
g. Paid interest on the note payable, $80.
h. Purchased land as a future building site, $19,500.
i. Paid dividends, $2,500.

Instructions

1. Indicate the effect of each transaction and the balances after each transaction, using the integrated financial statement framework.
2. Briefly explain why the stockholders' investments and revenues increased stockholders' equity, while dividends and expenses decreased stockholders' equity.
3. Prepare an income statement and retained earnings statement for July.
4. Prepare a balance sheet as of July 31, 2007.
5. Prepare a statement of cash flows for July.

Problem 2-2A

Transactions and financial statements

Goals **1, 2, 3**

1. Net income, $7,350

SPREADSHEET

Chris Darby established Top-Gun Computer Services on January 1, 2007. The effect of each transaction and the balances after each transaction for January are shown in the integrated financial statement framework at the top of the following page.

Instructions

1. Prepare an income statement for the month ended January 31, 2007.
2. Prepare a retained earnings statement for the month ended January 31, 2007.
3. Prepare a balance sheet as of January 31, 2007.
4. Prepare a statement of cash flows for the month ended January 31, 2007.

Statement of Cash Flows	Balance Sheet: Assets		= Liabilities	+ Stockholders' Equity		Income Statement
	Cash	+ Land	= Notes Payable	+ Capital Stock	+ Retained Earnings	
a. Investment	25,000			25,000		
b. Fees earned	15,000				15,000	b.
Balances	40,000			25,000	15,000	
c. Rent expense	−2,500				−2,500	c.
Balances	37,500			25,000	12,500	
d. Issued notes payable	10,000		10,000			
Balances	47,500		10,000	25,000	12,500	
e. Purchased land	−30,000	30,000				
Balances	17,500	30,000	10,000	25,000	12,500	
f. Paid expenses	−1,650				−1,650	f.
Balances	15,850	30,000	10,000	25,000	10,850	
g. Paid salary expense	−3,500				−3,500	g.
Balances	12,350	30,000	10,000	25,000	7,350	
i. Paid dividends	−1,500				−1,500	
Balances, Jan. 31	10,850	30,000	10,000	25,000	5,850	

Statement of Cash Flows

a. Financing	25,000
b. Operating	15,000
c. Operating	−2,500
d. Financing	10,000
e. Investing	−30,000
f. Operating	−1,650
g. Operating	−3,500
i. Financing	−1,500
Increase in cash	10,850

INTEGRATED FINANCIAL STATEMENT FRAMEWORK

Income Statement

b.	15,000	Fees earned
c.	−2,500	Rent expense
f.	−950	Auto expense
f.	−700	Misc. expense
g.	−3,500	Salary expense
	7,350	Net income

Problem 2-3A

Financial statements

Goals **4, 5**

1. Net income, $115,500

SPREADSHEET

The following amounts were taken from the accounting records of Lisko Services, Inc., as of December 31, 2007. Lisko Services began its operations on January 1, 2007.

Capital stock	$ 14,000
Cash	38,500
Dividends	7,000
Fees earned	321,300
Interest expense	1,680
Land	105,000
Miscellaneous expense	9,520
Notes payable	21,000
Rent expense	33,600
Salaries expense	91,000
Taxes expense	25,200
Utilities expense	44,800

Instructions

1. Prepare an income statement for the year ending December 31, 2007.
2. Prepare a retained earnings statement for the year ending December 31, 2007.
3. Prepare a balance sheet as of December 31, 2007.
4. Prepare a statement of cash flows for the year ending December 31, 2007.

Problem 2-4A

Financial statements

Goal 5

1. Net income, $128,100

SPREADSHEET

After its second year of operations, the following amounts were taken from the accounting records of Lisko Services, Inc., as of December 31, 2008. Lisko Services began its operations on January 1, 2007 (see Problem 2-3A).

Capital stock	$ 35,000
Cash	?
Dividends	21,000
Fees earned	355,740
Interest expense	2,240
Land	196,000
Miscellaneous expense	9,800
Notes payable	28,000
Rent expense	39,200
Salaries expense	98,000
Taxes expense	28,000
Utilities expense	50,400

Instructions

1. Prepare an income statement for the year ending December 31, 2008.
2. Prepare a retained earnings statement for the year ending December 31, 2008. (*Note:* The retained earnings at January 1, 2008, was $108,500.)
3. Prepare a balance sheet as of December 31, 2008.
4. Prepare a statement of cash flows for the year ending December 31, 2008. (*Hint:* You should compare the asset and liability amounts of December 31, 2008, with those of December 31, 2007, to determine cash used in investing and financing activities. See Problem 2-3A for the December 31, 2007, balance sheet amounts.)

Problem 2-5A

Missing amounts from financial statements

Goals 3, 5

a. $19,500

SPREADSHEET

The financial statements at the end of Sciatic Realty, Inc.'s first month of operation are shown below. By analyzing the interrelationships between the financial statements, fill in the proper amounts for (a) through (s).

Sciatic Realty, Inc.
Income Statement
For the Month Ended July 31, 2007

Fees earned		$ (a)
Operating expenses:		
Wages expense	$5,520	
Rent expense	3,000	
Utilities expense	(b)	
Interest expense	300	
Miscellaneous expense	660	
Total operating expenses		11,250
Net income		$ (c)

Sciatic Realty, Inc.
Retained Earnings Statement
For the Month Ended July 31, 2007

Retained earnings, July 1, 2007		$ (d)
Net income for July	$8,250	
Less dividends	(e)	(f)
Retained earnings, July 31, 2007		$ (g)

Sciatic Realty, Inc.
Balance Sheet
July 31, 2007

Assets		
Cash		$ (h)
Land		30,000
Total assets		$39,750
Liabilities		
Notes payable		$18,000
Stockholders' Equity		
Capital stock	$ (i)	
Retained earnings	(j)	(k)
Total liabilities and stockholders' equity		$ (l)

Sciatic Realty, Inc.
Statement of Cash Flows
For the Month Ended July 31, 2007

Cash flows from operating activities:			
Cash received from customers		$ 19,500	
Deduct cash payments for expenses		11,250	
Net cash flows from operating activities			$ (m)
Cash flows from investing activities:			
Cash payment for purchase of land			$(30,000)
Cash flows from financing activities:			
Cash received from sale of capital stock	$15,000		
Cash received from notes payable	(n)	$ (o)	
Deduct cash dividends		1,500	
Net cash flows from financing activities			(p)
Net increase in cash			$ (q)
July 1, 2007, cash balance			(r)
July 31, 2007, cash balance			$ (s)

Problem 2-6A

Financial statements

Goals **3, 5**

Crazy Creek Realty, Inc., organized October 1, 2007, is operated by Jane Eckhart. How many errors can you find in the following financial statements for Crazy Creek Realty, Inc., prepared after its first month of operation?

Crazy Creek Realty, Inc.
Income Statement
October 31, 2007

Sales commissions		$92,200
Operating expenses:		
Office salaries expense	$16,300	
Rent expense	7,600	
Automobile expense	3,500	
Dividends	2,000	
Miscellaneous expense	1,550	
Total operating expenses		30,950
Net income		$41,250

Jane Eckhart
Retained Earnings Statement
October 31, 2006

Net income for the month	$41,250
Retained earnings, October 31, 2007	$41,250

Balance Sheet
For the Month Ended October 31, 2007

Assets		
Cash		$ 60,850
Notes payable		20,000
Total assets		$ 80,850
Liabilities		
Land		$ 40,400
Stockholders' Equity		
Capital stock	$20,000	
Retained earnings	41,250	61,250
Total liabilities and stockholders' equity		$101,650

Crazy Creek Realty, Inc. **Statement of Cash Flows** October 31, 2007	
Cash flows from operating activities:	
Cash receipts from sales commissions	$ 92,200
Cash flows from investing activities:	
Cash payments for land	(40,400)
Cash flows from financing activities:	
Cash receipts from retained earnings	81,250
Net increase in cash during October	$133,050
Cash as of October 1, 2007	0
Cash as of October 31, 2007	$133,050

ALTERNATE ACCOUNTING APPLICATION PROBLEMS

Alternate Problem 2-1B

Transactions and financial statements

Goals **1, 2, 3**

3. Net income, $6,250

SPREADSHEET

GENERAL LEDGER

Whitney Tomas established a real estate agency on March 1, 2007, and completed the following transactions during March:

a. Opened a business bank account in the name of Tomas Realty, Inc., with a deposit of $25,000 in exchange for capital stock.
b. Borrowed $15,000 by issuing a note payable.
c. Received cash from commissions earned, $11,500.
d. Paid rent on office and equipment for the month, $2,200.
e. Paid automobile expense for month, $1,050, and miscellaneous expense, $500.
f. Paid office salaries, $1,400.
g. Paid interest on the note payable, $100.
h. Purchased land as a future building site, $22,600.
i. Paid dividends, $1,500.

Instructions

1. Indicate the effect of each transaction and the balances after each transaction, using the integrated financial statement framework.
2. Briefly explain why the stockholders' investments and revenues increased stockholders' equity, while dividends and expenses decreased stockholders' equity.
3. Prepare an income statement and retained earnings statement for March.
4. Prepare a balance sheet as of March 31, 2007.
5. Prepare a statement of cash flows for March.

Alternate Problem 2-2B

Transactions and financial statements

Goals **1, 2, 3**

1. Net income, $6,550

SPREADSHEET

Kay Larsh established Kodiak Architectural Services on October 1, 2007. The effect of each transaction and the balances after each transaction for October are shown in the integrated financial statement framework at the top of the following page.

Instructions

1. Prepare an income statement for the month ended October 31, 2007.
2. Prepare a retained earnings statement for the month ended October 31, 2007.
3. Prepare a balance sheet as of October 31, 2007.
4. Prepare a statement of cash flows for the month ended October 31, 2007.

Statement of Cash Flows	Balance Sheet: Assets: Cash	+	Land	=	Liabilities: Notes Payable	+	Stockholders' Equity: Capital Stock	+	Retained Earnings	Income Statement
a. Investment	20,000						20,000			
b. Fees earned	12,800								12,800	b.
Balances	32,800						20,000		12,800	
c. Rent expense	−2,000								−2,000	c.
Balances	30,800						20,000		10,800	
d. Issued note payable	18,000				18,000					
Balances	48,800				18,000		20,000		10,800	
e. Purchased land	−27,000		27,000							
Balances	21,800		27,000		18,000		20,000		10,800	
f. Paid expenses	−1,500								−1,500	f.
Balances	20,300		27,000		18,000		20,000		9,300	
g. Paid salary expense	−2,750								−2,750	g.
Balances	17,550		27,000		18,000		20,000		6,550	
i. Paid dividends	−1,500								−1,500	
Balances, Oct. 31	16,050		27,000		18,000		20,000		5,050	

Statement of Cash Flows

a. Financing	20,000
b. Operating	12,800
c. Operating	−2,000
d. Financing	18,000
e. Investing	−27,000
f. Operating	−1,500
g. Operating	−2,750
i. Financing	−1,500
Increase in cash	16,050

INTEGRATED FINANCIAL STATEMENT FRAMEWORK

Income Statement

b.	12,800	Fees earned
c.	−2,000	Rent expense
f.	−1,000	Auto expense
f.	−500	Misc. expense
g.	−2,750	Salary expense
	6,550	Net income

Alternate Problem 2-3B

Financial statements

Goals **4, 5**

1. Net income, $280,000

SPREADSHEET

The following amounts were taken from the accounting records of Rainbow Consulting Services, Inc., as of July 31, 2007. Rainbow Consulting Services began its operations on August 1, 2006.

Capital stock	$ 20,000
Cash	79,000
Dividends	50,000
Fees earned	676,600
Interest expense	9,600
Land	251,000
Miscellaneous expense	15,000
Notes payable	80,000
Rent expense	72,000
Salaries expense	160,000
Taxes expense	60,000
Utilities expense	80,000

Instructions

1. Prepare an income statement for the year ending July 31, 2007.
2. Prepare a retained earnings statement for the year ending July 31, 2007.
3. Prepare a balance sheet as of July 31, 2007.
4. Prepare a statement of cash flows for the year ending July 31, 2007.

Alternate Problem 2-4B

Financial statements

Goals **4, 5**

1. Net income, $160,000

SPREADSHEET

After its second year of operations, the following amounts were taken from the accounting records of Rainbow Consulting Services, Inc., as of July 31, 2008. Rainbow Consulting Services began its operations on August 1, 2006 (see Problem 2-3B).

Capital stock	$ 40,000
Cash	?
Dividends	40,000
Fees earned	578,000
Interest expense	12,000
Land	342,000
Miscellaneous expense	16,000
Notes payable	100,000
Rent expense	80,000
Salaries expense	180,000
Taxes expense	40,000
Utilities expense	90,000

Instructions

1. Prepare an income statement for the year ending July 31, 2008.
2. Prepare a retained earnings statement for the year ending July 31, 2008. (*Note:* The retained earnings at August 1, 2007, was $230,000.)
3. Prepare a balance sheet as of July 31, 2008.
4. Prepare a statement of cash flows for the year ending July 31, 2008. (*Hint:* You should compare the asset and liability amounts of July 31, 2008, with those of July 31, 2007, to determine cash used in investing and financing activities. See Problem 2-3B for the July 31, 2007, balance sheet amounts.)

Alternate Problem 2-5B

Missing amounts from financial statements

Goals **3, 5**

a. $55,500

SPREADSHEET

The financial statements at the end of Flagstone Consulting, Inc.'s first month of operation are shown below. By analyzing the interrelationships between the financial statements, fill in the proper amounts for (a) through (t).

Flagstone Consulting, Inc.
Income Statement
For the Month Ended June 30, 2007

Fees earned		$ (a)
Operating expenses:		
Wages expense	$13,500	
Rent expense	8,400	
Utilities expense	5,700	
Interest expense	600	
Miscellaneous expense	1,800	
Total operating expenses		30,000
Net income		$ (b)

Flagstone Consulting, Inc.
Retained Earnings Statement
For the Month Ended June 30, 2007

Retained earnings, June 1, 2007		$ (c)
Net income for June	$ (d)	
Less dividends	(e)	(f)
Retained earnings, June 30, 2007		$ (g)

Flagstone Consulting, Inc.
Balance Sheet
June 30, 2007

Assets		
Cash		$ (h)
Land		54,000
Total assets		$139,500
Liabilities		
Notes payable		$ 45,000
Stockholders' Equity		
Capital stock	$75,000	
Retained earnings	(i)	(j)
Total liabilities and stockholders' equity		$ (k)

Flagstone Consulting, Inc.
Statement of Cash Flows
For the Month Ended June 30, 2007

Cash flows from operating activities:			
Cash received from customers			$ (l)
Deduct cash payments for expenses			(m)
Net cash flows from operating activities			$ 25,500
Cash flows from investing activities:			
Cash payment for purchase of land			$(54,000)
Cash flows from financing activities:			
Cash received from sale of capital stock	$ (n)		
Cash received from notes payable	(o)	$ (p)	
Deduct cash dividends		6,000	
Net cash flows from financing activities			(q)
Net increase in cash			$ (r)
June 1, 2007, cash balance			(s)
June 30, 2007, cash balance			$ (t)

Alternate Problem 2-6B

Financial statements

Goals 3, 5

Pulmonary Consulting, Inc., organized April 1, 2007, is operated by Dr. Tobin. How many errors can you find in the following financial statements for Pulmonary Consulting, Inc., prepared after its first month of operation?

Pulmonary Consulting, Inc.
Income Statement
April 30, 2007

Fees earned		$92,500
Operating expenses:		
Office salaries expense	$42,500	
Rent expense	12,500	
Automobile expense	8,750	
Dividends	5,000	
Miscellaneous expense	2,750	
Total operating expenses		77,500
Net income		$15,000

Pulmonary Consulting, Inc.
Retained Earnings Statement
April 30, 2008

Net income for the month	$15,000
Retained earnings, April 30, 2007	$15,000

Dr. Tobin
Balance Sheet
For the Month Ended April 30, 2007

Assets		
Cash		$ 31,000
Notes payable		50,000
Total assets		$ 81,000
Liabilities		
Land		$ 65,000
Stockholders' Equity		
Capital stock	$25,000	
Retained earnings	15,000	40,000
Total liabilities and stockholders' equity		$105,000

Statement of Cash Flows April 30, 2007	
Cash flows from operating activities:	
Cash receipts from fees earned	$ 92,500
Net cash from operating activities	$ 92,500
Cash flows from investing activities:	
Cash payments for land	65,000
Cash flows from financing activities:	
Cash receipts from issuance of capital stock	25,000
Net increase in cash during April	$182,500
Cash as of April 1, 2007	0
Cash as of April 30, 2007	$182,500

FINANCIAL ANALYSIS AND REPORTING CASES

Case 2-1

Accounting equation

Condensed financial statements for Wm. Wrigley Jr. Company for 2004 and 2003 are shown in Exhibits 9 and 10 of this chapter. Based upon these financial statements, answer the following questions:

1. Using the accounting equation, Assets = Liabilities + Stockholders' Equity, fill in the amounts for 2003. Express the amounts in millions.
2. If during 2004, assets increased by $646 and liabilities increased by $288, determine the increase or decrease in stockholders' equity during 2004.
3. Based upon your answers to (1) and (2), determine the total stockholders' equity as of December 31, 2004. Does this amount agree with Wrigley's balance sheet shown in Exhibit 9?
4. Based upon Exhibit 9, what percent of Wrigley's total assets was financed by debt during 2004? Assuming you are a long-term creditor of Wrigley, interpret this percent in terms of the chances that you will be repaid by Wrigley.
5. Assuming that in (4) you are a short-term creditor of Wrigley, would your interpretation and analysis of your chances of being repaid change?

Case 2-2

Vertical analysis

SPREADSHEET

The balance sheets (in millions), on the following page, were adapted from the December 31, 2004 and 2003 financial statements of Boeing Co.

Instructions

1. Prepare a comparative vertical analysis of the balance sheets for 2004 and 2003. Round to one decimal place.
2. Based upon (1), what is your analysis of Boeing's financial condition in 2004 as compared to 2003?

	December 31, 2004	December 31, 2003
Assets:		
Cash	$ 3,204	$ 4,633
Receivables	7,260	6,430
Inventories	4,247	5,338
Property, plant, and equipment	8,443	8,432
Intangible assets and goodwill	2,903	2,948
Prepaid pension cost	12,588	8,542
Investments	13,754	12,951
Other assets	1,564	3,761
TOTAL ASSETS	$53,963	$53,035
Liabilities and Stockholders' Equity:		
Accounts payable	$17,989	$17,304
Notes payable	12,200	14,443
Other liabilities	12,488	13,149
Total liabilities	$42,677	$44,896
Stockholders' equity	11,286	8,139
TOTAL LIABILITIES AND STOCKHOLDERS' EQUITY	$53,963	$53,035

Case 2-3

Vertical analysis

The following income statement data (in millions) for Dell Computer Corporation and Apple Computer Inc. were taken from their recent annual reports:

	Dell	Apple
Net sales	$49,205	$8,279
Cost of goods sold	40,190	6,020
Gross profit	$ 9,015	$2,259
Operating expenses	4,761	1,933
Operating income (loss)	$ 4,254	$ 326

1. Prepare a vertical analysis of the income statement for Dell. Round to one decimal place.
2. Prepare a vertical analysis of the income statement for Apple. Round to one decimal place.
3. Based upon (1) and (2), how does Dell compare to Apple?

Case 2-4

Financial information

Yahoo.com's finance Internet site provides summary financial information about public companies, such as stock quotes, recent financial filings with the Securities and Exchange Commission, and recent news stories. Go to Yahoo.com's financial Web site (http://finance.yahoo.com/) and enter Wm. Wrigley Jr. Company's stock symbol, WWY. Answer the following questions concerning Wm. Wrigley Jr. Company by clicking on the various items under the tab "More on WWY."

1. At what price did Wrigley's stock last trade?
2. What is the 52-week range of Wrigley's stock?
3. When was the last time Wrigley's stock hit a 52-week high?
4. Over the last six months, has there been any insider selling or buying of Wrigley's stock?
5. Who is the president of Wm. Wrigley Jr. Company, and how old is the president?

6. What was the salary of the president of Wm. Wrigley Jr. Company?
7. What is the annual dividend of Wrigley's stock?
8. How many current broker recommendations are strong buy, buy, hold, sell, or strong sell? What is the average of the broker recommendations?
9. What is the net cash flow from operations for this year?
10. What is the operating margin for this year?

Case 2-5

Analyzing financial information

In the March 30, 2005, issue of *The Chicago Sun Times*, there is an article by Eric Herman, entitled "Wrigley Opening Facilities Here and Around the World." Read the article and answer the following questions:

1. Is the article favorable, neutral, or unfavorable regarding future prospects for Wm. Wrigley Jr. Company?
2. Would you invest in Wm. Wrigley Jr. Company's stock based only upon this article? If not, what additional information would you want?
3. Would it be a prudent investment strategy to only rely upon published financial statements in deciding to invest in a company's stock?
4. What sources do you think financial analysts use in making investment decisions and recommendations?

Case 2-6

Vertical analysis

The following comparative income statement information was provided by AMR Corp., the parent company of American Airlines for the years ended December 31, 2004 and 2003.

(in millions)	December 31, 2004	December 31, 2003
Revenues:		
Passenger—American Airlines	$ 15,021	$14,332
Regional affiliates	1,876	1,519
Cargo	625	558
Other revenues	1,123	1,031
Total operating revenues	$ 18,645	$17,440
Expenses:		
Wages, salaries, and benefits	$ 6,719	$ 7,264
Aircraft fuel	3,969	2,772
Depreciation and amortization	1,292	1,377
Other rentals and landing fees	1,187	1,173
Commissions, booking fees, and credit card expense	1,107	1,063
Maintenance, materials, and repairs	971	860
Aircraft rentals	609	687
Food service	558	611
Other operating expenses	2,366	2,428
Special charges	11	407
U.S. government grant	—	(358)
Total operating expenses	$ 18,789	$18,284
Operating loss	$ (144)	$ (844)

1. Provide a vertical analysis for the comparative years.
2. Interpret your results.

BUSINESS ACTIVITIES AND RESPONSIBILITY ISSUES

Activity 2-1

Business emphasis

GROUP ACTIVITY

Assume that you are considering developing a nationwide chain of women's clothing stores. You have contacted a Houston-based firm that specializes in financing new business ventures and enterprises. Such firms, called venture capital firms, finance new businesses in exchange for a percentage of the ownership.

1. In groups of four or five, discuss the different business emphases that you might use in your venture.
2. For each emphasis you listed in (1), provide an example of a real world business using the same strategy.
3. What percentage of the ownership would you be willing to give the venture capital firm in exchange for its financing?

Activity 2-2

Cash accounting

Kristin Stokes and Marikay Blair both graduated from State University in June 2007. After graduation, Marikay took a job as a staff accountant in the Chicago office of PricewaterhouseCoopers, an international public accounting firm. Kristin began working as a manager in Kleen Electronics, a wholesale computer hardware and software company, but left after only six months to start her own consulting business. The following conversation took place between Kristin and Marikay at their first annual alumni function:

Kristin: Marikay, good to see you again.
Marikay: Yes. It doesn't seem like it's been almost a year since we graduated.
Kristin: That's for sure. It seems like only yesterday we were listening to that boring commencement speaker. I don't even remember his name . . . Robert somebody. Are you still working for PricewaterhouseCoopers?
Marikay: Yes, it's been a great year. I've worked on 13 companies . . . it's been a fantastic learning experience. Each client has a different culture, management team, problems, and personality. I've learned something new every day. How about you? Are you still working for Kleen Electronics?
Kristin: No, I quit after six months. My customers really didn't know what they needed for computer systems . . . so . . . I quit and started a consulting business. I feel like I'm helping my customers more now than I did before. Besides, I like being my own boss.
Marikay: What's the name of your business?
Kristin: Stokes Consulting. It's been amazing. I started with my savings of $5,000 six months ago. My last bank statement showed I've got more than $45,000—"pure profit" of $40,000 in only six months.
Marikay: That's unbelievable! If you ever need a CPA firm, keep us in mind.
Kristin: Sure. What are friends for anyway?

Comment on Kristin's statement that she's earned $40,000 "pure profit" in only six months.

Activity 2-3

Cash flows

Amazon.com, an Internet retailer, was incorporated in the early 1990s and opened its virtual doors on the Web shortly thereafter. On the statement of cash flows, would you expect Amazon.com's net cash flows from operating, investing, and financing activities to be positive or negative for its first three years of operation? Use the following format for your answers, and briefly explain your logic.

	Year 1	Year 2	Year 3
Net cash flows from operating activities	negative		
Net cash flows from investing activities			
Net cash flows from financing activities			

Activity 2-4

Opportunities for accountants

The increasing complexity of the current business and regulatory environment has created an increased demand for accountants who can analyze business transactions and interpret their effects on the financial statements. In addition, a basic ability to analyze the effects of transactions is necessary to be successful in all fields of business as well as in other disciplines, such as law. To better understand the importance of accounting in today's environment, search the Internet or your local newspaper for job opportunities. One possible Internet site is http://www.jobweb.com. Then do one of the following:

1. Print a listing of at least two ads for accounting jobs. Alternatively, bring to class at least two newspaper ads for accounting jobs.
2. Print a listing of at least two ads for nonaccounting jobs for which some knowledge of accounting is preferred or necessary. Alternatively, bring to class at least two newspaper ads for such jobs.

ANSWERS TO SELF-STUDY QUESTIONS

1. **D** Even though a recording error has been made, the accounting equation will balance (answer D). However, assets (cash) will be overstated by $50,000, and liabilities (notes payable) will be overstated by $50,000. Answer A is incorrect because although cash is overstated by $50,000, the accounting equation will balance. Answer B is incorrect because although notes payable are overstated by $50,000, the accounting equation will balance. Answer C is incorrect because the accounting equation will balance and assets will not exceed liabilities.

2. **C** Total assets will exceed total liabilities and stockholders' equity by $16,000. This is because stockholders' equity (retained earnings) was decreased instead of increased by $8,000. Thus, stockholders' equity will be understated by a total of $16,000.

3. **C** The accounting equation is:

Assets = Liabilities + Stockholders' Equity

Therefore, if assets increased by $20,000 and liabilities increased by $12,000, stockholders' equity must have increased by $8,000 (answer C), as indicated in the following computation:

Assets	=	Liabilities	+	Stockholders' Equity
+ $20,000	=	$12,000	+	Stockholders' Equity
+ $20,000 − $12,000	=			Stockholders' Equity
+ $8,000	=			Stockholders' Equity

4. **B** Net income is the excess of revenue over expenses, or $7,500 (answer B). If expenses exceed revenue, the difference is a net loss. Dividends are the opposite of the stockholders' investing in the business and do not affect the amount of net income or net loss.

5. **B** The purchase of land for cash changes the mix of assets and does not affect liabilities or stockholders' equity (answer B). Borrowing cash from a bank (answer A) increases assets and liabilities. Receiving cash for fees earned (answer C) increases cash and stockholders' equity (retained earnings). Paying office salaries (answer D) decreases cash and stockholders' equity (retained earnings).

3 Accrual Accounting Concepts

Learning Goals

1. Describe basic accrual accounting concepts, including the matching concept.
2. Use accrual concepts of accounting to analyze, record, and summarize transactions.
3. Describe and illustrate the end-of-the-period adjustment process.
4. Prepare financial statements using accrual concepts of accounting, including a classified balance sheet.
5. Describe how the accrual basis of accounting enhances the interpretation of financial statements.
6. Describe the accounting cycle for the accrual basis of accounting.
7. Describe and illustrate how common-sized financial statements can be used to analyze and evaluate a company's performance.

Wendy's

Do you subscribe to any magazines? Most of us subscribe to one or more magazines such as *Cosmopolitan*, *Sports Illustrated*, *Golf Digest*, *Newsweek*, or *Rolling Stone*. Magazines usually require us to prepay the yearly subscription price before we receive any issues. When should the magazine company record revenue from the subscriptions? As we discussed in Chapter 2, sometimes revenues are earned and expenses are incurred at the point cash changes hands. However, for many transactions, such as magazine subscriptions, the revenue is earned when the magazine is delivered. Large corporations are required to account for revenues and expense when the benefit is substantially provided or consumed, which may not necessarily occur when cash is either received or paid.

For example, Wendy's International records revenues when cash is received at the cash register from meal sales. However, the ingredient costs associated with each meal are recorded at the time the meal is sold, not when the various ingredients are purchased. With over 4,000 restaurants, Wendy's has become a successful company, climbing to the third largest fast-food chain in the United States.

How did Wendy's succeed in the highly competitive fast-food industry? First, through innovation. Wendy's was the first restaurant to feature a salad bar. This was a radical change in the fast-food industry. Second, the company created a family-friendly atmosphere by decorating with glass lamps and bentwood chairs. Third, it emphasized the importance of making each sandwich fresh, never frozen, and offering customers a choice of toppings. Fourth, it is continually responding to customer taste changes, such as introducing the "combo choices" program, which lets customers replace french fries with side dishes such as a baked potato or chili.

COURTESY WENDY'S INTERNATIONAL INC.

In this chapter, we continue our discussion of financial statements and financial reporting systems. In doing so, we focus on accrual concepts of accounting that are used by all major businesses, such as Wendy's. Our discussions will include how to record transactions under accrual accounting concepts, update accounting records, and prepare accrual financial statements. Because all large companies, and many small ones, use accrual concepts of accounting, a thorough understanding of this topic is important for your business studies and future career.

Sources: Richard Bloom, "Wendy's Strives to Refresh Stale Brand," *The Globe and Mail*, January 6, 2005.

Describe basic accrual accounting concepts, including the matching concept.

BASIC ACCRUAL ACCOUNTING CONCEPTS INCLUDING THE MATCHING CONCEPT

In Chapter 2, we illustrated the recording of transactions for Family Health Care for the months of September and October. In these illustrations, we used many of the accounting concepts described in Chapter 1. For example, under the business entity concept, we accounted for Family Health Care as a separate entity, independent of the owner-manager, Dr. Lee Landry. Under the cost concept, we recorded the purchase of land at the amount paid for it. Consistent with the going concern concept, we did not revalue the land for increases or decreases in its market value, but retained the land in the accounting records at its original cost. We also employed the accounting period, full disclosure, objectivity, and unit of measurement concepts in preparing financial statements for Family Health Care.

The one accounting concept that we did not emphasize in Chapter 2 was the matching concept. This is because all the transactions in Chapter 2 were structured so that cash was either received or paid. We did this to simplify the recording of transactions and the preparation of financial statements. For example, all revenues were received in cash at the time the services were rendered and all expenses were paid in cash at the time they were incurred.

In the real world, cash may be received or paid at a different time from when revenues are earned or expenses are incurred. In fact, companies often earn revenues before or after cash is received and incur expense before or after cash is paid. For example, a company might spend months or years developing land for a business complex or subdivision. During the development of the land, the company has to pay for materials, wages, insurance, and other construction items. At the same time, cash might not be received until portions of the development are sold. Thus, if revenues were recorded only when cash is received and expenses recorded only when cash is paid, the company would report a series of losses on its income statement during the development of the land. In this case, the income statements would not provide a realistic picture of the company's operations. In fact, the development might be highly successful and the early losses misleading.

Accrual accounting concepts are designed to reflect a company's financial performance during a period and avoid misleading results that could arise from the timing of cash receipts and payments such as those described in the preceding paragraph. At the same time, accrual accounting recognizes the importance of reporting cash flows through its emphasis on preparing and reporting the statement of cash flows.

Q. J. C. Clark, attorney at law, drafted a will and estate documents for Max Winder on April 30. Clark billed Winder $1,200 for these services on May 20 and received payment on June 4. In what month should Clark record the revenue under the accrual concepts of accounting?

A. *April*

Under the accrual concepts of accounting, transactions are recorded as they occur and thus affect the accounting equation (assets, liabilities, and stockholders' equity). Since the receipt or payment of cash affects assets (cash), all cash receipts and payments are recorded in the accounts under accrual concepts. However, under the accrual concepts, transactions are also recorded even though cash is not received or paid until a later point. For example, Family Health Care may provide services to patients who are covered by health insurance. It then files a claim with the insurance company for the payment. In this case, revenue is recognized when the services are provided, and the services are said to be provided "on account." Likewise, a business may purchase supplies from a vendor, with terms that allow the business to pay for the purchase within a time period, such as 10 days. In this case, the supplies are said to be purchased "on account." Each of the preceding illustrations represents a business transaction that affects elements of the accounting equation and is therefore recorded under accrual concepts, *even though cash is not received or paid* at the time of the transaction.

In accounting, we often use the term "recognized" to refer to when a transaction is recorded. *Under accrual concepts of accounting, revenue is recognized when it is earned.*

HOW BUSINESSES MAKE MONEY

Not Cutting Corners

Have you ever ordered a hamburger from **Wendy's** and noticed that the meat patty is square? The square meat patty reflects a business emphasis instilled in Wendy's by its founder, Dave Thomas. Mr. Thomas emphasized offering high-quality products at a fair price in a friendly atmosphere, without "cutting corners;" hence, the square meat patty. In the highly competitive fast-food industry, Dave Thomas's approach has enabled Wendy's to become the third largest fast-food restaurant chain in the world, with annual sales of over $7 billion.

Source: Douglas Martin, "Dave Thomas, 69, Wendy's Founder, Dies," *The New York Times*, January 9, 2002.

For Family Health Care, revenue is earned when services have been provided to the patient. At this point, the revenue earning process is complete, and the patient is legally obligated to pay for the services.

Under the accrual concepts, the matching concept plays an important role in determining when expenses are recorded. When revenues are earned and recorded, all expenses incurred in generating the revenues must also be recorded, regardless of whether cash has been paid. In this way, revenues and expenses are matched and the net income or net loss for the period can be determined. This is an application of the matching concept that we discussed in Chapter 1. That is, expenses are recognized and recorded in the same period as the related revenues that they generated and, thus, net income (loss) can be accurately determined.

Accrual concepts recognize liabilities at the time the business incurs the obligation to pay for the services or goods purchased. For example, the purchase of supplies on account would be recorded when the supplies are received and the business has incurred the obligation to pay for the supplies.

Use accrual concepts of accounting to analyze, record, and summarize transactions.

USING ACCRUAL CONCEPTS OF ACCOUNTING FOR FAMILY HEALTH CARE'S NOVEMBER TRANSACTIONS

To illustrate accrual concepts of accounting, we will use the following November 2007 Family Health Care transactions.

a. On November 1, received $1,800 from ILS Company as rent for the use of Family Health Care's land as a temporary parking lot from November 2007 through March 2008.
b. On November 1, paid $2,400 for an insurance premium on a two-year, general business policy.
c. On November 1, paid $6,000 for an insurance premium on a six-month medical malpractice policy.
d. Dr. Landry invested an additional $5,000 in the business in exchange for capital stock.
e. Purchased supplies for $240 on account.
f. Purchased $8,500 of office equipment. Paid $1,700 cash as a down payment, with the remaining $6,800 ($8,500 − $1,700) due in five monthly installments of $1,360 ($6,800/5) beginning January 1.

g. Provided services of $6,100 to patients on account.
h. Received $5,500 for services provided to patients who paid cash.
i. Received $4,200 from insurance companies, which paid on patients' accounts for services that have been provided.
j. Paid $100 on account for supplies that had been purchased.
k. Expenses paid during November were as follows: wages, $2,790; rent, $800; utilities, $580; interest, $100; and miscellaneous, $420.
l. Paid dividends of $1,200 to stockholders (Dr. Landry).

In analyzing and recording the November transactions for Family Health Care, we use the integrated financial statement framework that we used in Chapter 2. In so doing, we record increases and decreases for each financial statement element. These separate elements are referred to as **accounts**.

Transaction a. *On November 1, received $1,800 from ILS Company as rent for the use of Family Health Care's land as a temporary parking lot from November 2007 through March 2008.* In this transaction, Family Health Care entered into a rental agreement for the use of its land. The agreement required the payment of the rental fee of $1,800 in advance. The rental agreement also gives ILS Company the option of renewing the agreement for another four months.

How does this transaction affect the accounts (elements) of the balance sheet, and how should it be recorded? Since cash has been received, cash is increased by $1,800, but what other account should be increased or decreased? Family Health Care has agreed to rent the land to ILS Company for five months and thus has incurred a liability to provide this service—rental of the land. If Family Health Care canceled the agreement on November 1, after accepting the $1,800, it would have to repay that amount to ILS Company. Thus, Family Health Care should record this transaction as an increase in cash and an increase in a liability for $1,800. Because the liability relates to rent that has been paid in cash, but not yet earned, it is recorded as **unearned revenue**, as shown below.

Statement of Cash Flows	Balance Sheet						Income Statement
	Assets		= Liabilities		+ Stockholders' Equity		
	Cash +	Land =	Notes Payable +	Unearned Revenue +	Capital Stock +	Retained Earnings	
Balances, Nov. 1	7,320	12,000	10,000		6,000	3,320	
a. Received rent in advance	1,800			1,800			
Balances	9,120	12,000	10,000	1,800	6,000	3,320	

Statement of Cash Flows		Income Statement
a. Operating	1,800	

As time passes, the liability will decrease, and Family Health Care will earn rental revenue. For example, at the end of November, one-fifth of the $1,800 ($360) will have been earned. Later in this chapter, we will discuss how to record the $360 of earned rent revenue at the end of November.

You should note that the November 1 balances shown in the preceding integrated financial statement spreadsheet are the ending balances from October. That is, the cash balance of $7,320 is the ending cash balance as of October 31, 2007. Likewise, the other balances are carried forward from the preceding month. In this sense, the accounting equation represents a cumulative history of the financial results of the business. In addition, the receipt of cash has the effect of increasing cash flows from operating activities on the statement of cash flows.

Transaction b. *On November 1, paid $2,400 for an insurance premium on a two-year, general business policy.* This insurance policy covers a variety of possible risks to the business, such as fire and theft. By paying the premium, Family Health Care has purchased an asset, insurance coverage, in exchange for cash. Thus, the mix of assets has changed and cash flows from operating activities decreases by $2,400. However, the prepaid insurance coverage is unique in that it expires with the passage of time. At the end of the two-year period, the asset will have been used up, and the insurance policy will be completely expired. Such assets are called **prepaid expenses** or **deferred expenses**. Thus, the purchase of the insurance coverage is recorded as prepaid insurance, as shown below.

Statement of Cash Flows	Balance Sheet							Income Statement
	Assets			= Liabilities		+ Stockholders' Equity		
	Cash	+ Prepaid Insurance	+ Land	= Notes Payable	+ Unearned Revenue	+ Capital Stock	+ Retained Earnings	
Balances	9,120		12,000	10,000	1,800	6,000	3,320	
b. Paid insurance for 2 yrs.	−2,400	2,400						
Balances	6,720	2,400	12,000	10,000	1,800	6,000	3,320	

Statement of Cash Flows	
b. Operating	−2,400

Income Statement

Later in this illustration, we will discuss how such accounts are updated at the end of an accounting period to reflect the portion of the asset that has expired.

Transaction c. *On November 1, paid $6,000 for an insurance premium on a six-month medical malpractice policy.* This transaction is similar to transaction (b), except that Family Health Care has purchased medical malpractice insurance that is renewable every six months. The transaction is recorded as follows:

Statement of Cash Flows	Balance Sheet							Income Statement
	Assets			= Liabilities		+ Stockholders' Equity		
	Cash	+ Prepaid Insurance	+ Land	= Notes Payable	+ Unearned Revenue	+ Capital Stock	+ Retained Earnings	
Balances	6,720	2,400	12,000	10,000	1,800	6,000	3,320	
c. Paid insurance for 6 mos.	−6,000	6,000						
Balances	720	8,400	12,000	10,000	1,800	6,000	3,320	

Statement of Cash Flows	
c. Operating	−6,000

Income Statement

Transaction d. *Dr. Landry invested an additional $5,000 in the business in exchange for capital stock.* This transaction is similar to the one in which Dr. Landry initially established Family Health Care. It is recorded as shown below.

Statement of Cash Flows	Balance Sheet							Income Statement
	Assets			= Liabilities		+ Stockholders' Equity		
	Cash	+ Prepaid Insurance	+ Land	= Notes Payable	+ Unearned Revenue	+ Capital Stock	+ Retained Earnings	
Balances	720	8,400	12,000	10,000	1,800	6,000	3,320	
d. Issued capital stock	5,000					5,000		
Balances	5,720	8,400	12,000	10,000	1,800	11,000	3,320	

Statement of Cash Flows		Income Statement
d. Financing	5,000	

Transaction e. *Purchased supplies for $240 on account.* This transaction is similar to transactions (b) and (c), in that purchased supplies are assets until they are used up in generating revenue. Family Health Care has purchased and received the supplies, with a promise to pay in the near future. Such liabilities that are incurred in the normal operations of the business are called **accounts payable**. The transaction is recorded by increasing the asset supplies and increasing the liability accounts payable, as shown below.

Statement of Cash Flows	Balance Sheet									Income Statement
	Assets				= Liabilities			+ Stockholders' Equity		
	Cash	+ Prepaid Insurance	+ Supplies	+ Land	= Notes Payable	+ Accounts Payable	+ Unearned Revenue	+ Capital Stock	+ Retained Earnings	
Balances	5,720	8,400		12,000	10,000		1,800	11,000	3,320	
e. Purchased supplies			240			240				
Balances	5,720	8,400	240	12,000	10,000	240	1,800	11,000	3,320	

Statement of Cash Flows	Income Statement

Transaction f. *Purchased $8,500 of office equipment. Paid $1,700 cash as a down payment, with the remaining $6,800 (8,500 − $1,700) due in five monthly installments of $1,360 ($6,800/5) beginning January 1.* In this transaction, the asset office equipment is increased by $8,500, cash is decreased by $1,700, notes payable is increased by $6,800, and cash flows from investing activities is decreased by $1,700. The transaction is recorded as follows:

Statement of Cash Flows	Balance Sheet										Income Statement
	Assets					= Liabilities			+ Stockholders' Equity		
	Cash	+ Prepaid Insur.	+ Supp.	+ Office Equip.	+ Land	= Notes Pay.	+ Accts. Pay.	+ Unearned Revenue	+ Capital Stock	+ Retained Earnings	
Balances	5,720	8,400	240		12,000	10,000	240	1,800	11,000	3,320	
f. Purchased office equip.	−1,700			8,500		6,800					
Balances	4,020	8,400	240	8,500	12,000	16,800	240	1,800	11,000	3,320	

Statement of Cash Flows		Income Statement
f. Investing	−1,700	

Transaction g. *Provided services of $6,100 to patients on account.* This transaction is similar to the revenue transactions that we recorded in September and October, except that the services have been provided on account. Family Health Care will collect cash from the patients' insurance companies in the future. Such amounts that are to be collected in the future and that arise from the normal operations of a business are called **accounts receivable**. Since a valid claim exists for future collection, accounts receivable are assets, and the transaction would be recorded as shown below.

Statement of Cash Flows	Balance Sheet											Income Statement
	Assets						= Liabilities			+ Stockholders' Equity		
	Cash	+ Accts. Rec.	+ Prepaid Insur.	+ Supp.	+ Office Equip.	+ Land	= Notes Pay.	+ Accts. Pay.	+ Unearned Revenue	+ Capital Stock	+ Retained Earnings	
Balances	4,020		8,400	240	8,500	12,000	16,800	240	1,800	11,000	3,320	
g. Fees earned on acct.		6,100									6,100	g.
Balances	4,020	6,100	8,400	240	8,500	12,000	16,800	240	1,800	11,000	9,420	

Statement of Cash Flows

Income Statement

g. 6,100 Fees earned

Transaction h. *Received $5,500 for services provided to patients who paid cash.* This transaction is similar to the revenue transactions that we recorded in September and October and is recorded as shown below.

Statement of Cash Flows	Balance Sheet											Income Statement
	Assets						= Liabilities			+ Stockholders' Equity		
	Cash	+ Accts. Rec.	+ Prepaid Insur.	+ Supp.	+ Office Equip.	+ Land	= Notes Pay.	+ Accts. Pay.	+ Unearned Revenue	+ Capital Stock	+ Retained Earnings	
Balances	4,020	6,100	8,400	240	8,500	12,000	16,800	240	1,800	11,000	9,420	
h. Fees earned for cash	5,500										5,500	h.
Balances	9,520	6,100	8,400	240	8,500	12,000	16,800	240	1,800	11,000	14,920	

Statement of Cash Flows

h. Operating 5,500

Income Statement

h. 5,500 Fees earned

Transaction i. *Received $4,200 from insurance companies, which paid on patients' accounts for services that have been provided.* In this transaction, cash is increased and the accounts receivable is decreased by $4,200. Thus, only the mix of assets changes, and the transaction is recorded as shown below.

Statement of Cash Flows	Balance Sheet											Income Statement
	Assets						= Liabilities			+ Stockholders' Equity		
	Cash	+ Accts. Rec.	+ Prepaid Insur.	+ Supp.	+ Office Equip.	+ Land	= Notes Pay.	+ Accts. Pay.	+ Unearned Revenue	+ Capital Stock	+ Retained Earnings	
Balances	9,520	6,100	8,400	240	8,500	12,000	16,800	240	1,800	11,000	14,920	
i. Collected cash on acct.	4,200	−4,200										
Balances	13,720	1,900	8,400	240	8,500	12,000	16,800	240	1,800	11,000	14,920	

Statement of Cash Flows

i. Operating 4,200

Income Statement

Transaction j. *Paid $100 on account for supplies that had been purchased.* This transaction reduces the cash and the accounts payable by $100, as shown below.

Statement of Cash Flows	Balance Sheet											Income Statement
	Assets						= Liabilities			+ Stockholders' Equity		
	Cash +	Accts. Rec. +	Prepaid Insur. +	Supp. +	Office Equip. +	Land =	Notes Pay. +	Accts. Pay. +	Unearned Revenue +	Capital Stock +	Retained Earnings	
Balances	13,720	1,900	8,400	240	8,500	12,000	16,800	240	1,800	11,000	14,920	
j. Paid on account	−100							−100				
Balances	13,620	1,900	8,400	240	8,500	12,000	16,800	140	1,800	11,000	14,920	

Statement of Cash Flows	
j. Operating	−100

Income Statement

Q. Assume that you cancel a $300 airline ticket that, though nonrefundable, may be applied to another ticket within one year. When should the airline transfer the $300 from unearned revenue to revenue?

A. *After one year, or when the $300 is applied to another ticket and you use that ticket.*

Transaction k. *Expenses paid during November were as follows: wages, $2,790; rent, $800; utilities, $580; interest, $100; and miscellaneous, $420.* This transaction is similar to the expense transaction that we recorded for Family Health Care in September and October. It is recorded as shown below.

Statement of Cash Flows	Balance Sheet											Income Statement
	Assets						= Liabilities			+ Stockholders' Equity		
	Cash +	Accts. Rec. +	Prepaid Insur. +	Supp. +	Office Equip. +	Land =	Notes Pay. +	Accts. Pay. +	Unearned Revenue +	Capital Stock +	Retained Earnings	
Balances	13,620	1,900	8,400	240	8,500	12,000	16,800	140	1,800	11,000	14,920	
k. Paid expenses	−4,690										−4,690	k.
Balances	8,930	1,900	8,400	240	8,500	12,000	16,800	140	1,800	11,000	10,230	

Statement of Cash Flows	
k. Operating	−4,690

Income Statement	
k. −2,790	Wages expense
−800	Rent expense
−580	Utilities expense
−100	Interest expense
−420	Misc. expense

Transaction l. *Paid dividends of $1,200 to stockholders (Dr. Landry).* This transaction is similar to the dividends transactions of September and October. It is recorded as shown on the next page.

Statement of Cash Flows	Balance Sheet											Income Statement
	Assets						= Liabilities			+ Stockholders' Equity		
	Cash +	Accts. Rec. +	Prepaid Insur. +	Supp. +	Office Equip. +	Land =	Notes Pay. +	Accts. Pay. +	Unearned Revenue +	Capital Stock +	Retained Earnings	
Balances	8,930	1,900	8,400	240	8,500	12,000	16,800	140	1,800	11,000	10,230	
I. Paid dividends	−1,200										−1,200	
Balances	7,730	1,900	8,400	240	8,500	12,000	16,800	140	1,800	11,000	9,030	

Statement of Cash Flows	
I. Financing	−1,200

Income Statement

Describe and illustrate the end-of-the-period adjustment process.

THE ADJUSTMENT PROCESS

Accrual concepts of accounting require the accounting records to be updated prior to preparing financial statements. This updating process, called the **adjustment process**, is necessary to properly match revenues and expenses. This is an application of the matching concept.

Adjustments are necessary because, at any point in time, some accounts (elements) of the accounting equation will not be up to date. For example, as time passes, prepaid insurance will expire and supplies will be used in operations. However, it is not efficient to record the daily expiration of prepaid insurance or the daily usage of supplies. Rather, the accounting records are normally updated just prior to preparing the financial statements.

You may wonder why we were able to prepare the September and October financial statements for Family Health Care in Chapter 2 without recording any adjustments. The answer is that in September and October, Family Health Care only entered into cash transactions. When all of a party's transactions are cash transactions, no adjustments are necessary. However, Family Health Care had accrual transactions in November. Thus, we must now address the adjustment process.

Deferrals and Accruals

The financial statements are affected by two types of adjustments—deferrals and accruals. Whether a deferral or an accrual, each adjustment will affect a balance sheet account and an income statement account.

Deferrals are created by recording a transaction in a way that delays or defers the recognition of an expense or a revenue. Common examples of deferrals are described below.

- **Prepaid expenses** or deferred expenses are items that initially have been recorded as assets but are expected to become expenses over time or through the normal operations of the business. For Family Health Care, prepaid insurance is an example of a deferral that will normally require adjustment. Other examples include supplies, prepaid advertising, and prepaid interest. McDonald's

Corporation reported over $300 million of prepaid expenses and other current assets on a recent balance sheet.

- **Unearned revenues** or **deferred revenues** are items that initially have been recorded as liabilities but are expected to become revenues over time or through the normal operations of the business. For Family Health Care, unearned rent is an example of a deferred revenue. Other examples include tuition received in advance by a school, an annual retainer fee received by an attorney, premiums received in advance by an insurance company, and magazine subscriptions received in advance by a publisher. On a recent balance sheet, Microsoft Corporation reported almost $5 billion of deferred revenue related to its software. Likewise, Time-Warner Inc. reported over a billion dollars of deferred revenue on a recent balance sheet.

Accruals are created when a revenue or expense has been earned or incurred, but has not been recorded at the end of the accounting period. Accruals are normally the result of revenue being earned or an expense being incurred before any cash is received or paid. One such situation where employees earn wages before the end of the year, but are not paid until after year-end. For example, employee wages may be paid and recorded every Friday, but the accounting period may end on a Tuesday. Thus, at the end of the accounting period, the company owes the employees for their wages on Monday and Tuesday that will be paid on the following Friday. At the end of the accounting period, these wages have been incurred by the company, but have not yet been recorded or paid. Thus, the amount of the wages for Monday and Tuesday is an accrual. Other examples of accruals are described below.

Q. Assume that you take advantage of an offer by a local funeral home to prepay your funeral, burial, and related expenses. How would the funeral home account for the prepayment?

A. *Increase cash and deferred (unearned) revenue.*

- **Accrued expenses** or accrued liabilities are expenses that have been incurred but have not been recorded in the accounts. An example of an accrued expense is accrued interest on notes payable at the end of a period. Other examples include accrued utility expenses and taxes. On a recent balance sheet, Home Depot reported over $600 million of accrued salaries and related expenses and over a billion dollars of other accrued expenses.
- **Accrued revenues** or accrued assets are revenues that have been earned but have not been recorded in the accounts. An example of an accrued revenue is fees for services that an attorney has provided but has not billed to the client at the end of the period. Other examples include accrued interest on notes receivable and accrued rent on property rented to others. In notes to a recent balance sheet, General Motors reported over $1 billion of accrued interest and rent receivables.

INTEGRITY, OBJECTIVITY, AND ETHICS IN BUSINESS

Dave's Legacy

When Dave Thomas, founder of **Wendy's**, died in 2002, he left behind a corporate culture of integrity and high ethical conduct. When asked to comment on Dave's death, Jack Schuessler, chairman and chief executive officer of Wendy's, stated:

". . . people (could) relate to Dave, that he was honest and has integrity and he really cares about people. . . . there is no replacing Dave Thomas . . . . So you are left with . . . the values that he gave us . . . and you take care of the customer every day like Dave would want us to and good things will happen."

". . . he's (Dave Thomas) taught us so much that when we get stuck, we can always look back and ask ourselves, how would Dave handle it?"

In a recent discussion of corporate earnings with analysts, Kerrii Anderson, chief financial officer of Wendy's, stated: ". . . we're confident about the future and because of our unwavering commitment to our core values, such as quality food, superior restaurant operations, continuous improvement, and *integrity to doing the right thing* (emphasis added)."

Sources: Neil Cavuto, "Wendy's CEO—Interview," *Fox News: Your World*, February 11, 2002; "Q1 2003 Wendy's International Earnings Conference Call—Final," *Financial Disclosure Wire*, April 24, 2003.

Exhibit 1

Deferrals and Accruals

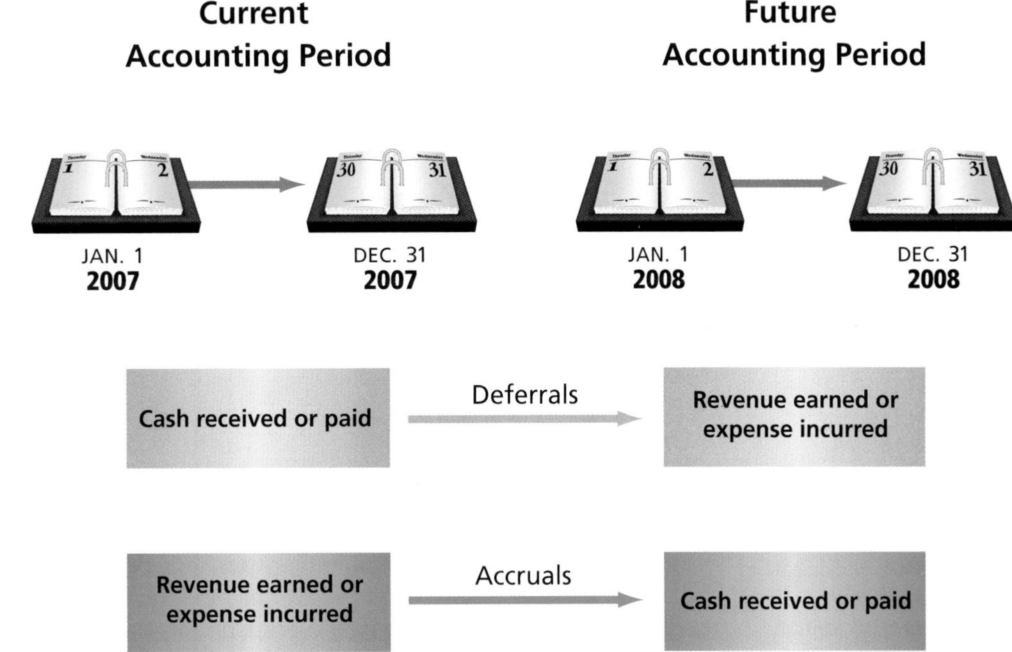

Exhibit 1 summarizes the nature of deferrals and accruals and the need for adjustments in order to prepare financial statements.

Adjustments for Family Health Care

We now analyze the accounts for Family Health Care at the end of November to determine whether any adjustments are necessary. Specifically, we will focus on the following adjustment data, which are typical for most businesses.

Deferred expenses:

1. Prepaid insurance expired, $1,100.
2. Supplies used, $150.
3. Depreciation on office equipment, $160.

Deferred revenue:

4. Unearned revenue earned, $360.

Accrued expense:

5. Wages owed but not paid to employees, $220.

Accrued revenue:

6. Services provided but not billed to insurance companies, $750.

Adjustment 1 (Prepaid Insurance). This first adjustment recognizes that a portion of the prepaid insurance purchased November 1 expired during November. Family Health Care prepaid two policies—a general business policy for $2,400 (transaction b) and a malpractice policy for $6,000 (transaction c). The general business policy is a two-year policy expiring at a rate of $100 ($2,400 ÷ 24) per month. The malpractice policy is a six-month policy that expires at a rate of $1,000 ($6,000 ÷ 6) per month. The total expired prepaid insurance is thus $1,100 ($100 + $1,000). This adjustment is recorded as shown on the next page.

Statement of Cash Flows	Balance Sheet											Income Statement
	Assets						= Liabilities			+ Stockholders' Equity		
	Cash +	Accts. Rec. +	Prepaid Insur. +	Supp. +	Office Equip. +	Land =	Notes Pay. +	Accts. Pay. +	Unearned Revenue +	Capital Stock +	Retained Earnings	
Balances	7,730	1,900	8,400	240	8,500	12,000	16,800	140	1,800	11,000	9,030	
a1. Insurance expense			−1,100								−1,100	a1.
Balances	7,730	1,900	7,300	240	8,500	12,000	16,800	140	1,800	11,000	7,930	

Statement of Cash Flows

Income Statement

a1. −1,100 Insurance exp.

Q. As of January 1, $450 of supplies are on hand. During January, $1,250 of supplies were purchased on account, and on January 31, $175 of supplies are on hand. What is the supplies expense for January?

A. *$1,525 ($450 + $1,250 − $175)*

Adjustment 2 (Supplies). This adjustment recognizes the portion of the $240 of supplies purchased during November that have been used. For November, $150 of the supplies were used, leaving $90 of supplies remaining for use during the coming months. Thus, after recording the adjustment, the accounting records should show supplies expense of $150 for November and supplies on hand (an asset) of $90. The second adjustment is recorded as shown below.

Statement of Cash Flows	Balance Sheet											Income Statement
	Assets						= Liabilities			+ Stockholders' Equity		
	Cash +	Accts. Rec. +	Prepaid Insur. +	Supp. +	Office Equip. +	Land =	Notes Pay. +	Accts. Pay. +	Unearned Revenue +	Capital Stock +	Retained Earnings	
Balances	7,730	1,900	7,300	240	8,500	12,000	16,800	140	1,800	11,000	7,930	
a2. Supplies expense				−150							−150	a2.
Balances	7,730	1,900	7,300	90	8,500	12,000	16,800	140	1,800	11,000	7,780	

Statement of Cash Flows

Income Statement

a2. −150 Supplies exp.

Adjustment 3 (Depreciation). This adjustment recognizes that fixed assets such as office equipment lose their ability to provide service over time. This reduction in the ability of a fixed asset to provide service is called **depreciation**. However, it is difficult to objectively determine the physical decline in the ability of fixed assets to provide service. For this reason, accountants estimate the amount of the cost of long-term assets that becomes expense over the asset's useful life. In a later chapter, we will discuss methods of estimating depreciation. In this chapter, we simply assume that the amount of November depreciation for the office equipment is $160.

To maintain a record of the initial cost of a fixed asset for tax and other purposes, the fixed asset (office equipment) is not reduced directly. Instead, an offsetting or contra asset account, called **accumulated depreciation**, is included in the accounting equation. On the balance sheet, the accumulated depreciation will be subtracted from the original cost of the fixed asset. Thus, the third adjustment is recorded as shown on the next page.

Statement of Cash Flows	Cash	+ Accts. Rec.	+ Prepaid Insur.	+ Supp.	+ Office Equip.	– Acc. Dep.	+ Land	= Notes Pay.	+ Accts. Pay.	+ Unearned Revenue	+ Capital Stock	+ Retained Earnings	Income Statement
Balances	7,730	1,900	7,300	90	8,500		12,000	16,800	140	1,800	11,000	7,780	
a3. Depreciation exp.						−160						−160	a3.
Balances	7,730	1,900	7,300	90	8,500	−160	12,000	16,800	140	1,800	11,000	7,620	

(Balance Sheet: Assets = Liabilities + Stockholders' Equity)

Statement of Cash Flows

Income Statement
a3. −160 Depreciation exp.

Note that the accumulated depreciation account is subtracted in determining the total assets. We should also note three other points related to Adjustment 3. First, land is not depreciated, since it usually does not lose its ability to provide service. Second, the cost of the equipment can be thought of as a deferred expense, since it is recognized as an expense over the equipment's useful life. Third, the cost of the fixed asset less the balance of its accumulated depreciation is called the asset's *carrying value* or *book value*. For example, the carrying value of the office equipment, after the preceding adjustment, is $8,340 ($8,500 − $160).

Adjustment 4 (Unearned Rent). This adjustment recognizes that a portion of the unearned revenue is earned by the end of November. That is, of the $1,800 received for rental of the land for five months (November through March), one-fifth, or $360, would have been earned as of November 30. The fourth adjustment recognizes this decrease in the unearned revenue and the increase in the rental revenue, as shown below.

Statement of Cash Flows	Cash	+ Accts. Rec.	+ Prepaid Insur.	+ Supp.	+ Office Equip.	– Acc. Dep.	+ Land	= Notes Pay.	+ Accts. Pay.	+ Unearned Revenue	+ Capital Stock	+ Retained Earnings	Income Statement
Balances	7,730	1,900	7,300	90	8,500	−160	12,000	16,800	140	1,800	11,000	7,620	
a4. Rent revenue										−360		360	a4.
Balances	7,730	1,900	7,300	90	8,500	−160	12,000	16,800	140	1,440	11,000	7,980	

(Balance Sheet: Assets = Liabilities + Stockholders' Equity)

Statement of Cash Flows

Income Statement
a4. 360 Rent revenue

Q. During August, wages expense of $18,950 was reported. If wages payable at August 1 was $1,100, and wages of $18,500 were paid during August, how much was accrued wages payable on August 31?

A. $1,550 ($18,500 − $1,100 = $17,400; $18,950 − $17,400 = $1,550); Or, $1,100 + $18,950 − $18,500

Adjustment 5 (Accrued Wages Expense). This adjustment recognizes that as of November 30, employees of Family Health Care may have worked one or more days for which they have not been paid. It is rare that the employees are paid the same day that the accounting period ends. Thus, at the end of an accounting period, it is normal for businesses to owe wages to their employees. This is what we defined as an accrued expense earlier in our discussion. The fifth adjustment is recorded by increasing wages payable, a liability, and deducting wages expense from retained earnings, as shown at the top of the next page.

Statement of Cash Flows	Balance Sheet													Income Statement
	Assets							= Liabilities				+ Stockholders' Equity		
	Cash +	Accts. Rec. +	Prepaid Insur. +	Supp. +	Office Equip. −	Acc. Dep. +	Land =	Notes Pay. +	Accts. Pay. +	Wages Pay. +	Unearned Revenue +	Capital Stock +	Retained Earnings	
Balances	7,730	1,900	7,300	90	8,500	−160	12,000	16,800	140		1,440	11,000	7,980	
a5. Wages exp.										220			−220	a5.
Balances	7,730	1,900	7,300	90	8,500	−160	12,000	16,800	140	220	1,440	11,000	7,760	

Statement of Cash Flows

Income Statement

a5. −220 Wages expense

Adjustment 6 (Accrued Fees Earned). This adjustment recognizes that Family Health Care has provided services to patients that have not yet been billed. Such services are usually provided near the end of the month. This adjustment is recorded by increasing accounts receivable and fees earned, as shown below.

Statement of Cash Flows	Balance Sheet													Income Statement
	Assets							= Liabilities				+ Stockholders' Equity		
	Cash +	Accts. Rec. +	Prepaid Insur. +	Supp. +	Office Equip. −	Acc. Dep. +	Land =	Notes Pay. +	Accts. Pay. +	Wages Pay. +	Unearned Revenue +	Capital Stock +	Retained Earnings	
Balances	7,730	1,900	7,300	90	8,500	−160	12,000	16,800	140	220	1,440	11,000	7,760	
a6. Fees earned		750											750	a6.
Balances	7,730	2,650	7,300	90	8,500	−160	12,000	16,800	140	220	1,440	11,000	8,510	

Statement of Cash Flows

Income Statement

a6. 750 Fees earned

The November transactions and adjustments for Family Health Care are summarized in Exhibit 2.

Prepare financial statements using accrual concepts of accounting, including a classified balance sheet.

FINANCIAL STATEMENTS

In Chapter 2, we prepared financial statements for Family Health Care for September and October. In this section, we describe and illustrate financial statements for November, using accrual concepts of accounting. These financial statements are shown in Exhibits 3, 4, 5, and 6. They are based on the summary of transactions and adjustments shown in Exhibit 2.

Income Statement

The income statement is prepared by summarizing the revenue and expense transactions listed under the income statement column of Exhibit 2. The operating income is

Exhibit 2

Family Health Care Summary of Transactions and Adjustments for November

Statement of Cash Flows	Balance Sheet													Income Statement
	Assets							= Liabilities				+ Stockholders' Equity		
	Cash +	Accts. Rec. +	Prepaid Insur. +	Supp. +	Office Equip. −	Acc. Dep. +	Land =	Notes Pay. +	Accts. Pay. +	Wages Pay. +	Unearned Revenue +	Capital Stock +	Retained Earnings	
Balances, Nov. 1	7,320						12,000	10,000				6,000	3,320	
a. Rental rev.	1,800										1,800			
b. Paid insurance	−2,400		2,400											
c. Paid insurance	−6,000		6,000											
d. Investment	5,000											5,000		
e. Pur. supplies				240					240					
f. Pur. off. equip.	−1,700				8,500			6,800						
g. Fees earned		6,100											6,100	g.
h. Fees earned	5,500												5,500	h.
i. Collected cash	4,200	−4,200												
j. Paid on acct.	−100								−100					
k. Paid expenses	−4,690												−4,690	k.
l. Dividends	−1,200												−1,200	
a1. Insurance exp.			−1,100										−1,100	a1.
a2. Supplies exp.				−150									−150	a2.
a3. Deprec. exp.						−160							−160	a3.
a4. Rental revenue											−360		360	a4.
a5. Wages exp.										220			−220	a5.
a6. Fees earned		750											750	a6.
Balances, Nov. 30	7,730	2,650	7,300	90	8,500	−160	12,000	16,800	140	220	1,440	11,000	8,510	

Statement of Cash Flows

a.	Operating	1,800
b.	Operating	−2,400
c.	Operating	−6,000
d.	Financing	5,000
f.	Investing	−1,700
h.	Operating	5,500
i.	Operating	4,200
j.	Operating	−100
k.	Operating	−4,690
l.	Financing	−1,200
Increase in cash		410
Nov. 1 cash bal.		7,320
Nov. 30 cash bal.		7,730

INTEGRATED FINANCIAL STATEMENT FRAMEWORK

Income Statement

g.	6,100	Fees earned
h.	5,500	Fees earned
k.	−2,790	Wages exp.
	−800	Rent exp.
	−580	Utilities exp.
	−100	Interest exp.
	−420	Misc. exp.
a1.	−1,100	Insur. exp.
a2.	−150	Supp. exp.
a3.	−160	Deprec. exp.
a4.	360	Rental rev.
a5.	−220	Wages exp.
a6.	750	Fees earned
	6,390	Net income

determined by deducting the operating expenses from the fees earned from normal operations. The other income—rental revenue—is then added to determine the net income for November.

As reported on the income statement, *revenues* are a result of providing services or selling products to customers. Examples of revenues include fees earned, fares earned, commissions revenue, interest revenue, and rent revenue.

Revenues from the primary operations of the business are normally reported separately from other revenue. For example, Family Health Care has two types of revenues for November, fees earned and rental revenue. Since the primary operation of the business is providing services to patients, rental revenue is reported under the heading of "Other income."

Expenses on the income statement are assets used up or services consumed in the process of generating revenues. Expenses are matched against their related revenues to determine the net income or net loss for a period. Examples of typical expenses include wages expense, rent expense, utilities expense, supplies expense, and miscellaneous expense. Expenses not related to the primary operations of the business are sometimes reported as "Other expense." Interest expense is an example of an expense that may be reported separately as an Other expense.

Exhibit 3

Family Health Care Income Statement for November

Family Health Care, P.C.
Income Statement
For the Month Ended November 30, 2007

Fees earned		$12,350
Operating expenses:		
Wages expense	$3,010	
Insurance expense	1,100	
Rent expense	800	
Utilities expense	580	
Depreciation expense	160	
Supplies expense	150	
Interest expense	100	
Miscellaneous expense	420	
Total operating expenses		6,320
Operating income		$ 6,030
Other income:		
Rental revenue		360
Net income		$ 6,390

Exhibit 4

Family Health Care Retained Earnings Statement for November

Family Health Care, P.C.
Retained Earnings Statement
For the Month Ended November 30, 2007

Retained earnings, November 1, 2007		$3,320
Net income for November	$6,390	
Less dividends	1,200	5,190
Retained earnings, November 30, 2007		$8,510

Retained Earnings Statement

The retained earnings statement shown in Exhibit 4 is prepared by adding the November net income (from the income statement), less the November dividends, to the beginning amount of retained earnings. This ending amount of retained earnings is included on the balance sheet.

Balance Sheet

The balance sheet shown in Exhibit 5 is prepared from the ending balances shown in the Balance Sheet columns of Exhibit 2. The balance sheet shown in Exhibit 3 is a **classified balance sheet**. As the term implies, a classified balance sheet is prepared with various sections, subsections, and captions that aid in its interpretation

Exhibit 5

Family Health Care Balance Sheet for November

Family Health Care, P.C.
Balance Sheet
November 30, 2007

Assets			
Current assets:			
Cash		$ 7,730	
Accounts receivable		2,650	
Prepaid insurance		7,300	
Supplies		90	
Total current assets			$17,770
Fixed assets:			
Office equipment	$8,500		
Less accumulated depreciation	160	$ 8,340	
Land		12,000	
Total fixed assets			20,340
Total assets			$38,110
Liabilities			
Current liabilities:			
Accounts payable		$ 140	
Wages payable		220	
Notes payable		6,800	
Unearned revenue		1,440	
Total current liabilities			$ 8,600
Long-term liabilities:			
Notes payable			10,000
Total liabilities			$18,600
Stockholders' Equity			
Capital stock		$11,000	
Retained earnings		8,510	
Total stockholders' equity			19,510
Total liabilities and stockholders' equity			$38,110

and analysis. In the following paragraphs, we describe some of these sections and subsections.

Assets are resources such as physical items or rights that are owned by the business. Examples of physical assets include cash, supplies, buildings, equipment, and land. Examples of rights are patent rights or rights to services (prepaid items). Physical assets of a long-term nature are referred to as **fixed assets**. Rights that are long term in nature are called **intangible assets**.

Assets are normally divided into classes in preparing a classified balance sheet. Three of these classes are (1) current assets, (2) fixed assets, and (3) intangible assets.

Cash and other assets that are expected to be converted to cash or sold or used up within one year or less, through the normal operations of the business, are called **current assets**. In addition to cash, the current assets normally include accounts receivable, notes receivable, supplies, and other prepaid expenses. Accounts receivable and notes receivable are current assets because they will usually be converted to cash within one year or less. **Notes receivable** are written claims against debtors who promise to pay the amount of the note and interest at an agreed-upon rate. A note receivable is the creditor's view of a note payable transaction. As shown in Exhibit 5, Family Health Care has current assets of cash, accounts receivable, prepaid insurance, and supplies as of November 30, 2007.

The fixed assets section may also be labeled as property, plant, and equipment, or plant assets. Fixed assets include equipment, machinery, buildings, and land. Except for land, such fixed assets depreciate over a period of time, as we discussed earlier in this chapter. The cost less accumulated depreciation for each major type of fixed asset is normally reported on the classified balance sheet. As of November 30, 2007, Family Health Care's fixed assets consist of office equipment and land.

Intangible assets represent rights, such as patent rights, copyrights, and goodwill. Goodwill arises from such factors as name recognition, location, product quality, reputation, and managerial skill. Goodwill is recorded and reported on the balance sheet when a company purchases another company at a premium price above the normal cost of the purchased company's assets. For example, goodwill was recognized when eBay, Inc., purchased PayPal, Inc. Family Health Care has no intangible assets as of November 30.

Liabilities are amounts owed to outsiders (creditors). Liabilities are often identified on the balance sheet by titles that include the word *payable*. Examples of liabilities include notes payable and wages payable.

Liabilities are normally divided into two classes on a classified balance sheet. These classes are (1) current liabilities and (2) long-term liabilities.

International Perspective
Under International Accounting Standards (IASs), noncurrent assets appear above current assets on the balance sheet, while current liabilities appear above noncurrent liabilities. The current asset and current liability accounts are then netted in the middle of the balance sheet on a summary line called "Net current assets."

Liabilities that will be due within a short time (usually one year or less) and that are to be paid out of current assets are called **current liabilities**. The most common current liabilities are notes payable and accounts payable. Other current liabilities reported on the classified balance sheet include wages payable, interest payable, taxes payable, and unearned revenue.

Liabilities that will not be due for a long time (usually more than one year) are called **long-term liabilities**. Long-term liabilities are reported below the current liabilities. As long-term liabilities come due and are to be paid within one year, they are reported as current liabilities. If they are to be renewed rather than paid, they would continue to be classified as long term. When an asset is pledged as security for a long-term liability, the obligation may be called a *mortgage note payable* or a *mortgage payable*.

Family Health Care's current and long-term liabilities as of November 30, 2007, are shown in Exhibit 5. You should note that $6,800 of the notes payable is due within the next year and therefore is reported as a current liability. The remainder of the notes payable, $10,000, is not due until 2012 and thus is reported as a long-term liability.

Family Health Care's other current liabilities consist of accounts payable, wages payable, and unearned revenue.

Stockholders' equity is the stockholders' rights to the assets of the business. For a corporation, the stockholders' equity consists of capital stock and retained earnings. The stockholders' equity section of a classified balance sheet reports each of these two financial statement accounts separately. The capital stock amount on the balance sheet of $11,000 results from adding the additional investment during November of $5,000 to the beginning amount of capital stock of $6,000. The ending retained earnings of $8,510 comes from the retained earnings statement.

Statement of Cash Flows

The statement of cash flows shown in Exhibit 6 is prepared by summarizing the cash transactions shown in the statement of cash flows column of Exhibit 2. The net cash flow from operations is computed by adding the cash receipts from revenue transactions and subtracting the cash payments for operating transactions. These items are identified in the statement of cash flows column of Exhibit 2 as operating activities. The cash received from revenue transactions consists of $9,700 ($5,500 + $4,200) received from patients and $1,800 received from rental of the land. The cash payments for operating transactions of $13,190 ($2,400 + $6,000 + $100 + $4,690) is determined by adding the negative cash payments related to operating activities shown in the statement of cash flows column of Exhibit 2. The purchase of the office equipment is treated as a separate cash outflow from investment activities. The receipt of the additional investment and the payment of dividends are reported as cash flows from financing activities.

Exhibit 6

Family Health Care Statement of Cash Flows for November

Family Health Care, P.C.
Statement of Cash Flows
For the Month Ended November 30, 2007

Cash flows from operating activities:		
Cash received from patients	$ 9,700	
Cash received from rental of land	1,800	$ 11,500
Deduct cash payments for expenses		(13,190)
Net cash flow used in operating activities		$ (1,690)
Cash flows from investing activities:		
Purchase of office equipment		(1,700)
Cash flows from financing activities:		
Additional issuance of capital stock	$ 5,000	
Deduct cash dividends	(1,200)	
Net cash flow from financing activities		3,800
Net increase in cash		$ 410
November 1, 2007, cash balance		7,320
November 30, 2007, cash balance		$ 7,730

Integration of Financial Statements

Exhibit 7 shows the integration of Family Health Care's financial statements for November. The reconciliation of net income and net cash flows from operations is shown in the appendix at the end of this chapter.

Exhibit 7

Integrated Financial Statements—Family Health Care

Family Health Care
Balance Sheet
November 30, 2007

Assets	=	Liabilities	+	Stockholders' Equity	
Cash				Capital Stock	Retained Earnings
⋮		⋮		⋮	⋮
$7,730		$18,600		$11,000	$8,510
$38,110 Total Assets	=	$38,110 Total Liabilities + Stockholders' Equity			

Family Health Care
Statement of Cash Flows
For the Month Ended Nov. 30, 2007

Operating act.	$(1,690)
Investing act.	(1,700)
Financing act.	3,800
Increase in cash	$ 410
Cash, Nov. 1	7,320
Cash, Nov. 30	$ 7,730

Family Health Care
Income Statement
For the Month Ended Nov. 30, 2007

Revenues	$12,350
Expenses	6,320
Operating income	$ 6,030
Other income	360
Net income	$ 6,390

Family Health Care
Retained Earnings Statement
For the Month Ended Nov. 30, 2007

RE, Nov. 1	$ 3,320
Net income	6,390
Dividends	(1,200)
RE, Nov. 30	$ 8,510

Reconciliation of cash flows from operations and net income (see appendix to this chapter)

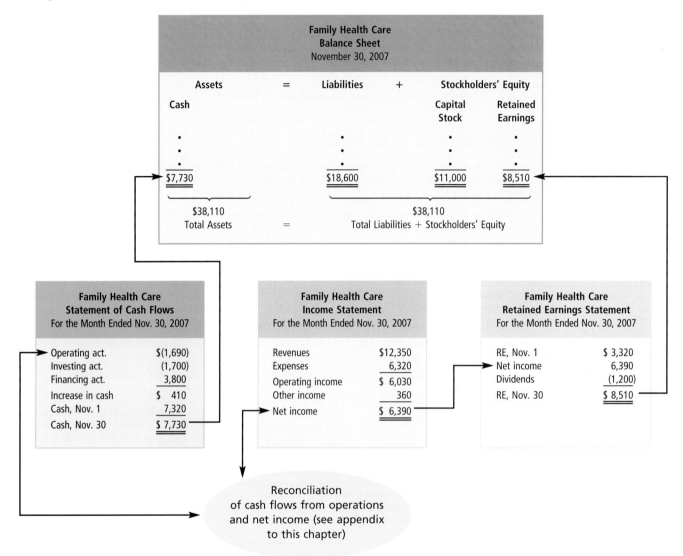

Describe how the accrual basis of accounting enhances the interpretation of financial statements.

ACCRUAL AND CASH BASES OF ACCOUNTING

The financial statements of Family Health Care for November were prepared under accrual accounting concepts. Entities that use accrual accounting concepts for recording transactions and preparing financial statements are said to use the *accrual basis of accounting*. The accrual basis of accounting is used by large businesses and is required of publicly held corporations such as Amazon.com, eBay, and Wm. Wrigley Jr. Company.

Entities that record transactions only when cash is received or paid are said to use the cash basis of accounting. Individuals and small businesses often use the *cash basis of accounting*.[1] For example, you probably use a cash basis because your checkbook is

1 Some businesses use modified-cash bases of accounting. These bases of accounting are covered in advanced accounting texts.

your primary accounting record. You keep track of your deposits (cash receipts) and checks (cash payments). Periodically, your bank sends you a statement that you use to verify the accuracy of your record keeping.

© RYAN MCVAY/PHOTODISC/GETTY IMAGES

Using the Cash Basis of Accounting

Under the **cash basis of accounting**, a business records only transactions involving increases or decreases of its cash. To illustrate, assume that a real estate agency sells a $300,000 piece of property on December 28, 2006. In selling the property, the agency earns a commission of 8% of the selling price. However, the agency does not receive the $24,000 commission check until January 3, 2007. Under the cash basis, the real estate agency will not record the commission (revenue) until January 3, 2007.

Under the cash basis, expenses are recorded only when cash is paid. For example, a December cellular phone bill that is paid in January would be recorded as a January expense, not a December expense. Thus, under the cash basis, the matching concept does not determine when expenses are recorded. That is, expenses are recorded when paid in cash, not necessarily in the period when the revenue is earned. As a result, adjusting entries are not required under the cash basis.

Q. On June 30, a lawyer billed a client for $4,000 for legal services provided during June. The client paid $1,500 in July and $2,500 in August. Under the cash basis, when are the fees earned recorded?

A. *June, $0; July, $1,500; August, $2,500*

Using the Accrual Basis of Accounting

Under the **accrual basis of accounting**, revenue is recorded as it is earned, regardless of when cash is received. To illustrate, using the preceding example, the real estate agency would record the commissions (revenue) of $24,000 as earned on December 28, 2006, even though the check (cash) is not received until January 3, 2007. Once revenue has been earned and recorded, any expenses that have been incurred in generating the revenue are recorded and thus matched against that revenue. For example, a December cellular phone bill would be recorded in December as an increase in expenses and liabilities, even though it is not paid until January. In this way, the December phone expense is matched against the revenue it helped generate in December. We used the accrual basis of accounting to record the November transactions of Family Health Care. In addition, as we illustrated earlier in this chapter, the accrual basis requires adjusting entries to update the accounting records at the end of the period. Exhibit 8 summarizes the basic differences of how revenue and expenses are recorded under the cash and accrual bases of accounting.

© STOCKBYTE PLATINUM/GETTY IMAGES

Exhibit 8

Cash versus Accrual Accounting

	Cash Basis	Accrual Basis
Revenue is recorded	When cash is received	When revenue is earned
Expense is recorded	When cash is paid	When expense is incurred in generating revenue
Adjusting entries	Not required	Required in order to prepare financial statements

Family Health Care Under the Cash and Accrual Bases of Accounting

All the transactions for Family Health Care in Chapter 2 involved the receipt or payment of cash. As a result, the financial statements shown in Chapter 2 for Family Health Care would be the same as that reported under the cash basis of accounting. In this chapter, however, Family Health Care entered into transactions that used accrual accounting concepts. As a result, the November financial statements shown in Exhibits 3 through 6 differ from those prepared using the cash basis of accounting.

One of the major differences in financial statements prepared under the accrual and cash bases of accounting involves the reporting of net income and net cash flows from operations. Under the cash basis of accounting, net income and net cash flows from operations are the same. For example, in Chapter 2, net income and net cash flows from operations for September and October for Family Health Care were $2,600 and $3,220. In contrast, under the accrual basis of accounting, net income and net cash flows from operations may be significantly different. This is shown in Exhibit 3 where Family Health Care reports net income of $6,390 for November while reporting net cash flows from operations of ($1,690). This difference is due to the effects of accrual and deferrals.[2]

Importance of Accrual Basis of Accounting

The use of the accrual basis of accounting is essential for assessing and interpreting the financial performance of an entity. To illustrate, we have summarized the net cash flows from operations and net income for Family Health Care below.

	Net Cash Flow from Operations	Net Income
September	$ 2,600	$2,600
October	3,220	3,220
November	(1,690)	6,390

Under the cash basis, the cash flows from operating activities and the net income for November would be reported as a negative amount (loss) of $1,690. While this might be interpreted as an unfavorable trend, the accrual basis better reflects what is really happening to Family Health Care. Since September, revenues have more than doubled, increasing from $5,500 to $12,350, and net income has more than doubled. Thus, the accrual basis reflects Family Health Care as a profitable, rapidly expanding business. This illustrates why net income is generally a better predictor of the long-term profitability of a business than is net cash flows from operations.

Such differences between the cash basis and the accrual basis illustrate why generally accepted accounting principles require the accrual basis for all but the very smallest businesses. You should recognize, however, that the net cash flow from operating activities is an important amount that is useful to readers of the financial statements. For this reason, generally accepted accounting principles require reporting cash flows. For example, in the long run, a business will go bankrupt if it continually

2 A formal reconciliation of net cash flows from operations and the net income is shown in the appendix at the end of this chapter.

experiences negative cash flows from operations, even though it may report net income. In other words, a business must generate positive cash flows from operations in order to survive. In the case of Family Health Care, the negative cash flows from operations for November was due in large measure to prepaying insurance premiums of $8,400. Thus, the negative cash flows from operations is temporary for Family Health Care and not a matter of major concern. This illustrates why the financial statements must be analyzed and interpreted together, rather than individually and why we use the integrated financial statements approach throughout this text. For example, long-run profitability is best analyzed by focusing on the net income reported under the accrual basis, while the availability of cash to pay debts as they become due is best analyzed by focusing on the net cash flows from operating activities.

Describe the accounting cycle for the accrual basis of accounting.

THE ACCOUNTING CYCLE

The process that begins with analyzing transactions and ends with preparing the accounting records for the next accounting period is called the **accounting cycle**. The most important output of the accounting cycle is the financial statements. The basic steps in the accounting cycle are listed below.

1. *Identifying, analyzing, and recording* the effects of transactions on the accounting equation (financial statement accounts).
2. *Identifying, analyzing, and recording* adjustment data.
3. *Preparing* financial statements.
4. *Preparing* the accounting records for the next accounting period.

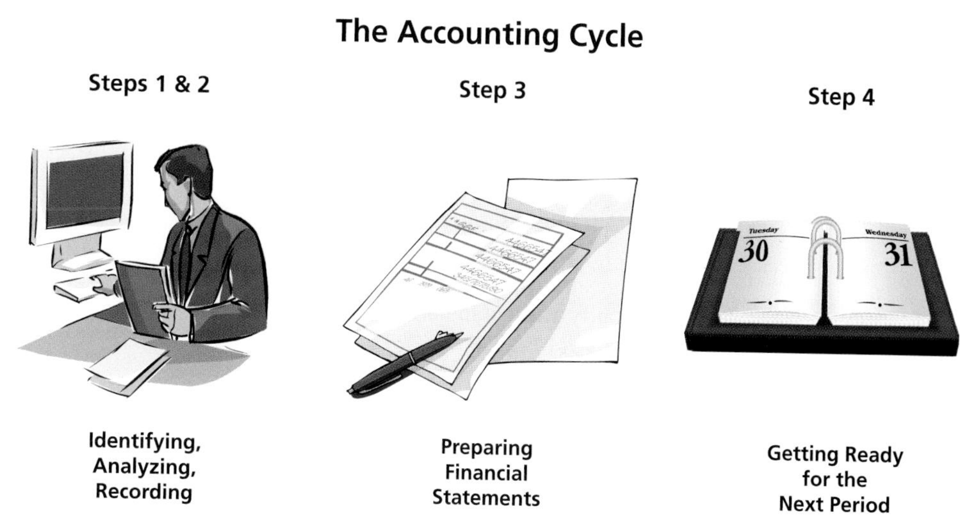

We have described and illustrated steps 1–3 in this chapter. In Chapter 4, we complete the discussion of the accounting cycle by describing how the accounting records are prepared for the next accounting period using closing entries.

Describe and illustrate how common-sized financial statements can be used to analyze and evaluate a company's performance.

COMMON-SIZED FINANCIAL STATEMENTS

Common-sized financial statements are often useful in comparing one company to another. In **common-sized financial statements**, all items are expressed in percentages. Such statements are useful in comparing the current period with prior periods, individual businesses, or one business with industry percentages. Industry data are often available from trade associations or financial information services.

To illustrate, common-sized income statement and balance sheet data for Wendy's and McDonald's Corporation are shown in Exhibit 9.[3] The income statement data are expressed as a percent of revenues; thus, Exhibit 9 indicates revenues for both companies as 100%. This, in turn, allows for analysis of the income statement components on

Exhibit 9

Common-Sized Financial Statements: Wendy's and McDonald's

Income Statements for the Year Ending December 31, 2004	Wendy's OLD FASHIONED HAMBURGERS	McDonald's
Revenues	100.0%	100.0%
Operating expenses	93.8	81.4
Operating income	6.2%	18.6%
Other expenses	1.2	1.8
Income before income taxes	5.0%	16.8%
Income taxes	3.6	4.8
Net income	1.4%	12.0%

Balance Sheets as of December 31, 2004	Wendy's OLD FASHIONED HAMBURGERS	McDonald's
Current assets:		
Cash and equivalents	5.5%	5.0%
Accounts and notes receivable	4.0	2.7
Inventories, prepaid, and other assets	4.8	2.6
Total current assets	14.3%	10.3%
Other long-term assets	12.2	15.4
Property and equipment	73.5	74.3
Total assets	100.0%	100.0%
Total current liabilities	21.5%	12.6%
Other liabilities	24.8	36.3
Total stockholders' equity	53.7	51.1
Total liabilities and stockholders' equity	100.0%	100.0%

3 The financial statements for Wendy's and McDonald's shown in Exhibit 9 were adapted from 10-K Securities and Exchange Commission filings.

a common basis. Without a common basis, it is difficult to compare companies. For example, Wendy's total operating expenses are $3,408,834,000 compared to McDonald's $15,524,200,000. So, does this mean that Wendy's has an advantage because of its lower total operating expenses? Exhibit 9 reveals that this is not the case. In fact, Wendy's operating expenses are 93.8% of sales in comparison to 81.4% for McDonald's. As a result, Wendy's operating income is significantly less as a percent of sales, 6.2%, compared to McDonald's 18.6%.

Based upon Exhibit 9, further analyses are called for to determine why Wendy's operating expenses as a percent of sales are significantly higher than McDonald's. For example, the higher operating expenses may be related to the fact that 19.2% of Wendy's revenues come from its franchise restaurants, while 25.4% of McDonald's revenues come from franchise restaurants.

Exhibit 9 also reports common-sized balance sheet information for Wendy's and McDonald's. The balance sheet data are expressed as a percentage of total assets. The common-sized balance sheets provide information about the relative composition of balance sheet categories to the total. Exhibit 9 indicates that Wendy's keeps a higher percent of its assets in the form of current assets, 14.3%, as compared to 10.3% for McDonald's. This can mostly be explained by Wendy's higher percent of receivables and inventory compared to McDonald's. The percent of property and equipment is nearly the same, while other assets are 12.2% of total assets compared to McDonald's 15.4%. Exhibit 9 also reveals that Wendy's finances more of its operations through stockholders' equity, 53.7%, than does McDonald's, 51.1%. In addition, the relative composition of their liabilities is quite different. Wendy's has current and long-term liabilities representing 21.5% and 24.8% of total assets, while McDonald's is 12.6% and 36.3%, respectively. McDonald's appears to require less relative current liabilities but more long-term debt to support its operations than does Wendy's.

As Exhibit 9 shows, common-sized financial statements facilitate company comparisons and analyses. Such statements are often a starting point for further investigation and analyses of major differences between companies in similar industries. For example, based upon the preceding comparison, further inquiries might be made into why Wendy's operating expenses are a higher percent of sales and why Wendy's maintains a higher percent of its total assets in accounts receivable and inventory than does McDonald's.

APPENDIX

Reconciliation: Net Cash Flows from Operations and Net Income[4]

In Chapter 2, we illustrated financial statements for Family Health Care for September and October 2007. Because all the September and October transactions were cash transactions, the net cash flows from operating activities shown on the statement of cash flows equals the net income shown in the income statements. For example, Exhibits 4 and 7 in Chapter 2 report net cash flows from operating activities and net income of $2,600 and $3,220 for September and October. When all of an entity's transactions have cash transactions or when an entity uses the cash basis of accounting, net cash flows from operating activities will always equal net income. This is not true, however, under the accrual basis of accounting.

4 In a later chapter, this reconciliation will be referred to as the indirect method of reporting cash flows from operations.

During November and December, Family Health Care used the accrual basis of accounting. The November financial statements are illustrated in Exhibits 3 through 6 of this chapter. The December financial statements for Family Health Care are illustrated in the Illustrative Problem at the end of this chapter. The net cash flows from operating activities and net income for November and December are shown below.

	Net Cash Flows from Operating Activities	Net Income
November	$(1,690)	$ 6,390
December	8,760	10,825

Under the accrual basis, net cash flows from operating activities will normally not be the same as net income. The difference can be reconciled by considering the effects of accruals and deferrals on the income statement. Exhibit 10 illustrates the November reconciliation of Family Health Care's net income with operating cash flows from operations.

In Exhibit 10, we begin with net income. We then add or deduct the effects of accruals or deferrals that influenced net income under the accrual basis but did not result in the receipt or payment of cash. We thus arrive at net cash flows from operating activities.

The effect of an accrual or deferral on the income statement and net income is reflected in its net increase or decrease during the period. For example, during November, depreciation expense of $160 was recorded (a deferred expense) and thus deducted in arriving at net income. Yet, no cash was paid. Thus, to arrive at cash flows from operations, depreciation expense is added back to net income. Likewise, accounts payable increased during November by $140, and a related expense was recorded. But again, no cash was paid. Similarly, wages payable increased during November by $220, and the related wages expense was deducted in arriving at net income. However, the $220 was not paid until the next month. Thus, for November, the increases of $140 in accounts payable and $220 in wages payable are added back to net income.

The increase in unearned revenue of $1,440 represents unearned revenue for four months for land rented to ILS Company. ILS Company initially paid Family Health Care $1,800 in advance. Of the $1,800, one-fifth ($360) was recorded as revenue for November. However, under the cash basis, the entire $1,800 would have been recorded as revenue. Therefore, $1,440 (the increase in the unearned revenue) is added back to net income to arrive at cash flows from operations.

During November, accounts receivable increased by $2,650 and thus was recorded as part of revenue in arriving at net income. However, no cash was received. Thus, this increase in accounts receivable is deducted in arriving at cash flows from operations.

Exhibit 10

November's Reconciliation of Net Income and Cash Flows from Operations

Net income		$ 6,390
Add:		
Depreciation expense	$ 160	
Increase in accounts payable	140	
Increase in wages payable	220	
Increase in unearned revenue	1,440	1,960
Deduct:		
Increase in accounts receivable	$(2,650)	
Increase in prepaid insurance	(7,300)	
Increase in supplies	(90)	(10,040)
Net cash flows from operating activities		$ (1,690)

The increase in prepaid insurance represents an $8,400 payment of cash for insurance premiums. During November, only $1,100 of the premiums is deducted in arriving at net income. Therefore, the remaining $7,300 (the increase in prepaid insurance) is deducted in arriving at cash flows from operations. Similarly, the increase in supplies of $90 is deducted.

You may have noticed a pattern in how we reconciled net income to net cash flows from operations. First, depreciation expense was added. Next, increases in current assets related to operations were deducted, while increases in current liabilities related to operations were added. The increase in the current liability for notes payable of $6,800 was not included in the reconciliation. This is because the notes payable is related to the purchase of office equipment, which, in the statement of cash flows, is an investing activity rather than an operating activity.

During November, all the current asset and liability accruals and deferrals related to operations were increases. This was because Family Health Care used the cash basis during October, so there were no deferrals or accruals at the beginning of November. In future periods, there would be both increases and decreases in these items. These increases and decreases would be added or subtracted to arrive at cash flows from operations, as shown in Exhibit 11.

Exhibit 11

Reconciling Items

Net income		$XXX
Add:		
Depreciation expense	$XXX	
Increases in current liabilities from operations	XXX	
Decreases in current assets from operations	XXX	XXX
Deduct:		
Increases in current assets from operations	$XXX	
Decreases in current liabilities from operations	XXX	XXX
Net cash flows from operations		$XXX

For example, a decrease in accounts receivable implies that cash was collected and thus would be added. In contrast, a decrease in accounts payable implies that cash was paid and thus would be deducted.

SUMMARY OF LEARNING GOALS

1. **Describe basic accrual accounting concepts, including the matching concept.** Under accrual concepts of accounting, revenue is recognized when it is earned. When revenues are earned and recorded, all expenses incurred in generating the revenues are recorded so that revenues and expenses are properly matched in determining the net income or loss for the period. Liabilities are recorded at the time a business incurs the obligation to pay for the services or goods purchased.

2. **Use accrual concepts of accounting to analyze, record, and summarize transactions.** Using the integrated financial statement framework, November transactions for Family Health Care are recorded. Family Health Care's November transactions involve accrual accounting transactions.

3. **Describe and illustrate the end-of-the-period adjustment process.** The accrual concepts of accounting require the accounting records to be updated prior to preparing financial statements. This updating process, called the adjustment process, is necessary to match revenues and expenses. The adjustment process involves two types of adjustments—deferrals and accruals. Adjustments for deferrals may involve deferred expenses or deferred revenues. Adjustments for accruals may involve accrued expenses or accrued revenues.

4. **Prepare financial statements using accrual concepts of accounting, including a classified balance sheet.**

A classified balance sheet includes sections for current assets; property, plant and equipment (fixed assets); and intangible assets. Liabilities are classified as current liabilities or long-term liabilities. The income statement normally reports sections for revenues, operating expenses, other income and expense, and net income.

5 **Describe how the accrual basis of accounting enhances the interpretation of financial statements.** The net cash flows from operating activities and net income will differ under the accrual basis of accounting. Under the accrual basis, net income is a better indicator of the long-term profitability of a business. For this reason, the accrual basis of accounting is required by generally accepted accounting principles, except for very small businesses. The accrual basis reports the effects of operations on cash flows through the reporting of net cash flows from operating activities on the statement of cash flows.

6 **Describe the accounting cycle for the accrual basis of accounting.** The accounting cycle is the process that begins with the analysis of transactions and ends with preparing the accounting records for the next accounting period. The basic steps in the accounting cycle are (1) identifying, analyzing, and recording the effects of transactions on the accounting equation; (2) identifying, analyzing, and recording adjustment data; (3) preparing financial statements; and (4) preparing the accounting records for the next accounting period.

7 **Describe and illustrate how common-sized financial statements can be used to analyze and evaluate a company's performance.** Common-sized financial statements are often useful in comparing one company to another. In common-sized financial statements, all items are expressed in percentages. Such statements are useful in comparing the current period with prior periods, individual businesses, or one business with industry percentages.

GLOSSARY

Account A record for summarizing increases and decreases in a financial statement element.

Accounting cycle The process that begins with the analysis of transactions and ends with preparing the accounting records for the next accounting period.

Accounts payable A liability for an amount incurred from purchases of products or services in the normal operations of a business.

Accounts receivable An asset for amounts due from customers in the normal operations of a business.

Accrual basis of accounting A system of accounting in which revenue is recorded as it is earned and expenses are recorded when they generate revenue.

Accruals A revenue or an expense that has not been recorded.

Accrued expense An expense that has been incurred at the end of an accounting period but has not been recorded in the accounts; sometimes called an accrued liability.

Accrued revenue A revenue that has been earned at the end of an accounting period but has not been recorded in the accounts; sometimes called an accrued asset.

Accumulated depreciation An offsetting or contra asset account used to record depreciation on a fixed asset.

Adjustment process A process required by the accrual basis of accounting in which the accounts are updated prior to preparing financial statements.

Cash basis of accounting A system of accounting in which only transactions involving increases or decreases of the entity's cash are recorded.

Classified balance sheet A balance sheet prepared with various sections, subsections, and captions that aid in its interpretation and analysis.

Common-sized financial statement A financial statement in which all items are expressed in percentages.

Current assets Cash and other assets that are expected to be converted to cash or sold or used up within one year or less, through the normal operations of the business.

Current liabilities Liabilities that will be due within a short time (usually one year or less) and that are to be paid out of current assets.

Deferrals The delayed recording of an expense or revenue.

Deferred expenses Items that are initially recorded as assets but are expected to become expenses over time or through the normal operations of the business; sometimes called prepaid expenses.

Deferred revenues Items that are initially recorded as liabilities but are expected to become revenues over time or through the normal operations of the business; sometimes called unearned revenues.

Depreciation The reduction in the ability of a fixed asset to provide service.

Fixed assets Physical assets of a long-term nature; sometimes called plant assets.

Intangible assets Assets that are rights of a long-term nature.

Liabilities Amounts owed to creditors.

Long-term liabilities Liabilities that will not be due for a long time (usually more than one year).

Notes receivable Written claims against debtors who promise to pay the amount of the note plus interest at an agreed-upon rate.

Prepaid expenses Items that are initially recorded as assets but are expected to become expenses over time or through the normal operations of the business; often called deferred expenses.

Stockholders' equity The stockholders' rights to the assets of a business.

Unearned revenues Items that are initially recorded as liabilities but are expected to become revenues over time or through the normal operation of the business; often called deferred revenues.

ILLUSTRATIVE ACCOUNTING APPLICATION PROBLEM

Assume that the December transactions for Family Health Care are as follows:

a. Received cash of $1,900 from patients for services provided on account during November.
b. Provided services of $10,800 on account.
c. Received $6,500 for services provided for patients who paid cash.
d. Purchased supplies on account, $400.
e. Received $6,900 from insurance companies that paid on patients' accounts for services that had been previously billed.
f. Paid $310 on account for supplies that had been purchased.
g. Expenses paid during December were as follows: wages, $4,200, including $220 accrued at the end of November; rent, $800; utilities, $610; interest, $100; and miscellaneous, $520.
h. Paid dividends of $1,200 to stockholders (Dr. Landry).

Instructions

1. Record the December transactions, using the integrated financial statement framework as shown below. The beginning balances of December 1 have already been entered. After each transaction, you should enter a balance for each item. The transactions are recorded similarly to those for November. You should note that in transaction (g), the $4,200 of wages paid includes wages of $220 that were accrued at the end of November. Thus, only $3,980 ($4,200 − $220) should be recorded as wages expense for December. The remaining $220 reduces the wages payable. You should also note that the balance of retained earnings on December 1, $8,510, is the balance on November 30.

Statement of Cash Flows	Balance Sheet													Income Statement
	Assets							= Liabilities				+ Stockholders' Equity		
	Cash +	Accts. Rec. +	Prepaid Insur. +	Supp. +	Office Equip. −	Acc. Dep. +	Land =	Notes Pay. +	Accts. Pay. +	Wages Pay. +	Unearned Revenue +	Capital Stock +	Retained Earnings	
Balances, Dec. 1	7,730	2,650	7,300	90	8,500	−160	12,000	16,800	140	220	1,440	11,000	8,510	
Statement of Cash Flows														Income Statement

2. The adjustment data for December are as follows:

   Deferred expenses:
   1. Prepaid insurance expired, $1,100.
   2. Supplies used, $275.
   3. Depreciation on office equipment, $160.

Deferred revenues:
4. Unearned revenue earned, $360.

Accrued expense:
5. Wages owed employees but not paid, $340.

Accrued revenue:
6. Services provided but not billed to insurance companies, $1,050.

Enter the adjustments in the integrated financial statement framework. Identify each adjustment by "a" and the number of the related adjustment item. For example, the adjustment for prepaid insurance should be identified as (a1).

3. Prepare the December financial statements, including the income statement, retained earnings statement, balance sheet, and statement of cash flows.
4. (Appendix) Reconcile the December net income with the net cash flows from operations. (*Note:* In computing increases and decreases in amounts, use adjusted balances.)

Solution

[Solutions to (1) and (2) are found on page 128. Solution to (3) is found below and on page 127.]

3.

Family Health Care, P.C.
Income Statement
For the Month Ended December 31, 2007

Fees earned		$18,350
Operating expenses:		
Wages expense	$4,320	
Insurance expense	1,100	
Rent expense	800	
Utilities expense	610	
Supplies expense	275	
Depreciation expense	160	
Interest expense	100	
Miscellaneous expense	520	
Total operating expenses		7,885
Operating income		$10,465
Other income:		
Rental revenue		360
Net income		$10,825

Family Health Care, P.C.
Retained Earnings Statement
For the Month Ended December 31, 2007

Retained earnings, December 1, 2007		$ 8,510
Net income for December	$10,825	
Less dividends	1,200	9,625
Retained earnings, December 31, 2007		$18,135

Family Health Care, P.C.
Statement of Cash Flows
For the Month Ended December 31, 2007

Cash flows from operating activities:	
Cash received from patients	$15,300
Deduct cash payments for expenses	(6,540)
Net cash flows from operating activities	$ 8,760
Cash flows from financing activities:	
Deduct cash dividends	(1,200)
Net increase in cash	$ 7,560
December 1, 2007, cash balance	7,730
December 31, 2007, cash balance	$15,290

Family Health Care, P.C.
Balance Sheet
December 31, 2007

Assets			
Current assets:			
Cash		$15,290	
Accounts receivable		5,700	
Prepaid insurance		6,200	
Supplies		215	
Total current assets			$27,405
Fixed assets:			
Office equipment	$8,500		
Less accumulated depreciation	320	$ 8,180	
Land		12,000	
Total fixed assets			20,180
Total assets			$47,585
Liabilities			
Current liabilities:			
Accounts payable		$ 230	
Wages payable		340	
Notes payable		6,800	
Unearned revenue		1,080	
Total current liabilities			$ 8,450
Long-term liabilities:			
Notes payable			10,000
Total liabilities			$18,450
Stockholders' Equity			
Capital stock		$11,000	
Retained earnings		18,135	
Total stockholders' equity			29,135
Total liabilities and stockholders' equity			$47,585

1 and 2. Family Health Care Summary of Transactions and Adjustments for December

Statement of Cash Flows	Balance Sheet													Income Statement
	Assets							= Liabilities			+ Stockholders' Equity			
	Cash +	Accts. Rec. +	Prepaid Insur. +	Supp. +	Office Equip. −	Acc. Dep. +	Land =	Notes Pay. +	Accts. Pay. +	Wages Pay. +	Unearned Revenue +	Capital Stock +	Retained Earnings	
Balances, Dec. 1	7,730	2,650	7,300	90	8,500	−160	12,000	16,800	140	220	1,440	11,000	8,510	
a. Collected cash	1,900	−1,900												
Balances	9,630	750	7,300	90	8,500	−160	12,000	16,800	140	220	1,440	11,000	8,510	
b. Fees earned		10,800											10,800	b.
Balances	9,630	11,550	7,300	90	8,500	−160	12,000	16,800	140	220	1,440	11,000	19,310	
c. Fees earned	6,500												6,500	c.
Balances	16,130	11,550	7,300	90	8,500	−160	12,000	16,800	140	220	1,440	11,000	25,810	
d. Pur. supplies				400					400					
Balances	16,130	11,550	7,300	490	8,500	−160	12,000	16,800	540	220	1,440	11,000	25,810	
e. Collected cash	6,900	−6,900												
Balances	23,030	4,650	7,300	490	8,500	−160	12,000	16,800	540	220	1,440	11,000	25,810	
f. Paid accts. pay.	−310								−310					
Balances	22,720	4,650	7,300	490	8,500	−160	12,000	16,800	230	220	1,440	11,000	25,810	
g. Paid expenses	−6,230									−220			−6,010	g.
Balances	16,490	4,650	7,300	490	8,500	−160	12,000	16,800	230	0	1,440	11,000	19,800	
h. Paid dividends	−1,200												−1,200	
Balances	15,290	4,650	7,300	490	8,500	−160	12,000	16,800	230	0	1,440	11,000	18,600	
a1. Insurance exp.			−1,100										−1,100	a1.
Balances	15,290	4,650	6,200	490	8,500	−160	12,000	16,800	230	0	1,440	11,000	17,500	
a2. Supplies exp.				−275									−275	a2.
Balances	15,290	4,650	6,200	215	8,500	−160	12,000	16,800	230	0	1,440	11,000	17,225	
a3. Deprec. exp.						−160							−160	a3.
Balances	15,290	4,650	6,200	215	8,500	−320	12,000	16,800	230	0	1,440	11,000	17,065	
a4. Rental revenue											−360		360	a4.
Balances	15,290	4,650	6,200	215	8,500	−320	12,000	16,800	230	0	1,080	11,000	17,425	
a5. Wages exp.										340			−340	a5.
Balances	15,290	4,650	6,200	215	8,500	−320	12,000	16,800	230	340	1,080	11,000	17,085	
a6. Fees earned		1,050											1,050	a6.
Balances, Dec. 31	15,290	5,700	6,200	215	8,500	−320	12,000	16,800	230	340	1,080	11,000	18,135	

Statement of Cash Flows

a. Operating	1,900
c. Operating	6,500
e. Operating	6,900
f. Operating	−310
g. Operating	−6,230
h. Financing	−1,200
Net increase in cash	7,560
Beginning cash bal.	7,730
Ending cash bal.	15,290

INTEGRATED FINANCIAL STATEMENT FRAMEWORK

Income Statement

b.	10,800	Fees earned
c.	6,500	Fees earned
g.	−3,980	Wages exp.
	−800	Rent exp.
	−610	Utilities exp.
	−100	Interest exp.
	−520	Misc. exp.
a1.	−1,100	Insur. exp.
a2.	−275	Supp. exp.
a3.	−160	Deprec. exp.
a4.	360	Rental rev.
a5.	−340	Wages exp.
a6.	1,050	Fees earned
	10,825	Net income

4. December's Reconciliation of Net Income with Net Cash Flows from Operations

Net income		$10,825
Add:		
Depreciation expense	$ 160	
Increase in accounts payable	90	
Increase in wages payable	120	
Decrease in prepaid insurance	1,100	1,470
Deduct:		
Increase in accounts receivable	$(3,050)	
Increase in supplies	(125)	
Decrease in unearned revenue	(360)	(3,535)
Net cash flows from operating activities		$ 8,760

SELF-STUDY QUESTIONS

Answers at end of chapter

1. Assume that a lawyer bills her clients $15,000 on June 30, 2007, for services rendered during June. The lawyer collects $8,500 of the billings during July and the remainder in August. Under the accrual basis of accounting, when would the lawyer record the revenue for the fees?
   A. June, $15,000; July, $0; and August, $0
   B. June, $0; July, $6,500; and August, $8,500
   C. June, $8,500; July, $6,500; and August, $0
   D. June, $0; July, $8,500; and August, $6,500

2. On January 24, 2007, Niche Consulting collected $5,700 it had billed its clients for services rendered on December 31, 2006. How would you record the January 24 transaction, using the accrual basis?
   A. Increase Cash, $5,700; decrease Fees Earned, $5,700
   B. Increase Accounts Receivable, $5,700; increase Fees Earned, $5,700
   C. Increase Cash, $5,700; decrease Accounts Receivable, $5,700
   D. Increase Cash, $5,700; increase Fees Earned, $5,700

3. Which of the following items represents a deferral?
   A. Prepaid insurance
   B. Wages payable
   C. Fees earned
   D. Accumulated depreciation

4. If the supplies account indicated a balance of $2,250 before adjustment on May 31 and supplies on hand at May 31 totaled $950, the adjustment would be:
   A. increase Supplies, $950; decrease Supplies Expense, $950.
   B. increase Supplies, $1,300; decrease Supplies Expense, $1,300.
   C. increase Supplies Expense, $950; decrease Supplies, $950.
   D. increase Supplies Expense, $1,300; decrease Supplies, $1,300.

5. The balance in the unearned rent account for Jones Co. as of December 31 is $1,200. If Jones Co. failed to record the adjusting entry for $600 of rent earned during December, the effect on the balance sheet and income statement for December would be:
   A. assets understated by $600; net income overstated by $600.
   B. liabilities understated by $600; net income understated by $600.
   C. liabilities overstated by $600; net income understated by $600.
   D. liabilities overstated by $600; net income overstated by $600.

DISCUSSION QUESTIONS

1. Would General Electric and Xerox use the cash basis or the accrual basis of accounting? Explain.
2. How are revenues and expenses reported on the income statement under (a) the cash basis of accounting and (b) the accrual basis of accounting?
3. Fees for services provided are billed to a customer during 2006. The customer remits the amount owed in 2007. During which year would the revenues be reported on the income statement under (a) the cash basis? (b) the accrual basis?

4. Employees performed services in 2006, but the wages were not paid until 2007. During which year would the wages expense be reported on the income statement under (a) the cash basis? (b) the accrual basis?
5. Which of the following accounts would appear only in an accrual basis accounting system, and which could appear in either a cash basis or an accrual basis accounting system? (a) Capital Stock, (b) Fees Earned, (c) Accounts Payable, (d) Land, (e) Utilities Expense, and (f) Accounts Receivable.
6. Is the land balance before the accounts have been adjusted the amount that should normally be reported on the balance sheet? Explain.
7. Is the supplies balance before the accounts have been adjusted the amount that should normally be reported on the balance sheet? Explain.
8. Why are adjustments needed at the end of an accounting period?
9. Identify the four different categories of adjustments frequently required at the end of an accounting period.
10. If the effect of an adjustment is to increase the balance of a liability account, which of the following statements describes the effect of the adjustment on the other account?
    a. Increases the balance of a revenue account.
    b. Increases the balance of an expense account.
    c. Increases the balance of an asset account.
11. If the effect of an adjustment is to increase the balance of an asset account, which of the following statements describes the effect of the adjustment on the other account?
    a. Increases the balance of a revenue account.
    b. Increases the balance of a liability account.
    c. Increases the balance of an expense account.
12. Does every adjustment have an effect on determining the amount of net income for a period? Explain.
13. (a) Explain the purpose of the two accounts: Depreciation Expense and Accumulated Depreciation. (b) Is it customary for the balances of the two accounts to be equal? (c) In what financial statements, if any, will each account appear?
14. Describe the nature of the assets that compose the following sections of a balance sheet: (a) current assets, (b) property, plant, and equipment.
15. (a) What are common-sized financial statements? (b) Why are common-sized financial statements useful in interpreting and analyzing financial statements?

EXERCISES

Exercise 3-1

Transactions using accrual accounting

Goal **2**

Chico Urgent Care is owned and operated by Dr. Janet Scanlon, the sole stockholder. During July 2007, Chico Urgent Care entered into the following transactions:

a. Dr. Scanlon invested $10,000 in Chico Urgent Care in exchange for capital stock.
b. Paid $3,600 for an insurance premium on a one-year policy.
c. Purchased supplies on account, $500.
d. Received fees of $18,650 during July.
e. Paid expenses as follows: wages, $5,240; rent, $2,500; utilities, $1,100; and miscellaneous, $880.
f. Paid dividends of $1,000.

Record the preceding transactions using the integrated financial statement framework. After each transaction, you should enter a balance for each item.

Exercise 3-2

Adjustment process

Goal **3**

SPREADSHEET

Using the data from Exercise 3-1, record the adjusting entries at the end of July to record the insurance expense and supplies expense. There were $280 of supplies on hand as of July 31. Identify the adjusting entry for insurance as (a1) and supplies as (a2).

Exercise 3-3

Financial statements

Goal **4**

SPREADSHEET

Using the data from Exercises 3-1 and 3-2, prepare financial statements for July, including income statement, retained earnings statement, balance sheet, and statement of cash flows.

Exercise 3-4

Reconcile net income and net cash flows from operations.

Appendix

Using the income statement and statement of cash flows you prepared in Exercise 3-3, reconcile net income with the net cash flows from operations.

Exercise 3-5

Accrual basis of accounting

Goal 2

Neal Hastings established Ember Services, P.C., a professional corporation, on January 1 of the current year. Ember Services offers financial planning advice to its clients. The effect of each transaction on the balance sheet and the balances after each transaction for January are as follows. Each increase or decrease in stockholders' equity, except transaction (h), affects net income.

	Assets					=	Liabilities	+	Stockholders' Equity		
	Cash	+	Accounts Receivable	+	Supplies	=	Accounts Payable	+	Capital Stock	+	Retained Earnings
a.	+20,000								+20,000		
b.					+900		+900				
Bal.	20,000				900		900		20,000		
c.	−775						−775				
Bal.	19,225				900		125		20,000		
d.	+11,500										+11,500
Bal.	30,725				900		125		20,000		11,500
e.	−7,500										−7,500
Bal.	23,225				900		125		20,000		4,000
f.					−625						−625
Bal.	23,225				275		125		20,000		3,375
g.			+3,000								+3,000
Bal.	23,225		3,000		275		125		20,000		6,375
h.	−1,000										−1,000
Bal.	22,225		3,000		275		125		20,000		5,375

a. Describe each transaction.
b. What is the amount of the net income for January?

Exercise 3-6

Classify accruals and deferrals

Goal 3

Classify the following items as (a) deferred expense (prepaid expense), (b) deferred revenue (unearned revenue), (c) accrued expense (accrued liability), or (d) accrued revenue (accrued asset).

1. Fees earned but not yet received.
2. Taxes owed but payable in the following period.
3. Salary owed but not yet paid.
4. Supplies on hand.
5. Fees received but not yet earned.
6. Utilities owed but not yet paid.
7. A two-year premium paid on a fire insurance policy.
8. Subscriptions received in advance by a magazine publisher.

Exercise 3-7

Classify adjustments

Goal 3

The following accounts were taken from the unadjusted trial balance of Dobro Co., a congressional lobbying firm. Indicate whether or not each account would normally require an adjusting entry. If the account normally requires an adjusting entry, use the following notation to indicate the type of adjustment:

AE—Accrued Expense
AR—Accrued Revenue
DR—Deferred Revenue
DE—Deferred Expense

To illustrate, the answers for the first two accounts are shown below.

Account	Answer
Dividends	Does not normally require adjustment.
Accounts Receivable	Normally requires adjustment (AR).
Accumulated Depreciation	
Cash	

(continued)

Account	Answer
Interest Payable	
Interest Receivable	
Land	
Office Equipment	
Prepaid Insurance	
Supplies Expense	
Unearned Fees	
Wages Expense	

Exercise 3-8

Adjustment for supplies

Goal 3

a. $1,715

Answer each of the following independent questions concerning supplies and the adjustment for supplies. (a) The balance in the supplies account, before adjustment at the end of the year, is $2,100. What is the amount of the adjustment if the amount of supplies on hand at the end of the year is $385? (b) The supplies account has a balance of $675, and the supplies expense account has a balance of $1,310 at December 31, 2007. If 2007 was the first year of operations, what was the amount of supplies purchased during the year?

Exercise 3-9

Adjustment for prepaid insurance

Goal 3

The prepaid insurance account had a balance of $2,750 at the beginning of the year. The account was increased for $1,500 for premiums on policies purchased during the year. What is the adjustment required at the end of the year for each of the following independent situations: (a) the amount of unexpired insurance applicable to future periods is $3,000? (b) the amount of insurance expired during the year is $1,050? For (a) and (b), indicate each account affected, whether the account is increased or decreased, and the amount of the increase or decrease.

Exercise 3-10

Adjustment for unearned fees

Goal 3

The balance in the unearned fees account, before adjustment at the end of the year, is $9,750. What is the adjustment if the amount of unearned fees at the end of the year is $5,600? Indicate each account affected, whether the account is increased or decreased, and the amount of the increase or decrease.

Exercise 3-11

Adjustment for unearned revenue

Goal 3

For the years ending June 30, 2004 and 2003, Microsoft Corporation reported short-term unearned revenue of $6,514 million and $7,225 million, respectively. For the year ending June 30, 2004, Microsoft also reported total revenues of $36,835 million. (a) What adjustment for unearned revenue did Microsoft make at June 30, 2004? Indicate each account affected, whether the account is increased or decreased, and the amount of the increase or decrease. (b) What percentage of total revenues was the adjustment for unearned revenue?

Exercise 3-12

Effect of omitting adjustment

Goal 3

At the end of February, the first month of the business year, the usual adjustment transferring rent earned to a revenue account from the unearned rent account was omitted. Indicate which items will be incorrectly stated, because of the error, on (a) the income statement for February and (b) the balance sheet as of February 28. Also indicate whether the items in error will be overstated or understated.

Exercise 3-13

Adjustment for accrued salaries

Goal 3

Townes Realty Co. pays weekly salaries of $15,000 on Friday for a five-day week ending on that day. What is the adjustment at the end of the accounting period, assuming that the period ends (a) on Tuesday, (b) on Wednesday? Indicate each account affected, whether the account is increased or decreased, and the amount of the increase or decrease.

Exercise 3-14

Determine wages paid

Goal 3

The balances of the two wages accounts at December 31, after adjustments at the end of the first year of operations, are Wages Payable, $5,750, and Wages Expense, $133,400. Determine the amount of wages paid during the year.

Exercise 3-15

Effect of omitting adjustment

Goal 3

Accrued salaries of $2,180 owed to employees for December 30 and 31 are not considered in preparing the financial statements for the year ended December 31, 2006. Indicate which items will be erroneously stated, because of the error, on (a) the income statement for December 2006 and (b) the balance sheet as of December 31, 2006. Also indicate whether the items in error will be overstated or understated.

Exercise 3-16

Effect of omitting adjustment

Goal 3

Assume that the error in Exercise 3-15 was not corrected and that the $2,180 of accrued salaries was included in the first salary payment in January 2007. Indicate which items will be erroneously stated, because of failure to correct the initial error, on (a) the income statement for January 2007 and (b) the balance sheet as of January 31, 2007.

Exercise 3-17

Effects of errors on financial statements

Goal 3

For a recent period, Circuit City Stores reported accrued expenses of $202,675 thousand. For the same period, Circuit City reported a loss before income taxes of $1,240 thousand. If accrued expenses had not been recorded, what would have been the income (loss) before income taxes?

Exercise 3-18

Effects of errors on financial statements

Goal 3

The balance sheet for Ford Motor Company as of December 31, 2004, includes $31,187 million of accrued expenses as liabilities. Before taxes, Ford Motor Company reported a net income of $4,853 million. If the accruals had not been recorded at December 31, 2004, how much would net income or net loss before taxes have been for the year ended December 31, 2004?

Exercise 3-19

Effects of errors on financial statements

Goal 3

b. $175,840

The accountant for Glacier Medical Co., a medical services consulting firm, mistakenly omitted adjusting entries for (a) unearned revenue earned during the year ($6,900) and (b) accrued wages ($3,740). (a) Indicate the effect of each error, considered individually, on the income statement for the current year ended December 31. Also indicate the effect of each error on the December 31 balance sheet. Set up a table similar to the following, and record your answers by inserting the dollar amount in the appropriate spaces. Insert a zero if the error does not affect the item.

	Error (a)		Error (b)	
	Over-stated	Under-stated	Over-stated	Under-stated
1. Revenue for the year would be	$	$	$	$
2. Expenses for the year would be	$	$	$	$
3. Net income for the year would be	$	$	$	$
4. Assets at December 31 would be	$	$	$	$
5. Liabilities at December 31 would be	$	$	$	$
6. Stockholders' equity at December 31 would be	$	$	$	$

(b) If the net income for the current year had been $172,680, what would be the correct net income if the proper adjustments had been made?

Exercise 3-20

Adjustment for accrued fees

Goal 3

At the end of the current year, $11,310 of fees have been earned but have not been billed to clients.

a. What is the adjustment to record the accrued fees? Indicate each account affected, whether the account is increased or decreased, and the amount of the increase or decrease.
b. If the cash basis rather than the accrual basis had been used, would an adjustment have been necessary? Explain.

Exercise 3-21

Adjustments for unearned and accrued fees

Goal 3

The balance in the unearned fees account, before adjustment at the end of the year, is $67,250. Of these fees, $18,000 have been earned. In addition, $10,200 of fees have been earned but have not been billed. What are the adjustments (a) to adjust the unearned fees account and (b) to record the accrued fees? Indicate each account affected, whether the account is increased or decreased, and the amount of the increase or decrease.

Exercise 3-22

Effect of deferred revenue

Goal 3

a. $234 million

Time Warner Inc. reported short-term deferred revenue of $1,497 million and $1,731 million as of December 31, 2004 and 2003, respectively. For the year ending December 31, 2004, Time Warner reported total revenues of $42,089 million. (a) What was the amount of the adjustment for unearned revenue for 2004? (b) What would have been total revenues under the cash basis after considering the effect of (a)?

Exercise 3-23

Effect on financial statements of omitting adjustment

Goal 3

The adjustment for accrued fees was omitted at October 31, the end of the current year. Indicate which items will be in error, because of the omission, on (a) the income statement for the current year and (b) the balance sheet as of October 31. Also indicate whether the items in error will be overstated or understated.

Exercise 3-24

Adjustment for depreciation

Goal 3

The estimated amount of depreciation on equipment for the current year is $5,000. (a) How is the adjustment recorded? Indicate each account affected, whether the account is increased or decreased, and the amount of the increase or decrease. (b) If the adjustment in (a) was omitted, which items would be erroneously stated on (1) the income statement for the year and (2) the balance sheet as of December 31?

Exercise 3-25

Adjustments

Goal 3

The Quasar Company is a consulting firm specializing in pollution control. The following adjustments were made for The Quasar Company:

Account	Adjustments Increase (Decrease)
Accounts Receivable	$ 7,140
Supplies	(1,715)
Prepaid Insurance	(1,400)
Accumulated Depreciation—Equipment	2,520
Wages Payable	1,260
Unearned Rent	(3,500)
Fees Earned	7,140
Wages Expense	1,260
Supplies Expense	1,715
Rent Revenue	3,500
Insurance Expense	1,400
Depreciation Expense	2,520

Identify each of the six pairs of adjustments. For each adjustment, indicate the account, whether the account is increased or decreased, and the amount of the adjustment. No account is affected by more than one adjustment. Use the following format. The first adjustment is shown as an example.

Adjustment	Account	Increase or Decrease	Amount
1.	Accounts Receivable	Increase	$7,140
	Fees Earned	Increase	7,140

Exercise 3-26

Book value of fixed assets

Goal **4**

Barnes & Noble Inc. reported *Property, Plant, and Equipment* of $1,677,836,000 and *Accumulated Depreciation* of $991,187,000 at January 31, 2004.

a. What was the book value of the fixed assets at January 31, 2004?

b. Would the book values of Barnes & Noble's fixed assets normally approximate their fair market values?

Exercise 3-27

Classify assets

Goal **4**

Identify each of the following as (a) a current asset or (b) property, plant, and equipment:

1. Accounts Receivable
2. Building
3. Cash
4. Office Equipment
5. Prepaid Insurance
6. Supplies

Exercise 3-28

Balance sheet classification

Goal **4**

At the balance sheet date, a business owes a mortgage note payable of $775,000, the terms of which provide for monthly payments of $4,150. Explain how the liability should be classified on the balance sheet.

Exercise 3-29

Classified balance sheet

Goal **4**

Total assets, $126,650

Tudor Co. offers personal weight reduction consulting services to individuals. After all the accounts have been closed on April 30, 2006, the end of the current fiscal year, the balances of selected accounts from the ledger of Tudor Co. are as follows:

Accounts Payable	$ 9,500	Prepaid Insurance	$ 7,200
Accounts Receivable	21,850	Prepaid Rent	4,800
Accum. Depreciation—Equipment	21,100	Retained Earnings	74,200
Capital Stock	40,000	Salaries Payable	1,750
Cash	?	Supplies	1,800
Equipment	80,600	Unearned Fees	1,200

Prepare a classified balance sheet that includes the correct balance for Cash.

Exercise 3-30

Classified balance sheet

Goal **4**

Total assets, $1,047,496

La-Z-Boy Inc. is one of the world's largest manufacturers of furniture that is best known for its reclining chairs. The following data (in thousands) were adapted from the 2004 annual report of La-Z-Boy Inc.:

Accounts payable	$122,576
Accounts receivable	337,770
Accumulated depreciation	296,942
Capital stock	269,316

(continued)

Cash	$ 33,882
Intangible assets	96,005
Inventories	250,568
Debt due within one year*	42,563
Long-term debt**	181,807
Other assets*	31,454
Other assets**	85,078
Other liabilities*	118,182
Other long-term liabilities**	60,040
Property, plant, and equipment	509,681
Retained earnings	253,012

For the preceding items, (*) indicates that the item is current in nature, while (**) indicates that the item is long-term in nature.

Prepare a classified balance sheet as of April 24, 2004.

Exercise 3-31

Balance sheet

Goal 4

List the errors you find in the following balance sheet. Prepare a corrected balance sheet.

Warburg Services Co.
Balance Sheet
For the Year Ended May 31, 2006

Assets		
Current assets:		
Cash	$ 4,170	
Accounts payable	7,250	
Supplies	1,650	
Prepaid insurance	2,400	
Land	75,000	
Total current assets		$ 90,470
Property, plant, and equipment:		
Building	$55,500	
Equipment	28,280	
Total property, plant, and equipment		104,280
Total assets		$194,750
Liabilities		
Current liabilities:		
Accounts receivable	$12,500	
Accumulated depreciation—building	23,000	
Accumulated depreciation—equipment	16,000	
Net loss	10,000	
Total liabilities		$ 61,500
Stockholders' Equity		
Wages payable	$ 1,500	
Capital stock	35,000	
Retained earnings	96,750	
Total stockholders' equity		133,250
Total liabilities and stockholders' equity		$194,750

ACCOUNTING APPLICATION PROBLEMS

Problem 3-1A

Accrual basis accounting

Goal **2**

SPREADSHEET

GENERAL LEDGER

Wizard Health Care, Inc., is owned and operated by Dr. Chandra Rains, the sole stockholder. During January 2007, Wizard Health Care entered into the following transactions:

Jan.	1	Received $8,100 from Goulash Company as rent for the use of a vacant office in Wizard Health Care's building. Goulash paid the rent six months in advance.
	1	Paid $3,600 for an insurance premium on a one-year, general business policy.
	4	Purchased supplies of $950 on account.
	5	Collected $9,000 for services provided to customers on account.
	11	Paid creditors $1,600 on account.
	18	Invested an additional $45,000 in the business in exchange for capital stock.
	20	Billed patients $24,800 for services provided on account.
	25	Received $6,800 for services provided to customers who paid cash.
	29	Paid expenses as follows: wages, $12,600; utilities, $3,500; rent on medical equipment, $2,700; interest, $250; and miscellaneous, $650.
	29	Paid dividends of $2,000 to stockholders (Dr. Rains).

Instructions

Analyze and record the January transactions for Wizard Health Care, Inc., using the integrated financial statement framework. Record each transaction by date and show the balance for each item after each transaction. The January 1, 2007, balances for the balance sheet are shown below.

	Assets							=	Liabilities				+	Stockholders' Equity	
	Cash +	Accts. Rec. +	Pre. Ins. +	Supp. +	Building −	Acc. Dep. +	Land	=	Accts. Pay. +	Un. Rev. +	Wages Pay. +	Notes Pay.	+	Capital Stock +	Ret. Earn.
Bal., Jan. 1	10,400	13,500	360	560	90,000	−7,200	45,000		3,800	0	0	36,000		45,000	67,820

Problem 3-2A

Adjustment process

Goal **3**

SPREADSHEET

GENERAL LEDGER

Adjustment data for Wizard Health Care, Inc., for January are as follows:

1. Insurance expired, $300.
2. Supplies on hand on January 31, $585.
3. Depreciation on building, $1,800.
4. Unearned rent revenue earned, $1,350.
5. Wages owed employees but not paid, $1,440.
6. Services provided but not billed to patients, $3,850.

Instructions

Based upon the transactions recorded in January for Problem 3-1A, record the adjustments for January using the integrated financial statement framework.

Problem 3-3A

Financial statements

Goals **4, 6**

1. Net income, $12,635

SPREADSHEET

GENERAL LEDGER

Data for Wizard Health Care for January are provided in Problems 3-1A and 3-2A.

Instructions

Prepare an income statement, retained earnings statement, and a classified balance sheet for January. The notes payable is due in 2013.

Problem 3-4A

Statement of cash flows

Goal **4**

Net cash flows from operating activities, ($1,000)

SPREADSHEET

GENERAL LEDGER

Data for Wizard Health Care for January are provided in Problems 3-1A, 3-2A, and 3-3A.

Instructions

1. Prepare a statement of cash flows for January.
2. Reconcile the net cash flows from operating activities with the net income for January. (*Hint:* See the appendix to this chapter and use adjusted balances in computing increases and decreases in accounts.)

Problem 3-5A

Adjustments and errors

Goal **3**

Corrected net income, $127,900

SPREADSHEET

At the end of July, the first month of operations, the following selected data were taken from the financial statements of Kay Lopez, Attorney-at-Law, P.C.

Net income for July	$124,350
Total assets at July 31	500,000
Total liabilities at July 31	125,000
Total stockholders' equity at July 31	375,000

In preparing the financial statements, adjustments for the following data were overlooked:

a. Unbilled fees earned at July 31, $9,600.
b. Depreciation of equipment for July, $3,500.
c. Accrued wages at July 31, $1,450.
d. Supplies used during July, $1,100.

Instructions

Determine the correct amount of net income for July and the total assets, liabilities, and stockholders' equity at July 31. In addition to indicating the corrected amounts, indicate the effect of each omitted adjustment by setting up and completing a columnar table similar to the following. Adjustment (a) is presented as an example.

	Net Income	Total Assets	Total Liabilities	Total Stockholders' Equity
Reported amounts	$124,350	$500,000	$125,000	$375,000
Corrections:				
Adjustment (a)	+9,600	+9,600	0	+9,600
Adjustment (b)	______	______	______	______
Adjustment (c)	______	______	______	______
Adjustment (d)	______	______	______	______
Corrected amounts	______	______	______	______

Problem 3-6A

Adjustment process and financial statements

Goals **3, 4**

2. Net income, $123,700

SPREADSHEET

GENERAL LEDGER

Adjustment data for Nocturnal Laundry, Inc., for the year ended August 31, 2007, are as follows:

a. Wages accrued but not paid at August 31, $3,200.
b. Depreciation of equipment during the year, $15,000.
c. Laundry supplies on hand at August 31, $2,500.
d. Insurance premiums expired, $3,000.

Instructions

1. Using the integrated financial statement framework shown at the top of the following page, record each adjustment to the appropriate accounts identifying each adjustment by its letter. After all adjustments are recorded, determine the balances.
2. Prepare an income statement and retained earnings statement for the year ended August 31, 2007. The retained earnings balance as of September 1, 2006, was $30,300.

Statement of Cash Flows	Balance Sheet									Income Statement
	Assets					= Liabilities		+ Stockholders' Equity		
	Cash	+ Laundry Supplies	+ Prepaid Insurance	+ Laundry Equip.	− Acc. Deprec.	= Accts. Payable	+ Wages Payable	+ Capital Stock	+ Retained Earnings	
Balances, Aug. 31, 2007	25,000	6,000	4,800	225,000	−45,000	5,100	0	36,000	174,700	

Statement of Cash Flows

Operating (Revenues)	280,000
Financing (Capital Stock)	10,000
Operating (Expenses)	−160,000
Investing (Equipment)	−110,000
Financing (Dividends)	−4,000
Net increase in cash	16,000
Beginning cash balance	9,000
Ending cash balance	25,000

INTEGRATED FINANCIAL STATEMENT FRAMEWORK

Income Statement

Aug.	280,000	Laundry revenue
Aug.	−77,500	Wages expense
Aug.	−28,000	Rent expense
Aug.	−22,600	Utilities expense
Aug.	−3,500	Misc. expense

3. Prepare a classified balance sheet as of August 31, 2007.
4. Prepare a statement of cash flows for the year ended August 31, 2007.

ALTERNATE ACCOUNTING APPLICATION PROBLEMS

Alternate Problem 3-1B

Accrual basis accounting

Goal 2

SPREADSHEET

GENERAL LEDGER

Tyro Health Care, Inc., is owned and operated by Dr. Ricky Owens, the sole stockholder. During March, Tyro Health Care entered into the following transactions:

Mar. 2 Received $10,800 from Mutton Company as rent for the use of a vacant office in Tyro Health Care's building. Mutton prepays the rent six months in advance.
2 Paid $4,200 for an insurance premium on a one-year, general business policy.
3 Purchased supplies of $1,250 on account.
6 Collected $6,600 for services provided to customers on account.
9 Paid creditors $2,750 on account.
18 Invested an additional $15,000 in the business in exchange for capital stock.
23 Billed patients $17,800 for services provided on account.
25 Received $5,800 for services provided to customers who paid cash.
30 Paid expenses as follows: wages, $12,300; utilities, $4,500; rent on medical equipment, $3,000; interest, $150; and miscellaneous, $400.
31 Paid dividends of $1,000 to stockholders (Dr. Owens).

Instructions

Analyze and record the March transactions for Tyro Health Care, Inc., using the integrated financial statement framework. Record each transaction by date and show the balance for each account after each transaction. The March 1, 2007, balances for the balance sheet are shown below.

	Assets							= Liabilities				+ Stockholders' Equity	
	Cash	+ Accts. Rec.	+ Pre. Ins.	+ Supp.	+ Building	− Acc. Dep.	+ Land	= Accts. Pay.	+ Un. Rev.	+ Wages Pay.	+ Notes Pay.	+ Capital Stock	+ Ret. Earn.
Bal., Mar. 1	7,000	9,900	360	220	60,000	−4,800	30,000	5,100	0	0	25,000	50,000	22,580

Alternate Problem 3-2B

Adjustment process

Goal **3**

SPREADSHEET

GENERAL LEDGER

Adjustment data for Tyro Health Care Inc. for March are as follows:

1. Insurance expired, $360.
2. Supplies on hand on March 31, $870.
3. Depreciation on building, $1,200.
4. Unearned rent revenue earned, $1,800.
5. Wages owed employees but not paid, $850.
6. Services provided but not billed to patients, $6,000.

Instructions

Based upon the transactions recorded in March for Problem 3-1B, record the adjustments for March using the integrated financial statement framework.

Alternate Problem 3-3B

Financial statements and the closing process

Goals **4, 6**

1. Net income, $8,040

SPREADSHEET

GENERAL LEDGER

Data for Tyro Health Care Inc. for March are provided in Problems 3-1B and 3-2B.

Instructions

Prepare an income statement, retained earnings statement, and a classified balance sheet for March. The notes payable is due in 2018.

Alternate Problem 3-4B

Statement of cash flows

Goal **4**

1. Net cash flows from operating activities, ($4,100)

SPREADSHEET

GENERAL LEDGER

Data for Tyro Health Care for March are provided in Problems 3-1B, 3-2B, and 3-3B.

Instructions

1. Prepare a statement of cash flows for March.
2. Reconcile the net cash flows from operating activities with the net income for March. *Hint:* See the appendix to this chapter and use adjusted balances in computing increases and decreases in accounts.

Alternate Problem 3-5B

Adjustments and errors

Goal **3**

Corrected net income, $209,745

SPREADSHEET

At the end of November, the first month of operations, the following selected data were taken from the financial statements of Jaime McCune, Attorney-at-Law, P.C.

Net income for November	$207,320
Total assets at November 30	440,960
Total liabilities at November 30	29,720
Total stockholders' equity at November 30	411,240

In preparing the financial statements, adjustments for the following data were overlooked:

a. Supplies used during November, $1,025.
b. Unbilled fees earned at November 30, $7,650.
c. Depreciation of equipment for November, $3,100.
d. Accrued wages at November 30, $1,100.

Instructions

Determine the correct amount of net income for November and the total assets, liabilities, and stockholders' equity at November 30. In addition to indicating the corrected amounts, indicate the effect of each omitted adjustment by setting up and completing a columnar table similar to the following. Adjustment (a) is presented as an example.

	Net Income	Total Assets	Total Liabilities	Total Stockholders' Equity
Reported amounts	$207,320	$440,960	$29,720	$411,240
Corrections:				
Adjustment (a)	−1,025	−1,025	0	−1,025
Adjustment (b)	______	______	______	______
Adjustment (c)	______	______	______	______
Adjustment (d)	______	______	______	______
Corrected amounts	______	______	______	______

Alternate Problem 3-6B

Adjustment process and financial statements

Goals **3, 4**

2. Net income, $101,050

SPREADSHEET

GENERAL LEDGER

Adjustment data for Giddy Laundry, Inc., for the year ended July 31, 2007, are as follows:

a. Wages accrued but not paid at July 31, $2,000.
b. Depreciation of equipment during the year, $8,000.
c. Laundry supplies on hand at July 31, $1,250.
d. Insurance premiums expired during the year, $2,100.

Instructions

1. Using the integrated financial statement framework shown below, record each adjustment to the appropriate accounts identifying each adjustment by its letter. After all adjustments are recorded, determine the balances.

Statement of Cash Flows	Balance Sheet									Income Statement
	Assets					= Liabilities		+ Stockholders' Equity		
	Cash	+ Laundry Supplies	+ Prepaid Insurance	+ Laundry Equip.	− Acc. Deprec.	= Accts. Payable	+ Wages Payable	+ Capital Stock	+ Retained Earnings	
Balances, July 31, 2007	20,000	4,800	3,800	180,000	−36,000	4,100	0	30,000	138,500	

Statement of Cash Flows

Operating (Revenues)	225,000
Financing (Capital Stock)	7,500
Operating (Expenses)	−125,000
Investing (Equipment)	−90,000
Financing (Dividends)	−2,000
Net increase in cash	15,500
Beginning cash balance	4,500
Ending cash balance	20,000

INTEGRATED FINANCIAL STATEMENT FRAMEWORK

Income Statement

July	225,000	Laundry revenue
July	−65,000	Wages expense
July	−22,500	Rent expense
July	−18,000	Utilities expense
July	−2,800	Misc. expense

2. Prepare an income statement and retained earnings statement for the year ended July 31, 2007. The retained earnings balance as of August 1, 2006, was $23,800.
3. Prepare a classified balance sheet as of July 31, 2007.
4. Prepare a statement of cash flows for the year ended July 31, 2007.

FINANCIAL ANALYSIS AND REPORTING CASES

Case 3-1

Analysis of income statements

Walgreen Company and CVS Corporation operate national chains of drugstores that sell prescription drugs, over-the-counter drugs, and other general merchandise such as greeting cards, beauty and cosmetics, household items, food, and beverages. Walgreen operates 4,579 stores, while CVS Corporation operates 5,375 stores. The following operating data (in thousands) were adapted from the 2004 SEC 10-K filings of Walgreen and CVS.

	CVS	Walgreen
Net sales	$30,594,300	$37,508,200
Cost of sales	22,563,100	27,310,400
Gross profit	$ 8,031,200	$10,197,800
Selling, general, and administrative expenses	6,079,700	8,055,100
Operating income	$ 1,951,500	$ 2,142,700
Other income and (expense)	(555,100)	33,600
Income before taxes	$ 1,396,400	$ 2,176,300
Income taxes	477,600	816,100
Net income	$ 918,800	$ 1,360,200

1. Prepare common-sized income statements for CVS and Walgreen.
2. Compute the average sales per store for CVS and Walgreen. Round to the thousands.
3. Analyze and comment on your results in (1) and (2).
4. Broker recommendations are reported on Yahoo.com's financial Web site. The recommendations are ranked as follows:

Strong Buy	1
Buy	2
Hold	3
Sell	4
Strong Sell	5

Based upon your answers to (2) and (3), would you expect the average broker recommendation for CVS to be higher (less favorable), the same, or lower (more favorable) than for Walgreen? Compare your assessment with the average broker recommendation on Yahoo.com's financial Web site (http://finance.yahoo.com/). To find the broker recommendation, enter the stock symbols for CVS (CVS) and Walgreen (WAG) and click on "research."

Case 3-2

Cash basis income statement

The following operating data (in thousands) were adapted from the 2004 SEC 10-K filings of Walgreen and CVS:

	CVS		Walgreen	
	2004	2003	2004	2003
Accounts receivable	$2,007,300	$1,601,700	$1,169,100	$1,017,800
Accounts payable	3,942,600	3,166,000	4,077,900	3,420,500

1. Using the preceding data, adjust the operating income for CVS and Walgreen shown in Case 3-1 to an adjusted cash basis. (*Hint:* To convert to a cash basis, you need to compute the change in each accrual accounting item shown on preceding page and then either add or subtract the change to the operating income.)
2. Compute the net difference between the operating income under the accrual and cash bases.
3. Express the net difference in (2) as a percent of operating income under the accrual basis.
4. Which company's operating income, CVS's or Walgreen's, is closer to the cash basis?
5. Do you think most analysts focus on operating income or net income in assessing the long-term profitability of a company? Explain.

Case 3-3

Cash basis vs. accrual basis financial statements

The local minor league baseball team, *The Hampton Hounds*, began their season in late April, with five home dates (and no road games) in April. The team's owner is seeking a short-term loan from the local bank to help fund some improvements. As a result, a statement of cash receipts and disbursements was prepared for the bank for April.

The owner estimates that the average cash receipts from tickets and concessions is $20,000 per home date. The average operating cash disbursements is $4,000 per home date. Players are paid the 15th of every month during the regular season (until September 15) at an average rate of $16,000 per month per player. All 25 players receive their first paycheck on May 15. Rent is paid on the stadium on the first of every month during the playing season at a rate of $60,000 per month, with the first payment due on May 1 and the last payment due on September 1. In addition to individual game sales, the Hounds sold 1,000 season tickets during the month of April at $720 per ticket. There are 160 total games in the season, half of which are home dates.

1. Prepare a statement of cash receipts and disbursements for April.
2. Prepare an accrual basis income statement for April. (*Hint:* Translate expenses into a per-game basis and match against the revenue.)
3. Which statement best represents the results of operations for April?
4. Comment on management's intention to use the statement of cash receipts and disbursements to support the request for the bank loan rather than using an accrual-based income statement.

Case 3-4

Effect of events on financial statements

On September 11, 2001, two **United Airlines** aircraft were hijacked and destroyed in terrorist attacks on the World Trade Center in New York City and in a crash near Johnstown, Pennsylvania. In addition to the loss of all passengers and crew on board the aircraft, these attacks resulted in numerous deaths and injuries to persons on the ground and massive property damage. In the immediate aftermath of the attacks, the FAA ordered all aircraft operating in the United States grounded immediately. This grounding effectively lasted for three days, and United was able to operate only a portion of its scheduled flights for several days thereafter. Passenger traffic and yields on United's flights declined significantly when flights were permitted to resume, and United refunded significant numbers of tickets for the period from September 11 to September 25.

The following data for United were adapted (in millions) from the Securities and Exchange Commission 10-K filing for the years ending December 31, 2000 and 1999:

	Year Ending December 31,	
	2000	1999
Operating income	$ 673	$1,342
Net income	52	1,204
Net cash flows from operating activities	2,358	2,415

1. Based upon the preceding data, develop an expectation of what you believe the operating income, net income, and net cash flows from operating activities would be for United Airlines for the year ending December 31, 2001. Use the following format for your answers:

	Year Ending December 31, 2001
Operating income (loss)	$ ______
Net income	$ ______
Net cash flows from operating activities	$ ______

2. Would you report the loss related to the terrorist attacks separately in the income statement? If so, how?

Case 3-5

Analysis of income and cash flows

The following data (in millions) for 2004, 2003, and 2002 were taken from 10-K filings with the Securities and Exchange Commission:

	2004	2003	2002
Company A			
Revenues	$21,962	$21,044	$19,564
Operating income	5,698	5,221	5,458
Net income	4,847	4,347	3,050
Net cash flows from operating activities	5,968	5,456	4,742
Net cash flows from investing activities	(503)	(936)	(1,187)
Net cash flows from financing activities	(2,261)	(3,601)	(3,327)
Total assets	31,327	27,342	24,501
Company B			
Revenues	$15,002	$13,303	$13,305
Operating income (loss)	(3,308)	(786)	(1,309)
Net income (loss)	(5,198)	(773)	(1,272)
Net cash flows from operating activities	(1,123)	453	285
Net cash flows from investing activities	(220)	(260)	(1,109)
Net cash flows from financing activities	636	548	583
Total assets	21,801	26,356	24,720
Company C			
Revenues	$ 6,921	$ 5,264	$ 3,933
Operating income (loss)	440	271	64
Net income (loss)	588	35	(149)
Net cash flows from operating activities	567	392	174
Net cash flows from investing activities	(318)	237	(122)
Net cash flows from financing activities	(97)	(332)	107
Total assets	3,249	2,162	1,990
Company D			
Revenues	$53,791	$51,760	$50,098
Operating income (loss)	1,374	2,573	2,359
Net income (loss)	315	1,205	1,043
Net cash flows from operating activities	2,215	3,183	2,347
Net cash flows from investing activities	(2,026)	(1,907)	(1,914)
Net cash flows from financing activities	(201)	(1,266)	(433)
Total assets	20,184	20,102	19,087

1. Match each of the following companies with the data for Company A, B, C, or D:

   Amazon.com
   Coca-Cola Inc.
   Delta Air Lines
   Kroger

2. Explain the logic underlying your matches.

Case 3-6

Analysis of income statements

Home Depot and Lowe's operate national chains of home improvement stores that sell a wide assortment of building materials and home improvement, lawn, and garden products, such as lumber, paint, wall coverings, lawn mowers, plumbing, and electrical supplies. Home Depot operates approximately 1,707 stores, while Lowe's operates approximately 952 stores. The following operating data (in millions) were adapted from the 2004 SEC 10-K filings of Home Depot and Lowe's:

	Home Depot	Lowe's
Net sales	$64,816	$30,838
Cost of sales	44,236	21,231
Gross profit	$20,580	$ 9,607
Operating expenses	13,734	6,429
Operating income	$ 6,846	$ 3,178
Interest expense	62	180
Other income	59	15
Income before taxes	$ 6,843	$ 3,013
Income taxes	2,539	1,136
Net income	$ 4,304	$ 1,877

1. Prepare common-sized income statements for Home Depot and Lowe's.
2. Compute the average sales per store for Home Depot and Lowe's. Round to the thousands.
3. Analyze and comment on your results in (1) and (2).
4. Broker recommendations are reported on Yahoo.com's financial Web site. The recommendations are ranked as follows:

Strong Buy	1
Buy	2
Hold	3
Sell	4
Strong Sell	5

Based upon your answer to (3), would you expect the average broker recommendation for Home Depot to be higher (less favorable) or lower (more favorable) than for Lowe's? Compare your assessment with the average broker recommendation on Yahoo.com's financial Web site (http://finance.yahoo.com/). To find the broker recommendation, enter the stock symbols for Home Depot (HD) and Lowe's (LOW) and click on "research."

Case 3-7

Common-sized statements

SPREADSHEET

Comparative income statements for two video game developers, Activision, Inc., and Electronic Arts, Inc., are provided for a recent fiscal year as follows:

	Activision	Electronic Arts
Net revenues	$680,094	$2,957,141
Cost of goods sold	397,292	1,102,950
Gross profit	$282,802	$1,854,191
Sales and marketing expenses	$105,248	$ 370,468
General and administrative expenses	15,407	184,825
Product development expense	25,068	510,858
Other expenses	0	12,443
Operating income	$137,079	$ 775,597

The cost of goods sold represents the total cost of manufacturing and packaging a game, plus royalties and licenses paid to independent game developers. Product development costs are the costs incurred to design games.

1. Prepare common-sized income statements for both companies.
2. Interpret the significant differences in these common-sized statements.

BUSINESS ACTIVITIES AND RESPONSIBILITY ISSUES

Activity 3-1

Accrued expense

On December 30, 2006, you buy a Ford Expedition. It comes with a three-year, 36,000-mile warranty. On January 18, 2007, you return the Expedition to the dealership for some basic repairs covered under the warranty. The cost of the repairs to the dealership is $725. In what year, 2006 or 2007, should Ford Motor Co. recognize the cost of the warranty repairs as an expense?

Activity 3-2

Account for revenue

Omaha College requires students to pay tuition each term before classes begin. Students who have not paid their tuition are not allowed to enroll or to attend classes.

What accounts do you think would be used by Omaha College to record the receipt of the students' tuition payments? Describe the nature of each account.

Activity 3-3

Accrued revenue

The following is an excerpt from a conversation between Nathan Cisneros and Sonya Lucas just before they boarded a flight to Paris on American Airlines. They are going to Paris to attend their company's annual sales conference.

Nathan: Sonya, aren't you taking an introductory accounting course at college?
Sonya: Yes, I decided it's about time I learned something about accounting. You know, our annual bonuses are based upon the sales figures that come from the accounting department.
Nathan: I guess I never really thought about it.
Sonya: You should think about it! Last year, I placed a $300,000 order on December 23. But when I got my bonus, the $300,000 sale wasn't included. They said it hadn't been shipped until January 5, so it would have to count in next year's bonus.
Nathan: A real bummer!
Sonya: Right! I was counting on that bonus including the $300,000 sale.
Nathan: Did you complain?
Sonya: Yes, but it didn't do any good. Beth, the head accountant, said something about matching revenues and expenses. Also, something about not recording revenues until the sale is final. I figure I'd take the accounting course and find out whether she's just jerking me around.
Nathan: I never really thought about it. When do you think American Airlines will record its revenues from this flight?
Sonya: Mmm . . . I guess it could record the revenue when it sells the ticket . . . or . . . when the boarding passes are taken at the door . . . or . . . when we get off the plane . . . or when our company pays for the tickets . . . or . . . I don't know. I'll ask my accounting instructor.

Discuss when American Airlines should recognize the revenue from ticket sales to properly match revenues and expenses.

Activity 3-4

Adjustments for financial statements

Several years ago, your brother opened Chestnut Television Repair. He made a small initial investment and added money from his personal bank account as needed. He withdrew money for living expenses at irregular intervals. As the business grew, he hired an assistant. He is now considering adding more employees, purchasing additional service trucks, and purchasing the building he now rents. To secure funds for the expansion, your brother submitted a loan application to the bank and included the most recent financial statements (shown at the top of the following page) prepared from accounts maintained by a part-time bookkeeper.

Chestnut Television Repair **Income Statement** For the Year Ended August 31, 2006		
Service revenue		$83,280
Less: Rent paid	$20,000	
Wages paid	18,500	
Supplies paid	5,100	
Utilities paid	3,175	
Insurance paid	2,400	
Miscellaneous payments	2,150	51,325
Net income		$31,955

Chestnut Television Repair **Balance Sheet** August 31, 2006	
Assets	
Cash	$11,150
Amounts due from customers	6,100
Truck	30,000
Total assets	$47,250
Equities	
Stockholders' equity	$47,250

After reviewing the financial statements, the loan officer at the bank asked your brother if he used the accrual basis of accounting for revenues and expenses. Your brother responded that he did and that is why he included an account for "Amounts Due from Customers." The loan officer then asked whether or not the accounts were adjusted prior to the preparation of the statements. Your brother answered that they had not been adjusted.

1. Why do you think the loan officer suspected that the accounts had not been adjusted prior to the preparation of the statements?
2. Indicate possible accounts that might need to be adjusted before an accurate set of financial statements could be prepared.

Activity 3-5

Compare balance sheets

Compare the balance sheets of two different companies, and present to the class a summary of the similarities and differences of the two companies. You may obtain the balance sheets you need from one of the following sources:

1. Your school or local library.
2. The investor relations department of each company.
3. The company's Web site on the Internet.
4. EDGAR (Electronic Data Gathering, Analysis, and Retrieval), the electronic archives of financial statements filed with the Securities and Exchange Commission. The EDGAR address is http://www.sec.gov/edgarhp.htm. To obtain annual report information, click on "Search for Company Filings," then click on "Companies & other Filers." Type in a company name on the "EDGAR Company Search" form. EDGAR will list the reports available for the selected company. A company's annual report (along with other information) is provided

in its annual 10-K report to the SEC. Click on the 10-K (or 10-K405) report for the year you wish to download. If you wish, you can save the whole 10-K report to a file and then open it with your word processor.

Activity 3-6

Business emphasis

GROUP ACTIVITY

Assume that you and two friends are debating whether to open an automotive and service retail chain that will be called Auto-Mart. Initially, Auto-Mart will open three stores locally, but the business plan anticipates going nationwide within five years.

Currently, you and your future business partners are debating whether to focus Auto-Mart on a "do-it-yourself" or "do-it-for-me" business. A do-it-yourself business emphasizes the sale of retail auto parts that customers will use themselves to repair and service their cars. A do-it-for-me business emphasizes the offering of maintenance and service for customers.

1. In groups of three or four, discuss whether to implement a do-it-yourself or do-it-for-me business emphasis. List the advantages of each emphasis and arrive at a conclusion as to which emphasis to implement.
2. Provide examples of real world businesses that use do-it-yourself or do-it-for-me business emphases.

ANSWERS TO SELF-STUDY QUESTIONS

1. A Under the accrual basis of accounting, revenues are recorded when the services are rendered. Since the services were rendered during June, all the fees should be recorded on June 30 (answer A). This is an example of accrued revenue. Under the cash basis of accounting, revenues are recorded when the cash is collected, not necessarily when the fees are earned. Thus, no revenue would be recorded in June, $8,500 of revenue would be recorded in July, and $6,500 of revenue would be recorded in August (answer D). Answers B and C are incorrect and are not used under either the accrual or cash bases.

2. C The collection of a $5,700 accounts receivable is recorded as an increase in Cash, $5,700, and a decrease in Accounts Receivable, $5,700 (answer C). The initial recording of the fees earned on account is recorded as an increase in Accounts Receivable and an increase in Fees Earned (answer B). Services rendered for cash are recorded as an increase in Cash and an increase in Fees Earned (answer D). Answer A is incorrect and would result in the accounting equation being out of balance because total assets would exceed total liabilities and stockholders' equity by $11,400.

3. A A deferral is the delay in recording an expense already paid, such as prepaid insurance (answer A). Wages payable (answer B) is considered an accrued expense or accrued liability. Fees earned (answer C) is a revenue item. Accumulated depreciation (answer D) is a contra account to a fixed asset.

4. D The balance in the supplies account, before adjustment, represents the amount of supplies available during the period. From this amount ($2,250) is subtracted the amount of supplies on hand ($950) to determine the supplies used ($1,300). The used supplies is recorded as an increase in Supplies Expense, $1,300, and a decrease in Supplies, $1,300 (answer D).

5. C The failure to record the adjusting entry increasing Rent Revenue, $600, and decreasing Unearned Rent, $600, would have the effect of overstating liabilities by $600 and understating net income by $600 (answer C).

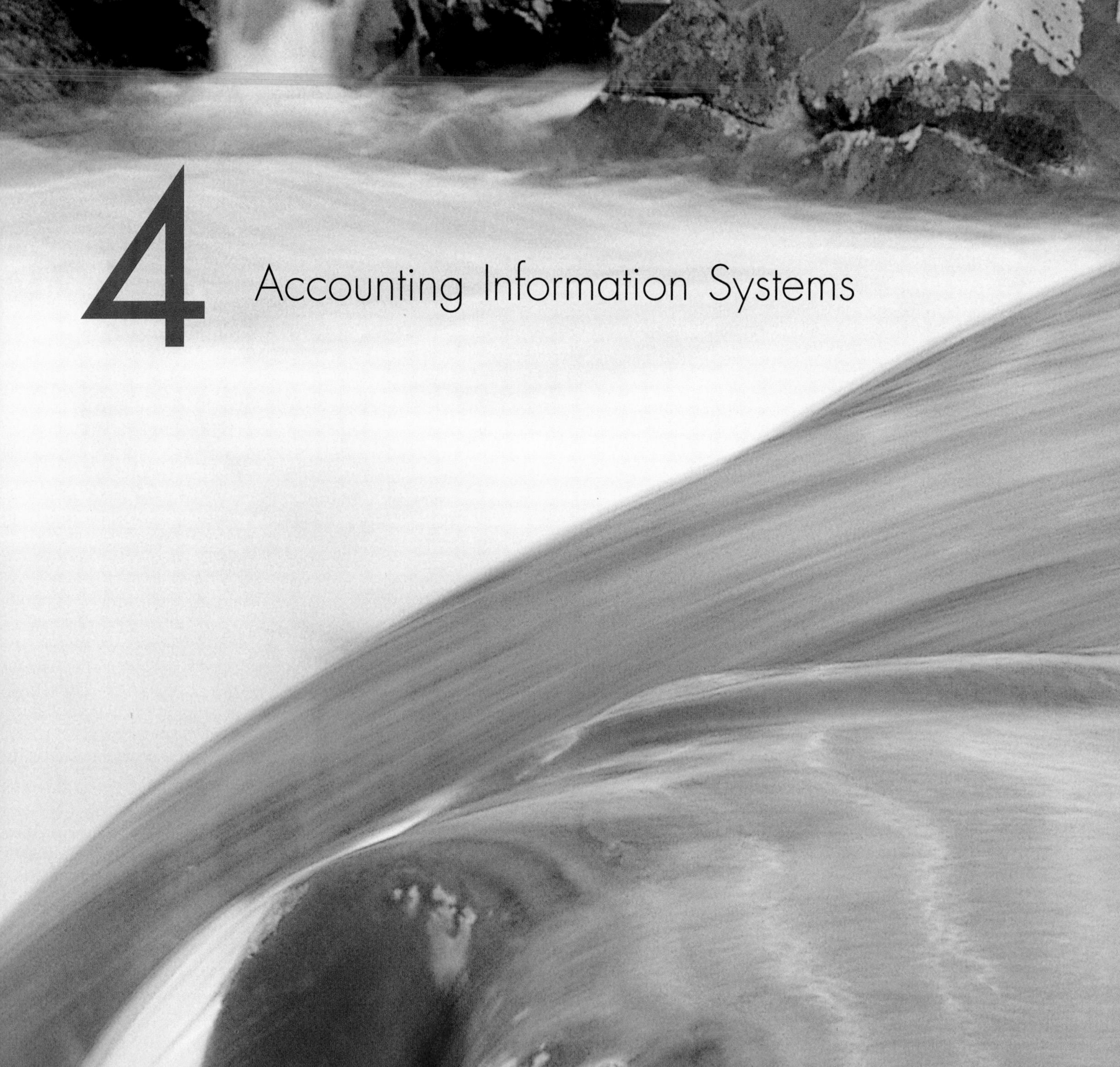

4 Accounting Information Systems

Learning Goals

1. Describe the nature of business information systems.
2. Describe the nature of accounting information systems.
3. Describe and illustrate the basic elements of transaction processing systems.
4. Describe and illustrate the basic elements of a financial reporting system.
5. Describe the accounting cycle for the double-entry accounting system.
6. Describe and illustrate the computation and use of earnings before interest, taxes, depreciation, and amortization (EBITDA).

Southwest Airlines

© JOSEPH KACZMAREK/AP PHOTO

You can organize music within your MP3 player according to various playlists, for example, your favorite songs, genre, artist, or album. Playlists allow you to quickly retrieve music for listening. Computer files are organized within folders for the same reason. Information, like music or digital files, is organized into categories to simplify retrieval and reporting. In the same way that you organize your digital information, a business also needs to organize their transactions. For example, when you shop at Wal-Mart or Target, buy gas at an ExxonMobil or BP station, buy groceries at Kroger or Supervalu, or buy a ticket to fly on Southwest Airlines or American Airlines, you enter into a transaction that is captured, processed, and recorded by the business. At Southwest Airlines, for example, most airline tickets are sold over the Internet through credit card transactions. But the transaction processing doesn't stop at this point. The credit card transaction records the cash received for the ticket and reserves space on a future flight. At the time the ticket is sold, the airline has recorded unearned revenue, because it still owes the service. When the passenger boards the plane, the ticket is scanned, and another transaction is recorded to earn the revenue.

While all airlines process transactions in similar ways, this doesn't mean that all airlines are created equal. Southwest Airlines has been one of the few profitable airlines in the United States. So what has been the key to Southwest's success over the years? Southwest, more than its competitors, has successfully developed a low-cost model that involves:

a. using only Boeing 737 aircraft to simplify maintenance and crew training.
b. using secondary airports in major cities to reduce ground costs.
c. maximizing airplane flying time by minimizing gate time.
d. avoiding commission-based ticket sales to travel agents.
e. minimizing baggage handling.

For example, Southwest's average passenger fare during 2004 was just over $88—and it earned a profit! Indeed, Southwest competes effectively with bus fares.

As a customer, understanding how transactions are processed by a business's information system is not usually important to you. If you own a business or work for a business, however, understanding the accounting information system is important. For example, you need to understand how to interpret and analyze business reports, which includes understanding how the reports were generated and whether the reports reflect all the relevant data necessary to make business decisions.

In this chapter, we begin by discussing the nature of business information systems. We then describe the nature of accounting information systems and their subsystems, including management reporting, transaction processing, and financial reporting systems. Our primary focus in this chapter is on the elements of transaction processing and financial reporting systems. The elements of these systems are the same for Southwest Airlines and Wal-Mart as for the local convenience store or hardware store.

Describe the nature of business information systems.

BUSINESS INFORMATION SYSTEMS

In prior chapters, we discussed how businesses report their financial condition and changes in financial condition through financial statements. We described and illustrated how small businesses and individuals often use the cash basis of accounting, while large, publicly held companies use the accrual basis of accounting. In those chapters, we used the integrated financial statement framework for recording and summarizing transactions and generating the resulting financial statements. While this framework may be used for a small number of transactions, it is not very efficient for recording millions of transactions daily by large corporations such as Home Depot or Wal-Mart.

In this chapter, we focus on how accounting information systems are designed to efficiently record a large number of transactions. We show how basic controls in the accounting system provide assurance that transactions are accurately recorded. We begin by describing generic business information systems.

A **business information system** collects and processes data and distributes the information to stakeholders. All business information systems share common elements that include data sources, data collection, data processing, database management, information, and stakeholders. These elements of business information systems are shown in Exhibit 1.

In designing a business information system, the end users of the information must first be identified and their information needs determined. Stakeholders can be classified as internal users, such as managers and operational employees, and external users, such as creditors, stockholders, regulatory agencies, suppliers, and customers. The information needs of internal users vary widely throughout the business in both form and content. In contrast, external users require information in standardized formats, such as tax forms, regulatory filings, and financial statements.

Once the information needs of users have been determined, the business information system must be designed to collect the necessary data and process the data into the required information. For example, a business's personnel information system requires data to be collected, such as anticipated and actual work schedules, training needs, accrued vacation time, sick leave, pay scales, and workmen's compensation requirements. Controls should be designed into the collection process to ensure that the data are accurate, timely, and complete. Likewise, controls should be designed into the information system so that errors in processing data are prevented and detected. For example, the personnel system should include a processing control that would prevent an employee from accruing vacation time beyond the total allowable by the business.

In practice, businesses have a variety of information systems. Examples of such systems include sales order, transportation, human resources, purchasing, and accounting systems. Each system should be linked to the other systems for operational efficiency and effectiveness. In the remainder of this chapter, we focus on accounting information systems.

Exhibit 1

Business Information Systems

Business Information System

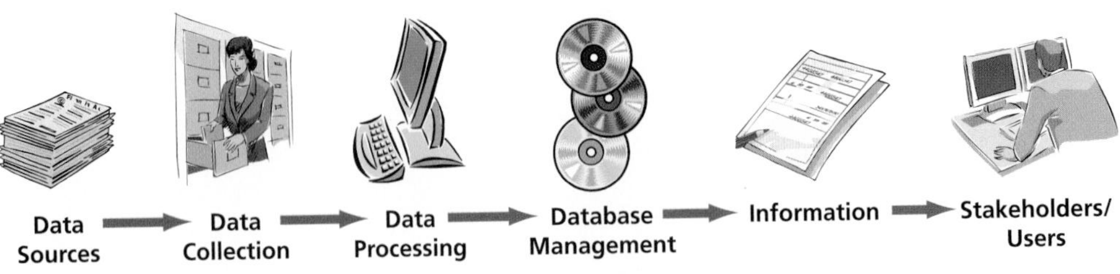

INTEGRITY, OBJECTIVITY, AND ETHICS IN BUSINESS

Integrity and Honesty Make a Difference

Herb Kelleher, chairman and former chief executive of **Southwest Airlines**, is known for his honesty and integrity among Southwest employees. In the mid-1990s, Kelleher negotiated a 10-year union contract with Southwest pilots in which the pilots agreed to freeze their wages for the first five years of the contract. A primary reason Kelleher was able to successfully negotiate the contract was that he constantly worked at building trust among his employees. When he was negotiating the contract, he told the pilots he would freeze his own pay for the same five years. The pilots' union believed him, knowing that Kelleher wouldn't ask them to do something he wouldn't do. Jackie Freiberg, co-author of the book, *Nuts! Southwest Airlines' Crazy Recipe for Business and Personal Success*, says: "Kelleher is a man of his word. He thinks straight and talks straight, so people respect and trust him."

Source: Steve Watkins, "Leaders and Success," *Investor's Business Daily*, November 5, 2004.

2 Describe the nature of accounting information systems.

BASIC ACCOUNTING SYSTEMS

An **accounting information system** processes financial and operational data into reports useful to internal and external stakeholders. As shown in Exhibit 2, accounting information systems normally consist of the following three subsystems: (1) the management reporting system, (2) the transaction processing system, and (3) the financial reporting system.

The **management reporting system** provides internal information to assist managers in making decisions. The form and content of the information will vary, depending upon the decisions. The information may include either financial information, such as the effects of a proposed acquisition on the financial statements, or nonfinancial information, such as the number of back orders, on-time deliveries, or customer returns. Examples of such reports could include budgets, variance analyses, cost-volume-profit analyses, sales mix analyses, and employee turnover. The area of accounting that focuses on developing management reporting systems is called *managerial accounting*.

The **transaction processing system** records and summarizes the effects of financial transactions on the business. Large businesses enter into thousands and, in some cases,

Exhibit 2

Accounting Information System

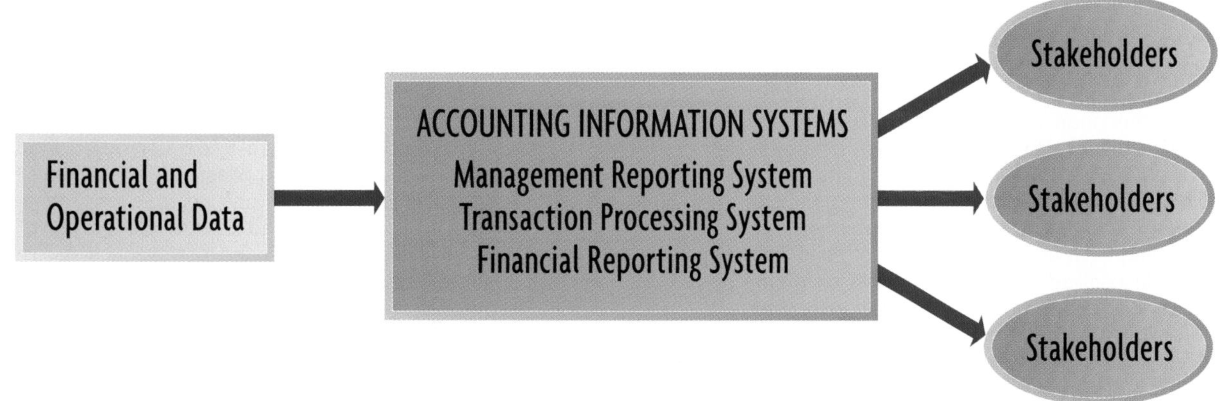

millions of transactions daily. To efficiently process such a large volume of transactions, most businesses group similar, repetitive transactions into transaction cycles. The most common transaction cycles are the revenue cycle, the purchasing cycle, the payroll cycle, the inventory cycle, and the treasury cycle.

Revenue cycle transactions involve providing services or selling products. They include collecting payments for the services or products. The *purchasing cycle* transactions involve buying assets or services for use in the normal operations of the business. Included in the purchasing cycle is the payment for the goods or services. *Payroll cycle* transactions involve paying employees. *Inventory cycle* transactions involve buying materials or finished products that eventually will be sold. Manufacturing businesses convert raw materials into finished products for sale. Merchandising businesses buy finished products ready for sale. *Treasury cycle* transactions involve financing the operations of the business. Examples of treasury cycle transactions include issuing capital stock or long-term debt. Paying dividends and redeeming long-term debt would also be types of treasury cycle transactions.

International Perspective International Accounting Standards rely on broad-based principles, rather than on detailed accounting rules. These rules provide general guidance on how transactions should be recorded, but they require the preparer to exercise considerable professional judgment in recording and reporting transactions.

The **financial reporting system** produces financial statements and other reports for external stakeholders. The financial reporting system is closely interrelated to the transaction processing system in that the financial statements summarize the effects of transactions on the financial condition and changes in financial condition of the business. The financial reporting system also summarizes transactions for other stakeholders in reports such as tax returns and other regulatory reports.

Our primary focus in this text is on the transaction processing and financial reporting systems. In this chapter, we describe and illustrate the basic elements of these two systems.

Describe and illustrate the basic elements of transaction processing systems.

TRANSACTION PROCESSING SYSTEMS

The basic elements of transaction processing systems have evolved over centuries, beginning with the earliest known economic activity and ending with today's highly computerized and integrated information systems. These elements include accounts

HOW BUSINESSES MAKE MONEY

Hub-and-Spoke or Point-to-Point?

Southwest Airlines uses a simple fare structure, featuring low, unrestricted, unlimited, everyday coach fares. These fares are made possible by Southwest's use of a point-to-point, rather than hub-and-spoke, business approach. **United**, **Delta**, and **American** employ a hub-and-spoke approach in which an airline establishes major hubs that serve as connecting links to other cities. For example, Delta has established major connecting hubs in Atlanta, Cincinnati, and Salt Lake City. In contrast, Southwest focuses on point-to-point service between selected cities with over 300 one-way, nonstop city pairs with an average length of 500 miles and average flying time of 1.5 hours. As a result, Southwest minimizes connections, delays, and total trip time. Southwest also focuses on serving conveniently located satellite or downtown airports, such as Dallas Love Field, Houston Hobby, and Chicago Midway. Because these airports are normally less congested than hub airports, Southwest is better able to maintain high employee productivity and reliable on-time performance. This permits the company to achieve high asset utilization of its fixed assets, such as its 737 aircraft. For example, aircraft are scheduled to spend only 25 minutes at the gate, thereby reducing the number of aircraft and gate facilities that would otherwise be required.

and rules for recording transactions in accounts, journals, and ledgers. In addition, the system should include controls to prevent and detect errors in the recording and summarization process.

The Account

In Chapters 2 and 3, we recorded and summarized transactions by using the integrated financial statement framework. Each financial statement item was represented. Transactions were recorded as pluses or minuses for each item affected by the transaction. Detecting and preventing errors in processing transactions was controlled by monitoring the equality of the balance sheet (accounting equation). That is, total assets must equal total liabilities plus stockholders' equity.

While the system illustrated in Chapters 2 and 3 allowed us to record and summarize transactions for a small business with few transactions, it would be inefficient for a large business. One element in which transactions are recorded efficiently is the *account*.

An **account**, in its simplest form, has three parts. First, each account has a title, which is the name of the item recorded in the account. Second, each account has a space for recording increases in the amount of the item. Third, each account has a space for recording decreases in the amount of the item. The account form presented below is called a *T account* because it resembles the letter T. The left side of the account is called the *debit* side, and the right side is called the *credit* side.

TITLE	
Left side	Right side
Debit	*Credit*

Amounts entered on the left side of an account, regardless of the account title, are called **debits** to the account. When debits are entered in an account, the account is said to be *debited* (or charged). Amounts entered on the right side of an account are called **credits**, and the account is said to be *credited*. Debits and credits are sometimes abbreviated as *Dr.* and *Cr.*

In the cash account that follows, transactions involving cash receipts are listed on the debit side of the account. The transactions involving cash payments are listed on the credit side. If at any time the total of cash receipts ($10,950) is needed, the entries on the debit side of the account are added. The total of the cash payments on the credit side, $6,850 in the example, is determined in a similar manner. Subtracting the payments from the receipts, $10,950 − $6,850, determines the amount of cash on hand, $4,100. This amount is called the **balance of an account**. This balance should be identified as a debit balance in some way, such as showing the balance on the debit side of the account or simply listing it as a debit balance.

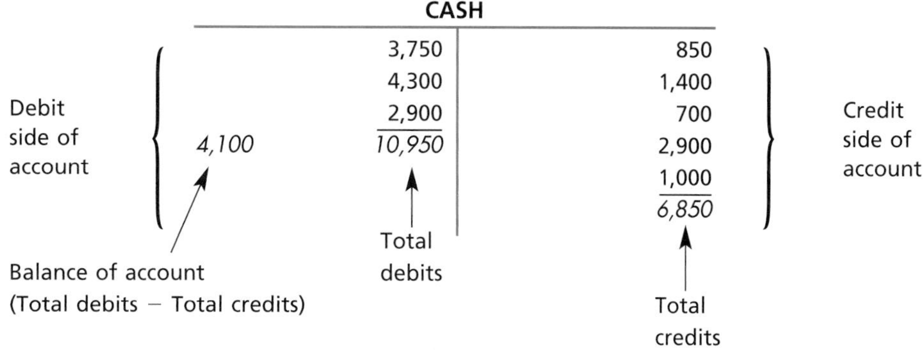

Rules of Debit and Credit

Why did we record increases in the cash account as debits and decreases as credits? The simple answer is because of convention. That is, a standardized method of recording increases and decreases in accounts is essential in order that businesses record transactions in a similar manner. If each business recorded transactions differently, the result would be chaotic and comparability between companies would be lost.

The standardized **rules of debit and credit** are incorporated into the accounting equation as shown in Exhibit 3. These standardized rules are used by all businesses—from the corner gas station to the largest public corporation.

Q. If $500 is debited to an account, on which side of the account is it entered? Is the account increased or decreased?

A. The $500 is entered on the left side of the account. Whether the $500 increases or decreases the account depends on what kind of account is involved.

Exhibit 3 shows three important characteristics of the rules of debit and credit. *First*, the **normal balance of an account** is the side of the account used to record increases. Thus, the normal balance of an asset account is a debit balance, while the normal balance of a liability account is a credit balance. This characteristic is often useful in detecting errors in the recording process. That is, when an account normally having a debit balance actually has a credit balance, or vice versa, an error may have occurred or an unusual situation may exist.

To illustrate, assume that at the end of the period the cash account has a credit balance. In this case, either an error has occurred or the company has overdrawn its bank account. Likewise, if accounts payable has a debit balance, then an error has occurred or the company has overpaid its accounts payable. On the other hand, a credit balance in the office equipment or land account can only result from an error in the recording process. That is, a company cannot have negative office equipment or land. Thus, the normal balances of accounts provide a degree of control in the recording process.

The *second* characteristic shown in Exhibit 3 is that accounts on the left side of the accounting equation (the assets side) are increased by debits and have normal debit balances, while accounts on the right side of the accounting equation (liability and stockholders' equity side) are increased by credits and have normal credit balances. On the asset (left-hand) side of the equation, the only exception to the preceding relationship is that some asset accounts, called contra asset accounts, are normally increased by credits and have normal credit balances. As the name contra asset implies, these accounts offset the normal debit balances of asset accounts. For example, accumulated depreciation, an offset to plant assets, is increased by credits and has a normal credit balance. Thus, accumulated depreciation is a contra asset account. We will discuss the concept of depreciation and accumulated depreciation in more depth in Chapter 9.

On the liability and stockholders' equity (right-hand) side of the equation, the only exceptions to the preceding relationship are the dividend and expense accounts. The payment of dividends decreases stockholders' equity (retained earnings); thus, the dividends account is increased by debits and has a normal debit balance. In this sense, the dividends account can be thought of as a type of offset to retained earnings.

Revenue increases stockholders' equity (retained earnings), and thus revenue accounts are increased by credits and have normal credit balances. In contrast, expenses decrease stockholders' equity (retained earnings). Thus, expense accounts are increased by debits and have a normal debit balance. Expense accounts can be thought of as a type of offset to revenues.

The *third* characteristic of the rules of debit and credit is that for each transaction the total debits will equal the total credits. That is, each transaction must be recorded so that the total debits for the transaction will equal the total credits. For example, assume that a company pays cash of $500 for supplies. The asset account Supplies will be debited (increased) by $500 and Cash will be credited (decreased) by $500. Likewise, if the company provides services and receives $2,000 from customers, Cash will be debited (increased) and Fees Earned will be credited (increased) by $2,000. Debits equaling the credits for each transaction provides a degree of control in the recording process. In addition, as shown in Exhibit 3, the equality of debits and credits for each transaction is built into the

Exhibit 3

Rules of Debit and Credit

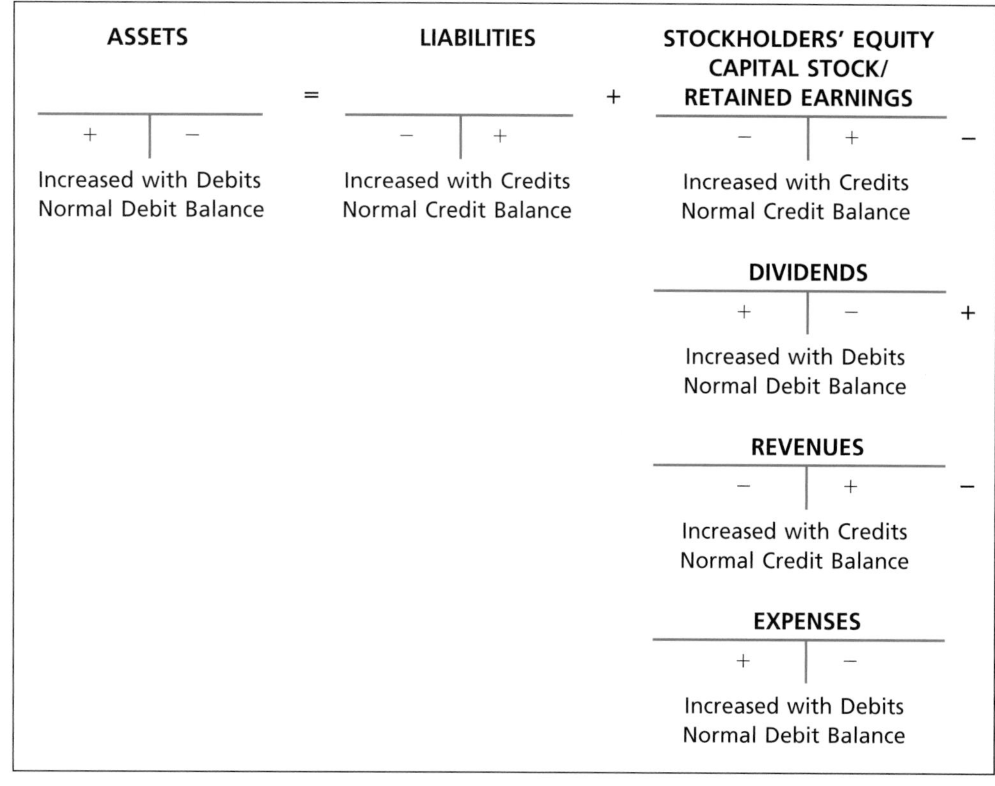

accounting equation: Assets = Liabilities + Stockholders' Equity. Because of this double equality, the system is referred to as the **double-entry accounting system**.

To summarize, each transaction is recorded under the rules shown in Exhibit 3. Under these rules, the total debits will equal the total credits for each transaction, because the equality of the debits and credits is built into the accounting equation: Assets = Liabilities + Stockholders' Equity.

Q. A credit balance in which of the following accounts—Cash, Dividends, or Unearned Revenue—would indicate that an error had occurred?

A. *Dividends. If Cash has a credit balance, the business may have overdrawn its bank account.*

The Journal

Each transaction is initially entered in chronological order in a record called a **journal**. In this way, the journal documents the history of the company. The process of recording transactions in the journal is called **journalizing**. The specific transaction record entered in the journal is called a **journal entry**.

In practice, most journal entries are automated with the transaction processing system. However, transactions that are unusual, correcting, or infrequent may require manual entries. We stress manual entries in this text to help you understand the automated framework.

A business may use a variety of formats for recording journal entries. It may use one all-purpose journal, sometimes called a *general journal*, or it may use several journals. In the latter case, a *special journal* is designed to record a single kind of transaction that occurs frequently. To simplify, we will use a basic, two-column general journal in the remainder of this chapter to illustrate the manual journalizing of transactions.

Assume that on November 1, 2007, Janet Moore organizes a corporation that will be known as Online Solutions. The first phase of Janet's business plan is to focus on building a service business that provides assistance to individuals and small businesses in developing Web pages and in configuring and installing application software. Janet

INTEGRITY, OBJECTIVITY, AND ETHICS IN BUSINESS

Will Journalizing Prevent Fraud?

While journalizing transactions reduces the possibility of fraud, it by no means eliminates it. For example, embezzlement can be hidden within the double-entry bookkeeping system by creating fictitious suppliers to whom checks are issued.

---

expects this initial phase of the business to last one to two years. During this period, Janet will gather information on the software and hardware needs of customers. During the second phase of the business plan, Janet plans to expand Online Solutions into an Internet-based retailer of software and hardware to individuals and small businesses.

To start the business, Janet deposits $25,000 in a bank account in the name of Online Solutions in return for shares of stock in the corporation. This first transaction increases cash and capital stock by $25,000. The transaction is entered in the general journal by first listing the date, then the title of the account to be debited, and the amount of the debit. Next, the title of the account to be credited is listed below and to the right of the debit, followed by the amount to be credited. The resulting journal entry follows.

2007				
Nov.	1	Cash	25,000	
		Capital Stock		25,000

The increase in the asset, cash, is debited to the cash account. The increase in stockholders' equity (capital stock) is credited to the capital stock account. As other assets are acquired, the increases are also recorded as debits to asset accounts. Likewise, other increases in stockholders' equity will be recorded as credits to stockholders' equity accounts.

Online Solutions entered into the following additional transactions during the remainder of November:

Nov.	5	Purchased land for $20,000, paying cash. The land is located in a new business park with convenient access to transportation facilities. Janet Moore plans to rent office space and equipment during the first phase of Online Solutions' business plan. During the second phase, Janet plans to build an office and warehouse on the land.
	10	Purchased supplies on account for $1,350.
	18	Received $7,500 for services provided to customers for cash.
	30	Paid expenses as follows: wages, $2,125; rent, $800; utilities, $450; and miscellaneous, $275.
	30	Paid creditors on account, $950.
	30	Paid stockholders (Janet Moore) dividends of $2,000.

The journal entries to record these transactions are shown at the top of the following page.

Effects of Journal Entries on the Financial Statements

Every transaction affects an element of the financial statements and, therefore, must be recorded. In Chapters 2 and 3, we recorded transactions using the integrated financial

SCF	BS	IS	Date	Account	Debit	Credit
I↓	A↑↓	—	Nov. 5	Land	20,000	
				Cash		20,000
—	A↑ L↑	—	10	Supplies	1,350	
				Accounts Payable		1,350
O↑	A↑ SE↑	R↑	18	Cash	7,500	
				Fees Earned		7,500
O↓	A↓ SE↓	E↑	30	Wages Expense	2,125	
				Rent Expense	800	
				Utilities Expense	450	
				Miscellaneous Expense	275	
				Cash		3,650
O↓	A↓ L↓	—	30	Accounts Payable	950	
				Cash		950
F↓	A↓ SE↓	—	30	Dividends	2,000	
				Cash		2,000

statement framework. In this chapter, we describe and illustrate the use of journal entries to record transactions. Both methods of recording transactions and their effects on the financial statements have advantages and disadvantages.

The integrated financial statement framework we used in Chapters 2–3 illustrates the effects of transactions on the financial statements and how the financial statements are integrated. In the real world, however, the double-entry accounting system, including journal entries and debits and credits, is used because it is more efficient and is common practice.

Since the double-entry accounting system is used in virtually all accounting systems, we use journal entries to record transactions in the remainder of this text. However, we supplement each journal entry with the following margin notation adapted from the integrated financial statement framework. We do this so that you can better see the effects of transactions on the financial statements and how transactions are integrated in the financial statements.

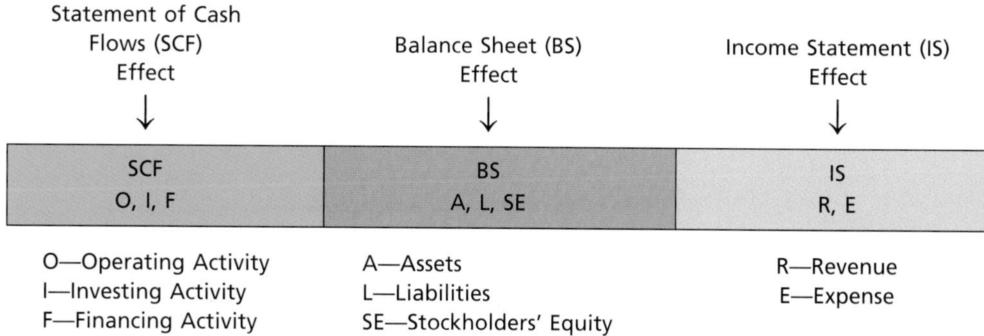

Upward or downward arrows show increases in each financial statement element. For example, the November 5 transaction of Online Solutions is accompanied by the following notation:

SCF	BS	IS
I↓	A↑↓	—

This notation indicates that the transaction has the effect of decreasing cash from investing activities on the statement of cash flows (I↓), increasing and decreasing assets by the same amount on the balance sheet (A↑↓), and that the transaction had no effect on the income statement (—). Because assets must always equal liabilities plus stockholders' equity, the effects of transactions on the balance sheet must always be equal. For example, in the preceding transaction, the increase in assets equals the decrease in assets.

The November 10 transaction is accompanied by the following margin notation:

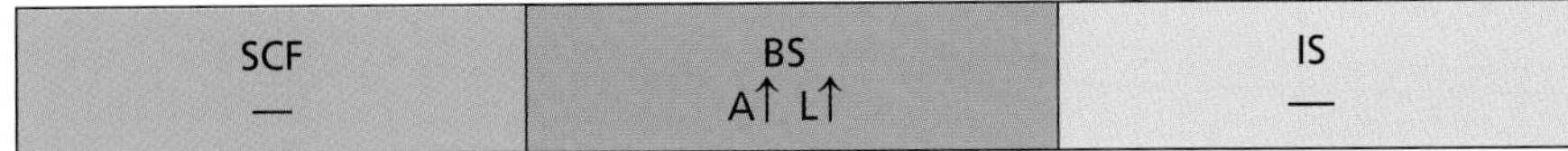

This notation indicates that the transaction has no effect on the statement of cash flows (—), that assets and liabilities were increased on the balance sheet (A↑ L↑), and there was no effect on the income statement (—).

The November 18 transaction is accompanied by the following margin notation:

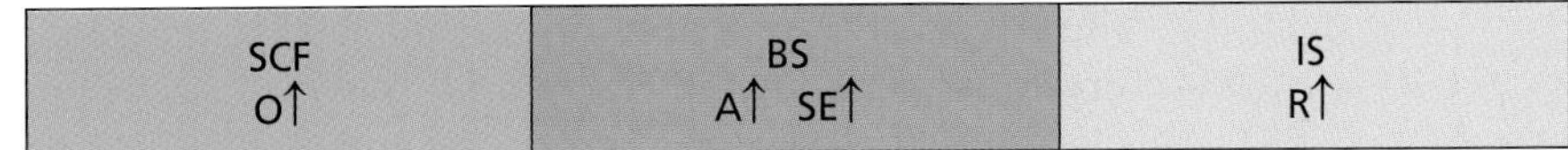

This notation indicates that the transaction increased cash from operating activities on the statement of cash flows (O↑), increased assets and stockholders' equity on the balance sheet (A↑ SE↑), and increased revenues on the income statement (R↑).

The journal entries in this chapter and the remainder of this text are accompanied by similar notation to indicate their effect on the financial statements. We do not show this notation for closing entries, since closing entries are only used to prepare the accounting records for the next period and do not reflect underlying transactions. Closing entries are described and illustrated later in this chapter.

Posting to the Ledger

As we discussed in the preceding section, a transaction is first recorded in the journal. The journal thus provides a chronological history of transactions. Periodically, the journal entries must be transferred to the accounts so that financial statements can be prepared. The group of accounts for a business is called its **general ledger**. The list of accounts in the general ledger is called the **chart of accounts**. The accounts are normally listed in the order in which they appear in the financial statements, beginning with the balance sheet and concluding with the income statement. The chart of accounts for Online Solutions is shown in Exhibit 4.

The process of transferring the debits and credits from the journal entries to the accounts in the ledger is called **posting**. To illustrate the posting process, Online Solutions' November 1 transaction, along with its posting to the cash and capital stock accounts, is shown in Exhibit 5.

Exhibit 4

Chart of Accounts for Online Solutions

Balance Sheet Accounts	Income Statement Accounts
Assets	Revenue
Cash	Fees Earned
Accounts Receivable	Rent Revenue
Supplies	Expenses
Prepaid Insurance	Wages Expense
Office Equipment	Rent Expense
Accumulated Depreciation	Depreciation Expense
Land	Utilities Expense
Liabilities	Supplies Expense
Accounts Payable	Insurance Expense
Wages Payable	Miscellaneous Expense
Unearned Rent	
Stockholders' Equity	
Capital Stock	
Retained Earnings	
Dividends	

Exhibit 5

Posting a Journal Entry

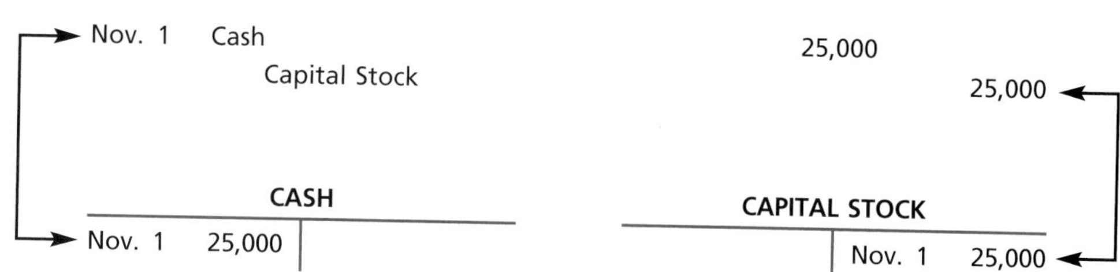

The debits and credits for each journal entry are posted to the accounts in the order in which they occur in the journal. In posting to the accounts, the date is entered followed by the amount of the entry. After the journal entries are posted, the ledger becomes a chronological history of transactions *by account*. The posting of Online Solutions' remaining journal entries is shown in Exhibit 6. Posting is performed automatically in computerized systems. In Exhibit 6, however, we illustrate the concept by posting manually.

Q. Cash of $450 was received on account, but was recorded as a $540 debit to Cash and a $540 debit to Accounts Receivable. Would the trial balance totals be equal?

A. *No. The debit total would exceed the credit total by $1,080.*

Trial Balance

How can you be sure that you have not made an error in posting the debits and credits to the ledger? One way is to make sure that the total of the debit account balances in the ledger equals the total of the credit account balances. This equality should be proved at the end of each accounting period, if not more often. Such a proof, called a **trial balance**, may be in the form of a computer printout or in the form shown in Exhibit 7, which lists the balances shown in Exhibit 6.

The trial balance does not provide complete proof of accuracy of the ledger. It indicates only that the debits and the credits are equal. This proof is of value, however, because errors often affect the equality of debits and credits. If the two totals of a trial balance are not equal, an error has occurred. In such a case, the error must be located and corrected before financial statements are prepared.

Exhibit 6

Ledger for Online Solutions—November

CASH

Nov. 1	25,000	Nov. 5	20,000
18	7,500	30	3,650
		30	950
		30	2,000
30 Bal.	5,900		

FEES EARNED

		Nov. 18	7,500

SUPPLIES

Nov. 10	1,350		

WAGES EXPENSE

Nov. 30	2,125		

LAND

Nov. 5	20,000		

RENT EXPENSE

Nov. 30	800		

ACCOUNTS PAYABLE

Nov. 30	950	Nov. 10	1,350
		30 Bal.	400

UTILITIES EXPENSE

Nov. 30	450		

CAPITAL STOCK

		Nov. 1	25,000

MISCELLANEOUS EXPENSE

Nov. 30	275		

DIVIDENDS

Nov. 30	2,000		

Exhibit 7

Trial Balance

Online Solutions
Trial Balance
November 30, 2007

	Debit Balances	Credit Balances
Cash	5,900	
Supplies	1,350	
Land	20,000	
Accounts Payable		400
Capital Stock		25,000
Dividends	2,000	
Fees Earned		7,500
Wages Expense	2,125	
Rent Expense	800	
Utilities Expense	450	
Miscellaneous Expense	275	
	32,900	32,900

Describe and illustrate the basic elements of a financial reporting system.

FINANCIAL REPORTING SYSTEM

In the prior section, we described and illustrated the basic elements of a transaction processing system. In this section, we continue this illustration to include the basic elements of a financial reporting system. These elements include adjusting entries, financial statements, and closing entries.

As a review of transaction processing systems and as a basis for illustrating a double-entry accounting financial reporting system, we continue our illustration of Online Solutions. During December, assume that Online Solutions entered into the following transactions:

Dec. 1 Paid a premium of $2,400 for a comprehensive insurance policy covering liability, theft, and fire. The policy covers a two-year period.

1 Paid rent for December, $800. The company from which Online Solutions is renting its store space now requires the payment of rent on the first of each month, rather than at the end of the month.

1 Received an offer from a local retailer to rent the land purchased on November 5. The retailer plans to use the land as a parking lot for its employees and customers. Online Solutions agreed to rent the land to the retailer for three months, with the rent payable in advance. Online Solutions received $360 for three months' rent beginning December 1.

4 Purchased office equipment on account from Executive Supply Co. for $1,800.

6 Paid $180 for a newspaper advertisement.

11 Paid creditors $400.

13 Paid a receptionist and a part-time assistant $950 for two weeks' wages.

16 Received $3,100 from fees earned for the first half of December.

16 Earned fees on account totaling $1,750 for the first half of December.

20 Paid $1,800 to Executive Supply Co. on the debt owed from the December 4 transaction.

21 Received $650 from customers in payment of their accounts.

23 Purchased $1,450 of supplies by paying $550 cash and charging the remainder on account.

27 Paid the receptionist and the part-time assistant $1,200 for two weeks' wages.

31 Paid $310 telephone bill for the month.

31 Paid $225 electric bill for the month.

31 Received $2,870 from fees earned for the second half of December.

31 Earned fees on account totaling $1,120 for the second half of December.

31 Paid dividends of $2,000 to stockholders.

The journal entries for the December transactions are shown in Exhibit 8. The posting of the journal entries to the ledger accounts is shown in Exhibit 15 (on pages 170–171).

Adjusting Entries

In Chapter 3, we described and illustrated various adjustments necessary in preparing financial statements. In this section, we illustrate this process for Online Solutions, using the double-entry accounting system. However, before we begin this process, we prepare the trial balance shown in Exhibit 9 (on page 165) to make sure that no error has occurred in posting December transactions to the general ledger.

The adjustment data for Online Solutions as of December 31, 2007, are as follows:

Supplies on hand at December 31, $760. Used supplies of $2,040 ($2,800 – $760).
Insurance premiums expired during December, $100.

(continued)

Exhibit 8

Journal Entries: December Transactions for Online Solutions

SCF	BS	IS				Debit	Credit
O↓	A↑↓	—	Dec.	1	Prepaid Insurance Cash	2,400	 2,400
O↓	A↓ SE↓	E↑		1	Rent Expense Cash	800	 800
O↑	A↑ L↑	—		1	Cash Unearned Rent	360	 360
—	A↑ L↑	—		4	Office Equipment Accounts Payable	1,800	 1,800
O↓	A↓ SE↓	E↑		6	Miscellaneous Expense Cash	180	 180
O↓	A↓ L↓	—		11	Accounts Payable Cash	400	 400
O↓	A↓ SE↓	E↑		13	Wages Expense Cash	950	 950
O↑	A↑ SE↑	R↑		16	Cash Fees Earned	3,100	 3,100
—	A↑ SE↑	R↑		16	Accounts Receivable Fees Earned	1,750	 1,750
O↓	A↓ L↓	—		20	Accounts Payable Cash	1,800	 1,800
O↑	A↑↓	—		21	Cash Accounts Receivable	650	 650

O↓	A↑↓ L↑	—		23	Supplies
					  Cash
					  Accounts Payable
						1,450	
							550
							900

O↓	A↓ SE↓	E↑		27	Wages Expense Cash	1,200	 1,200
O↓	A↓ SE↓	E↑		31	Utilities Expense Cash	310	 310
O↓	A↓ SE↓	E↑		31	Utilities Expense Cash	225	 225
O↑	A↑ SE↑	R↑		31	Cash Fees Earned	2,870	 2,870
—	A↑ SE↑	R↑		31	Accounts Receivable Fees Earned	1,120	 1,120
F↓	A↓ SE↓	—		31	Dividends Cash	2,000	 2,000

Unearned rent earned during December, $120.
Wages accrued, but not paid at December 31, $250.
Fees revenue earned, but not yet billed, $500.
Depreciation of office equipment during December, $50.

Based upon the preceding adjustment data, the adjusting entries for Online Solutions are shown in Exhibit 10.

Like other journal entries, Online Solutions' **adjusting entries** should be posted to the general ledger, as shown in Exhibit 15 (on pages 170–171). After these entries have been posted, we compute adjusted balances and prepare an **adjusted trial balance** prior to preparing the financial statements. This verifies that no errors have occurred in posting the adjustments. The adjusted trial balance for Online Solutions is shown in Exhibit 11.

Exhibit 9

Trial Balance for Online Solutions

Online Solutions Trial Balance December 31, 2007	Debit Balances	Credit Balances
Cash	2,065	
Accounts Receivable	2,220	
Supplies	2,800	
Prepaid Insurance	2,400	
Office Equipment	1,800	
Land	20,000	
Accounts Payable		900
Unearned Rent		360
Capital Stock		25,000
Dividends	4,000	
Fees Earned		16,340
Wages Expense	4,275	
Rent Expense	1,600	
Utilities Expense	985	
Miscellaneous Expense	455	
	42,600	42,600

Exhibit 10

Adjusting Entries for Online Solutions

SCF	BS	IS	Date	Account	Debit	Credit
—	A↓ SE↓	E↑	Dec. 31	Supplies Expense	2,040	
				Supplies		2,040
—	A↓ SE↓	E↑	31	Insurance Expense	100	
				Prepaid Insurance		100
—	L↓ SE↑	R↑	31	Unearned Rent	120	
				Rent Revenue		120
—	L↑ SE↓	E↑	31	Wages Expense	250	
				Wages Payable		250
—	A↑ SE↑	R↑	31	Accounts Receivable	500	
				Fees Earned		500
—	A↓ SE↓	E↑	31	Depreciation Expense	50	
				Accumulated Depreciation—Office Equipment		50

Financial Statements

Using the adjusted trial balance shown in Exhibit 11, the financial statements for Online Solutions for the two months ending December 31, 2007, can be prepared. The income statement, retained earnings statement, balance sheet, and statement of cash flows for Online Solutions are shown in Exhibit 12.

The income statement, retained earnings statement, and balance sheet for Online Solutions can be prepared directly from the adjusted trial balance shown in Exhibit 11. The statement of cash flows is more complex and requires additional analysis of November and December transactions. In the appendix at the end of this chapter, we describe and illustrate how Online Solutions' statement of cash flows is prepared.

Exhibit 11

Adjusted Trial Balance for Online Solutions

Online Solutions
Adjusted Trial Balance
December 31, 2007

	Debit Balances	Credit Balances
Cash	2,065	
Accounts Receivable	2,720	
Supplies	760	
Prepaid Insurance	2,300	
Office Equipment	1,800	
Accumulated Depreciation		50
Land	20,000	
Accounts Payable		900
Wages Payable		250
Unearned Rent		240
Capital Stock		25,000
Dividends	4,000	
Fees Earned		16,840
Rent Revenue		120
Wages Expense	4,525	
Supplies Expense	2,040	
Rent Expense	1,600	
Utilities Expense	985	
Insurance Expense	100	
Depreciation Expense	50	
Miscellaneous Expense	455	
	43,400	43,400

Exhibit 12

Financial Statements for Online Solutions

Online Solutions
Income Statement
For the Two Months Ended December 31, 2007

Fees earned		$16,840
Operating expenses:		
Wages expense	$4,525	
Supplies expense	2,040	
Rent expense	1,600	
Utilities expense	985	
Insurance expense	100	
Depreciation expense	50	
Miscellaneous expense	455	
Total operating expenses		9,755
Operating income		$ 7,085
Other income		120
Net income		$ 7,205

Online Solutions
Retained Earnings Statement
For the Two Months Ended December 31, 2007

Net income for November and December	$7,205
Less dividends	4,000
Retained earnings, December 31, 2007	$3,205

Exhibit 12
Concluded

Online Solutions
Balance Sheet
December 31, 2007

Assets			
Current assets:			
Cash		$ 2,065	
Accounts receivable		2,720	
Supplies		760	
Prepaid insurance		2,300	
Total current assets			$ 7,845
Property, plant, and equipment:			
Office equipment	$1,800		
Less accumulated depreciation	50	$ 1,750	
Land		20,000	
Total fixed assets			21,750
Total assets			$29,595
Liabilities			
Current liabilities:			
Accounts payable		$ 900	
Wages payable		250	
Unearned rent		240	
Total liabilities			$ 1,390
Stockholders' Equity			
Capital stock		$25,000	
Retained earnings		3,205	
Total stockholders' equity			28,205
Total liabilities and stockholders' equity			$29,595

Online Solutions
Statement of Cash Flows
For the Two Months Ended December 31, 2007

Cash flows from operating activities:		
Cash received from customers	$ 14,120	
Cash received from renting land	360	$14,480
Deduct cash payments for expenses		11,615
Net cash flows from operating activities		$ 2,865
Cash flows used for investing activities:		
Purchase of land	$(20,000)	
Purchase of office equipment	(1,800)	
Net cash flows used in investing activities		(21,800)
Cash flows from financing activities:		
Issuance of capital stock	$ 25,000	
Payment of dividends	(4,000)	
Net cash flows from financing activities		21,000
Net increase in cash		$ 2,065
November 1, 2007, cash balance		0
December 31, 2007, cash balance		$ 2,065

Exhibit 13 shows the integration of Online Solutions' financial statements. The reconciliation of net income and net cash flows from operations is shown in the appendix at the end of this chapter.

Exhibit 13

Integrated Financial Statements for Online Solutions

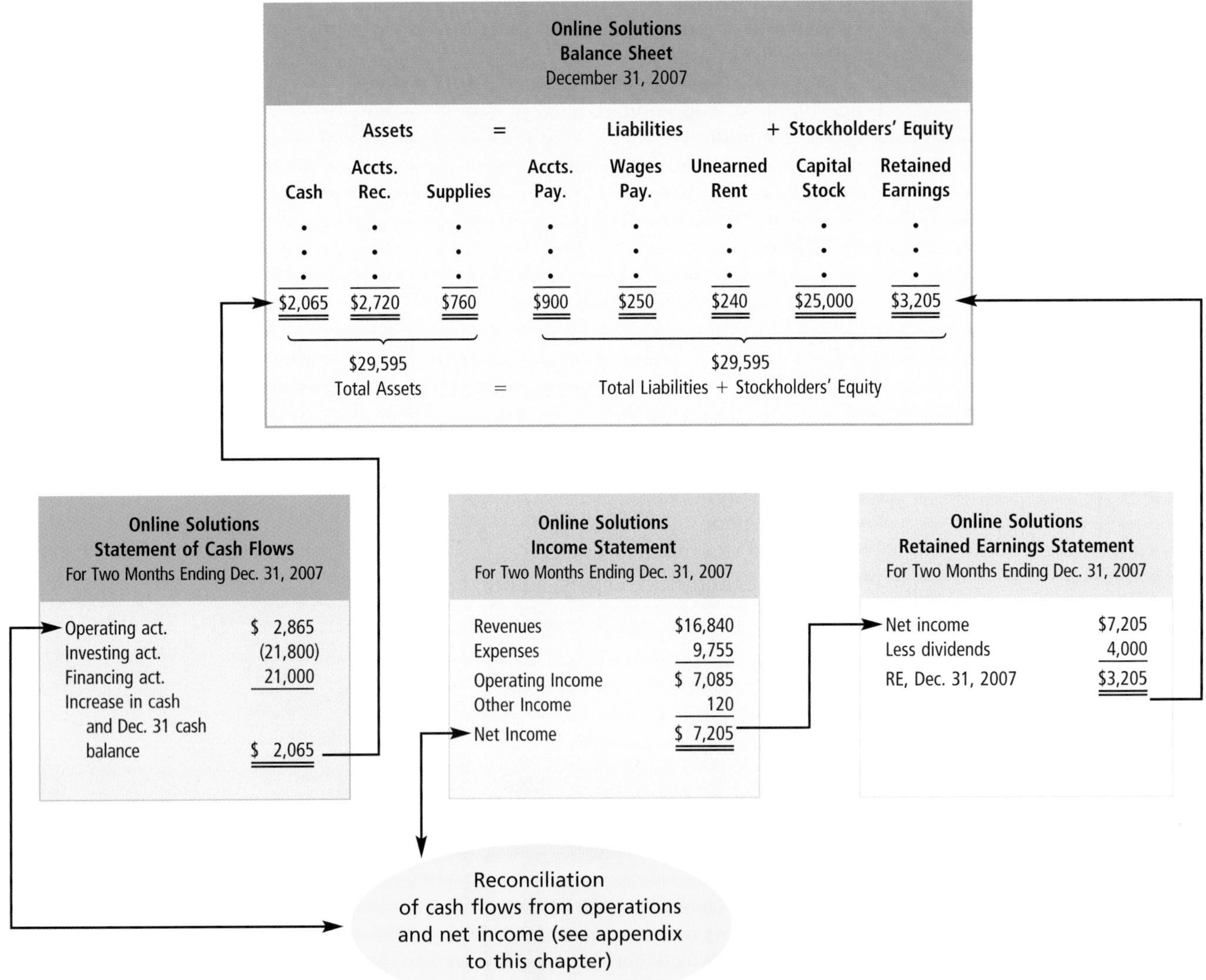

Fiscal Year

In the Online Solutions' illustration, operations began on November 1 and the accounting period was for two months, November and December. Janet Moore, the sole stockholder, decided to adopt a calendar-year accounting period. In future years, the financial statements for Online Solutions will be prepared for 12 months, ending on December 31 each year.

The annual accounting period adopted by a business is known as its **fiscal year**. Fiscal years begin with the first day of the month selected and end on the last day of the following twelfth month. The period most commonly used is the calendar year. Other periods are not unusual, especially for businesses organized as corporations. For example, a corporation may adopt a fiscal year that ends when business activities have reached the lowest point in its annual operating cycle. Such a fiscal year is called the **natural business year**. At the low point in its operating cycle, a business has more time to analyze the results of operations and to prepare financial statements. For example, Wal-Mart, Dell Inc. and The Gap Inc. have natural business years (fiscal periods) that end at the end of January after the busy holiday season.

Closing Entries

After the adjusting entries have been posted to Online Solutions' ledger, shown in Exhibit 15, the ledger is in agreement with the data reported on the financial statements. The balances of the accounts reported on the balance sheet are carried forward from period to period. Because the balances are maintained between periods, these accounts are called **permanent accounts**. In order for the net income for each period to be determined, the balances reported on the income statement are not carried forward from period to period. Likewise, the balance of the dividends account, which is reported in the retained earnings statement, is not carried forward. Because these accounts report amounts for only one period, they are called **temporary accounts**.

To report amounts for only one period, temporary accounts should have zero balances at the beginning of a period. How are these balances converted to zero? The balances of revenue, expense, and dividends accounts are transferred to retained earnings. The entries that transfer these balances to retained earnings are called **closing entries**. The transfer process is called the **closing process**. This closing process is diagrammed below.

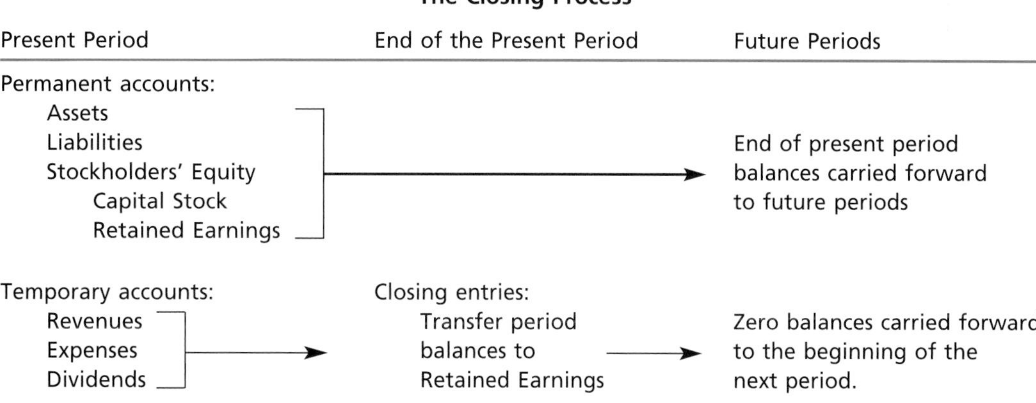

In a double-entry accounting system, a closing entry is normally prepared for each of the three categories of accounts that are closed. That is, three separate closing entries are prepared for revenues, expenses, and dividends. For Online Solutions, these three closing entries are shown in Exhibit 14.

After the closing entries have been posted to the ledger, as shown in Exhibit 15, the balance of the retained earnings account will agree with the amount reported on the retained earnings statement and the balance sheet. In addition, the revenue, expense, and dividends accounts will have zero balances.

Exhibit 14

Closing Entries for Online Solutions

Date	Account	Debit	Credit
Dec. 31	Fees Earned	16,840	
	Rent Revenue	120	
	Retained Earnings		16,960
31	Retained Earnings	9,755	
	Wages Expense		4,525
	Rent Expense		1,600
	Depreciation Expense		50
	Utilities Expense		985
	Supplies Expense		2,040
	Insurance Expense		100
	Miscellaneous Expense		455
31	Retained Earnings	4,000	
	Dividends		4,000

Exhibit 15

Ledger for Online Solutions—December

CASH

Date	Item	Debit	Date	Item	Credit
Dec. 1	Balance	5,900	Dec. 1		2,400
1		360	1		800
16		3,100	6		180
21		650	11		400
31		2,870	13		950
			20		1,800
			23		550
			27		1,200
			31		310
			31		225
			31		2,000
Dec. 31	Balance	2,065			

ACCOUNTS RECEIVABLE

Date	Item	Debit	Date	Item	Credit
Dec. 16		1,750	Dec. 21		650
31		1,120			
Dec. 31	Balance	2,220			
31	Adjusting	500			
Dec. 31	Adj. Bal.	2,720			

SUPPLIES

Date	Item	Debit	Date	Item	Credit
Dec. 1	Balance	1,350	Dec. 31	Adjusting	2,040
23		1,450			
31	Balance	2,800			
Dec. 31	Adj. Bal.	760			

PREPAID INSURANCE

Date	Item	Debit	Date	Item	Credit
Dec. 1		2,400	Dec. 31	Adjusting	100
Dec. 31	Adj. Bal.	2,300			

OFFICE EQUIPMENT

Date	Item	Debit	Date	Item	Credit
Dec. 4		1,800			

ACCUMULATED DEPRECIATION

Date	Item	Debit	Date	Item	Credit
			Dec. 31	Adjusting	50

LAND

Date	Item	Debit	Date	Item	Credit
Dec. 1	Balance	20,000			

ACCOUNTS PAYABLE

Date	Item	Debit	Date	Item	Credit
Dec. 11		400	Dec. 1	Balance	400
20		1,800	4		1,800
			23		900
			Dec. 31	Balance	900

WAGES PAYABLE

Date	Item	Debit	Date	Item	Credit
			Dec. 31	Adjusting	250

UNEARNED RENT

Date	Item	Debit	Date	Item	Credit
Dec. 31	Adjusting	120	Dec. 1		360
			Dec. 31	Adj. Bal.	240

CAPITAL STOCK

Date	Item	Debit	Date	Item	Credit
			Dec. 1	Balance	25,000

Exhibit 15
Concluded

RETAINED EARNINGS

Date	Item	Debit	Date	Item	Credit
Dec. 31	Closing	9,755	Dec. 31	Closing	16,960
31	Closing	4,000			
			Dec. 31	Balance	3,205

DIVIDENDS

Date	Item	Debit	Date	Item	Credit
Dec. 1	Balance	2,000	Dec. 31	Closing	4,000
31		2,000			
Dec. 31	Balance	4,000			
31	Balance	0			

FEES EARNED

Date	Item	Debit	Date	Item	Credit
Dec. 31	Closing	16,840	Dec. 1	Balance	7,500
			16		3,100
			16		1,750
			31		2,870
			31		1,120
			Dec. 31	Balance	16,340
			31	Adjusting	500
			Dec. 31	Adj. Bal.	16,840
			Dec. 31	Balance	0

RENT REVENUE

Date	Item	Debit	Date	Item	Credit
Dec. 31	Closing	120	Dec. 31	Adjusting	120
			Dec. 31	Balance	0

WAGES EXPENSE

Date	Item	Debit	Date	Item	Credit
Dec. 1	Balance	2,125	Dec. 31	Closing	4,525
13		950			
27		1,200			
Dec. 31	Balance	4,275			
31	Adjusting	250			
Dec. 31	Adj. Bal.	4,525			
31	Balance	0			

SUPPLIES EXPENSE

Date	Item	Debit	Date	Item	Credit
Dec. 1	Adjusting	2,040	Dec. 31	Closing	2,040
31	Adj. Bal.	2,040			
Dec. 31	Balance	0			

RENT EXPENSE

Date	Item	Debit	Date	Item	Credit
Dec. 1	Balance	800	Dec. 31	Closing	1,600
1		800			
Dec. 31	Balance	1,600			
Dec. 31	Balance	0			

UTILITIES EXPENSE

Date	Item	Debit	Date	Item	Credit
Dec. 1	Balance	450	Dec. 31	Closing	985
31		310			
31		225			
Dec. 31	Balance	985			
Dec. 31	Balance	0			

INSURANCE EXPENSE

Date	Item	Debit	Date	Item	Credit
Dec. 31	Adjusting	100	Dec. 31	Closing	100
Dec. 31	Balance	0			

DEPRECIATION EXPENSE

Date	Item	Debit	Date	Item	Credit
Dec. 31	Adjusting	50	Dec. 31	Closing	50
Dec. 31	Balance	0			

MISCELLANEOUS EXPENSE

Date	Item	Debit	Date	Item	Credit
Dec. 1	Balance	275	Dec. 31	Closing	455
6		180			
Dec. 31	Balance	455			
Dec. 31	Balance	0			

Post-Closing Trial Balance

A **post-closing trial balance** is normally prepared after the closing entries have been posted to the ledger. This is to make sure that no errors have been made in the posting process and that the ledger is in balance at the beginning of the next period. The accounts and amounts should agree exactly with the accounts and amounts listed on the balance sheet at the end of the period. The post-closing trial balance for Online Solutions is shown in Exhibit 16.

Exhibit 16

Post-Closing Trial Balance for Online Solutions

Online Solutions Post-Closing Trial Balance December 31, 2007		
	Debit Balances	**Credit Balances**
Cash	2,065	
Accounts Receivable	2,720	
Supplies	760	
Prepaid Insurance	2,300	
Office Equipment	1,800	
Accumulated Depreciation		50
Land	20,000	
Accounts Payable		900
Wages Payable		250
Unearned Rent		240
Capital Stock		25,000
Retained Earnings		3,205
Dividends	0	
Fees Earned		0
Rent Revenue		0
Wages Expense	0	
Supplies Expense	0	
Rent Expense	0	
Utilities Expense	0	
Insurance Expense	0	
Depreciation Expense	0	
Miscellaneous Expense	0	
	29,645	29,645

Describe the accounting cycle for the double-entry accounting system.

THE ACCOUNTING CYCLE

In Chapter 3, we briefly described the accounting cycle in a general sense as the process that begins with analyzing transactions, adjusts the accounting records, prepares financial statements, and ends with preparing the accounting records for the next period. In this section, we expand our discussion to include features of the double-entry accounting system. These features include the journal, ledger, unadjusted trial balance, adjusted trial balance, closing entries, and post-closing trial balance.

The basic steps of the accounting cycle for the double-entry accounting system are listed below. The accounting cycle begins with transactions that are supported by source documents and ends with the post-closing trial balance. We completed each of these steps for Online Solutions in this chapter.

1. Transactions are analyzed from source documents and are recorded in the journal using the rules of debit and credit.
2. Transactions recorded in the journal are posted to the ledger accounts.
3. An unadjusted trial balance is prepared.
4. Adjustment data are assembled and analyzed.
5. Adjusting entries are prepared and recorded in the journal.
6. Adjusting entries recorded in the journal are posted to the ledger accounts.

7. An adjusted trial balance is prepared.
8. The financial statements are prepared.
9. Closing entries are prepared and recorded in the journal.
10. Closing entries recorded in the journal are posted to the ledger accounts.
11. A post-closing trial balance is prepared.

EBITDA

Describe and illustrate the computation and use of earnings before interest, taxes, depreciation, and amortization (EBITDA).

In this chapter, we have illustrated the basic elements of transaction processing and financial reporting accounting systems. The financial statements, which are used by the company's stakeholders, are the major product of these systems. However, stakeholders often adjust financial statement data for use in their analyses. Such adjustments are called pro forma or "as if" computations. Because these pro forma computations are adjustments to financial statements, they are not in conformity with generally accepted accounting principles (GAAP). However, a company may report non-GAAP pro forma computations if it explains to investors why the additional disclosure would be useful to users. One common type of pro forma computation that is used and reported is **earnings before interest, taxes, depreciation, and amortization (EBITDA)**.

© TIM SLOAN/AFP/GETTY IMAGES

Bernard J. Ebbers, former WorldCom chief executive, appeared before the U.S. House Committee on Financial Services on July 8, 2002. His trial resulted in a conviction and a 25-year prison sentence for fraud, conspiracy, and false filings with securities regulators.

Many companies, such as AT&T, Time Warner, and Goodyear Tire and Rubber, have debt terms that require them to maintain some multiple of EBITDA. Thus, financial analysts often use EBITDA as a rough estimate of operating cash flows available to pay interest and other fixed charges.

Because the computation of EBITDA is not required by generally accepted accounting principles, its computation is not subject to standardized rules, and thus may vary from company to company. For example, Safeway Stores stated the following regarding its computation of EBITDA in its disclosures to the Securities and Exchange Commission: "Other companies may define Adjusted EBITDA differently and, as a result, such measures may not be comparable to Safeway's Adjusted EBITDA."

INTEGRITY, OBJECTIVITY, AND ETHICS IN BUSINESS

WorldCom, Inc.

In their public earnings announcements, companies have recently focused on reporting EBITDA to outside investors. This was done under the belief that EBITDA would be a more realistic measure of earning power in some industries with large depreciation expenses, such as telecommunications. However, alleged accounting fraud at **WorldCom, Inc.**, has changed perceptions. WorldCom is alleged to have caused nearly $4 billion in costs to disappear when reporting EBITDA. As stated recently by Chuck Hill, Director of Research at data provider Thomson Financial/First Call, "I think the days of having EBITDA being the focus of an earnings release are probably numbered."

Source: "Days May Be Numbered for EBITDA Numbers," *The Wall Street Journal*, July 5, 2002.

The computations of EBITDA (in millions) for Continental Airlines and Southwest Airlines for the year ended December 31, 2004, are shown below (in millions).

	Southwest Airlines	Continental Airlines
Operating income (loss) before interest and taxes	$554	$(229)
Depreciation and amortization	431	414
EBITDA	$985	$ 185

The preceding computations reveal that Southwest has a much higher EBITDA than Continental Airlines, even though Southwest is a smaller airline with $6.5 billion in revenue compared to Continental's $9.7 billion in revenue. Southwest is generating more cash from its operations to pay interest and other fixed charges than is Continental.

© RYAN MCVAY/PHOTODISC/GETTY IMAGES

As we pointed out earlier, EBITDA is only used as a rough estimate of cash flow. You should be careful not to confuse EBITDA with net cash flows from operating activities. For example, Southwest and Continental reported positive net cash flows from operating activities for 2004 of $1,157 million and $236 million, respectively. In contrast, the EBITDA for Southwest and Continental was $985 million and $185 million, respectively. These differences reflect that net cash flows from operating activities is computed using generally accepted accounting principles. These principles require the consideration of factors other than just interest, taxes, depreciation, and amortization in determining cash flows from operations. For example, increases or decreases in accounts receivable and inventories affect the amount of cash flows from operations. For this reason, EBITDA should be interpreted only as a rough estimate of the cash available to pay interest and other fixed charges, rather than as an estimate of cash flows from operations.

APPENDIX

The Statement of Cash Flows

The income statement, retained earnings statement, balance sheet, and statement of cash flows for Online Solutions are shown in Exhibit 12. The income statement, retained earnings statement, and balance sheet can be prepared directly from the adjusted trial balance shown in Exhibit 11. Preparing the statement of cash flows, however, is more complex.

The statement of cash flows for Online Solutions can be prepared by analyzing the cash account shown in Exhibits 6 and 15. Each of the transactions posted to the cash account should be classified as affecting cash flows from operating, investing, or financing activities. This analysis of the cash transactions in chronological order is shown on the following page.

Date	Transaction Description	Cash Flow Activity Increase (Decrease) Operating Activity	Investing Activity	Financing Activity
Nov. 1	Issued capital stock			$25,000
5	Purchased land		$(20,000)	
18	Earned cash fees	$7,500		
30	Paid $3,650 for:			
	Wages	(2,125)		
	Rent	(800)		
	Utilities	(450)		
	Miscellaneous	(275)		
30	Paid creditors on account for supplies	(950)		
30	Paid dividends			(2,000)
Dec. 1	Paid insurance premiums	(2,400)		
1	Paid rent	(800)		
1	Received cash for renting land	360		
6	Paid for adverstisement (misc. expense)	(180)		
11	Paid creditors on account for supplies	(400)		
13	Paid employee wages	(950)		
16	Earned cash fees	3,100		
20	Paid creditors on account for office equipment		(1,800)	
21	Received cash from customers on account for fees earned	650		
23	Paid for supplies	(550)		
27	Paid employee wages	(1,200)		
31	Paid telephone bill (utilities expense)	(310)		
31	Paid electric bill (utilities expense)	(225)		
31	Earned cash fees	2,870		
31	Paid dividends			(2,000)
Totals		$2,865	$(21,800)	$21,000

The statement of cash flows can be prepared from the preceding analysis by grouping the cash receipts and payments for each of the cash flow activities. The resulting statement for Online Solutions is shown in Exhibit 17.

You should note that the net cash flows from operating activities of $2,865 is not the same as the net income of $7,205. As discussed in Chapter 3, this difference is due to the effect of accruals and deferrals on determining net income under the accrual basis of accounting. In the appendix to Chapter 3, we showed how the net cash flows from operations can be reconciled with net income. This reconciliation is illustrated in Exhibit 18 for Online Solutions.

Exhibit 17

Statement of Cash Flows for Online Solutions

Online Solutions
Statement of Cash Flows
For the Two Months Ended December 31, 2007

Cash flows from operating activities:		
Cash received from customers	$ 14,120 (a)	
Cash received from renting land	360	$14,480
Deduct cash payments for expenses		11,615 (b)
Net cash flows from operating activities		$ 2,865
Cash flows used for investing activities:		
Purchase of land	$(20,000)	
Purchase of office equipment	(1,800)	
Net cash flows used in investing activities		(21,800)
Cash flows from financing activities:		
Issuance of capital stock	$ 25,000	
Payment of dividends	(4,000)	
Net cash flows from financing activities		21,000
Net increase in cash		$ 2,065
November 1, 2007, cash balance		0
December 31, 2007, cash balance		$ 2,065

Computational Notes:

(a) $14,120 = $7,500 + $3,100 + $650 + $2,870

(b) Wages ($2,125 + $950 + $1,200)	$ 4,275
Insurance	2,400
Supplies ($950 + $400 + $550)	1,900
Rent ($800 + $800)	1,600
Utilities ($450 + $310 + $225)	985
Miscellaneous ($275 + $180)	455
Total cash payments for expenses	$11,615

Exhibit 18

Reconciliation of Net Income with Net Cash Flows from Operating Activities

Online Solutions
Reconciliation of Net Income
with Net Cash Flows from Operating Activities
For the Two Months Ended December 31, 2007

Net income		$7,205
Add:		
Depreciation expense	$ 50	
Increase in accounts payable	900	
Increase in wages payable	250	
Increase in unearned rent	240	1,440
Deduct:		
Increase in accounts receivable	$(2,720)	
Increase in supplies	(760)	
Increase in prepaid insurance	(2,300)	(5,780)
Net cash flows from operating activities		$2,865

SUMMARY OF LEARNING GOALS

1 Describe the nature of business information systems. A business information system collects and processes data into information that is distributed to stakeholders/users. Business information systems share common elements that include data sources, data collection, data processing, database management, information generation, and stakeholders/users.

2 Describe the nature of accounting information systems. An accounting information system is a type of business information system that processes financial and operational data into reports useful to internal and external stakeholders. Accounting information systems consist of the (1) management reporting system, (2) the transaction processing system, and (3) the financial reporting system.

3 Describe and illustrate the basic elements of transaction processing systems. The basic elements of transaction processing systems include accounts and rules for recording transactions in accounts, journals, and ledgers. In addition, the processing system should include controls to prevent and detect errors in the recording and summarization process. An account is used to record increases and decreases in financial statement elements. The rules of debit and credit are used to determine how increases and decreases are recorded in the various accounts. A journal is a chronological record of each transaction. The ledger is the summary of all the accounts for a business. The trial balance provides the control that the total of accounts with debit balances must equal the total of accounts with credit balances.

4 Describe and illustrate the basic elements of a financial reporting system. The basic elements of a financial reporting system include adjusting entries, financial statements, and closing entries. Adjusting entries are necessary under the accrual basis of accounting to bring the accounts up to date for preparing financial statements. Closing entries transfer the balances of the revenue, expense, and dividend accounts to retained earnings.

5 Describe the accounting cycle for the double-entry accounting system. The accounting cycle of the double-entry accounting system includes the journal, ledger, unadjusted trial balance, adjusted trial balance, closing entries, and post-closing trial balance. The basic steps of the accounting cycle for the double-entry accounting system are listed on pages 172 and 173.

6 Describe and illustrate the computation and use of earnings before interest, taxes, depreciation, and amortization (EBITDA). Earnings before interest, taxes, depreciation, and amortization (EBITDA) is a type of pro forma computation used by financial analysts as a rough estimate of operating cash flows that are available to pay interest and other fixed charges.

GLOSSARY

Account The element of an accounting system that summarizes the increases and decreases in each financial statement item.

Accounting information system An information system that consists of management reporting, transaction processing, and financial reporting subsystems that processes financial and operational data into reports useful to internal and external stakeholders.

Adjusted trial balance The trial balance prepared after the adjusting entries have been posted to the ledger.

Adjusting entries The entries necessary to bring the accounts up to date before preparing financial statements.

Balance of an account The amount of the difference between the debits and the credits that have been entered into an account.

Business information system A system that collects and processes company data into information that is distributed to users.

Chart of accounts The list of accounts in the general ledger.

Closing entries The entries necessary at the end of an accounting period to transfer the balances of revenue, expense, and dividend accounts to retained earnings.

Closing process The process of transferring the balances of revenue, expense, and dividend accounts to retained earnings in preparation for recording transactions of the next period.

Credits Amounts entered on the right side of an account.

Debits Amounts entered on the left side of an account.

Double-entry accounting system A system of accounting for transactions, based on recording increases and decreases in accounts so that debits equal credits and Assets = Liabilities + Stockholders' Equity.

Earnings before interest, taxes, depreciation, and amortization (EBITDA) A type of pro forma computation used by financial analysts as a rough estimate of operating cash flows that are available to pay interest and other fixed charges.

Financial reporting system A subsystem of accounting that produces financial statements and other reports for external stakeholders.

Fiscal year The annual accounting period adopted by a business.

General ledger The group of accounts of a business.

Journal The record in which the effects of transactions are recorded in chronological order.

Journal entry The transaction record entered in the journal.

Journalizing The process of recording transactions in the journal.

Management reporting system A subsystem of accounting that provides internal information to assist managers in making decisions.

Natural business year The fiscal year that ends when a business's activities reach their lowest point in the operating cycle.

Normal balance of an account The debit or credit side of an account used to record increases.

Permanent accounts Accounts that are reported on the balance sheet and whose balances carry forward from period to period.

Post-closing trial balance The trial balance prepared after the closing entries have been posted to the ledger.

Posting The process of transferring the debits and credits from the journal entries to the accounts in the ledger.

Rules of debit and credit Standardized rules for recording increases and decreases in accounts.

Temporary accounts Revenue, expense, and dividend accounts whose balances are transferred to retained earnings at the end of the period.

Transaction processing system A subsystem of accounting that records and summarizes the effects of financial transactions on the business.

Trial balance A summary listing of the accounts and their balances in the ledger.

ILLUSTRATIVE ACCOUNTING APPLICATION PROBLEM

J. F. Outz, M.D., has been practicing as a cardiologist for three years in a professional corporation known as Hearts, P.C. During April 2007, Hearts completed the following transactions.

Apr. 1 Paid office rent for April, $800.
3 Purchased equipment on account, $1,575.
5 Received cash on account from patients, $3,150.
8 Purchased X-ray film and other supplies on account, $245.
9 One of the items of equipment purchased on April 3 was defective. It was returned with the permission of the supplier, who agreed to reduce the account for the amount charged for the item, $325.
12 Paid cash to equipment supplier on account, $1,250.
17 Paid cash for renewal of a six-month property insurance policy, $370.
20 Paid cash to laboratory on account, $200.
24 Paid cash for laboratory analysis, $545.
25 Recorded fees charged to patients on account for services performed in April, $5,145.
27 Paid cash dividends, $1,250.
28 Recorded the cash received in payment for services provided to patients during April, $1,720.
28 Paid salaries of receptionist and nurses, $1,725.
30 Paid various utility expenses, $360.
30 Paid miscellaneous expenses, $132.

Hearts' accounts and balances (all normal balances) as of April 1 are listed as follows: Cash, $4,123; Accounts Receivable, $4,725; Supplies, $290; Prepaid Insurance, $465; Equipment, $21,745; Accumulated Depreciation, $3,100; Accounts Payable, $765; Salary Payable; Capital Stock, $10,000; Retained Earnings, $17,483; Dividends; Professional Fees; Salary Expense; Rent Expense; Laboratory Expense; Insurance Expense; Utilities Expense; Supplies Expense; Depreciation Expense; Miscellaneous Expense.

Instructions

1. Enter the April 1 balances in standard T accounts. Identify each amount as "Balance." (*Hint:* Verify the equality of the debit and credit balances in the ledger before proceeding with the next instruction.)

2. Journalize each transaction in a two-column journal. Show the effects of each transaction on the financial statements using the margin notation illustrated in this chapter.
3. Post the journal entries to the T accounts, placing the date to the left of each amount to identify the transaction. Determine the account balances after all posting is complete.
4. Prepare an unadjusted trial balance as of April 30, 2007.
5. Data necessary to determine the end-of-month adjustments are as follows:
   a. Supplies on hand at April 30, $185.
   b. Professional fees accrued on April 30, $1,375.
   c. Insurance premiums expired during April, $435.
   d. Depreciation on equipment during April, $80.
   e. Salaries accrued at April 30, $300.
   Journalize and post the necessary adjusting entries for April. Identify each adjusting entry in the account as "Adjusting." Show the effects of each transaction on the financial statements using the margin notation illustrated in this chapter. For the adjusted accounts, determine an adjusted balance.
6. Prepare an adjusted trial balance as of April 30, 2007.
7. Prepare an income statement, a retained earnings statement, and a classified balance sheet.
8. Journalize and post the closing entries for April. Identify each entry in the accounts as "Closing."
9. Prepare a post-closing trial balance as of April 30, 2007.
10. (Appendix) Prepare a statement of cash flows for April. Note that the April 12 payment of $1,250 on account was for the equipment purchase. The April 20 payment of $200 on account was for laboratory expense.
11. (Appendix) Reconcile net income with net cash flows from operations for April. Note that only $45 of the increase in Accounts Payable represents operating activities. The remaining $525 increase in Accounts Payable relates to the purchase of equipment, an investing activity.

Solution to Illustrative Problem

2.

SCF	BS	IS	Date	Account	Debit	Credit
O↓	A↓SE↓	E↑	Apr. 1	Rent Expense	800	
				Cash		800
—	A↑L↑	—	3	Equipment	1,575	
				Accounts Payable		1,575
O↑	A↓↑	—	5	Cash	3,150	
				Accounts Receivable		3,150
—	A↑L↑	—	8	Supplies	245	
				Accounts Payable		245
—	A↓L↓	—	9	Accounts Payable	325	
				Equipment		325
O↓	A↓L↓	—	12	Accounts Payable	1,250	
				Cash		1,250
O↓	A↑↓	—	17	Prepaid Insurance	370	
				Cash		370
O↓	A↓L↓	—	20	Accounts Payable	200	
				Cash		200
O↓	A↓SE↓	E↑	24	Laboratory Expense	545	
				Cash		545
—	A↑SE↑	R↑	25	Accounts Receivable	5,145	
				Professional Fees		5,145
F↓	A↓SE↓	—	27	Dividends	1,250	
				Cash		1,250
O↑	A↑SE↑	R↑	28	Cash	1,720	
				Professional Fees		1,720

(continued)

SCF	BS	IS	Date	Account	Debit	Credit
O↓	A↓SE↓	E↑	Apr. 28	Salary Expense	1,725	
				Cash		1,725
O↓	A↓SE↓	E↑	30	Utilities Expense	360	
				Cash		360
O↓	A↓SE↓	E↑	30	Miscellaneous Expense	132	
				Cash		132

1. and 3.

CASH

April 1	Balance	4,123	April 1		800
5		3,150	12		1,250
28		1,720	17		370
			20		200
			24		545
			27		1,250
			28		1,725
			30		360
			30		132
April 30	Balance	2,361			

ACCOUNTS RECEIVABLE

April 1	Balance	4,725	April 5		3,150
25		5,145			
April 30	Balance	6,720			
30	Adjusting	1,375			
April 30	Adj. Bal.	8,095			

SUPPLIES

April 1	Balance	290			
8		245			
April 30	Balance	535	April 30	Adjusting	350
April 30	Adj. Bal.	185			

PREPAID INSURANCE

April 1	Balance	465			
17		370			
April 30	Balance	835	April 30	Adjusting	435
April 30	Adj. Bal.	400			

EQUIPMENT

April 1	Balance	21,745	April 9		325
3		1,575			
April 30	Balance	22,995			

ACCUMULATED DEPRECIATION

			April 30	Balance	3,100
			30	Adjusting	80
			April 30	Adj. Bal.	3,180

ACCOUNTS PAYABLE

April 9		325	April 1	Balance	765
12		1,250	3		1,575
20		200	8		245
			April 30	Balance	810

SALARY PAYABLE

			April 30	Adjusting	300

CAPITAL STOCK

			April 1	Balance	10,000

RETAINED EARNINGS

April 30	Closing	4,727	April 1	Balance	17,483
30	Closing	1,250	30	Closing	8,240
			April 30	Balance	19,746

DIVIDENDS

April 27		1,250	April 30	Closing	1,250
April 30	Balance	0			

PROFESSIONAL FEES

			April 25		5,145
			28		1,720
			30	Balance	6,865
			30	Adjusting	1,375
April 30	Closing	8,240	April 30	Adj. Bal.	8,240
			April 30	Balance	0

SALARY EXPENSE

April 28		1,725			
30	Adjusting	300			
April 30	Adj. Bal.	2,025	April 30	Closing	2,025
April 30	Balance	0			

RENT EXPENSE

April 1		800	April 30	Closing	800
April 30	Balance	0			

LABORATORY EXPENSE

April 24		545	April 30	Closing	545
April 30	Balance	0			

INSURANCE EXPENSE

April 30	Adjusting	435	April 30	Closing	435
April 30	Balance	0			

UTILITIES EXPENSE

April 30		360	April 30	Closing	360
April 30	Balance	0			

SUPPLIES EXPENSE

April 30	Adjusting	350	April 30	Closing	350
April 30	Balance	0			

DEPRECIATION EXPENSE

April 30	Adjusting	80	April 30	Closing	80
April 30	Balance	0			

MISCELLANEOUS EXPENSE

April 30		132	April 30	Closing	132
April 30	Balance	0			

4.

Hearts, P.C.
Unadjusted Trial Balance
April 30, 2007

	Debit Balances	Credit Balances
Cash	2,361	
Accounts Receivable	6,720	
Supplies	535	
Prepaid Insurance	835	
Equipment	22,995	
Accumulated Depreciation		3,100
Accounts Payable		810
Capital Stock		10,000
Retained Earnings		17,483
Dividends	1,250	
Professional Fees		6,865
Salary Expense	1,725	
Rent Expense	800	
Laboratory Expense	545	
Utilities Expense	360	
Miscellaneous Expense	132	
	38,258	38,258

5.

SCF	BS	IS				
—	A↓SE↓	E↑	a.	Supplies Expense	350	
				Supplies		350
—	A↑SE↑	R↑	b.	Accounts Receivable	1,375	
				Professional Fees		1,375
—	A↓SE↓	E↑	c.	Insurance Expense	435	
				Prepaid Insurance		435

(continued)

SCF	BS	IS				
—	A↓SE↓	E↑	d.	Depreciation Expense	80	
				Accumulated Depreciation		80
—	L↑SE↓	E↑	e.	Salary Expense	300	
				Salary Payable		300

6.

Hearts, P.C.
Adjusted Trial Balance
April 30, 2007

	Debit Balances	Credit Balances
Cash	2,361	
Accounts Receivable	8,095	
Supplies	185	
Prepaid Insurance	400	
Equipment	22,995	
Accumulated Depreciation		3,180
Accounts Payable		810
Salary Payable		300
Capital Stock		10,000
Retained Earnings		17,483
Dividends	1,250	
Professional Fees		8,240
Salary Expense	2,025	
Rent Expense	800	
Laboratory Expense	545	
Insurance Expense	435	
Utilities Expense	360	
Supplies Expense	350	
Depreciation Expense	80	
Miscellaneous Expense	132	
	40,013	40,013

7.

Hearts, P.C.
Income Statement
For the Month Ended April 30, 2007

Professional fees		$8,240
Operating expenses:		
Salary expense	$2,025	
Rent expense	800	
Laboratory expense	545	
Insurance expense	435	
Utilities expense	360	
Supplies expense	350	
Depreciation expense	80	
Miscellaneous expense	132	
Total operating expenses		4,727
Net income		$3,513

Hearts, P.C.
Retained Earnings Statement
For the Month Ended April 30, 2007

Retained earnings, April 1, 2007		$17,483
Net income for April	$3,513	
Less dividends	1,250	
Increase in retained earnings		2,263
Retained earnings, April 30, 2007		$19,746

Hearts, P.C.
Balance Sheet
April 30, 2007

Assets		
Current assets:		
Cash	$ 2,361	
Accounts receivable	8,095	
Supplies	185	
Prepaid insurance	400	
Total current assets		$11,041
Property, plant, and equipment:		
Equipment	$22,995	
Less accumulated depreciation	3,180	
Total property, plant, and equipment		19,815
Total assets		$30,856
Liabilities		
Current liabilities:		
Accounts payable	$ 810	
Salary payable	300	
Total liabilities		$ 1,110
Stockholders' Equity		
Capital stock	$10,000	
Retained earnings	19,746	
Total stockholders' equity		29,746
Total liabilities and stockholders' equity		$30,856

8.

Professional Fees	8,240	
Retained Earnings		8,240
Retained Earnings	4,727	
Salary Expense		2,025
Rent Expense		800
Laboratory Expense		545
Insurance Expense		435
Utilities Expense		360
Supplies Expense		350
Depreciation Expense		80
Miscellaneous Expense		132
Retained Earnings	1,250	
Dividends		1,250

9.

Hearts, P.C.
Post–Closing Trial Balance
April 30, 2007

	Debit Balances	Credit Balances
Cash	2,361	
Accounts Receivable	8,095	
Supplies	185	
Prepaid Insurance	400	
Equipment	22,995	
Accumulated Depreciation		3,180
Accounts Payable		810
Salary Payable		300
Capital Stock		10,000
Retained Earnings		19,746
	34,036	34,036

10.

Hearts, P.C.
Statement of Cash Flows
For the Month Ended April 30, 2007

Cash flows from operating activities:	
Cash received from customers	$ 4,870 (a)
Deduct cash payments for operating expenses	4,132 (b)
Net cash flows from operating activities	$ 738
Net cash flows used for investing activities:	
Purchase of equipment	(1,250)
Net cash flows used for financing activities:	
Payment of dividends	(1,250)
Net decrease in cash	$(1,762)
April 1, 2007, cash balance	4,123
April 30, 2007, cash balance	$ 2,361

Computational Notes:
(a) $3,150 + $1,720

(b) Salary	$1,725
Rent	800
Laboratory ($545 + $200)	745
Utilities	360
Insurance	370
Miscellaneous	132
Total cash payments for expenses	$4,132

11.

Net income		$3,513
Add:		
Depreciation	$ 80	
Decrease in supplies	105	
Decrease in prepaid insurance	65	
Increase in accounts payable (from operations)	45	
Increase in salary payable	300	595
Deduct:		
Increase in accounts receivable		3,370
Net cash flows from operating activities		$ 738

SELF-STUDY QUESTIONS

Answers at end of chapter

1. A debit may signify a(n):
   A. increase in an asset account.
   B. decrease in an asset account.
   C. increase in a liability account.
   D. increase in the capital stock account.
2. The type of account with a normal credit balance is:
   A. an asset.
   B. dividends.
   C. a revenue.
   D. an expense.
3. A debit balance in which of the following accounts would indicate a likely error?
   A. Accounts Receivable
   B. Cash
   C. Fees Earned
   D. Miscellaneous Expense
4. Which of the following entries closes the dividends account at the end of the period?
   A. Debit the dividends account, credit the capital stock account.
   B. Debit the retained earnings account, credit the dividends account.
   C. Debit the capital stock account, credit the dividends account.
   D. Debit the dividends account, credit the retained earnings account.
5. Which of the following accounts would not be closed to the retained earnings account at the end of a period?
   A. Fees Earned
   B. Wages Expense
   C. Rent Expense
   D. Accumulated Depreciation

DISCUSSION QUESTIONS

1. When you registered for this class and paid your tuition, you interacted with the college's information systems. (a) Are the registration and tuition payment systems business information systems? (b) Which system is part of the college's accounting system?
2. What is the difference between an account and a ledger?
3. Do the terms *debit* and *credit* signify increase or decrease, or can they signify either? Explain.
4. What is the effect (increase or decrease) of a debit to an expense account (a) in terms of stockholders' equity and (b) in terms of expense?
5. What is the effect (increase or decrease) of a credit to a revenue account (a) in terms of stockholders' equity and (b) in terms of revenue?
6. Regan Company adheres to a policy of depositing all cash receipts in a bank account and making all payments by check. The cash account as of August 31 has a credit balance of $1,200, and there is no undeposited cash on hand. (a) Assuming that no errors occurred during journalizing or posting, what caused this unusual balance? (b) Is the $1,200 credit balance in the cash account an asset, a liability, stockholders' equity, a revenue, or an expense?
7. Tull Company performed services in June for a specific customer for a fee of $2,230. Payment was received the following July. (a) Was the revenue earned in June or July? (b) What accounts should be debited and credited in (1) June and (2) July?

8. What proof is provided by a trial balance?
9. If the two totals of a trial balance are equal, does it mean that there are no errors in the accounting records? Explain.
10. Assume that when a purchase of supplies of $1,030 for cash was recorded, both the debit and the credit were journalized and posted as $1,300. (a) Would this error cause the trial balance to be out of balance? (b) Would the trial balance be out of balance if the $1,030 entry had been journalized correctly, but the credit to Cash had been posted as $1,300?
11. Banks rely heavily upon customers' deposits as a source of funds. Demand deposits normally pay interest to the customer, who is entitled to withdraw at any time without prior notice to the bank. Checking and NOW (negotiable order of withdrawal) accounts are the most common form of demand deposits for banks. Assume that LaDuke Storage has a checking account at City Savings Bank. What type of account (asset, liability, stockholders' equity, revenue, expense, dividends) does the account balance of $15,500 represent from the viewpoint of (a) LaDuke Storage and (b) City Savings Bank?
12. Why are closing entries required at the end of an accounting period?
13. What is the difference between adjusting entries and closing entries?
14. What types of accounts are closed by transferring their balances (a) as a debit to Retained Earnings, (b) as a credit to Retained Earnings?
15. What is the purpose of the post-closing trial balance?
16. The fiscal years for several well-known companies were as follows:

Company	Fiscal Year Ending
Wal-Mart	January 31
JCPenney	January 26
Best Buy	February 28
The Gap Inc.	January 31
Federated Department Stores	February 3
The Limited, Inc.	January 31

What general characteristic shared by these companies explains why they do not have fiscal years ending December 31?

EXERCISES

Exercise 4-1

Chart of accounts

Goal 3

The following accounts appeared in recent financial statements of Continental Airlines:

Accounts Payable
Aircraft Fuel Expense
Air Traffic Liability
Cargo and Mail Revenue
Commissions
Flight Equipment
Landing Fees
Passenger Revenue
Purchase Deposits for Flight Equipment
Spare Parts and Supplies

Identify each account as either a balance sheet account or an income statement account. For each balance sheet account, identify it as an asset, a liability, or stockholders' equity. For each income statement account, identify it as a revenue or an expense.

Exercise 4-2

Normal account balances

Goal 3

For each account listed in Exercise 4-1, indicate whether its normal balance is a debit or a credit.

Exercise 4-3

Chart of accounts

Goal 3

The following accounts have been adapted from recent financial statements of Time Warner:

Accounts Receivable
Accumulated Depreciation
Advertising Revenues
Cable Television Equipment
Compact Discs and DVD Merchandise
Interest Expense
Music Catalogs and Copyrights
Notes Payable (due December 6, 2019)
Property, Plant, and Equipment

Retained Earnings
Royalties and Programming Costs Payable
Selling, General, and Administrative Expense
Short-Term Investments
Unearned Subscriptions

Identify each account as either a balance sheet account or an income statement account. For each balance sheet account, identify it as an asset, a liability, or stockholders' equity. For each income statement account, identify it as a revenue or an expense.

Exercise 4-4

Normal account balances

Goal 3

For each account listed in Exercise 4-3, indicate whether its normal balance is a debit or a credit.

Exercise 4-5

Normal entries for accounts

Goal 3

During the month, Gilbert Labs Co. has a substantial number of transactions affecting each of the following accounts. State for each account whether it is likely to have (a) debit entries only, (b) credit entries only, or (c) both debit and credit entries.

1. Accounts Payable
2. Accounts Receivable
3. Cash
4. Fees Earned
5. Dividends
6. Miscellaneous Expense
7. Supplies Expense

Exercise 4-6

Normal balances of accounts

Goal 3

Identify each of the following accounts of Haifa Services Co. as asset, liability, stockholders' equity, revenue, or expense, and state in each case whether the normal balance is a debit or a credit.

a. Accounts Payable
b. Accounts Receivable
c. Cash
d. Capital Stock
e. Dividends
f. Equipment
g. Fees Earned
h. Rent Expense
i. Salary Expense
j. Supplies

Exercise 4-7

Rules of debit and credit

Goal 3

The following table summarizes the rules of debit and credit. For each of the items (a) through (n), indicate whether the proper answer is a debit or a credit.

	Increase	Decrease	Normal Balance
Balance sheet accounts:			
Asset	Debit	Credit	(a)
Liability	(b)	(c)	(d)
Stockholders' Equity:			
Capital Stock	(e)	(f)	Credit
Retained Earnings	Credit	(g)	(h)
Dividends	(i)	Credit	(j)
Income statement accounts:			
Revenue	(k)	Debit	(l)
Expense	(m)	Credit	(n)

Exercise 4-8

Identifying transactions

Goals 3, 4

Malta Co. is a travel agency. The nine transactions recorded by Malta during February 2006, its first month of operations, are indicated in the following T accounts:

CASH

Debit	Credit
(1) 40,000	(2) 1,800
(7) 9,500	(3) 9,000
	(4) 3,050
	(6) 7,500
	(8) 5,000

EQUIPMENT

Debit	Credit
(3) 24,000	

DIVIDENDS

Debit	Credit
(8) 5,000	

ACCOUNTS RECEIVABLE

Debit	Credit
(5) 12,000	(7) 9,500

ACCOUNTS PAYABLE

Debit	Credit
(6) 7,500	(3) 15,000

SERVICE REVENUE

Debit	Credit
	(5) 12,000

SUPPLIES

Debit	Credit
(2) 1,800	(9) 1,050

CAPITAL STOCK

Debit	Credit
	(1) 40,000

OPERATING EXPENSES

Debit	Credit
(4) 3,050	
(9) 1,050	

Indicate for each debit and each credit: (a) whether an asset, liability, stockholders' equity, dividends, revenue, or expense account was affected and (b) whether the account was increased (+) or decreased (–). Present your answers in the following form, with transaction (1) given as an example:

	Account Debited		Account Credited	
Transaction	Type	Effect	Type	Effect
(1)	asset	+	stockholders' equity	+

Exercise 4-9

Journal entries

Goals 3, 4

Based upon the T accounts in Exercise 4–8, prepare the nine journal entries from which the postings were made.

Exercise 4-10

Trial balance

Goals 3, 4

Based upon the data presented in Exercise 4–8, prepare a trial balance, listing the accounts in their proper order.

Exercise 4-11

Classification of accounts, normal balances

Goals 3, 4

The following accounts (in millions) were adapted from the financial statements of Apple Computer, Inc., for the year ending September 25, 2004:

Accounts Payable	$2,680	Other Assets	$ 651
Accounts Receivable	1,005	Other Income (net)	57
Capital Stock	2,406	Other Liabilities	294
Cash	2,969	Other Operating Expenses	23
Cost of Sales	6,020	Property, Plant, and Equipment	707
Goodwill and Other Intangible Assets	122	Research and Development Expenses	489
Income Tax Expense	107	Retained Earnings, September 27, 2003	2,394
Inventories	101	Sales	8,279
Investments	2,495	Selling, General, and Administrative Expenses	1,421

(a) Identify each account as either a balance sheet account or an income statement account. (b) For each balance sheet account, identify it as an asset, a liability, or stockholders' equity. For each income statement account, identify it as a revenue or an expense. (c) Indicate the normal balance of the account.

Exercise 4-12

Trial balance

Goals 3, 4

Total debit column, $16,110

Using the data from Exercise 4-11, prepare a trial balance for Apple Computer, Inc., as of September 25, 2004. List the accounts in the order they would appear in the ledger of Apple Computer.

Exercise 4-13

Income statement, retained earnings statement

Goals 3, 4

Net income, $276

Using the data from Exercises 4-11 and 4-12, prepare (a) an income statement and (b) a retained earnings statement for the year ending September 25, 2004, for Apple Computer, Inc.

Exercise 4-14

Closing entries, post-closing trial balance

Goals 3, 4

Total debit column, $8,050

Using the data from Exercises 4-11 and 4-12, (a) journalize the closing entries and (b) prepare a post-closing trial balance for Apple Computer, Inc.

Exercise 4-15

Cash account balance

Goals 3, 4

b. 7,550

During the month, Wembley Co. received $212,500 in cash and paid out $183,750 in cash.

a. Do the data indicate that Wembley Co. earned $28,750 during the month? Explain.
b. If the balance of the cash account is $36,300 at the end of the month, what was the cash balance at the beginning of the month?

Exercise 4-16

Account balances

Goals 3, 4

a. $40,550

a. On April 1, the cash account balance was $7,850. During April, cash receipts totaled $41,850, and the April 30 balance was $9,150. Determine the cash payments made during April.
b. On July 1, the accounts receivable account balance was $15,500. During July, $61,000 was collected from customers on account. Assuming the July 31 balance was $17,500, determine the fees billed to customers on account during July.
c. During January, $40,500 was paid to creditors on account, and purchases on account were $57,700. Assuming the January 31 balance of Accounts Payable was $38,000, determine the account balance on January 1.

Exercise 4-17

Transactions

Goals 3, 4

The Zuni Co. has the following accounts in its ledger: Cash; Accounts Receivable; Supplies; Office Equipment; Accounts Payable; Capital Stock; Dividends; Fees Earned; Rent Expense; Advertising Expense; Utilities Expense; Miscellaneous Expense.

Journalize the following selected transactions in a journal. Show the effects of each transaction on the financial statements using the margin notation illustrated in this chapter.

Aug.	1	Paid rent for the month, $1,500.
	2	Paid advertising expense, $700.
	4	Paid cash for supplies, $1,050.
	6	Purchased office equipment on account, $7,500.
	8	Received cash from customers on account, $3,600.
	12	Paid creditor on account, $1,150.
	20	Paid dividends, $1,000.
	25	Paid cash for repairs to office equipment, $500.
	30	Paid telephone bill for the month, $195.
	31	Fees earned and billed to customers for the month, $10,150.
	31	Paid electricity bill for the month, $380.

Exercise 4-18

Journalizing and posting

Goals 3, 4

On October 27, 2006, Lintel Co. purchased $1,320 of supplies on account.

a. Journalize the October 27, 2006, transaction.
b. Prepare a T account for Supplies. Enter a debit balance of $585 as of October 1, 2006.
c. Prepare a T account for Accounts Payable. Enter a credit balance of $6,150 as of October 1, 2006.
d. Post the October 27, 2006, transaction to the accounts and determine account balances.

Exercise 4-19

Transactions and T accounts

Goals 3, 4

SPREADSHEET

The following selected transactions were completed during May of the current year:

1. Billed customers for fees earned, $12,190.
2. Purchased supplies on account, $1,250.
3. Received cash from customers on account, $9,150.
4. Paid creditors on account, $750.

a. Journalize the above transactions in a two-column journal, using the appropriate number to identify the transactions.
b. Post the entries prepared in (a) to the following T accounts: Cash, Supplies, Accounts Receivable, Accounts Payable, Fees Earned. To the left of each amount posted in the accounts, place the appropriate number to identify the transactions.

Exercise 4-20

Trial balance

Goals 3, 4

SPREADSHEET

The accounts in the ledger of Haleakala Park Co. as of March 31, 2006, are listed in alphabetical order, as follows. All accounts have normal balances. The balance of the cash account has been intentionally omitted.

Accounts Payable	$ 18,710	Notes Payable	$ 40,000
Accounts Receivable	37,500	Prepaid Insurance	3,000
Capital Stock	50,000	Rent Expense	60,000
Cash	?	Retained Earnings	36,640
Dividends	20,000	Supplies	2,100
Fees Earned	310,000	Supplies Expense	7,900
Insurance Expense	6,000	Unearned Rent	9,000
Land	85,000	Utilities Expense	41,500
Miscellaneous Expense	8,900	Wages Expense	175,000

Prepare a trial balance, listing the accounts in their proper order and inserting the missing figure for cash.

Exercise 4-21

Effect of errors on trial balance

Goals 3, 4

Indicate which of the following errors, each considered individually, would cause the trial balance totals to be unequal:

a. A payment of $7,000 for equipment purchased was posted as a debit of $700 to Equipment and a credit of $700 to Cash.
b. Payment of a cash dividend of $12,000 was journalized and posted as a debit of $21,000 to Salary Expense and a credit of $12,000 to Cash.
c. A fee of $1,850 earned and due from a client was not debited to Accounts Receivable or credited to a revenue account, because the cash had not been received.
d. A payment of $1,475 to a creditor was posted as a debit of $1,475 to Accounts Payable and a debit of $1,475 to Cash.
e. A receipt of $325 from an account receivable was journalized and posted as a debit of $325 to Cash and a credit of $325 to Fees Earned.

Exercise 4-22

Errors in trial balance

Goals 3, 4

Total debit column, $181,600

SPREADSHEET

The following preliminary trial balance of Escalade Co., a sports ticket agency, does not balance:

Escalade Co.
Trial Balance
December 31, 2006

	Debit Balances	Credit Balances
Cash	47,350	
Accounts Receivable	22,100	
Prepaid Insurance		8,000
Equipment	57,000	
Accounts Payable		12,980
Unearned Rent		4,520
Capital Stock	25,000	
Retained Earnings	57,420	
Dividends	10,000	
Service Revenue		83,750
Wages Expense		42,000
Advertising Expense	7,200	
Miscellaneous Expense		1,425
	226,070	152,675

When the ledger and other records are reviewed, you discover the following: (1) the debits and credits in the cash account total $47,350 and $33,975, respectively; (2) a billing of $2,500 to a customer on account was not posted to the accounts receivable account; (3) a payment of $1,800 made to a creditor on account was not posted to the accounts payable account; (4) the balance of the unearned rent account is $4,250; (5) the correct balance of the equipment account is $75,000; and (6) each account has a normal balance.

Prepare a corrected trial balance.

Exercise 4-23

Effect of errors on trial balance

Goals 3, 4

The following errors occurred in posting from a two-column journal:

1. A debit of $1,250 to Supplies was posted twice.
2. A debit of $3,575 to Wages Expense was posted as $3,557.
3. A credit of $4,175 to Accounts Payable was not posted.
4. A debit of $400 to Accounts Payable was posted as a credit.
5. An entry debiting Accounts Receivable and crediting Fees Earned for $6,000 was not posted.
6. A credit of $350 to Cash was posted as $530.
7. A debit of $1,000 to Cash was posted to Miscellaneous Expense.

Considering each case individually (i.e., assuming that no other errors had occurred), indicate: (a) by "yes" or "no" whether the trial balance would be out of balance; (b) if answer to (a) is "yes," the amount by which the trial balance totals would differ; and (c) whether the debit or credit column of the trial balance would have the larger total. Answers should be presented in the following form, with error (1) given as an example:

Error	(a) Out of Balance	(b) Difference	(c) Larger Total
1.	yes	$1,250	debit

Exercise 4-24

Errors in trial balance

Goals **3, 4**

How many errors can you find in the following trial balance? All accounts have normal balances.

Dinero Co.
Trial Balance
For the Month Ending January 31, 2006

	Debit Balances	Credit Balances
Cash	7,500	
Accounts Receivable		16,400
Prepaid Insurance	3,600	
Equipment	50,000	
Accounts Payable	1,850	
Salaries Payable		1,250
Capital Stock		5,000
Retained Earnings		38,200
Dividends		6,000
Service Revenue		78,700
Salary Expense	32,810	
Advertising Expense		7,200
Miscellaneous Expense	1,490	
	152,750	152,750

Exercise 4-25

Adjusting entries

Goals **3, 4**

On January 31, the end of the current year, the following data were accumulated to assist the accountant in preparing the adjusting entries for Edsel Realty:

a. The supplies account balance on January 31 is $2,750. The supplies on hand on January 31 are $645.
b. The unearned rent account balance on January 31 is $9,450, representing the receipt of an advance payment on January 1 of three months' rent from tenants.
c. Wages accrued but not paid at January 31 are $2,150.
d. Fees accrued but unbilled at January 31 are $13,340.
e. Depreciation of office equipment for the year is $2,900.

Journalize the adjusting entries required at January 31.

Exercise 4-26

Adjusting entries

Goals **3, 4**

SPREADSHEET

Ithaca Services Co. offers cleaning services to business clients. The trial balance for Ithaca Services Co. before adjustments is shown on the next page.

Ithaca Services Co.
Unadjusted Trial Balance
January 31, 2006

	Debit Balances	Credit Balances
Cash	8	
Accounts Receivable	50	
Supplies	8	
Prepaid Insurance	12	
Land	50	
Equipment	32	
Accumulated Depreciation—Equipment		2
Accounts Payable		26
Wages Payable		0
Capital Stock		20
Retained Earnings		92
Dividends	8	
Fees Earned		60
Wages Expense	16	
Rent Expense	8	
Insurance Expense	0	
Utilities Expense	6	
Depreciation Expense	0	
Supplies Expense	0	
Miscellaneous Expense	2	
Totals	200	200

The data for year-end adjustments are as follows:

a. Fees earned but not yet billed, $7.
b. Supplies on hand, $3.
c. Insurance premiums expired, $6.
d. Depreciation expense, $5.
e. Wages accrued but not paid, $1.

Prepare the adjusting entries for Ithaca Services Co.

Exercise 4-27

Adjusting trial balance

Goals **3, 4**

Total debit column, $213

SPREADSHEET

Based upon the data in Exercise 4-26, adjust the account balances shown and prepare an adjusted trial balance for Ithaca Services Co.

Exercise 4-28

Financial statements

Goal **4**

Net income, $18

SPREADSHEET

Based upon the data in Exercise 4-27, prepare an income statement, retained earnings statement, and balance sheet for Ithaca Services Co.

Exercise 4-29

Closing entries

Goal **4**

Based upon the data in Exercises 4-26 and 4-27, prepare the closing entries for Ithaca Services Co.

Exercise 4-30

Statement of retained earnings

Goals **3, 4**

SPREADSHEET

Synthesis Systems Co. offers its services to residents in the Dillon City area. Selected accounts from the ledger of Synthesis Systems Co. for the current fiscal year ended October 31, 2006, are as follows:

RETAINED EARNINGS

Oct. 31	12,000	Bal., Nov. 1, 2005	173,750
31	277,150	Oct. 31	321,400
		Bal., Oct. 31, 2006	206,000

DIVIDENDS

Jan. 31	3,000	Oct. 31	12,000
Apr. 30	3,000		
July 31	3,000		
Oct. 31	3,000		

Prepare a retained earnings statement for the year ending October 31, 2006.

Exercise 4-31

Statement of retained earnings, net loss

Goals **3, 4**

SPREADSHEET

Selected accounts from the ledger of Bobcat Sports for the current fiscal year ended August 31, 2006, are as follows:

RETAINED EARNINGS

Aug. 31	16,000	Bal., Sept. 1, 2005	210,300
31	224,900	Aug. 31	175,250
		Bal., Aug. 31, 2006	144,650

DIVIDENDS

Nov. 30	4,000	Aug. 31	16,000
Feb. 28	4,000		
May 31	4,000		
Aug. 31	4,000		

Prepare a retained earnings statement for the year.

Exercise 4-32

Accounting cycle

Goal **5**

Rearrange the following steps of the accounting cycle in proper sequence.

a. Adjusting entries recorded in the journal are posted to the ledger accounts.
b. Closing entries are prepared and recorded in the journal.
c. An unadjusted trial balance is prepared.
d. A post-closing trial balance is prepared.
e. Transactions are analyzed from source documents and are recorded in the journal using the rules of debit and credit.
f. Adjustment data are assembled and analyzed.
g. Transactions recorded in the journal are posted to the ledger accounts.
h. Adjusting entries are prepared and recorded in the journal.
i. The financial statements are prepared.
j. Closing entries recorded in the journal are posted to the ledger accounts.
k. An adjusted trial balance is prepared.

Exercise 4-33

EBITDA

Goal 6

The Digital Express Company disclosed a net income of $12,000 on revenues of $400,000 for fiscal year ending December 31, 2007. The company had $500,000 of 6% debt outstanding during the year. In addition, the company had depreciation and amortization expenses of $32,000. The company's 2007 tax rate was 40%. The management believes a pro forma disclosure of EBITDA would be useful to investors.

a. Determine EBITDA for 2007.
b. Determine net income divided by sales and EBITDA divided by sales for 2007.
c. What disclosure must management provide in addition to the pro forma EBITDA calculations?

Exercise 4-34

EBITDA

Goal 6

Condensed income statements for Comcast Corp., the largest U.S. cable operator, and DirecTV Group, Inc., a satellite-based entertainment company, for a recent year are provided below (in millions).

	Comcast Corp.	DirecTV Group Inc.
Revenues	$20,307	$11,360
Operating expenses (excluding depreciation)	$ 7,462	$ 8,668
Selling, general, and administrative expenses	5,314	3,973
Depreciation expense	3,420	670
Amortization expense	1,203	168
Total expenses	$17,399	$13,479
Operating income (loss)	$ 2,908	$ (2,119)
Interest income (expense)	(1,112)	359
Income (loss) before tax	$ 1,796	$ (1,760)
Income tax (expense) benefit	(826)	704
Net income	$ 970	$ (1,056)

a. Determine EBITDA for each company.
b. Determine EBITDA divided by revenues for each company.
c. Compare and contrast Comcast with DirecTV based on your answers to parts (a) and (b).

ACCOUNTING APPLICATION PROBLEMS

Problem 4-1A

Journal entries and trial balance

Goal 3

3. Total debit column, $25,000

SPREADSHEET

GENERAL LEDGER

On March 1, 2006, Tim Cochran established Star Realty, which completed the following transactions during the month:

a. Tim Cochran transferred cash from a personal bank account to an account to be used for the business in exchange for capital stock, $12,000.
b. Purchased supplies on account, $850.
c. Earned sales commissions, receiving cash, $12,600.
d. Paid rent on office and equipment for the month, $2,000.
e. Paid creditor on account, $450.
f. Paid dividends, $1,500.
g. Paid automobile expenses (including rental charge) for month, $1,700, and miscellaneous expenses, $375.
h. Paid office salaries, $3,000.
i. Determined that the cost of supplies used was $605.

Instructions

1. Journalize entries for transactions (a) through (i), using the following accounts: Cash; Supplies; Accounts Payable; Capital Stock; Dividends; Sales Commissions Earned; Office Salaries Expense; Rent Expense; Automobile Expense; Supplies Expense; Miscellaneous Expense. Show the effects of each transaction on the financial statements using the margin notation illustrated in this chapter.

(continued)

2. Post the journal entries to T accounts, placing the appropriate letter to the left of each amount to identify the transactions. Determine the account balances, after all posting is complete.
3. Prepare a trial balance as of March 31, 2006.
4. Determine the following:
   a. Amount of total revenue recorded in the ledger.
   b. Amount of total expenses recorded in the ledger.
   c. Assuming that no adjustments are necessary, what is the amount of net income for March?

Problem 4-2A

Journal entries and trial balance

Goal **3**

3. Total debit column, $40,880

SPREADSHEET

GENERAL LEDGER

On July 1, 2006, Leon Cruz established an interior decorating business, Ingres Designs. During the remainder of the month, Leon Cruz completed the following transactions related to the business:

July 1 Leon transferred cash from a personal bank account to an account to be used for the business in exchange for capital stock, $18,000.
5 Paid rent for the period of July 5 to the end of the month, $1,500.
10 Purchased a truck for $15,000, paying $5,000 cash and giving a note payable for the remainder.
13 Purchased equipment on account, $4,500.
14 Purchased supplies for cash, $975.
15 Paid annual premiums on property and casualty insurance, $3,000.
15 Received cash for job completed, $4,100.
21 Paid creditor a portion of the amount owed for equipment purchased on July 13, $2,400.
24 Recorded jobs completed on account and sent invoices to customers, $6,100.
26 Received an invoice for truck expenses, to be paid in August, $580.
27 Paid utilities expense, $950.
27 Paid miscellaneous expense, $315.
29 Received cash from customers on account, $3,420.
30 Paid wages of employees, $2,500.
31 Paid dividends, $2,000.

Instructions

1. Journalize each transaction in a two-column journal, referring to the following chart of accounts in selecting the accounts to be debited and credited.

Cash	Capital Stock
Accounts Receivable	Dividends
Supplies	Fees Earned
Prepaid Insurance	Wages Expense
Equipment	Rent Expense
Truck	Utilities Expense
Notes Payable	Truck Expense
Accounts Payable	Miscellaneous Expense

2. Post the journal to a ledger of T accounts. For accounts with more than one posting, determine the account balance.
3. Prepare a trial balance for Ingres Designs as of July 31, 2006.

Problem 4-3A

Journal entries and trial balance

Goal **4**

Socket Realty acts as an agent in buying, selling, renting, and managing real estate. The account balances at the end of May 2007 of the current year are as shown at the top of the following page:

4. Total debit column, $97,520

SPREADSHEET

GENERAL LEDGER

	Debit Balances	Credit Balances
Cash	4,920	
Accounts Receivable	15,000	
Prepaid Insurance	1,440	
Office Supplies	960	
Land	0	
Office Equipment	10,480	
Accumulated Depreciation		2,880
Accounts Payable		640
Salary and Commissions Payable		0
Unearned Fees		1,440
Notes Payable		0
Capital Stock		20,000
Retained Earnings		7,840
Dividends	0	
Fees Earned		0
Salary and Commission Expense	0	
Rent Expense	0	
Office Supplies Expense	0	
Advertising Expense	0	
Automobile Expense	0	
Insurance Expense	0	
Depreciation Expense	0	
Miscellaneous Expense	0	
	32,800	32,800

The following business transactions were completed by Socket Realty during June 2007:

June 1 Paid rent on office for June, $2,000.
2 Purchased office supplies on account, $1,100.
5 Paid annual insurance premiums, $1,920.
8 Received cash from clients on account, $13,040.
10 Purchased land for a future building site for $48,000, paying $4,800 in cash and giving a non-interest-bearing note payable due in 2009 for the remainder.
16 Paid creditors on account, $640.
18 Returned a portion of the office supplies purchased on June 2, receiving full credit for their cost, $140.
24 Paid advertising expense, $680.
25 Billed clients for fees earned, $18,800.
27 Paid salaries and commissions, $6,000
28 Paid automobile expense (including rental charges for an automobile), $600.
29 Paid miscellaneous expenses, $200.
30 Received cash from client for fees earned, $2,400.
30 Paid dividends, $800.

Instructions

1. Record the June 1 balance of each account in the appropriate column of a T account. Write *Balance* to identify the opening amounts.
2. Journalize the transactions for June in a two-column journal.
3. Post the journal entries to the T accounts, placing the date to the left of each amount to identify the transaction. Determine the balances for all accounts with more than one posting.
4. Prepare an unadjusted trial balance of the ledger as of June 30, 2007.

Problem 4-4A

Adjusting entries, financial statements, closing entries

Goal **3, 4**

3. Total debit column, $99,200

SPREADSHEET

GENERAL LEDGER

The data necessary to adjust Socket Realty accounts from Problem 4-3A as of June 30, 2007, are as follows:

a. Prepaid insurance expired during June, $280.
b. Office supplies on hand at June 30, $580.
c. Depreciation on office equipment, $160.
d. Unearned fees earned during June, $480.
e. Accrued fees as of June 30, $960.
f. Accrued salary and commissions as of June 30, $560.

Instructions

1. Journalize the necessary adjusting entries for June.
2. Post the adjusting entries to T accounts. Identify each adjusting entry as "Adjusting." For those accounts that were adjusted, determine an adjusted balance.
3. Prepare an adjusted trial balance as of June 30.
4. Prepare an income statement, a retained earnings statement, and a classified balance sheet.
5. Journalize and post the closing entries for June. Identify each entry as "Closing." Determine post-closing balances.
6. Prepare a post-closing trial balance as of June 30, 2007.
7. (Appendix) Prepare a statement of cash flows for June. Note that the June 16 payment on account of $640 was for a May purchase of supplies on account.
8. (Appendix) Reconcile net income with net cash flows from operations for June.

Problem 4–5A

Adjustments and financial statements

Goals **3, 4**

2. Total debit column, $509,720

SPREADSHEET

GENERAL LEDGER

Heritage Company offers legal consulting advice to death-row inmates. Heritage Company prepared the following trial balance at April 30, 2006, the end of the current fiscal year:

Heritage Company
Trial Balance
April 30, 2006

	Debit Balances	Credit Balances
Cash	3,200	
Accounts Receivable	10,500	
Prepaid Insurance	1,800	
Supplies	1,350	
Land	50,000	
Building	136,500	
Accumulated Depreciation—Building		50,700
Equipment	92,700	
Accumulated Depreciation—Equipment		36,300
Accounts Payable		6,500
Unearned Rent		3,000
Capital Stock		50,000
Retained Earnings		162,500
Dividends	10,000	
Fees Revenue		191,000
Salaries and Wages Expense	96,200	
Advertising Expense	63,200	
Utilities Expense	18,000	
Repairs Expense	12,500	
Miscellaneous Expense	4,050	
	500,000	500,000

The data needed to determine year-end adjustments are as follows:

a. Accrued fees revenue at April 30 are $2,800.
b. Insurance expired during the year is $450.
c. Supplies on hand at April 30 are $650.
d. Depreciation of building for the year is $1,620.
e. Depreciation of equipment for the year is $3,500.
f. Accrued salaries and wages at April 30 are $1,800.
g. Unearned rent at April 30 is $1,500.

Instructions

1. Prepare the adjusting entries.
2. Based upon (1), prepare an adjusted trial balance.
3. Prepare an income statement for the year ended April 30, 2006.
4. Prepare a retained earnings statement for the year ended April 30, 2006.
5. Prepare a classified balance sheet as of April 30, 2006.
6. Prepare the closing entries.
7. Prepare a post-closing trial balance.

ALTERNATE ACCOUNTING APPLICATION PROBLEMS

Alternate Problem 4-1B

Journal entries and trial balance

Goal 3

3. Total debit column, $20,160

SPREADSHEET

GENERAL LEDGER

On January 2, 2006, Lela Peterson established Acadia Realty, which completed the following transactions during the month:

a. Lela Peterson transferred cash from a personal bank account to an account to be used for the business in exchange for capital stock, $9,000.
b. Paid rent on office and equipment for the month, $2,000.
c. Purchased supplies on account, $700.
d. Paid creditor on account, $290.
e. Earned sales commissions, receiving cash, $10,750.
f. Paid automobile expenses (including rental charge) for month, $1,400, and miscellaneous expenses, $480.
g. Paid office salaries, $2,500.
h. Determined that the cost of supplies used was $575.
i. Paid dividends, $1,000.

Instructions

1. Journalize entries for transactions (a) through (i), using the following accounts: Cash; Supplies; Accounts Payable; Capital Stock; Dividends; Sales Commissions Earned; Rent Expense; Office Salaries Expense; Automobile Expense; Supplies Expense; Miscellaneous Expense. Show the effects of each transaction on the financial statements using the margin notation illustrated in this chapter.
2. Post the journal entries to T accounts, placing the appropriate letter to the left of each amount to identify the transactions. Determine the account balances, after all posting is complete.
3. Prepare a trial balance as of January 31, 2006.
4. Determine the following:
   a. Amount of total revenue recorded in the ledger.
   b. Amount of total expenses recorded in the ledger.
   c. Assuming that no adjustments are necessary, what is the amount of net income for January?

Alternate Problem 4-2B

Journal entries and trial balance

Goal 3

3. Total debit column, $41,425

SPREADSHEET

GENERAL LEDGER

On November 2, 2006, Nicole Oliver established an interior decorating business, Devon Designs. During the remainder of the month, Nicole completed the following transactions related to the business:

Nov.	2	Nicole transferred cash from a personal bank account to an account to be used for the business in exchange for capital stock, $15,000.
	5	Paid rent for the period of November 5 to end of month, $1,750.
	6	Purchased office equipment on account, $8,500.
	8	Purchased a used truck for $18,000, paying $10,000 cash and giving a note payable for the remainder.
	10	Purchased supplies for cash, $1,115.
	12	Received cash for job completed, $7,500.
	15	Paid annual premiums on property and casualty insurance, $2,400.
	23	Recorded jobs completed on account and sent invoices to customers, $3,950.
	24	Received an invoice for truck expenses, to be paid in December, $600.
	29	Paid utilities expense, $750.
	29	Paid miscellaneous expenses, $310.
	30	Received cash from customers on account, $2,200.
	30	Paid wages of employees, $2,700.
	30	Paid creditor a portion of the amount owed for equipment purchased on November 6, $2,125.
	30	Paid dividends, $1,400.

Instructions

1. Journalize each transaction in a two-column journal, referring to the following chart of accounts in selecting the accounts to be debited and credited.

Cash	Capital Stock
Accounts Receivable	Dividends
Supplies	Fees Earned
Prepaid Insurance	Wages Expense
Equipment	Rent Expense
Truck	Utilities Expense
Notes Payable	Truck Expense
Accounts Payable	Miscellaneous Expense

2. Post the journal to a ledger of T accounts. For accounts with more than one posting, determine the account balance.
3. Prepare a trial balance for Devon Designs as of November 30, 2006.

Alternate Problem 4-3B

Journal entries and trial balance

Goal 3

4. Total debit column, $317,300

SPREADSHEET

GENERAL LEDGER

Gypsum Realty acts as an agent in buying, selling, renting, and managing real estate. The account balances at the end of March 2007 of the current year are as follows:

	Debit Balances	Credit Balances
Cash	16,300	
Accounts Receivable	57,500	
Prepaid Insurance	2,200	
Office Supplies	2,100	
Land	0	
Office Equipment	17,000	
Accumulated Depreciation		4,800
Accounts Payable		1,800
Salary and Commissions Payable		0
Unearned Fees		3,000
Notes Payable		0
Capital Stock		20,000
Retained Earnings		65,500
Dividends	0	
Fees Earned		0
Salary and Commission Expense	0	
Rent Expense	0	
Office Supplies Expense	0	
Advertising Expense	0	
Automobile Expense	0	
Insurance Expense	0	
Depreciation Expense	0	
Miscellaneous Expense	0	
	95,100	95,100

The following business transactions were completed by Gypsum Realty during April 2007:

Apr.	1	Paid rent on office for April, $8,000.
	2	Purchased office supplies on account, $2,750.
	5	Paid annual insurance premiums, $3,300.
	8	Received cash from clients on account, $55,000.
	15	Purchased land for a future building site for $150,000, paying $15,000 in cash and giving a non-interest-bearing note payable due in 2011 for the remainder.
	17	Paid creditors of April 2 purchase on account, $1,800.
	20	Returned a portion of the office supplies purchased on April 2, receiving full credit for their cost, $550.
	24	Paid advertising expense, $2,200.
	25	Billed clients for fees earned, $76,800.
	27	Paid salaries and commissions, $23,000.
	28	Paid automobile expense (including rental charges for an automobile), $1,430.
	29	Paid miscellaneous expense, $430.
	30	Received cash from client for fees earned, $10,000.
	30	Paid dividends, $4,000.

Instructions

1. Record the April 1 balance of each account in the appropriate column of a T account. Write *Balance* to identify the opening amounts.
2. Journalize the transactions for April in a two-column journal.
3. Post the journal entries to the T accounts, placing the date to the left of each amount to identify the transaction. Determine the balances for all accounts with more than one posting.
4. Prepare an unadjusted trial balance of the ledger as of April 30.

Alternate Problem 4-4B

Adjusting entries, financial statements, closing entries

Goals **3, 4**

3. Total debit column, $321,850

SPREADSHEET
GENERAL LEDGER

The data necessary to adjust Gypsum Realty accounts from Alternate Problem 4-3B as of April 30, 2007, are as follows:

a. Prepaid insurance expired during April, $500.
b. Office supplies on hand at April 30, $1,750.
c. Depreciation on office equipment, $250.
d. Unearned fees earned during April, $1,000.
e. Accrued fees as of April 30, $2,800.
f. Accrued salary and commissions as of April 30, $1,500.

Instructions

1. Journalize the necessary adjusting entries for April.
2. Post the adjusting entries to T accounts. Identify each adjusting entry as "Adjusting." For those accounts that were adjusted, determine an adjusted balance.
3. Prepare an adjusted trial balance as of April 30.
4. Prepare an income statement, a retained earnings statement, and a classified balance sheet.
5. Journalize and post the closing entries for April. Identify each entry as "Closing." Determine post-closing balances.
6. Prepare a post-closing trial balance as of April 30, 2007.
7. (Appendix) Prepare a statement of cash flows for April. Note that the April 17 payment on account of $1,800 was for a March purchase of supplies on account.
8. (Appendix) Reconcile net income with net cash flows from operations for April.

Alternate Problem 4-5B

Adjustments and financial statements

Goals **3, 4**

2. Total debit column, $384,980

SPREADSHEET

GENERAL LEDGER

Flamingo Company maintains and repairs warning lights, such as those found on radio towers and lighthouses. Flamingo Company prepared the following trial balance at July 31, 2006, the end of the current fiscal year:

Flamingo Company
Trial Balance
July 31, 2006

	Debit Balances	Credit Balances
Cash	4,500	
Accounts Receivable	13,500	
Prepaid Insurance	3,000	
Supplies	1,950	
Land	70,000	
Building	100,500	
Accumulated Depreciation—Building		71,700
Equipment	71,400	
Accumulated Depreciation—Equipment		60,800
Accounts Payable		4,100
Unearned Rent		1,500
Capital Stock		5,000
Retained Earnings		50,700
Dividends	4,000	
Fees Revenue		181,200
Salaries and Wages Expense	73,200	
Advertising Expense	15,500	
Utilities Expense	8,100	
Repairs Expense	6,300	
Miscellaneous Expense	3,050	
	375,000	375,000

The data needed to determine year-end adjustments are as follows:

a. Fees revenue accrued at July 31 is $3,500.
b. Insurance expired during the year is $2,000.
c. Supplies on hand at July 31 are $350.
d. Depreciation of building for the year is $1,520.
e. Depreciation of equipment for the year is $2,160.
f. Accrued salaries and wages at July 31 are $2,800.
g. Unearned rent at July 31 is $500.

Instructions

1. Prepare the adjusting entries.
2. Based upon (1), prepare an adjusted trial balance.
3. Prepare an income statement for the year ended July 31, 2006.
4. Prepare a retained earnings statement for the year ended July 31, 2006.
5. Prepare a classified balance sheet as of July 31, 2006.
6. Prepare the closing entries.
7. Prepare a post-closing trial balance.

FINANCIAL ANALYSIS AND REPORTING CASES

Case 4-1

The Gap Inc. is a global specialty retailer operating stores selling casual apparel, personal care, and other accessories for men, women, and children under The Gap, Banana Republic, and Old Navy brands. The Gap Inc. designs virtually all of its products, which are manufactured by independent sources and sold under The Gap's name brands.

The following operating data (in millions) were adapted from the 2005 SEC 10-K filings of The Gap Inc. for the years ending January 29, 2005, and January 31, 2004:

	2005	2004
Net sales	$16,267	$15,854
Costs and expenses:		
Cost of goods sold	9,886	9,885
Other expenses	4,509	4,285
Operating income	$ 1,872	$ 1,684
Income taxes	722	653
Net income (loss)	$ 1,150	$ 1,031
Depreciation and amortization	$ 620	$ 675
Interest expense	$ 167	$ 234

1. Compute EBITDA for 2005 and 2004.
2. Compute the ratio of EBITDA to interest expense for 2005 and 2004. Round to one decimal place.
3. Based upon (1) and (2), discuss the trends in EBITDA and the ratio of EBITDA to interest expense.
4. Is EBITDA normally the same as the amount reported for net cash flows from operating activities? Explain.

Case 4-2

Assume that The Gap Inc. has credit agreements that require a long-term liability to EBITDA ratio that does not exceed 3:1. Financial requirements such as this are called loan or credit covenants. The violation of a loan or credit covenant can result in the debt becoming due immediately, as well as requirements to pay additional interest and penalties. The long-term liabilities of The Gap Inc. at the end of 2005 and 2004 were $2,870 and $3,518 respectively.

1. Based upon your answer to Case 4-1, determine whether The Gap Inc. is in compliance with the loan covenant for 2005 and 2004. Round to one decimal place.
2. Assume that long-term debt does not change during 2006. Also, assume the following operating data for 2006:

Interest expense	$200
Depreciation and amortization	650
Income before income taxes	300

   Given this information, will The Gap Inc. violate its loan covenant in 2006? Show your computations. Round to one decimal place.
3. Assuming that during 2006 the long-term debt does not change, how much would EBITDA have to decline before The Gap Inc. would violate the covenant?

Case 4-3

The following income statement (in millions) is adapted from the 2004 10-K filing of Time Warner:

Revenues	$42,089
Cost of revenues	24,449
Gross profit	$17,640
Selling, administrative, and other expenses	10,300
Amortization of goodwill and other intangible assets	626
Other costs and expenses	549
Operating income	$ 6,165
Interest expense	1,754
Other nonrecurring income	651
Income before taxes	$ 5,062
Income tax expense	1,698
Net income	$ 3,364

Included in the preceding income statement is depreciation of property, plant, and equipment of $6,132.

1. Compute the EBITDA for 2004.
2. Compute the percentage of EBITDA to total revenues for 2004. Round to one decimal place after converting to a percentage.
3. Compute the ratio of EBITDA to interest expense for 2004. Round to one decimal place.
4. Compute the ratio of long-term debt to EBITDA for 2004. The long-term debt as of December 31, 2004, was $20,703. Round to one decimal place.
5. Comment on the ability of Time Warner to meet its interest obligations.

Case 4-4

The following income statement (in thousands) is from the Securities and Exchange Commission 10-K filing by Amazon.com for the year ending December 31, 2004:

Net sales		$6,921,124
Cost of sales		5,319,127
Gross profit		$1,601,997
Operating expenses:		
Fulfillment expenses	$590,397	
Marketing expenses	158,022	
Technology and content expenses	251,195	
General and administrative expenses	112,220	
Stock-based compensation expense	57,702	
Other operating (income) expense	(7,964)	
Total operating expenses		1,161,572
Income from operations before interest and taxes		$ 440,425

Included in the preceding income statement is depreciation and amortization expense of $75,724.

1. Compute the EBITDA for 2004.
2. Based upon (1), comment on Amazon.com's EBITDA.

Case 4-5

SPREADSHEET

WorldCom, Inc., allegedly reported nearly $4 billion as fixed assets on its balance sheet, rather than as operating expense on its income statement. Of this amount, $3.06 billion should have been expensed in 2001, rather than debited as a fixed asset. As a result of this discovery, WorldCom lost credibility with investors, and its common stock lost nearly all of its value. WorldCom made public disclosures of its net income, as required, but also focused its earning announcements on EBITDA. The income statement for the year ended December 31, 2001, reported the following:

WorldCom, Inc.
Income Statement
For the Year Ended December 31, 2001

	(in millions)
Revenues	$35,179
Operating expenses:	
Line costs	$14,739
Selling, general, and administrative	11,046
Depreciation and amortization	5,880
Total	$31,665
Operating income	$ 3,514
Other income (expense):	
Interest expense	(1,533)
Miscellaneous income	447
Income before income taxes	$ 2,428
Provision for income taxes	927
Net income	$ 1,501

1. Determine EBITDA, using the reported figures.
2. Determine EBITDA as it should have been reported in 2001 if costs were properly expensed, rather than debited as a fixed asset.
3. Assume that fixed assets are depreciated on the straight-line basis for five years. Under this assumption, what would be the correct net income (loss) before income taxes for 2001?

Case 4-6

On the Internet, go to the google.com Web site and perform an advanced search for "EBITDA." Review the articles for a discussion of the advantages and disadvantages of using EBITDA as a financial analysis tool. Pick one or more articles, read them, and summarize your findings.

Case 4-7

The income statements for Amazon.com, Google, Inc., and Borders, Inc., for a recent year are provided below.

	Amazon.com	Google, Inc.	Borders, Inc.
Net sales	$6,921	$3,189	$3,903
Cost of sales	5,319	1,457	2,804
Gross profit	$1,602	$1,732	$1,099
Selling, general, and administrative expenses	1,162	1,092	883
Operating income	$ 440	$ 640	$ 216
Interest expense (income)	84	(10)	9
Income before income taxes	$ 356	$ 650	$ 207
Income taxes expense (benefit)	(232)	251	76
Net income	$ 588	$ 399	$ 131

In addition, the statement of cash flows revealed the following line item in the cash flows from operations section of the statement:

	Amazon.com	Google, Inc.	Borders, Inc.
Depreciation and amortization	$76	$148	$113

1. Determine EBITDA (earnings before interest, taxes, depreciation, and amortization) for each company.
2. Why is the EBITDA for Amazon.com actually less than the net income?
3. Would you conclude that the EBITDA performance of Amazon.com is more like an Internet company such as Google, Inc., or more like a book retailer like Borders, Inc.? Explain. *Hint:* Compute EBITDA as a percent of net sales.
4. How is EBITDA different than cash flows from operations?

BUSINESS ACTIVITIES AND RESPONSIBILITY ISSUES

Activity 4-1

Business emphasis

Mohawk Industries is a leading distributor of carpets and rugs in the United States. The company sells its carpets and rugs to locally owned, independent carpet retailers, home centers such as Home Depot and Lowe's, and department stores such as Sears. Mohawk's carpets are marketed under the brand names that include "Aladdin, Mohawk Home, Bigelow, Custom Weave, Durkan, Karastan, and Townhouse."

1. List some factors that increase the demand for carpet.
2. Do you think Mohawk should view itself as a carpet or floor-covering manufacturer? Discuss the advantages and disadvantages of Mohawk viewing itself as a floor-covering manufacturer rather than just a carpet manufacturer.
3. Read Mohawk's latest 10-K filing with the Securities and Exchange Commission by using EdgarScan (http://edgarscan.pwcglobal.com). Does Mohawk view itself as a carpet manufacturer or as a floor-covering manufacturer? Explain.

Activity 4-2

Ethics and professional conduct in business

At the end of the current month, Ross Heimlich prepared a trial balance for Main Street Motor Co. The credit side of the trial balance exceeds the debit side by a significant amount. Ross has decided to add the difference to the balance of the miscellaneous expense account in order to complete the preparation of the current month's financial statements by a 5 o'clock deadline. Ross will look for the difference next week when he has more time.

Discuss whether Ross is behaving in a professional manner.

Activity 4-3

Recording transactions

The following discussion took place between Heather Sims, the office manager of Sedgemoor Data Company, and a new accountant, Ed Hahn.

Ed: I've been thinking about our method of recording entries. It seems that it's inefficient.
Heather: In what way?
Ed: Well—correct me if I'm wrong—it seems like we have unnecessary steps in the process. We could easily develop a trial balance by posting our transactions directly into the ledger and bypassing the journal altogether. In this way we could combine the recording and posting processes into one step and save ourselves a lot of time. What do you think?
Heather: We need to have a talk.

What should Heather say to Ed?

Activity 4-4

Debits and credits

GROUP ACTIVITY

The following excerpt is from a conversation between Peter Kaiser, the president and chief operating officer of Sprocket Construction Co., and his neighbor, Doris Nesmith:

Doris: Peter, I'm taking a course in night school, "Intro to Accounting." I was wondering—could you answer a couple of questions for me?
Peter: Well, I will if I can.
Doris: Okay, our instructor says that it's critical we understand the basic concepts of accounting, or we'll never get beyond the first test. My problem is with those rules of debit and credit . . . you know, assets increase with debits, decrease with credits, etc.
Peter: Yes, pretty basic stuff. You just have to memorize the rules. It shouldn't be too difficult.
Doris: Sure, I can memorize the rules, but my problem is I want to be sure I understand the basic concepts behind the rules.

For example, why can't assets be increased with credits and decreased with debits like revenue? As long as everyone did it that way, why not? It would seem easier if we had the same rules for all increases and decreases in accounts.

Also, why is the left side of an account called the debit side? Why couldn't it be called something simple . . . like the "LE" for Left Entry? The right side could be called just "RE" for Right Entry.

Finally, why are there just two sides to an entry? Why can't there be three or four sides to an entry?

In a group of four or five, select one person to play the role of Peter and one person to play the role of Doris.

1. After listening to the conversation between Peter and Doris, help Peter answer Doris's questions.
2. What information (other than just debit and credit journal entries) could the accounting system gather that might be useful to Peter in managing Sprocket Construction Co.?

Activity 4-5

Financial statements

The following is an excerpt from a telephone conversation between Pedro Mendoza, president of Goliath Supplies Co., and Natalie Weich, owner of Flint Employment Co.:

Pedro: Natalie, you're going to have to do a better job of finding me a new computer programmer. That last guy was great at programming, but he didn't have any common sense.

Natalie: What do you mean? The guy had a master's degree with straight A's.

Pedro: Yes, well, last month he developed a new financial reporting system. He said we could do away with manually preparing financial statements. The computer would automatically generate our financial statements with "a push of a button."

Natalie: So what's the big deal? Sounds to me like it would save you time and effort.

Pedro: Right! The balance sheet showed a minus for supplies!

Natalie: Minus supplies? How can that be?

Pedro: That's what I asked.

Natalie: So, what did he say?

Pedro: Well, after he checked the program, he said that it must be right. The minuses were greater than the pluses . . .

Natalie: Didn't he know that supplies can't have a credit balance—it must have a debit balance?

Pedro: He asked me what a debit and credit were.

Natalie: I see your point.

1. Comment on (a) the desirability of computerizing Goliath Supplies Co.'s financial reporting system and (b) the computer programmer's lack of accounting knowledge.
2. Explain to the programmer why supplies could not have a credit balance.

Activity 4-6

Financial statements

Assume that you recently accepted a position with the Bozeman National Bank as an assistant loan officer. As one of your first duties, you have been assigned the responsibility of evaluating a loan request for $150,000 from Sasquatch.com, a small corporation. In support of the loan application, Samantha Joyner, owner, submitted a "statement of accounts" (trial balance) for the first year of operations ended December 31, 2006.

1. Explain to Samantha Joyner why a set of financial statements (income statement, statement of retained earnings, balance sheet, and statement of cash flows) would be useful to you in evaluating the loan request.
2. In discussing the statement of accounts with Samantha Joyner, you discovered that the accounts had not been adjusted at December 31. Analyze the statement of accounts (shown at the top of the following page) and indicate possible adjusting entries that might be necessary before an accurate set of financial statements could be prepared.
3. Assuming that an accurate set of financial statements will be submitted by Samantha Joyner in a few days, what other considerations or information would you require before making a decision on the loan request?

Sasquatch.com
Statement of Accounts
December 31, 2006

Cash	4,100	
Billings Due from Others	30,150	
Supplies (chemicals, etc.)	14,950	
Trucks	52,750	
Equipment	16,150	
Amounts Owed to Others		5,700
Investment in Business		47,000
Service Revenue		147,300
Wages Expense	60,100	
Utilities Expense	14,660	
Rent Expense	4,800	
Insurance Expense	1,400	
Other Expenses	940	
	200,000	200,000

ANSWERS TO SELF-STUDY QUESTIONS

1. A A debit may signify an increase in an asset account (answer A) or a decrease in a liability or capital stock account. A credit may signify a decrease in an asset account (answer B) or an increase in a liability or capital stock account (answers C and D).

2. C Liability, capital stock, and revenue (answer C) accounts have normal credit balances. Asset (answer A), dividends (answer B), and expense (answer D) accounts have normal debit balances.

3. C Accounts Receivable (answer A), Cash (answer B), and Miscellaneous Expense (answer D) would all normally have debit balances. Fees Earned should normally have a credit balance. Hence, a debit balance in Fees Earned (answer C) would indicate a likely error in the recording process.

4. B The entry to close the dividends account is to debit the retained earnings account and credit the dividends account (answer B).

5. D Since all revenue and expense accounts are closed at the end of the period, Fees Earned (answer A), Wages Expense (answer B), and Rent Expense (answer C) would all be closed to Retained Earnings. Accumulated Depreciation (answer D) is a contra asset account that is not closed.

5 Accounting for Merchandise Operations

Learning Goals

1. Distinguish the activities and financial statements of a service business from those of a merchandise business.
2. Describe and illustrate the financial statements of a merchandising business.
3. Describe the accounting for the sale of merchandise.
4. Describe the accounting for the purchase of merchandise.
5. Describe the accounting for transportation costs and sales taxes.
6. Illustrate the dual nature of merchandising transactions.
7. Describe the accounting for merchandise shrinkage.
8. Describe and illustrate the effects of inventory misstatements on the financial statements.
9. Describe and illustrate the use of gross profit and operating income in analyzing a company's operations.

JCPenney

Twenty years ago, music was purchased at the "record store." Not any more. Today, CDs can be purchased at retail stores such as Best Buy, Borders, Wal-Mart, Sam Goody's, and Disc Exchange; through online retainers such as CDUniverse and CDNow; and as individual MP3 downloads from services such as Apple's iTunes® and Real's Rhapsody®. The way we buy goods (and services) has undergone significant changes and will continue to change with consumer tastes and technology. For example, an established retailer like JCPenney is faced with a rapidly changing competitive landscape through the emergence of (1) discount merchandising, (2) category killers, and (3) Internet retailing.

Over the last two decades, Wal-Mart has virtually reinvented *discount merchandising*, thus becoming the world's largest retailer. Wal-Mart's growth is centered on providing the consumer with everyday discount pricing over a broad array of household products. *Category killers* include Toys"R"Us (toys), Best Buy (electronics), Home Depot (home improvement), and Office Depot (office supplies), which provide a wide selection of attractively priced goods within a particular product segment. *Internet retailers*, such as Amazon.com and Lands' End (now part of Sears), allow time-conscious consumers to shop quickly and effortlessly.

JCPenney has had to adapt its retailing model in order to respond to all these changes. JCPenney is competing with the discounters by providing more assortment and quality than a discounter, but at a better price than a specialty retailer. JCPenney deals with category killers by eliminating hard goods and focusing on soft goods, such as clothes. JCPenney has had to adapt its retailing model in order to respond to these new competitors. The company's new business emphasis focuses on providing more assortment and quality than a discounter, but at a better price than a specialty retailer.

© PHOTODISC/GETTY IMAGES

Merchandising will undoubtedly continue to evolve as consumer lifestyles and technologies change in the future. In this chapter, we introduce you to the accounting issues unique to merchandisers. We emphasize merchandisers at this point in the text because merchandising is significant in its own right, and because even nonmerchandisers have similar accounting issues to those discussed in this chapter.

Distinguish the activities and financial statements of a service business from those of a merchandise business.

MERCHANDISE OPERATIONS

In prior chapters, we described and illustrated how businesses report their financial condition and changes in financial condition using the cash and accrual bases of accounting. In these prior chapters, we focused on service businesses. In this chapter, we describe and illustrate the accounting for merchandise operations.

How do the operating activities of a service business, such as a consulting firm, law practice, or architectural firm, differ from a merchandising business, such as Home Depot Inc. or Wal-Mart? The differences are best illustrated by focusing on the income statements of the two types of businesses.

The condensed income statement of H&R Block Inc. is shown in Exhibit 1.[1] H&R Block is a service business that primarily offers tax planning and preparation to its customers.

The condensed income statement of Home Depot is shown in Exhibit 2.[2] Home Depot is the world's largest home improvement retailer and the second largest retailer in the United States, based on net sales volume.

Q. Assume that operating income is $45,000, gross profit is $100,000, and the cost of goods sold is $525,000. What are the net sales and the total operating expenses?

A. *Net sales: $625,000 ($100,000 + $525,000) Operating expenses: $55,000 ($100,000 – $45,000)*

The revenue activities of a service business involve providing services to customers. On the income statement for a service business, the revenues from services are reported as revenues or fees earned. The operating expenses incurred in providing services are subtracted from the revenues to arrive at operating income. Any other income or expense is then added or subtracted to arrive at income before taxes. Net income is determined by subtracting income taxes. Exhibit 1 shows that H&R Block earned operating profits of $1,052 (in thousands) based upon revenue of $4,420 (in thousands). Adding other income and subtracting income taxes results in net income of $636 (in thousands).

In contrast, the revenue activities of a merchandising business involve the buying and selling of merchandise. A merchandise business must first purchase merchandise to sell to its customers. The revenue received for merchandise sold to customers less any merchandise returned or any discounts is reported as **net sales**. The related **cost of merchandise sold** is then determined and matched against the net sales. **Gross profit** is determined by subtracting the cost of merchandise sold from net sales. Gross profit gets its name from the fact that it is the profit before deducting operating expenses. Operating expenses are then subtracted in arriving at operating income. Like a service business, other income or expense is then added or subtracted to arrive at income before taxes. Subtracting income taxes yields net income.

Exhibit 1

H&R Block Income Statement

H&R Block Inc.
Condensed Income Statement
For the Year Ending April 30, 2005
(in thousands)

Revenue	$4,420
Operating expenses	3,368
Operating income	$1,052
Other income and (expense)	(34)
Income before taxes	$1,018
Income taxes	382
Net income	$ 636

1 Adapted from H&R Block's 10-K filing with the Securities and Exchange Commission.

2 Adapted from Home Depot's 10-K filing with the Securities and Exchange Commission.

HOW BUSINESSES MAKE MONEY

Under One Roof at JCPenney

Most businesses cannot be all things to all people. Businesses must seek a position in the marketplace to serve a unique customer need. Companies that are unable to do this can be squeezed out of the marketplace. The mall-based department store has been under pressure from both ends of the retail spectrum. At the discount store end of the market, **Wal-Mart** has been a formidable competitor. At the high end, specialty retailers have established a strong presence in identifiable niches, such as electronics and apparel. Over a decade ago, **JCPenney** abandoned its "hard goods," such as electronics and sporting goods, in favor of providing "soft goods" because of the emerging strength of specialty retailers in the hard goods segments. JCPenney is positioning itself against these forces by *"exceeding the fashion, quality, selection, and service components of the discounter, equaling the merchandise intensity of the specialty store, and providing the selection and 'under one roof' shopping convenience of the department store."* JCPenney merchandise emphasis is focused toward customers it terms the "modern spender" and "starting outs." It views these segments as most likely to value its higher-end merchandise offered under the convenience of "one roof."

Exhibit 2

Home Depot Income Statement

Home Depot Inc.
Condensed Income Statement
For the Year Ending January 30, 2005
(in millions)

Net sales	$73,094
Cost of merchandise sold	48,664
Gross profit	$24,430
Operating expenses	16,504
Operating income	$ 7,926
Other income and (expense)	(14)
Income before taxes	$ 7,912
Income taxes	2,911
Net income	$ 5,001

Exhibit 2 shows that Home Depot earned a gross profit of $24,430 million, based upon net sales of $73,094 million. Operating expenses reduce gross profit to an operating income of $7,926 million. Adding other income and subtracting income taxes results in net income of $5,001 million.

In addition to operating and income statement differences, merchandise inventory on hand (not sold) at the end of the accounting period is reported on the balance sheet as **merchandise inventory**. Since merchandise is normally sold within a year, it is reported as a current asset on the balance sheet.

Describe and illustrate the financial statements of a merchandising business.

FINANCIAL STATEMENTS FOR A MERCHANDISING BUSINESS

In this section, we continue the illustration from Chapter 4, illustrating the financial statements for Online Solutions after it becomes a retailer of computer hardware and software. These financial statements are similar to those for a service business.

During 2008, we assume that Janet Moore implemented the second phase of Online Solutions' business plan. Accordingly, Janet notified clients that beginning January 1,

2009, Online Solutions would be terminating its consulting services, and changing its business emphasis to an Internet-based retailer.

Online's business strategy is to focus on offering customized computer systems to individuals and small businesses who are upgrading or purchasing new computer systems. Online's personal service before the sale will include a no-obligation assessment of the customer's needs. By providing tailor-made solutions, personalized service, and follow-up, Janet feels that Online can compete effectively against larger retailers, such as Dell Inc. or Gateway. Initially, Janet plans to grow Online Solutions regionally. If successful, Janet plans to take the company public.

Multiple-Step Income Statement

The 2010 income statement for Online Solutions' second year as an Internet retailer is shown in Exhibit 3.[3] This form of income statement, called a **multiple-step income statement**, contains several sections, subsections, and subtotals.

Exhibit 3

Multiple-Step Income Statement

Online Solutions Income Statement For the Year Ended December 31, 2010			
Revenue from sales:			
Sales		$720,185	
Less: Sales returns and allowances	$ 6,140		
Sales discounts	5,790	11,930	
Net sales			$708,255
Cost of merchandise sold			525,305
Gross profit			$182,950
Operating expenses:			
Selling expenses:			
Sales salaries expense	$56,230		
Advertising expense	10,860		
Depr. expense—store equipment	3,100		
Miscellaneous selling expense	630		
Total selling expenses		$ 70,820	
Administrative expenses:			
Office salaries expense	$21,020		
Rent expense	8,100		
Depr. expense—office equipment	2,490		
Insurance expense	1,910		
Office supplies expense	610		
Misc. administrative expense	760		
Total administrative expenses		34,890	
Total operating expenses			105,710
Income from operations			$ 77,240
Other income and (expense):			
Rent revenue		$ 600	
Interest expense		(2,440)	(1,840)
Income before taxes			$ 75,400
Income taxes			15,000
Net income			$ 60,400

3 We use the Online Solutions income statement for 2010 as a basis for illustration because, as will be shown, it allows us to better illustrate the computation of the cost of merchandise sold.

Net sales for Online Solutions is determined as follows:

Sales		$720,185
Less: Sales returns and allowances	$6,140	
Sales discounts	5,790	11,930
Net sales		$708,255

Sales is the total amount charged customers for merchandise sold, including cash sales and sales on account. Both sales returns and allowances and sales discounts are subtracted in arriving at net sales.

Sales returns and allowances are granted by the seller to customers for damaged or defective merchandise. For example, rather than have a buyer return merchandise, a seller may offer a $500 allowance to the customer as compensation for damaged merchandise. Sales returns and allowances are recorded when the merchandise is returned or when the allowance is granted by the seller.

Q. Assume that sales are $790,000, sales discounts are $35,000, and net sales are $680,000. What are the sales returns and allowances?

A. *$75,000 ($790,000 − $35,000 − $680,000)*

Sales discounts are granted by the seller to customers for early payment of amounts owed. For example, a seller may offer a customer a 2% discount on a sale of $10,000 if the customer pays within 10 days. If the customer pays within the 10-day period, the seller receives cash of $9,800, and the buyer receives a discount of $200 ($10,000 × 2%). Sales discounts are recorded when the customer pays the bill.

Cost of merchandise sold is the cost of the merchandise sold to customers. To illustrate the determination of the cost of merchandise sold, assume that Online Solutions purchased $340,000 of merchandise during 2009. If the inventory at December 31, 2009, the end of the year, is $59,700, the cost of the merchandise sold during 2009 is determined as shown below.

Purchases	$340,000
Less merchandise inventory, December 31, 2009	59,700
Cost of merchandise sold	$280,300

As we discussed in the preceding section, sellers may offer customers sales discounts for early payment of their bills. Such discounts are referred to as **purchases discounts** by the buyer. Purchase discounts reduce the cost of merchandise. A buyer may return merchandise to the seller (a **purchase return**), or the buyer may receive a reduction in the initial price at which the merchandise was purchased (a **purchase allowance**). Like purchase discounts, purchases returns and allowances reduce the cost of merchandise purchased during a period. In addition, transportation costs paid by the buyer for merchandise, referred to as *transportation in*, also increase the cost of merchandise purchased.

Q. Assume that purchases are $480,000, purchases returns and allowances are $25,000, and purchases discounts are $60,000. What are the net purchases?

A. *$395,000 ($480,000 − $25,000 − $60,000)*

To continue the illustration, assume that during 2010 Online Solutions purchased additional merchandise of $521,980. It received credit for purchases returns and allowances of $9,100, took purchases discounts of $2,525, and paid transportation costs of $17,400. The purchases returns and allowances and the purchases discounts are deducted from the total purchases to yield the *net purchases*. The transportation costs are added to the net purchases to yield the *cost of merchandise purchased*, as shown below.

Purchases		$521,980
Less: Purchases returns and allowances	$9,100	
Purchases discounts	2,525	11,625
Net purchases		$510,355
Add transportation in		17,400
Cost of merchandise purchased		$527,755

The ending inventory of Online Solutions on December 31, 2009, $59,700, becomes the beginning inventory for 2010. This beginning inventory is added to the cost of merchandise purchased to yield **merchandise available for sale**. The ending inventory, which is assumed to be $62,150, is then subtracted from the merchandise available for sale to yield the cost of merchandise sold, as shown in Exhibit 4.

Exhibit 4

Cost of Merchandise Sold

Merchandise inventory, January 1, 2010			$ 59,700
Purchases		$521,980	
Less: Purchases returns and allowances	$9,100		
Purchases discounts	2,525	11,625	
Net purchases		$510,355	
Add transportation in		17,400	
Cost of merchandise purchased			527,755
Merchandise available for sale			$587,455
Less merchandise inventory, Dec. 31, 2010			62,150
Cost of merchandise sold			$525,305

The cost of merchandise sold was determined by deducting the merchandise on hand at the end of the period from the merchandise available for sale during the period. The merchandise on hand at the end of the period is determined by taking a physical count of inventory on hand. This method of determining the cost of merchandise sold and the amount of merchandise on hand is called the **periodic inventory method** of accounting for merchandise inventory. This flow of costs in the periodic inventory method is illustrated below.

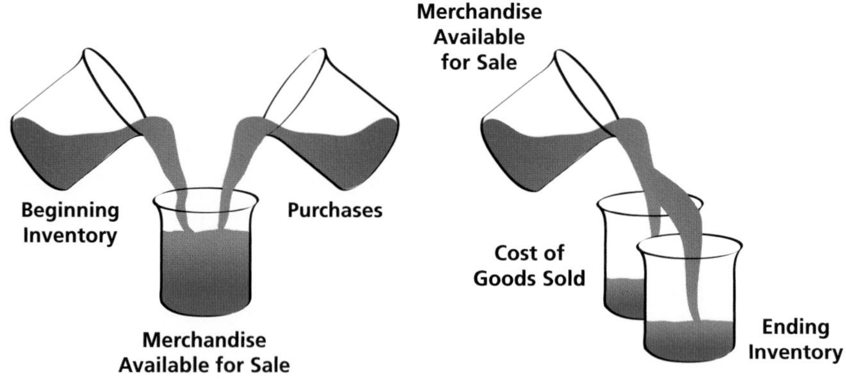

Q. If merchandise available for sale is $1,375,000 and the cost of merchandise sold is $950,000, what is the ending merchandise inventory?

A. *$425,000 ($1,375,000 – $950,000)*

Under the periodic method, the inventory records do not show the amount available for sale or the amount sold during the period. In contrast, under the **perpetual inventory method** of accounting for merchandise inventory, each purchase and sale of merchandise is recorded in the inventory and the cost of merchandise sold accounts. As a result, the amount of merchandise available for sale and the amount sold are continuously (perpetually) disclosed in the inventory records.

Most large retailers and many small merchandising businesses use computerized perpetual inventory systems. Such systems normally use bar codes, such as the one on the back of this textbook. An optical scanner reads the bar code to record merchandise purchased and sold. Merchandise businesses using a perpetual inventory system report the cost of merchandise sold as a single line on the income statement, as shown in Exhibit 3 for Online Solutions. Merchandise businesses using the periodic inventory method report the cost of merchandise sold by using the format shown in Exhibit 4.

Because of its wide use, we will use the perpetual inventory method throughout the remainder of this chapter.

Exhibit 3 shows that Online Solutions reported gross profit of $182,950 in 2010. *Operating income*, sometimes called **income from operations**, is determined by subtracting operating expenses from gross profit. Most merchandising businesses classify operating expenses as either selling expenses or administrative expenses. Expenses that are incurred directly in the selling of merchandise are **selling expenses**. They include such expenses as salespersons' salaries, store supplies used, depreciation of store equipment, and advertising. Expenses incurred in the administration or general operations of the business are **administrative expenses** or *general expenses*. Examples of these expenses are office salaries, depreciation of office equipment, and office supplies used. Credit card expense is also normally classified as an administrative expense. Although selling and administrative expenses may be reported separately, as shown in Exhibit 3, many companies report operating expenses as a single item.

International Perspective
To promote international consistency in financial reporting, the International Accounting Standards Board and the U.S. Financial Accounting Standards Board have joined forces on an accounting convergence project. The goal of the project is to improve consistency in how transactions are accounted for under U.S. GAAP and IAS.

As we will illustrate later in this chapter, operating income is often used in financial analysis to judge the efficiency and profitability of operations. For example, operating income divided by total assets or net sales is often used in comparing merchandise businesses.

Online Solutions' income statement in Exhibit 3 also reports other income and expense. Revenue from sources other than the primary operating activity of a business is classified as **other income**. In a merchandising business, these items include income from interest, rent, and gains resulting from the sale of fixed assets.

Expenses that cannot be traced directly to operations are identified as **other expense**. Interest expense that results from financing activities and losses incurred in the disposal of fixed assets are examples of these items.

Other income and other expense are offset against each other on the income statement, as shown in Exhibit 3. If the total of other income exceeds the total of other expense, the difference is added to income from operations. If the reverse is true, the difference is subtracted from income from operations.

Deducting income taxes from income before taxes yields the net income. As we illustrated in Chapter 4, net income or loss is closed to Retained Earnings at the end of the period.

Single-Step Income Statement

An alternate form of income statement is the **single-step income statement**. As shown in Exhibit 5, the income statement for Online Solutions deducts the total of all expenses *in one step* from the total of all revenues.

Exhibit 5

Single-Step Income Statement

Online Solutions
Income Statement
For the Year Ended December 31, 2010

Revenue:		
Net sales		$708,255
Expenses:		
Cost of merchandise sold	$525,305	
Operating expenses	105,710	
Income taxes	15,000	
Other income and expense (net)	1,840	647,855
Net income		$ 60,400

The single-step form emphasizes total revenues and total expenses as the factors that determine net income. A criticism of the single-step form is that such amounts as gross profit and income from operations are not readily available for analysis.

Retained Earnings Statement

The retained earnings statement for Online Solutions is shown in Exhibit 6. This statement is prepared in the same manner that we described previously for a service business.

Exhibit 6

Retained Earnings Statement

Online Solutions
Retained Earnings Statement
For the Year Ended December 31, 2010

Retained earnings, January 1, 2010		$128,800
Net income for the year	$60,400	
Less dividends	18,000	
Increase in retained earnings		42,400
Retained earnings, December 31, 2010		$171,200

Balance Sheet

As we discussed and illustrated in previous chapters, the balance sheet may be presented in a downward sequence in three sections, beginning with the assets. This form of balance sheet is called the **report form**.[4] The 2010 balance sheet for Online Solutions is shown in Exhibit 7. In this balance sheet, note that merchandise inventory at the end of the period is reported as a current asset and that the current portion of the note payable is $5,000.

Statement of Cash Flows

The statement of cash flows for Online Solutions is shown in Exhibit 8. It indicates that cash increased during 2010 by $11,450. This increase is generated from a positive cash flow from operating activities of $47,120, which is partially offset by negative cash flows from investing and financing activities of $12,670 and $23,000, respectively.

Finally, you should note that the December 31, 2010, cash balance reported on the statement of cash flows agrees with the amount reported for cash on the December 31, 2010, balance sheet shown in Exhibit 7.

Integration of Financial Statements

Exhibit 9 (on page 220) shows the integration of Online Solutions' financial statements. The preparation of the "cash flows from operating activities" section of the statement of cash flows shown in Exhibit 8 is discussed and illustrated in the appendix at the end of this chapter. This discussion includes the reconciliation of net income and net cash flows from operations.

4 The balance sheet may also be presented in an account form, with assets on the left-hand side and the liabilities and stockholders' equity on the right-hand side.

Exhibit 7

Balance Sheet

Online Solutions
Balance Sheet
December 31, 2010

Assets			
Current assets:			
Cash		$ 52,950	
Accounts receivable		76,080	
Merchandise inventory		62,150	
Office supplies		480	
Prepaid insurance		2,650	
Total current assets			$194,310
Property, plant, and equipment:			
Land		$ 20,000	
Store equipment	$27,100		
Less accumulated depreciation	5,700	21,400	
Office equipment	$15,570		
Less accumulated depreciation	4,720	10,850	
Total property, plant, and equipment			52,250
Total assets			$246,560
Liabilities			
Current liabilities:			
Accounts payable		$ 22,420	
Note payable (current portion)		5,000	
Salaries payable		1,140	
Unearned rent		1,800	
Total current liabilities			$ 30,360
Long-term liabilities:			
Note payable (final payment due 2020)			20,000
Total liabilities			$ 50,360
Stockholders' Equity			
Capital stock		$ 25,000	
Retained earnings		171,200	
Total stockholders' equity			196,200
Total liabilities and stockholders' equity			$246,560

Exhibit 8

Statement of Cash Flows for Merchandising Business

Online Solutions
Statement of Cash Flows
For the Year Ended December 31, 2010

Cash flows from operating activities:		
Net cash flows from operating activities		$ 47,120
Cash flows from investing activities:		
Purchase of store equipment	$ (7,100)	
Purchase of office equipment	(5,570)	
Net cash flows used in investing activities		(12,670)
Cash flows from financing activities:		
Payment of note payable	$ (5,000)	
Payment of dividends	(18,000)	
Net cash flows used in financing activities		(23,000)
Net increase in cash		$ 11,450
January 1, 2010, cash balance		41,500
December 31, 2010, cash balance		$ 52,950

Exhibit 9

Integrated Financial Statements for Online Solutions

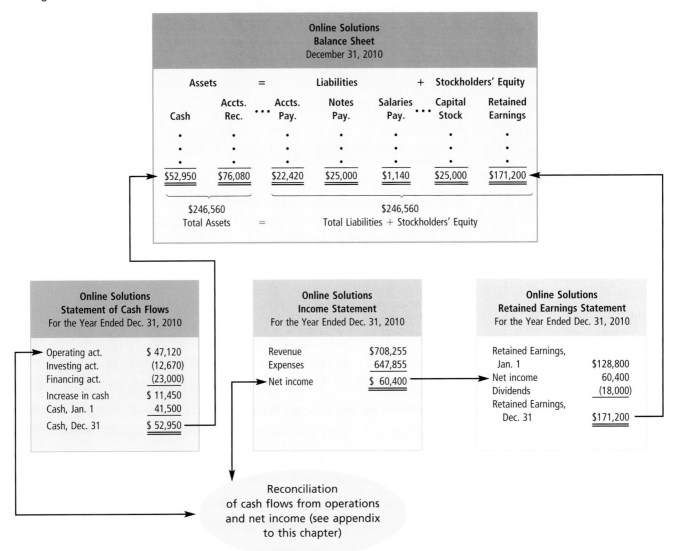

Online Solutions
Balance Sheet
December 31, 2010

Assets			=	Liabilities			+	Stockholders' Equity	
Cash	Accts. Rec.	...		Accts. Pay.	Notes Pay.	Salaries Pay.	...	Capital Stock	Retained Earnings
$52,950	$76,080			$22,420	$25,000	$1,140		$25,000	$171,200
$246,560 Total Assets			=	$246,560 Total Liabilities + Stockholders' Equity					

Online Solutions
Statement of Cash Flows
For the Year Ended Dec. 31, 2010

Operating act.	$ 47,120
Investing act.	(12,670)
Financing act.	(23,000)
Increase in cash	$ 11,450
Cash, Jan. 1	41,500
Cash, Dec. 31	$ 52,950

Online Solutions
Income Statement
For the Year Ended Dec. 31, 2010

Revenue	$708,255
Expenses	647,855
Net income	$ 60,400

Online Solutions
Retained Earnings Statement
For the Year Ended Dec. 31, 2010

Retained Earnings, Jan. 1	$128,800
Net income	60,400
Dividends	(18,000)
Retained Earnings, Dec. 31	$171,200

Reconciliation of cash flows from operations and net income (see appendix to this chapter)

Describe the accounting for the sale of merchandise.

SALES TRANSACTIONS

In the remainder of this chapter, we illustrate transactions that affect the financial statements of a merchandising business. These transactions affect the reporting of net sales, cost of merchandise sold, gross profit, and merchandise inventory.

Sales of merchandise are recorded in a journal and posted to the accounts in a ledger, using the rules of debit and credit that we illustrated in Chapter 4. The only difference between the illustrations in Chapter 4 and those in this chapter is that we are now focusing on sales of merchandise rather than services. Because the operating activities of a merchandise business differ from those of a service business, the chart of accounts will also differ. For example, instead of fees earned, sales of merchandise are recorded in a sales account.

To illustrate, assume that on January 3 Online Solutions sells merchandise costing $1,200 for $1,800, with the customer paying in cash. The entry to record the sale of $1,800 is as follows:

SCF	BS	IS
O↑	A↑ SE↑	R↑

Jan. 3	Cash	1,800	
	Sales		1,800

Under the perpetual inventory system, the cost of merchandise sold and the reduction of merchandise inventory on hand are recorded at the time of sale. In this way, the merchandise inventory account indicates the amount of merchandise on hand at all times. Thus, on January 3, Online Solutions also updates the merchandise inventory account with the following entry:

SCF	BS	IS
—	A↓ SE↓	E↑

Jan. 3	Cost of Merchandise Sold	1,200	
	Merchandise Inventory		1,200

In recent years, a large percentage of retail sales has increasingly been made to customers who use credit cards such as VISA or MasterCard. How do merchandise businesses record sales made with VISA or MasterCard? Such sales are recorded as cash sales. This is because the retailer normally receives payment within a few days of making the sale. Specifically, such sales are normally processed by a clearing-house that contacts the bank that issued the card. The issuing bank then electronically transfers cash directly to the retailer's bank account. Thus, if the customer in the preceding sale had used MasterCard to pay for their purchase, the sale would be recorded exactly as shown above. Any fees charged by the clearing-house or issuing bank are periodically recorded as an expense.

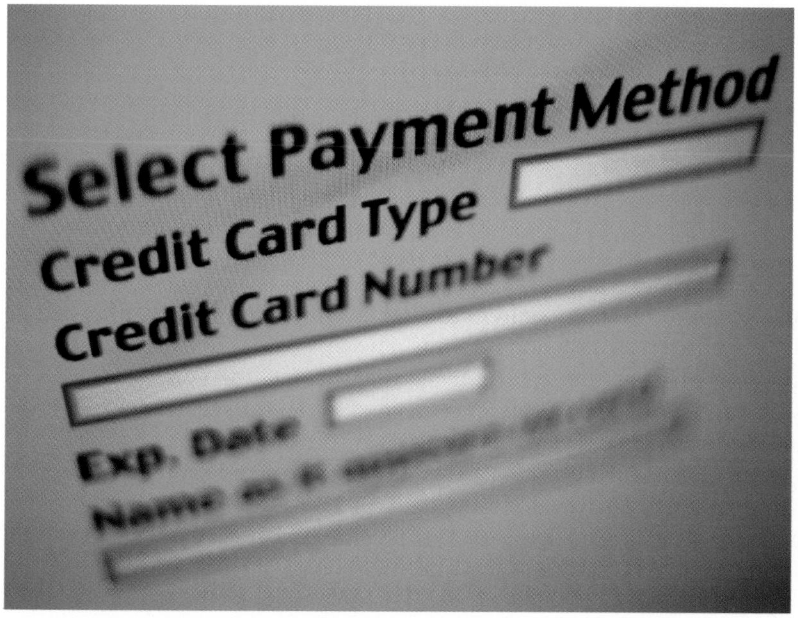

© DON FARRALL/PHOTODISC/GETTY IMAGES

Sales of merchandise on account would be recorded in the same manner as cash sales, except that Accounts Receivable rather than Cash is debited at the time of sale. An individual account for each customer is maintained in a **subsidiary ledger**. The total of the subsidiary ledger is represented in the general ledger by a **controlling account**. In the case of the accounts receivable subsidiary ledger, the accounts receivable account is the controlling account. Likewise, a subsidiary ledger is also maintained for other accounts, such as the merchandise inventory and accounts payable accounts. The relationship between the general ledger, controlling accounts, and subsidiary ledgers is shown in Exhibit 10 for Online Solutions.

Exhibit 10

General Ledger, Controlling Accounts, and Subsidiary Ledgers for Online Solutions

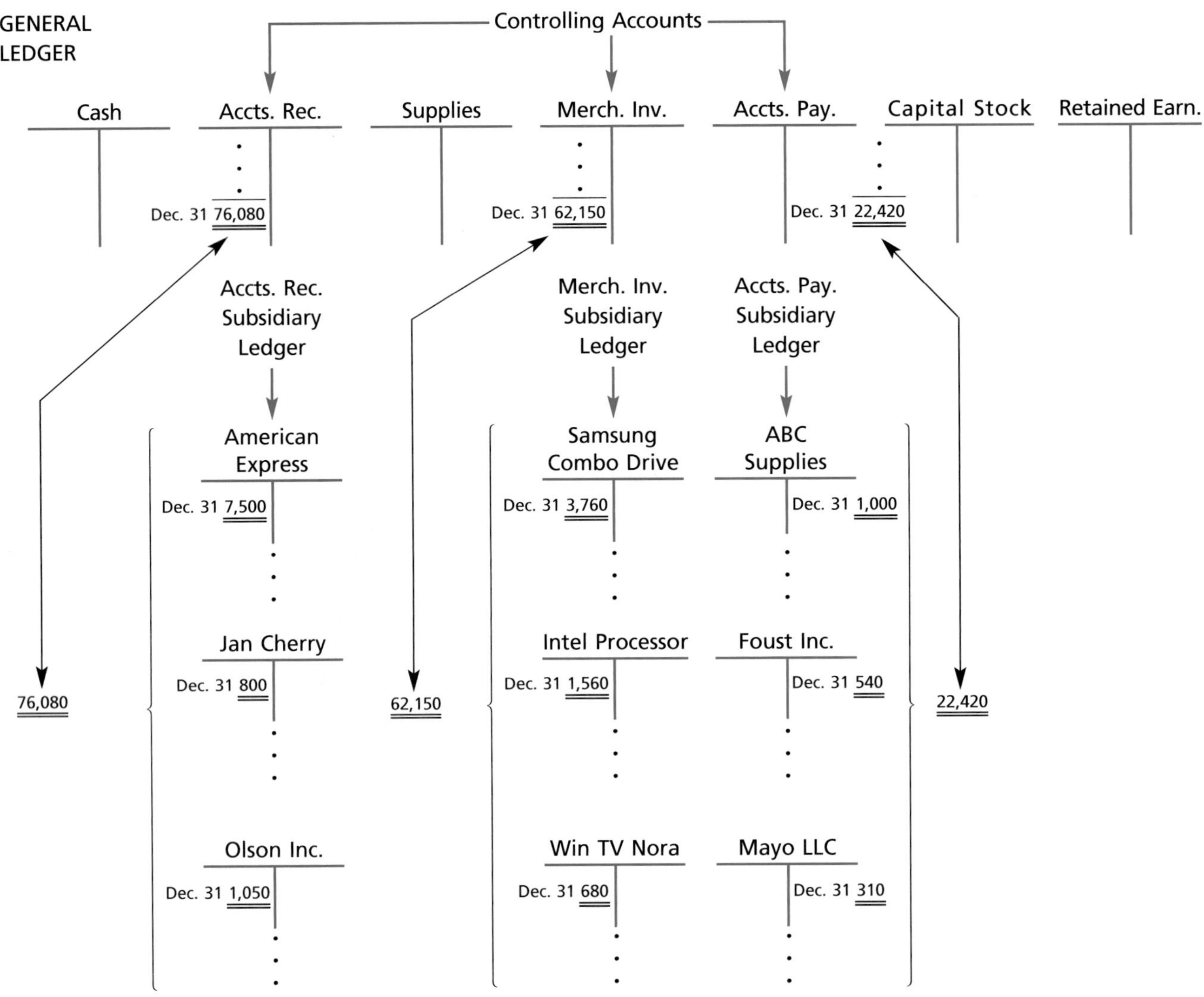

A sale to a customer who uses a credit card that is not issued by a bank, such as **American Express**, is recorded as a sale on account. The seller or a clearing-house must collect the receivable. Upon receiving notice of the sale, the issuing company, such as American Express, periodically remits the amount of sales less a service fee. The service fee is recorded as an expense.

To illustrate, assume that during January Online Solutions sold merchandise costing \$68,000 to American Express customers for \$100,000. At the end of January, Online submitted a bill to American Express and received cash less a 4% service fee on February 15. The entries to record the sales and the receipt of cash are shown at the top of the next page.

SCF	BS	IS
—	A↑ SE↑	R↑
—	A↓ SE↓	E↑
O↑	A↑↓SE↓	E↑

Jan. 31	Accounts Receivable—American Express	100,000	
	Sales		100,000
31	Cost of Merchandise Sold	68,000	
	Merchandise Inventory		68,000
Feb. 15	Cash	96,000	
	Credit Card Expense	4,000	
	Accounts Receivable—American Express		100,000

Sales Discounts

The **credit terms** of a sale on account are normally indicated on the **invoice** or bill that the seller sends to the customer. If payment is required on delivery, the terms are *cash* or *net cash*. Otherwise, the buyer is allowed an amount of time, known as the **credit period**, in which to pay. The credit period usually begins with the date of the sale as shown on the invoice. If payment is due within a stated number of days after the date of the invoice, such as 30 days, the terms are *net 30 days*. These terms may be written as *n/30*. If payment is due by the end of the month in which the sale was made, the terms are written as *n/eom*.

© PHOTODISC COLLECTION/GETTY IMAGES

As a means of encouraging the buyer to pay before the end of the credit period, the seller may offer a discount, called a *sales discount*. For example, a seller may offer a 2% discount if the buyer pays within 10 days of the invoice date. If the buyer does not take the discount, the total amount is due within 30 days. These terms are expressed as *2/10, n/30* and are read as *2% discount if paid within 10 days, net amount due within 30 days*.

Sales discounts reduce sales and, therefore, the sales account could be debited. However, managers may want to know the amount of the sales discounts for a period in deciding whether to change credit terms. For this reason, the seller records the sales discounts in a separate account. The sales discounts account is a *contra* (or *offsetting*) account to Sales.

To illustrate, assume that Online Solutions receives cash within the discount period from a $1,500 credit sale to Omega Technologies. The sale of merchandise costing $850 was made on January 12, with the terms 2/10, n/30. The initial sale and the receipt of the cash are recorded as follows:

SCF	BS	IS
—	A↑ SE↑	R↑
—	A↓SE↓	E↑
O↑	A↑↓SE↓	R↓

Jan. 12	Accounts Receivable—Omega Technologies	1,500	
	Sales		1,500
12	Cost of Merchandise Sold	850	
	Merchandise Inventory		850
22	Cash	1,470	
	Sales Discounts	30	
	Accounts Receivable—Omega Technologies		1,500

Sales Returns and Allowances

Merchandise that has been sold may be returned to the seller (*sales return*). In addition, because of defects or for other reasons, the seller may reduce the initial price at which the goods were sold (*sales allowance*). If the return or allowance is for a sale on account,

INTEGRITY, OBJECTIVITY, AND ETHICS IN BUSINESS

The Case of the Fraudulent Price Tags

One of the challenges for a retailer is policing its sales return policy. Customers can unethically or illegally abuse such policies in many ways. For example, someone could attach **JCPenney** store price tags to cheaper merchandise bought or obtained elsewhere. They could then return the cheaper goods and receive the substantially higher refund amount. In one such case for another retailer, company security officials discovered the fraud and had a couple arrested after they had allegedly bilked the company for over $1 million.

Q. $10,000 of merchandise is purchased 2/10, n/30; $4,500 is returned; and the invoice is paid within the discount period. What was the amount paid?

A. *$5,390 [$5,500 – ($5,500 × 2%)]*

the seller normally issues a **credit memorandum**. This memorandum is sent to the customer and indicates the amount the seller is crediting the customer's account receivable for the return or allowance.

Sales returns and allowances reduce sales revenue. They also result in additional shipping and other expenses. Since managers often want to know the amount of returns and allowances for a period, the seller records sales returns and allowances in a separate sales returns and allowances account. Sales Returns and Allowances may be viewed as a *contra* (or *offsetting*) account to Sales.

To illustrate, assume that on January 13 Online Solutions issued a $2,000 credit memorandum to Krier Company for merchandise that was returned. The merchandise was sold on account and the cost of the merchandise sold was $1,200. The entries to record the issuance of the credit memorandum and the receipt of the returned merchandise are as follows:

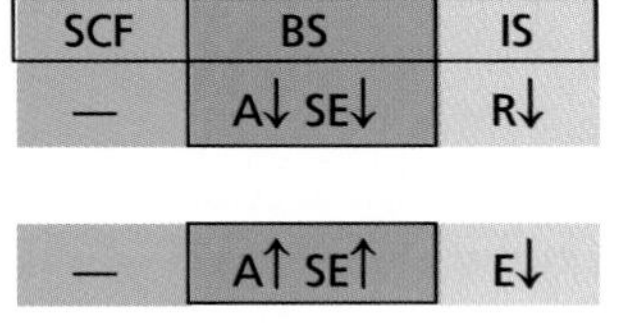

Jan.	13	Sales Returns and Allowances	2,000	
		Accounts Receivable—Krier Company		2,000
	13	Merchandise Inventory	1,200	
		Cost of Merchandise Sold		1,200

Using a perpetual inventory system, the second entry is necessary so that the merchandise inventory account is up to date and reflects the actual merchandise on hand.

What if the customer pays for the merchandise and later returns the merchandise? In this case, the seller issues a credit memorandum, and the credit may be applied against other accounts receivable owed by the customer, or cash may be refunded. If cash is refunded, the seller credits Cash, rather than Accounts Receivable, for the amount of the refund.

Describe the accounting for the purchase of merchandise.

PURCHASE TRANSACTIONS

As we indicated earlier in this chapter, most large retailers and many small merchandising businesses use computerized perpetual inventory systems. Under the perpetual inventory system, cash purchases of merchandise are recorded as follows:

SCF	BS	IS
O↓	A↑↓	—

Jan.	3	Merchandise Inventory	2,500	
		Cash		2,500

Purchases of merchandise on account are recorded as follows:

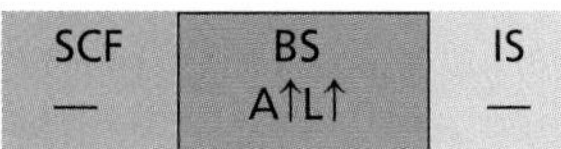

Jan. 6	Merchandise Inventory	1,800	
	Accounts Payable—Smith Corporation		1,800

Purchase Discounts

As we mentioned in our discussion of sales transactions, a seller may offer the buyer credit terms that include a discount for early payment. The buyer refers to such discounts as *purchases discounts*, which reduce the cost of merchandise purchased. Under the perpetual inventory system, the buyer initially debits the merchandise inventory account for the amount of the invoice. When paying the invoice, the buyer credits the merchandise inventory account for the amount of the discount. In this way, the merchandise inventory shows the *net* cost to the buyer.

To illustrate, assume that Online Solutions purchased the $1,800 merchandise from Smith Corporation in the preceding entry on January 6 under the terms 1/15, n/30. The entry to record the payment within the discount period is as follows:

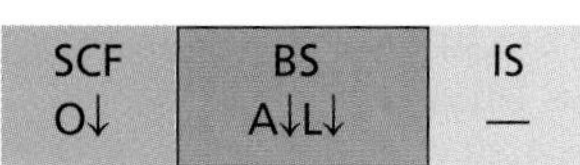

Jan. 21	Accounts Payable—Smith Corporation	1,800	
	Merchandise Inventory		18
	Cash		1,782

If Online Solutions does not pay within the discount period, the entry to record the payment is as follows:

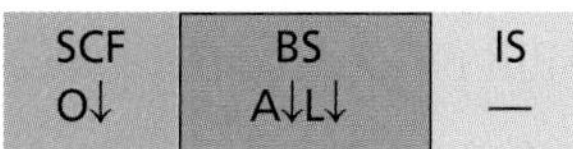

Feb. 5	Accounts Payable—Smith Corporation	1,800	
	Cash		1,800

Purchases Returns and Allowances

When merchandise is returned (*purchase return*) or a price adjustment is requested (*purchase allowance*), the buyer (debtor) usually sends the seller a letter or a debit memorandum. A **debit memorandum** informs the seller of the amount the buyer proposes to *debit* to the account payable due the seller. It also states the reasons for the return or the request for a price reduction.

The buyer may use a copy of the debit memorandum as the basis for recording the return or allowance or wait for approval from the seller (creditor). To illustrate, assume that on January 22 Online Solutions returns $5,000 of merchandise purchased from Quantum Inc. and issues an accompanying debit memorandum. The return is recorded as follows:

SCF —
BS A↓L↓
IS —

Jan. 22	Accounts Payable—Quantum Inc.	5,000	
	Merchandise Inventory		5,000

When a buyer returns merchandise or has been granted an allowance prior to paying the invoice, the amount of the debit memorandum is deducted from the invoice amount. The amount is deducted before any purchase discount is computed. For example, assume that the merchandise returned to Quantum on January 22 was only part of an overall purchase of $9,000 with terms 2/10, n/30. If Online pays within the discount period, it would deduct a discount of $80, or ($9,000 − $5,000) × 2%.

TRANSPORTATION COSTS AND SALES TAXES

Describe the accounting for transportation costs and sales taxes.

Merchandise businesses incur transportation costs in selling and purchasing merchandise. In addition, a retailer must also collect sales taxes in most states. In this section, we briefly discuss the unique aspects of accounting for transportation costs and sales taxes.

Transportation Costs

Does the buyer or the seller pay transportation costs? It depends upon when the ownership (title) of the merchandise passes from the seller to the buyer.[5] The terms of a sale should indicate when the ownership (title) of the merchandise passes to the buyer. The ownership of the merchandise may pass to the buyer when the seller delivers the merchandise to the transportation company or freight carrier. For example, DaimlerChrysler records the sale and the transfer of ownership of its vehicles to dealers when the vehicles are shipped. In this case, the terms are said to be **FOB (free on board) shipping point**. This term means that DaimlerChrysler is responsible for the transportation charges to the shipping point, which is where the shipment originates. The dealer then pays the transportation costs to the final destination. Such costs are part of the dealer's total cost of purchasing inventory and should be added to the cost of the inventory by debiting Merchandise Inventory.

To illustrate, assume that on January 19, Online Solutions buys merchandise from Data Max on account, $2,900, terms FOB shipping point, and prepays the transportation cost of $150. Online records these two transactions as follows:

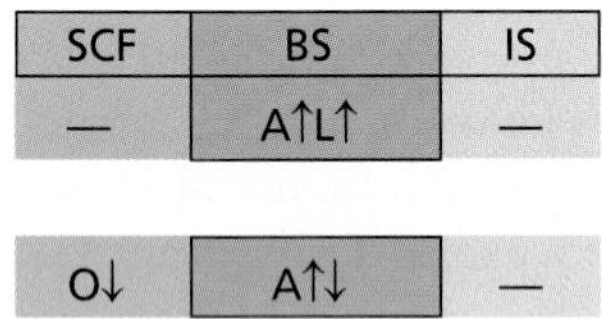

SCF	BS	IS
—	A↑L↑	—
O↓	A↑↓	—

Jan. 19	Merchandise Inventory	2,900	
	Accounts Payable—Data Max		2,900
19	Merchandise Inventory	150	
	Cash		150

The ownership of the merchandise may pass to the buyer when the buyer receives the merchandise. In this case, the terms are said to be **FOB (free on board) destination**. This term means that the seller delivers the merchandise to the buyer's final destination, free of transportation charges to the buyer. The seller thus pays the transportation costs to the final destination. The seller debits Transportation Out or Delivery Expense, which is reported on the seller's income statement as an expense.

5 The transfer of ownership (title) also determines whether the buyer or seller must pay other costs, such as the cost of insurance while the merchandise is in transit.

To illustrate, assume that on January 24, Online Solutions sells merchandise to Miller Company on account, $4,700, terms FOB destination. The cost of the merchandise sold is $2,750, and Online pays the transportation cost of $350. Online records the sale, the cost of the sale, and the transportation cost as shown below.

SCF	BS	IS
—	A↑SE↑	R↑
—	A↓SE↓	E↑
O↓	A↓SE↓	E↑

Jan. 24	Accounts Receivable—Miller Company	4,700	
	Sales		4,700
24	Cost of Merchandise Sold	2,750	
	Merchandise Inventory		2,750
24	Transportation Out	350	
	Cash		350

Sometimes FOB shipping point and FOB destination are expressed in terms of the location at which the title to the merchandise passes to the buyer. For example, if Toyota Motor Co.'s assembly plant in Osaka, Japan, sells automobiles to a dealer in Chicago, FOB shipping point could be expressed as FOB Osaka. Likewise, FOB destination could be expressed as FOB Chicago.

Shipping terms, the passage of title, and whether the buyer or seller pays the transportation costs are summarized in Exhibit 11.

As a convenience to the buyer, the seller may prepay the transportation costs, even though the terms are FOB shipping point. The seller will then add the transportation costs to the invoice. The buyer will debit Merchandise Inventory for the total amount of the invoice, including the transportation costs.

To illustrate, assume that on January 14, Online Solutions sells merchandise to Golden Company on account, $8,000, terms 2/10, n/30, FOB shipping point. Online

Exhibit 11

Transportation Terms

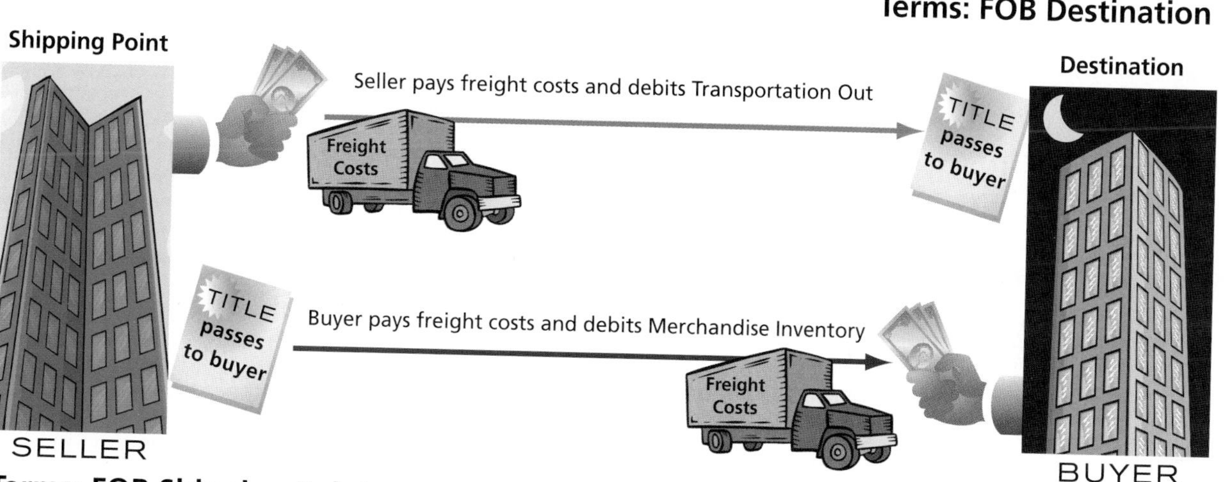

pays the transportation cost of $500 and adds it to the invoice. The cost of the merchandise sold is $4,800. Online records these transactions as follows:

SCF	BS	IS
—	A↑SE↑	R↑
—	A↓SE↓	E↑
O↓	A↑↓	—

Jan. 14	Accounts Receivable—Golden Company	8,000	
	Sales		8,000
14	Cost of Merchandise Sold	4,800	
	Merchandise Inventory		4,800
14	Accounts Receivable—Golden Company	500	
	Cash		500

Q. $8,000 of merchandise is purchased 1/15, n/30, FOB shipping point. The seller pays $500 shipping charges as an accommodation. If paid within the discount period, how much will the buyer remit?

A. *$8,420 [$8,000 − ($8,000 × 1%) + $500]*

When the seller prepays transportation costs for the buyer, any sales discount applies only to the amount of the merchandise sale. For example, if Golden Company pays within the discount period, it would remit cash of $8,340 [$8,000 − ($8,000 × 2%) + $500].

Sales Taxes

Almost all states and many other taxing units levy a tax on sales of merchandise.[6] The liability for the sales tax is incurred when the sale is made.

At the time of a cash sale, the seller collects the sales tax. When a sale is made on account, the seller charges the tax to the buyer by debiting Accounts Receivable. The seller credits the sales account for the amount of the sale and credits the tax to Sales Taxes Payable. Normally on a regular basis, the seller pays the amount of the sales tax collected to the taxing unit. The seller records such a payment by debiting Sales Taxes Payable and crediting Cash.

HOW BUSINESSES MAKE MONEY

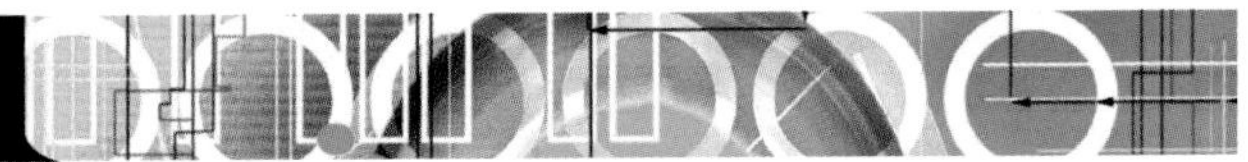

The Cost of Employee Theft

A recent survey reported that the 24 largest retail store chains, including **JCPenney**, have lost over $2 billion to shoplifting and employee theft. Of this amount, only 4.6% of the losses resulted in any recovery. The stores apprehended over 370,000 shoplifters and 35,500 dishonest employees during 2003. Approximately one out of every 28 employees was apprehended for theft from his or her employer. Each dishonest employee stole approximately 4.8 times the amount stolen by shoplifters ($660 vs. $137).

Source: Jack L. Hayes International, *Sixteenth Annual Retail Theft Survey*, 2004.

Illustrate the dual nature of merchandising transactions.

DUAL NATURE OF MERCHANDISE TRANSACTIONS

Each merchandising transaction affects a buyer and a seller. In the illustration on the next page, we show how the same transactions would be recorded by both the seller and the buyer. In this example, the seller is Scully Company and the buyer is Burton Co.

6 Businesses that purchase merchandise for resale to others are normally exempt from paying sales taxes on their purchases. Only final buyers of merchandise normally pay sales taxes.

Transaction	Scully Company (Seller)			Burton Co. (Buyer)		
July 1. Scully Company sold merchandise on account to Burton Co., $7,500, terms FOB shipping point, n/45. The cost of the merchandise sold was $4,500.	Accounts Receivable—Burton Co.	7,500		Merchandise Inventory	7,500	
	Sales		7,500	Accounts Payable—Scully Co.		7,500
	Cost of Merchandise Sold	4,500				
	Merchandise Inventory		4,500			
July 2. Burton Co. paid transportation charges of $150 on July 1 purchase from Scully Company.	No entry.			Merchandise Inventory	150	
				Cash		150
July 5. Scully Company sold merchandise on account to Burton Co., $5,000, terms FOB destination, n/30. The cost of the merchandise sold was $3,500.	Accounts Receivable—Burton Co.	5,000		Merchandise Inventory	5,000	
	Sales		5,000	Accounts Payable—Scully Co.		5,000
	Cost of Merchandise Sold	3,500				
	Merchandise Inventory		3,500			
July 7. Scully Company paid transportation costs of $250 for delivery of merchandise sold to Burton Co. on July 5.	Transportation Out	250		No entry.		
	Cash		250			
July 13. Scully Company issued Burton Co. a credit memorandum for merchandise returned, $1,000. The merchandise had been purchased by Burton Co. on account on July 5. The cost of the merchandise returned was $700.	Sales Returns & Allowances	1,000		Accounts Payable—Scully Co.	1,000	
	Accounts Receivable—Burton Co.		1,000	Merchandise Inventory		1,000
	Merchandise Inventory	700				
	Cost of Merchandise Sold		700			
July 15. Scully Company received payment from Burton Co. for purchase of July 5.	Cash	4,000		Accounts Payable—Scully Co.	4,000	
	Accounts Receivable—Burton Co.		4,000	Cash		4,000
July 18. Scully Company sold merchandise on account to Burton Co., $12,000, terms FOB shipping point, 2/10, n/eom. Scully Company prepaid transportation costs of $500, which were added to the invoice. The cost of the merchandise sold was $7,200.	Accounts Receivable—Burton Co.	12,000		Merchandise Inventory	12,500	
	Sales		12,000	Accounts Payable—Scully Co.		12,500
	Accounts Receivable—Burton Co.	500				
	Cash		500			
	Cost of Merchandise Sold	7,200				
	Merchandise Inventory		7,200			
July 28. Scully Company received payment from Burton Co. for purchase of July 18, less discount (2% × $12,000).	Cash	12,260		Accounts Payable—Scully Co.	12,500	
	Sales Discounts	240		Merchandise Inventory		240
	Accounts Receivable—Burton Co.		12,500	Cash		12,260

MERCHANDISE SHRINKAGE

Describe the accounting for merchandise shrinkage.

Under the perpetual inventory system, a separate merchandise inventory account is maintained in the ledger. During the accounting period, this account shows the amount of merchandise for sale at any time. However, merchandising businesses may experience some loss of inventory due to shoplifting, employee theft, or errors in recording or counting inventory. As a result, the **physical inventory** taken at the end of the accounting period may differ from the amount of inventory shown in the inventory records. Normally, the amount of merchandise for sale, as indicated by the balance of the merchandise inventory account, is larger than the total amount of merchandise counted during the physical inventory. For this reason, the difference is often called **inventory shrinkage** or *inventory shortage*. One recent study estimated that inventory shrinkage exceeds 1.7% of annual sales or $32 billion annually in the United States.[7]

To illustrate, Online Solutions' inventory records, called the **book inventory**, indicate that $63,950 of merchandise should be available for sale on December 31, 2010. The physical inventory taken on December 31, 2010, however, indicates that only $62,150 of merchandise is actually available for sale. The inventory shrinkage for the year ending December 31, 2010, is $1,800, as shown below.

December 31, 2010, unadjusted book inventory	$63,950
December 31, 2010, physical inventory	62,150
Inventory shrinkage	$ 1,800

The adjusting entry to record the shrinkage is as follows:

SCF	BS	IS
—	A↓SE↓	E↑

Dec. 31	Cost of Merchandise Sold	1,800	
	Merchandise Inventory		1,800

After this entry has been recorded, the adjusted Merchandise Inventory (book inventory) in the accounting records agrees with the actual physical inventory at the end of the period. Since no system of procedures and safeguards can totally eliminate it, inventory shrinkage is often considered a normal cost of operations. If the amount of the shrinkage is abnormally large, it may be disclosed separately on the income statement. In such cases, the shrinkage may be recorded in a separate account, such as Loss from Merchandise Inventory Shrinkage.

7 Richard C. Holling, *National Retail Security Survey*, 2003.

Describe and illustrate the effects of inventory misstatements on the financial statements.

EFFECTS OF INVENTORY MISSTATEMENTS ON THE FINANCIAL STATEMENTS

Any error in the physical inventory count at the end of the accounting period affects the income statement and balance sheet. This is because the physical inventory count is the basis for determining the amount of inventory shrinkage. As we illustrated in the preceding section, the adjusting entry for inventory shrinkage affects the cost of merchandise sold and merchandise inventory. Thus, if the physical inventory is misstated, then the amount of inventory shrinkage is misstated and the cost of merchandise sold will be misstated after the inventory shrinkage adjustment is recorded. Because net income is closed to Retained Earnings at the end of the accounting period, retained earnings and total assets are misstated. This misstatement of total assets, current assets, and merchandise inventory equals the misstatement of stockholders' equity. These effects are shown in Exhibit 12.

Exhibit 12

Effects of Inventory Misstatements

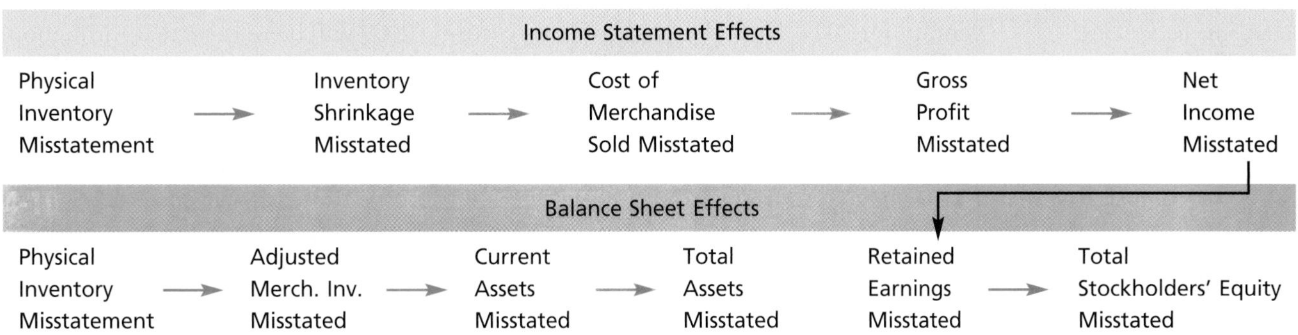

To illustrate, assume that in taking the physical inventory on December 31, 2008, Sapra Company incorrectly counted its physical inventory as $115,000 instead of $125,000. Because the ending physical inventory is understated, the inventory shrinkage and the cost of merchandise sold will be overstated by $10,000, as shown below.

	Amount of Misstatement Overstated (Understated)
December 31, 2008, unadjusted book inventory	Correct
Less December 31, 2008, physical inventory	$(10,000)
Inventory shrinkage (cost of merchandise sold)	$ 10,000

Recall from the preceding section that the amount of inventory shrinkage is recorded by adjusting the cost of merchandise sold. Thus, an overstatement of the inventory shrinkage overstates the cost of merchandise sold. Because the cost of merchandise sold is overstated, gross profit and net income for 2008 will be understated by $10,000. Since net income is closed to Retained Earnings at the end of 2008, the total stockholders' equity on the December 31, 2008, balance sheet will also be understated by $10,000.

As we discussed, the ending physical inventory determines the ending (adjusted) merchandise inventory reported on the balance sheet. Thus, on the December 31, 2008, balance sheet, merchandise inventory, current assets, and total assets are understated by $10,000 ($125,000 − $115,000).

The effects of the misstatement on Sapra Company's 2008 financial statements are summarized below.

2008 Financial Statements	**Amount of Misstatement Overstated (Understated)**
Balance sheet as of December 31, 2008:	
Merchandise inventory	$(10,000)
Current assets	(10,000)
Total assets	(10,000)
Total stockholders' equity (retained earnings)	(10,000)
Income statement for year ended December 31, 2008:	
Cost of merchandise sold	$ 10,000
Gross profit	(10,000)
Net income	(10,000)

Q. If the ending physical inventory is understated by $6,000, what is the effect on total assets, retained earnings, the cost of merchandise sold, and gross profit?

A. Total assets: understated $6,000; Retained earnings: understated $6,000; Cost of merchandise sold: overstated $6,000; Gross profit: understated $6,000.

If the $10,000 understatement of merchandise inventory at the end of 2008 is not detected, the misstatement will also affect the 2009 financial statements. This is because the merchandise inventory at the end of 2008 becomes the beginning merchandise inventory for 2009. Thus, the book inventory during 2009 will be understated throughout the year, and as a result, the unadjusted book inventory on December 31, 2009, will be understated by $10,000. Assuming that the physical inventory count at the end of 2009 is correct, the merchandise shrinkage will be understated by $10,000, as shown below.

	Amount of Misstatement Overstated (Understated)
December 31, 2009, unadjusted book inventory	$ (10,000)
Less December 31, 2009, physical inventory	Correct
Inventory shrinkage (cost of merchandise sold)	$(10,000)

Since inventory shrinkage is understated by $10,000, the cost of merchandise sold will be understated and gross profit will be overstated by $10,000 for 2009. Because the December 31, 2009, physical inventory is correct and the accounting records are adjusted to the physical count, the adjusted balance of merchandise inventory will be correct on the December 31, 2009, balance sheet. Likewise, the 2009 overstatement of net income offsets the 2008 understatement of net income, with the result that the December 31, 2009, stockholders' equity (retained earnings) is correct. Thus, the effects of inventory misstatements if not detected reverse themselves in the following period, and the balance sheet at the end of the second period will be correct, as shown below.

2009 Financial Statements	**Amount of Misstatement Overstated (Understated)**
Balance sheet as of December 31, 2009:	
Merchandise inventory	Correct
Current assets	Correct
Total assets	Correct
Total stockholders' equity (retained earnings)	Correct
Income statement for year ended December 31, 2009:	
Cost of merchandise sold	$(10,000)
Gross profit	10,000
Net income	10,000

In the examples of inventory misstatements, we assumed that an error occurred in the physical inventory count. This could occur because the quantities of inventory were miscounted or summarized (added) incorrectly. Other types of errors that could misstate the inventory could include using incorrect costs or including items not owned by the business. For example, merchandise businesses often carry items on consignment from other retailers. Items on **consignment** are owned by another retailer, called a **consignor**. The retailer carrying the item is a **consignee**. The consignee normally earns a commission or fee when the consigned goods are sold. Since consigned merchandise is normally displayed along with the consignee's own merchandise, consigned merchandise on hand at the end of the year may be incorrectly included in the consignee's physical inventory. This would overstate the ending physical inventory and misstate the financial statements. Likewise, merchandise out on consignment might be overlooked in counting the consignor's inventory, and thus understate the consignor's physical inventory.

Inventory misstatements may also arise for merchandise in transit at year-end. For example, merchandise may be ordered FOB shipping point near the end of the year. In such cases, it is likely that the merchandise is in transit at year-end. In determining the ending physical inventory it would be easy to overlook this merchandise in transit, since it is not on hand. The result would be that the physical inventory is understated. Similarly, merchandise sold FOB destination could be in transit at year-end. Even though the merchandise is not on hand, it is still owned by the seller and should be included in the seller's ending physical inventory.

Describe and illustrate the use of gross profit and operating income in analyzing a company's operations.

GROSS PROFIT AND OPERATING PROFIT ANALYSIS

Gross profit and operating income are two important profitability measures analysts use in assessing the efficiency and effectiveness of a merchandiser's operations. In this section, we use these measures to assess JCPenney's operating performance for the past several years against Saks Incorporated, which operates several major department stores.

Like many financial statement measures, sometimes referred to as performance metrics, gross profit and operating income are normally compared to competitors and analyzed over time as a percent rather than as dollar amounts.

Gross profit and operating profit as a percent of net sales for JCPenney are shown in Exhibit 13. The data (in millions), shown for three recent years, are taken from the Securities and Exchange Commission annual filings (Form 10-K). In addition, similar data (in millions) are shown for Saks for comparison in 2004.

As you can see in Exhibit 13, the gross profit as a percent of sales for JCPenney has gradually improved over the three-year period, to reach its peak in fiscal year 2004. Likewise, the operating income to sales has also improved in the three-year period. The operating income to sales ratio in 2004 is more than twice the ratio in 2002. In addition, JCPenney appears to have outperformed Saks Incorporated in 2004. JCPenney's gross profit and operating profit as a percent of sales in 2004 exceed the equivalent ratios for Saks, with the operating income to sales ratio a significant 2.5 percentage points above Saks (5.5%−3%). Obviously, JCPenney made significant improvements from 2002 to 2004. Management credits the improvement to compelling products, a more appealing and attractive shopping environment, and improved information technology that supports store operations.

Exhibit 13

Operating Ratios—JCPenney and Saks Incorporated

	JCPenney			Saks Incorporated
Fiscal Years' Ending	**2004**	**2003**	**2002**	**2004**
Net sales	$18,424	$17,786	$17,633	$6,437
Cost of merchandise sold	11,285	11,166	11,299	3,999
Gross profit	$ 7,139	$ 6,620	$ 6,334	$2,438
Operating expense	6,119	6,074	5,919	2,243
Operating income	$ 1,020	$ 546	$ 415	$ 195
Gross profit as a percent of net sales	38.7%	37.2%	35.9%	37.9%
Operating income as a percent of net sales	5.5%	3.1%	2.4%	3.0%

APPENDIX

Statement of Cash Flows: The Indirect Method

Online Solutions' statement of cash flows for the year ended December 31, 2010, is shown in Exhibit 8. The operating activities section is shown in summary form with net cash flows from operating activities of $47,120. In this appendix, we illustrate how to prepare the operating activities section of the statement of cash flows using the **indirect method**. This method is used by over 90% of publicly held companies.

The use of the indirect method only affects net cash flows from operating activities. The other method of preparing the net cash flows from operating activities section is called the **direct method**. The direct method analyzes each transaction and its effect on cash flows.[8] In contrast, the indirect method analyzes only the changes in accounts. However, regardless of whether the direct or indirect method is used, the net cash flows from operating activities is the same. In other words, use of the direct or indirect method affects the method of calculating and reporting cash flows from operating activities but not the amount of net cash flows from operating activities.

A major reason that the indirect method is so popular is that it is normally less costly to prepare. However, regardless of whether the indirect or direct method is used, the reporting of net cash flows from investing and financing activities is not affected.

The indirect method reconciles net income with net cash flows from operating activities. Net income is adjusted for the effects of accruals and deferrals that affected the net income but did not result in the receipt or payment of cash. The resulting amount is the net cash flows from operating activities.

The indirect method converts net income determined under the accrual basis of accounting to what it would have been under the cash basis of accounting. In other words, net cash flows from operating activities is equivalent to net income using the cash basis of accounting.

To illustrate, assume that accounts receivable increases during the period by $10,000. This increase is included in the period's revenue and thus increases net income. However, cash was not collected. Thus, an increase in accounts receivable must be deducted from net income under the indirect method. Likewise, depreciation expense is deducted in arriving at net income, but does not involve any cash payments. Therefore, depreciation expense is added to net income under the indirect method.

---

8 We used the direct method to prepare the statement of cash flows in Chapters 2 and 3 and in the appendix to Chapter 4.

The typical adjustments to convert net income to net cash flows from operating activities, using the indirect method, are shown in Exhibit 14.

Exhibit 14

Indirect Method Adjustments

Net income			$XXX
Add:	Depreciation	$XXX	
	Decreases in current assets (accounts receivable, inventories, prepaid expenses)	XXX	
	Increases in current liabilities (accounts payable, notes payable, accrued expenses)	XXX	XXX
Deduct:	Increases in current assets (accounts receivable, inventories, prepaid expenses)	$XXX	
	Decreases in current liabilities (accounts payable, notes payable, accrued expenses)	XXX	XXX
Net cash flows from operating activities			$XXX

You should note that, except for depreciation, the adjustments in Exhibit 14 are for changes in the current assets and current liabilities. This is because changes in the current assets and current liabilities are related to operations and thus net income. For example, changes in inventories are related to sales, while changes in accounts payable are related to expenses.

Cash Flows from Operating Activities

The statement of cash flows shown in Exhibit 8 for Online Solutions was prepared using the indirect method. To prepare the operating activities section, we need to determine depreciation and the changes in the current assets and the liabilities during the year. This information is included in Exhibit 15, which shows the comparative balance sheets for Online Solutions as of December 31, 2010 and 2009, and related changes.

Based on Exhibit 15, the net cash flows from operating activities is shown below.

Net income			$ 60,400
Add:	Depreciation expense—store equipment	$ 3,100	
	Depreciation expense—office equipment	2,490	
	Decrease in office supplies	120	
	Decrease in prepaid insurance	350	
	Increase in accounts payable	8,150	14,210
Deduct:			
	Increase in accounts receivable	$(24,080)	
	Increase in merchandise inventory	(2,450)	
	Decrease in salaries payable	(360)	
	Decrease in unearned rent	(600)	(27,490)
Net cash flows from operating activities			$ 47,120

The depreciation expense of $3,100 for store equipment is determined from the increase in the accumulated depreciation for store equipment. Likewise, the depreciation expense of $2,490 for office equipment is determined from the increase in the accumulated depreciation for office equipment. The changes in the current assets and current liabilities are also taken from Exhibit 15.

Cash Flows Used for Investing Activities

The cash flows for investing activities section can also be prepared by analyzing the changes in the accounts shown in Exhibit 15. For Online Solutions, the cash flows used for investing activities is composed of two items. First, additional store equipment of $7,100 was purchased, as shown by the increase in the store equipment. Likewise,

Exhibit 15

Online Solutions' Comparative Balance Sheets

Online Solutions
Balance sheets

	December 31,		Changes
	2010	2009	Increase (Decrease)
Assets			
Current assets:			
Cash	$ 52,950	$ 41,500	$11,450
Accounts receivable	76,080	52,000	24,080
Merchandise inventory	62,150	59,700	2,450
Office supplies	480	600	(120)
Prepaid insurance	2,650	3,000	(350)
Total current assets	$194,310	$156,800	$37,510
Property, plant, and equipment:			
Land	$ 20,000	$ 20,000	$ 0
Store equipment	27,100	20,000	7,100
Accumulated depreciation—store equipment	(5,700)	(2,600)	(3,100)
Office equipment	15,570	10,000	5,570
Accumulated depreciation—office equipment	(4,720)	(2,230)	(2,490)
Total property, plant, and equipment	$ 52,250	$ 45,170	$ 7,080
Total assets	$246,560	$201,970	$44,590
Liabilities			
Current liabilities:			
Accounts payable	$ 22,420	$ 14,270	$ 8,150
Notes payable (current portion)	5,000	5,000	0
Salaries payable	1,140	1,500	(360)
Unearned rent	1,800	2,400	(600)
Total current liabilities	$ 30,360	$ 23,170	$ 7,190
Long-term liabilities:			
Notes payable (final payment due 2020)	20,000	25,000	(5,000)
Total liabilities	$ 50,360	$ 48,170	$ 2,190
Stockholders' Equity			
Capital stock	$ 25,000	$ 25,000	$ 0
Retained earnings	171,200	128,800	42,400
Total stockholders' equity	$196,200	$153,800	$42,400
Total liabilities and stockholders' equity	$246,560	$201,970	$44,590

additional office equipment of $5,570 was purchased. Thus, cash of $12,670 was used for investing activities, as shown in Exhibit 8.

Cash Flows Used for Financing Activities

The cash flows for financing activities can also be determined from Exhibit 15. For Online Solutions, the cash flows used for financing activities is composed of two items. First, dividends of $18,000 are reported on the retained earnings statement shown in

Exhibit 6. Since no dividends payable appears on the balance sheets, cash dividends of $18,000 must have been paid during the year. In addition, notes payable decreased by $5,000 during the year. Thus, cash must have been used in paying off $5,000 of the notes. As a result, cash of $23,000 was used for financing activities, as shown in Exhibit 8.

SUMMARY OF LEARNING GOALS

1 **Distinguish the activities and financial statements of a service business from those of a merchandise business.** The revenue activities of a service enterprise involve providing services to customers. In contrast, the revenue activities of a merchandising business involve the buying and selling of merchandise.

2 **Describe and illustrate the financial statements of a merchandising business.** The multiple-step income statement of a merchandiser reports sales, sales returns and allowances, sales discounts, and net sales. The cost of the merchandise sold is subtracted from net sales to determine the gross profit. The cost of merchandise sold is determined by using either the periodic or perpetual method. Operating income is determined by subtracting operating expenses from gross profit. Operating expenses are normally classified as selling or administrative expenses. Net income is determined by subtracting income taxes and other expense and adding other income. The income statement may also be reported in a single-step form. The retained earnings statement and the statement of cash flows are similar to those for a service business. The balance sheet reports merchandise inventory at the end of the period as a current asset.

3 **Describe the accounting for the sale of merchandise.** Sales of merchandise for cash or on account are recorded by crediting Sales. The cost of merchandise sold and the reduction in merchandise inventory are also recorded for the sale. For sales of merchandise on account, the credit terms may allow sales discounts for early payment. Such discounts are recorded by the seller as a debit to Sales Discounts. Sales discounts are reported as a deduction from the amount initially recorded in Sales. Likewise, when merchandise is returned or a price adjustment is granted, the seller debits Sales Returns and Allowances. For sales on account, a subsidiary ledger is maintained for individual customer accounts receivable.

Under the perpetual inventory system, the cost of merchandise sold and the reduction of merchandise inventory on hand are recorded at the time of sale. In this way, the merchandise inventory account indicates the amount of merchandise on hand at all times. Likewise, any returned merchandise is recorded in the merchandise inventory account, with a related reduction in the cost of merchandise sold.

4 **Describe the accounting for the purchase of merchandise.** Purchases of merchandise for cash or on account are recorded by debiting Merchandise Inventory. For purchases of merchandise on account, the credit terms may allow cash discounts for early payment. Such purchases discounts are viewed as a reduction in the cost of the merchandise purchased. When merchandise is returned or a price adjustment is granted, the buyer credits Merchandise Inventory.

5 **Describe the accounting for transportation costs and sales taxes.** When merchandise is shipped FOB shipping point, the buyer pays the transportation costs and debits Merchandise Inventory. When merchandise is shipped FOB destination, the seller pays the transportation costs and debits Transportation Out or Delivery Expense. If the seller prepays transportation costs as a convenience to the buyer, the seller debits Accounts Receivable for the costs.

The liability for sales tax is incurred when the sale is made and recorded by the seller as a credit to the sales taxes payable account. When the amount of the sales tax is paid to the taxing unit, Sales Taxes Payable is debited and Cash is credited.

6 **Illustrate the dual nature of merchandising transactions.** Each merchandising transaction affects a buyer and a seller. The illustration in this chapter shows how the same transactions would be recorded by both.

7 **Describe the accounting for merchandise shrinkage.** The physical inventory taken at the end of the accounting period may differ from the amount of inventory shown in the inventory records. The difference, called inventory shrinkage, requires an adjusting entry debiting Cost of Merchandise Sold and crediting Merchandise Inventory. After this entry has been recorded, the adjusted Merchandise Inventory (book inventory) in the accounting records agrees with the actual physical inventory at the end of the period.

8 **Describe and illustrate the effects of inventory misstatements on the financial statements.** Any errors in the physical inventory count at the end of the accounting period affect the income statement and balance sheet. If the physical inventory is misstated, the amount of inventory shrinkage is misstated and the cost of merchandise sold will be misstated after the inventory shrinkage adjustment is recorded. Because net income is closed to Retained Earnings at the end of the accounting period, the retained

earnings and total stockholders' equity are also misstated. Likewise, merchandise inventory, current assets, and total assets are misstated. This misstatement of total assets, current assets, and merchandise inventory equals the misstatement of stockholders' equity. The effects of inventory misstatements on the financial statements are shown in Exhibit 12.

9 Describe and illustrate the use of gross profit and operating income in analyzing a company's operations. Gross profit and operating income are two important profitability measures analysts use in assessing the efficiency and effectiveness of a merchandiser's operations. Gross profit and operating income are normally analyzed over time as a percent of net sales.

GLOSSARY

Administrative expenses Expenses incurred in the administration or general operations of the business.

Book inventory The amount of inventory recorded in the accounting records.

Consignee The retailer carrying an item for sale (consignment) that is owned by another retailer (consignor).

Consignment Merchandise owned by a retailer (consignor) that is being carried for sale by another retailer (consignee).

Consignor A retailer who allows another retailer (consignee) to carry and sell its merchandise (consignment).

Controlling account The account in the general ledger that summarizes the balances of the accounts in a subsidiary ledger.

Cost of merchandise sold The cost that is reported as an expense when merchandise is sold.

Credit memorandum A form used by a seller to inform the buyer of the amount the seller proposes to credit to the account receivable due from the buyer.

Credit period The amount of time the buyer is allowed in which to pay the seller.

Credit terms Terms for payment on account by the buyer to the seller.

Debit memorandum A form used by a buyer to inform the seller of the amount the buyer proposes to debit to the account payable due the seller.

Direct method A method of preparing the statement of cash flows that analyzes each transaction and its effect on cash flows.

FOB (free on board) destination Freight terms in which the seller pays the transportation costs from the shipping point to the final destination.

FOB (free on board) shipping point Freight terms in which the buyer pays the transportation costs from the shipping point to the final destination.

Gross profit Sales minus the cost of merchandise sold.

Income from operations (operating income) The excess of gross profit over total operating expenses.

Indirect method A method of preparing the statement of cash flows that reconciles net income with net cash flows from operating activities.

Inventory shrinkage The amount by which the merchandise for sale, as indicated by the balance of the merchandise inventory account, is larger than the total amount of merchandise counted during the physical inventory.

Invoice The bill that the seller sends to the buyer.

Merchandise available for sale The cost of merchandise available for sale to customers.

Merchandise inventory Merchandise on hand (not sold) at the end of an accounting period.

Multiple-step income statement A form of income statement that contains several sections, subsections, and subtotals.

Net sales Revenue received for merchandise sold to customers less any sales returns and allowances and sales discounts.

Other expense Expenses that cannot be traced directly to operations.

Other income Revenue from sources other than the primary operating activity of a business.

Periodic inventory method The inventory method in which the inventory records do not show the amount available for sale or sold during the period.

Perpetual inventory method The inventory method in which each purchase and sale of merchandise is recorded in an inventory account.

Physical inventory A detailed listing of the merchandise for sale at the end of an accounting period.

Purchase return or allowance From the buyer's perspective, returned merchandise or an adjustment for defective merchandise.

Purchases discounts Discounts taken by the buyer for early payment of an invoice.

Report form The form of balance sheet in which assets, liabilities, and stockholders' equity are reported in a downward sequence.

Sales The total amount charged to customers for merchandise sold, including cash sales and sales on account.

Sales discounts From the seller's perspective, discounts that a seller may offer the buyer for early payment.

Sales returns and allowances From the seller's perspective, returned merchandise or an adjustment for defective merchandise.

Selling expenses Expenses that are incurred directly in the selling of merchandise.

Single-step income statement A form of income statement in which the total of all expenses is deducted from the total of all revenues.

Subsidiary ledger A ledger containing individual accounts with a common characteristic.

ILLUSTRATIVE ACCOUNTING APPLICATION PROBLEM

The following transactions were completed by Montrose Company during May of the current year. Montrose Company uses a perpetual inventory system.

May 3	Purchased merchandise on account from Floyd Co., $4,000, terms FOB shipping point, 2/10, n/30, with prepaid transportation costs of $120 added to the invoice.
5	Purchased merchandise on account from Kramer Co., $8,500, terms FOB destination, 1/10, n/30.
6	Sold merchandise on account to C. F. Howell Co., $2,800, terms 2/10, n/30. The cost of the merchandise sold was $1,125.
8	Purchased office supplies for cash, $150.
10	Returned merchandise purchased on May 5 from Kramer Co., $1,300.
13	Paid Floyd Co. on account for purchase of May 3, less discount.
14	Purchased merchandise for cash, $10,500.
15	Paid Kramer Co. on account for purchase of May 5, less return of May 10 and discount.
16	Received cash on account from sale of May 6 to C. F. Howell Co., less discount.
19	Sold merchandise on nonbank credit cards and reported accounts to the card company, American Express, $2,450. The cost of the merchandise sold was $980.
22	Sold merchandise on account to Comer Co., $3,480, terms 2/10, n/30. The cost of the merchandise sold was $1,400.
24	Sold merchandise for cash, $4,350. The cost of the merchandise sold was $1,750.
25	Received merchandise returned by Comer Co. from sale on May 22, $1,480. The cost of the returned merchandise was $600.
31	Received cash from card company for nonbank credit card sales of May 19, less $140 service fee.

Instructions

1. Journalize the preceding transactions.
2. Journalize the adjusting entry for merchandise inventory shrinkage, $3,750.

Solution

1.

May 3	Merchandise Inventory	4,120	
	Accounts Payable—Floyd Co.		4,120
5	Merchandise Inventory	8,500	
	Accounts Payable—Kramer Co.		8,500

(continued)

May 6	Accounts Receivable—C. F. Howell Co.	2,800	
	Sales		2,800
6	Cost of Merchandise Sold	1,125	
	Merchandise Inventory		1,125
8	Office Supplies	150	
	Cash		150
10	Accounts Payable—Kramer Co.	1,300	
	Merchandise Inventory		1,300
13	Accounts Payable—Floyd Co.	4,120	
	Merchandise Inventory		80
	Cash		4,040
	[$4,000 – (2% × $4,000) + $120]		
14	Merchandise Inventory	10,500	
	Cash		10,500
15	Accounts Payable—Kramer Co.	7,200	
	Merchandise Inventory		72
	Cash		7,128
	[($8,500 – $1,300) × 1% = $72; $8,500 – $1,300 – $72 = $7,128]		
16	Cash	2,744	
	Sales Discounts	56	
	Accounts Receivable—C. F. Howell Co.		2,800
19	Accounts Receivable—American Express	2,450	
	Sales		2,450
19	Cost of Merchandise Sold	980	
	Merchandise Inventory		980
22	Accounts Receivable—Comer Co.	3,480	
	Sales		3,480
22	Cost of Merchandise Sold	1,400	
	Merchandise Inventory		1,400
24	Cash	4,350	
	Sales		4,350
24	Cost of Merchandise Sold	1,750	
	Merchandise Inventory		1,750
25	Sales Returns and Allowances	1,480	
	Accounts Receivable—Comer Co.		1,480
25	Merchandise Inventory	600	
	Cost of Merchandise Sold		600
31	Cash	2,310	
	Credit Card Expense	140	
	Accounts Receivable—American Express		2,450

2.

May 31	Cost of Merchandise Sold	3,750	
	Merchandise Inventory		3,750

SELF-STUDY QUESTIONS

Answers at end of chapter

1. If merchandise purchased on account is returned, the buyer may inform the seller of the details by issuing a(n):
   A. debit memorandum
   B. credit memorandum
   C. invoice
   D. bill

2. If merchandise is sold on account to a customer for $1,000, terms FOB shipping point, 1/10, n/30, and the seller prepays $50 in transportation costs, the amount of the discount for early payment would be:
   A. $0 C. $10.00
   B. $5.00 D. $10.50

3. The income statement in which the total of all expenses is deducted from the total of all revenues is termed:
   A. multiple-step form C. direct form
   B. single-step form D. report form

4. On a multiple-step income statement, the excess of net sales over the cost of merchandise sold is called:
   A. operating income
   B. income from operations
   C. gross profit
   D. net income

5. As of December 31, 2007, Ames Corporation incorrectly counted its physical inventory as $275,000 instead of $300,000. The effect on the income statement is:
   A. Cost of merchandise sold is understated by $25,000
   B. Gross profit is overstated by $25,000
   C. Operating income is understated by $25,000
   D. Inventory shrinkage is understated by $25,000

DISCUSSION QUESTIONS

1. What distinguishes a merchandising business from a service business?
2. Can a business earn a gross profit but incur a net loss? Explain.
3. What is the difference between the cost of merchandise purchased and the cost of merchandise available for sale? Can they be the same amount? Explain.
4. What is the difference between the cost of merchandise available for sale and the cost of merchandise sold? Can they be the same amount? Explain.
5. Name at least three accounts that would normally appear in the financial statements of a merchandising business, but would not appear in the chart of accounts of a service business.
6. How does the accounting for sales to customers using bank credit cards, such as MasterCard and VISA, differ from accounting for sales to customers using nonbank credit cards, such as American Express? Explain.
7. Sometimes a retailer will not accept American Express, but will accept MasterCard or VISA. Why would a retailer accept one and not the other?
8. At some Texaco, Chevron, or Conoco gasoline stations, the cash price per gallon is 3 or 4 cents less than the credit price per gallon. As a result, many customers pay cash rather than use their credit cards. Why would a gasoline station owner establish such a policy?
9. Assume that you purchased merchandise with credit terms 2/10, n/30. On the date the invoice is due, you don't have the cash to pay the invoice. However, you can borrow the necessary money at an 8% annual interest rate. Should you borrow the money to pay the invoice? Explain.
10. What is the nature of (a) a credit memorandum issued by the seller of merchandise, (b) a debit memorandum issued by the buyer of merchandise?
11. Who bears the transportation costs when the terms of sale are (a) FOB shipping point, (b) FOB destination?
12. When you purchase a new car, the "sticker price" includes a "destination" charge. Are you purchasing the car FOB shipping point or FOB destination? Explain.
13. Bernard Office Equipment, which uses a perpetual inventory system, experienced a normal inventory shrinkage of $19,290. (a) What accounts would be debited and credited to record the adjustment for the inventory shrinkage at the end of the accounting period? (b) What are some causes of inventory shrinkage?
14. Assume that Bernard Office Equipment in Question 13 experienced an abnormal inventory shrinkage of $315,750. It has decided to record the abnormal inventory shrinkage so that it would be separately disclosed on the income statement. What account would be debited for the abnormal inventory shrinkage?
15. Assume that Joist Inc. (the consignee) included $40,000 of inventory held on consignment for Dory Company (the consignor) as part of its physical inventory. (a) What is the effect of this error on Joist's financial statements? (b) Would Joist's error also cause a misstatement in Dory's financial statements? Explain.

EXERCISES

Exercise 5-1

Determining gross profit

Goals **1, 9**

a. $8,031,200

CVS Corporation operates drugstores throughout the United States, selling prescription drugs, general merchandise, cosmetics, greeting cards, food, and beverages. For 2004, CVS reported (in thousands) net sales of $30,594,300, cost of sales of $22,563,100, and operating income of $1,454,700.

a. Determine CVS's gross profit.
b. Determine the gross profit as a percent of net sales. Round to one decimal place.
c. Determine the operating income as a percent of net sales. Round to one decimal place.

Exercise 5-2

Determining gross profit

Goals **1, 9**

a. $10,197,800

Walgreen Company operates drugstores throughout the United States, selling prescription drugs, general merchandise, cosmetics, food, and beverages. For 2004, Walgreen reported (in thousands) net sales of $37,508,200, cost of sales of $27,310,400, and operating income of $2,126,100.

a. Determine Walgreen's gross profit.
b. Determine the gross profit as a percent of net sales. Round to one decimal place.
c. Determine the operating income as a percent of net sales. Round to one decimal place.

Exercise 5-3

Analyzing gross profit and operating income

Goals **1, 9**

Based upon the data shown in Exercises 5–1 and 5–2, comment on the operating performance of CVS in comparison to Walgreen.

Exercise 5-4

Determining gross profit

Goals **1, 9**

a. $345,000

During the current year, merchandise is sold for $200,000 cash and for $950,000 on account. The cost of the merchandise sold is $805,000.

a. What is the amount of the gross profit?
b. Compute the gross profit as a percent of sales.
c. Will the income statement necessarily report a net income? Explain.

Exercise 5-5

Determining gross profit

Goals **1, 9**

a. $9,308,560

Office Depot operates a chain of office supply stores throughout the United States. For 2004, Office Depot reported (in thousands) net sales of $13,564,699, gross profit of $4,256,139, and operating income of $529,977.

a. Determine the cost of goods sold.
b. Determine the cost of goods sold as a percent of net sales. Round to one decimal place.
c. Determine the gross profit as a percent of net sales. Round to one decimal place.
d. Determine the operating income as a percent of net sales. Round to one decimal place.
e. What is the difference between the gross profit as a percent of net sales and the operating income as a percent of net sales? Explain.

Exercise 5-6

Income statement for merchandiser

Goal **2**

For the fiscal year, sales were $3,570,000, sales discounts were $320,000, sales returns and allowances were $240,000, and the cost of merchandise sold was $2,142,000. What was the amount of net sales and gross profit?

Exercise 5-7

Identify items missing in determining cost of merchandise sold

Goal 2

For (a) through (d), identify the items designated by X.

a. Purchases − (X + X) = Net purchases.
b. Net purchases + X = Cost of merchandise purchased.
c. Merchandise inventory (beginning) + Cost of merchandise purchased = X.
d. Merchandise available for sale − X = Cost of merchandise sold.

Exercise 5-8

Cost of merchandise sold and related items

Goal 2

a. Cost of merchandise sold, $931,000

SPREADSHEET

The following data were extracted from the accounting records of Meniscus Company for the year ended April 30, 2006:

Merchandise inventory, May 1, 2005	$ 121,200
Merchandise inventory, April 30, 2006	142,000
Purchases	985,000
Purchases returns and allowances	23,500
Purchases discounts	21,000
Sales	1,420,000
Transportation in	11,300

a. Prepare the cost of merchandise sold section of the income statement for the year ended April 30, 2006, using the periodic inventory method.
b. Determine the gross profit to be reported on the income statement for the year ended April 30, 2006.

Exercise 5-9

Cost of merchandise sold

Goal 2

Correct cost of merchandise sold, $599,500

Identify the errors in the following schedule of cost of merchandise sold for the current year ended December 31, 2006:

Cost of merchandise sold:			
Merchandise inventory, December 31, 2006			$120,000
Purchases		$600,000	
Plus: Purchases returns and allowances	$14,000		
Purchases discounts	6,000	20,000	
Gross purchases		$620,000	
Less transportation in		7,500	
Cost of merchandise purchased			612,500
Merchandise available for sale			$732,500
Less merchandise inventory, January 1, 2006			132,000
Cost of merchandise sold			$600,500

Exercise 5-10

Income statement for merchandiser

Goal 2

The following expenses were incurred by a merchandising business during the year. In which expense section of the income statement should each be reported: (a) selling or (b) administrative?

1. Advertising expense.
2. Depreciation expense on office equipment.
3. Insurance expense on store equipment.
4. Office supplies used.
5. Rent expense on office building.
6. Salaries of office personnel.
7. Salary of sales manager.

Exercise 5-11

Single-step income statement

Goal 2

Net income: $1,362,500

Summary operating data for The Meriden Company during the current year ended June 30, 2006, are as follows: cost of merchandise sold, $3,240,000; administrative expenses, $300,000; interest expense, $47,500; rent revenue, $30,000; net sales, $5,400,000; and selling expenses, $480,000. Prepare a single-step income statement.

Exercise 5-12

Determining amounts for items omitted from income statement

Goal 2

a. $25,000

Two items are omitted in each of the following four lists of income statement data. Determine the amounts of the missing items, identifying them by letter.

Sales	$393,000	$500,000	$930,000	$ (g)
Sales returns and allowances	(a)	15,000	(e)	30,500
Sales discounts	18,000	8,000	30,000	37,000
Net sales	350,000	(c)	860,000	(h)
Cost of merchandise sold	(b)	285,000	(f)	540,000
Gross profit	140,000	(d)	340,000	150,000

Exercise 5-13

Multiple-step income statement

Goal 2

How many errors can you find in the following income statement?

The Plautus Company
Income Statement
For the Year Ended October 31, 2006

Revenue from sales:			
Sales		$4,200,000	
Add: Sales returns and			
allowances	$81,200		
Sales discounts	20,300	101,500	
Gross sales			$4,301,500
Cost of merchandise sold			2,093,000
Income from operations			$2,208,500
Operating expenses:			
Selling expenses		$ 203,000	
Transportation out		7,500	
Administrative expenses		122,000	
Total operating expenses			332,500
			$1,876,000
Other expense:			
Interest revenue			66,500
Gross profit			$1,809,500

Exercise 5-14

Multiple-step income statement

Goal 2

a. Net income, $77,500

SPREADSHEET

On January 31, 2006, the balances of the accounts appearing in the ledger of Calloway Company, a furniture wholesaler, are as follows:

Administrative Expenses	$ 80,000	Office Supplies	$ 10,600
Building	512,500	Retained Earnings	528,580
Capital Stock	100,000	Salaries Payable	3,220
Cash	48,500	Sales	925,000
Cost of Merchandise Sold	560,000	Sales Discounts	20,000
Dividends	25,000	Sales Returns and Allowances	60,000
Interest Expense	7,500	Selling Expenses	120,000
Merchandise Inventory	130,000	Store Supplies	7,700
Notes Payable	25,000		

a. Prepare a multiple-step income statement for the year ended January 31, 2006.
b. Compare the major advantages and disadvantages of the multiple-step and single-step forms of income statements.

Exercise 5-15

Sales-related transactions, including the use of credit cards

Goal 3

Journalize the entries for the following transactions:

a. Sold merchandise for cash, $6,900. The cost of the merchandise sold was $4,830.
b. Sold merchandise on account, $7,500. The cost of the merchandise sold was $5,625.
c. Sold merchandise to customers who used MasterCard and VISA, $10,200. The cost of the merchandise sold was $6,630.
d. Sold merchandise to customers who used American Express, $7,200. The cost of the merchandise sold was $5,040.
e. Paid an invoice from City National Bank for $675, representing a service fee for processing MasterCard and VISA sales.
f. Received $6,875 from American Express Company after a $325 collection fee had been deducted.

Exercise 5-16

Sales returns and allowances

Goal 3

During the year, sales returns and allowances totaled $235,750. The cost of the merchandise returned was $141,450. The accountant recorded all the returns and allowances by debiting the sales account and crediting Cost of Merchandise Sold for $235,750.

Was the accountant's method of recording returns acceptable? Explain. In your explanation, include the advantages of using a sales returns and allowances account.

Exercise 5-17

Sales-related transactions

Goal 3

After the amount due on a sale of $7,500, terms 2/10, n/eom, is received from a customer within the discount period, the seller consents to the return of the entire shipment. The cost of the merchandise returned was $4,500. (a) What is the amount of the refund owed to the customer? (b) Journalize the entries made by the seller to record the return and the refund.

Exercise 5-18

Sales-related transactions

Goal 3

The debits and credits for three related transactions are presented in the following T accounts. Describe each transaction.

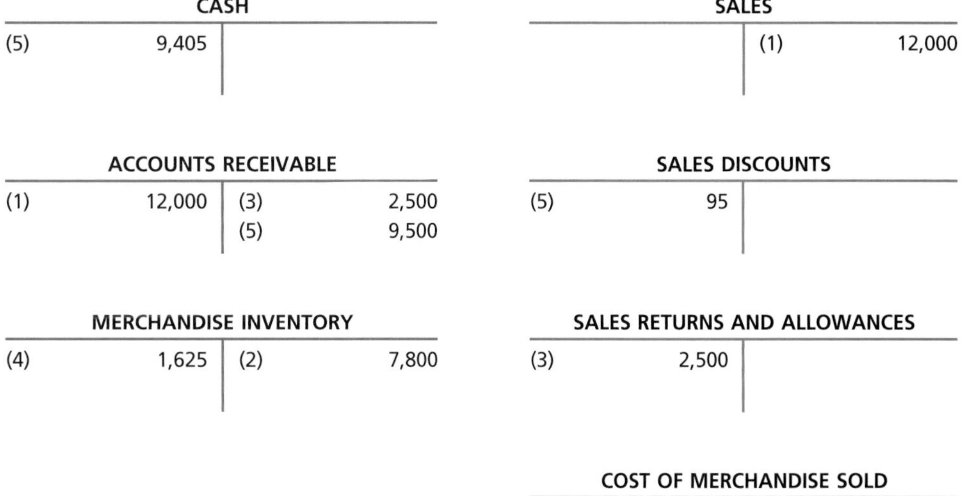

CASH

	Debit		Credit
(5)	9,405		

SALES

	Debit		Credit
		(1)	12,000

ACCOUNTS RECEIVABLE

	Debit		Credit
(1)	12,000	(3)	2,500
		(5)	9,500

SALES DISCOUNTS

	Debit		Credit
(5)	95		

MERCHANDISE INVENTORY

	Debit		Credit
(4)	1,625	(2)	7,800

SALES RETURNS AND ALLOWANCES

	Debit		Credit
(3)	2,500		

COST OF MERCHANDISE SOLD

	Debit		Credit
(2)	7,800	(4)	1,625

Exercise 5-19

Sales-related transactions

Goal 3

Merchandise is sold on account to a customer for $18,000, terms FOB shipping point, 3/10, n/30. The seller paid the transportation costs of $375. Determine the following: (a) amount of the sale, (b) amount debited to Accounts Receivable, (c) amount of the discount for early payment, and (d) amount due within the discount period.

Exercise 5-20

Purchase-related transaction

Goal 4

Cheddar Company purchased merchandise on account from a supplier for $8,500, terms 2/10, n/30. Before payment was due, Cheddar Company returned $800 of the merchandise and received full credit.

a. If Cheddar Company pays the invoice within the discount period, what is the amount of cash required for the payment?
b. Under a perpetual inventory system, what account is credited by Cheddar Company to record the return?

Exercise 5-21

Determining amounts to be paid on invoices

Goal 4

a. $10,500

Determine the amount to be paid in full settlement of each of the following invoices, assuming that credit for returns and allowances was received prior to payment and that all invoices were paid within the discount period.

	Merchandise	Transportation Paid by Seller		Returns and Allowances
a.	$12,000	—	FOB destination, n/30	$1,500
b.	4,500	$200	FOB shipping point, 1/10, n/30	500
c.	5,000	—	FOB destination, 2/10, n/30	—
d.	5,000	—	FOB shipping point, 1/10, n/30	1,000
e.	1,500	50	FOB shipping point, 2/10, n/30	700

Exercise 5-22

Purchase-related transactions

Goal 4

A retailer is considering the purchase of 100 units of a specific item from either of two suppliers. Their offers are as follows:

A: $400 a unit, total of $40,000, 2/10, n/30, plus transportation costs of $625.
B: $403 a unit, total of $40,300, 1/10, n/30, no charge for transportation.

Which of the two offers, A or B, yields the lower price?

Exercise 5-23

Purchase-related transactions

Goal 4

The debits and credits from four related transactions are presented in the following T accounts. Describe each transaction.

CASH

		(2)	175
		(4)	6,860

ACCOUNTS PAYABLE

(3)	1,000	(1)	8,000
(4)	7,000		

MERCHANDISE INVENTORY

(1)	8,000	(3)	1,000
(2)	175	(4)	140

Exercise 5-24

Purchase-related transactions

Goal 4

Enid Co., a women's clothing store, purchased $7,500 of merchandise from a supplier on account, terms FOB destination, 2/10, n/30. Enid Co. returned $1,200 of the merchandise, receiving a credit memorandum, and then paid the amount due within the discount period. Journalize Enid Co.'s entries to record (a) the purchase, (b) the merchandise return, and (c) the payment.

Exercise 5-25

Purchase-related transactions

Goal 4

Journalize entries for the following related transactions of Regius Company:

a. Purchased $12,000 of merchandise from Loew Co. on account, terms 2/10, n/30.
b. Paid the amount owed on the invoice within the discount period.
c. Discovered that $3,000 of the merchandise was defective and returned items, receiving credit.

d. Purchased $2,000 of merchandise from Loew Co. on account, terms n/30.
e. Received a check for the balance owed from the return in (c), after deducting for the purchase in (d).

Exercise 5-26

Sales tax

Goal **5**

A sale of merchandise on account for $4,000 is subject to a 7% sales tax. (a) Should the sales tax be recorded at the time of sale or when payment is received? (b) What is the amount of the sale? (c) What is the amount debited to Accounts Receivable? (d) What is the title of the account to which the $280 is credited?

Exercise 5-27

Sales tax transactions

Goal **5**

Journalize the entries to record the following selected transactions:

a. Sold $9,000 of merchandise on account, subject to a sales tax of 8%. The cost of the merchandise sold was $6,300.
b. Paid $9,175 to the state sales tax department for taxes collected.

Exercise 5-28

Sales-related transactions

Goals **3, 6**

Superior Co., a furniture wholesaler, sells merchandise to Beta Co. on account, $11,500, terms 2/15, n/30. The cost of the merchandise sold is $6,900. Superior Co. issues a credit memorandum for $900 for merchandise returned and subsequently receives the amount due within the discount period. The cost of the merchandise returned is $540. Journalize Superior Co.'s entries for (a) the sale, including the cost of the merchandise sold, (b) the credit memorandum, including the cost of the returned merchandise, and (c) the receipt of the check for the amount due from Beta Co.

Exercise 5-29

Purchase-related transactions

Goals **4, 6**

Based on the data presented in Exercise 5-28, journalize Beta Co.'s entries for (a) the purchase, (b) the return of the merchandise for credit, and (c) the payment of the invoice within the discount period.

Exercise 5-30

Normal balances of merchandise accounts

Goals **3, 4, 5, 6**

What is the normal balance of the following accounts: (a) Cost of Merchandise Sold, (b) Merchandise Inventory, (c) Sales, (d) Sales Discounts, (e) Sales Returns and Allowances, (f) Transportation Out?

Exercise 5-31

Adjusting entry for merchandise inventory shrinkage

Goal **7**

Jaguar Inc.'s perpetual inventory records indicate that $584,000 of merchandise should be on hand on July 31, 2007. The physical inventory indicates that $560,000 of merchandise is actually on hand. Journalize the adjusting entry for the inventory shrinkage for Jaguar Inc. for the year ended July 31, 2007.

Exercise 5-32

Effects of inventory misstatements

Goal 8

1. 2006 net income overstated, $20,000

Following are descriptions of two independent situations that involve inventory misstatements.

1. Ending merchandise inventory is overstated by $20,000 on December 31, 2006. Ending merchandise inventory is correct on December 31, 2007.
2. Ending merchandise inventory is understated by $13,000 on December 31, 2006. Ending merchandise inventory is overstated by $16,000 on December 31, 2007.

For each situation, indicate the effects of the misstatements on the financial statements for 2006 and 2007. Use the following format for your answers:

	Amount of Misstatement Overstatement (Understatement)	
	2006	**2007**
Balance sheet (December 31):		
Merchandise inventory	____	____
Current assets	____	____
Total assets	____	____
Retained earnings	____	____
Total stockholders' equity	____	____
Income statement:		
Cost of merchandise sold	____	____
Gross profit	____	____
Net income	____	____

Exercise 5-33

Effects of inventory misstatements

Goal 8

1. 2007 net income overstated, $2,500

Following are descriptions of two independent situations that involve inventory misstatements.

1. Ending merchandise inventory is overstated by $7,500 on December 31, 2006. Ending merchandise inventory is overstated by $10,000 on December 31, 2007.
2. Ending merchandise inventory is understated by $11,000 on December 31, 2006. Ending merchandise inventory is understated by $9,000 on December 31, 2007.

For each situation, indicate the effects of the misstatements on the financial statements for 2006 and 2007. Use the following format for your answers:

	Amount of Misstatement Overstatement (Understatement)	
	2006	**2007**
Balance sheet (December 31):		
Merchandise inventory	____	____
Current assets	____	____
Total assets	____	____
Retained earnings	____	____
Total stockholders' equity	____	____
Income statement:		
Cost of merchandise sold	____	____
Gross profit	____	____
Net income	____	____

Exercise 5-34

Effects of inventory misstatements

Goal 8

Merchandise of $65,000 was ordered on December 26, 2006, FOB destination, and was received on December 30, 2006. The invoice from the vendor was not received until January 7, 2007, and the related accounts payable journal entry was not recorded until January 7, 2007. However, since the merchandise was on hand at December 31, 2006, it was included in the physical inventory and properly assigned a cost.

Assume that the accounts payable was recorded on January 7, 2007, as a debit to Merchandise Inventory and a credit to Accounts Payable for $65,000. Also, assume that the December 31, 2007, physical inventory is correct. Indicate the effects of the inventory misstatements on the financial statements for 2006 and 2007, using the following format for your answers:

	Amount of Misstatement Overstatement (Understatement)	
	2006	**2007**
Balance sheet (December 31):		
Merchandise inventory	____	____
Total assets	____	____
Accounts payable	____	____
Total liabilities	____	____
Retained earnings	____	____
Total stockholders' equity	____	____
Income statement:		
Cost of merchandise sold	____	____
Gross profit	____	____
Net income	____	____

Exercise 5-35

Effects of inventory misstatements

Goal 8

Merchandise of $38,000 was ordered on December 29, 2006, FOB shipping point. The vendor paid the shipping charges of $1,000 as an accommodation to the buyer. The invoice from the vendor was not received until January 3, 2007, and the related accounts payable journal entry was not recorded until January 3, 2007. The merchandise was shipped on December 30, 2006, and was received on January 5, 2007. Since the merchandise was in transit, it was not included in the physical count of inventory on December 31, 2006.

Assume that the accounts payable was recorded on January 3, 2007, as a debit to Merchandise Inventory and a credit to Accounts Payable for $39,000. Also, assume that the December 31, 2007, physical inventory is correct. Indicate the effects of the inventory misstatements on the financial statements for 2006 and 2007, using the following format for your answers:

	Amount of Misstatement Overstatement (Understatement)	
	2006	**2007**
Balance sheet (December 31):		
Merchandise inventory	____	____
Total assets	____	____
Accounts payable	____	____
Total liabilities	____	____
Retained earnings	____	____
Total stockholders' equity	____	____
Income statement:		
Cost of merchandise sold	____	____
Gross profit	____	____
Net income	____	____

Exercise 5-36

Gross profit and operating income

Goal 9

Staples, Inc., operates a chain of office supply stores throughout the United States. For 2004 and 2003, Staples reported (in thousands) the following operating data:

	2004	**2003**
Net sales	$14,448,378	$13,181,222
Cost of goods sold	10,343,643	9,559,123
Gross profit	$ 4,104,735	$ 3,622,099
Operating income	$ 1,125,873	$ 798,288

a. Compute the percent of gross profit and operating income to net sales. Round to one decimal place.
b. Based upon (a), comment on Staples' operating performance in 2004 as compared to 2003.

ACCOUNTING APPLICATION PROBLEMS

Problem 5-1A

Multiple-step income statement, retained earnings statement, and report form of balance sheet

Goal 2

1. Net income, $81,600

SPREADSHEET

The following selected accounts and their current balances appear in the ledger of Sombrero Co. for the fiscal year ended November 30, 2006:

Cash	$ 91,800	Sales	$1,802,400
Accounts Receivable	74,400	Sales Returns and Allowances	25,200
Merchandise Inventory	120,000	Sales Discounts	13,200
Office Supplies	3,120	Cost of Merchandise Sold	1,284,000
Prepaid Insurance	8,160	Sales Salaries Expense	252,000
Office Equipment	76,800	Advertising Expense	33,960
Accumulated Depreciation— Office Equipment	12,960	Depreciation Expense— Store Equipment	5,520
Store Equipment	141,000	Miscellaneous Selling Expense	1,320
Accumulated Depreciation— Store Equipment	58,320	Office Salaries Expense	49,200
		Rent Expense	26,580
Accounts Payable	32,400	Insurance Expense	15,300
Salaries Payable	2,400	Depreciation Expense— Office Equipment	10,800
Note Payable (final payment due 2016)	36,000	Office Supplies Expense	1,080
Capital Stock	60,000	Miscellaneous Administrative Expense	1,440
Retained Earnings	261,600		
Dividends	30,000	Interest Expense	1,200

Instructions

1. Prepare a multiple-step income statement.
2. Prepare a retained earnings statement.
3. Prepare a report form of balance sheet, assuming that the current portion of the note payable is $3,000.
4. Briefly explain how multiple-step and single-step income statements differ.

Problem 5-2A

Single-step income statement and retained earnings statement

Goal 2

SPREADSHEET

Selected accounts and related amounts for Sombrero Co. for the fiscal year ended March 30, 2006, are presented in Problem 5-1A.

Instructions

1. Prepare a single-step income statement.
2. Prepare a retained earnings statement.

Problem 5-3A

Sales-related transactions

Goals 3, 5

GENERAL LEDGER

The following selected transactions were completed by Interstate Supplies Co., which sells irrigation supplies primarily to wholesalers and occasionally to retail customers:

Mar. 1 Sold merchandise on account to Babcock Co., $7,500, terms FOB shipping point, n/eom. The cost of the merchandise sold was $4,500.

2 Sold merchandise for $8,000 plus 6% sales tax to cash customers. The cost of merchandise sold was $4,750.

5 Sold merchandise on account to North Star Company, $16,000, terms FOB destination 1/10, n/30. The cost of merchandise sold was $10,500.

8 Sold merchandise for $6,150 plus 6% sales tax to customers who used VISA cards. Deposited credit card receipts into the bank. The cost of merchandise sold was $3,700.

13 Sold merchandise to customers who used American Express cards, $6,500. The cost of merchandise sold was $3,600.

Mar. 14 Sold merchandise on account to Blech Co., $7,500, terms FOB shipping point, 1/10, n/30. The cost of merchandise sold was $4,000.
15 Received check for amount due from North Star Company for sale on March 5.
16 Issued credit memorandum for $800 to Blech Co. for merchandise returned from sale on March 14. The cost of the merchandise returned was $360.
18 Sold merchandise on account to Westech Company, $6,850, terms FOB shipping point, 2/10, n/30. Paid $210 for transportation costs and added them to the invoice. The cost of merchandise sold was $4,100.
24 Received check for amount due from Blech Co. for sale on March 14 less credit memorandum of March 16 and discount.
27 Received $7,680 from American Express for $8,000 of sales reported March 1–12.
28 Received check for amount due from Westech Company for sale of March 18.
31 Paid Downtown Delivery Service $1,275 for merchandise delivered during March to customers under shipping terms of FOB destination.
31 Received check for amount due from Babcock Co. for sale of March 1.
Apr. 3 Paid First National Bank $725 for service fees for handling VISA sales during March.
10 Paid $2,800 to state sales tax division for taxes owed on March sales.

Instructions

Journalize the entries to record the transactions of Interstate Supplies Co.

Problem 5-4A

Purchase-related transactions

Goals **4, 5**

GENERAL LEDGER

The following selected transactions were completed by Petunia Co. during August of the current year:

Aug. 1 Purchased merchandise from Fisher Co., $8,500, terms FOB shipping point, 2/10, n/eom. Prepaid transportation costs of $250 were added to the invoice.
5 Purchased merchandise from Byrd Co., $10,400, terms FOB destination, n/30.
10 Paid Fisher Co. for invoice of August 1, less discount.
13 Purchased merchandise from Mickle Co., $7,500, terms FOB destination, 1/10, n/30.
14 Issued debit memorandum to Mickle Co. for $2,500 of merchandise returned from purchase on August 13.
18 Purchased merchandise from Lanning Company, $10,000, terms FOB shipping point, n/eom.
18 Paid transportation charges of $150 on August 18 purchase from Lanning Company.
19 Purchased merchandise from Hatcher Co., $7,500, terms FOB destination, 2/10, n/30.
23 Paid Mickle Co. for invoice of August 13, less debit memorandum of August 14 and discount.
29 Paid Hatcher Co. for invoice of August 19, less discount.
31 Paid Lanning Company for invoice of August 18.
31 Paid Byrd Co. for invoice of August 5.

Instructions

Journalize the entries to record the transactions of Petunia Co. for August.

Problem 5-5A

Sales-related and purchase-related transactions

Goals **3, 4, 5, 6**

GENERAL LEDGER

The following were selected from among the transactions completed by Ingress Company during January of the current year:

Jan. 3 Purchased merchandise on account from Pynn Co., $10,400, terms FOB shipping point, 2/10, n/30, with prepaid transportation costs of $320 added to the invoice.
5 Purchased merchandise on account from Wilhelm Co., $8,000, terms FOB destination, 1/10, n/30.

Jan.	6	Sold merchandise on acount to Sievert Co., $7,500, terms 2/10, n/30. The cost of the merchandise sold was $4,500.
	7	Returned $1,800 of merchandise purchased on January 5 from Wilhelm Co.
	13	Paid Pynn Co. on account for purchase of January 3, less discount.
	15	Paid Wilhelm Co. on account for purchase of January 5, less return of January 7 and discount.
	16	Received cash on account from sale of January 6 to Sievert Co., less discount.
	19	Sold merchandise on nonbank credit cards and reported accounts to the card company, American Express, $6,450. The cost of the merchandise sold was $3,950.
	22	Sold merchandise on account to Elk River Co., $3,480, terms 2/10, n/30. The cost of the merchandise sold was $1,400.
	23	Sold merchandise for cash, $9,350. The cost of the merchandise sold was $5,750.
	25	Received merchandise returned by Elk River Co. from sale on January 22, $1,480. The cost of the returned merchandise was $600.
	31	Received cash from American Express for nonbank credit sales of January 19, less $225 service fee.

Instructions

Journalize the transactions.

Problem 5-6A

Sales-related and purchase-related transactions for seller and buyer

Goals **3, 4, 5, 6**

GENERAL LEDGER

The following selected transactions were completed during June between Schnaps Company and Brandy Company:

June	2	Schnaps Company sold merchandise on account to Brandy Company, $14,000, terms FOB shipping point, 2/10, n/30. Schnaps Company paid transportation costs of $350, which were added to the invoice. The cost of the merchandise sold was $8,000.
	8	Schnaps Company sold merchandise on account to Brandy Company $12,500, terms FOB destination, 1/15, n/eom. The cost of the merchandise sold was $7,500.
	8	Schnaps Company paid transportation costs of $550 for delivery of merchandise sold to Brandy Company on June 8.
	12	Brandy Company returned $3,000 of merchandise purchased on account on June 8 from Schnaps Company. The cost of the merchandise returned was $1,800.
	12	Brandy Company paid Schnaps Company for purchase of June 2, less discount.
	23	Brandy Company paid Schnaps Company for purchase of June 8, less discount and less return of June 12.
	24	Schnaps Company sold merchandise on account to Brandy Company, $10,000, terms FOB shipping point, n/eom. The cost of the merchandise sold was $6,000.
	26	Brandy Company paid transportation charges of $310 on June 24 purchase from Schnaps Company.
	30	Brandy Company paid Schnaps Company on account for purchase of June 24.

Instructions

Journalize the June transactions for (1) Schnaps Company and (2) Brandy Company.

Appendix Problem 5-7A

Statement of cash flows using indirect method

For the year ending December 31, 2007, Chippendale Systems Inc. reported net income of $48,320 and paid dividends of $14,400. Comparative balance sheets as of December 31, 2007 and 2006, are as follows:

Chippendale Systems Inc.
Balance Sheets

	December 31, 2007	December 31, 2006	Changes Increase (Decrease)
Assets			
Current assets:			
Cash	$ 42,360	$ 33,200	$ 9,160
Accounts receivable	60,864	41,600	19,264
Merchandise inventory	49,720	47,760	1,960
Office supplies	384	480	(96)
Prepaid insurance	2,120	2,400	(280)
Total current assets	$155,448	$125,440	$30,008
Property, plant, and equipment:			
Land	$ 16,000	$ 16,000	$ 0
Store equipment	21,680	16,000	5,680
Accumulated depreciation—store equipment	(4,560)	(2,080)	(2,480)
Office equipment	12,456	8,000	4,456
Accumulated depreciation—office equipment	(3,776)	(1,784)	(1,992)
Total property, plant, and equipment	$ 41,800	$ 36,136	$ 5,664
Total assets	$197,248	$161,576	$35,672
Liabilities			
Current liabilities:			
Accounts payable	$ 17,936	$ 11,416	$ 6,520
Notes payable (current portion)	4,000	4,000	0
Salaries payable	912	1,200	(288)
Unearned rent	1,440	1,920	(480)
Total current liabilities	$ 24,288	$ 18,536	$ 5,752
Long-term liabilities:			
Notes payable (final payment due 2012)	16,000	20,000	(4,000)
Total liabilities	$ 40,288	$ 38,536	$ 1,752
Stockholders' Equity			
Capital stock	$ 20,000	$ 20,000	$ 0
Retained earnings	136,960	103,040	33,920
Total stockholders' equity	$156,960	$123,040	$33,920
Total liabilities and stockholders' equity	$197,248	$161,576	$35,672

1. Net cash flows from operating activities, $37,696

SPREADSHEET

Instructions

1. Prepare a statement of cash flows, using the indirect method.
2. Why is depreciation added to net income in determining net cash flows from operating activities? Explain.

ALTERNATE ACCOUNTING APPLICATION PROBLEMS

Alternate Problem 5-1B

Multiple-step income statement, retained earnings statement, and report form of balance sheet

Goal **2**

1. Net income, $80,000

SPREADSHEET

The following selected accounts and their current balances appear in the ledger of Sciatic Co. for the fiscal year ended July 31, 2006:

Cash	$123,000	Sales	$1,028,000
Accounts Receivable	96,800	Sales Returns and Allowances	18,480
Merchandise Inventory	140,000	Sales Discounts	17,520
Office Supplies	4,480	Cost of Merchandise Sold	620,000
Prepaid Insurance	2,720	Sales Salaries Expense	138,560
Office Equipment	68,000	Advertising Expense	35,040
Accumulated Depreciation— Office Equipment	10,240	Depreciation Expense— Store Equipment	5,120
Store Equipment	122,400	Miscellaneous Selling Expense	1,280
Accumulated Depreciation— Store Equipment	27,360	Office Salaries Expense	67,320
Accounts Payable	44,480	Rent Expense	25,080
Salaries Payable	1,920	Depreciation Expense— Office Equipment	10,160
Note Payable (final payment due 2016)	44,800	Insurance Expense	3,120
Capital Stock	75,000	Office Supplies Expense	1,040
Retained Earnings	301,600	Miscellaneous Administrative Expense	1,280
Dividends	28,000	Interest Expense	4,000

Instructions

1. Prepare a multiple-step income statement.
2. Prepare a retained earnings statement.
3. Prepare a report form of balance sheet, assuming that the current portion of the note payable is $6,000.
4. Briefly explain how multiple-step and single-step income statements differ.

Alternate Problem 5-2B

Single-step income statement and retained earnings statement

Goal **2**

SPREADSHEET

Selected accounts and related amounts for Sciatic Co. for the fiscal year ended July 31, 2006, are presented in Alternate Problem 5-1B.

Instructions

1. Prepare a single-step income statement.
2. Prepare a retained earnings statement.

Alternate Problem 5-3B

Sales-related transactions

Goals **3, 5**

GENERAL LEDGER

The following selected transactions were completed by Holistic Supply Co., which sells office supplies primarily to wholesalers and occasionally to retail customers:

Aug. 2 Sold merchandise on account to Runyan Co., $12,800, terms FOB destination, 2/10, n/30. The cost of merchandise sold was $7,600.

3 Sold merchandise for $5,000 plus 7% sales tax to cash customers. The cost of merchandise sold was $3,000.

4 Sold merchandise on account to McNutt Co., $2,800, terms FOB shipping point, n/eom. The cost of merchandise sold was $1,800.

5 Sold merchandise for $4,400 plus 7% sales tax to customers who used MasterCard. Deposited credit card receipts into the bank. The cost of merchandise sold was $2,500.

12 Received check for amount due from Runyan Co. for sale on August 2.

14 Sold merchandise to customers who used American Express cards, $15,000. The cost of merchandise sold was $9,200.

Aug. 16 Sold merchandise on account to Westpack Co., $12,000, terms FOB shipping point, 1/10, n/30. The cost of merchandise sold was $7,200.
18 Issued credit memorandum for $3,000 to Westpack Co. for merchandise returned from sale on August 16. The cost of the merchandise returned was $1,800.
19 Sold merchandise on account to DeGroot Co., $9,500, terms FOB shipping point, 1/10, n/30. Added $200 to the invoice for transportation costs prepaid. The cost of merchandise sold was $5,700.
26 Received check for amount due from Westpark Co. for sale on August 16 less credit memorandum of August 18 and discount.
27 Received $7,680 from American Express for $8,000 of sales reported August 1–12.
28 Received check for amount due from DeGroot Co. for sale of August 19.
31 Received check for amount due from McNutt Co. for sale of August 4.
31 Paid Fast Delivery Service $1,050 for delivering merchandise during August to customers under shipping terms of FOB destination.
Sept. 3 Paid First City Bank $850 for service fees for handling MasterCard sales during August.
15 Paid $4,100 to state sales tax division for taxes owed on August sales.

Instructions

Journalize the entries to record the transactions of Holistic Supply Co.

Alternate Problem 5-4B

Purchase-related transactions

Goals **4, 5**

GENERAL LEDGER

The following selected transactions were completed by Daffodil Company during March of the current year:

Mar. 1 Purchased merchandise from Fastow Co., $16,000, terms FOB destination, n/30.
3 Purchased merchandise from Moss Co., $9,000, terms FOB shipping point, 2/10, n/eom. Prepaid transportation costs of $150 were added to the invoice.
4 Purchased merchandise from Picadilly Co., $7,500, terms FOB destination, 2/10, n/30.
6 Issued debit memorandum to Picadilly Co. for $1,000 of merchandise returned from purchase on March 4.
13 Paid Moss Co. for invoice of March 3, less discount.
14 Paid Picadilly Co. for invoice of March 4, less debit memorandum of March 6 and discount.
19 Purchased merchandise from Reardon Co., $12,000, terms FOB shipping point, n/eom.
19 Paid transportation charges of $500 on March 19 purchase from Reardon Co.
20 Purchased merchandise from Hatcher Co., $8,000, terms FOB destination, 1/10, n/30.
30 Paid Hatcher Co. for invoice of March 20, less discount.
31 Paid Fastow Co. for invoice of Marth 1.
31 Paid Reardon Co. for invoice of March 19.

Instructions

Journalize the entries to record the transactions of Daffodil Company for March.

Alternate Problem 5-5B

Sales-related and purchase-related transactions

Goals **3, 4, 5, 6**

GENERAL LEDGER

The following were selected from among the transactions completed by Girder Company during November of the current year:

Nov. 3 Purchased merchandise on account from Whiting Co., $20,000, terms FOB destination, 2/10, n/30.
4 Sold merchandise for cash, $7,100. The cost of the merchandise sold was $4,150.
5 Purchased merchandise on account from Alamosa Co., $10,500, terms FOB shipping point, 2/10, n/30, with prepaid transportation costs of $300 added to the invoice.
6 Returned $5,000 of merchandise purchased on November 3 from Whiting Co.
11 Sold merchandise on account to Bowles Co., $1,800, terms 1/10, n/30. The cost of the merchandise sold was $1,050.
13 Paid Whiting Co. on account for purchase of November 3, less return of November 6 and discount.

Nov. 14 Sold merchandise on nonbank credit cards and reported accounts to the card company, American Express, $9,850. The cost of the merchandise sold was $5,900.
15 Paid Alamosa Co. on account for purchase of November 5, less discount.
21 Received cash on account from sale of November 11 to Bowles Co., less discount.
24 Sold merchandise on account to Kapinos Co., $4,200, terms 1/10, n/30. The cost of the merchandise sold was $1,850.
28 Received cash from American Express for nonbank credit card sales of November 14, less $440 service fee.
30 Received merchandise returned by Kapinos Co. from sale on November 24, $1,100. The cost of the returned merchandise was $600.

Instructions

Journalize the transactions.

Alternate Problem 5-6B

Sales-related and purchase-related transactions for seller and buyer

Goals **3, 4, 5, 6**

GENERAL LEDGER

The following selected transactions were completed during March between Snyder Company and Brooks Co.:

Mar. 1 Snyder Company sold merchandise on account to Brooks Co., $12,750, terms FOB destination, 2/15, n/eom. The cost of the merchandise sold was $6,000.
2 Snyder Company paid transportation costs of $150 for delivery of merchandise sold to Brooks Co. on March 1.
5 Snyder Company sold merchandise on account to Brooks Co., $18,500, terms FOB shipping point, n/eom. The cost of the merchandise sold was $11,000.
6 Brooks Co. returned $2,000 of merchandise purchased on account on March 1 from Snyder Company. The cost of the merchandise returned was $1,200.
9 Brooks Co. paid transportation charges of $180 on March 5 purchase from Snyder Company.
15 Snyder Company sold merchandise on account to Brooks Co., $20,000, terms FOB shipping point, 1/10, n/30. Snyder Company paid transportation costs of $1,750, which were added to the invoice. The cost of the merchandise sold was $12,000.
16 Brooks Co. paid Snyder Company for purchase of March 1, less discount and less return of March 6.
25 Brooks Co. paid Snyder Company on account for purchase of March 15, less discount.
31 Brooks Co. paid Snyder Company on account for purchase of March 5.

Instructions

Journalize the March transactions for (1) Snyder Company and (2) Brooks Co.

Appendix Alternate Problem 5-7B

Statement of cash flows using indirect method

1. Net cash flows from operating activities, $188,480

SPREADSHEET

For the year ending December 31, 2007, Guru Systems Inc. reported net income of $241,600 and paid dividends of $72,000. Comparative balance sheets as of December 31, 2007 and 2006, are as follows:

Guru Systems Inc.
Balance Sheets

	December 31, 2007	December 31, 2006	Changes Increase (Decrease)
Assets			
Current assets:			
Cash	$211,800	$166,000	$ 45,800
Accounts receivable	304,320	208,000	96,320
Merchandise inventory	248,600	238,800	9,800
Office supplies	1,920	2,400	(480)
Prepaid insurance	10,600	12,000	(1,400)
Total current assets	$777,240	$627,200	$150,040
Property, plant, and equipment:			
Land	$ 80,000	$ 80,000	$ 0
Store equipment	108,400	80,000	28,400
Accumulated depreciation—store equipment	(22,800)	(10,400)	(12,400)
Office equipment	62,280	40,000	22,280
Accumulated depreciation—office equipment	(18,880)	(8,920)	(9,960)
Total property, plant, and equipment	$209,000	$180,680	$ 28,320
Total assets	$986,240	$807,880	$178,360
Liabilities			
Current liabilities:			
Accounts payable	$ 89,680	57,080	$ 32,600
Notes payable (current portion)	20,000	20,000	0
Salaries payable	4,560	6,000	(1,440)
Unearned rent	7,200	9,600	(2,400)
Total current liabilities	$121,440	$ 92,680	$ 28,760
Long-term liabilities:			
Notes payable (final payment due 2012)	80,000	100,000	(20,000)
Total liabilities	$201,440	$192,680	$ 8,760
Stockholders' Equity			
Capital stock	$100,000	$100,000	$ 0
Retained earnings	684,800	515,200	169,600
Total stockholders' equity	$784,800	$615,200	$169,600
Total liabilities and stockholders' equity	$986,240	$807,880	$178,360

Instructions

1. Prepare a statement of cash flows, using the indirect method.
2. Under the indirect method, why is net income adjusted for changes in accruals and deferrals? Explain.

FINANCIAL ANALYSIS AND REPORTING CASES

Case 5-1

Analysis of gross profit and operating income

Federated Department Stores, Inc., is one of the leading operators of full-line department stores in the United States, operating under the names Bloomingdale's, The Bon Marche, Burdines, Goldsmith's, Lazarus, Macy's, and Rich's. The following operating data (in millions) for the past three years are taken from Federated's income statement:

	For the Years Ended		
	Jan. 29, 2005	Jan. 31, 2004	Feb. 1, 2003
Net sales	$15,630	$15,264	$15,435
Cost of merchandise sold	9,297	9,099	9,255
Operating expenses	4,933	4,824	4,837

1. Compute the gross profit for each year.
2. Compute the operating income for each year.
3. Compute the gross profit as a percentage of net sales for each year. Round to one decimal place.
4. Compute the operating income as a percentage of net sales for each year. Round to one decimal place.
5. Based upon this analysis, comment on the trends in operating performance for the past three years.
6. Based upon this analysis, compare Federated's operating performance with JCPenney's performance shown in this chapter (see Exhibit 13).

Case 5-2

Analysis of gross profit and operating income

SPREADSHEET

Nordstrom, Inc., is a fashion specialty retailer offering a wide selection of high-quality apparel, shoes, and accessories for women, men, and children in the United States through 150 stores located in 27 states. The following operating data (in thousands) were taken from 10K filings with the Securities and Exchange Commission:

	For Year Ending January 31		
	2004	2003	2002
Net sales	$6,491,673	$5,975,076	$5,634,130
Cost of goods sold	4,213,955	3,971,372	3,765,859
Gross profit	$2,277,718	$2,003,704	$1,868,271
Selling, general, admin. exp.	1,943,715	1,813,968	1,722,635
Operating income	$ 334,003	$ 189,736	$ 145,636

1. Compute gross profit as a percent of net sales for each year. Round to one decimal place.
2. Compute operating income as a percent of net sales for each year. Round to one decimal place.
3. Based upon (1) and (2), comment on Nordstrom's operating performance.

Case 5-3

Analysis of gross profit and operating income

Target Corporation is a general merchandise discount retailer. Target has 1,304 stores located in 47 states. The following operating data (in millions) were taken from 10K filings with the Securities and Exchange Commission:

	For Year Ending		
	Jan. 31, 2004	Feb. 1, 2003	Feb. 2, 2002
Net sales	$48,163	$43,917	$39,888
Cost of goods sold	31,790	29,260	27,246
Gross profit	$16,373	$14,657	$12,642
Operating income	$ 3,519	$ 3,264	$ 2,680

1. Compute gross profit as a percent of net sales for each year. Round to one decimal place.
2. Compute operating income as a percent of net sales for each year. Round to one decimal place.
3. Based upon (1) and (2), comment on Target's operating performance.

Case 5-4

Comparative analysis of operating performance

Using the data provided in Cases 5–2 and 5–3, compare the operating performances of Nordstrom and Target.

Case 5-5

Effects of inventory misstatements

Following are descriptions of two independent situations that involve inventory misstatements.

Saunders Corporation

On December 30, 2006, Saunders Corporation sold merchandise that cost $63,000 for $112,500, FOB shipping point. During the morning of December 31, 2006, the merchandise was counted as part of the physical inventory since it was still on hand. Late in the afternoon of December 31, the merchandise was picked up by the freight company hired by the customer to deliver the merchandise. Saunders Corporation's accounting department did not record the sale and related cost of merchandise sold until January 3, 2007. Saunders Corporation did not discover the preceding errors in 2007, and the customer paid the receivable later in January 2007.

Bjork Jewelry

On December 31, 2006, Bjork Jewelry failed to include in its inventory count $127,500 of its inventory that was out on consignment with other jewelers. Of this amount, $45,000 was sold the last week of December 2006 for $108,000. Bjork Jewelry was notified of these consignment sales on January 3, and, as a result, recorded the $108,000 of sales on January 3, 2007. On January 20, the consignee remitted the $108,000 to Bjork Jewelry. On December 31, 2007, Bjork again failed to include in its inventory count $115,000 of its inventory that was out on consignment with other jewelers. None of the jewelry out on consignment on December 31, 2007, had been sold as of that date. Bjork had not discovered any of the errors.

For each of the companies, indicate the effects of the inventory misstatements on the financial statements for 2006 and 2007.

Case 5-6

Comparative analysis of operating performance

Two major consumer electronics retailers are Best Buy and Circuit City Stores, Inc. Recent fiscal year-end income statements for both companies for a three-year period shown below and at the top of page 260.

1. Prepare a graph displaying the years 2002, 2003, and 2004 on the x-axis and the gross profit to sales ratio for Best Buy and Circuit City on the y-axis. Connect the ratio for each company with a line. Thus, the graph will display two lines, one for each company.
2. Prepare a second graph displaying the years 2002, 2003, and 2004 on the x-axis and the operating profit to sales ratio for Best Buy and Circuit City on the y-axis. Connect the ratio for each company with a line. Thus, the graph will display two lines, one for each company.
3. Interpret your graphs.

Best Buy
Income Statements
Fiscal Years Ending 2002, 2003, and 2004
(in millions)

	2004	2003	2002
Net sales	$27,433	$24,548	$20,943
Cost of merchandise sold	20,938	18,677	15,998
Gross profit	$ 6,495	$ 5,871	$ 4,945
Selling, general, and administrative expenses	5,053	4,567	3,935
Operating income	$ 1,442	$ 1,304	$ 1,010

Circuit City Stores, Inc.
Income Statements
Fiscal Years Ending 2002, 2003, and 2004
(in millions)

	2004	2003	2002
Net sales	$10,472	$9,857	$9,953
Cost of merchandise sold	7,903	7,573	7,603
Gross profit	$ 2,569	$2,284	$2,350
Selling, general, and administrative expenses	2,457	2,278	2,329
Operating income	$ 112	$ 6	$ 21

BUSINESS ACTIVITIES AND RESPONSIBILITY ISSUES

Activity 5-1

Ethics and professional conduct in business

On December 1, 2006, Cardinal Company, a garden retailer, purchased $20,000 of corn seed, terms 2/10, n/30, from Iowa Farm Co. Even though the discount period had expired, Sandi Kurtz subtracted the discount of $400 when she processed the documents for payment on December 15, 2006.

Discuss whether Sandi Kurtz behaved in a professional manner by subtracting the discount, even though the discount period had expired.

Activity 5-2

Purchases discounts and accounts payable

The Video Store Co. is owned and operated by Todd Shovic. The following is an excerpt from a conversation between Todd Shovic and Susan Mastin, the chief accountant for The Video Store.

Todd: Susan, I've got a question about this recent balance sheet.
Susan: Sure, what's your question?
Todd: Well, as you know, I'm applying for a bank loan to finance our new store in Three Forks, and I noticed that the accounts payable are listed as $110,000.
Susan: That's right. Approximately $90,000 of that represents amounts due our suppliers, and the remainder is miscellaneous payables to creditors for utilities, office equipment, supplies, etc.
Todd: That's what I thought. But as you know, we normally receive a 2% discount from our suppliers for earlier payment, and we always try to take the discount.
Susan: That's right. I can't remember the last time we missed a discount.
Todd: Well, in that case, it seems to me the accounts payable should be listed minus the 2% discount. Let's list the accounts payable due suppliers as $88,200, rather than $90,000. Every little bit helps. You never know. It might make the difference between getting the loan and not.

How would you respond to Todd Shovic's request?

Activity 5-3

Determining cost of purchase

The following is an excerpt from a conversation between Brad Hass and Terry Mann. Brad is debating whether to buy a stereo system from Radiant Sound, a locally owned electronics store, or Audio Pro Electronics, a mail-order electronics company.

Brad: Terry, I don't know what to do about buying my new stereo.
Terry: What's the problem?
Brad: Well, I can buy it locally at Radiant Sound for $395.00. However, Audio Pro Electronics has the same system listed for $399.99.
Terry: So what's the big deal? Buy it from Radiant Sound.
Brad: It's not quite that simple. Audio Pro said something about not having to pay sales tax, since I was out-of-state.

Terry: Yes, that's a good point. If you buy it at Radiant Sound, they'll charge you 6% sales tax.
Brad: But Audio Pro Electronics charges $12.50 for shipping and handling. If I have them send it next-day air, it'll cost $25 for shipping and handling.
Terry: I guess it is a little confusing.
Brad: That's not all. Radiant Sound will give an additional 1% discount if I pay cash. Otherwise, they will let me use my MasterCard, or I can pay it off in three monthly installments.
Terry: Anything else???
Brad: Well . . . Audio Pro says I have to charge it on my MasterCard. They don't accept checks.
Terry: I am not surprised. Many mail-order houses don't accept checks.
Brad: I give up. What would you do?

1. Assuming that Audio Pro Electronics doesn't charge sales tax on the sale to Brad, which company is offering the best buy?
2. What might be some considerations other than price that might influence Brad's decision on where to buy the stereo system?

Activity 5-4

Sales discounts

Your sister operates Callender Parts Company, a mail-order boat parts distributorship that is in its third year of operation. The following income statement was recently prepared for the year ended March 31, 2006:

Callender Parts Company
Income Statement
For the Year Ended March 31, 2006

Revenues:		
Net sales		$960,000
Interest revenue		8,000
Total revenues		$968,000
Expenses:		
Cost of merchandise sold	$672,000	
Selling expenses	105,600	
Administrative expenses	54,400	
Interest expense	16,000	
Total expenses		848,000
Net income		$120,000

Your sister is considering a proposal to increase net income by offering sales discounts of 2/15, n/30, and by shipping all merchandise FOB shipping point. Currently, no sales discounts are allowed and merchandise is shipped FOB destination. It is estimated that these credit terms will increase net sales by 10%. The ratio of the cost of merchandise sold to net sales is expected to be 70%. All selling and administrative expenses are expected to remain unchanged, except for store supplies, miscellaneous selling, office supplies, and miscellaneous administrative expenses, which are expected to increase proportionately with increased net sales. The amounts of these preceding items for the year ended March 31, 2006, were as follows:

Store supplies expense	$8,000
Miscellaneous selling expense	3,200
Office supplies expense	1,600
Miscellaneous administrative expense	2,880

The other income and other expense items will remain unchanged. The shipment of all merchandise FOB shipping point will eliminate all transportation out expenses, which for the year ended March 31, 2006, were $32,240.

1. Prepare a projected single-step income statement for the year ending March 31, 2007, based on the proposal. Assume all sales are collected within the discount period.
2. a. Based on the projected income statement in (1), would you recommend the implementation of the proposed changes?
   b. Describe any possible concerns you may have related to the proposed changes described in (1).

Activity 5-5

Shopping for a television

GROUP ACTIVITY

Assume that you are planning to purchase a 50-inch Plasma television. In groups of three or four, determine the lowest cost for the television, considering the available alternatives and the advantages and disadvantages of each alternative. For example, you could purchase locally, through mail order, or through an Internet shopping service. Consider such factors as delivery charges, interest-free financing, discounts, coupons, and availability of warranty services. Prepare a report for presentation to the class.

ANSWERS TO SELF-STUDY QUESTIONS

1. A A debit memorandum (answer A), issued by the buyer, indicates the amount the buyer proposes to debit to the accounts payable account. A credit memorandum (answer B), issued by the seller, indicates the amount the seller proposes to credit to the accounts receivable account. An invoice (answer C) or a bill (answer D), issued by the seller, indicates the amount and terms of the sale.

2. C The amount of discount for early payment is $10 (answer C), or 1% of $1,000. Although the $50 of transportation costs paid by the seller is debited to the customer's account, the customer is not entitled to a discount on that amount.

3. B The single-step form of income statement (answer B) is so named because the total of all expenses is deducted in one step from the total of all revenues. The multiple-step form (answer A) includes numerous sections and subsections with several subtotals. The report form (answer D) is a common form of the balance sheet.

4. C Gross profit (answer C) is the excess of net sales over the cost of merchandise sold. Operating income (answer A) or income from operations (answer B) is the excess of gross profit over operating expenses. Net income (answer D) is the final figure on the income statement after all revenues and expenses have been reported.

5. C Operating income is understated by $25,000 (answer C). The cost of merchandise sold is overstated, not understated (answer A). Gross profit is understated, not overstated (answer B). Inventory shrinkage is overstated, not understated (answer D).

6 Inventories

Learning Goals

1. Identify the types of inventory used by merchandisers and manufacturers.
2. Summarize and provide examples of control procedures that apply to inventories.
3. Describe three inventory cost flow assumptions and how they impact the income statement and balance sheet.
4. Determine the cost of inventory under the perpetual inventory system, using the first-in, first-out; last-in, first-out; and average cost methods.
5. Determine the cost of inventory under the periodic inventory system, using the first-in, first-out; last-in, first-out; and average cost methods.
6. Compare and contrast the use of the three inventory costing methods.
7. Determine the proper valuation of inventory at other than cost, using the lower-of-cost-or-market and net realizable value concepts.
8. Describe how inventories are being reduced through quick response.
9. Determine and interpret the inventory turnover ratio and the number of days' sales in inventory.

Best Buy

When you go to the store, it is common to purchase things like paper products and beverages in large quantities. In this way, you can store these products for future needs and not have to run back out to the store. After all, when you want a "cold one" (soft drink, that is), you don't want to always jump into the car. These at home shelf items can be thought of as your inventory.

Just as inventory offers you convenience, a business also uses inventory to support its business needs. From a consumer's perspective, inventory allows us to compare products, touch products, purchase on impulse, and take immediate delivery of a product upon purchase. For example, Best Buy has an inventory of TVs available for viewing prior to purchase. In other cases, consumers are willing to wait for the product to be produced to their unique specifications. Boeing, for example, builds aircraft only after an order is received.

© KIICHIRO SATO/AP PHOTO

The inventory held by a retailer must fit the target consumer audience. For example, Best Buy holds inventories of computer games, DVD movies, CD music, and computer software in order to create repeat consumer traffic. As a result, when a consumer wishes to purchase more expensive consumer electronic hardware, he or she will naturally consider Best Buy due to past familiarity. However, Best Buy does not carry lawn mowers because they do not fit its merchandising emphasis.

Beyond customer benefits, inventory provides protection against disruptions in production, transportation, or other processes. For example, an unexpected strike by a supplier's employees can halt production for a manufacturer or cause lost sales for a merchandiser. Inventory also allows a business to meet unexpected increases in the demand for its product. For example, Best Buy carries extra inventory in advance of holidays and sales events.

In addition to the benefits of inventory, there are costs to holding inventory. These include the costs to acquire, hold, store, handle, and finance inventory. Inventories are also subject to obsolescence. For example, electronic consumer products, like those sold at Best Buy, are subject to quick technical obsolescence. Thus, management must balance the benefits of holding inventory against these costs.

In this chapter, we will define inventory for manufacturers and merchandisers, illustrate inventory valuation approaches, and introduce ratios used to analyze management's effective use of inventory.

Identify the types of inventory used by merchandisers and manufacturers.

INVENTORY CLASSIFICATION FOR MERCHANDISERS AND MANUFACTURERS

In Chapter 5, we defined a merchandiser as a company that purchases products for resale, such as apparel, consumer electronics, hardware, or food items. We stated that the merchandise on hand (not sold) at the end of the period was a current asset called **merchandise inventory**. Inventory sold becomes the *cost of merchandise sold*. Merchandise inventory is a significant current asset for most merchandising companies, as illustrated for four well-known merchandising companies in Exhibit 1.

Exhibit 1

Size of Merchandise Inventory for Merchandising Businesses

	Merchandise Inventory as a Percent of Current Assets	Merchandise Inventory as a Percent of Total Assets
Wal-Mart	77%	25%
Best Buy	41	28
Home Depot	68	26
Kroger	74	21

What costs should be included in merchandise inventory? As we illustrated in earlier chapters, the cost of merchandise is its purchase price, less any purchases discounts. These costs are usually the largest portion of the inventory cost. Merchandise inventory also includes other costs, such as transportation, import duties, property taxes, and insurance costs. The underlying accounting concept is that the inventory cost must include all the costs of ownership. For example, the CarMax division of Circuit City Stores, Inc., states:

> *Parts and labor used to recondition vehicles, as well as transportation and other incremental expenses associated with acquiring vehicles, are included in the CarMax Group's inventory.*

In contrast, manufacturing companies convert raw materials into final products, which are often sold to merchandising businesses. A manufacturing company has three types of inventory, as illustrated in Exhibit 2.

Materials inventory consists of the cost of raw materials used in manufacturing a product. For example, Hershey Foods Corporation uses cocoa and sugar in making chocolate. The cost of cocoa and sugar held in the storage silos at the end of the period would be reported on the balance sheet as materials inventory.

Work-in-process inventory consists of the costs for partially completed product. These costs include the *direct materials*, which are a product's component materials that are introduced into the manufacturing process. For example, Hershey introduces cocoa and sugar in the process of making chocolate. Other costs are also added in the manufacturing process, such as direct labor and factory overhead costs. *Direct labor costs* are the wages of factory workers directly involved with making a product. *Factory overhead costs* are all factory costs other than direct labor and materials, such as equipment depreciation, supervisory salaries, and power costs. The balance sheet reports the work-in-process inventory at the end of the period as a current asset.

Finished goods inventory consists of the costs of direct materials, direct labor, and factory overhead for completed production. The finished goods inventory for Hershey Foods is the cost of packaged chocolate held in a finished goods warehouse at the end of the period. When the finished goods are sold, the costs are transferred to the **cost of goods sold** or the *cost of merchandise sold* on the income statement.

Exhibit 2

Manufacturing Inventories

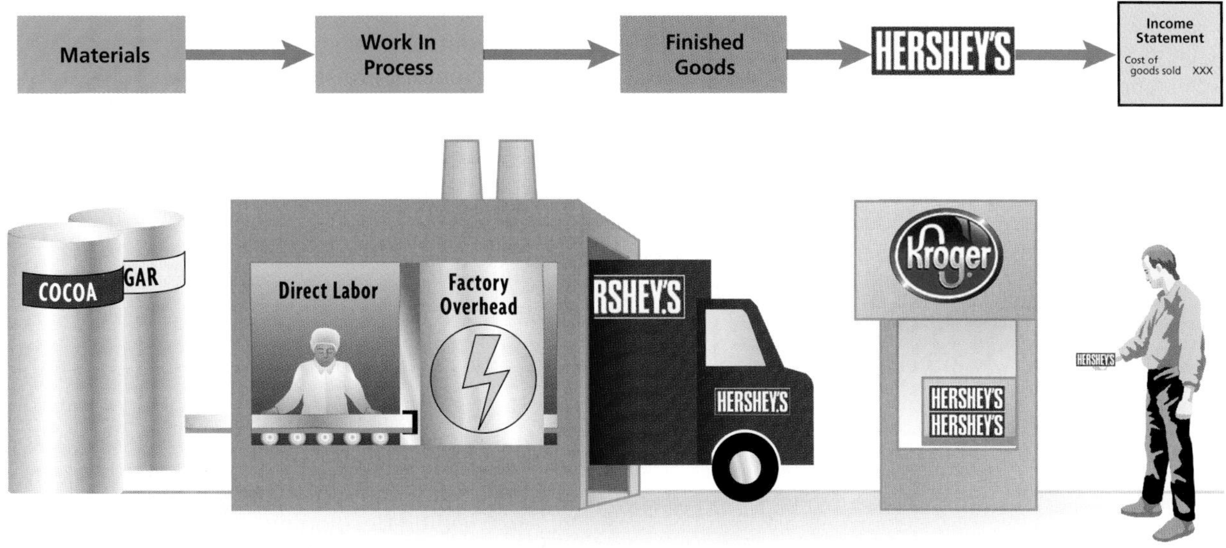

Manufacturing inventories are often disclosed in the footnotes to the financial statements of a manufacturer. For example, Hershey Foods Corporation reported inventories of $621,347,000 with the following footnote detail:

Materials	$166,813,000
Work-in-process	70,440,000
Finished goods	384,094,000
Total inventories	$621,347,000

In this chapter, we will illustrate inventory accounting and analysis issues from the perspective of the merchandising business. However, many of the points apply equally well to a manufacturer. The accounting for manufacturing inventories is covered in a managerial accounting course.

HOW BUSINESSES MAKE MONEY

The Consumer Electronic Wars: Best Buy v. Circuit City

How does **Best Buy** compete against **Circuit City Stores, Inc.** in the intensely competitive consumer electronics market? It doesn't just follow a "me too" method but approaches the market by trying to find a way to distinguish itself from Circuit City. First, a warmer color and lighting scheme, featuring light yellows, was chosen over Circuit City's darker color scheme. Second, it opened up bigger stores to provide extra space for the "software" of home electronics. Best Buy believes that more space devoted to CD music, DVD movies, and computer software creates customer foot traffic that eventually translates into other sales. Third, Best Buy introduced a "do-it-yourself" strategy on the sales floor. Rather than using commissioned salespersons, Best Buy believes that noncommissioned sales personnel can support floor sales. That is, it believes that customers don't need an expert to sell them a product. As a result, the selling expenses as a percent of revenues are reduced. Has the strategy worked? Over the last five years, Best Buy has grown from $15,189 million to $27,433 million in sales, an 81% increase, while Circuit City's sales have decreased by 1%.

Summarize and provide examples of control procedures that apply to inventories.

CONTROL OF INVENTORY

For companies such as Best Buy, good control over inventory must be maintained. Two primary objectives of control over inventory are safeguarding the inventory and properly reporting it in the financial statements. These controls can be either preventive or detective in nature. A preventive control is designed to prevent errors or misstatements from occurring. A detective control is designed to detect an error or misstatement after it has occurred.

Control over inventory should begin as soon as the inventory is received. Receiving reports should be completed by the company's receiving department in order to establish initial accountability for the inventory. To make sure the inventory received is what was ordered, each receiving report should agree with the company's original purchase order for the merchandise. Likewise, the price at which the inventory was ordered, as shown on the purchase order, should be compared to the price at which the vendor billed the company, as shown on the vendor's invoice. After the receiving report, purchase order, and vendor's invoice have been reconciled, the company should record the inventory and related account payable in the accounting records.

Controls for safeguarding inventory include developing and using security measures to prevent inventory damage or customer or employee theft. For example, inventory should be stored in a warehouse or other area to which access is restricted to authorized employees. When shopping, you may have noticed how retail stores protect inventory from customer theft. Retail stores often use such devices as two-way mirrors, cameras, and security guards. High-priced items are often displayed in locked cabinets. Retail clothing stores often place plastic alarm tags on valuable items such as leather coats. Sensors at the exit doors set off alarms if the tags have not been removed by the clerk. These controls are designed to prevent customers from shoplifting.

Using a perpetual inventory system for merchandise also provides an effective means of control over inventory. The amount of each type of merchandise is always readily available in a subsidiary **inventory ledger**. In addition, the subsidiary ledger can be an aid in maintaining inventory quantities at proper levels. Frequently, comparing balances with predetermined maximum and minimum levels allows for the timely reordering of merchandise and prevents the ordering of excess inventory.

To ensure the accuracy of the amount of inventory reported in the financial statements, a merchandising business should take a **physical inventory** (i.e., count the merchandise). In a perpetual inventory system, the physical inventory is compared to the recorded inventory in order to determine the amount of shrinkage or shortage. If the inventory shrinkage is unusually large, management can investigate further and take any necessary corrective action. Knowing that a physical inventory will be taken also helps prevent employee thefts or misuses of inventory.

Most companies take their physical inventories when their inventory levels are the lowest. For example, most retailers take their physical inventories in late January or early February, which is after the holiday selling season but before restocking for spring.

Describe three inventory cost flow assumptions and how they impact the income statement and balance sheet.

INVENTORY COST FLOW ASSUMPTIONS

When you arrive in line to purchase a movie ticket, the tickets are sold on a first-in, first-out (fifo) order. That is, those who arrive first in line purchase their tickets before those who arrive later. In this section, we will see how this ordering concept is used to value inventory. This issue arises when identical units of merchandise are acquired at different unit costs during a period. When the company sells one of these identical items, it must determine a unit cost so that it can record the proper accounting entry. To illustrate, assume that three identical units of Item X are purchased during May, as shown below.

		Item X	Units	Cost
May	10	Purchase	1	$ 9
	18	Purchase	1	13
	24	Purchase	1	14
	Total		3	$36
	Average cost per unit			$12

Assume that the company sells one unit on May 30 for $20. If this unit can be identified with a specific purchase, the *specific identification method* can be used to determine the cost of the unit sold. For example, if the unit sold was purchased on May 18, the cost assigned to the unit would be $13, and the gross profit would be $7 ($20 − $13). If, however, the unit sold was purchased on May 10, the cost assigned to the unit would be $9, and the gross profit would be $11 ($20 − $9). The specific identification method is normally used by companies that sell relatively expensive items, such as jewelry or automobiles. For example, Oakwood Homes Corp., a manufacturer and seller of mobile homes, stated in the footnotes to its annual report:

> *Inventories are valued at the lower of cost or market, with cost determined using the specific identification method for new and used manufactured homes. . . .*

The specific identification method is not practical unless each unit can be identified accurately. An automobile dealer, for example, may be able to use this method, since each automobile has a unique serial number. For many businesses, however, identical units cannot be separately identified, and a cost flow must be assumed. That is, which units have been sold and which units are still in inventory must be assumed.

Three common cost flow assumptions are used in business. Each of these assumptions is identified with an inventory costing method, as shown below.

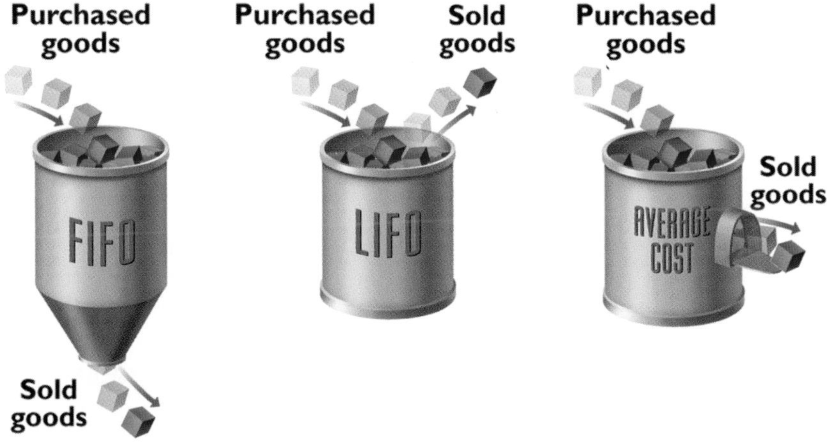

When the **first-in, first-out (fifo) method** is used, the ending inventory is made up of the most recent costs. When the **last-in, first-out (lifo) method** is used, the ending inventory is made up of the earliest costs. When the **average cost method** is used, the cost of the units in inventory is an average of the purchase costs.

To illustrate, we use the preceding example to prepare the income statement for May and the balance sheet as of May 31 for each of the cost flow methods. These financial statements are shown in Exhibit 3.

Exhibit 3

Effect of Inventory Costing Methods on Financial Statements

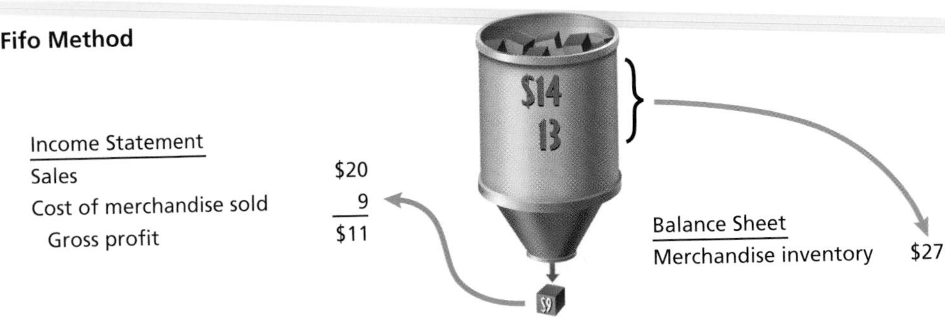

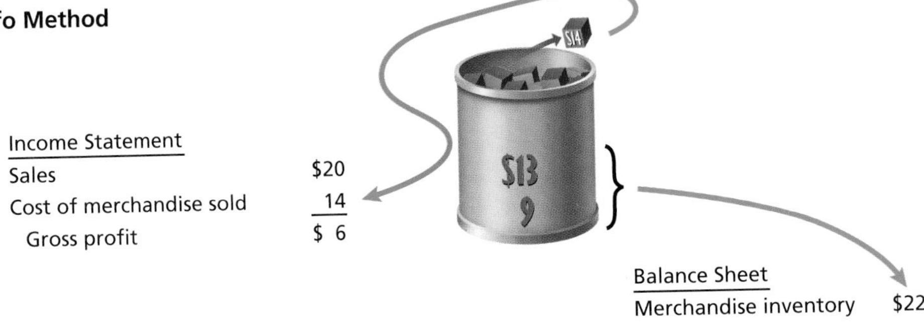

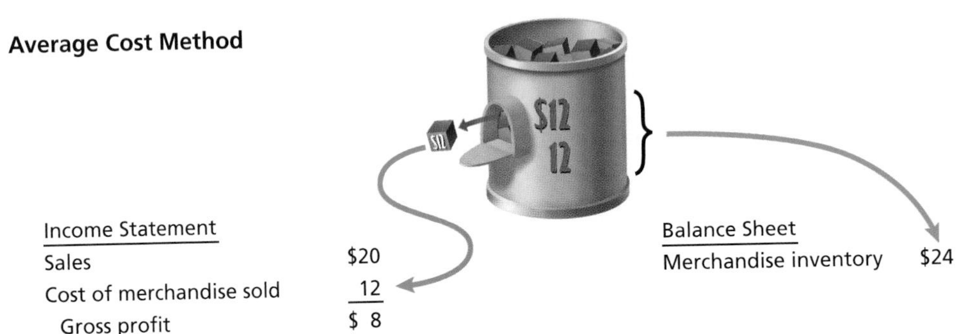

As you can see, selecting an inventory costing method can have a significant impact on the financial statements. For this reason, the selection has important implications for managers and others in analyzing and interpreting the financial statements. The chart in Exhibit 4 shows the frequency with which fifo, lifo, and the average methods are used in practice for firms exceeding $1 billion in sales.

INTEGRITY, OBJECTIVITY, AND ETHICS IN BUSINESS

Facilitating Others

Best Buy is focusing on growing from within (based upon the strength of its employees) and building a strength-based company. Brad Anderson, chief executive officer and vice chairman of Best Buy, stated:

. . . being a leader is not so much what you do, but what you facilitate from others. . . . [Best Buy is committed to]. . . show respect, humility and integrity; learn from challenge and change; have fun while being best and unleash the power of our people.

Source: Laura Heller, "Best Buy Chief Learns Valuable Lessons in First Year in Office," *Discount Store News*, Monday, July 7, 2003.

Exhibit 4

*Inventory Costing Methods**

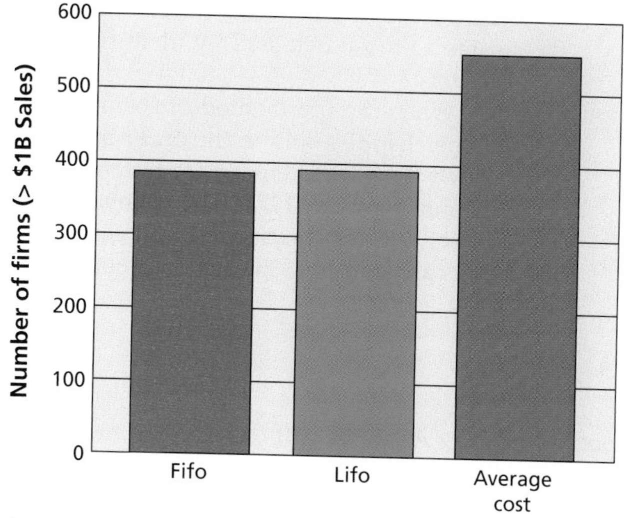

Source: Derived from Disclosure financial database.
*Firms may be counted more than once for using multiple methods.

Determine the cost of inventory under the perpetual inventory system, using the first-in, first-out; last-in, first-out; and average cost methods.

INVENTORY COSTING METHODS UNDER A PERPETUAL INVENTORY SYSTEM

In a perpetual inventory system, all merchandise increases and decreases are recorded in a manner similar to recording increases and decreases in cash. The merchandise inventory account at the beginning of an accounting period indicates the merchandise in stock on that date. Purchases are recorded by debiting *Merchandise Inventory* and crediting *Cash* or *Accounts Payable*. On the date of each sale, the cost of the merchandise sold is recorded by debiting *Cost of Merchandise Sold* and crediting *Merchandise Inventory*.

As we illustrated in the preceding section, a cost flow must be assumed when identical units of an item are purchased at different unit costs during a period. In such cases, the fifo, lifo, or average cost method is used. We illustrate each of these methods, using the data for Item 127B, shown below.

	Item 127B	Units	Cost
Jan. 1	Inventory	10	$20
4	Sale	7	
10	Purchase	8	21
22	Sale	4	
28	Sale	2	
30	Purchase	10	22

First-In, First-Out Method

Most businesses dispose of goods in the order in which the goods are purchased. This would be especially true of perishables and goods whose styles or models often change. For example, grocery stores shelve their milk products by expiration dates. Likewise, men's and women's clothing stores display clothes by season. At the end of a season, they often have sales to clear their stores of off-season or out-of-style clothing. Thus, the fifo method is often consistent with the *physical flow* or movement of merchandise.

To the extent that this is the case, the fifo method provides results that are about the same as those obtained by identifying the specific costs of each item sold and in inventory.

When the fifo method of costing inventory is used, costs are included in the cost of merchandise sold in the order in which they were incurred. To illustrate, Exhibit 5 shows the journal entries for purchases and sales and the inventory subsidiary ledger account for Item 127B. The number of units in inventory after each transaction, together with total costs and unit costs, are shown in the account. We assume that the units are sold for $30 each on account.

Exhibit 5

Entries and Perpetual Inventory Account (Fifo)

Date	Account	Debit	Credit
Jan. 4	Accounts Receivable	210	
	Sales		210
4	Cost of Merchandise Sold	140	
	Merchandise Inventory		140
10	Merchandise Inventory	168	
	Accounts Payable		168
22	Accounts Receivable	120	
	Sales		120
22	Cost of Merchandise Sold	81	
	Merchandise Inventory		81
28	Accounts Receivable	60	
	Sales		60
28	Cost of Merchandise Sold	42	
	Merchandise Inventory		42
30	Merchandise Inventory	220	
	Accounts Payable		220

Item 127B

	Purchases			Cost of Merchandise Sold			Inventory		
Date	Quantity	Unit Cost	Total Cost	Quantity	Unit Cost	Total Cost	Quantity	Unit Cost	Total Cost
Jan. 1							10	20	200
4				7	20	140	3	20	60
10	8	21	168				3	20	60
							8	21	168
22				3	20	60			
				1	21	21	7	21	147
28				2	21	42	5	21	105
30	10	22	220				5	21	105
							10	22	220

You should note that after the 7 units were sold on January 4, there was an inventory of 3 units at $20 each. The 8 units purchased on January 10 were acquired at a unit cost of $21. Therefore, the inventory after the January 10 purchase is reported on two lines: 3 units at $20 each and 8 units at $21 each. Next, note that the $81 cost of the 4 units sold on January 22 is made up of the remaining 3 units at $20 each and 1 unit at $21. At this point, 7 units are in inventory at a cost of $21 per unit. The remainder of the illustration is explained in a similar manner.

Last-In, First-Out Method

When the lifo method is used in a perpetual inventory system, the cost of the units sold is the cost of the most recent purchases. To illustrate, Exhibit 6 shows the journal entries for purchases and sales and the subsidiary ledger account for Item 127B, prepared on a lifo basis.

If you compare the ledger accounts for the fifo perpetual system and the lifo perpetual system, you should discover that the accounts are the same through the January 10 purchase. Using lifo, however, the cost of the 4 units sold on January 22 is the cost

Exhibit 6

Entries and Perpetual Inventory Account (Lifo)

Date	Account	Debit	Credit
Jan. 4	Accounts Receivable	210	
	Sales		210
4	Cost of Merchandise Sold	140	
	Merchandise Inventory		140
10	Merchandise Inventory	168	
	Accounts Payable		168
22	Accounts Receivable	120	
	Sales		120
22	Cost of Merchandise Sold	84	
	Merchandise Inventory		84
28	Accounts Receivable	60	
	Sales		60
28	Cost of Merchandise Sold	42	
	Merchandise Inventory		42
30	Merchandise Inventory	220	
	Accounts Payable		220

Item 127B

	Purchases			Cost of Merchandise Sold			Inventory		
Date	Quantity	Unit Cost	Total Cost	Quantity	Unit Cost	Total Cost	Quantity	Unit Cost	Total Cost
Jan. 1							10	20	200
4				7	20	140	3	20	60
10	8	21	168				3	20	60
							8	21	168
22				4	21	84	3	20	60
							4	21	84
28				2	21	42	3	20	60
							2	21	42
30	10	22	220				3	20	60
							2	21	42
							10	22	220

of the units from the January 10 purchase ($21 per unit). The cost of the 7 units in inventory after the sale on January 22 is the cost of the 3 units remaining from the beginning inventory and the cost of the 4 units remaining from the January 10 purchase. The remainder of the lifo illustration is explained in a similar manner.

When the lifo method is used, the inventory ledger is sometimes maintained in units only. The units are converted to dollars when the financial statements are prepared at the end of the period.

The use of the lifo method was originally limited to rare situations in which the units sold were taken from the most recently acquired goods. For tax reasons, which we will discuss later, its use has greatly increased during the past few decades. Lifo is now often used, even when it does not represent the physical flow of goods.

Average Cost Method

When the average cost method is used in a perpetual inventory system, an average unit cost for each type of item is computed each time a purchase is made. This unit cost is then used to determine the cost of each sale until another purchase is made and a new average is computed. This averaging technique is called a *moving average*. Since the average cost method is rarely used in a perpetual inventory system, we do not illustrate it in this chapter.

Computerized Perpetual Inventory Systems

The records for a perpetual inventory system may be maintained manually. However, such a system is costly and time consuming for businesses with a large number of inventory items with many purchase and sales transactions. In most cases, the record keeping for perpetual inventory systems is computerized.

An example of using computers in maintaining perpetual inventory records for retail stores is described below.

1. The relevant details for each inventory item, such as a description, quantity, and unit size, are stored in an inventory record. The individual inventory records make up the computerized inventory file, the total of which agrees with the balance of the inventory ledger account.
2. Each time an item is purchased or returned by a customer, the inventory data are entered into the computer's inventory records and files.
3. Each time an item is sold, a salesclerk scans the item's bar code with an optical scanner. The scanner reads the magnetic code and rings up the sale on the cash register. The inventory records and files are then updated for the cost of goods sold. For example, Best Buy, Wal-Mart, Target, Sears, and other retailers use bar code scanners to update inventory records and sales.
4. After a physical inventory is taken, the inventory count data are entered into the computer. These data are compared with the current balances, and a listing of the overages and shortages is printed. The inventory balances are then adjusted to the quantities determined by the physical count.

Such systems can be extended to aid managers in controlling and managing inventory quantities. For example, items that are selling fast can be reordered before the stock is depleted. Past sales patterns can be analyzed to determine when to mark down merchandise for sales and when to restock seasonal merchandise. In addition, such systems can provide managers with data for developing and fine-tuning their marketing strategies. For example, such data can be used to evaluate the effectiveness of advertising campaigns and sales promotions.

Determine the cost of inventory under the periodic inventory system, using the first-in, first-out; last-in, first-out; and average cost methods.

INVENTORY COSTING METHODS UNDER A PERIODIC INVENTORY SYSTEM

When the periodic inventory system is used, only revenue is recorded each time a sale is made. No entry is made at the time of the sale to record the cost of the merchandise sold. At the end of the accounting period, a physical inventory is taken to determine the cost of the inventory and the cost of the merchandise sold. Like the perpetual inventory system, a cost flow assumption must be made when identical units are acquired at different unit costs during a period. In such cases, the fifo, lifo, or average cost method is used.

First-In, First-Out Method

To illustrate the use of the fifo method in a periodic inventory system, we assume the following data:

Jan. 1	Inventory:	200 units at	$ 9	$ 1,800
Mar. 10	Purchase:	300 units at	10	3,000
Sept. 21	Purchase:	400 units at	11	4,400
Nov. 18	Purchase:	100 units at	12	1,200
Available for sale during year		1,000		$10,400

Q. What is the cost of merchandise sold if the beginning inventory is $50,000, the ending inventory is $65,000, the net purchases are $400,000, and the transportation in is $12,000?

A. *$397,000 ($50,000 + $400,000 + $12,000 – $65,000)*

The physical count on December 31 shows that 300 units have not been sold. Using the fifo method, the cost of the 700 units sold is determined as follows:

Earliest costs, Jan. 1:	200 units at	$ 9	$1,800
Next earliest costs, Mar. 10:	300 units at	10	3,000
Next earliest costs, Sept. 21:	200 units at	11	2,200
Cost of merchandise sold:	700		$7,000

Deducting the cost of merchandise sold of $7,000 from the $10,400 of merchandise available for sale yields $3,400 as the cost of the inventory at December 31. The $3,400 inventory is made up of the most recent costs incurred for this item. Exhibit 7 shows the relationship of the cost of merchandise sold during the year and the inventory at December 31.

Exhibit 7

First-In, First-Out Flow of Costs

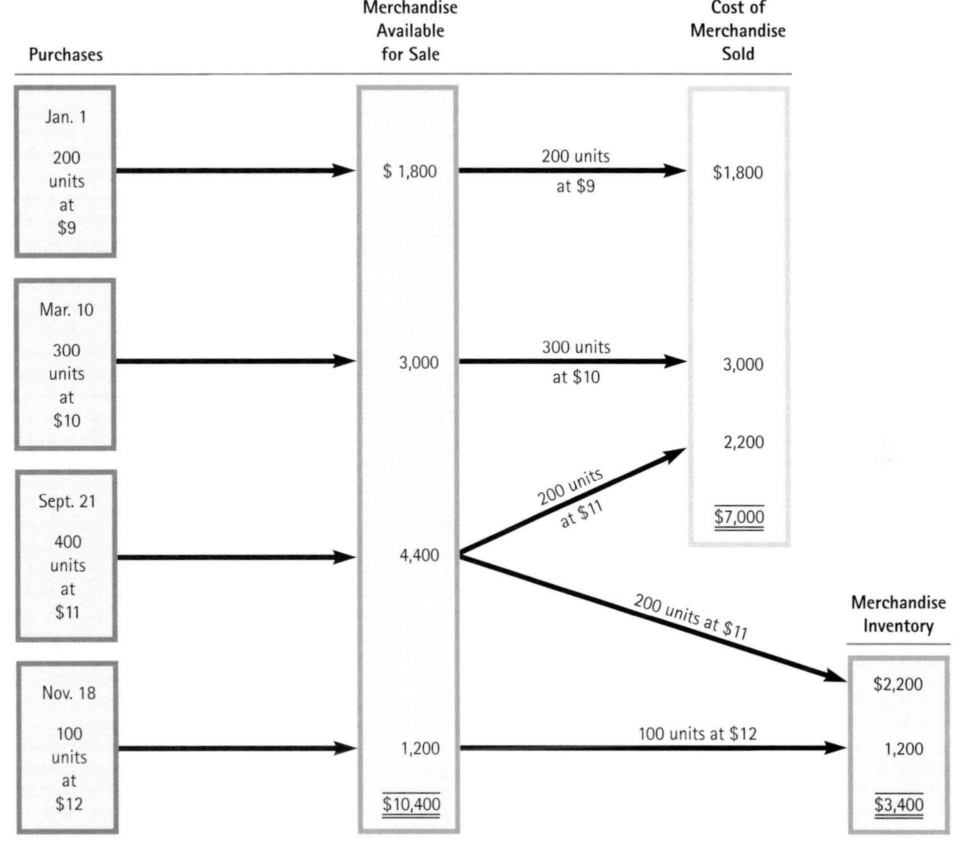

Last-In, First-Out Method

When the lifo method is used, the cost of merchandise sold is made up of the most recent costs. Based on the data in the fifo example, the cost of the 700 units of inventory is determined as follows:

Most recent costs, Nov. 18:	100 units at	$12	$1,200
Next most recent costs, Sept. 21:	400 units at	11	4,400
Next most recent costs, Mar. 10:	200 units at	10	2,000
Cost of merchandise sold:	700		$7,600

Deducting the cost of merchandise sold of $7,600 from the $10,400 of merchandise available for sale yields $2,800 as the cost of the inventory at December 31. The $2,800 inventory is made up of the earliest costs incurred for this item. Exhibit 8 shows the relationship of the cost of merchandise sold during the year and the inventory at December 31.

Exhibit 8

Last-In, First-Out Flow of Costs

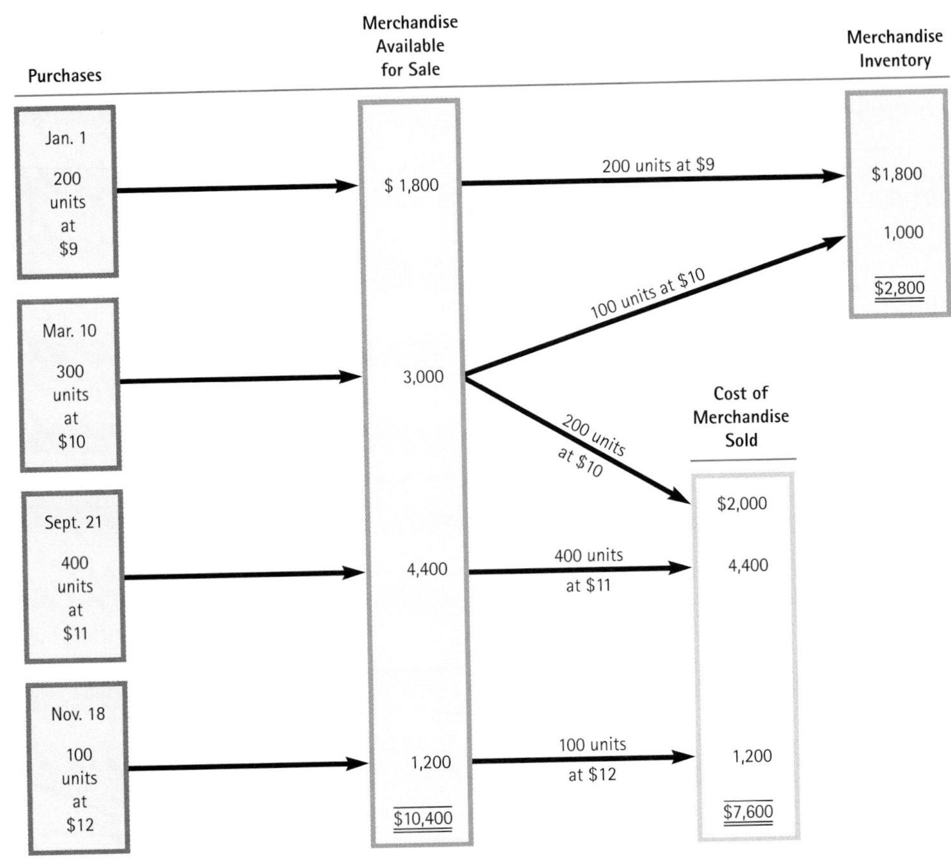

Average Cost Method

The average cost method is sometimes called the *weighted average method*. When this method is used, costs are matched against revenue according to an average of the unit cost of the goods sold. The same weighted average unit costs are used in determining the cost of the merchandise inventory at the end of the period. For businesses in which merchandise sales may be made up of various purchases of identical units, the average method approximates the physical flow of goods.

The weighted average unit cost is determined by dividing the total cost of the units of each item available for sale during the period by the related number of units of that item. Using the same cost data as in the fifo and lifo examples, the average cost of the 1,000 units, $10.40, and the cost of the 700 units, $7,280, are determined as follows:

Average unit cost: $10,400 ÷ 1,000 units = $10.40
Cost of merchandise sold: 700 units at $10.40 = $7,280

Deducting the cost of merchandise sold of $7,280 from the $10,400 of merchandise available for sale yields $3,120 as the cost of the inventory at December 31.

Compare and contrast the use of the three inventory costing methods.

COMPARING INVENTORY COSTING METHODS

As we have illustrated, a different cost flow is assumed for each of the three alternative methods of costing inventories. You should note that if the cost of units had remained stable, all three methods would have yielded the same results. Since prices do change, however, the three methods will normally yield different amounts for (1) the cost of the merchandise sold for the period, (2) the gross profit (and net income) for the period, and (3) the ending inventory. Using the preceding examples for the periodic inventory system and assuming that net sales were $15,000, the partial income statements shown below indicate the effects of each method when prices are rising.[1]

As these partial income statements show, the fifo method yielded the lowest amount for the cost of merchandise sold and the highest amount for gross profit (and net income). It also yielded the highest amount for the ending inventory. On the other hand, the lifo method yielded the highest amount for the cost of merchandise sold, the lowest amount for gross profit (and net income), and the lowest amount for ending inventory. The average cost method yielded results that were between those of fifo and lifo.

Partial Income Statements

	First-In, First-Out		Average Cost		Last-In, First-Out	
Net sales		$15,000		$15,000		$15,000
Cost of merchandise sold:						
Beginning inventory	$ 1,800		$ 1,800		$ 1,800	
Purchases	8,600		8,600		8,600	
Merchandise available for sale	$10,400		$10,400		$10,400	
Less ending inventory	3,400		3,120		2,800	
Cost of merchandise sold		7,000		7,280		7,600
Gross profit		$ 8,000		$ 7,720		$ 7,400

Use of the First-In, First-Out Method

When the fifo method is used during a period of inflation or rising prices, the earlier unit costs are lower than the more recent unit costs, as shown in the preceding fifo example. Much of the benefit of the larger amount of gross profit is lost, however, because the inventory must be replaced at ever higher prices. In fact, the balance sheet will report the ending merchandise inventory at an amount that is about the same as its current replacement cost. When prices are increasing, the larger gross profits that result from the fifo method are often called *inventory profits* or *illusory profits*. You should note that in a period of deflation or declining prices, the effect is just the opposite.

1 Similar results would also occur when comparing inventory costing methods under a perpetual inventory system.

Use of the Last-In, First-Out Method

International Perspective International Accounting Standards (IASs) do not allow companies to use the lifo method for costing inventory.

When the lifo method is used during a period of inflation or rising prices, the results are opposite those of the other two methods. As shown in the preceding example, the lifo method will yield a higher amount of cost of merchandise sold, a lower amount of gross profit, and a lower amount of inventory at the end of the period than the other two methods. The reason for these effects is that the cost of the most recently acquired units is about the same as the cost of their replacement. In a period of inflation, the more recent unit costs are higher than the earlier unit costs. Thus, it can be argued that the lifo method more nearly matches current costs with current revenues earnings reports. For example, DaimlerChrysler's reason for changing from the fifo method to the lifo method was stated in the following note that accompanied its financial statements:

> *DaimlerChrysler changed its method of accounting from first-in, first-out (fifo) to last-in, first-out (lifo) for substantially all of its domestic productive inventories. The change to lifo was made to more accurately match current costs with current revenues.*

The rules used for external financial reporting need not be the same as those used for income tax reporting. One exception to this general rule is the use of lifo. If a firm elects to use lifo inventory valuation for tax purposes, then the business must also use lifo for external financial reporting. This is called the **lifo conformity rule**. Thus, in periods of rising prices, lifo offers an income tax savings because it reports the lowest amount of net income of the three methods. Many managers elect to use lifo because of the tax savings, even though the reported earnings will be lower.

© M. VAZQUEZ/AFP/GETTY IMAGES

The ending inventory on the balance sheet may be quite different from its current replacement cost (or fifo estimate).[2] In such cases, the financial statements will include a note that states the estimated difference between the lifo inventory and the inventory if fifo had been used. This difference is called the **lifo reserve**. An example of such a note for Deere & Company is shown below.

> *Most inventories owned by (John) Deere & Company and its United States equipment subsidiaries are valued at cost, on the last-in, first-out (LIFO) basis. . . . If all inventories had been valued on a FIFO basis, estimated inventories by major classification at October 31 in millions of dollars would have been as follows:*

	2004	2003
Raw materials and supplies	$ 589	$ 496
Work-in-process	408	388
Finished machines and parts	2,004	1,432
Total FIFO value	$3,001	$2,316
Less (lifo reserve) adjustment to LIFO value	1,002	950
Inventories	$1,999	$1,366

2 The fifo equivalent is replacement cost, which is often similar to fifo.

As shown on page 278, the lifo reserve may be quite large for some companies. To illustrate, the inventory, lifo reserve, and relative size of the lifo reserve for some well-known companies are listed below.

	(In millions)			
Company	**Lifo Reported Inventory**	**Lifo Reserve**	**Fifo Equivalent**	**Percent Lifo Reserve to Fifo**
ChevronTexaco Corporation	$ 2,983	$3,036	$ 6,019	50.4%
United States Steel Corporation	1,197	770	1,967	39.1%
Caterpillar Inc.	4,675	2,124	6,799	31.2%
General Motors Corporation	11,717	1,442	13,159	11.0%
Ford Motor Company	10,766	1,001	11,767	8.5%
The Kroger Company	4,356	373	4,729	7.9%
General Electric Company	9,589	661	10,250	6.4%
Tiffany & Co.	1,057	64	1,121	5.7%

The wide differences in the percent of lifo reserve to lifo are a result of two major factors: (1) price inflation of the inventory and (2) the age of the inventory. Generally, old lifo inventory combined with rapid price inflation will result in large lifo reserves, such as those seen in the natural resources industry.

If a business sells some of its old lifo inventory, the lifo reserve is said to be liquidated. Since old lifo inventory is normally at low prices, selling old lifo inventory will result in a lower cost of merchandise sold and a higher gross profit and net income. For example, United States Steel Corporation reported the following in a note to its financial statements.

> *Cost of revenues was reduced and income (loss) from operations was improved by $16 million and $9 million in 2004 and 2003, respectively, . . . as a result of liquidations of LIFO inventories.*

Whenever lifo inventory is liquidated, investors and analysts should be careful in interpreting the income statement. In such cases, most investors and analysts will adjust earnings to what they would have been under fifo.

Use of the Average Cost Method

As you might have already reasoned, the average cost method is, in a sense, a compromise between fifo and lifo. The effect of price trends is averaged in determining the cost of merchandise sold and the ending inventory. For a series of purchases, the average cost will be the same, regardless of the direction of price trends. For example, reversing the sequence of unit costs presented in the preceding illustration would not affect the reported cost of merchandise sold, gross profit, or ending inventory.

Determine the proper valuation of inventory at other than cost, using the lower-of-cost-or-market and net realizable value concepts.

VALUATION OF INVENTORY AT OTHER THAN COST

Merchandise inventory is usually presented in the Current Assets section of the balance sheet, following receivables. The method of determining the cost of the inventory (fifo, lifo, or average) should be shown. It is not unusual for large businesses with varied activities to use different costing methods for different segments of their inventories. The details may be disclosed in parentheses on the balance sheet or in a footnote to the financial statements.

Inventory is valued at other than cost when (1) the cost of replacing items in inventory is below the recorded cost, and (2) the inventory is not salable at normal sales prices. This latter case may be due to imperfections, shop wear, style changes, or other causes. In either situation, the method of valuing the inventories (cost or lower of cost or market) should also be disclosed on the balance sheet.

Valuation at Lower of Cost or Market

If the cost of replacing an item in inventory is lower than the original purchase cost, the **lower-of-cost-or-market (LCM) method** is used to value the inventory. *Market*, as used in *lower of cost or market*, is the cost to replace the merchandise on the inventory date. This market value is based on quantities normally purchased from the usual source of supply. In businesses where inflation is the norm, market prices rarely decline. In businesses where technology changes rapidly (e.g., microcomputers and televisions), market declines are common. The primary advantage of the lower-of-cost-or-market method is that the gross profit (and net income) is reduced in the period in which the market decline occurred, rather than waiting until the inventory is sold.

Q. If the cost of an item is $410, its current replacement cost is $400, and its selling price is $525, at what amount should the item be included in the inventory according to the LCM method?

A. *$400*

In applying the lower-of-cost-or-market method, the cost and replacement cost can be determined in one of three ways. Cost and replacement cost can be determined for (1) each item in the inventory, (2) major classes or categories of inventory, or (3) the inventory as a whole. In practice, the cost and replacement cost of each item are usually determined.

To illustrate, assume that 400 identical units of Item A are in inventory, acquired at a unit cost of $10.25 each. If at the inventory date the item would cost $10.50 to replace, the cost price of $10.25 would be multiplied by 400 to determine the inventory value. On the other hand, if the item could be replaced at $9.50 a unit, the replacement cost of $9.50 would be used for valuation purposes.

Exhibit 9 illustrates a method of organizing inventory data and applying lower-of-cost-or-market to each inventory item. The amount of the market decline, $450 ($15,520 − $15,070), may be reported as a separate item on the income statement or included in the cost of merchandise sold. Regardless, net income will be reduced by the amount of the market decline.

Exhibit 9

Determining Inventory at Lower of Cost or Market

Commodity	Inventory Quantity	Unit Cost Price	Unit Market Price	Total Cost	Total Market	Total Lower of C or M
A	400	$10.25	$ 9.50	$ 4,100	$ 3,800	$ 3,800
B	120	22.50	24.10	2,700	2,892	2,700
C	600	8.00	7.75	4,800	4,650	4,650
D	280	14.00	14.75	3,920	4,130	3,920
Total				$15,520	$15,472	$15,070

Valuation at Net Realizable Value

As you would expect, merchandise that is out of date, spoiled, or damaged or that can be sold only at prices below cost should be written down. Such merchandise should be valued at net realizable value. **Net realizable value** is the estimated selling price less any direct cost of disposal, such as sales commissions. For example, assume that damaged merchandise costing $1,000 can be sold for only $800, and direct selling expenses are estimated to be $150. This inventory should be valued at $650 ($800 − $150), which is its net realizable value. For example, Digital Theater Systems Inc. provides

International Perspective
In Japan, inventories are generally valued at cost rather than lower of cost or net realizable value.

digital entertainment technologies, products, and services to the motion picture, consumer electronics, and professional audio industries. In the notes to its recent financial statements, Digital Theater reported the following write-downs of its monochrome projector inventory:

> *Inventories are stated at the lower of cost or market. Cost is determined using the first-in, first-out method. The Company evaluates its ending inventories for estimated excess quantities and obsolescence. The Company's evaluation includes the analysis of future sales demand by product, within specific time horizons. Inventories in excess of projected future demand are written down to net realizable value. In addition, the Company assesses the impact of changing technology on inventory balances and writes down inventories that are considered obsolete. The Company recorded an inventory write-down of $3,871 (thousands) related to its monochrome projector inventory during the year ended December 31, 2004 due to declines in future demand and technological obsolescence.*

Describe how inventories are being reduced through quick response.

QUICK RESPONSE

To satisfy consumer demand, with the least amount of inventory and inefficiency, merchandisers and manufacturers are embracing **quick response** or *efficient consumer response* strategies. Quick response is used to optimize inventory levels by electronically sharing common forecast, inventory, sales, and payment information between manufacturers and merchandisers, using the Internet or other electronic means. Using quick response, a merchandiser electronically transmits daily sales information to the manufacturer. The manufacturer uses this sales information to ship replacement stock to the merchandiser, usually within days of receiving the sales information. Shared forecasts are used to help the manufacturer plan for sales promotions or other seasonal factors that may require more or less goods than the replaced amounts. For example, VF Corporation, the manufacturer of Wrangler® jeans, reduced its inventory and increased sales by entering into a quick response program with Federated Department Stores (Bloomingdale's, Macy's). Under this program, VF receives sales information from Federated cash register scanners in the morning and ships goods directly to the retail store within 24 hours.

Prior to the quick response program, VF took about 30 days to deliver product to the selling floor after an order was received. Both VF and Federated saw significant improvements from the quick response strategy. VF estimated that jean sales improved by 40% as a result of having the right colors and sizes on Federated's shelves, while Federated eliminated over $100 million in inefficient paperwork by using electronic ordering. Both firms saw significant reduction in inventories.

Throughout the last two decades, inventory management techniques, such as quick response, have reduced the relative size of inventory by 35% for U.S. firms.[3] This has caused the economy to respond more quickly to changes in consumer demand and to be less wasteful in inventory costs. Managing inventory efficiently requires that the amount of inventory be known at all times. Accountants provide this information to managers to help guide inventory policy, so that the costs identified above are minimized.

3 Bernard DeGrove and Kevin Mellyn, "The Argument for Financial-Chain Management," *eCFO*, December 2000.

INVENTORY ANALYSIS AND INTERPRETATION

Determine and interpret the inventory turnover ratio and the number of days' sales in inventory.

As with many types of financial analyses, the efficiency and effectiveness of managing inventory can be analyzed by using more than one measure. Two such measures are the inventory turnover and the number of days' sales in inventory.

Inventory turnover (or inventory turns) measures the relationship between the volume of goods (merchandise) sold and the amount of inventory carried during the period. It is computed as follows:

$$\text{Inventory Turnover} = \frac{\text{Cost of Merchandise Sold*}}{\text{Average Inventory}}$$

* For a manufacturing company, the numerator would be Cost of Goods Sold.

We determine the average inventory by dividing the sum of the inventories at the beginning and end of the year by 2. To illustrate, the following data have been taken from recent annual reports for Best Buy and Circuit City Stores, Inc. (amounts in millions, except ratio):

	Best Buy	Circuit City
a. Cost of merchandise sold	$18,350	$7,904
Merchandise inventories:		
Beginning of year	$ 2,077	$1,517
End of year	2,607	1,459
Total	$ 4,684	$2,976
b. Average (total ÷ 2)	$ 2,342	$1,488
Inventory turnover (a ÷ b)	7.84	5.31

© JOHN A. RIZZO/PHOTODISC/GETTY IMAGES

The inventory turnover is 7.84 for Best Buy and 5.31 for Circuit City. That is, for every dollar of inventory, Best Buy is able to support $7.84 of cost of merchandise sold. Thus, a larger inventory turnover is associated with more efficient and effective management of the inventory. It appears that Best Buy is achieving greater inventory efficiency than is Circuit City. Best Buy's management explains its inventory efficiency efforts as follows:

> *By working more closely with our suppliers, we expect to reduce inefficiencies while creating more flexibility for responding to customer needs. As a result, we hope to ensure that we have the right product at the right location at the right time. Thus, we expect to improve our in-stock percentage, customer satisfaction, inventory turns and overall profitability.*

Differences in companies and industries are too great to allow specific statements as to what is a good inventory turnover. For example, Zale Corporation, a jewelry retailer, had a recent inventory turnover ratio of 1.38, which is slower than the inventory turnover of an electronics retailer. Such a difference would be expected, since jewelry is not subject to the same obsolescence as are consumer electronic products.

The **number of days' sales in inventory** approximates the length of time it takes to acquire, sell, and replace the inventory. It is computed as follows:

FOCUS ON CASH FLOW

Inventories and Cash Flows

If a company increases its inventory balances from period to period, then the amount of cash invested in inventory is increasing. In contrast, if the inventory balances are decreasing, cash is being returned to the business. This is why companies use inventory reduction strategies, such as quick response, in order to capture one-time cash benefits from reducing inventory. On the other hand, if management grows inventory in anticipation of sales that do not materialize, then cash will be used.

The impact of changes in inventory balances is shown in the operating activities section of the statement of cash flows. For example, **Best Buy** reported the following (in millions):

Net income	$ 984
Inventory, February 28, 2004	2,611
Inventory, February 26, 2005	2,851

The operating section of the statement of cash flows is reproduced for Best Buy below, with the shaded area showing the impact of inventory changes.

(in millions) For the Fiscal Year Ended	Feb. 26, 2005
Operating activities:	
Net income	$ 984
Depreciation	459
Other adjustments to net income	(33)
Changes in operating assets and liabilities:	
Receivables	(30)
Merchandise inventories	(240)
Liabilities	891
Other operating activities	(190)
Total cash provided by operating activities	$1,841

As you can see, the increase in inventory from $2,611 to $2,851 is reflected as a use of $240 cash on the statement of cash flows. Best Buy is a growing business; thus, using cash to increase inventories would be expected.

$$\text{Number of Days' Sales in Inventory} = \frac{\text{Average Inventory}}{\text{Average Daily Cost of Merchandise Sold}}$$

The average daily cost of merchandise sold is determined by dividing the cost of merchandise sold by 365. The number of days' sales in inventory for Best Buy and Circuit City is computed as shown below.

	Best Buy	Circuit City
Average daily cost of merchandise sold:		
$18,350/365	$50.27	
$7,904/365		$21.65
Average inventory	$2,342	$1,488
Number of days' sales in inventory	47 days	69 days

Generally, the lower the number of days' sales in inventory, the better. The number of days' sales in inventory confirms the inventory turnover ratio, namely, Best Buy is managing its inventory more efficiently than is Circuit City. As with inventory turnover, we should expect differences among industries, such as those for Best Buy and Zale, whose number of days' sales in inventory is 243 days.

Inventory ratios can also be used to evaluate inventory performance trends over time. For example, Best Buy has improved its inventory turnover over the last eight years from 4.6 turns to 7.8 turns. Best Buy has credited this improvement to quick response policies, lower markdowns, and faster-moving product assortments.

SUMMARY OF LEARNING GOALS

1 **Identify the types of inventory used by merchandisers and manufacturers.** The inventory of a merchandiser is called merchandise inventory. The cost of merchandise inventory that is sold is reported on the income statement. Manufacturers typically have three types of inventory: materials, work-in-process, and finished goods. When finished goods are sold, the cost is reported on the income statement as cost of goods sold.

2 Summarize and provide examples of control procedures that apply to inventories. Control procedures for inventories include those developed to protect the inventories from damage, employee theft, and customer theft. In addition, a physical inventory count should be taken periodically to detect shortages as well as to deter employee thefts.

3 Describe three inventory cost flow assumptions and how they impact the income statement and balance sheet. The three common cost flow assumptions used in business are the (1) first-in, first-out method, (2) last-in, first-out method, and (3) average cost method. Each method normally yields different amounts for the cost of merchandise sold and the ending merchandise inventory. Thus, the choice of a cost flow assumption directly affects the income statement and balance sheet.

4 Determine the cost of inventory under the perpetual inventory system, using the first-in, first-out; last-in, first-out; and average cost methods. In a perpetual inventory system, the number of units and the cost of each type of merchandise are recorded in a subsidiary inventory ledger, with a separate account for each type of merchandise. Inventory costs and the amounts charged against revenue are illustrated using the fifo and lifo methods.

5 Determine the cost of inventory under the periodic inventory system, using the first-in, first-out; last-in, first-out; and average cost methods. In a periodic inventory system, a physical inventory is taken to determine the cost of the inventory and the cost of merchandise sold. Inventory costs and the amounts charged against revenue are illustrated using fifo, lifo, and average cost methods.

6 Compare and contrast the use of the three inventory costing methods. The three inventory costing methods will normally yield different amounts for (1) the ending inventory, (2) the cost of the merchandise sold for the period, and (3) the gross profit (and net income) for the period. During periods of inflation, the fifo method yields the lowest amount for the cost of merchandise sold, the highest amount for gross profit (and net income), and the highest amount for the ending inventory. The lifo method yields the opposite results. During periods of deflation, the preceding effects are reversed. The average cost method yields results that are between those of fifo and lifo.

7 Determine the proper valuation of inventory at other than cost, using the lower-of-cost-or-market and net realizable value concepts. If the market price of an item of inventory is lower than its cost, the lower market price is used to compute the value of the item. Market price is the cost to replace the merchandise on the inventory date. It is possible to apply the lower of cost or market to each item in the inventory, to major classes or categories, or to the inventory as a whole.

Merchandise that can be sold only at prices below cost should be valued at net realizable value, which is the estimated selling price less any direct costs of disposal.

8 Describe how inventories are being reduced through quick response. Quick response is used to optimize inventory levels by electronically sharing common forecast, inventory, sales, and payment information between manufacturers and merchandisers, using the Internet or other electronic means. Using shared information in this way allows manufacturers to more quickly ship goods to replace sold items on the retailer's shelves.

9 Determine and interpret the inventory turnover ratio and the number of days' sales in inventory. The inventory turnover ratio, computed as the cost of merchandise sold divided by the average inventory, measures the relationship between the volume of goods (merchandise) sold and the amount of inventory carried during the period. The number of days' sales in inventory, computed as the average inventory divided by the average daily cost of merchandise sold, measures the length of time it takes to acquire, sell, and replace the inventory.

GLOSSARY

Average cost method The method of inventory costing that is based upon the assumption that costs should be charged against revenue by using the weighted average unit cost of the items sold.

Cost of goods sold The cost of product sold.

Finished goods inventory The cost of finished products on hand that have not been sold.

First-in, first-out (fifo) method A method of inventory costing based on the assumption that the costs of merchandise sold should be charged against revenue in the order in which the costs were incurred.

Inventory ledger The subsidiary ledger that shows the amount of each type of inventory.

Inventory turnover A ratio that measures the relationship between the volume of goods (merchandise) sold and the amount of inventory carried during the period.

Last-in, first-out (lifo) method A method of inventory costing based on the assumption that the most recent merchandise inventory costs should be charged against revenue.

Lifo conformity rule A financial reporting rule requiring a firm that elects to use lifo inventory valuation for tax purposes to also use lifo for external financial reporting.

Lifo reserve A required disclosure for lifo firms, showing the difference between inventory valued under fifo and inventory valued under lifo.

Lower-of-cost-or-market (LCM) method A method of valuing inventory that reports the inventory at the lower of its cost or current market value (replacement cost).

Materials inventory The cost of materials that have not yet entered into the manufacturing process.

Merchandise inventory Merchandise on hand and available for sale to customers.

Net realizable value The estimated selling price of an item of inventory less any direct costs of disposal, such as sales commissions.

Number of days' sales in inventory A measure of the length of time it takes to acquire, sell, and replace the inventory.

Physical inventory The detailed listing of merchandise on hand.

Quick response A method for optimizing inventory levels in the value chain by electronically sharing common forecast, inventory, sales, and payment information between manufacturers and merchandisers, using the Internet or other electronic means.

Work-in-process inventory The direct materials costs, the direct labor costs, and the factory overhead costs that have entered into the manufacturing process, but are associated with product that has not been finished.

ILLUSTRATIVE ACCOUNTING APPLICATION PROBLEM

Stewart Co.'s beginning inventory and purchases during the year ended December 31, 2008, were as follows:

		Units	Unit Cost	Total Cost
January 1	Inventory	1,000	$50.00	$ 50,000
March 10	Purchase	1,200	52.50	63,000
June 25	Sold 800 units			
August 30	Purchase	800	55.00	44,000
October 5	Sold 1,500 units			
November 26	Purchase	2,000	56.00	112,000
December 31	Sold 1,000 units			
Total		5,000		$269,000

Instructions

1. Determine the cost of inventory on December 31, 2008, using the perpetual inventory system and each of the following inventory costing methods:
   a. first-in, first-out
   b. last-in, first-out
2. Determine the cost of inventory on December 31, 2008, using the periodic inventory system and each of the following inventory costing methods:
   a. first-in, first-out
   b. last-in, first-out
   c. average cost
3. Assume that the cost of merchandise sold was $173,800 for 2008 and the inventory valuation is as determined in (1a). Determine the:
   a. inventory turnover ratio
   b. number of days' sales in inventory ratio

Solution

1. a. First-in, first-out method: $95,200

	Purchases			Cost of Merchandise Sold			Inventory		
Date	Quantity	Unit Cost	Total Cost	Quantity	Unit Cost	Total Cost	Quantity	Unit Cost	Total Cost
2008 Jan. 1							1,000	50.00	50,000
Mar. 10	1,200	52.50	63,000				1,000	50.00	50,000
							1,200	52.50	63,000
June 25				800	50.00	40,000	200	50.00	10,000
							1,200	52.50	63,000
Aug. 30	800	55.00	44,000				200	50.00	10,000
							1,200	52.50	63,000
							800	55.00	44,000
Oct. 5				200	50.00	10,000	700	55.00	38,500
				1,200	52.50	63,000			
				100	55.00	5,500			
Nov. 26	2,000	56.00	112,000				700	55.00	38,500
							2,000	56.00	112,000
Dec. 31				700	55.00	38,500	1,700	56.00	95,200
				300	56.00	16,800			

b. Last-in, first-out method: $91,000 ($35,000 + $56,000)

	Purchases			Cost of Merchandise Sold			Inventory		
Date	Quantity	Unit Cost	Total Cost	Quantity	Unit Cost	Total Cost	Quantity	Unit Cost	Total Cost
2008 Jan. 1							1,000	50.00	50,000
Mar. 10	1,200	52.50	63,000				1,000	50.00	50,000
							1,200	52.50	63,000
June 25				800	52.50	42,000	1,000	50.00	50,000
							400	52.50	21,000
Aug. 30	800	55.00	44,000				1,000	50.00	50,000
							400	52.50	21,000
							800	55.00	44,000
Oct. 5				800	55.00	44,000	700	50.00	35,000
				400	52.50	21,000			
				300	50.00	15,000			
Nov. 26	2,000	56.00	112,000				700	50.00	35,000
							2,000	56.00	112,000
Dec. 31				1,000	56.00	56,000	700	50.00	35,000
							1,000	56.00	56,000

2. a. First-in, first-out method: 1,700 units at $56 = $95,200
   b. Last-in, first-out method:

1,000 units at $50.00	$50,000
700 units at $52.50	36,750
1,700	$86,750

   c. Average cost method:
   Average cost per unit: $269,000 ÷ 5,000 units = $53.80
   Inventory, December 31, 2008: 1,700 units at $53.80 = $91,460

3. a. $\text{Inventory Turnover} = \dfrac{\text{Cost of Merchandise Sold}}{\text{Average Inventory}}$

$\text{Inventory Turnover} = \dfrac{\$173{,}800}{(\$50{,}000 + \$95{,}200)/2}$

Inventory Turnover = 2.39

b. $\text{Number of Days' Sales in Inventory} = \dfrac{\text{Average Inventory}}{\text{Average Daily Cost of Merchandise Sold}}$

$\text{Number of Days' Sales in Inventory} = \dfrac{(\$50{,}000 + \$95{,}200)/2}{\$173{,}800/365}$

Number of Days' Sales in Inventory = 152.5 days

SELF-STUDY QUESTIONS

Answers at end of chapter

1. The direct labor cost should be recognized first in which inventory account?
   A. Materials Inventory
   B. Merchandise Inventory
   C. Finished Goods Inventory
   D. Work-in-Process Inventory

2. The following units of a particular item were purchased and sold during the period:

Beginning inventory	40 units at $20
First purchase	50 units at $21
Second purchase	50 units at $22
First sale	110 units
Third purchase	50 units at $23
Second sale	45 units

What is the cost of the 35 units on hand at the end of the period as determined under the perpetual inventory system by the lifo costing method?
A. $715 C. $700
B. $705 D. $805

3. The following units of a particular item were available for sale during the period:

Beginning inventory	40 units at $20
First purchase	50 units at $21
Second purchase	50 units at $22
Third purchase	50 units at $23

What is the unit cost of the 35 units on hand at the end of the period as determined under the periodic inventory system by the fifo costing method?
A. $20 C. $22
B. $21 D. $23

4. If merchandise inventory is being valued at cost and the price level is steadily rising, the method of costing that will yield the highest net income is:
   A. lifo C. average
   B. fifo D. periodic

5. The average inventory is $50,000, and the cost of merchandise sold is $175,000. Determine the inventory turnover ratio.
   A. 2.92 C. 3.7
   B. 3.5 D. 4.375

DISCUSSION QUESTIONS

1. How are manufacturing inventories different than those of a merchandiser?
2. What security measures may be used by retailers to protect merchandise inventory from customer theft?
3. Which inventory system (perpetual or periodic) provides the more effective means of controlling inventories? Why?
4. Before inventory purchases are recorded, the receiving report should be reconciled to what documents?
5. Why is it important to periodically take a physical inventory if the perpetual system is used?
6. Do the terms *fifo* and *lifo* refer to techniques used in determining quantities of the various classes of merchandise on hand? Explain.
7. Does the term *last-in* in the lifo method mean that the items in the inventory are assumed to be the most recent (last) acquisitions? Explain.

8. If merchandise inventory is being valued at cost and the price level is steadily rising, which of the three methods of costing—fifo, lifo, or average cost—will yield (a) the highest inventory cost, (b) the lowest inventory cost, (c) the highest gross profit, (d) the lowest gross profit?
9. Which of the three methods of inventory costing—fifo, lifo, or average cost—will in general yield an inventory cost most nearly approximating current replacement cost?
10. If inventory is being valued at cost and the price level is steadily rising, which of the three methods of costing—fifo, lifo, or average cost—will yield the lowest annual income tax expense? Explain.
11. Can a company change its method of costing inventory? Explain.
12. Because of imperfections, an item of merchandise cannot be sold at its normal selling price. How should this item be valued for financial statement purposes?
13. How is the method of determining the cost of inventory and the method of valuing it disclosed in the financial statements?
14. What is the lifo reserve, and why would an analyst be careful in interpreting the earnings of a company that has liquidated some of its lifo reserve?
15. Why would a company such as Target Corporation prefer a quick response inventory policy?

EXERCISES

Exercise 6-1

Manufacturing inventories

Goal 1

Qualcomm Incorporated is a leading developer and manufacturer of digital wireless telecommunications products and services. Qualcomm reported the following inventories on September 30, 2004, in the notes to its financial statements:

	(In millions) September 30, 2004
Raw materials	$ 20
Work-in-process	3
Finished goods	131
	$154

a. Why does Qualcomm report three different inventories?
b. What costs are included in each of the three classes of inventory?

Exercise 6-2

Television costs of Walt Disney Company

Goal 1

The Walt Disney Company shows "television costs" as an asset on its balance sheet. In the notes to its financial statements, the following television cost disclosure was made:

	Sept. 30, 2004	Sept. 30, 2003
Television costs:		
Released, less amortization	$ 893	$ 961
Completed, not released	175	126
In-process	292	283
In development or pre-production	24	11
	$1,384	$1,381

a. Interpret the four television cost asset categories.
b. How are these classifications similar or dissimilar to the inventory classifications used in a manufacturing firm?

Exercise 6-3

Control of inventories

Goal 2

Onsite Hardware Store currently uses a periodic inventory system. Dana Cogburn, the owner, is considering the purchase of a computer system that would make it feasible to switch to a perpetual inventory system.

Dana is unhappy with the periodic inventory system because it does not provide timely information on inventory levels. Dana has noticed on several occasions that the store runs out of good-selling items, while too many poor-selling items are on hand.

Dana is also concerned about lost sales while a physical inventory is being taken. Onsite Hardware currently takes a physical inventory twice a year. To minimize distractions, the store is closed on the day inventory is taken. Dana believes that closing the store is the only way to get an accurate inventory count.

Will switching to a perpetual inventory system strengthen Onsite Hardware's control over inventory items? Will switching to a perpetual inventory system eliminate the need for a physical inventory count? Explain.

Exercise 6-4

Control of inventories

Goal **2**

Pacific Luggage Shop is a small retail establishment located in a large shopping mall. This shop has implemented the following procedures regarding inventory items.

a. Whenever Pacific receives a shipment of new inventory, the items are taken directly to the stockroom. Pacific's accountant uses the vendor's invoice to record the amount of inventory received.
b. Since the shop carries mostly high-quality, designer luggage, all inventory items are tagged with a control device that activates an alarm if a tagged item is removed from the store.
c. Since the display area of the store is limited, only a sample of each piece of luggage is kept on the selling floor. Whenever a customer selects a piece of luggage, the salesclerk gets the appropriate piece from the store's stockroom. Since all salesclerks need access to the stockroom, it is not locked. The stockroom is adjacent to the break room used by all mall employees.

State whether each of these procedures is an appropriate or inappropriate control procedure. If it is inappropriate, explain why.

Exercise 6-5

Perpetual inventory using fifo

Goals **3, 4**

Inventory balance, April 30, $802

SPREADSHEET

Beginning inventory, purchases, and sales data for portable CD players are as follows:

April 1	Inventory	35 units at $50
5	Sale	26 units
11	Purchase	15 units at $53
21	Sale	12 units
28	Sale	4 units
30	Purchase	7 units at $54

The business maintains a perpetual inventory system, costing by the first-in, first-out method. Determine the cost of the merchandise sold for each sale and the inventory balance after each sale, presenting the data in the form illustrated in Exhibit 5.

Exercise 6-6

Perpetual inventory using lifo

Goals **3, 4**

Inventory balance, April 30, $778

SPREADSHEET

Assume that the business in Exercise 6-5 maintains a perpetual inventory system, costing by the last-in, first-out method. Determine the cost of merchandise sold for each sale and the inventory balance after each sale, presenting the data in the form illustrated in Exhibit 6.

Exercise 6-7

Perpetual inventory using lifo

Goals **3, 4**

Inventory balance, March 31, $1,295

SPREADSHEET

Beginning inventory, purchases, and sales data for cell phones for March are as follows:

Inventory		Purchases		Sales	
Mar. 1	25 Units at $90	Mar. 5	20 units at $94	Mar. 9	18 Units
		21	15 units at $95	13	20 units
				31	8 units

Assuming that the perpetual inventory system is used, costing by the lifo method, determine the cost of merchandise sold for each sale and the inventory balance after each sale, presenting the data in the form illustrated in Exhibit 6.

Exercise 6-8

Perpetual inventory using fifo

Goals **3, 4**

Inventory balance, March 31, $1,330

SPREADSHEET

Assume that the business in Exercise 6-7 maintains a perpetual inventory system, costing by the first-in, first-out method. Determine the cost of merchandise sold for each sale and the inventory balance after each sale, presenting the data in the form illustrated in Exhibit 5.

Exercise 6-9

Fifo, lifo costs under perpetual inventory system

Goals **3, 4**

a. $700

The following units of a particular item were available for sale during the year:

Beginning inventory	20 units at $45
Sale	15 units at $80
First purchase	31 units at $47
Sale	27 units at $80
Second purchase	40 units at $50
Sale	35 units at $80

The firm uses the perpetual inventory system, and there are 14 units of the item on hand at the end of the year. What is the total cost of the ending inventory according to (a) fifo, (b) lifo?

Exercise 6-10

Periodic inventory by three methods

Goals **3, 5, 6**

b. $318

The units of an item available for sale during the year were as follows:

Jan. 1	Inventory	6 units at $28
Feb. 4	Purchase	12 units at $30
July 20	Purchase	14 units at $32
Dec. 30	Purchase	8 units at $33

There are 11 units of the item in the physical inventory at December 31. The periodic inventory system is used. Determine the inventory cost by (a) the first-in, first-out method, (b) the last-in, first-out method, and (c) the average cost method.

Exercise 6-11

Periodic inventory by three methods; cost of merchandise sold

Goals **3, 5, 6**

a. Inventory, $5,016

The units of an item available for sale during the year were as follows:

Jan. 1	Inventory	42 units at $120
Mar. 4	Purchase	58 units at $130
Aug. 7	Purchase	20 units at $136
Nov. 15	Purchase	30 units at $140

There are 36 units of the item in the physical inventory at December 31. The periodic inventory system is used. Determine the inventory cost and the cost of merchandise sold by three methods, presenting your answers in the following form:

	Cost	
Inventory Method	**Merchandise Inventory**	**Merchandise Sold**
a. First-in, first-out	$	$
b. Last-in, first-out		
c. Average cost		

Exercise 6-12

Comparing inventory methods

Goal **6**

Assume that a firm separately determined inventory under fifo and lifo and then compared the results.

1. In each space below, place the correct sign [less than (<), greater than (>), or equal (=)] for each comparison, assuming periods of rising prices.

a. Lifo inventory	________	Fifo Inventory
b. Lifo cost of goods sold	________	Fifo cost of goods sold
c. Lifo net income	________	Fifo net income
d. Lifo income tax	________	Fifo income tax

2. Why would management prefer to use lifo over fifo in periods of rising prices?

Exercise 6-13

Lower-of-cost-or-market inventory

Goal **7**

LCM: $8,325

SPREADSHEET

On the basis of the following data, determine the value of the inventory at the lower of cost or market. Assemble the data in the form illustrated in Exhibit 9.

Commodity	Inventory Quantity	Unit Cost Price	Unit Market Price
M76	8	$150	$160
T53	20	75	70
A19	10	275	260
J81	15	50	40
K10	25	101	105

Exercise 6-14

Merchandise inventory on the balance sheet

Goal **7**

Based on the data in Exercise 6-13 and assuming that cost was determined by the fifo method, show how the merchandise inventory would appear on the balance sheet.

Exercise 6-15

Quick response

Goal **8**

Assume that a company initiated a quick response program.

a. What impact would the program have on the inventory balance and cash flow?
b. What impact would the program have on cost of goods sold, assuming that the firm used lifo?

Exercise 6-16

Inventory turnover

Goal **9**

The following data were taken from recent annual reports of Dell Inc., a vendor of personal computers and related technology products, and Boeing Co., a manufacturer of jet aircraft and aerospace products:

	Dell Inc. (in millions)	Boeing Co. (in millions)
Cost of goods sold	$40,190	$44,675
Inventory, end of year	459	4,247
Inventory, beginning of the year	327	5,338

a. Determine the inventory turnover for Dell and Boeing. Round to one decimal place.
b. Would you expect Boeing's inventory turnover to be higher or lower than Dell's? Why?

Exercise 6-17

Manufacturing inventories and analysis

Goals **1, 9**

Number of days' sales in inventory of raw materials, 14.7

The inventories (in millions) of Anheuser-Busch Companies, Inc., were recently reported on its December 31, 2004 and 2003, balance sheets as follows:

	Dec. 31, 2004	Dec. 31, 2003
Raw materials	$405.0	$320.3
Work-in-process	80.0	81.9
Finished goods	205.3	185.3
Total	$690.3	$587.5

The cost of goods sold reported on the income statement was $8,983 million.

a. What do the three inventory classes on Anheuser-Busch's balance sheet represent?
b. Calculate the number of days' sales in inventory for raw materials and finished goods and for the total inventory. Round to one decimal place.
c. Interpret your calculations in (b).

Exercise 6-18

Inventory turnover and number of days' sales in inventory

Goal 9

a. Kroger, 38.4 days

Kroger Co., Safeway Inc., and Winn-Dixie Stores, Inc., are three large grocery chains in the United States. Inventory management is an important aspect of the grocery retail business. The balance sheets for these three companies indicated the following merchandise inventory information:

	Merchandise Inventory	
	Fiscal 2004 End-of-Year Balance (in millions)	**Fiscal 2003 End-of-Year Balance (in millions)**
Kroger	$4,169	$4,175
Safeway	2,741	2,642
Winn-Dixie	992	1,047

The cost of goods sold for each company during fiscal year 2004 was:

	Cost of Goods Sold for Fiscal Year 2004 (in millions)
Kroger	$39,637
Safeway	25,228
Winn-Dixie	7,819

a. Determine the number of days' sales in inventory and inventory turnover for the three companies for fiscal year 2004. Round to one decimal place.
b. Interpret your results in (a).

ACCOUNTING APPLICATION PROBLEMS

Problem 6-1A

Fifo perpetual inventory

Goals 3, 4

3. $240,100

SPREADSHEET

The beginning inventory of drift boats at Heritage Float Co. and data on purchases and sales for a three-month period are as follows:

Date	Transaction	Number of Units	Per Unit	Total
Aug. 1	Inventory	22	$2,200	$48,400
8	Purchase	18	2,250	40,500
11	Sale	12	4,800	57,600
22	Sale	11	4,800	52,800
Sept. 3	Purchase	16	2,300	36,800
10	Sale	10	5,000	50,000
21	Sale	5	5,000	25,000
30	Purchase	20	2,350	47,000
Oct. 5	Sale	20	5,250	105,000
13	Sale	12	5,250	63,000
21	Purchase	30	2,400	72,000
28	Sale	15	5,400	81,000

Instructions

1. Record the inventory, purchases, and cost of merchandise sold data in a perpetual inventory record similar to the one illustrated in Exhibit 5, using the first-in, first-out method.
2. Determine the total sales and the total cost of drift boats sold for the period. Journalize the entries in the sales and cost of merchandise sold accounts. Assume that all sales were on account.
3. Determine the gross profit from sales of drift boats for the period.
4. Determine the ending inventory cost.

Problem 6-2A

Lifo perpetual inventory

Goals **3, 4**

2. Gross profit, $238,900

SPREADSHEET

The beginning inventory of drift boats and data on purchases and sales for a three-month period are shown in Problem 6-1A.

Instructions

1. Record the inventory, purchases, and cost of merchandise sold data in a perpetual inventory record similar to the one illustrated in Exhibit 6, using the last-in, first-out method.
2. Determine the total sales, the total cost of drift boats sold, and the gross profit from sales for the period.
3. Determine the ending inventory cost.

Problem 6-3A

Periodic inventory by three methods

Goals **3, 5**

1. $12,701

SPREADSHEET

Henning Appliances use the periodic inventory system. Details regarding the inventory of appliances at January 1, 2006, purchases invoices during the year, and the inventory count at December 31, 2006, are summarized as follows:

Model	Inventory, January 1	Purchase Invoices 1st	2nd	3rd	Inventory Count, December 31
231T	3 at $208	3 at $212	5 at $213	4 at $225	6
673W	2 at 520	2 at 527	2 at 530	2 at 535	4
193Q	6 at 520	8 at 531	4 at 549	6 at 542	7
144Z	9 at 213	7 at 215	6 at 222	6 at 225	11
160M	6 at 305	3 at 310	3 at 316	4 at 317	5
180X	—	4 at 222	4 at 232	—	2
971K	4 at 140	6 at 144	8 at 148	7 at 156	6

Instructions

1. Determine the cost of the inventory on December 31, 2006, by the first-in, first-out method. Present data in columnar form, using the following headings:

Model	Quantity	Unit Cost	Total Cost

   If the inventory of a particular model comprises one entire purchase plus a portion of another purchase acquired at a different unit cost, use a separate line for each purchase.
2. Determine the cost of the inventory on December 31, 2006, by the last-in, first-out method, following the procedures indicated in (1).
3. Determine the cost of the inventory on December 31, 2006, by the average cost method, using the columnar headings indicated in (1).
4. Discuss which method (fifo or lifo) would be preferred for income tax purposes in periods of (a) rising prices and (b) declining prices.

Problem 6-4A

Lower-of-cost-or-market inventory

Goal **7**

Total LCM, $38,238

SPREADSHEET

Data on the physical inventory of Timberline Company as of December 31, 2007, are presented below.

Description	Inventory Quantity	Unit Market Price
A90	35	$ 57
C18	16	200
D41	24	140
E34	125	26
F17	18	550
G68	60	15
K41	5	390
Q79	375	6
R72	100	17
S60	6	235
W21	140	18
Z35	9	700

Quantity and cost data from the last purchase invoice of the year and the next-to-the-last purchase invoice are summarized as follows:

	Last Purchases Invoice		Next-to-the-Last Purchases Invoice	
Description	**Quantity Purchased**	**Unit Cost**	**Quantity Purchased**	**Unit Cost**
A90	25	$ 59	40	$ 58
C18	25	188	15	191
D41	16	145	15	142
E34	150	25	100	27
F17	6	550	15	540
G68	75	14	100	13
K41	8	400	4	398
Q79	500	6	500	7
R72	70	18	50	16
S60	5	250	4	260
W21	120	20	115	17
Z35	8	701	7	699

Instructions

Determine the inventory at cost and also at the lower of cost or market, using the first-in, first-out method. Record the appropriate unit costs on an inventory sheet and complete the pricing of the inventory. When there are two different unit costs applicable to an item, proceed as follows:

1. Draw a line through the quantity, and insert the quantity and unit cost of the last purchase.
2. On the following line, insert the quantity and unit cost of the next-to-the-last purchase.
3. Total the cost and market columns and insert the lower of the two totals in the Lower of C or M column. The first item on the inventory sheet has been completed below as an example.

Inventory Sheet
December 31, 2007

				Total		
Description	**Inventory Quantity**	**Unit Cost Price**	**Unit Market Price**	**Cost**	**Market**	**Lower of C or M**
A90	~~35~~ 25	$59	$57	$1,475	$1,425	
	10	58		580	570	
				$2,055	$1,995	$1,995

ALTERNATE ACCOUNTING APPLICATION PROBLEMS

Alternate Problem 6-1B

Fifo perpetual inventory

Goals 3, 4

3. $4,895

SPREADSHEET

The beginning inventory of floor mats at Intermountain Office Supplies and data on purchases and sales for a three-month period are as follows:

Date		Transaction	Number of Units	Per Unit	Total
Apr.	1	Inventory	200	$2.10	$ 420
	8	Purchase	800	2.20	1,760
	20	Sale	350	4.00	1,400
	30	Sale	450	4.00	1,800
May	8	Sale	50	4.10	205
	10	Purchase	500	2.30	1,150
	27	Sale	350	4.20	1,470
	31	Sale	200	4.50	900

(continued)

Date		Transaction	Number of Units	Per Unit	Total
June	5	Purchase	750	$2.40	$1,800
	13	Sale	350	5.00	1,750
	23	Purchase	400	2.60	1,040
	30	Sale	500	5.00	2,500

Instructions

1. Record the inventory, purchases, and cost of merchandise sold data in a perpetual inventory record similar to the one illustrated in Exhibit 5, using the first-in, first-out method.
2. Determine the total sales and the total cost of floor mats sold for the period. Journalize the entries in the sales and cost of merchandise sold accounts. Assume that all sales were on account.
3. Determine the gross profit from sales for the period.
4. Determine the ending inventory cost.

Alternate Problem 6-2B

Lifo perpetual inventory

Goals **3, 4**

2. Gross profit, $4,785

SPREADSHEET

The beginning inventory of floor mats at International Office Supplies and data on purchases and sales for a three-month period are shown in Alternate Problem 6-1B.

Instructions

1. Record the inventory, purchases, and cost of merchandise sold data in a perpetual inventory record similar to the one illustrated in Exhibit 6, using the last-in, first-out method.
2. Determine the total sales, the total cost of floor mats sold, and the gross profit from sales for the period.
3. Determine the ending inventory cost.

Alternate Problem 6-3B

Periodic inventory by three methods

Goals **3, 5**

1. $8,053

SPREADSHEET

Three Forks Appliances uses the periodic inventory system. Details regarding the inventory of appliances at May 1, 2005, purchases invoices during the year, and the inventory count at April 30, 2006, are summarized follows.

Model	Inventory, May 1	Purchase Invoices 1st	Purchase Invoices 2nd	Purchase Invoices 3rd	Inventory Count, April 30
AC54	2 at $250	2 at $260	4 at $271	4 at $272	6
BH43	6 at 80	5 at 82	8 at 89	8 at 90	6
G113	2 at 108	2 at 110	3 at 128	3 at 130	5
K243	8 at 88	4 at 79	3 at 85	6 at 92	8
PM18	7 at 242	6 at 250	5 at 260	10 at 259	8
Q661	5 at 160	4 at 170	4 at 175	7 at 180	8
W490	—	4 at 150	4 at 200	4 at 202	5

Instructions

1. Determine the cost of the inventory on April 30, 2006, by the first-in, first-out method. Present data in columnar form, using the following headings:

Model	Quantity	Unit Cost	Total Cost

   If the inventory of a particular model comprises one entire purchase plus a portion of another purchase acquired at a different unit cost, use a separate line for each purchase.
2. Determine the cost of the inventory on April 30, 2006, by the last-in, first-out method, following the procedures indicated in (1).
3. Determine the cost of the inventory on April 30, 2006, by the average cost method, using the columnar headings indicated in (1).
4. Discuss which method (fifo or lifo) would be preferred for income tax purposes in periods of (a) rising prices and (b) declining prices.

Alternate Problem 6-4B

Lower-of-cost-or-market inventory

Goal 7

Total LCM, $38,585

SPREADSHEET

Data on the physical inventory of Cinnabar Co. as of December 31, 2007, are presented below.

Description	Inventory Quantity	Unit Market Price
A90	35	$ 57
C18	16	200
D41	24	140
E34	125	26
F17	18	550
G68	60	15
K41	5	390
Q79	375	6
R72	100	17
S60	6	235
W21	140	18
Z35	9	700

Quantity and cost data from the last purchases invoice of the year and the next-to-the-last purchases invoice are summarized as follows:

	Last Purchases Invoice		Next-to-the-Last Purchases Invoice	
Description	Quantity Purchased	Unit Cost	Quantity Purchased	Unit Cost
A90	25	$ 59	30	$ 58
C18	35	206	20	205
D41	10	144	25	142
E34	150	25	100	24
F17	10	565	10	560
G68	100	15	100	14
K41	10	385	5	384
Q79	500	6	500	6
R72	80	20	50	18
S60	5	250	4	260
W21	100	20	75	19
Z35	7	701	6	699

Instructions

Determine the inventory at cost and also at the lower of cost or market, using the first-in, first-out method. Record the appropriate unit costs on an inventory sheet and complete the pricing of the inventory. When there are two different unit costs applicable to an item, proceed as follows:

1. Draw a line through the quantity, and insert the quantity and unit cost of the last purchase.
2. On the following line, insert the quantity and unit cost of the next-to-the-last purchase.
3. Total the cost and market columns and insert the lower of the two totals in the Lower of C or M column. The first item on the inventory sheet has been completed below as an example.

Inventory Sheet
December 31, 2007

				Total		
Description	Inventory Quantity	Unit Cost Price	Unit Market Price	Cost	Market	Lower of C or M
A90	~~35~~ 25	$59	$57	$1,475	$1,425	
	10	58		580	570	
				$2,055	$1,995	$1,995

FINANCIAL ANALYSIS AND REPORTING CASES

Case 6-1

Fifo vs. lifo

The following note was taken from the 2004 financial statements of Walgreen Company:

Inventories are valued on a . . . last-in, first-out (lifo) cost . . . basis. At August 31, 2004 and 2003, inventories would have been greater by $736,400,000 and $729,700,000 respectively, if they had been valued on a lower of first-in, first-out (fifo) cost or market basis.

Additional data are as follows:

Earnings before income taxes, 2004	$2,176,300,000
Total lifo inventories, August 31, 2004	4,738,600,000

Based on the preceding data, determine (a) what the total inventories at August 31, 2004, would have been, using the fifo method, and (b) what the earnings before income taxes for the year ended August 31, 2004, would have been if fifo had been used instead of lifo.

Case 6-2

Comparing inventory ratios for two companies

The Neiman Marcus Group, Inc., is a high-end specialty retailer, while Amazon.com uses its e-commerce services, features, and technologies to sell its products through the Internet. The balance sheet inventory disclosures for Neiman Marcus and Amazon.com are as follows for financial statements dated in 2004:

	End-of-Period Inventory	Beginning-of-Period Inventory
Neiman Marcus Group, Inc.	$720,277,000	$687,062,000
Amazon.com	479,709,000	293,917,000

The cost of merchandise sold reported by each company for the fiscal 2004 period was:

	Neiman Marcus Group, Inc.	Amazon.com
Cost of merchandise sold	$2,321,110,000	$5,319,127,000

a. Determine the inventory turnover and number of days' sales in inventory for Neiman Marcus and Amazon.com.
b. Interpret your results.

Case 6-3

Saks Incorporated inventory note

Saks Incorporated disclosed the following note regarding its merchandise inventories for its January 31, 2004, financial statements:

Merchandise Inventories and Cost of Sales
Merchandise inventories are valued by the retail method and are stated at the lower of cost (last-in, first-out "LIFO"), or market and include freight, buying and distribution costs. The Company takes markdowns related to slow moving inventory, ensuring the appropriate inventory valuation. At January 31, 2004 and February 1, 2003, the LIFO value of inventories exceeded market value and, as a result, inventory was stated at the lower market amount.

Consignment merchandise on hand of $127,861 and $112,435 at January 31, 2004 and February 1, 2003, respectively, is not reflected in the consolidated balance sheets.

a. Why were inventories recorded at market value?
b. What are consignment inventories, and why were they excluded from the balance sheet valuation?

Case 6-4

Inventory turnover and number of days' sales in inventory—Wal-Mart

Wal-Mart's annual reports showed the following inventory and cost of goods sold data (in millions) for the years ended January 31, 2005 and 2004:

	2005	2004
Cost of goods sold	$219,793	$198,747
Inventory	29,447	26,612

The following graphs were taken from EdgarScan™ Benchmarking Assistant for the past 10 years:

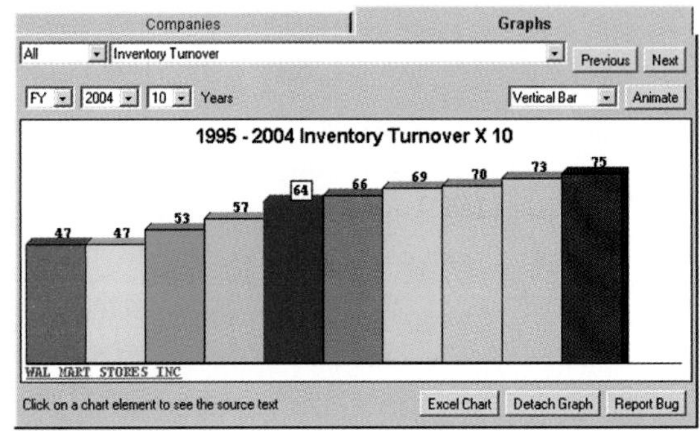

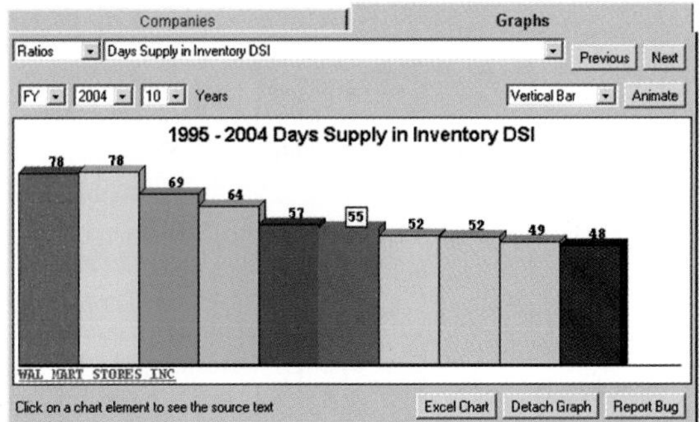

a. Using the preceding cost of goods sold and inventory data, compute the inventory turnover for 2005. Does it agree with the amount shown in the preceding graph? (*Hint:* The graph is based upon using ending rather than average inventory.)

b. Using the preceding cost of goods sold and inventory data, compute the days' sales in inventory for 2005. Does it agree with the amount shown in the preceding graph?

c. Comment on the preceding graphs.

Case 6-5

Inventory ratios for Dell and HP

Dell Inc. and Hewlett-Packard Company (HP) are both manufacturers of computer equipment and peripherals. However, the two companies follow two different approaches. Dell follows a build-to-order approach, where the consumer orders the computer from a Web page. The order is then manufactured and shipped to the customer within days of the order. In contrast, HP follows a build-to-stock approach, where the computer is first built for inventory, then sold from inventory to retailers, such as **Best Buy**. The following financial statement information is provided for Dell and HP for fiscal year 2004 (in millions):

	Dell	HP
Inventory, end of period	$ 459	$ 7,071
Inventory, beginning of period	327	6,065
Cost of goods sold	40,190	60,150

The two approaches can be seen in the difference between the inventory turnover and number of days' sales in inventory ratio for the two companies.

a. Determine the inventory turnover ratio and number of days' sales in inventory ratio for each company. Round to one decimal place.
b. Interpret the difference between the ratios for the two companies.

Case 6-6

Costing inventory

Feedbag Company began operations in 2005 by selling a single product. Data on purchases and sales for the year were as follows:

Purchases:

Date	Units Purchased	Unit Cost	Total Cost
April 3	7,750	$24.40	$ 189,100
May 15	8,250	26.00	214,500
June 6	10,000	26.40	264,000
July 10	10,000	28.00	280,000
August 3	6,800	28.50	193,800
October 5	3,200	29.00	92,800
November 1	2,000	29.90	59,800
December 10	2,000	32.00	64,000
	50,000		$1,358,000

Sales:

April	4,000 Units
May	4,000
June	5,000
July	6,000
August	7,000
September	7,000
October	4,500
November	2,500
December	2,000
Total units	42,000
Total sales	$1,300,000

On January 3, 2006, the president of the company, Heather Ola, asked for your advice on costing the 8,000-unit physical inventory that was taken on December 31, 2005. Moreover, since the firm plans to expand its product line, she asked for your advice on the use of a perpetual inventory system in the future.

1. Determine the cost of the December 31, 2005, inventory under the periodic system, using the (a) first-in, first-out method, (b) last-in, first-out method, and (c) average cost method.
2. Determine the gross profit for the year under each of the three methods in (1).

(continued)

3. a. Explain varying viewpoints why each of the three inventory costing methods may best reflect the results of operations for 2005.
   b. Which of the three inventory costing methods may best reflect the replacement cost of the inventory on the balance sheet as of December 31, 2005?
   c. Which inventory costing method would you choose to use for income tax purposes? Why?
   d. Discuss the advantages and disadvantages of using a perpetual inventory system. From the data presented in this case, is there any indication of the adequacy of inventory levels during the year?

Case 6-7

SPREADSHEET

The general merchandise retail industry has a number of segments represented by the following companies:

Company Name	Merchandise Concept
Costco Wholesale Corporation	Membership warehouse
Wal-Mart	Discount general merchandise
JCPenney	Department store

For a recent year, the following cost of merchandise sold and beginning and ending inventories have been provided from corporate annual reports for these three companies:

	Costco	Wal-Mart	JCPenney
Cost of merchandise sold	$42,092	$219,793	$11,285
Merchandise inventory, beginning	3,339	26,612	3,156
Merchandise inventory, ending	3,644	29,447	3,169

a. Determine the inventory turnover ratio for all three companies.
b. Determine the number of day's sales in inventory for all three companies.
c. Interpret these results based upon each company's merchandise concept.

BUSINESS ACTIVITIES AND RESPONSIBILITY ISSUES

Activity 6-1

Ethics and professional conduct in business

Follicle Co. is experiencing a decrease in sales and operating income for the fiscal year ending December 31, 2006. Preston Shipley, controller of Follicle Co., has suggested that all orders received before the end of the fiscal year be shipped by midnight, December 31, 2006, even if the shipping department must work overtime. Since Follicle Co. ships all merchandise FOB shipping point, it would record all such shipments as sales for the year ending December 31, 2006, thereby offsetting some of the decreases in sales and operating income.

Discuss whether Preston Shipley is behaving in a professional manner.

Activity 6-2

Lifo and inventory flow

The following is an excerpt from a conversation between Jaime Noll, the warehouse manager for Baltic Wholesale Co., and its accountant, Tara Stroud. Baltic Wholesale operates a large regional warehouse that supplies produce and other grocery products to grocery stores in smaller communities.

Jaime: Tara, can you explain what's going on here with these monthly statements?
Tara: Sure, Jaime. How can I help you?
Jaime: I don't understand this last-in, first-out inventory procedure. It just doesn't make sense.
Tara: Well, what it means is that we assume that the last goods we receive are the first ones sold. So the inventory is made up of the items we purchased first.
Jaime: Yes, but that's my problem. It doesn't work that way! We always distribute the oldest produce first. Some of that produce is perishable! We can't keep any of it very long or it'll spoil.
Tara: Jaime, you don't understand. We only *assume* that the products we distribute are the last ones received. We don't actually have to distribute the goods in this way.
Jaime: I always thought that accounting was supposed to show what really happened. It all sounds like "make believe" to me! Why not report what really happens?

Respond to Jaime's concerns.

Activity 6-3

Observe controls over inventory

GROUP ACTIVITY

Select a business in your community and observe its controls over inventory. In groups of three or four, identify and discuss the similarities and differences in each business's inventory controls. Prepare a written summary of your findings.

Activity 6-4

Compare inventory cost flow assumptions

GROUP ACTIVITY

In groups of three or four, examine the financial statements of a well-known retailing business. You may obtain the financial statements you need from one of the following sources:

1. Your school or local library.
2. The investor relations department of the company.
3. The company's Web site on the Internet.
4. EDGAR (Electronic Data Gathering, Analysis, and Retrieval), the electronic archives of financial statements filed with the Securities and Exchange Commission. SEC documents can be retrieved using the EdgarScan service from PricewaterhouseCoopers at http://edgarscan.pwcglobal.com. To obtain annual report information, type in a company name in the appropriate space. EdgarScan will list the reports available to you for the company you've selected. Select the most recent annual report filing, identified as a 10-K or 10-K405. EdgarScan provides an outline of the report, including the separate financial statements. You can double-click the income statement and balance sheet for the selected company into an Excel spreadsheet for further analysis.

Determine the cost flow assumption(s) that the company is using for its inventory, and determine whether the company is using the lower-of-cost-or-market rule. Prepare a written summary of your findings.

ANSWERS TO SELF-STUDY QUESTIONS

1. **D** The direct labor costs are introduced into production initially as work in process. Once the units are completed, these costs are transferred to finished goods inventory (answer C). Materials inventory (answer A) includes only material costs, not direct labor cost. Merchandise inventory (answer B) is not used in a manufacturing setting, hence does not include direct labor cost.

2. **A** The lifo method of costing is based on the assumption that costs should be charged against revenue in the reverse order in which costs were incurred. Thus, the oldest costs are assigned to inventory. Thirty of the 35 units would be assigned a unit cost of $20 (since 110 of the beginning inventory units were sold on the first sale), and the remaining 5 units would be assigned a cost of $23, for a total of $715 (answer A).

3. **D** The fifo method of costing is based on the assumption that costs should be charged against revenue in the order in which they were incurred (first-in, first-out). Thus, the most recent costs are assigned to inventory. The 35 units would be assigned a unit cost of $23 (answer D).

4. **B** When the price level is steadily rising, the earlier unit costs are lower than recent unit costs. Under the fifo method (answer B), these earlier costs are matched against revenue to yield the highest possible net income. The periodic inventory system (answer D) is a system and not a method of costing.

5. **B** The inventory turnover ratio is computed as follows:

$$\text{Inventory turnover} = \frac{\text{Cost of Merchandise Sold}}{\text{Average Inventory}}$$

$$\text{Inventory turnover} = \frac{\$175{,}000}{\$50{,}000} = 3.5$$

7 Sarbanes-Oxley, Internal Control, and Cash

Learning Goals

1. Describe the Sarbanes-Oxley Act of 2002 and its impact on internal controls and financial reporting.
2. Describe and illustrate the objectives and elements of internal control.
3. Describe and illustrate the application of internal controls to cash.
4. Describe the nature of a bank account and its use in
5. Describe and illustrate the use of a bank reconciliation in controlling cash.
6. Describe the accounting for special-purpose cash funds.
7. Describe and illustrate the reporting of cash and cash equivalents in the financial statements.
8. Describe, illustrate, and interpret the cash flow to net in-

The Walt Disney Company

Once a month, you may receive a bank statement that lists the deposits and withdrawals that have been added to and subtracted from your account balance. If you wrote any checks, the statement may also be accompanied by copies of your canceled checks.

New forms of payment are now arising that don't involve checks at all. Retailers, such as grocery stores, now allow customers to pay for merchandise by swiping their bank cards at check-out, causing an immediate transfer of funds out of a bank account. Banks are allowing regular monthly bills, such as utility bills, to be paid directly out of a checking account, using electronic fund transfers. Internet payments can be made by using services such as PayPal®, which will make payments to third parties directly out of a checking account. In all of these cases, you need to verify actual fund transfers with the correct amounts by comparing your bank statement with electronic invoices, receipts, and other evidence of payment.

Many banks are making real-time checking account information available on the Internet to account owners. Thus, account owners using this feature are now able to manage and control their accounts in a more timely way.

Like individuals, businesses must control their cash and other assets to guard against errors and fraud. For example, The Walt Disney Company has extensive cash collection and control activities at its theme parks. Cash is collected, counted, and deposited from the parking lot, admissions office, and on-site retail shops.

© RICHARD DREW/AP PHOTO

Disney also accepts credit card payments at its theme parks and mall-based Disney stores. In addition, Disney collects cash in the form of checks and electronic fund transfers for advertising revenues on the ABC, A&E, and ESPN networks and for ticket sales from theatrical releases of motion pictures that are paid by the movie exhibitors.

In this chapter, we will discuss how companies like Walt Disney control their cash and other assets. We begin by discussing the importance of the Sarbanes-Oxley Act that was passed by Congress to improve the financial controls and reporting practices of companies.

Describe the Sarbanes-Oxley Act of 2002 and its impact on internal controls and financial reporting.

SARBANES-OXLEY ACT OF 2002

During the Enron, WorldCom, Tyco, Adelphia, and other financial scandals of the early 2000s, stockholders, creditors, and other investors lost millions and in some cases billions of dollars.[1] The resulting public outcry led Congress to pass the **Sarbanes-Oxley Act of 2002**. This act, referred to simply as *Sarbanes-Oxley*, is considered one of the most important and significant laws affecting publicly held companies in recent history. Although Sarbanes-Oxley applies only to companies whose stock is traded on public exchanges, referred to as *publicly held companies*, it has become the standard for assessing the financial controls and reporting of all companies.

Sarbanes-Oxley's purpose is to restore public confidence and trust in the financial statements of companies. In doing so, Sarbanes-Oxley emphasizes the importance of effective internal control.[2] **Internal control** is broadly defined as the procedures and processes used by a company to safeguard its assets, process information accurately, and ensure compliance with laws and regulations.

Sarbanes-Oxley requires companies to maintain strong and effective internal controls over the recording of transactions and the preparing of financial statements. Such controls are important because they deter fraud and prevent misleading financial statements as shown in the following illustration:

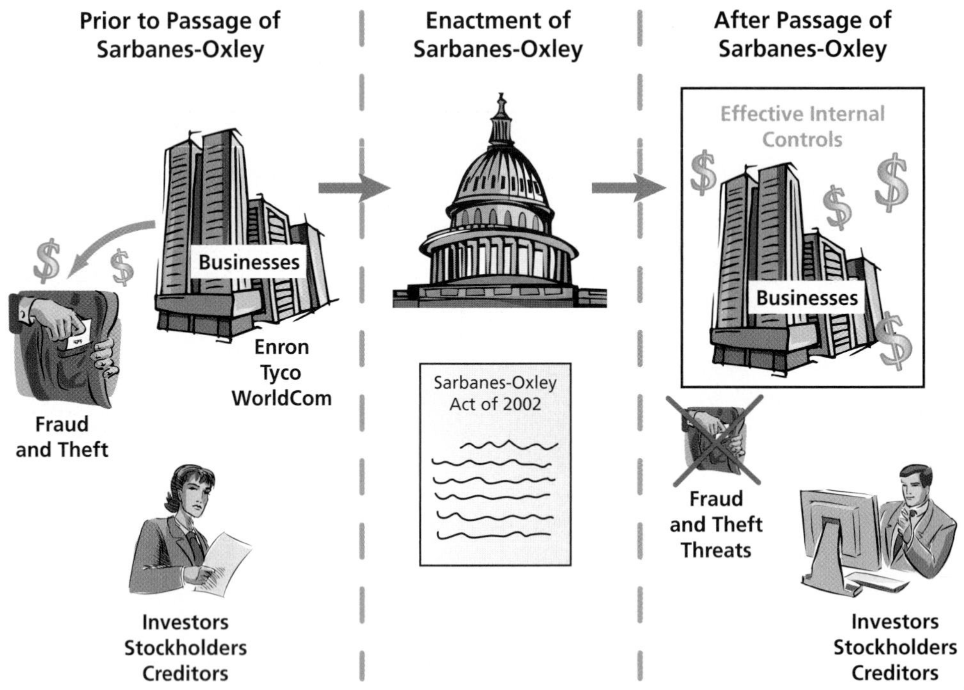

Sarbanes-Oxley not only requires companies to maintain strong and effective internal controls, but it also requires companies and their independent accountants to

1 Exhibit 9 in Chapter 1 briefly summarizes these scandals.

2 Sarbanes-Oxley also has important implications for corporate governance and the regulation of the public accounting profession. In this chapter, we focus on the internal control implications of Sarbanes-Oxley.

report on the effectiveness of the company's internal controls.[3] These reports are required to be filed with the company's annual 10-K report with the Securities and Exchange Commission. The act also encourages companies to include these reports in their annual reports to stockholders. An example of such a report by the management of General Electric Company (GE) is shown in Exhibit 1.

Exhibit 1

Sarbanes-Oxley Report General Electric Company

Management's Annual Report on Internal Control over Financial Reporting

The management of General Electric Company is responsible for establishing and maintaining adequate internal control over financial reporting for the company. With the participation of the Chief Executive Officer and the Chief Financial Officer, our management conducted an evaluation of the effectiveness of our internal control over financial reporting based on the framework and criteria established in *Internal Control—Integrated Framework*, issued by the Committee of Sponsoring Organizations. . . . Based on this evaluation, our management has concluded that our internal control over financial reporting was effective as of December 31, 2004.

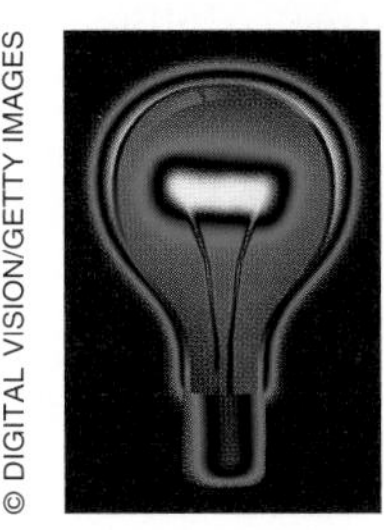

© DIGITAL VISION/GETTY IMAGES

General Electric Company's independent [accountant] auditor, KPMG LLP, a registered public accounting firm, has [also] issued an audit report on our management's assessment of our internal control over financial reporting.

JEFFREY R. IMMELT
Chairman of the Board
and Chief Executive Officer

KEITH S. SHERIN
Senior Vice President, Finance
and Chief Financial Officer

GE based its assessment and evaluation of internal controls upon *Internal Control—Integrated Framework,* which was issued by the Committee of Sponsoring Organizations. This framework is the widely accepted standard by which companies design, analyze, and evaluate internal controls. For this reason, we use this framework in the next section of this chapter as a basis for our discussion of internal controls.

Describe and illustrate the objectives and elements of internal control.

INTERNAL CONTROL

As indicated in the prior section, effective internal controls are required by Sarbanes-Oxley. In addition, effective internal controls help businesses guide their operations and prevent theft and other abuses. For example, assume that you own and manage a lawn care service. Your business uses several employee teams, and you provide each team with vehicle and lawn equipment. What issues might you face as a manager in controlling the operations of this business? Below are some examples.

- Lawn care must be provided on time.
- The quality of lawn care services must meet customer expectations.
- Employees must provide work for the hours they are paid.
- Lawn care equipment should be used for business purposes only.
- Vehicles should be used for business purposes only.
- Customers must be billed and payments collected for services rendered.

3 These reporting requirements are required under Section 404 of the act. As a result, these requirements and reports are often referred to as 404 requirements and 404 reports.

How would you address these issues? You could, for example, develop a schedule at the beginning of each day and then inspect the work at the end of the day to verify that it was completed according to quality standards. You could have "surprise" inspections by arriving on site at random times to verify that the teams are working according to schedule. You could require employees to "clock in" at the beginning of the day and "clock out" at the end of the day to make sure that they are paid for hours worked. You could require the work teams to return the vehicles and equipment to a central location to prevent unauthorized use. You could keep a log of odometer readings at the end of each day to verify that the vehicles have not been used for "joy riding." You could bill customers after you have inspected the work and then monitor the collection of all receivables. All of these are examples of internal control.

In this section, we describe and illustrate internal control using the framework developed by the Committee of Sponsoring Organizations, which was formed by five major business associations. The committee's deliberations were published in *Internal Control—Integrated Framework*.[4] This framework, cited by GE in Exhibit 1, has become the standard by which companies design, analyze, and evaluate internal control. We describe and illustrate the framework by first describing the objectives of internal control and then showing how these objectives can be achieved through the five elements of internal control.

Objectives of Internal Control

The objectives of internal control are to provide reasonable assurance that: (1) assets are safeguarded and used for business purposes, (2) business information is accurate, and (3) employees comply with laws and regulations. These objectives are illustrated below.

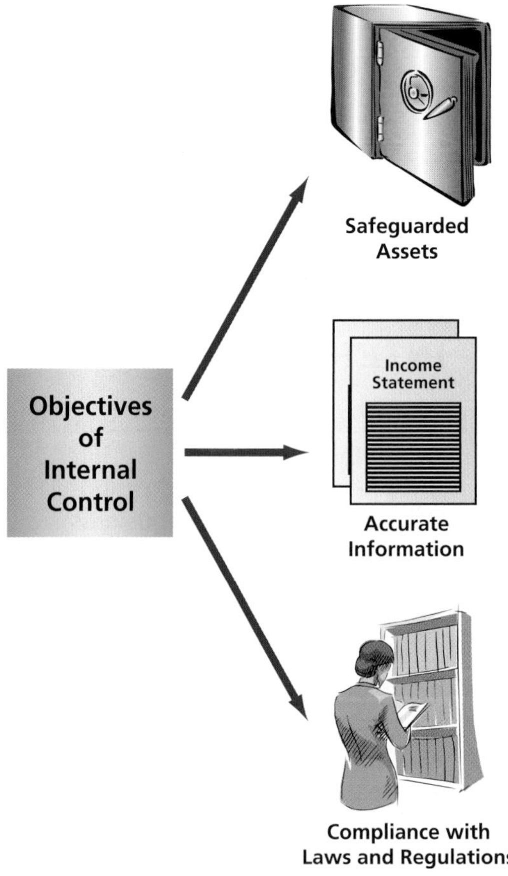

4 *Internal Control—Integrated Framework* by the Committee of Sponsoring Organizations (COSO) of the Treadway Commission, 1992.

Internal control can safeguard assets by preventing theft, fraud, misuse, or misplacement. One of the most serious breaches of internal control is employee fraud. **Employee fraud** is the intentional act of deceiving an employer for personal gain. Such deception may range from purposely overstating expenses on a travel expense report to embezzling millions of dollars through complex schemes.

Accurate information is necessary for operating a business successfully. The safeguarding of assets and accurate information often go hand-in-hand. The reason is that employees attempting to defraud a business will also need to adjust the accounting records in order to hide the fraud.

Businesses must comply with applicable laws, regulations, and financial reporting standards. Examples of such standards and laws include environmental regulations, contract terms, safety regulations, and generally accepted accounting principles (GAAP).

Elements of Internal Control

How does management achieve its internal control objectives? Management is responsible for designing and applying five **elements of internal control** to meet the three internal control objectives. These elements are (1) the control environment, (2) risk assessment, (3) control procedures, (4) monitoring, and (5) information and communication.[5]

The elements of internal control are illustrated in Exhibit 2. In this exhibit, these elements form an umbrella over the business to protect it from control threats. The

Exhibit 2

Elements of Internal Control

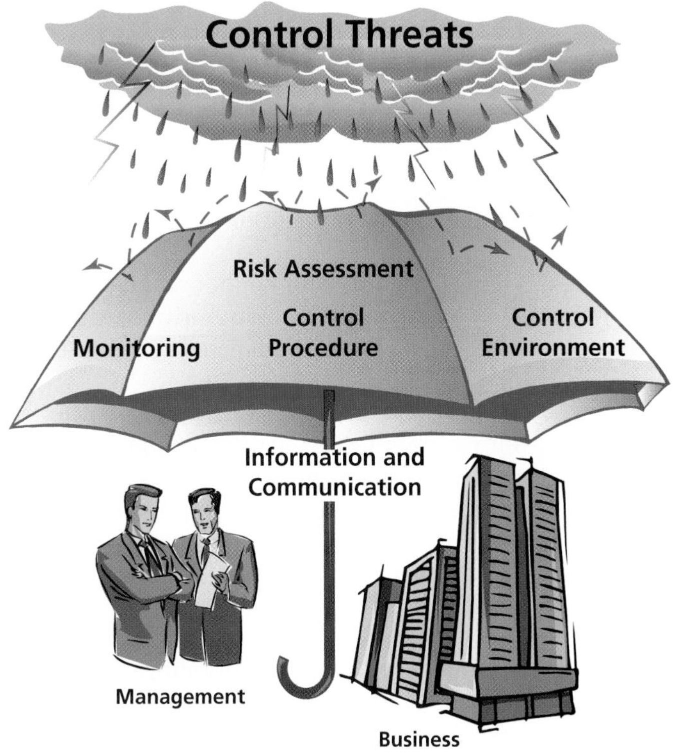

5 Ibid., 12–14.

business's control environment is represented by the size of the umbrella. Risk assessment, control procedures, and monitoring are the fabric that keeps the umbrella from leaking. Information and communication link the umbrella to management. In the following paragraphs, we discuss each of these elements.

Control Environment

A business's control environment is the overall attitude of management and employees about the importance of controls. One of the factors that influences the control environment is *management's philosophy and operating style.* A management that overemphasizes operating goals and deviates from control policies may indirectly encourage employees to ignore controls. For example, the pressure to achieve revenue targets may encourage employees to fraudulently record sham sales. On the other hand, a management that emphasizes the importance of controls and encourages adherence to control policies will create an effective control environment.

Control Environment

CEO

employees

Management's Philosophy and Operating Style

Organizational Structure

Personnel Policies

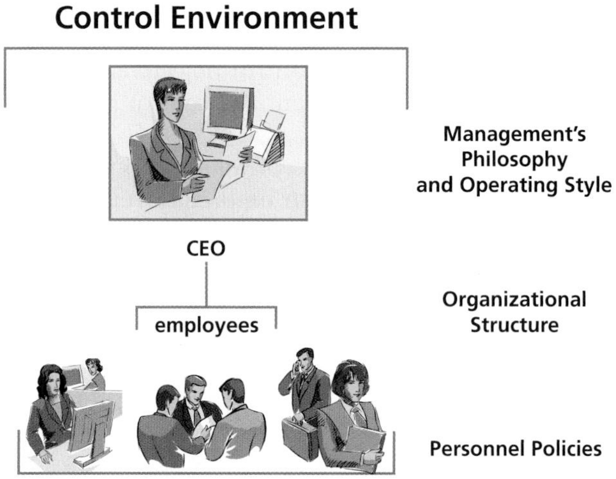

The business's *organizational structure,* which is the framework for planning and controlling operations, also influences the control environment. For example, a department store chain might organize each of its stores as separate business units. Each store manager has full authority over pricing and other operating activities. In such a structure, each store manager has the responsibility for establishing an effective control environment.

Personnel policies also affect the control environment. Personnel policies involve the hiring, training, evaluation, compensation, and promotion of employees. In addition, job descriptions, employee codes of ethics, and conflict-of-interest policies are part of the personnel policies. Such policies can enhance the internal control environment if they provide reasonable assurance that only competent, honest employees are hired and retained.

To illustrate the importance of the control environment, consider the case where the head of a bank's loan department perpetrated a fraud by accepting kickbacks from customers with poor credit ratings. As a result, the bank lost thousands of dollars from bad loans. After discovering the fraud, the bank president improved the bank's control environment by implementing a program that allowed employees to report suspicious conduct anonymously. In addition to encouraging employees to report suspicious conduct, the employees were warned that employee fraud might occur anywhere and involve anyone.

Risk Assessment

All organizations face risks. Examples of risk include changes in customer requirements, competitive threats, regulatory changes, changes in economic factors such as interest rates, and employee violations of company policies and procedures. Management should assess these risks and take necessary actions to control them, so that the objectives of internal control can be achieved.

Once risks are identified, they can be analyzed to estimate their significance, to assess their likelihood of occurring, and to determine actions that will minimize them. For example, the manager of a warehouse operation may analyze the risk of employee back injuries, which might give rise to lawsuits. If the manager determines that the risk is significant, the company may purchase back support braces for its warehouse employees and require them to wear the braces.

Control Procedures

Control procedures are established to provide reasonable assurance that business goals will be achieved, including the prevention of fraud. In the following paragraphs, we will briefly discuss control procedures that can be integrated throughout the accounting system. These procedures are listed in Exhibit 3.

Exhibit 3

Internal Control Procedures

Competent Personnel, Rotating Duties, and Mandatory Vacations. The successful operation of an accounting system requires procedures to ensure that people are able to perform the duties to which they are assigned. Hence, it is necessary that all accounting employees be adequately trained and supervised in performing their jobs. It may also be advisable to rotate duties of clerical personnel and mandate vacations for nonclerical personnel. These policies encourage employees to adhere to prescribed procedures. In addition, existing errors or fraud may be detected. For example, numerous cases of employee

INTEGRITY, OBJECTIVITY, AND ETHICS IN BUSINESS

Tips on Preventing Employee Fraud in Small Companies

- Do not have the same employee write company checks and keep the books. Look for payments to vendors you don't know or payments to vendors whose names appear to be misspelled.
- If your business has a computer system, restrict access to accounting files as much as possible. Also, keep a backup copy of your accounting files and store it at an off-site location.
- Be wary of anybody working in finance that declines to take vacations. They may be afraid that a replacement will uncover fraud.
- Require and monitor supporting documentation (such as vendor invoices) before signing checks.
- Track the number of credit card bills you sign monthly.
- Limit and monitor access to important documents and supplies, such as blank checks and signature stamps.
- Check W-2 forms against your payroll annually to make sure you're not carrying any fictitious employees.
- Rely on yourself, not on your accountant, to spot fraud.

Source: Steve Kaufman, "Embezzlement Common at Small Companies," Knight-Ridder Newspapers, reported in *Athens Daily News/Athens Banner-Herald*, March 10, 1996, page 4D.

fraud have been discovered after a long-term employee, who never took vacations, missed work because of an illness or other unavoidable reasons.

To illustrate, consider the case where a bank officer who was not required to take vacations stole approximately $5 million over 16 years by printing fake certificates of deposit. The officer would then issue the fake certificate to the customer and pocket the customer's money. After discovering the theft, the bank began requiring all employees to take vacations.

Separating Responsibilities for Related Operations. To decrease the possibility of inefficiency, errors, and fraud, the responsibility for related operations should be divided among two or more persons. For example, the responsibilities for purchasing, receiving, and paying for computer supplies should be divided among three persons or departments. If the same person orders supplies, verifies the receipt of the supplies, and pays the supplier, the following abuses are possible:

1. Orders may be placed on the basis of friendship with a supplier, rather than on price, quality, and other objective factors.
2. The quantity and quality of supplies received may not be verified, thus causing payment for supplies not received or poor-quality supplies.
3. Supplies may be stolen by the employee.
4. The validity and accuracy of invoices may be verified carelessly, thus causing the payment of false or inaccurate invoices.

The "checks and balances" provided by dividing responsibilities among various departments requires no duplication of effort. The business documents prepared by one department are designed to coordinate with and support those prepared by other departments.

To illustrate, consider the case where an accounts payable clerk created false invoices and submitted them for payment. The clerk obtained the resulting checks, opened a bank account, and cashed the checks under an assumed name. The clerk was able to steal thousands of dollars because no one was required to approve the payments other than the accounts payable clerk.

Separating Operations, Custody of Assets, and Accounting. Control policies should establish the responsibilities for various business activities. To reduce the possibility of errors and fraud, the responsibilities for operations, custody of assets, and accounting should be separated. The accounting records then serve as an independent check on the individuals who have custody of the assets and who engage in the business operations. For example, the employees entrusted with handling cash receipts from credit customers should not record cash receipts in the accounting records. To do so would allow employees to borrow or steal cash and hide the theft in the records. Likewise, if those engaged in operating activities also record the results of operations, they could distort the accounting reports to show favorable results. For example, a store manager whose year-end bonus is based upon operating profits might be tempted to record fictitious sales in order to receive a larger bonus.

To illustrate, consider the case where a payroll clerk was responsible for preparing the payroll and distributing the payroll checks. The clerk stole almost $40,000 over two months by preparing duplicate payroll checks and checks for fictitious part-time employees. After the theft was detected, the duties of preparing payroll checks and distributing payroll checks were assigned to separate employees.

Proofs and Security Measures. Proofs and security measures should be used to safeguard assets and ensure reliable accounting data. This control procedure applies to many different techniques, such as authorization, approval, and reconciliation procedures. For example, employees who travel on company business may be required to obtain a department manager's approval on a travel request form.

Other examples of control procedures include the use of bank accounts and other measures to ensure the safety of cash and valuable documents. A cash register that displays the amount recorded for each sale and provides the customer a printed receipt can be an effective part of the internal control structure. An all-night convenience store could use the following security measures to deter robberies:

1. Locate the cash register near the door, so that it is fully visible from outside the store; have two employees work late hours; employ a security guard.
2. Deposit cash in the bank daily, before 5 p.m.
3. Keep only small amounts of cash on hand after 5 p.m. by depositing excess cash in a store safe that can't be opened by employees on duty.
4. Install cameras and alarm systems.

To illustrate, consider the case where someone stole thousands of dollars in parking fines from a small town. Citizens would pay their parking fines by placing money in ticket envelopes and putting them in a locked box outside the town hall. The key to the locked box was not safeguarded and was readily available to a variety of people. As a result, the person who stole the money was never discovered. The town later gave one person the responsibility of safeguarding the key and emptying the locked box.

Monitoring

Monitoring the internal control system locates weaknesses and improves control effectiveness. The internal control system can be monitored through either ongoing efforts by management or by separate evaluations. Ongoing monitoring efforts may include observing both employee behavior and warning signs from the accounting system. The indicators shown in Exhibit 4 may be clues to internal control problems.[6]

Separate monitoring evaluations are generally performed when there are major changes in strategy, senior management, business structure, or operations. In large businesses, internal auditors who are independent of operations normally are responsible for monitoring the internal control system. Internal auditors can report issues and concerns to an audit committee of the board of directors, who are independent of management. In addition, external auditors also evaluate internal control as a normal part of their annual financial statement audit.

Information and Communication

Information and communication are essential elements of internal control. Information about the control environment, risk assessment, control procedures, and monitoring is

6 Edwin C. Bliss, "Employee Theft," *Boardroom Reports*, July 15, 1994, pp. 5–6.

Exhibit 4

Indicators of Internal Control Problems

CLUES TO POTENTIAL PROBLEMS

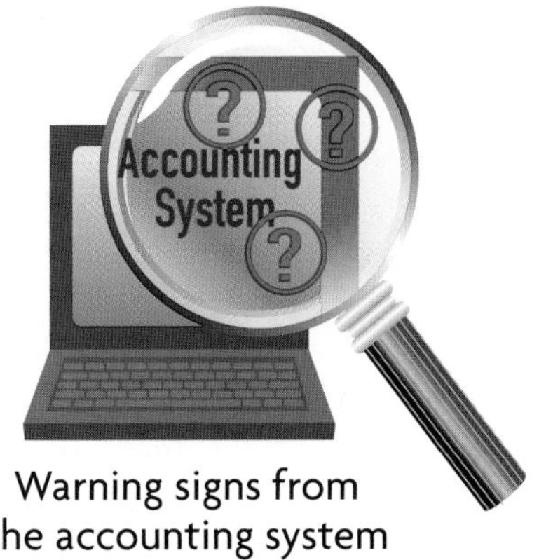

Warning signs with regard to people

1. Abrupt change in lifestyle (without winning the lottery).
2. Close social relationships with suppliers.
3. Refusing to take a vacation.
4. Frequent borrowing from other employees.
5. Excessive use of alcohol or drugs.

Warning signs from the accounting system

1. Missing documents or gaps in transaction numbers (could mean documents are being used for fraudulent transactions).
2. An unusual increase in customer refunds (refunds may be phony).
3. Differences between daily cash receipts and bank deposits (could mean receipts are being pocketed before being deposited).
4. Sudden increase in slow payments (employee may be pocketing the payment).
5. Backlog in recording transactions (possibly an attempt to delay detection of fraud).

needed by management to guide operations and ensure compliance with reporting, legal, and regulatory requirements. Management can also use external information to assess events and conditions that impact decision making and external reporting. For example, management uses information from the Financial Accounting Standards Board (FASB) to assess the impact of possible changes in reporting standards.

INTEGRITY, OBJECTIVITY, AND ETHICS IN BUSINESS

You Really Don't Understand

Michael S. Ovitz, former president of **The Walt Disney Company**, is involved in a bitter lawsuit with shareholders who are seeking the return of his $140 million severance package from Disney. The lawsuit asserts that Mr. Ovitz should have been fired for gross negligence rather than being terminated without cause.

During testimony, allegations of improper conduct include hundreds of thousands of dollars of gifts and charitable contributions made by Mr. Ovitz on behalf of Disney. The gifts include Disney character toys, over $600 in jewelry and food he gave talk-show host David Letterman, and a $25,000 gift to the Museum of Modern Art where he served as a trustee.

In response, Mr. Ovitz is quoted as saying:

"The entertainment business is very much about favors. . . . In our world people do things that are very unorthodox. . . . You just don't really understand the television business. . . ."

Sources: Rita K. Farrell, "Ovitz Defends Costs of Gifts Dispensed by Him at Disney," *The New York Times*, November 2, 2004; and Laura M. Holson, "Ovitz Defends His Brief Record at Disney," *The New York Times*, October 29, 2004.

Describe and illustrate the application of internal controls to cash.

CASH CONTROLS OVER RECEIPTS AND PAYMENTS

Cash includes coins, currency (paper money), checks, money orders, and money on deposit that is available for unrestricted withdrawal from banks and other financial institutions. Normally, you can think of cash as anything that a bank would accept for deposit in your account. For example, a check made payable to you could normally be deposited in a bank and thus is considered cash.

We will assume in this chapter that a business maintains only *one* bank account, represented in the ledger as *Cash*. In practice, however, a business may have several bank accounts, such as one for general cash payments and another for payroll. For each of its bank accounts, the business will maintain a ledger account, one of which may be called *Cash in Bank—First Bank*, for example. It will also maintain separate ledger accounts for special-purpose cash funds, such as travel reimbursements. We will introduce some of these other cash accounts later in this chapter.

Because of the ease with which money can be transferred, cash is the asset most likely to be diverted and used improperly by employees. In addition, many transactions either directly or indirectly affect the receipt or the payment of cash. Businesses must therefore design and use controls that safeguard cash and control the authorization of cash transactions. In the following paragraphs, we will discuss these controls.

Control of Cash Receipts

To protect cash from theft and misuse, a business must control cash from the time it is received until it is deposited in a bank. Businesses normally receive cash from two main sources: (1) customers purchasing products or services and (2) customers making payments on account. For example, fast-food restaurants, such as McDonald's, Wendy's, and Burger King, receive cash primarily from over-the-counter sales to customers. Mail-order and Internet retailers, such as Lands' End, Orvis, L.L. Bean, and Amazon.com, receive cash primarily through electronic funds transfers from credit card companies.

Cash Received from Cash Sales. Regardless of the source of cash receipts, every business must properly safeguard and record its cash receipts. One of the most important controls to protect cash received in over-the-counter sales is a cash register. When a clerk (cashier) enters the amount of a sale, the cash register normally displays the amount. This is a control to ensure that the clerk has charged you the correct amount. You also receive a receipt to verify the accuracy of the amount.

At the beginning of a work shift, each cash register clerk is given a cash drawer that contains a predetermined amount of cash for making change for customers. The amount in each drawer is sometimes called a *change fund*. At the end of the shift, the clerk and the supervisor count the cash in that clerk's cash drawer. The amount of cash in each drawer should equal the beginning amount of cash plus the cash sales for the day. However, errors in recording cash sales or errors in making change cause the amount of cash on hand to differ from this amount. Such differences are recorded in a **cash short and over account**.

At the end of the accounting period, a debit balance in the cash short and over account is included in Miscellaneous Expense in the income statement. A credit balance is included in the Other Income section. If a clerk consistently has significant cash short and over amounts, the supervisor may require the clerk to take additional training.

Q. A cash register begins with $300, recorded cash sales are $13,644, and cash of $13,959 is on hand. What is the cash short or over?

A. Cash over is $15.

After a cash register clerk's cash has been counted and recorded on a memorandum form, the cash is then placed in a store safe in the Cashier's Department until it can be deposited in the bank. The supervisor forwards the clerk's cash register receipts to the Accounting Department, where they serve as the basis for recording the transactions for the day as shown below.

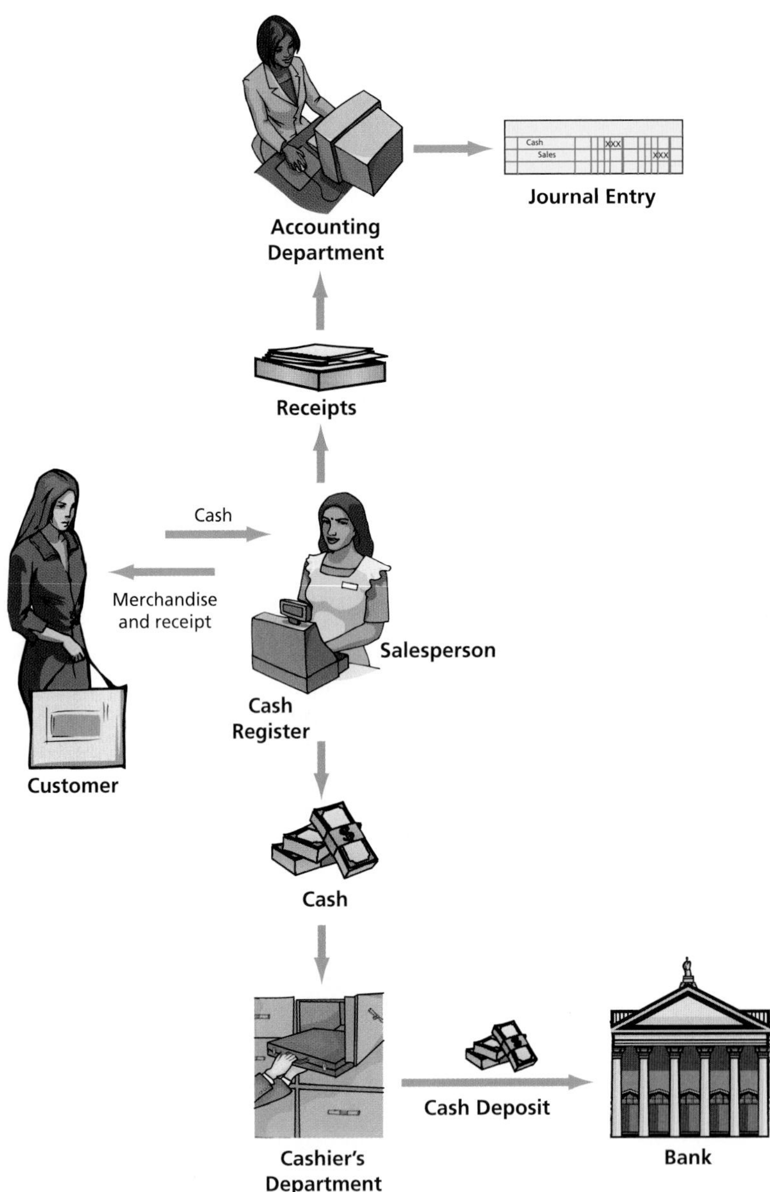

Some retail companies use debit card systems to transfer and record the receipt of cash. In a debit card system, a customer pays for goods at the time of purchase by presenting a plastic card. The card authorizes the electronic transfer of cash from the customer's checking account to the retailer's bank account.

Cash Received in the Mail. Cash is received in the mail when customers pay their bills. This cash is usually in the form of checks and money orders. Most companies' invoices are designed so that customers return a portion of the invoice, called a *remittance*

HOW BUSINESSES MAKE MONEY

The Lion King

How many ways does **The Walt Disney Company** earn revenues from *The Lion King*?

The answer includes ticket sales for the animated motion picture and any sequels, DVD sales, music soundtrack sales, ticket sales for the Broadway play, tickets and concession sales for Disney on Ice®, merchandise and apparel sales, theme park attractions, cable television programming, and video game sales—to name just a few. Disney's business approach is to develop a character, such as the Lion King, and then develop multiple ways to earn revenues from this key asset. Often, Disney will develop new channels of distribution in order to support the breadth of product offshoots, such as a cable channel, merchandise store, Broadway theater, or theme park.

Overall, the preceding approach has been very successful in earning money for Disney. However, this approach is based on continual development of new characters from which to build a product universe. This is Disney's key challenge as it moves toward the world of computer animation, which is now dominated by **Pixar**.

Source: Adrian J. Slywotzky, David J. Morrison, and Bob Andelman, *The Profit Zone: How Strategic Business Design Will Lead You to Tomorrow's Profits* (New York: Random House, 1997).

---

advice, with their payment. The employee who opens the incoming mail should initially compare the amount of cash received with the amount shown on the remittance advice. If a customer does not return a remittance advice, an employee prepares one. Like the cash register, the remittance advice serves as a record of cash initially received. It also helps ensure that the posting to the customer's account is accurate. Finally, as a control, the employee opening the mail normally also stamps checks and money orders "For Deposit Only" in the bank account of the business.

All cash received in the mail is sent to the Cashier's Department. An employee there combines it with the receipts from cash sales and prepares a bank deposit ticket. The remittance advices and their summary totals are delivered to the Accounting Department. An accounting clerk then prepares the records of the transactions and posts them to the customer accounts.

When cash is deposited in the bank, the bank normally stamps a duplicate copy of the deposit ticket with the amount received. This bank receipt is returned to the Accounting Department, where a clerk compares the receipt with the total amount that should have been deposited. This control helps ensure that all the cash is deposited and that no cash is lost or stolen on the way to the bank. Any shortages are thus promptly detected.

Separating the duties of the Cashier's Department, which handles cash, and the Accounting Department, which records cash, is a control. If Accounting Department employees both handle and record cash, an employee could steal cash and change the accounting records to hide the theft.

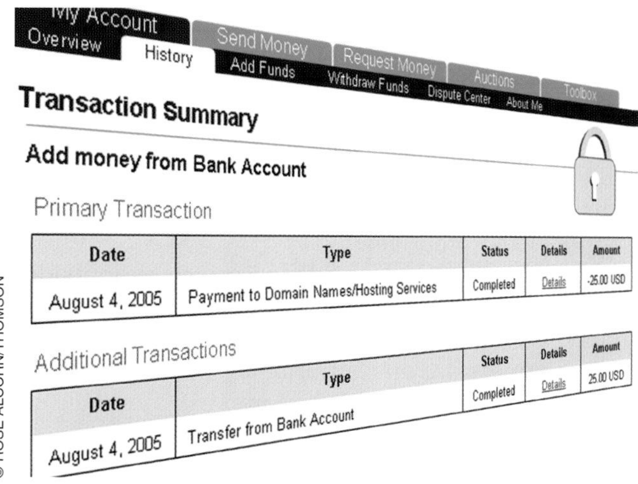

Cash Received by EFT. Cash may also be received from customers through **electronic funds transfers**. For example, customers may authorize automatic electronic transfers from their checking accounts to pay monthly bills for such items as cell phone, cable, Internet, and electric services. In such cases, the company sends the customer's bank a signed form from the customer authorizing the monthly electronic transfers from the customer's checking acount to the company's bank account. Each month, the company electronically notifies the customer's bank of the amount of the transfer and the date the transfer should take place. On the due date, the company records the electronic transfer as a receipt of cash to its bank account and posts the amount paid to the customer's account.

Most companies encourage automatic electronic transfers by customers for several reasons. First, electronic transfers are less costly than receiving cash payments through the mail since the employee handling of cash is eliminated. Second, electronic transfers enhance internal controls over cash since the cash is received directly by the bank without the handling of cash by employees. Thus, potential theft of cash is eliminated. Finally, electronic transfers reduce late payments from customers and speed up the processing of cash receipts.

Control of Cash Payments

The control of cash payments should provide reasonable assurance that payments are made for only authorized transactions. In addition, controls should ensure that cash is used efficiently. For example, controls should ensure that all available discounts, such as purchase discounts, are taken.

In a small business, an owner/manager may authorize payments based upon personal knowledge of goods and services purchased. In a large business, however, the duties of purchasing goods, inspecting the goods received, and verifying the invoices are usually performed by different employees. These duties must be coordinated to ensure that checks for proper payments are made to creditors. One system used for this purpose is the voucher system.

Voucher System. A **voucher system** is a set of procedures for authorizing and recording liabilities and cash payments. A **voucher** is any document that serves as proof of authority to pay cash or issue an electronic funds transfer. For example, an invoice properly approved for payment could be considered a voucher. In many businesses, however, a voucher is a special form for recording relevant data about a liability and the details of its payment.

A voucher is normally prepared after all necessary supporting documents have been received. For example, when a voucher is prepared for the purchase of goods, the voucher should be supported by the supplier's invoice, a purchase order, and a receiving report. After a voucher is prepared, it is submitted to the proper manager for approval. Once approved, the voucher is recorded in the accounts and filed by due date. Upon payment, the voucher is recorded in the same manner as the payment of an account payable.

A voucher system may be either manual or computerized. In a computerized system, properly approved supporting documents (such as purchase orders and receiving reports) would be entered directly into computer files. At the due date, the checks would be automatically generated and mailed to creditors. At that time, the voucher would be automatically transferred to a paid voucher file.

Cash Paid by EFT. Cash can also be paid by electronic funds transfer systems by using computers rather than paper money or checks. For example, a company may pay its employees by means of EFT. Under such a system, employees may authorize the deposit of their payroll checks directly into checking accounts. Each pay period, the business electronically transfers the employees' net pay to their checking accounts through the use of computer systems and networks. Likewise, many companies are using EFT systems to pay their suppliers and other vendors.

Electronic funds payments are also becoming more widely accepted by individuals. For example, **TeleCheck Services, Inc.**, and **PayPal** offer online real-time check payment options for purchases made over the Internet. "It is apparent from the rapid growth of online sales that many consumers are as comfortable writing checks for Internet purchases as they are at their local brick-and-mortar store," explains the chief executive officer of TeleCheck.

Describe the nature of a bank account and its use in controlling cash.

BANK ACCOUNTS

Most of you are familiar with bank accounts. You probably have a checking account at a local bank, credit union, savings and loan association, or other financial institution. In this section, we discuss the use of bank accounts by businesses. We then discuss the use of bank accounts as an additional control over cash.

Use of Bank Accounts

A business often maintains several bank accounts. For example, a business with several branches or retail outlets such as Sears or The Gap Inc. will often maintain a bank account for each location. In addition, businesses usually maintain a separate bank account for payroll and other special purposes.

A major reason that businesses use bank accounts is for control purposes. Use of bank accounts reduces the amount of cash on hand at any one time. For example, many merchandise businesses deposit cash receipts twice daily to reduce the amount of cash on hand that is susceptible to theft. Likewise, using a payroll account allows for paying employees by check or electronic funds transfer rather than by distributing a large amount of cash each payroll period.

In addition to reducing the amount of cash on hand, bank accounts provide an independent recording of cash transactions that can be used as a verification of the business's recording of transactions. That is, the use of bank accounts provides a double recording of cash transactions. The company's cash account corresponds to the bank's liability (deposit) account for the company. As we will discuss and illustrate in the next section, this double recording of cash transactions allows for a reconciliation of the cash account on the company's records with the cash balance recorded by the bank.

Finally, the use of bank accounts facilitates the transfer of funds. For example, electronic funds transfer systems require bank accounts for the transfer of funds between companies. Within a company, cash can be transferred between bank accounts through the use of wire transfers. In addition, online banking allows companies to transfer funds and pay bills electronically as well as monitor their cash balances on a real-time basis.

Bank Statement

Banks usually maintain a record of all checking account transactions. A summary of all transactions, called a **bank statement**, is mailed to the depositor or made available online, usually each month. Like any account with a customer or a creditor, the bank statement shows the beginning balance, additions, deductions, and the balance at the end of the period. A typical bank statement is shown in Exhibit 5.

The depositor's checks or copies of the checks received by the bank during the period may accompany the bank statement, arranged in order of payment. If paid checks are returned, they are stamped "Paid," together with the date of payment. Many banks no longer return checks or check copies with bank statements. Instead, the check payment information is available online. Other entries that the bank has made in the depositor's account are described as debit or credit memorandums on the statement.

The depositor's checking account balance *in the bank records* is a liability; thus, in the bank's records, the depositor's account has a credit balance. Since the bank statement is prepared from the bank's point of view, a credit memorandum entry on the bank statement indicates an increase (a credit) in the depositor's account. Likewise, a

Exhibit 5
Bank Statement

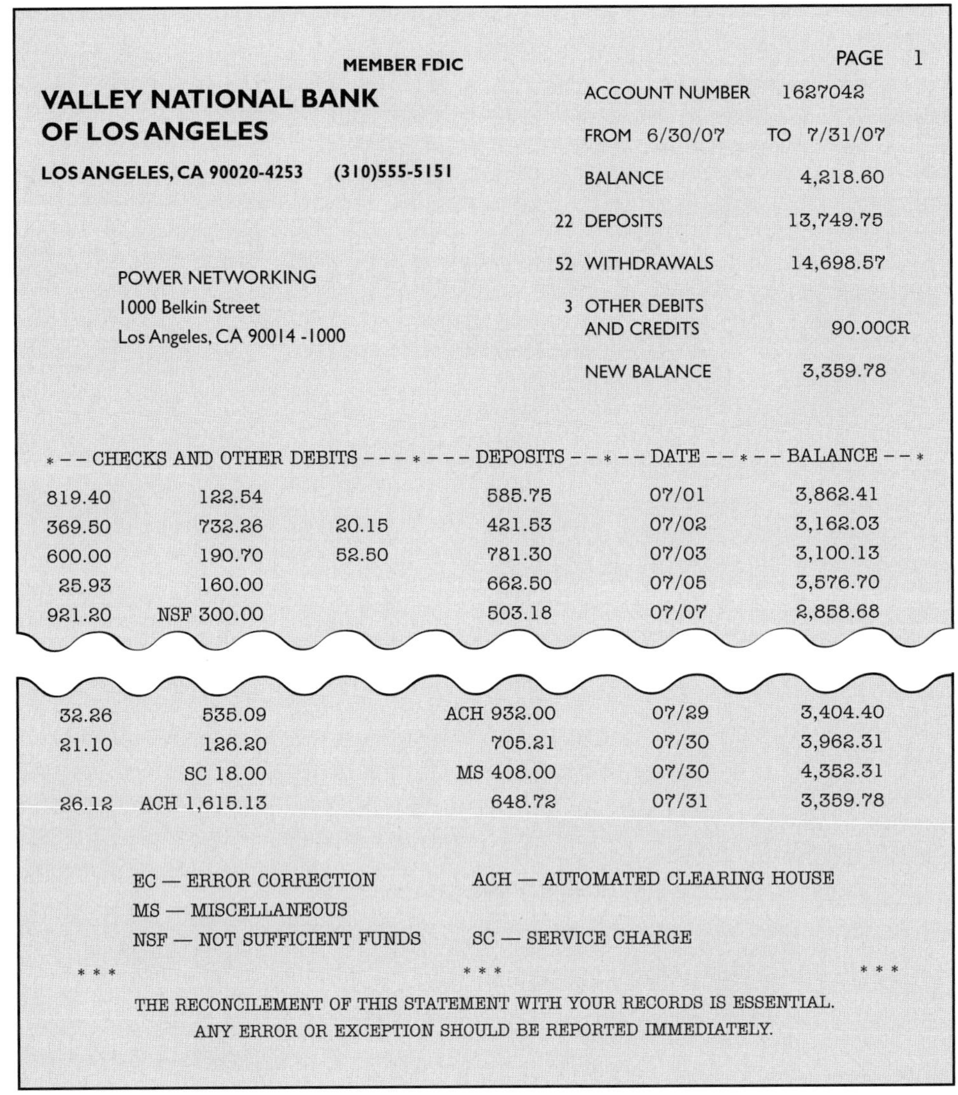

MEMBER FDIC

VALLEY NATIONAL BANK OF LOS ANGELES

LOS ANGELES, CA 90020-4253 (310)555-5151

PAGE 1

	ACCOUNT NUMBER	1627042
	FROM 6/30/07	TO 7/31/07
	BALANCE	4,218.60
22	DEPOSITS	13,749.75
52	WITHDRAWALS	14,698.57
3	OTHER DEBITS AND CREDITS	90.00CR
	NEW BALANCE	3,359.78

POWER NETWORKING
1000 Belkin Street
Los Angeles, CA 90014 -1000

CHECKS AND OTHER DEBITS			DEPOSITS	DATE	BALANCE
819.40	122.54		585.75	07/01	3,862.41
369.50	732.26	20.15	421.53	07/02	3,162.03
600.00	190.70	52.50	781.30	07/03	3,100.13
25.93	160.00		662.50	07/05	3,576.70
921.20	NSF 300.00		503.18	07/07	2,858.68
32.26	535.09		ACH 932.00	07/29	3,404.40
21.10	126.20		705.21	07/30	3,962.31
	SC 18.00		MS 408.00	07/30	4,352.31
26.12	ACH 1,615.13		648.72	07/31	3,359.78

EC — ERROR CORRECTION
ACH — AUTOMATED CLEARING HOUSE
MS — MISCELLANEOUS
NSF — NOT SUFFICIENT FUNDS
SC — SERVICE CHARGE

* * * * * * * * *

THE RECONCILEMENT OF THIS STATEMENT WITH YOUR RECORDS IS ESSENTIAL. ANY ERROR OR EXCEPTION SHOULD BE REPORTED IMMEDIATELY.

debit memorandum entry on the bank statement indicates a decrease (a debit) in the depositor's account. This relationship is shown below.

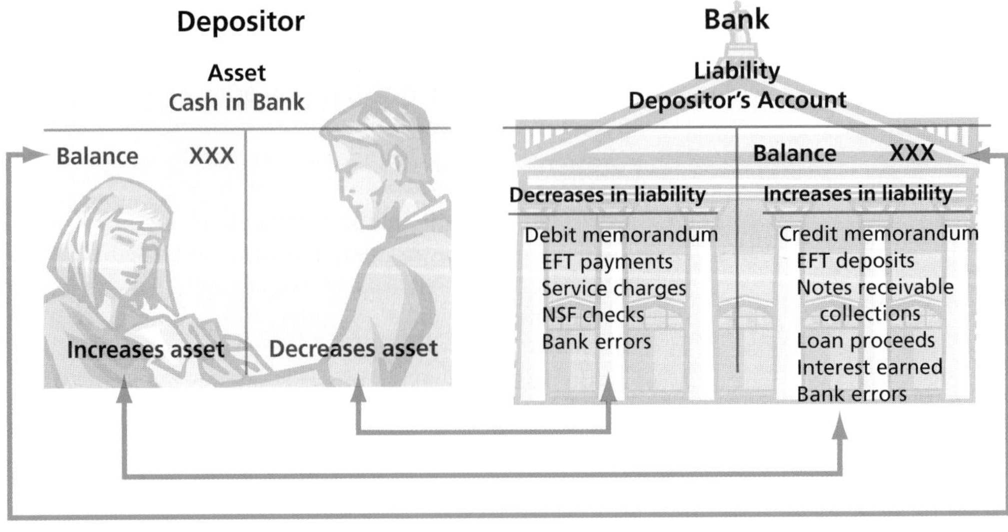

A bank makes credit entries (issues credit memoranda) for deposits made by electronic funds transfer, for collections of note receivable for the depositor, for proceeds for a loan to the depositor, for interest earned on the depositor's account, and to correct bank errors. A bank makes debit entries (issues debit memoranda) for payments made by electronic funds transfer, for service charges, for customers' checks returned for not sufficient funds, and to correct bank errors.

Customers' checks returned for not sufficient funds, called *NSF checks*, are checks that were initially deposited, but were not paid when they were presented to the customer's bank for payment. Since the bank initially credited the check to the depositor's account when it was deposited, the bank debits (issues a debit memorandum) when the check is returned without payment. We discuss the accounting for NSF checks later in this chapter.

The reason for a credit or debit memorandum entry is indicated on the bank statement. For example, Exhibit 5 identifies the following types of credit and debit memorandum entries:

EC — Error correction to correct bank error.
NSF — Not sufficient funds check.
SC — Service charge.
ACH — Automated Clearing House entry for electronic funds transfer.
MS — Miscellaneous item such as collection of a note receivable on behalf of the depositor or receipt of loan proceeds by the depositor from the bank.

Q. On the bank's records, are customer service charges recorded as a debit or a credit to the depositor's account?

A. *Debit.*

In the preceding list, we have included the notation "ACH" for electronic funds transfers. ACH is a network for clearing of electronic funds transfers among individuals, companies, and banks.[7] Because electronic funds transfers may be either deposits or payments, ACH entries may indicate either a debit or credit entry to the depositor's account. Likewise, entries to correct bank errors and miscellaneous items may indicate a debit or credit entry to the depositor's account.

Bank Accounts as a Control Over Cash

As we mentioned earlier, a bank account is one of the primary tools a company uses to control cash. For example, companies often require that all cash receipts be initially deposited in a bank account. Likewise, companies usually use checks or bank account transfers to make all cash payments, except for very small amounts. When such a system is used, there is a double record of cash transactions—one by the company and the other by the bank.

A company can use a bank statement to compare the cash transactions recorded in its accounting records to those recorded by the bank. The cash balance shown by a bank statement is usually different from the cash balance shown in the accounting records of the company, as shown in Exhibit 6.

This difference may be the result of a delay by either party in recording transactions. For example, there is a time lag of one day or more between the date a check is written and the date that it is presented to the bank for payment. If the company mails deposits to the bank or uses the night depository, a time lag between the date of the deposit and the date that it is recorded by the bank is also probable. The bank may also debit or credit the company's account for transactions about which the company will not be informed until later.

The difference may be the result of errors made by either the company or the bank in recording transactions. For example, the company may incorrectly post to Cash a check written for $4,500 as $450. Likewise, a bank may incorrectly record the amount of a check.

7 For further information on ACH, see http://www.nacha.org/About/what_is_ach_.htm.

Exhibit 6

Power Networking's Records and Bank Statement

Bank Statement

Beginning Balance		$ 4,218.60
Additions:		
Deposits	$13,749.75	
Miscellaneous	408.00	14,157.75
Deductions:		
Checks	$14,698.57	
NSF Check	300	
Service Charge	18	15,016.57
Ending Balance		$ 3,359.78

Power Networking Records

Beginning Balance	$ 4,227.60
Deposits	14,565.95
Checks	16,243.56
Ending Balance	$ 2,549.99

Power Networking should determine the reason for the difference in these two amounts.

INTEGRITY, OBJECTIVITY, AND ETHICS IN BUSINESS

Check Fraud

Check fraud involves counterfeiting, altering, or otherwise manipulating the information on checks in order to fraudulently cash a check. According to the **National Check Fraud Center**, check fraud and counterfeiting are among the fastest growing problems affecting the financial system, generating over $10 billion in losses annually. Criminals perpetrate the fraud by taking blank checks from your checkbook, finding a canceled check in the garbage, or removing a check you have mailed to pay bills. Consumers can prevent check fraud by carefully storing blank checks, placing outgoing mail in postal mailboxes, and shredding canceled checks.

Describe and illustrate the use of a bank reconciliation in controlling cash.

BANK RECONCILIATION

For effective control, the reasons for the difference between the cash balance on the bank statement and the cash balance in the accounting records should be analyzed by preparing a bank reconciliation. A **bank reconciliation** is an analysis of the items and amounts that cause the cash balance reported in the bank statement to differ from the balance of the cash account in the ledger in order to determine the adjusted cash balance.

A bank reconciliation is usually divided into two sections. The first section, referred to as the bank section, begins with the cash balance according to the bank statement and ends with the adjusted balance. The second section, referred to as the company section, begins with the cash balance according to the company's records and ends with the adjusted balance. The two amounts designated as the adjusted balance must be equal. The content of the bank reconciliation is shown on the next page.

The following steps are useful in finding the reconciling items and determining the adjusted balance of Cash:

1. Compare each deposit listed on the bank statement with unrecorded deposits appearing in the preceding period's reconciliation and with the current period's

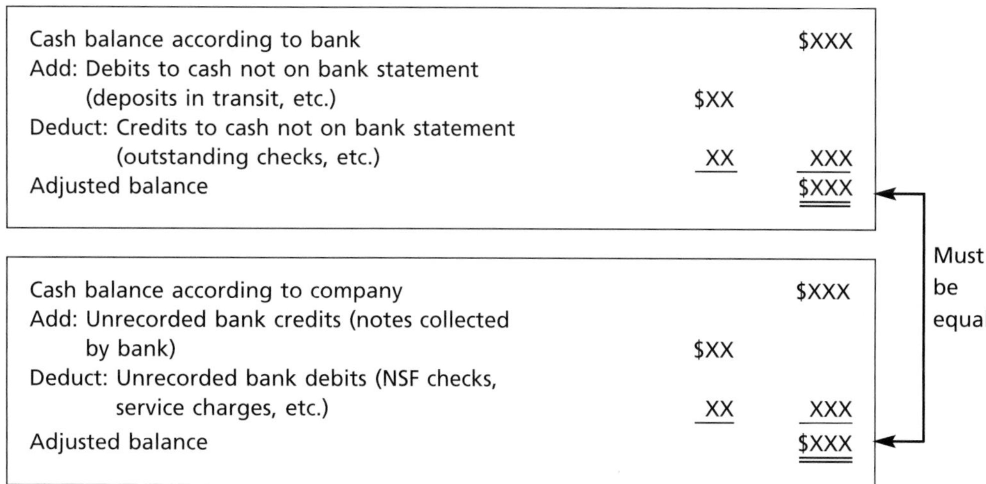

Cash balance according to bank		$XXX
Add: Debits to cash not on bank statement (deposits in transit, etc.)	$XX	
Deduct: Credits to cash not on bank statement (outstanding checks, etc.)	XX	XXX
Adjusted balance		$XXX

Cash balance according to company		$XXX
Add: Unrecorded bank credits (notes collected by bank)	$XX	
Deduct: Unrecorded bank debits (NSF checks, service charges, etc.)	XX	XXX
Adjusted balance		$XXX

deposits. *Add deposits not recorded by the bank to the balance according to the bank statement.*

2. Compare paid checks with outstanding checks appearing on the preceding period's reconciliation and with recorded checks. *Deduct checks outstanding that have not been paid by the bank from the balance according to the bank statement.*
3. Compare bank credit memorandums to entries in the journal. For example, a bank would issue a credit memorandum for a note receivable and interest that it collected for a company. *Add credit memorandums that have not been recorded to the balance according to the company's records.*
4. Compare bank debit memorandums to entries recording cash payments. For example, a bank normally issues debit memorandums for service charges and check printing charges. A bank also issues debit memorandums for not sufficient funds checks. NSF checks are normally charged back to the customer as an account receivable. *Deduct debit memorandums that have not been recorded from the balance according to the company's records.*
5. List any errors discovered during the preceding steps. For example, if an amount has been recorded incorrectly by the company, the amount of the error should be added to or deducted from the cash balance according to the company's records. Similarly, errors by the bank should be added to or deducted from the cash balance according to the bank statement.

Q. Is an NSF check added to or deducted from the bank balace according to the company's records?

A. *Deducted*

To illustrate a bank reconciliation, we will use the bank statement for Power Networking in Exhibit 5. This bank statement shows a balance of $3,359.78 as of July 31. The cash balance in Power Networking's ledger as of the same date is $2,549.99. The following reconciling items are revealed by using the steps outlined above:

Deposit of July 31, not recorded on bank statement	$ 816.20
Checks outstanding: No. 812, $1,061.00; No. 878, $435.39; No. 883, $48.60	1,544.99
Note plus interest of $8 collected by bank (credit memorandum), not recorded in the journal	408.00
Check from customer (Thomas Ivey) returned by bank because of insufficient funds (NSF)	300.00
Bank service charges (debit memorandum), not recorded in the journal	18.00
Check No. 879 for $732.26 to Taylor Co. on account, recorded in the journal as $723.26	9.00

The bank reconciliation, based on the bank statement and the reconciling items, is shown in Exhibit 7.

Exhibit 7

Bank Reconciliation for Power Networking

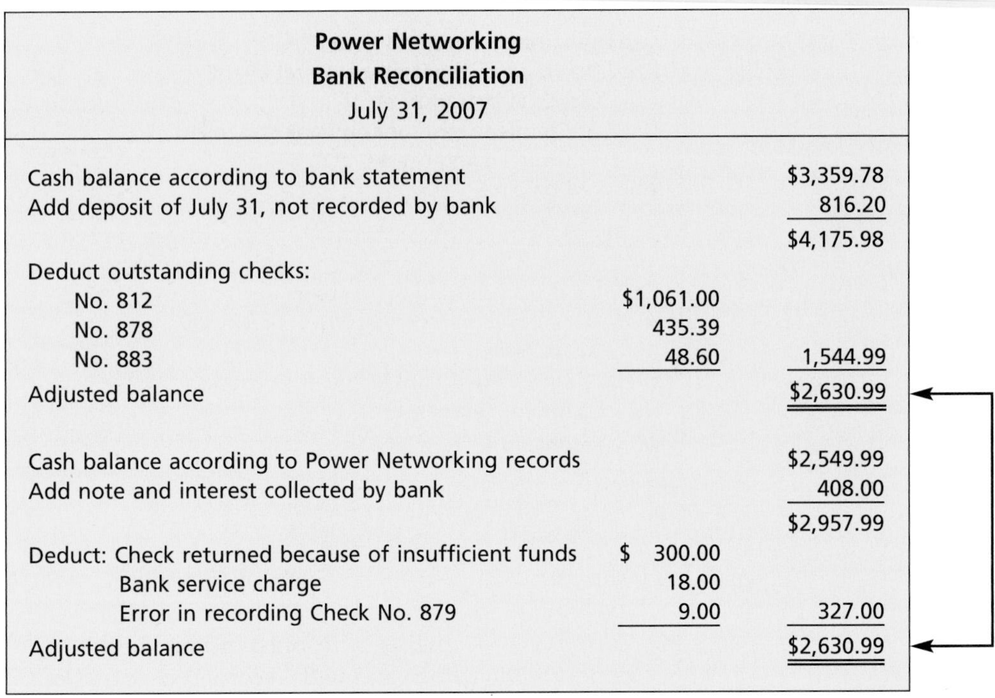

Power Networking
Bank Reconciliation
July 31, 2007

Cash balance according to bank statement		$3,359.78
Add deposit of July 31, not recorded by bank		816.20
		$4,175.98
Deduct outstanding checks:		
No. 812	$1,061.00	
No. 878	435.39	
No. 883	48.60	1,544.99
Adjusted balance		$2,630.99
Cash balance according to Power Networking records		$2,549.99
Add note and interest collected by bank		408.00
		$2,957.99
Deduct: Check returned because of insufficient funds	$ 300.00	
Bank service charge	18.00	
Error in recording Check No. 879	9.00	327.00
Adjusted balance		$2,630.99

No entries are necessary on the company's records as a result of the information included in the bank section of the reconciliation. This section begins with the cash balance according to the bank statement. However, the bank should be notified of any errors that need to be corrected on its records.

Any items in the company's section of the bank reconciliation must be recorded in the company's accounts. For example, journal entries should be made for any unrecorded bank memorandums and any company errors. The journal entries for Power Networking, based on the preceding bank reconciliation, are as follows:

SCF	BS	IS
O↑	A↑↓SE↑	R↑
O↓	A↑↓L↓SE↓	E↑

July 31	Cash	408	
	Notes Receivable		400
	Interest Income		8
31	Accounts Receivable—Thomas Ivey	300	
	Miscellaneous Expense	18	
	Accounts Payable—Taylor Co.	9	
	Cash		327

After the entries above have been posted, the cash account will have a debit balance of $2,630.99. This balance agrees with the adjusted cash balance shown on the bank reconciliation. This is the amount of cash available as of July 31 and the amount that would be reported on Power Networking's July 31 balance sheet.

Although businesses may reconcile their bank accounts in a slightly different format from what we described above, the objective is the same: to control cash by reconciling the company's records to the records of an independent outside source, the bank. In doing so, any errors or misuse of cash may be detected.

INTEGRITY, OBJECTIVITY, AND ETHICS IN BUSINESS

Bank Error in Your Favor

You may sometime have a bank error in your favor, such as a misposted deposit. Such errors are not a case of "found money," as in the Monopoly® game. Bank control systems quickly discover most errors and make automatic adjustments. Even so, you have a legal responsibility to report the error and return the money to the bank.

For effective control, the bank reconciliation should be prepared by an employee who does not take part in or record cash transactions. When these duties are not properly separated, mistakes are likely to occur, and it is more likely that cash will be stolen or otherwise misapplied. For example, an employee who takes part in all of these duties could prepare and cash an unauthorized check, omit it from the accounts, and omit it from the reconciliation.

Describe the accounting for special-purpose cash funds.

SPECIAL-PURPOSE CASH FUNDS

It is usually not practical for a business to write checks to pay small amounts, such as postage. Yet, these small payments may occur often enough to add up to a significant total amount. Thus, it is desirable to control such payments. For this purpose, a special cash fund, called a **petty cash fund**, is used.

A petty cash fund is established by first estimating the amount of cash needed for payments from the fund during a period, such as a week or a month. After necessary approvals, a check is written and cashed for this amount. The money obtained from cashing the check is then given to an employee, called the petty cash custodian, who is authorized to disburse monies from the fund. For control purposes, the company may place restrictions on the maximum amount and the types of payments that can be made from the fund. Each time monies are paid from petty cash, the custodian records the details of the payment on a petty cash receipt form.

The petty cash fund is normally replenished at periodic intervals or when it is depleted or reaches a minimum amount. When a petty cash fund is replenished, the accounts debited are determined by summarizing the petty cash receipts. A check is then written for this amount, payable to petty cash.

To illustrate normal petty cash fund entries, assume that a petty cash fund of $500 is established on August 1. The entry to record this transaction is as follows:

SCF	BS	IS
—	A↑↓	—

Aug. 1	Petty Cash	500	
	Cash		500

At the end of August, the petty cash receipts indicate expenditures for the following items: office supplies, $380; postage (office supplies), $22; store supplies, $35; and miscellaneous administrative expense, $30. The entry to replenish the petty cash fund on August 31 is as follows:

SCF	BS	IS
O↓	A↑↓SE↓	E↑

Aug. 31	Office Supplies	402	
	Store Supplies	35	
	Miscellaneous Administrative Expense	30	
	Cash		467

Q. If the petty cash account has a balance of $200, the cash in the fund totals $20, and the petty cash receipts total $180 at the end of a period, what account is credited and what is the amount of the credit in the entry to replenish the fund?

A. *Cash is credited for $180.*

Replenishing the petty cash fund restores it to its original amount of $500. You should note that there is no entry in Petty Cash when the fund is replenished. Petty Cash is debited only when the fund is initially set up or when the amount of the fund is increased at a later time. Petty Cash is credited if it is being decreased.

In addition, businesses often use other cash funds to meet special needs, such as travel expenses for salespersons. For example, each salesperson might be given $200 for travel-related expenses. Periodically, the salesperson submits a detailed expense report and the travel funds are replenished. Also, as we discussed earlier in this chapter, retail businesses use change funds for making change for customers. Finally, most businesses use a payroll bank account to pay employees. Such cash funds are called **special-purpose funds.**

A special-purpose cash fund is initially established by first estimating the amount of cash needed for payments from the fund during a period, such as a week or a month. After necessary approvals, a check is written and cashed for this amount. The money obtained from cashing the check is then given to an employee, called the custodian, who is authorized to disburse monies from the fund. For control purposes, the company may place restrictions on the maximum amount and the types of payments that can be made from the fund.

Describe and illustrate the reporting of cash and cash equivalents in the financial statements.

FINANCIAL STATEMENT REPORTING OF CASH

Cash is the most liquid asset, and therefore it is listed as the first asset in the Current Assets section of the balance sheet. Most companies present only a single cash amount on the balance sheet by combining all their bank and cash fund accounts.

A company may have cash in excess of its operating needs. In such cases, the company normally invests in highly liquid investments in order to earn interest. These investments are called **cash equivalents.**[8] Examples of cash equivalents include U.S. Treasury Bills, notes issued by major corporations (referred to as commercial paper), and money market funds. Companies that have invested excess cash in cash equivalents usually report *Cash and cash equivalents* as one amount on the balance sheet.

International Perspective
In the United Kingdom, the statement of cash flows is prepared using a narrower definition of "cash" than in the United States. Specifically, the United Kingdom does not include cash equivalents, such as certificates of deposit, in its definition of cash as does the United States.

To illustrate, Microsoft Corp. disclosed the details of its cash and cash equivalents in the notes to its financial statements as follows:

(in millions)	June 30, 2004	June 30, 2005
Cash and cash equivalents:		
Cash	$ 1,812	$1,911
Money market mutual funds	3,595	817
Commercial paper	4,109	1,570
Certificates of deposit	330	453
U.S. government and agency securities	4,083	—
Corporate notes and bonds	98	80
Municipal securities	277	20
	$14,304	$4,851

8 To be classified a cash equivalent, according to FASB Statement 95, the investment is expected to be converted to cash within 90 days.

Banks may require companies to maintain minimum cash balances in their bank accounts. Such a balance is called a *compensating balance*. This requirement is often imposed by the bank as a part of a loan agreement or line of credit. A *line of credit* is a preapproved amount the bank is willing to lend to a customer upon request. If significant, compensating balance requirements should be disclosed in notes to the financial statements.

CASH RATIOS

Describe, illustrate, and interpret the cash flow to net income ratio and the cash to monthly cash expenses ratio.

Analyzing cash and cash flows is essential to interpreting financial statements. The statement of cash flows reports cash flows from operating, investing, and financing activities. In addition, two cash ratios useful for analyzing and interpreting operating performance are (1) cash flow to net income and (2) cash to monthly cash expenses.

Ratio of Cash Flow to Net Income

The accrual basis of accounting is used by all public companies in determining and reporting net income. As we illustrate throughout this text, accrual accounting records revenues when earned and expenses when incurred and not necessarily when cash is received or paid. This process gives rise to accruals and deferrals that are updated and adjusted at the end of each reporting period. As a result, net cash flows from operations is rarely the same as net income.

When the amount of accruals and deferrals is large, the difference between net cash flows from operations and net income will also be large. The effect of accruals and deferrals on net income can be measured by the ratio of net cash flows from operations to net income. Accordingly, significant changes in this ratio from year to year should be investigated for the underlying causes. For example, implementing a new accounting standard may significantly affect net income and comparability between years. Likewise, management could change methods of estimating and recording accruals, deferrals, and depreciation. Such changes also affect the current period's net income comparability with prior years.

The ratio of cash flow to net income is computed as follows:

$$\text{Ratio of Cash Flow to Net Income} = \frac{\text{Net Cash Flows from Operations}}{\text{Net Income}}$$

To illustrate, the ratio of cash flow to net income for The Walt Disney Company for 2004 and 2003, respectively, is shown below. Amounts are in millions.

	2004	2003
Net cash flows from operations	$4,370	$2,901
Net income	$2,345	$1,267
Cash flow ratio	1.86	2.29

The cash flow ratio declined from 2.29 in 2003 to 1.86 in 2004. Cash flows from operations increased at a smaller relative amount than did the net income. Why did this happen? A review of the statement of cash flows for Disney reveals that during 2004 Disney used cash to support operations. Such changes in the ratio are usually of little concern. However, large ratios, or large changes in the ratio between years, may warrant further analysis of the underlying accruals and deferrals, giving rise to the size or change in the ratio.

Ratio of Cash to Monthly Cash Expenses

As we illustrated for The Walt Disney Company, the cash flow ratio is useful for identifying when significant changes may have occurred in accrual accounting methods. Another cash ratio that is especially useful for startup companies is the ratio of cash to monthly cash expenses.

For companies that are either starting up or in financial distress, cash is critical for their survival. In their first few years of operations, startup companies often report losses and negative net cash flows. In these cases, the ratio of cash to monthly cash expenses (negative cash flow for operating activities) is useful for assessing how long a company can continue to operate without additional financing or without generating positive cash flows from operations. Likewise, this ratio can be used to assess how long a business may continue to operate when experiencing financial distress. In computing cash to monthly cash expenses, the amount of cash on hand can be taken from the balance sheet, while the monthly cash expenses can be estimated from the operating activities section of the statement of cash flows.

The ratio of cash to monthly cash expenses is computed by first determining the monthly cash expenses. The monthly cash expenses are determined as follows:

$$\text{Monthly Cash Expenses} = \frac{\text{Negative Cash Flows from Operations}}{12}$$

The ratio of cash to monthly cash expenses can then be computed as follows:

$$\text{Ratio of Cash to Monthly Cash Expenses} = \frac{\text{Cash and Cash Equivalent as of Year-End}}{\text{Monthly Cash Expenses}}$$

To illustrate these ratios, we use Gateway Inc., a manufacturer of personal computer products. For the year ending December 31, 2004, Gateway reported the following data (in millions):

Negative cash flows from operations	$(434.2)
Cash and cash equivalent as of December 31, 2004	383.0

Based upon the preceding data, the monthly cash expenses, sometimes referred to as cash burn, were $36.2 per month ($434.2 ÷ 12). Thus, as of December 31, 2004, the cash to monthly cash expenses ratio was 10.6 ($383.0 ÷ $36.2). That is, as of December 31, 2004, Gateway would run out of cash in less than 11 months unless it changes its operations, sells investments, or raises additional financing.

FOCUS ON CASH FLOW

Reconciling Net Income and Cash Flows from Operating Activities

In preparing the statement of cash flows, generally accepted accounting principles require a company to reconcile net income with cash flows from operating activities. This reconciliation for **The Walt Disney Company** is shown below for the year ended September 30, 2004.

	Year Ended September 30, 2004 (in thousands)
Net income	$2,345,000
Operating activities, cash flows provided by or used in:	
Depreciation	1,210,000
Adjustments to net income	866,000
Changes in accounts receivable	(115,000)
Changes in liabilities	237,000
Changes in inventories	(84,000)
Changes in other operating activities	(89,000)
Total cash flow from operating activities	$4,370,000

The preceding reconciliation begins by adding back depreciation of $1,210,000. This is because depreciation is deducted as an expense in arriving at net income, but it does not impact cash. That is, no cash related to yearly depreciation is paid.

The other reconciling items involve increases or decreases in other financial statement accounts. The logic behind including these reconciling items involves the accounting equation. Specifically, the accounting equation must always balance.

$$\text{Assets} = \text{Liabilities} + \text{Stockholders' Equity}$$

Therefore, changes in the cash account can be determined by analyzing changes in the other accounts:

$$\text{Changes in Cash} = \begin{array}{l}\text{Changes in Liabilities} + \\ \text{Changes in Stockholders' Equity} - \\ \text{Changes in Noncash Assets}\end{array}$$

As shown in the illustration for The Walt Disney Company, some changes in the noncash accounts affect the reporting of cash flows from operating activities. Changes in noncash accounts also affect the reporting of cash flows from financing and investing activities.

SUMMARY OF LEARNING GOALS

(1) **Describe the Sarbanes-Oxley Act of 2002 and its impact on internal controls and financial reporting.** The purpose of the Sarbanes-Oxley Act of 2002 is to restore public confidence and trust in the financial statements of companies. Sarbanes-Oxley requires companies to maintain strong and effective internal controls over the recording of transactions and the preparing of financial statements. Sarbanes-Oxley also requires companies and their independent accountants to report on the effectiveness of a company's internal controls.

(2) **Describe and illustrate the objectives and elements of internal control.** The objectives of internal control are to provide reasonable assurance that (1) assets are safeguarded and used for business purposes, (2) business information is accurate, and (3) laws and regulations are complied with. The elements of internal control are the control environment, risk assessment, control procedures, monitoring, and information and communication.

(3) **Describe and illustrate the application of internal controls to cash.** One of the most important controls to protect cash received in over-the-counter sales is a cash register. A remittance advice is a control for cash received through the mail. Separating the duties of handling cash and recording cash is also a control. A voucher system is a control system for cash payments that uses a set of procedures for authorizing and recording liabilities and cash payments. Many companies use electronic funds transfers to enhance their control over cash receipts and cash payments.

(4) **Describe the nature of a bank account and its use in controlling cash.** Businesses use bank accounts as a means of controlling cash. Bank accounts reduce the amount of cash on hand and facilitate the transfer of cash between businesses and locations. In addition, banks send monthly statements to their customers, summarizing all of the transactions for the month. The bank statement allows a business to reconcile the cash transactions recorded in the accounting records to those recorded by the bank.

(5) **Describe and illustrate the use of a bank reconciliation in controlling cash.** The first section of the bank reconciliation begins with the cash balance according to the bank statement. This balance is adjusted for the company's changes in cash that do not appear on the bank statement and for any bank errors. The second section begins with the cash balance according to the company's records. This

balance is adjusted for the bank's changes in cash that do not appear on the company's records and for any company's errors. The adjusted balances for the two sections must be equal. No entries are necessary on the company's records as a result of the information included in the bank section of the bank reconciliation. However, the items in the company section must be journalized on the company's records.

6 **Describe the accounting for special-purpose cash funds.** Businesses often use special-purpose cash funds, such as a petty cash fund or travel funds, to meet specific needs. Each fund is initially established by cashing a check for the amount of cash needed. The cash is then given to a custodian who is authorized to disburse monies from the fund. At periodic intervals or when it is depleted or reaches a minimum amount, the fund is replenished and the disbursements recorded.

7 **Describe and illustrate the reporting of cash and cash equivalents in the financial statements.** Cash is listed as the first asset in the Current Assets section of the balance sheet. Companies that have invested excess cash in highly liquid investments usually report *Cash and cash equivalents* on the balance sheet.

8 **Describe, illustrate, and interpret the cash flow to net income ratio and the cash to monthly cash expenses ratio.** Two cash ratios useful for analyzing and interpreting operating performance are (1) cash flow to net income and (2) cash to monthly cash expenses. The effect of accruals and deferrals on net income can be measured by the ratio of net cash flows from operations to net income. The ratio of cash to monthly cash expenses is useful for assessing how long a company can continue to operate without additional financing or without generating positive cash flows from operations.

GLOSSARY

Bank reconciliation The analysis of the items responsible for the difference between the cash balance reported in the bank statement and the balance of the cash account in the company's ledger in order to determine the adjusted cash balance.

Bank statement A summary of all transactions is mailed to the depositor by the bank each month.

Cash Coins, currency (paper money), checks, money orders, and money on deposit that is available for unrestricted withdrawal from banks and other financial institutions.

Cash equivalents Highly liquid investments that are usually reported with cash on the balance sheet.

Cash short and over account An account used to record the difference between the amount of cash in a cash register and the amount of cash that should be on hand according to the records.

Electronic funds transfer (EFT) A system in which computers rather than paper (money, checks, etc.) are used to effect cash transactions.

Elements of internal control The control environment, risk assessment, control activities, information and communication, and monitoring.

Employee fraud The intentional act of deceiving an employer for personal gain.

Internal controls The procedures and processes used by a company to safeguard its assets, process information accurately, and ensure compliance with laws and regulations.

Petty cash fund A special-purpose cash fund to pay relatively small amounts.

Sarbanes-Oxley Act of 2002 An act passed by Congress to restore public confidence and trust in the financial statements of companies.

Special-purpose fund A cash fund used for a special business need.

Voucher Any document that serves as proof of authority to pay cash.

Voucher system A set of procedures for authorizing and recording liabilities and cash payments.

ILLUSTRATIVE ACCOUNTING APPLICATION PROBLEM

The bank statement for Urethane Company for June 30, 2007, indicates a balance of $9,143.11. All cash receipts are deposited each evening in a night depository, after banking hours. The accounting records indicate the following summary data for cash receipts and payments for June:

Cash balance as of June 1	$ 3,943.50
Total cash receipts for June	28,971.60
Total amount of checks issued in June	28,388.85

Comparing the bank statement and the accompanying canceled checks and memorandums with the records reveals the following reconciling items:

a. The bank had collected for Urethane Company $1,030 on a note left for collection. The face of the note was $1,000.
b. A deposit of $1,852.21, representing receipts of June 30, had been made too late to appear on the bank statement.
c. Checks outstanding totaled $5,265.27.
d. A check drawn for $139 had been incorrectly charged by the bank as $157.
e. A check for $30 returned with the statement had been recorded in the company's records as $240. The check was for the payment of an obligation to Avery Equipment Company for the purchase of office supplies on account.
f. Bank service charges for June amounted to $18.20.

Instructions

1. Prepare a bank reconciliation for June.
2. Journalize the entries that should be made by Urethane Company.

Solution

1.

Urethane Company
Bank Reconciliation
June 30, 2007

Cash balance according to bank statement		$ 9,143.11
Add: Deposit of June 30 not recorded by bank	$1,852.21	
Bank error in charging check as $157 instead of $139	18.00	1,870.21
		$11,013.32
Deduct: Outstanding checks		5,265.27
Adjusted balance		$ 5,748.05
Cash balance according to company's records		$ 4,526.25*
Add: Proceeds of note collected by bank, including $30 interest	$1,030.00	
Error in recording check	210.00	1,240.00
		$ 5,766.25
Deduct: Bank service charges		18.20
Adjusted balance		$ 5,748.05

*$3,943.50 + $28,971.60 − $28,388.85

2.

Cash	1,240.00	
Notes Receivable		1,000.00
Interest Revenue		30.00
Accounts Payable–Avery Equipment Company		210.00
Miscellaneous Administrative Expense	18.20	
Cash		18.20

SELF-STUDY QUESTIONS

Answers at end of chapter

1. Which of the following is *not* an element of internal control?
   A. Control environment
   B. Monitoring
   C. Compliance with laws and regulations
   D. Control procedures
2. The policies and procedures used by management to protect assets from misuse, ensure accurate business information, and ensure compliance with laws and regulations are called:
   A. internal controls.
   B. systems analysis.
   C. systems design.
   D. systems implementation.
3. In preparing a bank reconciliation, the amount of checks outstanding would be:
   A. added to the cash balance according to the bank statement.
   B. deducted from the cash balance according to the bank statement.
   C. added to the cash balance according to the company's records.
   D. deducted from the cash balance according to the company's records.
4. Journal entries based on the bank reconciliation are required for:
   A. additions to the cash balance according to the company's records.
   B. deductions from the cash balance according to the company's records.
   C. both A and B.
   D. neither A nor B.
5. A petty cash fund is:
   A. used to pay relatively small amounts.
   B. established by estimating the amount of cash needed for disbursements of relatively small amounts during a specified period.
   C. reimbursed when the amount of money in the fund is reduced to a predetermined minimum amount.
   D. all of the above.

DISCUSSION QUESTIONS

1. (a) Why did Congress pass the Sarbanes-Oxley Act of 2002? (b) What was the purpose of the Sarbanes-Oxley Act of 2002?
2. Define *internal control.*
3. (a) Name and describe the five elements of internal control. (b) Is any one element of internal control more important than another?
4. How does a policy of rotating clerical employees from job to job aid in strengthening the control procedures within the control environment? Explain.
5. Why should the responsibility for a sequence of related operations be divided among different persons? Explain.
6. Why should the employee who handles cash receipts not have the responsibility for maintaining the accounts receivable records? Explain.
7. In an attempt to improve operating efficiency, one employee was made responsible for all purchasing, receiving, and storing of supplies. Is this organizational change wise from an internal control standpoint? Explain.
8. The ticket seller at a movie theater doubles as a ticket taker for a few minutes each day while the ticket taker is on a break. Which control procedure of a business's system of internal control is violated in this situation?
9. Why should the responsibility for maintaining the accounting records be separated from the responsibility for operations? Explain.
10. Assume that Julee Shiver, accounts payable clerk for Galaxy Inc., stole $110,000 by paying fictitious invoices for goods that were never received. The clerk set up

accounts in the names of the fictitious companies and cashed the checks at a local bank. Describe a control procedure that would have prevented or detected the fraud.

11. Before a voucher for the purchase of merchandise is approved for payment, supporting documents should be compared to verify the accuracy of the liability. Give an example of a supporting document for the purchase of merchandise.
12. The accounting clerk pays all obligations by prenumbered checks. What are the strengths and weaknesses in the internal control over cash payments in this situation?
13. The balance of Cash is likely to differ from the bank statement balance. What two factors are likely to be responsible for the difference?
14. What is the purpose of preparing a bank reconciliation?
15. Do items reported as credits on the bank statement represent (a) additions made by the bank to the company's balance or (b) deductions made by the bank from the company's balance? Explain.
16. Spectacle Inc. has a petty cash fund of $2,000. (a) Since the petty cash fund is only $2,000, should Spectacle Inc. implement controls over petty cash? (b) What controls, if any, could be used for the petty cash fund?
17. (a) How are cash equivalents reported in the financial statements? (b) What are some examples of cash equivalents?

EXERCISES

Exercise 7-1

Sarbanes-Oxley internal control report

Goal 1

Using the http://www.google.com Advanced Search feature, enter "Sarbanes-Oxley" and click on Google Search. Click on "Summary of Sarbanes-Oxley Act of 2002" that appears as part of the aipca.org Web site. Scan the summary of the act and read Section 404. What does Section 404 require of management's internal control report?

Exercise 7-2

Internal controls

Goals 2, 3

Barbara Holmes has recently been hired as the manager of Fresh Start Coffee. Fresh Start Coffee is a national chain of franchised coffee shops. During her first month as store manager, Barbara encountered the following internal control situations:

a. Fresh Start Coffee has one cash register. Prior to Barbara's joining the coffee shop, each employee working on a shift would take a customer order, accept payment, and then prepare the order. Barbara made one employee on each shift responsible for taking orders and accepting the customer's payment. Other employees prepare the orders.
b. Since only one employee uses the cash register, that employee is responsible for counting the cash at the end of the shift and verifying that the cash in the drawer matches the amount of cash sales recorded by the cash register. Barbara expects each cashier to balance the drawer to the penny *every* time—no exceptions.
c. Barbara caught an employee putting a box of 100 single-serving tea bags in his car. Not wanting to create a scene, Barbara smiled and said. "I don't think you're putting those tea bags on the right shelf. Don't they belong inside the coffee shop?" The employee returned the tea bags to the stockroom.

State whether you agree or disagree with Barbara's method of handling each situation and explain your answer.

Exercise 7-3

Internal controls

Goals 2, 3

Elegance by Elaine is a retail store specializing in women's clothing. The store has established a liberal return policy for the holiday season in order to encourage gift purchases. Any item purchased during November and December may be returned through January 31, with a receipt, for cash or exchange. If the customer does not have a receipt, cash will still be refunded for any item under $50. If the item is more than $50, a check is mailed to the customer.

Whenever an item is returned, a store clerk completes a return slip, which the customer signs. The return slip is placed in a special box. The store manager visits the return counter approximately once every two hours to authorize the return slips. Clerks are instructed to place the returned merchandise on the proper rack on the selling floor as soon as possible.

This year, returns at Elegance by Elaine have reached an all-time high. There are a large number of returns under $50 without receipts.

a. How can sales clerks employed at Elegance by Elaine use the store's return policy to steal money from the cash register?
b. What internal control weaknesses do you see in the return policy that make cash thefts easier?
c. Would issuing a store credit in place of a cash refund for all merchandise returned without a receipt reduce the possibility of theft? List some advantages and disadvantages of issuing a store credit in place of cash refund.
d. Assume that Elegance by Elaine is committed to the current policy of issuing cash refunds without a receipt. What changes could be made in the store's procedures regarding customer refunds in order to improve internal control?

Exercise 7-4

Internal controls for bank lending

Goals **2, 3**

First Charter Bank provides loans to businesses in the community through its Commercial Lending Department. Small loans (less than $100,000) may be approved by an individual loan officer, while larger loans (greater than $100,000) must be approved by a board of loan officers. Once a loan is approved, the funds are made available to the loan applicant under agreed-upon terms. The president of First Charter Bank has instituted a policy whereby she has the individual authority to approve loans up to $5,000,000. The president believes that this policy will allow flexibility to approve loans to valued clients much quicker than under the previous policy.

As an internal auditor of First Charter Bank, how would you respond to this change in policy?

Exercise 7-5

Internal controls

Goals **2, 3**

One of the largest fraud losses in history involved a securities trader for the Singapore office of Barings Bank, a British merchant bank. The trader established an unauthorized account number that was used to hide $1.4 billion in losses. Even after Barings' internal auditors noted that the trader both executed trades and recorded them, management did not take action. As a result, a lone individual in a remote office bankrupted an internationally recognized firm overnight.

What general weaknesses in Barings' internal controls contributed to the occurrence and size of the fraud?

Exercise 7-6

Internal controls

Goals **2, 3**

An employee of JHT Holdings Inc., a trucking company, was responsible for resolving roadway accident claims under $25,000. The employee created fake accident claims and wrote settlement checks of between $5,000 and $25,000 to friends or acquaintances acting as phony "victims." One friend recruited subordinates at his place of work to cash some of the checks. Beyond this, the JHT employee also recruited lawyers, who he paid to represent both the trucking company and the fake victims in the bogus accident settlements. When the lawyers cashed the checks, they allegedly split the money with the corrupt JHT employee. This fraud went undetected for two years.

Why would it take so long to discover such a fraud?

Exercise 7-7

Internal controls

Goals **2, 3**

Event Sound Co. discovered a fraud whereby one of its front office administrative employees used company funds to purchase goods, such as computers, digital cameras, compact disk players, and other electronic items for her own use. The fraud was discovered when employees noticed an increase in delivery frequency from vendors and the use of unusual vendors. After some investigation, it was discovered that the employee would alter the description or change the quantity on an invoice in order to explain the cost on the bill.

What general internal control weaknesses contributed to this fraud?

Exercise 7-8

Financial statement fraud

Goals **2, 3**

A former chairman, CFO, and controller of Donnkenny, an apparel company that makes sportswear for Pierre Cardin and Victoria Jones, pleaded guilty to financial statement fraud. These managers used false journal entries to record fictitious sales, hid inventory in public warehouses so that it could be recorded as "sold," and required sales orders to be backdated so that the sale could be moved back to an earlier period. The combined effect of these actions caused \$25 million out of \$40 million in quarterly sales to be phony.

a. Why might control procedures listed in this chapter be insufficient in stopping this type of fraud?
b. How could this type of fraud be stopped?

Exercise 7-9

Internal control of cash receipts

Goals **2, 3**

The procedures used for over-the-counter receipts are as follows. At the close of each day's business, the sales clerks count the cash in their respective cash drawers, after which they determine the amount recorded by the cash register and prepare the memorandum cash form, noting any discrepancies. An employee from the cashier's office counts the cash, compares the total with the memorandum, and takes the cash to the cashier's office.

a. Indicate the weak link in internal control.
b. How can the weakness be corrected?

Exercise 7-10

Internal control of cash receipts

Goals **1, 2, 3**

Deana Crisman works at the drive-through window of Awesome Burgers. Occasionally, when a drive-through customer orders, Deana fills the order and pockets the customer's money. She does not ring up the order on the cash register.

Identify the internal control weaknesses that exist at Awesome Burgers, and discuss what can be done to prevent this theft.

Exercise 7-11

Internal control of cash receipts

Goals **2, 3**

The mailroom employees send all remittances and remittance advices to the cashier. The cashier deposits the cash in the bank and forwards the remittance advices and duplicate deposit slips to the Accounting Department.

a. Indicate the weak link in internal control in the handling of cash receipts.
b. How can the weakness be corrected?

Exercise 7-12

Entry for cash sales; cash short

Goals **2, 3**

The actual cash received from cash sales was \$17,572.40, and the amount indicated by the cash register total was \$17,589.65. Journalize the entry to record the cash receipts and cash sales.

Exercise 7-13

Entry for cash sales; cash over

Goals **2, 3**

The actual cash received from cash sales was \$6,973.60, and the amount indicated by the cash register total was \$6,932.15. Journalize the entry to record the cash receipts and cash sales.

Exercise 7-14

Internal control of cash payments

Goals **2, 3**

Migraine Co. is a medium-size merchandising company. An investigation revealed that in spite of a sufficient bank balance, a significant amount of available cash discounts had been lost because of failure to make timely payments. In addition, it was discovered that the invoices for several purchases had been paid twice.

Outline procedures for the payment of vendors' invoices, so that the possibilities of losing available cash discounts and of paying an invoice a second time will be minimized.

Exercise 7-15

Internal control of cash payments

Goals **2, 3**

Satchell Company, a communications equipment manufacturer, recently fell victim to an embezzlement scheme masterminded by one of its employees. To understand the scheme, it is necessary to review Satchell's procedures for the purchase of services.

The purchasing agent is responsible for ordering services (such as repairs to a photocopy machine or office cleaning) after receiving a service requisition from an authorized manager. However, since no tangible goods are delivered, a receiving report is not prepared. When the Accounting Department receives an invoice billing Satchell for a service call, the accounts payable clerk calls the manager who requested the service in order to verify that it was performed.

The embezzlement scheme involves Drew Brogan, the manager of plant and facilities. Drew arranged for his uncle's company, Brogan Industrial Supply and Service, to be placed on Satchell's approved vendor list. Drew did not disclose the family relationship.

On several occasions, Drew would submit a requisition for services to be provided by Brogan Industrial Supply and Service. However, the service requested was really not needed, and it was never performed. Brogan would bill Satchell for the service and then split the cash payment with Drew.

Explain what changes should be made to Satchell's procedures for ordering and paying for services in order to prevent such occurrences in the future.

Exercise 7-16

Bank reconciliation

Goals **4, 5**

Identify each of the following reconciling items as: (a) an addition to the cash balance according to the bank statement, (b) a deduction from the cash balance according to the bank statement, (c) an addition to the cash balance according to the company's records, or (d) a deduction from the cash balance according to the company's records. (None of the transactions reported by bank debit and credit memorandums have been recorded by the company.)

1. Check drawn by company for $300 but incorrectly recorded as $3,000.
2. Check of a customer returned by bank to company because of insufficient funds, $775.
3. Bank service charges, $35.
4. Check for $129 incorrectly charged by bank as $219.
5. Outstanding checks, $6,137.68.
6. Deposit in transit, $7,500.
7. Note collected by bank, $12,000.

Exercise 7-17

Entries based on bank reconciliation

Goals **4, 5**

Which of the reconciling items listed in Exercise 7-16 require an entry in the company's accounts?

Exercise 7-18

Bank reconciliation

Goals **4, 5**

Adjusted balance: $7,961.45

SPREADSHEET

The following data were accumulated for use in reconciling the bank account of Kidstock Co. for March:

a. Cash balance according to the company's records at March 31, $7,671.45.
b. Cash balance according to the bank statement at March 31, $4,457.25.
c. Checks outstanding, $2,276.20.
d. Deposit in transit, not recorded by bank, $5,780.40.
e. A check for $145 in payment of an account was erroneously recorded in the check register at $451.
f. Bank debit memorandum for service charges, $16.00.

Prepare a bank reconciliation, using the format shown in Exhibit 7.

Exercise 7-19

Entries for bank reconciliation

Goals **4, 5**

Using the data presented in Exercise 7-18, journalize the entry or entries that should be made by the company.

Exercise 7-20

Entries for note collected by bank

Goals **4, 5**

Accompanying a bank statement for Covershot Company is a credit memorandum for $15,300, representing the principal ($15,000) and interest ($300) on a note that had been collected by the bank. The company had been notified by the bank at the time of the collection but had made no entries. Journalize the entry that should be made by the company to bring the accounting records up to date.

Exercise 7-21

Bank reconciliation

Goals **4, 5**

Adjusted balance: $14,452.75

SPREADSHEET

An accounting clerk for Dubitzky Co. prepared the following bank reconciliation:

Dubitzky Co.
Bank Reconciliation
July 31, 2008

Cash balance according to company's records		$ 8,100.75
Add: Outstanding checks	$6,557.12	
Error by Dubitzky Co. in recording Check No. 4217 as $6,315 instead of $3,615	2,700.00	
Note for $3,600 collected by bank, including interest	3,672.00	12,929.12
		$21,029.87
Deduct: Deposit in transit on July 31	$7,150.00	
Bank service charges	20.00	7,170.00
Cash balance according to bank statement		$13,859.87

a. From the data in the above bank reconciliation, prepare a new bank reconciliation for Dubitzky Co., using the format shown in the illustrative problem.

b. If a balance sheet were prepared for Dubitzky Co. on July 31, 2008, what amount should be reported for cash?

Exercise 7-22

Bank reconciliation

Goals **4, 5**

Corrected adjusted balance: $8,898.02

Identify the errors in the following bank reconciliation. Prepare a corrected bank reconciliation.

Imaging Services Co.
Bank Reconciliation
For the Month Ended April 30, 2008

Cash balance according to bank statement			$ 9,767.76
Add outstanding checks:			
No. 821		$ 345.95	
839		272.75	
843		759.60	
844		501.50	1,879.80
			$11,647.56
Deduct deposit of April 30, not recorded by bank			1,010.06
Adjusted balance			$ 9,637.50
Cash balance according to company's records			$ 1,118.32
Add: Proceeds of note collected by bank:			
Principal	$8,000.00		
Interest	280.00	$8,280.00	
Service charges		18.00	8,298.00
			$ 9,416.32
Deduct: Check returned because of insufficient funds		$ 752.30	
Error in recording April 10 deposit of $4,850 as $4,580		270.00	1,022.30
Adjusted balance			$ 8,394.02

Exercise 7-23

Using bank reconciliation to determine cash receipts stolen

Goals **4, 5**

Prometheus Co. records all cash receipts on the basis of its cash register receipts. Prometheus Co. discovered during April 2006 that one of its sales clerks had stolen an undetermined amount of cash receipts when she took the daily deposits to the bank. The following data have been gathered for April:

Cash in bank according to the general ledger	$12,573.22
Cash according to the April 30, 2006, bank statement	13,271.14
Outstanding checks as of April 30, 2006	1,750.20
Bank service charge for April	45.10
Note receivable, including interest collected by bank in April	5,200.00

No deposits were in transit on April 30, which fell on a Sunday.

a. Determine the amount of cash receipts stolen by the sales clerk.
b. What accounting controls would have prevented or detected this theft?

Exercise 7-24

Petty cash fund entries

Goal **6**

Journalize the entries to record the following:

a. Established a petty cash fund of $750.
b. The amount of cash in the petty cash fund is now $119.57. Replenished the fund, based on the following summary of petty cash receipts: office supplies, $415.83; miscellaneous selling expense, $126.50; miscellaneous administrative expense, $88.10.

Exercise 7-25

Petty cash fund entries

Goal **6**

Journalize the entries to record the following:

a. Established a petty cash fund of $500.
b. The amount of cash in the petty cash fund is now $89.60. Replenished the fund, based on the following summary of petty cash receipts: office supplies, $267.25; miscellaneous selling expense, $110.85; miscellaneous administrative expense, $32.30.

Exercise 7-26

Variation in cash flows

Goal **7**

Toys"R"Us is one of the world's leading retailers of toys, children's apparel, and baby products, operating over 1,500 retail stores. For a recent year, Toys"R"Us reported the following net cash flows from operating activities (in thousands):

First quarter ending May 1, 2004	$(246,000)
Second quarter ending July 31, 2004	(63,000)
Third quarter ending October 30, 2004	(415,000)
Year ending January 29, 2005	746,000

Explain how Toys"R"Us can report negative net cash flows from operating activities during the first three quarters yet report net positive cash flows for the year.

Exercise 7-27

Cash flow to net income ratio

Goal **8**

a. 2004: 1.0

Avon Products Inc. is a global manufacturer and marketer of beauty products. Avon distributes its products to customers in the United States through independent sales representatives. The following operating results (in thousands) are for years ending December 31:

	2004	2003
Net cash flows from operating activities	$882,600	$745,300
Net income	846,100	664,800

a. Compute the ratio of cash flow to net income for each year. Round to one decimal place.
b. Is there a significant difference between the ratios for 2004 and 2003? If so, what are some possible causes for the difference?

Exercise 7-28

Cash flow to net income ratio

Goal 8

a. 2004: 1.3

Colgate-Palmolive is a consumer products company with the leading toothpaste brand in the United States. In addition, Colgate sells bar and liquid hand soaps, shower gels, shampoos, conditioners, deodorants, antiperspirants, and shaving products. The following operating results (in thousands) are for years ending December 31:

	2004	2003
Net cash flows from operating activities	$1,754,300	$1,767,700
Net income	1,327,100	1,421,300

a. Compute the ratio of cash flow to net income for each year. Round to one decimal place.
b. Is there a significant difference between the ratios for 2004 and 2003? If so, what are some possible causes for the difference?

Exercise 7-29

Cash flow to net income ratio

Goal 8

Time Warner Inc. (Time Warner) is a media and entertainment company that includes America Online, cable systems, film entertainment, television networks, and publishing. The following operating results (in millions) are for the years ending December 31:

	2004	2003
Net cash flows from operating activities	$6,618	$6,601
Net income	3,364	2,639

a. Compute the ratio of cash flow to net income for each year. Round to one decimal place.
b. Is there a significant difference between the ratios for 2004 and 2003? If so, what are some possible causes for the difference?

Exercise 7-30

Cash to monthly cash expenses ratio

Goal 8

During 2007, Kinetic Inc. has monthly cash expenses of $175,000. On December 31, 2007, the cash balance is $1,575,000.

a. Compute the ratio of cash to monthly cash expenses.
b. Based upon (a), what are the implications for Kinetic Inc.?

Exercise 7-31

Cash to monthly cash expenses ratio

Goal 8

Delta Air Lines is one of the major airlines in the United States and the world. It provides passengers and cargo services for 219 domestic U.S. cities as well as 53 international cities in 35 countries. It operates a fleet of 845 aircraft and is headquartered in Atlanta, Georgia. Delta reported the following financial data (in millions) for the year ended December 31, 2004:

Net cash flows from operating activities	$(1,123)
Cash, December 31, 2004	1,811

a. Determine the monthly cash expenses. Round to one decimal place.
b. Determine the ratio of cash to monthly expenses. Round to one decimal place.
c. Based upon your analysis, do you believe that Delta will remain in business?

Exercise 7-32

Cash to monthly cash expenses ratio

Goal 8

HyperSpace Communications Inc. engages in the development, manufacture, and marketing of network acceleration and data compression software worldwide. Its software products speed up the delivery of information over computer networks, including the Internet, wireless, broadband, private, and dial-up networks. HyperSpace reported the following data (in thousands) for the years ending December 31:

	2004	2003
Net cash flows from operating activities	$(2,558)	($624)
Cash, December 31	5,875	27

a. Determine the monthly cash expenses for 2004 and 2003. Round to one decimal place.
b. Determine the ratio of cash to monthly expenses for December 31, 2004 and 2003. Round to one decimal place.
c. Based upon (a) and (b), why do you think HyperSpace's cash to monthly expenses ratio improved so much by the end of 2004?

ACCOUNTING APPLICATION PROBLEMS

Problem 7-1A

Evaluate internal control of cash

Goals **2, 3**

The following procedures were recently installed by The Geodesic Company:

a. All sales are rung up on the cash register, and a receipt is given to the customer. All sales are recorded on a record locked inside the cash register.
b. Vouchers and all supporting documents are perforated with a PAID designation after being paid by the treasurer.
c. Checks received through the mail are given daily to the accounts receivable clerk for recording collections on account and for depositing in the bank.
d. At the end of a shift, each cashier counts the cash in his or her cash register, unlocks the cash register record, and compares the amount of cash with the amount on the record to determine cash shortages and overages.
e. Each cashier is assigned a separate cash register drawer to which no other cashier has access.
f. The bank reconciliation is prepared by the accounts receivable clerk.
g. Disbursements are made from the petty cash fund only after a petty cash receipt has been completed and signed by the payee.

Instructions

Indicate whether each of the procedures of internal control over cash represents (1) a strength or (2) a weakness. For each weakness, indicate why it exists.

Problem 7-2A

Bank reconciliation and entries

Goals **4, 5**

1. Adjusted balance: $26,315.40

SPREADSHEET

The cash account for Showtime Systems at February 28, 2006, indicated a balance of $19,144.15. The bank statement indicated a balance of $31,391.40 on February 28, 2006. Comparing the bank statement and the accompanying canceled checks and memorandums with the records reveals the following reconciling items:

a. Checks outstanding totaled $11,021.50.
b. A deposit of $6,215.50, representing receipts of February 28, had been made too late to appear on the bank statement.
c. The bank had collected $6,300 on a note left for collection. The face of the note was $6,000.
d. A check for $1,275 returned with the statement had been incorrectly recorded by Showtime Systems as $2,175. The check was for the payment of an obligation to Wilson Co. for the purchase of office supplies on account.
e. A check drawn for $855 had been incorrectly charged by the bank as $585.
f. Bank service charges for February amounted to $28.75.

Instructions

1. Prepare a bank reconciliation.
2. Journalize the necessary entries. The accounts have not been closed.

Problem 7-3A

Bank reconciliation and entries

Goals **4, 5**

1. Adjusted balance: $16,821.88

SPREADSHEET

The cash account for Alpine Sports Co. on April 1, 2006, indicated a balance of $16,911.95. During April, the total cash deposited was $65,500.40, and checks written totaled $68,127.47. The bank statement indicated a balance of $18,880.45 on April 30, 2006. Comparing the bank statement, the canceled checks, and the accompanying memorandums with the records revealed the following reconciling items:

a. Checks outstanding totaled $5,180.27.
b. A deposit of $3,481.70, representing receipts of April 30, had been made too late to appear on the bank statement.
c. A check for $620 had been incorrectly charged by the bank as $260.
d. A check for $479.30 returned with the statement had been recorded by Alpine Sports Co. as $497.30. The check was for the payment of an obligation to Bray & Son on account.
e. The bank had collected for Alpine Sports Co. $3,424 on a note left for collection. The face of the note was $3,200.
f. Bank service charges for April amounted to $25.
g. A check for $880 from Shuler Co. was returned by the bank because of insufficient funds.

Instructions

1. Prepare a bank reconciliation as of April 30.
2. Journalize the necessary entries. The accounts have not been closed.

Problem 7-4A

Bank reconciliation and entries

Goals **4, 5**

1. Adjusted balance: $14,244.09

SPREADSHEET

Rocky Mountain Interiors deposits all cash receipts each Wednesday and Friday in a night depository after banking hours. The data required to reconcile the bank statement as of May 31 have been taken from various documents and records and are reproduced as follows. The sources of the data are printed in capital letters. All checks were written for payments on account.

BANK RECONCILIATION PRECEDING MONTH (DATED APRIL 30):

Cash balance according to bank statement		$10,422.80
Add deposit of April 30, not recorded by bank		780.80
		$11,203.60
Deduct outstanding checks:		
No. 580	$310.10	
No. 602	85.50	
No. 612	92.50	
No. 613	137.50	625.60
Adjusted balance		$10,578.00
Cash balance according to company's records		$10,605.70
Deduct service charges		27.70
Adjusted balance		$10,578.00

CASH ACCOUNT:

Balance as of May 1 $10,578.00

CHECKS WRITTEN:

Number and amount of each check issued in May:

Check No.	Amount	Check No.	Amount	Check No.	Amount
614	$243.50	621	$309.50	628	$ 837.70
615	350.10	622	Void	629	329.90
616	279.90	623	Void	630	882.80
617	395.50	624	707.01	631	1,081.56
618	435.40	625	158.63	632	624.00
619	320.10	626	550.03	633	310.08
620	238.87	627	318.73	634	303.30

Total amount of checks issued in May $8,676.61

MAY BANK STATEMENT:

AMERICAN NATIONAL BANK OF DETROIT
MEMBER FDIC
DETROIT, MI 48201-2500 (313)555-8547

PAGE 1

ACCOUNT NUMBER
FROM 5/01/20– TO 5/31/20–

	BALANCE	10,422.80
9	DEPOSITS	6,086.35
20	WITHDRAWALS	7,514.11
4	OTHER DEBITS AND CREDITS	5,150.50CR
	NEW BALANCE	14,145.54

ROCKY MOUNTAIN INTERIORS

CHECKS AND OTHER DEBITS					DEPOSITS	DATE	BALANCE
No.580	310.10	No.612	92.50		780.80	05/01	10,801.00
No.613	137.50	No.614	243.50		569.50	05/03	10,989.50
No.615	350.10	No.616	279.90		701.80	05/06	11,061.30
No.617	395.50	No.618	435.40		819.24	05/11	11,049.64
No.619	320.10	No.620	238.87		580.70	05/13	11,071.37
No.621	309.50	No.624	707.01		MS 5,000.00	05/14	15,054.86
No.625	158.63	No.626	550.03		MS 400.00	05/14	14,746.20
No.627	318.73	No.629	329.90		600.10	05/17	14,697.67
No.630	882.80	No.631	1,081.56	NSF 225.40		05/20	12,507.91
No.632	62.40	No.633	310.08		701.26	05/21	12,836.69
					731.45	05/24	13,568.14
					601.50	05/28	14,169.64
		SC	24.10			05/31	14,145.54

EC — ERROR CORRECTION
MS — MISCELLANEOUS
NSF — NOT SUFFICIENT FUNDS
OD — OVERDRAFT
PS — PAYMENT STOPPED
SC — SERVICE CHARGE

* * * * * * * * *

THE RECONCILEMENT OF THIS STATEMENT WITH YOUR RECORDS IS ESSENTIAL.
ANY ERROR OR EXCEPTION SHOULD BE REPORTED IMMEDIATELY.

CASH RECEIPTS FOR MONTH OF MAY $6,630.60

DUPLICATE DEPOSIT TICKETS:

Date and amount of each deposit in May:

Date	Amount	Date	Amount	Date	Amount
May 2	$569.50	May 12	$580.70	May 23	$ 731.45
5	701.80	16	600.10	26	601.50
9	819.24	19	701.26	31	1,325.05

Instructions

1. Prepare a bank reconciliation as on May 31. If errors in recording deposits or checks are discovered, assume that the errors were made by the company. Assume that all deposits are from cash sales. All checks are written to satisfy accounts payable.
2. Journalize the necessary entries. The accounts have not been closed.
3. What is the amount of cash that should appear on the balance sheet as of May 31?
4. Assume that a canceled check for $1,375 has been incorrectly recorded by the bank as $1,735. Briefly explain how the error would be included in a bank reconciliation and how it should be corrected.

ALTERNATE ACCOUNTING APPLICATION PROBLEMS

Alternate Problem 7-1B

Evaluating internal control of cash

Goals **2, 3**

The following procedures were recently installed by Pancreas Company:

a. At the end of each day, an accounting clerk compares the duplicate copy of the daily cash deposit slip with the deposit receipt obtained from the bank.
b. The bank reconciliation is prepared by the cashier, who works under the supervision of the treasurer.
c. At the end of the day, cash register clerks are required to use their own funds to make up any cash shortages in their registers.
d. Along with petty cash expense receipts for postage, office supplies, etc., several post-dated employee checks are in the petty cash fund.
e. The accounts payable clerk prepares a voucher for each disbursement. The voucher along with the supporting documentation is forwarded to the treasurer's office for approval.
f. All mail is opened by the mail clerk, who forwards all cash remittances to the cashier. The cashier prepares a listing of the cash receipts and forwards a copy of the list to the accounts receivable clerk for recording in the accounts.
g. After necessary approvals have been obtained for the payment of a voucher, the treasurer signs and mails the check. The treasurer then stamps the voucher and supporting documentation as paid and returns the voucher and supporting documentation to the accounts payable clerk for filing.
h. At the end of each day, any deposited cash receipts are placed in the bank's night depository.

Instructions

Indicate whether each of the procedures of internal control over cash represents (1) a strength or (2) a weakness. For each weakness, indicate why it exists.

Alternate Problem 7-2B

Bank reconciliation and entries

Goals **4, 5**

1. Adjusted balance: $16,215.95

SPREADSHEET

The cash account for Pickron Co. at April 30, 2006, indicated a balance of $13,290.95. The bank statement indicated a balance of $18,016.30 on April 30, 2006. Comparing the bank statement and the accompanying canceled checks and memorandums with the records revealed the following reconciling items:

a. Checks outstanding totaled $7,169.75.
b. A deposit of $5,189.40, representing receipts of April 30, had been made too late to appear on the bank statement.
c. The bank had collected $3,240 on a note left for collection. The face of the note was $3,000.
d. A check for $1,960 returned with the statement had been incorrectly recorded by Pickron Co. as $1,690. The check was for the payment of an obligation to Jones Co. for the purchase of office equipment on account.
e. A check drawn for $1,680 had been erroneously charged by the bank as $1,860.
f. Bank service charges for April amounted to $45.00.

Instructions

1. Prepare a bank reconciliation.
2. Journalize the necessary entries. The accounts have not been closed.

Alternate Problem 7-3B

Bank reconciliation and entries

Goals **4, 5**

1. Adjusted balance: $5,689.87

SPREADSHEET

The cash account for Seal-Tek Co. at December 1, 2006, indicated a balance of $3,945.90. During December, the total cash deposited was $31,077.75, and checks written totaled $30,395.78. The bank statement indicated a balance of $5,465.50 on December 31. Comparing the bank statement, the canceled checks, and the accompanying memorandums with the records revealed the following reconciling items:

a. Checks outstanding totaled $3,003.84.
b. A deposit of $2,148.21, representing receipts of December 31, had been made too late to appear on the bank statement.
c. The bank had collected for Seal-Tek Co. $1,908 on a note left for collection. The face of the note was $1,800.

d. A check for $120 returned with the statement had been incorrectly charged by the bank as $1,200.
e. A check for $318 returned with the statement had been recorded by Seal-Tek Co. as $138. The check was for the payment of an obligation to Kenyon Co. on account.
f. Bank service charges for December amounted to $30.
g. A check for $636 from Fontana Co. was returned by the bank because of insufficient funds.

Instructions

1. Prepare a bank reconciliation as of December 31.
2. Journalize the necessary entries. The accounts have been closed.

Alternate Problem 7-4B

Bank reconciliation and entries

Goals **4, 5**

1. Adjusted balance: $10,322.02

SPREADSHEET

Heritage Furniture Company deposits all cash receipts each Wednesday and Friday in a night depository, after banking hours. The data required to reconcile the bank statement as of November 30 have been taken from various documents and records and are reproduced as follows. The sources of the data are printed in capital letters. All checks were written for payments on account.

NOVEMBER BANK STATEMENT:

MEMBER FDIC

AMERICAN NATIONAL BANK OF DETROIT

DETROIT, MI 48201-2500 (313)555-8547

HERITAGE FURNITURE COMPANY

PAGE 1

	ACCOUNT NUMBER	
	FROM 11/01/20–	TO 11/30/20–
	BALANCE	7,447.20
9	DEPOSITS	8,691.77
20	WITHDRAWALS	7,345.91
4	OTHER DEBITS AND CREDITS	2,298.70CR
	NEW BALANCE	11,091.76

CHECKS AND OTHER DEBITS				DEPOSITS	DATE	BALANCE
No.731	162.15	No.738	251.40	690.25	11/01	7,723.90
No.739	60.55	No.740	237.50	1,080.50	11/02	8,506.35
No.741	495.15	No.742	501.90	854.17	11/04	8,363.47
No.743	671.30	No.744	506.88	840.50	11/09	8,025.79
No.745	117.25	No.746	298.66	MS 2,500.00	11/09	10,109.88
No.748	450.90	No.749	640.13	MS 125.00	11/09	9,143.85
No.750	276.77	No.751	299.37	896.61	11/11	9,464.32
No.752	537.01	No.753	380.95	882.95	11/16	9,429.31
No.754	449.75	No.756	113.95	1,606.74	11/18	10,472.35
No.757	407.95	No.760	486.39	897.34	11/23	10,475.35
				942.71	11/25	11,418.06
		NSF	291.90		11/28	11,126.16
		SC	34.40		11/30	11,091.76

EC — ERROR CORRECTION
MS — MISCELLANEOUS
NSF — NOT SUFFICIENT FUNDS
OD — OVERDRAFT
PS — PAYMENT STOPPED
SC — SERVICE CHARGE

* * * * * * * * *

THE RECONCILEMENT OF THIS STATEMENT WITH YOUR RECORDS IS ESSENTIAL.
ANY ERROR OR EXCEPTION SHOULD BE REPORTED IMMEDIATELY.

CASH ACCOUNT

Balance as of November 1	$7,317.40
CASH RECEIPTS FOR MONTH OF NOVEMBER	$8,651.58

DUPLICATE DEPOSIT TICKETS:

Date and amount of each deposit in November:

Date	Amount	Date	Amount	Date	Amount
Nov. 1	$1,080.50	Nov. 10	$ 896.61	Nov. 22	$ 537.34
3	854.17	15	882.95	24	942.71
8	840.50	17	1,606.74	29	1,010.06

CHECKS WRITTEN:

Number and amount of each check issued in November:

Check No.	Amount	Check No.	Amount	Check No.	Amount
740	$237.50	747	Void	754	$ 449.75
741	495.15	748	$450.90	755	272.75
742	501.90	749	640.13	756	113.95
743	671.30	750	276.77	757	407.95
744	506.88	751	299.37	758	259.60
745	117.25	752	337.01	759	901.50
746	298.66	753	380.95	760	486.39

Total amount of checks issued in November $8,105.66

BANK RECONCILIATION FOR PRECEDING MONTH:

Heritage Furniture Company
Bank Reconciliation
October 31, 20—

Cash balance according to bank statement		$7,447.20
Add deposit for October 31, not recorded by bank		690.25
		$8,137.45
Deduct outstanding checks:		
No. 731	$162.15	
736	345.95	
738	251.40	
739	60.55	820.05
Adjusted balance		$7,317.40
Cash balance according to company's records		$7,352.50
Deduct service charges		35.10
Adjusted balance		$7,317.40

Instructions

1. Prepare a bank reconciliation as of November 30. If errors in recording deposits or checks are discovered, assume that the errors were made by the company. Assume that all deposits are from cash sales. All checks are written to satisfy accounts payable.
2. Journalize the necessary entries. The accounts have not been closed.
3. What is the amount of cash that should appear on the balance sheet as of November 30?
4. Assume that a canceled check for $580 has been incorrectly recorded by the bank as $850. Briefly explain how the error would be included in a bank reconciliation and how it should be corrected.

FINANCIAL ANALYSIS AND REPORTING CASES

Case 7-1

Sarbanes-Oxley internal control report

Using the Web site http://edgarscan.pwcglobal.com/servlets/edgarscan, enter "Hershey Foods." Click on Hershey Foods Corp. and then click on 10-K 2004–12–31. Fetch the entire 10-K filing by clicking on text rich (724K). Once the 10-K filing appears, find the "Management Report on Internal Control over Financial Reporting" by searching the document for the key words "internal control" using the Word "Find" command, and answer the following questions:

1. How many times is "internal control" mentioned in Hershey's 10-K?
2. Are there any recent changes in internal control over financial reporting?
3. What criteria were used by management to analyze and assess internal control as a basis for the "Management Report on Internal Control over Financial Reporting"?
4. Who signed the "Management Report on Internal Control over Financial Reporting" on behalf of Hershey's management?
5. Do Hershey's internal controls guarantee its financial reporting is complete and accurate?
6. Who is Hershey's independent public accounting firm?
7. What do 10-K Exhibits 31.1 and 31.2 say about the possible existence of fraud?

Case 7-2

Control environment of a public corporation

eBay Inc. operates an Internet-based community in which buyers and sellers are brought together to buy and sell almost anything. The eBay online service permits sellers to list items for sale, buyers to bid on items of interest, and all eBay users to browse through listed items in a fully automated, topically arranged service that is available online seven days a week. Through the PayPal service, the company enables any business or consumer with e-mail in 38 countries to send and receive online payments. For the year ending December 31, 2004, eBay reported sales of almost $3.3 billion and net income of $778 million. For corporations such as eBay, maintaining a strong control environment is an everyday challenge. One method of maintaining a strong control environment is to have a strong Board of Directors that is actively engaged in overseeing the business.

Using the Internet, access the eBay December 30, 2004 10-K filing with the Securities and Exchange Commission. You can use the PricewaterhouseCoopers Web site, http://edgarscan.pwcglobal.com, to search for company filings by name. Based upon the 10-K filing, answer the following questions:

1. List the members of the Board of Directors of eBay, their age, and their title.
2. Based upon your answer to (1), what percentage of the Board is not part of eBay's management team? Round to one decimal place.
3. Based upon your answer to (1), what is the average age of a Board member of eBay?
4. Based upon your answer to (3), do you think the average age of a Board member of eBay is higher or lower than the average age of a Board member of American Express?
5. What are the purpose and policy of the Audit Committee of eBay? *Hint:* You can find this information by going to eBay's Web site at http://investor.ebay.com/governance/home.cfm and clicking on the Charter of the Audit Committee.
6. List the members of the Board of Directors who belong to the Audit Committee.
7. Are any members of the Audit Committee also members of eBay's management team?
8. Search eBay's 10-K for the certifications required by the Sarbanes-Oxley Act of 2002. Read the certifications. Who signed the Sarbanes-Oxley certifications for eBay?
9. Based upon your answers to (1) through (8), do you believe that eBay has a sound control environment?

Case 7-3

Responsibility for internal controls of a public corporation

CVS Corporation is a leader in the retail drugstore industry in the United States, with net sales of $30.6 billion in fiscal 2004. As of January 1, 2005, CVS operated over 5,375 retail and specialty pharmacy stores in 36 states and the District of Columbia.

Using the Internet, access the CVS January 1, 2005 10-K filing with the Securities and Exchange Commission. You can use the PricewaterhouseCoopers Web site, http://edgarscan.pwcglobal.com, to search for company filings by name. Based upon the 10-K filing, answer the following questions:

1. Who is responsible for the integrity and objectivity of the financial statements of CVS?
2. What is the system of internal controls of CVS designed to accomplish?

3. In addition to management, who reviews the system of internal controls for improvements and modifications necessary because of changing business conditions?
4. Were there any changes in the internal controls over financial reporting in 2004?
5. Who are the independent auditors of CVS?
6. Do you think having the chief executive officer and chief financial officer of CVS serve on its Audit Committee is a good way to foster an effective control environment?
7. Do members of the management team of CVS serve on the Audit Committee of the Board of Directors?

Case 7-4

Ratio of cash flow to net income

SPREADSHEET

The operating activities section of the statement of cash flows for General Motors Corporation is provided below for three recent years.

General Motors Corporation
Operating Activities Section—Statement of Cash Flows (annotated)
For the Years Ended December 31, 2004, 2003, 2002
(in millions)

	2004	2003	2002
Net income	$ 2,805	$ 2,862	$ 1,975
Selected adjustments to reconcile income to net cash provided by operating activities:			
Depreciation and amortization expenses	14,152	13,513	11,569
Pension contributions	(13,511)	(24,704)	(9,490)
Pension and retiree health benefit expense	7,023	8,011	5,888
Change in other operating assets and liabilities	(1,628)	(2,277)	(3,391)
Other	4,220	5,551	4,524
Net cash provided by operating activities	$ 13,061	$ 2,956	$11,075

A large expense for General Motors is its pension expense. Under pension accounting, the pension expense is recognized in the period that the pension is earned. However, the company has latitude regarding the funding of the pension benefit. That is, the expense and the related cash flow to fund the future benefit need not occur in the same period.

1. Calculate General Motors' ratio of cash flow to net income for all three comparative years. Round to two decimal places.
2. Interpret the magnitude and year-to-year changes in the ratio.

Case 7-5

Ratio of cash flow to net income

Estée Lauder Inc. is one of the world's leading manufacturers and marketers of skin care, makeup, and hair products. Estée Lauder products are sold in over 130 countries and territories under such brand names as Clinique, Rodan, Tommy Hilfiger, and Donna Karan. The following data (in thousands) were taken from the 10-K filings with the Securities and Exchange Commission for the years ending June 30, 2004 and 2003:

	2004	2003
Cash flow from operating activities	$667,300	$548,500
Net income	342,100	319,800

1. Compute the ratio of cash flow to net income for 2004 and 2003. Round to one decimal place.
2. In 2004, Estée Lauder reported a loss from discontinued operations of $33.3 million. Compute the ratio of cash flow to net income for 2004 taking into consideration the impact of the discontinued operations on net income. Round to one decimal place.
3. Based upon (2), is the ratio of cash flow to net income comparable between 2004 and 2003?

Case 7-6

Ratio of cash flow to net income

Best Buy is a specialty retailer of consumer electronics, home office products, entertainment software, appliances, and related services. The following data (in millions) were taken from the 10-K filings with the Securities and Exchange Commission for the years ending February 28, 2004, and March 2, 2003:

	2004	2003
Cash flow from operating activities	$1,361	$667
Net income	705	99

1. Compute the ratio of cash flow to net income for 2004 and 2003. Round to one decimal place.
2. In 2004, Best Buy reported a loss from discontinued operations of $95 million. In 2003, Best Buy reported a loss from discontinued operations of $441 million and a reduction of income from an accounting change of $82 million. Compute the ratio of cash flow to net income for 2004 and 2003 taking into consideration the impact of the discontinued operations and accounting change on net income. Round to one decimal place.
3. Based upon (2), is the ratio of cash flow to net income comparable between 2004 and 2003?
4. Further review of the statement of cash flows reveals that inventories increased by $282 million in 2004 over the level of change in 2003. In addition, operating liabilities increased by $588 million over the level of change in 2003. Taking into account this change in inventory and operating liabilities on cash flows and your results from (2), compute the ratio of cash flow to net income for 2004.
5. Based upon (4), is the ratio of cash flow to net income for 2004 more comparable to the ratio for 2003 computed in (2)?

Case 7-7

Cash to monthly cash expenses ratio

OccuLogix Inc. provides treatments for eye diseases, including age-related macular degeneration (AMD). The company's treatment system, called the RHEO system, consists of an Octonova pump and disposable treatment sets that improve microcirculation in the eye by filtering high molecular weight proteins and other macromolecules from the patient's plasma. OccuLogix reported the following data (in thousands) for the years ending December 31, 2004, 2003, and 2002:

	2004	2003	2002
Cash as of December 31*	$60,040	$1,239	$ 603
Net cash flows from operating activities	(5,382)	(2,375)	(2,126)

* Includes cash equivalents and short-term investments.

1. Determine the monthly cash expenses for 2004, 2003, and 2002. Round to one decimal place.
2. Determine the ratio of cash to monthly expenses as of December 31, 2004, 2003, and 2002. Round to one decimal place.
3. Based upon (1) and (2), comment on OccuLogix's ratio of cash to monthly operating expenses for 2004, 2003, and 2002.

Case 7-8

Cash to monthly cash expenses ratio

Acusphere Inc. is a specialty pharmaceutical company that develops new drugs and improved formulations of existing drugs using its proprietary microparticle technology. Currently, the company has three products in development in the areas of cardiology, oncology, and asthma. Acusphere reported the following data (in thousands) for the years ending December 31, 2004, 2003, and 2002.

	2004	2003	2002
Cash as of December 31*	$45,180	$54,562	$ 7,992
Net cash flows from operating activities	(19,319)	(15,507)	(17,682)

* Includes cash equivalents and short-term investments.

1. Determine the monthly cash expenses for 2004, 2003, and 2002. Round to one decimal place.
2. Determine the ratio of cash to monthly expenses as of December 31, 2004, 2003, and 2002. Round to one decimal place.
3. Based upon (1) and (2), comment on Acusphere's ratio of cash to monthly operating expenses for 2004, 2003, and 2002.

BUSINESS ACTIVITIES AND RESPONSIBILITY ISSUES

Activity 7-1

Ethics and professional conduct in business

Lee Garrett sells security systems for Guardsman Security Co. Garrett has a monthly sales quota of $40,000. If Garrett exceeds this quota, he is awarded a bonus. In measuring the quota, a sale is credited to the salesperson when a customer signs a contract for installation of a security system. Through the 25th of the current month, Garrett has sold $30,000 in security systems.

Vortex Co., a business rumored to be on the verge of bankruptcy, contacted Garrett on the 26th of the month about having a security system installed. Garret estimates that the contract would yield about $14,000 worth of business for Guardsman Security Co. In addition, this contract would be large enough to put Garrett "over the top" for a bonus in the current month. However, Garrett is concerned that Vortex Co. will not be able to make the contract payment after the security system is installed. In fact, Garrett has heard rumors that a competing security services company refused to install a system for Vortex Co. because of these concerns.

Upon further consideration, Garrett concluded that his job is to sell security systems and that it's someone else's problem to collect the resulting accounts receivable. Thus, Garrett wrote the contract with Vortex Co. and received a bonus for the month.

1. Discuss whether Lee Garrett was acting in an ethical manner.
2. How might Guardsman Security Co. use internal controls to prevent this scenario from occurring?

Activity 7-2

Ethics and financial statement fraud

WorldCom, the second largest telecommunications company in the United States, became the largest bankruptcy in history due to financial reporting irregularities and misstatements of nearly $7 billion. WorldCom's controller, director of general accounting, and director of management reporting all pleaded guilty to financial reporting fraud. These employees all stated that they were ordered by superiors to adjust the records to artificially boost the company's profits. Under protest, these employees made the adjustments.

1. Should these employees be held responsible for their actions, since they were "following orders"?
2. How should an employee respond to questionable or unethical requests from superiors?

Activity 7-3

Ethics and professional conduct in business

During the preparation of the bank reconciliation for The Image Co., Chris Renees, the assistant controller, discovered that Empire National Bank incorrectly recorded a $936 check written by The Image Co. as $396. Chris has decided not to notify the bank but wait for the bank to detect the error. Chris plans to record the $540 error as Other Income if the bank fails to detect the error within the next three months.

Discuss whether Chris is behaving in a professional manner.

Activity 7-4

Internal controls

The following is an excerpt from a conversation between two sales clerks, Carol Dickson and Jill Kesner. Both Carol and Jill are employed by Reboot Electronics, a locally owned and operated computer retail store.

Carol: Did you hear the news?
Jill: What news?
Carol: Candis and Albert were both arrested this morning.
Jill: What? Arrested? You're putting me on!
Carol: No, really! The police arrested them first thing this morning. Put them in handcuffs, read them their rights—the whole works. It was unreal!
Jill: What did they do?
Carol: Well, apparently they were filling out merchandise refund forms for fictitious customers and then taking the cash.

Jill: I guess I never thought of that. How did they catch them?

Carol: The store manager noticed that returns were twice that of last year and seemed to be increasing. When he confronted Candis, she became flustered and admitted to taking the cash, apparently over $2,800 in just three months. They're going over the last six months' transactions to try to determine how much Albert stole. He apparently started stealing first.

Suggest appropriate control procedures that would have prevented or detected the theft of cash.

Activity 7-5

Internal controls

The following is an excerpt from a conversation between the store manager of Piper Grocery Stores, Bill Dowell, and Cary Wynne, president of Piper Grocery Stores.

Cary: Bill, I'm concerned about this new scanning system.

Bill: What's the problem?

Cary: Well, how do we know the clerks are ringing up all the merchandise?

Bill: That's one of the strong points about the system. The scanner automatically rings up each item, based on its bar code. We update the prices daily, so we're sure that the sale is rung up for the right price.

Cary: That's not my concern. What keeps a clerk from pretending to scan items and then simply not charging his friends? If his friends were buying 10–15 items, it would be easy for the clerk to pass through several items with his finger over the bar code or just pass the merchandise through the scanner with the wrong side showing. It would look normal for anyone observing. In the old days, we at least could hear the cash register ringing up each sale.

Bill: I see your point.

Suggest ways that Piper Grocery Stores could prevent or detect the theft of merchandise as described.

Activity 7-6

Ethics and professional conduct in business

Tim Jost and Kerri Stein are both cash register clerks for Frontier Markets. Kathy Rostad is the store manager for Frontier Markets. The following is an excerpt of a conversation between Tim and Kerri:

Tim: Kerri, how long have you been working for Frontier Markets?

Kerri: Almost five years this August. You just started two weeks ago . . . right?

Tim: Yes. Do you mind if I ask you a question?

Kerri: No, go ahead.

Tim: What I want to know is, have they always had this rule that if your cash register is short at the end of the day, you have to make up the shortage out of your own pocket?

Kerri: Yes, as long as I've been working here.

Tim: Well, it's the pits. Last week I had to pay in almost $30.

Kerri: It's not that big a deal. I just make sure that I'm not short at the end of the day.

Tim: How do you do that?

Kerri: I just short-change a few customers early in the day. There are a few jerks that deserve it anyway. Most of the time, their attention is elsewhere and they don't think to check their change.

Tim: What happens if you're over at the end of the day?

Kerri: Rostad lets me keep it as long as it doesn't get to be too large. I've not been short in over a year. I usually clear about $20 to $30 extra per day.

Discuss this case from the viewpoint of proper controls and professional behavior.

Activity 7-7

Bank reconciliation and internal control

The records of Lumberjack Company indicate a July 31 cash balance of $9,806.05, which includes undeposited receipts for July 30 and 31. The cash balance on the bank statement as of July 31 is $6,004.95. This balance includes a note of $4,000 plus $240 interest collected by the bank but not recorded in the journal. Checks outstanding on July 31 were as follows: No 670, $781.20; No. 679, $610; No. 690, $716.50; No. 1996, $127.40; No. 1997, $520; and No. 1999, $851.50.

On July 3, the cashier resigned, effective at the end of the month. Before leaving on July 31, the cashier prepared the following bank reconciliation:

Cash balance per books, July 31		$ 9,806.05
Add outstanding checks:		
No. 1996	$127.40	
1997	520.00	
1999	851.50	1,198.90
		$11,004.95
Less undeposited receipts		5,000.00
Cash balance per bank, July 31		$ 6,004.95
Deduct unrecorded note with interest		4,240.00
True cash, July 31		$ 1,764.95

Calculator Tape of Outstanding Checks:
0.00*
127.40 +
520.00 +
851.50 +
1,198.90*

Subsequently, the owner of Lumberjack Company discovered that the cashier had stolen an unknown amount of undeposited receipts, leaving only $5,000 to be deposited on July 31. The owner, a close family friend, has asked your help in determining the amount that the former cashier has stolen.

1. Determine the amount the cashier stole from Lumberjack Company. Show your computations in good form.
2. How did the cashier attempt to conceal the theft?
3. a. Identify two major weaknesses in internal controls which allowed the cashier to steal the undeposited cash receipts.
   b. Recommend improvements in internal controls, so that similar types of thefts of undeposited cash receipts can be prevented.

Activity 7-8

Observe internal controls over cash

GROUP ACTIVITY

Select a business in your community and observe its internal controls over cash receipts and cash payments. The business could be a bank or a bookstore, restaurant, department store, or other retailer. In groups of three or four, identify and discuss the similarities and differences in each business's cash internal controls.

Activity 7-9

Invest excess cash

Assume that you have just received a $100,000 check! Go to the Web site of (or visit) a local bank and collect information about the savings and checking options that are available. Identify the option that is best for you and why it is best.

ANSWERS TO SELF-STUDY QUESTIONS

1. **C** Compliance with laws and regulations (answer C) is an objective, not an element, of internal control. The control environment (answer A), monitoring (answer B), control procedures (answer D), risk assessment, and information and communication are the five elements of internal control.

2. **A** The polices and procedures that are established to safeguard assets, ensure accurate business information, and ensure compliance with laws and regulations are called internal controls (answer A). The three steps in setting up an accounting system are (1) analysis (answer B), (2) design (answer C), and (3) implementation (answer D).

3. **B** On any specific date, the cash account in a company's ledger may not agree with the account in the bank's ledger because of delays and/or errors by either party in recording transactions. The purpose of a bank reconciliation, therefore, is to determine the reasons for any differences between the two account balances. All errors should then be corrected by the company or the bank, as appropriate. In arriving at the adjusted cash balance according to the bank statement, outstanding checks must be deducted (answer B) to adjust for checks that have been written by the company but that have not yet been presented to the bank for payment.

4. **C** All reconciling items that are added to and deducted from the cash balance according to the company's records on the bank reconciliation (answer C) require that journal entries be made by the company to correct errors made in recording transactions or to bring the cash account up to date for delays in recording transactions.

5. **D** To avoid the delay, annoyance, and expense that is associated with paying all obligations by check, relatively small amounts (answer A) are paid from a petty cash fund. The fund is established by estimating the amount of cash needed to pay these small amounts during a specified period (answer B), and it is then reimbursed when the amount of money in the fund is reduced to a predetermined minimum amount (answer C).

8 Receivables

Learning Goals

1. Describe the common classifications of receivables.
2. Describe the nature of and the accounting for uncollectible receivables.
3. Describe the direct write-off method of accounting for uncollectible receivables.
4. Describe the allowance method of accounting for uncollectible receivables.
5. Compare the direct write-off and allowance methods of accounting for uncollectible accounts.
6. Describe the nature, characteristics, and accounting for notes receivable.
7. Describe the reporting of receivables on the balance sheet.
8. Describe the principles of managing accounts receivable.
9. Compute and interpret the accounts receivable turnover and the number of days' sales in receivables.

Starbucks Corporation

© PHOTODISC/GETTY IMAGES

The sale and purchase of goods and services typically involve the exchange of goods and services for money. The point at which money changes hands, however, can vary greatly depending on the circumstances. In the simplest arrangement, the purchaser makes payment and receives goods at the time of the transaction. For example, if you purchased a grande latte from Starbucks Corporation, you would pay for and receive the beverage at the same time. Starbucks would not need to rely on you for future payment, since you are making payment at the same time you receive the latte.

At other times, however, the transaction elements do not occur at the same time; that is, one party delays in either providing the cash or the product. This is most common when companies do business with each other. Unlike the individual consumer purchasing coffee, a person purchasing for a business does not have control of the business checkbook. Rather, the supplier will invoice the customer for payment at a later time. This delay in payment facilitates internal control by separating the purchase decision from payment. For example, Starbucks will invoice local businesses for providing on-premises coffee service. Local businesses will pay for the coffee service after delivery according to the terms of the invoice. This gives local businesses time to process the invoice. Starbucks trusts the local business to pay the invoice because of its successful history as business partners, coupled with its financial strength. Indeed, as an individual you might be able to move from cash-based transactions to transactions on a personal account with some businesses. For example, a copy shop might agree to an account relationship after establishing trust from a history of cash-basis transactions.

Starbucks has built its business on trust—trust in its employees, suppliers, and customers. As a result, Starbucks has been voted one of the most admired companies in the United States.

Trust is a large part of business. Trust allows companies to avoid simultaneous cash transactions and use trade credit. Trade credit gives rise to accounts receivable for the seller, which is often a significant current asset for many businesses. In this chapter, we will discuss how to account for, disclose, manage, and analyze accounts and notes receivable.

Describe the common classifications of receivables.

CLASSIFICATION OF RECEIVABLES

Many companies sell on credit in order to sell more services or products. The receivables that result from such sales are normally classified as accounts receivable or notes receivable. The term **receivables** includes all money claims against other entities, including people, business firms, and other organizations. These receivables are usually a significant portion of the total current assets. For example, an annual report of La-Z-Boy Chair Company reported that receivables made up over 40% of La-Z-Boy's current assets.

Accounts Receivable

The most common transaction creating a receivable is selling merchandise or services on credit. The receivable is recorded as a debit to the accounts receivable account. Such **accounts receivable** are normally expected to be collected within a relatively short period, such as 30 or 60 days. They are classified on the balance sheet as a current asset.

Notes Receivable

Notes receivable are amounts that customers owe for which a formal, written instrument of credit has been issued. As long as notes receivable are expected to be collected within a year, they are normally classified on the balance sheet as a current asset.

Notes are often used for credit periods of more than 60 days. For example, a furniture dealer may require a down payment at the time of sale and accept a note or a series of notes for the remainder. Such arrangements usually provide for monthly payments. For example, if you have purchased furniture on credit, you probably signed a note. From your viewpoint, the note is a note payable. From the creditor's viewpoint, the note is a note receivable.

Notes may be used to settle a customer's account receivable. Notes and accounts receivable that result from sales transactions are sometimes called *trade receivables*. Unless stated otherwise, we will assume that all notes and accounts receivable in this chapter are from sales transactions.

HOW BUSINESSES MAKE MONEY

Coffee Anyone?

Starbucks' strategic goal is to establish the Starbucks name as the most recognized and respected brand in the world. To achieve this goal, the company focuses on two core areas of business: retail coffee stores and nonretail sales. When planning new retail stores, Starbucks focuses on high-traffic, high-visibility locations that offer convenient access for pedestrians and drivers. Starbucks varies the size and format of its stores to fit the location. As a result, you may find Starbucks in a variety of locations, including downtown and suburban retail centers, office buildings, and university campuses. The company's specialty operations further develop the Starbucks brand through alternative supply channels and new products. For example, the company has recently expanded coffee sales to grocery stores, warehouse clubs, and restaurants. Other activities include joint ventures with companies, such as **PepsiCo, Inc.** and **Dreyer's Grand Ice Cream**, to market food products such as Frappucino and Dreyer's Ice Cream under the Starbucks name. Finally, Starbucks has recently extended its brand-building activities to nonfood items by offering a Starbucks credit card in conjunction with **Banc One** and music through the Starbucks Hear Music channel on XMSR.

Source: Starbucks Corporation Form 10-K filing with the Securities and Exchange Commission for the year ending October 3, 2004.

Other Receivables

Other receivables are normally listed separately on the balance sheet. If they are expected to be collected within one year, they are classified as current assets. If collection is expected beyond one year, they are classified as noncurrent assets and reported under the caption *Investments*. *Other receivables* include interest receivable, taxes receivable, and receivables from officers or employees.

Describe the nature of and the accounting for uncollectible receivables.

UNCOLLECTIBLE RECEIVABLES

In prior chapters, we described and illustrated the accounting for transactions involving sales of merchandise or services on credit. A major issue that we have not yet discussed is that some customers will not pay their accounts. That is, some accounts receivable will be uncollectible.

Many retail businesses may shift the risk of uncollectible receivables to other companies. For example, some retailers do not accept sales on account, but will only accept cash or credit cards. Such policies shift the risk to the credit card companies.

Companies may also sell their receivables to other companies. This is often the case when a company issues its own credit card. For example, Macy's, Sears, and JCPenney issue their own credit cards. Selling receivables is called *factoring* the receivables, and the buyer of the receivables is called a *factor*. An advantage of factoring is that the company selling its receivables receives immediate cash for operating and other needs. In addition, depending upon the factoring agreement, some of the risk of uncollectible accounts may be shifted to the factor.

Regardless of the care used in granting credit and the collection procedures used, a part of the credit sales will not be collectible. The operating expense recorded from uncollectible receivables is called **bad debt expense**, *uncollectible accounts expense*, or *doubtful accounts expense*.

When does an account or a note become uncollectible? There is no general rule for determining when an account is uncollectible. Once a receivable is past due, a company should first notify the customer and try to collect the account. If after repeated attempts the customer doesn't pay, the company may turn the account over to a collection agency. After the collection agency attempts collection, any remaining balance in the account is considered worthless. One of the most significant indications of partial or complete uncollectibility occurs when the debtor goes into bankruptcy. Other indications include the closing of the customer's business and an inability to locate or contact the customer.

There are two methods of accounting for receivables that appear to be uncollectible: the direct write-off method and the allowance method. The **direct write-off method** records bad debt expense only when an account is judged to be worthless. The **allowance method** records bad debt expense by estimating uncollectible accounts at the end of the accounting period.

In the next sections of this chapter, we describe and illustrate the accounting for bad debt expense using the direct write-off method and the allowance method. We begin by describing and illustrating the direct write-off method since it is simpler and easier to understand. The direct write-off method is used by smaller companies and by companies with few receivables.[1] Generally accepted accounting principles, however, require companies with a large amount of receivables to use the allowance method.

1 The direct write-off method is also required for federal income tax purposes.

Describe the direct write-off method of accounting for uncollectible receivables.

DIRECT WRITE-OFF METHOD FOR UNCOLLECTIBLE ACCOUNTS

Under the direct write-off method, bad debt expense is not recorded until the customer's account is determined to be worthless. At that time, the customer's account receivable is written off. To illustrate, assume that a $4,200 account receivable from D. L. Ross has been determined to be uncollectible. The entry to write off the account is as follows:

SCF	BS	IS
—	A↓ SE↓	E↑

May 10	Bad Debt Expense	4,200	
	Accounts Receivable—D. L. Ross		4,200

What happens if an account receivable that has been written off is later collected? In such cases, the account is reinstated by an entry that reverses the write-off entry. The cash received in payment is then recorded as a receipt on account.

To illustrate, assume that the D. L. Ross account of $4,200 written off on May 10 in the preceding entry is later collected on November 21. The reinstatement and receipt of cash is recorded as follows:

SCF	BS	IS
—	A↑ SE↑	E↓
O↑	A↑↓	—

Nov. 21	Accounts Receivable—D. L. Ross	4,200	
	Bad Debt Expense		4,200
21	Cash	4,200	
	Accounts Receivable—D. L. Ross		4,200

The direct write-off method is used by businesses that sell most of their goods or services for cash and accept only MasterCard or VISA, which are recorded as cash sales. In such cases, receivables are a small part of the current assets and any bad debt expense would be small. Examples of such businesses are a restaurant, a convenience store, and a small retail store.

Describe the allowance method of accounting for uncollectible receivables.

ALLOWANCE METHOD FOR UNCOLLECTIBLE ACCOUNTS

As we mentioned earlier, the allowance method is required by generally accepted accounting principles for companies with large accounts receivable. As a result, most well-known companies such as General Electric, PepsiCo, Inc., Intel, and Federal Express use the allowance method.

© STOCKDISC CLASSIC/GETTY IMAGES

As discussed in the preceding section, the direct write-off method records bad debt expense only when an account is determined to be worthless. In contrast, the allowance method estimates the accounts receivable that will not be collected and records bad debt expense for this estimate at the end of each accounting period. Based upon this estimate, bad debt expense is then recorded by an adjusting entry.

To illustrate, assume that ExTone Company began operations in August and chose to use the calendar year as its fiscal year. As of December 31, 2007, ExTone Company has an accounts receivable balance of $1,000,000 that includes some accounts that are past due. However,

ExTone doesn't know which customer accounts will be uncollectible. Based upon industry data, ExTone estimates that $40,000 of its accounts receivable will be uncollectible. Using this estimate, the following adjusting entry is made on December 31:

SCF	BS	IS
—	A↓ SE↓	E↑

Dec. 31	Bad Debt Expense	40,000	
	Allowance for Doubtful Accounts		40,000

Since the $40,000 reduction in accounts receivable is an estimate, specific customer accounts cannot be reduced or credited. Instead, a contra asset account entitled **Allowance for Doubtful Accounts** is credited.

As with all adjustments, the preceding adjusting entry affects the balance sheet and income statement. First, the adjusting entry records $40,000 of bad debt expense, which will be matched against the related revenues of the period on the income statement. Second, the adjusting entry reduces the value of the receivables to the amount of cash expected to be realized in the future. This amount, $960,000 ($1,000,000 − $40,000), is called the **net realizable value** of the receivables. The net realizable value of the receivables is reported on the balance sheet.

Q. If the balance of accounts receivable is $380,000 and the balance of the allowance for doubtful accounts is $56,000, what is the net realizable value of the receivables?

A. *$324,000 ($380,000 − $56,000)*

You should note that after the preceding adjusting entry has been recorded, Accounts Receivable still has a debit balance of $1,000,000. This balance represents the total amount owed by customers on account and is supported by the individual customer accounts in the accounts receivable subsidiary ledger. The accounts receivable contra account, Allowance for Doubtful Accounts, has a credit balance of $40,000.

Write-Offs to the Allowance Account

When a customer's account is identified as uncollectible, it is written off against the allowance account. This requires the company to remove the specific accounts receivable and an equal amount from the allowance account. For example, on January 21, 2008, John Parker's account of $6,000 with ExTone Company is written off as follows:

SCF	BS	IS
—	A↑↓	—

Jan. 21	Allowance for Doubtful Accounts	6,000	
	Accounts Receivable—John Parker		6,000

At the end of a period, the Allowance for Doubtful Accounts will normally have a balance. This is because the Allowance for Doubtful Accounts is based upon an estimate. As a result, the total write-offs to the allowance account during the period will rarely equal the balance of the account at the beginning of the period. The allowance account will have a credit balance at the end of the period if the write-offs during the period are less than the beginning balance. It will have a debit balance if the write-offs exceed the beginning balance.

To illustrate, assume that during 2008 ExTone Company writes off $36,750 of uncollectible accounts, including the $6,000 account of John Parker recorded on January 21. The Allowance for Doubtful Accounts will have a credit balance of $3,250 ($40,000 − $36,750), as shown below.

ALLOWANCE FOR DOUBTFUL ACCOUNTS

			Jan. 1, 2008 Bal.	40,000
Total accounts written off $36,750	Jan. 21	6,000		
	Feb. 2	3,900		
	⋮	⋮		
			Dec. 31, 2008 Unadjusted balance	3,250

If ExTone Company had written off $44,100 in accounts receivable during 2008, the Allowance for Doubtful Accounts would have a debit balance of $4,100, as shown below.

ALLOWANCE FOR DOUBTFUL ACCOUNTS

			Jan. 1, 2008 Bal.	40,000
Total accounts written off $44,100	Jan. 21	6,000		
	Feb. 2	3,900		
	.	.		
	.	.		
	.	.		
Dec. 31, 2008 Unadjusted balance		4,100		

You should note that the allowance account balances (credit balance of $3,250 and debit balance of $4,100) in the preceding illustrations are *before* the end-of-the-period adjusting entry. After the end-of-the-period adjusting entry is recorded, Allowance for Doubtful Accounts should always have a credit balance.

What happens if an account receivable that has been written off against the allowance account is later collected? Like the direct write-off method, the account is reinstated by an entry that reverses the write-off entry. The cash received in payment is then recorded as a receipt on account.

To illustrate, assume that Nancy Smith's account of $5,000 which was written off on April 2 is later collected on June 10. ExTone Company records the reinstatement and the collection as follows:

SCF	BS	IS
—	A↑↓	—
O↑	A↑↓	—

June 10	Accounts Receivable—Nancy Smith	5,000	
	Allowance for Doubtful Accounts		5,000
10	Cash	5,000	
	Accounts Receivable—Nancy Smith		5,000

Estimating Uncollectibles

As we indicated earlier in this section, the allowance method estimates bad debt expense at the end of the period. How is the amount of uncollectible accounts estimated? The estimate of uncollectibles at the end of a fiscal period is based on past experience and forecasts of the future. When the general economy is doing well, the estimate of bad debt expense is normally less than it would be when the economy is doing poorly.

Two methods are commonly used to estimate uncollectible accounts receivable at the end of the period. The estimate may be based upon (1) a percent of sales or (2) an analysis of the receivables. We describe and illustrate each method next.

Estimate Based on Percent of Sales. Since accounts receivable are created by credit sales, bad debt expense can be estimated as a percent of credit sales. To illustrate, assume that on December 31, 2008, the Allowance for Doubtful Accounts for ExTone Company has a credit balance of $3,250. In addition, ExTone estimates that $1\frac{1}{2}$% of 2008 credit sales will be uncollectible. If credit sales for the year are $3,000,000, the adjusting entry for uncollectible accounts on December 31 is as follows:

SCF	BS	IS
—	A↓ SE↓	E↑

Dec. 31	Bad Debt Expense	45,000	
	Allowance for Doubtful Accounts		45,000
	($3,000,000 × 0.015 = $45,000)		

After the preceding adjusting entry is posted to the ledger, Bad Debt Expense will have a balance of $45,000, and the Allowance for Doubtful Accounts will have a balance of $48,250, as shown on page 361.

BAD DEBT EXPENSE

Dec. 31	Adjusting entry	45,000	
Dec. 31	Adjusted balance	45,000	

ALLOWANCE FOR DOUBTFUL ACCOUNTS

			Jan. 1, 2008	Bal.	40,000
Total accounts written off $36,750	Jan. 21	6,000			
	Feb. 2	3,900			
	.	.			
			Dec. 31	Unadjusted balance	3,250
			Dec. 31	Adjusting entry	45,000
			Dec. 31	Adjusted balance	48,250

Q. Before the year-end adjustment, the Allowance for Doubtful Accounts has a credit balance of $45,000. Uncollectible accounts are estimated as 2% of credit sales of $1,200,000. The accounts receivable balance before adjustment is $290,000. What is (1) the bad debt expense for the period, (2) the balance of the Allowance for Doubtful Accounts after adjustment, and (3) the net realizable value of the receivables after adjustment?

A. *(1) $24,000 (2% × $1,200,000); (2) $69,000 ($24,000 + $45,000); and (3) $221,000 ($290,000 – $69,000)*

As shown above, after the adjusting entry is recorded, the Allowance for Doubtful Accounts has a credit balance of $48,250. If there had been a debit balance of $4,100 in the allowance account before the year-end adjustment, the amount of the adjustment would still have been $45,000. However, the December 31 ending balance of the allowance account would have been $40,900 ($45,000 – $4,100). In other words, under the percent of sales method, the bad debt expense is credited to whatever balance exists in the Allowance for Doubtful Accounts.

Estimate Based on Analysis of Receivables. The longer an account receivable is outstanding, the less likely that it will be collected. Thus, we can base the estimate of uncollectible accounts on how long specific accounts have been outstanding. For this purpose, we can use a process called **aging the receivables**.

Receivables are aged by preparing a schedule that classifies each customer's receivable by its due date. The number of days an account is past due is the number of days between the due date of the account and the date the aging schedule is prepared. To illustrate, assume that Rodriguez Company is preparing an aging schedule for its accounts receivable of $86,300 as of August 31, 2008. The $160 account receivable for Saxon Woods Company was due on May 29. As of August 31, Saxon's account is 94 days past due, as shown below.

Number of days past due in May	2 days	(31 – 29)
Number of days past due in June	30 days	
Number of days past due in July	31 days	
Number of days past due in August	31 days	
Total number of days past due	94 days	

A portion of the aging schedule for Rodriguez Company is shown in Exhibit 1. The schedule shows the total amount of receivables in each aging class.

Rodriguez Company uses a sliding scale of percentages, based on industry or company experience, to estimate the amount of uncollectibles in each aging class. As shown in Exhibit 2, the percent estimated as uncollectible increases the longer the account is past due. For accounts not past due, the percent is 2%, while for accounts over 365 days past due the percent is 80%. The total of these amounts is the desired end-of-the-period balance for the Allowance for Doubtful Accounts. For Rodriguez Company, the desired August 31 balance of the Allowance for Doubtful Accounts is $3,390.

Comparing the estimate of $3,390 with the unadjusted balance of the allowance account determines the amount of the adjustment for bad debt expense. For example, assume that the unadjusted balance of the allowance account is a credit balance of

Exhibit 1

Aging of Accounts Receivable

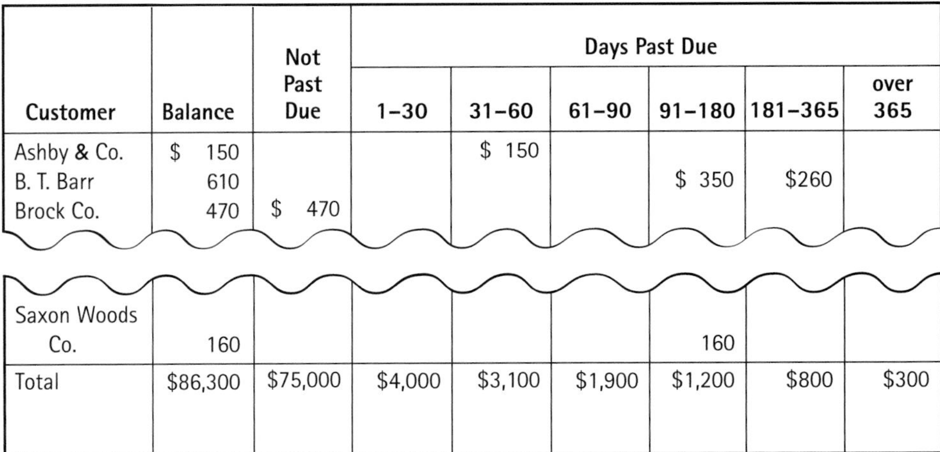

Customer	Balance	Not Past Due	Days Past Due					
			1–30	31–60	61–90	91–180	181–365	over 365
Ashby & Co.	$ 150			$ 150				
B. T. Barr	610					$ 350	$260	
Brock Co.	470	$ 470						
Saxon Woods Co.	160					160		
Total	$86,300	$75,000	$4,000	$3,100	$1,900	$1,200	$800	$300

Exhibit 2

Estimate of Uncollectible Accounts

Age Interval	Balance	Estimated Uncollectible Accounts Percent	Estimated Uncollectible Accounts Amount
Not past due	$75,000	2%	$1,500
1–30 days past due	4,000	5	200
31–60 days past due	3,100	10	310
61–90 days past due	1,900	20	380
91–180 days past due	1,200	30	360
181–365 days past due	800	50	400
Over 365 days past due	300	80	240
Total	$86,300		$3,390

$510. The amount to be added to this balance is therefore $2,880 ($3,390 − $510), and the adjusting entry is as follows:

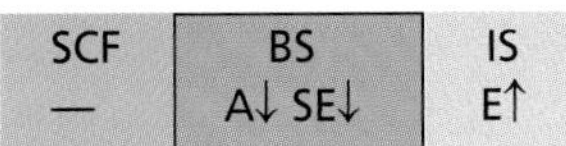

SCF	BS	IS
—	A↓ SE↓	E↑

Aug. 31	Bad Debt Expense	2,880	
	Allowance for Doubtful Accounts		2,880

After the preceding adjusting entry is posted to the ledger, Bad Debt Expense will have a balance of $2,880, and the Allowance for Doubtful Accounts will have a balance of $3,390, as shown below.

BAD DEBT EXPENSE

Aug. 31	Adjusting entry	2,880	
Aug. 31	Adjusted balance	2,880	

ALLOWANCE FOR DOUBTFUL ACCOUNTS

	Aug. 31	Unadusted balance	510
	Aug. 31	Adjusting entry	2,880
	Aug. 31	Adjusted balance	3,390

As shown above, after the adjustment is recorded, the balance of the bad debt expense account is $2,880, and the balance of the allowance account is $3,390. The net realizable value of the receivables is $82,910 ($86,300 − $3,390).

If the unadjusted balance of the allowance account had been a debit balance of $300, the amount of the adjustment would have been $3,690 ($3,390 + $300). In this case, the bad debt expense account would have a $3,690 balance, but the balance of the allowance account would still have been $3,390, as shown below.

BAD DEBT EXPENSE

		Debit			Credit
Aug. 31	Adjusting entry	3,690			
Aug. 31	Adjusted balance	3,690			

ALLOWANCE FOR DOUBTFUL ACCOUNTS

		Debit			Credit
Aug. 31	Unadjusted balance	300			
			Aug. 31	Adjusting entry	3,690
			Aug. 31	Adjusted balance	3,390

Q. Before the year-end adjustment, the Allowance for Doubtful Accounts has a debit balance of $3,000. Using the aging-of-receivables method, the desired balance of the allowance for doubtful accounts is estimated as $55,000. The accounts receivable balance before adjustment is $290,000. What is (1) the bad debt expense for the period, (2) the balance of the Allowance for Doubtful Accounts after adjustment, and (3) the net realizable value of the receivables after adjustment?

A. (1) $58,000 ($3,000 + $55,000); (2) $55,000; and (3) $235,000 ($290,000 − $55,000)

Comparing Estimation Methods. The percent of sales and analysis of receivables methods of estimating uncollectible accounts can be compared in two different ways. First, the methods can be compared based on their financial statement emphasis. Second, the methods can be compared based on whether bad debt expense or the Allowance for Doubtful Accounts is the focus of the estimate.

The percent of sales method emphasizes the matching of bad debts expense with the related credit sales of the period. In doing so, the percent of sales method places more emphasis on the income statement. The analysis of receivables method emphasizes the end-of-the-period net realizable value of the receivables and the related balance of the allowance account. Thus, the analysis of receivables method places more emphasis on the balance sheet.

Under the percent of sales method, bad debt expense is the focus of the estimation process. In other words, the percent of sales method emphasizes obtaining the best estimate for bad debt expense for the period. The ending balance for Allowance for Doubtful Accounts becomes the end result of estimating bad debt expense. For example, in the ExTone Company illustration, bad debt expense was estimated as $45,000 ($3,000,000 × $1\frac{1}{2}$%). In recording this estimate, $45,000 was credited to the Allowance for Doubtful Accounts. Since the Allowance for Doubtful Accounts had an unadjusted credit balance of $3,250, its ending balance became a credit balance of $48,250.

In contrast, the analysis of receivables method focuses the estimation process on obtaining the best estimate for the Allowance for Doubtful Accounts. Bad debt expense becomes the end result of estimating the Allowance for Doubtful Accounts. For example, in the Rodriguez Company illustration, the adjusted balance for the Allowance for Doubtful Accounts was estimated using the aging method as $3,390. Since the Allowance for Doubtful Accounts had an unadjusted credit balance of $510, it was credited for $2,880 ($3,390 − $510). The corresponding debit of $2,880 was to Bad Debt Expense. Thus, the ending balance of Bad Debt Expense becomes $2,880.

The following table summarizes the differences between the percent of sales and the analysis of receivables methods.

	Percent of Sales Method	Analysis of Receivables Method
Financial statement emphasis	Income statement	Balance sheet
Focus of estimate	Bad debt expense	Allowance for doubtful accounts
End result of estimate	Balance of Allowance for Doubtful Accounts	Bad debt expense

Compare the direct write-off and allowance methods of accounting for uncollectible accounts.

COMPARING DIRECT WRITE-OFF AND ALLOWANCE METHODS

In this section, we will illustrate the journal entries for the direct write-off and allowance methods. As a basis for our illustration, we will use the following selected transactions, which were taken from the records of Hobbs Company for the year ending December 31, 2007:

Mar. 1	Wrote off account of C. York, $3,650.	
Apr. 12	Received $2,250 as partial payment on the $5,500 account of Cary Bradshaw. Wrote off the remaining balance as uncollectible.	
June 22	Received the $3,650 from C. York, which had been written off on March 1. Reinstated the account and recorded the cash receipt.	
Sept. 7	Wrote off the following accounts as uncollectible (record as one journal entry):	
	Jason Bigg	$1,100
	Steve Bradey	2,220
	Samantha Neeley	775
	Stanford Noonan	1,360
	Aiden Wyman	990
Dec. 31	Hobbs Company uses the percent of credit sales method of estimating uncollectible expenses. Based upon past history and industry averages, 1.25% of credit sales are expected to be uncollectible. Hobbs recorded $3,400,000 of credit sales during 2007.	

Exhibit 3 illustrates the journal entries that would have been recorded for Hobbs Company using the direct write-off method and the allowance method. Using the direct write-off method, there is no adjusting entry on December 31 for uncollectible accounts.

Exhibit 3

Comparing Direct Write-Off and Allowance Methods

Date	Direct Write-Off Method			Allowance Method		
Mar. 1	Bad Debt Expense	3,650		Allowance for Doubtful Accounts	3,650	
	Accounts Receivable—C. York		3,650	Accounts Receivable—C. York		3,650
Apr. 12	Cash	2,250		Cash	2,250	
	Bad Debt Expense	3,250		Allowance for Doubtful Accounts	3,250	
	Accounts Receivable—Cary Bradshaw		5,500	Accounts Receivable—Cary Bradshaw		5,500
June 22	Accounts Receivable—C. York	3,650		Accounts Receivable—C. York	3,650	
	Bad Debt Expense		3,650	Allowance for Doubtful Accounts		3,650
22	Cash	3,650		Cash	3,650	
	Accounts Receivable—C. York		3,650	Accounts Receivable—C. York		3,650
Sept. 7	Bad Debt Expense	6,445		Allowance for Doubtful Accounts	6,445	
	Accounts Receivable—Jason Bigg		1,100	Accounts Receivable—Jason Bigg		1,100
	Accounts Receivable—Steve Bradey		2,220	Accounts Receivable—Steve Bradey		2,220
	Accounts Receivable—Samantha Neeley		775	Accounts Receivable—Samantha Neeley		775
	Accounts Receivable—Stanford Noonan		1,360	Accounts Receivable—Stanford Noonan		1,360
	Accounts Receivable—Aiden Wyman		990	Accounts Receivable—Aiden Wyman		990
Dec. 31	No entry			Bad Debt Expense	42,500	
				Allowance for Doubtful Accounts		42,500
				($3,400,000 × 0.0125 = $42,500)		

In contrast, the allowance method records an adjusting entry for estimated uncollectible accounts of $42,500.

The primary differences between these two methods are summarized in the table below.

Comparing the Direct Write-Off and Allowance Methods

	Direct Write-Off Method	**Allowance Method**
Amount of bad debt expense recorded	When the actual accounts receivable determined to be uncollectible	Using estimate based on either (1) a percent of sales or (2) analysis of receivables
Allowance account	No allowance account is used	The allowance account is used
Primary users	Small companies and companies with relatively few receivables	Large companies and those with a large amount of receivables

INTEGRITY, OBJECTIVITY, AND ETHICS IN BUSINESS

Receivables Fraud

Financial reporting frauds are often tied to accounts receivable, because receivables allow companies to record revenue before cash is received. Take, for example, the case of entrepreneur Michael Weinstein, who acquired **Coated Sales, Inc.** with the dream of growing the small specialty company into a major corporation. To acquire funding that would facilitate this growth, Weinstein had to artificially boost the company's sales. He accomplished this by adding millions in false accounts receivable to existing customer accounts.

The company's auditors began to sense a problem when they called one of the Company's customers to confirm a large order. When the customer denied placing the order, the auditors began to investigate the company's receivables more closely. Their analysis revealed a fraud which overstated profits by $55 million and forced the company into bankruptcy, costing investors and creditors over $160 million.

Source: Joseph T. Wells, "Follow Fraud to the Likely Perpetrator," *The Journal of Accountancy*, March 2001.

Describe the nature, characteristics, and accounting for notes receivable.

NOTES RECEIVABLE

A claim supported by a note has some advantages over a claim in the form of an account receivable. By signing a note, the debtor recognizes the debt and agrees to pay it according to the terms listed. A note is thus a stronger legal claim.

Characteristics of Notes Receivable

A note receivable, or promissory note, is a written promise to pay a sum of money (face amount) on demand or at a definite time. It can be payable either to an individual or a business, or to the bearer or holder of the note. It is signed by the person or firm that makes the promise. The one to whose order the note is payable is called the *payee*, and the one making the promise is called the *maker*.

The date a note is to be paid is called the *due date* or *maturity date*. The period of time between the issuance date and the due date of a short-term note may be stated in either days or months. When the term of a note is stated in days, the due date is the specified number of days after its issuance. To illustrate, the due date of a 90-day note dated March 16 is June 14, as shown below.

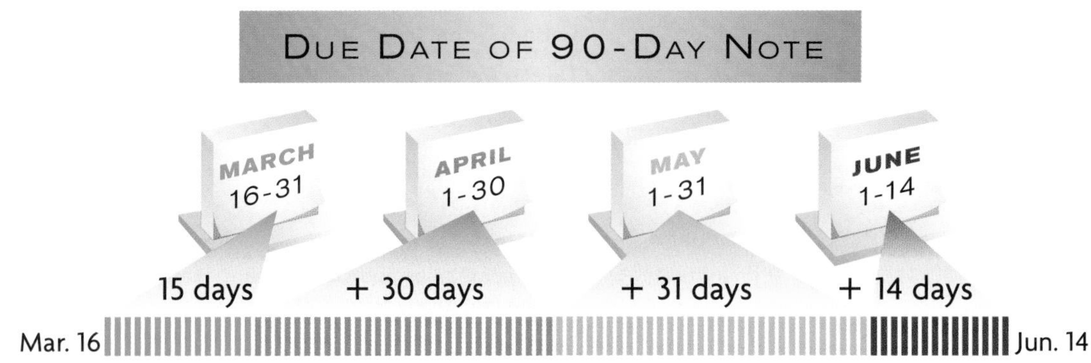

Q. What is the due date of a 120-day note receivable dated September 9?

A. *January 7 [21 days in September (30 days − 9 days) + 31 days in October + 30 days in November + 31 days in December + 7 days in January = 120 days]*

Q. What is the maturity value of a $15,000, 90-day, 12% note?

A. *$15,450 [$15,000 + ($15,000 × 0.12 × 90/360)]*

The term of a note may be stated as a certain number of months after the issuance date. In such cases, the due date is determined by counting the number of months from the issuance date. For example, a three-month note dated June 5 would be due on September 5. A two-month note dated July 31 would be due on September 30.

A note normally specifies that interest be paid for the period between the issuance date and the due date.[2] Notes covering a period of time longer than one year normally provide for interest to be paid annually, semiannually, quarterly, or monthly. When the term of the note is less than one year, the interest is usually payable at the time the note is paid.

The interest rate on notes is normally stated in terms of a year, regardless of the actual period of time involved. Thus, the interest on $2,000 for one year at 12% is $240 (12% × $2,000). The interest on $2,000 for 90 days at 12% is $60 ($2,000 × 12% × 90/360). To simplify computations, we will use 360 days per year. In practice, companies such as banks and mortgage companies use the exact number of days in a year, 365.

The amount that is due at the maturity or due date of a note receivable is its **maturity value**. The maturity value of a note is the sum of the face amount and the interest. For example, the maturity value of a $25,000, 9%, 120-day note receivable is $25,750 [$25,000 + ($25,000 × 9% × 120/360)].

Accounting for Notes Receivable

A customer may use a note to replace an account receivable. To illustrate, assume that a company accepts a 30-day, 12% note dated November 21, 2008, in settlement of the account of W. A. Bunn Co., which is past due and has a balance of $6,000. The company records the receipt of the note as follows:

SCF	BS	IS
—	A↑↓	—

Nov. 21	Notes Receivable—W. A. Bunn Co.	6,000	
	Accounts Receivable—W. A. Bunn Co.		6,000

2 You may occasionally see references to non-interest-bearing notes receivable. Such notes are not widely used and carry an assumed or implicit interest rate.

When the note matures, the company records the receipt of $6,060 ($6,000 principal plus $60 interest) as follows:

Dec. 21	Cash	6,060	
	Notes Receivable—W. A. Bunn Co.		6,000
	Interest Revenue		60

If the maker of a note fails to pay the debt on the due date, the note is a **dishonored note receivable**. A company that holds a dishonored note transfers the face value of the note plus any interest due back to an accounts receivable account. For example, assume that the $6,000, 30-day, 12% note received from W. A. Bunn Co. and recorded on November 21 is dishonored at maturity. The company holding the note transfers the note and interest back to the customer's account as follows:

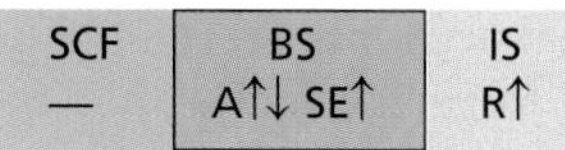

Dec. 21	Accounts Receivable—W. A. Bunn Co.	6,060	
	Notes Receivable—W. A. Bunn Co.		6,000
	Interest Revenue		60

The company has earned the interest of $60, even though the note is dishonored. If the account receivable is uncollectible, the company will write off $6,060 against the Allowance for Doubtful Accounts.

If a note matures in a later fiscal period, the company holding the note records an adjustment for the interest accrued in the period in which the note is received. For example, assume that Crawford Company uses a 90-day, 12% note dated December 1, 2008, to settle its account, which has a balance of $4,000. Assuming that the accounting period ends on December 31, the holder of the note records the transactions as follows:

SCF	BS	IS
—	A↑↓	—
—	A↑ SE↑	R↑
O↑	A↑↓ SE↑	R↑

2008				
Dec.	1	Notes Receivable—Crawford Company	4,000	
		Accounts Receivable—Crawford Company		4,000
	31	Interest Receivable	40	
		Interest Revenue		40
2009				
Mar.	1	Cash	4,120	
		Notes Receivable—Crawford Company		4,000
		Interest Receivable		40
		Interest Revenue		80

The interest revenue account is closed at the end of each accounting period. The amount of interest revenue is normally reported in the Other Income section of the income statement.

Describe the reporting of receivables on the balance sheet.

REPORTING RECEIVABLES ON THE BALANCE SHEET

All receivables expected to be realized in cash within a year are presented in the Current Assets section of the balance sheet. These assets are normally listed in the order of their liquidity, that is, the order in which they are expected to be converted to

International Perspective Under International Accounting Standards, current assets are shown in reverse order of liquidity on the balance sheet. As a result, inventories are typically one of the first assets displayed in the Current Assets section, and cash and cash equivalents is typically the last item displayed.

cash during normal operations. The receivables are presented on Starbucks' balance sheet, as shown below.[3]

Assets (in millions)	Oct. 3, 2004	Sept. 28, 2003
Current assets:		
Cash and cash equivalents	$ 299.1	$200.9
Marketable securities	353.8	149.1
Accounts receivable, net of allowances of $2.2 and $4.8, respectively	140.2	114.4
Inventories	422.7	342.9
Prepaid expenses and other current assets	135.0	102.6
Total current assets	$1,350.8	$909.9

Starbucks reports net accounts receivable of $140.2 and $114.5. The allowances for doubtful accounts of $2.2 and $4.8 are subtracted from the total accounts receivable to arrive at the net receivables. Alternatively, the allowances for each year could be shown in a note to the financial statements.

Other disclosures related to receivables are presented either on the face of the financial statements or in the accompanying notes.[4] Such disclosures include the market (fair) value of the receivables if significantly different from the reported value. In addition, if unusual credit risks exist within the receivables, the nature of the risks should be disclosed. For example, if the majority of the receivables are due from one customer or are due from customers located in one area of the country or one industry, these facts should be disclosed.

Starbucks did not report any unusual credit risks related to its receivables. However, the following credit risk disclosure appeared in the 2004 financial statements of Deere & Company:

> *Trade accounts and notes receivable have significant concentrations of credit risk in the agricultural, commercial and consumer, and construction and forestry sectors. The portion of credit receivables related to the agricultural business was 57%, that related to commercial and consumer business was 25%, and that related to the construction and forestry business was 18%. On a geographic basis, there is not a disproportionate concentration of credit risk in any area.*

Describe the principles of managing accounts receivable.

MANAGING ACCOUNTS RECEIVABLE

Businesses grant credit in order to earn additional profits from customers who would otherwise not purchase the company's goods or services. Thus, the overall objective of managing accounts receivable is to help the company earn profits. The basic steps in managing accounts receivable include the following:

1. Screening customers
2. Determining credit terms
3. Monitoring collections

3 Adapted from Starbucks Corporation amended 10-K for the year ended October 3, 2004.

4 *Statement of Financial Accounting Standards No. 105*, "Disclosures of Information about Financial Instruments with Off-Balance Sheet Risk and Financial Instruments with Concentrations of Credit Risk," and *No. 107*, "Disclosures about Fair Value of Financial Instruments" (Norwalk, CT: Financial Accounting Standards Board).

Screening Customers

Screening customers involves assessing which customers should be granted credit. Too strict a credit-screening process causes the company to lose revenues and profits from customers who would otherwise pay their accounts on time. Too loose a credit-screening process causes the company to extend credit to customers who do not pay. Not only does the company lose any profits on nonpaying customers, but the company also incurs the expense of providing the goods or services to the customers as well as the additional expense of trying to collect the amounts due. For this reason, too loose a credit-screening process can be more costly than too tight a policy.

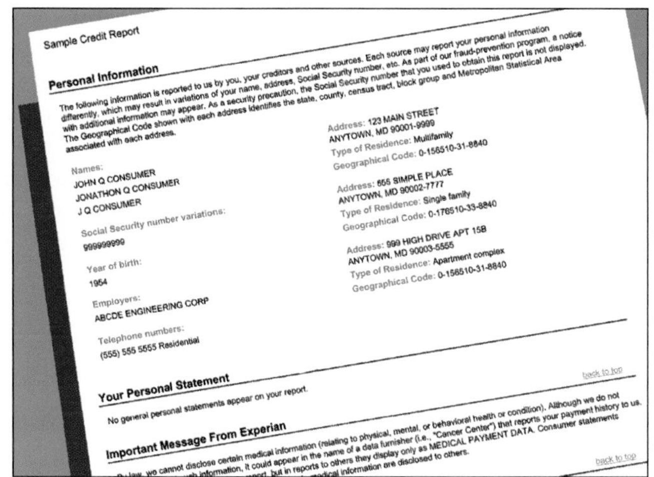

Most businesses have formal credit-screening procedures that include customer-submitted documentation of creditworthiness. For example, if you apply for a credit card, you have to fill out an application form. Likewise, if you apply for a student loan or home mortgage, you have to fill out a loan application form. In addition, loan applications normally require the customer to also submit other documents, such as recent tax returns or bank statements.

Business customers that apply for credit often are asked to submit recent financial statements with their credit applications. Sometimes the seller will also require a letter of credit from the business's bank. The letter of credit documents that the business has funds available to pay the seller. Letters of credit are often required when a buyer is purchasing goods from overseas sellers. In rare cases, a seller may also require the customer's bank to guarantee the credit of the buyer.

Once the seller receives the buyer's credit application and documents, the seller analyzes the buyer's creditworthiness. In addition to analyzing the application and documents submitted by the buyer, the seller usually requests an independent credit report and often will contact the buyer's banking and other credit references. The *Dun & Bradstreet Reference Book of American Business* provides credit ratings for many business customers. The amount of analysis for a customer will, of course, vary with the size of the buyer's purchases. For example, credit card applications with credit limits of $1,500 do not receive as much analysis and independent verification as a business's credit application for a $500,000 purchase.

Determining Credit Terms

Once a seller has decided to grant credit to a buyer, the seller must determine credit terms for the sale. Credit terms include determining the amount of credit, called the *credit limit*, and the payment terms. The credit limit is set consistent with the creditworthiness of the customer. New customers often receive a small limit that is increased over time as the customer pays accounts and thus establishes a good credit history with the seller.

The payment terms are often set so that they are consistent with the seller's industry and competitors. For example, MasterCard and VISA's payment terms require full or partial payment within 30 days. Any amounts due after 30 days are subject to interest charges. Likewise, businesses often set payment terms of 2/10, n/30. As we discussed in Chapter 5, these terms offer the buyer a 2% discount if the invoice is paid within 10 days, with the entire amount due within 30 days. Regardless of the payment terms, the seller should communicate them to the buyer at the time of sale. In most cases, the payment terms are stated on the sales invoice.

Monitoring Collections

Effective internal controls over receivables and credit granting require the seller to monitor collections of receivables on a routine basis. One means of monitoring receivables and collections is to prepare an aging schedule. We illustrated the aging of receivables earlier in this chapter.

In some cases, a company in financial distress will still try to purchase goods and services on account. In these cases, sellers must be careful in advancing credit to such companies, because trade creditors have low priority in the event of bankruptcy. To help sellers avoid extending credit to such companies, third-party services specialize in evaluating financially distressed customers. These services analyze the credit risk of buyers by evaluating recent management payment decisions (who is getting paid and when), court actions (if in bankruptcy), and other supplier credit tightening or suspension actions. Such information helps a seller monitor and determine trade credit amounts and terms with financially distressed customers.

Compute and interpret the accounts receivable turnover and the number of days' sales in receivables.

ACCOUNTS RECEIVABLE TURNOVER AND DAYS' SALES IN RECEIVABLES

In addition to preparing an aging of receivables schedule and monitoring concentrations of credit risk, several financial statement ratios are also useful in monitoring receivables and their collection. Two of these ratios are described and illustrated in the following paragraphs.

Businesses granting long credit terms normally have relatively greater amounts committed to accounts receivable than those granting short credit terms. In either case, businesses normally desire to collect receivables as promptly as possible. The cash collected from receivables improves solvency and lessens the risk of loss from uncollectible accounts. Two financial measures that are especially useful in evaluating efficiency in collecting receivables are (1) the accounts receivable turnover and (2) the number of days' sales in receivables.

The **accounts receivable turnover** measures how frequently during the year the accounts receivable are being converted to cash. For example, with credit terms of 2/10, n/30, the accounts receivable should turn over more than 12 times per year. The accounts receivable turnover is computed as follows:[5]

$$\text{Accounts Receivable Turnover} = \frac{\text{Net Sales}}{\text{Average Accounts Receivable}}$$

The average accounts receivable can be determined by using monthly data or by simply adding the beginning and ending accounts receivable balances and dividing by two. For example, using the following financial data (in millions) for Starbucks, the 2004 accounts receivable turnover is computed as 41.6.

5 If known, credit sales can be used in the numerator. However, because credit sales are not normally disclosed to external users, most analysts use net sales in the numerator.

	Oct. 3, 2004	Sept. 28, 2003	Sept. 29, 2002
Net sales	$5,294.2	$4,075.5	—
Net accounts receivable	140.2	114.4	$97.6

$$\text{Accounts Receivable Turnover} = \frac{\text{Net Sales}}{\text{Average Accounts Receivable}}$$

$$= \frac{\$5{,}294.2}{(\$140.2 + \$114.4)/2} = 41.6$$

By computing the accounts receivable turnover for the prior year, shown below, we can determine whether Starbucks' management of accounts receivable has improved.

$$\text{Accounts Receivable Turnover} = \frac{\text{Net Sales}}{\text{Average Accounts Receivable}}$$

$$= \frac{\$4{,}075.5}{(\$114.4 + \$97.6)/2} = 38.5$$

The 2003 accounts receivable turnover for Starbucks is 38.5. Thus, Starbucks improved its management of accounts receivable slightly during fiscal year 2004.

The **number of days' sales in receivables** is an estimate of the length of time the accounts receivable have been outstanding. With credit terms of 2/10, n/30, the number of days' sales in receivables should be less than 20 days. It is computed as follows:

$$\text{Number of Days' Sales in Receivables} = \frac{\text{Average Accounts Receivable}}{\text{Average Daily Sales}}$$

Average daily sales are determined by dividing net sales by 365 days. For example, using the preceding data for Starbucks, the number of days' sales in receivables is 8.8 days and 9.5 days for 2004 and 2003, as shown below.

	2004	2003
Net sales	$5,294.2	$4,075.5
Accounts receivable	140.2	114.4
Average accounts receivable	127.3 [($140.2 + 114.4) ÷ 2]	106.0 [($114.4 + $97.6) ÷ 2]
Accounts receivable turnover	41.6 ($5,294.2 ÷ $127.3)	38.5 ($4,075.5 ÷ 106)
Average daily sales	14.5 ($5,294.2 ÷ 365)	11.2 ($4,075.5 ÷ 365)
Days' sales in receivables	8.8 ($127.3 ÷ 14.5)	9.5 ($106 ÷ 11.2)

The number of days' sales in receivables confirms the accounts receivable turnover by declining slightly during 2004. Generally, this would be viewed as a favorable trend. That is, the efficiency in collecting accounts receivable has improved when the number of days' sales in receivables decreases. However, these measures should also be compared with similar companies within the industry. For example, Peet's Coffee and Tea Inc. is a specialty coffee roaster, wholesaler, and retailer. Peet's reports an accounts receivable turnover of 41.6 and 8.8 days' sales in receivables. Thus, Peet's accounts receivable turnover and days' sales in receivables are virtually identical to that of Starbucks, indicating a very similar accounts receivable collection experience between the two companies.

FOCUS ON CASH FLOW

Accounts Receivable and Cash Flows

Most retail companies sell merchandise for cash and on account. When merchandise is sold on account, an account receivable is recorded. If accounts receivable increase from one period to the next, then the amount of revenue shown on the income statement does not represent the amount of cash received from revenue during the period. Instead, part of the revenue includes sales on account (accounts receivable) not collected during the period. Thus, to determine the cash flows from revenue activities, any increase or decrease in accounts receivable must be considered.

For example, assume that Bower Company reports total revenues of $760,000 during 2008 and that accounts receivable increased during the year from $45,000 to $63,000. Thus, the amount of cash received from Bower's revenues during 2008 is not $760,000, but rather $742,000. That is, of the $760,000 of total revenue during the year, $18,000 ($63,000 − $45,000) represents revenue that was created by increasing sales on account. Likewise, assume that instead of increasing by $18,000, Bower's accounts receivable had decreased by $15,000 (from $45,000 to $30,000) during 2008. In this case, the cash received from revenue activities would have been $775,000 ($760,000 + $15,000).

In reporting cash flows from operating activities on the statement of cash flows, companies are required to reconcile net income with cash flows from operating activities. In doing so, companies must consider the effect of increases and decreases of their accounts receivable on their cash flows from revenue activities. As illustrated above, if accounts receivable increase, the increase must be deducted in arriving at cash flows. During 2004, **Starbucks'** accounts receivable increased by $25.8 ($140.2 − $114.4). Thus, on its statement of cash flows, Starbucks must deduct this increase to arrive at cash flows from operating activities, as shown below.[6]

(in millions)	
Net earnings	$390.6
Increase in accounts receivable	(25.8)
~~	
Net cash provided by operating activities	820.2

6 Adapted from Starbucks Corporation Form 10-K filing with the Securities and Exchange Commission. Small differences in reported amounts may appear due to reclassifications within the financial statements.

SUMMARY OF LEARNING GOALS

(1) **Describe the common classifications of receivables.** The term *receivables* includes all money claims against other entities, including people, business firms, and other organizations. Receivables are normally classified as accounts receivable, notes receivable, or other receivables.

(2) **Describe the nature of and the accounting for uncollectible receivables.** The two methods of accounting for uncollectible receivables are the direct write-off method and the allowance method. The direct write-off method recognizes the expense only when the account is judged to be uncollectible. The allowance method provides in advance for uncollectible receivables.

(3) **Describe the direct write-off method of accounting for uncollectible receivables.** Under the direct write-off method, the entry to write off an account debits Bad Debt Expense and credits Accounts Receivable. Neither an allowance account nor an adjusting entry is needed at the end of the period.

(4) **Describe the allowance method of accounting for uncollectible receivables.** A year-end adjusting entry provides for (1) the reduction of the value of the receivables to the amount of cash expected to be realized from them in the future and (2) the allocation to the current period of the expected expense resulting from such reduction. The adjusting entry debits Bad Debt Expense and credits Allowance for Doubtful Accounts. When an account is believed to be uncollectible, it is written off against the allowance account.

When the estimate of uncollectibles is based on the amount of sales for the period, the adjusting entry is made without regard to the balance of the allowance account. When the estimate of uncollectibles is based on the amount and the age of the receivable accounts at the end of the period, the adjusting entry is recorded so that the balance of the allowance account will equal the estimated uncollectibles at the end of the period.

The allowance account, which will have a credit balance after the adjusting entry has been posted, is a contra asset account. The bad debt expense is generally reported on the income statement as an administrative expense.

5 Compare the direct write-off and allowance methods of accounting for uncollectible accounts. The two methods of accounting for uncollectible accounts are recorded differently in the accounts and presented differently in the financial statements. Under the direct write-off method, bad debt expense is equal to the amount of accounts receivable written off during the period. Alternatively, under the allowance method, bad debt expense is estimated based on either a percent of sales or an analysis of receivables.

6 Describe the nature, characteristics, and accounting for notes receivable. A note is a written promise to pay a sum of money on demand or at a definite time. Characteristics of notes that affect how they are recorded and reported include the due date, interest rate, and maturity value. The due date is the date a note is to be paid, and the period of time between the issuance date and the due date is normally stated in either days or months. The maturity value of a note is the sum of the face amount and the interest.

A note received in settlement of an account receivable is recorded as a debit to Notes Receivable and a credit to Accounts Receivable. When a note matures, Cash is debited, Notes Receivable is credited, and Interest Revenue is credited. If the maker of a note fails to pay the debt on the due date, the note is said to be dishonored. The holder of a dishonored note debits an accounts receivable account for the amount of the claim against the maker of the note.

7 Describe the reporting of receivables on the balance sheet. All receivables that are expected to be realized in cash within a year are presented in the Current Assets section of the balance sheet. It is normal to list the assets in the order of their liquidity, which is the order in which they can be converted to cash in normal operations. In addition to the allowance for doubtful accounts, additional receivable disclosures include the market (fair) value and unusual credit risks.

8 Describe the principles of managing accounts receivable. Businesses grant credit in order to earn additional profits from customers who would otherwise not purchase the company's goods or services. Thus, the overall objective of managing accounts receivable is to help the company earn profits. The basic steps in managing accounts receivable include (1) screening customers, (2) determining credit terms, and (3) monitoring collections.

9 Compute and interpret the accounts receivable turnover and the number of days' sales in receivables. The accounts receivable turnover is net sales divided by average accounts receivable. It measures how frequently accounts receivable are being converted into cash. The number of days' sales in receivables is the end-of-year accounts receivable divided by the average daily sales. It measures the length of time the accounts receivable have been outstanding.

GLOSSARY

Accounts receivable A receivable created by selling merchandise or services on credit.

Accounts receivable turnover Measures how frequently during the year the accounts receivable are being converted to cash.

Aging the receivables The process of analyzing the accounts receivable and classifying them according to various age groupings, with the due date being the base point for determining age.

Allowance for Doubtful Accounts The contra asset account for accounts receivable.

Allowance method The method of accounting for uncollectible accounts that provides an expense for uncollectible receivables in advance of their write-off.

Bad debt expense The operating expense incurred because of the failure to collect receivables.

Direct write-off method The method of accounting for uncollectible accounts that recognizes the expense only when accounts are judged to be worthless.

Dishonored note receivable A note that the maker fails to pay on the due date.

Maturity value The amount that is due at the maturity or due date of a note.

Net realizable value The amount of cash expected to be realized in the future from a receivable.

Notes receivable Amounts customers owe, for which a formal, written instrument of credit has been issued.

Number of days' sales in receivables An estimate of the length of time the accounts receivable have been outstanding.

Receivables All money claims against other entities, including people, business firms, and other organizations.

ILLUSTRATIVE ACCOUNTING APPLICATION PROBLEM

Ditzler Company, a construction supply company, uses the allowance method of accounting for uncollectible accounts receivable. Selected transactions completed by Ditzler Company are as follows:

Feb. 1	Sold merchandise on account to Ames Co., $8,000. The cost of the merchandise sold was $4,500.
Mar. 15	Accepted a 60-day, 12% note for $8,000 from Ames Co. on account.
Apr. 9	Wrote off a $2,500 account from Dorset Co. as uncollectible.
21	Loaned $7,500 cash to Jill Klein, receiving a 90-day, 14% note.
May 14	Received the interest due from Ames Co. and a new 90-day, 14% note as a renewal of the loan. (Record both the debit and the credit to the notes receivable account.)
June 13	Reinstated the account of Dorset Co., written off on April 9, and received $2,500 in full payment.
July 20	Jill Klein dishonored her note.
Aug. 12	Received from Ames Co. the amount due on its note of May 14.
19	Received from Jill Klein the amount owed on the dishonored note, plus interest for 30 days at 15%, computed on the maturity value of the note.
Dec. 16	Accepted a 60-day, 12% note for $12,000 from Global Company on account.
31	It is estimated that 3% of the credit sales of $1,375,000 for the year ended December 31 will be uncollectible.

Instructions

1. Journalize the transactions.
2. Journalize the adjusting entry to record the accrued interest on December 31 on the Global Company note.

Solution

1.

Feb. 1	Accounts Receivable—Ames Co.	8,000	
	Sales		8,000
1	Cost of Merchandise Sold	4,500	
	Merchandise Inventory		4,500
Mar. 15	Notes Receivable—Ames Co.	8,000	
	Accounts Receivable—Ames Co.		8,000
Apr. 9	Allowance for Doubtful Accounts	2,500	
	Accounts Receivable—Dorset Co.		2,500
21	Notes Receivable—Jill Klein	7,500	
	Cash		7,500
May 14	Notes Receivable—Ames Co.	8,000	
	Cash	160	
	Notes Receivable—Ames Co.		8,000
	Interest Revenue		160
June 13	Accounts Receivable—Dorset Co.	2,500	
	Allowance for Doubtful Accounts		2,500
13	Cash	2,500	
	Accounts Receivable—Dorset Co.		2,500
July 20	Accounts Receivable—Jill Klein	7,762.50	
	Notes Receivable—Jill Klein		7,500.00
	Interest Revenue		262.50
Aug. 12	Cash	8,280	
	Notes Receivable—Ames Co.		8,000
	Interest Revenue		280

Aug. 19	Cash	7,859.53	
	Accounts Receivable—Jill Klein		7,762.50
	Interest Revenue		97.03
	($7,762.50 × 15% × 30/360)		
Dec. 16	Notes Receivable—Global Company	12,000	
	Accounts Receivable—Global Company		12,000
31	Bad Debt Expense	41,250	
	Allowance for Doubtful Accounts		41,250

2.

Dec. 31	Interest Receivable	60	
	Interest Revenue		60
	($12,000 × 12% × 15/360)		

SELF-STUDY QUESTIONS

Answers at end of chapter

1. At the end of the fiscal year, before the accounts are adjusted, Accounts Receivable has a balance of $200,000 and Allowance for Doubtful Accounts has a credit balance of $2,500. If the estimate of uncollectible accounts determined by aging the receivables is $8,500, the amount of bad debt expense is:
   A. $2,500
   B. $6,000
   C. $8,500
   D. $11,000

2. At the end of the fiscal year, Accounts Receivable has a balance of $100,000 and Allowance for Doubtful Accounts has a balance of $7,000. The expected net realizable value of the accounts receivable is:
   A. $7,000
   B. $93,000
   C. $100,000
   D. $107,000

3. What is the maturity value of a 90-day, 12% note for $10,000?
   A. $8,800
   B. $10,000
   C. $10,300
   D. $11,200

4. What is the due date of a $12,000, 90-day, 8% note receivable dated August 5?
   A. October 31
   B. November 2
   C. November 3
   D. November 4

5. When a note receivable is dishonored, Accounts Receivable is debited for what amount?
   A. The face value of the note
   B. The maturity value of the note
   C. The maturity value of the note less accrued interest
   D. The maturity value of the note plus accrued interest

DISCUSSION QUESTIONS

1. What are the three classifications of receivables?
2. What types of transactions give rise to accounts receivable?
3. In what section of the balance sheet should a note receivable be listed if its term is (a) 120 days, (b) six years?
4. Give two examples of other receivables.
5. Wilson's Hardware is a small hardware store in the rural township of Struggleville that rarely extends credit to its customers in the form of an account receivable. The few customers that are allowed to carry accounts receivable are long-time residents of Struggleville and have a history of doing business at Wilson's. What method of accounting for uncollectible receivables should Wilson's Hardware use? Why?
6. Which of the two methods of accounting for uncollectible accounts provides for the recognition of the expense at the earlier date?
7. What kind of an account (asset, liability, etc.) is Allowance for Doubtful Accounts, and is its normal balance a debit or a credit?
8. After the accounts are adjusted and closed at the end of the fiscal year, Accounts Receivable has a balance of $783,150 and Allowance for Doubtful Accounts has a balance of $41,694. Describe how the accounts receivable and the allowance for doubtful accounts are reported on the balance sheet.
9. A firm has consistently adjusted its allowance account at the end of the fiscal year by adding a fixed percent of the period's net sales on account. After five years, the balance in Allowance for Doubtful Accounts has become very large in relationship to the balance in Accounts Receivable. Give two possible explanations.

10. Which of the two methods of estimating uncollectibles provides for the most accurate estimate of the current net realizable value of the receivables?
11. For a business, what are the advantages of a note receivable in comparison to an account receivable?
12. Tecan Company issued a note receivable to Bauer Company. (a) Who is the payee? (b) What is the title of the account used by Bauer Company in recording the note?
13. If a note provides for payment of principal of $75,000 and interest at the rate of 8%, will the interest amount to $6,000? Explain.
14. The maker of a $6,000, 10%, 120-day note receivable failed to pay the note on the due date of April 30. What accounts should be debited and credited by the payee to record the dishonored note receivable?
15. The note receivable dishonored in Question 14 is paid on May 30 by the maker, plus interest for 30 days, 9%. What entry should be made to record the receipt of the payment?
16. Under what section should accounts receivable be reported on the balance sheet?
17. To reduce its bad debt expense, Adang Inc. decided to quit granting credit to customers. Is this a wise decision by Adang Inc.? Explain.
18. The accounts receivable turnover increased, while the number of days' sales in receivables decreased for the current year for Nackerud Co. Are changes for the current year good or bad? Explain.

EXERCISES

Exercise 8-1

Classifications of receivables

Goal **1**

The Boeing Company is one of the world's major aerospace firms, with operations involving commercial aircraft, military aircraft, missiles, satellite systems, and information and battle management systems. As of December 31, 2004, Boeing had $2,701 million of receivables involving U.S. government contracts and $985 million of receivables involving commercial aircraft customers, such as Delta Air Lines and United Airlines. Should Boeing report these receivables separately in the financial statements, or combine them into one overall accounts receivable amount? Explain.

Exercise 8-2

Nature of uncollectible accounts

Goal **2**

a. 5.4%

Mandalay Resort Group owns and operates casinos at several of its hotels, located primarily in Nevada. At the end of one fiscal year, the following accounts and notes receivable were reported (in thousands):

Hotel accounts and notes receivable	$31,724	
Less: Allowance for doubtful accounts	1,699	
		$30,025
Casino accounts receivable	$44,139	
Less: Allowance for doubtful accounts	12,300	
		31,839

a. Compute the percentage of the allowance for doubtful accounts to the gross hotel accounts and notes receivable for the end of the fiscal year.
b. Compute the percentage of the allowance for doubtful accounts to the gross casino accounts receivable for the end of the fiscal year.
c. Discuss possible reasons for the difference in the two ratios computed in (a) and (b).

Exercise 8-3

Number of days past due

Goal **4**

The Body Shop, 58 days

Douglas Auto Supply distributes new and used automobile parts to local dealers throughout the Southeast. Douglas's credit terms are n/30. As of the end of business on July 31, the following accounts receivable were past due.

Account	Due Date	Amount
The Body Shop	June 3	$3,000
Custom Auto	July 1	2,500
Hometown Repair	March 22	500
Jake's Auto Repair	May 19	1,000
Like New	June 18	750
Sally's	April 12	1,800
Uptown Auto	May 8	500
Westside Repair & Tow	May 31	1,100

Determine the number of days each account is past due.

Exercise 8-4

Aging-of-receivables schedule

Goal **4**

The accounts receivable clerk for Vandalay Industries prepared the following partially completed aging-of-receivables schedule as of the end of business on November 30:

			Days Past Due			
Customer	**Balance**	**Not Past Due**	**1–30**	**31–60**	**61–90**	**Over 90**
Aaron Brothers Inc.	2,000	2,000				
Abell Company	1,500		1,500			
Zollo Company	5,000			5,000		
Subtotals	872,500	540,000	180,000	78,500	42,300	31,700

The following accounts were unintentionally omitted from the aging schedule and not included in the subtotals above:

Customer	Balance	Due Date
Tamika Industries	$25,000	August 24
Ruppert Company	8,500	September 3
Welborne Inc.	35,000	October 17
Kristi Company	6,500	November 5
Simrill Company	12,000	December 3

a. Determine the number of days past due for each of the preceding accounts.
b. Complete the aging-of-receivables schedule by including the omitted accounts.

Exercise 8-5

Estimating allowance for doubtful accounts

Goal **4**

$78,290

SPREADSHEET

Vandalay Industries has a past history of uncollectible accounts, as shown below. Estimate the allowance for doubtful accounts, based on the aging-of-receivables schedule you completed in Exercise 8-4.

Age Class	Percentage Uncollectible
Not past due	3%
1–30 days past due	5
31–60 days past due	15
61–90 days past due	25
Over 90 days past due	40

Exercise 8-6

Adjustment for uncollectible accounts

Goal **4**

Using data in Exercise 8-4, assume that the allowance for doubtful accounts for Vandalay Industries has a credit balance of $8,195 before adjustment on November 30. Journalize the adjusting entry for uncollectible accounts as of November 30.

Exercise 8-7

Estimating doubtful accounts

Goal **4**

Phoenician Co. is a wholesaler of office supplies. An aging of the company's accounts receivable on December 31, 2007, and a historical analysis of the percentage of uncollectible accounts in each age category are as follows:

Age Interval	Balance	Percent Uncollectible
Not past due	$350,000	1%
1–30 days past due	90,000	2
31–60 days past due	17,000	5
61–90 days past due	13,000	10
91–180 days past due	9,400	70
Over 180 days past due	3,600	90
	$483,000	

Estimate what the proper balance of the allowance for doubtful accounts should be as of December 31, 2007.

Exercise 8-8

Entry for uncollectible accounts

Goal **4**

Using the data in Exercise 8-7, assume that the allowance for doubtful accounts for Phoenician Co. had a debit balance of $2,760 as of December 31, 2007.

Journalize the adjusting entry for uncollectible accounts as of December 31, 2007.

Exercise 8-9

Providing for doubtful accounts

Goal **4**

a. $15,000
b. $14,600

At the end of the current year, the accounts receivable account has a debit balance of $775,000, and net sales for the year total $6,000,000. Determine the amount of the adjusting entry to provide for doubtful accounts under each of the following assumptions:

a. The allowance account before adjustment has a credit balance of $4,750. Bad debt expense is estimated at $\frac{1}{4}$ of 1% of net sales.
b. The allowance account before adjustment has a credit balance of $3,750. An aging of the accounts in the customer ledger indicates estimated doubtful accounts of $18,350.
c. The allowance account before adjustment has a debit balance of $5,050. Bad debt expense is estimated at $\frac{1}{2}$ of 1% of net sales.
d. The allowance account before adjustment has a debit balance of $5,050. An aging of the accounts in the customer ledger indicates estimated doubtful accounts of $31,400.

Exercise 8-10

Entries to write off accounts receivable

Goals **3, 4**

Jadelis Resources, a computer consulting firm, has decided to write off the $12,500 balance of an account owed by a customer. Journalize the entry to record the write-off, assuming that (a) the direct write-off method is used, and (b) the allowance method is used.

Exercise 8-11

Entries for uncollectible accounts, using direct write-off method

Goal 3

Journalize the following transactions in the accounts of Simmons Co., a medical equipment company that uses the direct write-off method of accounting for uncollectible receivables:

Aug. 8	Sold merchandise on account to Dr. Pete Baker, $21,400. The cost of the merchandise sold was $12,600.
Sept. 7	Received $13,000 from Dr. Pete Baker and wrote off the remainder owed on the sale of August 8 as uncollectible.
Dec. 20	Reinstated the account of Dr. Pete Baker that had been written off on September 7 and received $8,400 cash in full payment.

Exercise 8-12

Entries for uncollectible receivables, using allowance method

Goal 4

Journalize the following transactions in the accounts of Simply Yummy Company, a restaurant supply company that uses the allowance method of accounting for uncollectible receivables:

Jan. 13	Sold merchandise on account to Lynn Berry, $16,000. The cost of the merchandise sold was $9,400.
Feb. 12	Received $4,000 from Lynn Berry and wrote off the remainder owed on the sale of January 13 as uncollectible.
July 3	Reinstated the account of Lynn Berry that had been written off on February 12 and received $12,000 cash in full payment.

Exercise 8-13

Effect of doubtful accounts on net income

Goals 3, 4

During its first year of operations, West Plumbing Supply Co. had net sales of $1,800,000, wrote off $51,000 of accounts as uncollectible using the direct write-off method, and reported net income of $125,000. Determine what the net income would have been if the allowance method had been used, and the company estimated that 3% of net sales would be uncollectible.

Exercise 8-14

Effect of doubtful accounts on net income

Goals 3, 4

Using the data in Exercise 8-13, assume that during the second year of operations West Plumbing Supply Co. had net sales of $2,200,000, wrote off $61,500 of accounts as uncollectible using the direct write-off method, and reported net income of $143,500.

a. Determine what net income would have been in the second year if the allowance method (using 3% of net sales) had been used in both the first and second years.

b. Determine what the balance of the allowance for doubtful accounts would have been at the end of the second year if the allowance method had been used in both the first and second years.

Exercise 8-15

Entries for bad debt expense under the direct write-off and allowance methods

Goal 5

Becker wrote off the following accounts receivable as uncollectible for the first year of its operations ending December 31, 2008:

Customer	Amount
Skip Simon	$20,000
Clarence Watson	13,500
Bill Jacks	7,300
Matt Putnam	4,200
Total	$45,000

a. Journalize the write-offs for 2008 under the direct write-off method.

b. Journalize the write-offs for 2008 under the allowance method. Also, journalize the estimate of bad debts. The company recorded $2,000,000 of credit sales during 2008. Based on past history and industry averages, 3% of credit sales are expected to be uncollectible.

c. How much higher (lower) would Becker's 2008 net income have been under the direct write-off method than under the allowance method?

Exercise 8-16

Entries for bad debt expense under the direct write-off and allowance methods

Goal 5

Hazard wrote off the following accounts receivable as uncollectible for the year ending December 31, 2008:

Customer	Amount
Boss Hogg	$ 5,000
Daisy Duke	3,500
Bo Duke	6,300
Luke Duke	4,200
Total	$19,000

The company has provided the following aging schedule for its accounts receivable on December 31, 2008:

Aging Class (Number of Days Past Due)	Receivables Balance on December 31	Estimate of the Percentage of Receivables That Will Become Uncollectible
0–30 days	$380,000	2%
31–60 days	70,000	5
61–90 days	30,000	15
91–120 days	25,000	25
More than 120 days	10,000	50
Total receivables	$515,000	

a. Journalize the write-offs for 2008 under the direct write-off method.
b. Journalize the write-offs and the year-end adjusting entry for 2008 under the allowance method, presuming that the allowance account had a beginning balance of $18,000 and the company uses the analysis of receivables method.
c. Does the write-off of bad debts affect cash under the direct write-off and allowance methods?

Exercise 8-17

Entries for bad debt expense under the direct write-off and allowance methods

Goal 5

The following selected transactions were taken from the records of Shaw Company for the first year of its operations ending December 31, 2008.

Jan. 31	Wrote off account of B. Roberts, $2,400.
Mar. 26	Received $1,500 as partial payment on the $3,500 account of Carol Castellino. Wrote off the remaining balance as uncollectible.
July 7	Received $2,400 from B. Roberts, which had been written off on January 31. Reinstated the account and recorded the cash receipt.
Oct. 12	Wrote off the following accounts as uncollectible (record as one journal entry):

Julie Lindley	$1,350
Mark Black	950
Jennifer Kerlin	525
Beth Chalhoub	1,125
Allison Fain	725

Dec. 31	Shaw Company uses the percent of credit sales method of estimating uncollectible accounts expense. Based upon past history and industry averages, 2% of credit sales are expected to be uncollectible. Shaw recorded $750,000 of credit sales during 2008.

a. Journalize the transactions for 2008 under the direct write-off method.
b. Journalize the transactions for 2008 under the allowance method.
c. How much higher (lower) would Shaw's 2008 net income have been under the direct write-off method than under the allowance method?

Exercise 8-18

Entries for bad debt expense under the direct write-off and allowance methods

Goal 5

The following selected transactions were taken from the records of Kemper Company for the year ending December 31, 2008:

Feb. 2 Wrote off account of L. Armstrong, $7,250.

May 10 Received $4,150 as partial payment on the $8,500 account of Jill Knapp. Wrote off the remaining balance as uncollectible.

Aug. 12 Received the $7,250 from L. Armstrong, which had been written off on February 2. Reinstated the account and recorded the cash receipt.

Sep. 27 Wrote off the following accounts as uncollectible (record as one journal entry):

Kim Whalen	$4,400
Brad Johnson	2,210
Angelina Quan	1,375
Tammy Newsome	2,850
Donna Short	1,690

Dec. 31 The company provided the following aging schedule for its accounts receivable:

Aging Class (Number of Days Past Due)	Receivables Balance on December 31	Estimate of the Percentage of Receivables That Will Become Uncollectible
0–30 days	$160,000	3%
31–60 days	40,000	10
61–90 days	18,000	20
91–120 days	11,000	40
More than 120 days	6,500	75
Total receivables	$235,500	

a. Journalize the transactions for 2008 under the direct write-off method.

b. Journalize the transactions for 2008 under the allowance method, presuming that the allowance account had a beginning balance of $18,000 and the company uses the analysis of receivables method.

c. How much higher (lower) would Kemper's 2008 net income have been under the direct write-off method than under the allowance method?

Exercise 8-19

Determine due date and interest on notes

Goal 6

a. May 5, $225

Determine the due date and the amount of interest due at maturity on the following notes:

	Date of Note	Face Amount	Term of Note	Interest Rate
a.	March 6	$15,000	60 days	9%
b.	May 20	8,000	60 days	10
c.	June 2	5,000	90 days	12
d.	August 30	18,000	120 days	10
e.	October 1	10,500	60 days	12

Exercise 8-20

Entries for notes receivable

Goal 6

b. $25,562.50

Holsten Interior Decorators issued a 90-day, 9% note for $25,000, dated April 6, to Maderia Furniture Company on account.

a. Determine the due date of the note.

b. Determine the maturity value of the note.

c. Journalize the entries to record the following: (1) receipt of the note by the payee and (2) receipt by the payee of payment of the note at maturity.

Exercise 8-21

Entries for notes receivable

Goal 6

The series of seven transactions recorded in the following T-accounts were related to a sale to a customer on account and the receipt of the amount owed. Briefly describe each transaction.

CASH

(7)	23,028		

NOTES RECEIVABLE

(5)	22,000	(6)	22,000

ACCOUNTS RECEIVABLE

(1)	25,000	(3)	3,000
(6)	22,725	(5)	22,000
		(7)	22,725

SALES RETURNS AND ALLOWANCES

(3)	3,000		

MERCHANDISE INVENTORY

(4)	1,800	(2)	15,000

COST OF MERCHANDISE SOLD

(2)	15,000	(4)	1,800

SALES

		(1)	25,000

INTEREST REVENUE

		(6)	725
		(7)	303

Exercise 8-22

Entries for notes receivable, including year-end entries

Goal 6

The following selected transactions were completed by Lupine Co., a supplier of elastic bands for clothing:

2006

Dec. 13 Received from Stout Co., on account, a $30,000, 120-day, 9% note dated December 13.

31 Recorded an adjusting entry for accrued interest on the note of December 13.

2007

Apr. 12 Received payment of note and interest from Stout Co.

Journalize the transactions.

Exercise 8-23

Entries for receipt and dishonor of note receivable

Goal 6

Journalize the following transactions of Theres Productions:

July 3 Received a $150,000, 90-day, 8% note dated July 3 from Hermes Company on account.

Oct. 1 The note is dishonored by Hermes Company.

31 Received the amount due on the dishonored note plus interest for 30 days at 10% on the total amount charged to Hermes Company on October 1.

Exercise 8-24

Entries for receipt and dishonor of notes receivable

Goals 4, 6

Journalize the following transactions in the accounts of Dimitrious Co., which operates a riverboat casino:

Apr. 1 Received a $10,000, 30-day, 6% note dated April 1 from Wilcox Co. on account.

18 Received a $12,000, 30-day, 9% note dated April 18 from Aaron Co. on account.

May 1 The note dated April 1 from Wilcox Co. is dishonored, and the customer's account is charged for the note, including interest.

June 17 The note dated April 18 from Aaron Co. is dishonored, and the customer's account is charged for the note, including interest.

July 30 Cash is received for the amount due on the dishonored note dated April 1 plus interest for 90 days at 8% on the total amount debited to Wilcox Co. on May 1.

Sept. 3 Wrote off against the allowance account the amount charged to Aaron Co. on June 17 for the dishonored note dated April 18.

Exercise 8-25

Receivables in the balance sheet

Goal 7

List any errors you can find in the following partial balance sheet.

Mishkie Company
Balance Sheet
December 31, 2007

Assets

Current assets:		
Cash		$127,500
Notes receivable	$400,000	
Less interest receivable	24,000	376,000
Accounts receivable	$529,200	
Plus allowance for doubtful accounts	42,000	571,200

Exercise 8-26

Accounts receivable turnover

Goal 9

a. 2004: 7.1

May Department Stores is a large retailer that operates such brands as Hecht's, Lord & Taylor, Marshall Field's, and David's Bridal. May reported the following data (in millions) for fiscal years ending:

	Jan. 29, 2005	Jan. 31, 2004
Net sales	$14,441	$13,343
Accounts receivable	2,294	1,788

Assume that accounts receivable (in millions) were $1,776 on January 31, 2003.

a. Compute the accounts receivable turnover for the year ended January 29, 2005, and the year ended January 31, 2004. Round to one decimal place.
b. What conclusions can be drawn from these analyses regarding May Department Stores' efficiency in collecting receivables?

Exercise 8-27

Days' sales in receivables

Goal 9

a. 2004: 51.5 days

Use the May Department Stores data in Exercise 8-26 to analyze days' sales in receivables.

a. Compute the days' sales in receivables for the years ended January 29, 2005, and January 31, 2004. Round to one decimal place.
b. What conclusions can be drawn from these analyses regarding May Department Stores' efficiency in collecting receivables?

Exercise 8-28

Accounts receivable turnover and days' sales in receivables

Goal 9

a. 2004: 5.8

Polo Ralph Lauren Corporation designs, markets, and distributes a variety of apparel, home decor, accessory, and fragrance products. The company's products include such brands as Polo by Ralph Lauren, Ralph Lauren Purple Label, Ralph Lauren, Polo Jeans Co., and Chaps. For fiscal years 2004 and 2003, Polo Ralph Lauren reported the following (in thousands):

	For the Period Ending	
	Oct. 31, 2004	Oct. 31, 2003
Net sales	$2,380,844	$2,189,321
Accounts receivable	441,724	375,823

Assume that accounts receivable (in millions) were $353,608 at the end of fiscal 2002.

a. Compute the accounts receivable turnover for 2004 and 2003. Round to one decimal place.
b. Compute the days' sales in receivables for 2004 and 2003. Round to one decimal place.
c. What conclusions can be drawn from these analyses regarding Ralph Lauren's efficiency in collecting receivables?

Exercise 8-29

Accounts receivable turnover and days' sales in receivables

Goal 9

a. 2004: 7.5

H.J. Heinz Company was founded in 1869 at Sharpsburg, Pennsylvania, by Henry J. Heinz. The company manufactures and markets food products throughout the world, including ketchup, condiments and sauces, frozen food, pet food, soups, and tuna. For the fiscal years 2004 and 2003, H.J. Heinz reported the following (in thousands):

	Year Ending	
	April 28, 2004	April 30, 2003
Net sales	$8,414,538	$8,236,836
Account receivable	1,093,155	1,165,460

Assume that the accounts receivable (in thousands) were $1,125,200 at the beginning of the 2003 fiscal year.

a. Compute the accounts receivable turnover for 2004 and 2003. Round to one decimal place.
b. Compute the days' sales in receivables at the end of 2004 and 2003. Round to one decimal place.
c. What conclusions can be drawn from these analyses regarding Heinz's efficiency in collecting receivables?

Exercise 8-30

Accounts receivable turnover and days' sales in receivables

Goal 9

The Limited Inc. sells women's and men's clothing through specialty retail stores, including Structure, The Limited, Express, Lane Bryant, and Lerner New York. The Limited sells women's intimate apparel and personal care products through Victoria Secret and Bath & Body Works stores. For fiscal 2004 and 2003, The Limited reported the following (in millions):

	For the Period Ending	
	Jan. 29, 2005	Jan. 31, 2004
Net sales	$9,408	$8,934
Accounts receivable	128	112

Assume that accounts receivable (in millions) were $151 on February 1, 2003.

a. Compute the accounts receivable turnover for 2004 and 2003. Round to one decimal place.
b. Compute the day's sales in receivables for 2004 and 2003. Round to one decimal place.
c. What conclusions can be drawn from these analyses regarding The Limited's efficiency in collecting receivables?

Exercise 8-31

Accounts receivable turnover

Goal 9

Use the data in Exercises 8-29 and 8-30 to analyze the accounts receivable turnover ratios of H.J. Heinz Company and The Limited Inc.

a. Compute the average accounts receivable turnover ratio for The Limited Inc. and H.J. Heinz Company for the years shown in Exercises 8-29 and 8-30.
b. Does The Limited or H.J. Heinz Company have the higher average accounts receivable turnover ratio?
c. Explain the logic underlying your answer in (b).

ACCOUNTING APPLICATION PROBLEMS

Problem 8-1A

Entries related to uncollectible accounts

Goal 4

3. $837,250

GENERAL LEDGER

The following transactions were completed by The Corion Gallery during the current fiscal year ended December 31:

Feb. 21	Reinstated the account of Tony Marshal, which had been written off in the preceding year as uncollectible. Journalized the receipt of $4,050 cash in full payment of Marshal's account.
Mar. 31	Wrote off the $5,500 balance owed by Amos Co., which is bankrupt.
July 7	Received 35% of the $10,000 balance owed by Morton Co., a bankrupt business, and wrote off the remainder as uncollectible.

Aug. 29 Reinstated the account of Louis Sabo, which had been written off two years earlier as uncollectible. Recorded the receipt of $2,400 cash in full payment.

Dec. 31 Wrote off the following accounts as uncollectible (compound entry): Dailey Co., $10,050; Sun Co., $7,260; Zheng Furniture, $3,775; Carey Wenzel, $2,820.

31 Based on an analysis of the $875,250 of accounts receivable, it was estimated that $38,000 will be uncollectible. Journalized the adjusting entry.

Instructions

1. Record the January 1 credit balance of $32,000 in a T-account for Allowance for Doubtful Accounts.
2. Journalize the transactions. Post each entry that affects the following T-accounts and determine the new balances:

   Allowance for Doubtful Accounts
   Bad Debt Expense

3. Determine the expected net realizable value of the accounts receivable as of December 31.
4. Assuming that instead of basing the provision for uncollectible accounts on an analysis of receivables, the adjusting entry on December 31 had been based on an estimated expense of $\frac{1}{2}$ of 1% of the net sales of $7,750,000 for the year, determine the following:
   a. Bad debt expense for the year.
   b. Balance in the allowance account after the adjustment of December 31.
   c. Expected net realizable value of the accounts receivable as of December 31.

Problem 8-2A

Aging of receivables; estimating allowance for doubtful accounts

Goal 4

3. $65,038.50

SPREADSHEET

Miller Wigs Company supplies wigs and hair care products to beauty salons throughout California and the Pacific Northwest. The accounts receivable clerk for Miller Wigs prepared the following partially completed aging-of-receivables schedule as of the end of business on December 31, 2007:

			Days Past Due				
Customer	Balance	Not Past Due	1–30	31–60	61–90	91–120	Over 120
Daytime Beauty	$20,000	$20,000					
Blount Wigs	$11,000			$11,000			
Zabka's	2,900		2,900				
Subtotals	780,000	398,600	197,250	98,750	33,300	29,950	22,150

The following accounts were unintentionally omitted from the aging schedule:

Customer	Due Date	Balance
Houseal Uniquely Yours	July 1, 2007	$ 900
Country Designs	Aug. 2, 2007	4,000
Treat's	Sept. 9, 2007	1,200
Molina's Beauty Store	Sept. 29, 2007	1,100
Ginburg Supreme	Oct. 10, 2007	1,500
Steve's Hair Products	Oct. 17, 2007	600
Hairy's Hair Care	Oct. 31, 2007	2,000
VanDiver's Images	Nov. 18, 2007	700
Lopez Hair Styling	Nov. 28, 2007	1,800
Josset Ritz	Nov. 30, 2007	3,500
Cool Designs	Dec. 1, 2007	1,000
Buttram Images	Jan. 3, 2008	6,200

Miller Wigs has a past history of uncollectible accounts by age category, as follows:

Age Class	Percentage Uncollectible
Not past due	2%
1–30 days past due	4
31–60 days past due	10
61–90 days past due	15
91–120 days past due	35
Over 120 days past due	80

Instructions

1. Determine the number of days past due for each of the preceding accounts.
2. Complete the aging-of-receivables schedule.
3. Estimate the allowance for doubtful accounts, based on the aging-of-receivables schedule.
4. Assume that the allowance for doubtful accounts for Miller Wigs has a credit balance of $11,350 before adjustment on December 31, 2007. Illustrate the effect on the accounts and financial statements of the adjustment for uncollectible accounts.

Problem 8-3A

Compare two methods of accounting for uncollectible receivables

Goals **3, 4**

1. Year 4: Balance of allowance account, end of year, $5,050

SPREADSHEET

Baron Company, which operates a chain of 30 electronics supply stores, has just completed its fourth year of operations. The direct write-off method of recording bad debt expense has been used during the entire period. Because of substantial increases in sales volume and the amount of uncollectible accounts, the firm is considering changing to the allowance method. Information is requested as to the effect that an annual provision of $\frac{1}{2}$% of sales would have had on the amount of bad debt expense reported for each of the past four years. It is also considered desirable to know what the balance of Allowance for Doubtful Accounts would have been at the end of each year. The following data have been obtained from the accounts:

		Uncollectible Accounts Written	Year of Origin of Accounts Receivable Written Off as Uncollectible			
Year	Sales	Off	1st	2nd	3rd	4th
1st	$ 500,000	$ 600	$ 600			
2nd	750,000	1,500	700	$ 800		
3rd	1,150,000	6,500	1,900	1,500	$3,100	
4th	2,100,000	8,850		2,000	3,050	$3,800

Instructions

1. Assemble the desired data, using the following column headings:

	Bad Debt Expense			
Year	Expense Actually Reported	Expense Based on Estimate	Increase (Decrease) in Amount of Expense	Balance of Allowance Account, End of Year

2. Experience during the first four years of operations indicated that the receivables were either collected within two years or had to be written off as uncollectible. Does the estimate of $\frac{1}{2}$% of sales appear to be reasonably close to the actual experience with uncollectible accounts originating during the first two years? Explain.

Problem 8-4A

Details of notes receivable and related entries

Goal **6**

Abdou Co. produces advertising videos. During the last six months of the current fiscal year, Abdou Co. received the following notes:

	Date	Face Amount	Term	Interest Rate
1.	May 17	$12,000	45 days	9%
2.	July 9	10,000	60 days	8

1. Note 2: Due date, Sept. 7;

Interest due at maturity, $133.33

	Date	Face Amount	Term	Interest Rate
3.	Aug. 1	$16,500	90 days	7%
4.	Sept. 4	20,000	90 days	6
5.	Nov. 26	18,000	60 days	8
6.	Dec. 16	36,000	60 days	13

Instructions

1. Determine for each note (a) the due date and (b) the amount of interest due at maturity, identifying each note by number.
2. Journalize the entry to record the dishonor of Note (3) on its due date.
3. Journalize the adjusting entry to record the accrued interest on Notes (5) and (6) on December 31.
4. Journalize the entries to record the receipt of the amounts due on Notes (5) and (6) in January and February.

Problem 8-5A

Notes receivable entries

Goal **6**

GENERAL LEDGER

The following data relate to notes receivable and interest for Vidovich Co., a financial services company. (All notes are dated as of the day they are received.)

Mar.	1	Received a $13,000, 9%, 60-day note on account.
	21	Received a $7,500, 8%, 90-day note on account.
Apr.	30	Received $13,195 on note of March 1.
May	16	Received a $40,000, 7%, 90-day note on account.
	31	Received a $6,000, 8%, 30-day note on account.
June	19	Received $7,650 on note of March 21.
	30	Received $6,040 on note of May 31.
July	1	Received a $5,000, 12%, 30-day note on account.
	31	Received $5,050 on note of July 1.
Aug.	14	Received $40,700 on note of May 16.

Instructions

Journalize the entries to record the transactions.

Problem 8-6A

Sales and notes receivable transactions

Goal **6**

GENERAL LEDGER

The following were selected from among the transactions completed during the current year by Hackworth Co., an appliance wholesale company:

Jan.	7	Sold merchandise on account to Dewit Co., $12,300. The cost of merchandise sold was $3,800.
Mar.	8	Accepted a 60-day, 8% note for $12,300 from Dewit Co. on account.
May	7	Received from Dewit Co. the amount due on the note of March 8.
June	1	Sold merchandise on account to Kihl's for $15,000. The cost of merchandise sold was $10,750.
	5	Loaned $18,000 cash to Michele Hobson, receiving a 30-day, 6% note.
	11	Received from Kihl's the amount due on the invoice of June 1, less 2% discount.
July	5	Received the interest due from Michele Hobson and a new 60-day, 9% note as a renewal of the loan of June 5. (Record both the debit and the credit to the notes receivable account.)
Sept.	3	Received from Michele Hobson the amount due on her note of July 5.
	4	Sold merchandise on account to Wood Co., $9,000. The cost of merchandise sold was $6,250.
Oct.	4	Accepted a 60-day, 6% note for $9,000 from Wood Co. on account.
Dec.	3	Wood Co. dishonored the note dated October 4.
	29	Received from Wood Co. the amount owed on the dishonored note, plus interest for 26 days at 6% computed on the maturity value of the note.

Instructions

Journalize the transactions. Round to the nearest dollar.

ALTERNATE ACCOUNTING APPLICATION PROBLEMS

Alternate Problem 8-1B

Entries related to uncollectible accounts

Goal 4

3. $643,750

GENERAL LEDGER

The following transactions were completed by Clark Management Company during the current fiscal year ended December 31:

Mar. 17 Received 70% of the $21,000 balance owed by Baxter Co., a bankrupt business, and wrote off the remainder as uncollectible.

Apr. 20 Reinstated the account of Bart Tiffany, which had been written off in the preceding year as uncollectible. Journalized the receipt of $4,875 cash in full payment of Tiffany's account.

July 29 Wrote off the $4,500 balance owed by Ski Time Co., which has no assets.

Oct. 31 Reinstated the account of Kirby Co., which had been written off in the preceding year as uncollectible. Journalized the receipt of $7,750 cash in full payment of the account.

Dec. 31 Wrote off the following accounts as uncollectible (compound entry): Maxie Co., $2,150; Nance Co., $2,600; Powell Distributors, $3,500; J.J. Levi, $5,500.

31 Based on an analysis of the $657,250 of accounts receivable, it was estimated that $13,500 will be uncollectible. Journalized the adjusting entry.

Instructions

1. Record the January 1 credit balance of $11,050 in a T-account for Allowance for Doubtful Accounts.
2. Journalize the transactions. Post each entry that affects the following selected T-accounts and determine the new balances:

   Allowance for Doubtful Accounts
   Bad Debt Expense

3. Determine the expected net realizable value of the accounts receivable as of December 31.
4. Assuming that instead of basing the provision for uncollectible accounts on an analysis of receivables, the adjusting entry on December 31 had been based on an estimated expense of $\frac{1}{4}$ of 1% of the net sales of $5,350,000 for the year, determine the following:
   a. Bad debt expense for the year.
   b. Balance in the allowance account after the adjustment of December 31.
   c. Expected net realizable value of the accounts receivable as of December 31.

Alternate Problem 8-2B

Aging of receivables; estimating allowance for doubtful accounts

Goal 4

3. $80,646

SPREADSHEET

Zahovik Company supplies flies and fishing gear to sporting goods stores and outfitters throughout the western United States. The accounts receivable clerk for Zahovik prepared the following partially completed aging-of-receivables schedule as of the end of business on December 31, 2007:

			Days Past Due				
Customer	Balance	Not Past Due	1–30	31–60	61–90	91–120	Over 120
Alexandra Fishery	15,000	15,000					
Cutthroat Sports	5,500			5,500			
Yellowstone Sports	2,900		2,900				
Subtotals	880,000	448,600	247,250	98,750	33,300	29,950	22,150

The following accounts were unintentionally omitted from the aging schedule.

Customer	Due Date	Balance
Adel Sports & Flies	June 21, 2007	$1,500
Buzzer Sports	July 30, 2007	3,000
Marabou Flies	Sept. 9, 2007	2,500
Midge Co.	Sept. 30, 2007	1,100
Adventure Outfitters	Oct. 10, 2007	2,500
Pheasant Tail Sports	Oct. 17, 2007	600
Red Tag Sporting Goods	Oct. 30, 2007	2,000
Ross Sports	Nov. 18, 2007	500
Sawyer's Pheasant Tail	Nov. 28, 2007	1,800
Tent Caddis Outfitters	Nov. 30, 2007	3,500
Wulff Company	Dec. 1, 2007	1,000
Zug Bug Sports	Jan. 6, 2008	6,200

Zahovik Company has a past history of uncollectible accounts by age category, as follows:

Age Class	Percentage Uncollectible
Not past due	2%
1–30 days past due	5
31–60 days past due	10
61–90 days past due	25
91–120 days past due	45
Over 120 days past due	90

Instructions

1. Determine the number of days past due for each of the preceding accounts.
2. Complete the aging-of-receivables schedule.
3. Estimate the allowance for doubtful accounts, based on the aging-of-receivables schedule.
4. Assume that the allowance for doubtful accounts for Zahovik Company has a debit balance of $2,600 before adjustment on December 31, 2007. Journalize the adjusting entry for uncollectible accounts.

Alternate Problem 8-3B

Compare two methods of accounting for uncollectible receivables

Goals **3, 4**

1. Year 4: Balance of allowance account, end of year, $12,250

SPREADSHEET

Franklin Company, a telephone service and supply company, has just completed its fourth year of operations. The direct write-off method of recording bad debt expense has been used during the entire period. Because of substantial increases in sales volume and the amount of uncollectible accounts, the firm is considering changing to the allowance method. Information is requested as to the effect that an annual provision of $\frac{3}{4}$% of sales would have had on the amount of bad debt expense reported for each of the past four years. It is also considered desirable to know what the balance of Allowance for Doubtful Accounts would have been at the end of each year. The following data have been obtained from the accounts:

			Year of Origin of Accounts Receivable Written Off as Uncollectible			
Year	Sales	Uncollectible Accounts Written Off	1st	2nd	3rd	4th
1st	$ 650,000	$2,500	$2,500			
2nd	760,000	2,950	1,900	$1,050		
3rd	950,000	5,700	700	4,000	$1,000	
4th	1,800,000	7,800		1,200	2,550	$4,050

Instructions

1. Assemble the desired data, using the following column headings:

	Bad Debt Expense			
Year	Expense Actually Reported	Expense Based on Estimate	Increase (Decrease) in Amount of Expense	Balance of Allowance Account, End of Year

2. Experience during the first four years of operations indicated that the receivables were either collected within two years or had to be written off as uncollectible. Does the estimate of $\frac{3}{4}$% of sales appear to be reasonably close to the actual experience with uncollectible accounts originating during the first two years? Explain.

Alternate Problem 8-4B

Details of notes receivable and related entries

Goal 6

1. Note 2: Due date, July 15; Interest due at maturity, $190

Gentry Co. wholesales bathroom fixtures. During the current fiscal year, Gentry Co. received the following notes:

	Date	Face Amount	Term	Interest Rate
1.	March 3	$32,000	60 days	8%
2.	June 15	19,000	30 days	12
3.	Aug. 20	10,800	120 days	6
4.	Oct. 31	11,500	60 days	9
5.	Nov. 23	15,000	60 days	6
6.	Dec. 27	8,500	30 days	12

Instructions

1. Determine for each note (a) the due date and (b) the amount of interest due at maturity, identifying each note by number.
2. Journalize the entry to record the dishonor of Note (3) on its due date.
3. Journalize the adjusting entry to record the accrued interest on Notes (5) and (6) on December 31.
4. Journalize the entries to record the receipt of the amounts due on Notes (5) and (6) in January.

Alternate Problem 8-5B

Notes receivable entries

Goal 6

GENERAL LEDGER

The following data relate to notes receivable and interest for Generic Optic Co., a cable manufacturer and supplier. (All notes are dated as of the day they are received.)

June	1	Received a $15,800, 9%, 60-day note on account.
July	16	Received a $30,000, 10%, 120-day note on account.
	31	Received $16,037 on note of June 1.
Sept.	1	Received a $24,000, 9%, 60-day note on account.
Oct.	31	Received $24,360 on note of September 1.
Nov.	8	Received a $24,000, 7%, 30-day note on account.
	13	Received $31,000 on note of July 16.
	30	Received a $15,000, 10%, 30-day note on account.
Dec.	8	Received $24,140 on note of November 8.
	30	Received $15,125 on note of November 30.

Instructions

Journalize entries to record the transactions.

Alternate Problem 8-6B

Sales and notes receivable transactions

Goal 6

GENERAL LEDGER

The following were selected from among the transactions completed by Hunter Co. during the current year. Hunter Co. sells and installs home and business security systems.

Jan.	8	Loaned $8,500 cash to Mark Tift, receiving a 90-day, 8% note.
Feb.	3	Sold merchandise on account to Messina and Son, $16,000. The cost of the merchandise sold was $9,000.
Feb.	12	Sold merchandise on account to Gwyn Co., $27,500. The cost of merchandise sold was $15,750.
Mar.	5	Accepted a 60-day, 6% note for $16,000 from Messina and Son on account.
	14	Accepted a 60-day, 12% note for $27,500 from Gwyn Co. on account.
Apr.	9	Received the interest due from Mark Tift and a new 90-day, 9% note as a renewal of the loan of January 8. (Record both the debit and the credit to the notes receivable account.)
May	4	Received from Messina and Son the amount due on the note of March 5.
	13	Gwyn Co. dishonored its note dated March 14.
June	12	Received from Gwyn Co. the amount owed on the dishonored note, plus interest for 30 days at 12% computed on the maturity value of the note.
July	8	Received from Mark Tift the amount due on his note of April 9.
Aug.	23	Sold merchandise on account to MacKenzie Co., $10,000. The cost of the merchandise sold was $6,500.
Sept.	2	Received from MacKenzie Co. the amount of the invoice of August 23, less 1% discount.

Instructions

Journalize the transactions.

FINANCIAL ANALYSIS AND REPORTING CASES

Case 8-1

Accounts receivable turnover and days' sales in receivables

Best Buy is a specialty retailer of consumer electronics, including personal computers, entertainment software, and appliances. Best Buy operates retail stores in addition to the Best Buy, Media Play, On Cue, and Magnolia Hi-Fi Web sites. For the years ending February 26, 2005, and February 28, 2004, Best Buy reported the following (in millions):

	Year Ending	
	Feb. 26, 2005	Feb. 28, 2004
Net sales	$27,433	$24,548
Accounts receivable at end of year	375	343

Assume that the accounts receivable (in millions) were $312 at the beginning of the year ending February 28, 2004.

1. Compute the accounts receivable turnover for 2005 and 2004. Round to one decimal place.
2. Compute the days' sales in receivables at the end of 2005 and 2004.
3. What conclusions can be drawn from (1) and (2) regarding Best Buy's efficiency in collecting receivables?
4. For its years ending in 2005 and 2004, Circuit City has an accounts receivable turnover of 61.0 and 56.3, respectively. Compare Best Buy's efficiency in collecting receivables with that of Circuit City.
5. What assumption did we make about sales for the Circuit City and Best Buy ratio computations that might distort the two company ratios and therefore cause the ratios not to be comparable?

Case 8-2

Accounts receivable turnover and days' sales in receivables

Apple Computer Inc. designs, manufactures, and markets personal computers and related personal computing and communicating solutions for sale primarily to education, creative, consumer, and business customers. Substantially all of the company's net sales over the last five years are from sales of its Apple Macintosh line of personal computers and related software and peripherals. For the fiscal years ending September 25, 2004 and September 27, 2003, Apple reported the following (in millions):

	Year Ending	
	Sept. 25, 2004	**Sept 27, 2003**
Net sales	$8,279	$6,207
Accounts receivable at end of year	774	766

Assume that the accounts receivable (in millions) were $565 at the beginning of the 2003 fiscal year.

1. Compute the accounts receivable turnover for 2004 and 2003. Round to one decimal place.
2. Compute the days' sales in receivables at the end of 2004 and 2003.
3. What conclusions can be drawn from (1) and (2) regarding Apple's efficiency in collecting receivables?
4. Using the Internet, access the Apple September 25, 2004, 10-K filing with the Securities and Exchange Commission. You can use the PricewaterhouseCoopers Web site at http://edgarscan.pwcglobal.com to search for company filings by name. Search the 10-K filing for the term "receivable." Identify one company that had accounts receivable with Apple at the end of fiscal years 2004 and 2003.

Case 8-3

Accounts receivable turnover and days' sales in receivables

SPREADSHEET

Earthlink, Inc., is a nationwide Internet Service Provider (ISP). Earthlink provides a variety of services to its customers, including narrowband access, broadband or high-speed access, and Web hosting services. For the years ending December 31, 2004 and 2003, Earthlink reported the following (in thousands):

	Year Ending December 31,	
	2004	**2003**
Net sales	$1,382,202	$1,401,930
Accounts receivable at end of year	30,733	35,585

Assume that the accounts receivable (in thousands) were $53,496 at January 1, 2003.

1. Compute the accounts receivable turnover for 2004 and 2003. Round to one decimal place.
2. Compute the days' sales in receivables at the end of 2004 and 2003.
3. What conclusions can be drawn from (1) and (2) regarding Earthlink's efficiency in collecting receivables?
4. Given the nature of Earthlink's operations, do you believe Earthlink's accounts receivable turnover ratio would be higher or lower than a typical manufacturing company, such as Boeing or Kellogg's? Explain.

Case 8–4

Account receivable turnover

General Electric (GE) is one of the largest and most diversified industrial corporations in the world. GE's products include major appliances, lighting products, medical diagnostic imaging equipment, motors, locomotives, and commercial and military aircraft jet engines. Through the

National Broadcasting Company (NBC), GE offers network television services, operates television stations, and provides cable, Internet, and programming services. Through General Electric Capital Services (GECS), GE offers consumer financing, commercial and industrial financing, real estate financing, asset management and leasing, mortgage services, and insurance services.

For the years ending December 31, 2004 and 2003, GE reported the following data (in millions):

	December 31,	
	2004	**2003**
GE (without GECS):		
Total accounts receivable from sales of goods and services	$15,271	$ 11,459
Allowance for doubtful accounts	738	486
Net accounts receivable	$14,533	$ 10,973
GECS:		
Total accounts receivable from financing	$288,347	$254,370
Allowance for doubtful accounts	5,648	6,256
Net accounts receivable	$282,699	$248,114
Sales for GE (without GECS) for year ending December 31, 2004		$ 85,769
Revenue for GECS from services for year ending December 31, 2004		$ 67,097

1. Compute the accounts receivable turnover for GE, excluding GECS, for 2004. Use net accounts receivable and round to one decimal place in your computations.
2. Compute the accounts receivable turnover for GECS for 2004. Use net accounts receivable and round to one decimal place in your computations.
3. Comment on the interpretation of the accounts receivable turnover for GECS.
4. As of December 31, 2004 and 2003, compute the percent of the allowance for doubtful accounts to total accounts receivable for GE, without GECS. Round to one decimal place.
5. As of December 31, 2004 and 2003, compute the percent of the allowance for doubtful accounts to total accounts receivable for GECS. Round to one decimal place.
6. Compare (4) and (5) and explain why one percentage is higher than the other.

Case 8-5

Accounts receivable turnover

The accounts receivable turnover ratio will vary across companies, depending upon the nature of the company's operations. For example, an accounts receivable turnover of six for an Internet Services Provider is unacceptable but might be excellent for a manufacturer of specialty milling equipment. A list of well-known companies is listed below.

Alcoa	The Coca-Cola Company	Kroger
AutoZone	Delta Air Lines	Procter & Gamble
Barnes & Noble	Home Depot	Wal-Mart
Caterpillar	IBM	Whirlpool

1. Using the PricewaterhouseCoopers Web site, http://edgarscan.pwcglobal.com, look up each company by entering its name. Click on each company's name and then scroll down to the bottom of the page to "Set Preferences." Select "Receivables Turnover" in the Ratios list. Then click "Save Preferences."
2. Categorize each of the preceding companies as to whether its turnover ratio is above or below 15.
3. Based upon (2), identify a characteristic of companies with accounts receivable turnover ratios above 15.

BUSINESS ACTIVITIES AND RESPONSIBILITY ISSUES

Activity 8-1

Ethics and professional conduct in business

Tricia Fenton, vice president of operations for Billings National Bank, has instructed the bank's computer programmer to use a 365-day year to compute interest on depository accounts (payables). Tricia also instructed the programmer to use a 360-day year to compute interest on loans (receivables).

Discuss whether Tricia is behaving in a professional manner.

Activity 8-2

Collecting accounts receivable

The following is an excerpt from a conversation between the office manager, Jamie Luthi, and the president of Jefferson Construction Supplies Co., David King. Jefferson sells building supplies to local contractors.

Jamie: David, we're going to have to do something about these overdue accounts receivable. One-third of our accounts are over 60 days past due, and I've had accounts that have stayed open for almost a year!

David: I didn't realize it was that bad. Any ideas?

Jamie: Well, we could stop giving credit. Make everyone pay with cash or a credit card. We accept MasterCard and Visa already, but only the walk-in customers use them. Almost all of the contractors put purchases on their bills.

David: Yes, but we've been allowing credit for years. As far as I know, all of our competitors allow contractors credit. If we stopped giving credit, we'd lose many of our contractors. They'd just go elsewhere. You know, some of these guys run up bills as high as $40,000 or $60,000. There's no way they could put that kind of money on a credit card.

Jamie: That's a good point. But we've got to do something.

David: How many of the contractor accounts do you actually end up writing off as uncollectible?

Jamie: Not many. Almost all eventually pay. It's just that they take so long!

Suggest one or more solutions to Jefferson's problem concerning the collection of accounts receivable.

Activity 8-3

Value of receivables

The following is an excerpt from a conversation between Kay Kinder, the president and owner of Retriever Wholesale Co., and Michele Stephens, Retriever's controller. The conversation took place on January 4, 2007 shortly after Michele began preparing the financial statements for the year ending December 31, 2006.

Michele: Kay, I've completed my analysis of the collectibility of our accounts receivable. My staff and I estimate that the allowance for doubtful accounts should be somewhere between $60,000 and $90,000. Right now, the balance of the allowance account is $18,000.

Kay: Oh, no! We are already below the estimated earnings projection I gave the bank last year. We used that as a basis for convincing the bank to loan us $100,000. They're going to be upset! Is there any way we can increase the allowance without the adjustment increasing expenses?

Michele: I'm afraid not. The allowance can only be increased by debiting the bad debt expense account.

Kay: Well, I guess we're stuck. The bank will just have to live with it. But let's increase the allowance by only $42,000. That gets us into our range of estimates with the minimum expense increase.

Michele: Kay, there is one more thing we need to discuss.

Kay: What now?

Michele: Jill, my staff accountant, noticed that you haven't made any payments on your receivable for over a year. Also, it has increased from $20,000 last year to $80,000. Jill thinks we ought to reclassify it as a noncurrent asset and report it as an "other receivable."

Kay: What's the problem? Didn't we just include it in accounts receivable last year?

Michele: Yes, but last year it was immaterial.

Kay: Look, I'll make a $60,000 payment next week. So let's report it as we did last year.

If you were Michele, how would you address Kay's suggestions?

Activity 8-4

Estimate uncollectible accounts

For several years, sales have been on a "cash only" basis. On January 1, 2004, however, Sheepshank Co. began offering credit on terms of n/30. The amount of the adjusting entry to record the estimated uncollectible receivables at the end of each year has been $\frac{1}{4}$ of 1% of credit sales, which is the rate reported as the average for the industry. Credit sales and the year-end credit balances in Allowance for Doubtful Accounts for the past four years are as follows:

Year	Credit Sales	Allowance for Doubtful Accounts
2004	$7,800,000	$ 5,100
2005	8,000,000	11,100
2006	8,100,000	16,850
2007	9,250,000	25,375

Carisa Parker, president of Sheepshank Co., is concerned that the method used to account for and write off uncollectible receivables is unsatisfactory. She has asked for your advice in the analysis of past operations in this area and for recommendations for change.

1. Determine the amount of (a) the addition to Allowance for Doubtful Accounts and (b) the accounts written off for each of the four years.
2. **a.** Advise Carisa Parker as to whether the estimate of $\frac{1}{4}$ of 1% of credit sales appears reasonable.
   b. Assume that after discussing (a) with Carisa Parker, she asked you what action might be taken to determine what the balance of Allowance for Doubtful Accounts should be at December 31, 2007, and what possible changes, if any, you might recommend in accounting for uncollectible receivables. How would you respond?

Activity 8-5

Granting credit

GROUP ACTIVITY

In groups of three or four, determine how credit is typically granted to customers. Interview an individual responsible for granting credit for a bank, a department store, an automobile dealer, or other business in your community. You should ask such questions as the following:

1. What procedures are used to decide whether to grant credit to a customer?
2. What procedures are used to try to collect from customers who are delinquent in their payments?
3. Approximately what percentage of customers' accounts are written off as uncollectible in a year?

Summarize your findings in a report to the class.

Activity 8-6

Collection of receivables

Go to the Web page of two department store chains, Federated Department Stores Inc. and Dillard's Inc. The Internet sites for these companies are:

http://www.federated-fds.com
http://www.dillards.com

Using the financial information provided at each site, calculate the most recent accounts receivable turnover for each company, and identify which company is collecting its receivables faster.

ANSWERS TO SELF-STUDY QUESTIONS

1. **B** The estimate of uncollectible accounts, $8,500 (answer C), is the amount of the desired balance of Allowance for Doubtful Accounts after adjustment. The amount of the current provision to be made for bad debt expense is thus $6,000 (answer B), which is the amount that must be added to the Allowance for Doubtful Accounts credit balance of $2,500 (answer A), so that the account will have the desired balance of $8,500.

2. **B** The amount expected to be realized from accounts receivable is the balance of Accounts Receivable, $100,000, less

the balance of Allowance for Doubtful Accounts, $7,000, or $93,000 (answer B).

3. C Maturity value is the amount that is due at the maturity or due date. The maturity value of $10,300 (answer C) is determined as follows:

Face amount of note	$10,000
Plus interest ($10,000 × 0.12 × 90/360)	300
Maturity value of note	$10,300

4. C November 3 is the due date of a $12,000, 90-day, 8% note receivable dated August 5 [26 days in August (31 days − 5 days) + 30 days in September + 31 days in October + 3 days in November].

5. B If a note is dishonored, Accounts Receivable is debited for the maturity value of the note (answer B). The maturity value of the note is its face value (answer A) plus the accrued interest. The maturity value of the note less accrued interest (answer C) is equal to the face value of the note. The maturity value of the note plus accrued interest (answer D) is incorrect, since the interest would be added twice.

9 Fixed Assets and Intangible Assets

Learning Goals

1. Define, classify, and account for the cost of fixed assets.
2. Compute depreciation, using the following methods: straight-line, units-of-production, and declining-balance.
3. Account for the disposal of fixed assets.
4. Describe and account for intangible assets, such as patents, copyrights, and goodwill.
5. Describe how depreciation expense is reported in an income statement, and prepare a balance sheet that includes fixed assets and intangible assets.
6. Analyze the utilization of fixed assets.

Marriott International, Inc.

© MARK LENNIHAN/AP WIDE WORLD PHOTO

Some things are timeless, like heirlooms, a good book, an antique, or real estate. Unfortunately, for most things, time is an enemy. In other words, they just wear out. Automobiles, boats, houses, audio and video equipment, cell phones, and the like all eventually need to be repaired or replaced. Sometimes, as in the case of an automobile or a boat, the mere use consumes the benefits. They just wear out as we use them. Other times, as in the case of electronic equipment, new functions will cause the equipment to become obsolete before it wears out. For example, would you buy a VHS tape player today? They're disappearing, not because they are broken, but because DVDs and digital cable are fast replacing VHS technology. Thus, as individuals, we purchase fixed assets with the intent of using them until either they become obsolete or wear out.

In the same way, fixed assets are a key element of a business's strategy. Many businesses need fixed assets in order to operate. For example, Marriott International, Inc., the largest lodging company in the world, needs hotel rooms in order to operate. Since fixed assets, such as hotel properties, use significant business resources, managers must clearly understand their business goals and strategies before making significant fixed asset purchases.

A business strives to have the right quantity and the right type of fixed assets. For example, the financial success of a lodging (hotel) company, such as Marriott, depends upon properly balancing the supply and demand for rooms. This is because hotel properties become a long-term commitment once they are built. Thus, unlike a manufacturing company, a lodging company cannot easily or quickly reduce the supply of rooms if demand falls, or quickly increase the supply of rooms when demand increases. For this reason, developing hotel properties with attractive long-term prospects is critical to Marriott's or any other lodging company's success.

Excess fixed asset capacity caused by either overinvesting in fixed assets or losing customers can lead a company into financial difficulty. For example, many argue that some Internet companies (e.g., eB2B Commerce, eToys, and Webvan) failed because they invested significant resources in fixed assets without a clear strategy for earning profits. Trump Hotels and Casino Resorts, Inc. lost customers because it failed to competitively maintain its three Atlantic City hotels and casinos. As a result, the company had to declare bankruptcy in 2004. In contrast, underinvesting in fixed assets can limit a business. For example, Apple Computer Inc. recently suffered shortages of its popular iPod® during the critical holiday shopping period as a result of inadequate manufacturing capacity.

In this chapter, we will focus on the accounting for and reporting of fixed assets, such as a hotel. We describe and illustrate determining the cost of a fixed asset, depreciation methods, fixed asset disposals, and how to analyze the efficiency of fixed asset usage.

Define, classify, and account for the cost of fixed assets.

NATURE OF FIXED ASSETS

Why is a "major purchase" different than other expenditures that you make? More than likely, the purchase is expensive and long-lived. As a result, you are careful when making these types of purchases. The same is true for a business. A business makes major purchases of equipment, furniture, tools, machinery, buildings, and land. These assets, which are called **fixed assets**, are long-term or relatively permanent assets. They are tangible assets because they exist physically. They are owned and used by the business and are not offered for sale as part of normal operations. Other descriptive titles for these assets are *plant assets* or *property, plant, and equipment.*

The fixed assets of a business can be a significant part of the total assets. Exhibit 1 shows the percent of fixed assets to total assets for some select companies, divided between service, manufacturing, and merchandising firms. As you can see, the fixed assets for most firms comprise a significant proportion of their total assets. In contrast, Computer Associates is a consulting firm that relies more on people rather than fixed assets to deliver value to customers.

Exhibit 1

Fixed Assets as a Percent of Total Assets—Selected Companies

	Fixed Assets as a Percent of Total Assets
Service Firms:	
Computer Associates	6%
Marriott International, Inc.	31
Verizon Communications Inc.	45
Manufacturing Firms:	
Alcoa Inc.	40%
Ford Motor Company	35
ExxonMobil Corporation	60
Merchandising Firms:	
Kroger Company	55%
Walgreen Co.	46
Wal-Mart	53

Q. St. Mary's Hospital maintains an auxiliary generator for use in electrical outages. Such outages are rare, and the generator has not been used for the past two years. Should the generator be reported as a fixed asset on St. Mary's balance sheet?

A. Yes. Even though the generator has not been used recently, it should be reported as a fixed asset.

Classifying Costs

Exhibit 2 displays questions that help classify costs. If the purchased item is long-lived, then it should be capitalized, which means it should appear on the balance sheet as an asset. Otherwise, the cost should be reported as an expense on the income statement. Capitalized costs are normally expected to last more than a year. If the asset is also used for a productive purpose, which involves a repeated use or benefit, then it should be classified as a fixed asset, such as land, buildings, or equipment. An asset need not actually be used on an ongoing basis or even often. For example, standby equipment for use in the event of a breakdown of regular equipment or for use only during peak periods is included in fixed assets. Fixed assets that have been abandoned or are no longer used should not be classified as a fixed asset.

Fixed assets are owned and used by the business and are not offered for resale. Long-lived assets held for resale are not classified as fixed assets, but should be listed on the balance sheet in a section entitled *investments*. For example, undeveloped land acquired as an investment for resale would be classified as an investment, not land.

Exhibit 2
Classifying Costs

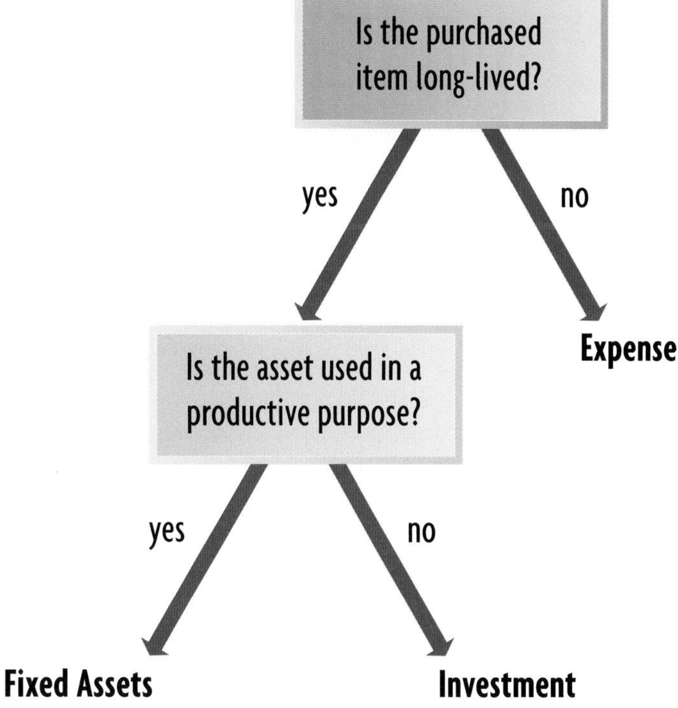

The Cost of Fixed Assets

The costs of acquiring fixed assets include all amounts spent to position and prepare the asset for use. For example, freight costs and the costs of installing equipment are added to the purchase price in determining the equipment's total cost.

Exhibit 3 summarizes some of the common costs of acquiring fixed assets. These costs should be recorded by debiting the related fixed asset account, such as Land,[1] Building, Land Improvements, or Machinery and Equipment.

HOW BUSINESSES MAKE MONEY

Fixed Assets as Barriers to Competition

One of the largest hotel complexes built in the United States is the new Gaylord Texan Resort & Convention Center outside of Dallas, Texas. The hotel has over 2.5 million square feet with 1,500 rooms and 150 acres and boasts a staff of 2,000. The hotel was built and is operated by **Gaylord Entertainment Co.** Following Gaylord's highly successful Grand Ole Opry hotel concept in Nashville, the hotel is designed to place all resort amenities under one roof, including restaurants, shopping, and entertainment. Texan Resort promotes a Texas theme, complete with saddle barstools, longhorn steers, Lone Star symbols, and a San Antonio Riverwalk representation. The company builds these massive projects primarily to attract large conventions. "What they are doing is taking the Las Vegas model and doing it in other cities," says one analyst. The hotel costs around $480 million to build. Unlike most hotel companies, Gaylord develops and builds the properties on its own. Such a large price tag helps keep the competition away. As noted by one analyst, "It requires $500 million of capital—that immediately eliminates most hotel developers around the world." As a result, Gaylord is able to use the size of the project as a strategic barrier, which allows the company to acquire and operate prime hotel locations without threat of rivals.

Source: Ryan Chittum, "What's Not Big at the Texan Hotel? Tourists." August 11, 2004, *The Wall Street Journal*, p. B1.

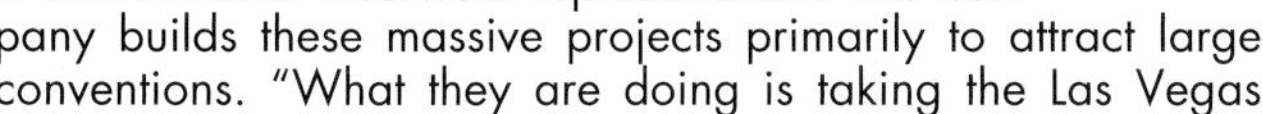

1 As discussed here, land is assumed to be used only as a location or site and not for its mineral deposits or other natural resources.

Exhibit 3

Costs of Acquiring Fixed Assets

Land

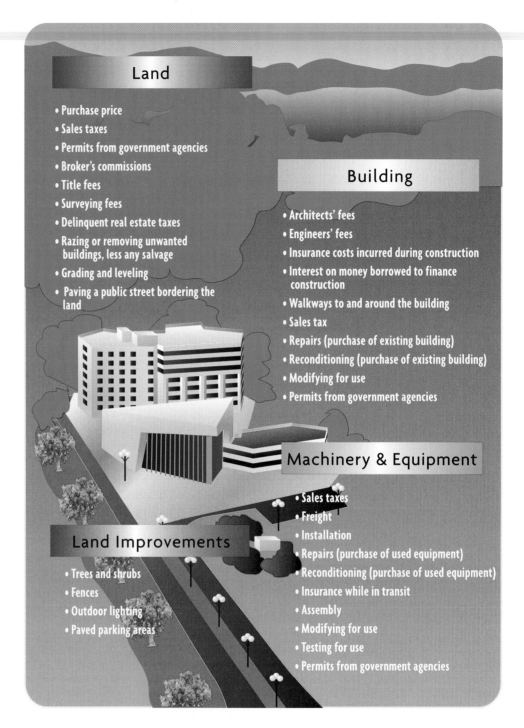

- Purchase price
- Sales taxes
- Permits from government agencies
- Broker's commissions
- Title fees
- Surveying fees
- Delinquent real estate taxes
- Razing or removing unwanted buildings, less any salvage
- Grading and leveling
- Paving a public street bordering the land

Building

- Architects' fees
- Engineers' fees
- Insurance costs incurred during construction
- Interest on money borrowed to finance construction
- Walkways to and around the building
- Sales tax
- Repairs (purchase of existing building)
- Reconditioning (purchase of existing building)
- Modifying for use
- Permits from government agencies

Machinery & Equipment

- Sales taxes
- Freight
- Installation
- Repairs (purchase of used equipment)
- Reconditioning (purchase of used equipment)
- Insurance while in transit
- Assembly
- Modifying for use
- Testing for use
- Permits from government agencies

Land Improvements

- Trees and shrubs
- Fences
- Outdoor lighting
- Paved parking areas

Q. Glacier Co. is purchasing property (building and land) for use as a warehouse. In purchasing the land, Glacier has agreed to pay the prior owner's delinquent property taxes. Should the cost of paying the delinquent property taxes be included as part of the cost of the property?

A. Yes. All costs of acquiring the property, including the delinquent property taxes, should be included as part of the total cost of the property.

Only costs necessary for preparing a long-lived asset for use should be included as a cost of the asset. Unnecessary costs that do not increase the asset's usefulness are recorded as an expense. For example, the following costs are treated as an expense:

- Vandalism
- Mistakes in installation
- Uninsured theft
- Damage during unpacking and installing
- Fines for not obtaining proper permits from governmental agencies

Capital and Revenue Expenditures

Once a fixed asset has been acquired and placed in service, expenditures may be incurred for ordinary maintenance and repairs. In addition, expenditures may be incurred for improving an asset or for extraordinary repairs that extend the asset's useful life. Expenditures that benefit only the current period are called **revenue expenditures**. Expenditures that improve the asset or extend its useful life are **capital expenditures**.

Ordinary Maintenance and Repairs. Expenditures related to the ordinary maintenance and repairs of a fixed asset are recorded as an expense of the current period. Such expenditures are *revenue expenditures* and are recorded as increases to Repairs and Maintenance Expense. For example, $300 paid for a tune-up of a delivery truck would be recorded as follows:

SCF	BS	IS
O↓	A↓ SE↓	E↑

Repairs and Maintenance Expense	300	
Cash		300

Asset Improvements. After a fixed asset has been placed in service, expenditures may be incurred to improve an asset. For example, the service value of a delivery truck might be improved by adding a $5,500 hydraulic lift to allow for easier and quicker loading of heavy cargo. Such expenditures are *capital expenditures* and are recorded as increases to the fixed asset account. In the case of the hydraulic lift, the expenditure is recorded as follows:

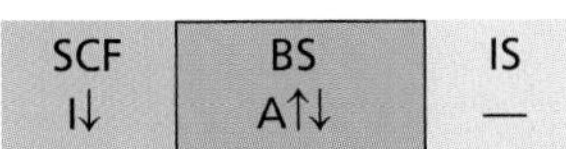

Delivery Truck	5,500	
Cash		5,500

Because the cost of the delivery truck has increased, depreciation for the truck would also change over its remaining useful life.

Extraordinary Repairs. After a fixed asset has been placed in service, expenditures may be incurred to extend the asset's useful life. For example, the engine of a forklift that is near the end of its useful life may be overhauled at a cost of $4,500, which would extend its useful life by eight years. Such expenditures are *capital expenditures* and are recorded as a decrease in an accumulated depreciation account. In the case of the forklift, the expenditure is recorded as follows:

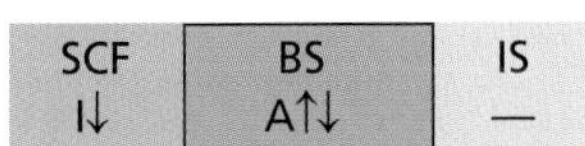

Accumulated Depreciation—Forklift	4,500	
Cash		4,500

Because the forklift's remaining useful life has changed, depreciation for the forklift would also change based upon the new book value of the forklift.

INTEGRITY, OBJECTIVITY, AND ETHICS IN BUSINESS

Capital Crime

One of the largest alleged accounting frauds in history involved the improper accounting for capital expenditures. **WorldCom, Inc.**, the second largest telecommunications company in the United States, improperly treated maintenance expenditures on its telecommunications network as capital expenditures. As a result, the company had to restate its prior years' earnings downward by nearly $4 billion to correct this error. The company declared bankruptcy within months of disclosing the error, and the CEO was sentenced to 25 years in prison.

The accounting for revenue and capital expenditures is summarized below.

Expenditure

Revenue Expenditure	Capital Expenditure	
Ordinary Repairs and Maintenance	Asset Improvement	Extraordinary Repair
Benefits only current period	Benefits current and future periods	Benefits current and future periods
	Adds service value to the asset	Extends the assest's useful life
Increase repairs and maintenance expense	Increase fixed assets	Decrease account depreciation
	Revise depreciation for current and future periods	Revise depreciation for current and future periods

Compute depreciation, using the following methods: straight-line, units-of-production, and declining-balance.

ACCOUNTING FOR DEPRECIATION

As we have discussed in earlier chapters, land has an unlimited life and therefore can provide unlimited services. In contrast, other fixed assets such as equipment, buildings, and land improvements lose their ability, over time, to provide services. As a result, the cost of equipment, buildings, and land improvements should be transferred to expense accounts in a systematic manner during their expected useful lives. This periodic transfer of cost to expense is called **depreciation**.

The adjusting entry to record depreciation is usually made at the end of each month or at the end of the year. This entry debits Depreciation Expense and credits a contra asset account entitled Accumulated Depreciation or Allowance for Depreciation. Recall, a contra asset account is disclosed in the asset section as a subtracted amount, thus the normal balance is a credit. The use of a contra asset account allows the original cost to remain unchanged in the fixed asset account.

Factors that cause a decline in a fixed asset's ability to provide services may be identified as physical depreciation or functional depreciation. Physical depreciation occurs from wear and tear from use and from the effects of weather conditions. Functional depreciation occurs when a fixed asset is no longer able to provide services at the level for which it was intended. Advances in technology have made functional depreciation an increasingly important cause of depreciation. For example, a personal computer made in the 1990s is not able to provide a wireless Internet connection, significantly decreasing its value.

The term *depreciation* as used in accounting is often misunderstood because the same term is also used in business to mean a decline in the market value of an asset. However, the amount of a fixed asset's unexpired cost reported in the balance sheet usually does not agree with the amount that could be realized from its sale. Fixed assets are held for use in a business rather than for sale. Since the business is assumed to be a going concern, a decision to dispose of a fixed asset is based mainly on the usefulness of the asset to the business and not on its market value.

Another common misunderstanding is that depreciation provides cash needed to replace fixed assets as they wear out. This misunderstanding probably occurs because depreciation, unlike most expenses, does not require an outlay of cash in the period in which it is recorded. The cash account is neither increased nor decreased by the periodic entries that transfer the cost of fixed assets to depreciation expense accounts. Rather, the cash outflow occurs when the fixed asset is originally purchased.

Factors in Computing Depreciation Expense

Three factors are considered in determining the amount of depreciation expense to be recognized each period. These three factors are (a) the fixed asset's initial cost, (b) its expected useful life, and (c) its estimated value at the end of its useful life. This third factor is called the **residual value**, *scrap value*, *salvage value*, or *trade-in value*.

A fixed asset's residual value at the end of its expected useful life must be estimated at the time the asset is placed in service. If a fixed asset is expected to have little or no residual value when it is taken out of service, then its initial cost should be spread over its expected useful life as depreciation expense. If, however, a fixed asset is expected to have a significant residual value, the difference between its initial cost and its residual value, called the asset's *depreciable cost*, is the amount that is spread over the asset's useful life as depreciation expense. Exhibit 4 shows the relationship among the factors used to compute periodic depreciation expense.

A fixed asset's *expected useful life* must also be estimated at the time the asset is placed in service. Estimates of expected useful lives are available from various trade associations and other publications. It is not uncommon for different companies to have different useful lives for similar assets. For example, the primary useful life for buildings is 50 years for JCPenney, while the useful life for buildings for Tandy Corporation, which operates Radio Shack, varies from 10 to 40 years. For federal income tax purposes, the Internal Revenue Service (IRS) has established guidelines for useful lives. For example, the IRS useful life guideline for most vehicles is five years, while the designated life for most machinery and equipment is seven years. These

Exhibit 4
Factors that Determine Depreciation Expense

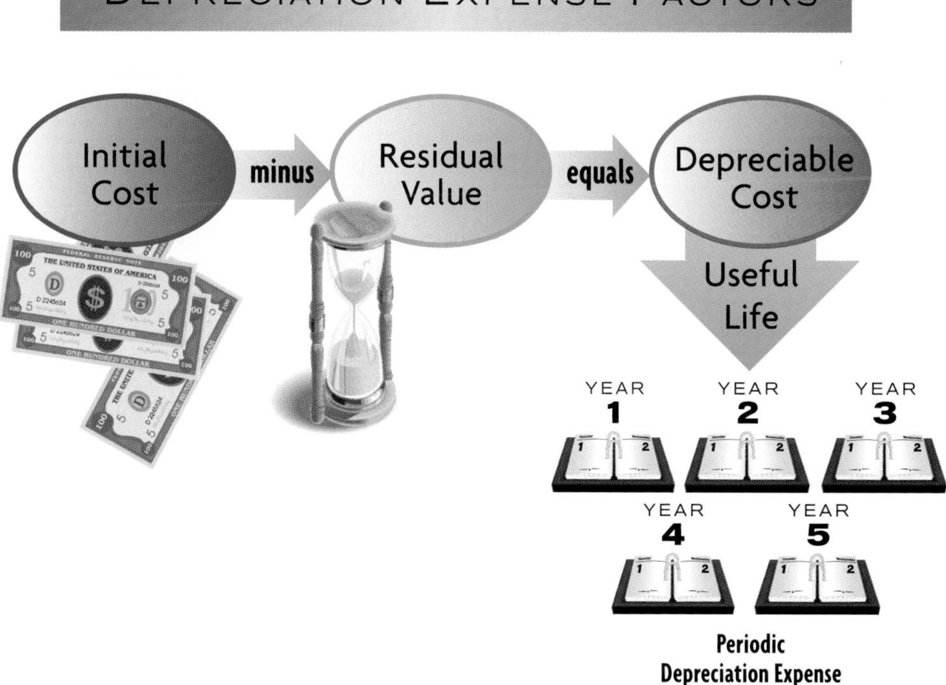

guidelines may also be helpful in determining depreciation for financial reporting purposes. Companies often use different useful lives for similar assets.

Guidelines are also necessary for determining when an asset is placed into and out of service. In practice, many businesses assume that assets placed in or taken out of service during the first half of a month are treated as if the event occurred on the first day of that month. That is, these businesses compute depreciation on these assets for the entire month. Likewise, all fixed asset additions and deductions during the second half of a month are treated as if the event occurred on the first day of the next month. We will follow this practice in this chapter.

A business is not required to use a single method of computing depreciation for all its depreciable assets. The methods used in the accounts and financial statements may also differ from the methods used in determining income taxes and property taxes. The three methods used most often are (1) straight-line, (2) units-of-production, and (3) declining-balance. Exhibit 5 shows the extent of the use of these methods in financial statements.

Exhibit 5

Use of Depreciation Methods

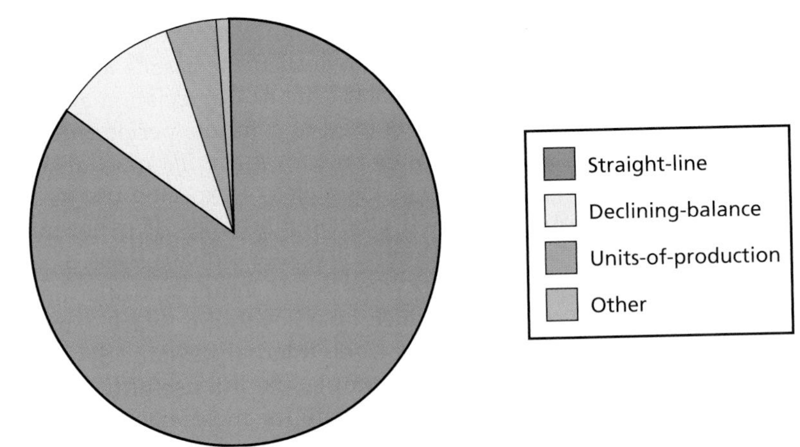

Source: Accounting Trends and Techniques, AICPA, 58th edition, 2004.

Q. A truck that cost $35,000 has a residual value of $5,000 and a useful life of 12 years. What are (a) the depreciable cost, (b) the straight-line rate, and (c) the annual straight-line depreciation?

A. *(a) $30,000 ($35,000–$5,000), (b) 8 1/3%(1/12), (c) $2,500 ($30,000 × 8 1/3%)*

Straight-Line Method

The **straight-line method** provides for the same amount of depreciation expense for each year of the asset's useful life. For example, assume that the initial cost of a depreciable asset is $24,000, its estimated residual value is $2,000, and its estimated life is five years. The annual depreciation is computed as follows:

$$\frac{\$24{,}000 \text{ Initial Cost} - \$2{,}000 \text{ Estimated Residual Value}}{\text{5-Year Estimated Life}} = \$4{,}400 \text{ Annual Depreciation}$$

The adjusting entry for depreciation would be recorded as follows:

SCF	BS	IS
—	A↓ SE↓	E↑

Dec. 31	Depreciation Expense	4,400	
	Accumulated Depreciation		4,400

When an asset is used for only part of a year, the annual depreciation is prorated. For example, assume that the fiscal year ends on December 31 and that the asset in the above example is placed in service on October 1. The depreciation for the first fiscal year of use would be $1,100 ($4,400 × $\frac{3}{12}$).

© EDMOND VAN HOORICK/PHOTODISC/GETTY IMAGES

For ease in applying the straight-line method, the annual depreciation may be converted to a percentage of the depreciable cost. This percentage is determined by dividing 100% by the number of years of useful life. For example, a useful life of 20 years converts to a 5% rate (100% ÷ 20 years), eight years converts to a 12.5% rate (100% ÷ 8 years), and so on.[2] In the above example, the annual depreciation of $4,400 can be computed by multiplying the depreciable cost of $22,000 by 20% (100% ÷ 5 years).

The straight-line method is simple and is widely used. It provides a reasonable transfer of costs to periodic expense when the asset's use and the related revenues from its use are about the same from period to period.

Units-of-Production Method

Sometimes the use of the fixed asset varies significantly from period to period, such as might be the case for vehicles, aircraft, or construction equipment. When the amount of use of a fixed asset varies from year to year, the units-of-production method may be more appropriate than the straight-line method. In such cases, the units-of-production method better matches the depreciation expense with the related revenue.

Q. A truck that cost $35,000 has a residual value of $5,000 and a useful life of 125,000 miles. What are (a) the depreciation rate per mile and (b) the first year's depreciatiion if 18,000 miles were driven?

A. (a) $0.24 per mile [($35,000 – $5,000) ÷ 125,000 miles], (b) $4,320 (18,000 miles × $0.24 per mile)

The **units-of-production method** provides for the same amount of depreciation expense for each unit produced or each unit of capacity used by the asset. For example, Norfolk Southern Corporation depreciates train engines on the basis of hours of operation, which is its unit of capacity.

To apply this method, the useful life of the asset is expressed in terms of units of productive capacity, such as hours or miles. The total depreciation expense for each accounting period is then determined by multiplying the unit depreciation by the number of units produced or used during the period. For example, assume that a machine with an initial cost of $24,000 and an estimated residual value of $2,000 is expected to have an estimated life of 10,000 operating hours. The depreciation for a unit of one hour is computed as follows:

$$\frac{\$24{,}000 \text{ Initial Cost} - \$2{,}000 \text{ Estimated Residual Value}}{10{,}000 \text{ Estimated Hours}} = \$2.20 \text{ Hourly Depreciation}$$

Assuming that the machine was in operation for 2,100 hours during a year, the depreciation for that year would be $4,620 ($2.20 × 2,100 hours).

Declining-Balance Method

The **declining-balance method** provides for a declining periodic expense over the estimated useful life of the asset. To apply this method, the annual depreciation rate is often expressed as a multiple of the straight-line rate. When the rate is doubled, the declining-balance method is called the *double-declining-balance method.* For example, the double-declining-balance rate for an asset with an estimated life of five years is 40%, which is double the straight-line rate of 20% (100% ÷ 5 years).

For the first year of use, the cost of the asset is multiplied by the declining-balance rate. After the first year, the declining **book value** or net book value (initial asset cost

2 The depreciation rate may also be expressed as a fraction. For example, the annual straight-line rate for an asset with a three-year useful life is $\frac{1}{3}$.

minus accumulated depreciation) of the asset is multiplied by this rate. To illustrate, the amount of annual double-declining-balance depreciation for an asset with an estimated five-year life and a cost of $24,000 is shown below.

Year	Cost	Accum. Depr. at Beginning of Year	Book Value at Beginning of Year	Rate	Depreciation for Year	Book Value at End of Year
1	$24,000		$24,000.00	40%	$9,600.00	$14,400.00
2	24,000	$ 9,600.00	14,400.00	40	5,760.00	8,640.00
3	24,000	15,360.00	8,640.00	40	3,456.00	5,184.00
4	24,000	18,816.00	5,184.00	40	2,073.60	3,110.40
5	24,000	20,889.60	3,110.40	—	1,110.40	2,000.00

Q&A

Q. A truck that cost $35,000 has a residual value of $5,000 and a useful life of 12 years. What is the double-declining-balance depreciation for the second full year of use?

A. *$4,861 {[$35,000 – ($35,000 × 16⅔%)] × 16⅔%}*

You should note that when using the declining-balance method, the estimated residual value is not considered in determining the depreciation rate. It is also ignored in computing the periodic depreciation. However, the asset should not be depreciated below its estimated residual value. In the above example, the estimated residual value was $2,000. Therefore, the depreciation for the fifth year is $1,110.40 ($3,110.40 – $2,000.00) instead of $1,244.16 (40% × $3,110.40).

In the example, we assumed that the first use of the asset occurred at the beginning of the fiscal year. This is normally not the case in practice, however, and depreciation for the first partial year of use must be computed. For example, assume that the asset above was in service at the end of the third month of the fiscal year. In this case, only a portion ($\frac{9}{12}$) of the first full year's depreciation of $9,600 is allocated to the first fiscal year. Thus, depreciation of $7,200 ($\frac{9}{12}$ × $9,600) is allocated to the first partial year of use. The depreciation for the second fiscal year would then be $6,720 [40% × ($24,000 – $7,200)].

Comparing Depreciation Methods

The three depreciation methods can be compared as shown in Exhibit 6. All three methods assign a portion of the total cost of an asset to an accounting period, while never depreciating an asset below its residual value. The straight-line and declining-balance methods assign depreciation to the period on the basis of the life of the asset, while the units-of-production method assigns cost on the basis of use. The straight-line method provides for the same periodic amounts of depreciation expense over the life of the asset. The units-of-production method provides for periodic amounts of depreciation expense that vary, depending upon the amount the asset is used.

The declining-balance method provides for a higher depreciation amount in the first year of the asset's use, followed by a gradually declining amount. For this reason

Exhibit 6

Comparing Depreciation Methods

Method	Asset Life Expressed in	Asset Cost Depreciated	Depreciation Rate	Depreciation Expense Pattern over Time
Straight-line	Years	Cost less residual value	100% ÷ Estimated Life	Level
Units-of-production	Total estimated units produced or used	Cost less residual value	(Cost – Residual Value) ÷ Total Estimated Units Produced or Used	Variable
Declining-balance	Years	Declining book value, but not below residual value	(100% ÷ Estimated Life) × 2	Declining

the declining-balance method is called an **accelerated depreciation method**. This method is most appropriate when the decline in an asset's productivity or earning power is greater in the early years of its use than in later years. Further, using this method is often justified because repairs tend to increase with the age of an asset. The reduced amounts of depreciation in later years are thus offset to some extent by increased repair expenses.

Depreciation for Federal Income Tax

The Internal Revenue Code specifies the *Modified Accelerated Cost Recovery System (MACRS)* for use by businesses in computing depreciation for tax purposes. MACRS specifies eight classes of useful life and depreciation rates for each class. The two most common classes, other than real estate, are the five-year class and the seven-year class.[3] The five-year class includes automobiles and light-duty trucks, and the seven-year class includes most machinery and equipment. The depreciation deduction for these two classes is similar to that computed using the declining-balance method in that larger depreciation amounts are recorded in earlier periods.

In using the MACRS rates, residual value is ignored, and all fixed assets are assumed to be put in and taken out of service in the middle of the year. For the five-year-class assets, depreciation is spread over six years, as shown in the following MACRS schedule of depreciation rates:

Q&A

Q. What is the third-year MACRS depreciation for an automobile that cost $26,000 and has a residual value of $6,500?

A. *$4,992 ($26,000 × 19.2%)*

Year	5-Year-Class Depreciation Rates
1	20.0%
2	32.0
3	19.2
4	11.5
5	11.5
6	5.8
	100.0%

To simplify its record keeping, a business will sometimes use the MACRS method for both financial statement and tax purposes. This is acceptable if MACRS does not result in significantly different amounts than would have been reported using one of the three depreciation methods discussed earlier in this chapter.

Revising Depreciation Estimates

Revising the estimates of the residual value and the useful life is normal. When these estimates are revised, they are used to determine the depreciation expense in future periods. They do not affect the amounts of depreciation expense recorded in earlier years.

To illustrate, assume that a fixed asset purchased for $140,000 was originally estimated to have a useful life of five years and a residual value of $10,000. The asset has been depreciated for two years by the straight-line method at a rate of $26,000 per year [($140,000 − $10,000) ÷ 5 years]. At the end of two years, the asset's book value (undepreciated cost) is $88,000, determined as follows:

Asset cost	$140,000
Less accumulated depreciation ($26,000 per year × 2 years)	52,000
Book value (undepreciated cost), end of second year	$ 88,000

3 Real estate is in $27\frac{1}{2}$-year and $31\frac{1}{2}$-year classes and is depreciated by the straight-line method.

Exhibit 7

Book Value of Asset with Change in Estimate

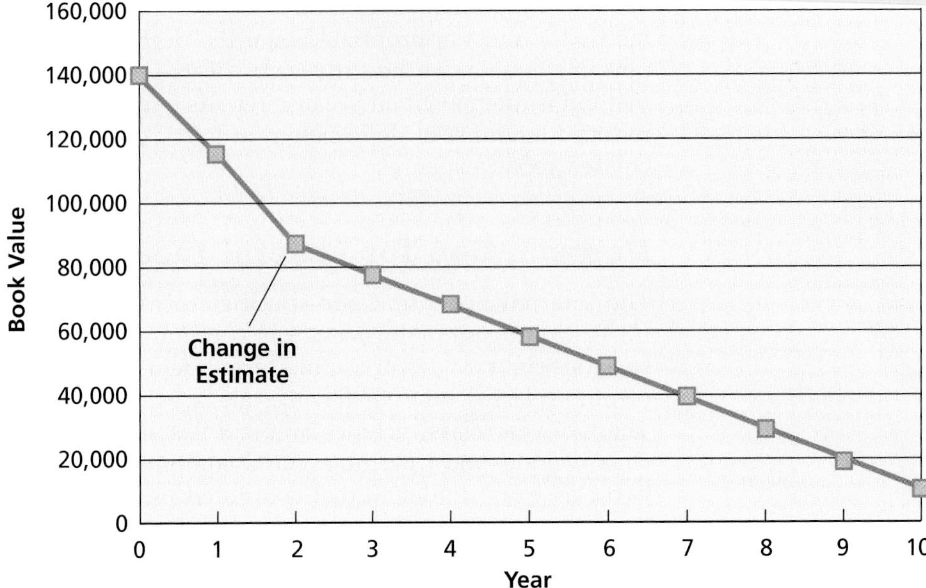

Q&A

Q. An asset with an original cost of $80,000 and a residual value of $12,000 was estimated to have an eight-year life. After three years, the asset is estimated to have a remaining life of 10 years, with no change in residual value. What is the revised depreciation expense for the fourth year?

A. *$4,250. The depreciation expense per year for the first three years is $8,500 per year [($80,000 − $12,000) ÷ 8]. The book value at the end of the third year is $54,500 [$80,000 − (3 × $8,500)]. The remaining book value less the residual value divided by the remaining life is [($54,500 − $12,000) ÷ 10].*

During the third year, the company estimates that the remaining useful life is eight years (instead of three) and that the residual value is $8,000 (instead of $10,000). The depreciation expense for each of the remaining eight years is $10,000, computed as follows:

Book value (undepreciated cost), end of second year	$88,000
Less revised estimated residual value	8,000
Revised remaining depreciable cost	$80,000
Revised annual depreciation expense ($80,000 ÷ 8 years)	$10,000

Exhibit 7 shows the book value of the asset over its original and revised lives. Notice that the book value declines at a slower rate beginning at the end of year 2 and continuing until it reaches the residual value of $8,000 at the end of year 10, which is the revised end of the asset's useful life.

A change in estimate should be disclosed in the notes to the financial statements. An example of such a disclosure is shown for St. Paul Companies as follows:

> *Acceleration of Software Depreciation . . . . The resulting strategy to standardize technology throughout . . . and maintain one data center in St. Paul, Minnesota, resulted in the identification of duplicate software applications. As a result, the estimated useful life for that software was shortened, resulting in an additional charge to earnings.*

3

Account for the disposal of fixed assets.

FIXED ASSET DISPOSALS

Fixed assets that are no longer useful may be discarded, sold, or exchanged for other fixed assets.[4] Often, such transactions will give rise to gains and losses upon disposal. The details of the entry to record a disposal will vary. In all cases, however, the book

4 Accounting for fixed asset exchanges (trades) is a topic covered in advanced accounting courses.

value of the asset is removed from the accounts. The entry to record the disposal of a fixed asset debits the asset's accumulated depreciation account for its balance on the date of disposal and credits the asset account for the cost of the asset.

If the asset is still used by the business, the cost and accumulated depreciation remain in the ledger. This maintains accountability for the asset in the ledger. If the book value of the asset is removed from the ledger, the accounts contain no evidence of the continued existence of the asset. In addition, the cost and accumulated depreciation data on such assets are often needed for property tax and income tax reports.

Discarding Fixed Assets

When fixed assets are no longer useful to the business and have no residual or market value, they are discarded. To illustrate, assume that an item of equipment acquired at a cost of $25,000 is fully depreciated, with no residual value at December 31, the end of the preceding fiscal year. On February 14, the equipment is discarded. The entry to record this is as follows:

SCF	BS	IS
—	A↓↑	—

Feb. 14	Accumulated Depreciation	25,000	
	Equipment		25,000

If an asset has not been fully depreciated, depreciation should be recorded prior to removing it from service and from the accounting records. To illustrate, assume that equipment costing $6,000 is depreciated at an annual straight-line rate of 10%. In addition, assume that on December 31 of the preceding fiscal year, the accumulated depreciation balance, after adjusting entries, is $4,750. Finally, assume that the asset is removed from service on the following March 24. The entry to record the depreciation for the three months of the current period prior to the asset's removal from service is as follows:

SCF	BS	IS
—	A↓ SE↓	E↑

Mar. 24	Depreciation Expense—Equipment	150	
	Accumulated Depreciation—Equipment		150
	To record current depreciation on equipment discarded ($600 × $\frac{3}{12}$).		

The discarding of the equipment is then recorded by the following entry:

SCF	BS	IS
—	A↑↓ SE↓	E↑

Mar. 24	Accumulated Depreciation—Equipment	4,900	
	Loss on Disposal of Fixed Assets	1,100	
	Equipment		6,000

The loss of $1,100 is recorded because the balance of the accumulated depreciation account ($4,900) is less than the balance in the equipment account ($6,000) which represents the undepreciated portion of the discarded asset. Losses on the discarding of fixed assets are nonoperating items and are normally reported in the Other Expense section of the income statement.

Selling Fixed Assets

The entry to record the sale of a fixed asset is similar to the entry illustrated above, except that the cash or other asset received must also be recorded. If the selling price is more than the book value of the asset, the transaction results in a gain. If the selling price is less than the book value, there is a loss. For example, H.J. Heinz Company recognized a gain of $18.2 million on the sale of an office building in the United Kingdom because the selling price exceeded the book value.

To illustrate a sale transaction, assume that equipment is acquired at a cost of $10,000, has no residual value, and is depreciated at an annual straight-line rate of 10%. The building is sold for cash on October 12 of the eighth year of its use. The balance of the accumulated depreciation account as of the preceding December 31 is $7,600. The depreciation for the nine months of the current year is $750 ($\$10{,}000 \times 10\% \times \frac{9}{12}$). The entry to update the depreciation on October 12 is as follows:

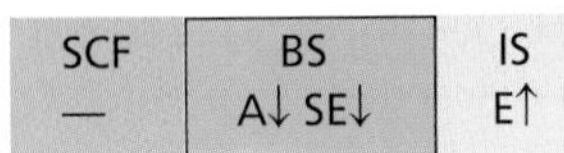

Oct. 12	Depreciation Expense	750	
	Accumulated Depreciation		750

After the current depreciation is recorded, the book value of the asset is $2,250 ($10,000 – $7,750). The entry to record the sale, assuming the asset was sold for $1,000 is as follows:

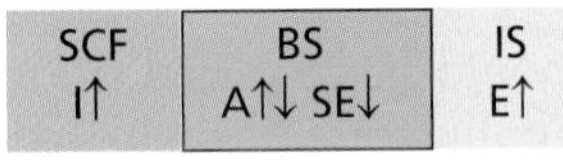

Oct. 12	Cash	1,000	
	Accumulated Depreciation	7,750	
	Loss on Disposal of Fixed Asset	1,250	
	Equipment		10,000

Q&A

Q. Provide the journal entry if the asset described in the text illustration was sold for $2,800.

A. Oct. 12

Cash	2,800	
Accum. Depr.	7,750	
Gain on Disposal of Fixed Asset		550
Equipment		10,000

The loss can be verified as the difference between the cash proceeds upon sale and the book value of the asset, as follows:

Cash proceeds		$1,000
Less: Equipment initial cost	$10,000	
Accumulated depreciation	7,750	
Equipment book value		2,250
Loss on disposal of fixed asset		$1,250

Describe and account for intangible assets, such as patents, copyrights, and goodwill.

INTANGIBLE ASSETS

Patents, copyrights, trademarks, and goodwill are long-lived assets that are useful in the operations of a business and are not held for sale. These assets are called **intangible assets** because they do not exist physically.

The basic principles of accounting for intangible assets are like those described earlier for fixed assets. The major concerns are determining (1) the initial cost and (2) the **amortization**—the amount of cost to transfer to expense. Amortization results from the passage of time or a decline in the usefulness of the intangible asset.

Patents

Manufacturers may acquire exclusive rights to produce and sell goods with one or more unique features. Such rights are granted by **patents**, which the federal government issues to inventors. These rights continue in effect for 20 years. A business may purchase patent rights from others, or it may obtain patents developed by its own research and development efforts.

The initial cost of a purchased patent, including any related legal fees, is debited to an asset account. This cost is written off, or amortized, over the years of the patent's expected usefulness. This period of time may be less than the remaining legal life of the patent. The estimated useful life of the patent may also change as technology or consumer tastes change.

The straight-line method is normally used to determine the periodic amortization. When the amortization is recorded, it is debited to an expense account and credited directly to the patents account. A separate contra asset account is usually not used for intangible assets.

To illustrate, assume that at the beginning of its fiscal year, a business acquires patent rights for $100,000. The patent had been granted six years earlier by the Federal Patent Office. Although the patent will not expire for 14 years, its remaining useful life is estimated as five years. The adjusting entry to amortize the patent at the end of the fiscal year is as follows:

SCF	BS	IS
—	A↓ SE↓	E↑

Dec. 31	Amortization Expense—Patents	20,000	
	Patents		20,000

Rather than purchase patent rights, a business may incur significant costs in developing patents through its own research and development efforts. Such research and development costs are usually accounted for as current operating expenses in the period in which they are incurred. Expensing research and development costs is justified because the future benefits from research and development efforts are highly uncertain.

Copyrights and Trademarks

The exclusive right to publish and sell a literary, artistic, or musical composition is granted by a **copyright**. Copyrights are issued by the federal government and extend for 70 years beyond the author's death. The costs of a copyright include all costs of creating the work plus any administrative or legal costs of obtaining the copyright. A copyright that is purchased from another should be recorded at the price paid for it. Copyrights are amortized over their estimated useful lives. For example, Sony Corporation states the following amortization policy with respect to its artistic and music intangible assets:

> *Intangibles, which mainly consist of artist contracts and music catalogs, are being amortized on a straight-line basis principally over 16 years and 21 years, respectively.*

A **trademark** is a name, term, or symbol used to identify a business and its products. For example, the distinctive red-and-white Coca-Cola logo is an example of a trademark. Most businesses identify their trademarks with ® in their advertisements and on their products. Under federal law, businesses can protect against others using their trademarks by registering them for 10 years and renewing the registration for 10-year periods thereafter. Like a copyright, the costs of acquiring a trademark are

INTEGRITY, OBJECTIVITY, AND ETHICS IN BUSINESS

21st Century Pirates

Pirated software is a major concern of software companies. For example, during a recent global sweep, **Microsoft** seized nearly 5 million units of counterfeit Microsoft software with an estimated retail value of $1.7 billion. U.S. copyright laws and practices are sometimes ignored or disputed in other parts of the world.

Businesses must honor the copyrights held by software companies by eliminating pirated software from corporate computers. The **Business Software Alliance (BSA)** represents the largest software companies in campaigns to investigate illegal use of unlicensed software by businesses. The BSA estimates software industry losses of nearly $12 billion annually from software piracy. Employees using pirated software on business assets risk bringing legal penalties to themselves and their employers.

recorded as an asset. Thus, even though the Coca-Cola trademarks are extremely valuable, they are not shown on the balance sheet because the costs for establishing these trademarks are immaterial. If, however, a trademark is purchased from another business, the cost of its purchase is recorded as an asset. The cost of a trademark is in most cases considered to have an indefinite useful life. Thus, trademarks are not amortized over a useful life, as are the previously discussed intangible assets. Rather, trademarks should be tested periodically for impaired value. When a trademark is impaired from competitive threats or other circumstances, the trademark should be written down and a loss recognized.

Goodwill

In business, **goodwill** refers to an intangible asset of a business that is created from such favorable factors as location, product quality, reputation, and managerial skill. Generally accepted accounting principles permit goodwill to be recorded in the accounts only if it is objectively determined by a transaction. An example of such a transaction is the purchase of a business at a price in excess of the net assets (assets − liabilities) of the acquired business. The excess is recorded as goodwill and reported as an intangible asset. Similar to trademarks, goodwill is not amortized because it has an indefinite life. However, a loss should be recorded if the business prospects of the acquired firm become significantly impaired. This loss would normally be disclosed in the Other Expense section of the income statement. To illustrate, Time Warner, Inc., recorded one of the largest losses in corporate history of nearly $54 billion for the write-down of goodwill associated with the AOL and Time Warner merger. The entry is recorded as follows:

SCF	BS	IS
—	A↓ SE↓	E↑

Loss from Impaired Goodwill	54,000,000,000	
Goodwill		54,000,000,000

Exhibit 8 shows the frequency of intangible asset disclosures for a sample of 600 large firms. As you can see, goodwill is the most frequently reported intangible asset. This is because goodwill arises from merger transactions, which are very common.

Exhibit 9 summarizes the characteristics of intangible assets discussed in this section. Patents and copyrights are examples of intangible assets with finite lives and are thus subject to periodic amortization based upon their estimated useful lives. Trademarks and goodwill are examples of intangible assets with indefinite lives and are thus not subject to periodic amortization. Rather, intangible assets with indefinite lives are tested periodically for impairment. If the intangible asset is impaired, then the intangible asset carrying value is written down, and an impairment loss is recognized for the period.

Exhibit 8

Frequency of Intangible Asset Disclosures for 600 Firms

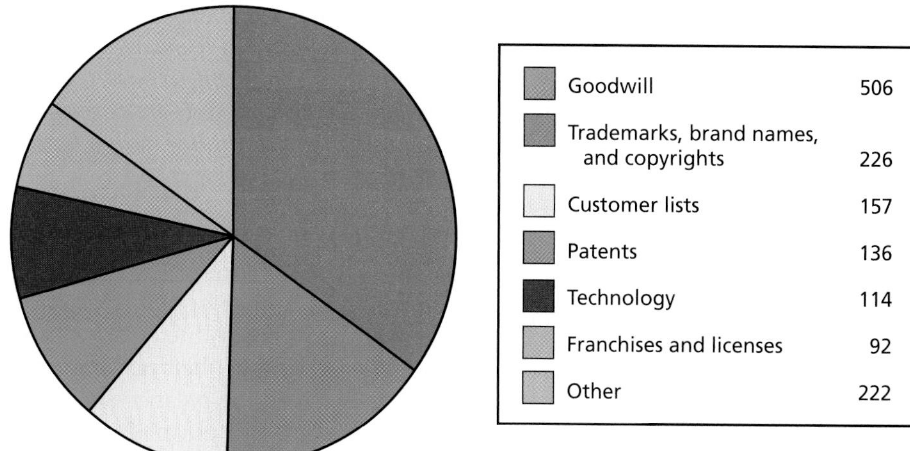

Source: *Accounting Trends and Techniques,* 58th ed., American Institute of Certified Public Accountants, New York, 2004. *Note:* Some firms have multiple disclosures.

Exhibit 9

Comparison of Intangible Assets

Intangible Asset	Description	Amortization Period	Periodic Expense
Patent	Exclusive right to benefit from an innovation.	Estimated useful life not to exceed legal life.	Amortization expense.
Copyright	Exclusive right to benefit from a literary, artistic, or musical composition.	Estimated useful life not to exceed legal life.	Amortization expense.
Trademark	Exclusive use of a name, term, or symbol.	None	Impairment loss if fair value less than carrying value (impaired).
Goodwill	Excess of purchase price of a business over its net assets.	None	Impairment loss if fair value less than carrying value (impaired).

INTEGRITY, OBJECTIVITY, AND ETHICS IN BUSINESS

When Does Goodwill Become Worthless?

The timing and amount of goodwill write-offs can be very subjective. Managers and their accountants should fairly estimate the value of goodwill and record goodwill impairment when it occurs. It would be unethical to delay a write-down of goodwill when it is determined that the asset is impaired.

5 Describe how depreciation expense is reported in an income statement, and prepare a balance sheet that includes fixed assets and intangible assets.

REPORTING FIXED ASSETS AND INTANGIBLE ASSETS

The amount of depreciation and amortization expense for a period should be reported separately in the income statement or disclosed in a note. A general description of the capitalization and depreciation policies should also be reported, as illustrated below for Marriott International, Inc.

We capitalize the cost of improvements that extend the useful life of property and equipment when incurred. These capitalized costs may include structural costs, equipment, fixtures, floor and wall coverings and paint. All repair and maintenance costs are expensed as incurred. We compute depreciation using the straight-line method over the estimated useful lives of the assets (three to 40 years).

The amount of each major class of fixed assets should be disclosed in the balance sheet or in notes. The related accumulated depreciation should also be disclosed, either by major class or in total. The fixed assets may be shown at their book value (cost less accumulated depreciation), which can also be described as their net amount. Alternatively, a single amount may be presented in the balance sheet, supported by a separate detailed listing. Fixed assets are normally presented under the more descriptive caption of *property, plant, and equipment*. Property, plant, and equipment may include construction in progress. This account accumulates the costs associated with fixed assets under construction which have yet to be placed into service. For growing companies, construction in progress can be significant. For example, XM Satellite Radio Holdings Inc. recently disclosed $92.5 million of satellite system construction in progress, which was 12% of its total fixed assets.

Intangible assets are usually reported in the balance sheet in a separate section immediately following the fixed assets. The balance of each major class of intangible assets should be disclosed at an amount net of the amortization taken to date. Exhibit 10 is a partial balance sheet that shows the reporting of fixed assets and intangible assets for Marriott International, Inc.

Exhibit 10

Fixed Assets and Intangible Assets in the Balance Sheet

Marriott International, Inc.
Partial Balance Sheet
December 31, 2004

	In Millions
Property, Plant, and Equipment:	
Land	$ 371
Buildings	642
Furniture and equipment	771
Timeshare properties	1,186
Construction in progress	100
	$3,070
Less: Accumulated depreciation	681
	$2,389
Intangible Assets:	
Franchise and licenses	$ 513
Goodwill	923
	$1,436

Analyze the utilization of fixed assets.

ANALYZING FIXED ASSETS

Business success for many firms is influenced by the utilization of fixed assets. Fixed assets that sit idle do not generate revenue and, hence, do not provide a return on investment. Thus, analysts examine the utilization of the fixed assets. The two major types of analyses are operational utilization analysis and financial utilization analysis.

Operational Utilization Analysis

The operating statistics of fixed assets for some fixed asset-intensive industries are provided by the reports filed with the SEC (Securities and Exchange Commission) and, hence, are publicly available for analysis. These operational measures are typically determined by the following general ratio:

$$\text{Operational Utilization (general ratio)} = \frac{\text{Annual Usage of the Fixed Asset}}{\text{Total Annual Fixed Asset Capacity}}$$

The closer the operational utilization approaches 100%, the more efficient the fixed assets. Naturally, a 100% utilization would be rare; however, much smaller percentages could indicate a problem. Exhibit 11 provides the ratio name and calculation for several operational utilization ratios for a number of industries.

Exhibit 11

Operational Utilization Ratio Examples

Industry	Ratio Name	Ratio Calculation
Airline	Load factor	Seat miles sold ÷ Available seat miles
Cable	Penetration	Subscribers ÷ Potential connections on network
Hospital (operating room)	Utilization	Utilized hours ÷ Available hours
Hotel	Occupancy	Nights sold ÷ Available nights
Power generation	Utilization	Net generating output ÷ Total generating capacity

To illustrate, the occupancy rate reported to the SEC for Starwood Hotels & Resorts (Sheraton® and Westin® hotel brands) was 68.5%. This percentage is determined by dividing the total room nights sold by the total available nights. The available nights are the number of rooms multiplied by 365 operating days in the year. The comparable ratio for Marriott International, Inc., was 71.8%. We could conclude that Marriott has utilized its hotel assets more efficiently than Starwood because more room nights were sold as a percent of available nights.

HOW BUSINESSES MAKE MONEY

Rent or Own?

You might hire a copy shop to copy a school paper, rather than acquiring a copy machine to make your own copies. In the same way, companies must decide which activities they should perform and which activities they should hire other companies to perform for them. The activities that are performed internally usually require fixed assets. Fixed assets, in turn, place a firm at risk, since these assets must be used in order to have a financial return. Thus, some firms limit internal activities to their core competencies, or those activities that provide the company a strategic comparative advantage. Under this philosophy, non-core activities are purchased from others. **Sara Lee Corporation** embraced this strategic philosophy by becoming "an asset-less company." That is, Sara Lee has retained only its core activities and has asked suppliers to perform its non-core activities, such as manufacturing. In contrast, **General Mills**, a Sara Lee competitor, owns its manufacturing facilities. This difference in strategic philosophy can be seen in the companies' respective fixed asset turnover ratios, 6.0 for Sara Lee and 3.6 for General Mills.

Financial Utilization Analysis

Fixed assets can also be evaluated by their ability to generate revenue. One measure of the revenue-generating efficiency of fixed assets is the fixed asset turnover ratio. The **fixed asset turnover ratio** measures the number of dollars of revenue earned per dollar of fixed assets and is calculated as follows:

$$\text{Fixed Asset Turnover Ratio} = \frac{\text{Revenue}}{\text{Average Book Value of Fixed Assets}}$$

To illustrate the calculation, the following fixed asset balance sheet information is available for Marriott International, Inc.:

	December 31, 2004 (in millions)	January 2, 2004 (in millions)
Property and equipment (net)	\$2,389	\$2,513

In addition, Marriott reported revenue of \$10,099 million for 2004. Thus, the fixed asset turnover ratio is calculated as follows:

$$\text{Fixed Asset Turnover Ratio} = \frac{\$10{,}099}{(\$2{,}389 + \$2{,}513)/2} = 4.12$$

For every dollar of fixed assets, Marriott earns \$4.12 of revenue. The larger this ratio, the more efficiently a business is using its fixed assets. This ratio can be compared across time within a single firm or to other companies in the industry to evaluate overall fixed asset turnover performance. For example, the fixed asset turnover ratios for Starwood Hotels & Resorts and Choice Hotels are 0.76 and 8.4, respectively. Marriott is operating its hotel assets at an efficiency level between that of Starwood and Choice. Choice's high fixed asset turnover ratio can be explained by its aggressive franchising strategy, which allows it to earn revenues in the form of franchising fees without owning hotel fixed assets.

Exhibit 12 shows the fixed asset turnover ratio for a number of different businesses. The smaller ratios are associated with companies that require large fixed asset investments. The larger fixed asset turnover ratios are associated with firms that are more labor-intensive and require smaller fixed asset investments.

Exhibit 12

Fixed Asset Turnover Ratios

Company (industry)	Fixed Asset Turnover Ratio
Comcast Corp. (cable)	1.00
Computer Associates International Inc. (consulting)	5.00
Google Inc. (Internet)	12.15
Manpower, Inc. (temporary employment)	65.15
Norfolk Southern Corporation (railroad)	0.35
Ruby Tuesday, Inc. (restaurant)	1.47
Southwest Airlines Co. (airline)	0.84

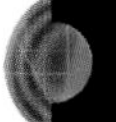

FOCUS ON CASH FLOW

Fixed Assets, Depreciation, and Cash Flow

Depreciation and amortization are deducted from revenues in determining the net income. However, depreciation and amortization expense do not reduce cash. Thus, in the Operating Activities section of the statement of cash flows under the indirect method, the depreciation and amortization expense for the period should be added back to net income in order to adjust the accrual net income amount to reflect operating cash flow.

In addition, proceeds from the sale of fixed assets are included in the Investing Activities section of the statement of cash flows.

To illustrate these disclosures, the partial Operating Activities section of the statement of cash flows for **Marriott International, Inc.**, shows depreciation adjustments in order to reconcile net income to cash generated by operating activities.

Marriott International, Inc.
Partial Statement of Cash Flows—Operating Activities
For the Year Ended December 31, 2004

Cash flows from operating activities:	
Net income	$594
Adjustments to reconcile net income to net cash provided by operating activities:	
Depreciation and amortization	166
Other adjustments	131
Net cash provided by operating activities	$891

The proceeds from the sale of fixed assets and the cash used to purchase fixed assets are disclosed in the Investing Activities section of the statement of cash flows. These are both illustrated for Marriott as follows:

Marriott International, Inc.
Partial Statement of Cash Flows—Investing Activities
For the Year Ended December 31, 2004

Cash flows from investing activities:	
Purchase of fixed assets	$(181)
Proceeds from sale of fixed assets	402
Other	66
Net cash provided by investing activities	$ 287

SUMMARY OF LEARNING GOALS

1 **Define, classify, and account for the cost of fixed assets.** Fixed assets are long-term tangible assets that are owned by a business and are used in the normal operations of the business. Examples of fixed assets are equipment, buildings, and land. The initial cost of a fixed asset includes all amounts spent to get the asset in place and ready for use. For example, sales tax, freight, insurance in transit, and installation costs are all included in the cost of a fixed asset. Once a fixed asset is placed in service, expenditures can be made to repair, improve, or extend the asset's life. Expenditures to repair an asset are treated as revenue expenditures, and expenditures to improve or extend the asset's life are treated as capital expenditures.

2 Compute depreciation, using the following methods: straight-line, units-of-production, and declining-balance. As time passes, all fixed assets except land lose their ability to provide services. As a result, the cost of a fixed asset should be transferred to an expense account, in a systematic manner, during the asset's expected useful life. This periodic transfer of cost to expense is called *depreciation*. In computing depreciation, three factors need to be considered: (1) the fixed asset's initial cost, (2) the useful life of the asset, and (3) the residual value of the asset.

The straight-line method spreads the initial cost less the residual value equally over the useful life. The units-of-production method spreads the initial cost less the residual value equally over the units expected to be produced by the asset during its useful life. The declining-balance method is applied by multiplying the declining book value of the asset by a multiple of the straight-line rate.

3 Account for the disposal of fixed assets. The journal entries to record disposals of fixed assets will vary. In all cases, however, any depreciation for the current period should be recorded, and the book value of the asset is then removed from the accounts. The entry to remove the book value from the accounts is a debit to the asset's accumulated depreciation account and a credit to the asset account for the cost of the asset. For assets retired from service, a loss may be recorded for any remaining book value of the asset.

When a fixed asset is sold, the book value is removed, and the cash or other asset received is also recorded. If the selling price is more than the book value of the asset, the transaction results in a gain. If the selling price is less than the book value, a loss occurs.

4 Describe and account for intangible assets, such as patents, copyrights, and goodwill. Long-term assets that are without physical attributes but are used in the business are classified as intangible assets. Examples of intangible assets are patents, copyrights, trademarks, and goodwill. The initial cost of an intangible asset should be debited to an asset account. For patents and copyrights, this cost should be written off, or amortized, over the years of the asset's expected usefulness by debiting an expense account and crediting the intangible asset account. Trademarks and goodwill are not amortized, but are written down only upon impairment.

5 Describe how depreciation expense is reported in an income statement, and prepare a balance sheet that includes fixed assets and intangible assets. The amount of depreciation expense and the method or methods used in computing depreciation should be disclosed in the financial statements. In addition, each major class of fixed assets should be disclosed, along with the related accumulated depreciation. Intangible assets are usually presented in the balance sheet in a separate section immediately following the fixed assets. Each major class of intangible assets should be disclosed at an amount net of the amortization recorded to date.

6 Analyze the utilization of fixed assets. Business success for many firms is influenced by the utilization of their fixed assets. Fixed asset utilization can be measured using operational and financial data. Operational utilization statistics evaluate the used portion of fixed assets to the total fixed asset capacity. A financial measure of asset utilization is the fixed asset turnover ratio, which is calculated as revenue divided by the average book value of fixed assets.

GLOSSARY

Accelerated depreciation method A depreciation method that provides for a higher depreciation amount in the first year of the asset's use, followed by a gradually declining amount of depreciation.

Amortization The periodic transfer of the cost of an intangible asset to expense.

Book value The cost of a fixed asset minus accumulated depreciation on the asset.

Capital expenditures The cost of acquiring fixed assets, improving an asset, or extending the asset's life.

Copyright An exclusive right to publish and sell a literary, artistic, or musical composition.

Declining-balance method A method of depreciation that provides periodic depreciation expense based on the declining book value of a fixed asset over its estimated life.

Depreciation The systematic periodic transfer of the cost of a fixed asset to an expense account during its expected useful life.

Fixed asset turnover ratio A ratio that measures the number of dollars of revenue earned per dollar of fixed assets and is calculated as total revenue divided by the average book value of fixed assets.

Fixed assets Long-lived or relatively permanent tangible assets that are used in the normal business operations.

Goodwill An intangible asset of a business that is created from such favorable factors as location, product quality, reputation, and managerial skill, as verified from a merger transaction.

Intangible assets Long-lived assets that are useful in the operations of a business, are not held for sale, and are without physical qualities.

Patents Exclusive rights to produce and sell goods with one or more unique features.

Residual value The estimated value of a fixed asset at the end of its useful life.

Revenue expenditures Costs that benefit only the current period or costs incurred for normal maintenance and repairs of fixed assets.

Straight-line method A method of depreciation that provides for equal periodic depreciation expense over the estimated life of a fixed asset.

Trademark A name, term, or symbol used to identify a business and its products.

Units-of-production method A method of depreciation that provides for depreciation expense based on the expected productive capacity of a fixed asset.

ILLUSTRATIVE ACCOUNTING APPLICATION PROBLEM

McCollum Company, a furniture wholesaler, acquired new equipment at a cost of $150,000 at the beginning of the fiscal year. The equipment has an estimated life of five years and an estimated residual value of $12,000. Ellen McCollum, the president, has requested information regarding alternative depreciation methods.

Instructions

1. Determine the annual depreciation for each of the five years of estimated useful life of the equipment, the accumulated depreciation at the end of each year, and the book value of the equipment at the end of each year by using (a) the straight-line method and (b) the declining-balance method (at twice the straight-line rate).
2. Assume that the equipment was depreciated under the declining-balance method. In the first week of the fifth year, the equipment was sold for $25,000. Record the entry for the sale.

Solution

1.

	Year	Depreciation Expense	Accumulated Depreciation, End of Year	Book Value, End of Year
a.	1	$27,600*	$ 27,600	$122,400
	2	27,600	55,200	94,800
	3	27,600	82,800	67,200
	4	27,600	110,400	39,600
	5	27,600	138,000	12,000

*$27,600 = ($150,000 − $12,000) ÷ 5

	Year	Depreciation Expense	Accumulated Depreciation, End of Year	Book Value, End of Year
b.	1	$60,000**	$ 60,000	$ 90,000
	2	36,000	96,000	54,000
	3	21,600	117,600	32,400
	4	12,960	130,560	19,440
	5	7,440***	138,000	12,000

**$60,000 = $150,000 × 40%

***The asset is not depreciated below the estimated residual value of $12,000.

2.

Cash	25,000	
Accumulated Depreciation—Equipment	130,560	
Equipment		150,000
Gain on Disposal of Fixed Assets		5,560

SELF-STUDY QUESTIONS

Answers at end of chapter

1. Which of the following expenditures incurred in connection with acquiring machinery is a proper charge to the asset account?
   A. Freight
   B. Installation costs
   C. Both A and B
   D. Neither A nor B

2. What is the amount of depreciation using the declining-balance method (twice the straight-line rate) for the second year of use for equipment costing $9,000, with an estimated residual value of $600 and an estimated life of three years?
   A. $6,000
   B. $3,000
   C. $2,000
   D. $400

3. An example of an accelerated depreciation method is:
   A. Straight-line
   B. Declining-balance
   C. Units-of-production
   D. Depletion

4. A fixed asset with a book value of $5,000 has its life extended at the beginning of the year with an overhaul capitalized at a cost of $40,000. The overhaul extended the life of the fixed asset by five years. How much is accumulated depreciation decreased for the year?
   A. $8,000
   B. $9,000
   C. $31,000
   D. $40,000

5. A company shows the book value of fixed assets at the beginning of the year of $80,000 and a balance at the end of the year of $120,000. Total revenues were $500,000 for the year. What is the fixed asset turnover ratio?
   A. 0.20
   B. 4.0
   C. 5.0
   D. 6.0

DISCUSSION QUESTIONS

1. Which of the following qualities are characteristics of fixed assets? (a) tangible, (b) capable of repeated use in the operations of the business, (c) held for sale in the normal course of business, (d) used continuously in the operations of the business, (e) long-lived
2. Penguin Office Equipment Co. has a fleet of automobiles and trucks for use by salespersons and for delivery of office supplies and equipment. Sioux City Auto Sales Co. has automobiles and trucks for sale. Under what caption would the automobiles and trucks be reported on the balance sheet of (a) Penguin Office Equipment Co., (b) Sioux City Auto Sales Co.?
3. Spiral Co. acquired an adjacent vacant lot with the hope of selling it in the future at a gain. The lot is not intended to be used in Spiral's business operations. Where should such real estate be listed in the balance sheet?
4. Tensile Company solicited bids from several contractors to construct an addition to its office building. The lowest bid received was for $340,000. Tensile Company decided to construct the addition itself at a cost of $325,000. What amount should be recorded in the building account?
5. Are the amounts at which fixed assets are reported in the balance sheet their approximate market values as of the balance sheet date? Discuss.
6. Differentiate between the accounting for capital expenditures and revenue expenditures.
7. Immediately after a used truck is acquired, a new motor is installed at a total cost of $4,750. Is this a capital expenditure or a revenue expenditure?
8. **a.** Does recognizing depreciation in the accounts provide a special cash fund for the replacement of fixed assets? Explain.
   b. Describe the nature of depreciation as the term is used in accounting.
9. Name the three factors that need to be considered in determining the amount of periodic depreciation.
10. Trigger Company purchased a machine that has a manufacturer's suggested life of 15 years. The company plans to use the machine on a special project that will last 11 years. At the completion of the project, the machine will be sold. Over how many years should the machine be depreciated?
11. Is it necessary for a business to use the same method of computing depreciation (a) for all classes of its depreciable assets, (b) in the financial statements and in determining income taxes?
12. Of the three common depreciation methods, which is most widely used?
13. **a.** Why is an accelerated depreciation method often used for income tax purposes?
    b. What is the Modified Accelerated Cost Recovery System (MACRS), and under what conditions is it used?
14. A company revised the estimated useful lives of its fixed assets, which resulted in an increase in the remaining lives of several assets. Does GAAP permit the company to include, as income of the current period, the cumulative effect of the changes, which reduces the depreciation expense of past periods? Discuss.
15. For some of the fixed assets of a business, the balance in Accumulated Depreciation is exactly equal to the cost of the asset. (a) Is it permissible to record additional depreciation on the assets if they are still useful to the business? Explain. (b) When should an entry be made to remove the cost and the accumulated depreciation from the accounts?

16. In what sections of the income statement are gains and losses from the disposal of fixed assets presented?
17. a. Over what period of time should the cost of a patent acquired by purchase be amortized?
    b. In general, what is the required treatment for research and development costs?
    c. How should goodwill be amortized?
18. How would you evaluate the effective use of fixed assets?

EXERCISES

Exercise 9-1

Costs of acquiring fixed assets

Goal 1

Cristy Fleming owns and operates Quesenberry Print Co. During February, Quesenberry Print Co. incurred the following costs in acquiring two printing presses. One printing press was new, and the other was used by a business that recently filed for bankruptcy.

Costs related to the new printing press include the following:

1. Freight
2. Special foundation
3. Sales tax on purchase price
4. Insurance while in transit
5. Fee paid to factory representative for installation
6. New parts to replace those damaged in unloading

Costs related to the secondhand printing press include the following:

7. Repair of vandalism during installation
8. Replacement of worn-out parts
9. Freight
10. Installation
11. Repair of damage incurred in reconditioning the press
12. Fees paid to attorney to review purchase agreement

a. Indicate which costs incurred in acquiring the new printing press should be debited to the asset account.
b. Indicate which costs incurred in acquiring the secondhand printing press should be debited to the asset account.

Exercise 9-2

Determine cost of land

Goal 1

A company has developed a tract of land into a ski resort. The company has cut the trees, cleared and graded the land and hills, and constructed ski lifts. (a) Should the tree cutting, land clearing, and grading costs of constructing the ski slopes be debited to the land account? (b) If such costs are debited to Land, should they be depreciated?

Exercise 9-3

Determine cost of land

Goal 1

$188,000

Alligator Delivery Company acquired an adjacent lot to construct a new warehouse, paying $35,000 and giving a short-term note for $125,000. Legal fees paid were $1,100, delinquent taxes assumed were $12,500, and fees paid to remove an old building from the land were $18,000. Materials salvaged from the demolition of the building were sold for $3,600. A contractor was paid $512,500 to construct a new warehouse. Determine the cost of the land to be reported on the balance sheet.

Exercise 9-4

Nature of depreciation

Goal 1

Ball-Peen Metal Casting Co. reported $859,600 for equipment and $317,500 for accumulated depreciation—equipment on its balance sheet. Does this mean (a) that the replacement cost of the equipment is $859,600 and (b) that $317,500 is set aside in a special fund for the replacement of the equipment? Explain.

Exercise 9-5

Capital and revenue expenditures

Goal 1

Hicks Co. incurred the following costs related to trucks and vans used in operating its delivery service:

1. Removed a two-way radio from one of the trucks and installed a new radio with a greater range of communication.
2. Overhauled the engine on one of the trucks that had been purchased three years ago.
3. Changed the oil and greased the joints of all the trucks and vans.
4. Installed security systems on four of the newer trucks.
5. Changed the radiator fluid on a truck that had been in service for the past four years.
6. Installed a hydraulic lift to a van.
7. Tinted the back and side windows of one of the vans to discourage theft of contents.
8. Repaired a flat tire on one of the vans.
9. Rebuilt the transmission on one of the vans that had been driven 40,000 miles. The van was no longer under warranty.
10. Replace the trucks' suspension system with a new suspension system that allows for the delivery of heavier loads.

Classify each of the costs as a capital expenditure or a revenue expenditure. For those costs identified as capital expenditures, classify each as an expenditure improving an asset or extending the life of an asset.

Exercise 9-6

Capital and revenue expenditures

Goal 1

Felix Little owns and operates Big Sky Transport Co. During the past year, Felix incurred the following costs related to his 18-wheel truck.

1. Replaced a headlight that had burned out.
2. Removed the old CB radio and replaced it with a newer model with a greater range.
3. Replaced a shock absorber that had worn out.
4. Installed a television in the sleeping compartment of the truck.
5. Replaced the old radar detector with a newer model that detects the KA frequencies now used by many of the state patrol radar guns. The detector is wired directly into the cab, so that it is partially hidden. In addition, Felix fastened the detector to the truck with a locking device that prevents its removal.
6. Installed fog and cab lights.
7. Installed a wind deflector on top of the cab to increase fuel mileage.
8. Modified the factory-installed turbo charger with a special-order kit designed to add 50 more horsepower to the engine performance.
9. Replaced the hydraulic brake system that had begun to fail during his latest trip through the Rocky Mountains.
10. Overhauled the engine.

Classify each of the costs as a capital expenditure or a revenue expenditure. For those costs identified as capital expenditures, classify each as an expenditure improving an asset or extending the life of an asset.

Exercise 9-7

Fixed asset improvement

Goal 1

Jacobs Company owned a warehouse that had an expected remaining life of 30 years and a book value of $360,000 on January 1, 2008. The company added a sprinkler system to its warehouse to provide fire prevention. The sprinkler system cost $34,000 to install on January 8, 2008. The salvage value of the warehouse was $19,000. The sprinkler system did not change the salvage value or the estimated life of the warehouse.

a. Record the cost of the new sprinkler system on January 8, 2008.
b. Record the annual depreciation expense adjusting entry for the warehouse on December 31, 2008, under the straight-line method.

Exercise 9-8

Fixed asset improvement

Goal 1

b. $5,500

Dale's Winning Edge, Inc., purchased and installed an alarm system for its retail store on January 1, 1999, at a cost of $50,000. The alarm system was estimated to have a 10-year life with no residual value. On January 1, 2006, the alarm system was enhanced with wireless monitors. The new monitors cost $40,000. In addition, the alarm system was estimated to have a remaining life of 10 years, with no residual value, on January 1, 2006. Dale's Winning Edge uses the straight-line depreciation method.

a. Record the cost of the new alarm system enhancements on January 1, 2006.
b. Determine the total depreciation expense reported in the income statement in 2006 from this transaction.

Exercise 9-9

Fixed asset extraordinary repair

Goal 1

c. $200,750

Northeast Railroad Company overhauled a diesel motor on one of its railroad engines at a cost of $110,000 on June 30, 2006. The engine was purchased on January 1, 2000, for $280,000, with an estimated original useful life of 20,000 hours and a residual value of $50,000. As of June 30, 2006, the engine had been used 15,000 hours since its original purchase. The overhaul increased the remaining useful life of the engine to 24,000 hours with no change in residual value. After the overhaul, the engine was used for 2,400 hours for the remainder of 2006.

a. Record the journal entry for the overhaul costs incurred during June 2006.
b. Record the journal entry for the depreciation expense on the overhauled engine for the remainder of 2006.
c. Determine the book value of the engine on December 31, 2006.

Exercise 9-10

Fixed asset improvement and extraordinary repair

Goal 1

c. Transmission system, $113,900

On October 1, 2007, Tri-State Power Company added transmission lines costing $25,000 to improve transmission capacity on a transmission system having a book value of $90,000. The transmission system has 25 years of estimated remaining life with a $5,000 residual value on October 1. In addition, on October 1, a generator with an original cost of $40,000 and accumulated depreciation of $36,000 was overhauled at a cost of $20,000. The overhaul extended the remaining life of the generator to 12 years with no residual value.

a. Record the journal entries on October 1 for the transmission system improvement and generator extraordinary repair.
b. Record the adjusting journal entry on December 31 to record the depreciation expense for the two fixed assets.
c. Determine the book value of the two fixed assets on December 31.

Exercise 9-11

Straight-line depreciation rates

Goal 2

a. 5%

Convert each of the following estimates of useful life to a straight-line depreciation rate, stated as a percentage, assuming that the residual value of the fixed asset is to be ignored: (a) 20 years, (b) 25 years, (c) 40 years, (d) 4 years, (e) 5 years, (f) 10 years, (g) 50 years.

Exercise 9-12

Straight-line depreciation

Goal 2

$18,000

A refrigerator used by a meat processor has a cost of $312,000, an estimated residual value of $42,000, and an estimated useful life of 15 years. What is the amount of the annual depreciation computed by the straight-line method?

Exercise 9-13

Depreciation by units-of-production method

Goal 2

$5,450

A diesel-powered generator with a cost of $345,000 and estimated residual value of $18,000 is expected to have a useful operating life of 75,000 hours. During July, the generator was operated 1,250 hours. Determine the depreciation for the month using the units-of-production method.

Exercise 9-14

Depreciation by units-of-production method

Goal 2

Prior to adjustment at the end of the year, the balance in Trucks is $182,600 and the balance in Accumulated Depreciation—Trucks is $74,950. Details of the subsidiary ledger are as follows:

a. Truck #1, credit Accumulated Depreciation, $8,000

Truck No.	Cost	Estimated Residual Value	Estimated Useful Life	Accumulated Depreciation at Beginning of Year	Miles Operated During Year
1	$68,000	$8,000	300,000 miles	$27,000	40,000 miles
2	48,600	6,600	200,000	39,900	12,000
3	38,000	3,000	200,000	8,050	36,000
4	28,000	4,000	120,000	—	21,000

a. Determine the depreciation rates per mile and the amount to be credited to the accumulated depreciation section of each of the subsidiary accounts for the miles operated during the current year.
b. Journalize the entry to record depreciation for the year.

Exercise 9-15

Depreciation by two methods

Goal 2

a. $7,000

A backhoe acquired on January 5 at a cost of $84,000 has an estimated useful life of 12 years. Assuming that it will have no residual value, determine the depreciation for each of the first two years (a) by the straight-line method and (b) by the declining-balance method, using twice the straight-line rate. Round to the nearest dollar.

Exercise 9-16

Depreciation by two methods

Goal 2

a. $9,100

A dairy storage tank acquired at the beginning of the fiscal year at a cost of $98,500 has an estimated residual value of $7,500 and an estimated useful life of 10 years. Determine the following: (a) the amount of annual depreciation by the straight-line method and (b) the amount of depreciation for the first and second years computed by the declining-balance method (at twice the straight-line rate).

Exercise 9-17

Partial-year depreciation

Goal 2

a. First year, $2,700

Sandblasting equipment acquired at a cost of $54,000 has an estimated residual value of $10,800 and an estimated useful life of 12 years. It was placed in service on April 1 of the current fiscal year, which ends on December 31. Determine the depreciation for the current fiscal year and for the following fiscal year by (a) the straight-line method and (b) the declining-balance method, at twice the straight-line rate.

Exercise 9-18

Change in estimate

Goal 2

a. $15,000

A warehouse with a cost of $800,000 has an estimated residual value of $200,000, an estimated useful life of 40 years, and is depreciated by the straight-line method. (a) What is the amount of the annual depreciation? (b) What is the book value at the end of the twentieth year of use? (c) If at the start of the twenty-first year it is estimated that the remaining life is 25 years and that the residual value is $150,000, what is the depreciation expense for each of the remaining 25 years?

Exercise 9-19

Book value of fixed assets

Goal 2

The following data were taken from recent annual reports of Interstate Bakeries Corporation (IBC). Interstate Bakeries produces, distributes, and sells fresh bakery products nationwide through supermarkets, convenience stores, and its 67 bakeries and 1,500 thrift stores.

	Current Year	Preceding Year
Land and buildings	$ 426,322,000	$ 418,928,000
Machinery and equipment	1,051,861,000	1,038,323,000
Accumulated depreciation	633,178,000	582,941,000

a. Compute the book value of the fixed assets for the current year and the preceding year and explain the differences, if any.
b. Would you normally expect the book value of fixed assets to increase or decrease during the year?

Exercise 9-20

Entries for sale of fixed asset

Goal 3

Metals Inc. acquired metal recycling equipment acquired on January 3, 2003, at a cost of $240,000, with an estimated useful life of 10 years, an estimated residual value of $15,000, and is depreciated by the straight-line method.

a. What was the book value of the equipment at December 31, 2006, the end of the fiscal year?
b. Assuming that the equipment was sold on July 1, 2007, for $135,000, journalize the entries to record (1) depreciation for the six months until the sale date and (2) the sale of the equipment.

Exercise 9-21

Disposal of fixed asset

Goal 3

b. $51,000

Equipment acquired on January 3, 2004, at a cost of $96,000, has an estimated useful life of six years and an estimated residual value of $6,000.

a. What was the annual amount of depreciation for the years 2004, 2005, and 2006, using the straight-line method of depreciation?
b. What was the book value of the equipment on January 1, 2007?
c. Assuming that the equipment was sold on January 2, 2007, for $38,000, journalize the entry to record the sale.
d. Assuming that the equipment had been sold on January 2, 2007, for $53,000 instead of $38,000, journalize the entry to record the sale.

Exercise 9-22

Amortization entries

Goal 4

a. $37,750

Colmey Company acquired patent rights on January 3, 2004, for $472,500. The patent has a useful life equal to its legal life of 15 years. On January 5, 2007, Colmey successfully defended the patent in a lawsuit at a cost of $75,000.

a. Determine the patent amortization expense for the current year ended December 31, 2007.
b. Journalize the adjusting entry to recognize the amortization.

Exercise 9-23

Goodwill impairment

Goal 4

a. $3,200,000

On July 1, 2005, Cumberland Products, Inc., purchased the assets of Jupiter Brands, Inc., for $12,000,000, a price reflecting a $3,200,000 goodwill premium. On December 31, 2007, Cumberland determined that the goodwill from the Jupiter acquisition was impaired and had a value of $1,000,000.

a. Determine the book value of the goodwill on December 31, 2007, prior to making the impairment adjusting entry.
b. Record the goodwill impairment adjusting entry for December 31, 2007.

Exercise 9-24

Patent and amortization entries

Goal 4

b. $207,000

During the first half of 2006, Hi-Def Electronics Company spent $450,000 on research and development efforts that resulted in a new product invention. During June, Hi-Def incurred $50,000 to prepare a patent application and an additional $10,000 for legal fees associated with a patent search, resulting in a pending patent award on July 1, 2006. Management expects the patent to have a life of 12 years. During December 2006, the patent was successfully defended in a legal proceeding which cost $149,500.

a. Record the year-end adjusting journal entry for patent amortization on December 31, 2006.
b. Determine the patent book value on December 31, 2006.
c. Record the year-end adjusting journal entry for patent amortization on December 31, 2007.

Exercise 9-25

Balance sheet presentation

Goal **4**

List the errors you find in the following partial balance sheet:

Kraftmaid Company
Balance Sheet
December 31, 2007

Assets

	Replacement Cost	Accumulated Depreciation	Book Value
Total current assets			$597,500
Property, plant, and equipment:			
Land	$ 100,000	$ 20,000	$ 80,000
Buildings	260,000	76,000	184,000
Factory equipment	550,000	292,000	258,000
Office equipment	120,000	80,000	40,000
Patents	80,000	—	80,000
Goodwill	45,000	5,000	40,000
Total property, plant, and equipment	$1,155,000	$473,000	$682,000

Exercise 9-26

Balance sheet presentation and analysis

Goals **4, 5**

The following are recent excerpts from the financial statements of Sirius Satellite Radio Inc., a company delivering national satellite audio entertainment services:

Balance Sheet—Property, Equipment, and Intangible Assets	(in millions)
Satellite system	$ 945.5
Terrestrial repeater network	72.0
Broadcast studio equipment	28.9
Furniture and fixtures	41.3
Other	69.9
Construction in progress	4.7
Property and equipment, gross	$1,162.3
Accumulated depreciation	(281.0)
Property and equipment, net	$ 881.3
FCC license	83.7
Total property, equipment, and intangible assets	$ 965.0
Depreciation Expense—Income Statement	$ 95.4

a. Estimate the average useful lives of depreciable property and equipment, assuming straight-line depreciation and no residual value. Round to the nearest year.

b. Estimate the percent of remaining life of depreciable property and equipment, assuming straight-line depreciation and no residual value. Round to one decimal place.

c. Sirius reports no amortization expense associated with the FCC (Federal Communication Commission) license. Why is this?

Exercise 9-27

Intangible assets and balance sheet presentation

Goals **4, 5**

The following financial statement note information was provided for two recent comparative years for Johnson & Johnson, one of the world's most comprehensive health-care products companies. Patents are a significant asset for Johnson & Johnson; thus, accumulated amortization information is provided in the notes to provide users additional disclosure beyond what is generally required.

	Jan. 2, 2005 (in millions)	Dec. 28, 2003 (in millions)
Patents	$3,974	$3,798
Accumulated amortization	(1,125)	(818)
Patents, net	$2,849	$2,980

Assume there were no patent sales during 2004.

a. Reproduce the journal entry of patent purchases recorded for 2004.
b. Reproduce the adjusting journal entry for amortization expense recorded for 2004.
c. Estimate the average life of patents using the January 2, 2005, patent balance and amortization expense determined in (b). Round to the nearest year.

Exercise 9-28

Fixed asset turnover ratio

Goal **6**

Verizon Communications Inc. is a major telecommunications company in the United States. Verizon's balance sheet disclosed the following information regarding fixed assets:

	Dec. 31, 2004 (in millions)	Dec. 31, 2003 (in millions)
Plant, property, and equipment	$185,522	$180,940
Less accumulated depreciation	111,398	105,638
	$ 74,124	$ 75,302

Verizon's revenue for 2004 was $71,283 million. The fixed asset turnover for the telecommunications industry averages 1.10.

a. Determine Verizon's fixed asset turnover ratio.
b. Interpret Verizon's fixed asset turnover ratio.

Exercise 9-29

Fixed asset utilization

Goal **6**

a. 808.5

Carnival Corporation, a vacation cruise line, measures the operating capacity of its business using available lower berth days (ALBDs). An ALBD is the passenger capacity assuming two passengers per room (berth) multiplied by the number of cruise days in a year. Carnival has a passenger capacity of 73 ships that can hold 118,040 passengers, assuming two passengers per room. Carnival ran its ships an average of 282 cruise days per year. Carnival actually carried 5,037,553 passengers during the period for 34,419,047 berth days.

a. Determine the average number of rooms (berths) per ship.
b. Determine the average length in days of a passenger cruise vacation.
c. Determine the utilization, or occupancy, percentage.

ACCOUNTING APPLICATION PROBLEMS

Problem 9-1A

Allocate payments and receipts to fixed asset accounts

Goal **1**

The following payments and receipts are related to land, land improvements, and buildings acquired for use in a wholesale apparel business. The receipts are identified by an asterisk.

a.	Finder's fee paid to real estate agency	$ 5,000
b.	Cost of real estate acquired as a plant site: Land	100,000
	Building	60,000
c.	Fee paid to attorney for title search	3,500
d.	Delinquent real estate taxes on property, assumed by purchaser	17,500
e.	Cost of razing and removing building	16,250
f.	Cost of filling and grading land	12,500
g.	Proceeds from sale of salvage materials from old building	4,500*
h.	Special assessment paid to city for extension of water main to the property	11,000
i.	Premium on one-year insurance policy during construction	7,200
j.	Architect's and engineer's fees for plans and supervision	50,000
k.	Cost of repairing windstorm damage during construction	2,500
l.	Cost of repairing vandalism damage during construction	1,800
m.	Cost of trees and shrubbery planted	12,000
n.	Cost of paving parking lot to be used by customers	18,500
o.	Proceeds from insurance company for windstorm and vandalism damage	4,000*

p.	Interest incurred on building loan during construction	$ 65,000
q.	Money borrowed to pay building contractor	1,000,000*
r.	Payment to building contractor for new building	1,250,000
s.	Refund of premium on insurance policy (i) canceled after 10 months	1,200*

Instructions

1. Assign each payment and receipt to Land (unlimited life), Land Improvements (limited life), Building, or Other Accounts. Indicate receipts by an asterisk. Identify each item by letter and list the amounts in columnar form, as follows:

Item	Land	Land Improvements	Building	Other Accounts

2. Determine the amount debited to Land, Land Improvements, and Building.
3. The costs assigned to the land, which is used as a plant site, will not be depreciated, while the costs assigned to land improvements will be depreciated. Explain this seemingly contradictory application of the concept of depreciation.

Problem 9-2A

Compare three depreciation methods

Goal 2

a. 2005: straight-line depreciation, $50,000

SPREADSHEET

Cero Company purchased waterproofing equipment on January 2, 2005, for $214,000. The equipment was expected to have a useful life of four years, or 31,250 operating hours, and a residual value of $14,000. The equipment was used for 10,750 hours during 2005, 9,500 hours in 2006, 6,000 hours in 2007, and 5,000 hours in 2008.

Instructions

Determine the amount of depreciation expense for the years ended December 31, 2005, 2006, 2007 and 2008, by (a) the straight-line method, (b) the units-of-production method, and (c) the declining-balance method, using twice the straight-line rate. Also determine the total depreciation expense for the four years by each method. The following columnar headings are suggested for recording the depreciation expense amounts:

	Depreciation Expense		
Year	Straight-Line Method	Units-of-Production Method	Declining-Balance Method

Problem 9-3A

Depreciation by three methods; partial years

Goal 2

a. 2005, $30,600

SPREADSHEET

Caribou Company purchased tool sharpening equipment on July 1, 2005, for $194,400. The equipment was expected to have a useful life of three years, or 22,950 operating hours, and a residual value of $10,800. The equipment was used for 4,650 hours during 2005, 7,500 hours in 2006, 7,350 hours in 2007, and 3,450 hours in 2008.

Instructions

Determine the amount of depreciation expense for the years ended December 31, 2005, 2006, 2007, and 2008, by (a) the straight-line method, (b) the units-of-production method, and (c) the declining-balance method, using twice the straight-line rate.

Problem 9-4A

Depreciation by two methods; sale of fixed asset

Goals 2, 3

1. b. Year 1, $80,000 depreciation expense

New tire retreading equipment, acquired at a cost of $160,000 at the beginning of a fiscal year, has an estimated useful life of four years and an estimated residual value of $16,000. The manager requested information regarding the effect of alternative methods on the amount of depreciation expense each year.

Instructions

1. Determine the annual depreciation expense for each of the estimated four years of use, the accumulated depreciation at the end of each year, and the book value of the equipment at the end of each year by (a) the straight-line method and (b) the declining-balance method (at twice the straight-line rate). The following columnar headings are suggested for each schedule:

Year	Depreciation Expense	Accumulated Depreciation, End of Year	Book Value, End of Year

2. On the basis of the data presented to the manager, the declining-balance method was selected. In the first week of the fourth year, the equipment was sold for $26,000. Record the entry for the sale.
3. Record the entry for the sale, assuming a sales price of $17,400.

Problem 9-5A

Transactions for fixed assets

Goals 1, 3, 4

GENERAL LEDGER

The following transactions, adjusting entries, and closing entries were completed by Trailways Furniture Co. during a three-year period. All are related to the use of delivery equipment. The declining-balance method (at twice the straight-line rate) of depreciation is used.

2005

Jan. 2 Purchased a used delivery truck for $39,000 paying cash.

5 Paid $1,250 for a new transmission for the truck. (Debit Delivery Equipment)

Apr. 7 Paid garage $125 for changing the oil, replacing the oil filter, and tuning the engine on the delivery truck.

Dec. 31 Recorded depreciation on the truck for the fiscal year. The estimated useful life of the truck is 8 years, with a residual value of $250.

2006

Jan. 1 Purchased a new truck for $80,000, paying cash.

Mar. 13 Paid garage $180 to tune the engine and make other minor repairs on the truck.

Mar. 31 Sold the used truck for $24,500. (Record depreciation to date in 2006 for the truck.)

Dec. 31 Recorded depreciation on the remaining truck. It has an estimated residual value of $2,000 and an estimated life of 10 years.

2007

July 1 Purchased a new truck for $45,000, paying cash.

Oct. 2 Sold the truck purchased Jan. 1, 2006, for $69,075. (Record depreciation for the year.)

Dec. 31 Recorded depreciation on the remaining truck. It has an estimated residual value of $4,500 and an estimated useful life of 10 years.

Instructions

Record the transactions and the adjusting entries.

Problem 9-6A

Intangible assets

Goal 6

Data related to the acquisition of intangible assets during the current year ended December 31 are as follows:

a. Goodwill arising from acquiring a business was purchased on January 9 for $29,500,000. The goodwill is estimated to have been impaired during the year, and thus was estimated to have a value of $9,400,000 on December 31.

b. Governmental and legal costs of $225,600 were incurred on July 5 in obtaining a patent with an estimated economic life of eight years.

c. Copyrights with an estimated life of 12 years were purchased for $90,000 on September 1.

Instructions

1. Record the acquisition of each intangible asset.
2. Record the December 31 adjusting entries for each intangible asset.
3. What impact will the transactions in (1) and (2) have on the statement of cash flows?

ALTERNATE ACCOUNTING APPLICATION PROBLEMS

Alternate Problem 9-1B

Allocate payments and receipts to fixed asset accounts

Goal 1

The following payments and receipts are related to land, land improvements, and buildings acquired for use in a wholesale ceramic business. The receipts are identified by an asterisk.

a.	Fee paid to attorney for title search	$ 2,500
b.	Cost of real estate acquired as a plant site: Land	150,000
	Building	40,000
c.	Delinquent real estate taxes on property, assumed by purchaser	13,750
d.	Cost of razing and removing building	4,800
e.	Special assessment paid to city for extension of water main to the property	10,200
f.	Proceeds from sale of salvage materials from old building	5,000*
g.	Cost of filling and grading land	29,700
h.	Premium on one-year insurance policy during construction	6,600
i.	Cost of repairing windstorm damage during construction	3,500
j.	Cost of paving parking lot to be used by customers	12,500
k.	Cost of trees and shrubbery planted	7,000
l.	Architect's and engineer's fees for plans and supervision	75,000
m.	Cost of repairing vandalism damage during construction	1,600
n.	Interest incurred on building loan during construction	30,000
o.	Cost of floodlights installed on parking lot	8,500
p.	Money borrowed to pay building contractor	500,000*
q.	Payment to building contractor for new building	750,000
r.	Proceeds from insurance company for windstorm and vandalism damage	4,000*
s.	Refund of premium on insurance policy (h) canceled after 11 months	550*

Instructions

1. Assign each payment and receipt to Land (unlimited life), Land Improvements (limited life), Building, or Other Accounts. Indicate receipts by an asterisk. Identify each item by letter and list the amounts in columnar form, as follows:

Item	Land	Land Improvements	Building	Other Accounts

2. Determine the amount debited to Land, Land Improvements, and Building.
3. The costs assigned to the land, which is used as a plant site, will not be depreciated, while the costs assigned to land improvements will be depreciated. Explain this seemingly contradictory application of the concept of depreciation.

Alternate Problem 9-2B

Compare three depreciation methods

Goal 2

a. 2005. Straight-line depreciation, $55,800

SPREADSHEET

Red Tiger Company purchased waterproofing equipment on January 3, 2005, for $180,000. The equipment was expected to have a useful life of three years, or 22,320 operating hours, and a residual value of $12,600. The equipment was used for 12,500 hours during 2005, 6,000 hours in 2006, and 3,820 hours in 2007.

Instructions

Determine the amount of depreciation expense for the years ended December 31, 2005, 2006, and 2007, by (a) the straight-line method, (b) the units-of-production method, and (c) the declining-balance method, using twice the straight-line rate. Also determine the total depreciation expense for the three years by each method. The following columnar headings are suggested for recording the depreciation expense amounts:

	Depreciation Expense		
Year	Straight-Line Method	Units-of-Production Method	Declining-Balance Method

Alternate Problem 9-3B

Depreciation by three methods; partial years

Goal **2**

a. 2005; $28,050

SPREADSHEET

Rhymer Company purchased plastic laminating equipment on July 1, 2005, for $174,000. The equipment was expected to have a useful life of three years, or 14,025 operating hours, and a residual value of $5,700. The equipment was used for 2,500 hours during 2005, 5,500 hours in 2006, 4,025 hours in 2007, and 2,000 hours in 2008.

Instructions

Determine the amount of depreciation expense for the years ended December 31, 2005, 2006, 2007, and 2008, by (a) the straight-line method, (b) the units-of-production method, and (c) the declining-balance method, using twice the straight-line rate. Round to the nearest dollar.

Alternate Problem 9-4B

Depreciation by two methods; sale of fixed asset

Goals **2, 3**

1. b. Year 1: $40,000 depreciation expense

New lithographic equipment, acquired at a cost of $100,000 at the beginning of a fiscal year, has an estimated useful life of five years and an estimated residual value of $8,000. The manager requested information regarding the effect of alternative methods on the amount of depreciation expense each year.

Instructions

1. Determine the annual depreciation expense for each of the estimated five years of use, the accumulated depreciation at the end of each year, and the book value of the equipment at the end of each year by (a) the straight-line method and (b) the declining-balance method (at twice the straight-line rate). The following columnar headings are suggested for each schedule:

Year	Depreciation Expense	Accumulated Depreciation, End of Year	Book Value, End of Year

2. On the basis of the data presented to the manager, the declining-balance method was selected. In the first week of the fifth year, the equipment was sold for $24,000. Record the entry for the sale.
3. Record the entry for the sale, assuming a sales price of $8,000.

Alternate Problem 9-5B

Transactions for fixed assets, including sale

Goals **1, 3, 4**

GENERAL LEDGER

The following transactions, adjusting entries, and closing entries were completed by Lodge Pole Pine Furniture Co. during a three-year period. All are related to the use of delivery equipment. The straight-line method of depreciation is used.

2005

Jan. 3	Purchased a used delivery truck for $26,500, paying cash.
5	Paid $4,000 for a new transmission for the truck. (Debit Delivery Equipment)
Aug. 16	Paid garage $285 for miscellaneous repairs to the truck.
Dec. 31	Recorded depreciation on the truck for the fiscal year. The estimated useful life of the truck is 4 years, with a residual value of $5,500.

2006

Jan. 1	Purchased a new truck for $65,000, paying cash.
June 30	Sold the used truck for $12,000. (Record depreciation to date in 2006 for the truck.)
Aug. 10	Paid garage $175 for miscellaneous repairs to the truck.
Dec. 31	Recorded depreciation on the truck. It has an estimated residual value of $7,500 and an estimated life of 5 years.

2007

July 1	Purchased a new truck for $84,000, paying cash.
Oct. 1	Sold the truck purchased January 1, 2006, for $26,750. (Record depreciation for the year.)
Dec. 31	Recorded depreciation on the remaining truck. It has an estimated residual value of $8,000 and an estimated useful life of 8 years.

Instructions

Record the transactions and the adjusting entries.

Alternate Problem 9-6B

Intangible assets

Goal 6

Data related to the acquisition of intangible assets during the current year ended December 31 are as follows:

a. Governmental and legal costs of $655,200 were incurred on January 4 in obtaining a patent with an estimated economic life of 12 years.
b. Goodwill arising from acquiring a business was purchased on July 1 for $8,400,000. The goodwill is estimated to have been impaired during the remainder of the year, and thus was estimated to have a value of $1,100,000 on December 31.
c. Copyrights with an estimated life of nine years were purchased for $450,000 on October 1.

Instructions

1. Record the acquisition of each intangible asset.
2. Record the December 31 adjusting entries for each intangible asset.
3. What impact will the transactions in (1) and (2) have on the statement of cash flows?

FINANCIAL ANALYSIS AND REPORTING CASES

Case 9-1

Comparing book value and depreciation expense for two companies

Micron Technology, Inc., is in the semiconductor industry. This industry requires extensive capital investments in fabrication facilities in order to maintain technological competitiveness. E. I. De Nemours DuPont & Co. is one of the leading chemical companies in the world. DuPont requires significant investment in chemical processing facilities. Chemical products have longer lives than do semiconductor products. The following selected fixed asset information is provided from recent financial statements (all numbers in millions):

	Plant and Equipment Initial Cost	Accumulated Depreciation	Depreciation Expense
Micron Technology	$ 8,998	$ 4,836	$1,158
DuPont	22,661	14,257	1,355

a. Determine the book value of the plant and equipment for each company.
b. Estimate the total useful life of the plant and equipment, assuming straight-line depreciation and no residual value.
c. Estimate the percent of accumulated depreciation to the total initial cost of property, plant, and equipment for each company. Round to one decimal place.
d. Interpret the differences between Micron and DuPont from your calculations in (b) and (c).

Case 9-2

Financial and operational analyses in the airline industry

SPREADSHEET

The financial performance of the airline industry is sensitive to aircraft utilization and cost control. The industry uses a number of common measures to evaluate financial performance. Three of these are as follows:

Passenger Load Factor = RPM/ASM
Operating Revenue per Available Seat Mile = Operating Revenue/ASM
Operating Cost per Available Seat Mile = Operating Cost/ASM

Available seat mile (ASM) is the total number of seats *available* for transporting passengers multiplied by the total number of miles flown during a reporting period. Revenue passenger mile (RPM) is the total number of seats *purchased* by passengers multiplied by the total number of miles flown during a reporting period.

The following table provides some recent operating statistics for four passenger airlines:

	Available Seat Miles (ASM) (in millions)	Revenue Passenger Miles (RPM) (in millions)	Operating Revenue (in millions)	Operating Cost (in millions)
Northwest Airlines	88,593	68,476	$ 7,936	$ 8,800
Delta Air Lines	134,383	98,674	13,303	14,089
U.S. Airways	51,494	37,741	5,536	5,850
Southwest Airlines	76,861	53,418	6,530	5,976

a. Prepare a table showing for each airline the load factor, operating revenue per ASM, operating cost per ASM, and operating margin (profit) per ASM. Round to four decimal places.

b. Interpret the results in (a) for the four airlines.

Case 9-3

Fixed asset turnover: three industries

The following table shows the revenues and average net fixed assets for a recent fiscal year for three different companies from three different industries: retailing, manufacturing, and communications.

	Revenues (in millions)	Average Net Fixed Assets (in millions)
Wal-Mart	$258,681	$51,686
Alcoa Inc.	21,504	12,333
Comcast Corp.	18,348	18,427

a. For each company, determine the fixed asset turnover ratio. Round to two decimal places.

b. Explain Wal-Mart's ratio relative to the other two companies.

Case 9-4

Interpreting railroad fixed asset efficiency

The freight statistics for Burlington Northern Santa Fe Corp.'s rail operations for three years are provided from public disclosures as follows:

	Year Ended December 31,		
	2004	2003	2002
Revenue ton miles (millions)	570,688	508,200	490,234
Freight revenue per thousand revenue ton miles	$18.82	$18.27	$18.10
Average haul per ton (miles)	1,045	1,014	992

a. Revenue ton miles is also sometimes termed *gross ton miles*. What is a *revenue ton mile*? (*Hint:* Note that the revenue ton miles are not expressed in dollar terms.)

b. How would you interpret the trend in *freight revenue per thousand revenue ton miles* over the three years indicated?

c. Estimate the number of tons moved in 2004.

d. Estimate Burlington Northern's total revenue for 2004.

Case 9-5

Operating utilization statistics—power generation

Duke Energy Corp. is an integrated energy and energy services provider that generates and distributes electricity in North Carolina and South Carolina. Operating statistics for electricity generation and sales are provided from its public reports for a recent fiscal year, as follows:

Sources of Electric Energy, GWh*	
Generated—net output:	
Coal	43,696
Nuclear	40,256
Hydro	2,101
Oil and gas	106
Total generation	86,159

*Gigawatt-hour

Electric Energy Sales, GWh*:	
Residential	$23,947
Nonresidential	58,459
Total GWh sales	$82,406**

*Gigawatt-hour
**The difference between generation and sales is caused by line losses and purchased power.

Duke operated eight coal-fired stations and seven oil and gas combustion turbine stations with a combined capacity of 7,699 MW (megawatts), three nuclear generating stations with a combined net capacity of 5,020 MW, 31 hydroelectric stations with a combined capacity of 2,806 MW, and seven combustion turbine stations with a combined capacity of 2,424 MW.

The megawatt (MW) rating is the capacity of the unit at a point in time. Translating this capacity into annual MWh (megawatt-hours) requires multiplying this amount times 24 hours per day times 340 days in the year (assuming 25 days for repair). A gigawatt is 1,000 megawatts.

a. Determine the utilization of the coal, nuclear, hydro, and oil and gas turbine generation assets. (*Hint:* You must translate the megawatt rating into gigawatt-hour capacity for 340 days.)
b. Why are the utilization statistics different across the different generating sources?
c. What percent of total electric sales (in GWh) is nonresidential?
d. Why are operating statistics like this useful to analysts?

Case 9-6

Effect of depreciation on net income

Five Points Construction Co. specializes in building replicas of historic houses. Sharon Higgs, president of Five Points, is considering the purchase of various items of equipment on July 1, 2004, for $120,000. The equipment would have a useful life of five years and no residual value. In the past, all equipment has been leased. For tax purposes, Sharon is considering depreciating the equipment by the straight-line method. She discussed the matter with her CPA and learned that, although the straight-line method could be elected, it was to her advantage to use the modified accelerated cost recovery system (MACRS) for tax purposes. She asked for your advice as to which method to use for tax purposes.

a. Compute depreciation for each of the years (2004, 2005, 2006, 2007, 2008, and 2009) of useful life by (a) the straight-line method and (b) MACRS. In using the straight-line method, one-half year's depreciation should be computed for 2004 and 2009. Use the MACRS rates presented in the chapter.
b. Assuming that income before depreciation and income tax is estimated to be $200,000 uniformly per year and that the income tax rate is 30%, compute the net income for each of the years 2004, 2005, 2006, 2007, 2008, and 2009 if (a) the straight-line method is used and (b) MACRS is used.
c. What factors would you present for Sharon's consideration in the selection of a depreciation method?

BUSINESS ACTIVITIES AND RESPONSIBILITY ISSUES

Activity 9-1

Ethics and professional conduct in business

Lizzie Paulk, CPA, is an assistant to the controller of Insignia Co. In her spare time, Lizzie also prepares tax returns and performs general accounting services for clients. Frequently, Lizzie performs these services after her normal working hours, using Insignia Co.'s computers and laser printers. Occasionally, Lizzie's clients will call her at the office during regular working hours.

Discuss whether Lizzie is performing in a professional manner.

Activity 9-2

Financial vs. tax depreciation

The following is an excerpt from a conversation between the employees of Ermine Co., Jody Terpin and Hal Graves. Jody is the accounts payable clerk, and Hal is the cashier.

Jody: Hal, could I get your opinion on something?
Hal: Sure, Jody.

Jody: Do you know Margaret, the fixed assets clerk?
Hal: I know who she is, but I don't know her real well. Why?
Jody: Well, I was talking to her at lunch last Monday about how she liked her job, etc. You know, the usual . . . and she mentioned something about having to keep two sets of books . . . one for taxes and one for the financial statements. That can't be good accounting, can it? What do you think?
Hal: Two sets of books? It doesn't sound right.
Jody: It doesn't seem right to me either. I was always taught that you had to use generally accepted accounting principles. How can there be two sets of books? What can be the difference between the two?

How would you respond to Hal and Jody if you were Margaret?

Activity 9-3

Integrity, Objectivity, and Ethics in Business

The following is an excerpt from a conversation between the chief executive officer, Rob Rameriz, and the chief financial officer, Maurice Chandler, of Nile Group, Inc.:

Rameriz (CEO): Maurice, as you know, the auditors are coming in to audit our year-end financial statements pretty soon. Do you see any problems on the horizon?
Chandler (CFO): Well, you know about our "famous" Hill Companies acquisition a couple of years ago. We booked $1,000,000 of goodwill from that acquisition, and the accounting rules require us to recognize any impairment of goodwill.
Rameriz (CEO): Uh oh.
Chandler (CFO): Yeah, right. We had to shut the old Hill Company operations down this year because those products were no longer selling. Thus, our auditor is going to insist that we write off the $1,000,000 of goodwill to reflect the impaired value.
Rameriz (CEO): We can't have that—at least not this year. Do everything you can to push back on this one. We just can't take that kind of a hit this year. The most we could stand is $200,000. Maurice, keep the write-off to $200,000 and promise anything in the future. Then we'll deal with that when we get there.

How should Chandler respond to the CEO?

Activity 9-4

Shopping for a delivery truck

GROUP ACTIVITY

You are planning to acquire a delivery truck for use in your business for three years. In groups of three or four, explore a local dealer's purchase and leasing options for the truck. Summarize the costs of purchasing versus leasing, and list other factors that might help you decide whether to buy or lease the truck.

Activity 9-5

Applying for patents, copyrights, and trademarks

Go to the Internet and review the procedures for applying for a patent, a copyright, or a trademark. One Internet site that is useful for this purpose is http://www.uspto.gov, which is linked to the text's Web site at http://warren.swlearning.com. Prepare a written summary of these procedures.

ANSWERS TO SELF-STUDY QUESTIONS

1. C All amounts spent to get a fixed asset (such as machinery) in place and ready for use are proper charges to the asset account. In the case of machinery acquired, the freight (answer A) and the installation costs (answer B) are both (answer C) proper charges to the machinery account.

2. C The periodic charge for depreciation under the declining-balance method (twice the straight-line rate) for the second year is determined by first computing the depreciation charge for the first year. The depreciation for the first year of $6,000 (answer A) is computed by multiplying the cost of the equipment, \$9,000, by $\frac{2}{3}$ (the straight-line rate of $\frac{1}{3}$ multiplied by 2). The depreciation for the second year of \$2,000 (answer C) is then determined by multiplying the book value at the end of the first year, \$3,000 (the cost of \$9,000 minus the first-year depreciation of \$6,000), by $\frac{2}{3}$. The third year's depreciation is \$400 (answer D). It is determined by multiplying the book value at the end of the second year, \$1,000, by $\frac{2}{3}$, thus yielding \$667. However, the equipment cannot be depreciated below its residual value of \$600; thus, the third-year depreciation is \$400 (\$1,000 − \$600).

3. B A depreciation method that provides for a higher depreciation amount in the first year of the use of an asset and a gradually declining periodic amount thereafter is called an accelerated depreciation method. The declining-balance method (answer B) is an example of such a method.

4. C The accumulated depreciation is debited for the overhaul cost of \$40,000. The book value of \$45,000 is depreciated over the five-year remaining life; thus, the net decrease in accumulated depreciation is \$31,000 (\$40,000 − \$9,000) (answer C)

5. C Fixed asset turnover ratio = Revenue ÷ Average book value of fixed assets, or {\$500,000/[(\$80,000 + \$120,000)/2]}, or 5.0 (answer C).

10 Liabilities

Learning Goals

1. Describe and illustrate current liabilities related to accounts payable, notes payable, and payroll transactions.
2. Describe the characteristics of long-term liabilities and apply present value concepts to bonds payable.
3. Describe and illustrate deferred liabilities related to
4. Identify the characteristics of contingent liabilities.
5. Illustrate the reporting of liabilities on the balance sheet.
6. Analyze and interpret liquidity using the current ratio, quick ratio, number of times interest charges earned, and ratio of total liabilities to total assets.

Barnes & Noble, Inc.

Banks and other financial institutions provide loans or credit to buyers for purchases of various items. Using credit is probably as old as commerce itself. The Babylonians were lending money as early as 1300 B.C. The use of credit provides individuals convenience and buying power. Credit cards provide individuals convenience by supporting Internet purchases, helping them avoid the hassles of checks or cash, and consolidating payments to a single credit card company. Credit also creates purchasing power by allowing individuals to purchase fixed assets, such as automobiles and houses, prior to having money for the total purchase price. Just imagine if you had to save the complete purchase price of a home prior to purchase. Most of us would only be able to buy a house by the time our families were already grown and gone. Thus, credit allows us to purchase assets whose benefits are consumed in the long term, such as houses and cars.

Like individuals, the use of debt can help a business reach its business objectives. For example, Barnes & Noble, Inc., a major media superstore in the United States, uses short-term credit to purchase books, music, and DVDs from publishers and studios. As these items are sold, cash is generated to pay the suppliers for these purchases. In addition, Barnes & Noble uses long-term debt to expand its business. As a result of Barnes & Noble's use of credit, it has become the No. 1 retail brand for quality, sold over 500 million books annually, become the second largest coffee house chain in the United States, and built a network of over 820 stores.

While debt can help a company achieve the kind of success that Barnes & Noble has, too much debt can be a financial burden that can even lead to bankruptcy. Just like individuals, businesses must manage debt wisely. In this chapter, we will discuss the nature of, accounting for, and analysis of both current and long-term debt.

CURRENT LIABILITIES

Describe and illustrate current liabilities related to accounts payable, notes payable, and payroll transactions.

When a business or a bank advances *credit*, it is making a loan. In these circumstances, it is called a **creditor** (or *lender*). Individuals or businesses that receive the credit are called **debtors** (or *borrowers*). Debt is an obligation that is recorded as a liability. *Long-term liabilities* are obligations due for a period of time greater than one year. Thus, a 30-year mortgage taken out to purchase property would be an example of a long-term liability. In contrast, *current liabilities* are obligations that will be paid out of current assets and are due within a short time, usually within one year.

Three types of current liabilities will be discussed in this section—accounts payable, notes payable, and payroll liabilities.

Accounts Payable

Accounts payable arise from purchasing goods or services for use in a company's operations or for purchasing merchandise for resale. For most businesses, this is often the largest current liability. Exhibit 1 illustrates the size of the accounts payable balance as a percent of total current liabilities for a number of different companies. The average percent of accounts payable to total current liabilities for large companies is 35.7%.[1]

Exhibit 1

Accounts Payable as a Percent of Total Current Liabilities

Company	Accounts Payable as a Percent of Total Current Liabilities
Alcoa Inc.	39%
BellSouth	16
The Gap Inc.	47
IBM	22
Nissan Motor Co.	25
Rite-Aid Corp.	51
Chevron Texaco	54

Notes Payable

A second type of current liability is notes payable. A note payable may be issued when merchandise or other assets are purchased, or a note may be issued in exchange for cash from a bank. A note may also be issued to creditors to temporarily satisfy an account payable created earlier. For example, assume that a business issues a 90-day, 12% note for $1,000, dated August 1, 2007, to Murray Co. for a $1,000 overdue account. The issuance of the note is recorded as follows:

SCF	BS	IS
—	L↑↓	—

Aug. 1	Accounts Payable—Murray Co.	1,000	
	Notes Payable		1,000

When the note matures, the entry to record the payment of the $1,000 principal plus $30 interest ($\$1,000 \times 12\% \times 90/360$) is as follows:

1 Determined from analysis of public companies exceeding $10 billion in sales.

SCF	BS	IS
O↓	A↓ L↓ SE↓	E↑

Oct. 30	Notes Payable	1,000	
	Interest Expense	30	
	Cash		1,030

The interest expense is reported in the Other Expense section of the income statement for the year ended December 31, 2007. The interest expense account is closed at December 31.

The preceding entries for notes payable are similar to those we discussed in Chapter 8 for notes receivable. Notes payable entries are presented from the viewpoint of the borrower, while notes receivable entries are presented from the viewpoint of the creditor or lender. To illustrate, the following entries are journalized for a borrower (Bowden Co.), who issues a note payable to a creditor (Coker Co.):

	Bowden Co. (Borrower)			**Coker Co. (Creditor)**		
May 1. Bowden Co. purchased merchandise on account from Coker Co., $10,000, 2/10, n/30. The merchandise cost Coker Co. $7,500.	Merchandise Inventory	10,000		Accounts Receivable	10,000	
	Accounts Payable		10,000	Sales		10,000
				Cost of Merchandise Sold	7,500	
				Merchandise Inventory		7,500
May 31. Bowden Co. issued a 60-day, 12% note for $10,000 to Coker Co. on account.	Accounts Payable	10,000		Notes Receivable	10,000	
	Notes Payable		10,000	Accounts Receivable		10,000
July 30. Bowden Co. paid Coker Co. the amount due on the note of May 31. Interest: $10,000 × 12% × 60/360.	Notes Payable	10,000		Cash	10,200	
	Interest Expense	200		Notes Receivable		10,000
	Cash		10,200	Interest Revenue		200

Q. In buying a used delivery truck, a business issues an $8,000, 60-day note dated July 15, which the truck's seller discounts at 12%. What is the cost of the truck (the proceeds)?

A. *$7,840 [$8,000 − ($8,000 × 12% × 60/360)]*

Sometimes a borrower will issue a creditor a discounted note rather than an interest-bearing note. Although such a note does not specify an interest rate, the creditor sets a rate of interest and deducts the interest from the face amount of the note. This interest is called the **discount**. The rate used in computing the discount is called the **discount rate**. The borrower is given the remainder, called the **proceeds**.

To illustrate, assume that on August 10, Cary Company issues a $20,000, 90-day note to Seinfeld Company in exchange for inventory. Seinfeld discounts the note at a rate of 15%. The amount of the discount, $750, is debited to *Interest Expense*. The proceeds, $19,250, are debited to *Merchandise Inventory*. *Notes Payable* is credited for the face amount of the note, which is also its maturity value. This entry is shown below.

SCF	BS	IS
—	A↑ L↑ SE↓	E↑

Aug. 10	Merchandise Inventory	19,250	
	Interest Expense	750	
	Notes Payable		20,000

When the note is paid, the entry is recorded as follows:[2]

SCF	BS	IS
O↓	A↓ L↓	—

Nov. 8	Notes Payable	20,000	
	Cash		20,000

2 If the accounting period ends before a discounted note is paid, an adjusting entry should record the prepaid (deferred) interest that is not yet an expense. This deferred interest would be deducted from Notes Payable.

Payroll Liabilities

A third type of current liability is the payroll liability. In accounting, the term **payroll** refers to the amount paid to employees for the services they provide during a period. A business's payroll is usually significant for several reasons. First, the payroll and related payroll taxes have a significant effect on net income. Second, the payroll is subject to various federal and state regulations. Finally, the payroll usually has a significant effect on employee morale.

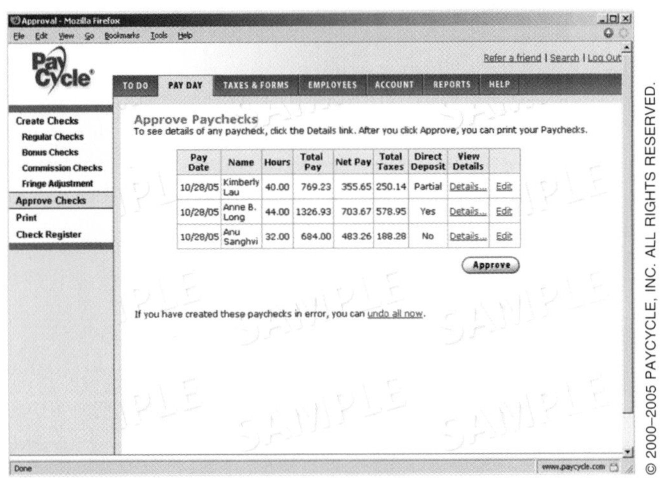

Recording Payroll. Employee salaries and wages are expenses to an employer. The total earnings of an employee for a payroll period, including bonuses and overtime pay, are called **gross pay**. From this amount, one or more *deductions* are subtracted to arrive at the net pay. **Net pay** is the amount the employer must pay the employee. The deductions for federal taxes are usually the largest deduction. Deductions may also be required for state or local income taxes. Other deductions may be made for FICA, medical insurance, contributions to pensions, and items authorized by individual employees.

Most of us have Federal Insurance Contributions Act (FICA) tax withheld from our payroll checks. Employers are required to withhold a portion of the earnings of each employee. The amount of **FICA tax** withheld is the employee's contribution to two federal programs: Social Security and Medicare. The FICA tax rate and the amounts subject to the tax are established annually by law.[3]

To illustrate recording payroll, assume that McDermott Co. had a gross payroll of \$13,800 for the week ending April 11. Assume that the FICA tax was 7.5% of the gross payroll, and that federal and state withholding was \$1,655 and \$280, respectively. The McDermott Co. payroll is recorded below.

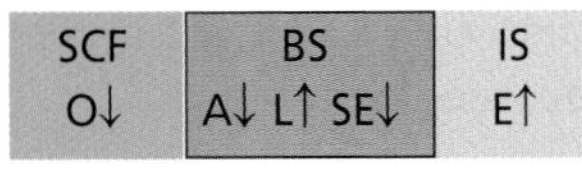

Apr. 11	Wage and Salary Expense	13,800	
	FICA Tax Payable (\$13,800 × 0.075)		1,035
	Employees Federal Income Tax Payable		1,655
	Employees State Income Tax Payable		280
	Cash		10,830

The FICA, federal, and state taxes withheld from the employees' earnings are not expenses to the employer. Rather, these amounts are withheld on behalf of employees.

Liability for Employer Payroll Taxes. In addition to amounts withheld on behalf of employees, most employers are also subject to federal and state payroll taxes based on the amount paid to their employees. Such taxes are an operating expense of the business. Exhibit 2 summarizes the responsibility for employee and employer payroll taxes.

---

3 The Social Security portion of the FICA tax is limited to a specified amount of annual compensation for each individual. The 2005 limitation is \$90,000. The Medicare portion is not subject to a limitation. Throughout this text, we will simplify by assuming that all compensation is within the Social Security limitation. Under this assumption, the Social Security and Medicare tax rates can be combined into a single tax rate, termed FICA tax.

Exhibit 2

Responsibility for Tax Payments

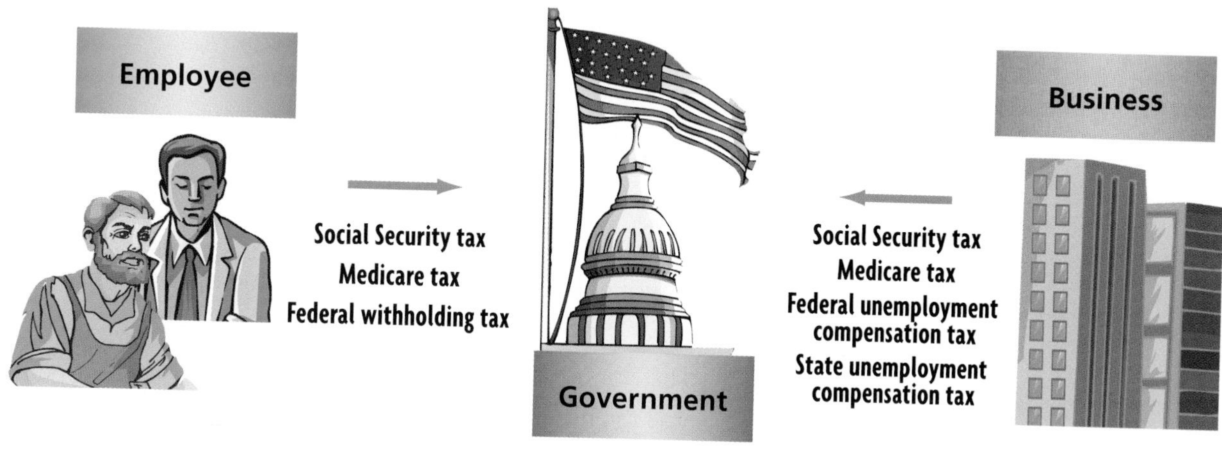

FICA Tax Employers are required to contribute to the Social Security and Medicare programs for each employee. The employer must match the employee's contribution to each program.

Federal Unemployment Compensation Tax The Federal Unemployment Tax Act (FUTA) provides for temporary payments to those who become unemployed as a result of layoffs due to economic causes beyond their control. Types of employment subject to this program are similar to those covered by FICA taxes. The FUTA tax rate and maximum earnings of each employee subject to the tax are established annually by law.

State Unemployment Compensation Tax State Unemployment Tax Acts (SUTA) also provide for payments to unemployed workers. The amounts paid as benefits are obtained, for the most part, from a tax levied upon employers only. The employment experience and the status of each employer's tax account are reviewed annually, and the tax rates are adjusted accordingly.

Recording and Paying Payroll Taxes. The employer's payroll taxes become liabilities when the related payroll is *paid* to employees. The payroll information of McDermott Co. indicates that the amount of FICA tax withheld is $1,035 on April 11. Since the employer must match the employees' FICA contributions, the employer's

INTEGRITY, OBJECTIVITY, AND ETHICS IN BUSINESS

Phantom Employees

Companies must guard against the fraudulent creation and cashing of payroll checks. Numerous payroll frauds involve supervisors adding fictitious employees to or failing to remove departing employees from the payroll, and then cashing the check. Requiring proper authorization and approval of employee additions, removals, or changes in pay rate can minimize this type of fraud.

Social Security payroll tax will also be $1,035. Further, assume that the SUTA and FUTA taxes are $145 and $25, respectively. The entry to record the payroll tax expense for the week and the liability for the taxes accrued is shown below.

SCF	BS	IS
—	L↑ SE↓	E↑

Apr. 11	Payroll Tax Expense	1,205	
	FICA Tax Payable		1,035
	SUTA Tax Payable		145
	FUTA Tax Payable		25

Payroll tax liabilities are paid to appropriate taxing authorities on a quarterly basis. The quarterly entry would debit the various taxes payable and credit Cash.

Employees' Fringe Benefits. Many companies provide their employees a variety of benefits in addition to salary and wages earned. Such **fringe benefits** may take many forms, including vacations, medical benefits, and post-retirement benefits such as pension plans. When the employer pays part or all of the cost of the fringe benefits, these costs must be recognized as expenses. To properly match revenues and expenses, the estimated cost of these benefits should be recorded as an expense during the period in which the employee earns the benefit.

Exhibit 3 shows benefit dollars as a percent of total benefits for 864 companies surveyed by the U.S. Chamber of Commerce.

Exhibit 3

Benefit Dollars as a Percent of Total

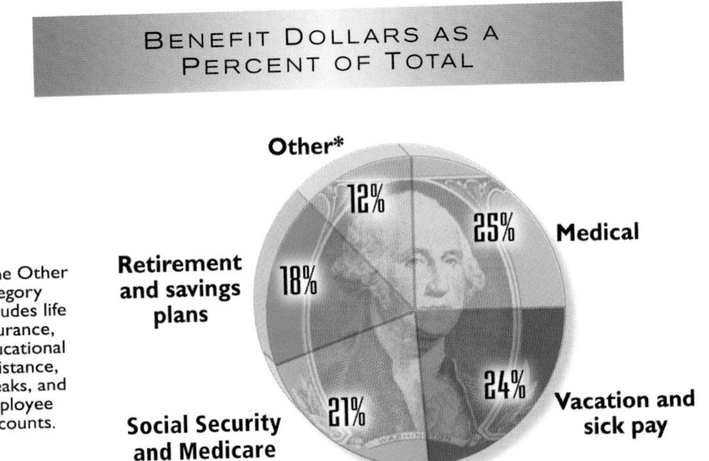

Source: U.S Chamber of Commerce.

We will use vacation pay to illustrate fringe benefit accounting. Most employers grant vacation rights, sometimes called *compensated absences*, to their employees. Such rights give rise to a recordable contingent liability. The liability for employees' vacation pay should be accrued as a liability as the vacation rights are earned. The entry to accrue vacation pay may be recorded in total at the end of each fiscal year, or it may be recorded at the end of each pay period. To illustrate this latter case, assume that employees earn one day of vacation for each month worked during the year. Assume also that the estimated vacation pay for the payroll period ending May 5 is $2,000. The entry to record the accrued vacation pay for this pay period is shown as follows:

SCF	BS	IS
—	L↑ SE↓	E↑

May 5	Vacation Pay Expense	2,000	
	Vacation Pay Payable		2,000

HOW BUSINESSES MAKE MONEY 

Barnes & Noble, Inc.: More Than Just a Book Seller

Barnes & Noble, Inc., is the largest bookstore chain in the United States. In addition to selling books at its retail stores, Barnes & Noble also sells books through the Internet and computer games through its GameStop subsidiary. In recent years, the company has expanded into the publishing business, focusing on out-of-print classic books, study aids, and how-to books. Barnes & Noble's approach of expanding into new lines of business has the potential to increase profits as well as differentiate it from competitors such as **Borders, Inc.**

If employees are required to take all their vacation time within one year, the vacation pay payable is reported on the balance sheet as a current liability. If employees are allowed to accumulate their vacation time, the estimated vacation pay liability that is applicable to time that will *not* be taken within one year is a long-term liability.

When payroll is prepared for the period in which employees have taken vacations, the vacation pay payable is reduced. The entry debits *Vacation Pay Payable* and credits *Salaries Payable* and the other related accounts for taxes and withholdings.

Describe the characteristics of long-term liabilities and apply present value concepts to bonds payable.

LONG-TERM LIABILITIES

Most of us have or will finance (purchase on credit) an automobile, a computer, or a home. Similarly, corporations often finance their operations by purchasing on credit through long-term borrowing. The most common form of long-term borrowing for a corporation is by issuing **bonds**, which are simply a form of a long-term, interest-bearing note. Like a note, a bond requires periodic interest payments, and the face amount must be repaid, or redeemed, at the maturity date. Bondholders are creditors of the issuing corporation, and their claims on the assets of the corporation rank ahead of stockholders.

A corporation that issues bonds enters into a contract, called a **bond indenture** or trust indenture, with the bondholders. A bond issue is normally divided into a number of individual bonds. Usually, the face value of each bond, called the *principal*, is $1,000 or a multiple of $1,000. The **interest** on bonds may be payable annually, semiannually, or quarterly. Most bonds pay interest semiannually.

The price of a bond is quoted as a percentage of the bond's face value. Thus, investors could purchase or sell Time Warner bonds quoted at $109\frac{7}{8}$ for $1,098.75. Likewise, bonds quoted at 109 could be purchased or sold for $1,090.

When all bonds of an issue mature at the same time, they are called **term bonds**. If the maturities are spread over several dates, they are called **serial bonds**. For example, one-tenth of an issue of $1,000,000 bonds, or $100,000, may mature 16 years from the issue date, another $100,000 in the 17th year, and so on, until the final $100,000 matures in the 25th year.

Bonds that may be exchanged for other securities, such as common stock, are called **convertible bonds**. Bonds that a corporation reserves the right to redeem before their maturity are called **callable bonds**. Bonds issued on the basis of the general credit of the corporation are called **debenture bonds**.

Once bonds are issued, periodic interest payments and repayment of the face value of the bonds are required. If these payments are not made, the bondholders could seek court action and force the company into bankruptcy. For example, Atkins Nutritionals, Inc., the company that made low-carb dieting famous, recently filed for Chapter 11 bankruptcy protection. While the Atkins diet was initially popular because of its appealing approach and relatively fast results, criticism by health experts about the safety of the diet led to a sharp drop in revenues and cash flow. As cash flows diminished, the company was unable to meet $300 million in principal and interest payments. As a result, creditors forced the company into Chapter 11 bankruptcy and, thus, became the new owners.[4]

In a related example, Krispy Kreme Doughnuts, the popular doughnut franchise, defaulted on its debts recently as a result of a downturn in revenues that were insufficient to support interest and debt payments. The company cited the popularity of the Atkins diet as a key factor that contributed to the downturn in its revenues.

When a corporation issues bonds, the price that buyers are willing to pay for the bonds depends upon present value concepts. For this reason, we discuss present value concepts next.

Present Value Concepts

Because of the ability to earn interest, money received in the future is not worth as much as it is today. That is, money has time value. For example, if Apex Corp. deposited $55,840 in the bank today at 6% annual interest, it would accumulate to $100,000 in 10 periods. In contrast, if Apex did not receive the $55,840 until the end of the 10 periods, the $44,160 ($100,000 − $55,840) of interest would not have been earned. In other words, $55,840 received or paid in the future is not the same as $55,840 received today. Thus, comparing $55,840 to be received today to $55,840 to be received in 10 years is like comparing apples to oranges, as shown in Exhibit 4.

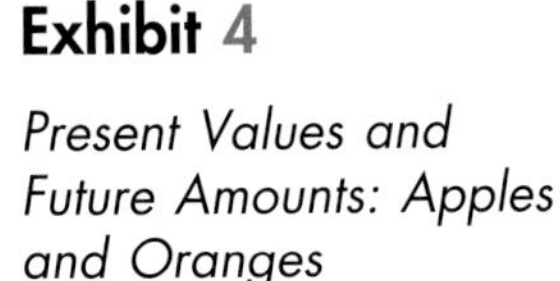

Exhibit 4

Present Values and Future Amounts: Apples and Oranges

How then do we compare current and future dollars? We do this by using present value. **Present value** is the current value today of dollars to be received or paid in the future. That is, present value computes today's value of amounts to be received in the future by considering the effects of interest.

Present Value of an Amount to Be Received in the Future. The present value of a future amount is determined by (1) the interest rate and (2) the number of periods until the future amount is received or paid. To calculate present value, the future amount is multiplied by the present value of $1 factor for the interest rate and time period. **Present value of $1** factors are found in the present value tables included in Appendix A at the end of this text. An excerpt from these tables is illustrated in Exhibit 5.

In Exhibit 5, the columns represent interest rates, and the rows represent the number of periods. For example, the present value of $1, 10 periods hence at an interest rate of 6%, which we will denote as Present Value of $\$1_{6\%,\ n\ =\ 10}$, is 0.55840. Thus, the present value of $100,000 to be received 10 years in the future can be calculated by

4 Elizabeth Lesure, "Atkins Company, Leader in Low-Carb Diet Craze, Files for Bankruptcy," *Associated Press*, August 1, 2005.

Exhibit 5

Present Value of $1 Factors

Periods	5%	$5\frac{1}{2}$%	6%	$6\frac{1}{2}$%	7%	10%	11%	12%	13%	14%
1	0.95238	0.94787	0.94340	0.93897	0.93458	0.90909	0.90090	0.89286	0.88496	0.87719
2	0.90703	0.89845	0.89000	0.88166	0.87344	0.82645	0.81162	0.79719	0.78315	0.76947
3	0.86384	0.85161	0.83962	0.82785	0.81630	0.75132	0.73119	0.71178	0.69305	0.67497
4	0.82270	0.80722	0.79209	0.77732	0.76290	0.68301	0.65873	0.63552	0.61332	0.59208
5	0.78353	0.76513	0.74726	0.72988	0.71299	0.62092	0.59345	0.56743	0.54276	0.51937
6	0.74622	0.72525	0.70496	0.68533	0.66634	0.56447	0.53464	0.50663	0.48032	0.45559
7	0.71068	0.68744	0.66506	0.64351	0.62275	0.51316	0.48166	0.45235	0.42506	0.39964
8	0.67684	0.65160	0.62741	0.60423	0.58201	0.46651	0.43393	0.40388	0.37616	0.35056
9	0.64461	0.61763	0.59190	0.56735	0.54393	0.42410	0.39092	0.36061	0.33288	0.30751
10	0.61391	0.58543	0.55840	0.53273	0.50835	0.38554	0.35218	0.32197	0.29459	0.26974

multiplying the $100,000 by the present value of $1 factor for 10 periods at 6% annual interest, as shown below.

Present Value = Future Amount × Present Value of $\$1_{6\%,\ n\ =\ 10}$
$55,840 = $100,000 × 0.55840

In this case, $100,000 to be received 10 years in the future is worth $55,840 today. This process of converting a future amount into a present value is called **discounting**. Discounting converts future dollars into current dollars as shown in Exhibit 6.

Exhibit 6

Converting a Future Amount to Its Present Value

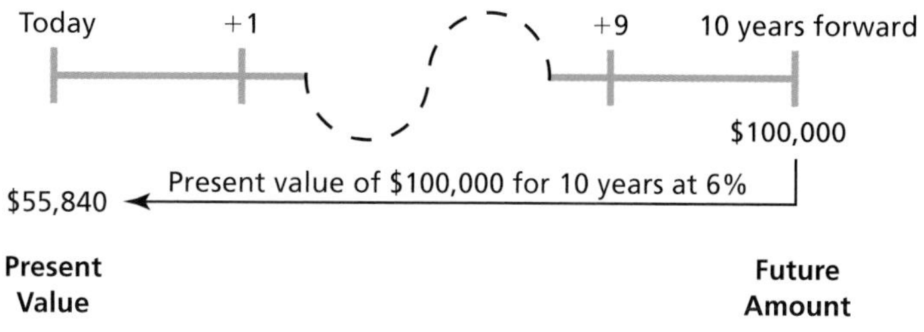

In other words, if $55,840 is invested today at 6% annual interest, it will be worth $100,000 in 10 years.

Present Value of a Series of Payments to Be Received in the Future. Up to this point, we have discussed the present value of $1 to be received in the future. Assume, however, that several amounts are to be received in the future. For example, assume that you inherit $60,000, to be received in 10 annual payments of $6,000, with the first payment being received one year from today. How much would your inheritance be worth in today's dollars assuming 6% annual interest?

One way to determine the present value of this stream of cash receipts is to add the present values of the individual future amounts. Using the present value of $1 table in Exhibit 5, your inheritance has a present value of $44,160.54, as shown in Exhibit 7.

Exhibit 7

Present Value of a Stream of Cash Receipts

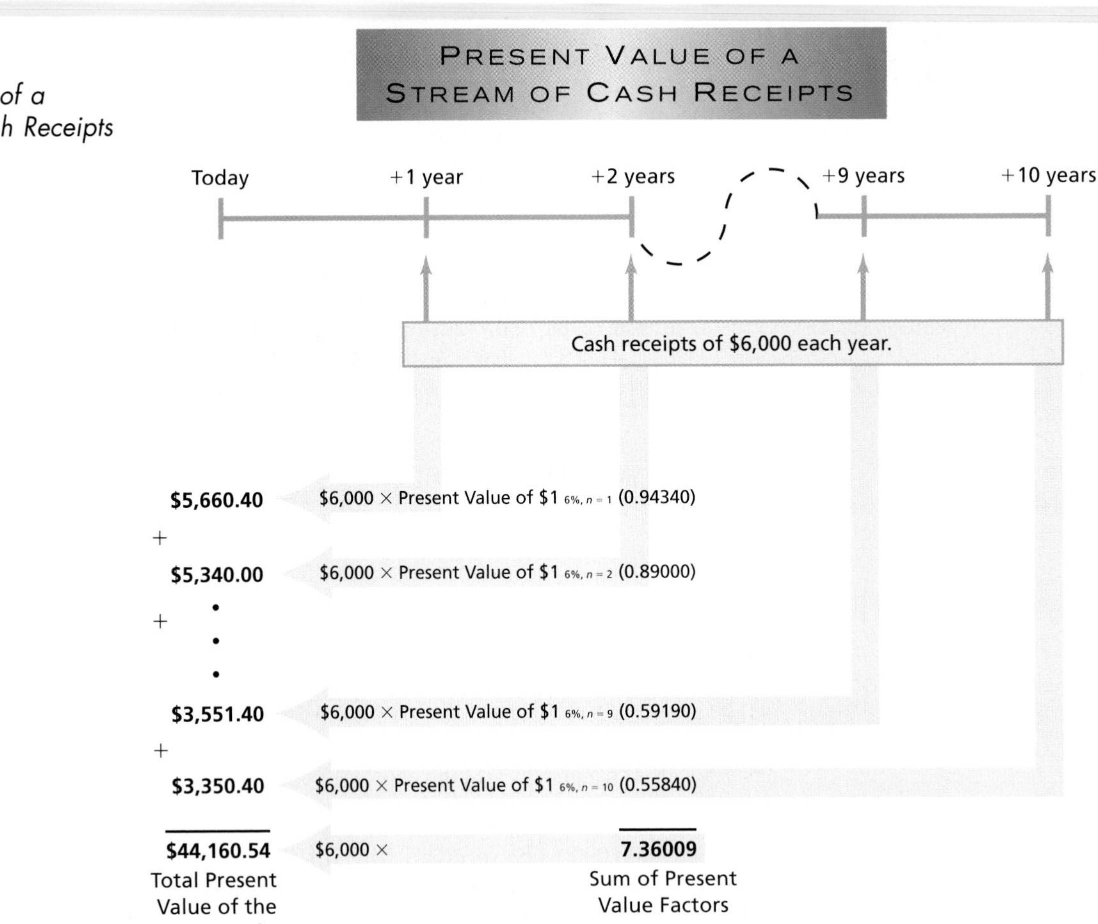

In the preceding case, the periodic cash flows of $6,000 are called an **annuity**. An annuity is a series of cash payments or receipts (called **annuity payments**), spaced equally in time, as illustrated in Exhibit 8.

Exhibit 8

The Concept of an Annuity

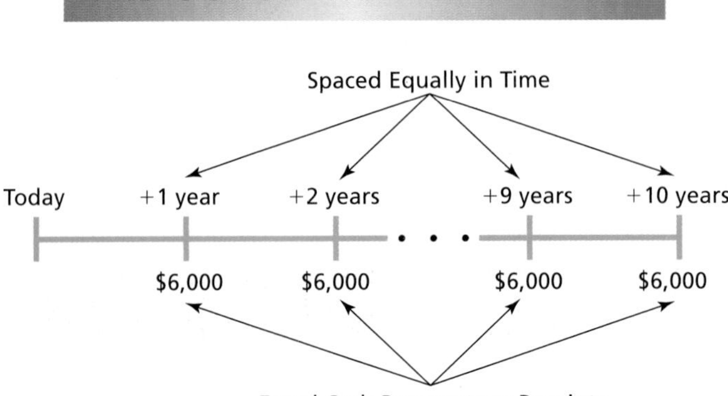

The present value calculation for an annuity can be simplified using **Present Value of an Annuity of $1** tables. An excerpt of a present value of an annuity of $1 table is shown in Exhibit 9.

For example, the present value of an annuity of $1 for 10 periods at an interest rate of 6% we will denote as Present Value of an Annuity of $\$1_{6\%, n = 10}$, which from the table

Exhibit 9

Present Value of an Annuity of $1

Periods	5%	$5\frac{1}{2}$%	6%	$6\frac{1}{2}$%	7%	10%	11%	12%	13%	14%
1	0.95238	0.94787	0.94340	0.93897	0.93458	0.90909	0.90090	0.89286	0.88496	0.87719
2	1.85941	1.84632	1.83339	1.82063	1.80802	1.73554	1.71252	1.69005	1.66810	1.64666
3	2.72325	2.69793	2.67301	2.64848	2.62432	2.48685	2.44371	2.40183	2.36115	2.32163
4	3.54595	3.50515	3.46511	3.42580	3.38721	3.16987	3.10245	3.03735	2.97447	2.91371
5	4.32948	4.27028	4.21236	4.15568	4.10020	3.79079	3.69590	3.60478	3.51723	3.43308
6	5.07569	4.99553	4.91732	4.84101	4.76654	4.35526	4.23054	4.11141	3.99755	3.88867
7	5.78637	5.68297	5.58238	5.48452	5.38929	4.86842	4.71220	4.56376	4.42261	4.28830
8	6.46321	6.33457	6.20979	6.08875	5.97130	5.33493	5.14612	4.96764	4.79677	4.63886
9	7.10782	6.95220	6.80169	6.65610	6.51523	5.75902	5.53705	5.32825	5.13166	4.94637
10	7.72174	7.53763	7.36009	7.18883	7.02358	6.14457	5.88923	5.65022	5.42624	5.21612

is 7.36009. Thus, the present value of the preceding $6,000 per year annuity using the present value of an annuity of $1 for 10 periods at 6% is calculated as follows:

Present Value of the Annuity	=	Cash Flow or Annuity Payment	×	Present Value of an Annuity of $\$1_{6\%,\ 10}$
$44,160.54*	=	$6,000	×	7.36009

* Because the present value tables are rounded to five decimal places, minor rounding differences may appear in the illustrations.

You should note that using the present value of an annuity of $1 table yields the same present value, $44,160.54, as our prior computation that calculated present values of each annual receipt of $6,000. In addition, you should note that the *sum of the present value of $1 factors* from the previous calculation and illustrated in Exhibit 9, 7.36009, equals the present value annuity of $1 factor.

Bonds Issued at Face Value

We now use the preceding present value concepts in determining the issue price of a bond. When a corporation issues bonds, the price that buyers are willing to pay for the bonds depends upon the following three factors:

1. The face amount of the bonds, which is the amount due at the maturity date.
2. The periodic interest to be paid on the bonds.
3. The market rate of interest.

The face amount and the periodic interest to be paid on the bonds are identified in the bond indenture. The periodic interest is expressed as a percentage of the face amount of the bond. This percentage or rate of interest is called the **contract rate**, or coupon rate. The **market rate** or effective rate of interest is determined by transactions between buyers and sellers of similar bonds. This is the rate of return that investors demand for bonds of a similar quality and duration. The market rate is affected by a variety of factors such as investors' assessment of current economic conditions and the company's credit quality.

If the contract rate of interest equals the market rate of interest, the bonds will sell at their face amount. If the market rate is *higher* than the contract rate, the bonds will sell at a **discount**, or less than their face amount. If the market rate is *lower* than the contract rate, the bonds will sell at a **premium**, or more than their face amount.

Why is this the case? Buyers are not willing to pay the face amount for bonds whose contract rate is lower than the market rate. The discount, in effect, represents the amount necessary to make up for the difference in the market and the contract interest rates. In contrast, if the market rate is lower than the contract rate, the bonds will sell at a premium, or for more than their face amount. In this case, buyers are willing to pay more than the face amount for bonds whose contract rate is higher than the market rate.

The face amount of the bonds and the periodic interest on the bonds represent cash to be received in the future. The buyer determines how much to pay for the bonds by computing the present value of these future cash receipts, using the market rate of interest. Thus, the price of a bond is computed by adding (1) the present value of the face amount and (2) the present value of the interest payments, as illustrated in Exhibit 10. The contract rate determines the *amount* of periodic interest payments, while the market rate determines the *present value factor* to be used to discount the bond's cash flows.

Exhibit 10

Calculating the Price of a Bond

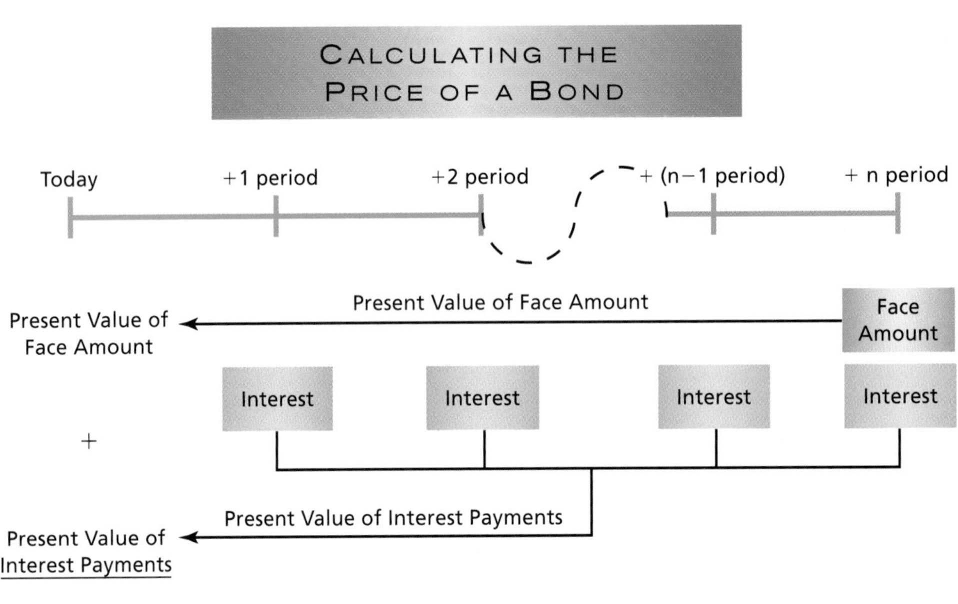

Often, bonds will pay interest every six months. When this is the case, the contract rate will be expressed as an annual interest rate to be paid semiannually. Thus, the annual interest rate must be converted to a semiannual rate by multiplying the rate by $\frac{1}{2}$. For example, on January 1, 2007, Moore Co. issues $100,000, 12%, five-year corporate bonds that pay interest semiannually on June 30 and December 31. The 12% bonds pay a semiannual rate of 6%. Thus, the amount of interest paid every six months is $6,000 ($100,000 × 6%).

Using the example above, assume that Moore Co. issues the $100,000, 12%, five-year bonds when the market rate of interest is 12%. The price of the bond issue is computed by adding the present value of the face amount of $100,000 and the present value of the interest payments of $6,000. As illustrated in Exhibit 11, the combined present value, or price, of the Moore Co. bonds is its face value, $100,000. This is because the market rate of interest equals the contract rate of interest, so the bonds will sell at their face amount.

Exhibit 11

Present Value of Bonds Issued at Face Amount

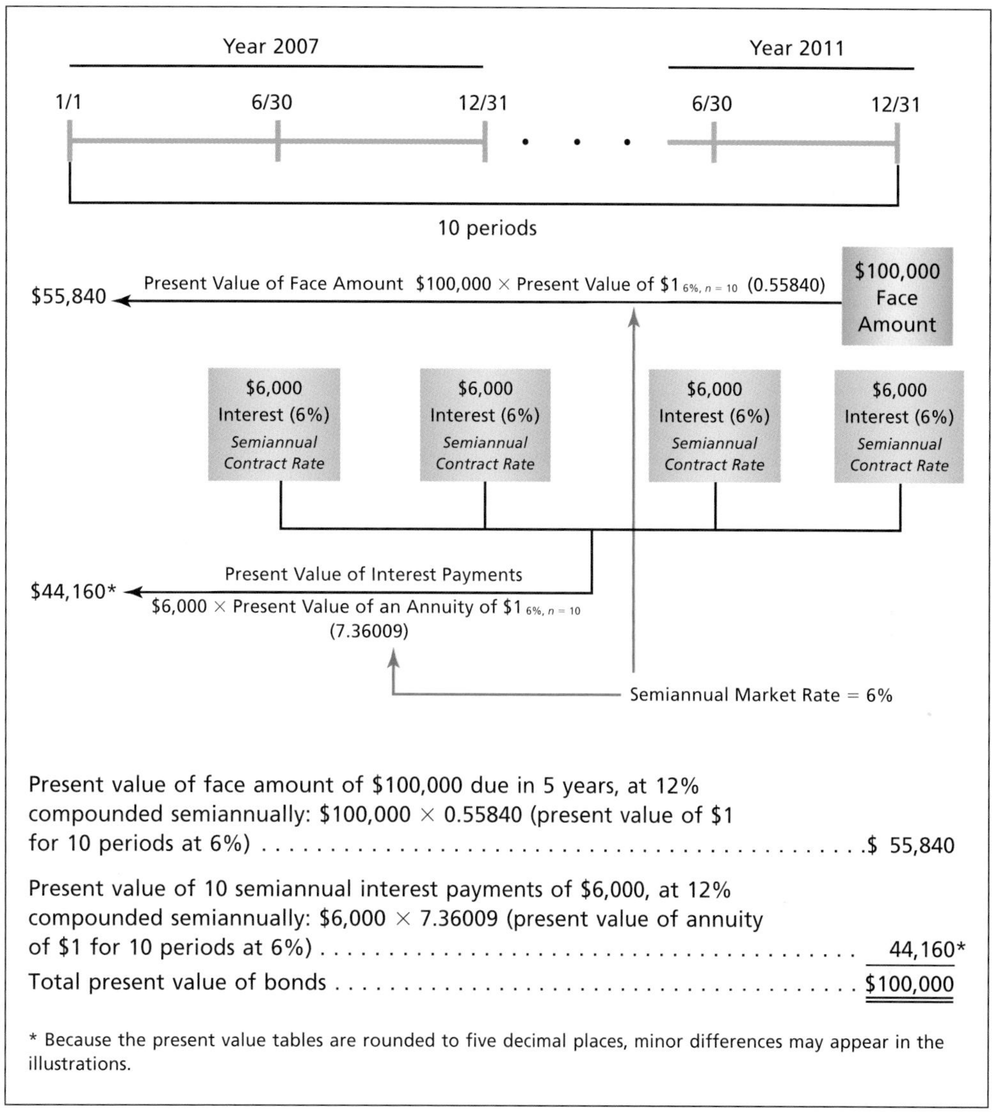

The following journal entry records the $100,000 bonds issued at their face amount:

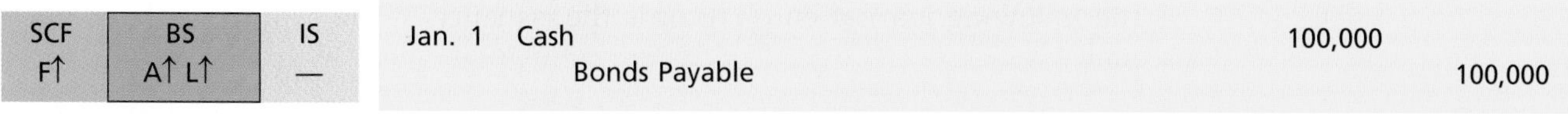

SCF	BS	IS
F↑	A↑ L↑	—

		Debit	Credit
Jan. 1	Cash	100,000	
	Bonds Payable		100,000

INTEGRITY, OBJECTIVITY, AND ETHICS IN BUSINESS

Credit Quality

The market rate of interest for a corporate bond is influenced by a number of factors, including the credit quality of the issuer. In June 2002, **WorldCom** disclosed a massive accounting fraud within the company, prompting credit rating agencies and bond investors to drastically lower their assessment of the company's credit quality. As a result, the price of WorldCom's $30 billion in bond debt dropped to 15 cents on the dollar, or $4.5 billion in a few short weeks.

Every six months after the bonds are issued, interest payments of $6,000 are made, beginning on June 30. As we discuss in Chapter 13, interest payments are reported in the operating activities section of the statement of cash flows. The first interest payment is recorded as shown below.

SCF	BS	IS
O↓	A↓ SE↓	E↑

June 30	Interest Expense	6,000	
	Cash		6,000

At the maturity date, the payment of the $100,000 principal is recorded as follows:

SCF	BS	IS
F↓	A↓ L↓	—

Dec. 31	Bonds Payable	100,000	
	Cash		100,000

Bonds Issued at Discount

If the market rate is *higher* than the contract rate, the bonds will sell at a discount, or for less than their face amount. This is because buyers are not willing to pay the full face amount for bonds which pay a lower rate of interest (contract rate) than they could earn on similar bonds. The discount, in effect, represents the amount necessary to make up for the difference between the market rate of interest and the contract rate of interest.

Continuing with our prior example, assume that the Moore Co. $100,000, 12%, five-year bonds were issued when the market rate of interest was 13% instead of 12%. As shown in Exhibit 12, the semiannual interest payments are not affected by the change in the market rate of interest. However, the market rate of interest of 13% requires different present value factors for discounting the interest payments and the face value of the bonds. As a result, the price of the bonds drops to $96,406, as shown in Exhibit 13. As discussed previously, the difference between the price of the bonds and their face value of $3,594 is called the bond *discount*.

Face Value of Bond	$100,000
− Price of the Bond	− 96,406
Discount on Bond	$ 3,594

Q. **General Motors** issued $500,000 of 8% five-year bonds that pay interest annually when the annual market rate of interest is 10%. What is the price of the bonds?

A. *Interest Payment = $500,000 × 8% (contract rate) = $40,000*
Price = [$500,000 × (.62092)] + [$40,000 × (3.79079)**]*
Price = $310,460 + $151,632 = $462,092

* Present Value of $\$1_{10\%,\ 5}$
** Present Value of Annuity of $\$1_{10\%,\ 5}$

The following journal entry records the issuance of the Moore Co. bonds at a discount:

SCF	BS	IS
F↑	A↑ L↑	—

Jan. 1	Cash	96,406	
	Discount on Bonds Payable	3,594	
	Bonds Payable		100,000

The $3,594 discount may be viewed as the amount that is needed to convince investors to accept a contract rate below the market rate. You may think of the discount as the market's way of adjusting a bond's contract rate of interest to the higher market rate of interest. Using this logic, generally accepted accounting principles require that bond discounts be amortized as interest expense over the life of the bond.

Exhibit 12
Present Value of Bonds Issued at Discount

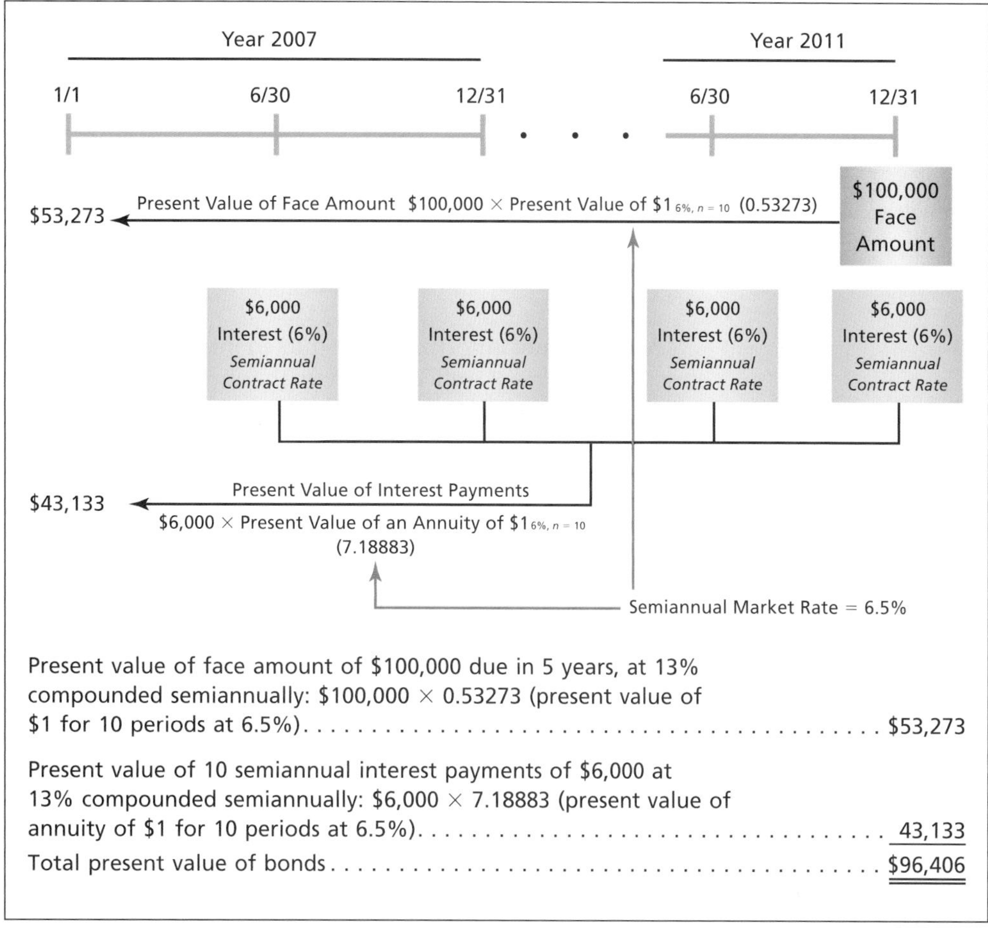

Present value of face amount of $100,000 due in 5 years, at 13% compounded semiannually: $100,000 × 0.53273 (present value of $1 for 10 periods at 6.5%)	$53,273
Present value of 10 semiannual interest payments of $6,000 at 13% compounded semiannually: $6,000 × 7.18883 (present value of annuity of $1 for 10 periods at 6.5%)	43,133
Total present value of bonds	$96,406

Bond Discount Amortization

Because a bond discount increases the effective interest rate of the bond issue, the discount must be reflected in the bond's periodic interest expense. This is accomplished through amortization of the bond discount. Amortization allocates a portion of the bond discount to each interest payment period, increasing periodic interest expense to reflect the higher market rate of interest at which the bonds were issued.

The two methods of amortizing a bond discount or premium are (1) the **straight-line method** and (2) the **effective interest rate method**, often called the *interest method*.[5] Both methods amortize the same total amount of discount over the life of the bonds. The interest method is required by generally accepted accounting principles. However, the straight-line method is acceptable if the results obtained do not materially differ from the results that would be obtained by using the interest method. Because the straight-line method illustrates the basic concept of amortizing discounts and is simpler, we will use it in this chapter.

The straight-line method allocates the same amount of bond discount to each period. Applying this method to the preceding example yields amortization of $\frac{1}{10}$ of

5 The interest method is discussed in the appendix to this chapter.

$3,594, or $359.40, each six months. The entry to record the first interest payment and the amortization of the related discount is shown below.

June 30	Interest Expense	6,359.40	
	Discount on Bonds Payable		359.40
	Cash		6,000.00

Thus, discount amortization results in interest expense that is greater than the periodic coupon payment, reflecting the higher market rate of interest at which the bonds were issued. The periodic amortization and interest expense on the bonds is the same, $6,359.40 ($6,000 + $359.40) for each half-year.

Bonds Issued at a Premium

If the market rate is *lower* than the contract rate on the date of issuance, the bonds will sell for more than their face amount, or at a premium. The premium represents the additional amount that buyers are willing to pay for the bonds because of the higher contract rate of interest. In the example above, assume that the Moore Co. $100,000, 12%, five-year bonds were issued when the market rate of interest was 11%. In this case, the lower market rate of interest causes the price of the Moore Co. bonds to be $3,769 higher than their face value, as shown in Exhibit 13.

As computed at the top of page 457, the $3,769 is the bond **premium**, which investors are willing to pay because the bonds pay a higher rate of interest than they could earn on similar bonds.

Exhibit 13

Present Value of Bonds Issued at Premium

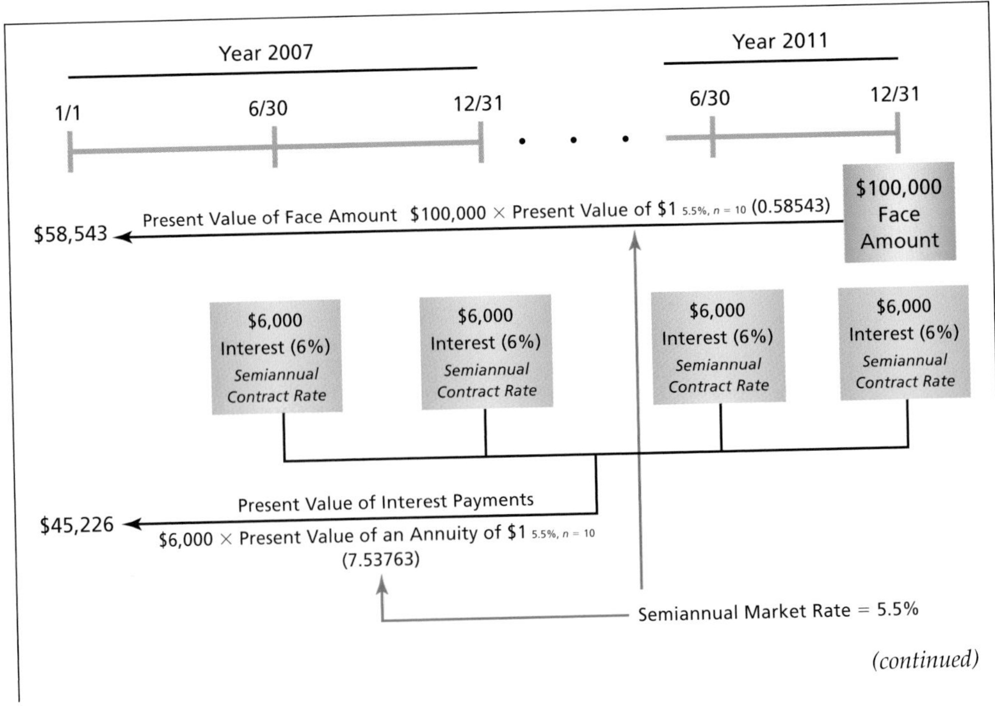

(continued)

Exhibit 13
Concluded

Present value of face amount of $100,000 due in 5 years, at 11% compounded semiannually: $100,000 × 0.58543 (present value of $1 for 10 periods at 5.5%)	$ 58,543
Present value of 10 semiannual interest payments of $6,000, at 11% compounded semiannually: $6,000 × 7.53763 (present value of annuity of $1 for 10 periods at 5.5%)	45,226
Total present value of bonds	$103,769

Price of the Bond	$103,769
−Face Value of the Bond	−100,000
Premium on the Bond	$ 3,769

The issuance of the bonds is recorded as follows:

SCF	BS	IS
F↑	A↑ L↑	—

Jan. 1	Cash	103,769	
	Bonds Payable		100,000
	Premium on Bonds Payable		3,769

Amortizing a Bond Premium

As with bond discounts, the bond premium must be amortized and reflected in the bond's periodic interest expense. Premium amortization, however, reduces interest expense below the amount of the cash coupon payment. In the above example, the straight-line method yields amortization of $\frac{1}{10}$ of $3,769, or $376.90, each half year. The entry to record the first interest payment and the amortization of the related premium is as follows:

SCF	BS	IS
O↓	A↓ L↓ SE↓	E↑

June 30	Interest Expense	5,623.10	
	Premium on Bonds Payable	376.90	
	Cash		6,000.00

Thus, premium amortization results in interest expense that is lower than the periodic coupon payment, reflecting the lower market rate of interest at which the bonds were issued. As with a discount, the periodic amortization and interest expense on the bonds is the same, $5,623.10 ($6,000.00 − $376.90) for each half-year.

Bond Redemption

A corporation may call or redeem bonds before they mature. This is often done if the market rate of interest declines significantly after the bonds have been issued. In this situation, the corporation may sell new bonds at a lower interest rate and use the funds to redeem the original bond issue. The corporation can thus save on future interest expenses.

A corporation often issues callable bonds to protect itself against significant declines in future interest rates. However, callable bonds are more risky for investors, who may not be able to replace the called bonds with investments paying an equal amount of interest.

Callable bonds can be redeemed by the issuing corporation within the period of time and at the price stated in the bond indenture. Normally, the call price is above

International Perspective
International Accounting Standards give companies the option of recording certain financial instruments such as bonds at either their fair value or their amortized cost.

the face value. A corporation may also redeem its bonds by purchasing them on the open market.

A corporation usually redeems its bonds at a price different from that of the carrying amount (or book value) of the bonds. The carrying amount of bonds payable is the balance of the bonds payable account (face amount of the bonds) less any unamortized discount or plus any unamortized premium. If the price paid for redemption is below the bond carrying amount, the difference in these two amounts is recorded as a gain. If the price paid for the redemption is above the carrying amount, a loss is recorded. Gains and losses on the redemption of bonds are reported on the income statement.[6]

To illustrate, assume that on June 30, a corporation has a bond issue of $100,000 outstanding, on which there is an unamortized premium of $4,000. If the corporation calls the entire bond issue for $105,000 on June 30, the redemption is recorded as follows:

SCF	BS	IS
F↓	A↓ L↓ SE↓	E↑

June 30	Bonds Payable	100,000	
	Premium on Bonds Payable	4,000	
	Loss on Bonds Payable	1,000	
	Cash		105,000

Instead of calling the entire bond issue, assume that the corporation purchases one-fourth ($25,000) of the bonds for $24,000 on June 30, the redemption is recorded as follows:

SCF	BS	IS
F↓	A↓ L↓ SE↑	R↑

June 30	Bonds Payable	25,000	
	Premium on Bonds Payable	1,000	
	Cash		24,000
	Gain on Redemption of Bonds		2,000

In the preceding entry, only a portion of the premium relating to the redeemed bonds is written off. The difference between the carrying amount of the bonds purchased, $26,000 ($25,000 + $1,000), and the price paid for the redemption, $24,000, is recorded as a gain.

Zero-Coupon Bonds

Some corporations issue bonds that provide for only the payment of the face amount at the maturity date. Such bonds are called zero-coupon bonds. Because they do not provide for interest payments, these bonds sell at a large discount. For example, $1,000 of General Motor Acceptance Corp. (GMAC) face value zero-coupon bonds maturing in 2015 were selling for $465.50 on November 8, 2005.

The accounting for zero-coupon bonds is similar to that for interest-bearing bonds that have been sold at a discount. The discount is amortized as interest expense over the life of the bonds. To illustrate, assume that a $100,000 zero-coupon bond due in 5 years is issued at $53,273 on January 1, 2007. The entry to record the issuing of the bonds follows on the next page.

6 As we will discuss in Chapter 12, gains and losses on bond redemptions are reported separately on the income statement as extraordinary items.

SCF	BS	IS
F↑	A↑ L↑	—

		Debit	Credit
2007			
Jan. 1	Cash	53,273	
	Discount on Bonds Payable	46,727	
	Bonds Payable		100,000

The adjusting entry to record the interest expense on December 31, 2007, is as follows:

SCF	BS	IS
—	L↑ SE↓	E↑

		Debit	Credit
2007			
Dec. 31	Interest Expense ($46,727 ÷ 5)	9,345	
	Discount on Bonds Payable		9,345

Describe and illustrate deferred liabilities related to deferred revenue and deferred taxes.

DEFERRED LIABILITIES

Deferred liabilities are created when a transaction delays or defers (1) the recognition of *revenue* or (2) the payment of cash related to an *expense*. Thus, deferred liabilities are classified as either deferred revenues or deferred expenses.

Deferred Revenue

Deferred revenue, often referred to as unearned revenue, is created when cash is received from a transaction prior to recording revenue. This occurs when a company receives payment before providing the goods or services. These transactions are initially recorded as liabilities and become revenue at a later date when the company delivers the product or provides the service. For example, airlines often have large amounts of deferred (unearned) revenues because plane tickets are typically paid for in full before passengers take a flight. In this case, the airline does not earn the revenue until the customer completes the last leg of their flight. Other common examples of deferred (unearned) revenues include tuition received in advance by a school, magazine subscriptions received in advance, and rent received at the beginning of the period.

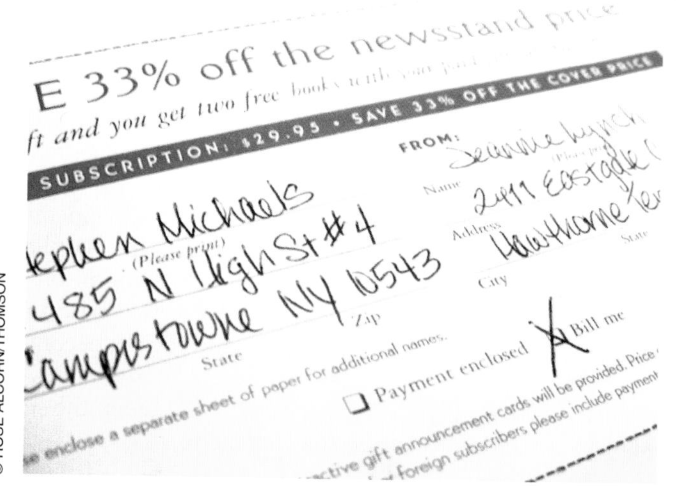

Deferred Expense

A **deferred expense** arises when an expense is recorded prior to the related cash payment. For example, tax expense is often recorded before the cash payment for taxes is made to the government. This occurs because the *taxable income* of a corporation is determined according to the tax laws and is reported to taxing authorities on the corporation's tax return. Taxable income is often different from the income before income taxes reported in the income statement according to generally accepted accounting principles. As a result, the income tax based on taxable income (tax return) usually differs from the income tax based on income before taxes (income statement), as shown in Exhibit 14.

To illustrate, assume that at the end of the first year of operations a corporation reports $300,000 income before income taxes on its income statement. If we assume an income tax rate of 40%, the income tax expense reported on the income statement is

Exhibit 14

Tax Differences between Tax Return and Income Statement

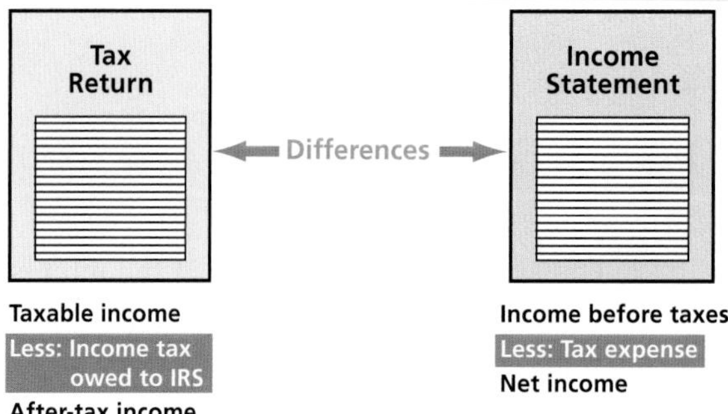

$120,000 ($300,000 × 40%). However, to reduce the amount owed for current income taxes, the corporation uses tax planning to reduce the taxable income to $100,000. Thus, the income tax actually due for the year is only $40,000 ($100,000 × 40%), and $80,000 of income tax is deferred to future years, calculated as follows:

Income tax based on $300,000 reported income at 40%	$120,000
Income tax based on $100,000 taxable income at 40%	40,000
Income tax deferred to future years	$ 80,000

The difference between taxable income and income before taxes is deferred to future periods. This allows the current year's tax expense to be matched against the current year's revenues on the income statement, using the following journal entry.

SCF	BS	IS
—	L↑ SE↓	E↑

Income Tax Expense	120,000	
Income Tax Payable		40,000
Deferred Income Tax Expense		80,000

The income tax expense reported on the income statement is the total tax, $120,000, expected to be paid on the income for the year. The actual amount owed currently is the $40,000 shown on the tax return.

The $80,000 ($120,000 − $40,000) difference between the tax expense on the income statement and the amount owed on the tax return is often temporary. That is, tax planning often delays the tax recognition of revenue and accelerates the tax recognition of expenses. In future years, the $80,000 in Deferred Income Tax Expense will be transferred to Income Tax Payable as the temporary differences reverse and the tax becomes due.

For example, if the $48,000 of the deferred tax reverses and becomes due in the second year, the following journal entry would be made in the second year:

SCF	BS	IS
—	L↑↓	—

Deferred Income Tax Expense	48,000	
Income Tax Payable		48,000

The deferred income tax expense account represents the portion of income tax expense that will be paid to the government at a later date and appears on the balance sheet as a deferred liability. The deferred liability appears as a long-term liability if it will not reverse within the next year. When the deferred expense is due to reverse within one year, it is classified on the balance sheet as a current liability.

CONTINGENT LIABILITIES

Identify the characteristics of contingent liabilities.

Some past transactions will result in liabilities if certain events occur in the future. These potential obligations are called **contingent liabilities**. For example, Ford Motor Company would have a contingent liability for the estimated costs associated with warranty work on new car sales. The obligation is contingent upon a future event, namely, a customer requiring warranty work on a vehicle. The obligation is the result of a past transaction, which is the original sale of the vehicle.

If a contingent liability is probable and the amount of the liability can be reasonably estimated, it should be recorded in the accounts. Ford Motor Company's vehicle warranty costs are an example of a contingent liability that is recorded. The warranty costs are probable because warranty repairs will be required on some vehicles. In addition, the costs can be estimated from past warranty experience.

To illustrate, assume that during June a company sells a product for $60,000 on which there is a 36-month warranty for repairing defects. Past experience indicates that the average cost to repair defects is 5% of the sales price over the warranty period. The entry to record the estimated product warranty expense for June is as follows:

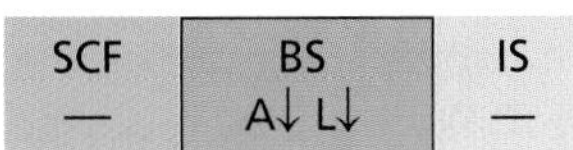

June 30	Product Warranty Expense	3,000	
	Product Warranty Payable		3,000

This transaction matches revenues and expenses properly by recording warranty costs in the same period in which the sale is recorded. When the defective product is repaired, the repair costs are recorded by debiting Product Warranty Payable and crediting Cash, Supplies, or other appropriate accounts. Thus, if a customer required a $200 part replacement on August 16, the entry is as follows:

SCF	BS	IS
—	A↓ L↓	—

Aug. 16	Product Warranty Payable	200	
	Supplies		200

If a contingent liability is probable but cannot be reasonably estimated or is only possible, then the nature of the contingent liability should be disclosed in the notes to the financial statements. The accounting treatment of contingent liabilities is summarized in Exhibit 15.

Q. A business sells to a customer $120,000 of commercial audio equipment with a one-year repair and replacement warranty. Historically, the average cost to repair or replace is 2% of sales. How is this contingent liability recorded?

A. A debit to Product Warranty Expense for $2,400 and a credit to Product Warranty Payable for $2,400.

Exhibit 15

Accounting Treatment of Contingent Liabilities

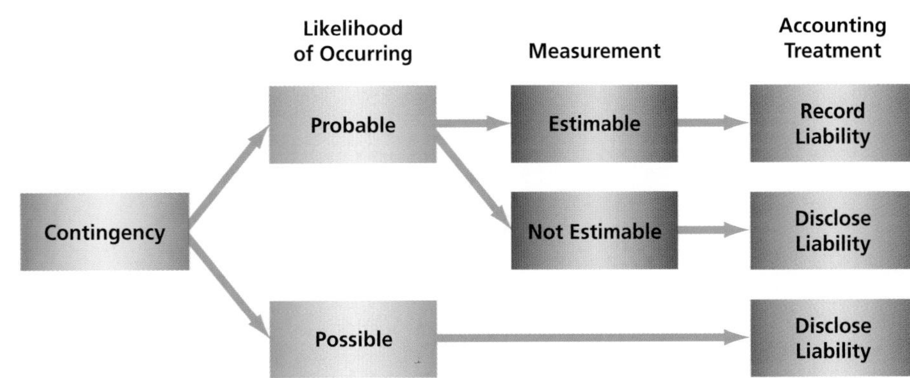

REPORTING LIABILITIES

Illustrate the reporting of liabilities on the balance sheet.

Liabilities are reported on the balance sheet in the order of liquidity, that is, in the order in which cash is going to be required to make payment for the liability. In addition to the amounts reported on the balance sheet, additional information on liabilities may be included in the financial statement notes. Examples of liability disclosures that are often found in the notes to the financial statements are current maturities of long-term debt, long-term liability disclosures, and contingent liabilities. These are each discussed briefly below.

Current Maturities of Long-Term Debt

Long-term liability maturities that are due within the coming year must be classified as a current liability. The total amount of the loan due after the coming year is classified as a long-term liability. To illustrate, Starbucks Corporation reported the following scheduled debt payments in the notes to its annual report for the fiscal year ending October 3, 2004:

Fiscal Year Ending	(in thousands)
2005	$ 735
2006	748
2007	762
2008	775
2009	790
Thereafter	543
Total principal payments	$4,353

The debt of $735 due in 2005 would be reported as a current liability on the October 3, 2004, balance sheet. The remaining debt of $3,618 ($4,353 − $735) would be reported as a long-term liability on the balance sheet.

Long-Term Liability Disclosures

The carrying value, interest rate, and maturity of long-term liabilities must also be disclosed on the financial statements or in the notes to the financial statements. To illustrate, The Coca-Cola Company disclosed the following long-term debt in the notes to its financial statements:

	(in millions)	
December 31,	2004	2003
Variable rate euro notes due 2004	$ 0	$ 296
$5\frac{7}{8}$% euro notes due 2005	663	591
4% U.S. dollar notes due 2005	750	749
$5\frac{3}{4}$% U.S. dollar notes due 2009	399	399
$5\frac{3}{4}$% U.S. dollar notes due 2011	499	498
$7\frac{3}{8}$% U.S. dollar notes due 2093	116	116
Other, due through 2013	220	191
	$2,647	$2,840
Less current portion	1,490	323
	$1,157	$2,517

Coca-Cola uses the term "notes," which is similar to a bond. Notice also that the current maturities are subtracted from the long-term debt total. As discussed previously, this is done because the current maturities are included as current liabilities.

Contingent Liabilities

As discussed earlier, contingent liabilities that are both probable and reasonably estimated are reported on the balance sheet. Professional judgment is required in distinguishing between contingent liabilities that are probable versus those that are only possible. Common examples of contingent liabilities disclosed in notes to the financial statements are litigation, environmental matters, guarantees, and sales of receivables. The following example of a contingency disclosure, related to litigation, was taken from a recent annual report of Ford Motor Company:

> *Various legal actions, governmental investigations and proceedings and claims are pending or may be instituted or asserted in the future against us, including those arising out of alleged defects in our products; governmental regulations relating to safety, emissions and fuel economy . . . Some of the foregoing matters involve or may involve compensatory, punitive, or antitrust or other treble damage claims in very large amounts, or demands for recall campaigns, environmental remediation programs, sanctions, or other relief, which, if granted, would require very large expenditures . . . We have established accruals for certain of the matters discussed . . . where losses are deemed probable and reasonably estimable. It is reasonably possible, however, that some of the matters discussed in the foregoing paragraph for which accruals have not been established could be decided unfavorably to us and could require us to pay damages or make other expenditures in amounts or a range of amounts that cannot be estimated at December 31, 2004.*

At the time, Ford did not anticipate that these matters would have a material effect on future financial statements, but acknowledged that material losses were possible.

Analyze and interpret liquidity using the current ratio, quick ratio, number of times interest charges earned, and ratio of total liabilities to total assets.

LIQUIDITY ANALYSIS

A company's current and long-term liquidity can be analyzed from financial statement information. Current liquidity is analyzed using the current and quick ratios. Long-term liquidity is analyzed using the number of times interest charges earned and ratio of total liabilities to total assets.

Current Liquidity Analysis

Current liabilities are evaluated in relation to current assets, because current assets are normally used to pay current liabilities. When current assets are not deemed sufficient to pay current liabilities, the current liabilities may be refinanced through long-term debt. Using long-term debt in this way is generally considered undesirable. The current assets and current liabilities sections of recent balance sheets for Barnes & Noble, Inc., and Borders, Inc., are shown in Exhibit 16.

Exhibit 16

Partial Balance Sheets for Barnes & Noble, Inc., and Borders, Inc.

	Barnes & Noble, Inc. Jan. 29, 2005 (in millions)	Borders, Inc. Jan. 23, 2005 (in millions)
Current assets:		
Cash and cash equivalents	$ 535.7	$ 244.8
Temporary investments	—	95.4
Receivables, net	74.6	118.3
Merchandise inventories	1,274.6	1,306.9
Prepaid expenses and other current assets	85.1	0.0
Total current assets	$1,970.0	$1,765.4
Current liabilities:		
Short-term debt and current portion of long-term debt	$ 0.0	$ 141.2
Accounts payable	745.1	615.1
Accrued liabilities	580.5	439.7
Total current liabilities	$1,325.6	$1,196.0

Current Ratio. Financial ratios that measure the degree to which current assets are available to satisfy current liabilities are called **liquidity** ratios. One of the most popular liquidity ratios is the **current ratio**, which is calculated as follows:

$$\text{Current Ratio} = \frac{\text{Current Assets}}{\text{Current Liabilities}}$$

The current ratio measures the degree to which current assets are available to pay the current liabilities. For example, a current ratio of 2.0 would indicate that current assets are twice as large as current liabilities. A current ratio exceeding 2.0 would generally indicate favorable liquidity, although this guideline may differ across industries.

Quick Ratio. A second liquidity ratio used by analysts is the **quick ratio**, or acid-test ratio, which is calculated as follows:

$$\text{Quick Ratio} = \frac{\text{Quick Assets}}{\text{Current Liabilities}}$$

Quick assets are cash, cash equivalents, temporary investments, and receivables that can be quickly converted into cash. Notice that inventories and prepaid items are excluded from the numerator. Thus, the quick ratio measures the "instant" current debt-paying ability of a company. A quick ratio exceeding 1.0 is often considered desirable, which again may differ for some industries. A ratio less than 1.0 would indicate that current liabilities cannot be covered by cash and "near cash" assets.

Illustration of Current and Quick Ratios. To illustrate the current and quick ratios, refer to the partial balance sheet information for Barnes & Noble, Inc., and Borders, Inc., in Exhibit 16. The current ratio for Barnes & Noble and Borders would be calculated as follows:

$$\text{Barnes \& Noble, Inc.: } \frac{\$1{,}970.0}{\$1{,}325.6} = 1.49$$

$$\text{Borders, Inc.: } \frac{\$1{,}765.4}{\$1{,}196.0} = 1.48$$

The quick ratio for both companies would be computed as shown:

$$\text{Barnes \& Noble, Inc.: } \frac{\$535.7 + \$74.6}{\$1{,}325.6} = 0.46$$

$$\text{Borders, Inc.: } \frac{\$244.8 + \$95.4 + \$118.3}{\$1{,}196.0} = 0.38$$

Both companies' ratios are less than the "rule of thumb" guidelines. This is not surprising, since retail bookselling companies, such as Barnes & Noble and Borders, are not expected to have large accounts receivable balances. Most of their sales would be cash and credit card; thus, they can satisfy current liabilities as sales are made, without having to wait for collections.

In comparing the two companies, the current ratio is nearly identical, while Barnes & Noble has a slightly larger quick ratio, indicating a slightly stronger quick asset position.

Long-Term Liability Analysis

As an individual, if you have an annual salary of $50,000, you should not borrow $500,000 for a new house. Your monthly income cannot support the monthly debt payments. Similarly, managers set long-term debt levels that can be supported by the company's income. The ability of a business to meet its fixed financial obligations (debts) is called **leverage**. We will describe two leverage ratios.

Number of Times Interest Charges Are Earned. The first leverage ratio measures the relationship between a company's income and its interest expense on debt. The ratio is called the **number of times interest charges are earned** during the year (or interest coverage ratio) and is calculated as follows:

$$\text{Number of Times Interest Charges Are Earned} = \frac{\text{Income Before Income Tax} + \text{Interest Expense}}{\text{Interest Expense}}$$

The calculation uses "income before income tax" in the numerator, because the amount available to make interest payments is not affected by taxes on income. This is because interest is deductible in determining taxable income. In interpreting the ratio, the higher the ratio, the higher the likelihood that interest payments will continue to be made if earnings decrease. In contrast, the lower the ratio, the lower the likelihood the company will be able to support its required interest payments from current period earnings.

To illustrate this ratio, the following financial statement information was taken from the fiscal 2004 annual reports for Barnes & Noble and Borders:

	Barnes & Noble, Inc. (in millions)	Borders, Inc. (in millions)
Interest expense	$ 14.5	$ 9.1
Income before taxes	218.6	207.6

The number of times interest charges are earned for Barnes & Noble and Borders is 16.1 and 23.8, respectively, calculated using the formula above as follows:

$$\text{Number of Times Interest Charges Are Earned} = \frac{\$218.6 + \$14.5}{\$14.5} = 16.1$$

$$\text{Number of Times Interest Charges Are Earned} = \frac{\$207.6 + \$9.1}{\$9.1} = 23.8$$

The number of times interest charges are earned indicates that both companies have excellent coverage, with slight favoring of Borders. Lenders will generally be concerned if this ratio drops below 2.

Ratio of Total Liabilities to Total Assets. The second leverage measure compares the total liabilities to the amount of total assets. To illustrate, assume that you borrowed $80,000 and used $20,000 of your own funds to purchase a $100,000 house. Your debt as a percentage of the total value of the house would be 80% ($80,000 ÷ $100,000). In a similar way, analysts can measure a company's relative use of debt by measuring the ratio of the total liabilities to the total assets. The **ratio of total liabilities to total assets** is calculated as shown:[7]

$$\text{Ratio of Total Liabilities to Total Assets} = \frac{\text{Total Liabilities}}{\text{Total Assets}}$$

To illustrate, fiscal 2004 annual reports for Barnes & Noble and Borders disclosed the following:

	Barnes & Noble, Inc.	Borders, Inc.
Total liabilities	$2,135.6	$1,538.5
Total assets	3,301.5	2,628.8

The ratio of total liabilities to total assets for Barnes & Noble and Borders is 0.65 and 0.59, respectively, calculated as follows:

$$\text{Ratio of Total Liabilities to Total Assets} = \frac{\$2{,}135.6}{\$3{,}301.5} = 0.65$$

$$\text{Ratio of Total Liabilities to Total Assets} = \frac{\$1{,}538.5}{\$2{,}628.8} = 0.59$$

Barnes & Noble has slightly more relative debt as a percent of total assets than does Borders. This is the likely reason for Barnes & Noble's smaller interest coverage. Regardless, both companies appear to be having little difficulty managing their debt.

---

7 The ratio of total liabilities to total stockholders' equity is another common leverage measure. This ratio is algebraically related to the ratio of total liabilities to total assets and thus conveys the same relative information.

FOCUS ON CASH FLOW

Liabilities

In the statement of cash flows, the net income is adjusted by the change in current liabilities in determining the cash flows from operating activities. That is, increases in current liabilities are added to net income, while decreases in current liabilities are deducted from net income. The Operating Activities section of the statement of cash flows is reproduced below for **Cendant Corporation** for a recent year.

Cendant Corporation
Partial Statement of Cash Flows—Operating Activities Section

	(in millions)
Net income (loss)	$1,172
Adjustments to reconcile net income (loss) to net cash provided by (used in) operating activities	(142)
Changes in operating assets and liabilities:	
Accounts receivable	(214)
Deferred income taxes	(121)
Other current assets	44
Accounts payable and other current liabilities	401
Current portion of long-term debt	1,599
Deferred income taxes	174
Net cash provided by (used in) operating activities	$2,913

The shaded area shows the changes in current liability adjustments to net income. In this case, all the changes were increases, which were added to net income in order to obtain the net cash used in operating activities.

The Financing Activities section of the statement of cash flows will disclose the increases and decreases in cash from long-term liability financing. Increases in long-term liabilities will result in an increase in cash, while a decrease will result in a use of cash. This disclosure is shown below for Cendant Corporation.

The shaded area shows both proceeds from issuing new debt and the use of cash from retiring debt.

Cendant Corporation
Partial Statement of Cash Flows—Financing Activities Section

	(in millions)
Proceeds from borrowings	$ 2,593
Principal payments on borrowings	(3,479)
Issuances of common stock	446
Repurchases of common stock	(1,090)
Other, net	(86)
Net cash provided by (used in) financing activities	$(1,616)

APPENDIX

Effective Interest Rate Method of Amortization

The effective interest rate method of amortizing discounts and premiums provides for a constant rate of interest on the carrying amount of the bonds at the beginning of each period. This is in contrast to the straight-line method, which provides for a constant amount of interest expense.

The interest rate used in the interest method of amortization is the market rate on the date the bonds are issued. The carrying amount of the bonds to which the interest rate is applied is the face amount of the bonds minus any unamortized discount or plus any unamortized premium. Under the interest method, the interest expense to be reported on the income statement is computed by multiplying the effective interest rate by the carrying amount of the bonds. The difference between the interest expense computed in this way and the periodic interest payment is the amount of discount or premium to be amortized for the period.

Amortization of Discount by the Interest Method

To illustrate the interest method for amortizing bond discounts, we assume the following data from the chapter illustration of issuing $100,000 bonds at a discount:

Face value of 12%, five-year bonds, interest compounded semiannually	$100,000
Present value of bonds at effective (market) rate of interest of 13%	96,406
Discount on bonds payable	$ 3,594

Applying the interest method to these data yields the amortization table in Exhibit 17. You should note the following items in this table:

1. The interest paid (Column A) remains constant at 6% of $100,000, the face amount of the bonds.
2. The interest expense (Column B) is computed at 6½% of the bond carrying amount at the beginning of each period. This results in an increasing interest expense each period.
3. The excess of the interest expense over the interest payment of $6,000 is the amount of discount to be amortized (Column C).
4. The unamortized discount (Column D) decreases from the initial balance, $3,594, to a zero balance at the maturity date of the bonds.
5. The carrying amount (Column E) increases from $96,406, the amount received for the bonds, to $100,000 at maturity.

Exhibit 17

Amortization of Discount on Bonds Payable

Interest Payment	A Interest Paid (6% of Face Amount)	B Interest Expense (6½% of Bond Carrying Amount)	C Discount Amortization (B − A)	D Unamortized Discount (D − C)	E Bond Carrying Amount ($100,000 − D)
				$3,594	$ 96,406
1	$6,000	$6,266 (6½% of $96,406)	$266	3,328	96,672
2	6,000	6,284 (6½% of $96,672)	284	3,044	96,956
3	6,000	6,302 (6½% of $96,956)	302	2,742	97,258
4	6,000	6,322 (6½% of $97,258)	322	2,420	97,580
5	6,000	6,343 (6½% of $97,580)	343	2,077	97,923
6	6,000	6,365 (6½% of $97,923)	365	1,712	98,288
7	6,000	6,389 (6½% of $98,288)	389	1,323	98,677
8	6,000	6,414 (6½% of $98,677)	414	909	99,091
9	6,000	6,441 (6½% of $99,091)	441	468	99,532
10	6,000	6,470 (6½% of $99,532)	468*	—	100,000

* Cannot exceed unamortized discount.

The entry to record the first interest payment on June 30, 2007, and the related discount amortization is as follows:

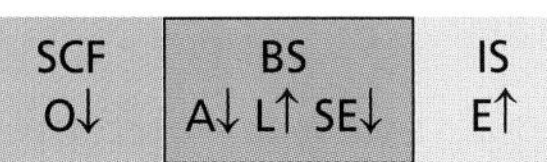

2007			
June 30	Interest Expense	6,266	
	Discount on Bonds Payable		266
	Cash		6,000

If the amortization is recorded only at the end of the year, the amount of the discount amortized on December 31 would be $550. This is the sum of the first two semiannual amortization amounts ($266 and $284) from Exhibit 17.

Amortization of Premium by the Interest Method

To illustrate the interest method for amortizing bond premiums, we assume the following data from the chapter illustration of issuing $100,000 bonds at a premium:

Present value of bonds at effective (market) rate of interest of 11%	$103,769
Face value of 12% five-year bonds, interest compounded semiannually	100,000
Premium on bonds payable	$ 3,769

Using the interest method to amortize the above premium yields the amortization table in Exhibit 18. You should note the following items in this table:

1. The interest paid (Column A) remains constant at 6% of $100,000, the face amount of the bonds.
2. The interest expense (Column B) is computed at $5\frac{1}{2}$% of the bond carrying amount at the beginning of each period. This results in a decreasing interest expense each period.

Exhibit 18

Amortization of Premium on Bonds Payable

Interest Payment	A Interest Paid (6% of Face Amount)	B Interest Expense ($5\frac{1}{2}$% of Bond Carrying Amount)	C Premium Amortization (A − B)	D Unamortized Premium (D − C)	E Bond Carrying Amount ($100,000 + D)
				$3,769	$103,769
1	$6,000	$5,707 ($5\frac{1}{2}$% of $103,769)	$293	3,476	103,476
2	6,000	5,691 ($5\frac{1}{2}$% of $103,476)	309	3,167	103,167
3	6,000	5,674 ($5\frac{1}{2}$% of $103,167)	326	2,841	102,841
4	6,000	5,656 ($5\frac{1}{2}$% of $102,841)	344	2,497	102,497
5	6,000	5,637 ($5\frac{1}{2}$% of $102,497)	363	2,134	102,134
6	6,000	5,617 ($5\frac{1}{2}$% of $102,134)	383	1,751	101,751
7	6,000	5,596 ($5\frac{1}{2}$% of $101,751)	404	1,347	101,347
8	6,000	5,574 ($5\frac{1}{2}$% of $101,347)	426	921	100,921
9	6,000	5,551 ($5\frac{1}{2}$% of $100,921)	449	472	100,472
10	6,000	5,526 ($5\frac{1}{2}$% of $100,472)	472*	—	100,000

* Cannot exceed unamortized premium.

3. The excess of the periodic interest payment of $6,000 over the interest expense is the amount of premium to be amortized (Column C).
4. The unamortized premium (Column D) decreases from the initial balance, $3,769, to a zero balance at the maturity date of the bonds.
5. The carrying amount (Column E) decreases from $103,769, the amount received for the bonds, to $100,000 at maturity.

The entry to record the first interest payment on June 30, 2007, and the related premium amortization is as follows:

SCF	BS	IS
O↓	A↓ L↓ SE↓	E↑

2007			
June 30	Interest Expense	5,707	
	Premium on Bonds Payable	293	
	Cash		6,000

If the amortization is recorded only at the end of the year, the amount of the premium amortized on December 31, 2008, would be $602. This is the sum of the first two semiannual amortization amounts ($293 and $309) from Exhibit 18.

SUMMARY OF LEARNING GOALS

1 Describe and illustrate current liabilities related to accounts payable, notes payable, and payroll transactions. Current liabilities are obligations that are to be paid out of current assets and are due within a short time, usually within one year. The three primary types of current liabilities are accounts payable, notes payable, and payroll liabilities.

Accounts payable is typically the largest current liability. Notes payable may be issued when merchandise is purchased or to temporarily satisfy an account payable. Notes payable require the recording of interest expense. Notes may also be discounted at a bank. The employer's liability for payroll includes the wages payable plus deductions from employees' gross pay. In addition, the employer's liability includes employer taxes, such as the employer's share of FICA plus federal and state unemployment insurance. Employers may also incur employment-related expenses and associated liabilities for fringe benefits, such as vacation pay, pensions, and medical benefits.

2 Describe the characteristics of long-term liabilities and apply present value concepts to bonds payable. The most common form of long-term borrowing for a corporation is bonds, which are simply a form of a long-term, interest-bearing note. Like a note, a bond requires periodic interest payments, and the face amount must be repaid at the maturity date. Once bonds are issued, periodic interest payments and repayment of the face value of the bonds are required.

When a corporation issues bonds, the price that buyers are willing to pay for the bonds depends upon the following three factors: (1) the face amount of the bonds, which is the amount due at the maturity date; (2) the periodic interest to be paid on the bonds; and (3) the rate of return demanded by investors who will buy these bonds in the market. Using present value concepts, bonds may be issued at their face value, a discount, or a premium.

A discount on bonds payable is amortized to interest expense over the life of the bonds by debiting Interest Expense and crediting Discount on Bonds Payable. The entry to amortize a premium debits Premium on Bonds Payable and credits Interest Expense.

If a corporation redeems bonds, Bonds Payable is debited for the face amount of the bonds, the premium (discount) on bonds account is debited (credited) for its balance, Cash is credited, and any gain or loss on the redemption is recorded.

3 Describe and illustrate deferred liabilities related to deferred revenue and deferred taxes. Deferred liabilities are created when a transaction is recorded in a way that delays or defers (1) the recognition of *revenue* or (2) the payment of cash related to an *expense*. Thus, deferred liabilities are classified as either deferred (unearned) revenues or deferred expense. Two of the most common deferred liabilities are deferred (unearned) revenue and deferred income taxes.

4 Identify the characteristics of contingent liabilities. A contingent liability is a potential obligation that results from a past transaction but depends on a future event. If the contingent liability is both probable and estimable, the liability should be recorded. If the contingent liability is reasonably possible or is not estimable, it should be disclosed in the footnotes to the financial statements.

(5) **Illustrate the reporting of liabilities on the balance sheet.** Liabilities are reported on the balance sheet in the order of liquidity, that is, in the order in which cash is going to be required to make payment for the liability. In addition to the amounts reported on the balance sheet, additional information on liabilities may be included in the financial statement footnotes.

(6) **Analyze and interpret liquidity using the current ratio, quick ratio, number of times interest charges earned, and ratio of total liabilities to total assets.** The current position is analyzed by the current ratio (current assets ÷ current liabilities) and the quick ratio (quick assets ÷ current liabilities). The number of times interest charges are earned during the year is a measure of the risk that interest payments to debtholders will continue to be made if earnings decrease. It is computed by dividing income before income tax plus interest expense by interest expense. The ratio of total liabilities to total assets measures the percent of total assets funded by debt. The larger this ratio, the greater the leverage risk.

GLOSSARY

Annuity A series of cash flows that are (1) equal in amount and (2) spaced equally in time.

Annuity payment The dollar amount of the equal periodic cash flows in an annuity.

Bond A form of interest-bearing note used by corporations to borrow on a long-term basis.

Bond indenture The contract between a corporation issuing bonds and the bondholders.

Callable bonds Bonds that a corporation reserves the right to redeem before their maturity.

Contingent liability An obligation from a past transaction that is contingent upon a future event. An example would be product warranty payable.

Contract rate The periodic interest to be paid on the bonds that is identified in the bond indenture; expressed as a percentage of the face amount of the bond.

Convertible bonds Bonds that may be exchanged for other securities.

Creditor A lender of money, such as a bank or bondholder.

Current ratio A financial ratio that is computed by dividing current assets by current liabilities.

Debenture bonds Bonds issued on the basis of the general credit of the corporation.

Debtor A borrower of money.

Deferred expense An item that has initially been recorded as an asset but is expected to become an expense over time or through the normal operations of the business.

Deferred (unearned) revenue A liability that occurs when a company receives cash payment from a transaction before providing goods or services.

Discount The interest deducted from the maturity value of a note or the excess of the face amount of bonds over their issue price.

Discount rate The rate used in computing the interest to be deducted from the maturity value of a note.

Discounting The process of converting a future amount into a present value.

Effective interest rate method A method of amortizing a bond discount or premium, using present value techniques.

FICA tax Federal Insurance Contributions Act tax used to finance federal programs for old-age and disability benefits (Social Security) and health insurance for the aged (Medicare).

Fringe benefits Benefits provided to employees in addition to wages and salaries.

Gross pay The total earnings of an employee for a payroll period.

Interest The cost of borrowing or lending money.

Leverage The ability of a business to meet its fixed financial obligations (debts).

Liquidity Measures the ability of a business to pay or otherwise satisfy its current liabilities.

Market rate The rate of return that investors demand for bonds of a specific quality and duration.

Net pay Gross pay less payroll deductions; the amount the employer is obligated to pay the employee.

Number of times interest charges are earned A ratio that measures the risk that interest payments to debtholders will continue to be made if earnings decrease.

Payroll The total amount paid to employees for a certain period.

Premium The excess of the issue price of bonds over their face amount.

Present value The current value of dollars received in the future, after considering the effects of compound interest.

Present value of $1 The present value interest factor for a single sum. This amount is used to convert a single lump sum of money at some point in the future to its value in today's dollars.

Present value of an annuity of $1 The present value interest factor for an annuity. This amount is used to convert an annuity to its value in terms of a single sum in today's dollars.

Proceeds The net amount available from discounting a note payable.

Quick assets Cash, cash equivalents, and receivables that can be quickly converted into cash.

Quick ratio A financial ratio that measures the ability to pay current liabilities with quick assets (cash, marketable securities, accounts receivable).

Ratio of total liabilities to total assets The percent of total assets that are funded by total liabilities; a measure of solvency.

Serial bonds Bonds whose maturities are spread over several dates.

Straight-line method A method of amortizing a bond discount or premium in equal periodic amounts.

Term bonds Bonds of an issue that mature at the same time.

ILLUSTRATIVE ACCOUNTING APPLICATION PROBLEM

The fiscal year of Russell Inc., a manufacturer of acoustical supplies, ends December 31. Selected transactions for the period 2007 through 2014, involving bonds payable issued by Russell Inc., are as follows:

2007

June 30	Issued $2,000,000 of 15-year, 10% callable bonds dated June 30, 2007, when the market rate of interest was 12%. Interest is payable semiannually on June 30 and December 31.
Dec. 31	Paid the semiannual interest on the bonds.
31	Recorded amortization of the bond discount using the straight-line method.

2008

June 30	Paid the semiannual interest on the bonds, and recorded amortization of the bond discount using the straight-line method.
Dec. 31	Paid the semiannual interest on the bonds, and recorded amortization of the bond discount using the straight-line method.

2014

June 30	Recorded the redemption of the bonds, which were called at $101\frac{1}{2}$ after the payment of interest and amortization of discount have been recorded. (Record the redemption only.)

Instructions

1. Calculate the selling price of the bonds, the amount of the bond discount or premium, and the semiannual bond discount or premium amortization. Use the present value tables in Appendix A. Round to the nearest dollar.
2. Record the entries for the preceding transactions.
3. Determine the amount of interest expense for 2007 and 2008.
4. Determine the carrying amount of the bonds as of December 31, 2008.

Solution

1. Sales Price of the Bonds

Present value of bond principal:	
Principal × Present Value of $\$1_{i = 6\%, n = 30}$	
$2,000,000 × 0.17411 =	$ 348,220
Present value of bond interest:	
Principal × Present Value of Annuity of $\$1_{i = 6\%, n = 30}$	
$100,000 × 13.76483 =	1,376,483
Sales price of the bonds	$1,724,703
Calculation of Bond Discount and Discount Amortization	
Face Value of Bonds	$2,000,000
Sales Price of the Bonds	1,724,703
Bond Discount	$ 275,297
Bond Discount	$ 275,297
Amortization period (15 years)	÷ 15
Annual bond discount amortization	$ 18,353
Semiannual interest periods (semiannual periods per year)	÷ 2
Semiannual bond discount amortization	$ 9,177

2.

2007			
June 30	Cash	1,724,703	
	Discount on Bonds Payable	275,297	
	Bonds Payable		2,000,000
Dec. 31	Interest Expense	100,000	
	Cash		100,000
31	Interest Expense	9,177	
	Discount on Bonds Payable		9,177
2008			
June 30	Interest Expense	100,000	
	Cash		100,000
31	Interest Expense	9,177	
	Discount on Bonds Payable		9,177
Dec. 31	Interest Expense	100,000	
	Cash		100,000
31	Interest Expense	9,177	
	Discount on Bonds Payable		9,177
2014			
June 30	Bonds Payable	2,000,000	
	Loss on Redemption of Bonds Payable	176,819**	
	Discount on Bonds Payable		146,819*
	Cash		2,030,000

3. 2007—$109,177
2008—$218,354

4.

Initial carrying amount of bonds	$1,724,703
Discount amortized on December 31, 2007	9,177
Discount amortized on December 31, 2008	18,354
Carrying amount of bonds, December 31, 2008	$1,752,234

* Calculation of Unamortized Bond Discount on June 30, 2014

Unamortized discount on June 30, 2007		$ 275,297
Semiannual discount amortization	$9,177	
Number of years since issuance (2007 to 2014)	× 7 years	
Two semiannual periods per year	× 2	
Discount amortization between June 30, 2007, and June 30, 2014		128,478
Unamortized discount on June 30, 2014		$ 146,819

** Calculation of Loss on Redemption of Bonds Payable

Bonds payable	$2,000,000
Less: Unamortized bond discount on June 30, 2014	146,819
Carrying value of bonds redeemed on June 30, 2014	$1,853,181
Cash required to redeem the bonds	2,030,000
Loss on redemption of bonds payable	$ 176,819

SELF-STUDY QUESTIONS

Answers at end of chapter

1. A business issued a $5,000, 60-day note to a supplier, which discounted the note at 12%. The proceeds are:
   A. $4,400.
   B. $4,900.
   C. $5,000.
   D. $5,100.

2. Which of the following taxes are employers usually not required to withhold from employees?
   A. Federal income tax
   B. Federal unemployment compensation tax
   C. Medicare tax
   D. State and local income taxes

3. A firm's current assets include $100,000 cash, $300,000 accounts receivable, and $400,000 inventory. The current liabilities are $200,000. What are the current and quick ratios?
   A. 0.5, 2.0
   B. 4.0, 0.5
   C. 2.0, 4.0
   D. 4.0, 2.0
4. A company issues $200,000 of 10% bonds that pay interest annually and have a five-year term. What will the selling price and the discount or premium of the bonds be if the market rate of interest is 9% on the date the bonds are issued? Use the present value tables in Appendix A.
   A. $129,986 selling price, $70,014 discount
   B. $207,779 selling price, $7,779 premium
   C. $207,779 selling price, $7,779 discount
   D. $200,000 selling price, $7,779 discount
5. A firm reported net income before tax of $500,000 and paid dividends of $200,000. The firm has $1,000,000 face value 10% bonds outstanding. What is the number of times interest charges are earned?
   A. 3.0
   B. 4.0
   C. 5.0
   D. 6.0

DISCUSSION QUESTIONS

1. What two types of transactions cause most current liabilities?
2. When are short-term notes payable issued?
3. The "Questions and Answers Technical Hotline" in the *Journal of Accountancy* included the following question:

   Several years ago, Company B instituted legal action against Company A. Under a memorandum of settlement and agreement, Company A agreed to pay Company B a total of $17,500 in three installments—$5,000 on March 1, $7,500 on July 1, and the remaining $5,000 on December 31. Company A paid the first two installments during its fiscal year ended September 30. Should the unpaid amount of $5,000 be presented as a current liability at September 30?

   How would you answer this question?
4. What programs are funded by the FICA (Federal Insurance Contributions Act) tax?
5. For each of the following payroll-related taxes, indicate whether it generally applies to (a) employees only, (b) employers only, (c) both employees and employers:
   1. Social Security tax
   2. Medicare tax
   3. Federal income tax
   4. Federal unemployment compensation tax
   5. State unemployment compensation tax
6. To match revenues and expenses properly, should the expense for employee vacation pay be recorded in the period during which the vacation privilege is earned or during the period in which the vacation is taken? Discuss.
7. What is interest? How does simple interest differ from compound interest?
8. What key characteristics define an annuity? What is the present value of a $500, three-year annuity, where the first payment is received one year from today and the relevant interest rate is 8%? Use the present value tables in Appendix A.
9. What is discounting?
10. Bill expects to receive $3,000 from his grandfather when he graduates from college three years from today. What is the present value of the $3,000 if the relevant interest rate is 6% compounded anually?
11. Describe the two distinct obligations incurred by a corporation when issuing bonds.
12. If you asked your broker to purchase for you a 6% bond when the market interest rate for such bonds was 7%, would you expect to pay more or less than the face amount for the bond? Explain.
13. A corporation issues $10,000,000 of 6% bonds to yield interest at the rate of 5%. (a) Was the amount of cash received from the sale of the bonds greater or less than $10,000,000? (b) Identify the following terms related to the bond issue: (1) face amount, (2) market or effective rate of interest, (3) contract rate of interest, and (4) maturity amount.
14. If bonds issued by a corporation are sold at a premium, is the market rate of interest greater or less than the contract rate?
15. The following data relate to a $1,000,000, 6% bond issue for a selected semiannual interest period:

Bond carrying amount at beginning of period	$1,150,000
Interest paid at end of period	30,000
Interest expense allocable to the period	28,750

   (a) Were the bonds issued at a discount or at a premium? (b) What is the unamortized amount of the discount or premium account at the beginning of the period? (c) What account was debited to amortize the discount or premium?
16. Would a zero-coupon bond ever sell for its face amount?
17. Bonds Payable has a balance of $750,000, and Discount on Bonds Payable has a balance of $12,500. If the issuing corporation redeems the bonds at 99, is there a gain or loss on the bond redemption?
18. When should the liability associated with a product warranty be recorded? Discuss.
19. Hewlett-Packard reported $1,494 million of product warranties in the current liabilities section of a recent balance sheet. How would costs of repairing a defective product be recorded?
20. How would you interpret a four-year trend in the current ratio, which has declined from 2.0 to 0.50?
21. What is the number of times interest charges are earned if the business has net income before taxes of $600,000 and a $1,500,000 face value bond payable with a coupon rate of 10%?

EXERCISES

Exercise 10-1

Current liabilities

Goal 1

Total current liabilities, $273,750

SPREADSHEET

Ski World Magazine Inc. sold 5,200 annual subscriptions of *Ski World* for $50 each during December 2006. These new subscribers will receive monthly issues, beginning in January 2007. In addition, the business had taxable income of $225,000 during the first calendar quarter of 2007. The federal tax rate is 35%. A quarterly tax payment will be made on April 7, 2007.

Prepare the Current Liabilities section of the balance sheet for Ski World Magazine Inc. on March 31, 2007. Ignore deferred taxes.

Exercise 10-2

Entries for discounting notes payable

Goal 1

Collins Lighting Co. issues a 90-day note for $600,000 to Wolfman Supply Co. for merchandise inventory. Wolfman discounts the note at 10%.

a. Journalize Collins' entries to record:
   1. The issuance of the note.
   2. The payment of the note at maturity.

b. Journalize Wolfman's entries to record:
   1. The receipt of the note.
   2. The receipt of the payment of the note at maturity.

Exercise 10-3

Evaluate alternative notes

Goal 1

A borrower has two alternatives for a loan: (1) issue a $75,000, 90-day, 7% note or (2) issue a $75,000, 90-day note that the creditor discounts at 7%.

a. Calculate the amount of the interest expense for each option.
b. Determine the proceeds received by the borrower in each situation.
c. Which alternative is more favorable to the borrower? Explain.

Exercise 10-4

Entries for notes payable

Goal 1

A business issued a 60-day, 8% note for $60,000 to a creditor on account. Record the entries for (a) the issuance of the note and (b) the payment of the note at maturity, including interest.

Exercise 10-5

Fixed asset purchases with note

Goal 1

On June 30, Zahovik Game Company purchased land for $125,000 and a building for $365,000, paying $190,000 cash and issuing an 8% note for the balance, secured by a mortgage on the property. The terms of the note provide for 20 semiannual payments of $15,000 on the principal plus the interest accrued from the date of the preceding payment. Record the entries for (a) the transaction on June 30, (b) the payment of the first installment on December 31, and (c) the payment of the second installment the following June 30.

Exercise 10-6

Notes payable and maturities currently due

Goal 1

The Sun Construction Company borrowed $1,200,000 on July 1, 2007, at an annual interest rate of 12%. The note payable is to be repaid in annual installments of $300,000, plus accrued interest, on each June 30th beginning June 30, 2008, until the note is paid in full (on June 30, 2011). Determine the current liabilities disclosed on the December 31, 2007, balance related to this transaction.

Exercise 10-7

Calculate payroll

Goal 1

b. Net pay, $1,218

An employee earns $32 per hour and $1\frac{1}{2}$ times that rate for all hours in excess of 40 hours per week. Assume that the employee worked 50 hours during the week. Assume further that the FICA tax rate was 7.5% and federal income tax to be withheld was $410.

a. Determine the gross pay for the week.
b. Determine the net pay for the week.

Exercise 10-8

Summary payroll data

Goal 1

a. (3) Total earnings, $211,000

In the following summary of data for a payroll period, some amounts have been intentionally omitted:

Earnings:	
1. At regular rate	?
2. At overtime rate	$ 32,500
3. Total earnings	?
Deductions:	
4. FICA tax	15,165
5. Income tax withheld	29,500
6. Medical insurance	3,150
7. Union dues	?
8. Total deductions	50,000
9. Net amount paid	161,000
Accounts debited:	
10. Factory Wages	121,600
11. Sales Salaries	?
12. Office Salaries	34,300

a. Calculate the amounts omitted in lines (1), (3), (7), and (11).
b. Record the entry for the payroll accrual.
c. Record the entry for paying the payroll.

Exercise 10-9

Payroll tax entries

Goal 1

a. Payroll Taxes, $60,892.50

According to a summary of the payroll of Pendant Publishing Co., $800,000 of payroll was subject to the 7.5% FICA tax. Also, $17,500 was subject to state and federal unemployment taxes.

a. Calculate the employer's payroll taxes using the following rates: state unemployment, 4.3%; federal unemployment, 0.8%.
b. Record the entry for the accrual of payroll taxes.

Exercise 10-10

Recording payroll and payroll taxes

Goal 1

Tower Controls Co. had a gross salary payroll of $750,000 for the month ending March 31. The complete payroll is subject to a FICA tax rate of 7.5%. Only $30,000 of this payroll is subject to state and federal unemployment taxes of 4% and 0.5%, respectively. The employees' income tax withholding is $142,500.

a. Record the March 31 payroll.
b. Record the March 31 payroll taxes.

Exercise 10-11

Accrued vacation pay

Goal 1

A business provides its employees with varying amounts of vacation per year, depending on the length of employment. The estimated amount of the current year's vacation pay is $325,600. Record the adjusting entry required on January 31, the end of the first month of the current year, to accrue the vacation pay.

Exercise 10-12

Present value

Goal 2

2. $16,775.20

Using the present value tables in Appendix A, calculate the present value of the following:

1. $250,000 to be received three years from today, assuming an annual interest rate of 6%.
2. $2,500 to be received annually at the end of each of 10 periods, discounted at 8%.
3. $4,000 receivable at the end of each of the next five periods when the market rate of interest is 5%.

Exercise 10-13

Bond price

Goal 2

General Motors' 8.375% bonds due in 2033 were reported in *The Wall Street Journal* as selling for 100.245 on February 18, 2005.

Were the bonds selling at a premium or at a discount on February 18, 2005? Explain.

Exercise 10-14

Entries for issuing bonds

Goal 2

SPREADSHEET

Hic-Tec Co. produces and distributes fiber-optic cable for use by telecommunications companies. Hic-Tec Co. issued $10,000,000 of 20-year, 9% bonds on April 1 of the current year, with interest payable on April 1 and October 1. The fiscal year of the company is the calendar year. Record the entries for the following selected transactions for the current year:

Apr. 1	Issued the bonds for cash at their face amount.
Oct. 1	Paid the interest on the bonds.
Dec. 31	Recorded accrued interest for three months.

Exercise 10-15

Computing bond proceeds, entries for bond issuing, and amortizing premium by straight-line method

Goal 2

Fajitas Corporation wholesales oil and grease products to equipment manufacturers. On March 1, 2006, Fajitas Corporation issued $10,000,000 of five-year, 11% bonds. The bonds were issued for $10,386,057 to yield an effective interest rate of 10%. Interest is payable semiannually on March 1 and September 1. Record the entries for the following:

a. Sale of bonds on March 1, 2006.
b. First interest payment on September 1, 2006, and amortization of bond premium for six months, using the straight-line method. Round to the nearest dollar.

Exercise 10-16

Computing bond proceeds, entries for issuing bonds, and amortizing discount by straight-line method

Goal 2

b. $615,677.76

On the first day of its fiscal year, Jones Company issued $6,000,000 of five-year, 8% bonds to finance its operations of producing and selling home electronics equipment. Interest is payable semiannually. The bonds were issued at an effective interest rate of 11%. Refer to the tables in Appendix A for present value factors.

a. Record the entries for the following:
   1. Sale of the bonds.
   2. First semiannual interest payment. (Amortization of discount is to be recorded annually.)
   3. Second semiannual interest payment.
   4. Amortization of discount at the end of the first year, using the straight-line method. Round to the nearest dollar.
b. Determine the amount of the bond interest expense for the first year.

Exercise 10-17

Calculating bond price, calculating bond discount/premium, entries for issuing bonds

Goal 2

JTD Corporation issued $800,000 of 20-year, 12% bonds on January 1, 2006, when the market rate of interest was 10%. Interest is payable annually on December 31. Use the present values tables in Appendix A.

a. Calculate the price of the bonds on January 1, 2006, the date the bonds were issued.
b. Calculate the bond discount or premium that arises upon issuance.
c. Prepare the journal entry to record the issuance of the bonds on January 1, 2006.

Exercise 10-18

Entries for issuing and calling bonds; loss

Goal 2

Farouk Corp., a wholesaler of office furniture, issued $8,000,000 of 30-year, 9% callable bonds on March 1, 2006, with interest payable on March 1 and September 1. The fiscal year of the company is the calendar year. Record the entries for the following selected transactions:

2006

Mar. 1	Issued the bonds for cash at their face amount.
Sept. 1	Paid the interest on the bonds.

2010

Sept. 1	Called the bond issue at 102, the rate provided in the bond indenture. (Omit entry for payment of interest.)

Exercise 10-19

Entries for issuing and calling bonds; gain

Goal 2

Loumos Corp. produces and sells automotive and aircraft safety belts. To finance its operations, Loumos Corp. issued $15,000,000 of 25-year, 8% callable bonds on June 1, 2006, with interest payable on June 1 and December 1. The fiscal year of the company is the calendar year. Record the entries for the following selected transactions:

2006

June 1	Issued the bonds for cash at their face amount.
Dec. 1	Paid the interest on the bonds.

2011

Dec. 1	Called the bond issue at 98, the rate provided in the bond indenture. (Omit entry for payment of interest.)

Exercise 10-20

Deferred income taxes

Goal 3

Integrated Systems, Inc., recognized service revenue of $300,000 on its financial statements in 2007. Assume, however, that the Tax Code requires this amount to be recognized for tax purposes in 2008. The taxable income for 2007 and 2008 is $2,000,000 and $2,500,000, respectively. Assume a tax rate of 40%.

Prepare the journal entries to record the tax expense, deferred taxes, and taxes payable for 2007 and 2008, respectively.

Exercise 10-21

Accrued product warranty

Goal 4

In-Tune Audio Company warrants its products for one year. The estimated product warranty is 3% of sales. Assume that sales were $400,000 for January. In February, a customer received warranty repairs requiring $205 of parts and $300 of labor.

a. Record the adjusting entry required at January 31, the end of the first month of the current year, to record the accrued product warranty.
b. Record the entry for the warranty work provided in February.

Exercise 10-22

Accrued product warranty

Goal 4

a. 2.07%

During a recent year, Motorola, Inc., had sales of $31,323,000,000. An analysis of Motorola's product warranty payable account for the year was as follows:

Product warranty payable, January 1	$ 359,000,000
Product warranty expense	648,000,000
Warranty claims paid*	(507,000,000)
Product warranty payable, December 31	$ 500,000,000

* The amount reported for Warranty Claims Paid includes other adjustments.

a. Determine the product warranty expense as a percent of sales. Round to two decimal places.
b. Record the adjusting entry for the product warranty expense for the year.

Exercise 10-23

Contingent liabilities

Goal 4

Several months ago, Endurance Battery Company experienced a hazardous materials spill at one of its plants. As a result, the Environmental Protection Agency (EPA) fined the company $200,000. The company is contesting the fine. In addition, an employee is seeking $600,000 damages related to the spill. Lastly, a homeowner has sued the company for $150,000. The homeowner lives 20 miles from the plant, but believes that the incident has reduced her home's resale value by $150,000.

Endurance Battery's legal counsel believes that it is probable that the EPA fine will stand. In addition, counsel indicates that an out-of-court settlement of $250,000 has recently been reached with the employee. The final papers will be signed next week. Counsel believes that the homeowner's case is much weaker and will be decided in favor of Endurance. Other litigation related to the spill is possible, but the damage amounts are uncertain.

a. Record the contingent liabilities associated with the hazardous materials spill.
b. Prepare a note disclosure relating to this incident.

Exercise 10-24

Current and quick ratios

Goal 6

a. Apple Computer Inc. current ratio, 2.63

The current assets and current liabilities for Apple Computer Inc. and Gateway Inc. are shown as follows at the end of a recent fiscal period:

	Apple Computer Inc. (in thousands) Sept. 29, 2004	Gateway Inc. (in thousands) Dec. 31, 2004
Current assets:		
Cash and cash equivalents	$2,969,000	$ 358,633
Short-term investments	2,495,000	284,876
Accounts receivable	774,000	342,121
Inventories	101,000	196,324
Other current assets*	716,000	217,663
Total current assets	$7,055,000	$1,399,617
Current liabilities:		
Accounts payable	$1,451,000	$ 532,329
Accrued and other current liabilities	1,229,000	590,323
Total current liabilities	$2,680,000	$1,122,652

* These represent deferred tax assets, prepaid expenses, and other nonquick current assets.

a. Determine the current and quick ratios for both companies. Round to two decimal places.
b. Interpret the ratio differences between the two companies.

Exercise 10-25

Number of times interest charges earned

Goal 6

The following data were taken from recent annual reports of Trump Hotels and Casino Resorts, Inc., which owns and operates casino-based entertainment resorts in Atlantic City, New Jersey.

	2004	2003
Interest expense	$221,048,000	$225,867,000
Income before income tax	(15,496,000)	(90,570,000)

a. Determine the number of times interest charges were earned for the current and preceding years. Round to two decimal places.
b. What conclusions can you draw?

Exercise 10-26

Long-term solvency ratios for comparative years

Goal 6

Yum! Brands, Inc., is a nationwide restaurant company whose brands include Taco Bell, KFC, and Pizza Hut. Selected balance sheet information is as follows for two comparative dates.

	Dec. 25, 2004	Dec. 27, 2003
Total liabilities	$4,101	$4,500
Capital stock	659	916
Retained earnings	936	204

In addition, the income statement for these two periods showed the following income before tax and interest expense information:

	For the Year Ended	
	Dec. 25, 2004	Dec. 27, 2003
Interest expense	$ 129	$173
Income before income tax	1026	886

a. Determine the ratio of total liabilities to total assets at the end of the two accounting periods. Round to two decimal places.
b. Determine the number of times interest charges were earned for the two fiscal years.
c. Interpret the change in the two ratios across the two periods.

Exercise 10-27

Appendix: Compute bond price, discount, and journalize entries.

Appendix

Motley Corporation issued $4,000,000, five-year, 8% bonds on January 1, 2007. The bonds were issued at an effective interest rate of 11%, resulting in Motley Corporation receiving cash proceeds of $3,547,740.80. The company uses the effective interest rate method to amortize bond discounts and premiums.

a. Using the present value tables in Appendix A, journalize the entries to record the following:
   1. Sale of the bonds.
   2. First semiannual interest payment (amortization of discount is to be recorded semiannually using the interest method of amortization).
   3. Second semiannual interest payment.
b. Compute the amount of bond interest expense for the first year. (Round to the nearest penny.)

Exercise 10-28

Appendix: Compute bond price, premium, and journalize entries.

Appendix

On March 1, 2006, Fulton Corporation issued $5,000,000, five-year, 11% bonds at an effective interest rate of 10%, receiving cash proceeds of $5,193,028.50. Interest is paid semiannually on March 1 and September 1. Fulton Corporation's fiscal year begins on March 1. The company uses the effective interest rate method to amortize bond discounts and premiums.

a. Using the present value tables in Appendix A, journalize the entries to record the following:
   1. Sale of the bonds.
   2. First semiannual interest payment on September 1, 2006 (amortization of premium is to be recorded semiannually using the interest method of amortization).
   3. Second semiannual interest payment on March 1, 2007.

b. Compute the amount of bond interest expense for the first year. (Round to the nearest penny.)

ACCOUNTING APPLICATION PROBLEMS

Problem 10-1A

Current liability transactions

Goal 1

GENERAL LEDGER

The following items were selected from among the transactions completed by Wiggins Manufacturing during the current year:

Apr.	7	Borrowed $30,000 from First Financial Corporation, issuing a 60-day, 12% note for that amount.
May	10	Purchased equipment by issuing a $90,000, 120-day note to Brown Equipment Co., which discounted the note at the rate of 10%.
June	6	Paid First Financial Corporation the interest due on the note of April 7 and renewed the loan by issuing a new 30-day, 16% note for $30,000. (Record both the debit and credit to the notes payable account.)
July	6	Paid First Financial Corporation the amount due on the note of June 6.
Aug.	3	Purchased merchandise on account from Webb Co., $48,000, terms, n/30.
Sept.	2	Issued a 60-day, 15% note for $48,000 to Webb Co., on account.
	7	Paid Brown Equipment Co. the amount due on the note of May 10.
Nov.	1	Paid Webb Co. the amount owed on the note of September 2.
	15	Purchased store equipment from Shingo Equipment Co. for $150,000, paying $62,000 and issuing a series of eight 12% notes for $11,000 each, coming due at 30-day intervals.
Dec.	15	Paid the amount due Shingo Equipment Co. on the first note in the series issued on November 15.
	21	Settled a product liability lawsuit with a customer for $83,000, to be paid in January. Wiggins Manufacturing accrued the loss in a litigation claims payable account.

Instructions

1. Record the transactions.
2. Record the adjusting entry for each of the following accrued expenses at the end of the current year:
   a. Product warranty cost, $16,800.
   b. Interest on the seven remaining notes owed to Shingo Equipment Co.

Problem 10-2A

Payroll accounts and year-end entries

Goal 1

GENERAL LEDGER

The following accounts, with the balances indicated, appear in the ledger of Roan Outdoor Equipment Company on December 1 of the current year:

Salaries Payable	—
FICA Tax Payable	$ 6,667
Employees Federal Income Tax Payable	8,566
Employees State Income Tax Payable	8,334
State Unemployment Tax Payable	840
Federal Unemployment Tax Payable	210
Bond Deductions Payable	1,400
Medical Insurance Payable	3,600
Sales Salaries Expense	640,200
Officers Salaries Expense	283,800
Office Salaries Expense	94,600
Payroll Taxes Expense	79,114

The following transactions relating to payroll, payroll deductions, and payroll taxes occurred during December:

Dec. 1 Issued Check No. 728 to Blue Ridge Insurance Company for $3,600, in payment of the semiannual premium on the group medical insurance policy.

2 Issued Check No. 729 to Montreat National Bank for $15,233, in payment for $6,667 of FICA tax and $8,566 of employees' federal income tax due.

3 Issued Check No. 730 for $1,400 to Montreat National Bank to purchase U.S. savings bonds for employees.

14 Recorded the entry for the biweekly payroll. A summary of the payroll record follows:

Salary distribution:		
Sales	$29,000	
Officers	13,200	
Office	4,500	$46,700
Deductions:		
FICA tax	$ 3,270	
Federal income tax withheld	8,313	
State income tax withheld	2,102	
Savings bond deductions	700	
Medical insurance deductions	600	14,985
Net amount		$31,715

14 Issued Check No. 738 in payment of the net amount of the biweekly payroll.

14 Recorded the entry for payroll taxes on employees' earnings of December 14: FICA tax, $3,270; state unemployment tax, $180; federal unemployment tax, $45.

17 Issued Check No. 744 to Montreat National Bank for $14,853, in payment for $6,540 of FICA tax and $8,313 of employees' federal income tax due.

28 Recorded the entry for the biweekly payroll. A summary of the payroll record follows:

Salary distribution:		
Sales	$29,500	
Officers	13,100	
Office	4,400	$47,000
Deductions:		
FICA tax	$ 3,243	
Federal income tax withheld	8,366	
State income tax withheld	2,115	
Savings bond deductions	700	14,424
Net amount		$32,576

28 Issued Check No. 782 for the net amount of the biweekly payroll.

28 Recorded the entry for payroll taxes on employees' earnings of December 28: FICA tax, $3,243; state unemployment tax, $110; federal unemployment tax, $28.

30 Issued Check No. 791 for $12,551 to Montreat National Bank in payment of employees' state income tax due on December 31.

30 Issued Check No. 792 to Montreat National Bank for $1,400 to purchase U.S. savings bonds for employees.

Instructions

1. Record the transactions.
2. Record the following adjusting entries on December 31:
   a. Salaries accrued: sales salaries, $2,950; officers' salaries, $1,310; office salaries, $440. The payroll taxes are immaterial and are not accrued.
   b. Vacation pay, $12,900.

Problem 10-3A

Bond premium; entries for bonds payable transactions

Goal **2**

4. $726,381.91

Mitchell Inc. produces and sells voltage regulators. On July 1, 2006, Mitchell Inc. issued $14,000,000 of 10-year, 11% bonds priced to yield an effective interest rate of 10%. Interest on the bonds is payable semiannually on December 31 and June 30. The fiscal year of the company is the calendar year.

Instructions

1. Calculate the selling price of the bonds and the amount of bond premium or discount upon issuance. Use the present value tables in Appendix A.
2. Record the entry for the amount of the cash proceeds from the sale of the bonds.
3. Record the entries for the following:
   a. The first semiannual interest payment on December 31, 2006, including the amortization of the bond premium, using the straight-line method.
   b. The interest payment on June 30, 2007, and the amortization of the bond premium, using the straight-line method.
4. Determine the total interest expense for 2006.
5. Will the bond proceeds always be greater than the face amount of the bonds when the contract rate is greater than the market rate of interest? Explain.

Problem 10-4A

Bond discount; entries for bonds payable transactions

Goal **2**

4. $536,026.80

On July 1, 2006, Brushy Mountain Communications Equipment Inc. issued $10,000,000 of 10-year, 9% bonds when the market rate of interest was 12%. Interest on the bonds is payable semiannually on December 31 and June 30. The fiscal year of the company is the calendar year.

Instructions

1. Calculate the selling price of the bond issue and the bond discount or premium on the issue date. Use the present value tables in Appendix A.
2. Record the entry for the amount of the cash proceeds from the sale of the bonds.
3. Record the entries for the following:
   a. The first semiannual interest payment on December 31, 2006, and the amortization of the bond discount, using the straight-line method. (Round to the nearest dollar.)
   b. The interest payment on June 30, 2007, and the amortization of the bond discount, using the straight-line method.
4. Determine the total interest expense for 2006.
5. Will the bond proceeds always be less than the face amount of the bonds when the contract rate is less than the market rate of interest? Explain.

Problem 10-5A

Entries for bonds payable transactions

Goal **2**

3. a. $939,590.55

SPREADSHEET

GENERAL LEDGER

Topspin Co. produces and sells synthetic string for tennis rackets. The following transactions were completed by Topspin Co., whose fiscal year is the calendar year:

2006

July 1 Issued $15,000,000 of five-year, 14% callable bonds dated July 1, 2006, at an effective rate of 12%. Interest is payable semiannually on December 31 and June 30.

Dec. 31 Paid the semiannual interest on the bonds.

31 Recorded bond premium amortization, which was determined by using the straight-line method.

2007

June 30 Paid the semiannual interest on the bonds. (Amortization of discount or premium is to be recorded annually.)

Dec. 31 Paid the semiannual interest on the bonds.

31 Recorded bond premium amortization, which was determined by using the straight-line method.

2008

July 1 Recorded the redemption of the bonds, which were called at 102. The balance in the bond premium account is $662,456.70 after the payment of interest and amortization of premium have been recorded. (Record the redemption only.)

Instructions

1. Calculate the selling price of the bond issue and the amount of the bond discount or premium at issuance. Use the present value tables in Appendix A.

2. Record the entries for the foregoing transactions.
3. Indicate the amount of the interest expense in (a) 2006 and (b) 2007.
4. Determine the carrying amount of the bonds as of December 31, 2007.

ALTERNATE ACCOUNTING APPLICATION PROBLEMS

Alternate Problem 10-1B

Liability transactions

Goal 1

GENERAL LEDGER

The following items were selected from among the transactions completed by Davidson Co. during the current year:

Feb.	15	Purchased merchandise on account from Ranier Co., $36,000, terms n/30.
Mar.	17	Issued a 30-day, 8% note for $36,000 to Ranier Co., on account.
Apr.	16	Paid Ranier Co. the amount owed on the note of March 17.
July	15	Borrowed $40,000 from Black Mountain Bank, issuing a 90-day, 8% note.
	25	Purchased tools by issuing an $80,000, 120-day note to Sun Supply Co., which discounted the note at the rate of 7%.
Oct.	13	Paid Black Mountain Bank the interest due on the note of July 15 and renewed the loan by issuing a new 30-day, 9% note for $40,000. (Record both the debit and credit to the notes payable account.)
Nov.	12	Paid Black Mountain Bank the amount due on the note of October 13.
	22	Paid Sun Supply Co. the amount due on the note of July 25.
Dec.	1	Purchased office equipment from Valley Equipment Co. for $125,000, paying $25,000 and issuing a series of ten 12% notes for $10,000 each, coming due at 30-day intervals.
	17	Settled a product liability lawsuit with a customer for $52,000, payable in January. Renaissance accrued the loss in a litigation claims payable account.
	31	Paid the amount due Valley Equipment Co. on the first note in the series issued on December 1.

Instructions

1. Record the transactions.
2. Record the adjusting entry for each of the following accrued expenses at the end of the current year: (a) product warranty cost, $22,500; (b) interest on the nine remaining notes owed to Valley Equipment Co.

Alternate Problem 10-2B

Payroll accounts and year-end entries

Goal 1

GENERAL LEDGER

The following accounts, with the balances indicated, appear in the ledger of South Mountain CableView Co. on December 1 of the current year:

Salaries Payable	—
FICA Tax Payable	$ 9,657
Employees Federal Income Tax Payable	12,321
Employees State Income Tax Payable	11,988
State Unemployment Tax Payable	1,180
Federal Unemployment Tax Payable	310
Bond Deductions Payable	1,200
Medical Insurance Payable	6,000
Operations Salaries Expense	847,000
Officers Salaries Expense	376,200
Office Salaries Expense	242,000
Payroll Taxes Expense	113,689

The following transactions relating to payroll, payroll deductions, and payroll taxes occurred during December:

Dec.	2	Issued Check No. 728 for $1,200 to Cullowee National Bank to purchase U.S. savings bonds for employees.
	3	Issued Check No. 729 to Cullowee National Bank for $21,978, in payment of $9,657 of FICA tax and $12,321 of employees' federal income tax due.

Dec. 14 Record the entry for the biweekly payroll. A summary of the payroll record follows:

Salary distribution:		
Operations	$38,000	
Officers	17,400	
Office	10,800	$66,200
Deductions:		
FICA tax	$ 4,634	
Federal income tax withheld	11,784	
State income tax withheld	2,979	
Savings bond deductions	600	
Medical insurance deductions	1,000	20,997
Net amount		$45,203

14 Issued Check No. 738 in payment of the net amount of the biweekly payroll.
14 Record the entry for payroll taxes on employees' earnings of December 14: FICA tax, $4,634; state unemployment tax, $285; federal unemployment tax, $75.
17 Issued Check No. 744 to Cullowee National Bank for $21,052, in payment of $9,268 of social security tax and $11,784 of employees' federal income tax due.
18 Issued Check No. 750 to Bent Creek Insurance Company for $6,000, in payment of the semiannual premium on the group medical insurance policy.
28 Record the entry for the biweekly payroll. A summary of the payroll record follows:

Salary distribution:		
Operations	$39,000	
Officers	17,500	
Office	11,000	$67,500
Deductions:		
FICA tax	$ 4,658	
Federal income tax withheld	12,015	
State income tax withheld	3,038	
Savings bond deductions	600	20,311
Net amount		$47,189

28 Issued Check No. 782 in payment of the net amount of the biweekly payroll.
28 Record the entry for payroll taxes on employees' earnings of December 28: FICA tax, $4,658; state unemployment tax, $171; federal unemployment tax, $43.
30 Issued Check No. 791 to Cullowee National Bank for $1,200 to purchase U.S. savings bonds for employees.
30 Issued Check No. 792 for $18,005 to Cullowee National Bank in payment of employees' state income tax due on December 31.

Instructions

1. Record the transactions.
2. Record the following adjusting entries on December 31:
   a. Salaries accrued: operations salaries, $3,900; officers' salaries, $1,750; office salaries, $1,100. The payroll taxes are immaterial and are not accrued.
   b. Vacation pay, $11,000.

Alternate Problem 10-3B

Bond premium; entries for bonds payable transactions

Goal **2**

1. Selling Price = $12,717,033.60

Canton Corporation produces and sells ski equipment. On July 1, 2006, Canton Corporation issued $12,000,000 of 10-year, 12% bonds priced to yield an effective interest rate of 11%. Interest on the bonds is payable semiannually on December 31 and June 30. The fiscal year of the company is the calendar year.

Instructions

1. Calculate the selling price and the amount of discount or premium of the bond issue. Use the present value tables in Appendix A.
2. Record the entry for the amount of the cash proceeds from the sale of the bonds.

3. Record the entries for the following:
   a. The first semiannual interest payment on December 31, 2006, and the amortization of the bond premium, using the straight-line method. (Round to the nearest dollar.)
   b. The interest payment on June 30, 2007, and the amortization of the bond premium, using the straight-line method.
4. Determine the total interest expense for 2006.
5. Will the bond proceeds always be greater than the face amount of the bonds when the contract rate is greater than the market rate of interest? Explain.

Alternate Problem 10-4B

Bond discount; entries for bonds payable transactions

Goal **2**

4. $436,977.94

On July 1, 2006, Cougar Corporation, a wholesaler of used robotic equipment, issued $7,500,000 of 10-year, 10% bonds when the market rate of interest was 13%. Interest on the bonds is payable semiannually on December 31 and June 30. The fiscal year of the company is the calendar year.

Instructions

1. Calculate the selling price and the amount or discount of premium of the bond issue. Use the present value tables in Appendix A.
2. Record the entry for the amount of the cash proceeds from the sale of the bonds.
3. Record the entries for the following:
   a. The first semiannual interest payment on December 31, 2006, and the amortization of the bond discount, using the straight-line method. (Round to the nearest dollar.)
   b. The interest payment on June 30, 2007, and the amortization of the bond discount, using the straight-line method.
4. Determine the total interest expense for 2006.
5. Will the bond proceeds always be less than the face amount of the bonds when the contract rate is less than the market rate of interest? Explain.

Alternate Problem 10-5B

Entries for bonds payable transactions

Goal **2**

3. a. $1,193,051

SPREADSHEET

GENERAL LEDGER

The following transactions were completed by Douthett Inc., whose fiscal year is the calendar year:

2006

July 1 Issued $25,000,000 of five-year, 8% callable bonds dated July 1, 2006, at an effective rate of 10%. Interest is payable semiannually on December 31 and June 30.

Dec. 31 Paid the semiannual interest on the bonds.

31 Recorded bond discount amortization, which was determined by using the straight-line method.

2007

June 30 Paid the semiannual interest on the bonds. (Amortization of discount or premium is to be recorded annually.)

Dec. 31 Paid the semiannual interest on the bonds.

31 Recorded bond discount amortization, which was determined by using the straight-line method.

2008

June 30 Recorded the redemption of the bonds, which were called at $98\frac{1}{2}$. The balance in the bond discount account is $1,158,306 after payment of interest and amortization of discount have been recorded. (Record the redemption only.)

Instructions

1. Calculate the selling price and the amount of the discount or premium for the bond issue. Use the present value tables in Appendix A.
2. Record the entries for the foregoing transactions.
3. Indicate the amount of the interest expense in (a) 2006 and (b) 2007.
4. Determine the carrying amount of the bonds as of December 31, 2007.

FINANCIAL ANALYSIS AND REPORTING CASES

Case 10-1

Time value of money

Present value involves converting dollars received or paid in the future to their value in today's dollars. Use your knowledge of present value and the time value of money to analyze the following scenarios.

Scenario A

Barry Bonds, a highly successful baseball player, has recently become a free agent. Assume his agent has negotiated potential contracts with three different ball clubs. The details of these compensation packages are outlined below. For purposes of your analysis, analyze these options as of today, the beginning of the calendar year.

San Francisco Giants

- A $1,000,000 signing bonus payable today.
- $2,000,000 per year for three years. The annual payments are payable at the end of the calendar year, with the first payment occurring at the end of this year.

Chicago Cubs

- A $2,000,000 signing bonus payable at the end of the calendar year.
- $1,000,000 per year for three years. The annual payments are payable at the end of the calendar year, with the first payment occurring at the end of this year.
- A $1,000,000 payment at the end of three years if he completes all three seasons with the Cubs and does not retire prior to the end of his contract. You can assume for this exercise that he intends to meet this condition of his contract.

Milwaukee Brewers

- No signing bonus.
- $1,500,000 per year for three years. The annual payments are payable at the end of the calendar year, with the first payment occurring at the end of this year.
- A local endorsement contract that will pay $1,200,000 at the end of the first calendar year.

Which contract should Barry sign if the only relevant factor in his decision-making process is the total value of the contract and he can earn 8% interest? Explain your answer and provide any necessary supporting calculations.

Scenario B

Kristen Nash recently won the jackpot in the New Jersey lottery while she was visiting her parents. When she arrived at the lottery office to collect her winnings, she was offered the following two payout options:

- Receive $5,000,000 in cash today.
- Receive $2,000,000 today and $600,000 per year for 10 years, with the first $600,000 payment being received one year from today.
- Receive $1,000,000 per year for 10 years, with the first payment being received one year from today.

Assuming that the market rate of interest is 9%, which payout option should Kristen select? Explain your answer and provide any necessary supporting calculations.

Case 10-2

Bond issuance, convertible bonds

Giant Jumbo, Inc., is a manufacturer of recreational vehicles located in upstate New York. In recent years the company has experienced a huge spike in sales volume, but has had difficulty meeting demand because of limited manufacturing capacity. Backlogs have reached periods in excess of six months, and the company has had to turn away an increasing amount of business because of order backlogs. On November 1, 2005, Giant Jumbo issued $250 million of 10%

convertible bonds due in 10 years. The bond issue generated proceeds of $275 million dollars, which the company will use to build a second manufacturing facility on the west coast. Each $1,000 bond is convertible into 20 shares of common stock, and may be converted at any time prior to maturity.

1. Were the bonds issued at a premium or a discount?
2. What is the face value, contract rate of interest, and maturity date of the bonds?
3. What are convertible bonds? Why might a company issue convertible bonds rather than typical term bonds?
4. At what stock price would it be worthwhile for bond holders to convert the bonds into shares of common stock?

Case 10-3

Contingent liability disclosure

A contingent liability note from DuPont Co.'s 2003 financial statements is reproduced below.

> *The company is also subject to contingencies pursuant to environmental laws and regulations that in the future may require the company to take further action to correct the effects on the environment of prior disposal practices or releases of chemical or petroleum substances by the company or other parties. The company accrues for environmental remediation activities . . . . At December 31, 2003, the company's Consolidated Balance Sheet includes a liability of $380 relating to these matters and, in management's opinion, is appropriate based on existing facts and circumstances. The average time frame over which the accrued or presently unrecognized amounts may be paid, based on past history, is estimated to be 15–20 years. Considerable uncertainty exists with respect to these costs and, under adverse changes in circumstances, potential liability may range up to two to three times the amount accrued as of December 31, 2003.*

On September 10, 2004, *The Wall Street Journal* reported the following:

> *In a proposed settlement of a class-action lawsuit that could involve payouts of more than $300 million, DuPont Co. is betting that science is on its side.*
>
> *The nation's No. 2 chemical maker yesterday agreed to settle allegations that it contaminated water supplies with a toxic chemical used to make Teflon, a slippery substance that can be found in everything from cookware to clothing. It requires the company to pay plaintiffs $85 million, plus other expenditures, as well as pay attorney's fees and expenses of $22.6 million.*
>
> *But its payments could rise by another $235 million depending on whether a $5 million study the company will fund finds a probable link between exposure to the chemical and any diseases.*

1. How would the $380 million in environmental liabilities be reported on DuPont's financial statements, assuming that $270 million of this amount was estimated to be paid in fiscal 2004? Provide the journal entry.
2. How would DuPont account for the Teflon settlement payments during 2004, assuming the cost was accrued in the prior year? How would this answer differ if the costs had not previously been accrued?
3. What are the different ways in which the company could handle the additional $235 million in potential payments related to the environmental study? How would you account for these costs?

Case 10-4

Current and quick ratios—industry comparison

Summary financial information is provided below for BellSouth Corp., a telecommunications company, and Belk, Inc., a general department store retailer. The financial information for these companies is similar to that of most companies in the telephone communications and department store industries, respectively.

	BellSouth Corp. (in millions) Dec. 31, 2004		Belk, Inc. (in thousands) Jan. 29, 2005	
	Amount	**%**	**Amount**	**%**
Cash	$ 696	12.2%	$ 232,264	21.2%
Accounts receivable	2,559	44.9%	319,706	29.1%
Merchandise inventory	—	—	527,860	48.1%
Materials and supplies	321	5.6%	—	—
Other	2,123	37.3%	17,302	1.6%
Total current assets	$ 5,699	100.0%	$1,097,132	100.0%
Accounts payable	$ 1,047	10.1%	$ 177,793	57.6%
Short-term debt	5,475	52.8%	8,199	2.7%
Other	3,848	37.1%	122,397	39.7%
Total current liabilities	$10,370	100.0%	$ 308,389	100.0%
Current ratio	0.550		3.558	
Quick ratio	0.314		1.790	

	BellSouth Corp.	Belk, Inc.	Difference
Current Ratio	0.550	3.558	3.008
Quick Ratio	0.314	1.790	1.476
Difference	0.236	1.768	

1. Why is the current ratio of the department store 3.008 greater than the current ratio of the telecommunications company?
2. Why is the quick ratio of the department store 1.476 greater than the quick ratio of the telecommunications company?
3. Why are the differences between the current and quick ratios much larger for the department store than they are for the telecommunications company (1.768 vs. 0.236)?

Case 10-5

Current and quick ratios across time

The current assets and current liabilities for Texas Instruments Inc. for five recent years are shown as follows (in millions):

	2004	2003	2002	2001	2000
Cash and cash equivalents	$ 2,668	$1,818	$ 949	$ 431	$ 745
Short-term investments	3,690	2,511	2,063	2,513	3,258
Accounts receivable	1,696	1,451	1,217	1,078	2,204
Inventories	1,256	984	790	751	1,233
Other current assets	880	945	1,107	1,002	675
Total current assets	$10,190	$7,709	$6,126	$5,775	$8,115
Notes payable	$ 11	$ 437	$ 422	$ 38	$ 148
Accounts payable and accrued expenses	1,444	1,496	1,204	1,205	1,921
Other current liabilities	470	267	308	337	744
Total current liabilities	$ 1,925	$2,200	$1,934	$1,580	$2,813

1. Calculate and graph the current and quick ratios for the five comparative years. Round to two decimal places.
2. Interpret your graph.

Case 10-6

Long-term solvency measures for two aerospace companies

The Lockheed Martin Corp. and Northrop Grumman Corp. are two major defense contractors. A partial balance sheet for the end of a recent fiscal year is shown as follows (in millions):

SPREADSHEET

	Lockheed Martin 12/31/04	Northrop Grumman 12/31/04
Liabilities and stockholders' equity:		
Total current liabilities	$ 8,566	$ 6,223
Long-term debt	5,104	5,116
Post-retirement benefit liabilities	2,896	3,736
Deferred income taxes	0	506
Other non-current liabilities	1,967	1,080
Total stockholders' equity	7,021	16,700
Total liabilities and stockholders' equity	$25,554	$33,361

The interest expense, income tax expense, and net income (before unusual items) were as follows for both companies:

	Lockheed Martin 2004	Northrop Grumman 2004
Interest expense	$ 425	$ 431
Income tax expense	398	522
Net income from continuing operations	1,266	1,093

1. Determine the total liabilities to total assets ratio for each company. Round to two decimal places.
2. Determine the number of times interest charges are earned for each company.
3. Interpret your results.

Case 10-7

Ratio of total liabilities to total assets—banking industry

The ratio of total liabilities to total assets for the 12 largest bank holding companies for a recent year are shown in the table below. The average ratio of total liabilities to total assets for the group is 91.1%. This means that the average debt held by these banks is over 91% of their total assets, which is much more than in any other industry.

Bank Holding Company	Ratio of Total Liabilities to Total Assets
Citigroup Inc.	0.925
J.P. Morgan Chase	0.908
Bank of America Corporation	0.910
Wachovia Corporation	0.898
Wells Fargo & Company	0.911
Taunus Corporation	0.987
U.S. Bancorp	0.900
Suntrust Banks, Inc.	0.896
National City Corporation	0.906
Citizens Financial Group, Inc.	0.848
ABN AMRO North America Holding Company	0.939
Countrywide Financial Corporation	0.906
Average	0.911

Why are these ratios so large?

BUSINESS ACTIVITIES AND RESPONSIBILITY ISSUES

Activity 10-1

Business emphasis

One reason that PepsiCo, Inc., purchased Quaker Oats in 2001 was to acquire the rights to its sports drink, Gatorade. However, Gatorade is under increasing pressure from its competitors, including Coca-Cola's Powerade. As a result, PepsiCo is initiating an aggressive advertising campaign to promote and grow sales of Gatorade.

GROUP ACTIVITY

In groups of three or four, answer the following questions:

1. Go to the Gatorade Web site at http://gatorade.com. (a) How and why was Gatorade developed? (b) What is Gatorade's share of the sports-drink market?
2. Drinks can be labeled as sports, lifestyle, or active thirst drinks. (a) How would you describe each of these drink labels? (b) Give an example of what you would label a sports, lifestyle, and active thirst drink.
3. Do you think PepsiCo's advertising campaign will focus on Gatorade as a sports, lifestyle, or active thirst drink? Explain.

Activity 10-2

Employment ethics

Marge McMaster is a certified public accountant (CPA) and a staff assistant for Tester and Morris, a local CPA firm. The firm's policy had been to provide a holiday bonus equal to two weeks' salary to all employees. The firm's new management team announced on November 25 that a bonus equal to only one week's salary would be made available to employees this year. Marge thought that this policy was unfair because she and her coworkers planned on the full two-week bonus. The two-week bonus had been given for 10 straight years, so it seemed as though the firm had breached an implied commitment. Thus, Marge decided that she would make up the lost bonus week by working an extra six hours of overtime per week over the next five weeks until the end of the year. Tester and Morris's policy is to pay overtime at 150% of straight time.

Marge's supervisor was surprised to see overtime being reported, since there is generally very little additional or unusual client service demands at the end of the calendar year. However, the overtime was not questioned, since firm employees are on the "honor system" in reporting their overtime.

Discuss whether the firm is acting in an ethical manner by changing the bonus. Is Marge behaving in an ethical manner?

Activity 10-3

Salary survey

Several Internet services provide career guidance, classified employment ads, placement services, résumé posting, career questionnaires, and salary surveys. Select one of the following Internet sites to determine current average salary levels for one of your career options:

http://www.salaryexpert.com/seco/index.cfm?cobrandid=90	Accounting salary information
http://www.spherion.com	Links to computer, engineering, finance, marketing, and accounting salary information
http://www.monster.com	Online Career Center, with links to salary information
http://www.imanet.org	Institute of Management Accountants salary survey information (see Career Center)

Activity 10-4

General Electric bond issuance

General Electric Capital, a division of General Electric, uses long-term debt extensively. In early 2002, GE Capital issued $11 billion in long-term debt to investors, then within days filed legal documents to prepare for another $50 billion long-term debt issue. As a result of the $50 billion filing, the price of the initial $11 billion offering declined (due to higher risk of more debt).

> *Bill Gross, a manager of a bond investment fund, "denounced a 'lack in candor' related to GE's recent debt deal. 'It was the most recent and most egregious example of how bondholders are mistreated.' Gross argued that GE was not forthright when GE Capital recently issued $11 billion in bonds, one of the largest issues ever from a U.S. corporation. What bothered Gross is that three days after the issue the company announced its intention to sell as much as $50 billion in additional debt, warrants, preferred stock, guarantees, letters of credit and promissory notes at some future date."*

In your opinion, did GE Capital act unethically by selling $11 billion of long-term debt without telling those investors that a few days later it would be filing documents to prepare for another $50 billion debt offering?

Source: Jennifer Ablan, "Gross Shakes the Bond Market: GE Claims It, a Bit," *Barron's*, March 25, 2002.

Activity 10-5

Investing in bonds

GROUP ACTIVITY

During fiscal 2004, Georgia-Pacific Company called the following bond issuances:

$243 million	9.875% bonds	due November 1, 2021
$250 million	9.625% bonds	due March 15, 2022
$250 million	9.500% bonds	due May 15, 2022
$240 million	9.125% bonds	due July 1, 2022
$250 million	8.250% bonds	due March 1, 2023
$250 million	8.125% bonds	due June 15, 2023

In groups of three or four:

1. Identify the face value, coupon rate, and maturity of each of the bond issues.
2. Discuss some of the potential reasons that Georgia-Pacific may have had for deciding to call these bond issues early.

Activity 10-6

Bond ratings

Moody's Investors Service maintains a Web site at http://www.Moodys.com. One of the services offered at this site is a listing of announcements of recent bond rating changes. Visit this site and read over some of these announcements. Write down several of the reasons provided for rating downgrades and upgrades. If you were a bond investor or bond issuer, would you care if Moody's changed the rating on your bonds? Why or why not?

ANSWERS TO SELF-STUDY QUESTIONS

1. **B** The net amount available to a borrower from discounting a note payable is called the proceeds. The proceeds of $4,900 (answer B) is determined as follows:

Face amount of note	$5,000
Less discount ($5,000 × 12% × 60/360)	100
Proceeds	$4,900

2. **B** Employers are usually required to withhold a portion of their employees' earnings for payment of federal income taxes (answer A), Medicare tax (answer C), and state and local income taxes (answer D). Generally, federal unemployment compensation taxes (answer B) are levied against the employer only and thus are not deducted from employee earnings.

3. **D** Current ratio: $800,000/$200,000 = 4.0
Quick ratio: ($100,000 + $300,000)/$200,000 = 2.0

4. **B**

Sales Price of the Bonds:

Present value of bond principle:	
Principle × Present Value of $\$1_{i = 9\%, n = 5}$	
$200,000 × 0.64993 =	$129,986
Present value of bond interest:	
Principle × Present Value of Annuity of $\$1_{i = 9\%, n = 5}$	
$20,000 × 3.88965	77,793
	$207,779

Calculation of bond premium:	
Selling price of the bonds	$207,779
Face value of the bonds	200,000
Bond premium (Selling price > Face value)	$ 7,779

5. **D** The number of times interest charges are earned is determined as: ($500,000 + $100,000)/$100,000, or 6.0.

11 Stockholders' Equity: Capital Stock and Dividends

Learning Goals

1. Describe the nature of the corporate form of organization.
2. List the major sources of paid-in capital, including the various classes of stock.
3. Describe the financial statement effects of issuing stock.
4. Describe the financial statement effects of treasury stock transactions.
5. Describe the effect of stock splits on the financial statements.
6. Analyze the impact of issuing common stock or bonds.
7. Describe the financial statement effects of cash dividends and stock dividends.
8. Describe financial statement presentations of stockholders' equity.
9. Compute and interpret the dividend yield and dividend payout ratio on common stock.

Mattel, Inc.

If you purchased 100 shares of Mattel, Inc., you would own a small interest in the company. Thus, you would own a small amount of the future financial prospects of the company that has already sold over 1 billion Barbie® dolls in over 150 different countries. These shares might increase or decrease in value, depending upon the market's perception of the future earnings prospects of Barbie, American Girl®, Fisher Price® toys, and other Mattel products. In addition, the number of shares outstanding might impact the value of your shares. You would want the financial statements to inform you of any changes in your underlying ownership. For example, new issues of common stock would dilute your interest in the firm, while reductions in the outstanding stock would increase your interest in the firm.

The shares might also pay a dividend, which is a return of cash to the stockholders. Mattel pays a dividend of $0.45 per share. Thus, a holder of 100 shares would receive dividend payments equal to $45.00 per year. Would you invest in a company that didn't pay any dividends? Many companies do not pay dividends, yet they remain attractive investments. The reason is that many companies have excellent investment opportunities for funds that might otherwise be paid out as dividends. This is why growth companies, such as Google and Cisco Systems, do not pay any dividends, while more mature companies, such as Procter & Gamble, The Coca-Cola Company, and Bank of America, do pay dividends.

In this chapter, we will present accounting for common stock and dividends. We will also present some analysis tools for evaluating common stock and dividend policy.

Describe the nature of the corporate form of organization.

NATURE OF A CORPORATION

More than 70% of all businesses are proprietorships, and 10% are partnerships. Most of these businesses are small businesses. The remaining 20% of businesses are corporations. Many corporations are large, and, as a result, they generate more than 90% of the total business dollars in the United States.

Characteristics of a Corporation

Corporations have several advantages and disadvantages over proprietorships or partnerships as shown in Exhibit 1. A corporation is a separate legal entity that can be used to raise large amounts of capital that is easily transferable among shareholders, while limiting the liability of the stockholders to their investment. However, owners are normally separate from management, are subject to double taxation, and have higher regulatory costs than other forms of business organization.

Exhibit 1

Advantages and Disadvantages of the Corporate Form

Advantages	Explanation
Separate legal existence	A corporation exists separately from its owners.
Continuous life	A corporation's life is separate from its owners; therefore, it exists indefinitely.
Raising large amounts of capital	The corporate form is suited for raising large amounts of money from shareholders.
Ownership rights easily transferred	A corporation sells shares of ownership, called *stock*. The stockholders of a public company can transfer their shares of stock to other stockholders through stock markets, such as the New York Stock Exchange.
Limited liability	A corporation's creditors usually may not go beyond the assets of the corporation to satisfy their claims. Thus, the financial loss that a stockholder may suffer is limited to the amount invested.
Disadvantages	
Owner is separate from management	Stockholders control management through a board of directors. The board of directors should represent shareholder interests; however, when the board is not sufficiently independent of management, it is possible for shareholder interests to be poorly represented.
Double taxation of dividends	As a separate legal entity, a corporation is subject to taxation. Thus, net income distributed as dividends will be taxed once at the corporation level, and then again at the individual level.
Regulatory costs	Corporations must satisfy many regulatory requirements, including internal control assessments as required by the Sarbanes-Oxley Act of 2002.[1]

Forming a Corporation

The first step in forming a corporation is to file an *application of incorporation* with the state. State incorporation laws differ, and corporations often organize in those states with the more favorable laws. For this reason, more than half of the largest companies are incorporated in Delaware. Exhibit 2 lists some corporations that you may be familiar with, their states of incorporation, and the location of their headquarters.

1 A Financial Executive International survey estimated the total cost of Sarbanes-Oxley compliance for the average public company at $3.14 million per year.

INTEGRITY, OBJECTIVITY AND ETHICS IN BUSINESS

The Responsible Board

Recent accounting scandals, such as those involving **Enron**, **WorldCom**, and **Fannie Mae**, have highlighted the roles of boards of directors in executing their responsibilities. For example, eighteen of Enron's former directors and their insurance providers have settled shareholder litigation for $168 million, of which $13 million is to come from the directors' personal assets. Board members are now on notice that their directorship responsibilities are being taken seriously by stockholders.

© DAVID T. PHILLIP/AP WIDE WORLD PHOTO

Exhibit 2

Examples of Corporations and Their States of Incorporation

Corporation	State of Incorporation	Headquarters
Caterpillar, Inc.	Delaware	Peoria, Ill.
Delta Air Lines	Delaware	Atlanta, Ga.
Dow Chemical Company	Delaware	Midland, Mich.
General Electric Company	New York	Fairfield, Conn.
The Home Depot	Delaware	Atlanta, Ga.
Kellogg Company	Delaware	Battle Creek, Mich.
3M	Delaware	St. Paul, Minn.
RJ Reynolds Tobacco	Delaware	Winston-Salem, N.C.
Starbucks Corporation	Washington	Seattle, Washington
Sun Microsystems, Inc.	Delaware	Palo Alto, Calif.
The Washington Post Company	Delaware	Washington, D.C.
Whirlpool Corporation	Delaware	Benton Harbor, Mich.

After the application of incorporation has been approved, the state grants a *charter* or *articles of incorporation*. The articles of incorporation formally create the corporation.[2] The corporate management and board of directors then prepare a set of *bylaws*, which are the rules and procedures for conducting the corporation's affairs.

2 The articles of incorporation may also restrict a corporation's activities in certain areas, such as owning certain types of real estate, conducting certain types of business activities, or purchasing its own stock.

INTEGRITY, OBJECTIVITY, AND ETHICS IN BUSINESS

Not-for-Profit, or Not?

Corporations can be formed for not-for-profit purposes by making a request to the Internal Revenue Service under *Internal Revenue Code* section 501(c)3. Such corporations are exempt from federal taxes. Forming businesses inside a 501(c)3 exempt organization that competes with profit-making (and hence, tax-paying) businesses is very controversial. For example, should the local YMCA receive a tax exemption for providing similar services as the local health club business? The IRS is now challenging such businesses and is withholding 501(c)3 status to many organizations due to this issue.

Significant costs may be incurred in organizing a corporation. These costs include legal fees, taxes, state incorporation fees, license fees, and promotional costs. Such costs are recorded as an expense for the period incurred.

List the major sources of paid-in capital, including the various classes of stock.

SOURCES OF PAID-IN CAPITAL

The managers of a corporation are responsible for establishing the capital structure of a company. The *capital structure* of a company is the percentage of total assets that is financed by creditors, as discussed in the previous chapter, and the percentage that is financed by owners. The financing from owners comes from two main sources of stockholders' equity: (1) paid-in capital (or contributed capital) and (2) retained earnings. The main source of paid-in capital is from issuing stock, which we will discuss in the next sections.

Common Stock

When only one class of stock is issued, it is called **common stock**. In this case, each share of common stock has equal rights. The major rights that accompany ownership of a share of stock are as follows:

1. The right to vote in matters concerning the corporation.
2. The right to share in distributions of earnings.
3. The right to share in assets upon liquidation.

The distribution of earnings is called a *dividend*. The board of directors of a corporation has the sole authority to distribute dividends to the stockholders. When such action is taken, the directors are said to declare a dividend. Since dividends are normally based on earnings, a corporation cannot guarantee dividends. For example, CIGNA Corp., a major insurance company, recently slashed its dividend by 90% due to financial constraints.

The shares of a company can be categorized as follows:

- *Authorized:* The amount of shares available to be issued as stated in the corporate charter.
- *Issued:* The actual amount of shares that have been sold to shareholders.
- *Outstanding:* The issued shares, less the amount of previously issued stock reacquired by the company, that are remaining in the hands of shareholders.

Authorized
Issued
Outstanding

Number of shares authorized, issued, and outstanding

The relationship between authorized, issued, and **outstanding stock** is shown in the graphic at the left.

Shares of stock are often assigned a monetary amount, called **par**. Often, this amount is related to state laws requiring a minimum stockholder contribution, called *legal capital*. Stock may also be issued without par, in which case, it is called *no-par stock*. Some states require the board of directors to assign a **stated value** to no-par stock.

Market for Common Stock

A public company may sell common stock to the general public, which can then be traded on a stock exchange. Three major types of stock market transactions are possible:

1. *An initial public offering (IPO)*. An IPO is a company's first issue of common stock to the public, and thus the first step to becoming a publicly owned company. For example, Google sold 10% of its common shares at an IPO price of $85 per share.[3] In addition, IPOs are common for corporate spin-offs into separately held companies. For example, DreamWorks LLC sold DreamWorks Animation Inc. to the public through an IPO. In either case, the issuing company will often use investment bankers, such as Merrill Lynch, to help sell an IPO to the general public, which is called the *primary market*.
2. *Additional shares sold by an established public company*. Established publicly owned companies can raise additional equity capital by selling common stock to the public. Like IPOs, such shares are sold by investment bankers in the primary market.
3. *Market exchanges between owners of a publicly held company*. By far, the most widespread stock market transactions occur between buyers and sellers of outstanding common stock. These transactions occur on the secondary market. The largest secondary markets in the United States are the New York Stock Exchange (NYSE) and National Association of Security Dealers Automated Quotation (NASDAQ). The market price can be determined for any company listed on an organized exchange from numerous Internet sites and from daily financial publications. A sample quotation from *The Wall Street Journal* for Wal-Mart is explained as follows:

YTD	52 Weeks					Yld		Vol		Net
% CHG	Hi	Lo	Stock	Sym	Div	%	PE	100s	LAST	Chg
0.9	61^{31}	51^{08}	WalMart	WMT	.52	1.0	23	82260	53^{29}	+0.07

The preceding quotation is interpreted as follows:

YTD % CHG	The year-to-date cumulative percentage change in the price
Hi	Highest price during the past 52 weeks
Lo	Lowest price during the past 52 weeks
Stock	Name of the company
Sym	Stock exchange symbol (WMT for Wal-Mart)
Div	Dividends paid per share during the past year
Yld %	Annual dividend yield per share, based on the closing price (Wal-Mart's 1% yield on common stock is computed as $0.52/$53.29)
PE	Price-earnings ratio on common stock (price ÷ earnings per share)
Vol	The volume of stock traded in 100s for that day
LAST	Closing price for the day
Net Chg	The net change in price from the previous day

---

3 Google broke tradition by issuing its IPO shares using an auction approach, rather than investment bankers. This may become more popular in the future.

INTEGRITY, OBJECTIVITY, AND ETHICS IN BUSINESS

What's the Real Value?

Stock fraud often involves illegal methods to sell stock or other investments at a price that is higher than its actual value. This can be done through illegally manipulating the stock price, selling stock in nonexistent companies, or using the proceeds of later investors to pay off earlier investors (pyramid scheme). You can avoid these kinds of fraud by following three rules:

1. Don't invest in small new companies that have market prices below $1, based on hot tips from unsolicited e-mails or phone calls.
2. Don't invest on advice from acquaintances in social or religious groups, without checking the merits yourself.
3. Don't invest in unsolicited "risk-free" and "guaranteed" investments that promise quick profits if you act immediately.

Preferred Stock

To appeal to a broader investment market, a corporation may issue one or more classes of stock with various preference rights. A common example of such a right is the preference to dividends. Such a stock is generally called a **preferred stock**. Similar to common stock, preferred stock trades in the secondary markets, such as the New York Stock Exchange.

The dividend rights of preferred stock are usually stated in monetary terms or as a percent of par. For example, *$4 preferred stock* has a right to an annual $4 per share dividend. If the par value of the preferred stock was $50, the same right to dividends could be stated as *8% ($4/$50) preferred stock.*

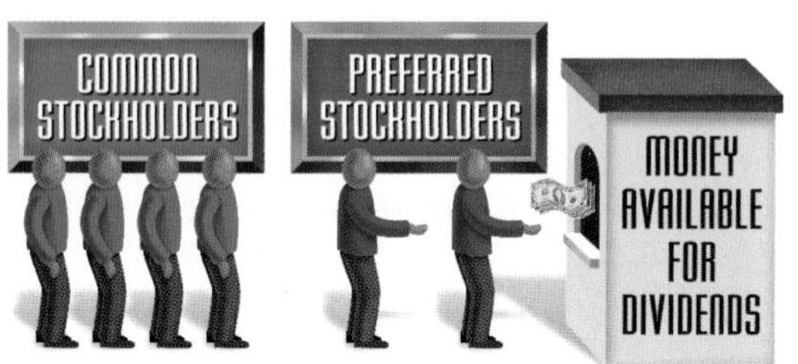

A corporation cannot guarantee dividends, even to preferred stockholders. However, because they have first rights to any dividends, the preferred stockholders have a greater chance of receiving regular dividends than do the common stockholders.

Cumulative preferred stock has a right to receive regular dividends that have been passed (not declared) before any common stock dividends are paid. Noncumulative preferred stock does not have this right. Dividends that have been passed are said to be *in arrears*. Such dividends should be disclosed, normally in a footnote to the financial statements.

To illustrate how dividends on cumulative preferred stock are calculated, assume that a corporation has 1,000 shares of $4 cumulative preferred stock and 4,000 shares of common stock outstanding, and that no dividends were paid in 2006 and 2007. In 2008, the board of directors declares dividends of $22,000. Exhibit 3 shows how the dividends paid in 2008 are distributed between the preferred and common stockholders.

Exhibit 3

Dividends to Cumulative Preferred Stock

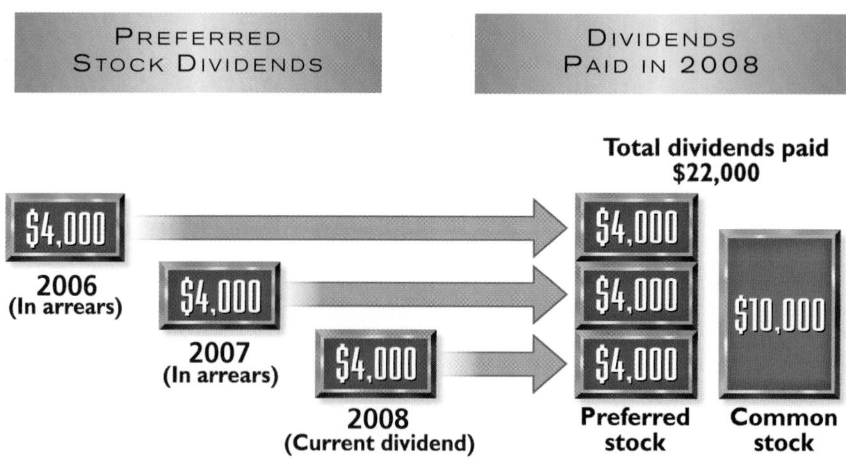

Exhibit 3
Concluded

Amount distributed		$22,000
Preferred dividend (1,000 shares):		
2006 dividend in arrears	$4,000	
2007 dividend in arrears	4,000	
2008 dividend	4,000	12,000
Common dividend (4,000 shares)		$10,000
Dividends per share:		
Preferred		$ 12.00
Common		2.50

ISSUING STOCK

Describe the financial statement effects of issuing stock.

A separate account is used for recording the amount of each class of stock issued to investors in a corporation. For example, assume that a corporation is authorized to issue 10,000 shares of preferred stock, $100 par, and 100,000 shares of common stock, $20 par. One-half of each class of authorized shares is issued at par for cash. The corporation's stock issue is recorded as follows:[4]

SCF	BS	IS
F↑	A↑ SE↑	—

Cash	1,500,000	
Preferred Stock		500,000
Common Stock		1,000,000

Stock is often issued by a corporation at a price other than its par. This is because the par value of a stock is simply its legal capital. The price at which stock can be sold by a corporation depends on a variety of factors, such as the following:

1. The financial condition, earnings record, and dividend record of the corporation.
2. Investor expectations of the corporation's potential earning power.
3. General business and economic conditions and prospects.

Premium on Stock

When stock is issued for a price that is more than its par, the stock has sold at a **premium**. Thus, if stock with a par of $1 is issued for a price of $55, the stock has sold at a premium of $54.

When stock is issued at a premium, Cash or other asset accounts are debited for the amount received. Common Stock or Preferred Stock is then credited for the par amount. The excess of the amount paid over par is a part of the total investment of the stockholders in the corporation. Therefore, such an amount in excess of par should be classified as a part of the paid-in capital. An account entitled *Paid-In Capital in Excess of Par* is usually credited for this amount.

To illustrate, assume that Caldwell Company issues 2,000 shares of $1 par common stock for cash at $55. This transaction is recorded as follows:

4 The accounting for investments in stocks from the point of view of the investor is discussed in the next chapter.

SCF	BS	IS
F↑	A↑ SE↑	—

Cash	110,000	
Common Stock		2,000
Paid-In Capital in Excess of Par—Common Stock		108,000

When stock is issued in exchange for assets other than cash, such as land, buildings, and equipment, the assets acquired should be recorded at their fair market value. If this value cannot be objectively determined, the fair market price of the stock issued may be used.

To illustrate, assume that a corporation acquired land for which the fair market value cannot be determined. In exchange, the corporation issued 10,000 shares of its $10 par preferred stock. Assuming that the stock has a current market price of $12 per share, this transaction is recorded as follows:

SCF	BS	IS
—	A↑ SE↑	—

Land	120,000	
Common Stock		100,000
Paid-In Capital in Excess of Par—Preferred Stock		20,000

No-Par Stock

In most states, both preferred and common stock may be issued without a par value. When no-par stock is issued, the entire proceeds are credited to the stock account. This is true, even though the issue price varies from time to time. For example, assume that a corporation issues 10,000 shares of no-par common stock at $40 a share, and at a later date issues 1,000 additional shares at $36. The no-par stock is recorded as follows:

SCF	BS	IS
F↑	A↑ SE↑	—
F↑	A↑ SE↑	—

Cash	400,000	
Common Stock		400,000
Cash	36,000	
Common Stock		36,000

Some states require that the entire proceeds from the issue of no-par stock be recorded as legal capital. In this case, the preceding entries would be proper. In other states, no-par stock may be assigned a *stated value per share*. The stated value is recorded like par value. Assuming a stated value of $25 per share, 10,000 shares issued for $40 per share, and at a later date 1,000 additional shares issued at $36 per share, are recorded as follows:

SCF	BS	IS
F↑	A↑ SE↑	—
F↑	A↑ SE↑	—

Cash	400,000	
Common Stock		250,000
Paid-In Capital in Excess of Stated Value		150,000
Cash	36,000	
Common Stock		25,000
Paid-In Capital in Excess of Stated Value		11,000

Stock Options

One method of motivating employees to behave in the best interest of the owners is to provide the employees with common stock at a discount from the market price. A common method for doing this is by way of an employee **stock option**. Over 95% of large companies use stock option plans to reward employees. Stock options can be very lucrative for senior executives. For example, stock option gains frequently represent over half of total chief executive officer (CEO) compensation. Barry Diller, CEO of InterActive Corp., cashed in over $151 million in stock options in 2003, making him the highest paid CEO in that year. Such high compensation through stock options has led to new requirements to recognize options as an expense on the income statement.

Stock options grant an employee the right to purchase common stock at a fixed price for a limited period of time, as illustrated below. The stock option price is called the *exercise price*, and the limited time period is called the *exercise period*. Stock options are often granted to employees at an exercise price equal to the market price on the grant date. If the market price of the stock exceeds the exercise price at any time during the exercise period, it is beneficial for the employee to exercise the option. Exercising the stock option allows the employee to purchase the common stock at a price below the prevailing market price, which may then be sold to realize gains.

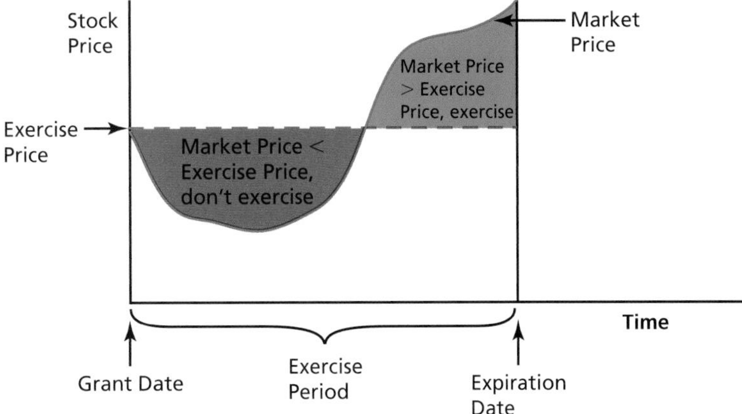

Stock options can have many unique features. For example, the employee receiving the stock option may be required to hold the option for a period of time until it can be exercised. Such a waiting period is called a *vesting period*. Due to the complex nature of stock options, their accounting treatment is covered in advanced accounting courses.

Describe the financial statement effects of treasury stock transactions.

TREASURY STOCK

A corporation may buy its own stock to provide shares for resale to employees, for reissuing shares as a bonus to employees, or for supporting the market price of the stock. For example, General Motors bought back its common stock and stated that two primary uses of this stock would be for stock option plans and employee savings plans. Such stock that a corporation has once issued and then reacquired is called

treasury stock. The 2004 edition of *Accounting Trends & Techniques* indicated that over 67% of the companies surveyed reported treasury stock.

A commonly used method of accounting for the purchase and resale of treasury stock is the *cost method*.[5] When the stock is purchased by the corporation, the account *Treasury Stock* is debited for its cost (the price paid for it). The par value and the price at which the stock was originally issued are ignored. When the stock is resold. Treasury Stock is credited for its cost, and any difference between the cost and the selling price is normally debited or credited to *Paid-In Capital from Sale of Treasury Stock.*

To illustrate, assume that the paid-in capital of a corporation is as follows:

Common stock, $25 par (20,000 shares authorized and issued)	$500,000	
Excess of issue price over par	150,000	$650,000

The purchase of 1,000 shares of treasury stock at a price of $45 per share is recorded as follows:

SCF	BS	IS
F↓	A↓ SE↓	—

Treasury Stock	45,000	
Cash		45,000

If 200 shares of treasury stock were resold at $60 per share, it is recorded as follows:

SCF	BS	IS
F↑	A↑ SE↑	—

Cash	12,000	
Treasury Stock		9,000
Paid-In Capital from Sale of Treasury Stock		3,000

If at a later date another 200 shares of treasury stock are sold for $40 per share, it would be recorded as follows:

SCF	BS	IS
F↑	A↑ SE↑	—

Cash	8,000	
Paid-In Capital from Sale of Treasury Stock	1,000	
Treasury Stock		9,000

As shown above, a sale of treasury stock may result in a decrease in paid-in capital. To the extent that Paid-In Capital from Sale of Treasury Stock has a credit balance, it should be debited for any decrease. Any remaining decrease should then be debited to the retained earnings account.

At the end of the period, the balance in the treasury stock account is reported as a deduction from the total of the paid-in capital and retained earnings. The balance of Paid-In Capital from Sale of Treasury Stock is reported as part of the paid-in capital, as shown in Exhibit 4.

---

5 Another method that is infrequently used, called the *par value method*, is discussed in advanced accounting texts.

Exhibit 4

Stockholders' Equity Section with Treasury Stock

Stockholders' Equity			
Paid-in capital:			
Common stock, $25 par (20,000 shares authorized and issued)	$500,000		
Paid-in capital in excess of par—common	150,000		
Paid-in capital—treasury stock	2,000		
Total paid-in capital		$652,000	
Retained earnings		130,000	
Total		$782,000	
Deduct treasury stock (600 shares at cost)		27,000	
Total stockholders' equity			$755,000

Describe the effect of stock splits on the financial statements.

STOCK SPLITS

Corporations sometimes reduce the par or stated value of their common stock and issue a proportionate number of additional shares. When this is done, a corporation is said to have split its stock, and the process is called a **stock split**.

When stock is split, the reduction in par or stated value applies to all shares, including the unissued, issued, and treasury shares. A major objective of a stock split is to reduce the market price per share of the stock. This, in turn, should attract more investors to enter the market for the stock and broaden the types and numbers of stockholders.

To illustrate a stock split, assume that Rojek Corporation has 10,000 shares of $100 par common stock outstanding with a current market price of $150 per share. The board of directors declares a 5-for-1 stock split, which reduces the par to $20, and increases the number of shares to 50,000. The amount of common stock outstanding is $1,000,000 both before and after the stock split. Only the number of shares and the par value per share are changed. Each Rojek Corporation shareholder owns the same total par amount of stock before and after the stock split. For example, a stockholder who owned four shares of $100 par stock before the split (total par of $400) would own 20 shares of $20 par stock after the split (total par of $400).

Since there are more shares outstanding after the stock split, we would expect the market price of the stock to fall. In the preceding example, there would be five times as many shares outstanding after the split. Thus, we would expect the market price of the stock to fall from $150 to approximately $30 ($150 ÷ 5).

Since a stock split changes only the par or stated value and the number of shares outstanding, it is not recorded by a journal entry. Although the accounts are not affected, the details of stock splits are normally disclosed in the notes to the financial statements.

Q. LTM Corporation announced a 4-for-1 stock split of its $50 par value common stock, which is currently trading for $120 per share. What is the new par value and the estimated market price of the stock after the split?

A. *$12.50 ($50 ÷ 4) par value; $30 ($120 ÷ 4) estimated market price.*

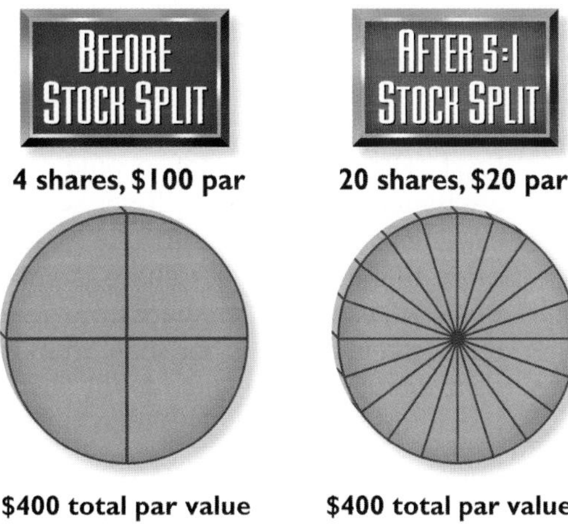

HOW BUSINESSES MAKE MONEY

The "Razor Blade" Tactic

A popular and effective business tactic is to link a base product to its accessories, often termed the "razor blade" tactic. Under this approach, the base product is often sold for a low profit margin, while the profits are earned on the accessories. The key to this approach is eliminating competition for the accessory products by technically or psychologically linking them to the base product. Examples of this tactic include razors and blades, printers and printer cartridges, electronic game consoles and games, and movie tickets and concession items. This is also **Mattel, Inc.**'s business strategy for Barbie®. The Barbie doll is the base product, while all of Barbie's accessories are the major source of Mattel's profitability. The size of Barbie's "pink aisle" at the local toy store reveals the power of Mattel's razor blade tactic.

6 Analyze the impact of issuing common stock or bonds.

ANALYZING FINANCING ALTERNATIVES

Significant changes in the capital stock accounts can impact a shareholder's ownership interest in the firm. Such changes in the capital accounts can occur when there are significant corporate financing transactions. Shareholders should analyze the impact of proposed financing alternatives in order to evaluate the status of their ownership interests. To illustrate, assume that Manning International, Inc. has 500,000 shares of common stock outstanding and is seeking additional financing to support a $1,500,000 investment at the beginning of the year. The additional financing can be obtained by either issuing common stock at a price of $15 per share or by issuing 10% bonds with a $1,500,000 face value. Assume that the earnings before interest and taxes (EBIT) for the year is $1,220,000 without the impact of the financing. During the year, we assume that the financing will be invested to earn a 12% pretax return on investment. Which financing alternative is most beneficial to the stockholders? One consideration is the impact of financing alternatives on earnings per share. Earnings per share is the net income of the company divided by the outstanding shares during a period. Thus, the earnings per share is the earnings for each share of stock. Earnings per share is commonly used by stockholders to evaluate earnings across different companies, time periods, and alternatives. We will use earnings per share to evaluate different financing alternatives in the paragraphs to follow. In the next chapter, we will discuss earnings per share as it is used to evaluate different companies and time periods.

Exhibit 5 shows the impact on earnings per share for the two financing options compared to no financing. Both financing options create funds that can be invested to produce a pretax return of $180,000 ($1,500,000 × 12%). In the first column, there is no impact on income except for the before-tax return on investment. That is, the common stock issuance does not result in any reduction in net income. Taxes are deducted from the EBIT to obtain a net income of $840,000. Assume the additional 100,000 shares are issued at a price of $15 per share to obtain the $1,500,000 financing objective. The earnings per share is thus $1.40 ($840,000 ÷ 600,000 shares). Compared to the third column, this earnings per share is smaller than the $1.46 ($732,000 ÷ 500,000 shares, rounded) earnings per share from assuming that the financing was never obtained. The reduction in earnings per share from issuing more common stock is termed *earnings per share dilution*. Shareholders will wish to avoid dilution. Shareholders can avoid dilution in this case when common stock is issued at a higher price (reducing the number of shares offered), or the investment earns a higher return on investment. For example, if the common stock was issued at a price of $50 per share, an additional 30,000 shares ($1,500,000 ÷ $50 per share) would be issued. Under this assumed share price, the

Exhibit 5

Common Stock and Bond Financing Alternatives on Earnings per Share

	$15 per Share Common Stock Financing	10% Bond Financing	No Financing
Earnings before interest and taxes—base case (EBIT)	$1,220,000	$1,220,000	$1,220,000
Return on investment (12% × $1,500,000)	180,000	180,000	—
Interest on bonds (10% × $1,500,000)	—	(150,000)	—
Earnings before taxes	$1,400,000	$1,250,000	$1,220,000
Income tax (@40%)	560,000	500,000	488,000
Net income	$ 840,000	$ 750,000	$ 732,000
Base number of shares outstanding	500,000	500,000	500,000
Plus additional shares issued	100,000		
Total shares outstanding	600,000	500,000	500,000
Earnings per share (EPS)	$ 1.40	$ 1.50	$ 1.46

earnings per share would increase from $1.46 in the base case to $1.58 ($840,000 ÷ 530,000 shares, rounded). This increase in earnings per share is termed *accretion*.

The second column shows the earnings per share from issuing bonds. In addition to the $180,000 return on investment, the bond interest expense of $150,000 (10% × $1,500,000) must be deducted from the EBIT before deducting taxes. The net income after deducting taxes would be $750,000. With bond financing, the number of common shares outstanding would remain unchanged. Thus, the earnings would be $1.50 per share ($750,000 ÷ 500,000 shares). As can be seen in this example, the bond alternative avoids dilution.[6] For bond financing, the EPS will fall below the no financing option (third column) whenever the return on investment is less than the interest on the bonds. Thus, firms would not borrow money to invest in projects with investment returns less than the interest rate.

Describe the financial statement effects of cash dividends and stock dividends.

ACCOUNTING FOR DIVIDENDS

When a board of directors declares a cash dividend, it authorizes the distribution of a portion of the corporation's cash to stockholders. When a board of directors declares a stock dividend, it authorizes the distribution of a portion of its stock. In both cases, the declaration of a dividend reduces the retained earnings of the corporation.[7]

Cash Dividends

A cash distribution of earnings by a corporation to its shareholders is called a **cash dividend**. Although dividends may be paid in the form of other assets, cash dividends are the most common form.

6 A bond or other security that avoids dilution is also called "antidilutive."

7 In rare cases, when a corporation is reducing its operations or going out of business, a dividend may be a distribution of paid-in capital. Such a dividend is called a *liquidating dividend*.

A corporation must usually meet the following three conditions in order to pay a cash dividend:

1. Sufficient retained earnings
2. Sufficient cash
3. Formal action by the board of directors

A large amount of retained earnings does not always mean that a corporation is able to pay dividends. As we indicated earlier in the chapter, the balances of the cash and retained earnings accounts are often unrelated. Thus, a large retained earnings account does not mean that there is cash available to pay dividends.

A corporation's board of directors is not required by law to declare dividends. This is true, even if both retained earnings and cash are large enough to justify a dividend. However, many corporations try to maintain a stable dividend record in order to make their stock attractive to investors. Although dividends may be paid once a year or semiannually, most corporations pay dividends quarterly. In years of high profits, a corporation may declare a *special* or *extra* dividend.

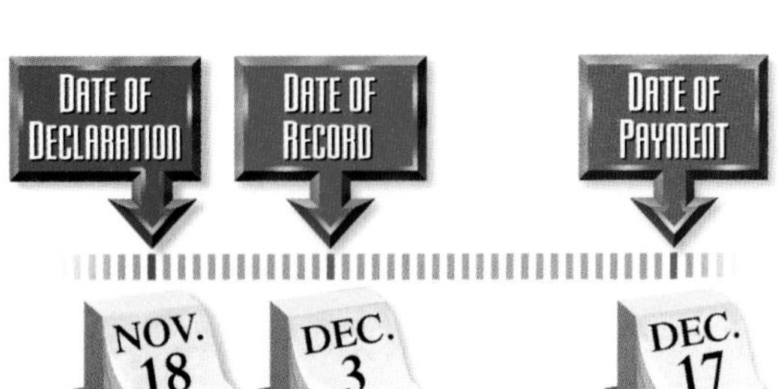

Board of directors takes action to declare dividends.

ENTRY:
Debit *Cash Dividends*
Credit *Cash Dividends Payable*

Ownership of shares determines who receives dividend (no entry required).

Dividend is paid.

ENTRY:
Debit *Cash Dividends Payable*
Credit *Cash*

You may have seen announcements of dividend declarations in financial newspapers or investor services. An example of such an announcement is shown below.

On November 18, the board of directors of Mattel Inc. declared a quarterly cash dividend of $0.45 per share payable on December 17 to shareholders of record on December 3.

This announcement includes three important dates: the *date of declaration* (November 18), the *date of record* (December 3), and the *date of payment* (December 17). During the period of time between the record date and the payment date, the stock price is usually quoted as selling *ex-dividends*. This means that, since the date of record has passed, a new investor will not receive the dividend.

To illustrate, assume that on *December 1* the board of directors of Hiber Corporation declares the following quarterly cash dividends. The date of record is *December 10*, and the date of payment is *January 2*.

	Dividend per Share	Total Dividends
Preferred Stock, $100 par, 5,000 shares outstanding	$2.50	$12,500
Common stock, $10 par, 100,000 shares outstanding	0.30	30,000
Total		$42,500

Hiber Corporation records the $42,500 liability for the dividends on December 1, the declaration date, as follows:[8]

Dec. 1	Retained Earnings	42,500	
	Cash Dividends Payable		42,500

8 Alternatively, the debit could be to "Cash Dividends," which is then closed to Retained Earnings.

No entry is required on the date of record, December 10, since this date merely determines which stockholders will receive the dividend. On the date of payment, January 2, the corporation records the $42,500 payment of the dividends as follows:

SCF	BS	IS
F↓	A↓ L↓	—

Jan. 2	Cash Dividends Payable	42,500	
	Cash		42,500

If Hiber Corporation's fiscal year ends December 31, Cash Dividends Payable will be listed on the December 31 balance sheet as a current liability.

If a corporation that holds treasury stock declares a cash dividend, the dividends are not paid on the treasury shares. To do so would place the corporation in the position of earning income through dealing with itself. For example, if Hiber Corporation in the preceding illustration had held 5,000 shares of its own common stock, the cash dividends on the common stock would have been $28,500 [(100,000 − 5,000) × $0.30] instead of $30,000.

© PHOTODISC COLLECTION/GETTY IMAGES

Stock Dividends

A distribution of shares of stock to stockholders is called a **stock dividend**. Usually, such distributions are in common stock and are issued to holders of common stock. Stock dividends are different from cash dividends, in that there is no distribution of cash or other assets to stockholders.

The effect of a stock dividend on the stockholders' equity of the issuing corporation is to transfer retained earnings to paid-in capital. For public corporations, the amount transferred from retained earnings to paid-in capital is normally the *fair value* (market price) of the shares issued in the stock dividend.[9] To illustrate, assume that the stockholders' equity accounts of Hendrix Corporation as of December 15 are as follows:

Common stock, $20 par (2,000,000 shares issued)	$40,000,000
Paid-in capital in excess of par—common stock	9,000,000
Retained earnings	26,600,000

On December 15, the board of directors declares a stock dividend of 5% or 100,000 shares (2,000,000 shares × 5%) to be issued on January 10 to stockholders of record on December 31. The market price of the stock on the declaration date is $31 a share. The declaration is recorded as follows:[10]

SCF	BS	IS
—	SE↑↓	—

Retained Earnings	3,100,000*	
Stock Dividends Distributable		2,000,000**
Paid-In Capital in Excess of Par—Common Stock		1,100,000

* (100,000 shares × $31 market price)
** (100,000 × $20 par)

The stock dividends distributable account is listed in the Paid-In Capital section of the balance sheet. Thus, the effect of the stock dividend is to transfer $3,100,000 of retained earnings to paid-in capital.

9 The use of fair market value is justified as long as the number of shares issued for the stock dividend is small (less than 25% of the shares outstanding).

10 Alternatively, the debit could be to "Stock Dividend," which is then closed to Retained Earnings.

On January 10, the number of shares outstanding is increased by 100,000 by the following entry to record the issue of the stock:

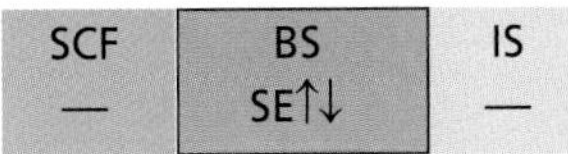

Jan. 10	Stock Dividends Distributable	2,000,000	
	Common Stock		2,000,000

A stock dividend does not change the assets, liabilities, or total stockholders' equity of the corporation. Likewise, it does not change a stockholder's proportionate interest (equity) in the corporation. For example, if a stockholder owned 1,000 of a corporation's 10,000 shares outstanding, the stockholder owns 10% (1,000/10,000) of the corporation. After declaring a 6% stock dividend, the corporation will issue 600 additional shares (10,000 shares × 6%), and the total shares outstanding will be 10,600. The stockholder of 1,000 shares will receive 60 additional shares and will now own 1,060 shares, which is still a 10% equity interest.

Describe financial statement presentations of stockholders' equity.

REPORTING STOCKHOLDERS' EQUITY

Significant changes in stockholders' equity are reported for the period in which they occur. These changes are reported in a **statement of stockholders' equity**. This statement is often prepared in a columnar format, where each column represents a major stockholders' equity classification. Changes in each classification are then described in the left-hand column, starting with the beginning balance in the first row and ending with the ending balance in the last row. Exhibit 6 illustrates the statement of stockholders' equity for Mattel, Inc. Most corporations report changes in retained earnings by preparing a separate Retained Earnings column in the statement of stockholders' equity, as shown for Mattel in Exhibit 6. The beginning balance of the retained earnings is adjusted for net income (add) or loss (deduct) and dividends (deduct). Mattel, Inc., earned $573 million and paid dividends of $187 million during 2004, which caused Retained Earnings to increase by $386 million ($573 − $187).

Accumulated Other Comprehensive Income (Loss)

Note that one of the columns in Exhibit 6 is *Accumulated Other Comprehensive Income (Loss)*. This column includes an addition for other comprehensive income of $17 million. **Other comprehensive income (loss)** items include foreign currency items, pension liability adjustments, and unrealized gains and losses on investments.[11] GAAP requires these items to be separately disclosed from earnings. The cumulative effects of other comprehensive income items must be reported separately from retained earnings and paid-in capital on the balance sheet as **accumulated other comprehensive income (loss)**. In addition, companies must report **comprehensive income (loss)** for the period, which is the sum of traditional net income plus other comprehensive income. Comprehensive income for Mattel, Inc., was $590 million ($573 million + $17 million). When other comprehensive income items are not present, the income state-

11 We will illustrate the accounting for other comprehensive income for unrealized gains and losses on investments in the next chapter.

Exhibit 6

Statement of Stockholders' Equity

Mattel, Inc.
Statement of Stockholders' Equity
For the Year Ended December 31, 2004 (in millions)

	Common Stock	Additional Paid-In Capital	Treasury Stock	Retained Earnings	Accumulated Other Comprehensive Loss	Total Stockholders' Equity
Balance, December 31, 2003	$441.00	$1,599.00	$(244)	$ 707	$(287)	$2,216
Comprehensive income:						
Net income				573		573
Other comprehensive income items					17	17
Comprehensive income				573	17	590
Purchase of treasury stock			(255)			(255)
Issuance of treasury stock		(6)	26			20
Issuance of common stock for exercise of stock options	0.20	1.80				2
Dividends declared on common stock				(187)		(187)
Balance, December 31, 2004	$441.20	$1,594.80	$(473)	$1,093	$(270)	$2,386

ment and balance sheet formats are similar to those we have illustrated in this and preceding chapters.

In the 2004 edition of *Accounting Trends & Techniques*, over 97% of the surveyed companies reported other comprehensive income. Over 80% of these companies disclosed other comprehensive income in the statement of stockholders' equity, such as illustrated for Mattel. Alternatively, companies may report comprehensive income on the income statement or in a separate statement of comprehensive income.

Reporting Stockholders' Equity on the Balance Sheet

International Perspective Balance sheets prepared under International Accounting Standards report a line item for net assets, which is the difference between a company's assets and liabilities.

The Stockholders' Equity section of the balance sheet is illustrated for Mattel, Inc., in Exhibit 7. Notice that the balances shown in the last row of the statement of stockholders' equity in Exhibit 6 are the balances that are disclosed on the balance sheet in Exhibit 7. The balance sheet also commonly discloses the authorized, issued, and outstanding shares, as well as the par value of various classes of stock. In addition, relevant rights and privileges of the various classes of stock outstanding must be disclosed.[12] Examples of types of information that must be disclosed include dividend and liquidation preferences, rights to participate in earnings, conversion rights, and redemption rights. Such information may be disclosed on the face of the balance sheet or in the accompanying notes.

12 *Statement of Financial Accounting Standards No. 129*, "Disclosure Information about Capital Structure" (Norwalk, CT: Financial Accounting Standards Board, 1997).

Exhibit 7

Stockholders' Equity Section of the Balance Sheet

Mattel, Inc.
Stockholders' Equity
December 31, 2004 (in millions)

Common stock, $1.00 par value, 1.0 billion shares authorized; 441.2 million shares issued	$ 441.2
Additional paid-in capital	1,594.8
Treasury stock at cost; 26 million shares	(473.0)
Retained earnings	1,093.0
Accumulated other comprehensive loss	(270.0)
Total stockholders' equity	$ 2,386.0

Compute and interpret the dividend yield and dividend payout ratio on common stock.

ANALYZE DIVIDENDS

Shareholders and analysts evaluate both the *amount* of dividends paid and the likelihood that the dividends will be *maintained* in the future. The dividend yield measures the amount, while the dividend payout ratio can be used to evaluate dividend maintenance.

Dividend Yield

The amount of the cash dividend can be evaluated as a rate of return on the value of an investment. This rate of return is called a **dividend yield**. Although the dividend yield can be computed for both preferred and common stock, it is most often computed for common stock. This is because most preferred stock has a stated dividend rate or amount. In contrast, the dividend and market price of common stock normally varies with the profitability of the corporation.

The dividend yield is computed by dividing the annual dividend paid per share of common stock by the market price per share of common stock at a specific date, as shown below.

$$\text{Dividend Yield} = \frac{\text{Annual Cash Dividend per Share of Common Stock}}{\text{Market Price per Share of Common Stock}}$$

To illustrate, the market price of Mattel, Inc., common stock was $18.89 as of the close of business, January 10, 2005. During the past year, Mattel had paid dividends of $0.45 per share. Thus, the dividend yield of Mattel's common stock is 2.38% ($0.45/$18.89). Because the market price of a corporation's stock will vary from day to day, its dividend yield will also vary from day to day. Fortunately, the dividend yield is provided with newspaper listings of market prices and most Internet quotation services, such as from Yahoo's Finance Web site.

The recent dividend yields for some selected companies are as follows:

Company	Dividend Yield (%)
AT&T Corporation	5.06
Duke Energy Corporation	4.46
General Motors	8.10
Hewlett-Packard Company	1.05
Home Depot Inc.	0.82
Oracle Corporation	None
The Coca-Cola Company	1.00

As can be seen, the dividend yield varies widely across firms. Which dividend yield is right for an investor? The answer depends on the investor's objectives. The dividend yield on common stock is of special interest to investors whose main objective is to receive a current dividend return on their investment. In addition, a stock with a healthy dividend yield should be less likely to decline significantly in market price, because the increasing yield would attract buyers. However, a high dividend yield also restricts a company's growth because cash is used for dividends rather than for business objectives. Investors must also be careful in purchasing common stock with very high dividend yields, such as with General Motors. Such high dividends may be "too good to be true." The high dividend yield may not be *safe*, meaning that financial difficulties may force management to reduce the dividend in the future.

In contrast, investors whose main objective is a rapid increase in the market price of their investments may not desire a high dividend yield. For example, growth companies often do not pay dividends, but instead, reinvest their earnings in research and development, such as with Oracle Corporation. Investors expect such stocks to increase in market price as a result of this reinvestment. Since many factors affect stock prices, an investment tactic relying solely on increases in market prices is more risky than a tactic based on dividend yields.

Dividend Payout Ratio

Investors purchasing common stock for their dividends need to assess the likelihood that the existing dividend can be maintained, which is termed *dividend safety*. While evaluating the safety of the dividend involves many considerations, one important measure is the amount of the dividend as a percent of net income. The **dividend payout ratio** is the ratio of the cash dividend to the net income of the company, determined as follows:

$$\text{Dividend Payout Ratio} = \frac{\text{Annual Cash Dividends}}{\text{Annual Net Income}} \text{ or } \frac{\text{Annual Cash Dividend per Share}}{\text{Annual Earnings per Share}}$$

To illustrate, Mattel, Inc., recently reported earnings of \$537.6 million and paid cash dividends of \$171.3 million. The dividend payout ratio would be as follows:

$$\frac{\$171.3}{\$537.6} = 31.9\%$$

This ratio means that Mattel paid out more than 30 percent of its annual earnings in dividends. This is a reasonable payout ratio that would be considered maintainable. In contrast, General Motors is paying dividends in the midst of losses, which might not be considered sustainable in the long term.

Exhibit 8 shows the dividend payout ratios for a number of different industries. As can be seen, the dividend policies are not consistent across industries. Indeed, some industries, such as telecommunications, are paying out more in dividends than they are earning. They cannot sustain this payout ratio in the long term. As of this writing, some telecommunication companies are experiencing low profitability, while dividends have yet to be cut to reflect this reality. In contrast, software and consumer electronics industries have very small payout ratios, which reflect their high internal growth prospects. That is, management from these industries choose to retain earnings for financing growth, rather than pay them out as dividends.

Exhibit 8

Dividend Payout Ratios for Selected Industries

Industry (large companies only)	Dividend Payout Ratio (%)
Airlines	0*
Automotive	19
Consumer electronics	5
Consumer products	34
Electric and gas utilities	21
Electronic manufacturing	9
Financial services	11
Food and beverage	8
Petrochemical	4
Retail	9
Software	2
Telecommunications	186

* Due to losses, the industry pays no dividends

FOCUS ON CASH FLOW

Capital Stock and Dividends

Changes in the stockholders' equity accounts can have a significant impact on cash flows. Issuing common stock will increase cash flows, while purchasing treasury stock will reduce cash flows. In addition, cash dividends reduce cash flows. Changes in stockholders' equity and dividends are disclosed in the Financing Activities section of the statement of cash flows, as illustrated for **Mattel, Inc.**, below.

Mattel, Inc.
Partial Statement of Cash Flows—Financing Activities
For the Year Ended December 31, 2004 (in millions)

Cash Flows from Financing Activities:	
Payments of short-term borrowings, net	$ 6.3
Payments of long-term debt	(52.3)
Purchase of treasury stock	(255.0)
Payment of dividends on common stock	(187.0)
Proceeds from exercise of stock options and sale of treasury stock	22.0
Net cash flows used for financing activities	$(466.0)

As can be seen from the figures in color, Mattel has paid over $187 million in dividends and another $255 million to purchase treasury stock. The $22 million received from exercising stock options and issuing treasury stock are proceeds from common stock issuances paid by employees exercising stock options.

SUMMARY OF LEARNING GOALS

1 **Describe the nature of the corporate form of organization.** Corporations have a separate legal existence, transferable units of stock, and limited stockholders' liability. Corporations are subject to federal income tax.

The documents included in forming a corporation include an application of incorporation, articles of incorporation, and bylaws. Costs often incurred in organizing a corporation include legal fees, taxes, state incorporation fees, and promotional costs. Such costs are treated as an expense.

2 List the major sources of paid-in capital, including the various classes of stock. The main source of paid-in capital is from issuing stock. The two primary classes of stock are common stock and preferred stock. Preferred stock may be cumulative or noncumulative. In addition to the issuance of stock, paid-in capital may arise from treasury stock transactions.

3 Describe the financial statement effects of issuing stock. When a corporation issues stock at par for cash, the cash account is debited and the class of stock issued is credited for its par amount. When a corporation issues stock at more than par, Paid-In Capital in Excess of Par is credited for the difference between the cash received and the par value of the stock. When stock is issued in exchange for assets other than cash, the assets acquired should be recorded at their fair market value.

When no-par stock is issued, the entire proceeds are credited to the stock account. No-par stock may be assigned a stated value per share, and the excess of the proceeds over the stated value may be credited to Paid-In Capital in Excess of Stated Value.

4 Describe the financial statement effects of treasury stock transactions. When a corporation buys its own stock, the cost method of accounting is normally used. Treasury Stock is debited for its cost, and Cash is credited. If the stock is resold, Treasury Stock is credited for its cost, and any difference between the cost and the selling price is normally debited or credited to Paid-In Capital from Sale of Treasury Stock.

5 Describe the effect of stock splits on the financial statements. When a corporation reduces the par or stated value of its common stock and issues a proportionate number of additional shares, a stock split has occurred. There are no changes in the balances of any corporation accounts, and no entry is required for a stock split.

6 Analyze the impact of issuing common stock or bonds. Common stock dilution occurs when a common stock issuance results in an earnings per share decline. Dilution can be avoided by issuing common stock when the stock price is high. When capital is raised through debt, a return in excess of the interest rate will cause earnings per share to increase. In comparing the earnings per share between a debt or common stock offering, the common stock offering will be favored when the stock price is high. The opposite is the case when the common stock price is low.

7 Describe the financial statement effects of cash dividends and stock dividends. The entry to record a declaration of cash dividends debits Retained Earnings and credits Dividends Payable for each class of stock. The payment of dividends is recorded in the normal manner. When a stock dividend is declared, Retained Earnings is debited for the fair value of the stock to be issued. Stock Dividends Distributable is credited for the par or stated value of the common stock to be issued. The difference between the fair value of the stock and its par or stated value is credited to Paid-In Capital in Excess of Par–Common Stock. When the stock is issued on the date of payment, Stock Dividends Distributable is debited, and Common Stock is credited for the par or stated value of the stock issued.

8 Describe financial statement presentations of stockholders' equity. The statement of stockholders' equity discloses changes in the stockholders' equity accounts, in columnar format. The balance of each account at the bottom of the column reconciles with the balance sheet disclosure of each account. The statement of stockholders' equity will often include a column for accumulated other comprehensive income (loss), which identifies the other comprehensive income (loss) items for the period. These items include foreign currency items, pension liability adjustments, and unrealized gains and losses on investments. These items are recognized for their impact on stockholders' equity directly, rather than as net income on retained earnings.

9 Compute and interpret the dividend yield and dividend payout ratio on common stock. The dividend yield indicates the rate of return to stockholders in terms of cash dividend distributions. It is computed by dividing the annual dividends paid per share of common stock by the market price per share at a specific date. This ratio is of special interest to investors whose main objective is to receive a current dividend return on their investment.

The dividend payout ratio measures dividend safety by computing the percentage of net income paid out in dividends. When this ratio is high, or exceeds 1.0, it suggests a dividend rate that will be difficult to maintain.

GLOSSARY

Accumulated other comprehensive income (loss) The cumulative effect of other comprehensive income items disclosed in the Stockholders' Equity section of the balance sheet.

Cash dividend A cash distribution of earnings by a corporation to its shareholders.

Common stock The stock outstanding when a corporation has issued only one class of stock.

Comprehensive income (loss) Net income and other comphensive income items combined together. Often disclosed on the statement of stockholders' equity.

Cumulative preferred stock A class of preferred stock that has a right to receive regular dividends that have been passed (not declared) before any common stock dividends are paid.

Dividend payout ratio A ratio computed by dividing the annual cash dividends (per share) by the annual net income (per share); indicates dividend safety.

Dividend yield A ratio computed by dividing the annual dividends paid per share of common stock by the market price per share at a specific date; indicates the rate of return to stockholders in terms of cash dividend distributions.

Other comprehensive income (loss) Required disclosures that change the stockholders' equity, but are not disclosed as net income or retained earnings. These items include foreign currency items, pension liability adjustments, and unrealized gains and losses on investments.

Outstanding stock The stock in the hands of stockholders.

Par The monetary amount printed on a stock certificate.

Preferred stock A class of stock with preferential rights over common stock.

Premium The excess of the issue price of a stock over its par value.

Stated value A value, similar to par value, approved by the board of directors of a corporation for no-par stock.

Statement of stockholders' equity This statement is often prepared in a columnar format, where each column shows the change in each major stockholders' equity classification.

Stock dividend A distribution of shares of stock to stockholders.

Stock option The right to purchase common stock at a fixed price over a limited period of time, often used to provide employee incentives to enhance stock price.

Stock split A reduction in the par or stated value of a common stock and the issuance of a proportionate number of additional shares.

Treasury stock Stock that a corporation has once issued and then reacquires.

ILLUSTRATIVE ACCOUNTING APPLICATION PROBLEM

Altenburg Inc. is a lighting fixture wholesaler located in Arizona. During its current fiscal year, ended December 31, 2007, Altenburg Inc. completed the following selected transactions:

Feb. 3	Purchased 2,500 shares of its own common stock at $26, recording the stock at cost. (Prior to the purchase, there were 40,000 shares of $20 par common stock outstanding.)
May 1	Declared a semiannual dividend of $1 on the 10,000 shares of preferred stock and a 30¢ dividend on the common stock to stockholders of record on May 31, payable on June 15.
June 15	Paid the cash dividends.
Sept. 23	Sold 1,000 shares of treasury stock at $28, receiving cash.
Nov. 1	Declared semiannual dividends of $1 on the preferred stock and 30¢ on the common stock. In addition, a 5% common stock dividend was declared on the common stock outstanding, to be capitalized at the fair market value of the common stock, which is estimated at $30.
Dec. 1	Paid the cash dividends and issued the certificates for the common stock dividend.

Instructions

Journalize the entries to record the transactions for Altenburg Inc.

Solution

2007			
Feb. 3	Treasury Stock	65,000	
	Cash		65,000
May 1	Retained Earnings	21,250	
	Cash Dividends Payable		21,250
	(10,000 × $1) + [(40,000 − 2,500) × $0.30]		

June 15	Cash Dividends Payable	21,250	
	Cash		21,250
Sept. 23	Cash	28,000	
	Treasury Stock		26,000
	Paid-In Capital from Sale of Treasury Stock		2,000
Nov. 1	Retained Earnings	21,550	
	Cash Dividends Payable		21,550
	(10,000 × $1) + [(40,000 − 1,500) × $0.30]		
1	Retained Earnings	57,750	
	Stock Dividends Distributable		38,500
	Paid-In Capital in Excess of Par		19,250
	(40,000 − 1,500) × 5% × $30		
Dec. 1	Cash Dividends Payable	21,550	
	Stock Dividends Distributable	38,500	
	Cash		21,550
	Common Stock		38,500

SELF-STUDY QUESTIONS

Answers at end of chapter

1. If a corporation has outstanding 1,000 shares of $9 cumulative preferred stock of $100 par and dividends have been passed for the preceding three years, what is the amount of preferred dividends that must be declared in the current year before a dividend can be declared on common stock?
   A. $9,000 C. $36,000
   B. $27,000 D. $45,000
2. Paid-in capital for a corporation may arise from which of the following sources?
   A. Issuing cumulative preferred stock
   B. Declaring a stock dividend
   C. Selling the corporation's treasury stock
   D. All of the above
3. If a corporation reacquires its own stock, the stock is listed on the balance sheet in the:
   A. Current Assets section.
   B. Long-Term Liabilities section.
   C. Stockholders' Equity section.
   D. Investments section.
4. A corporation has issued 25,000 shares of $100 par common stock and holds 3,000 of these shares as treasury stock. If the corporation declares a $2 per share cash dividend, what amount will be recorded as cash dividends?
   A. $22,000 C. $44,000
   B. $25,000 D. $50,000
5. A corporation declares a cash dividend of $2.40 per common share for the current year. The market price of common stock is $48 per share at the end of the year, while the book value (stockholders' equity divided by shares outstanding) per share is $32 per share. The earnings per share is $4.00 for the current year. Determine the dividend yield and dividend payout ratio (in that order).
   A. 60%, 5% C. 5%, 60%
   B. 5%, 67% D. 7.5%, 60%

DISCUSSION QUESTIONS

1. Describe the stockholders' liability to creditors of a corporation.
2. Why is it said that the earnings of a corporation are subject to *double taxation*? Discuss.
3. Why are most large businesses organized as corporations?
4. Of two corporations organized at approximately the same time and engaged in competing businesses, one issued $50 par common stock, and the other issued $1 par common stock. Do the par designations provide any indication as to which stock is preferable as an investment? Explain.
5. **a.** Differentiate between common stock and preferred stock.
   b. Describe briefly cumulative preferred stock.

6. A stockbroker advises a client to "buy cumulative preferred stock . . . . With that type of stock, . . . [you] will never have to worry about losing the dividends." Is the broker right?
7. What is the difference between the primary and secondary markets?
8. If common stock of $100 par is sold for $130, what is the $30 difference between the issue price and par called?
9. What are some factors that influence the market price of a corporation's stock?
10. When a corporation issues stock at a premium, is the premium income? Explain.
11. Land is acquired by a corporation for 15,000 shares of its $25 par common stock, which is currently selling for $70 per share on a national stock exchange. What accounts should be credited to record the transaction?
12. Indicate which of the following accounts would be reported as part of paid-in capital on the balance sheet:
    a. Retained Earnings
    b. Common Stock
    c. Preferred Stock
13. a. In what respect does treasury stock differ from unissued stock?
    b. How should treasury stock be presented on the balance sheet?
14. A corporation reacquires 5,000 shares of its own $40 par common stock for $370,000, recording it at cost. (a) What effect does this transaction have on revenue or expense of the period? (b) What effect does it have on stockholders' equity?
15. The treasury stock in Question 14 is resold for $400,000. (a) What is the effect on the corporation's revenue of the period? (b) What is the effect on stockholders' equity?
16. What is the primary purpose of a stock split?
17. Explain how shareholders can avoid earnings per share dilution from common stock issuances?
18. What are the conditions for declaring and paying a cash dividend?
19. The dates associated with a cash dividend are October 1, November 15, and December 30. Identify each date.
20. A corporation with both cumulative preferred stock and common stock outstanding has a substantial credit balance in its retained earnings account at the beginning of the current fiscal year. Although net income for the current year is sufficient to pay the preferred dividend of $100,000 each quarter and a common dividend of $300,000 each quarter, the board of directors declares dividends only on the preferred stock. Suggest possible reasons for passing the dividends on the common stock.
21. An owner of 200 shares of Dunston Company common stock receives a stock dividend of four shares. (a) What is the effect of the stock dividend on the stockholder's proportionate interest (equity) in the corporation? (b) How does the total equity of 204 shares compare with the total equity of 200 shares before the stock dividend?
22. a. Where should a declared but unpaid cash dividend be reported on the balance sheet?
    b. Where should a declared but unissued stock dividend be reported on the balance sheet?
23. What is the purpose of the statement of stockholders' equity?
24. What is other comprehensive income, and how is it disclosed?

EXERCISES

Exercise 11-1

Market for common stock

Goals **2, 9**

Use either the Internet or the newspaper to determine the following for The Coca-Cola Company:

a. What stock exchange trades the common stock?
b. What is the exchange abbreviation for the common stock?
c. What is the annual dividend per share?
d. What is the current market price?
e. What is the current dividend yield? Round percent to one decimal place.

Exercise 11-2

Dividends per share

Goal **2**

Preferred stock, 3rd year: $1.40

SPREADSHEET

Fiji Inc., a developer of radiology equipment, has stock outstanding as follows: 25,000 shares of 1% cumulative preferred stock of $100 par, and 250,000 shares of $50 par common. During its first five years of operations, the following amounts were distributed as dividends: first year, none; second year, $40,000; third year, $80,000; fourth year, $120,000; fifth year, $140,000. Calculate the dividends per share on each class of stock for each of the five years.

Exercise 11-3

Dividends per share

Goal 2

Preferred stock, 3rd year: $0.75

SPREADSHEET

Infinity.com, a software development firm, has stock outstanding as follows: 100,000 shares of 2% cumulative preferred stock of $20 par, and 50,000 shares of $100 par common. During its first five years of operations, the following amounts were distributed as dividends: first year, none; second year, $45,000; third year, $110,000; fourth year, $130,000; fifth year, $180,000. Calculate the dividends per share on each class of stock for each of the five years.

Exercise 11-4

Entries for issuing par stock

Goal 3

On July 7, Sloth Inc., a marble contractor, issued for cash 40,000 shares of $25 par common stock at $40, and on October 20, it issued for cash 15,000 shares of $100 par preferred stock at $120.

a. Journalize the entries for July 7 and October 20.
b. What is the total amount invested (total paid-in capital) by all stockholders as of October 20?

Exercise 11-5

Entries for issuing no-par stock

Goal 3

On February 20, Mudguard Corp., a carpet wholesaler, issued for cash 100,000 shares of no-par common stock (with a stated value of $10) at $15, and on April 30, it issued for cash 4,000 shares of $25 par preferred stock at $30.

a. Journalize the entries for February 20 and April 30, assuming that the common stock is to be credited with the stated value.
b. What is the total amount invested (total paid-in capital) by all stockholders as of April 30?

Exercise 11-6

Issuing stock for assets other than cash

Goal 3

On August 29, Welch Corporation, a wholesaler of hydraulic lifts, acquired land in exchange for 10,000 shares of $15 par common stock with a current market price of $28. Journalize the entry to record the transaction.

Exercise 11-7

Issuing stock

Goal 3

Pearl.com, with an authorization of 50,000 shares of preferred stock and 200,000 shares of common stock, completed several transactions involving its stock on May 1, the first day of operations. The trial balance at the close of the day follows:

Cash	475,000	
Land	45,000	
Buildings	80,000	
Preferred 4% Stock, $50 par		100,000
Paid-In Capital in Excess of Par—Preferred Stock		25,000
Common Stock, $100 par		400,000
Paid-In Capital in Excess of Par—Common Stock		75,000
	600,000	600,000

All shares within each class of stock were sold at the same price. The preferred stock was issued in exchange for the land and buildings.

Journalize the two entries to record the transactions summarized in the trial balance.

Exercise 11-8

Issuing stock

Goal 3

Calvert Products Inc., a wholesaler of office products, was organized on January 5 of the current year, with an authorization of 80,000 shares of 2% noncumulative preferred stock, $50 par and 250,000 shares of $100 par common stock. The following selected transactions were completed during the first year of operations.

Jan.	5	Issued 10,000 shares of common stock at par for cash.
	18	Issued 100 shares of common stock at par to an attorney in payment of legal fees for organizing the corporation.
Feb.	13	Issued 4,250 shares of common stock in exchange for land, buildings, and equipment with fair market prices of $50,000, $280,000, and $120,000, respectively.
Apr.	1	Issued 3,500 shares of preferred stock at $52 for cash.

Journalize the transactions.

Exercise 11-9

Issuing an IPO

Goals **2, 3**

On December 15, 2004, Las Vegas Sands Corp., owner of the Venetian Hotel in Las Vegas, conducted an initial public offering of 23.8 million shares of $0.001 par value common stock at a price of $29 per share. The price of the common stock rose to $46.56 by the end of the day's trading on the New York Stock Exchange. Goldman Sachs Group, Inc., and Citicorp were the lead underwriters of the initial public offering.

a. Journalize the entry for the initial public offering, assuming an underwriting fee of 0.5% of the IPO proceeds to be paid to the underwriters.
b. What services do Goldman Sachs Group, Inc., and Citigroup provide in the IPO?
c. Describe the primary and secondary markets in this transaction.
d. Who received the increase in share price on the first day of trading, and what was their percentage return?

Exercise 11-10

Treasury stock transactions

Goal **4**

b. $5,500 credit

Crystal Springs Inc. bottles and distributes spring water. On June 1 of the current year, Crystal reacquired 2,500 shares of its common stock at $60 per share. On July 8, Crystal sold 1,500 of the reacquired shares at $65 per share. The remaining 1,000 shares were sold at $58 per share on November 2.

a. Journalize the transactions of June 1, July 8, and November 2.
b. What is the balance in Paid-In Capital from Sale of Treasury Stock on December 31 of the current year?
c. For what reasons might Crystal Springs have purchased the treasury stock?

Exercise 11-11

Treasury stock transactions

Goals **4, 8**

b. $50,000 credit

Geyser Inc. develops and produces spraying equipment for lawn maintenance and industrial uses. On March 3 of the current year, Geyser Inc. reacquired 7,500 shares of its common stock at $120 per share. On August 11, 4,000 of the reacquired shares were sold at $130 per share, and on October 3, 2,500 of the reacquired shares were sold at $124.

a. Journalize the transactions of March 3, August 11, and October 3.
b. What is the balance in Paid-In Capital from Sale of Treasury Stock on December 31 of the current year?
c. What is the balance in Treasury Stock on December 31 of the current year?
d. How will the balance in Treasury Stock be reported on the balance sheet?

Exercise 11-12

Treasury stock transactions

Goals **4, 8**

b. $1,500 credit

Aspen Inc. manages resort properties. On August 1 of the current year, Aspen Inc. reacquired 12,000 shares of its common stock at $36 per share. On September 23, Aspen Inc. sold 7,500 of the reacquired shares at $38 per share. The remaining 4,500 shares were sold at $33 per share on December 29.

a. Journalize the transactions of August 1, September 23, and December 29.
b. What is the balance in Paid-In Capital from Sale of Treasury Stock on December 31 of the current year?

c. Where will the balance in Paid-In Capital from Sale of Treasury Stock be reported on the balance sheet?
d. For what reasons might Aspen Inc. have purchased the treasury stock?

Exercise 11-13

Effect of stock split

Goal 5

Golden Hearth Corporation wholesales ovens and ranges to restaurants throughout the Midwest. Golden Hearth Corporation, which had 25,000 shares of common stock outstanding, declared a 5-for-1 stock split (4 additional shares for each share issued).

a. What will be the number of shares outstanding after the split?
b. If the common stock had a market price of $165 per share before the stock split, what would be an approximate market price per share after the split?

Exercise 11-14

Common stock dilution

Goal 6

Triangle Media Group, Inc., issued 15,000 shares of $0.10 par value common stock at a price of $50 per share on January 1, 2007. The proceeds will be used to invest in a project that is expected to generate a 12% annual return. The base earnings per share without the impact of the new investment is $4.00 for each of the 135,000 common shares. Ignore income taxes.

a. Determine the estimated earnings per share for 2007, including the impact of the new investment.
b. Assume the return on the investment was only 4%. What would be the impact on earnings per share under this assumption?

Exercise 11-15

Common stock and bond financing alternatives

Goal 6

SPREADSHEET

Sunrise Developments, Inc., is considering two financing alternatives for a $9,500,000 retail complex. One option is to issue 250,000 shares of common stock at a price of $38 per share. The second option is to borrow $9,500,000 at an interest rate of 6%. The new complex is expected to yield a before-tax return of 10%. The before-tax earnings before considering either financing alternative is $6,250,000. There are 2,000,000 shares of common stock outstanding prior to considering financing alternatives. The tax rate is 20%.

a. Determine the estimated earnings per share impact from the two financing alternatives.
b. Which alternative has the most favorable impact on earnings per share?

Exercise 11-16

Effect of cash dividend and stock split

Goals 5, 7

Indicate whether the following actions would (+) increase, (−) decrease, or (0) not affect Indigo Inc.'s total assets, liabilities, and stockholders' equity:

	Assets	Liabilities	Stockholders' Equity
(1) Declaring a cash dividend	______	______	______
(2) Paying the cash dividend declared in (1)	______	______	______
(3) Authorizing and issuing stock certificates in a stock split	______	______	______
(4) Declaring a stock dividend	______	______	______
(5) Issuing stock certificates for the stock dividend declared in (4)	______	______	______

Exercise 11-17

Entries for cash dividends

Goal 7

The important dates in connection with a cash dividend of $120,000 on a corporation's common stock are February 13, March 15, and April 10. Record the entries required on each date.

Exercise 11-18

Entries for stock dividends

Goal **7**

b. (1) $13,250,000

(3) $43,828,000

Health Co. is an HMO for 12 businesses in the Chicago area. The following account balances appear on the balance sheet of Health Co.: Common stock (250,000 shares authorized), $100 par, $12,500,000; Paid-in capital in excess of par—common stock, $750,000; and Retained earnings, $30,578,000. The board of directors declared a 2% stock dividend when the market price of the stock was $110 per share. Health Co, reported no income or loss for the current year.

a. Journalize the entries for (1) the declaration of the dividend, capitalizing an amount equal to market value, and (2) the issuance of the stock certificates.

b. Determine the following amounts before the stock dividend was declared: (1) total paid-in capital, (2) total retained earnings, and (3) total stockholders' equity.

c. Determine the following amounts after the stock dividend was declared and closing entries were recorded at the end of the year: (1) total paid-in capital, (2) total retained earnings, and (3) total stockholders' equity.

Exercise 11-19

Selected stock and dividend transactions

Goals **5, 7**

Selected transactions completed by Indy Boating Supply Corporation during the current fiscal year are as follows:

Feb. 9 Split the common stock 3 for 1 and reduced the par from $120 to $40 per share. After the split, there were 900,000 common shares outstanding.

Apr. 10 Declared semiannual dividends of $1 on 12,000 shares of preferred stock and $0.05 on the common stock to stockholders of record on April 20, payable on May 1.

May 1 Paid the cash dividends.

Oct. 12 Declared semiannual dividends of $1 on the preferred stock and $0.15 on the common stock (before the stock dividend). In addition, a 1% common stock dividend was declared on the common stock outstanding. The fair market value of the common stock is estimated at $48.

Nov. 14 Paid the cash dividends and issued the certificates for the common stock dividend.

Journalize the transactions.

Exercise 11-20

Other comprehensive income

Goal **8**

A recent statement of comprehensive income for Caterpillar, Inc., was disclosed as follows (all amounts in millions):

Caterpillar, Inc.
Statement of Comprehensive Income
December 31, 2004

Net earnings	$ 2,035
Other comprehensive income:	
Foreign currency translation	141
Pension adjustment	(59)
Unrealized gains on investments	11
Total comprehensive income	$ 2,128

The balance sheet dated December 31, 2003, showed a retained earnings balance of $8,450 and an accumulated other comprehensive loss of $517. The company declared $548 in dividends during the fiscal year.

a. What is the total other comprehensive income or loss for Caterpillar for the fiscal year ended December 31, 2004?

b. What percent of total comprehensive income consists of other comprehensive income items? Round percent to one decimal place.

c. What was the December 31, 2004, balance of (1) Retained Earnings and (2) Accumulated Other Comprehensive Loss?

Exercise 11-21

Stockholders' Equity section of balance sheet

Goal **8**

Total stockholders' equity, $5,193,000

SPREADSHEET

Big Boy Toys Inc. retails racing products for BMWs, Porsches, and Ferraris. The following accounts and their balances appear in the ledger of Big Boy Toys Inc. on October 31, the end of the current year:

Common Stock, $4 par	$ 600,000
Paid-In Capital in Excess of Par—Common Stock	210,000
Paid-In Capital in Excess of Par—Preferred Stock	78,000
Paid-In Capital from Sale of Treasury Stock—Common	42,000
Preferred 2% Stock, $100 par	480,000
Retained Earnings	3,903,000
Treasury Stock—Common	120,000

Ten thousand shares of preferred and 250,000 shares of common stock are authorized. There are 12,000 shares of common stock held as treasury stock.

Prepare the Stockholders' Equity section of the balance sheet as of October 31, the end of the current year.

Exercise 11-22

Statement of stockholders' equity

Goal **8**

Total stockholders' equity, Dec. 31, $2,285,000

SPREADSHEET

The stockholders' equity T-accounts of Tender Heart Greeting Cards Inc. for the current fiscal year ended December 31, 2007, are as follows. Prepare a statement of stockholders' equity for the fiscal year ended December 31, 2007.

COMMON STOCK

			Jan. 1	Balance	500,000
			Mar. 13	Issued 50,000 shares	100,000
			Dec. 31	Balance	600,000

PAID-IN CAPITAL IN EXCESS OF PAR

			Jan. 1	Balance	400,000
			Mar. 13	Issued 50,000 shares	45,000
			Dec. 31	Balance	445,000

TREASURY STOCK

Apr. 30	Purchased 10,000 shares	25,000			

RETAINED EARNINGS

June 30	Dividend	25,000	Jan. 1	Balance	1,075,000
Dec. 30	Dividend	25,000	Dec. 31	Closing (net income)	240,000
			Dec. 31	Balance	1,265,000

Exercise 11-23

Statement of stockholders' equity and cash flows

Goals **8, 9**

Procter & Gamble is the largest manufacturer of consumer household products in the United States. The selected entries at the top of the following page were disclosed on the statement of stockholders' equity for a recent year:

(in 000,000s)	Common Stock	Preferred Stock	Additional Paid-In Capital	Accumulated Other Comprehensive Income	Retained Earnings	Total
Net earnings					$ 6,481	$ 6,481
Dividends to:						
Common shareholders					(2,408)	(2,408)
Preferred shareholders					(131)	(131)
Treasury purchases	$(80)		$ 33		(4,023)	(4,070)
Common stock issuances (option plan)	23		711			734
Other comprehensive income				$461		461

a. For all items except net earnings and other comprehensive income, identify the disclosure location, amount, and direction (inflow or outflow) on the statement of cash flows.
b. Determine the dividend payout ratio. Round percentage to one decimal place.
c. Determine the comprehensive income (loss).

Exercise 11-24

Interpret stock exchange listing

Goals **2, 9**

a. $110

The Wall Street Journal reported the following stock exchange information for General Electric Co. on January 18, 2005:

YTD % CHG	52 Weeks Hi	52 Weeks Lo	Stock	Sym	Div	Yld%	PE	Vol 100s	LAST	Net Chg
−1.5	37^{75}	28^{88}	GenElec	GE	.88	2.4	24	198977	35^{96}	+0.44

a. If you owned 500 shares of GE, what amount would you receive as a quarterly dividend?
b. Calculate and prove the dividend yield. Round to two decimal places.
c. What is GE's percentage change in market price from the January 17, 2005, close? Round to two decimal places.
d. What was the price of GE common stock at the beginning of the first trading day of the year? (*Hint:* Use the YTD % CHG column and the current price.)
e. If you bought 500 shares of GE at the close price on January 18, 2005, how much would it cost, and who gets the money?

Exercise 11-25

Dividend yield and dividend payout ratio

Goal **9**

At the market close of January 19, 2005, Bank of America Corp. had a closing stock price of $44.97. In addition, Bank of America had earnings per share of $3.76 and dividend per share was $1.80. Determine Bank of America's (a) dividend yield and (b) dividend payout ratio. Round percentages to one decimal place.

Exercise 11-26

Dividend yield and dividend payout ratio

Goal **9**

SPREADSHEET

General Motors Corporation had earnings per share of $5.62 for 2003 and $4.95 for 2004. In addition, the dividend was $2.00 per share during these two years. The market price for GM closed at $40.17 per share on December 31, 2004.

a. Determine the dividend yield for General Motors on December 31, 2004. Round percentages to two decimal places.
b. Determine the 2003 and 2004 dividend payout ratio for General Motors. Round percentages to one decimal place.
c. Interpret these measures.

Exercise 11-27

Dividend yield

Goal 9

SPREADSHEET

eBay Inc. developed a Web-based marketplace at http://www.ebay.com, in which individuals can buy and sell a variety of items. eBay also acquired PayPal, an online payments system that allows businesses and individuals to send and receive online payments securely. In a recent annual report, eBay published the following dividend policy:

> *We have never paid cash dividends on our stock, and currently anticipate that we will continue to retain any future earnings to finance the growth of our business.*

Given eBay's dividend policy, why would an investor be attracted to its stock?

ACCOUNTING APPLICATION PROBLEMS

Problem 11-1A

Dividends on preferred and common stock

Goal 2

1. Common dividends in 2003: $10,000

SPREADSHEET

Lemonds Corp. manufactures mountain bikes and distributes them through retail outlets in Oregon and Washington. Lemonds Corp. has declared the following annual dividends over a six-year period: 2003, $40,000; 2004, $18,000; 2005, $24,000; 2006, $27,000; 2007, $65,000; and 2008, $54,000. During the entire period, the outstanding stock of the company was composed of 25,000 shares of cumulative, 6% preferred stock, $20 par, and 40,000 shares of common stock, $1 par.

Instructions

1. Calculate the total dividends and the per-share dividends declared on each class of stock for each of the six years. There were no dividends in arrears on January 1, 2003. Summarize the data in tabular form, using the following column headings:

		Preferred Dividends		Common Dividends	
Year	**Total Dividends**	**Total**	**Per Share**	**Total**	**Per Share**
2003	$40,000				
2004	18,000				
2005	24,000				
2006	27,000				
2007	65,000				
2008	54,000				

2. Calculate the average annual dividend per share for each class of stock for the six-year period.
3. Assuming that the preferred stock was sold at par and common stock was sold at $8 at the beginning of the six-year period, calculate the average annual percentage return on initial shareholders' investment, based on the average annual dividend per share (a) for preferred stock and (b) for common stock.

Problem 11-2A

Stock transaction for corporate expansion

Goal 3

Diamond Optics produces medical lasers for use in hospitals. The following accounts and their balances appear in the ledger of Diamond Optics on September 30 of the current year:

Preferred 5% Stock, $100 par (20,000 shares authorized, 12,000 shares issued)	$1,200,000
Paid-In Capital in Excess of Par—Preferred Stock	180,000
Common Stock, $25 par (100,000 shares authorized, 72,000 shares issued)	1,800,000
Paid-In Capital in Excess of Par—Common Stock	240,000
Retained Earnings	3,572,500

At the annual stockholders' meeting on October 19, the board of directors presented a plan for modernizing and expanding plant operations at a cost of approximately $2,500,000. The plan provided (a) that the corporation borrow $780,000, (b) that 6,000 shares of the unissued preferred stock be issued through an underwriter, and (c) that a building, valued at $900,000, and the land on which it is located, valued at $120,000, be acquired in accordance with preliminary negotiations by the issuance of 24,000 shares of common stock. The plan was approved by the stockholders and accomplished by the following transactions:

Nov.	5	Borrowed $780,000 from Bozeman National Bank, giving a 7% mortgage note.
	20	Issued 6,000 shares of preferred stock, receiving $120 per share in cash from the underwriter.
	23	Issued 24,000 shares of common stock in exchange for land and a building, according to the plan.

No other transactions occurred during November.

Instructions

Journalize the entries to record the foregoing transactions.

Problem 11-3A

Selected stock transactions

Goals **3, 4, 7**

GENERAL LEDGER

Elk River Corporation sells and services pipe welding equipment in Wyoming. The following selected accounts appear in the ledger of Elk River Corporation on January 1, 2007, the beginning of the current fiscal year:

Preferred 2% Stock, $100 par (80,000 shares authorized, 18,000 shares issued)	$1,800,000
Paid-In Capital in Excess of Par—Preferred Stock	172,500
Common Stock, $10 par (800,000 shares authorized, 500,000 shares issued)	5,000,000
Paid-In Capital in Excess of Par—Common Stock	1,236,000
Retained Earnings	6,450,000

During the year, the corporation completed a number of transactions affecting the stockholders' equity. They are summarized as follows:

a. Purchased 60,000 shares of treasury common for $1,080,000.
b. Sold 20,000 shares of treasury common for $420,000.
c. Sold 7,000 shares of preferred 2% stock at $108.
d. Issued 40,000 shares of common stock at $23, receiving cash.
e. Sold 35,000 shares of treasury common for $595,000.
f. Declared cash dividends of $2 per share on preferred stock and $0.16 per share on common stock.
g. Paid the cash dividends.

Instructions

Journalize the entries to record the transactions. Identify each entry by letter.

Problem 11-4A

Entries for selected corporate transactions

Goals **3, 4, 7, 8**

Aerotronics Enterprises Inc. produces aeronautical navigation equipment. The stockholders' equity accounts of Aerotronics Enterprises Inc., with balances on January 1, 2007, are as follows:

Common Stock, $10 stated value (100,000 shares authorized, 60,000 shares issued)	$600,000
Paid-In Capital in Excess of Stated Value	150,000
Retained Earnings	497,750
Treasury Stock (7,500 shares, at cost)	120,000

4. Total stockholders' equity, $1,796,950

SPREADSHEET

GENERAL LEDGER

The following selected transactions occurred during the year:

Jan. 19	Paid cash dividends of $0.60 per share on the common stock. The dividend had been properly recorded when declared on December 28 of the preceding fiscal year for $31,500.
Feb. 2	Sold all of the treasury stock for $150,000.
Mar. 15	Issued 20,000 shares of common stock for $480,000.
July 30	Declared a 2% stock dividend on common stock, to be capitalized at the market price of the stock, which is $25 a share.
Aug. 30	Issued the certificates for the dividend declared on July 30.
Oct. 10	Purchased 5,000 shares of treasury stock for $105,000.
Dec. 30	Declared a $0.50-per-share dividend on common stock.

In addition, net income was $182,500 for the year.

Instructions

1. Enter the January 1 balances in T-accounts for the stockholders' equity accounts listed. Also prepare T-accounts for the following: Paid-In Capital from Sale of Treasury Stock; Stock Dividends Distributable.
2. Journalize the entries to record the transactions, and post to the six selected accounts.
3. Prepare a retained earnings statement for the year ended December 31, 2007.
4. Prepare the Stockholders' Equity section of the December 31, 2007, balance sheet.

Problem 11-5A

Entries for selected corporate transactions

Goals **3, 4, 5, 7**

SPREADSHEET

GENERAL LEDGER

Serra do Mar Corporation manufactures and distributes leisure clothing. Selected transactions completed by Serra do Mar during the current fiscal year are as follows:

Jan. 8	Split the common stock 3 for 1 and reduced the par from $18 to $6 per share. After the split, there were 600,000 common shares outstanding.
Mar. 20	Declared semiannual dividends of $1 on 20,000 shares of preferred stock and $0.14 on the 600,000 shares of $10 par common stock to stockholders of record on March 31, payable on April 20.
Apr. 20	Paid the cash dividends.
May 8	Purchased 50,000 shares of the corporation's own common stock at $48, recording the stock at cost.
Aug. 2	Sold 30,000 shares of treasury stock at $56, receiving cash.
Sept. 15	Declared semiannual dividends of $1 on the preferred stock and $0.07 on the common stock (before the stock dividend). In addition, a 1% common stock dividend was declared on the common stock outstanding, to be capitalized at the fair market value of the common stock, which is estimated at $52.
Oct. 15	Paid the cash dividends and issued the certificates for the common stock dividend.

Instructions

Journalize the transactions.

ALTERNATE ACCOUNTING APPLICATION PROBLEMS

Alternate Problem 11-1B

Dividends on preferred and common stock

Da Show Inc. owns and operates movie theaters throughout Texas and California. Da Show has declared the following annual dividends over a six-year period: 2003, $18,000; 2004, $54,000; 2005, $70,000; 2006, $75,000; 2007, $80,000; and 2008, $90,000. During the entire period, the outstanding stock of the company was composed of 20,000 shares of cumulative, 2% preferred stock, $100 par, and 25,000 shares of common stock, $10 par.

Goal **2**

1. Common dividends in 2005: $22,000

SPREADSHEET

Instructions

1. Calculate the total dividends and the per-share dividends declared on each class of stock for each of the six years. There were no dividends in arrears on January 1, 2003. Summarize the data in tabular form, using the following column headings:

	Total	Preferred Dividends		Common Dividends	
Year	Dividends	Total	Per Share	Total	Per Share
2003	$18,000				
2004	54,000				
2005	70,000				
2006	75,000				
2007	80,000				
2008	90,000				

2. Calculate the average annual dividend per share for each class of stock for the six-year period.
3. Assuming that the preferred stock was sold at par and common stock was sold at $39.20 at the beginning of the six-year period, calculate the average annual percentage return on initial shareholders' investment, based on the average annual dividend per share (a) for preferred stock and (b) for common stock.

Alternate Problem 11-2B

Stock transactions for corporate expansion

Goal **3**

On January 1 of the current year, the following accounts and their balances appear in the ledger of Dahof Corp., a meat processor:

Preferred 4% Stock, $100 par (20,000 shares authorized, 6,000 shares issued)	$ 600,000
Paid-In Capital in Excess of Par—Preferred Stock	120,000
Common Stock, $50 par (100,000 shares authorized, 50,000 shares issued)	2,500,000
Paid-In Capital In Excess of Par—Common Stock	320,000
Retained Earnings	1,675,000

At the annual stockholders' meeting on March 6, the board of directors presented a plan for modernizing and expanding plant operations at a cost of approximately $800,000. The plan provided (a) that a building, valued at $225,000, and the land on which it is located, valued at $45,000, be acquired in accordance with preliminary negotiations by the issuance of 4,800 shares of common stock, (b) that 3,000 shares of the unissued preferred stock be issued through an underwriter, and (c) that the corporation borrow $155,000. The plan was approved by the stockholders and accomplished by the following transactions:

Apr. 3 Issued 4,800 shares of common stock in exchange for land and a building, according to the plan.

18 Issued 3,000 shares of preferred stock, receiving $125 per share in cash from the underwriter.

28 Borrowed $155,000 from Northeast National Bank, giving an 8% mortgage note.

No other transactions occurred during April.

Instructions

Journalize the entries to record the foregoing transactions.

Alternate Problem 11-3B

Selected stock transactions

Goals **3, 4, 7**

GENERAL LEDGER

The following selected accounts appear in the ledger of Kingfisher Environmental Corporation on March 1, 2007, the beginning of the current fiscal year:

Preferred 2% Stock, $75 par (10,000 shares authorized, 8,000 shares issued)	$ 600,000
Paid-In Capital in Excess of Par—Preferred Stock	100,000
Common Stock, $10 par (50,000 shares authorized, 35,000 shares issued)	350,000
Paid-In Capital in Excess of Par—Common Stock	85,000
Retained Earnings	1,050,000

During the year, the corporation completed a number of transactions affecting the stockholders' equity. They are summarized as follows:

a. Issued 7,500 shares of common stock at $24, receiving cash.
b. Sold 800 shares of preferred 2% stock at $81.
c. Purchased 3,000 shares of treasury common for $66,000.
d. Sold 1,800 shares of treasury common for $50,400.
e. Sold 750 shares of treasury common for $14,250.
f. Declared cash dividends of $1.50 per share on preferred stock and $0.40 per share on common stock.
g. Paid the cash dividends.

Instructions

Journalize the entries to record the transactions. Identify each entry by letter.

Alternate Problem 11-4B

Entries for selected corporate transactions

Goals **3, 4, 7, 8**

4. Total stockholders' equity, $2,859,825

SPREADSHEET

GENERAL LEDGER

Shoshone Enterprises Inc. manufactures bathroom fixtures. The stockholders' equity accounts of Shoshone Enterprises Inc., with balances on January 1, 2007, are as follows:

Common Stock, $20 stated value (100,000 shares authorized, 75,000 shares issued)	$1,500,000
Paid-In Capital in Excess of Stated Value	180,000
Retained Earnings	725,000
Treasury Stock (5,000 shares, at cost)	140,000

The following selected transactions occurred during the year:

Jan. 28	Paid cash dividends of $0.80 per share on the common stock. The dividend had been properly recorded when declared on December 30 of the preceding fiscal year for $56,000.
Mar. 21	Issued 15,000 shares of common stock for $480,000.
May 10	Sold all of the treasury stock for $165,000.
July 1	Declared a 4% stock dividend on common stock, to be capitalized at the market price of the stock, which is $36 a share.
Aug. 11	Issued the certificates for the dividend declared on July 1.
Oct. 20	Purchased 7,500 shares of treasury stock for $255,000.
Dec. 27	Declared a $0.75-per-share dividend on common stock.

In addition, Shoshone had net income of $269,400 during the current year.

Instructions

1. Enter the January 1 balances in T-accounts for the stockholders' equity accounts listed. Also prepare T-accounts for the following: Paid-In Capital from Sale of Treasury Stock; Stock Dividends Distributable.
2. Journalize the entries to record the transactions, and post to the six selected accounts.
3. Prepare a retained earnings statement for the year ended December 31, 2007.
4. Prepare the Stockholders' Equity section of the December 31, 2007, balance sheet.

Alternate Problem 11-5B

Entries for selected corporate transactions

Goals **3, 4, 5, 7**

SPREADSHEET

GENERAL LEDGER

Selected transactions completed by Mead Boating Supply Corporation during the current fiscal year are as follows:

Jan. 20	Split the common stock 5 for 1 and reduced the par from $50 to $10 per share. After the split, there were 500,000 common shares outstanding.
Apr. 1	Purchased 20,000 shares of the corporation's own common stock at $30 recording the stock at cost.
May 1	Declared semiannual dividends of $1.50 on 24,000 shares of preferred stock and $0.15 on the common stock to stockholders of record on May 20, payable on June 1.
June 1	Paid the cash dividends.

Aug. 7 Sold 12,000 shares of treasury stock at $38, receiving cash.
Nov. 15 Declared semiannual dividends of $1.50 on the preferred stock and $0.08 on the common stock (before the stock dividend). In addition, a 2% common stock dividend was declared on the common stock outstanding. The fair market value of the common stock is estimated at $35.
Dec. 15 Paid the cash dividends and issued the certificates for the common stock dividend.

Instructions

Journalize the transactions.

FINANCIAL ANALYSIS AND REPORTING CASES

Case 11-1

Campbell Soup Dividend Policy

SPREADSHEET

The following dividend announcement was made by Campbell Soup Company on November 18, 2004:

> *Campbell Soup Company today announced that the Company's Board of Directors declared a regular quarterly dividend on its capital stock of $.17 per share. The dividend is payable January 31, 2005 to shareholders of record at the close of business on January 3, 2005.*

Campbell Soup had 410,000,000 common shares issued and outstanding on the dividend record date. The most recent annual earnings were $647,000,000. Campbell's stock price at the time of the dividend record date was $30 per share.

a. What is the business purpose of a dividend?
b. Record Campbell Soup's quarterly dividend declaration.
c. How is Campbell Soup's dividend reported?
d. Calculate and interpret Campbell Soup's annualized dividend yield and dividend payout ratio to one place after the decimal point.

Case 11-2

Dividend information on the Internet

Yahoo's Web portal provides stock market information for publicly traded companies. Go to http://finance.yahoo.com on the Internet. Enter the symbol for Chevron Texaco Corp. using the "Symbol Lookup" feature. Double-click on the symbol for the detailed market information for Chevron Texaco. Once at the detailed Chevron Texaco page view, answer the follow questions:

a. What is Chevron Texaco's historical, trailing 12 months (ttm) earnings per share?
b. What is Chevron Texaco's annual dividend per share?
c. What is Chevron Texaco's closing stock price?
d. Calculate Chevron Texaco's dividend yield, using the closing stock price from (c).
e. What calendar date is the dividend "ex-dividend," and what does this mean?
f. What calendar date is the dividend date, and what does this mean?

Case 11-3

Capital stock dilution

Phoenix Footwear Group, Inc., designs and distributes shoes under the SoftWalk® and Trotters® brand names. The company made the following announcement in July 2004:

> *Phoenix Footwear Group, Inc. announced the pricing of its public offering of 2,500,000 shares of common stock at a price of $12.50 per share . . . . The Company plans to use the net offering proceeds to pay a portion of the price for the pending Altama acquisition.*

Altama Delta Corporation manufactures high performance tactical and combat boots for the Department of Defense. The acquisition was completed for a price of $39 million soon after the successful common stock offering. Altama is estimated to generate annual net income of $4.5 million for 2004. Prior to the common stock offering, Phoenix had 4,460,000 shares of $0.01 par value common stock issued and outstanding on December 31, 2003. Net income was $941,000 for 2003.

a. Provide the journal entry for the common stock issue in July 2004.
b. Determine the expected (pro forma) earnings per share from the acquisition assuming the acquisition was included in operations for all of 2004 and there were no other changes in operations. Assume the difference in the acquisition price and the common stock proceeds was financed by the proceeds of 6% (after-tax) long-term debt.
c. Is the answer in (b) dilutive to earnings per share?

Case 11-4

Dividend yield

The recent market price per share and dividend per share are provided for five large financial services and insurance companies traded on the New York Stock Exchange in the following table:

Company	Market Price per Share	Dividend per Share
American International Group (AIG)	$67.11	$0.50
Prudential Financial Inc.	53.99	0.63
Lincoln National	45.76	1.46
Hartford Financial Services Group	66.61	1.16
ING Groep, NV	28.81	0.99

a. Determine the dividend yield for the five companies. Round percentages to two decimal places.
b. Why are the dividend yields different, even though these companies are from the same industry?
c. Should you avoid investing in a company with a low dividend yield?

Case 11-5

Statement of Stockholders' Equity—Thomas Nelson, Inc.

Thomas Nelson, Inc., is a publisher of Bibles and other religious materials. Thomas Nelson, Inc., had the following statement of stockholders' equity for the fiscal year ended March 31, 2004:

Thomas Nelson, Inc.
Statement of Stockholders' Equity
For the Fiscal Year Ended March 31, 2004
(in thousands, except per-share data)

	Common Stock	Class B Common Stock	Additional Paid-In Capital	Retained Earnings	Total
Balance at March 31, 2003	$13,350	$1,025	$44,064	$29,385	$ 87,824
Net and comprehensive income				16,165	16,165
Class B stock converted to common	62	(62)			—
Common stock issued:					
Option plans—90,823 common shares	91		633		724
Dividends declared—$0.12 per share				(1,731)	(1,731)
Balance at March 31, 2004	$13,503	$ 963	$44,697	$43,819	$102,982

a. What is the par value of the common stock? Round to the nearest dollar.
b. How much did employees pay per share for common stock under the option plan? Round to the nearest cent.
c. Record the entry for the common stock issuance under the option plan. (*Hint:* The issuance is recorded as illustrated in the text for a common stock issuance.)
d. Record the summary entry for the dividends declared during the year.
e. Does the dividend seem sustainable?

Case 11-6

Capitalizing a development stage company

The following chart shows the retained earnings (deficits) balance for Amazon.com, Inc., from its initial public offering date until December 31, 2004:

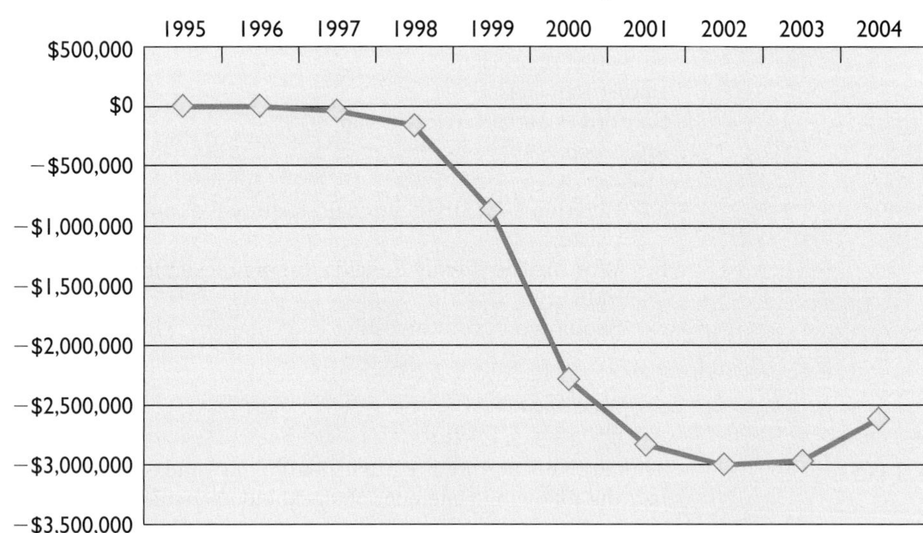

As can be seen, Amazon.com has accumulated deficits during its complete life as a public company. Below is the Liabilities and Stockholders' Equity section of Amazon.com's December 31, 2004, balance sheet.

Current liabilities	$ 1,252,701
Long-term liabilities	1,945,439
Paid-in capital	1,903,403
Accumulated deficit	(2,974,428)
Total stockholders' equity	$(1,071,025)
Total liabilities and stockholders' equity	$ 2,127,115

a. Would you expect Amazon.com to be paying a dividend?
b. Go to Yahoo Finance at finance.yahoo.com and determine the current market value of Amazon.com from the Amazon quotes and information page. Type AMZN in the blank indicated by "Get Quotes." Explain the difference between the total stockholders' equity shown on the balance sheet and the market valuation.
c. Where does Amazon.com obtain the funds to stay in business?

BUSINESS ACTIVITIES AND RESPONSIBILITY ISSUES

Activity 11-1

Business emphasis

7-Eleven operates more than 24,000 convenience food stores worldwide. 7-Eleven stores are normally less than 3,000 square feet and carry a variety of items, including soft drinks, candy and snacks, cigarettes, milk, and t-shirts. Many stores also sell CITGO-brand gasoline. 7-Eleven faces increasing competition from other convenience store chains as well as from grocery and supermarket chains, grocery wholesalers and buying clubs, gasoline/miniconvenience stores, food stores, fast food chains, and variety, drug, and candy stores. In groups of three to four, answer the following questions:

1. Go to the 7-Eleven Web site, which is linked to the text's Web site at http://duchac.swlearning.com. How did the name 7-Eleven originate?
2. How many items do you think an average 7-Eleven carries?
3. What percent of total sales is represented by gasoline sales?
4. Describe some ways that you think 7-Eleven can increase its same-store sales in the face of increasing competition.

Activity 11-2

Board of directors' actions

In early 2002, Bernie Ebbers, then CEO of WorldCom Group, a major telecommunications company, was having personal financial troubles. Ebbers pledged a large stake of his WorldCom stock as security for some personal loans. As the price of WorldCom stock sank, Ebbers' bankers threatened to sell his stock in order to protect their loans. To avoid having his stock sold, Ebbers asked the board of directors of WorldCom to loan him nearly $400 million of corporate assets at 2.5% interest to pay off his bankers. The board agreed to lend him the money.

Comment on the decision of the board of directors in this situation.

Activity 11-3

Ethics and professional conduct in business

Lois Heck and Keith Ryan are organizing Beaufort Unlimited Inc. to undertake a high-risk gold-mining venture in Canada. Lois and Keith tentatively plan to request authorization for 80,000,000 shares of common stock to be sold to the general public. Lois and Keith have decided to establish par of $1 per share in order to appeal to a wide variety of potential investors. Lois and Keith feel that investors would be more willing to invest in the company if they received a large quantity of shares for what might appear to be a "bargain" price.

Discuss whether Lois and Keith are behaving in a professional manner.

Activity 11-4

Issuing stock

Kilimanjaro Inc. began operations on January 6, 2007, with the issuance of 400,000 shares of $50 par common stock. The sole stockholders of Kilimanjaro Inc. are Donna White and Dr. Larry Klein, who organized Kilimanjaro Inc. with the objective of developing a new flu vaccine. Dr. Klein claims that the flu vaccine, which is nearing the final development stage, will protect individuals against 98% of the flu types that have been medically identified. To complete the project, Kilimanjaro Inc. needs $20,000,000 of additional funds. The local banks have been unwilling to loan the funds because of the lack of sufficient collateral and the riskiness of the business.

The following is a conversation between Donna White, the chief executive officer of Kilimanjaro Inc., and Dr. Larry Klein, the leading researcher.

White: What are we going to do? The banks won't loan us any more money, and we've got to have $20 million to complete the project. We are so close! It would be a disaster to quit now. The only thing I can think of is to issue additional stock. Do you have any suggestions?

Klein: I guess you're right. But if the banks won't loan us any more money, how do you think we can find any investors to buy stock?

White: I've been thinking about that. What if we promise the investors that we will pay them 2% of net sales until they have received an amount equal to what they paid for the stock?

Klein: What happens when we pay back the $20 million? Do the investors get to keep the stock? If they do, it'll dilute our ownership.

White: How about, if after we pay back the $20 million, we make them turn in their stock for $100 per share? That's twice what they paid for it, plus they would have already gotten all their money back. That's a $100 profit per share for the investors.

Klein: It could work. We get our money, but don't have to pay any interest, dividends, or the $100 until we start generating net sales. At the same time, the investors could get their money back plus $100 per share.

White: We'll need current financial statements for the new investors. I'll get our accountant working on them and contact our attorney to draw up a legally binding contract for the new investors. Yes, this could work.

In late 2007, the attorney and the various regulatory authorities approved the new stock offering, and 400,000 shares of common stock were privately sold to new investors at the stock's par of $50.

In preparing financial statements for 2007, Donna White and Anita Sparks, the controller for Kilimanjaro Inc., have the following conversation.

Sparks: Donna, I've got a problem.

White: What's that, Anita?

Sparks: Issuing common stock to raise that additional $20 million was a great idea. But . . .

White: But what?

Sparks: I've got to prepare the 2007 annual financial statements, and I am not sure how to classify the common stock.

White: What do you mean? It's common stock.

Sparks: I'm not so sure. I called the auditor and explained how we are contractually obligated to pay the new stockholders 2% of net sales until $50 per share is paid. Then, we may be obligated to pay them $100 per share.

White: So . . .

Sparks: So the auditor thinks that we should classify the additional issuance of $20 million as debt, not stock! And, if we put the $20 million on the balance sheet as debt, we will violate our other loan agreements with the banks. And, if these agreements are violated, the banks may call in all our debt immediately. If they do that, we are in deep trouble. We'll probably have to file for bankruptcy. We just don't have the cash to pay off the banks.

1. Discuss the arguments for and against classifying the issuance of the $20 million of stock as debt.
2. What do you think might be a practical solution to this classification problem?

Activity 11-5

Dividends

Matterhorn Inc. has paid quarterly cash dividends since 1993. These dividends have steadily increased from $0.05 per share to the latest dividend declaration of $0.40 per share. The board of directors would like to continue this trend and is hesitant to suspend or decrease the amount of quarterly dividends. Unfortunately, sales dropped sharply in the fourth quarter of 2007 because of worsening economic conditions and increased competition. As a result, the board is uncertain as to whether it should declare a dividend for the last quarter of 2007.

On November 1, 2007, Matterhorn Inc. borrowed $400,000 from Cheyenne National Bank to use in modernizing its retail stores and to expand its product line in reaction to its competition. The terms of the 10-year, 12% loan require Matterhorn Inc. to:

a. Pay monthly interest on the last day of the month.
b. Pay $40,000 of the principal each November 1, beginning in 2008.
c. Maintain a current ratio (current assets ÷ current liabilities) of 2.
d. Maintain a minimum balance (a compensating balance) of $20,000 in its Cheyenne National Bank account.

On December 31, 2007, $100,000 of the $400,000 loan had been disbursed in modernization of the retail stores and in expansion of the product line. Matterhorn Inc.'s balance sheet as of December 31, 2007, is as follows:

Matterhorn Inc.
Balance Sheet
December 31, 2007

Assets			
Current assets:			
Cash		$ 32,000	
Marketable securities		300,000	
Accounts receivable	$ 73,200		
Less allowance for doubtful accounts	5,200	68,000	
Merchandise inventory		100,000	
Prepaid expenses		3,600	
Total current assets			$ 503,600
Property, plant, and equipment:			
Land		$120,000	
Buildings	$760,000		
Less accumulated depreciation	172,000	588,000	
Equipment	$368,000		
Less accumulated depreciation	88,000	280,000	
Total property, plant, and equipment			988,000
Total assets			$1,491,600
Liabilities			
Current liabilities:			
Accounts payable		$ 57,440	
Notes payable (Cheyenne National Bank)		40,000	
Salaries payable		2,560	
Total current liabilities			$ 100,000
Long-term liabilities:			
Notes payable (Cheyenne National Bank)			360,000
Total liabilities			$ 460,000
Stockholders' Equity			
Paid-in capital:			
Common stock, $20 par (50,000 shares authorized, 20,000 shares issued)	$400,000		
Excess of issue price over par	32,000		
Total paid-in capital		$432,000	
Retained earnings		599,600	
Total stockholders' equity			1,031,600
Total liabilities and stockholders' equity			$1,491,600

The board of directors is scheduled to meet January 6, 2008, to discuss the results of operations for 2007 and to consider the declaration of dividends for the fourth quarter of 2007. The chairman of the board has asked for your advice on the declaration of dividends.

1. What factors should the board consider in deciding whether to declare a cash dividend?
2. The board is considering the declaration of a stock dividend instead of a cash dividend. Discuss the issuance of a stock dividend from the point of view of (a) a stockholder and (b) the board of directors.

Activity 11-6

Profiling a corporation

Select a public corporation you are familiar with or which interests you. Using the Internet, your school library, and other sources, develop a short (two to five pages) profile of the corporation. Include in your profile the following information:

GROUP ACTIVITY

1. Name of the corporation.
2. State of incorporation.
3. Nature of its operations.
4. Total assets for the most recent balance sheet.
5. Total revenues for the most recent income statement.
6. Net income for the most recent income statement.
7. Classes of stock outstanding.
8. Market price of the stock outstanding.
9. High and low price of the stock for the past year.
10. Dividends paid for each share of stock during the past year.

In groups of three or four, discuss each corporate profile. Select one of the corporations, assuming that your group has $100,000 to invest in its stock. Summarize why your group selected the corporation it did and how financial accounting information may have affected your decision. Keep track of the performance of your corporation's stock for the remainder of the term.

Note: Most major corporations maintain home pages on the Internet. This home page provides a variety of information on the corporation and often includes the corporation's financial statements. In addition, the New York Stock Exchange Web site (http://www.nyse.com) includes links to the home pages of many listed companies. Financial statements can also be accessed using EDGAR, the electronic archives of financial statements filed with the Securities and Exchange Commission (SEC).

SEC documents can also be retrieved using the EdgarScan™ service from PricewaterhouseCoopers at http://edgarscan.pwcglobal.com. To obtain annual report information, key in a company name in the appropriate space. EdgarScan will list the reports, available to you for the company you've selected. Select the most recent annual report filing, identified as a 10-K or 10-K405. EdgarScan provides an outline of the report, including the separate financial statements, which can also be selected in an Excel® spreadsheet.

ANSWERS TO SELF-STUDY QUESTIONS

1. **C** If a corporation has cumulative preferred stock outstanding, dividends that have been passed for prior years plus the dividend for the current year must be paid before dividends may be declared on common stock. In this case, dividends of $27,000 ($9,000 × 3) have been passed for the preceding three years, and the current year's dividends are $9,000, making a total of $36,000 (answer C) that must be paid to preferred stockholders before dividends can be declared on common stock.

2. **D** Paid-in capital is one of the two major subdivisions of the stockholders' equity of a corporation. It may result from many sources, including the issuance of cumulative preferred stock (answer A), declaring a stock dividend (answer B), or the sale of a corporation's treasury stock (answer C).

3. **C** Reacquired stock, known as treasury stock, should be listed in the Stockholders' Equity section (answer C) of the balance sheet. The price paid for the treasury stock is deducted from the total of all the stockholders' equity accounts.

4. **C** If a corporation that holds treasury stock declares a cash dividend, the dividends are not paid on the treasury shares. To do so would place the corporation in the position of earning income through dealing with itself. Thus, the corporation will record $44,000 (answer C) as cash dividends [(25,000 shares issued less 3,000 shares held as treasury stock) × $2 per share dividend].

5. **C** The dividend yield is 5% ($2.40 ÷ $48.00). The dividend payout ratio is 60% ($2.40 ÷ $4.00). The book value per share is not used in any of the calculations.

12 Special Income and Investment Reporting Issues

Learning Goals

1. Prepare an income statement reporting the following unusual items: fixed asset impairments, restructuring charges, discontinued operations, extraordinary items, and cumulative changes in accounting principles.

4. Record entries for the purchase, interest, discount and premium amortization, and sale of bond investments.

5. Compute and interpret the price-earnings and price-book

eBay Inc.

If you go to a bank to apply for a loan, the bank will often ask for several years' tax returns as evidence of income. Why would the bank ask for more than the latest tax return? Several years' tax returns would help the bank evaluate your normal income. For example, suppose you won a $50,000 lottery (congratulations!), increasing your taxable income for that year to $75,000, including $25,000 income from employment. Upon review of several years' tax returns, the bank would be able to determine that the lottery year contained an unusual event that would not likely be repeated in future years. That is, the normal income is closer to $25,000 per year, even though actual income for one year was $75,000. As a result, the bank may discount the $50,000 lottery proceeds when estimating your future debt repayment capacity.

In the same way, companies must identify unusual items of income or expense, so as to provide financial statement users insight to normal earnings. Thus, defining and reporting earnings is an important part of the financial reporting process. As a user of financial statements, you will need to evaluate the reported earnings numbers to understand the earning power of the company.

For example, eBay Inc., the online auction company, has earnings power from over 125 million registered users that host up to 350 million listings for over 45,000 different categories. Over 10,000 full-time traders operate on eBay. Over 21 million items are for sale at any one time, and the site was visited by over 30% of all active Internet users in a recent month. Clearly, eBay is an Internet retail powerhouse. These normal aspects of eBay are part of its ongoing operations. Infrequent or unusual events should be separately disclosed so that the normal earnings trends can be estimated.

© PR NEWSPHOTO/EBAY INC. (AP WIDE WORLD PHOTO)

In this chapter, we will discuss a number of special topics that impact earnings disclosure. In addition, we will discuss investment reporting issues.

Sources: Adapted from David Sheets, "Fact Is Really Much Better Than Fiction in Rise of eBay" *Everyday Magazine*, June 26, 2002; Kara Swisher, "Boom Town: eBay Founder Is Bidding on a Sense of Community—Omidyar Plans to Use Wealth to Apply His Firm's Model to the Real Global Village," *The Wall Street Journal*, October 29, 2001, p. B-1; and "How eBay Made Net Profit," *The Guardian*, October 16, 2004.

Prepare an income statement reporting the following unusual items: fixed asset impairments, restructuring charges, discontinued operations, extraordinary items, and cumulative changes in accounting principles.

UNUSUAL ITEMS AFFECTING THE INCOME STATEMENT

Generally accepted accounting principles require that certain unusual items be reported separately on the income statement. These items can be classified into the following two categories:

1. Unusual items that are subtracted from gross profit in determining income from continuing operations. These items are reported *above* income from continuing operations.
2. Unusual items that adjust income from continuing operations in determining net income. These items are reported *below* income from continuing operations.

In the following paragraphs, we discuss each of these unusual items.

Unusual Items Reported Above Income from Continuing Operations

Some unusual items are deducted from gross profit in arriving at income from continuing operations. These unusual items consist of fixed asset impairments and restructuring charges; these are sometimes termed *special charges* when combined together.

Fixed Asset Impairments. A **fixed asset impairment** occurs when the fair value of a fixed asset falls below its book value and is not expected to recover.[1] Examples of events that might cause an asset impairment are (1) decreases in the market price of fixed assets, (2) significant changes in the business or regulations related to fixed assets, (3) adverse conditions affecting the use of fixed assets, or (4) expected cash flow losses from using fixed assets.[2] For example, on March 1, assume that Jones Corporation consolidates operations by closing a factory. As a result of the closing, plant and equipment is impaired by $750,000. The journal entry to record the impairment is as follows:

SCF	BS	IS
—	A↓ SE↓	E↓

Mar. 1	Loss on Fixed Asset Impairment	750,000	
	Fixed Assets—Plant and Equipment		750,000

The loss on fixed asset impairment is reported as a separate expense item deducted from gross profit in determining income from continuing operations, as illustrated for Jones Corporation in Exhibit 1. In addition, note disclosure should describe the nature of the asset impaired and the cause of the impairment.

The loss reduces the book value of the fixed asset and thus reduces the depreciation expense for future periods. If the asset could be salvaged for sale, the gain or loss on the sale would be based on the lower book value. Therefore, asset impairment accounting recognizes the loss when it is first identified, rather than at a later sale date.

1 Fixed assets that are discontinued components, such as an operating segment, subsidiary, or asset group, should be treated as discontinued items as discussed in a later section.

2 *Statement of Financial Accounting Standards No. 144*, "Accounting for the Impairment or Disposal of Long-Lived Assets" (Norwalk, CT: Financial Accounting Standards Board, 2001).

Exhibit 1

Unusual Items in Income Statement

Jones Corporation
Income Statement
For the Year Ended December 31, 2007

Net sales		$12,350,000
Cost of merchandise sold		5,800,000
Gross profit		$ 6,550,000
Operating expenses	$3,490,000	
Restructuring charge	1,000,000	
Loss from asset impairment	750,000	5,240,000
Income from continuing operations before income tax		$ 1,310,000
Income tax expense		620,000
Income from continuing operations		$ 690,000
Loss on discontinued operations (net of applicable income tax benefit of $50,000)		100,000
Income before extraordinary items and cumulative effect of a change in accounting principle (net of applicable income tax of $88,000)		$ 590,000
Extraordinary item:		
Gain on condemnation of land, net of applicable income tax of $65,000		150,000
Cumulative effect on prior years of changing to a different depreciation method		92,000
Net income		$ 832,000

INTEGRITY, OBJECTIVITY, AND ETHICS IN BUSINESS

When Is an Asset Impaired?

The asset impairment principle is designed to reduce the subjectivity of timing asset write-downs. That is, write-downs should occur when the impairment is deemed permanent. In practice, however, judgment is still needed in determining when such impairment has occurred. Ethical managers will recognize asset write-downs when they occur, not when it is most convenient. For example, the SEC investigated **Avon Corporation** for delaying the write-off of a computer software project. In settling the formal investigation, Avon had to restate its earnings to reflect the earlier write-off date.

Restructuring Charges. **Restructuring charges** are costs incurred with actions such as canceling contracts, laying off or relocating employees, and combining operations. Often, these events incur initial one-time costs in order to obtain long-term savings. For example, terminated employees often receive a one-time termination or severance benefit at the time of their dismissal. Employee termination benefits are normally the most significant restructuring charges; thus, they will be the focus of this section.

Employee termination benefits arise when a plan specifying the number of terminated employees, the benefit, and the benefit timing has been authorized by senior management and communicated to the employees.[3] To illustrate, assume that the management of Jones Corporation communicates a plan to terminate 200 employees from the closed manufacturing plant on March 1. The plan calls for a termination benefit of $5,000 per employee. Once the plan is communicated to employees, they have the legal

3 *Statement of Financial Accounting Standards No. 146,* "Accounting for Costs Associated with Exit or Disposal Activities" (Norwalk, CT: Financial Accounting Standards Board, 2002).

right to work for 60 days but may elect to leave the firm earlier. That is, employees may be paid severance at the end of 60 days or at any time in between. The expense and liability to provide employee benefits should be recognized at its fair value on the plan communication date.[4] The fair value of this plan would be $1,000,000 (200 × $5,000), which is the aggregate expected cost of terminating the employees. Thus, the $1,000,000 restructuring charge would be recorded as follows:

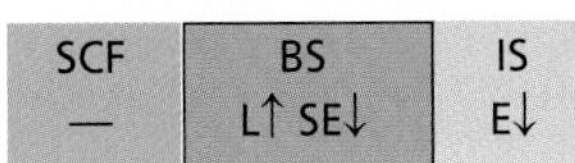

Mar. 1	Restructuring Charge	1,000,000	
	Employee Termination Obligation		1,000,000

The restructuring charge is reported as a separate expense deducted from gross profit in determining income from continuing operations, as shown in Exhibit 1. The employee termination obligation would be shown as a current liability. If the plan called for expected severance payments beyond one year, then a long-term liability would be recognized. In addition, a note should disclose the nature and cause of the restructuring event and the costs associated with the type of restructuring event.

The actual benefits paid to terminated employees should be debited to the liability as employees leave the firm. For example, assume that 25 employees find other employment and leave the company on March 25. The entry to record the severance payment to these employees would be as follows:

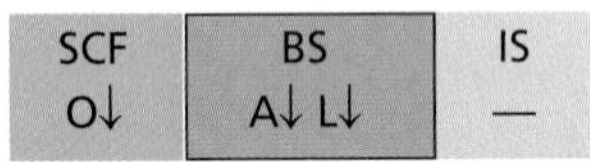

Mar. 25	Employee Termination Obligation	125,000	
	Cash		125,000

Unusual Items Reported Below Income from Continuing Operations

Some unusual items are deducted from income from continuing operations in arriving at net income. These unusual items consist of discontinued operations, extraordinary items, and changes in accounting principles.

INTEGRITY, OBJECTIVITY, AND ETHICS IN BUSINESS

Ethics in Action

The **eBay Inc.** community is noted for the following principles:

- We believe people are basically good.
- We believe everyone has something to contribute.
- We believe that an honest, open environment can bring out the best in people.
- We recognize and respect everyone as a unique individual.
- We encourage you to treat others the way you want to be treated.

Unfortunately, there are a few bad apples in every barrel, and eBay is not without its share. As a result of increasing fraud, eBay has introduced feedback, escrow services, buyer protection plans, a warranty program, and over 800 "fraud-busters." Even so, online fraud escalates as eBay's popularity grows.

Source: http://www.ebay.com

4 For longer-term severance agreements, present value concepts may be required to determine fair value. We will assume short-term agreements where the time value of money is assumed to be immaterial. Present value concepts are discussed in Chapter 10.

International Perspective International Accounting Standards (IASs) do not allow for the reporting of extraordinary items on the income statement.

Discontinued Operations. A gain or loss from disposing of a business segment or component of an entity is reported on the income statement as a gain or loss from **discontinued operations**. The term *business segment* refers to a major line of business for a company, such as a division or a department or a certain class of customer. A *component* of an entity is the lowest level at which the operations and cash flows can be clearly distinguished, operationally and for financial reporting purposes, from the rest of the entity.[5] Examples would be a store for a retailer, a territory for a sales organization, or a product category for a consumer products company. To illustrate the disclosure, assume that Jones Corporation has separate divisions that produce electrical products, hardware supplies, and lawn equipment. Jones sells its electrical products division at a loss. As shown in Exhibit 1, this loss is deducted from Jones' income from continuing operations (income from its hardware and lawn equipment divisions). In addition, a note should disclose the identity of the segment sold, the disposal date, a description of the segment's assets and liabilities, and the manner of disposal.

Extraordinary Items. An **extraordinary item** results from events and transactions that (1) are significantly different (unusual) from the typical or the normal operating activities of the business *and* (2) occur infrequently. The gains and losses resulting from natural disasters that occur infrequently, such as floods, earthquakes, and fires, are extraordinary items. Gains or losses from condemning land or buildings for public use are also extraordinary. Such gains and losses, other than those from disposing of a business segment, should be reported in the income statement as extraordinary items, as shown in Exhibit 1.

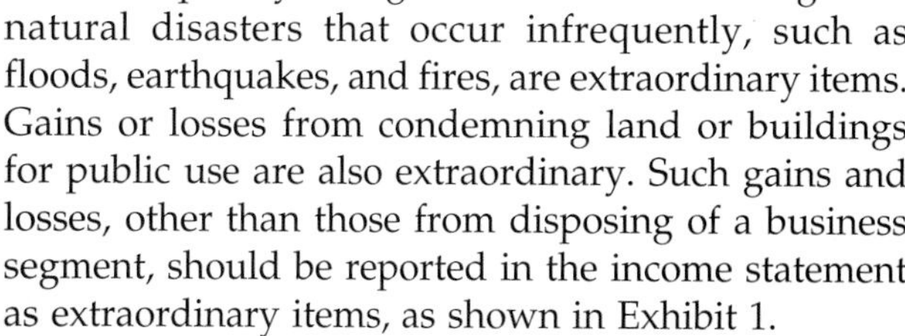

Sometimes extraordinary items result in unusual financial results. For example, Delta Air Lines once reported an extraordinary gain of over $5.5 million as the result of the crash of one of its 727s. The plane that crashed was insured for $6.5 million, but its book value in Delta's accounting records was $962,000.

Gains and losses on the disposal of fixed assets are *not* extraordinary items. This is because (1) they are not unusual and (2) they recur from time to time in the normal operations of a business. Likewise, gains and losses from the sale of investments are usual and recurring for most businesses.

International Perspective Under IASs, changes in accounting methods are not recorded on the income statement, but are handled by presenting prior-period financial statements as if the new accounting method had been used during prior periods.

Changes in Accounting Principles. Businesses are often required to change their accounting principles when the Financial Accounting Standards Board (FASB) issues a new accounting standard. In addition, a business may voluntarily change from one generally accepted accounting principle to another. For example, a corporation may change from the FIFO to the LIFO method of costing inventory to better match revenues and expenses. Changes in generally accepted accounting principles should be disclosed in the financial statements (or in notes to the statements) of the period in which they occur. This disclosure should include the following information:

1. The nature of the change.
2. The justification for the change.
3. The effect on the current year's net income.
4. The cumulative effect of the change on the net income of prior periods.

---

5 *Statement of Financial Accounting Standards No. 144*, op. cit., par. 41.

To illustrate, assume that one of Jones Corporation's divisions changes from the declining-balance method to the straight-line method of depreciation. As shown in Exhibit 1, the cumulative effect of this change is reported after the extraordinary items. If financial statements for prior periods are also presented, they should be restated as if the change had been made in the prior periods, and the effect of the restatement should be reported either on the face of the statements or in a note.

Reporting unusual items separately on the income statement allows investors to isolate the effects of these items on income and cash flows. In addition to reporting these three items separately, their related tax effects should also be reported either with the item with which they are associated or in the notes to the statement. Approximately 19% of U.S. companies reported one of these unusual items on their income statement for a recent fiscal year.[6] By reporting such items separately, investors and other users of the financial statements can consider such factors in assessing a business's future income and cash flows.

HOW BUSINESSES MAKE MONEY

Winner-Take-All Emphasis

In the winner-take-all emphasis, the business that is first able to achieve significant size can often drive out competition and, thus, dominate the market. Success breeds even more success. This emphasis is most effective with businesses that offer a product or service that gains value through use within a community of networked customers. One example is **Microsoft**'s office productivity software. Products like Word® gain value because users can swap files with each other. This feature reduces rival word processing software from gaining a competitive foothold. **eBay Inc.** also uses this emphasis. eBay's network offers more goods, more sellers, and more potential buyers than a start-up rival. Hence, in every country that eBay enters, it tries to acquire or establish initial market dominance knowing that once it is established, rivals will be hard pressed to compete.

Prepare an income statement reporting earnings per share data.

EARNINGS PER COMMON SHARE

The amount of net income is often used by investors and creditors in evaluating a company's profitability. However, net income by itself is difficult to use in comparing companies of different sizes. Also, trends in net income may be difficult to evaluate, using only net income, if there have been significant changes in a company's stockholders' equity. Thus, the profitability of companies is often expressed as earnings per share. **Earnings per common share (EPS)**, sometimes called *basic earnings per share*, is the net income per share of common stock outstanding during a period.

Because of its importance, earnings per share is reported in the financial press and by various investor services, such as Moody's and Standard & Poor's. Changes in earnings per share can lead to significant changes in the price of a corporation's stock in the marketplace. For example, the stock of eBay Inc. fell by over 19% to $83.33 per share after the company announced earnings per share of 33¢ as compared to Wall Street analysts' estimate of 34¢ per share.

6 Determined from U.S. firms in excess of $5 billion sales on Thomson Research® database.

Corporations whose stock is traded in a public market must report earnings per common share on their income statements.[7] If no preferred stock is outstanding, the earnings per common share is calculated as follows:

$$\text{Earnings per Common Share} = \frac{\text{Net Income}}{\text{Number of Common Shares Outstanding}}$$

When the number of common shares outstanding has changed during the period, a weighted average number of shares outstanding is used. If a company has preferred stock outstanding, the net income must be reduced by the amount of any preferred dividends, as shown below.

$$\text{Earnings per Common Share} = \frac{\text{Net Income} - \text{Preferred Stock Dividends}}{\text{Number of Common Shares Outstanding}}$$

Comparing the earnings per share of two or more years, based on only the net incomes of those years, could be misleading. For example, assume that Jones Corporation, whose partial income statement was presented in Exhibit 1, reported $700,000 net income for 2006. Also assume that no extraordinary or other unusual items were reported in 2006. Jones has no preferred stock outstanding and has 200,000 common shares outstanding in 2006 and 2007. The earnings per common share is $3.50 ($700,000/200,000 shares) for 2006 and $4.16 ($832,000/200,000 shares) for 2007. Comparing the two earnings per share amounts suggests that operations have improved. However, the 2007 earnings per share number that is comparable to the $3.50 is $3.45, which is the income from continuing operations of $690,000 divided by 200,000 shares. The latter amount indicates a slight downturn in normal earnings.

When unusual items reported *below* income from continuing operations exist, earnings per common share should be reported for those items. To illustrate, a partial income statement for Jones Corporation, showing earnings per common share, is shown in Exhibit 2. In this income statement, Jones reports all the earnings per common share amounts on the face of the income statement. However, only earnings per share amounts

Exhibit 2

Income Statement with Earnings per Share

Jones Corporation
Income Statement
For the Year Ended December 31, 2007

Earnings per common share:	
Income from continuing operations	$3.45
Loss on discontinued operations	0.50
Income before extraordinary items and cumulative effect of a change in accounting principle	$2.95
Extraordinary item:	
Gain on condemnation of land, net of applicable income tax of $65,000	0.75
Cumulative effect on prior years of changing to a different depreciation method	0.46
Net income	$4.16

7 *Statement of Financial Accounting Standards No. 128*, "Earnings per Share" (Norwalk, CT: Financial Accounting Standards Board, 1997).

for income from continuing operations and net income are required to be presented on the face of the statement. The other per-share amounts may be presented in the notes to the financial statements.[8]

In the preceding paragraphs, we have assumed a simple capital structure with only common stock or common stock and preferred stock outstanding. Often, however, corporations have complex capital structures with various types of securities outstanding, such as convertible preferred stock, options, warrants, and contingently issuable shares. In such cases, the possible effects of converting such securities to common stock must be calculated and reported as *earnings per common share assuming dilution or diluted earnings per share*.[9] This topic is discussed further in advanced accounting texts.

Describe the accounting for investments in stocks.

ACCOUNTING FOR INVESTMENTS IN STOCKS

Corporations not only issue stock, but they also purchase stock of other companies for investment purposes. Like individuals, businesses have a variety of reasons for investing in stock, called **equity securities**. A business may purchase stock as a means of earning a return (income) on excess cash that it does not need for its normal operations. Such investments are usually for a short period of time. In other cases, a business may purchase the stock of another company as a means of developing or maintaining business relationships with the other company. A business may also purchase common stock as a means of gaining control of another company's operations. In these two latter cases, the business usually intends to hold the investment for a long period of time.

© PHOTODISC COLLECTION/GETTY IMAGES

The equity securities in which a business invests may be classified as trading securities or available-for-sale securities. **Trading securities** are securities that management intends to actively trade for profit. Businesses holding trading securities are those whose normal operations involve buying and selling securities. Examples of such businesses include banks and insurance companies. **Available-for-sale securities** are securities that management expects to sell in the future but which are not actively traded for profit. For example, Warren Buffett, one of the wealthiest men in the world, invests through a public company called Berkshire Hathaway Inc. In a recent annual report, Berkshire Hathaway reported over $35 billion of equity investment holdings listed on its balance sheet as available-for-sale securities. Some of these investments include The Coca-Cola Company, McDonald's Corporation, and American Express. In this section, we describe and illustrate the accounting for available-for-sale equity securities. The accounting for trading securities is described and illustrated in advanced accounting texts.

Short-Term Investments in Stocks

Rather than allow excess cash to be idle until it is needed, a business may invest in available-for-sale securities. These investments are classified as **temporary investments** or *marketable securities*. Although such investments may be retained for several years,

8 Ibid., pars. 36 and 37.

9 Ibid., pars. 11–39.

they continue to be classified as temporary, provided they meet two conditions. First, the securities are readily marketable and can be sold for cash at any time. Second, management intends to sell the securities when the business needs cash for operations.

Temporary investments in available-for-sale securities are recorded in a current asset account, *Marketable Securities*, at their cost. This cost includes all amounts spent to acquire the securities, such as broker's commissions. Any dividends received on the investment are recorded as a debit to *Cash* and a credit to *Dividend Revenue*.[10]

To illustrate, assume that on June 1 Crabtree Co. purchased 2,000 shares of Inis Corporation common stock at $89.75 per share plus a brokerage fee of $500. On October 1, Inis declared a $0.90 per share cash dividend payable on November 30. Crabtree's entries to record the stock purchase and the receipt of the dividend are as follows:

SCF	BS	IS
O↑	A↑ SE↑	R↑

Date	Account	Debit	Credit
June 1	Marketable Securities	180,000	
	Cash		180,000
	Purchased 2,000 shares of Inis Corporation common stock [($89.75 × 2,000 shares) + $500].		
Nov. 30	Cash	1,800	
	Dividend Revenue		1,800
	Received dividend on Inis Corporation common stock (2,000 shares × $0.90).		

On the balance sheet, temporary investments are reported at their fair market value. Market values are normally available from stock quotations in financial newspapers, such as *The Wall Street Journal*. Any difference between the fair market values of the securities and their cost is an **unrealized holding gain or loss**. This gain or loss is termed "unrealized" because a transaction (the sale of the securities) is necessary before a gain or loss becomes real (realized).

To illustrate, assume that Crabtree Co.'s portfolio of temporary investments was purchased during 2007 and has the following fair market values and unrealized gains and losses on December 31, 2007:

Common Stock	Cost	Market	Unrealized Gain (Loss)
Edwards Inc.	$150,000	$190,000	$ 40,000
SWS Corp.	200,000	200,000	—
Inis Corporation	180,000	210,000	30,000
Bass Co.	160,000	150,000	(10,000)
Total	$690,000	$750,000	$ 60,000

If income taxes of $18,000 are allocated to the unrealized gain, Crabtree's temporary investments should be reported at their total cost of $690,000, plus the unrealized gain (net of applicable income tax) of $42,000 ($60,000 – $18,000), as shown in Exhibit 3.

The unrealized gain (net of applicable taxes) of $42,000 should also be reported as an *other comprehensive income item*, as we mentioned in the preceding chapter. For example, assume that Crabtree Co. has net income of $720,000 for the year ended December 31, 2007. Crabtree elects to report comprehensive income in the *statement of comprehensive income*, as shown in Exhibit 4. In addition, the accumulated other comprehensive income on the balance sheet would also be $42,000, representing the beginning balance of zero plus other comprehensive income of $42,000, as shown in Exhibit 3.

10 Stock dividends received on an investment are not journalized, since they have no effect on the investor's assets and revenues.

Exhibit 3

Temporary Investments on the Balance Sheet

Crabtree Co. Balance Sheet (selected items) December 31, 2007		
Assets		
Current assets:		
Cash		$119,500
Temporary investments in marketable securities at cost	$690,000	
Unrealized gain (net of applicable income tax of $18,000)	42,000	732,000
Stockholders' Equity		
Accumulated other comprehensive income		42,000

Exhibit 4

Statement of Comprehensive Income

Crabtree Co. Statement of Comprehensive Income For the Year Ended December 31, 2007	
Net income	$720,000
Other comprehensive income:	
Unrealized gain on temporary investments in marketable securities (net of applicable income tax of $18,000)	42,000
Comprehensive income	$762,000

Unrealized losses are reported in a similar manner. Unrealized gains and losses are reported as other comprehensive income items until the related securities are sold. When temporary securities are sold, the unrealized gains or losses become realized and are included in determining net income.

Long-Term Investments in Stocks

Long-term investments in stocks are not intended as a source of cash in the normal operations of the business. Rather, such investments are often held for their income, long-term gain potential, or influence over another business entity. They are reported in the balance sheet under the caption **Investments**, which usually follows the Current Assets section.

When the investor does not have a significant influence over the investee, the investment is treated as an available-for-sale security as illustrated in the preceding section for short-term available-for-sale securities. Thus, the investment is recorded at cost and reported at fair market value net of any applicable income tax effects. In addition, any unrealized gains and losses are reported as part of the comprehensive income.[11] For example, Delta Air Lines disclosed investments in Priceline.com preferred stock as a noncurrent investment at the appraised fair market value.

In some cases, however, the investor (the buyer of the stock) has significant influence over the operating and financing activities of the investee (company whose stock is owned). In this case, the **equity method** is used to account for the investment.

11 An exception to reporting unrealized gains and losses as part of comprehensive income is made if the decrease in the market value for a stock is considered permanent. In this case, the cost of the individual stock is written down (decreased), and the amount of the write-down is included in net income.

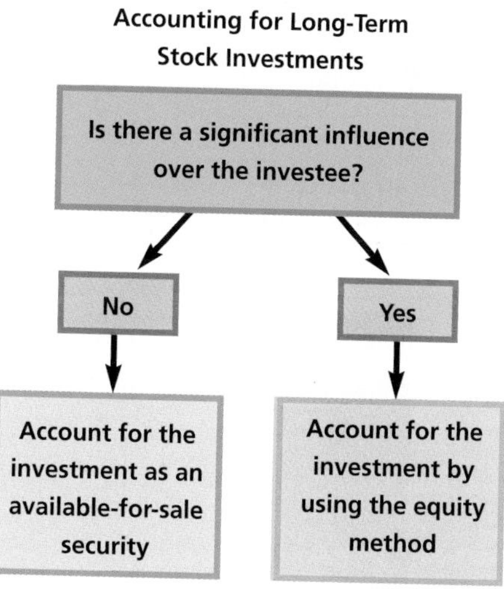
Accounting for Long-Term Stock Investments
Is there a significant influence over the investee?
No
Yes
Account for the investment as an available-for-sale security
Account for the investment by using the equity method

Evidence of significant influence includes the percentage of ownership, the existence of intercompany transactions, and the interchange of managerial personnel. Generally, if the investor owns 20% or more of the voting stock of the investee, it is assumed that the investor has significant influence over the investee.

Under the equity method, the stock purchase is recorded at cost but is *not* subsequently adjusted to fair value. Rather, the book value of the investment is adjusted as follows:

1. The investor's share of the periodic net income of the investee is recorded as an *increase in the investment account* and as *income for the period*. Likewise the investor's share of an investee's net loss is recorded as a *decrease in the investment account* and as a *loss for the period*.
2. The investor's share of cash dividends from the investee is recorded as an *increase in the cash account* and a *decrease in the investment account*.

To illustrate, assume that on January 2, Hally Inc. pays cash of $350,000 for 40% of the common stock and net assets of Brock Corporation. Assume also that, for the year ending December 31, Brock Corporation reports net income of $105,000 and declares and pays $45,000 in dividends. Using the equity method, Hally Inc. (the investor) records these transactions as follows:

SCF	BS	IS				
I↓	A↑↓	—	Jan. 2	Investment in Brock Corporation Stock	350,000	
				Cash		350,000
				Purchased 40% of Brock Corporation Stock.		
—	A↑ SE↑	R↑	Dec. 31	Investment in Brock Corporation Stock	42,000	
				Income of Brock Corporation		42,000
				Recorded 40% share of Brock Corporation net income of $105,000.		
I↑	A↑↓	—	Dec. 31	Cash	18,000	
				Investment in Brock Corporation Stock		18,000
				Recorded 40% share of Brock Corporation dividends.		

Q. Assume that Hally Inc. increased its ownership in Brock Corporation to 45% at the beginning of the next year. If Brock Corporation reported net income of $80,000 and declared dividends of $50,000, by how much would Hally Inc. adjust the Investment in Brock Corporation Stock?

A. *$13,500 [($80,000 × 45%) − ($50,000 × 45%)]*

The combined effect of recording 40% of Brock Corporation's net income and dividends is to increase Hally's interest in the net assets of Brock by $24,000 ($42,000 − $18,000), as shown at the top of the following page.

The equity method causes the investment account to reflect the changes in the book value of the investee. Thus, Brock Corporation's book value increased by $60,000 ($105,000 − $45,000), while the investment in Brock account increased by Hally's share of that increase, or $24,000 ($60,000 × 40%). Both the book value of Brock Corporation and Hally's investment in Brock increased at the same rate from the original cost.

Sale of Investments in Stocks

Accounting for the sale of stock is the same for both short- and long-term investments. When shares of stock are sold, the investment account is credited for the carrying amount (book value) of the shares sold. The cash or receivables account is debited for the proceeds (sales price less commission and other selling costs). Any difference between the proceeds and the carrying amount is recorded as a gain or loss on the sale and is included in determining net income.

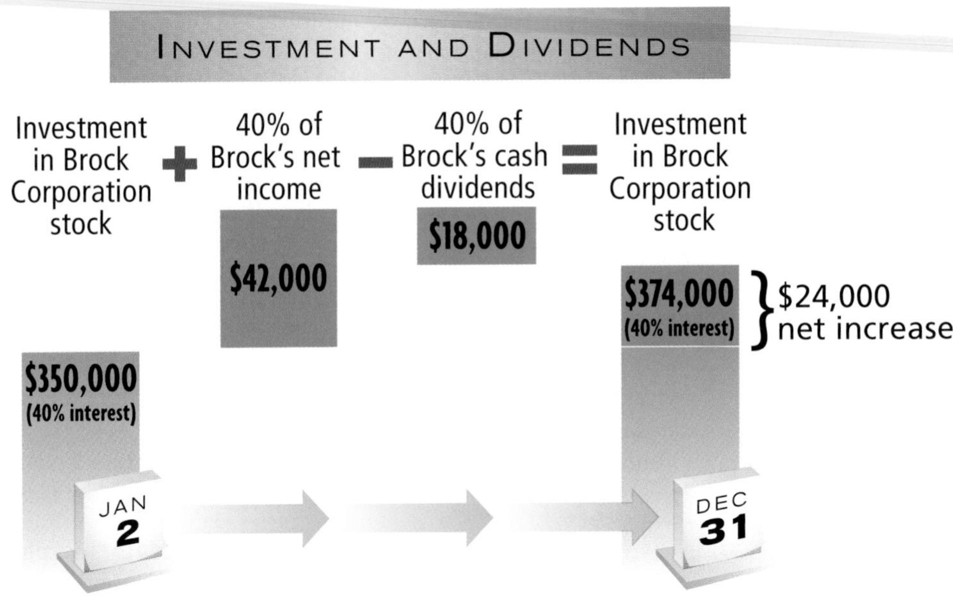

To illustrate, assume that an investment in Drey Inc. stock has a carrying amount of $15,700 when it is sold on March 1. If the proceeds from the sale of the stock are $17,500, the entry to record the transaction is as follows:

SCF	BS	IS
I↑	A↑↓ SE↑	R↑

Mar. 1	Cash	17,500	
	Investment in Drey Inc. Stock		15,700
	Gain on Sale of Investments		1,800

Once the security is sold, any unrealized gains or losses associated with that security will no longer be included in comprehensive income at the end of the period. This prevents gains or losses from being double-counted, once as unrealized, then again as realized.

Investment Reporting

To illustrate investment disclosures, eBay Inc. reported the following current and long-term investments on a recent balance sheet:

Current assets	
Short-term investments	$682,004
Noncurrent assets	
Long-term investments	$1,266,289

eBay's notes included the following additional disclosure:

> *Short- and long-term investments, which include marketable equity securities, municipal, government and corporate bonds, are classified as available-for-sale and reported at fair value using the specific identification method. Realized gains and losses are included in earnings and were immaterial in all periods presented. Unrealized gains*

and losses are excluded from earnings and reported as a component of other comprehensive income (loss), net of related estimated tax provisions or benefits.

eBay did not have any equity method investments. Thus, eBay accounted for all of their investments in marketable equity securities at fair (market) value.

Business Combinations

Businesses may combine in order to produce more efficiently or to diversify product lines. Business combinations occur when one corporation acquires a controlling share of the outstanding voting stock of another corporation by paying cash or exchanging stock. The corporation owning all or a majority of the voting stock of the other corporation is called the **parent company**. The corporation that is controlled is called the **subsidiary company**. For example, PayPal became a subsidiary of eBay when eBay exchanged eBay common stock for all the outstanding common stock of PayPal.

Although parent and subsidiary corporations may operate as a single economic unit, they continue to maintain separate accounting records and prepare their own periodic financial statements. At the end of the year, the financial statements of the parent and subsidiary are combined and reported as a single company. These combined financial statements are called **consolidated financial statements**. Such statements are usually identified by adding "and subsidiary(ies)" to the name of the parent corporation or by adding "consolidated" to the statement title. To the stockholders of the parent company, consolidated financial statements are more meaningful than separate statements for each corporation. This is because the parent company, in substance, controls the subsidiaries, even though the parent and its subsidiaries are separate entities.

Accounting for business combinations and preparing consolidated financial statements is discussed in greater detail in advanced accounting courses.

INTEGRITY, OBJECTIVITY, AND ETHICS IN BUSINESS

What Does It Take to Succeed in Life?

The answer to this question, according to Warren Buffett, the noted investment authority, is three magic ingredients; intelligence, energy, and integrity. According to Buffett, "If you lack the third ingredient, the other two will kill you." In other words, without integrity, your intelligence and energy may very well misguide you.

Source: Eric Clifford, *University of Tennessee Torchbearer*, Summer 2002.

Record entries for the purchase, interest, discount and premium amortization, and sale of bond investments.

INVESTMENTS IN BONDS

In the previous section, we discussed the accounting for investments in equity securities. A business may also make investments in municipal, government, or corporate bonds. If bonds are held for possible sale in managing the cash flow needs of the business, they should be accounted for as available-for-sale securities, as discussed in the previous section. If, however, the business intends and has the ability to hold the bonds for their entire life, then these securities should be accounted for as **held-to-maturity securities**. Held-to-maturity securities are disclosed on the balance sheet at amortized cost. In this section, we will illustrate accounting for bonds as held-to-maturity securities.

Accounting for Bond Investments—Purchase, Interest, and Amortization

Bonds may be purchased either directly from the issuing corporation or through an organized bond exchange. Bond exchanges publish daily bond quotations. These quotations normally include the bond interest rate, maturity date, volume of sales and the high, low, and closing prices for each corporation's bonds traded during the day. Prices for bonds are quoted as a percentage of the face amount. Thus, the price of a $1,000 bond quoted at 99.5 would be $995, while the price of a bond quoted at 104.25 would be $1,042.50.

As with other assets, the cost of a bond investment includes all costs related to the purchase. For example, for bonds purchased through an exchange, the amount paid as a broker's commission should be included as part of the cost of the investment.

When bonds are purchased between interest dates, the buyer normally pays the seller the interest accrued from the last interest payment date to the date of purchase. The amount of the interest paid is normally debited to *Interest Revenue,* since it is an offset against the amount that will be received at the next interest date.

To illustrate, assume that an investor purchases a $1,000 bond at 102 plus a brokerage fee of $5.30 and accrued interest of $10.20. The investor records the transaction as follows:

SCF	BS	IS
I↓	A↑↓ SE↓	R↓

2007			
Apr. 2	Investment in Lewis Co. Bonds	1,025.30	
	Interest Revenue	10.20	
	Cash		1,035.50

The cost of the bond is recorded in a single investment account. The face amount of the bond and the premium (or discount) are normally not recorded in separate accounts. This is different from the accounting for bonds payable. Separate premium and discount accounts are usually not used by investors.

When bonds held as long-term investments are purchased at a price other than the face amount, the premium or discount should be amortized over the remaining life of the bonds. The amortization of premiums and discounts affects the investment and interest accounts, as shown below.

Premium Amortization:			*Discount Amortization:*		
Interest Revenue	XXX		Investment in Bonds	XXX	
Investment in Bonds		XXX	Interest Revenue		XXX

The amount of the amortization can be determined by using the straight-line method. Unlike bonds payable, the amortization of premiums and discounts on bond investments is usually recorded at the end of the period, rather than when interest is received.

To illustrate the accounting for bond investments, assume that on July 1, 2007, Crenshaw Inc. purchases $50,000 of 8% bonds of Deitz Corporation, due in $8\frac{3}{4}$ years. Crenshaw Inc. purchases the bonds directly from Deitz Corporation to yield an effective interest rate of 11%. The purchase price is $41,706 plus interest of $1,000 ($50,000 × 8% × $\frac{3}{12}$) accrued from April 1, 2007, the date of the last semiannual interest payment. Entries in the accounts of Crenshaw Inc. at the time of purchase and for the remainder of the fiscal period ending December 31, 2007, are as follows:

SCF	BS	IS
I↓	A↑↓ SE↓	R↓

Date		Account	Debit	Credit
2007				
July	1	Investment in Deitz Corporation Bonds	41,706	
		Interest Revenue	1,000	
		Cash		42,706
		Purchased investment in bonds, plus accrued interest.[a]		
Oct.	1	Cash	2,000	
		Interest Revenue		2,000
		Received semiannual interest for April 1 to October 1.[b]		
Dec.	31	Interest Receivable	1,000	
		Interest Revenue		1,000
		Adjusting entry for interest accrued from October 1 to December 31.[c]		
	31	Investment in Deitz Corporation Bonds	474	
		Interest Revenue		474
		Adjusting entry for amortization of discount for July 1 to December 31.[d]		

Margin effects: Oct. 1 — SCF O↑, BS A↑ SE↑, IS R↑; Dec. 31 — SCF —, BS A↑ SE↑, IS R↑; Dec. 31 — SCF —, BS A↑ SE↑, IS R↑.

Calculations:

[a]Cost of $50,000 of Deitz Corporation bonds	$41,706
Interest accrued ($50,000 × 8% × $\frac{3}{12}$)	1,000
Total	$ 42,706

[b]$50,000 × 8% × $\frac{6}{12}$ = $2,000

[c]$50,000 × 8% × $\frac{3}{12}$ = $1,000

[d]Face value of bonds	$50,000
Cost of bond investment	41,706
Discount on bond investment	$ 8,294
Number of months to maturity (8$\frac{3}{4}$ years × 12)	105 months
Monthly amortization ($8,294/105 months, rounded to nearest dollar)	$79 per mo.
Amortization for 6 months ($79 × 6)	$474

Accounting for Bond Investments—Sale

Many long-term investments in bonds are sold before their maturity date. When this occurs, the seller receives the sales price (less commissions and other selling costs) plus any accrued interest since the last interest payment date. Before recording the cash proceeds, the seller should amortize any discount or premium for the current period up to the date of sale. Any gain or loss on the sale is then recorded when the cash proceeds are recorded. Such gains and losses are normally reported in the Other Income section of the income statement.

To illustrate, assume that the Deitz Corporation bonds in the preceding example are sold for $47,350 plus accrued interest on June 30, 2014. The *carrying amount* of the bonds (cost plus amortized discount) as of January 1, 2014 (78 months after their purchase) is $47,868 [$41,706 + ($79 per month × 78 months)]. The entries to amortize the discount for the current year and to record the sale of the bonds are shown at the top of the next page.

Q. If the Deitz Corporation bonds had been sold on September 30 instead of June 30, what would have been the amount of the loss?

A. *$1,229 {$47,350 − [$48,342 + ($79 × 3 months)]}*

SCF	BS	IS
—	A↑↓ SE↑	R↑

		Debit	Credit
2014			
June 30	Investment in Deitz Corporation Bonds	474	
	Interest Revenue		474
	Amortized discount for current year.[a]		

SCF	BS	IS
I↑	A↑↓ SE↑	R↑ E↓

		Debit	Credit
30	Cash	48,350	
	Loss on Sale of Investments	992	
	Interest Revenue		1,000
	Investment in Deitz Corporation Bonds[b]		48,342
	Received interest and proceeds from sale of bonds.		
	Interest for April 1 to June 30 = $\$50,000 \times 8\% \times \frac{3}{12} = \$1,000$		

Calculations:

[a]$79 × 6 months	$ 474
[b]Carrying amount of bonds on January 1, 2014	$47,868
Discount amortized, January 1 to June 30, 2014	474
Carrying amount of bonds on June 30, 2014	$ 48,342
Proceeds of sale	47,350
Loss on sale	$ 992

Compute and interpret the price-earnings and price-book ratios.

MARKET-BASED FINANCIAL MEASURES

Two ratios used by investors to compare the market price of common stock to an accounting measure are the price-earnings ratio and the market-to-book-value ratios.

Price-Earnings Ratio

A firm's growth potential and future earnings prospects are indicated by how much the market is willing to pay per dollar of a company's earnings. This ratio, called the **price-earnings ratio**, or *P/E ratio*, is commonly included in stock market quotations reported by the financial press. A high P/E ratio indicates that the market expects high growth and earnings in the future. Likewise, a low P/E ratio indicates lower growth and earnings expectations.

The price-earnings ratio on common stock is computed by dividing the stock's market price per share at a specific date by the company's annual basic earnings per share, as shown below.

$$\text{Price-Earnings Ratio} = \frac{\text{Market Price per Share of Common Stock}}{\text{Earnings per Share of Common Stock (basic)}}$$

Investors that invest in high price-earnings-ratio companies are often referred to as *growth* investors. Growth investors pay a high price for shares because they expect the company to grow and provide a superior return. That is, high price-earnings ratios can be related to investor optimism. Examples of growth companies are eBay Inc. (P/E 99), Red Hat, Inc. (P/E 53), and Genentech, Inc. (P/E 65). Growth companies are considered risky because high growth expectations are already reflected in the market price. Thus, if the company's high growth expectations are not realized, the stock price will likely fall.

In contrast, investors in low price-earnings-ratio companies are often referred to as *value* investors. Value investors seek companies with stable and predictable earnings. The value investor believes that the low price-earnings ratio investment is safer than high price-earnings investments, since the stock is priced at a "bargain" level. Value investing is generally considered the "tortoise" emphasis to the growth investor's "hare" emphasis. Examples of value stocks are Bank of America (P/E 12.5), U.S. Steel (P/E 6.2), and General Motors (P/E 5.6).

To illustrate the calculation and analysis of the price-earnings ratio, consider the following market price per share, earnings per share, and price-earnings ratio information for eBay Inc.

Dec. 31	Market Price per Share	Earnings per Share (Basic)	Price-Earnings Ratio
2002	33.91	0.43	79 ($33.91/$0.43)
2003	64.61	0.69	94 ($64.61/$0.69)
2004	116.34	1.18	99 ($116.34/$1.18)

As can be seen, eBay's price-earnings ratio has increased over the three-year period. Apparently, investors increased their growth expectations for this company, and the price-earnings ratio increased accordingly. This expectation is not without merit. Over the three-year period, earnings per share grew by 174% [(1.18 − 0.43)/0.43]. The price-earnings ratio for eBay can be compared to the price-earnings ratio of a market index, such as the Standard & Poor's 500®.[12] Exhibit 5 shows a graph of eBay's price-earnings ratio plotted with the price-earnings ratio of the Standard & Poor's 500 index. The exhibit shows that eBay's price-earnings ratio is much greater than the broader market, reflecting eBay's growth potential. Over this time period, eBay's price-earnings ratio actually increased, while the broader market declined.

Exhibit 5

Price-Earnings Ratios for eBay and the Standard & Poor's 500 Index

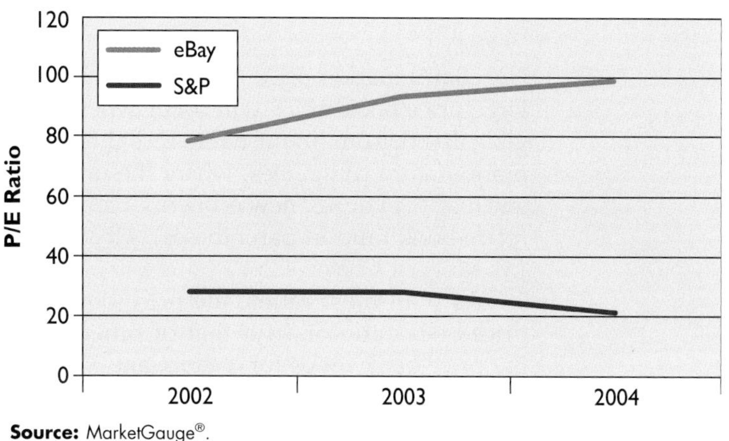

Source: MarketGauge®.

12 The Standard & Poor's 500 index is an index of the largest 500 companies in the United States. The price-earnings ratio for the index is determined by dividing the market price of the index by the total earnings per share of all the stocks within the index. This P/E ratio is a broad gauge of the market as a whole.

Price-Book Ratio

The **price-book ratio** is the ratio of the market value of a share of common stock to the book value of a share of common stock. A price-book value of 1.0 suggests that a company's market value is equal to the balance sheet estimate of the value (book value). Most companies would be expected to have a price-book ratio greater than 1.0. This is because the going concern value of the company should exceed the sum of the historical costs of the net assets. To illustrate the calculation, the market price per share of eBay Inc., on December 31, 2004, was $116 per share. The book value per share is determined by dividing the total shareholders' equity (book value) by the common shares outstanding, as shown below.

Total stockholders' equity	$6,728,341,000
Common shares outstanding—basic (balance sheet date)	659,729,000

$$\text{Book Value per Share} = \frac{\text{Total Stockholders' Equity}}{\text{Common Shares Outstanding}}$$

$$\text{Book Value per Share} = \frac{\$6{,}728{,}341{,}000}{659{,}729{,}000}, \text{ or } \$10.20 \text{ (rounded)}$$

Thus, the price-book ratio would be:

$$\text{Price-Book Ratio} = \frac{\text{Market Price per Share}}{\text{Book Value per Share}}$$

$$\text{Price-Book Ratio} = \frac{\$116}{\$10.20}$$

$$\text{Price-Book Ratio} = 11.37$$

eBay's market price is over 11 times greater than the book value per share. Such large price-book ratios will occur when a company has significant unrecorded intangible assets from brand name recognition, patents, or technologies. This differs from more mature companies, where the unrecorded intangible asset values will be much less than for young "new economy" companies. Examples of mature companies include (price-book ratio in parentheses) Alcoa Inc. (1.91), Ford Motor Company (1.71), and J.P. Morgan Chase (1.26).

As with most ratios, the price-book ratio can be compared to eBay's historical price-book ratio or with that of other firms in the Internet industry. For example, the price-book ratios for Yahoo! and Google are 8 and 20, respectively. Thus, eBay's large price-book ratio is consistent with other Internet businesses.

FOCUS ON CASH FLOW

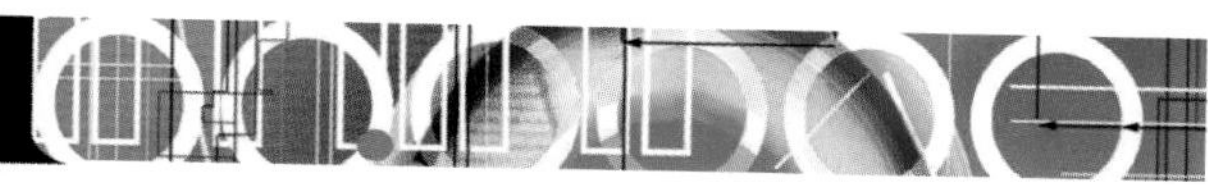

Investment and Cash Flows

Purchases and sales of investments are shown in the Investing Activities section of the statement of cash flows. Purchases of investments are a use of cash, while maturities and sales of investments provide cash. For example, the Investing Activities section of **eBay**'s statement of cash flows for 2004 and 2003 are as follows (in millions):

	2004	2003
Cash flows from investing activities:		
Purchases of property and equipment	$ (292,838)	$ (365,384)
Purchases of investments	(1,754,808)	(2,035,053)
Maturities and sales of investments	1,079,548	1,297,262
Proceeds from sale of assets	(8,646)	
Acquisitions, net of cash acquired	(1,036,476)	(216,367)
Net cash used in investing activities	$(2,013,220)	$(1,319,542)

As can be seen, eBay purchased more investments than were sold during 2003 and 2004. This reflects eBay's investment of excess cash flows into temporary investments. As a result, eBay's investments exceed $1.9 billion as of the end of 2004.

Under the equity method of accounting for income from an investment, the amount of income recognized on the income statement may exceed the amount received in cash as a dividend. This difference is termed the undistributed net earnings from equity investments. Since this amount does not impact cash flow, the Operating Activities section of the statement of cash flows must reduce the accrual net income number for undistributed net earnings from equity investments. However, eBay had no equity method investments, so it did not make this adjustment. eBay had permanent impairments that did not impact cash flow in 2003, thus requiring a positive adjustment to net income in determining cash flows from operations, shown as follows:

	2004	2003
Net income	$ 778,223	$441,771
Depreciation and amortization	253,690	159,003
Impairment of equity investments		1,230
Other items	415,338	231,777
Net changes in current assets and liabilities	(161,936)	40,338
Net cash provided by operating activities	$1,285,315	$874,119

SUMMARY OF LEARNING GOALS

(1) **Prepare an income statement reporting the following unusual items: fixed asset impairments, restructuring charges, discontinued operations, extraordinary items, and cumulative changes in accounting principles.** Fixed asset impairments occur when the fair value of a fixed asset falls below its book value and is not expected to recover. The asset is written down, and a loss is recognized. The loss is deducted from gross profit on the income statement.

Restructuring charges are costs associated with involuntarily terminating employees, terminating contracts, consolidating facilities, or relocating employees. The accrued expenses associated with such a plan are recognized in the period that senior executives approve and communicate the plan. The expense is deducted from gross profit on the income statement.

A gain or loss resulting from the disposal of a business segment, net of related tax, should be added to or deducted from income from continuing operations on the income statement.

Gains and losses may result from events and transactions that are unusual and occur infrequently. Such extraordinary items, net of related income tax, should be added to or deducted from income from continuing operations on the income statement.

A change in an accounting principle results from the adoption of a generally accepted accounting principle different from the one used previously for reporting purposes. The effect of the change in principle on net income in the current period, as well as the cumulative effect on income of prior periods, should be disclosed in the financial statements, net of tax, below income from continuing operations.

2 **Prepare an income statement reporting earnings per share data.** Earnings per share is reported on the income statements of public corporations. If there are unusual items below income from continuing operations on the income statement, the per-share amount should be presented for each of these items as well as net income.

3 **Describe the accounting for investments in stocks.** A business may purchase stocks as a means of earning a return (income) on excess cash that it does not need for its normal operations. Such investments are recorded in a marketable securities account. Their cost includes all amounts spent to acquire the securities. Any dividends received on an investment are recorded as a debit to Cash and a credit to Dividend Revenue. On the balance sheet, temporary investments are reported as available-for-sale securities at their fair market values. Any difference between the fair market values of the securities and their cost is an unrealized holding gain or loss (net of applicable taxes) that is reported as an other comprehensive income item.

Long-term investments in stocks are not intended as a source of cash in the normal operations of the business. They are reported in the balance sheet either as available-for-sale securities, and disclosed at fair value, or reported under the equity method if the investor has significant influence over the investee.

The accounting for the sale of stock is the same for both short- and long-term investments. The investment account is credited for the carrying amount (book value) of the shares sold, the cash or receivables account is debited for the proceeds, and any difference between the proceeds and the carrying amount is recorded as a gain or loss on the sale.

4 **Record entries for the purchase, interest, discount and premium amortization, and sale of bond investments.** A long-term investment in bonds is recorded by debiting Investment in Bonds. When bonds are purchased between interest dates, the amount of the interest paid should be debited to Interest Revenue. Any discount or premium on bond investments should be amortized, using the straight-line method. The amortization of a discount is recorded by debiting Investment in Bonds and crediting Interest Revenue. The amortization of a premium is recorded by debiting Interest Revenue and crediting Investment in Bonds.

When bonds held as long-term investments are sold, any discount or premium for the current period should first be amortized. Cash is then debited for the proceeds of the sale, Investment in Bonds is credited for its balance, and any gain or loss is recorded.

5 **Compute and interpret the price-earnings and price-book ratios.** The assessment of a firm's expected earnings growth is indicated by the price-earnings ratio, or P/E ratio. It is computed by dividing the stock's market price per share at a specific date by the company's annual earnings per share. The price-book ratio compares the market value of a share of common stock to the book value of a share of common stock. This ratio measures the degree to which the market value exceeds the net assets valued under historical cost principles.

GLOSSARY

Available-for-sale securities Securities that management expects to sell in the future but which are not actively traded for profit.

Consolidated financial statements Financial statements resulting from combining parent and subsidiary statements.

Discontinued operations Operations of a major line of business or component for a company, such as a division, a department, or a certain class of customer, that have been disposed of.

Earnings per common share (EPS) Net income per share of common stock outstanding during a period.

Equity method A method of accounting for an investment in common stock by which the investment account is adjusted for the investor's share of periodic net income and cash dividends of the investee.

Equity securities The common and preferred stock of a firm.

Extraordinary items Events and transactions that (1) are significantly different (unusual) from the typical or the normal operating activities of a business and (2) occur infrequently.

Fixed asset impairments A condition when the fair value of a fixed asset falls below its book value and is not expected to recover.

Held-to-maturity securities Debt securities intended to be held until maturity, which are disclosed at amortized cost.

Investments The balance sheet caption used to report long-term investments in stocks not intended as a source of cash in the normal operations of the business.

Parent company The corporation owning all or a majority of the voting stock of the other corporation.

Price-book ratio The ratio of the market value of a share of common stock to the book value of a share of common stock.

Price-earnings ratio The ratio computed by dividing a corporation's stock market price per share at a specific date by the company's annual earnings per share.

Restructuring charge The cost of accrued employee termination benefits associated with a management-approved employee termination plan.

Subsidiary company The corporation that is controlled by a parent company.

Temporary investments The balance sheet caption used to report investments in income-yielding securities that can be quickly sold and converted to cash as needed.

Trading securities Securities that management intends to actively trade for profit.

Unrealized holding gain or loss The difference between the fair market values of the securities and their cost.

ILLUSTRATIVE ACCOUNTING APPLICATION PROBLEM

The following data were selected from the records of Botanica Greenhouses Inc. for the current fiscal year ended August 31, 2007:

Administrative expenses	$ 82,200
Cost of merchandise sold	750,000
Fixed asset impairment	115,000
Gain on condemnation of land	25,000
Income tax:	
Applicable to continuing operations	27,200
Applicable to gain on condemnation of land	10,000
Applicable to loss on discontinued operations (reduction)	24,000
Interest expense	15,200
Loss on discontinued operations	60,200
Restructuring charge	40,000
Sales	1,252,500
Selling expenses	182,100

Instructions

Prepare a multiple-step income statement, concluding with a section for earnings per share in the form illustrated in this chapter. There were 10,000 shares of common stock (no preferred) outstanding throughout the year. Assume that the gain on condemnation of land is an extraordinary item.

Solution

Botanica Greenhouses Inc.
Income Statement
For the Year Ended August 31, 2007

Sales		$1,252,500
Cost of merchandise sold		750,000
Gross profit		$ 502,500
Operating expenses:		
Selling expenses	$182,100	
Administrative expenses	82,200	
Fixed asset impairment	115,000	
Restructuring charge	40,000	
Total operating expenses		419,300
Income from operations		$ 83,200
Other expense:		
Interest expense		15,200
Income from continuing operations before income tax		$ 68,000
Income tax expense		27,200
Income from continuing operations		$ 40,800
Loss on discontinued operations	$ 60,200	
Less applicable income tax	24,000	36,200
Income before extraordinary item		$ 4,600
Extraordinary item:		
Gain on condemnation of land	$ 25,000	
Less applicable income tax	10,000	15,000
Net income		$ 19,600
Earnings per share:		
Income from continuing operations		$4.08
Loss on discontinued operations		3.62
Income before extraordinary item		$0.46
Extraordinary item		1.50
Net income		$1.96

SELF-STUDY QUESTIONS

Answers at end of chapter

1. A material gain resulting from condemning land for public use would be reported on the income statement as:
   A. an extraordinary item.
   B. an other income item.
   C. revenue from sales.
   D. a change in estimate.

2. Gwinnett Corporation's temporary investments cost $100,000 and have a market value of $120,000 at the end of the accounting period. Assuming a tax rate of 40%, the difference between the cost and market value would be reported as a:
   A. $12,000 realized gain.
   B. $12,000 unrealized gain.
   C. $20,000 realized gain.
   D. $20,000 unrealized gain.

3. Cisneros Corporation owns 75% of Harrell Inc. During the current year, Harrell Inc. reported net income of $150,000 and declared dividends of $40,000. How much would Cisneros Corporation increase Investment in Harrell Inc. Stock for the current year?
   A. $0
   B. $30,000
   C. $82,500
   D. $110,000

4. Knowledge Warehouse Inc. purchased for cash $120,000 of 8% bonds on September 1, 2006, at 102 plus accrued interest, as an investment to be held to maturity. The bonds pay interest on July 1 and January 1. If $80 of premium on bond investment is amortized on December 31, 2006, how much total interest revenue should be recognized from these bonds in 2006?
   A. $1,680
   B. $3,120
   C. $3,280
   D. $4,720

5. Harkin Company has a market price of $60 per share on December 31. The total stockholders' equity is $2,400,000, and the net income is $600,000. There are 200,000 shares outstanding. The price-earnings and price-book ratios, respectively, are:
   A. 5, 20.
   B. 3, 5.
   C. 20, 5.
   D. 20, 12.

DISCUSSION QUESTIONS

1. Maxwell Company owns an equipped plant that has a book value of $150 million. Due to a permanent decline in consumer demand for the products produced by this plant, the market value of the plant and equipment is appraised at $20 million. Describe the accounting treatment for this impairment.
2. How should the severance costs of terminated employees be accounted for?
3. During the current year, 40 acres of land that cost $200,000 were condemned for construction of an interstate highway. Assuming that an award of $350,000 in cash was received and that the applicable income tax on this transaction is 40%, how would this information be presented in the income statement?
4. Corporation X realized a material gain when its facilities at a designated floodway were acquired by the urban renewal agency. How should the gain be reported in the income statement?
5. A recent annual report of Viacom, Inc., the parent company of CBS and MTV, disclosed the sale of Blockbuster, Inc. The estimated after-tax loss of these operations was $1.1 billion. Indicate how the loss from discontinued operations should be reported by Viacom on its income statement.
6. If significant changes are made in the accounting principles applied from one period to the next, why should the effect of these changes be disclosed in the financial statements?
7. A corporation reports earnings per share of $1.38 for the most recent year and $1.10 for the preceding year. The $1.38 includes a $0.45-per-share gain from insurance proceeds related to a fully depreciated asset that was destroyed by fire.
   a. Should the composition of the $1.38 be disclosed in the financial reports?
   b. On the basis of the limited information presented, would you conclude that operations had improved or declined?
8. The earnings per share impact from a restructuring charge was calculated as a loss of $0.22 per share for Gotham Company. How should this per share loss be disclosed on the income statement?
9. How should earnings per share be reported when there are unusual items disclosed below the income from continuing operations?
10. Why might a business invest in another company's stock?
11. How are temporary investments in marketable securities reported on the balance sheet?
12. How are unrealized gains and losses on temporary investments in marketable securities reported on the statement of comprehensive income?
13. a. What method of accounting is used for long-term investments in stock in which there is significant influence over the investee?
    b. Under what caption are long-term investments in stock reported on the balance sheet?
14. Plaster Inc. received a $0.15-per-share cash dividend on 50,000 shares of Gestalt Corporation common stock, which Plaster Inc. carries as a long-term investment. Assuming that Plaster Inc. uses the equity method of accounting for its investment in Gestalt Corporation, what account would be credited for the receipt of the $7,500 dividend?
15. An annual report of The Campbell Soup Company reported on its income statement $2.4 million as "equity in earnings of affiliates." Journalize the entry that Campbell would have made to record this equity in earnings of affiliates.
16. Where are investments in bonds that are classified as held-to-maturity securities reported on the balance sheet?
17. At what amount are held-to-maturity investments in bonds reported on the balance sheet?
18. Microsoft Corporation stock recently traded at $26 per share and had earnings per share of $0.92. Determine Microsoft's price-earnings ratio. Round to two decimal places.

EXERCISES

Exercise 12-1

Fixed asset impairment

Goal 1

a. $84,000,000

LightWave Communications, Inc., spent $100 million expanding its fiber optic communication network between Chicago and Los Angeles during 2005. The fiber optic network was assumed to have a 10-year life, with a $20 million salvage value, when it was put into service on January 1, 2006. The network is depreciated using the straight-line method. At the end of 2007, the expected traffic volume on the fiber optic network was only 60% of what was originally expected. The reduced traffic volume caused the fair market value of the asset to be estimated at $45 million on December 31, 2007. The loss is not expected to be recoverable.

a. Determine the book value of the network on December 31, 2007, prior to the impairment adjustment.
b. Provide the journal entry to record the fixed asset impairment on December 31, 2007.
c. Provide the balance sheet disclosure for fixed assets on December 31, 2007.

Exercise 12-2

Fixed asset impairment

Goal 1

Sunset Resorts, Inc., owns and manages resort properties. On January 15, 2007, one of its properties was found to be adjacent to a toxic chemical disposal site. As a result of the negative publicity, this property's bookings dropped 40% during 2007. On December 31, 2007, the accounts of the company showed the following details regarding the impaired property:

Land	$ 25,000,000
Buildings and improvements (net)	80,000,000
Equipment (net)	15,000,000
Total	$120,000,000

Management decides that closing the resort is the only option. As a result, it is estimated that the buildings and improvements will be written off completely. The land can be sold for other uses for $17 million, while the equipment can be disposed of for $4 million, net of disposal costs.

a. Journalize the entry to record the asset impairment on December 31, 2007.
b. Provide the note disclosure for the impairment.

Exercise 12-3

Restructuring charge

Goal 1

a. Restructuring charge, $3,600,000

Jen-King Company's board of directors approved and communicated an employee severance plan in response to a decline in demand for the company's products. The plan called for the elimination of 150 headquarters positions by providing a severance equal to 5% of the annual salary multiplied by the number of years of service. The average annual salary of the eliminated positions is $60,000. The average tenure of terminated employees is eight years. The plan was communicated to employees on November 1, 2007. Actual termination notices will be distributed over the period between December 1, 2007, and April 1, 2008. On December 15, 2007, 40 employees received a lay-off notice and were terminated with severance.

a. Provide the journal entry for the restructuring charge on November 1, 2007.
b. Provide the entry for the severance payment on December 15, 2007, assuming that the actual tenure and salary of terminated employees were consistent with the overall average.
c. Provide the balance sheet and note disclosures on December 31, 2007.

Exercise 12-4

Restructuring charge

Goal 1

a. Restructuring charge, $3,039,200

Mango Juice Company has been suffering a downturn in its juice business due to adverse publicity regarding the caffeine content of its drink products. As a result, the company has been required to restructure operations. The board of directors approved and communicated a plan on July 1, 2006, calling for the following actions.

1. Close a juice plant on October 15, 2006. Closing, equipment relocation, and employee relocation costs are expected to be $500,000 during October.
2. Eliminate 280 plant positions. A severance will be paid to the terminated employees equal to 400% of their estimated monthly earnings payable in four quarterly installments on October 15, 2006; January 15, 2007; April 15, 2007; and July 15, 2007.

3. Terminate a juice supply contract, activating a $120,000 cancellation penalty, payable upon notice of termination. The notice will be formally delivered to the supplier on August 15, 2006.

The 280 employees earn an average of $12 per hour. The average employee works 180 hours per month.

a. Determine the total restructuring charge.
b. Journalize the entry for the restructuring charge on July 1, 2006. (*Note:* Use Restructuring Obligation as the liability account, since the charges involve more than just employee terminations.)
c. Provide the journal entry for the October 15, 2006, employee severance payment.
d. Provide the balance sheet disclosure for December 31, 2006.
e. Provide a note disclosure for December 31, 2006.

Exercise 12-5

Restructuring charges and asset impairments

Goal **1**

a. Severance restructuring charge, $650,000

Conway Transportation Company has suffered losses due to increased competition in its service market from low-cost independent truckers. As a result, on December 31, 2006, the board of directors of the company approved and communicated a restructuring plan that calls for the elimination of 50 driver positions and 15 staff support positions. The market price for used tractor-trailers is depressed due to general overcapacity in the transportation industry. As a result, the market value of tractor-trailers is estimated to be only 40% of the book value of these assets. It is not believed that the impairment in fixed assets is recoverable. The cost and accumulated depreciation of the total tractor-trailer fleet on December 31 are $34 million and $9 million, respectively. The restructuring plan will provide a severance to the drivers and staff totaling $10,000 per employee, payable on March 14, 2007, which is the expected employee termination date.

a. Journalize the entries on December 31, 2006, for the fixed asset impairment and the employee severance costs.
b. Provide the balance sheet and note disclosure on December 31, 2006.
c. Journalize the entry for March 14, 2007.

Exercise 12-6

Restructuring charges

Goal **1**

The notes to recent financial statements of Xerox Corporation disclosed the following tabular information regarding restructuring charges. (Assume all restructuring charges were for employee termination benefits.)

	(in millions)
Ending balance, December 31, 2003	$221
Provision (net)	85
Charges against reserve	(189)
Ending balance, December 31, 2004	$117

a. What amount is shown on the December 31, 2004, balance sheet for the total estimated restructuring obligation?
b. Provide the journal entry for the 2004 restructuring charge.
c. Provide the journal entry for the employee termination benefit payments in 2004.

Exercise 12-7

Extraordinary item

Goal **2**

A company received life insurance proceeds on the death of its president before the end of its fiscal year. It intends to report the amount in its income statement as an extraordinary item.

Would this reporting be in conformity with generally accepted accounting principles? Discuss.

Exercise 12-8

Extraordinary item

Goal **1**

For the year ended December 31, 2002, Delta Air Lines, Inc., provided the following note to its financial statements:

> *On September 22, 2001, the Air Transportation Safety and System Stabilization Act (Stabilization Act) became effective. The Stabilization Act is intended to preserve the viability of the U.S. air transportation system following the terrorist attacks on September 11, 2001 by, among other things, (1) providing for payments from the U.S. Government totaling $5 billion to compensate U.S. air carriers for losses incurred from September 11, 2001, through December 31, 2001, as a result of the September 11 terrorist attacks and (2) permitting the Secretary of Transportation to sell insurance to U.S. air carriers.*
>
> *Our allocated portion of compensation under the Stabilization Act was $668 million. Due to uncertainties regarding the U.S. government's calculation of compensation, we recognized $634 million of this amount in our 2001 Consolidated Statement of Operations. We recognized the remaining $34 million of compensation in our 2002 Consolidated Statement of Operations. We received $112 million and $556 million in cash for the years ended December 31, 2002 and 2001, respectively, under the Stabilization Act.*

Do you believe that the income related to the Stabilization Act should be reported as an extraordinary item on the income statement of Delta Air Lines?

Exercise 12-9

Identifying extraordinary items

Goal **1**

Assume that the amount of each of the following items is material to the financial statements. Classify each item as either normally recurring (NR) or extraordinary (E).

a. Interest revenue on notes receivable.
b. Uninsured flood loss. (Flood insurance is unavailable because of periodic flooding in the area.)
c. Loss on sale of fixed assets.
d. Restructuring charge related to employee termination benefits.
e. Gain on sale of land condemned for public use.
f. Uncollectible accounts expense.
g. Uninsured loss on building due to hurricane damage. The firm was organized in 1920 and had not previously incurred hurricane damage.
h. Loss on disposal of equipment considered to be obsolete because of development of new technology.

Exercise 12-10

Income statement

Goals **1, 2**

Net income, $24,000

SPREADSHEET

Wave Runner, Inc., produces and distributes equipment for sailboats. On the basis of the following data for the current fiscal year ended June 30, 2006, prepare a multiple-step income statement for Wave Runner, including an analysis of earnings per share in the form illustrated in this chapter. There were 10,000 shares of $150 par common stock outstanding throughout the year.

Administrative expenses	$ 92,400
Cost of merchandise sold	431,900
Cumulative effect on prior years of changing to a different depreciation method (decrease in income)	60,000
Gain on condemnation of land (extraordinary item)	43,000
Income tax reduction applicable to change in depreciation method	24,000
Income tax applicable to gain on condemnation of land	17,200
Income tax reduction applicable to loss from discontinued operations	36,000
Income tax applicable to ordinary income	58,800
Loss on discontinued operations	90,000
Loss from fixed asset impairment	100,000
Restructuring charge	80,000
Sales	976,400
Selling expenses	125,100

Exercise 12-11

Income statement

Goals **1, 2**

Correct EPS for net income, $8.25

Audio Affection, Inc., sells automotive and home stereo equipment. It has 50,000 shares of $100 par common stock outstanding and 10,000 shares of $2, $100 par cumulative preferred stock outstanding as of December 31, 2006. List the errors you find in the following income statement for the year ended December 31, 2006.

Audio Affection, Inc.
Income Statement
For the Year Ended December 31, 2006

Net sales		$9,450,000
Cost of merchandise sold		7,100,000
Gross profit		$2,350,000
Operating expenses:		
Selling expenses	$820,000	
Administrative expenses	320,000	1,140,000
Income from continuing operations before income tax		$1,210,000
Income tax expense		420,000
Income from continuing operations		$ 790,000
Cumulative effect on prior years' income (decrease) of changing to a different depreciation method (net of applicable income tax of $86,000)		(204,000)
Fixed asset impairment		(30,000)
Income before condemnation of land, restructuring charge, and discontinued operations		$ 556,000
Extraordinary items:		
Gain on condemnation of land (net of applicable income tax of $80,000)		120,000
Restructuring charge (net of applicable income tax of $25,500)		(59,500)
Loss on discontinued operations (net of applicable income tax of $76,000)		(184,000)
Net income		$ 432,500
Earnings per common share:		
Income from continuing operations		$ 15.80
Cumulative effect on prior years' income (decrease) of changing to a different depreciation method		(4.08)
Fixed asset impairment		(0.60)
Income before extraordinary item and discontinued operations		$ 11.12
Extraordinary items:		
Gain on condemnation of land		2.40
Restructuring charge		(1.19)
Loss on discontinued operations		(3.68)
Net income		$ 8.65

Exercise 12-12

Earnings per share with preferred stock

Goal **3**

Glow-Rite Lighting Company had earnings for 2006 of $740,000. The company had 125,000 shares of common stock outstanding during the year. In addition, the company issued 50,000 shares of $100 par value preferred stock on January 5, 2006. The preferred stock has a dividend of $6 per share. There were no transactions in either common or preferred stock during 2006.

Determine the basic earnings per share for Glow-Rite.

Exercise 12-13

Earnings per share with preferred stock

Goal 3

Hazard Guard Insurance Company had 100,000 shares of $4, $100 par value preferred stock issued and outstanding during 2006. In addition, the company had 500,000 shares of common stock issued, of which 100,000 shares were held as Treasury stock. Hazard had $1,500,000 of income before taxes and extraordinary items. Hazard experienced earthquake damage to a regional sales office resulting in a before-tax extraordinary loss of $200,000. The income tax rate was 40%. Determine the earnings per share disclosure for Hazard Guard.

Exercise 12-14

Comprehensive income and temporary investments

Goal 3

c. $37,000

The statement of comprehensive income for the years ended December 31, 2006 and 2007, plus selected items from comparative balance sheets of McClain Wholesalers, Inc., are as follows:

McClain Wholesalers, Inc.
Statement of Comprehensive Income
For the Years Ended December 31, 2006 and 2007

	2006	2007
Net income	a.	$36,000
Other comprehensive income (loss), net of tax	b.	2,000
Total comprehensive income	c.	e.

McClain Wholesalers, Inc.
Selected Balance Sheet Items
December 31, 2005, 2006, and 2007

	Dec. 31, 2005	Dec. 31, 2006	Dec. 31, 2007
Temporary investments in marketable securities at fair market value, net of taxes on unrealized gains or losses	$ 26,000	d.	f.
Retained earnings	140,000	$180,000	g.
Accumulated other comprehensive income or (loss)	(5,000)	(8,000)	h.

There were no dividends or purchases or sales of temporary investments. Other comprehensive items included only after-tax unrealized gains and losses on investments.

Determine the missing lettered items.

Exercise 12-15

Comprehensive income and temporary investments

Goal 3

a. Total comprehensive income, $185,000

SPREADSHEET

During 2006, Cosby Corporation held a portfolio of available-for-sale securities having a cost of $260,000. There were no purchases or sales of investments during the year. The market values after adjusting for the impact of taxes, at the beginning and end of the year, were $200,000 and $240,000, respectively. The net income for 2006 was $145,000, and no dividends were paid during the year. The Stockholders' Equity section of the balance sheet was as follows on December 31, 2005:

Cosby Corporation
Stockholders' Equity
December 31, 2005

Common stock	$ 35,000
Paid-in capital in excess of par value	350,000
Retained earnings	435,000
Accumulated other comprehensive loss	(60,000)
Total	$760,000

a. Prepare a statement of comprehensive income for 2006.
b. Prepare the Stockholders' Equity section of the balance sheet for December 31, 2006.

Exercise 12-16

Temporary investments and other comprehensive income

Goal 3

a. 2007 unrealized gain, $60,000

The temporary investments of Secure Connections, Inc., include only 10,000 shares of Lambert Acres, Inc., common stock purchased on January 10, 2006, for $20 per share. As of the December 31, 2006, balance sheet date, assume that the share price declined to $17 per share. As of the December 31, 2007, balance sheet date, assume that the share price rose to $27 per share. The investment was held through December 31, 2007. Assume a tax rate of 40%.

a. Determine the net after-tax unrealized gain or loss from holding the Lambert Acres common stock for 2006 and 2007.
b. What is the balance of Accumulated Other Comprehensive Income or Loss for December 31, 2006, and December 31, 2007?
c. Where is Accumulated Other Comprehensive Income or Loss disclosed on the financial statements?

Exercise 12-17

Temporary investments in marketable securities

Goal 3

During 2006, its first year of operations, Lyon Research Corporation purchased the following securities as a temporary investment:

Security	Shares Purchased	Cost	Cash Dividends Received
M-Labs, Inc.	1,000	$29,000	$ 900
Spectrum Corp.	2,500	45,000	1,600

a. Record the purchase of the temporary investments for cash.
b. Record the receipt of the dividends.

Exercise 12-18

Financial statement reporting of temporary investments

Goal 3

b. Comprehensive income, $73,400

SPREADSHEET

Using the data for Lyon Research Corporation in Exercise 12-17, assume that as of December 31, 2006, the M-Labs, Inc., stock had a market value of $28 per share and the Spectrum Corp. stock had a market value of $14 per share. For the year ending December 31, 2006, Lyon Research Corporation had net income of $80,000. Its tax rate is 40%.

a. Prepare the balance sheet presentation for the temporary investments.
b. Prepare a statement of comprehensive income presentation for the temporary investments.

Exercise 12-19

Entries for investment in stock, receipt of dividends, and sale of shares

Goal 3

On February 27, Ball Corporation acquired 3,000 shares of the 50,000 outstanding shares of Beach Co. common stock at 40.75 plus commission charges of $150. On July 8, a cash dividend of $1.50 per share and a 2% stock dividend were received. On December 7, 1,000 shares were sold at 49, less commission charges of $60. Prepare the entries to record (a) the purchase of the stock, (b) the receipt of dividends, and (c) the sale of the 1,000 shares.

Exercise 12-20

Entries using equity method for stock investment

Goal 3

At a total cost of $1,820,000, Joshua Corporation acquired 70,000 shares of Caleb Corp. common stock as a long-term investment. Joshua Corporation uses the equity method of accounting for this investment. Caleb Corp. has 280,000 shares of common stock outstanding, including the shares acquired by Joshua Corporation. Journalize the entries by Joshua Corporation to record the following information:

a. Caleb Corp. reports net income of $2,500,000 for the current period.
b. A cash dividend of $3.40 per common share is paid by Caleb Corp. during the current period.

Exercise 12-21

Equity method for stock investment

Goal 3

Toys"R"Us Inc. is a major retailer of toys in the United States. A recent balance sheet disclosed a long-term investment in Toys-Japan, a public company trading on the Tokyo over-the-counter market. The balance sheet disclosure for two comparative years was as follows:

	Feb. 2, 2002	Feb. 3, 2001
Investment in Toys-Japan (in millions)	$123	$108

In addition, the Toys"R"Us income statement disclosed equity earnings in the Toys-Japan investment as follows (in millions):

	Feb. 2, 2002	Feb. 3, 2001
Equity in net earnings of Toys-Japan	$29	$31

The notes to the financial statements provided the following additional information about this investment:

The company accounts for its investment in the common stock of Toys-Japan under the "equity method" of accounting since the initial public offering on April 24, 2000. The quoted market value of the company's investment in Toys-Japan was $283 at February 2, 2002.

a. Explain the change in the investment in Toys-Japan account for fiscal year ended February 2, 2002.
b. Why is the Investment in Toys-Japan not recognized at market value?

Exercise 12-22

Equity method for stock investment

Goal 3

The following note to the consolidated financial statements for The Goodyear Tire and Rubber Co. relates to investments in affiliated companies:

Goodyear's investments in 20% to 50% owned companies in which it has the ability to exercise significant influence over operating and financial policies are accounted for by the equity method. Accordingly, Goodyear's share of the earnings of these companies is included in consolidated net income (loss).

Dividends received by the Company from its unconsolidated affiliates accounted for under the equity method was $2.8 million.

a. Is Goodyear required to use the equity method for these investments? Explain.
b. Journalize the entry for receipt of the dividend making the credit to Investment in Affiliates.

Exercise 12-23

Entries for purchase and sale of investment in bonds; loss

Goal 4

Laser Vision Co. sells optical supplies to opticians and ophthalmologists. Prepare the entries to record the following selected transactions of Laser Vision Co.:

a. Purchased for cash $450,000 of Pierce Co. 8% bonds at $101\frac{1}{2}$ plus accrued interest of $9,000.
b. Received first semiannual interest.
c. At the end of the first year, amortized $540 of the bond premium.
d. Sold the bonds at 99 plus accrued interest of $3,000. The bonds were carried at $453,750 at the time of the sale.

Exercise 12-24

Entries for purchase and sale of investment in bonds; gain

Goal 4

Inez Company develops and sells graphics software for use by architects. Prepare the entries to record the following selected transactions of Inez Company:

a. Purchased for cash $270,000 of Theisen Co. 5% bonds at 98 plus accrued interest of $2,250.
b. Received first semiannual interest.
c. Amortized $450 on the bond investment at the end of the first year.
d. Sold the bonds at 100 plus accrued interest of $4,500. The bonds were carried at $267,250 at the time of the sale.

Exercise 12-25

Price-earnings ratio

Goal **5**

The following comparative net income and earnings per share data are provided for Research in Motion Ltd., developer of the BlackBerry® wireless handheld device, for three recent fiscal years:

Year ended	Feb. 28, 2005	Feb. 28, 2004	Mar. 1, 2003
Net income	$213,387	$51,829	$(148,857)
Basic earnings per share	1.14	0.65	(1.92)
Diluted earnings per share	1.09	0.62	(1.92)

The stock market prices at the end of each of the three fiscal years were as follows:

March 1, 2003	$ 6.65
February 28, 2004	49.45
February 28, 2005	66.11

a. Determine the price-earnings ratio for Research in Motion for each of the three fiscal years, using basic earnings per share and the ending stock market price. Round to two decimal places.
b. What conclusions can you reach by considering the price-earnings ratio?
c. Why is the diluted earnings per share less than the basic earnings per share?

Exercise 12-26

Price-book ratio calculations

Goal **5**

a. Google, Inc., 12.73

Below are some financial statistics for Google, the Web search engine provider, and Burlington Northern Santa Fe, a large North American railroad (all numbers in thousands, except per share amounts).

	Google	Burlington Northern Santa Fe
Total stockholders' equity, Dec. 31, 2004	$2,929,056,000	$9,311,000,000
Common shares outstanding, Dec. 31, 2004	193,176,000	376,800,000
Market price, Dec. 31, 2004	$193 per share	$ 47 per share

a. Determine the price-book ratio for each company. Round to two decimal places.
b. Explain the difference in the price-book ratio between the two companies.

Exercise 12-27

Price-earnings and price-book ratio calculations

Goal **5**

a. 2004: 13.04

SPREADSHEET

ExxonMobil Corporation is one of the largest companies in the world. The company explores, develops, refines, and markets petroleum products. The basic earnings per share for three comparative years were as follows:

	Years Ended December 31,		
	2004	2003	2002
Basic earnings per share	$3.91	$3.24	$1.69

The company disclosed the following information from the statement of stockholders' equity (in millions):

	Dec. 31, 2004	Dec. 31, 2003	Dec. 31, 2002
Total stockholders' equity	$101,661	$89,915	$74,597
Common shares outstanding	6,401	6,568	6,700

The market price at the end of each year was $33, $40, and $51 for December 31, 2002, 2003, and 2004, respectively.

a. Determine the price-earnings ratio for 2002, 2003, and 2004. Round to two decimal places.
b. Determine the price-book ratio for 2002, 2003, 2004.
c. Interpret your results over the three years.

ACCOUNTING APPLICATION PROBLEMS

Problem 12-1A

Income tax, income statement

Goals **1, 2**

Net income, $180,100

SPREADSHEET

MotoSport, Inc., produces and sells off-road motorcycles and jeeps. The following data were selected from the records of MotoSport, Inc., for the current fiscal year ended October 31, 2006:

Advertising expense	$ 64,000
Cost of merchandise sold	612,400
Depreciation expense—office equipment	7,000
Depreciation expense—store equipment	23,000
Gain on condemnation of land	36,400
Income tax:	
Applicable to continuing operations	92,500
Applicable to loss from discontinued operations (reduction)	12,000
Applicable to gain on condemnation of land	13,400
Interest revenue	12,000
Loss from discontinued operations	31,000
Loss from fixed asset impairment	110,000
Miscellaneous administrative expense	12,000
Miscellaneous selling expense	5,500
Office salaries expense	75,000
Rent expense	24,000
Restructuring charge	14,000
Sales	1,350,000
Sales salaries expense	140,000
Store supplies expense	6,500
Unrealized loss (net of tax) on temporary investments	7,000

Instructions

Prepare a multiple-step income statement, concluding with a section for earnings per share (rounded to the nearest cent) in the form illustrated in this chapter. There were 25,000 shares of common stock (no preferred) outstanding throughout the year. Assume that the gain on the condemnation of land is an extraordinary item.

Problem 12-2A

Income statement, retained earnings statement, balance sheet

Goals **1, 2, 3**

Net income, $340,000

SPREADSHEET

The following data were taken from the records of Surf's Up Corporation for the year ended July 31, 2006:

Retained earnings and balance sheet data:	
Accounts payable	$ 9,500
Accounts receivable	276,050
Accumulated depreciation	3,050,000
Accumulated other comprehensive income	15,000
Allowance for doubtful accounts	11,500
Cash	115,500
Common stock, $10 par (500,000 shares authorized; 251,000 shares issued)	2,510,000
Deferred income taxes payable (current portion, $4,700)	65,700
Dividends:	
Cash dividends for common stock	80,000
Cash dividends for preferred stock	100,000
Stock dividends for common stock	40,000
Dividends payable	25,000
Employee termination benefit obligation (current)	90,000
Equipment	11,819,050
Income tax payable	55,900
Interest receivable	2,500
Merchandise inventory (July 31, 2006), at lower of cost (FIFO) or market	551,500

Paid-in capital from sale of Treasury stock	$ 5,000
Paid-in capital in excess of par—common stock	996,300
Paid-in capital in excess of par—preferred stock	240,000
Patents	85,000
Preferred $6\frac{2}{3}$% stock, $100 par (30,000 shares authorized; 15,000 shares issued)	1,500,000
Prepaid expenses	15,900
Retained earnings, August 1, 2005	4,231,600
Temporary investments in marketable equity securities (at cost)	95,000
Treasury stock (1,000 shares of common stock at cost of $40 per share)	40,000
Unrealized gain (net of tax) on marketable equity securities	15,000
Income statement data:	
Administrative expenses	$ 140,000
Cost of merchandise sold	984,000
Gain on condemnation of land	30,000
Income tax:	
Applicable to continuing operations	170,000
Applicable to loss from discontinued operations	24,000
Applicable to gain on condemnation of land	10,000
Interest expense	7,500
Interest revenue	1,500
Loss from disposal of discontinued operations	104,000
Loss from fixed asset impairment	60,000
Restructuring charge	300,000
Sales	2,600,000
Selling expenses	540,000

Instructions

1. Prepare a multiple-step income statement for the year ended July 31, 2006, concluding with earnings per share. In computing earnings per share, assume that the average number of common shares outstanding was 250,000 and preferred dividends were $100,000. Assume that the gain on the condemnation of land is an extraordinary item.
2. Prepare a retained earnings statement for the year ended July 31, 2006.
3. Prepare a balance sheet in report form as of July 31, 2006.

Problem 12-3A

Entries for investments in stock

Goal 3

GENERAL LEDGER

Theater Arts Company produces and sells theater costumes. The following transactions relate to certain securities acquired by Theater Arts Company, which has a fiscal year ending on December 31:

2006

Feb. 10	Purchased 4,000 shares of the 150,000 outstanding common shares of Haslam Corporation at 48 per share plus commission and other costs of $168.
June 15	Received the regular cash dividend of $0.70 a share on Haslam Corporation stock.
Dec. 15	Received the regular cash dividend of $0.70 a share plus an extra dividend of $0.05 a share on Haslam Corporation stock.

(Assume that all intervening transactions have been recorded properly and that the number of shares of stock owned have not changed from December 31, 2006, to December 31, 2009.)

2010

Jan. 3	Purchased an influential interest in Jacob, Inc. for $1,250,000 by purchasing 40,000 shares directly from the estate of the founder of Jacob. There are 100,000 shares of Jacob, Inc. stock outstanding.
Apr. 1	Received the regular cash dividend of $0.70 a share and a 2% stock dividend on the Haslam Corporation stock.
July 20	Sold 1,000 shares of Haslam Corporation stock at 41. The broker deducted commission and other costs of $50, remitting the balance.
Dec. 15	Received a cash dividend at the new rate of $0.80 a share on the Haslam Corporation stock.

(continued)

Dec. 31 Received $40,000 of cash dividends on Jacob, Inc., stock. Jacob, Inc., reported net income of $295,000 in 2010. Theater Arts uses the equity method of accounting for its investment in Jacob, Inc.

Instructions

Journalize the entries for the preceding transactions.

Problem 12-4A

Entries for bond investments

Goal **4**

SPREADSHEET

Danka, Inc., develops and leases databases of publicly available information. The following selected transactions relate to certain securities acquired as a long-term investment by Danka, Inc., whose fiscal year ends on December 31.

2006

Sept. 1 Purchased $480,000 of Sheehan Company 10-year, 8% bonds dated July 1, 2006, directly from the issuing company, for $494,750 plus accrued interest of $6,400.

Dec. 31 Received the semiannual interest on the Sheehan Company bonds.

31 Recorded bond premium amortization of $500 on the Sheehan Company bonds. The amortization amount was determined by using the straight-line method.

(Assume that all intervening transactions and adjustments have been properly recorded and that the number of bonds owned has not changed from December 31, 2006, to December 31, 2011.)

2012

June 30 Received the semiannual interest on the Sheehan Company bonds.

Aug. 31 Sold one-half of the Sheehan Company bonds at 102 plus accrued interest. The broker deducted $400 for commission, etc., remitting the balance. Prior to the sale, $500 of premium on one-half of the bonds is to be amortized, reducing the carrying amount of those bonds to $242,875.

Dec. 31 Received the semiannual interest on the Sheehan Company bonds.

31 Recorded bond premium amortization of $750 on the Sheehan Company bonds.

Instructions

Journalize the foregoing transactions.

ALTERNATE ACCOUNTING APPLICATION PROBLEMS

Alternate Problem 12-1B

Income tax, income statement

Goals **1, 2**

Net income, $82,000

SPREADSHEET

The following data were selected from the records of Healthy Pantry, Inc., for the current fiscal year ended June 30, 2006:

Advertising expense	$ 46,000
Cost of merchandise sold	279,000
Depreciation expense—office equipment	6,000
Depreciation expense—store equipment	31,000
Gain on discontinued operations	42,500
Income tax:	
Applicable to continuing operations	32,000
Applicable to gain on discontinued operations	16,000
Applicable to loss on condemnation of land (reduction)	8,000
Insurance expense	9,000
Interest expense	18,000
Loss from condemnation of land	24,500

Loss from fixed asset impairment	$ 90,000
Miscellaneous administrative expense	7,500
Miscellaneous selling expense	5,500
Office salaries expense	60,000
Rent expense	29,000
Restructuring charge	150,000
Sales	980,000
Sales commissions expense	145,000
Unrealized gain (net of tax) on temporary investments	25,000

Instructions

Prepare a multiple-step income statement, concluding with a section for earnings per share in the form illustrated in this chapter. There were 75,000 shares of common stock (no preferred) outstanding throughout the year. Assume that the loss on the condemnation of land is an extraordinary item.

Alternate Problem 12-2B

Income statement, retained earnings statement, balance sheet

Goals **1, 2, 3**

Net income, $277,000

SPREADSHEET

The following data were taken from the records of Skate N' Ski Corporation for the year ended October 31, 2006:

Income statement data:	
Administrative expenses	$ 100,000
Cost of merchandise sold	732,000
Gain on condemnation of land	60,000
Income tax:	
Applicable to continuing operations	206,000
Applicable to loss from discontinued operations	28,800
Applicable to gain on condemnation of land	24,000
Interest expense	8,000
Interest revenue	5,000
Loss from discontinued operations	76,800
Loss from fixed asset impairment	200,000
Restructuring charge	90,000
Sales	2,020,000
Selling expenses	400,000
Retained earnings and balance sheet data:	
Accounts payable	$ 89,500
Accounts receivable	309,050
Accumulated depreciation	3,050,000
Accumulated other comprehensive loss	24,000
Allowance for doubtful accounts	21,500
Cash	145,500
Common stock, $15 par (400,000 shares authorized; 152,000 shares issued)	2,280,000
Deferred income taxes payable (current portion, $4,700)	25,700
Dividends:	
Cash dividends for common stock	40,000
Cash dividends for preferred stock	100,000
Stock dividends for common stock	60,000
Dividends payable	30,000
Employee termination benefit obligation (current)	60,000
Equipment	9,541,050
Income tax payable	55,900
Interest receivable	2,500
Merchandise inventory (October 31, 2006), at lower of cost (FIFO) or market	425,000
Notes receivable	77,500
Paid-in capital from sale of Treasury stock	16,000
Paid-in capital in excess of par—common stock	894,750
Paid-in capital in excess of par—preferred stock	240,000

(continued)

Patents	$ 55,000
Preferred $6\frac{2}{3}$% stock, $100 par (30,000 shares authorized; 15,000 shares issued)	1,500,000
Prepaid expenses	15,900
Retained earnings, November 1, 2005	2,446,150
Temporary investment in marketable equity securities	145,000
Treasury stock (2,000 shares of common stock at cost of $35 per share)	70,000
Unrealized loss (net of tax) on temporary equity securities	24,000

Instructions

1. Prepare a multiple-step income statement for the year ended October 31, 2006, concluding with earnings per share. In computing earnings per share, assume that the average number of common shares outstanding was 150,000 and preferred dividends were $100,000. Assume that the gain on condemnation of land is an extraordinary item.
2. Prepare a retained earnings statement for the year ended October 31, 2006.
3. Prepare a balance sheet in report form as of October 31, 2006.

Alternate Problem 12-3B

Entries for investments in stock

Goal 3

GENERAL LEDGER

Samson Company is a wholesaler of men's hair products. The following transactions relate to certain securities acquired by Samson Company, which has a fiscal year ending on December 31:

2006

Jan. 3 Purchased 3,000 shares of the 40,000 outstanding common shares of Davidson Corporation at 67 per share plus commission and other costs of $468.

July 2 Received the regular cash dividend of $1.30 a share on Davidson Corporation stock.

Dec. 5 Received the regular cash dividend of $1.30 a share plus an extra dividend of $0.10 a share on Davidson Corporation stock.

(Assume that all intervening transactions have been recorded properly and that the number of shares of stock owned have not changed from December 31, 2006, to December 31, 2009.)

2010

Jan. 2 Purchased an influential interest in Comstock, Inc., for $760,000 by purchasing 24,000 shares directly from the estate of the founder of Comstock. There are 80,000 shares of Comstock, Inc., stock outstanding.

July 6 Received the regular cash dividend of $1.30 a share and a 3% stock dividend on the Davidson Corporation stock.

Oct. 23 Sold 750 shares of Davidson Corporation stock at 78. The broker deducted commission and other costs of $140, remitting the balance.

Dec. 10 Received a cash dividend at the new rate of $1.50 a share on the Davidson Corporation stock.

31 Received $32,000 of cash dividends on Comstock, Inc., stock. Comstock, Inc., reported net income of $350,000 in 2010. Samson uses the equity method of accounting for its investment in Comstock, Inc.

Instructions

Journalize the entries for the preceding transactions.

Alternate Problem 12-4B

Entries for bond investments

The following selected transactions relate to certain securities acquired by Wildflower Blueprints, Inc., whose fiscal year ends on December 31:

2006

Sept. 1 Purchased $400,000 of Churchill Company 20-year, 9% bonds dated July 1, 2006, directly from the issuing company, for $385,720 plus accrued interest of $6,000.

Goal 4

SPREADSHEET

Dec. 31 Received the semiannual interest on the Churchill Company bonds.
31 Recorded bond discount amortization of $240 on the Churchill Company bonds. The amortization amount was determined by using the straight-line method.

(Assume that all intervening transactions and adjustments have been properly recorded and that the number of bonds owned has not changed from December 31, 2006, to December 31, 2010.)

2011
June 30 Received the semiannual interest on the Churchill Company bonds.
Oct. 31 Sold one-half of the Churchill Company bonds at 96½ plus accrued interest. The broker deducted $400 for commission, etc., remitting the balance. Prior to the sale, $300 of discount on one-half of the bonds was amortized, reducing the carrying amount of those bonds to $194,720.
Dec. 31 Received the semiannual interest on the Churchill Company bonds.
31 Recorded bond discount amortization of $360 on the Churchill Company bonds.

Instructions

Journalize the foregoing transactions.

FINANCIAL ANALYSIS AND REPORTING CASES

Case 12-1

Market-based financial measures

Recent year-end market price and financial statement information for Wal-Mart Stores, Inc., the largest retailer in the world, is provided as follows:

Year	Year-End Market Price per Share	Net Income (basic, millions)	Common Stock Dividend per Share	Number of Common Shares Outstanding (weighted, millions)
2004	$52.33	$10,267	$0.52	4,259
2003	51.33	9,054	0.36	4,363
2002	48.75	7,955	0.30	4,430

a. How has the market price of Wal-Mart compared to earnings per share for 2002–2004? Round to two decimal places.
b. What information should be reported to compare earnings over time and across companies?

Case 12-2

Special charges

In the notes to its 2004 annual report, Boeing Co. provided the following information regarding the 717 airplane termination:

> *On January 12, 2005 we decided to conclude production of the 717 commercial airplane . . . due to the lack of overall market demand for the airplane. The decision is expected to result in total pre-tax charges of approximately $385, of which $280 is incorporated in the 2004 fourth quarter and year end results.*
>
> *Of the $280 charge . . . , supplier termination charges were $171; production disruption and related charges were $36; pension/post-retirement curtailment charges were $43; and severance charges were $30. The termination of the 717 line will result in $385 of cash expenditures that are expected to occur during 2005 through 2007.*

a. Record the $280 million charge for 2004 using account names suggested by the note.
b. Provide a brief description of the nature of each special charge.
b. Assume the severance charges are paid in cash in 2005. Record the appropriate entry in 2005.
c. Why wasn't the total $385 million expected cash expenditures recorded as a charge in 2004?

Case 12-3

Restructuring charges and fixed asset impairment disclosure

The notes to the financial statements for Maytag Corporation provided the following table of special charges.

Maytag Corporation
Schedule of Special Charges (annotated)
For the Year Ended January 1, 2005
(in thousands)

Description of Special Charge	Balance, Jan. 3, 2004	Charged to Earnings 2004	Cash Utilization	Noncash Utilization	Balance, Jan. 1, 2005
Severance and related expense	$15,326	$37,999	$(30,822)		$22,503
Moving of equipment		981	(981)		
Asset write-downs		30,174		$(30,174)	
Excess inventory		1,453		(1,453)	
Purchase commitment		1,610			1,610
Other		1,096	(1,096)		
Total	$15,326	$73,313	$(32,899)	$(31,627)	$24,113

The special charges include both severance-related and asset impairments. The columns of the table indicate the balances and change in balances of the balance sheet accounts affected by the restructuring events.

a. Journalize the entry for special charges for 2004.
b. What is meant by "noncash utilization"?
c. Provide the balance sheet disclosure for the restructuring obligation on January 1, 2005.

Case 12-4

Market-based financial measures

SPREADSHEET

Citigroup, Inc., one of the largest financial services firms in the world, disclosed the following retained earnings information in its statement of stockholders' equity:

	2004	2003	2002
Retained earnings balance, beginning of year	$ 93,483	$81,403	$69,803
Net income	17,046	17,853	15,276
Common dividends	(8,307)	(5,702)	(3,593)
Preferred dividends	(68)	(71)	(83)
Balance, end of year	$102,154	$93,483	$81,403

The average common shares for determining basic earnings per share for the three most recent years were as follows:

2004: 5,107.2
2003: 5,093.3
2002: 5,078.0

Total common stockholders' equity and the stock price at year-end were as follows:

	Dec. 31, 2004	Dec. 31, 2003	Dec. 31, 2002
Common stockholders' equity	$108,166	$96,889	$85,318
Common stock price	48.18	48.54	32.83

a. Determine the earnings per common share for all three years. Round to two decimal places.
b. Determine the book value per common share for all three years. Round to two decimal places.
c. Determine the price-earnings ratio for all three years. Round to two decimal places.
d. Determine the price-book ratio for all three years. Round to two decimal places.
e. Interpret the trend in price-earnings and price-book ratios for the three years.

Case 12-5

Unrealized gains and losses

Berkshire Hathaway, Inc., is a public company holding the investments of Warren Buffet, one of the wealthiest people in the world. Recent financial statements revealed the following:

Accumulated other comprehensive income:	
Unrealized appreciation of investments	$ 2,599
Applicable income taxes	(905)
Reclassification adjustment for appreciation included in net earnings	(1,569)
Applicable income taxes	549
Foreign currency translation adjustments	140
Applicable income taxes	134
Minimum pension liability adjustment	(38)
Applicable income taxes	3
Other	(34)
Other comprehensive income	$ 879
Net earnings	$ 7,308

Retained Earnings and Accumulated Other Comprehensive Income balances at the end of the year were $39,189 and $20,435, respectively.

a. Determine the total comprehensive income.
b. Determine the total other comprehensive income as a percent of comprehensive income for Berkshire Hathaway. Round to one decimal place. Discuss the meaning of this percent.
c. Why is unrealized appreciation (gain) included as part of other comprehensive income?
d. Why are the taxes for unrealized gains subtracted in determining other comprehensive income?

BUSINESS ACTIVITIES AND RESPONSIBILITY ISSUES

Activity 12-1

Ethics and professional conduct in business

Taylor Company made a long-term investment in 100,000 shares of Summit Company at $50 per share. This investment represented less than 1% of the outstanding shares of Summit. By year-end, the share price climbed to $75 per share for an appreciation of $2,500,000. Near the end of the year, the CEO, Bud Greene approached the CFO, Sasha Whitman, wishing to recognize the $2.5 million appreciation as a gain on the income statement. The CEO reasoned that the fair value of the Summit investment should be disclosed on the balance sheet with the associated appreciation in share price recognized on the income statement. How should Sasha respond to the CEO's assertion?

Activity 12-2

Ethics and professional conduct in business

Dillon Matthews is the president and chief operating officer of Ratchet Corporation, a developer of personal financial planning software. During the past year, Ratchet Corporation was forced to sell 10 acres of land to the city of Houston for expansion of a freeway exit. The corporation fought the sale, but after condemnation hearings, a judge ordered it to sell the land. Because of the location of the land and the fact that Ratchet Corporation had purchased the land over 15 years ago, the corporation recorded a $0.20-per-share gain on the sale. Always looking to turn a negative into a positive, Dillon has decided to announce the corporation's earnings per share of $1.05, without identifying the $0.20 impact of selling the land. Although he will retain majority ownership, Dillon plans on selling 20,000 of his shares in the corporation sometime within the next month. Are Dillon's plans to announce earnings per share of $1.05 without mentioning the $0.20 impact of selling the land ethical and professional?

Activity 12-3

Reporting extraordinary item

Fuhlmer, Inc., is in the process of preparing its annual financial statements. Fuhlmer, Inc., is a large citrus grower located in central Florida. The following is a discussion between Jason Kirk, the controller, and April Gwinn, the chief executive officer and president of Fuhlmer, Inc.

April: Jason, I've got a question about your rough draft of this year's financial statement.
Jason: Sure, April. What's your question?
April: Well, your draft shows a net loss of $750,000.
Jason: That's right. We'd have had a profit, except for this year's frost damage. I figured that the frost destroyed over 30% of our crop. We had a good year otherwise.
April: That's my concern. I estimated that if we eliminate the frost damage, we'd show a profit of . . . let's see . . . about $250,000.
Jason: That sounds about right.
April: This income statement seems misleading. Why can't we show the loss on the frost damage separately? That way the bank and our outside investors will be able to see that this year's loss is just temporary. I'd hate to get them upset over nothing.
Jason: Maybe we can do something. I recall from my accounting courses something about showing unusual items separately. Let's see . . . yes, I remember. They're called extraordinary items.
April: Well, we haven't had any frost damage in over five years. This year's damage is certainly extraordinary. Let's do it!

Discuss the appropriateness of revising Fuhlmer, Inc.'s income statement to report the frost damage separately as an extraordinary item.

Activity 12-4

Special charges analysis

The two-year comparative income statements and a note disclosure for Fleet Shoes, Inc., were as follows:

Fleet Shoes, Inc.
Income Statement
For the Years Ended December 31, 2006 and 2007

	2006	2007
Sales	$ 430,000	$ 510,000
Cost of merchandise sold	193,500	224,400
Gross profit	$ 236,500	$ 285,600
Selling and administrative expenses	(107,500)	(122,400)
Loss on fixed asset impairment		(102,000)
Income from operations	$ 129,000	$ 61,200
Income tax expense	51,600	24,480
Net income	$ 77,400	$ 36,720

Note: A fixed asset impairment of $102,000 was recognized in 2007 as the result of abandoning an order management software system. The system project was started in early 2006 and ran into significant delays and performance problems throughout 2007. It was determined that there was no incremental benefit from completing the system. Thus, the accumulated costs associated with the system were written off.

1. Construct a vertical analysis for 2006 and 2007 by determining for each line item its ratio as a percent of sales.
2. Interpret the performance of the company in 2007.

Activity 12-5

Extraordinary items and discontinued operations

GROUP ACTIVITY

In groups of three or four students, search company annual reports, news releases, or the Internet for extraordinary items and announcements of discontinued operations. Identify the most unusual extraordinary item in your group. Also, select a discontinued operation of a well-known company that might be familiar to other students or might interest them.

Prepare a brief analysis of the earnings per share impact of both the extraordinary item and the discontinued operation. Estimate the *potential* impact on the company's market price by multiplying the current price-earnings ratio by the earnings per share amount of each item.

One Internet site that has annual reports is EDGAR (Electronic Data Gathering, Analysis, and Retrieval), the electronic archives of financial statements filed with the Securities and Exchange Commission. SEC documents can be retrieved using the EdgarScan service from PricewaterhouseCoopers at http://edgarscan.pwcglobal.com.

To obtain annual report information, type in a company name in the appropriate space. EdgarScan will list the reports available to you for the company you've selected. Select the most recent annual report filing, identified as a 10-K or 10-K405. EdgarScan provides an outline of the report, including the separate financial statements. You can double click the income statement and balance sheet for the selected company into an Excel™ spreadsheet for further analysis.

ANSWERS TO SELF-STUDY QUESTIONS

1. A Events and transactions that are distinguished by their unusual nature and by the infrequency of their occurrence, such as a gain on condemning land for public use, are reported in the income statement as extraordinary items (answer A).

2. B The difference between the cost of temporary investments held as available-for-sale securities and their market value is reported as an unrealized gain, net of applicable income taxes, as shown below.

Market value of investments	$120,000
Cost of investments	100,000
	$ 20,000
Applicable taxes (40%)	8,000
Unrealized gain, net of taxes	$ 12,000

The unrealized gain of $12,000 (answer B) is reported on the balance sheet as an addition to the cost of the investments and as part of other comprehensive income.

3. C Under the equity method of accounting for investments in stocks, Cisneros Corporation records its share of both net income and dividends of Harrell Inc. in Investment in Harrell Inc. Stock. Thus, Investment in Harrell Inc. Stock would increase by $82,500 [($150,000 × 75%) − ($40,000 × 75%)] for the current year. $30,000 (answer B) is only Cisneros Corporation's share of Harrell's dividends for the current year, $110,000 (answer D) assumes 100% ownership of Harrell.

4. B The interest revenue is the total interest earned for four months (September through December), less the amount of amortized premium.

Interest revenue ($120,000 × 8% × $\frac{4}{12}$)	$ 3,200
Premium amortization	(80)
Total interest revenue	$3,120

The accrued interest purchased on September 1 is not interest revenue for the period.

5. C

$$\text{Price-Earnings Ratio: } \frac{\text{Market Price per Common Share}}{\text{Earnings per Share}},$$

$$\text{or } \frac{\$60}{\$600{,}000 \div 200{,}000} = 20$$

$$\text{Price-Book Ratio: } \frac{\text{Market Price per Share}}{\text{Book Value per Share}},$$

$$\text{or } \frac{\$60}{\$2{,}400{,}000 \div 200{,}000} = 5$$

13 Statement of Cash Flows

Learning Goals

1. Summarize the types of cash flow activities reported in the statement of cash flows.
2. Prepare a statement of cash flows, using the indirect method.
3. Prepare a statement of cash flows, using the direct method.
4. Calculate and interpret the cash conversion cycle, flow ratio, and free cash flow.

Dell Inc.

Is it possible to have too much cash? Clearly, most of us would answer no. However, a business views cash differently than either you or I would. Naturally, a business needs cash to develop and launch new products, expand markets, purchase plant and equipment, and acquire other businesses. However, some businesses have built up huge cash balances beyond even these needs. For example, both **Microsoft Corporation** and **Dell Inc.** have accumulated billions of dollars in cash and temporary investments, totaling in excess of 60% of their total assets. Such large cash balances can lower the return on total assets. As stated by one analyst, "when a company sits on cash (which earns 1% or 2%) and leaves equity outstanding . . . , it is tantamount to taking a loan at 15% and investing in a passbook savings account that earns 2%—it destroys value." So while having too much cash is a good problem to have, companies like Microsoft, **Cisco Systems**, **IBM**, **Apple Computer**, and Dell are under pressure to pay dividends or repurchase common stock. For example, Microsoft recently declared a $32 billion special dividend to distribute excess cash to shareholders.

How does a company grow into such a success that cash can actually be a problem? Consider the story of Michael Dell. Dell began the company that bears his name at the tender age of 19 in 1984. The business began in his college dorm room with $1,000 of his own money. Dell's transforming vision was to sell computers directly to the customer, without the middleman. After experiencing initial success, Dell knew he was on to something, so he said Goodbye to school and dedicated himself to the business. This initial idea is now the famous Dell Direct® model, which became even more powerful with the growth of the Internet. Today, Dell Inc. is valued at over $90 billion. Moving from $1,000 to $90 billion in 20 years, while being the best performing stock among large companies during the last decade, is extraordinary.

COURTESY OF DELL INC.

How a company generates cash and uses cash plays a critical role in the company's potential for success. As a result, understanding a company's cash flows is as important as understanding earnings power. In this chapter, we will illustrate how to determine and interpret the cash flows of a company using the statement of cash flows.

Sources: Dominic White, "Still Logging on to Prove Folks Wrong Despite a $13 Billion Fortune and Approaching Middle Age, Michael Dell Remains Eager to Defy Critics," *The Daily Telegraph*, September 18, 2004, p. 32; Marcelo Prince and Donna Fuscaldo, "Cash-Rich Tech Titans May Not Follow Microsoft's Example," *Dow Jones Newswire*, July 21, 2004.

Summarize the types of cash flow activities reported in the statement of cash flows.

REPORTING CASH FLOWS

We have already introduced and illustrated the statement of cash flows throughout this text. In this chapter, we will address this key financial statement in greater detail. Recall that the **statement of cash flows** reports a firm's major cash inflows and outflows for a period.[1] The statement of cash flows is a required financial statement that explains how a company generates and uses cash during an accounting period. It provides useful information about a firm's ability to generate cash from operations, maintain and expand its operating capacity, meet its financial obligations, and pay dividends. It is useful to managers in evaluating past operations and in planning future investing and financing activities. It is useful to investors, creditors, and others in assessing a firm's profit potential. In addition, cash flows are particularly important in evaluating firms in financial distress, because the ultimate cause of bankruptcy is lack of cash. Thus, the statement is also used to assess the firm's ability to pay its maturing debt.

The cash flow statement is made up of three sections. Each section reports the cash flows of a different type of activity:

1. **Cash flows from operating activities** are cash flows from transactions that affect net income. Examples of such transactions include the purchase and sale of merchandise by a retailer.
2. **Cash flows from investing activities** are cash flows from transactions that affect the investments in noncurrent assets. Examples of such transactions include the sale and purchase of fixed assets, such as equipment and buildings.
3. **Cash flows from financing activities** are cash flows from transactions that affect the equity and debt of the business. Examples of such transactions include issuing or retiring debt securities as well as paying dividends.

In the statement of cash flows, the cash flows from operating activities are normally presented first, followed by the cash flows from investing activities and financing activities. The total of the net cash flow from these activities is the net increase or decrease in cash for the period. The cash balance at the beginning of the period is added to the net increase or decrease in cash, resulting in the cash balance at the end of the period. The ending cash balance on the statement of cash flows equals the cash reported on the balance sheet.

Exhibit 1 shows common cash flow transactions reported in each of the three sections of the statement of cash flows. By reporting cash flows by operating, investing, and financing activities, significant relationships within and among the activities can be evaluated. For example, the cash receipts from issuing bonds can be related to repayments of borrowings when both are reported as financing activities. Also, the impact of each of the three activities (operating, investing, and financing) on cash flows can be identified. This allows investors and creditors to evaluate the effects of cash flows on a firm's profits and ability to pay debt.

International Perspective Under International Accounting Standards, interest received or paid can be reported as either a cash flow from operating activities, cash flow from investing activities, or cash flow from financing activities.

Cash Flows from Operating Activities

The most important cash flows of a business often relate to operating activities. The two alternative methods for reporting cash flows from operating activities in the statement of cash flows are (1) the direct method and (2) the indirect method.

The **direct method** reports the sources of operating cash and the uses of operating cash. The major source of operating cash is cash received from customers. The major

1 As used in this chapter, cash refers to cash and cash equivalents. Examples of cash equivalents include short-term, highly liquid investments, such as certificates of deposit, U.S. Treasury bills, and money market funds.

Exhibit 1
Cash Flows

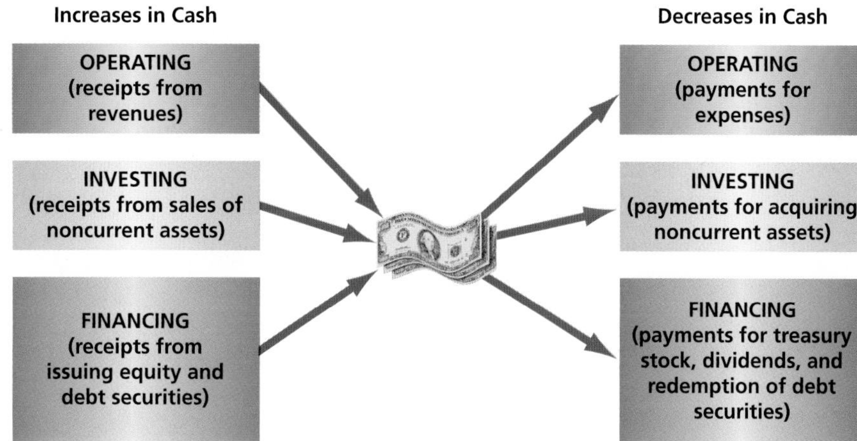

uses of operating cash include cash paid to suppliers for merchandise and services and cash paid to employees for wages. The difference between these operating cash receipts and cash payments is the net cash flow from operating activities.

The primary advantage of the direct method is that it reports the sources and uses of cash in the statement of cash flows. Its primary disadvantage is that the necessary data may not be readily available and may be costly to gather.

The **indirect method** reports the operating cash flows by beginning with net income and adjusting it for revenues and expenses that do not involve the receipt or payment of cash. In other words, accrual net income is adjusted to determine the net amount of cash flows from operating activities.

A major advantage of the indirect method is that it focuses on the differences between net income and cash flows from operations. In this sense, it shows the relationship between the income statement, the balance sheet, and the statement of cash flows. Because these data are readily available, the indirect method is normally less costly to use than the direct method. Because of these advantages, most firms use the indirect method to report cash flows from operations.

Exhibit 2 illustrates the cash flow from operating activities section of the statement of cash flows under the direct and indirect methods. Both statements are for Family Health Care for the month ended November 2007. The first statement was shown in Chapter 3, Exhibit 6, while the second statement was shown in Chapter 3, Exhibit 10. Both statements show the same amount of net cash flow from operating activities, regardless of the method. We will illustrate both methods in detail later in this chapter.

Cash Flows from Investing Activities

Cash inflows from investing activities normally arise from selling fixed assets, investments, and intangible assets. Cash outflows normally include payments to acquire fixed assets, investments, and intangible assets. For example, Oracle Corp. recently invested $10.3 billion cash to acquire PeopleSoft, Inc., to increase its customer base and strengthen its competitive position in enterprise computing.

Cash flows from investing activities are reported on the statement of cash flows by first listing the cash inflows. The cash outflows are then presented. If the inflows are greater than the outflows, *net cash flow provided by investing activities* is reported. If the inflows are less than the outflows, *net cash flow used for investing activities* is reported.

The cash flows from investing activities section in the statement of cash flows for Family Health Care is shown below.

Cash flows from investing activities:	
Purchase of office equipment	$(1,700)

Exhibit 2

Cash Flow from Operations: Direct and Indirect Methods

Family Health Care, PC
Cash Flows from Operating Activities (Direct and Indirect Methods)
For the Month Ended November 30, 2007

Direct Method		
Cash flows from operating activities:		
Cash received from patients	$9,700	
Cash received from rental of land	1,800	$ 11,500
Deduct cash payments for expenses:		
Insurance premiums	$8,400	
Supplies	100	
Wages	2,790	
Rent	800	
Utilities	580	
Interest	100	
Miscellaneous expense	420	(13,190)
Net cash flow from operating activities		$ (1,690)
Indirect Method		
Cash flows from operating activities:		
Net income, per income statement		$ 6,390
Add: Depreciation expense	$ 160	
Increase in accounts payable	140	
Increase in wages payable	220	
Increase in unearned revenue	1,440	1,960
		$ 8,350
Deduct: Increase in accounts receivable	$2,650	
Increase in prepaid insurance	7,300	
Increase in supplies	90	(10,040)
Net cash flow from operating activities		$ (1,690)

Cash Flows from Financing Activities

Cash inflows from financing activities normally arise from issuing debt or equity securities. Examples of such inflows include issuing bonds, notes payable, and preferred and common stocks. For example, Google Inc. recently received cash proceeds of $1.16 billion from its initial public offering of common stock. Often, companies that are expanding operations will seek cash from debt and equity offerings; such is the case with Google as it expands its internet services. Cash outflows from financing activities include paying cash dividends, repaying debt, and acquiring treasury stock. For example, Intel Corporation used $7.5 billion cash to acquire treasury stock to use for its stock option plans.

Cash flows from financing activities are reported on the statement of cash flows by first listing the cash inflows. The cash outflows are then presented. If the inflows are greater than the outflows, *net cash flow provided by financing activities* is reported. If the inflows are less than the outflows, *net cash flow used for financing activities* is reported.

The cash flows from financing activities section in the statement of cash flows for Family Health Care is shown below.

Cash flows from financing activities:	
Additional issuance of capital stock	$ 5,000
Deduct cash dividends	(1,200)
Net cash flow from financing activities	$ 3,800

Noncash Investing and Financing Activities

A business may enter into investing and financing activities that do not directly involve cash. For example, it may issue common stock to retire long-term debt. Such a

INTEGRITY, OBJECTIVITY, AND ETHICS IN BUSINESS

What Is the *Real* Cash Flow?

The Securities and Exchange Commission disagreed with a cash flow disclosure from a complex natural gas trading arrangement of **Dynegy Inc.**, a major energy provider and trader. As a result, the company was required to remove $300 million from cash flow from operations (a drop of 37%) and put it into the financing section. Although this change did not impact net cash flow from all sources, it did change the interpretation of cash flows. As quoted by one source, "The restatement is a big blow to the many investors who held onto the cash flow statement as a beacon of truth even as their faith in the earnings figure was shattered in recent months . . . ." Dynegy's share price dropped 67% within two months of this announcement.

Source: Henny Sender, "'Reliable' Cash Flow Has Shortcomings—Sums Aren't Always What They Seem." *The Wall Street Journal*, May 9, 2002.

© DIGITAL VISION/PHOTODISC/GETTY IMAGES

transaction does not have a direct effect on cash. However, the transaction does eliminate the need for future cash payments to pay interest and retire the bonds. Thus, because of their future effect on cash flows, such transactions should be reported to readers of the financial statements.

When noncash investing and financing transactions occur during a period, their effect is reported in a separate schedule. This schedule usually appears at the bottom of the statement of cash flows. For example, in such a schedule, Procter & Gamble Inc., disclosed the issuance of $55 billion in common stock for Gillette Co. Other examples of noncash investing and financing transactions include acquiring fixed assets by issuing bonds or capital stock and issuing common stock in exchange for convertible preferred stock.

No Cash Flow per Share

The term *cash flow per share* is sometimes reported in the financial press. Often, the term is used to mean "cash flow from operations per share." Such reporting may be misleading to users of the financial statements. For example, users might interpret cash flow per share as the amount available for dividends. This would not be the case if most of the cash generated by operations is required for repaying loans or for reinvesting in the business. Users might also think that cash flow per share is equivalent or perhaps superior to earnings per share. For these reasons, the financial statements, including the statement of cash flows, should not report cash flow per share.

HOW BUSINESSES MAKE MONEY

Dell Direct®

Dell Inc. invented the direct to consumer model for the computer industry. This model uses an assemble-to-order (ATO) manufacturing process, rather than a build-to-stock (BTS) process. Under ATO, the computer is not built until an order is received. Thus, no finished inventory is produced prior to an order being received. Dell is able to reduce inventory investment and obsolescence losses while eliminating retailer costs and margin. The ATO model requires Dell to assemble and ship the order quickly, often

within days of an Internet order being received. This is accomplished by positioning computer components near the assembly location. The ATO model allows customers to receive a custom computer directly to their location, at prices often less than shelf product. The only downside is that the consumer must wait a few days for delivery. The direct model is so attractive that other industries are considering it, such as automobiles, home appliances, and consumer electronics.

Prepare a statement of cash flows, using the indirect method.

STATEMENT OF CASH FLOWS—THE INDIRECT METHOD

The indirect method of reporting cash flows from operating activities is normally less costly and more efficient than the direct method. In addition, when the direct method is used, the indirect method must also be used in preparing a supplemental reconciliation of net income with cash flows from operations. The 2004 edition of *Accounting Trends & Techniques* reported that 593 out of 600 surveyed companies used the indirect method. For these reasons, we will discuss first the indirect method of preparing the statement of cash flows.

To collect the data for the statement of cash flows, all the cash receipts and cash payments for a period could be analyzed. However, this procedure is expensive and time-consuming. A more efficient approach is to analyze the changes in the noncash balance sheet accounts. The logic of this approach is that a change in any balance sheet account (including cash) can be analyzed in terms of changes in the other balance sheet accounts. To illustrate, the accounting equation is rewritten below to focus on the cash account:

$$\text{Assets} = \text{Liabilities} + \text{Stockholders' Equity}$$
$$\text{Cash} + \text{Noncash Assets} = \text{Liabilities} + \text{Stockholders' Equity}$$
$$\text{Cash} = \text{Liabilities} + \text{Stockholders' Equity} - \text{Noncash Assets}$$

Any change in the cash account results in a change in one or more noncash balance sheet accounts. That is, if the cash account changes, then a liability, stockholders' equity, or noncash asset account must also change.

Additional data are also obtained by analyzing the income statement accounts and supporting records. For example, since the net income or net loss for the period is closed to *Retained Earnings*, a change in the retained earnings account can be partially explained by the net income or net loss reported on the income statement.

There is no order in which the noncash balance sheet accounts must be analyzed. However, it is usually more efficient to analyze the accounts in the reverse order in which they appear on the balance sheet. Thus, the analysis of retained earnings provides the starting point for determining the cash flows from operating activities, which is the first section of the statement of cash flows.

The comparative balance sheet for Rundell Inc. on December 31, 2007 and 2006, is used to illustrate the indirect method. This balance sheet is shown in Exhibit 3. Selected ledger accounts and other data are presented as needed.

Retained Earnings

The comparative balance sheet for Rundell Inc. shows that retained earnings increased $80,000 during the year. Analyzing the entries posted to the retained earnings account indicates how this change occurred. The retained earnings account for Rundell Inc. is shown below.

The retained earnings account must be carefully analyzed because some of the entries to retained earnings may not affect cash. For example, a decrease in retained

RETAINED EARNINGS

Dec. 31	Cash dividends	28,000	Jan. 1	Balance	202,300
			Dec. 31	Net income	108,000
					310,300
			Dec. 31	Balance	282,300

Exhibit 3

Comparative Balance Sheet

Rundell Inc.
Comparative Balance Sheet
December 31, 2007 and 2006

	2007	2006	Increase Decrease*
Assets			
Cash	$ 97,500	$ 26,000	$ 71,500
Accounts receivable (net)	74,000	65,000	9,000
Inventories	172,000	180,000	8,000*
Land	80,000	125,000	45,000*
Building	260,000	200,000	60,000
Accumulated depreciation—building	(65,300)	(58,300)	(7,000)
Total assets	$618,200	$537,700	$ 80,500
Liabilities			
Accounts payable (merchandise creditors)	$ 43,500	$ 46,700	$ 3,200*
Accrued expenses payable (operating expenses)	26,500	24,300	2,200
Income taxes payable	7,900	8,400	500*
Dividends payable	14,000	10,000	4,000
Bonds payable	100,000	150,000	50,000*
Total liabilities	$191,900	$239,400	$ 47,500*
Stockholders' Equity			
Common stock ($2 par)	$ 24,000	$ 16,000	$ 8,000
Paid-in capital in excess of par	120,000	80,000	40,000
Retained earnings	282,300	202,300	80,000
Total stockholders' equity	$426,300	$298,300	$128,000
Total liabilities and stockholders' equity	$618,200	$537,700	$ 80,500

earnings resulting from issuing a stock dividend does not affect cash. Such transactions are not reported on the statement of cash flows.

For Rundell Inc., the retained earnings account indicates that the $80,000 change resulted from net income of $108,000 and cash dividends declared of $28,000. The effect of each of these items on cash flows is discussed in the following sections.

Cash Flows from Operating Activities

The net income of $108,000 reported by Rundell Inc. normally is not equal to the amount of cash generated from operations during the period. This is because net income is determined using the accrual method of accounting.

Under the accrual method of accounting, revenues and expenses are recorded at different times from when cash is received or paid. For example, merchandise may be sold on account and the cash received at a later date.

Likewise, insurance expense represents the amount of insurance expired during the period. The premiums for the insurance may have been paid in a prior period. Thus, the net income reported on the income statement must be adjusted in determining cash flows from operating activities. The typical adjustments to net income are summarized in Exhibit 4.[2]

2 Other items that also require adjustments to net income to obtain cash flow from operating activities include amortization of bonds payable discounts (add), losses on debt retirement (add), amortization of bonds payable premium (deduct), and gains on retirement of debt (deduct).

Exhibit 4

Adjustments to Net Income—Indirect Method

Net income, per income statement		$XX
Add: Depreciation of fixed assets and amortization of intangible assets	$XX	
Decreases in current assets (receivables, inventories, prepaid expenses)	XX	
Increases in current liabilities (accounts and notes payable, accrued liabilities)	XX	
Losses on disposal of assets	XX	XX
Deduct: Increases in current assets (receivables, inventories, prepaid expenses)	$XX	
Decreases in current liabilities (accounts and notes payable, accrued liabilities)	XX	
Gains on disposal of assets	XX	XX
Net cash flow from operating activities		$XX

Some of the adjustment items in Exhibit 4 are for expenses that affect noncurrent accounts but not cash. For example, depreciation of fixed assets and amortization of intangible assets are deducted from revenue but do not affect cash.

Some of the adjustment items in Exhibit 4 are for revenues and expenses that affect current assets and current liabilities but not cash flows. For example, a sale of $10,000 on account increases accounts receivable by $10,000. However, cash is not affected. Thus, the increase in accounts receivable of $10,000 between two balance sheet dates is deducted from net income in arriving at cash flows from operating activities.

Cash flows from operating activities should not include investing or financing transactions. For example, assume that land costing $50,000 was sold for $90,000 (a gain of $40,000). The sale should be reported as an investing activity: "Cash receipts from the sale of land, $90,000." However, the $40,000 gain on the sale of the land is included in net income on the income statement. Thus, the $40,000 gain is deducted from net income in determining cash flows from operations in order to avoid "double counting" the cash flow from the gain. Losses from the sale of fixed assets are added to net income in determining cash flows from operations.

The effect of dividends payable on cash flows from operating activities is omitted from Exhibit 4. Dividends payable is omitted because dividends do not affect net income. Later in the chapter, we will discuss how dividends are reported in the statement of cash flows. In the following paragraphs, we will discuss each of the adjustments that change Rundell Inc.'s net income to "Cash flows from operating activities."

Depreciation

The comparative balance sheet in Exhibit 3 indicates that Accumulated Depreciation—Building increased by $7,000. As shown below, this account indicates that depreciation for the year was $7,000 for the building.

ACCUMULATED DEPRECIATION—BUILDING

	Jan. 1	Balance	58,300
	Dec. 31	Depreciation for year	7,000
	Dec. 31	Balance	65,300

The $7,000 of depreciation expense reduced net income but did not require an outflow of cash. Thus, the $7,000 is added to net income in determining cash flows from operating activities, as follows:

Cash flows from operating activities:		
Net income	$108,000	
Add depreciation	7,000	$115,000

Q. Net income was $45,000 for the year. The accumulated depreciation balance increased by $15,000 over the year. There were no sales of fixed assets or changes in noncash current assets or liabilities. What is the cash flow from operations?

A. *$60,000 ($45,000 + $15,000)*

In a recent year, Delta Air Lines had a net loss of $773 million, but a positive cash flow from operating activities of $453 million. This difference was mostly due to $1,230 million of depreciation and amortization. Except for start-up enterprises, negative cash flows from operating activities would normally indicate financial distress.

Current Assets and Current Liabilities

As shown in Exhibit 4, decreases in noncash current assets and increases in current liabilities are added to net income. In contrast, increases in noncash current assets and decreases in current liabilities are deducted from net income. The current asset and current liability accounts for both comparative years and their change from 2006 to 2007 for Rundell Inc. are as follows:

	December 31		Increase
Accounts	**2007**	**2006**	**Decrease***
Accounts receivable (net)	$ 74,000	$ 65,000	$9,000
Inventories	172,000	180,000	8,000*
Accounts payable (merchandise creditors)	43,500	46,700	3,200*
Accrued expenses payable (operating expenses)	26,500	24,300	2,200
Income taxes payable	7,900	8,400	500*

The $9,000 increase in *accounts receivable* indicates that the sales on account during the year are $9,000 more than collections from customers on account. The amount reported as sales on the income statement therefore includes $9,000 that did not result in a cash inflow during the year. Thus, $9,000 is deducted from net income.

The $8,000 decrease in *inventories* indicates that the merchandise sold exceeds the cost of the merchandise purchased by $8,000. The amount deducted as cost of merchandise sold on the income statement therefore includes $8,000 that did not require a cash outflow during the year. Therefore, $8,000 is added to net income.

The $3,200 decrease in *accounts payable* indicates that the amount of cash payments for merchandise exceeds the merchandise purchased on account by $3,200. The amount reported on the income statement for cost of merchandise sold therefore excludes $3,200 that required a cash outflow during the year. Thus, $3,200 is deducted from net income.

Q. Net income was $36,000 for the year. Accounts receivable increased $3,000, and accounts payable increased $5,000. What is the cash flow from operations?

A. *$38,000 ($36,000 − $3,000 + $5,000)*

The $2,200 increase in *accrued expenses payable* indicates that the amount incurred during the year for operating expenses exceeds the cash payments by $2,200. The amount reported on the income statement for operating expenses therefore includes $2,200 that did not require a cash outflow during the year. Hence, $2,200 is added to net income.

The $500 decrease in *income taxes payable* indicates that the amount paid for taxes exceeds the amount incurred during the year by $500. The amount reported on the income statement for income tax therefore is less than the amount paid by $500. In this case, $500 is deducted from net income.

Gain on Sale of Land

The ledger or income statement of Rundell Inc. indicates that the sale of land resulted in a gain of $12,000. As we discussed previously, the sale proceeds, which include the gain and the carrying value of the land, are included in cash flows from investing

INTEGRITY, OBJECTIVITY, AND ETHICS IN BUSINESS

Backdating Contracts

PurchasePro.com, once high-flying Internet darling, crashed into bankruptcy in the early 2000s. Adding to this was a set of grand jury indictments against key executives of PurchasePro and **AOL** for allegedly inflating revenues by backdating contracts into earlier quarters. One executive allegedly stated, "the quarter ends when I say it ends" when discussing the timing of revenue with the accountants. Naturally, manipulating the timing of revenue is misleading and illegal. The cash flows from operations, however, would not be impacted by manipulating revenue timing. This is why many analysts evaluate the relationship between earnings and cash flows from operations to evaluate abnormal accruals.

activities.[3] The gain is also included in net income. To avoid double reporting, the gain of $12,000 is deducted from net income in determining cash flows from operating activities as follows:

Cash flows from operating activities:	
Net income	$108,000
Deduct gain on sale of land	12,000

Reporting Cash Flows from Operating Activities

We have now presented all the necessary adjustments to convert the net income to cash flows from operating activities for Rundell Inc. These adjustments are summarized in Exhibit 5 in a format suitable for the statement of cash flows.

Exhibit 5

Cash Flows from Operating Activities—Indirect Method

Rundell Inc.
Cash Flows from Operating Activities
For the Year Ended December 31, 2007

Cash flows from operating activities:			
Net income		$108,000	
Add: Depreciation	$ 7,000		
Decrease in inventories	8,000		
Increase in accrued expenses	2,200	17,200	
		$125,200	
Deduct: Increase in accounts receivable	$ 9,000		
Decrease in accounts payable	3,200		
Decrease in income taxes payable	500		
Gain on sale of land	12,000	24,700	
Net cash flow from operating activities			$100,500

Cash Flows Used for Payment of Dividends

According to the retained earnings account of Rundell Inc., shown earlier in the chapter, cash dividends of $28,000 were declared during the year. However, the dividends payable account, shown below, indicates that dividends of only $24,000 were paid during the year.

DIVIDENDS PAYABLE

Jan. 10	Cash paid	10,000	Jan. 1	Balance	10,000
July 10	Cash paid	14,000	June 20	Dividends declared	14,000
			Dec. 20	Dividends declared	14,000
		24,000			38,000
			Dec. 31	Balance	14,000

3 Reporting the proceeds (cash flows) from the sale of land as part of investing activities is discussed later in this chapter.

The $24,000 of dividend payments represents a cash outflow that is reported in the financing activities section as follows:

Cash flows from financing activities:	
Cash paid for dividends	$24,000

For some mature companies, cash outflows for dividends can be significant. For example, in a recent year Bank of America Corp. paid over $4.3 billion in dividends, which was equal to 18% of cash flows from operations.

Common Stock

The common stock account increased by $8,000, and the paid-in capital in excess of par–common stock account increased by $40,000, as shown below. These increases resulted from issuing 4,000 shares of common stock for $12 per share.

COMMON STOCK

	Jan. 1	Balance	16,000
	Nov. 1	4,000 shares issued for cash	8,000
	Dec. 31	Balance	24,000

PAID-IN CAPITAL IN EXCESS OF PAR

	Jan. 1	Balance	80,000
	Nov. 1	4,000 shares issued for cash	40,000
	Dec. 31	Balance	120,000

This cash inflow is reported in the financing activities section, as follows:

Cash flows from financing activities:	
Cash received from sale of common stock	$48,000

Bonds Payable

The bonds payable account decreased by $50,000, as shown below. This decrease resulted from retiring the bonds by a cash payment for their face amount.

BONDS PAYABLE

June 30	Retired by payment of cash at face amount	50,000	Jan. 1	Balance	150,000
			Dec. 31	Balance	100,000

This cash outflow is reported in the financing activities section, as follows:

Cash flows from financing activities:	
Cash paid to retire bonds payable	$50,000

Building

The building account increased by $60,000, and the accumulated depreciation—building account increased by $7,000, as shown on the next page.

BUILDING

Jan. 1	Balance	200,000			
Dec. 27	Purchased for cash	60,000			
Dec. 31	Balance	260,000			

ACCUMULATED DEPRECIATION—BUILDING

			Jan. 1	Balance	58,300
			Dec. 31	Depreciation for year	7,000
			Dec. 31	Balance	65,300

The purchase of a building for cash of $60,000 is reported as an outflow of cash in the investing activities section, as follows:

Cash flows from investing activities:	
Cash paid for purchase of building	$60,000

The credit in the accumulated depreciation—building account, shown earlier, represents depreciation expense for the year. This depreciation expense of $7,000 on the building has already been considered as an addition to net income in determining cash flows from operating activities, as reported in Exhibit 5.

Q&A

Q. A building with a cost of $145,000 and accumulated depreciation of $35,000 was sold for a $10,000 gain. How much cash was generated from this investing activity?

A. *$120,000 ($145,000 − $35,000 + $10,000)*

Land

The $45,000 decline in the land account resulted from two separate transactions, as shown below.

LAND

Jan. 1	Balance	125,000	June 8	Sold for $72,000 cash	60,000
Oct. 12	Purchased for cash	15,000			
		140,000			
Dec. 31	Balance	80,000			

The first transaction is the sale of land with a cost of $60,000 for $72,000 in cash. The $72,000 proceeds from the sale are reported in the investing activities section, as follows:

Cash flows from investing activities:	
Cash received from sale of land (includes $12,000 gain reported in net income)	$72,000

The proceeds of $72,000 include the $12,000 gain on the sale of land and the $60,000 cost (book value) of the land. As shown in Exhibit 5, the $12,000 gain is also deducted from net income in the cash flows from operating activities section. This is necessary so that the $12,000 cash inflow related to the gain is not included twice as a cash inflow.

The second transaction is the purchase of land for cash of $15,000. This transaction is reported as an outflow of cash in the investing activities section, as follows:

Cash flows from investing activities:	
Cash paid for purchase of land	$15,000

Preparing the Statement of Cash Flows

The statement of cash flows for Rundell Inc. is prepared from the data assembled and analyzed above, using the indirect method. Exhibit 6 shows the statement of cash flows prepared by Rundell Inc. The statement indicates that the cash position increased by $71,500 during the year. The most significant increase in net cash flows, $100,500, was from operating activities. The most significant use of cash, $26,000, was for financing activities.

Exhibit 6

Statement of Cash Flows—Indirect Method

Rundell Inc.
Statement of Cash Flows
For the Year Ended December 31, 2007

Cash flows from operating activities:			
Net income		$108,000	
Add: Depreciation	$ 7,000		
Decrease in inventories	8,000		
Increase in accrued expenses	2,200	17,200	
		$125,200	
Deduct: Increase in accounts receivable	$ 9,000		
Decrease in accounts payable	3,200		
Decrease in income taxes payable	500		
Gain on sale of land	12,000	24,700	
Net cash flow from operating activities			$100,500
Cash flows from investing activities:			
Cash from sale of land		$ 72,000	
Less: Cash paid to purchase land	$15,000		
Cash paid for purchase of building	60,000	75,000	
Net cash flow used for investing activities			(3,000)
Cash flows from financing activities:			
Cash received from sale of common stock		$ 48,000	
Less: Cash paid to retire bonds payable	$50,000		
Cash paid for dividends	24,000	74,000	
Net cash flow used for financing activities			(26,000)
Increase in cash			$ 71,500
Cash at the beginning of the year			26,000
Cash at the end of the year			$ 97,500

Prepare a statement of cash flows, using the direct method.

STATEMENT OF CASH FLOWS—THE DIRECT METHOD

As we discussed previously, the manner of reporting cash flows from investing and financing activities is the same under the direct and indirect methods. In addition, the direct method and the indirect method will report the same amount of cash flows from operating activities. However, the methods differ in how the cash flows from operating activities data are obtained, analyzed, and reported.

To illustrate the direct method, we will use the comparative balance sheet and the income statement for Rundell Inc. In this way, we can compare the statement of cash flows under the direct method and the indirect method.

Exhibit 7 shows the changes in the current asset and liability account balances for Rundell Inc. The income statement in Exhibit 7 shows additional data for Rundell Inc.

Exhibit 7

Balance Sheet and Income Statement Data for Direct Method

Rundell Inc.
Schedule of Changes in Current Accounts

Accounts	December 31 2007	December 31 2006	Increase Decrease*
Cash	$ 97,500	$ 26,000	$71,500
Accounts receivable (net)	74,000	65,000	9,000
Inventories	172,000	180,000	8,000*
Accounts payable (merchandise creditors)	43,500	46,700	3,200*
Accrued expenses payable (operating expenses)	26,500	24,300	2,200
Income taxes payable	7,900	8,400	500*
Dividends payable	14,000	10,000	4,000

Rundell Inc.
Income Statement
For the Year Ended December 31, 2007

Sales		$1,180,000
Cost of merchandise sold		790,000
Gross profit		$ 390,000
Operating expenses:		
Depreciation expense	$ 7,000	
Other operating expenses	196,000	
Total operating expenses		203,000
Income from operations		$ 187,000
Other income:		
Gain on sale of land	$ 12,000	
Other expense:		
Interest expense	8,000	4,000
Income before income tax		$ 191,000
Income tax expense		83,000
Net income		$ 108,000

The direct method reports cash flows from operating activities by major classes of operating cash receipts and operating cash payments. The difference between the major classes of total operating cash receipts and total operating cash payments is the net cash flow from operating activities.

Cash Received from Customers

The $1,180,000 of sales for Rundell Inc. is reported by using the accrual method. To determine the cash received from sales to customers, the $1,180,000 must be adjusted.

The adjustment necessary to convert the sales reported on the income statement to the cash received from customers is summarized below.

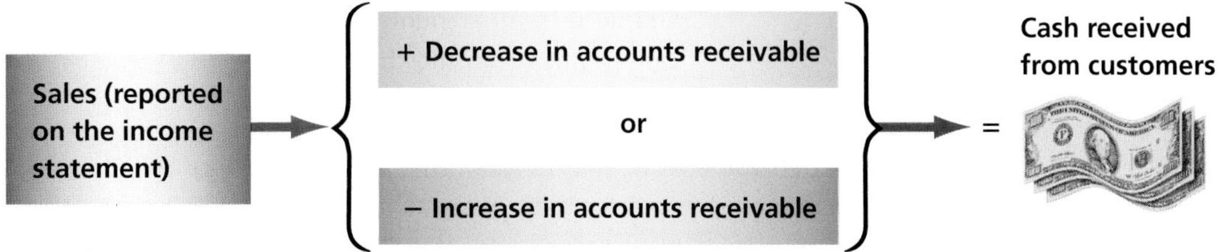

For Rundell Inc., the cash received from customers is $1,171,000, as shown below.

Sales	$1,180,000
Less increase in accounts receivable	9,000
Cash received from customers	$1,171,000

Q&A

Q. Sales reported on the income statement were $350,000. The accounts receivable balance declined $8,000 over the year. What was the amount of cash received from customers?

A. *$358,000 ($350,000 + $8,000)*

The additions to *accounts receivable* for sales on account during the year were $9,000 more than the amounts collected from customers on account. Sales reported on the income statement therefore included $9,000 that did not result in a cash inflow during the year. In other words, the increase of $9,000 in accounts receivable during 2007 indicates that sales on account exceeded cash received from customers by $9,000. Thus, $9,000 is deducted from sales to determine the cash received from customers. The $1,171,000 of cash received from customers is reported in the cash flows from operating activities section of the cash flow statement.

Cash Payments for Merchandise

The $790,000 of cost of merchandise sold is reported on the income statement for Rundell Inc., using the accrual method. The adjustments necessary to convert the cost of merchandise sold to cash payments for merchandise during 2007 are summarized below.

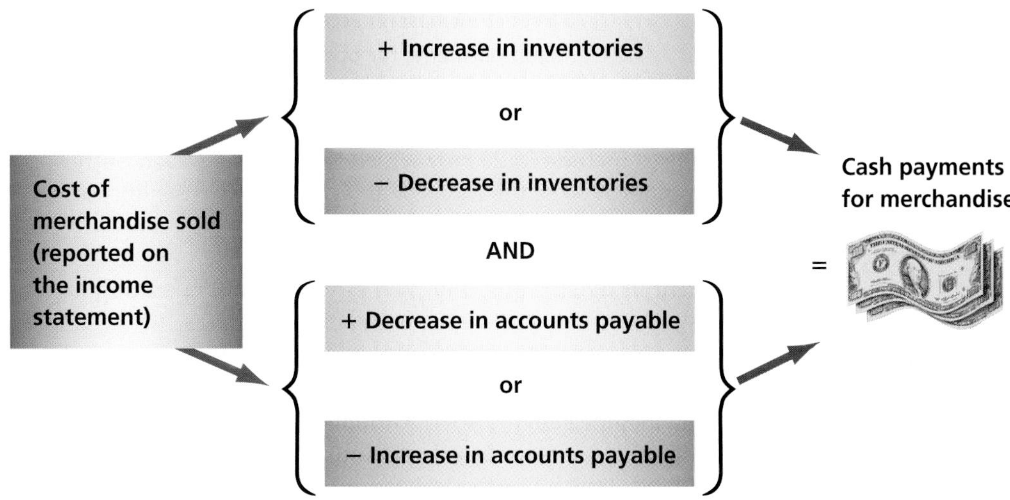

For Rundell Inc., the amount of cash payments for merchandise is $785,200, as determined below.

Cost of merchandise sold	$790,000
Deduct decrease in inventories	(8,000)
Add decrease in accounts payable	3,200
Cash payments for merchandise	$785,200

The $8,000 decrease in *inventories* indicates that the cost of merchandise sold exceeded the cost of the merchandise purchased by $8,000. The amount reported on the income statement for cost of merchandise sold therefore includes $8,000 that did not require a cash outflow during the year. Therefore, $8,000 is deducted from the cost of merchandise sold in determining the cash payments for merchandise.

The $3,200 decrease in *accounts payable* (merchandise creditors) indicates a cash outflow that is excluded from cost of merchandise sold. In other words, the decrease in accounts payable indicates that cash payments for merchandise were $3,200 more than the purchases on account during 2007. Thus, $3,200 is added to the cost of merchandise sold in determining the cash payments for merchandise.

Cash Payments for Operating Expenses

The $7,000 of depreciation expense reported on the income statement did not require a cash outflow. Under the direct method, it is not reported on the statement of cash flows. Instead, the $196,000 reported for other operating expenses is adjusted to reflect the cash payments for operating expenses, as summarized below.

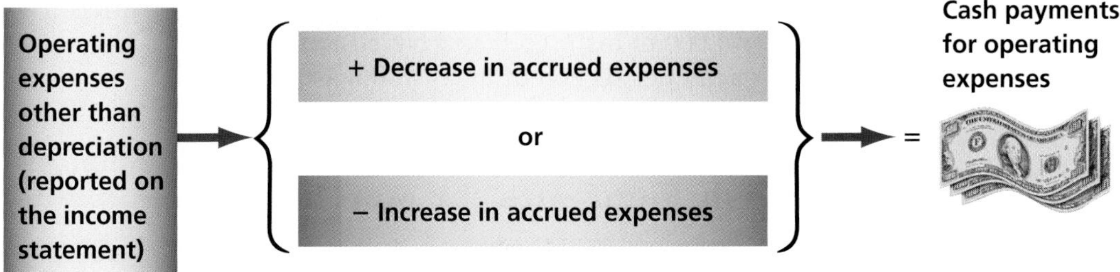

For Rundell Inc., the amount of cash payments for operating expenses is $193,800, determined as follows:

Operating expenses other than depreciation	$196,000
Deduct increase in accrued expenses	2,200
Cash payments for operating expenses	$193,800

The increase in *accrued expenses* (operating expenses) indicates that operating expenses include $2,200 for which there was no cash outflow (payment) during the year. In other words, the increase in accrued expenses indicates that the cash payments for operating expenses were $2,200 less than the amount reported as an expense during the year. Thus, $2,200 is deducted from the operating expenses on the income statement in determining the cash payments for operating expenses.

Gain on Sale of Land

The income statement for Rundell Inc. in Exhibit 7 reports a gain of $12,000 on the sale of land. As we discussed previously, the gain is included in the proceeds from the sale of land, which is reported as part of the cash flows from investing activities.

Interest Expense

The income statement for Rundell Inc. in Exhibit 7 reports interest expense of $8,000. The interest expense is related to the bonds payable that were outstanding during the year. We assume that interest on the bonds is paid on June 30 and December 31. Cash outflow for interest expense of $8,000 is reported on the statement of cash flows as an operating activity.

If interest payable had existed at the end of the year, the interest expense would be adjusted for any increase or decrease in interest payable from the beginning to the end of the year. That is, a decrease in interest payable would be added to interest expense and an increase in interest payable would be subtracted from interest expense. This is similar to the adjustment for changes in income taxes payable, which we will illustrate in the following paragraphs.

Cash Payments for Income Taxes

The adjustment to convert the income tax reported on the income statement to the cash basis is summarized below.

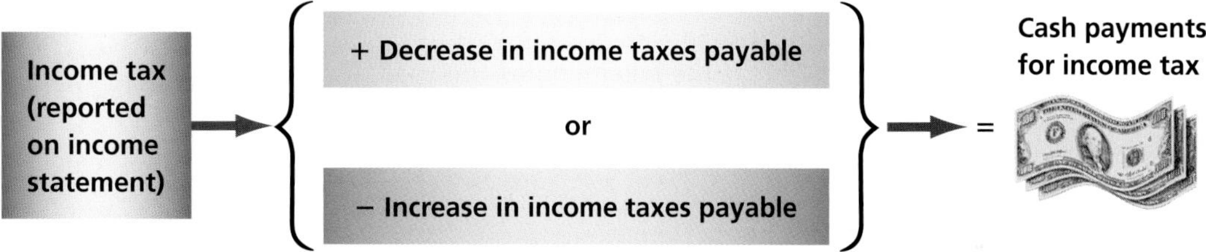

For Rundell Inc., cash payments for income tax are $83,500, determined as follows:

Income tax	$83,000
Add decrease in income taxes payable	500
Cash payments for income tax	$83,500

The cash outflow for income taxes exceeded the income tax deducted as an expense during the period by $500. Thus, $500 is added to the amount of income tax reported on the income statement in determining the cash payments for income tax.

Reporting Cash Flows from Operating Activities—Direct Method

Exhibit 8 is a complete statement of cash flows for Rundell Inc., using the direct method for reporting cash flows from operating activities. The portions of this statement that differ from the indirect method are highlighted in color. Exhibit 8 also includes the separate schedule reconciling net income and net cash flow from operating activities. This schedule must accompany the statement of cash flows when the direct method is used. This schedule is similar to the cash flows from operating activities section of the statement of cash flows prepared using the indirect method.

Exhibit 8

Statement of Cash Flows—Direct Method

Rundell Inc.
Statement of Cash Flows
For the Year Ended December 31, 2007

Cash flows from operating activities:			
Cash received from customers		$1,171,000	
Deduct: Cash payments for merchandise	$785,200		
Cash payments for operating expenses	193,800		
Cash payments for interest	8,000		
Cash payments for income taxes	83,500	1,070,500	
Net cash flow from operating activities			$100,500
Cash flows from investing activities:			
Cash from sale of land		$ 72,000	
Less: Cash paid to purchase land	$ 15,000		
Cash paid for purchase of building	60,000	75,000	
Net cash flow used for investing activities			(3,000)
Cash flows from financing activities:			
Cash received from sale of common stock		$ 48,000	
Less: Cash paid to retire bonds payable	$ 50,000		
Cash paid for dividends	24,000	74,000	
Net cash flow used for financing activities			(26,000)
Increase in cash			$ 71,500
Cash at the beginning of the year			26,000
Cash at the end of the year			$ 97,500
Schedule Reconciling Net Income with Cash Flows from Operating Activities:			
Net income, per income statement		$108,000	
Add: Depreciation	$ 7,000		
Decrease in inventories	8,000		
Increase in accrued expenses	2,200	17,200	
		$125,200	
Deduct: Increase in accounts receivable	$ 9,000		
Decrease in accounts payable	3,200		
Decrease in income taxes payable	500		
Gain on sale of land	12,000	24,700	
Net cash flow from operating activities		$100,500	

Calculate and interpret the cash conversion cycle, flow ratio, and free cash flow.

ANALYSIS AND INTERPRETATION OF CASH FLOWS

Managers want to generate cash from operations using a minimum of noncash working capital resources. The efficiency and cash generating ability of a firm can be measured by the cash conversion cycle and free cash flow.

Cash Conversion Cycle

Noncash working capital consists of current assets and liabilities, other than cash. One way to view noncash working capital efficiency is to view operations as a cycle—from initial purchase of inventory to the final collection upon sale. The cycle begins with a purchase of inventory on account followed by the account payment, after which the item is sold and the account collected. In each step, a current account is involved: inventory, accounts payable, and accounts receivable. These three balances can be translated into days of sales and used to measure how well a company efficiently manages noncash working capital. This measure is termed the **cash conversion cycle**, which is calculated as follows:

$$\text{Cash Conversion Cycle (in days)} = \text{Number of Days' Sales in Receivables} + \text{Number of Days' Sales in Inventory} - \text{Number of Days' Sales in Accounts Payable}$$

Where,

$$\text{Number of days' sales in accounts receivable} = \frac{\text{Average accounts receivable}}{\text{Average daily net sales}}$$

$$\text{Number of days' sales in inventory} = \frac{\text{Average inventory}}{\text{Average daily cost of merchandise (goods) sold}}$$

$$\text{Number of days' sales in accounts payable} = \frac{\text{Average accounts payable}}{\text{Average daily cost of merchandise (goods) sold}}$$

PURCHASE AGREEMENT AND ESCROW INSTRUCTIONS

THIS PURCHASE AGREEMENT AND ESCROW INSTRUCTIONS ("Agreement"), dated for reference purposes ______________ is entered into on this day by and between John Thompson, an individual ("Seller"), and Single Point Investors, LLC, a limited liability company ("Buyer").

ARTICLE 1. RECITALS

1.1 The Property. Seller is the owner of unimproved real property commonly known as 1035-1039 Single Point Lane, Temecula, California, located in the City of Temecula, County of Riverside, State of California. The Property is more particularly described on Exhibit "A" attached hereto (the "Land"). The Land, is also referred to as the "Property", which term shall also encompass, in addition to the Land, all of Seller's right, title and interest in and to any easements, rights of way, air rights, mineral, water and riparian rights appurtenant to the Land, and all permits, land use entitlements, development rights, sewer capacity, map approvals, and other rights or approvals relating to or authorizing the development, construction, ownership, or the operation of the Property.

1.2 Intention of the Parties. Buyer wishes to purchase the Property from Seller, and Seller is willing to sell the Property to Buyer, all on the terms and subject to the conditions of this Agreement.

ARTICLE 2. DEFINITIONS

2.1 Definitions. Unless the context otherwise indicates, whenever used in this Agreement:

2.1.1 "City" means the City of Temecula.

2.1.2 "Closing Date" means the date which is thirty days after the Contingency Date.

2.1.3 "Contingency Date" means the date which is the later of sixty days after the Effective Date, or thirty days following approval by the City of Buyer's preliminary development permit application.

2.1.4 "County" means the County of Riverside.

2.1.5 "Deposit" means the sum of $25,000.

2.1.6 "Effective Date" means the date on which both Buyer and Seller have signed this Purchase and Sale Agreement, or if signed on different dates, the date this Agreement was signed by the later signing signator.

2.1.7 "Escrow Holder" means Nationwide Title Insurance Company.

2.1.8 "Hazardous Materials" means any substance, material or other thing regulated by or pursuant to any federal, state or local statute or ordinance by reason of it potential for harm to human health or the environment, or because of its flammability, toxicity, reactivity or corrosiveness, including but not limited to those substances defined as "hazardous substances," "hazardous materials", or "toxic substances" in the Comprehensive Environmental Response, Compensation and Liability Act of 1980, as amended, 42 U.S.C. § 9601 et seq.; or the Hazardous Materials Transportation Act, 49 USC § 1801 et seq.; or the Resource Conservation and Recovery Act, 42 U.S.C. § 6901 et seq.; and also including those substances defined as "hazardous wastes" or as "hazardous substances" pursuant to the laws of the state of California; and in the regulations adopted and publications promulgated pursuant to all such current and future federal and state laws and local ordinances.

2.1.9 "Property Documents" means all reports, studies and information relating to the Property, including without limitation the items described in Paragraph 7.2.

2.1.10 "Purchase Price" means the sum of Seven Hundred Fifty Thousand Dollars ($750,000).

2.1.11 "Title Insurer" means Nationwide Title Insurance Company – Escrow Department.

The average account balance in the numerator is determined by adding the beginning and ending balances and dividing by two. The average in the denominator is determined by dividing the sales or cost of merchandise sold by 365 days.

One way to generate cash from operations is to reduce the amount of noncash current assets and increase the level of current liabilities. The more positive the cash conversion cycle, the less efficient is the firm's operations from a cash flow perspective. The smaller the cash conversion cycle, the leaner are the working capital requirements for a given level of operations, thus releasing cash for other purposes. Negative cash conversion cycles indicate a highly efficient use of noncash working capital.

To illustrate the cash conversion cycle, the following information was determined from recent annual reports for selected companies in the computer industry:

	Apple Computer	Dell Inc.	Gateway	Hewlett-Packard	Sun Microsystems
Number of days' sales in:					
Receivables	34	30	28	45	75
Inventory	5	4	17	50	26
Accounts payable	(79)	(74)	(52)	(70)	(63)
Cash conversion cycle	(40)	(40)	(7)	25	38

As can be seen from the table, Dell, Gateway, and Apple all have negative cash conversion cycles. For all three companies, their superior inventory management policies (low number of days' sales in inventory) explain this performance. Both Sun Microsystem's and Hewlett-Packard's accounts receivable and inventory appear high for the industry indicating that these companies inefficiently use cash to finance customers and inventory.

Free Cash Flow

Working capital efficiency explains how well a firm uses its working capital, but it does not indicate how much cash is actually being generated. A valuable tool for evaluating the cash flows of a business is free cash flow. **Free cash flow** is a measure of operating cash flow available for corporate purposes after providing sufficient fixed asset additions to maintain current productive capacity and dividends. Free cash flow can be calculated as follows:

Cash flow from operating activities	
Less: Investments in fixed assets to maintain current production	
Dividends	
Free cash flow	

Analysts often use free cash flow, rather than cash flows from operating activities, to measure the financial strength of a business. Many capital-intensive firms must aggressively reinvest to remain competitive. This can reduce free cash flow. For example, Motorola's free cash flow is less than 10% of its cash flow from operating activities. In contrast, Coca-Cola's free cash flow is approximately 75% of its cash flow from operating activities.

To illustrate, the cash flow from operating activities for Dell Inc. was $3,670 million in a recent fiscal year. The statement of cash flows indicated that the cash invested in property, plant, and equipment was $329 million and no dividends were paid. Assuming that the amount invested in property, plant, and equipment maintained existing operations, free cash flow would be calculated as follows (in millions):

Cash flow from operating activities	$3,670
Less: Investments in fixed assets to maintain current production	329
Dividends	
Free cash flow	$3,341

During this period, Dell generated free cash flow in excess of $3 billion, which was 91% of cash flows from operations and over 8% of sales. The free cash flows for several companies in the computer industry are shown for comparison purposes below (in millions).

	Apple Computer	Dell Inc.	Gateway	Hewlett-Packard	Sun Microsystems
Cash flow from operating activities	$934	$3,670	$73	$6,057	$2,226
Cash used to purchase property, plant, and equipment	(176)	(329)	(73)	(1,995)	(249)
Cash used to pay dividends			(9)	(977)	—
Free cash flow	$758	$3,341	$ (9)	$3,085	$1,977
Free cash flow as a percent of cash flow from operations	81%	91%	−12%	51%	89%
Free cash flow as a percent of sales	9%	8%	0%	4%	18%

Positive free cash flow is considered favorable. A company that has free cash flow is able to fund internal growth, retire debt, and enjoy financial flexibility. A company with no free cash flow is unable to maintain current productive capacity or dividend payments to stockholders. Lack of free cash flows can be an early indicator of liquidity problems. Thus, Gateway's negative free cash flow would be a concern to management and investors. As stated by one analyst, "Free cash flow gives the company firepower to reduce debt and ultimately generate consistent, actual income."[4]

4 Jill Krutick, *Fortune*, March 30, 1998, p. 106.

SUMMARY OF LEARNING GOALS

(1) **Summarize the types of cash flow activities reported in the statement of cash flows.** The statement of cash flows reports cash receipts and cash payments by three types of activities: operating activities, investing activities, and financing activities.

Cash flows from operating activities are cash flows from transactions that affect net income. The two methods of reporting cash flows from operating activities are (1) the direct method and (2) the indirect method.

Cash inflows from investing activities are cash flows from the sale of investments, fixed assets, and intangible assets. Cash outflows generally include payments to acquire investments, fixed assets, and intangible assets.

Cash inflows from financing activities include proceeds from issuing equity securities, such as preferred and common stock. Cash inflows also arise from issuing bonds, mortgage notes payable, and other long-term debt. Cash outflows from financing activities arise from paying cash dividends, purchasing treasury stock, and repaying amounts borrowed.

Investing and financing for a business may be affected by transactions that do not involve cash. The effect of such transactions should be reported in a separate schedule accompanying the statement of cash flows.

Because it may be misleading, cash flow per share is not reported in the statement of cash flows.

(2) **Prepare a statement of cash flows, using the indirect method.** To prepare the statement of cash flows, changes in the noncash balance sheet accounts are analyzed. This logic relies on the fact that a change in any balance sheet account can be analyzed in terms of changes in the other balance sheet accounts. Thus, by analyzing the noncash balance sheet accounts, those activities that resulted in cash flows can be identified. Although the noncash balance sheet accounts may be analyzed in any order, it is usually more efficient to begin with retained earnings. Additional data are obtained by analyzing the income statement accounts and supporting records.

(3) **Prepare a statement of cash flows, using the direct method.** The direct and indirect methods will report the same amount of cash flows from operating activities. Also, the manner of reporting cash flows from investing and financing activities is the same under both methods. The methods differ in how the cash flows from operating activities data are obtained, analyzed, and reported. The direct method reports cash flows from operating activities by major classes of operating cash receipts and cash payments. The difference between the major classes of total operating cash receipts and total operating cash payments is the net cash flow from operating activities.

The data for reporting cash flows from operating activities by the direct method can be obtained by analyzing the cash flows related to the revenues and expenses reported on the income statement. The revenues and expenses are adjusted from the accrual basis of accounting to the cash basis for purposes of preparing the statement of cash flows.

When the direct method is used, a reconciliation of net income and net cash flow from operating activities is reported in a separate schedule. This schedule is similar to the cash flows from operating activities section of the statement of cash flows prepared using the indirect method.

(4) **Calculate and interpret the cash conversion cycle, flow ratio, and free cash flow.** The cash conversion cycle and flow ratio measure the efficiency of using noncash working capital for operations. The cash conversion cycle is calculated as the number of days' sales in accounts receivable, plus the number of days' sales in inventory, less the number of days' sales in accounts payable. Low or negative values for the cash conversion cycle are considered very efficient. Free cash flow is the amount of operating cash flow remaining after replacing current productive capacity and maintaining current dividends. Free cash flow is the amount of cash available to reduce debt, expand the business, or return to shareholders through increased dividends or treasury stock purchases.

GLOSSARY

Cash conversion cycle The number of days' sales in accounts receivable, plus the number of days' sales in inventory, less the number of days' sales in accounts payable.

Cash flows from financing activities The section of the statement of cash flows that reports cash flows from transactions affecting the equity and debt of the business.

Cash flows from investing activities The section of the statement of cash flows that reports cash flows from transactions affecting investments in noncurrent assets.

Cash flows from operating activities The section of the statement of cash flows that reports the cash transactions affecting the determination of net income.

Direct method A method of reporting the cash flows from operating activities as the difference between the operating cash receipts and the operating cash payments.

Free cash flow The amount of operating cash flow remaining after replacing current productive capacity and maintaining current dividends.

Indirect method A method of reporting the cash flows from operating activities as the net income from operations adjusted for all deferrals of past cash receipts and payments and all accruals of expected future cash receipts and payments.

Statement of cash flows A summary of the major cash receipts and cash payments for a period.

ILLUSTRATIVE ACCOUNTING APPLICATION PROBLEM

The comparative balance sheet of Dowling Company for December 31, 2007 and 2006, is shown below.

An examination of the accounting records revealed the following additional information applicable to 2007:

a. Land costing $15,000 was sold for $15,000.
b. A mortgage note was issued for $40,000.
c. A building costing $115,000 was constructed.
d. 2,500 shares of common stock were issued at 40 in exchange for the bonds payable.
e. Cash dividends declared were $74,670.

Instructions

1. Prepare a statement of cash flows, using the indirect method of reporting cash flows from operating activities.
2. Prepare a statement of cash flows, using the direct method of reporting cash flows from operating activities.

Dowling Company
Comparative Balance Sheet
December 31, 2007 and 2006

	2007	2006
Assets		
Cash	$ 140,350	$ 95,900
Accounts receivable (net)	95,300	102,300
Inventories	165,200	157,900
Prepaid expenses	6,240	5,860
Investments (long-term)	35,700	84,700
Land	75,000	90,000
Buildings	375,000	260,000
Accumulated depreciation—buildings	(71,300)	(58,300)
Machinery and equipment	428,300	428,300
Accumulated depreciation—machinery and equipment	(148,500)	(138,000)
Patents	58,000	65,000
Total assets	$1,159,290	$1,093,660
Liabilities and Stockholders' Equity		
Accounts payable (merchandise creditors)	$ 43,500	$ 46,700
Accrued expenses (operating expenses)	14,000	12,500
Income taxes payable	7,900	8,400
Dividends payable	14,000	10,000
Mortgage note payable, due 2020	40,000	0
Bonds payable	150,000	250,000
Common stock, $30 par	450,000	375,000
Excess of issue price over par—common stock	66,250	41,250
Retained earnings	373,640	349,810
Total liabilities and stockholders' equity	$1,159,290	$1,093,660

The income statement for Dowling Company is shown at the top of the following page.

Dowling Company
Income Statement
For the Year Ended December 31, 2007

Sales		$1,100,000
Cost of merchandise sold		710,000
Gross profit		$ 390,000
Operating expenses:		
Depreciation expense	$ 23,500	
Patent amortization	7,000	
Other operating expenses	196,000	
Total operating expenses		226,500
Income from operations		$ 163,500
Other income:		
Gain on sale of investments	$ 11,000	
Other expense:		
Interest expense	26,000	(15,000)
Income before income tax		$ 148,500
Income tax expense		50,000
Net income		$ 98,500

Solution

1.

Dowling Company
Statement of Cash Flows—Indirect Method
For the Year Ended December 31, 2007

Cash flows from operating activities:			
Net income, per income statement		$ 98,500	
Add: Depreciation	$23,500		
Amortization of patents	7,000		
Decrease in accounts receivable	7,000		
Increase in accrued expenses	1,500	39,000	
		$137,500	
Deduct: Increase in inventories	$ 7,300		
Increase in prepaid expenses	380		
Decrease in accounts payable	3,200		
Decrease in income taxes payable	500		
Gain on sale of investments	11,000	22,380	
Net cash flow from operating activities			$115,120
Cash flows from investing activities:			
Cash received from sale of:			
Investments	$60,000		
Land	15,000	$ 75,000	
Less: Cash paid for construction of building		115,000	
Net cash flow used for investing activities			(40,000)
Cash flows from financing activities:			
Cash received from issuing mortgage note payable		$ 40,000	
Less: Cash paid for dividends		70,670	
Net cash flow used for financing activities			(30,670)
Increase in cash			$ 44,450
Cash at the beginning of the year			95,900
Cash at the end of the year			$140,350
Schedule of Noncash Investing and Financing Activities:			
Issued common stock to retire bonds payable			$100,000

2.

Dowling Company
Statement of Cash Flows—Direct Method
For the Year Ended December 31, 2007

Cash flows from operating activities:			
Cash received from customers[1]		$1,107,000	
Deduct: Cash paid for merchandise[2]	$720,500		
Cash paid for operating expenses[3]	194,880		
Cash paid for interest expense	26,000		
Cash paid for income tax[4]	50,500	991,880	
Net cash flow from operating activities			$115,120
Cash flows from investing activities:			
Cash received from sale of:			
Investments	$ 60,000		
Land	15,000	$ 75,000	
Less: Cash paid for construction of building		115,000	
Net cash flow used for investing activities			(40,000)
Cash flows from financing activities:			
Cash received from issuing mortgage note payable		$ 40,000	
Less: Cash paid for dividends[5]		70,670	
Net cash flow used for financing activities			(30,670)
Increase in cash			$ 44,450
Cash at the beginning of the year			95,900
Cash at the end of the year			$140,350
Schedule of Noncash Investing and Financing Activities:			
Issued common stock to retire bonds payable			$100,000

Computations:
[1]$1,100,000 + $7,000 = $1,107,000
[2]$710,000 + $3,200 + $7,300 = $720,500
[3]$196,000 + $380 − $1,500 = $194,880
[4]$50,000 + $500 = $50,500
[5]$74,670 + $10,000 − $14,000 = $70,670

SELF-STUDY QUESTIONS

Answers at end of chapter

1. An example of a cash flow from an investing activity is:
   - **A.** receipt of cash from the sale of equipment.
   - **B.** receipt of cash from the sale of stock.
   - **C.** payment of cash for dividends.
   - **D.** payment of cash to acquire treasury stock.

2. An example of a cash flow from a financing activity is:
   - **A.** receipt of cash from customers on account.
   - **B.** receipt of cash from the sale of equipment.
   - **C.** payment of cash for dividends.
   - **D.** payment of cash to acquire land.

3. Which of the following methods of reporting cash flows from operating activities adjusts net income for revenues and expenses not involving the receipt or payment of cash?
   - **A.** Direct method
   - **B.** Purchase method
   - **C.** Reciprocal method
   - **D.** Indirect method

4. The net income reported on the income statement for the year was $55,000, and depreciation of fixed assets for the year was $22,000. The balances of the current asset and current liability accounts at the beginning and end of the year are as follows:

	End	Beginning
Cash	$ 65,000	$ 70,000
Accounts receivable	100,000	90,000
Inventories	145,000	150,000
Prepaid expenses	7,500	8,000
Accounts payable (merchandise creditors)	51,000	58,000

The total amount reported for cash flows from operating activities in the statement of cash flows, using the indirect method, is:

A. $33,000.
B. $55,000.
C. $65,500.
D. $77,000.

5. An analysis of the balance sheet of Getty Company revealed the number of days' sales in accounts receivable and inventory of 30 and 45 days, respectively. The number of days' sales in accounts payable was 25 days. What is Getty's cash conversion cycle?
A. 100 days
B. −40 days
C. 50 days
D. 75 days

DISCUSSION QUESTIONS

1. What is the principal disadvantage of the direct method of reporting cash flows from operating activities?
2. What are the major advantages of the indirect method of reporting cash flows from operating activities?
3. A corporation issued $200,000 of common stock in exchange for $200,000 of fixed assets. Where would this transaction be reported on the statement of cash flows?
4. **a.** What is the effect on cash flows of declaring and issuing a stock dividend?
   b. Is the stock dividend reported on the statement of cash flows?
5. A retail business, using the accrual method of accounting, owed merchandise creditors (accounts payable) $290,000 at the beginning of the year and $315,000 at the end of the year. How would the $25,000 increase be used to adjust net income in determining the amount of cash flows from operating activities by the indirect method? Explain.
6. If salaries payable was $75,000 at the beginning of the year and $65,000 at the end of the year, should $10,000 be added to or deducted from income to determine the amount of cash flows from operating activities by the indirect method? Explain.
7. A long-term investment in bonds with a cost of $75,000 was sold for $80,000 cash. (a) What was the gain or loss on the sale? (b) What was the effect of the transaction on cash flows? (c) How should the transaction be reported in the statement of cash flows if cash flows from operating activities are reported by the indirect method?
8. A corporation issued $5,000,000 of 20-year bonds for cash at 105. How would the transaction be reported on the statement of cash flows?
9. Fully depreciated equipment costing $55,000 was discarded. What was the effect of the transaction on cash flows if (a) $5,000 cash is received, (b) no cash is received?
10. For the current year, Accord Company decided to switch from the indirect method to the direct method for reporting cash flows from operating activities on the statement of cash flows. Will the change cause the amount of net cash flow from operating activities to be (a) larger, (b) smaller, or (c) the same as if the indirect method had been used? Explain.
11. Name five common major classes of operating cash receipts or operating cash payments presented on the statement of cash flows when the cash flows from operating activities are reported by the direct method.
12. In a recent annual report, PepsiCo, Inc., reported that during the year it issued stock of $438 million for acquisitions. How would this be reported on the statement of cash flows?
13. Maytag Corporation has 49 days in accounts receivable, 46 days in inventory, and 49 days in accounts payable. What is Maytag's cash conversion cycle?

EXERCISES

Exercise 13-1

Cash flows from operating activities—net loss

Goal 1

On its income statement for a recent year, Time Warner reported a net *loss* of $4.9 billion from operations. On its statement of cash flows, it reported $5.3 billion of cash flows from operating activities.

Explain this apparent contradiction between the loss and the positive cash flows.

Exercise 13-2

Effect of transactions on cash flows

Goal 1

b. Cash receipt, $41,000

State the effect (cash receipt or payment and amount) of each of the following transactions, considered individually, on cash flows:

a. Sold 5,000 shares of $30 par common stock for $45 per share.
b. Sold equipment with a book value of $42,500 for $41,000.
c. Purchased land for $120,000 cash.
d. Purchased 5,000 shares of $30 par common stock as treasury stock at $50 per share.
e. Sold a new issue of $100,000 of bonds at 101.
f. Paid dividends of $1.50 per share. There were 30,000 shares issued and 5,000 shares of treasury stock.
g. Retired $500,000 of bonds, on which there was $2,500 of unamortized discount, for $501,000.
h. Purchased a building by paying $30,000 cash and issuing a $90,000 mortgage note payable.

Exercise 13-3

Classifying cash flows

Goal 1

Identify the type of cash flow activity for each of the following events (operating, investing, or financing):

a. Purchased patents.
b. Purchased buildings.
c. Purchased treasury stock.
d. Sold equipment.
e. Net income.
f. Issued preferred stock.
g. Redeemed bonds.
h. Paid cash dividends.
i. Sold long-term investments.
j. Issued common stock.
k. Issued bonds.

Exercise 13-4

Cash flows from operating activities—indirect method

Goal 2

The following quote was from the notes of a recent annual report of Qwest Communications International Inc.:

> "... in conjunction with our effort to sell certain assets, we determined that the carrying amounts were in excess of our expected sales price, which indicated that our investments in these assets may have been impaired at that date. In accordance with SFAS No. 144, the estimated fair value of the impaired assets becomes the new basis for accounting purposes. As such, approximately $122 million in accumulated depreciation was eliminated against the cost of these impaired assets in connection with the accounting for these impairments."

What impact would this asset impairment have on Qwest's statement of cash flows under the indirect method?

Exercise 13-5

Cash flows from operating activities—indirect method

Goal 2

Indicate whether each of the following would be added to or deducted from net income in determining net cash flow from operating activities by the indirect method:

a. Increase in notes payable due in 90 days to vendors
b. Loss on disposal of fixed assets
c. Decrease in accounts payable
d. Increase in notes receivable due in 90 days from customers
e. Decrease in salaries payable
f. Decrease in prepaid expenses
g. Depreciation of fixed assets
h. Decrease in accounts receivable
i. Amortization of patent
j. Increase in merchandise inventory
k. Gain on retirement of long-term debt

Exercise 13-6

Cash flows from operating activities—indirect method

Goals **1, 2**

a. Cash flows from operating activities, $292,100

SPREADSHEET

The net income reported on the income statement for the current year was $255,800. Depreciation recorded on equipment and a building amounted to $53,500 for the year. Balances of the current asset and current liability accounts at the beginning and end of the year are as follows:

	End of Year	Beginning of Year
Cash	$ 42,000	$ 44,200
Accounts receivable (net)	65,400	67,000
Inventories	125,900	112,600
Prepaid expenses	5,800	6,000
Accounts payable (merchandise creditors)	61,400	67,500
Salaries payable	8,300	7,900

a. Prepare the cash flows from operating activities section of the statement of cash flows, using the indirect method.

b. If the direct method had been used, would the net cash flow from operating activities have been the same? Explain.

Exercise 13-7

Cash flows from operating activities—indirect method

Goal **2**

Cash flows from operating activities, $96,400

SPREADSHEET

The net income reported on the income statement for the current year was $75,000. Depreciation recorded on store equipment for the year amounted to $22,500. Balances of the current asset and current liability accounts at the beginning and end of the year are as follows:

	End of Year	Beginning of Year
Cash	$46,700	$43,000
Accounts receivable (net)	28,800	32,500
Merchandise inventory	54,800	49,300
Prepaid expenses	4,000	3,600
Accounts payable (merchandise creditors)	40,500	42,400
Wages payable	25,500	22,500

Prepare the cash flows from operating activities section of the statement of cash flows, using the indirect method.

Exercise 13-8

Cash flows from operating activities—indirect method

Goal **2**

Colgate Palmolive Company is a major consumer health-care products company. The current assets and current liabilities from two recent balance sheet dates are reproduced below.

Colgate Palmolive Company
Current Assets and Current Liabilities
December 31, 2004 and 2003

(in millions)	Dec. 31, 2004	Dec. 31, 2003
Current assets:		
Cash and cash equivalents	$ 319.6	$ 265.3
Accounts receivable (less allowances of $47.2 and $43.6, respectively)	1,319.9	1,222.4
Inventories	845.5	718.3
Other current assets	254.9	290.5
Total current assets	$2,739.9	$2,496.5
Current liabilities:		
Notes and loans payable	$ 134.3	$ 103.6
Current portion of long-term debt	451.3	314.4
Accounts payable	864.4	753.6
Accrued income taxes	153.1	183.8
Other accruals	1,127.6	1,090.0
Total current liabilities	$2,730.7	$2,445.4

Assuming that there were no mergers, acquisitions, or divestitures that would impact consolidated current accounts during the year, prepare a schedule showing the impact of changes in current accounts in reconciling net income to cash flows from operating activities.

Exercise 13-9

Determining cash payments to stockholders

Goal 2

The board of directors declared cash dividends totaling $80,000 during the current year. The comparative balance sheet indicates dividends payable of $25,000 at the beginning of the year and $20,000 at the end of the year. What was the amount of cash payments to stockholders during the year?

Exercise 13-10

Reporting changes in equipment on statement of cash flows

Goal 2

An analysis of the general ledger accounts indicates that office equipment, which cost $30,000 and on which accumulated depreciation totaled $10,000 on the date of sale, was sold for $25,000 during the year. Using this information, indicate the items to be reported on the statement of cash flows.

Exercise 13-11

Reporting changes in equipment on statement of cash flows

Goal 2

An analysis of the general ledger accounts indicates that delivery equipment, which cost $120,000 and on which accumulated depreciation totaled $40,000 on the date of sale, was sold for $75,000 during the year. Using this information, indicate the items to be reported on the statement of cash flows.

Exercise 13-12

Reporting land transactions on statement of cash flows

Goal 2

On the basis, of the details of the following fixed asset account, indicate the items to be reported on the statement of cash flows:

LAND

Jan. 1	Balance	900,000	Oct. 30	Sold for $310,000	250,000
Feb. 5	Purchased for cash	300,000			
Dec. 31	Balance	950,000			

Exercise 13-13

Reporting stockholders' equity items on statement of cash flows

Goal 2

On the basis of the following stockholders' equity accounts, indicate the items, exclusive of net income, to be reported on the statement of cash flows. There were no unpaid dividends at either the beginning or the end of the year.

COMMON STOCK

	Date		
	Jan. 1	Balance, 70,000 shares	700,000
	Feb. 11	12,000 shares issued for cash	120,000
	June 30	4,100-share stock dividend	41,000
	Dec. 31	Balance	861,000

PAID-IN CAPITAL IN EXCESS OF PAR

	Date		
	Jan. 1	Balance	140,000
	Feb. 11	12,000 shares issued for cash	360,000
	June 30	Stock dividend	102,500
	Dec. 31	Balance	602,500

RETAINED EARNINGS

June 30	Stock dividend	143,500	Jan. 1	Balance	1,000,000
Dec. 30	Cash dividend	240,000	Dec. 31	Net income	800,000
			Dec. 31	Balance	1,416,500

Exercise 13-14

Reporting land acquisition for cash and mortgage note on statement of cash flows

Goal 2

On the basis of the details of the following fixed asset account, indicate the items to be reported on the statement of cash flows:

LAND

Jan. 1	Balance	160,000	
Feb. 10	Purchased for cash	290,000	
Nov. 20	Purchased with long-term mortgage note	200,000	
Dec. 31	Balance	650,000	

Exercise 13-15

Reporting issuance and retirement of long-term debt

Goal 2

On the basis of the details of the following bonds payable and related discount accounts, indicate the items to be reported in the financing section of the statement of cash flows, assuming no gain or loss on retiring the bonds:

BONDS PAYABLE

			Jan. 1	Balance	150,000
Jan. 3	Retire bonds	48,000	July 30	Issue bonds	200,000
			Dec. 31	Balance	302,000

DISCOUNT ON BONDS PAYABLE

Jan. 1	Balance	12,000	Jan. 3	Retire bonds	4,000
July 30	Issue bonds	15,000	Dec. 31	Amortize discount	1,200
Dec. 31	Balance	21,800			

Exercise 13-16

Determining net income from net cash flow from operating activities

Goal 2

Tiger Golf Inc. reported a net cash flow from operating activities of $105,700 on its statement of cash flows for the year ended December 31, 2006. The following information was reported in the cash flows from operating activities section of the statement of cash flows, using the indirect method:

Decrease in income taxes payable	$ 2,100
Decrease in inventories	6,400
Depreciation	11,000
Gain on sale of investments	3,600
Increase in accounts payable	4,700
Increase in prepaid expenses	2,000
Increase in accounts receivable	6,500

Determine the net income reported by Tiger Golf Inc. for the year ended December 31, 2006.

Exercise 13-17

Cash flows from operating activities

Goal 2

Selected data derived from the income statement and balance sheet of Williams Sonoma, Inc., a specialty retailer of kitchen products, for a recent year are as follows:

Income Statement Data (dollars in thousands):	
Net earnings	$75,096
Depreciation	81,594
Loss on sale of fixed assets	3,950
Other noncash income	7,242

(continued)

Cash flows from operating activities, $205,006

SPREADSHEET

Balance Sheet Data (dollars in thousands):

Decrease in accounts receivable	$ 6,025
Decrease in merchandise inventories	33,793
Increase in prepaid expense	4,511
Increase in accounts payable and other accrued expenses	4,156
Increase in income tax payable	12,145

Prepare the cash flows from operating activities section of the statement of cash flows (using the indirect method) for Williams Sonoma for the year.

Exercise 13-18

Cash flows from operating activities—direct method

Goal 3

a. $537,000

The cash flows from operating activities are reported by the direct method on the statement of cash flows. Determine the following:

a. If sales for the current year were $510,000 and accounts receivable decreased by $27,000 during the year, what was the amount of cash received from customers?
b. If income tax expense for the current year was $29,000 and income tax payable decreased by $3,900 during the year, what was the amount of cash payments for income tax?

Exercise 13-19

Cash paid for merchandise purchases

Goal 3

The cost of merchandise sold for Toys"R"Us, Inc., for a recent year was $7,604 million. The balance sheet showed the following current account balances (in millions):

	Balance, End of Year	Balance, Beginning of Year
Merchandise inventories	$2,041	$2,307
Accounts payable	878	1,152

Determine the amount of cash payments for merchandise.

Exercise 13-20

Determining selected amounts for cash flows from operating activities—direct method

Goal 3

b. $79,600

Selected data taken from the accounting records of Floral Escape, Inc., for the current year ended December 31 are as follows:

	Balance, December 31	Balance, January 1
Accrued expenses (operating expenses)	$ 4,300	$ 4,900
Accounts payable (merchandise creditors)	32,100	36,800
Inventories	59,500	71,200
Prepaid expenses	2,500	3,500

During the current year, the cost of merchandise sold was $450,000, and the operating expenses other than depreciation were $80,000. The direct method is used for presenting the cash flows from operating activities on the statement of cash flows.

Determine the amount reported on the statement of cash flows for (a) cash payments for merchandise and (b) cash payments for operating expenses.

Exercise 13-21

Cash flows from operating activities—direct method

Goal 3

Cash flows from operating activities, $97,000

SPREADSHEET

The income statement of Heart Grain Bakeries, Inc., for the current year ended June 30 is as follows:

Sales		$645,000
Cost of merchandise sold		367,800
Gross profit		$277,200
Operating expenses:		
Depreciation expense	$ 45,000	
Other operating expenses	155,400	
Total operating expenses		200,400

(continued)

Income before income tax	$ 76,800
Income tax expense	25,400
Net income	$ 51,400

Changes in the balances of selected accounts from the beginning to the end of the current year are as follows:

	Increase Decrease*
Accounts receivable (net)	$12,000*
Inventories	4,200
Prepaid expenses	2,500*
Accounts payable (merchandise creditors)	8,400*
Accrued expenses (operating expenses)	2,300
Income tax payable	3,600*

Prepare the cash flows from operating activities section of the statement of cash flows, using the direct method.

Exercise 13-22

Cash flows from operating activities—direct method

Goal 3

Cash flows from operating activities, $27,100

SPREADSHEET

The income statement for Wholly Bagel Company for the current year ended June 30 and balances of selected accounts at the beginning and the end of the year are as follows:

Sales		$265,000
Cost of merchandise sold		95,800
Gross profit		$169,200
Operating expenses:		
Depreciation expense	$ 12,500	
Other operating expenses	125,700	
Total operating expenses		138,200
Income before income tax		$ 31,000
Income tax expense		12,300
Net income		$ 18,700

	End of Year	Beginning of Year
Accounts receivable (net)	$14,800	$12,500
Inventories	38,100	32,800
Prepaid expenses	6,000	6,400
Accounts payable (merchandise creditors)	27,900	24,300
Accrued expenses (operating expenses)	7,900	8,400
Income tax payable	1,500	1,500

Prepare the cash flows from operating activities section of the statement of cash flows, using the direct method.

Exercise 13-23

Statement of cash flows

Goal 2

Net cash flow from operating activities, $29

SPREADSHEET

The comparative balance sheet of Contemporary Millworks, Inc., for December 31, 2008 and 2007, is shown at the top of the following page.

The following additional information is taken from the records:

a. Land was sold for $13.
b. Equipment was acquired for cash.
c. There were no disposals of equipment during the year.
d. The common stock was issued for cash.
e. There was a $30 credit to Retained Earnings for net income.
f. There was a $4 debit to Retained Earnings for cash dividends declared.

Prepare a statement of cash flows, using the indirect method of presenting cash flows from operating activities.

	Dec. 31, 2008	Dec. 31, 2007
Assets		
Cash	$ 50	$ 16
Accounts receivable (net)	30	32
Inventories	24	19
Land	35	50
Equipment	32	15
Accumulated depreciation—equipment	(9)	(6)
Total	$162	$126
Liabilities and Stockholders' Equity		
Accounts payable (merchandise creditors)	$ 17	$ 20
Dividends payable	1	—
Common stock, $1 par	4	2
Paid-in capital in excess of par—common stock	20	10
Retained earnings	120	94
Total	$162	$126

Exercise 13-24

Statement of cash flows

Goal 2

List the errors you find in the following statement of cash flows. The cash balance at the beginning of the year was $70,700. All other figures are correct, except the cash balance at the end of the year.

Healthy Choice Nutrition Products, Inc.
Statement of Cash Flows
For the Year Ended December 31, 2006

Cash flows from operating activities:			
Net income, per Income statement		$100,500	
Add: Depreciation	$ 49,000		
Increase in accounts receivable	10,500		
Gain on sale of investments	5,000	64,500	
		$165,000	
Deduct: Increase in accounts payable	$ 4,400		
Increase in inventories	18,300		
Decrease in accrued expenses	1,600	24,300	
Net cash flow from operating activities			$140,700
Cash flows from investing activities:			
Cash received from sale of investments		$ 85,000	
Less: Cash paid for purchase of land	$ 90,000		
Cash paid for purchase of equipment	150,100	240,100	
Net cash flow used for investing activities			(155,100)
Cash flows from financing activities:			
Cash received from sale of common stock		$107,000	
Cash paid for dividends		45,000	
Net cash flow provided by financing activities			152,000
Increase in cash			$137,600
Cash at the end of the year			105,300
Cash at the beginning of the year			$242,900

Exercise 13-25

Cash conversion cycle

Goal 4

The average accounts receivable, inventory, and accounts payable information for fiscal year 2004 for Home Depot Inc. and Lowe's Inc. is provided as follows (in millions):

	Home Depot Inc.	Lowe's Inc.
Average accounts receivable	$1,298	$ 78
Average inventory	9,576	5,283
Average accounts payable	5,462	2,450

In addition, the sales and cost of merchandise sold for each company were reported for 2004 as follows (in millions):

	Home Depot Inc.	Lowe's Inc.
Sales	$73,094	$36,464
Cost of merchandise sold	48,664	24,165

a. Calculate the cash conversion cycle for Home Depot and Lowe's. Round your calculations to the nearest whole day.
b. Interpret your results.

Exercise 13-26

Cash conversion cycle

Goal 4

The comparative current assets and current liabilities for Robert Mondavi Corp., a major California winery, are provided as follows:

Robert Mondavi Corp.
Selected Balance Sheet Information

(in thousands)	June 30, 2004	June 30, 2003
Current assets:		
Cash and cash equivalents	$ 48,960	$ 1,339
Accounts receivable, net	94,549	96,111
Inventories	387,940	392,635
Prepaid expenses and other current assets	7,025	12,545
Total current assets	$538,474	$502,630
Current liabilities:		
Accounts payable	$ 26,037	$ 28,727
Other accrued expenses	37,565	33,419
Current portion of long-term debt	18,910	9,837
Total current liabilities	$ 82,512	$ 71,983

The income statements indicated sales were $491,957 and the cost of goods sold was $283,849 for the fiscal year ended 2004 (in thousands).

a. Determine the cash conversion cycle for the fiscal year ending 2004. Round to the nearest whole day.
b. Interpret your results.

Exercise 13-27

Free cash flow

Goals 2, 4

Hacienda Tile Company has 100,000 shares of common stock issued and outstanding and 1,000 shares of 8%, $100 par value preferred stock issued and outstanding. Hacienda had cash flows from operating activities of $120,000. Cash flows used for investments in property, plant, and equipment totaled $45,000, of which 60% of this investment was used to replace existing capacity. A cash dividend of $0.20 per share was declared and paid on common stock.

Determine the free cash flow for Hacienda Tile Company.

Exercise 13-28

Free cash flow

Goal 4

The following information was available from selected financial statements of Paradise Hotels, Inc.:

Net income	$2,400,000
Depreciation expense	320,000
Cash flows provided by operating activities	3,000,000
Dividends paid	575,000
Cash used to purchase and improve fixed assets	510,000
Interest expense	52,000
Cash used to repay bank loans	225,000

Assume that the present capacity of the hotel chain can be maintained by investing an amount equal to 150% of depreciation expense. Determine Paradise Hotel's free cash flow.

Exercise 13-29

Calculate free cash flow

Goal 4

An annotated statement of cash flows for Sara Lee Corporation is shown below.

Sara Lee Corporation
Statement of Cash Flows
For the Years Ended July 3, 2004 and June 28, 2003

(annotated, in millions)	Fiscal Year 2004	Fiscal Year 2003
Net cash from operating activities	$ 2,042	$1,824
Investment activities:		
Purchases of property and equipment	(530)	(746)
Acquisitions of businesses and investments	—	(10)
Dispositions of businesses and investments	137	—
Other	209	82
Net cash used in investment activities	$ (184)	$ (674)
Financing activities:		
Issuances of common stock	$ 139	$ 98
Purchases of common stock	(350)	(305)
Redemption of preferred stock	—	(250)
Borrowings of long-term debt	1	1,773
Repayments of long-term debt	(1,288)	(995)
Short-term borrowings (repayments), net	15	(395)
Payments of dividends	(714)	(497)
Other	35	65
Net cash (used in) from financing activities	$(2,162)	$ (506)
(Decrease) increase in cash and equivalents	$ (304)	$ 644
Cash and equivalents at beginning of year	942	298
Cash and equivalents at end of year	$ 638	$ 942

a. From Sara Lee's statement of cash flows, determine the free cash flow for the fiscal years ended 2003 and 2004. Assume 60% of the acquisition of property, plant, and equipment is used to maintain productive capacity, while the remaining 40% adds to productive capacity. Round to the nearest dollar.
b. Determine the free cash flow as a percent of sales for both years. The sales were $19,566 and $18,291 for fiscal years 2004 and 2003, respectively (in millions). Round the percent to one decimal place.
c. Interpret your results.

ACCOUNTING APPLICATION PROBLEMS

Problem 13-1A

Statement of cash flows—indirect method

Goal 2

Net cash flow from operating activities, $163,300

SPREADSHEET

The comparative balance sheet of Winner's Edge Sporting Goods, Inc., for December 31, 2007 and 2006, is at the top of the following page.

The following additional information was taken from the records:

a. The investments were sold for $132,000 cash.
b. Equipment and land were acquired for cash.
c. There were no disposals of equipment during the year.
d. The common stock was issued for cash.
e. There was a $180,600 credit to Retained Earnings for net income.
f. There was a $56,000 debit to Retained Earnings for cash dividends declared.

Instructions

Prepare a statement of cash flows, using the indirect method of presenting cash flows from operating activities.

	Dec. 31, 2007	Dec. 31, 2006
Assets		
Cash	$ 464,100	$ 395,800
Accounts receivable (net)	163,200	145,700
Inventories	395,000	367,900
Investments	0	120,000
Land	160,000	0
Equipment	695,500	575,500
Accumulated depreciation—equipment	(194,000)	(168,000)
Total	$1,683,800	$1,436,900
Liabilities and Stockholders' Equity		
Accounts payable (merchandise creditors)	$ 228,700	$ 210,500
Accrued expenses (operating expenses)	16,500	21,400
Dividends payable	14,000	10,000
Common stock, $10 par	75,000	60,000
Paid-in capital in excess of par—common stock	265,000	175,000
Retained earnings	1,084,600	960,000
Total	$1,683,800	$1,436,900

Problem 13-2A

Statement of cash flows—indirect method

Goal 2

Net cash flow from operating activities, $78,400

SPREADSHEET

The comparative balance sheet of Medalist Athletic Apparel Co. at December 31, 2007 and 2006, is as follows:

	Dec. 31, 2007	Dec. 31, 2006
Assets		
Cash	$ 37,200	$ 45,300
Accounts receivable (net)	61,200	65,400
Merchandise inventory	91,000	85,600
Prepaid expenses	5,500	4,000
Equipment	190,500	155,500
Accumulated depreciation—equipment	(41,200)	(35,800)
Total	$344,200	$320,000
Liabilities and Stockholders' Equity		
Accounts payable (merchandise creditors)	$ 67,100	$ 65,400
Mortgage note payable	0	95,000
Common stock, $1 par	14,000	10,000
Paid-in capital in excess of par—common stock	200,000	100,000
Retained earnings	63,100	49,600
Total	$344,200	$320,000

Additional data obtained from the income statement and from an examination of the accounts in the ledger for 2007 are as follows:

a. Net income, $61,500.
b. Depreciation reported on the income statement, $17,900.
c. Equipment was purchased at a cost of $47,500, and fully depreciated equipment costing $12,500 was discarded, with no salvage realized.
d. The mortgage note payable was not due until 2011, but the terms permitted earlier payment without penalty.
e. 4,000 shares of common stock were issued at $26 for cash.
f. Cash dividends declared and paid, $48,000.

Instructions

Prepare a statement of cash flows, using the indirect method of presenting cash flows from operating activities.

Problem 13-3A

Statement of cash flows—indirect method

Goal 2

Net cash flow from operating activities, ($53,000)

SPREADSHEET

The comparative balance sheet of Sunrise Juice Co. at December 31, 2007 and 2006, is as follows:

	Dec. 31, 2007	Dec. 31, 2006
Assets		
Cash	$ 405,200	$ 432,100
Accounts receivable (net)	324,100	305,700
Inventories	602,300	576,900
Prepaid expenses	10,000	12,000
Land	100,000	190,000
Buildings	650,000	400,000
Accumulated depreciation—buildings	(172,500)	(155,000)
Equipment	225,600	210,700
Accumulated depreciation—equipment	(48,100)	(56,500)
Total	$2,096,600	$1,915,900
Liabilities and Stockholders' Equity		
Accounts payable (merchandise creditors)	$ 399,100	$ 402,600
Bonds payable	80,000	0
Common stock, $1 par	60,000	50,000
Paid-in capital in excess of par—common stock	350,000	200,000
Retained earnings	1,207,500	1,263,300
Total	$2,096,600	$1,915,900

The noncurrent asset, the noncurrent liability, and the stockholders' equity accounts for 2007 are as follows:

LAND

Date	Item	Debit	Date	Item	Credit
Jan. 1	Balance	190,000	April 20	Realized $81,000 cash from sale	90,000
Dec. 31	Balance	100,000			

BUILDINGS

Date	Item	Debit	Date	Item	Credit
Jan. 1	Balance	400,000			
Apr. 20	Acquired for cash	250,000			
Dec. 31	Balance	650,000			

ACCUMULATED DEPRECIATION—BUILDINGS

Date	Item	Debit	Date	Item	Credit
			Jan. 1	Balance	155,000
			Dec. 31	Depreciation for year	17,500
			Dec. 31	Balance	172,500

EQUIPMENT

Date	Item	Debit	Date	Item	Credit
Jan. 1	Balance	210,700	Jan. 26	Discarded, no salvage	18,000
Aug. 11	Purchased for cash	32,900			
Dec. 31	Balance	225,600			

ACCUMULATED DEPRECIATION—EQUIPMENT

Date	Item	Debit	Date	Item	Credit
Jan. 26	Discarded, no salvage	18,000	Jan. 1	Balance	56,500
			Dec. 31	Depreciation for year	9,600
			Dec. 31	Balance	48,100

BONDS PAYABLE

Date	Item	Debit	Date	Item	Credit
			May 1	Issued 20-year bonds	80,000
			Dec. 31	Balance	80,000

COMMON STOCK

		Jan. 1	Balance	50,000
		Dec. 7	Issued 10,000 shares of common stock for $16 per share	10,000
		Dec. 31	Balance	60,000

PAID-IN CAPITAL IN EXCESS OF PAR

		Jan. 1	Balance	200,000
		Dec. 7	Issued 10,000 shares of common stock for $16 per share	150,000
		Dec. 31	Balance	350,000

RETAINED EARNINGS

Dec. 31	Net loss	43,800	Jan. 1	Balance	1,263,300
Dec. 31	Cash dividends	12,000			
			Dec. 31	Balance	1,207,500

Instructions

Prepare a statement of cash flows, using the indirect method of presenting cash flows from operating activities.

Problem 13-4A

Statement of cash flows—direct method

Goal 3

Net cash flow from operating activities, $345,200

SPREADSHEET

The comparative balance sheet of Village Markets, Inc., for December 31, 2007 and 2006, is as follows:

	Dec. 31, 2007	Dec. 31, 2006
Assets		
Cash	$ 421,900	$ 456,700
Accounts receivable (net)	397,200	365,700
Inventories	658,900	623,100
Investments	—	175,000
Land	230,000	—
Equipment	590,000	450,000
Accumulated depreciation	(282,100)	(234,500)
Total	$2,015,900	$1,836,000
Liabilities and Stockholders' Equity		
Accounts payable (merchandise creditors)	$ 471,200	$ 456,300
Accrued expenses (operating expenses)	40,000	45,300
Dividends payable	61,000	58,000
Common stock, $1 par	23,000	20,000
Paid-in capital in excess of par—common stock	195,000	120,000
Retained earnings	1,225,700	1,136,400
Total	$2,015,900	$1,836,000

The income statement for the year ended December 31, 2007, is as follows:

Sales		$4,367,800
Cost of merchandise sold		2,532,000
Gross profit		$1,835,800
Operating expenses:		
Depreciation expense	$ 47,600	
Other operating expenses	1,257,900	
Total operating expenses		1,305,500

(continued)

Operating income	$ 530,300
Other expense:	
Loss on sale of investments	25,000
Income before income tax	$ 505,300
Income tax expense	175,000
Net income	$ 330,300

The following additional information was taken from the records:

a. Equipment and land were acquired for cash.
b. There were no disposals of equipment during the year.
c. The investments were sold for $150,000 cash.
d. The common stock was issued for cash.
e. There was a $241,000 debit to Retained Earnings for cash dividends declared.

Instructions

Prepare a statement of cash flows, using the direct method of presenting cash flows from operating activities.

Problem 13-5A

Statement of cash flows—direct method applied to Problem 13-1A

Goal 3

Net cash flow from operating activities, $163,300

SPREADSHEET

The comparative balance sheet of Winner's Edge Sporting Goods, Inc., for December 31, 2007 and 2006, is as follows:

	Dec. 31, 2007	Dec. 31, 2006
Assets		
Cash	$ 464,100	$ 395,800
Accounts receivable (net)	163,200	145,700
Inventories	395,000	367,900
Investments	0	120,000
Land	160,000	0
Equipment	695,500	575,500
Accumulated depreciation—equipment	(194,000)	(168,000)
Total	$1,683,800	$1,436,900
Liabilities and Stockholders' Equity		
Accounts payable (merchandise creditors)	$ 228,700	$ 210,500
Accrued expenses (operating expenses)	16,500	21,400
Dividends payable	14,000	10,000
Common stock, $10 par	75,000	60,000
Paid-in capital in excess of par—common stock	265,000	175,000
Retained earnings	1,084,600	960,000
Total	$1,683,800	$1,436,900

The income statement for the year ended December 31, 2007, is as follows:

Sales		$1,580,500
Cost of merchandise sold		957,300
Gross profit		$ 623,200
Operating expenses:		
Depreciation expense	$ 26,000	
Other operating expenses	329,400	
Total operating expenses		355,400
Operating income		$ 267,800
Other income:		
Gain on sale of investments		12,000
Income before income tax		$ 279,800
Income tax expense		99,200
Net income		$ 180,600

The following additional information was taken from the records:

a. The investments were sold for $132,000 cash.
b. Equipment and land were acquired for cash.
c. There were no disposals of equipment during the year.
d. The common stock was issued for cash.
e. There was a $56,000 debit to Retained Earnings for cash dividends declared.

Instructions

Prepare a statement of cash flows, using the direct method of presenting cash flows from operating activities.

ALTERNATE ACCOUNTING APPLICATION PROBLEMS

Alternate Problem 13-1B

Statement of cash flows—indirect method

Goal 2

Net cash flow from operating activities, $45,900

SPREADSHEET

The comparative balance sheet of True-Tread Flooring Co. for June 30, 2007 and 2006, is as follows:

	June 30, 2007	June 30, 2006
Assets		
Cash	$ 68,900	$ 53,700
Accounts receivable (net)	89,200	85,400
Inventories	145,800	132,700
Investments	0	45,000
Land	105,500	0
Equipment	210,800	185,600
Accumulated depreciation	(52,800)	(45,100)
Total	$567,400	$457,300
Liabilities and Stockholders' Equity		
Accounts payable (merchandise creditors)	$104,300	$100,200
Accrued expenses (operating expenses)	15,200	14,300
Dividends payable	12,000	10,000
Common stock, $11 par	55,000	50,000
Paid-in capital in excess of par—common stock	200,000	100,000
Retained earnings	180,900	182,800
Total	$567,400	$457,300

The following additional information was taken from the records of True-Tread Flooring Co.:

a. Equipment and land were acquired for cash.
b. There were no disposals of equipment during the year.
c. The investments were sold for $41,000 cash.
d. The common stock was issued for cash.
e. There was a $46,100 credit to Retained Earnings for net income.
f. There was a $48,000 debit to Retained Earnings for cash dividends declared.

Instructions

Prepare a statement of cash flows, using the indirect method of presenting cash flows from operating activities.

Alternate Problem 13-2B

Statement of cash flows—indirect method

Goal 2

Net cash flow from operating activities, $178,800

SPREADSHEET

The comparative balance sheet of Sky-Mate Luggage Company at December 31, 2007 and 2006, is as follows:

	Dec. 31, 2007	Dec. 31, 2006
Assets		
Cash	$ 184,200	$ 165,400
Accounts receivable (net)	252,100	224,300
Inventories	300,200	348,700
Prepaid expenses	9,500	8,000
Land	120,000	120,000
Buildings	600,000	425,000
Accumulated depreciation—buildings	(215,000)	(194,000)
Machinery and equipment	310,000	310,000
Accumulated depreciation—machinery & equipment	(83,500)	(75,000)
Patents	50,000	54,000
Total	$1,527,500	$1,386,400
Liabilities and Stockholders' Equity		
Accounts payable (merchandise creditors)	$ 284,300	$ 295,700
Dividends payable	15,000	10,000
Salaries payable	19,500	22,500
Mortgage note payable, due 2027	70,000	—
Bonds payable	—	102,000
Common stock, $1 par	22,000	20,000
Paid-in capital in excess of par—common stock	150,000	50,000
Retained earnings	966,700	886,200
Total	$1,527,500	$1,386,400

An examination of the income statement and the accounting records revealed the following additional information applicable to 2007:

a. Net income, $140,500.
b. Depreciation expense reported on the income statement: buildings, $21,000; machinery and equipment, $8,500.
c. Patent amortization reported on the income statement, $4,000.
d. A building was constructed for $175,000.
e. A mortgage note for $70,000 was issued for cash.
f. 2,000 shares of common stock were issued at $51 in exchange for the bonds payable.
g. Cash dividends declared, $60,000.

Instructions

Prepare a statement of cash flows, using the indirect method of presenting cash flows from operating activities.

Alternate Problem 13-3B

Statement of cash flows—indirect method

Goal 2

Net cash flow from operating activities, $71,400

SPREADSHEET

The comparative balance sheet of Builders' Supply Co. at December 31, 2007 and 2006, is as follows:

	Dec. 31, 2007	Dec. 31, 2006
Assets		
Cash	$ 40,400	$ 45,200
Accounts receivable (net)	95,100	87,900
Inventories	140,700	122,800
Prepaid expenses	3,900	5,000
Land	75,000	100,000
Buildings	315,000	140,000
Accumulated depreciation—buildings	(70,200)	(58,300)
Equipment	225,600	210,400
Accumulated depreciation—equipment	(81,400)	(85,900)
Total	$744,100	$567,100

(continued)

	Dec. 31, 2007	Dec. 31, 2006
Liabilities and Stockholders' Equity		
Accounts payable (merchandise creditors)	$ 97,000	$100,500
Income tax payable	7,100	6,400
Bonds payable	40,000	—
Common stock, $1 par	32,000	30,000
Paid-in capital in excess of par—common stock	200,000	120,000
Retained earnings	368,000	310,200
Total	$744,100	$567,100

The noncurrent asset, the noncurrent liability, and the stockholders' equity accounts for 2007 are as follows:

LAND

Jan. 1	Balance	100,000	Apr. 20	Realized $31,000 cash from sale	25,000
Dec. 31	Balance	75,000			

BUILDINGS

Jan. 1	Balance	140,000			
Apr. 20	Acquired for cash	175,000			
Dec. 31	Balance	315,000			

ACCUMULATED DEPRECIATION—BUILDINGS

			Jan. 1	Balance	58,300
			Dec. 31	Depreciation for year	11,900
			Dec. 31	Balance	70,200

EQUIPMENT

Jan. 1	Balance	210,400	Jan. 26	Discarded, no salvage	24,000
Aug. 11	Purchased for cash	39,200			
Dec. 31	Balance	225,600			

ACCUMULATED DEPRECIATION—EQUIPMENT

Jan. 26	Discarded, no salvage	24,000	Jan. 1	Balance	85,900
			Dec. 31	Depreciation for year	19,500
			Dec. 31	Balance	81,400

BONDS PAYABLE

			May 1	Issued 20-year bonds	40,000
			Dec. 31	Balance	40,000

COMMON STOCK

			Jan. 1	Balance	30,000
			Dec. 7	Issued 2,000 shares of common stock for $41 per share	2,000
			Dec. 31	Balance	32,000

PAID-IN CAPITAL IN EXCESS OF PAR

			Jan. 1	Balance	120,000
			Dec. 7	Issued 2,000 shares of common stock for $41 per share	80,000
			Dec. 31	Balance	200,000

RETAINED EARNINGS

Dec. 31	Cash dividends	15,000	Jan. 1	Balance	310,200
			Dec. 31	Net income	72,800
			Dec. 31	Balance	368,000

Instructions

Prepare a statement of cash flows, using the indirect method of presenting cash flows from operating activities.

Alternate Problem 13-4B

Statement of cash flows—direct method

Goal 3

Net cash flow from operating activities, $110,900

SPREADSHEET

The comparative balance sheet of Heaven's Bounty Nursery Inc. for December 31, 2006 and 2007, is as follows:

	Dec. 31, 2007	Dec. 31, 2006
Assets		
Cash	$ 134,200	$154,300
Accounts receivable (net)	203,200	189,700
Inventories	267,900	243,700
Investments	—	110,000
Land	140,000	—
Equipment	290,000	210,000
Accumulated depreciation	(112,300)	(93,400)
Total	$ 923,000	$814,300
Liabilities and Stockholders' Equity		
Accounts payable (merchandise creditors)	$ 192,100	$175,400
Accrued expenses (operating expenses)	12,400	14,600
Dividends payable	32,100	30,400
Common stock, $1 par	10,000	8,000
Paid-in capital in excess of par—common stock	180,000	100,000
Retained earnings	496,400	485,900
Total	$ 923,000	$814,300

The income statement for the year ended December 31, 2007, is as follows:

Sales		$965,000
Cost of merchandise sold		503,200
Gross profit		$461,800
Operating expenses:		
Depreciation expense	$ 18,900	
Other operating expenses	258,300	
Total operating expenses		277,200
Operating income		$184,600
Other income:		
Gain on sale of investments		22,000
Income before income tax		$206,600
Income tax expense		69,400
Net income		$137,200

The following additional information was taken from the records:

a. Equipment and land were acquired for cash.
b. There were no disposals of equipment during the year.
c. The investments were sold for $132,000 cash.
d. The common stock was issued for cash.
e. There was a $126,700 debit to Retained Earnings for cash dividends declared.

Instructions

Prepare a statement of cash flows, using the direct method of presenting cash flows from operating activities.

Alternate Problem 13-5B

Statement of cash flows—direct method applied to Alternate Problem 13-1B

Goal 3

Net cash flow from operating activities, $45,900

SPREADSHEET

The comparative balance sheet of True-Tread Flooring Co. for June 30, 2007 and 2006, is as follows:

	June 30, 2007	June 30, 2006
Assets		
Cash	$ 68,900	$ 53,700
Accounts receivable (net)	89,200	85,400
Inventories	145,800	132,700
Investments	0	45,000
Land	105,500	0
Equipment	210,800	185,600
Accumulated depreciation	(52,800)	(45,100)
Total	$567,400	$457,300
Liabilities and Stockholders' Equity		
Accounts payable (merchandise creditors)	$104,300	$100,200
Accrued expenses (operating expenses)	15,200	14,300
Dividends payable	12,000	10,000
Common stock, $11 par	55,000	50,000
Paid-in capital in excess of par—common stock	200,000	100,000
Retained earnings	180,900	182,800
Total	$567,400	$457,300

The income statement for the year ended June 30, 2007, is as follows:

Sales		$945,200
Cost of merchandise sold		665,900
Gross profit		$279,300
Operating expenses:		
Depreciation expense	$ 7,700	
Other operating expenses	193,400	
Total operating expenses		201,100
Operating income		$ 78,200
Other expenses:		
Loss on sale of investments		4,000
Income before income tax		$ 74,200
Income tax expense		28,100
Net income		$ 46,100

The following additional information was taken from the records:

a. Equipment and land were acquired for cash.
b. There were no disposals of equipment during the year.
c. The investments were sold for $41,000 cash.
d. The common stock was issued for cash.
e. There was a $48,000 debit to Retained Earnings for cash dividends declared.

Instructions

Prepare a statement of cash flows, using the direct method of presenting cash flows from operating activities.

FINANCIAL ANALYSIS AND REPORTING CASES

Case 13-1

Interpreting cash flows from operations

The operating activities section of the statement of cash flows for PepsiCo, Inc., owner of the Pepsi beverage brand, is shown as follows:

PepsiCo, Inc.
Statement of Cash Flows—Operating Activities (annotated)
For the Year Ended December 28, 2004

	(in millions)
Operating activities:	
Net income	$4,212
Adjustments to reconcile net income to net cash provided by operating activities:	
Depreciation and amortization	1,264
Stock-based compensation expense	368
Impairment and restructuring charges	150
Bottling equity income, net of dividends	(297)
Other noncash charges and credits, net	(230)
Changes in operating working capital, excluding effects of acquisitions and dispositions accounts and notes receivable:	(130)
Inventories	(100)
Prepaid expenses and other current assets	(31)
Accounts payable and other current liabilities	216
Income taxes payable	(268)
Net change in operating working capital	$ (313)
Other	$ (100)
Net cash provided by operating activities	$5,054

a. Why are impairment and restructuring charges added to the net income in determining cash flows provided by operating activities?
b. Why is the bottling equity income, net of dividends, subtracted from the net income in determining cash flows provided by operating activities?
c. What is "stock-based compensation expense," and why would it be added back to net income in determining cash flows provided by operating activities?

Case 13-2

Analysis of statement of cash flows

Lee O'Brien is the president and majority shareholder of Fluff N' Stuff, Inc., a small retail store chain. Recently, O'Brien submitted a loan application for Fluff N' Stuff, Inc., to Montvale National Bank. It called for a $300,000, 7%, 10-year loan to help finance the construction of a building and the purchase of store equipment, costing a total of $340,000, to enable Fluff N' Stuff, Inc., to open a store in Montvale. Land for this purpose was acquired last year. The bank's loan officer requested a statement of cash flows in addition to the most recent income statement, balance sheet, and retained earnings statement that O'Brien had submitted with the loan application.

As a close family friend, O'Brien asked you to prepare a statement of cash flows. From the records provided, you prepared the following statement.

Fluff N' Stuff, Inc.
Statement of Cash Flows
For the Year Ended December 31, 2007

Cash flows from operating activities:			
Net income, per income statement		$ 86,400	
Add: Depreciation	$31,000		
Decrease in accounts receivable	11,500	42,500	
		$128,900	
Deduct: Increase in inventory	$12,000		
Increase in prepaid expenses	1,500		
Decrease in accounts payable	3,000		
Gain on sale of investments	7,500	24,000	
Net cash flow from operating activities			$104,900
Cash flows from investing activities:			
Cash received from investments sold		$ 40,500	
Less cash paid for purchase of store equipment		31,000	
Net cash flow from investing activities			9,500
Cash flows from financing activities:			
Cash paid for dividends		$ 40,000	
Net cash flow used for financing activities			(40,000)
Increase in cash			$ 74,400
Cash at the beginning of the year			27,500
Cash at the end of the year			$101,900
Schedule of Noncash Financing and Investing Activities: Issued common stock at par for land			$ 40,000

After reviewing the statement, O'Brien telephoned you and commented, "Are you sure this statement is right?" O'Brien then raised the following questions:

1. "How can depreciation be a cash flow?"
2. "Issuing common stock for the land is listed in a separate schedule. This transaction has nothing to do with cash! Shouldn't this transaction be eliminated from the statement?"
3. "How can the gain on sale of investments be a deduction from net income in determining the cash flow from operating activities?"
4. "Why does the bank need this statement anyway? They can compute the increase in cash from the balance sheets for the last two years."

After jotting down O'Brien's questions, you assured him that this statement was "right." However, to alleviate O'Brien's concern, you arranged a meeting for the following day.

a. How would you respond to each of O'Brien's questions?
b. Do you think that the statement of cash flows enhances the chances of Fluff N' Stuff, Inc., receiving the loan? Discuss.

Case 13-3

Analyzing cash conversion cycle over time

A schedule of current assets and current liabilities for Lexmark International, Inc., a leading manufacturer of laser and inkjet printers, for three comparative years is as follows:

Lexmark International, Inc.
Schedule of Current Assets and Current Liabilities
December 31, 2004, 2003, and 2002

(in millions)	Dec. 31, 2004	Dec. 31, 2003	Dec. 31, 2002
Current assets:			
Cash and cash equivalents	$ 626.20	$ 744.60	$ 497.70
Marketable securities	940.50	451.50	
Accounts receivable, net of allowances	744.40	615.40	600.30
Inventories	464.90	437.00	410.30
Prepaid expenses and other current assets	224.90	195.30	290.50
Total current assets	$3,000.90	$2,443.80	$1,798.80
Current liabilities:			
Short-term debt	$ 1.50	$ 1.10	$ 12.30
Accounts payable	670.60	465.70	378.50
Accrued liabilities	795.60	716.50	708.20
Total current liabilities	$1,467.70	$1,183.30	$1,099.00

In addition, sales and cost of goods sold information for 2004 and 2003 are as follows (in millions):

	2004	2003
Revenue	$5,313.80	$4,754.70
Cost of goods sold	3,522.40	3,209.60

a. Determine the cash conversion cycles for 2003 and 2004. Round to the nearest whole day.
b. Interpret your findings.

Case 13-4

Analyzing noncash working capital efficiency—beer industry

The average accounts receivable, inventory, and accounts payable for Molson Coors Brewing Co., Anheuser-Busch Co., and Boston Beer Company are shown below for a recent fiscal year (in thousands).

	Molson Coors Brewing Co.	Anheuser-Busch Co.	Boston Beer Company
Average accounts receivable	$654,600	$ 682,500	$11,629
Average inventory	222,150	638,900	11,225
Average accounts payable	319,043	1,144,250	8,070

Sales and cost of goods sold information for the three companies are as follows (in thousands):

	Molson Coors Brewing Co.	Anheuser-Busch Co.	Boston Beer Company
Sales	$4,305,816	$14,934,200	$217,208
Cost of goods sold	2,741,694	8,982,500	87,973

a. Determine the cash conversion cycles for the three companies. Round to the nearest whole day.
b. Interpret your findings.

Case 13-5

Calculating free cash flow and interpreting the statement of cash flows

SPREADSHEET

The statement of cash flows for IAC InterActive Corp., a diversified Internet company providing services through the Ticketmaster, Expedia, Hotels.com, and Home Shopping Network brand names, is shown below.

IAC InterActive Corp.
Statement of Cash Flows (annotated)
For the Year Ended December 31, 2004

	(in millions)
Cash flows from operating activities:	
Net income	$ 185,761
Goodwill impairment	184,780
Depreciation	526,971
Amortization	330,507
Other	(111,591)
Net changes in current assets and liabilities	156,800
Net cash provided by operating activities	$1,273,228
Cash flows from investing activities:	
Acquisitions	$ (486,033)
Capital expenditures	(223,787)
Investments in securities, net	(43,374)
Net cash used in investing activities	$ (753,194)
Cash flows from financing activities:	
Borrowings, net	$ 19,039
Treasury stock purchases	(430,295)
Proceeds from issuing common stock	147,283
Preferred dividends	(13,053)
Other, net	17,380
Net cash used in financing activities	$ (259,646)
Net increase in cash flows from continuing operations	$ 260,388

a. Calculate the free cash flow.
b. Explain why the cash flow from operations is nearly 600% greater than the net income.
c. Identify the major sources and uses of cash and interpret.

Case 13-6

Free cash flow—semiconductors

The sales and statement of cash flows for Intel Corp., National Semiconductor, and Texas Instruments for a recent fiscal year are shown on the following page (in millions). These three companies are part of the semiconductor fabrication industry. Assume that investments made in property, plant, and equipment are to maintain productive capacity.

a. Determine the free cash flow for each company.
b. Determine the free cash flow as a percent of cash flow from operating activities and as a percent of sales for each company. Round to the nearest percent.
c. Interpret your results.

Statement of Cash Flows (annotated)
For a Recent Fiscal Year

	Intel	National Semi-conductor	Texas Instruments
Sales	$ 34,209	$ 1,983	$12,580
Cash flows provided by (used for) operating activities:			
Net income	$ 7,516.0	$ 282.8	$ 1,861.0
Adjustments to reconcile net income to net cash provided by operating activities:			
Depreciation and amortization	$ 4,889.0	$ 209.9	$ 1,549.0
Net loss on retirements and impairments of property, plant, and equipment	91.0	6.2	
Other	139.0	36.0	69.0
Changes in assets and liabilities:			
Marketable equity securities	(468.0)		
Accounts receivable	(39.0)	(50.4)	(238.0)
Inventories	(101.0)	(62.5)	(272.0)
Accounts payable	283.0	78.7	(71.0)
Accrued compensation and benefits	295.0		235.0
Income taxes payable	378.0	13.6	59.0
Other assets and liabilities	136.0	(36.6)	(46.0)
Total adjustments	$ 5,603.0	$ 194.9	$ 1,285.0
Net cash provided by operating activities	$13,119.0	$ 477.7	$ 3,146.0
Cash flows provided by (used for) investing activities:			
Additions to property, plant, and equipment	$ (3,843.0)	$(215.3)	$(1,298.0)
Acquisitions, net of cash acquired	(53.0)		
Purchases of available-for-sale investments	(16,618.0)	(386.7)	(3,674.0)
Maturities and sales of available-for-sale investments	15,633.0	359.0	3,809.0
Other investing activities	(151.0)	(9.2)	2.0
Net cash used for investing activities	$ (5,032.0)	$(252.2)	$(1,161.0)
Cash flows provided by (used for) financing activities:			
Repayments and retirement of debt	$ (31.0)	$ (2.1)	$ (435.0)
Proceeds from sale of common stock	894.0	211.9	192.0
Repurchase and retirement of common stock	(7,516.0)	(542.5)	(753.0)
Payment of dividends to stockholders	(1,022.0)		(154.0)
Other	24.0	(52.1)	15.0
Net cash used for financing activities	$ (7,651.0)	$(384.8)	$(1,135.0)
Net increase (decrease) in cash and cash equivalents	$ 436.0	$(159.3)	$ 850.0

BUSINESS ACTIVITIES AND RESPONSIBILITY ISSUES

Activity 13-1

Ethics and professional conduct in business

Toni Lance, president of Fine Fashions Inc., believes that reporting operating cash flow per share on the income statement would be a useful addition to the company's just completed financial statements. The following discussion took place between Toni Lance and Fine Fashions' controller, Tom Kee, in January, after the close of the fiscal year.

Toni: I have been reviewing our financial statements for the last year. I am disappointed that our net income per share has dropped by 10% from last year. This is not going to look good to our shareholders. Isn't there anything we can do about this?

Tom: What do you mean? The past is the past, and the numbers are in. There isn't much that can be done about it. Our financial statements were prepared according to generally accepted accounting principles, and I don't see much leeway for significant change at this point.

Toni: No, no. I'm not suggesting that we "cook the books." But look at the cash flow from operating activities on the statement of cash flows. The cash flow from operating activities has increased by 20%. This is very good news—and, I might add, useful information. The higher cash flow from operating activities will give our creditors comfort.

Tom: Well, the cash flow from operating activities is on the statement of cash flows, so I guess users will be able to see the improved cash flow figures there.

Toni: This is true, but somehow I feel that this information should be given a much higher profile. I don't like this information being "buried" in the statement of cash flows. You know as well as I do that many users will focus on the income statement. Therefore, I think we ought to include an operating cash flow per share number on the face of the income statement—someplace under the earnings per share number. In this way, users will get the complete picture of our operating performance. Yes, our earnings per share dropped this year, but our cash flow from operating activities improved! And all the information is in one place where users can see and compare the figures. What do you think?

Tom: I've never really thought about it like that before. I guess we could put the operating cash flow per share on the income statement, under the earnings per share. Users would really benefit from this disclosure. Thanks for the idea—I'll start working on it.

Toni: Glad to be of service.

How would you interpret this situation? Is Tom behaving in an ethical and professional manner?

Activity 13-2

Using the statement of cash flows

You are considering an investment in a new start-up Internet company, VideosToGo.com Inc. A review of the company's financial statements reveals a negative retained earnings. In addition, it appears as though the company has been running a negative cash flow from operating activities since the company's inception.

How is the company staying in business under these circumstances? Could this be a good investment?

Activity 13-3

Profit vs. cash flows and management decision making

The Retailing Division of Biltmore Company provided information on its cash flow from operations as shown below.

Net income	$ 450,000
Increase in accounts receivable	(340,000)
Increase in inventory	(300,000)
Decrease in accounts payable	(90,000)
Depreciation	100,000
Cash flow from operating activities	$(180,000)

The manager of the Retailing Division provided the accompanying memo with this report:

> *From: Senior Vice President, Retailing Division*
> *I am pleased to report that we had earnings of $450,000 over the last period. This resulted in a return on invested capital of 10%, which is near our target for this division. I have been aggressive in building the revenue volume in the division. As a result, I am happy to report that we have increased the number of new credit card customers as a result of an aggressive marketing campaign. In addition, we have found some excellent merchandise opportunities. Some of our suppliers have made some of their apparel merchandise available at a deep discount. We have purchased as much of these goods as possible in order to improve profitability. I'm also happy to report that our vendor payment problems have improved. We are nearly caught up on our overdue payables balances.*

Comment on the senior vice president's memo in light of the cash flow information.

Activity 13-4

Operating cash flow

Todd Manning is the president of Under Wraps, Inc., a chain of sandwich shops. Manning was meeting with his bank loan officer, Kim Wells. The following conversation took place:

Kim: Todd, I was looking at your income statement and you generated a loss during the last year. I'm really concerned about this.

Todd: I know, but you also need to look at the statement of cash flows. Our cash flow from operating activities was positive. Net income is just an accounting number. It's cash that's important. Wouldn't you agree?

Kim: Well, yes . . . cash is important. We want you to generate cash so you can pay back our loan. But your cash from operations, while positive, is not the end of the story.

Todd: What do you mean?

Kim: Well, don't you need cash for updating and replacing equipment in your shops? I don't think that's part of cash provided from operations.

Todd: I think that's why the accountant added back the depreciation. With the depreciation added back, we must be accounting for replacement of productive capacity somehow.

Is Kim's concern valid? Comment on Todd's analysis of Kim's concern.

Activity 13-5

Statement of cash flows

GROUP ACTIVITY

This activity will require two teams to retrieve cash flow statement information from the Internet. One team is to obtain the most recent year's statement of cash flows for Altria Group, Inc., a tobacco company, and the other team the most recent year's statement of cash flows for Delta Air Lines.

The statement of cash flows is included as part of the annual report information that is a required disclosure to the Securities and Exchange Commission (SEC). The SEC, in turn, provides this information online through its EDGAR service. EDGAR (Electronic Data Gathering, Analysis, and Retrieval) is the electronic archive of financial statements filed with the Securities and Exchange Commission (SEC). SEC documents can be retrieved using the EdgarScan service from Pricewaterhousecoopers at **http://edgarscan.pwcglobal.com**.

To obtain annual report information, type in a company name in the appropriate space. EdgarScan will list the reports available to you for the company you've selected. Select the most recent annual report filing, identified as a 10-K or 10-K405. EdgarScan provides an outline of the report, including the separate financial statements. You can double-click the income statement and balance sheet for the selected company into an Excel™ spreadsheet for further analysis.

As a group, compare the two statements of cash flows. How are Altria and Delta similar or different regarding cash flows?

ANSWERS TO SELF-STUDY QUESTIONS

1. **A** Cash flows from investing activities include receipts from the sale of noncurrent assets, such as equipment (answer A), and payments to acquire noncurrent assets. Receipts of cash from the sale of stock (answer B) and payments of cash for dividends (answer C) and to acquire treasury stock (answer D) are cash flows from financing activities.

2. **C** Payment of cash for dividends (answer C) is an example of a financing activity. The receipt of cash from customers on account (answer A) is an operating activity. The receipt of cash from the sale of equipment (answer B) is an investing activity. The payment of cash to acquire land (answer D) is an example of an investing activity.

3. **D** The indirect method (answer D) reports cash flows from operating activities by beginning with net income and adjusting it for revenues and expenses not involving the receipt or payment of cash.

4. **C** The cash flows from operating activities section of the statement of cash flows would report net cash flow from operating activities of $65,500, determined as follows:

Net income		$55,000
Add: Depreciation	$22,000	
Decrease in inventories	5,000	
Decrease in prepaid expenses	500	27,500
		$82,500
Deduct: Increase in accounts rec.	$10,000	
Decrease in accounts pay.	7,000	17,000
Net cash flow from operating activities		$65,500

5. **C** The cash conversion cycle is calculated as the number of days' sales in accounts receivable, plus the number of days' sales in inventory, less the number of days' sales in accounts payable. Or, 30 days + 45 days − 25 days = 50 days (answer C).

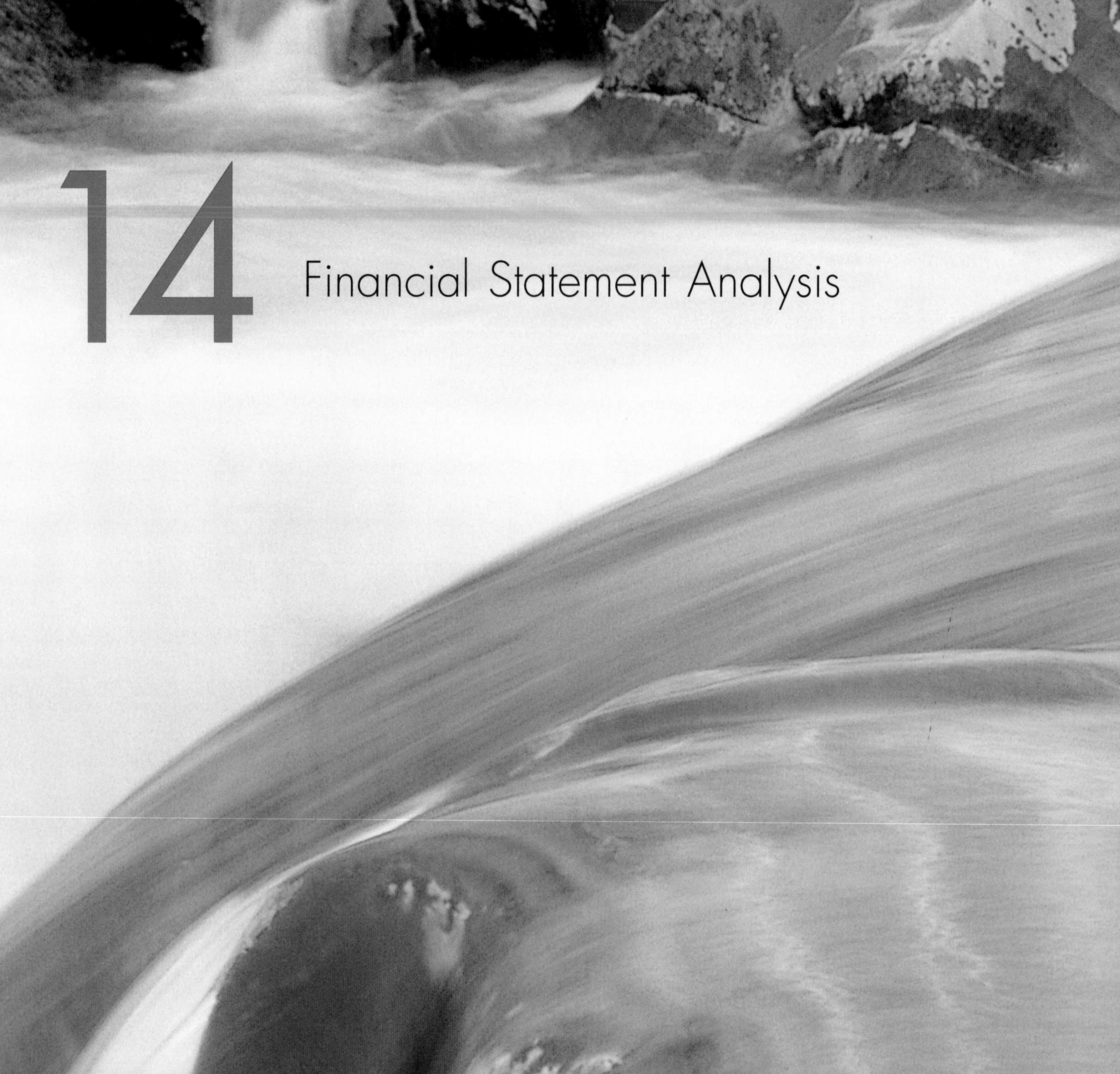

14 Financial Statement Analysis

Learning Goals

1. Construct and interpret horizontal and vertical analyses.
2. Calculate and interpret the rate earned on stockholders' equity and the rate earned on total assets.
3. Analyze the rate earned on total assets by evaluating the profit margin and the asset efficiency of a business.
4. Determine and interpret leverage.
5. Calculate and interpret shareholder ratios: earnings per share, price-earnings ratio, and dividend yield.
6. Summarize the uses and limitations of analytical measures.

Pixar

Microsoft Corporation is a well-known, international company. However, U.S. Airways, Kmart, WorldCom, Polaroid, Winn-Dixie Stores, Inc., and Planet Hollywood were also well-known companies. These latter companies share the common characteristic of having declared bankruptcy!

Obviously, being well-known is not necessarily a good basis for investing. For example, Planet Hollywood sought bankruptcy protection twice, even though it was owned and promoted by such prominent Hollywood stars as Bruce Willis, Whoopi Goldberg, and Arnold Schwarzenegger. Knowing that a company has a good product, by itself, may also be an inadequate basis for investing in the company. Even with a good product, a company may go bankrupt for a variety of reasons, such as inadequate financing.

How, then, does one decide on the companies in which to invest? Like any other significant purchase, you would need to do some research to guide your investment decision. If you were buying a car, for example, you might go to Edmunds.com to obtain reviews, ratings, prices, specifications, options, and fuel economy across a number of vehicle alternatives. You could research investment alternatives using financial analysis techniques. In this chapter, we will illustrate financial statement analysis with Pixar's financial statements.

Pixar has created six of the highest grossing animated features in the history of film, including *Toy Story, Finding Nemo, The Incredibles*, and *Cars*. Pixar essentially invented computer-animated feature films, thus making obsolete the traditional hand-drawn approach used for years by Disney. Pixar was born out of the creative energy of John Lasseter and the business vision of Steve Jobs, who is now CEO of both Apple Computer and Pixar. Today, Pixar is regarded as the most successful animation studio in the industry. Indeed, this success has been translated into a debt-free business with over $800 million in the bank.

Pixar's success is demonstrated by its Animation Time-Line:

- *Toy Story:* The first computer-animated feature film.
- *A Bug's Life:* Pixar simulated translucent leaves to create rounder, more organic forms. This required 12 times the computer power of *Toy Story*.
- *Monsters, Inc:* Unlike bugs and toys, Sulley is covered by 3 million hairs that had to look and move naturally. Some frames took 80 hours to render on the computer.
- *Finding Nemo:* Programmers learn to simulate waves, swells, currents, and underwater light movements. Nemo's tank has over 120,000 individual pebbles.
- *The Incredibles:* According to the director, "the more geometric the figure is, the easier it is to do with computer animation. The more organic something is the harder it is. Everything about a human is organic. The audience looks into the mirror every day, so if you don't get it right, it is obvious to them." To make humans lifelike, the animators first made the muscles over which a sheath of skin was placed. The muscle animation then caused the skin to move.

© MIKE WINTROATH/AP PHOTO (AP WIDE WORLD PHOTO)

While Pixar's movies are very successful, how can one determine the company's finanical success? This is the role of financial statements. In this chapter, we will focus on the important role that financial statements play in analyzing business operations as well as how those operations are financed. The basic financial statements provide much of the information users need to make economic decisions about businesses. We illustrate how to perform a complete analysis of Pixar's statements by integrating individual analytical measures. In addition, we discuss the contents of corporate annual reports.

Sources: Richard Corliss, "All Too Superhuman Breaking Rules, Making Megahits, the Pixar Team Now Unleashes a Family of Repressed Superheroes," reported by Desa Philadelphia/Emeryville, *Time*, October 25, 2004; Randall Stross, "Pixar's Mr. Incredible May Yet Rewrite the Apple Story," *The New York Times*, October 24, 2004.

HORIZONTAL AND VERTICAL ANALYSES

Construct and interpret horizontal and vertical analyses.

Basic financial statement analysis begins with evaluating the relative size of changes in account balances across time and the relative size of account balances within a statement. These are termed horizontal and vertical analyses.

Horizontal Analysis

The percentage analysis of increases and decreases in related items in comparative financial statements is called **horizontal analysis**. The amount of each item on the most recent statement is compared with the related item on one or more earlier statements. The amount of increase or decrease in the item is listed, along with the percent of increase or decrease. For example, cash of $150,000 on the current balance sheet may be compared with cash of $100,000 on the balance sheet of a year earlier. The current year's cash may be expressed as 1.5 or 150% of the earlier amount, or as an increase of 50% or $50,000.

The analysis of Pixar's and DreamWorks Animation's financial statements in this chapter is the authors' and is intended for instructional use, not for investment or valuation purposes.

When horizontal analysis compares two statements, the earlier statement is used as the base. Horizontal analysis may also compare three or more statements. In this case, the earliest date or period may be used as the base for comparing all later dates or periods. Alternatively, each statement may be compared to the immediately preceding statement. Exhibit 1 is a comparative balance sheet with horizontal analysis for two years for Pixar.

Exhibit 1

Comparative Balance Sheet—Horizontal Analysis

Pixar
Comparative Balance Sheets (In millions)
January 1, 2005, and January 3, 2004

			Increase (Decrease)	
	Jan. 1, 2005	**Jan. 3, 2004**	**Amount**	**Percent**
Assets				
Cash and cash equivalents	$ 28.7	$ 48.3	$ (19.6)	−40.6%
Investments	826.1	473.6	352.5	74.4
Accounts receivable, net	82.0	204.9	(122.9)	−60.0
Prepaid expenses and other assets	2.2	1.0	1.2	120.0
Total current assets	$ 939.0	$ 727.8	$ 211.2	29.0
Film inventory	140.0	107.7	32.3	30.0
Property and equipment, net	125.6	115.0	10.6	9.2
Other assets	70.4	51.5	18.9	36.7
Total assets	$ 1,275.0	$ 1,002.0	$ 273.0	27.2
Liabilities				
Accounts payable	$ 5.4	$ 1.8	$ 3.6	200.0
Income taxes payable	14.0	37.6	(23.6)	−62.8
Other accrued liabilities	27.0	13.0	14.0	107.7
Unearned revenue	8.5	9.1	(0.6)	−6.6
Total liabilities	$ 54.9	$ 61.5	$ (6.6)	−10.7
Stockholders' Equity				
Common stock, no par value	$ 687.4	$ 547.0	$ 140.4	25.7
Retained earnings	534.9	393.2	141.7	36.0
Accumulated other comprehensive income (loss)	(2.2)	0.3	(2.5)	−833.3
Total shareholders' equity	$ 1,220.1	$ 940.5	$ 279.6	29.7
Total liabilities and shareholders' equity	$ 1,275.0	$ 1,002.0	$ 273.0	27.2

We cannot fully evaluate the significance of the various increases and decreases in the items shown in Exhibit 1 without additional information. Total assets on January 1, 2005, were approximately $273 million (27.2%) greater than at the beginning of the year. This increase is largely the result of an increase in investments of $352.5 million (74.4%). This is mostly due to the operating success of the company, which can be seen by the 36.0% increase in retained earnings. In addition, stockholders' equity increased by 29.7% due to the issuance of additional common stock from exercise of employee stock options. Overall, the financial position of Pixar has improved over the year.

The remaining changes in the balance sheet accounts in Exhibit 1 appear favorable. The increase in cash is explained on the statement of cash flows. The accounts receivable declined 60.0% due to significant collections on amounts owed by Disney on its film partnership. Film inventories grew by 30.0% reflecting the costs incurred for new film projects. *Inventory* in this industry represents the costs associated with Pixar's film pipeline, which is classified as noncurrent because it exceeds one year.

Exhibit 2 shows the horizontal analysis for the income statement of Pixar. The last line of the statement indicates that Pixar had a $16.9 million (13.5%) increase in net income. This is a strong improvement. The rest of the income statement indicates how Pixar accomplished this. The net sales increased by 4.2%, while the cost of goods sold decreased by 21.3%, thus causing the gross profit to increase by 8.5%. The general and administrative expenses increased by 17.2%, while the research and development increased by 13.7%, causing total operating expenses to increase by 14.4%. Interest income increased by 18.1% from the increased investment shown on the balance sheet. The increase in gross profit and interest income more than offset the increase in operating expenses, causing net income to increase.

Exhibit 2

Comparative Income Statement—Horizontal Analysis

Pixar
Income Statement (In millions)
For Periods Ended January 1, 2005, and January 3, 2004

			Increase (Decrease)	
	2004	2003	Amount	Percent
Total revenue	$273.5	$262.5	$11.0	4.2%
Cost of goods sold	29.9	38.0	(8.1)	−21.3
Gross profit	$243.6	$224.5	$19.1	8.5
Research and development expenses	$ 17.4	$ 15.3	$ 2.1	13.7
Sales and marketing expenses	2.5	2.4	0.1	4.2
General and administrative expenses	15.0	12.8	2.2	17.2
Total operating expenses	$ 34.9	$ 30.5	$ 4.4	14.4
Income from operations	$208.7	$194.0	$14.7	7.6
Interest income and other	12.4	10.5	1.9	18.1
Income before income taxes	$221.1	$204.5	$16.6	8.1
Income tax expense	79.4	79.7	(0.3)	−0.4
Net income	$141.7	$124.8	$16.9	13.5

Vertical Analysis

A percentage analysis may also be used to show the relationship of each component to the total within a single statement. This type of analysis is called **vertical analysis**. To illustrate, assume that cash of $50,000 and inventories of $250,000 are included in the total assets of $1,000,000 on a balance sheet. In relative terms, the cash balance is 5% of the total assets, and the inventories are 25% of the total assets.

Like horizontal analysis, the statements may be prepared in either detailed or condensed form. In the latter case, additional details of the changes in individual items may be presented in supporting schedules. In such schedules, the percentage analysis may be based on either the total of the schedule or the statement total. Although vertical analysis is limited to an individual statement, its significance may be improved by preparing comparative statements.

In vertical analysis of the balance sheet, each asset item is stated as a percent of the total assets. Each liability and stockholders' equity item is stated as a percent of the total liabilities and stockholders' equity. Exhibit 3 is a condensed comparative balance sheet with vertical analysis for Pixar. On January 3, 2004, current assets were 72.6% of total assets, and property and equipment was 11.5% of total assets. On January 1, 2005, the current assets increased slightly to 73.6% of total assets, while property and equipment declined to 9.9% of total assets. The total liabilities as a percent of the total declined by 1.8% (from 6.1% to 4.3%), while stockholders' equity as a percent of the total increased by 1.8% (from 93.9% to 95.7%).

In a vertical analysis of the income statement, each item is stated as a percent of net sales. Exhibit 4 is a condensed comparative income statement with vertical analysis for Pixar. The vertical analysis indicates that the net income as a percentages of sales improved by 4.3% (51.8% − 47.5%) between the two years. This improvement is largely explained by the improvement in the gross profit as a percent of sales between the two years. The other income statement items had smaller relative changes as a percent of sales between the two years. Clearly, Pixar has experienced great success with its film production business, earning net income of approximately 50% of sales for the two years.

Exhibit 3

Comparative Balance Sheet—Vertical Analysis

Pixar
Comparative Balance Sheets (In millions)
January 1, 2005, and January 3, 2004

	Jan. 1, 2005		Jan. 3, 2004	
	Amount	**Percent**	**Amount**	**Percent**
Assets				
Cash and cash equivalents	$ 28.7	2.2%	$ 48.3	4.8%
Investments	826.1	64.8	473.6	47.2
Accounts receivable, net	82.0	6.4	204.9	20.5
Prepaid expenses and other assets	2.2	0.2	1.0	0.1
Total current assets	$ 939.0	73.6%	$ 727.8	72.6%
Film inventory	140.0	11.0	107.7	10.7
Property and equipment, net	125.6	9.9	115.0	11.5
Other assets	70.4	5.5	51.5	5.1
Total assets	$1,275.0	100.0%	$1,002.0	100.0%
Liabilities				
Accounts payable	$ 5.4	0.4%	$ 1.8	0.2%
Income taxes payable	14.0	1.1	37.6	3.7
Other accrued liabilities	27.0	2.1	13.0	1.3
Unearned revenue	8.5	0.7	9.1	0.9
Total liabilities	$ 54.9	4.3%	$ 61.5	6.1%
Stockholders' Equity				
Common stock, no par value	$ 687.4	53.9%	$ 547.0	54.7%
Retained earnings	534.9	42.0	393.2	39.2
Accumulated other comprehensive income (loss)	(2.2)	−0.2	0.3	0.0
Total shareholders' equity	$1,220.1	95.7%	$ 940.5	93.9%
Total liabilities and shareholders' equity	$1,275.0	100.0%	$1,002.0	100.0%

Pixar's balance sheet as reported to the Securities Exchange Commission (SEC) does not classify current assets separately. Our classification above is provided to illustrate ratios using the current asset designation, and represents the authors', and not Pixar's estimate of currency. For example, the investments could be either current or noncurrent based upon management judgment. The balance sheet for Pixar as reported to the SEC is reproduced in the back of the book for comparison purposes. Note that the actual titles for accounts used by Pixar have in some cases been simplified above for instructional purposes.

Exhibit 4

Comparative Income Statement—Vertical Analysis

Pixar
Income Statement (In millions)
For Periods Ended January 1, 2005, and January 3, 2004

	2004		2003	
	Amount	Percent	Amount	Percent
Total revenue	$273.5	100.0%	$262.5	100.0%
Cost of goods sold	29.9	10.9	38.0	14.5
Gross profit	$243.6	89.1%	$224.5	85.5%
Research and development expenses	$ 17.4	6.4%	$ 15.3	5.8%
Selling, general, and administrative expenses	17.5	6.4	15.2	5.8
Total operating expenses	$ 34.9	12.8%	$ 30.5	11.6%
Income from operations	$208.7	76.3%	$194.0	73.9%
Interest income and other	12.4	4.5	10.5	4.0
Income before income taxes	$221.1	80.8%	$204.5	77.9%
Income tax expense	79.4	29.0	79.7	30.4
Net income	$141.7	51.8%	$124.8	47.5%

Common-Size Statements

Horizontal and vertical analyses with both dollar and percentage amounts are useful in assessing relationships and trends in financial conditions and operations of a business. Vertical analysis with both dollar and percentage amounts is also useful in comparing one company with another or with industry averages. Such comparisons are easier to make with the use of common-size statements. In a **common-size statement**, all items are expressed in percentages. An example of common-size income statements for Pixar and DreamWorks Animation SKG, Inc., is shown later in this chapter.

Common-size statements are useful in comparing the current period with prior periods, individual businesses, or one business with industry percentages. Industry data are often available from trade associations and financial information services.

Other Analytical Measures

In addition to the preceding analyses, other relationships may be expressed in ratios and percentages. These relationships are described and illustrated in the following sections. Often, the items analyzed are taken from the financial statements, and thus the analysis is a type of vertical analysis. Comparing these items with items from earlier periods is a type of horizontal analysis.

HOW BUSINESSES MAKE MONEY

Blockbuster Strategy

Pixar employs the blockbuster emphasis, which is common in the film and pharmaceutical industries. This emphasis involves investing large up-front costs to develop a product with fewer additional costs after the product is launched. As a result, the success of the product is determined by the amount of sales after the product is developed. Blockbusters are very profitable under this strategy; however, box office bombs can result in large development and marketing write-offs. Pixar has earned over $3.2 billion in worldwide box office receipts from six feature films, achieving a blockbuster return on every film it has produced. As stated by an investment analyst, "Pixar is in the sweet spot, you can spend $100 million and get a $400 million profit."

PROFITABILITY ANALYSIS

Calculate and interpret the rate earned on stockholders' equity and the rate earned on total assets.

The relative profitability of a firm can be analyzed by combining both profitability and balance sheet information into a single ratio. Two relative profitability ratios constructed in this way are the rate earned on stockholders' equity and the rate earned on total assets.

Rate Earned on Stockholders' Equity

The stockholder desires a return on his or her investment. One measure of this return is the rate earned on stockholders' equity. The **rate earned on stockholders' equity** is calculated as the net income divided by the average stockholders' equity. The average stockholders' equity is often calculated as the sum of the beginning and ending balances of stockholders' equity, divided by two. Note that the average stockholders' equity is determined from the balance sheet and not by the market value of the common stock. To illustrate, the following information was provided in recent financial statements of Pixar and DreamWorks Animation SKG, Inc., a major competitor to Pixar in the filmed animation entertainment market.[1]

	Pixar (in millions) Year Ended Jan. 1, 2005	DreamWorks (in millions) Year Ended Dec. 31, 2004
a. Net income	$ 141.7	$333.0
Stockholders' equity:		
Beginning of year	$ 940.5	$ (12.4)
End of year	1,220.1	826.9
Total	$2,160.6	$814.5
b. Average (Total ÷ 2)	$1,080.3	$407.3
Rate earned on stockholders' equity (a ÷ b)	13.1%	81.8%

Pixar earned a 13.1% return on stockholders' equity, while DreamWorks earned 81.8%. DreamWorks' high return on stockholders' equity relative to Pixar is partially explained by strong earnings combined with a negative beginning stockholders' equity balance, caused by DreamWorks Animation's spinoff from DreamWorks.

1 We will shorten DreamWorks Animation SKG to DreamWorks in this chapter. However, this should not be confused with movie production company by the same name.

Rate Earned on Total Assets

The **rate earned on total assets** is computed by dividing net income by the average total assets.[2] The rate earned on total assets measures the profitability of total assets, without considering how the assets are financed. That is, the rate is not affected by whether assets are financed primarily by creditors or stockholders.

The rate earned on total assets by Pixar and DreamWorks for a recent year is computed as follows:

	Pixar (in millions) Year Ended Jan. 1, 2005	DreamWorks (in millions) Year Ended Dec. 31, 2004
a. Net income	$ 141.7	$ 333.0
Total assets:		
Beginning of year	$1,002.0	$ 681.4
End of year	1,275.0	1,200.0
Total	$2,277.0	$1,881.4
b. Average (Total ÷ 2)	$1,138.5	$ 940.7
Rate earned on total assets (a ÷ b)	12.4%	35.4%

The rate earned on total assets of Pixar was 12.4%, which is good, while DreamWorks was 35.4%. DreamWorks' high rate earned on total assets is from the successful DVD sales of *Shrek 2* during 2004. Pixar is earning good returns on its assets, with earnings coming from the launch of *The Incredibles* at the end of 2004. Much of the difference between Pixar and DreamWorks can be explained by differences in the relative timing of their film earning cycles. DreamWorks earned most of its revenues for *Shrek 2* in 2004, while Pixar still had much of the revenues for *The Incredibles* to be realized in 2005.

A company's objective is to generate a return on total assets that exceeds the cost of capital. The **cost of capital** is the cost of financing its operations from both debt and common stock, expressed in percentage terms. For example, if a company borrows money at an 8% interest rate, the invested funds must generate a rate of return in excess of 8% to be successful.[3] The rate earned on total assets is widely acknowledged as a good summary measure of managerial performance, since it measures the return on total assets under management care and control, regardless of the method of financing those assets.

Sometimes, it may be desirable to compute the rate of income from operations to total assets. This is especially true if significant amounts of nonoperating income and expense, such as interest income and expense, are reported on the income statement. In this case, any assets related to the nonoperating income and expense items should be excluded from total assets in computing the rate. In addition, using income from operations (which is before tax) has the advantage of eliminating the effects of any changes in the tax structure on the rate of earnings. When evaluating published data on rates earned on assets, you should be careful to determine the exact nature of the measure that is reported.

---

2 Alternatively, the numerator could be net income plus interest expense in order to remove the impact of the financing decision from the numerator. We select a simpler approach here to ease interpretation of the comprehensive analysis.

3 The cost of capital calculation is illustrated in finance textbooks.

Comprehensive Profitability Analysis

Exhibit 5 diagrams the comprehensive ratio relationships that can be used to analyze the rate earned on stockholders' equity. Reading left to right, the rate earned on stockholders' equity and rate earned on total assets as computed previously can be related to each other. Specifically, the rate earned on stockholders' equity is the product of the rate earned on total assets and the amount of debt, or **leverage**, held by the firm. The rate earned on stockholders' equity is normally higher than the rate earned on total assets when a company uses debt, or leverage, in its capital structure.

The relationship between the rate earned on stockholders' equity and the rate earned on total assets can be computed using the following **leverage formula**:

$$\text{Rate Earned on Stockholders' Equity} = \text{Rate Earned on Total Assets} \times \text{Leverage}$$

$$\frac{\text{Net Income}}{\text{Average Stockholders' Equity}} = \frac{\text{Net Income}}{\text{Average Total Assets}} \times \frac{\text{Average Total Assets}}{\text{Average Stockholders' Equity}}$$

The leverage formula for Pixar and DreamWorks Animation is as follows for fiscal year 2004:

	Rate Earned on Stockholders' Equity	=	Rate Earned on Total Assets	×	Leverage
Pixar	13.1%[a]	=	12.4% (p. 637)	×	1.05[b]
DreamWorks	81.8%	=	35.4% (p. 637)	×	2.31[c]

[a]Small differences in multiplication may occur due to rounding.
[b]$1,138.5 ÷ $1,080.3 = 1.05, from average total assets and stockholders' equity on pp. 636 and 637.
[c]$940.7 ÷ $407.3 = 2.31, from average total assets and stockholders' equity on pp. 636 and 637.

International Perspective International Accounting Standards provide a consistent financial reporting framework that allows users of financial statements to compare companies from different countries.

Pixar's leverage is 1.05 ($1,138.5 ÷ $1,080.3), while DreamWorks' is 2.31 ($940.7 ÷ $407.3). Thus, the rate earned on stockholders' equity using the leverage formula for Pixar is 13.1% (12.4% × 1.05), and for DreamWorks it is 81.8% (35.4% × 2.31). The leverage term (average total assets divided by average stockholders' equity) measures the number of asset dollars supported by each dollar of stockholders' equity. The larger the value of this measure, the greater the leverage. For example, if a firm had no debt, then this ratio would be 1.0, thus causing the rate earned on stockholders' equity to equal the rate earned on total assets. If the firm had average debt equal to 50% of average total assets, then this leverage ratio would be 2.0. It is clear that DreamWorks uses more leverage than does Pixar. We will discuss leverage in greater detail in a later section of this chapter.

Exhibit 5

Comprehensive Ratio Analysis

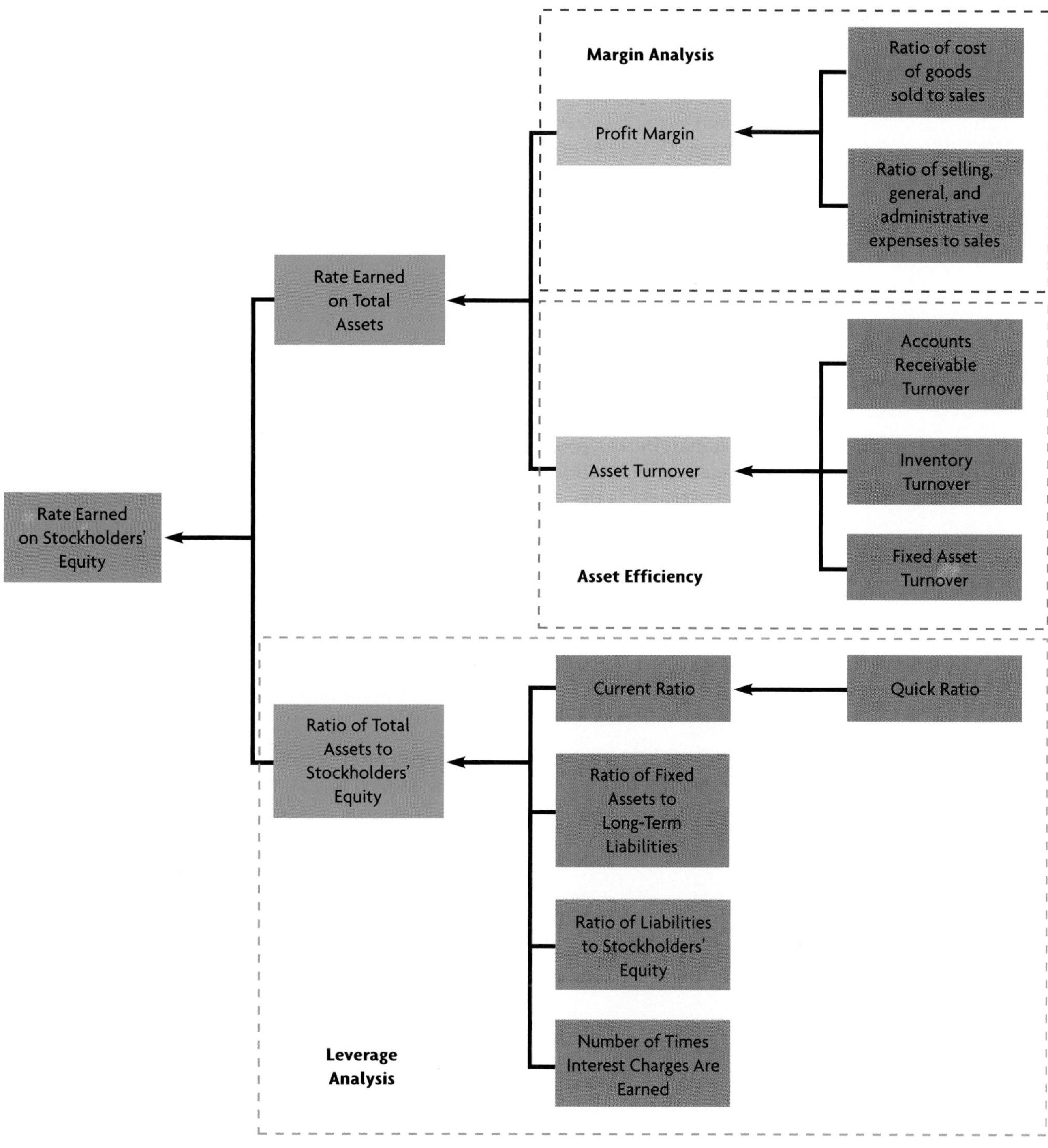

Analyze the rate earned on total assets by evaluating the profit margin and the asset efficiency of a business.

MARGIN ANALYSIS AND ASSET EFFICIENCY ANALYSIS

In the previous section, we noted that Pixar is earning 12.4% on its assets, while DreamWorks is earning 35.4% on its assets. In this section, we will more precisely explain this difference. The rate earned on total assets is the product of a firm's profit margin and the efficiency by which it uses its assets, as shown in Exhibit 5. One way to summarize this relationship is the DuPont formula. The **DuPont formula**, created by a financial executive of E.I. DuPont De Nemours & Co. in 1919, states that the rate earned on total assets is the product of two factors, the profit margin and the total asset turnover, shown as follows:

$$\text{Rate Earned on Total Assets} = \text{Profit Margin} \times \text{Asset Turnover}$$

$$\frac{\text{Net Income}}{\text{Average Total Assets}} = \frac{\text{Net Income}}{\text{Net Sales}} \times \frac{\text{Net Sales}}{\text{Average Total Assets}}$$

The first factor is the ratio of net income to net sales (or revenues), often called the net **profit margin**. The profit margin shows the profit earned as a percent of sales. The second factor is the ratio of net sales to average total assets, or the **asset turnover**. The asset turnover is the number of sales dollars earned for each dollar of total assets. The "profit machine" shown in Exhibit 6 illustrates the DuPont formula. Profits are earned by either increasing the profit margin (increasing the size of the opening) or increasing the asset turnover (turning the crank faster) or both.

The DuPont formula for Pixar and DreamWorks, with 2004 net sales for DreamWorks of $1,078.2, is as follows:

	Rate Earned on Total Assets	=	Profit Margin	×	Asset Turnover
Pixar	12.4%	=	51.8%[b]	×	0.24[c]
DreamWorks	35.4%[a]	=	30.9%[d]	×	1.15[e]

[a]Small differences in multiplication may occur due to rounding.
[b]$141.70/$273.50 [c]$273.50/$1,138.50
[d]$333/$1,078.20 [e]$1,078.20/$940.70

Exhibit 6
The "Profit Machine"

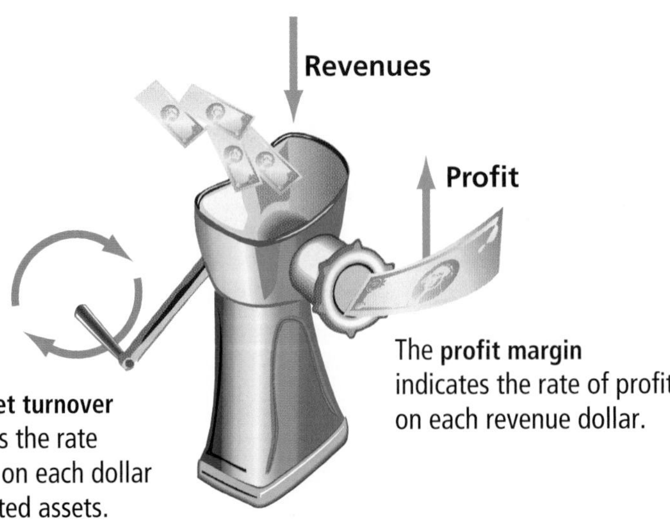
The "Profit Machine"
Revenues
Profit
The profit margin indicates the rate of profit on each revenue dollar.
The asset turnover indicates the rate of sales on each dollar of invested assets.

We now have more insight into the difference between Pixar and DreamWorks' rate earned on total assets. Pixar's profit margin is much better than DreamWorks', 51.8% compared to 30.9%. However, Pixar is much less efficient in using its assets. Pixar earns $0.24 in net sales for each dollar of total assets, while DreamWorks earns $1.15 in net sales for each dollar of total assets. This is a significant difference in asset efficiency. Multiplying these two factors together shows that DreamWorks' rate earned on total assets of 35.4% was stronger than Pixar's 12.4%. Apparently, Pixar's higher profit margin was not sufficient to compensate for its much lower asset turnover, when compared to DreamWorks.

Each of the two factors that determine the rate earned on total assets can be subjected to a more detailed analysis. The profit margin can be analyzed in more detail, using common-size information, while the total asset turnover can be segmented into a more detailed asset efficiency analysis.

Margin Analysis

Why is the profit margin of Pixar over 20 percentage points stronger than DreamWorks? This question can be addressed by analyzing the percentage of major expenses to net sales and comparing the percentages for the two companies.

Exhibit 7 is a comparative common-size income statement for Pixar and DreamWorks, wherein the major income statement items are translated into a percent of net sales (or revenues). Exhibit 7 indicates that Pixar has a much higher rate of gross profit (or lower cost of goods sold) as a percent of sales than does DreamWorks. Pixar's selling expenses are nearly the same as DreamWorks', but Pixar incurs expenses for research and development of proprietary animation software that is not incurred by DreamWorks. Pixar has interest income from its investments as a percent of sales, while DreamWorks incurs interest expense on debt. DreamWorks should review its cost of goods sold and determine if there might be better methods of producing films to better match Pixar's performance.

Asset Efficiency

We determined from the DuPont analysis that Pixar's total asset turnover was 0.24, while DreamWorks' was 1.146. What causes this difference? We can segment the total

Exhibit 7

Pixar and DreamWorks Animation SKG

Pixar and DreamWorks Animation SKG
Condensed Common-Size Income Statements
For the Year Ended January 1, 2005, and December 31, 2004

	Pixar	DreamWorks
Total revenue	100.0%	100.0%
Cost of goods sold	10.9	52.5
Gross profit	89.1%	47.5%
Research and development expenses	6.4	0.0
Selling, general, and administrative expenses	6.4	6.8
Income from operations	76.3%	40.7%
Net interest income or expense	4.5	(1.4)
Income before income taxes	80.8%	39.3%
Income tax expense	29.0	8.4
Net income	51.8%	30.9%

asset turnover into its component parts to address this question. The major components of total assets for many companies are accounts receivable, inventory, and fixed assets (property and equipment). Thus, the total asset turnover can be evaluated in terms of these three subcategories of assets.

Accounts Receivable Analysis

The size and makeup of accounts receivable change constantly during business operations. Sales on account increase accounts receivable, whereas collections from customers decrease accounts receivable. Firms that grant long credit terms usually have larger accounts receivable balances than those granting short credit terms. Increases or decreases in the volume of sales also affect the balance of accounts receivable.

Collecting receivables as promptly as possible is desirable. The cash collected from receivables improves liquidity. In addition, the cash generated by prompt collections from customers may be used in operations for such purposes as purchasing merchandise in large quantities at lower prices. The cash may also be used for payment of dividends to stockholders or for other investing or financing purposes. Prompt collection also lessens the risk of loss from uncollectible accounts.

Accounts Receivable Turnover. The relationship between credit sales and accounts receivable may be stated as the **accounts receivable turnover**. This ratio is computed by dividing net sales by the average net accounts receivable.[4] Basing the average on monthly balances, which allows for seasonal changes in sales, is desirable. When such data are not available, it may be necessary to use the average of the accounts receivable balance at the beginning and end of the year. If there are trade notes receivable as well as accounts, the two may be combined. The accounts receivable turnover data for Pixar and DreamWorks are as follows:

	Pixar (in millions, except ratio)	DreamWorks (in millions, except ratio)
a. Net sales	$ 273.50	$1,078.20
Accounts receivable (net):		
Beginning of year	$ 204.90	$ 132.30
End of year	82.00	386.10
Total	$ 286.90	$ 518.40
b. Average (Total ÷ 2)	$ 143.45	$ 259.20
Accounts receivable turnover (a ÷ b)	1.91	4.16

DreamWorks' accounts receivable turnover is much greater than that of Pixar. However, both companies turn their accounts reveivable very slowly.

Number of Days' Sales in Receivables. Another measure of the relationship between net sales and accounts receivable is the **number of days' sales in receivables**. This ratio is computed by dividing the net average accounts receivable by the average daily sales. Average daily sales is determined by dividing net sales by 365 days.

---

4 Alternatively, the net sales on account can be used for the calculation. However, this number may not be publicly available; thus, net sales must be used. When so doing, the analyst must be aware that cash sales could impact the interpretation of the analysis.

The number of days' sales in receivables is computed for Pixar and DreamWorks as follows:

	Pixar (in millions, except ratio)	DreamWorks (in millions, except ratio)
Accounts receivable (net):		
Beginning of year	$204.90	$ 132.30
End of year	82.00	386.10
Total	$286.90	$ 518.40
a. Average (Total ÷ 2)	$143.45	$ 259.20
Net sales	$273.50	$1,078.20
b. Average daily sales (Net sales ÷ 365)	$ 0.75	$ 2.95
Number of days' sales in receivables (a ÷ b)	191.3	87.9

The number of days' sales in receivables is an estimate of the length of time (in days) the accounts receivable have been outstanding. As can be seen, the number of days' sales outstanding in accounts receivable is very high for both companies. Why is this? The bulk of the accounts receivable for both companies is from film distribution companies, such as Disney or Universal. These companies distribute and market films to theaters and collect money from theaters. Payments are then made by the distribution companies to production companies, such as Pixar and DreamWorks. The distribution companies are apparently slow in making contractual payments to the production companies for the released films. For many firms, the number of day's sales in receivables should closely match their collection terms with their customers, which are often less than 60 days. For example, the number of days' sales in receivables for Procter & Gamble Company is 28.45 days.

Inventory Analysis

A business should keep enough inventory on hand to meet the needs of its customers and its operations. At the same time, however, an excessive amount of inventory reduces liquidity by tying up funds. Excess inventories also increase insurance expense, property taxes, storage costs, and other related expenses. These expenses further reduce funds that could be used elsewhere to improve operations. Finally, excess inventory also increases the risk of losses because of price declines or obsolescence of the inventory. Two measures that are useful for evaluating inventory efficiency are the inventory turnover and the number of days' sales in inventory.

Inventory Turnover. The relationship between the volume of goods (merchandise) sold and inventory may be stated as the **inventory turnover**. It is computed by dividing the cost of goods sold by the average inventory. If monthly data are not available, the average of the inventory at the beginning and the end of the year may be used. The inventory turnover for Pixar and DreamWorks is computed as follows:

	Pixar (in millions, except ratio)	DreamWorks (in millions, except ratio)
a. Cost of goods sold	$ 29.90	$566.20
Inventory:		
Beginning of year	$107.70	$427.50
End of year	140.00	519.90
Total	$247.70	$947.40
b. Average (Total ÷ 2)	$123.85	$473.70
Inventory turnover (a ÷ b)	0.24	1.2

© ROSE ALCORN/THOMSON

The inventory is often a significant asset category for many companies. Thus, inventory efficiency will be an important component of total asset efficiency. Pixar's inventory turnover is approximately one full turn slower than DreamWorks. That is, Pixar is less efficient in moving inventory than is DreamWorks.

Differences across inventories, companies, and industries are too great to allow a general statement on what is a good inventory turnover. For example, a firm selling food should have a higher turnover than a firm selling furniture or jewelry. Likewise, the perishable foods department of a supermarket should have a higher turnover than the soaps and cleansers department. For Pixar and DreamWorks, the inventory is the cost of films. Films have a much longer life cycle than, say, on-the-shelf consumer products. Thus, the inventory turnover is much slower than would be the case for a consumer products company, such as Procter & Gamble, which has an inventory turnover of 11.68. Each business or each department within a business has a reasonable turnover rate. A turnover lower than this rate could mean that inventory is not being managed properly.

Number of Days' Sales in Inventory. Another measure of the relationship between the cost of goods sold and inventory is the **number of days' sales in inventory**. This measure is computed by dividing the average inventory by the average daily cost of goods sold (cost of goods sold divided by 365). The number of days' sales in inventory for Pixar and DreamWorks is computed as follows:

	Pixar (in millions, except ratio)	DreamWorks (in millions, except ratio)
Inventory:		
Beginning of year	$107.70	$427.50
End of year	140.00	519.90
Total	$247.70	$947.40
a. Average (Total ÷ 2)	$123.85	$473.70
Cost of goods sold	$ 29.90	$566.20
b. Average daily cost of goods sold (COGS ÷ 365)	$ 0.08	$ 1.55
Number of days' sales in inventory (a ÷ b)	1,510	306

The number of days' sales in inventory is a rough measure of the length of time it takes to acquire, sell, and replace the inventory. For Pixar and Dreamworks, the number of days' sales in inventory is the approximate amount of days in a film's life cycle, from initial production to final exhibition. This cycle is approximately 1,510 days for Pixar, while for DreamWorks it is much shorter at 306 days. While there are a number of possible explanations for this difference, it does suggest that Pixar films have a longer production cycle than do DreamWorks films.

Fixed Asset Analysis

The fixed assets consist mostly of the property, plant, and equipment of a firm. These are usually the largest asset classification for most firms, especially manufacturing firms. Thus, the efficient deployment of fixed assets will significantly impact the overall asset efficiency of most firms. Businesses invest in fixed assets in order to create capacity to meet demand. If the capacity is not well matched to the demand, either in terms of product volume or mix, then the fixed asset turnover can suffer adversely.

A common financial measure of fixed asset efficiency is the **fixed asset turnover**. As in the other turnover measures, the fixed asset turnover measures the number of dollars of sales that are generated from each dollar of average fixed assets during the year. It is computed by dividing the net sales by the average fixed assets. If monthly data are not available, the average of the net fixed assets at the beginning and end of the year may be used. The fixed asset turnover for Pixar and DreamWorks is computed as follows:

	Pixar (in millions, except ratio)	DreamWorks (in millions, except ratio)
a. Net sales	$273.50	$1,078.20
Fixed assets (net):		
Beginning of year	$115.00	$ 89.80
End of year	125.60	86.00
Total	$240.60	$ 175.80
b. Average (Total ÷ 2)	$120.30	$ 87.90
Fixed asset turnover (a ÷ b)	2.27	12.27

For Pixar and DreamWorks, the fixed asset turnover measures how many dollars of sales are being made from investments in property and equipment. Pixar is able to generate $2.27 of revenue for each dollar invested in property and equipment, while DreamWorks is able to generate $12.27 per dollar invested in property and equipment. Again, this suggests that Pixar's efficiency in using its assets is much less than DreamWorks'.

Asset Efficiency Summary

The asset efficiency of the three major asset categories can now be compared for the two companies, as follows:

	Pixar	DreamWorks
Total asset turnover	0.24	1.15
Accounts receivable turnover	1.91	4.16
Inventory turnover	0.24	1.20
Fixed asset turnover	2.27	12.27

DreamWorks' total asset turnover is stronger than Pixar's because its accounts receivable, inventory, and fixed asset turnovers are stronger. Pixar should work toward increasing sales relative to the assets required to support those sales. This can be done through a number of short- and long-term strategies, including adding advertising, producing more films, earning revenue from character licenses, or improving film production methods.

Determine and interpret leverage.

LEVERAGE ANALYSIS

As we explained in a previous section, the excess of the rate earned by stockholders' equity over the rate earned on total assets is caused by leverage. Leverage measures the amount of debt used by a firm to finance its assets. Pixar's rate earned on stockholders' equity of 13.1% is only 0.7 percentage points greater than its rate of 12.4% earned on total assets, while DreamWorks' 81.8% rate earned on stockholders' equity is 46.4 percentage points higher than its rate of 35.4% earned on total assets.

Positive leverage will normally cause the rate earned on stockholders' equity to exceed the rate earned on total assets. This occurs when the rate earned on total assets is positive. Negative leverage will normally cause the rate earned on stockholders' equity to be less than the rate earned on total assets. This occurs when the rate earned on total assets is negative. Firms that have significant debt and negative leverage are candidates for bankruptcy. Highly leveraged commercial airlines, such as United Airlines and Delta Air Lines, faced this problem in the mid-2000s.

The rate earned on stockholders' equity can be compared to the rate earned on total assets by using the leverage formula, shown previously, where leverage is measured as the average total assets divided by the average stockholders' equity:

Rate Earned on Stockholders' Equity = Rate Earned on Total Assets × Leverage

Both Pixar and DreamWorks have debt, but both have positive leverage. The impact of leverage for these two companies is shown below. DreamWorks' rate earned on total assets was 23 percentage points (35.4 − 12.4) greater than Pixar's, indicating significantly stronger performance in asset efficiency (as discussed in the previous section). DreamWorks' rate earned on stockholders' equity, which is the ultimate concern of stockholders, is 68.7 percentage points (81.8 − 13.1) greater than Pixar's. Thus, DreamWorks supports more assets by each dollar of stockholders' equity than does Pixar (2.31 versus 1.05). That is, DreamWorks uses more leverage than does Pixar. As such, DreamWorks is able to turn its strong rate of return on asset performance into an even stronger rate of return on stockholders' equity performance as compared to Pixar.

	Rate Earned on Stockholders' Equity	=	Rate Earned on Total Assets	×	Leverage (Average Total Assets/Average Stockholders' Equity)
Pixar	13.1%	=	12.4%	×	1.054[a]
DreamWorks	81.8%	=	35.4%	×	2.310[b]

[a]$1,138.50 ÷ $1,080.30
[b]$940.70 ÷ $407.25

While positive leverage can improve a firm's financial performance for its stockholders, leverage also carries risk. A business that cannot pay its interest expense or debts on a timely basis may experience difficulty in obtaining further credit, and, thus, may be forced into liquidating assets, curtailing operations, or even filing for bankruptcy.

Leverage analysis focuses on the ability of a business to pay or otherwise satisfy its current and noncurrent liabilities. Thus, we can use leverage analysis to assess whether DreamWorks' use of leverage is too aggressive relative to its financial condition. Leverage is normally assessed by examining current and long-term balance sheet relationships, using the following major ratios:

Current balance sheet relationships
- Current ratio
- Quick ratio

Long-term balance sheet relationships
- The ratio of fixed assets to long-term liabilities
- The ratio of liabilities to stockholders' equity
- The number of times interest charges are earned

Current Ratio

To be useful in assessing solvency, a ratio or other financial measure must relate to a business's ability to pay or otherwise satisfy its liabilities. Using measures to assess a business's ability to pay its current liabilities is called *current position analysis.* Such analysis is of special interest to short-term creditors.

An analysis of a firm's current position normally includes determining the current ratio and the quick ratio. The current and quick ratios are most useful when analyzed together and compared to previous periods and other firms in the industry.

The **current ratio** is computed by dividing the total current assets by the total current liabilities. For Pixar and DreamWorks, the current ratios are shown below.

	Pixar (in millions, except ratio)	DreamWorks (in millions, except ratio)
a. Current assets	$939.00	$727.80
b. Current liabilities	54.90	152.90
Working capital (a − b)	$884.10	$574.90
Current ratio (a ÷ b)	17.10	4.76

While Pixar has slightly more working capital than DreamWorks, working capital is not a relative measure of current position when making comparisons between firms or across time. Rather, the current ratio is a relative measure of current position. This ratio is 17.10 for Pixar and 4.76 for DreamWorks. A current ratio greater than 1.0 would indicate that a firm has sufficient current assets to meet short-term claims. Thus, most analysts would expect a current ratio greater than 1.0. Current ratios that exceed 1.5 are often considered acceptable for most industries, while a current ratio in excess of 2.0 is excellent and would indicate capacity for short-term borrowing. Thus, both Pixar and DreamWorks have excellent current positions.

Quick Ratio

The current ratio does not consider the makeup of the current assets. To illustrate the importance of this consideration, the current position data for Lincoln Company and Jefferson Corporation as of December 31, 2006, are as follows:

	Lincoln Company	Jefferson Corporation
Current assets:		
Cash	$ 90,500	$ 45,500
Marketable securities	75,000	25,000
Accounts receivable (net)	115,000	90,000
Inventories	264,000	380,000
Prepaid expenses	5,500	9,500
Total current assets	$550,000	$550,000
Current liabilities	210,000	210,000
Working capital	$340,000	$340,000
Current ratio	2.6	2.6

Both companies have a working capital of $340,000 and a current ratio of 2.6. But the ability of each company to pay its current debts is significantly different. Jefferson Corporation has more of its current assets in inventories. Some of these inventories must be sold and the receivables collected before the current liabilities can be paid in full. Thus, a large amount of time may be necessary to convert these inventories into cash. Declines in market prices and a reduction in demand could also impair Jefferson's ability to pay current liabilities. In contrast, Lincoln Company has cash and current assets (marketable securities and accounts receivable) that can generally be converted to cash rather quickly to meet its current liabilities.

A ratio that measures the "instant" debt-paying ability of a company is called the **quick ratio** or *acid-test ratio*. It is the ratio of the total quick assets to the total current liabilities. **Quick assets** are cash and other current assets that can be quickly converted to cash. Quick assets normally include cash, marketable securities, and receivables. The quick ratios for Lincoln Company and Jefferson Corporation are 1.3 ($280,500 ÷ $210,000) and 0.76 ($160,500 ÷ $210,000), respectively. Quick ratios exceeding 1.0 are generally considered good.

The quick ratios for Pixar and DreamWorks are as follows:

	Pixar (in millions, except ratio)	DreamWorks (in millions, except ratio)
Quick assets:		
Cash	$ 28.70	$ 63.10
Temporary investments	826.10	0.00
Accounts receivable (net)	82.00	387.80
a. Total quick assets	$936.80	$450.90
b. Current liabilities	÷ $ 54.90	÷ $152.90
Quick ratio (a ÷ b)	17.06	2.95

Pixar's quick ratio (17.06) is stronger than DreamWorks' (2.95). The difference between the two quick ratios is caused by Pixar's strong temporary investment balance at 64.8% ($826.1 ÷ $1,275.0) of total assets, while DreamWorks has no temporary investments. DreamWorks' quick ratio is still not so small as to be of concern. DreamWorks' quick ratio is still above 1.0, which indicates a strong liquidity position. DreamWorks is a strong company and would be able to obtain cash easily through short-term borrowing if necessary.

Ratio of Fixed Assets to Long-Term Liabilities

Long-term notes and bonds are often secured by mortgages on fixed assets. The **ratio of fixed assets to long-term liabilities** is a leverage measure that indicates the margin of safety of the noteholders or bondholders. It also indicates the ability of the business to borrow additional funds on a long-term basis. The ratio of fixed assets to long-term liabilities for Pixar and DreamWorks is as follows:

	Pixar (in millions, except ratio)	DreamWorks (in millions, except ratio)
Fixed assets (net)	$125.60	$ 89.70
Long-term liabilities	÷$ 0	÷$217.20
Ratio of fixed assets to long-term liabilities	NA	0.41

The ratio of fixed assets to long-term liabilities is not applicable (NA) to Pixar, because it has no long-term debt. Thus, Pixar has long-term debt borrowing capacity available if the need arises. In contrast, DreamWorks' ratio of long-term debt to fixed assets is 0.41, indicating safety of only 41 cents of fixed assets for each dollar of long-term debt. This ratio shows the difference in leverage between the two companies. Pixar is not using long-term debt, while DreamWorks is using long-term debt more aggressively.

Given DreamWorks' profitability, this much long-term debt would not be considered reckless, and is actually an advantage to stockholders, due to positive leverage.

Ratio of Liabilities to Stockholders' Equity

Claims against the total assets of a business are divided into two groups: (1) claims of creditors and (2) claims of owners. The relationship between the total claims of the creditors and owners—the **ratio of liabilities to stockholders' equity**—is a leverage measure that indicates the margin of safety for creditors. This ratio is used widely to summarize a business's aggregate leverage. The ratio also indicates the ability of the business to withstand adverse business conditions. When the claims of creditors are large in relation to the equity of the stockholders, there are usually significant interest payments. If earnings decline to the point where the company is unable to meet its interest payments, the business may be taken over by the creditors. This is what happened at Kmart.

The relationship between creditor and stockholders' equity is shown in the vertical analysis of the balance sheet. For example, the balance sheet of Pixar in Exhibit 3 indicates that on January 1, 2005, total liabilities represented 4.3% and stockholders' equity represented 95.7% of the total liabilities and stockholders' equity (100.0%). Instead of expressing each item as a percent of the total, this relationship may be expressed as a ratio of one to the other, as follows, for both Pixar and DreamWorks:

	Pixar (in millions, except ratio)	DreamWorks (in millions, except ratio)
Total liabilities	$ 54.90	$373.10
Total stockholders' equity	÷ $1,220.10	÷ $826.90
Ratio of liabilities to stockholders' equity	0.04	0.45

The liability to stockholders' equity ratio of 1.0 occurs when half of the total assets are funded by debt and half are funded by stockholders' equity (that is, they are equal). This is an average ratio. Thus, Pixar's ratio would be interpreted as very conservative because it uses no long-term debt as discussed above. DreamWorks' ratio is also conservative and would not be cause for concern. Both Pixar and DreamWorks must be conservative with the use of debt because a string of box office failures could place either company in financial stress.

Number of Times Interest Charges Earned

Corporations in some industries, such as airlines, normally have high ratios of debt to stockholders' equity. For such corporations, the relative risk of the debtholders is normally measured as the **number of times interest charges are earned** during the year. The higher the ratio, the lower the risk that interest payments will not be made if earnings decrease. In other words, the higher the ratio, the greater the assurance that interest payments will be made on a continuing basis. This measure also indicates the general financial strength of the business, which is of interest to stockholders and employees as well as creditors.

The amount available to meet interest charges is not affected by taxes on income. This is because interest is deductible in determining taxable income. Thus, the number of times interest charges are earned for Pixar and DreamWorks is computed as shown on the following page.

	Pixar (in millions, except ratio)	DreamWorks (in millions, except ratio)
Net income	$141.7	$333.0
Add income tax expense	79.4	90.3
a. Add interest expense	0	15.0
b. Amount available to meet interest charges	$221.1	$438.3
Number of times interest charges earned (b ÷ a)	NA	29.2

Again, we see that the number of times interest earned ratio for Pixar does not apply, because it has no interest expense. DreamWorks' ratio is 29.2, which would be considered excellent interest charge coverage.

Leverage Summary

We began this section by noting DreamWorks' advantageous use of positive leverage. However, since there are limits to the use of leverage, we next asked if DreamWorks used too much leverage. After reviewing the additional leverage ratios in this section, DreamWorks' use of leverage is clearly not too aggressive. Pixar, on the other hand, is not using leverage as aggressively as it might. By avoiding debt, Pixar is forgoing the advantages to the stockholders in using leverage.

Calculate and interpret shareholder ratios: earnings per share, price-earnings ratio, and dividend yield.

STOCKHOLDER RATIOS

The analytical approaches in the previous sections help shareholders and managers analyze the financial statements of companies. In this section, we will describe and illustrate analytical approaches used by shareholders to evaluate the stock price and/or dividend performance of their equity investments. The stock price and dividends on the common stock are the primary means by which an investor earns a return. Thus, additional ratios that relate to stock price and dividend information are of interest to shareholders. Three common shareholder ratios are earnings per share, the price-earnings ratio, and dividend yield.

Earnings per Share

One of the profitability measures often quoted by the financial press is **earnings per share (EPS)**. It is also normally reported in the income statement in corporate annual reports. If a company has issued only one class of stock, the earnings per share is computed by dividing net income by the number of shares of stock outstanding. If preferred and common stock are outstanding, the net income is first reduced by the amount of preferred dividend requirements.[5]

The data on the earnings per share of common stock for Pixar and DreamWorks are as follows:

	Pixar (in millions, except ratio)	DreamWorks (in millions, except ratio)
Net income	$141.70	$333.00
Shares of common stock outstanding	÷ 56.76	÷ 81.43
Earnings per share on common stock	$ 2.50	$ 4.09

5 Additional details related to earnings per share were discussed in Chapter 12.

Earnings per share is difficult to interpret by itself. Rather, it should be compared to historical EPS trends and the stock price of a firm, as shown with the price-earnings ratio in the next section.

Price-Earnings Ratio

Another profitability measure quoted by the financial press is the **price-earnings (P/E) ratio** on common stock. The price-earnings ratio indicates a firm's future earnings prospects. It is computed by dividing the market price per share of common stock at a specific date by the annual earnings per share. To illustrate, the market prices per common share on March 1, 2005, for Pixar and DreamWorks were $90.06 and $37.44, respectively. Thus, the price-earnings ratio on common stock is computed as follows:

	Pixar	DreamWorks
Market price per share of common stock	$90.06	$37.44
Earning per share on common stock	÷ $ 2.50	÷ $ 4.09
Price-earnings ratio on common stock	36.02	9.15

The price-earnings ratio indicates that a share of common stock of Pixar sold for 36.02 times earnings, while for DreamWorks it was only 9.15 times earnings. At the time, the market average was approximately 16 times earnings. This means that market participants were optimistic about the future performance of Pixar and were willing to price the common stock at a premium on the underlying earnings per share. The price of DreamWorks' common stock appears to be discounted to the overall market because market participants believed that DreamWorks' earnings would decline from the historical performance of 2004.

Dividend Yield

Since the primary basis for dividends is earnings, dividends per share and earnings per share on common stock are commonly used by investors in assessing alternative stock investments. However, neither Pixar nor DreamWorks pays dividends.

Dividends per share can be reported with earnings per share to indicate the relationship between dividends and earnings. The ratio of these two per-share amounts, called the *dividend payout ratio*, indicates the extent to which the corporation is paying dividends to stockholders, versus retaining earnings for future growth. Since Pixar and DreamWorks pay no dividends, they are retaining all their earnings for future growth, and hence, have a zero dividend payout ratio.

The **dividend yield** on common stock shows the rate of return to common stockholders in terms of cash dividends. It is of special interest to investors whose main investment objective is to receive current returns (dividends) on an investment, rather than an increase in the market price of the investment. The dividend yield is computed by dividing the annual dividends paid per share of common stock by the market price per share on a specific date. Again, Pixar and DreamWorks offer no dividend yield. Shareholders anticipate low or no dividend yield for growth companies, because they expect reinvested earnings to return market price increases.

Summarize the uses and limitations of analytical measures.

SUMMARY OF ANALYTICAL MEASURES

Exhibit 8 presents a summary of the financial ratios that we have discussed for Pixar, DreamWorks, and the motion picture industry as a whole. Depending on the specific business being analyzed, some measures might be omitted or additional measures could be developed. The type of industry, the capital structure, and the diversity of the

Exhibit 8

Summary of Analytical Measures

	Equation	Pixar	DreamWorks Animation	Motion Picture Industry
Rate earned on stockholders' equity	$\frac{\text{Net income}}{\text{Average total stockholders' equity}}$	13.1%	81.8%	−13.6%
Rate earned on total assets	$\frac{\text{Net income}}{\text{Average total assets}}$	12.4%	35.4%	−4.7%
Leverage ratio	$\frac{\text{Average total assets}}{\text{Average stockholders' equity}}$	1.05	2.31	2.90
Profit margin	$\frac{\text{Net income}}{\text{Net sales}}$	51.8%	30.9%	−9.8%
Asset turnover	$\frac{\text{Net sales}}{\text{Average total assets}}$	0.24	1.15	0.5
Accounts receivable turnover	$\frac{\text{Net sales}}{\text{Average accounts receivable}}$	1.91	4.16	2.94
Number of days' sales in receivables	$\frac{\text{Average accounts receivable}}{\text{Average daily net sales}}$	191.3	87.9	124.1
Inventory turnover	$\frac{\text{Cost of goods sold}}{\text{Average inventory}}$	0.24	1.20	4.9
Number of days' sales in inventory	$\frac{\text{Average inventory}}{\text{Average daily cost of goods sold}}$	1,510	306	75.1
Fixed asset turnover	$\frac{\text{Net sales}}{\text{Average fixed assets, net}}$	2.27	12.27	10.8
Current ratio	$\frac{\text{Current assets}}{\text{Current liabilities}}$	17.10	4.76	1.1
Quick ratio	$\frac{\text{Quick assets}}{\text{Current liabilities}}$	17.06	2.95	0.65
Ratio of fixed assets to long-term liabilities	$\frac{\text{Fixed assets (net)}}{\text{Long-term liabilities}}$	NA	0.41	0.35
Ratio of liabilties to stockholders' equity	$\frac{\text{Total liabilities}}{\text{Total stockholders' equity}}$	0.04	0.45	1.9
Number of times interest charges earned	$\frac{\text{Income before income tax + Interest expense}}{\text{Interest expense}}$	NA	29.2	−0.8
Earnings per share	$\frac{\text{Net income − Preferred dividends}}{\text{Shares of common stock outstanding}}$	$2.50	$4.09	*
Price-earnings ratio	$\frac{\text{Market price per share of common stock}}{\text{Earnings per share of common stock}}$	36.02	9.15	Negative
Dividend yield	$\frac{\text{Dividends per share of common stock}}{\text{Market price per share of common stock}}$	NA	NA	0.3%

NA: Not applicable

* Earnings per share is not often compared to industry averages, since it is more meaningfully compared to stock price using the price-earnings ratio.

business's operations usually affect the measures used. For example, analysis for an airline might include revenue per passenger mile and cost per available seat as measures. Likewise, analysis for a hotel might focus on occupancy rates.

Percentage analyses, ratios, turnovers, and other measures of financial position and operating results are useful analytical measures. They are helpful in assessing a business's past performance and predicting its future. They are not, however, a substitute for sound judgment. In selecting and interpreting analytical measures, conditions peculiar to a business or its industry should be considered. In addition, the analytical measures are not ends in themselves. They are only guides in evaluating financial and operating data. Many other factors, such as trends in the industry and general economic conditions, should also be considered.

In determining trends, the interrelationship of the measures used in assessing a business should be carefully studied. Comparable indexes of earlier periods should also be studied. Data from competing businesses or the industry may be useful in assessing the efficiency of operations for the firm under analysis. For example, in Exhibit 8, it is clear that both DreamWorks and Pixar are performing better than the motion picture industry as a whole for this time period. The motion picture industry has been suffering losses as seen from the first three ratios. In addition, the industry as a whole uses more debt than does either Pixar or DreamWorks. In making such comparisons, however, the effects of differences in the accounting methods used by the businesses and multiple year comparisons should be considered.

Describe the contents of corporate annual reports.

CORPORATE ANNUAL REPORTS

Public corporations are required to issue annual reports to their stockholders and other interested parties. Such reports summarize the corporation's operating activities for the past year and plans for the future. There are many variations in the order and form for presenting the major sections of annual reports. However, one section of the annual report is devoted to the financial statements, including the accompanying notes. In addition, annual reports usually include the following sections:

1. Management Discussion and Analysis
2. Report on adequacy of internal control
3. Report on fairness of financial statements

In the following paragraphs, we describe these sections. Each section, as well as the financial statements, is illustrated in the annual report for Pixar on their Web site.

Management Discussion and Analysis

A required disclosure in the annual report filed with the Securities and Exchange Commission is the **Management Discussion and Analysis (MDA)**. The MDA provides critical information in interpreting the financial statements and assessing the future of the company.

The MDA includes an analysis of the results of operations and discusses management's opinion about future performance. It compares the prior year's income statement with the current year's to explain changes in sales, significant expenses, gross profit, and income from operations. For example, an increase in sales may be explained by referring to higher shipment volume or stronger prices.

The MDA also includes an analysis of the company's financial condition. It compares significant balance sheet items between successive years to explain changes in

INTEGRITY, OBJECTIVITY, AND ETHICS IN BUSINESS

One Bad Apple

A recent survey by *CFO* magazine reported that 17% of chief financial officers have been pressured by their chief executive officer to misrepresent financial results, while only 5% admit to knowingly violating generally accepted accounting principles.

Used with permission of see eye and Goodrich Corporation

liquidity and capital resources. In addition, the MDA discusses significant risk exposure. For example, Pixar has identified fluctuations in interest rates as a risk factor influencing the value of its investments.

A new subsection of the MDA required by the Sarbanes-Oxley Act must now include a section describing any "off-balance-sheet" arrangements. Such arrangements are discussed in advanced accounting courses.

Report on Adequacy of Internal Control

As discussed in Chapter 7, the Sarbanes-Oxley Act of 2002 requires management to provide a report stating their responsibility for establishing and maintaining internal control. In addition, the report must state management's conclusion concerning the effectiveness of internal controls over financial reporting. The act also requires a public accounting firm to examine and verify management's conclusions regarding internal control. Thus, public companies must provide two reports, one by management and one by a public accounting firm certifying the management report as accurate. Both reports for Pixar are included in the annual report on their Web site.

Report on Fairness of Financial Statements

In addition to a public accounting firm's internal control report, all publicly held corporations are also required to have an independent audit (examination) of their financial statements. For the financial statements of most companies, the CPAs who conduct the audit render an opinion on the fairness of the statements. An opinion stating that the financial statements fairly represent the financial condition of a public company is said to be an unqualified, or "clean," opinion. The Independent Auditors' Report for Pixar is included in the annual report on their Web site. Pixar's auditors gave the company an unqualified opinion.

SUMMARY OF LEARNING GOALS

(1) **Construct and interpret horizontal and vertical analyses.** The analysis of percentage increases and decreases in related items in comparative financial statements is called horizontal analysis. The analysis of percentages of component parts to the total in a single statement is called vertical analysis. Financial statements in which all amounts are expressed in percentages for purposes of analysis are called common-size statements.

(2) **Calculate and interpret the rate earned on stockholders' equity and the rate earned on total assets.** The rate earned on stockholders' equity, which is net income divided by average stockholders' equity, is a widely acknowledged summary measure of financial performance from the stockholders' perspective. The rate earned on total assets, which is net income divided by average total assets, is an acknowledged summary measure of management performance.

(3) **Analyze the rate earned on total assets by evaluating the profit margin and the asset efficiency of a business.** The rate earned on total assets is the product of the profit margin and the total asset turnover, as shown below.

$$\text{Rate Earned on Total Assets} = \text{Profit Margin} \times \text{Asset Turnover}$$

$$\frac{\text{Net Income}}{\text{Average Total Assets}} = \frac{\text{Net Income}}{\text{Net Sales}} \times \frac{\text{Net Sales}}{\text{Average Total Assets}}$$

Management can evaluate the rate earned on total assets by conducting a margin analysis, which segments the profit margin into a vertical analysis of the income statement. Alternatively, management may evaluate the rate earned on total assets by conducting an asset efficiency analysis, which segments the total asset turnover into sub-asset categories.

(4) **Determine and interpret leverage.** Leverage measures the amount of debt used by the firm to finance its assets. The proper use of leverage can cause the rate earned on stockholders' equity to exceed the rate earned on total assets. A firm must be careful to avoid excess leverage, since debt requires fixed periodic interest payments, and the debt must eventually be repaid. The rate earned on stockholders' equity can be compared to the rate earned on total assets by using the leverage formula, as follows:

$$\text{Rate Earned on Stockholders' Equity} = \text{Rate Earned on Total Assets} \times \text{Leverage}$$

Leverage analysis can be used to examine additional measures of current and long-term relationships, using the current ratio, the quick ratio, the ratio of fixed assets to long-term liabilities, the ratio of liabilities to stockholders' equity, and the number of times interest charges are earned.

(5) **Calculate and interpret shareholder ratios: earnings per share, price-earnings ratio, and dividend yield.** Shareholders are interested in making money on their stock investment. This return can come from stock appreciation or from dividends. Thus, earnings per share, the price-earnings ratio, and dividend yield, which relate to stock price and dividend information, are of interest to shareholders.

(6) **Summarize the uses and limitations of analytical measures.** In selecting and interpreting analytical measures, conditions peculiar to a business or its industry should be considered. For example, the type of industry, capital structure, and diversity of the business's operations affect the measures used. Thus, most analysts will compare a firm's ratios with competitors and averages for an industry. In addition, the influence of the general economic and business environment should be considered.

(7) **Describe the contents of corporate annual reports.** Corporate annual reports normally include financial statements and the following sections: Management Discussion and Analysis, reports on the adequacy of internal control, and a report on the fairness of financial statements.

GLOSSARY

Accounts receivable turnover The relationship between net sales and accounts receivable, computed by dividing net sales by the average net accounts receivable.

Asset turnover The number of sales dollars earned for each dollar of total assets, calculated as the ratio of net sales to total assets.

Common-size statement A financial statement in which all items are expressed only in percentages.

Cost of capital The cost of financing operations from both debt and common stock, expressed as a percentage rate.

Current ratio The ratio of current assets to current liabilities.

Dividend yield The rate of return to common stockholders in terms of cash dividends.

DuPont formula A formula that states that the rate earned on total assets is the product of two factors, the profit margin and the total asset turnover.

Earnings per share (EPS) The profitability ratio of net income available to common shareholders to the number of common shares outstanding.

Fixed asset turnover The number of dollars of sales that are generated from each dollar of average fixed assets during the year, computed by dividing the net sales by the average net fixed assets.

Horizontal analysis The percentage of increases and decreases in corresponding items in comparative financial statements.

Inventory turnover The relationship between the volume of goods sold and inventory, computed by dividing the cost of goods sold by the average inventory.

Leverage The amount of debt used by the firm to finance its assets; causes the rate earned on stockholders' equity to vary from the rate earned on total assets because the amount earned on assets acquired through the use of funds provided by creditors varies from the interest paid to these creditors.

Leverage formula A formula that states the rate earned on stockholders' equity as the product of the rate earned on total assets and the ratio of the average total assets divided by average stockholders' equity, or leverage.

Management Discussion and Analysis (MDA) An annual report disclosure that provides an analysis of the results of operations and financial condition.

Number of days' sales in inventory The relationship between the volume of sales and inventory, computed by dividing the inventory at the end of the year by the average daily cost of goods sold.

Number of days' sales in receivables The relationship between sales and accounts receivable, computed by dividing the net accounts receivable at the end of the year by the average daily sales.

Number of times interest charges are earned A ratio that measures creditor margin of safety for interest payments, calculated as income before interest and taxes divided by interest expense.

Price-earnings (P/E) ratio The ratio of the market price per share of common stock, at a specific date, to the annual earnings per share.

Profit margin A measure of the amount earned on each dollar of sales, calculated as the ratio of net income to net sales.

Quick assets Cash and other current assets that can he quickly converted to cash, such as cash, marketable securities, and receivables.

Quick ratio The ratio of the sum of cash, receivables, and marketable securities to current liabilities.

Rate earned on stockholders' equity A measure of profitability computed by dividing net income by total stockholders' equity.

Rate earned on total assets A measure of the profitability of assets, without regard to the equity of creditors and stockholders in the assets, calculated as the net income divided by average total assets.

Ratio of fixed assets to long-term liabilities A leverage ratio that measures the margin of safety of long-term creditors, calculated as the net fixed assets divided by the long-term liabilities.

Ratio of liabilities to stockholders' equity A comprehensive leverage ratio that measures the relationship of the claims of creditors to that of owners, calculated as total liabilities divided by total stockholders' equity.

Vertical analysis The percentage analysis of component parts in relation to the total of the parts in a single financial statement.

ILLUSTRATIVE ACCOUNTING APPLICATION PROBLEM

Rainbow Paint Co.'s comparative financial statements for the years ending December 31, 2007 and 2006, are as follows. The market price of Rainbow Paint Co.'s common stock was $30 on December 31, 2006, and $25 on December 31, 2007.

Rainbow Paint Co.
Comparative Retained Earnings Statement
For the Years Ended December 31, 2007 and 2006

	2007	2006
Retained earnings, January 1	$723,000	$581,800
Add net income for year	245,000	211,200
Total	$968,000	$793,000
Deduct dividends:		
On preferred stock	$ 40,000	$ 40,000
On common stock	45,000	30,000
Total	$ 85,000	$ 70,000
Retained earnings, December 31	$883,000	$723,000

Rainbow Paint Co.
Comparative Income Statement
For the Years Ended December 31, 2007 and 2006

	2007	2006
Net sales	$5,000,000	$3,200,000
Cost of goods sold	3,400,000	2,080,000
Gross profit	$1,600,000	$1,120,000
Selling expenses	$ 650,000	$ 464,000
Administrative expenses	325,000	224,000
Total operating expenses	$ 975,000	$ 688,000
Income from operations	$ 625,000	$ 432,000
Other income	25,000	19,200
	$ 650,000	$ 451,200
Other expense (interest)	105,000	64,000
Income before income tax	$ 545,000	$ 387,200
Income tax expense	300,000	176,000
Net income	$ 245,000	$ 211,200

Rainbow Paint Co.
Comparative Balance Sheet
December 31, 2007 and 2006

	Dec. 31, 2007	Dec. 31, 2006
Assets		
Current assets:		
Cash	$ 175,000	$ 125,000
Marketable securities	150,000	50,000
Accounts receivable (net)	425,000	325,000
Inventories	720,000	480,000
Prepaid expenses	30,000	20,000
Total current assets	$1,500,000	$1,000,000
Long-term investments	250,000	225,000
Property, plant, and equipment (net)	2,093,000	1,948,000
Total assets	$3,843,000	$3,173,000
Liabilities		
Current liabilities	$ 750,000	$ 650,000
Long-term liabilities:		
Mortgage note payable, 10%, due 2011	$ 410,000	$ —
Bonds payable, 8%, due 2014	800,000	800,000
Total long-term liabilities	$ 1,210,000	$ 800,000
Total liabilities	$ 1,960,000	$1,450,000
Stockholders' Equity		
Preferred 8% stock, $100 par	$ 500,000	$ 500,000
Common stock, $10 par	500,000	500,000
Retained earnings	883,000	723,000
Total stockholders' equity	$ 1,883,000	$1,723,000
Total liabilities and stockholders' equity	$ 3,843,000	$3,173,000

Instructions

a. Determine the following measures for 2007:
   1. Rate earned on stockholders' equity
   2. Rate earned on total assets
   3. Leverage ratio
   4. Profit margin
   5. Asset turnover
   6. Accounts receivable turnover
   7. Number of days' sales in receivables
   8. Inventory turnover
   9. Number of days' sales in inventory
   10. Fixed asset turnover
   11. Current ratio
   12. Quick ratio
   13. Ratio of fixed assets to long-term liabilities
   14. Ratio of liabilities to stockholders' equity
   15. Number of times interest charges earned
   16. Earnings per share
   17. Price-earnings ratio
   18. Dividend yield

b. Compute the DuPont formula for 2007.

Solution

(Ratios are rounded to the nearest single digit after the decimal point.)

a.
   1. Rate earned on stockholders' equity: 13.6%
      $245,000 ÷ [($1,883,000 + $1,723,000) ÷ 2]
   2. Rate earned on total assets: 7.0%
      $245,000 ÷ [($3,843,000 + $3,173,000) ÷ 2]
   3. Leverage ratio: 2.0
      [($3,843,000 + $3,173,000) ÷ 2] ÷ [($1,883,000 + $1,723,000) ÷ 2]
   4. Profit margin: 4.9%
      $245,000 ÷ $5,000,000
   5. Asset turnover: 1.4
      $5,000,000 ÷ [($3,843,000 + $3,173,000) ÷ 2]
   6. Accounts receivable turnover: 13.3
      $5,000,000 ÷ [($425,000 + $325,000) ÷ 2]
   7. Number of days' sales in receivables: 27.4 days
      $5,000,000 ÷ 365 = $13,699
      ($425,000 + $325,000)/2 ÷ $13,699
   8. Inventory turnover: 5.7
      $3,400,000 ÷ [($720,000 + $480,000) ÷ 2]
   9. Number of days' sales in inventory: 64.4 days
      $3,400,000 ÷ 365 = $9,315
      [($720,000 + $480,000) ÷ 2] ÷ $9,315
   10. Fixed asset turnover: 2.5
       $5,000,000 ÷ [($2,093,000 + $1,948,000) ÷ 2]
   11. Current ratio: 2.0
       $1,500,000 ÷ $750,000
   12. Quick ratio: 1.0
       $750,000 ÷ $750,000
   13. Ratio of fixed assets to long-term liabilities: 1.7
       $2,093,000 ÷ $1,210,000
   14. Ratio of liabilities to stockholders' equity: 1.0
       $1,960,000 ÷ $1,883,000
   15. Number of times interest charges earned: 6.2
       ($545,000 + $105,000) ÷ $105,000

16. Earnings per share: $4.10
    ($245,000 − $40,000) ÷ 50,000
17. Price-earnings ratio: 6.1
    $25 ÷ $4.10
18. Dividend yield: 3.6%
    $0.90 ÷ $25

b. DuPont formula:

Rate Earned on Total Assets = Profit Margin × Asset Turnover

$$\frac{\text{Net Income}}{\text{Average Total Assets}} = \frac{\text{Net Income}}{\text{Net Sales}} \times \frac{\text{Net Sales}}{\text{Average Total Assets}}$$

6.9% = 4.9% × 1.4

SELF-STUDY QUESTIONS

Answers at end of chapter

1. What type of analysis is indicated by the following?

	Amount	Percent
Current assets	$100,000	20%
Property, plant, and equipment	400,000	80
Total assets	$500,000	100%

   A. Vertical analysis
   B. Horizontal analysis
   C. Profitability analysis
   D. Asset efficiency analysis

2. Horizon Company has the following current account information for a recent balance sheet:

Cash	$ 25,000
Temporary investments	25,000
Accounts receivable	125,000
Merchandise inventory	100,000
Accounts payable	75,000
Accrued expenses	25,000

   What are the current and quick ratios?
   A. 1.75, 2.50 C. 2.75, 0.50
   B. 2.50, 1.50 D. 2.75, 1.75

3. Tiger Equipment Sales Co. had accounts receivable at the beginning and end of the year of $200,000 and $300,000, respectively. The net sales were $1,000,000. Determine the accounts receivable turnover and number of days' sales in accounts receivable.
   A. 3.3, 109 C. 4.0, 109
   B. 3.3, 91 D. 4.0, 91.25

4. The DuPont formula is:
   A. Rate Earned on Total Assets = Profit Margin × Asset Turnover
   B. Rate Earned on Total Stockholders' Equity = Rate Earned on Total Assets × Leverage
   C. Rate Earned on Total Assets = Rate Earned on Total Stockholders' Equity ÷ Leverage
   D. Rate Earned on Total Assets = Profit Margin × Leverage

5. A measure useful in evaluating the efficiency in the management of inventories is:
   A. working capital ratio.
   B. quick ratio.
   C. number of days' sales in inventory.
   D. ratio of fixed assets to long-term liabilities.

DISCUSSION QUESTIONS

1. The current year's amount of net income (after income tax) is 15% larger than that of the preceding year. Does this indicate an improved operating performance? Discuss.
2. How would you respond to a horizontal analysis that showed an expense increasing by over 100%?
3. a. What measure is used by stockholders to assess the profitability of the firm?
   b. How is the ratio in (a) calculated?
4. a. What measure is used by managers in assessing the profitability of the firm?
   b. How is the ratio in (a) calculated?

5. What is the DuPont formula?
6. A company that grants terms of n/30 on all sales has a yearly accounts receivable turnover, based on monthly averages, of 6. Is this a satisfactory turnover? Discuss.
7. What does an increase in the number of days' sales in receivables ordinarily indicate about the credit and collection policy of the firm?
8. a. Why is it advantageous to have a high inventory turnover?
   b. Is it possible for the inventory turnover to be too high? Discuss.
9. Would a railroad be expected to have a high fixed asset turnover?
10. a. What is financial leverage?
    b. What impact does positive leverage have on the rate earned on stockholders' equity compared to the rate earned on total assets?
11. How would the current and quick ratios of a service business compare?
12. For Lindsay Corporation, the working capital at the end of the current year is $5,000 greater than the working capital at the end of the preceding year, reported as follows:

	Current Year	Preceding Year
Current assets:		
Cash, marketable securities, and receivables	$34,000	$30,000
Inventories	51,000	32,500
Total current assets	$85,000	$62,500
Current liabilities	42,500	25,000
Working capital	$42,500	$37,500

Has the current position improved? Explain.

13. What do the following data taken from a comparative balance sheet indicate about the company's ability to borrow additional funds on a long-term basis in the current year as compared to the preceding year?

	Current Year	Preceding Year
Fixed assets (net)	$175,000	$170,000
Total long-term liabilities	70,000	85,000

14. What does a decrease in the ratio of liabilities to stockholders' equity indicate about the margin of safety for a firm's creditors and the ability of the firm to withstand adverse business conditions?
15. The price-earnings ratio for the common stock of Benoit Company was 10 at December 31, the end of the current fiscal year. What does the ratio indicate about the selling price of the common stock in relation to current earnings?
16. Why would the dividend yield differ significantly from the rate earned on common stockholders' equity?
17. Favorable business conditions may bring about certain seemingly unfavorable ratios, and unfavorable business operations may result in apparently favorable ratios. For example, Sanchez Company increased its sales and net income substantially for the current year; yet, the current ratio at the end of the year is lower than at the beginning of the year. Discuss some possible causes of the apparent weakening of the current position, while sales and net income have increased substantially.
18. Indicate the purpose of the Management Discussion and Analysis in a corporation's annual report.

EXERCISES

Exercise 14-1

Vertical analysis of income statement

Goal 1

2007 net income: $50,000; 10% of sales

SPREADSHEET

Revenue and expense data for Home-Mate Appliance Co. are as follows:

	2007	2006
Sales	$500,000	$450,000
Cost of goods sold	275,000	234,000
Selling expenses	90,000	94,500
Administrative expenses	60,000	63,000
Income tax expense	25,000	22,500

a. Prepare an income statement in comparative form, stating each item for both 2007 and 2006 as a percent of sales.
b. Comment on the significant changes disclosed by the comparative income statement.

Exercise 14-2

Vertical analysis of income statement

The following comparative income statement (in millions of dollars) for the fiscal years 2003 and 2004 was adapted from the annual report of Speedway Motorsports, Inc., owner and operator of several major motor speedways, such as the Atlanta, Texas, and Las Vegas Motor Speedways.

Goal 1

a. Fiscal year 2004 income from continuing operations, 26.7% of revenues

SPREADSHEET

Speedway Motorsports, Inc.
Comparative Income Statement (in millions of dollars)
For the Years Ended December 31, 2004 and 2003

	2004	2003
Revenues:		
Admissions	$156.7	$150.2
Event-related revenue	137.1	127.1
NASCAR broadcasting revenue	110.0	90.7
Other operating revenue	42.7	36.5
Total revenues	$446.5	$404.5
Expenses and other:		
Direct expense of events	$ 81.4	$ 78.0
NASCAR purse and sanction fees	78.4	69.7
Other direct operating expense	37.7	32.3
General and administrative	65.1	58.7
Depreciation and amortization	35.6	33.9
Other expenses	28.9	35.2
Total expenses and other	$327.1	$307.8
Income from continuing operations	$119.4	$ 96.7

a. Prepare a comparative income statement for fiscal years 2003 and 2004 in vertical form, stating each item as a percent of revenues. Round to one decimal place.
b. Comment on the significant changes.

Exercise 14-3

Common-size income statement

Goal 1

a. Horizon net income: $105,000; 7.5% of sales

SPREADSHEET

Revenue and expense data for the current calendar year for Horizon Publishing Company and for the publishing industry are as follows. The Horizon Publishing Company data are expressed in dollars. The publishing industry averages are expressed in percentages.

	Horizon Publishing Company	Publishing Industry Average
Sales	$1,414,000	101.0%
Sales returns and allowances	14,000	1.0
Cost of goods sold	504,000	40.0
Selling expenses	574,000	39.0
Administrative expenses	154,000	10.5
Other income	16,800	1.2
Other expense	23,800	1.7
Income tax expense	56,000	4.0

a. Prepare a common-size income statement comparing the results of operations for Horizon Publishing Company with the industry average. Round to one decimal place.
b. As far as the data permit, comment on significant relationships revealed by the comparisons.

Exercise 14-4

Vertical analysis of balance sheet

Goal 1

Retained earnings, Dec. 31, 2007, 46.25%

SPREADSHEET

Balance sheet data for Santa Fe Tile Company on December 31, the end of the fiscal year, are as follows:

	2007	2006
Current assets	$260,000	$200,000
Property, plant, and equipment	500,000	450,000
Intangible assets	40,000	50,000
Current liabilities	170,000	150,000
Long-term liabilities	210,000	200,000
Common stock	50,000	50,000
Retained earnings	370,000	300,000

Prepare a comparative balance sheet for 2007 and 2006, stating each asset as a percent of total assets and each liability and stockholders' equity item as a percent of the total liabilities and stockholders' equity. Round to two decimal places.

Exercise 14-5

Horizontal analysis of the income statement

Goal 1

a. Net income decrease, 77.5%

SPREADSHEET

Income statement data for Scribe Paper Company for the year ended December 31, 2007 and 2006, are as follows:

	2007	2006
Sales	$66,300	$85,000
Cost of goods sold	32,000	40,000
Gross profit	$34,300	$45,000
Selling expenses	$24,000	$25,000
Administrative expenses	7,500	6,000
Total operating expenses	$31,500	$31,000
Income before income tax	$ 2,800	$14,000
Income tax expense	1,000	6,000
Net income	$ 1,800	$ 8,000

a. Prepare a comparative income statement with horizontal analysis, indicating the increase (decrease) for 2007 when compared with 2006. Round to two decimal places.
b. What conclusions can be drawn from the horizontal analysis?

Exercise 14-6

Profitability ratios

Goal 2

a. Rate earned on total assets, 2008, 31.3%

SPREADSHEET

The following selected data were taken from the financial statements of Atlantic Resources, Inc., for December 31, 2008, 2007, and 2006:

	December 31, 2008	December 31, 2007	December 31, 2006
Total assets	$4,000,000	$2,400,000	$1,800,000
Common stock	800,000	800,000	800,000
Retained earnings	2,230,000	1,230,000	600,000

The 2008 net income was $1,000,000, and the 2007 net income was $630,000.

a. Determine the rate earned on total assets and the rate earned on stockholders' equity for the years 2007 and 2008. Round to one decimal place.
b. Relate the rate earned on stockholders' equity to the rate earned on total assets using the leverage ratio for fiscal year 2008. Round to a single decimal place.
c. What conclusions can be drawn from these data as to the company's profitability?

Exercise 14-7

Profitability ratios

Goal 2

a. 2004 rate earned on total assets, 4.9%

Ann Taylor Stores Corp. sells professional women's apparel through company-owned retail stores. Recent financial information for Ann Taylor is provided below (all numbers in millions).

	Fiscal Year Ended	
	Jan. 29, 2005	Jan. 31, 2004
Net income	$63.3	$100.7

	Jan. 29, 2005	Jan. 31, 2004	Feb. 1, 2003
Total assets	$1,327.3	$1,256.4	$1,008.5
Total stockholders' equity	926.7	818.9	714.4

The apparel retail industry average rate earned on total assets is 8.2%, and the average rate earned on stockholders' equity is 16.7% for fiscal year 2004 (mostly January 29, 2005-dated statements).

a. Determine the rate earned on total assets for Ann Taylor for the fiscal years ended January 29, 2005, and January 31, 2004. Round to one decimal place.
b. Determine the rate earned on stockholders' equity for Ann Taylor for the fiscal years ended January 29, 2005, and January 31, 2004. Round to one decimal place.
c. Evaluate the two-year trend for the profitability ratios determined in (a) and (b).
d. Evaluate Ann Taylor's profit performance relative to the industry.

Exercise 14-8

Profitability ratios

Goal 2

b. 2006 rate earned on total assets, 7.2%

The Imagination Studios, Inc., produces television shows. The company earned $300,000 and $400,000 in 2006 and 2007, respectively. The company had total assets of $4,000,000 and total liabilities of $1,000,000 on January 1, 2006. The company had no investing or financing transactions during 2006. On July 1, 2007, the company purchased studio property for $3,000,000 by issuing debt for the same amount.

a. Determine the average total assets and average stockholders' equity for 2006 and 2007.
b. Calculate the rate earned on total assets and rate earned on stockholders' equity for 2006 and 2007. Round to one decimal place.
c. Why did the profits increase from 2006 to 2007, but the rate earned on total assets decrease?
d. Why did the difference between the rate earned on stockholders' equity and rate earned on total assets increase from 2006 to 2007?

Exercise 14-9

DuPont formula

Goal 3

a. 2006 rate earned on total assets, 18%

The chief financial officer (CFO) of Beacon Publishing Company has asked for a DuPont analysis of the company over the last two years. The CFO has requested that the rate earned on total assets be broken into its profit margin and asset turnover components. The following information is available, from the financial statements:

	2006	2007
Sales	$360,000	$700,000
Net income	28,800	77,000

	December 31, 2005	December 31, 2006	December 31, 2007
Total assets	$120,000	$200,000	$360,000

a. Perform a DuPont analysis for 2006 and 2007.
b. Analyze the change in the rate earned on total assets for the two years.

Exercise 14-10

DuPont formula

Goal 3

a. Profit margin, fiscal 2005, 9.81%

Bed Bath and Beyond, Inc., is a major retailer of bed and bath products. During two recent fiscal years, the company reported the following information from the income statement (in millions):

	For the Year Ended	
	Feb. 26, 2005	Feb. 28, 2004
Sales	$5,147.7	$4,478.0
Net income	505.0	399.5

In addition, the balance sheet revealed the following information (in millions):

	Feb. 26, 2005	Feb. 28, 2004	Mar. 1, 2003
Total assets	$3,200.0	$2,865.0	$2,188.8
Total liabilities	996.2	874.2	736.9
Total stockholders' equity	2,203.8	1,990.8	1,451.9

a. Determine the profit margin for fiscal years ending February 26, 2005, and February 28, 2004. Round to two decimal places.
b. Determine the asset turnover for fiscal years ending February 26, 2005, and February 28, 2004. Round to two decimal places.
c. Use the DuPont formula to determine the rate earned on total assets from (a) and (b).
d. Interpret the change in the rate earned on total assets between the two fiscal periods.

Exercise 14-11

DuPont formula and margin analysis

Goal 3

a. Rate earned on total assets, 2006: 17.6%

SPREADSHEET

Prince Foods Company disclosed the following comparative income statement information:

	For the Year Ended	
	Dec. 31, 2007	Dec. 31, 2006
Sales	$600,000	$500,000
Cost of goods sold	252,000	190,000
Gross profit	$348,000	$310,000
Operating expenses	240,000	200,000
Income from operations	$108,000	$110,000

The asset turnover for both 2006 and 2007 was 0.80.

a. Determine the rate earned on total assets for 2006 and 2007, using the DuPont formula.
b. Prepare common-size income statements for 2006 and 2007.
c. Analyze the change in the rate earned on total assets between 2006 and 2007 by conducting a margin analysis on common-size statements.

Exercise 14-12

Accounts receivable analysis

Goal 3

a. Accounts receivable turnover, 2008, 7.1

The following data are taken from the financial statements of Ovation Industries Inc. Terms of all sales are 1/10, n/55.

	2008	2007
Accounts receivable, end of year	$ 48,219	$ 52,603
Monthly average accounts receivable (net)	45,070	46,154
Net sales	320,000	300,000

a. Determine for each year (1) the accounts receivable turnover and (2) the number of days' sales in receivables. Round to nearest dollar and to one decimal place.
b. What conclusions can be drawn from these data concerning accounts receivable and credit policies?

Exercise 14-13

Accounts receivable analysis

Goal 3

a. (1) Coca-Cola's accounts receivable turnover, 10.31

The Coca-Cola Company and PepsiCo, Inc., are the two largest beverage companies in the United States. Both companies offer credit to their customers. Information from the financial statements for both companies for a recent year is as follows (all numbers are in millions):

	Coca-Cola	PepsiCo
Sales	$21,962	$29,261
Accounts receivable (net)—ending balance	2,171	2,505
Accounts receivable (net)—beginning balance	2,091	2,309

a. Determine (1) the accounts receivable turnover and (2) the number of days' sales in receivables for both companies. Round to two decimal places.
b. Compare the two companies with regard to their accounts receivable efficiency.

Exercise 14-14

Inventory analysis

Goal 3

a. Inventory turnover, 2007, 8.0

The following data were extracted from the income statement of Mountain Sports Inc.:

	2007	2006
Sales	$656,000	$774,000
Beginning inventories	42,000	44,000
Cost of goods sold	328,000	430,000
Ending inventories	40,000	42,000

a. Determine for each year (1) the inventory turnover and (2) the number of days' sales in inventory. Round to nearest dollar and to two decimal places.
b. What conclusions can be drawn from these data concerning the inventories?

Exercise 14-15

Inventory analysis

Goal 3

a. (1) Dell inventory turnover, 99.5

Dell Inc. and Hewlett-Packard Corporation (HP) compete with each other in the personal computer market. Dell's strategy is to assemble computers to customer orders, rather than for inventory. For example, Dell will build and deliver a computer within four days of a customer entering an order on a Web page. Hewlett-Packard, in contrast, builds some computers prior to receiving an order, then sells from this inventory once an order is received. Below is selected financial information for both companies from a recent year's financial statements (in millions).

	Dell Inc.	Hewlett-Packard Corporation
Sales	$35,404	$45,955
Cost of goods sold	29,055	34,573
Inventory, beginning of period	278	5,204
Inventory, end of period	306	5,797

a. Determine for both companies (1) the inventory turnover and (2) the number of days' sales in inventory. Round to one decimal place.
b. Interpret the inventory ratios by considering Dell's and Hewlett-Packard's operating emphases.

Exercise 14-16

Fixed asset analysis

Goal 3

a. Media Networks, 0.45

The Walt Disney Co. reported segment information for a recent year as shown below.

	(in millions)			
	Media Networks	Parks and Resorts	Studio Entertainment	Consumer Products
Sales	$11,778	$ 7,750	$8,713	$2,511
Identifiable fixed assets, ending balance	26,193	15,221	6,954	1,037
Identifiable fixed assets, beginning balance	25,882	11,067	7,832	966

A brief description of each segment is as follows:

Media Networks: The ABC television and radio network, Disney channel, ESPN, A&E, E!, and Disney.com.
Parks and Resorts: Disney World, Disneyland, Disney Cruise Line, and other resort properties.
Studio Entertainment: Walt Disney Pictures, Touchstone Pictures, Hollywood Pictures, Miramax, and Disney theatrical productions.
Consumer Products: Character merchandising and licensing, Disney stores, books, and magazines.

a. Determine for each business segment the fixed asset turnover for the year. Round to two decimal places.
b. Analyze your results.

Exercise 14-17

Leverage formula

Goal 4

International Paper Company is one of the world's largest manufacturers of paper and wood products. The following information (in millions) was disclosed on recent two-year comparative income statements:

	2004	2003
Net income (loss)*	$(35)	$302

*Before discontinued operations, extraordinary items, and cumulative effect from change in accounting principle.

Information (in millions) from three-year comparative balance sheets is as follows:

	Dec. 31, 2004	Dec. 31, 2003	Dec. 31, 2002
Total assets	$34,217	$35,525	$33,792
Total stockholders' equity	8,254	8,237	7,374

a. Determine the rate earned on total assets for 2003 and 2004. Round to two decimal places.
b. Determine the rate earned on stockholders' equity, using the leverage formula, for 2003 and 2004. Round to two decimal places.
c. Analyze comparative ratios in (a) and (b) for the two years.

Exercise 14-18

Leverage formula

Goal 4

a. 8%

Celtic Arts, Inc., earned $50,000 in 2007 and $80,000 in 2008. The company began operations on January 1, 2007, with a $600,000 investment by stockholders and no debt. On June 30, 2008, the company borrowed $1,000,000 from a bank, payable in 10 years.

a. Determine the rate earned on total assets and the rate earned on total stockholders' equity for 2007. Round to two decimal places.
b. Determine the rate earned on total assets for 2008. Round to two decimal places.
c. Use the leverage formula to determine the rate earned on stockholders' equity for 2008.

Exercise 14-19

Current position analysis

Goal 4

2007 working capital, $625,000

The following data were taken from the balance sheet of Marine Equipment Company:

	Dec. 31, 2007	Dec. 31, 2006
Cash	$118,000	$ 95,000
Marketable securities	152,000	131,000
Accounts and notes receivable (net)	210,000	198,000
Inventories	345,000	326,000
Prepaid expenses	50,000	45,000
Accounts and notes payable (short-term)	190,000	208,000
Accrued liabilities	60,000	57,000

a. Determine for each year (1) the working capital, (2) the current ratio, and (3) the quick ratio. Round to one decimal place.
b. What conclusions can be drawn from these data as to the company's ability to meet its currently maturing debts?

Exercise 14-20

Leverage analysis: current position

Goal 4

a. (1) March 31, 2004, current ratio, 3.86

Tommy Hilfiger Corp., the fashion apparel company, had the following current assets and current liabilities at the end of two recent years:

	March 31, 2004 (in millions)	March 31, 2003 (in millions)
Cash and cash equivalents	$414.5	$420.8
Temporary investments	27.5	—
Accounts receivable	188.5	185.0
Inventories	206.3	229.7
Deferred tax and other current assets	92.8	80
Short-term borrowings	—	19.4
Current portion of long-term debt	0.7	151.9
Accounts payable	32.7	47.8
Accrued expenses and other current liabilities	207.2	185.9

a. Determine the (1) current ratio and (2) quick ratio for both years. Round to two decimal places. Treat the deferred tax and other current assets as nonquick assets.
b. What conclusions can you draw from these data?

Exercise 14-21

Current position analysis

Goal 4

The bond indenture for the 10-year, $9\frac{1}{2}\%$ debenture bonds dated January 2, 2007, required working capital of $350,000, a current ratio of 1.5, and a quick ratio of 1 at the end of each calendar year until the bonds mature. At December 31, 2008, the three measures were computed as follows:

1. Current assets:

Cash	$275,000	
Marketable securities	123,000	
Accounts and notes receivable (net)	172,000	
Inventories	295,000	
Prepaid expenses	35,000	
Goodwill	150,000	
Total current assets		$1,050,000
Current liabilities:		
Accounts and short-term notes payable	$375,000	
Accrued liabilities	250,000	
Total current liabilities		625,000
Working capital		$ 425,000

2. Current ratio = 1.68 ($1,050,000 ÷ $625,000)
3. Quick ratio = 1.52 ($570,000 ÷ $375,000)

a. List the errors in the determination of the three measures of current position analysis.
b. Is the company satisfying the terms of the bond indenture?

Exercise 14-22

Leverage analysis: long-term debt position

Goal 4

a. Ratio of liabilities to stockholders' equity, Dec. 31, 2007, 0.54

The following data were taken from the financial statements of Durable Structures, Inc., for December 31, 2007 and 2006:

	December 31, 2007	December 31, 2006
Accounts payable	$ 150,000	$ 140,000
Current maturities of serial bonds payable	200,000	200,000
Serial bonds payable, 8%, issued 2002, due 2012	1,000,000	1,200,000
Common stock, $1 par value	100,000	100,000
Paid-in capital in excess of par	500,000	500,000
Retained earnings	1,900,000	1,600,000

The income before income tax was $528,000 and $336,000 for the years 2007 and 2006, respectively.

a. Determine the ratio of liabilities to stockholders' equity at the end of each year. Round to two decimal places.
b. Determine the number of times the bond interest charges are earned during the year for both years.
c. What conclusions can be drawn from these data as to the company's ability to meet its currently maturing debts?

Exercise 14-23

Leverage analysis: long-term debt position

Goal 4

Dow Jones & Co., Inc., and New York Times Co. are major publishers of financial and general news and information. Condensed financial information for both companies for a recent year is as follows:

Recent year income statement information:

	Dow Jones	New York Times
Interest expense	$ 3.7	$ 41.8
Income tax expense	58.6	183.5
Net income	99.5	292.6

Recent year balance sheet information:

	Dow Jones	New York Times
Fixed assets	$1,023.2	$3,117.0
Total assets	1,380.2	3,949.9
Long-term liabilities	509.3	1,294.9
Total stockholders' equity	150.5	1,400.5

a. Determine the following ratios for each company (round to two decimal places):
   (1) Ratio of fixed assets to long-term liabilities.
   (2) Ratio of liabilities to stockholders' equity.
   (3) Number of times interest charges were earned.
b. Compare the debt position of the two companies from the ratios in part (a).

Exercise 14-24

Stockholder ratios

Goal 5

b. Price-earnings ratio, 20

The following information was taken from the financial statements of Fashion Cosmetics, Inc., for December 31 of the current fiscal year:

Common stock, $12 par value (no change during the year)	$2,400,000
Preferred $9 stock, $100 par, cumulative, nonparticipating (no change during year)	600,000

The net income was $444,000 and the declared dividends on the common stock were $156,000 for the current year. The market price of the common stock is $39 per share.

For the common stock, determine the (a) earnings per share, (b) price-earnings ratio, (c) dividends per share, and (d) dividend yield. Round to two decimal places.

Exercise 14-25

Stockholder ratios

Goal 5

b. Dividends per share, $0.38

AFLAC, Inc., is the largest accident and health insurer in the United States. The stockholders' equity section of the balance sheet disclosed the following for the ending date of a recent year:

Shareholders' equity (in millions):	
Common stock	$ 533
Retained earnings	6,992
Accumulated other comprehensive income, net of taxes	2,609
Less: Treasury stock	2,561
Total shareholders' equity	$7,573

The statement of stockholders' equity showed the following changes in the retained earnings balance for the year:

Retained earnings (in millions):	
Beginning of year	$5,885
Net income	1,299
Dividends declared on common stock	(192)
End of year	$6,992

There were 507,333,000 shares outstanding for computing earnings per share. The market price of the common stock averaged $40 per share during the year.

Determine for the common stock (rounding to two decimal places):

a. Earnings per share.
b. Dividends per share.
c. Price-earnings ratio.
d. Dividend yield.

Exercise 14-26

Earnings per share

Goal **5**

b. Earnings per share on common stock, $1.14

The net income reported on the income statement of Cincinnati Soap Co. was $890,000. There were 500,000 shares of $20 par common stock and 40,000 shares of $8 cumulative preferred stock outstanding throughout the current year. The income statement included two extraordinary items: a $256,000 gain from condemnation of land and a $166,000 loss arising from flood damage, both after applicable income tax. Determine the per-share figures for common stock for (a) income before extraordinary items and (b) net income.

Exercise 14-27

Price-earnings ratio; dividend yield

Goal **5**

The table below shows the stock price, earnings per share, and dividends per share for three companies as of a recent date:

	Price	Earnings per Share	Dividends per Share
Bank of America Corp.	$68.20	$5.91	$2.56
eBay Inc.	73.56	0.85	0.00
Coca-Cola Company	40.06	1.68	0.80

a. Determine the price-earnings ratio and dividend yield for the three companies. Round to two decimal places.
b. Explain the differences in these ratios across the three companies.

Exercise 14-28

Leverage of stockholder ratios

Goals **4, 5**

c. Price-earnings ratio, 20.83

The balance sheet for Collier Medical, Inc., at the end of the current fiscal year indicated the following:

Bonds payable, 12% (issued in 1996, due in 2016)	$1,500,000
Preferred $10 stock, $100 par	250,000
Common stock, $20 par	2,500,000

Income before income tax was $450,000, and income taxes were $125,000 for the current year. Cash dividends paid on common stock during the current year totaled $100,000. The common stock was selling for $50 per share at the end of the year. Determine each of the following: (a) number of times bond interest charges were earned, (b) earnings per share on common stock, (c) price-earnings ratio, (d) dividends per share of common stock, and (e) dividend yield. Round to two decimal places.

Exercise 14-29

Profitability and leverage ratios

Goals **2, 4**

c. Ratio of net sales to assets, 1.43

The following data were taken from the financial statements of Orion Systems Inc. for the current fiscal year:

Property, plant, and equipment (net)			$ 950,000
Liabilities:			
Current liabilities		$ 45,000	
Mortgage note payable, 7.5%, issued 1996, due 2011		680,000	
Total liabilities			$ 725,000
Stockholders' equity:			
Preferred $8 stock, $100 par, cumulative, nonparticipating (no change during year)			$ 200,000
Common stock, $10 par (no change during year)			650,000
Retained earnings:			
Balance, beginning of year	$500,000		
Net income	180,000	$680,000	
Preferred dividends	$ 16,000		
Common dividends	48,000	64,000	
Balance, end of year			616,000
Total stockholders' equity			$1,466,000
Net sales			$3,000,000
Interest expense			$ 51,000

Assuming that total assets were $2,009,000 at the beginning of the year, determine the following: (a) ratio of fixed assets to long-term liabilities, (b) ratio of liabilities to stockholders' equity, (c) asset turnover, (d) rate earned on total assets, and (e) rate earned on stockholders' equity. Round to two decimal places.

ACCOUNTING APPLICATION PROBLEMS

Problem 14-1A

Horizontal analysis for income statement

Goal **1**

1. Net sales, 12% increase

SPREADSHEET

For 2008, Turnberry Company reported its most significant decline in net income in years. At the end of the year, Hai Chow, the president, is presented with the following condensed comparative income statement:

Turnberry Company
Comparative Income Statement
For the Years Ended December 31, 2008 and 2007

	2008	2007
Sales	$482,000	$429,000
Sales returns and allowances	6,000	4,000
Net sales	$476,000	$425,000
Cost of goods sold	216,000	180,000
Gross profit	$260,000	$245,000
Selling expenses	$109,250	$ 95,000
Administrative expenses	52,500	30,000
Total operating expenses	$161,750	$125,000
Income from operations	$ 98,250	$120,000
Other income	2,000	2,000
Income before income tax	$100,250	$122,000
Income tax expense	30,000	40,000
Net income	$ 70,250	$ 82,000

Instructions

1. Prepare a comparative income statement with horizontal analysis for the two-year period, using 2007 as the base year. Round to two decimal places.
2. To the extent the data permit, comment on the significant relationships revealed by the horizontal analysis prepared in (1).

Problem 14-2A

Vertical analysis for income statement

Goal 1

1. Net income, 2008, 21.20%

SPREADSHEET

For 2008, Audio Tone Company initiated a sales promotion campaign that included the expenditure of an additional $13,800 for advertising. At the end of the year, Gordon Kincaid, the president, is presented with the following condensed comparative income statement:

Audio Tone Company
Comparative Income Statement
For the Years Ended December 31, 2008 and 2007

	2008	2007
Sales	$664,000	$526,000
Sales returns and allowances	4,000	6,000
Net sales	$660,000	$520,000
Cost of goods sold	257,400	213,200
Gross profit	$402,600	$306,800
Selling expenses	$138,600	$124,800
Administrative expenses	72,600	67,600
Total operating expenses	$211,200	$192,400
Income from operations	$191,400	$114,400
Other income	2,500	2,000
Income before income tax	$193,900	$116,400
Income tax expense	54,000	30,000
Net income	$139,900	$ 86,400

Instructions

1. Prepare a comparative income statement for the two-year period, presenting an analysis of each item in relationship to net sales for each of the years. Round to two decimal places.
2. To the extent the data permit, comment on the significant relationships revealed by the vertical analysis prepared in (1).

Problem 14-3A

Effect of transactions on current position analysis

Goal 4

1. Current ratio, 2.13

SPREADSHEET

Data pertaining to the current position of Anderson Lumber Company are as follows:

Cash	$240,000
Marketable securities	110,000
Accounts and notes receivable (net)	380,000
Inventories	495,000
Prepaid expenses	30,000
Accounts payable	390,000
Notes payable (short-term)	150,000
Accrued expenses	50,000

Instructions

1. Compute (a) the working capital, (b) the current ratio, and (c) the quick ratio. Round to two decimal places.
2. List the following captions on a sheet of paper:

Transaction	Working Capital	Current Ratio	Quick Ratio

Compute the working capital, the current ratio, and the quick ratio after each of the following transactions, and record the results in the appropriate columns. Consider each transaction separately and assume that only that transaction affects the data given above. Round to two decimal places.

a. Sold marketable securities at no gain or loss, $56,000.
b. Paid accounts payable, $60,000.
c. Purchased goods on account, $80,000.
d. Paid notes payable, $40,000.
e. Declared a cash dividend, $25,000.
f. Declared a common stock dividend, $28,500.
g. Borrowed cash from bank on a long-term note, $120,000.
h. Received cash on account, $164,000.
i. Issued additional shares of stock for cash, $250,000.
j. Paid cash for prepaid expenses, $10,000.

Problem 14-4A

Nineteen measures of solvency and profitability

Goals **2, 3, 4, 5**

5. Number of days' sales in receivables, 63.3

SPREADSHEET

The comparative financial statements of Vision International, Inc., are as follows. The market price of Vision International, Inc., common stock was $20 on December 31, 2007.

Vision International, Inc.
Comparative Retained Earnings Statement
For the Years Ended December 31, 2007 and 2006

	2007	2006
Retained earnings, January 1	$375,000	$327,000
Add net income for year	68,000	67,000
Total	$443,000	$394,000
Deduct dividends:		
On preferred stock	$ 15,000	$ 12,000
On common stock	7,000	7,000
Total	$ 22,000	$ 19,000
Retained earnings, December 31	$421,000	$375,000

Vision International, Inc.
Comparative Income Statement
For the Years Ended December 31, 2007 and 2006

	2007	2006
Net sales	$1,050,000	$960,000
Cost of goods sold	400,000	390,000
Gross profit	$ 650,000	$570,000
Selling expenses	$ 270,000	$275,000
Administrative expenses	195,000	165,000
Total operating expenses	$ 465,000	$440,000
Income from operations	$ 185,000	$130,000
Other income	20,000	15,000
	$ 205,000	$145,000
Other expense (interest)	96,000	48,000
Income before income tax	$ 109,000	$ 97,000
Income tax expense	41,000	30,000
Net income	$ 68,000	$ 67,000

Vision International, Inc.
Comparative Balance Sheet
December 31, 2007 and 2006

	Dec. 31, 2007	Dec. 31, 2006
Assets		
Current assets:		
Cash	$ 165,000	$ 126,000
Marketable securities	398,000	254,000
Accounts receivable (net)	199,000	165,000
Inventories	84,000	52,000
Prepaid expenses	25,000	18,000
Total current assets	$ 871,000	$ 615,000
Long-term investments	300,000	200,000
Property, plant, and equipment (net)	1,040,000	760,000
Total assets	$2,211,000	$1,575,000
Liabilities		
Current liabilities	$ 290,000	$ 250,000
Long-term liabilities:		
Mortgage note payable, 8%, due 2012	$ 300,000	—
Bonds payable, 12%, due 2016	600,000	$ 400,000
Total long-term liabilities	$ 900,000	$ 400,000
Total liabilities	$1,190,000	$ 650,000
Stockholders' Equity		
Preferred $6 stock, $100 par	$ 250,000	$ 200,000
Common stock, $10 par	350,000	350,000
Retained earnings	421,000	375,000
Total stockholders' equity	$1,021,000	$ 925,000
Total liabilities and stockholders' equity	$2,211,000	$1,575,000

Instructions

Determine the following measures for 2007, rounding to one decimal place:

1. Working capital
2. Current ratio
3. Quick ratio
4. Accounts receivable turnover
5. Number of days' sales in receivables
6. Inventory turnover
7. Number of days' sales in inventory
8. Ratio of fixed assets to long-term liabilities
9. Ratio of liabilities to stockholders' equity
10. Number of times interest charges earned
11. Asset turnover
12. Rate earned on total assets
13. Rate earned on stockholders' equity
14. Earnings per share on common stock
15. Price-earnings ratio
16. Dividends per share of common stock
17. Dividend yield
18. DuPont formula
19. Leverage formula

Problem 14-5A

Profitability and leverage trend analysis

Goals **2, 3**

Sage Software Company has provided the following comparative information:

	2008	2007	2006	2005	2004
Net income	$1,200,000	$ 800,000	$ 600,000	$ 400,000	$ 300,000
Interest expense	200,000	170,000	150,000	120,000	100,000
Income tax expense	360,000	240,000	180,000	120,000	90,000
Total assets (ending balance)	6,000,000	4,500,000	3,500,000	2,600,000	2,000,000
Total stockholders' equity (ending balance)	4,000,000	2,800,000	2,000,000	1,400,000	1,000,000
Average total assets	5,250,000	4,000,000	3,050,000	2,300,000	1,800,000
Average stockholders' equity	3,400,000	2,400,000	1,700,000	1,200,000	900,000

You have been asked to evaluate the historical performance of the company over the last five years.

Selected industry ratios have remained relatively steady at the following levels for the last five years:

	2004–2008
Rate earned on total assets	15%
Rate earned on stockholders' equity	25%
Number of times interest charges earned	3.0
Ratio of liabilities to stockholders' equity	1.5

Instructions

1. Prepare four line graphs with the ratio on the vertical axis and the years on the horizontal axis for the following four ratios (rounded to two decimal places):
   - **a.** Rate earned on total assets
   - **b.** Rate earned on stockholders' equity
   - **c.** Number of times interest charges earned
   - **d.** Ratio of liabilities to stockholders' equity

   Display both the company ratio and the industry benchmark on each graph. That is, each graph should have two lines.

2. Prepare an analysis of the graphs in (1).

ALTERNATIVE ACCOUNTING APPLICATION PROBLEMS

Alternate Problem 14-1B

Horizontal analysis for income statement

Goal **1**

1. Net sales, 25% increase

SPREADSHEET

For 2007, Pet Care, Inc., reported its most significant increase in net income in years. At the end of the year, Jeff Newton, the president, is presented with the condensed comparative income statement on the following page.

Instructions

1. Prepare a comparative income statement with horizontal analysis for the two-year period, using 2006 as the base year. Round to two decimal places.

2. To the extent the data permit, comment on the significant relationships revealed by the horizontal analysis prepared in (1).

Pet Care, Inc.
Comparative Income Statement
For the Years Ended December 31, 2007 and 2006

	2007	2006
Sales	$76,200	$61,000
Sales returns and allowances	1,200	1,000
Net sales	$75,000	$60,000
Cost of goods sold	42,000	35,000
Gross profit	$33,000	$25,000
Selling expenses	$13,800	$12,000
Administrative expenses	9,000	8,000
Total operating expenses	$22,800	$20,000
Income from operations	$10,200	$ 5,000
Other income	500	500
Income before income tax	$10,700	$ 5,500
Income tax expense	2,400	1,200
Net income	$ 8,300	$ 4,300

Alternate Problem 14-2B

Vertical analysis for income statement

Goal 1

1. Net loss, 2008, 4.28%

SPREADSHEET

For 2008, Industrial Sanitation Systems, Inc. initiated a sales promotion campaign that included the expenditure of an additional $26,000 for advertising. At the end of the year, Alex Gonzalez, the president, is presented with the condensed comparative income statement below.

Industrial Sanitation Systems, Inc.
Comparative Income Statement
For the Years Ended December 31, 2008 and 2007

	2008	2007
Sales	$144,000	$128,000
Sales returns and allowances	4,000	3,000
Net sales	$140,000	$125,000
Cost of goods sold	80,000	72,000
Gross profit	$ 60,000	$ 53,000
Selling expenses	$ 56,000	$ 30,000
Administrative expenses	14,000	12,000
Total operating expenses	$ 70,000	$ 42,000
Income from operations	$ (10,000)	$ 11,000
Other income	2,000	1,800
Income before income tax	$ (8,000)	$ 12,800
Income tax expense (benefit)	(2,000)	3,000
Net income (loss)	$ (6,000)	$ 9,800

Instructions

1. Prepare a comparative income statement for the two-year period, presenting an analysis of each item in relationship to net sales for each of the years. Round to two decimal places.
2. To the extent the data permit, comment on the significant relationships revealed by the vertical analysis prepared in (1).

Alternate Problem 14-3B

Effect of transactions on current position analysis

Goal 4

1. Quick ratio, 1.34

SPREADSHEET

Data pertaining to the current position of Around Town Clothing Co. are as follows:

Cash	$120,000
Marketable securities	56,000
Accounts and notes receivable (net)	185,000
Inventories	224,000
Prepaid expenses	9,000
Accounts payable	188,000
Notes payable (short-term)	55,000
Accrued expenses	26,000

Instructions

1. Compute (a) the working capital, (b) the current ratio, and (c) the quick ratio. Round to two decimal places.
2. List the following captions on a sheet of paper:

Transaction	Working Capital	Current Ratio	Quick Ratio

Compute the working capital, the current ratio, and the quick ratio after each of the following transactions, and record the results in the appropriate columns. Consider each transaction separately and assume that only that transaction affects the data given above. Round to two decimal places.

a. Sold marketable securities at no gain or loss, $34,000.
b. Paid accounts payable, $60,000.
c. Purchased goods on account, $40,000.
d. Paid notes payable, $20,000.
e. Declared a cash dividend, $25,000.
f. Declared a common stock dividend, $16,500.
g. Borrowed cash from bank on a long-term note, $120,000.
h. Received cash on account, $86,000.
i. Issued additional shares of stock for cash, $100,000.
j. Paid cash for prepaid expenses, $9,000.

Alternate Problem 14-4B

Profitability, asset efficiency, leverage, and stockholder ratios

Goals 2, 3, 4, 5

9. Ratio of liabilities to stockholders' equity, 0.6

SPREADSHEET

The comparative financial statements of Quest Polymers, Inc., are as follows. The market price of Quest Polymers, Inc., common stock was $64 on December 31, 2007.

Quest Polymers, Inc.
Comparative Retained Earnings Statement
For the Years Ended December 31, 2007 and 2006

	2007	2006
Retained earnings, January 1	$ 645,000	$512,000
Add net income for year	361,000	221,000
Total	$1,006,000	$733,000
Deduct dividends:		
On preferred stock	$ 32,000	$ 24,000
On common stock	64,000	64,000
Total	$ 96,000	$ 88,000
Retained earnings, December 31	$ 910,000	$645,000

Quest Polymers, Inc.
Comparative Income Statement
For the Years Ended December 31, 2007 and 2006

	2007	2006
Net sales	$2,800,000	$2,425,000
Cost of goods sold	1,250,000	1,150,000
Gross profit	$1,550,000	$1,275,000
Selling expenses	$ 605,000	$ 575,000
Administrative expenses	405,000	380,000
Total operating expenses	$1,010,000	$ 955,000
Income from operations	$ 540,000	$ 320,000
Other income	40,000	30,000
	$ 580,000	$ 350,000
Other expense (interest)	79,000	34,000
Income before income tax	$ 501,000	$ 316,000
Income tax expense	140,000	95,000
Net income	$ 361,000	$ 221,000

Quest Polymers, Inc.
Comparative Balance Sheet
December 31, 2007 and 2006

	Dec. 31, 2007	Dec. 31, 2006
Assets		
Current assets:		
Cash	$ 108,000	$ 96,000
Marketable securities	320,000	126,000
Accounts receivable (net)	172,000	158,000
Inventories	325,000	265,000
Prepaid expenses	20,000	25,000
Total current assets	$ 945,000	$ 670,000
Long-term investments	250,000	200,000
Property, plant, and equipment (net)	2,100,000	1,500,000
Total assets	$3,295,000	$2,370,000
Liabilities		
Current liabilities	$ 285,000	$ 225,000
Long-term liabilities:		
Mortgage note payable, 9%, due 2012	$ 500,000	$ —
Bonds payable, 8.5%, due 2016	400,000	400,000
Total long-term liabilities	$ 900,000	$ 400,000
Total liabilities	$1,185,000	$ 625,000
Stockholders' Equity		
Preferred $8 stock, $100 par	$ 400,000	$ 300,000
Common stock, $10 par	800,000	800,000
Retained earnings	910,000	645,000
Total stockholders' equity	$2,110,000	$1,745,000
Total liabilities and stockholders' equity	$3,295,000	$2,370,000

Instructions

Determine the following measures for 2007, rounding to nearest single digit after the decimal point:

1. Working capital
2. Current ratio
3. Quick ratio
4. Accounts receivable turnover
5. Number of days' sales in receivables
6. Inventory turnover
7. Number of days' sales in inventory
8. Ratio of fixed assets to long-term liabilities
9. Ratio of liabilities to stockholders' equity
10. Number of times interest charges earned
11. Asset turnover
12. Rate earned on total assets
13. Rate earned on stockholders' equity
14. Earnings per share on common stock
15. Price-earnings ratio
16. Dividends per share of common stock
17. Dividend yield
18. DuPont formula
19. Leverage formula

Alternate Problem 14-5B

Profitability and leverage trend analysis

Goals **2, 3**

Crane Plastics Company has provided the following comparative information:

	2008	2007	2006	2005	2004
Net income	$ 30,000	$ 50,000	$ 100,000	$ 150,000	$ 150,000
Interest expense	102,000	95,000	85,000	80,000	75,000
Income tax expense	9,000	15,000	30,000	45,000	45,000
Total assets (ending balance)	1,600,000	1,500,000	1,350,000	1,200,000	1,000,000
Total stockholders' equity (ending balance)	580,000	550,000	500,000	400,000	250,000
Average total assets	1,550,000	1,425,000	1,275,000	1,100,000	900,000
Average stockholders' equity	565,000	525,000	450,000	325,000	225,000

You have been asked to evaluate the historical performance of the company over the last five years.

Selected industry ratios have remained relatively steady at the following levels for the last five years:

	2004–2008
Rate earned on total assets	7%
Rate earned on stockholders' equity	20%
Number of times interest charges earned	3.0
Ratio of liabilities to stockholders' equity	2.0

Instructions

1. Prepare four line graphs with the ratio on the vertical axis and the years on the horizontal axis for the following four ratios (rounded to two decimal places):
   a. Rate earned on total assets
   b. Rate earned on stockholders' equity
   c. Number of times interest charges earned
   d. Ratio of liabilities to stockholders' equity

   Display both the company ratio and the industry benchmark on each graph. That is, each graph should have two lines.
2. Prepare an analysis of the graphs in (1).

FINANCIAL ANALYSIS AND REPORTING CASES

Case 14-1

Vertical analysis

The condensed income statements through income from operations for Apple Computer Co. and Dell Inc. are reproduced below for a recent fiscal year (in millions):

	Apple Computer Co.	Dell Inc.
Sales	$8,279	$49,205
Cost of goods sold	6,020	40,190
Gross profit	$2,259	$ 9,015
Operating expenses:		
Selling, general, and administrative expenses	$1,421	$ 4,298
Research and development expense	489	463
Other expenses	23	
Total operating expenses	$1,933	$ 4,761
Income from operations	$ 326	$ 4,254

Prepare comparative common-size statements, rounding to one decimal place. Interpret the analyses.

Case 14-2

Comprehensive leverage analysis

Marriott International, Inc. and Hilton Hotels Corp. are two major owners and managers of lodging and resort properties in the United States. Abstracted income statement information for the two companies is as follows for a recent year (in millions):

	Marriott	Hilton
Net income	$596	$238
Interest expense	99	274
Income tax expense	100	127

Balance sheet information at the end of the period is as follows (in millions):

	Marriott	Hilton
Total liabilities	$4,587	$5,674
Total stockholders' equity	4,081	2,568
Total liabilities and stockholders' equity	8,668	8,242

The average liabilities, stockholders' equity, and total assets for the year were as follows (in millions):

	Marriott	Hilton
Average total liabilities	$4,462	$5,808
Average total stockholders' equity	3,960	2,404
Average total assets	8,422	8,212

1. Determine the following ratios for both companies. (Round to two decimal places.)
   a. Rate earned on total assets
   b. Rate earned on total stockholders' equity
   c. Number of times interest charges earned
   d. Ratio of liabilities to stockholders' equity
2. Determine the leverage formula for both companies.
3. Analyze and compare the two companies, using the information in (1) and (2).

Case 14-3

Profitability and stockholder ratios

Ford Motor Company is the second largest automobile and truck manufacturer in the United States. In addition to manufacturing motor vehicles, Ford also provides vehicle-related financing, insurance, and leasing services. Historically, people purchase automobiles when the economy is strong and delay automobile purchases when the economy is faltering. For this reason, Ford is considered a cyclical company. This means that when the economy does well, Ford usually prospers, and when the economy is down, Ford usually suffers.

The following information is available for three recent years (in millions except per-share amounts):

	2004	2003	2002
Net income (loss)	$3,487	$495	$(980)
Preferred dividends	$0	$0	$15
Shares outstanding for computing earnings per share	1,830	1,832	1,819
Cash dividend per share	$0.40	$0.40	$0.40
Average total assets	$308,032	$293,678	$277,037
Average stockholders' equity	$13,848	$8,532	$6,511
Average stock price per share	$14.98	$11.95	$12.56

1. Calculate the following ratios for each year, rounding to one decimal place.
   a. Rate earned on total assets
   b. Rate earned on stockholders' equity
   c. Earnings per share
   d. Dividend yield (use average stock price)
   e. Price-earnings ratio (use average stock price)
2. Calculate the leverage formula for 2004.
3. Why does Ford have so much leverage?
4. Explain the direction of the dividend yield and price-earnings ratio in light of Ford's profitability trend.

Case 14-4

Profitability and leverage analysis

Cinemark USA Inc. is one of the largest exhibitors of motion pictures in the United States. The condensed liabilities and stockholders' equity portion of Cinemark's balance sheet for the end of a recent year is as follows (in millions):

Total current liabilities	$ 128.9
Long-term debt	687.1
Other items	16.7
Total liabilities	$ 832.7
Stockholders' equity (deficit):	
Common stock	$ 49.5
Additional paid-in capital	51.1
Accumulated other comprehensive loss	(77.1)
Retained earnings	169.6
Treasury stock	(24.2)
Total stockholders' equity	$ 168.9
Total liabilities and stockholders' equity	$1,001.6

Additional information:

Total assets, beginning of year: $960.7
Total stockholders' equity, beginning of year: $76.8

Cinemark's income statement for a recent year-end was as follows:

Revenues:	
Admissions	$ 647.0
Concession	321.6
Other	55.6
Total revenues	$1,024.2
Costs and expenses:	
Cost of operations:	
Film rentals and advertising	$ 348.8
Concession supplies	53.8
Salaries and wages	103.1

Facility lease expense	$ 126.6
Utilities and other	113.0
Total cost of operations	$ 745.30
General and administrative expenses	51.5
Depreciation and amortization	67.1
Other expenses	38.5
Total costs and expenses	$ 902.4
Operating income	$ 121.8
Other income (expense)	
Interest expense	$ 42.7
Other expense	7.6
Income before income taxes	$ 71.5
Income taxes	27.0
Net income	$ 44.5

1. Determine the following:
   a. DuPont formula
   b. Leverage formula
   c. Total operating profit as a percent of sales
   d. Concession gross profit as a percent of concession sales
   e. Number of times interest charges earned
2. Evaluate Cinemark's financial performance, using the calculations in (1).

Case 14-5

Comprehensive DuPont and asset efficiency ratios

Domino's Inc. and Papa John's International Inc. are the two largest pizza delivery companies in the United States. Both companies have both company-owned and franchise store locations, featuring a delivery-oriented store design. Franchised restaurants are owned by other entities that pay fees to the franchiser based upon franchise contract provisions. The accounts receivable are associated with these fees. Comparative condensed income statements for a recent fiscal year for both companies are as follows:

Domino's Inc. and Papa John's
Comparative Income Statements
(in millions)

	Domino's	Papa John's
Revenues	$1,446.5	$942.4
Cost of goods sold	1,092.8	756.6
Gross profit	$ 353.7	$185.8
General and administrative expenses	182.3	144.0
Income from operations	$ 171.4	$ 41.8
Other income and expenses	(71.4)	(4.6)
Income before taxes	$ 100.0	$ 37.2
Income tax expense	37.8	13.9
Net income	$ 62.2	$ 23.3

Average balances from comparative balance sheets for both companies were as follows for a recent year (in millions):

	Domino's	Papa John's
Average total assets	$449.7	$360.9
Average accounts receivable	68.9	21.5
Average inventory	20.5	20.1
Average fixed assets	132.0	200.5

1. Prepare a common-size income statement for both companies. Round to one decimal place.
2. Determine the DuPont formula for each company. Round to two decimal places.
3. Calculate the accounts receivable, inventory, and fixed asset turnover for each company. Round to two decimal places.
4. Analyze and compare the two companies, based on your answers in parts (1) through (3).

Case 14-6

Comprehensive DuPont and asset efficiency ratios

SPREADSHEET

United Parcel Service, Inc., is the world's largest package delivery company. Condensed income statement information for three recent comparative years is as follows:

United Parcel Service, Inc.
Comparative Income Statements
For the Years Ended December 31, 2004, 2003, 2002
(in millions)

	2004	2003	2002
Revenues	$36,582	$33,485	$31,272
Operating expenses:			
Compensation and benefits	$20,916	$19,328	$17,940
Other	10,677	9,712	9,236
	$31,593	$29,040	$27,176
Operating profit	$ 4,989	$ 4,445	$ 4,096
Other income (expense)	(67)	(75)	913
Income before income taxes	$ 4,922	$ 4,370	$ 5,009
Income taxes	1,589	1,472	1,755
Net income	$ 3,333	$ 2,898	$ 3,254

The average total assets of United Parcel Service, Inc., for comparative years were as follows:

	2004	2003	2002
Average total assets	$62,760	$56,091	$50,993

1. Prepare comparative income statements with vertical analysis for all three years. Round to one decimal place.
2. Calculate the DuPont formula for the three comparative years. Round to one decimal place.
3. Analyze the company's performance trend for the three comparative years, using the information in parts (1) and (2).

BUSINESS ACTIVITIES AND RESPONSIBILITY ISSUES

Activity 14-1

Ethics and professional conduct in business

Lee Camden, president of Camden Equipment Co., prepared a draft of the Management Discussion and Analysis to be included with Camden Equipment Co.'s 2007 annual report. The letter mentions a 10% increase in sales and a recent expansion of plant facilities, but fails to mention the net loss of $180,000 for the year. You have been asked to review the draft for the annual report.

How would you respond to the omission of the net loss of $180,000? Specifically, is such an action ethical?

Activity 14-2

Analysis of financing corporate growth

Assume that the president of Crest Brewery made the following statement to shareholders in Crest's most recent annual report:

> "The founding family and majority shareholders of the company do not believe in using debt to finance future growth. The founding family learned from hard experience during Prohibition and the Great Depression that debt can cause loss of flexibility and eventual loss of corporate control. The company will not place itself at such risk. As such, all future growth will be financed either by stock sales to the public or by internally generated resources."

As a public shareholder of this company, how would you respond to this policy?

Activity 14-3

Receivables and inventory turnover

Micro-Tek Company completed its fiscal year on December 31, 2007. The auditor, Ashley Blake, has approached the CFO, Gwen Williams, regarding the year-end receivables and inventory levels of Micro-Tek. The following conversation takes place:

Ashley: We are beginning our audit of Micro-Tek and have prepared ratio analyses to determine if there have been significant changes in operations or financial position. This helps us guide the audit process. This analysis indicates that the inventory turnover has decreased from 15 to 8.5, while the accounts receivable turnover has decreased from 12 to 8. I was wondering if you could explain this change in operations.

Gwen: There is little need for concern. The inventory represents computers that we were unable to sell during the holiday buying season. We are confident, however, that we will be able to sell these computers as we move into the next fiscal year.

Ashley: What gives you this confidence?

Gwen: We will increase our advertising and provide some very attractive price concessions to move these machines. We have no choice. Newer technology is already out there, and we have to unload this inventory.

Ashley: . . . and the receivables?

Gwen: As you may be aware, the company is under tremendous pressure to expand sales and profits. As a result, we lowered our credit standards to our commercial customers so that we would be able to sell products to a broader customer base. As a result of this policy change, we have been able to expand sales by 35%.

Ashley: Your responses have not been reassuring to me.

Gwen: I'm a little confused. Assets are good, right? Why don't you look at our current ratio? It has improved, hasn't it? I would think that you would view that very favorably.

Why is Ashley concerned about the inventory and accounts receivable turnover ratios and Gwen's responses to them? What action may Ashley need to take? How would you respond to Gwen's last comment?

Activity 14-4

Warren Buffet on investing

Warren Buffet, one of the most successful investors in the world, made the following comment about his investment emphasis: "We simply attempt to be fearful when others are greedy and to be greedy only when others are fearful."

What does Buffet mean by this quote?

Activity 14-5

Investing strategies

Use the Internet to research the difference between the following three popular investing strategies:

1. Value investing
2. Growth investing
3. Technical investing (or analysis)

Provide a brief paragraph explaining each investment approach.

ANSWERS TO SELF-STUDY QUESTIONS

1. **A** Percentage analysis indicating the relationship of the component parts to the total in a financial statement, such as the relationship of current assets to total assets (20% to 100%) in the question, is called vertical analysis (answer A). Percentage analysis of increases and decreases in corresponding items in comparative financial statements is called horizontal analysis (answer B). An example of horizontal analysis would be the presentation of the amount of current assets in the preceding balance sheet, along with the amount of current assets at the end of the current year, with the increase or decrease in current assets between the periods expressed as a percentage. Profitability analysis (answer C) is the analysis of a firm's ability to earn income. Asset efficiency analysis (answer D) segments the asset turnover ratio into subcategories of assets.

2. **D** Current Ratio:

$$\frac{\text{Current Assets}}{\text{Current Liabilities}} =$$

$$\frac{\$275{,}000}{\$100{,}000} = 2.75$$

Quick Ratio:

$$\frac{\text{Quick Assets}}{\text{Current Liabilities}} =$$

$$\frac{\$175{,}000}{\$100{,}000} = 1.75$$

3. **D** Accounts receivable turnover:

$$\frac{\text{Sales (net)}}{\text{Average Accounts Receivable (net)}} =$$

$$\frac{\$1{,}000{,}000}{(\$200{,}000 + \$300{,}000)/2} = 4.0$$

Number of days' sales in accounts receivable:

$$\frac{\text{Accounts Receivable, Average}}{\text{Average Daily Sales}} =$$

$$\frac{(\$200{,}000 + \$300{,}000)/2}{\$1{,}000{,}000 \div 365} = 91.25$$

4. **A** The DuPont ratio segments the rate earned on total assets into the product of the profit margin and the asset turnover (answer A). The rate earned on stockholders' equity is not explained by the DuPont ratio, but is explained by leverage. (Answers B and C are true statements, but they are not the Dupont formula.) Answer D is meaningless.

5. **C** The number of days' sales in inventory (answer C), which is determined by dividing the inventories at the end of the year by the average daily cost of goods sold, expresses the relationship between the cost of goods sold and inventory. It indicates the efficiency in the management of inventory. The working capital ratio (answer A) indicates the ability of the business to meet currently maturing obligations (debt). The quick ratio (answer B) indicates the "instant" debt-paying ability of the business. The ratio of fixed assets to long-term liabilities (answer D) indicates the margin of safety for long-term creditors.

Appendix A

Appendix A: Interest Tables

Present Value of $1 at Compound Interest Due in *n* Periods

n \ *i*	5%	5.5%	6%	6.5%	7%	8%
1	0.95238	0.94787	0.94334	0.93897	0.93458	0.92593
2	0.90703	0.89845	0.89000	0.88166	0.87344	0.85734
3	0.86384	0.85161	0.83962	0.82785	0.81630	0.79383
4	0.82270	0.80722	0.79209	0.77732	0.76290	0.73503
5	0.78353	0.76513	0.74726	0.72988	0.71290	0.68058
6	0.74622	0.72525	0.70496	0.68533	0.66634	0.63017
7	0.71068	0.68744	0.66506	0.64351	0.62275	0.58349
8	0.67684	0.65160	0.62741	0.60423	0.58201	0.54027
9	0.64461	0.61763	0.59190	0.56735	0.54393	0.50025
10	0.61391	0.58543	0.55840	0.53273	0.50835	0.46319
11	0.58468	0.55491	0.52679	0.50021	0.47509	0.42888
12	0.55684	0.52598	0.49697	0.46968	0.44401	0.39711
13	0.53032	0.49856	0.46884	0.44102	0.41496	0.36770
14	0.50507	0.47257	0.44230	0.41410	0.38782	0.34046
15	0.48102	0.44793	0.41726	0.38883	0.36245	0.31524
16	0.45811	0.42458	0.39365	0.36510	0.33874	0.29189
17	0.43630	0.40245	0.37136	0.34281	0.31657	0.27027
18	0.41552	0.38147	0.35034	0.32189	0.29586	0.25025
19	0.39573	0.36158	0.33051	0.30224	0.27651	0.23171
20	0.37689	0.34273	0.31180	0.28380	0.25842	0.21455
21	0.35894	0.32486	0.29416	0.26648	0.24151	0.19866
22	0.34185	0.30793	0.27750	0.25021	0.22571	0.18394
23	0.32557	0.29187	0.26180	0.23494	0.21095	0.17032
24	0.31007	0.27666	0.24698	0.22060	0.19715	0.15770
25	0.29530	0.26223	0.23300	0.20714	0.18425	0.14602
26	0.28124	0.24856	0.21981	0.19450	0.17211	0.13520
27	0.26785	0.23560	0.20737	0.18263	0.16093	0.12519
28	0.25509	0.22332	0.19563	0.17148	0.15040	0.11591
29	0.24295	0.21168	0.18456	0.16101	0.14056	0.10733
30	0.23138	0.20064	0.17411	0.15119	0.13137	0.09938
31	0.22036	0.19018	0.16426	0.14196	0.12277	0.09202
32	0.20987	0.18027	0.15496	0.13329	0.11474	0.08520
33	0.19987	0.17087	0.14619	0.12516	0.10724	0.07889
34	0.19036	0.16196	0.13791	0.11752	0.10022	0.07304
35	0.18129	0.15352	0.13010	0.11035	0.09366	0.06764
40	0.14205	0.11746	0.09722	0.08054	0.06678	0.04603
45	0.11130	0.08988	0.07265	0.05879	0.04761	0.03133
50	0.08720	0.06877	0.05429	0.04291	0.03395	0.02132

Present Value of $1 at Compound Interest Due in *n* Periods

n \ *i*	9%	10%	11%	12%	13%	14%
1	0.91743	0.90909	0.90090	0.89286	0.88496	0.87719
2	0.84168	0.82645	0.81162	0.79719	0.78315	0.76947
3	0.77218	0.75132	0.73119	0.71178	0.69305	0.67497
4	0.70842	0.68301	0.65873	0.63552	0.61332	0.59208
5	0.64993	0.62092	0.59345	0.56743	0.54276	0.51937
6	0.59627	0.56447	0.53464	0.50663	0.48032	0.45559
7	0.54703	0.51316	0.48166	0.45235	0.42506	0.39964
8	0.50187	0.46651	0.43393	0.40388	0.37616	0.35056
9	0.46043	0.42410	0.39092	0.36061	0.33288	0.30751
10	0.42241	0.38554	0.35218	0.32197	0.29459	0.26974
11	0.38753	0.35049	0.31728	0.28748	0.26070	0.23662
12	0.35554	0.31863	0.28584	0.25668	0.23071	0.20756
13	0.32618	0.28966	0.25751	0.22917	0.20416	0.18207
14	0.29925	0.26333	0.23199	0.20462	0.18068	0.15971
15	0.27454	0.23939	0.20900	0.18270	0.15989	0.14010
16	0.25187	0.21763	0.18829	0.16312	0.14150	0.12289
17	0.23107	0.19784	0.16963	0.14564	0.12522	0.10780
18	0.21199	0.17986	0.15282	0.13004	0.11081	0.09456
19	0.19449	0.16351	0.13768	0.11611	0.09806	0.08295
20	0.17843	0.14864	0.12403	0.10367	0.08678	0.07276
21	0.16370	0.13513	0.11174	0.09256	0.07680	0.06383
22	0.15018	0.12285	0.10067	0.08264	0.06796	0.05599
23	0.13778	0.11168	0.09069	0.07379	0.06014	0.04911
24	0.12640	0.10153	0.08170	0.06588	0.05323	0.04308
25	0.11597	0.09230	0.07361	0.05882	0.04710	0.03779
26	0.10639	0.08390	0.06631	0.05252	0.04168	0.03315
27	0.09761	0.07628	0.05974	0.04689	0.03689	0.02908
28	0.08955	0.06934	0.05382	0.04187	0.03264	0.02551
29	0.08216	0.06304	0.04849	0.03738	0.02889	0.02237
30	0.07537	0.05731	0.04368	0.03338	0.02557	0.01963
31	0.06915	0.05210	0.03935	0.02980	0.02262	0.01722
32	0.06344	0.04736	0.03545	0.02661	0.02002	0.01510
33	0.05820	0.04306	0.03194	0.02376	0.01772	0.01325
34	0.05331	0.03914	0.02878	0.02121	0.01568	0.01162
35	0.04899	0.03558	0.02592	0.01894	0.01388	0.01019
40	0.03184	0.02210	0.01538	0.01075	0.00753	0.00529
45	0.02069	0.01372	0.00913	0.00610	0.00409	0.00275
50	0.01345	0.00852	0.00542	0.00346	0.00222	0.00143

Present Value of Ordinary Annuity of $1 per Period

n \ i	5%	5.5%	6%	6.5%	7%	8%
1	0.95238	0.94787	0.94340	0.93897	0.93458	0.92593
2	1.85941	1.84632	1.83339	1.82063	1.80802	1.78326
3	2.72325	2.69793	2.67301	2.64848	2.62432	2.57710
4	3.54595	3.50515	3.46511	3.42580	3.38721	3.31213
5	4.32948	4.27028	4.21236	4.15568	4.10020	3.99271
6	5.07569	4.99553	4.91732	4.84101	4.76654	4.62288
7	5.78637	5.68297	5.58238	5.48452	5.38923	5.20637
8	6.46321	6.33457	6.20979	6.08875	5.97130	5.74664
9	7.10782	6.95220	6.80169	6.65610	6.51523	6.24689
10	7.72174	7.53763	7.36009	7.18883	7.02358	6.71008
11	8.30641	8.09254	7.88688	7.68904	7.49867	7.13896
12	8.86325	8.61852	8.38384	8.15873	7.94269	7.53608
13	9.39357	9.11708	8.85268	8.59974	8.35765	7.90378
14	9.89864	9.58965	9.29498	9.01384	8.74547	8.22424
15	10.37966	10.03758	9.71225	9.40267	9.10791	8.55948
16	10.83777	10.46216	10.10590	9.76776	9.44665	8.85137
17	11.27407	10.86461	10.47726	10.11058	9.76322	9.12164
18	11.68959	11.24607	10.82760	10.43247	10.05909	9.37189
19	12.08532	11.60765	11.15812	10.73471	10.33560	9.60360
20	12.46221	11.95038	11.46992	11.01851	10.59401	9.81815
21	12.82115	12.27524	11.76408	11.28498	10.83553	10.01680
22	13.16300	12.58317	12.04158	11.53520	11.06124	10.20074
23	13.48857	12.87504	12.30338	11.77014	11.27219	10.37106
24	13.79864	13.15170	12.55036	11.99074	11.46933	10.52876
25	14.09394	13.41393	12.78336	12.19788	11.65358	10.67478
26	14.37518	13.66250	13.00317	12.39237	11.82578	10.80998
27	14.64303	13.89810	13.21053	12.57500	11.98671	10.93516
28	14.89813	14.12142	13.40616	12.74648	12.13711	11.05108
29	15.14107	14.33310	13.59072	12.90749	12.27767	11.15841
30	15.37245	14.53375	13.76483	13.05868	12.40904	11.25778
31	15.59281	14.72393	13.92909	13.20063	12.53181	11.34980
32	15.80268	14.90420	14.08404	13.33393	12.64656	11.43500
33	16.00255	15.07507	14.23023	13.45909	12.75379	11.51389
34	16.19290	15.23703	14.36814	13.57661	12.85401	11.58693
35	16.37420	15.39055	14.49825	13.68696	12.94767	11.65457
40	17.15909	16.04612	15.04630	14.14553	13.33171	11.92461
45	17.77407	16.54773	15.45583	14.48023	13.60552	12.10840
50	18.25592	16.93152	15.76186	14.72452	13.80075	12.23348

Present Value of Ordinary Annuity of $1 per Period

n \ i	9%	10%	11%	12%	13%	14%
1	0.91743	0.90909	0.90090	0.89286	0.88496	0.87719
2	1.75911	1.73554	1.71252	1.69005	1.66810	1.64666
3	2.53130	2.48685	2.44371	2.40183	2.36115	2.32163
4	3.23972	3.16986	3.10245	3.03735	2.97447	2.91371
5	3.88965	3.79079	3.69590	3.60478	3.51723	3.43308
6	4.48592	4.35526	4.23054	4.11141	3.99755	3.88867
7	5.03295	4.86842	4.71220	4.56376	4.42261	4.28830
8	5.53482	5.33493	5.14612	4.96764	4.79677	4.63886
9	5.99525	5.75902	5.53705	5.32825	5.13166	4.94637
10	6.41766	6.14457	5.88923	5.65022	5.42624	5.21612
11	6.80519	6.49506	6.20652	5.93770	5.68694	5.45273
12	7.16072	6.81369	6.49236	6.19437	5.91765	5.66029
13	7.48690	7.10336	6.74987	6.42355	6.12181	5.84236
14	7.78615	7.36669	6.96187	6.62817	6.30249	6.00207
15	8.06069	7.60608	7.19087	6.81086	6.46238	6.14217
16	8.31256	7.82371	7.37916	6.97399	6.60388	6.26506
17	8.54363	8.02155	7.54879	7.11963	6.72909	6.37286
18	8.75562	8.20141	7.70162	7.24967	6.83991	6.46742
19	8.95012	8.36492	7.83929	7.36578	6.93797	6.55037
20	9.12855	8.51356	7.96333	7.46944	7.02475	6.62313
21	9.29224	8.64869	8.07507	7.56200	7.10155	6.68696
22	9.44242	8.77154	8.17574	7.64465	7.16951	6.74294
23	9.58021	8.88322	8.26643	7.71843	7.22966	6.79206
24	9.70661	8.98474	8.34814	7.78432	7.28288	6.83514
25	9.82258	9.07704	8.42174	7.84314	7.32998	6.87293
26	9.92897	9.16094	8.48806	7.89566	7.37167	6.90608
27	10.02658	9.23722	8.54780	7.94255	7.40856	6.93515
28	10.11613	9.30657	8.60162	7.98442	7.44120	6.96066
29	10.19828	9.36961	8.65011	8.02181	7.47009	6.98304
30	10.27365	9.42691	8.69379	8.05518	7.49565	7.00266
31	10.34280	9.47901	8.73315	8.08499	7.51828	7.01988
32	10.40624	9.52638	8.76860	8.11159	7.53830	7.03498
33	10.46444	9.56943	8.80054	8.13535	7.55602	7.04823
34	10.51784	9.60858	8.82932	8.15656	7.57170	7.05985
35	10.56682	9.64416	8.85524	8.17550	7.58557	7.07005
40	10.75736	9.77905	8.95105	8.24378	7.63438	7.10504
45	10.88118	9.86281	9.00791	8.28252	7.66086	7.12322
50	10.96168	9.91481	9.04165	8.30450	7.67524	7.13266

Glossary

Accelerated depreciation method A depreciation method that provides for a higher depreciation amount in the first year of the asset's use, followed by a gradual declining amount of depreciation. (p. 409)

Account The element of an accounting system that summarizes the increases and decreases in each financial statement item. (pp. 100, 155)

Accounting An information system that provides reports to stakeholders about the economic activities and condition of a business. (p. 13)

Accounting cycle The process that begins with the analysis of transactions and ends with preparing the accounting records for the next accounting period. (p. 119)

Accounting equation Assets = Liabilities + Stockholders' Equity. (p. 17)

Accounting information system An information system that consists of management reporting, transaction processing, and financial reporting subsystems that processes financial and operational data into reports useful to internal and external stakeholders. (p. 153)

Accounting period concept A concept of accounting in which accounting data are recorded and summarized in a periodic process. (p. 23)

Accounts payable A liability for an amount incurred from purchases of products or services in the normal operations of a business. (pp. 11, 102)

Accounts receivable A receivable created by selling merchandise or services on credit. (pp. 12, 103, 356)

Accounts receivable turnover The relationship between net sales and accounts receivable, computed by dividing net sales by the average net accounts receivable. (pp. 370, 642)

Accrual basis of accounting A system of accounting in which revenue is recorded as it is earned and expenses are recorded when they generate revenue. (p. 117)

Accruals A revenue or expense that has not been recorded. (p. 106)

Accrued expense An expense that has been incurred at the end of an accounting period but has not been recorded in the accounts; sometimes called an accrued liability. (p. 106)

Accrued revenue A revenue that has been earned at the end of an accounting period but has not been recorded in the accounts; sometimes called an accrued asset. (p. 106)

Accumulated depreciation An offsetting or contra asset account used to record depreciation on a fixed asset. (p. 108)

Accumulated other comprehensive income The cumulative effect of other comprehensive income items disclosed in the Stockholders' Equity section of the balance sheet. (p. 508)

Adequate disclosure concept A concept of accounting that requires that the financial statements include all relevant data a reader needs to understand the financial condition and performance of a business. (p. 23)

Adjusted trial balance The trial balance prepared after the adjusting entries have been posted to the ledger. (p. 164)

Adjusting entries The entries necessary to bring the accounts up to date before preparing financial statements. (p. 164)

Adjustment process A process required by the accrual basis of accounting in which the accounts are updated prior to preparing financial statements. (p. 105)

Administrative expenses Expenses incurred in the administration or general operations of the business. (p. 217)

Aging the receivables The process of analyzing the accounts receivable and classifying them according to various age groupings, with the due date being the base point for determining age. (p. 361)

Allowance for Doubtful Accounts The contra asset account for accounts receivable. (p. 359)

Allowance method The method of accounting for uncollectible accounts that provides an expense for uncollectible receivables in advance of their write-off. (p. 357)

Amortization The periodic transfer of the cost of an intangible asset to expense. (p. 412)

Annuity A series of cash flows that are (1) equal in amount and (2) spaced equally in time. (p. 450)

Annuity payments The dollar amount of the equal periodic payment in an annuity. (p. 450)

Asset turnover The number of sales dollars earned for each dollar of total assets, calculated as the ratio of net sales to total assets. (p. 640)

Assets The resources owned by a business. (p. 12)

Available-for-sale securities Securities that management expects to sell in the future but which are not actively traded for profit. (p. 544)

Average cost method The method of inventory costing that is based upon the assumption that costs should be charged against revenue by using the weighted average unit cost of the items sold. (p. 269)

Bad debt expense The operating expense incurred because of the failure to collect receivables. (p. 357)

Balance of an account The amount of the difference between the debits and the credits that have been entered into an account. (p. 155)

Balance sheet A list of the assets, liabilities, and stockholders' equity *as of a specific date*, usually at the close of the last day of a month or a year. (p. 15)

Bank reconciliation The analysis that details the items responsible for the difference between the cash balance reported in the bank statement and the balance of the cash account in the ledger. (p. 322)

Bank statement A summary of all transactions is mailed to the depositor by the bank each month. (p. 319)

Bond A form of interest-bearing note used by corporations to borrow on a long-term basis. (p. 447)

Bond indenture The contract between a corporation issuing bonds and the bondholders. (p. 447)

Bonds payable A type of long-term debt financing with a face amount that is due in the future with interest that is normally paid semiannually. (p. 11)

Book inventory The amount of inventory recorded in the accounting records. (p. 230)

Book value The cost of a fixed asset minus accumulated depreciation on the asset. (p. 407)

Business An organization in which basic resources (inputs), such as materials and labor, are assembled and processed to provide goods or services (outputs) to customers. (p. 4)

Business entity concept A concept of accounting that limits the economic data in the accounting system to data related directly to the activities of a specific business or entity. (p. 21)

Business information system A system that collects and processes company data into information that is distributed to users. (p. 152)

Business stakeholder A person or entity who has an interest in the economic performance of a business. (p. 8)

Callable bonds Bonds that a corporation reserves the right to redeem before their maturity. (p. 448)

Capital expenditures The cost of acquiring fixed assets, adding a component, or replacing a component of fixed assets. (p. 403)

Capital stock Types of stock a corporation may issue. (p. 11)

Cash Coins, currency (paper money), checks, money orders, and money on deposit that is available for unrestricted withdrawal from banks and other financial institutions. (p. 315)

Cash basis of accounting A system of accounting in which only transactions involving increases or decreases of the entity's cash are recorded. (p. 117)

Cash conversion cycle The number of days' sales in accounts receivable, plus the number of days' sales in inventory, less the number of days' sales in accounts payable. (p. 597)

Cash dividend A cash distribution of earnings by a corporation to its shareholders. (p. 505)

Cash equivalents Highly liquid investments that are usually reported with cash on the balance sheet. (p. 326)

Cash flows from financing activities The section of the statement of cash flows that reports cash flows from transactions affecting the equity and debt of the business. (p. 580)

Cash flows from investing activities The section of the statement of cash flows that reports cash flows from transactions affecting investments in noncurrent assets. (p. 580)

Cash flows from operating activities The section of the statement of cash flows that reports the cash transactions affecting the determination of net income. (p. 580)

Cash short and over account An account used to record the difference between the amount of cash in a cash register and the amount of cash that should be on hand according to the records. (p. 315)

Chart of accounts The list of accounts in the general ledger. (p. 160)

Classified balance sheet A balance sheet prepared with various sections, subsections, and captions that aid in its interpretation and analysis. (p. 113)

Closing entries The entries necessary at the end of an accounting period to transfer the balances of revenue, expense, and dividend accounts to retained earnings. (p. 169)

Closing process The process of transferring the balances of the revenue, expense, and dividends accounts to retained earnings in preparation for the next accounting period. (p. 169)

Common stock The stock outstanding when a corporation has issued only one class of stock. (pp. 11, 496)

Common-sized financial statement A financial statement in which all items are expressed only in percentages. (pp. 120, 635)

Comprehensive income All changes in stockholders' equity during a period except those resulting from dividends and stockholders' investments. (p. 508)

Consignee The retailer carrying an item for sale (consignment) that is owned by another retailer (consignor). (p. 233)

Consignment Merchandise that is owned by a retailer (consignor) that is being carried for sale by another retailer (consignee). (p. 233)

Consignor A retailer who allows another retailer (consignee) to carry and sale its merchandise (consignment). (p. 233)

Consolidated financial statements Financial statements resulting from combining parent and subsidiary statements. (p. 549)

Contingent liability An obligation from a past transaction that is contingent upon a future event. An example would be product warranty payable. (p. 461)

Contract rate The periodic interest to be paid on the bonds that is identified in the bond indenture; expressed as a percentage of the face amount of the bond. (p. 451)

Controlling account The account in the general ledger that summarizes the balances of the accounts in a subsidiary ledger. (p. 221)

Convertible bonds Bonds that may be exchanged for other securities. (p. 447)

Copyright An exclusive right to publish and sell a literary, artistic, or musical composition. (p. 413)

Corporation A business organized under state or federal statutes as a separate legal entity. (p. 5)

Cost concept A concept of accounting that determines the amount initially entered into the accounting records for purchases. (p. 22)

Cost of capital The cost of financing operations from both debt and common stock, expressed as a percentage rate. (p. 637)

Cost of goods sold The cost of product sold. (p. 266)

Cost of merchandise sold The cost that is reported as an expense when merchandise is sold. (p. 212)

Credit memorandum A form used by a seller to inform the buyer of the amount the seller proposes to credit to the account receivable due from the buyer. (p. 224)

Credit period The amount of time the buyer is allowed in which to pay the seller. (p. 223)

Credit terms Terms for payment on account by the buyer to the seller. (p. 223)

Creditor A lender of money, such as a bank or bondholder. (p. 442)

Credits Amounts entered on the right side of an account. (p. 155)

Cumulative preferred stock A class of preferred stock that has a right to receive regular dividends that have been passed (not declared) before any common stock dividends are paid. (p. 498)

Current assets Cash and other assets that are expected to be converted to cash or sold or used up within one year or less, through the normal operations of the business. (p. 114)

Current liabilities Liabilities that will be due within a short time (usually one year or less) and that are to be paid out of current assets. (p. 114)

Current ratio A financial ratio that is computed by dividing current assets by current liabilities. (pp. 464, 647)

Debenture bonds Bonds issued on the basis of the general credit of the corporation. (p. 448)

Debit memorandum A form used by a buyer to inform the seller of the amount the buyer proposes to debit to the account payable due the seller. (p. 225)

Debits Amounts entered on the left side of an account. (p. 155)

Debtor A borrower of money. (p. 442)

Declining-balance method A method of depreciation that provides periodic depreciation expense based on the declining book value of a fixed asset over its estimated life. (p. 407)

Deferrals The delayed recording of an expense or revenue. (p. 105)

Deferred expense Items that are initially recorded as assets but are expected to become expenses over time or through the normal operations of the business; sometimes called prepaid expenses. (p. 101, 459)

Deferred revenues Items that are initially recorded as liabilities but are expected to become revenues over time or through the normal operations of the business; sometimes called unearned revenues. (pp. 106, 459)

Depreciation The systematic periodic transfer of the cost of a fixed asset to an expense account during its expected useful life. (pp. 108, 404)

Direct method A method of reporting the cash flows from operating activities as the difference between the operating cash receipts and the operating cash payments. (pp. 234, 580)

Direct write-off method The method of accounting for uncollectible accounts that recognizes the expense only when accounts are judged to be worthless. (p. 357)

Discontinued operations Operations of a major line of business or component for a company, such as a division, a department, or a certain class of customer, that have been disposed of. (p. 541)

Discount The interest deducted from the maturity value of a note or the excess of the face amount of bonds over their issue price. (p. 443)

Discount rate The rate used in computing the interest to be deducted from the maturity value of a note. (p. 443)

Discounting The process of converting a future amount into a present value. (p. 449)

Dishonored note receivable A note that the maker fails to pay on the due date. (p. 367)

Dividend payout ratio A ratio computed by dividing the annual cash dividends (per share) by the annual net income (per share); indicates dividend safety. (p. 511)

Dividend yield A ratio computed by dividing the annual dividends paid per share of common stock by the market price per share at a specific date; indicates the rate of return to stockholders in terms of cash dividend distributions. (pp. 510, 651)

Dividends Distributions of earnings of a corporation to stockholders. (p. 12)

Double-entry accounting system A system of accounting for recording transactions, based on recording increases and decreases in accounts so that debits equal credits and Assets = Liabilities + Stockholders' Equity. (p. 157)

DuPont formula A formula that states that the rate earned on total assets is the product of two factors, the profit margin and the total asset turnover. (p. 640)

Earnings before interest, taxes, depreciation, and amortization (EBITDA) A type of pro forma computation used by financial analysts as a rough estimate of operating cash flows that are available to pay interest and other fixed charges. (p. 173)

Earnings per common share (EPS) The profitability ratio of net income available to common shareholders to the number of common shares outstanding. (pp. 542, 650)

Effective interest rate method A method of amortizing a bond discount or premium using present value techniques. (p. 455)

Electronic funds transfer (EFT) A system in which computers rather than paper (money, checks, etc.) are used to effect cash transactions. (p. 317)

Elements of internal control The control environment, risk assessment, control activities, information and communication, and monitoring. (p. 309)

Employee fraud The intentional act of deceiving an employer for personal gain. (p. 309)

Equity method A method of accounting for an investment in common stock by which the investment account is adjusted for the investor's share of periodic net income and cash dividends of the investee. (p. 546)

Equity securities The common and preferred stock of a firm. (p. 544)

Expenses Costs used to earn revenues. (p. 12)

Extraordinary items Events and transactions that (1) are significantly different (unusual) from the typical or the normal operating activities of a business and (2) occur infrequently. (p. 541)

FICA tax Federal Insurance Contributions Act tax used to finance federal programs for old-age and disability benefits (social security) and health insurance for the aged (Medicare). (p. 444)

Financial Accounting Standards Board (FASB) The authoritative body that has the primary responsibility for developing accounting principles. (p. 21)

Financial accounting system A system that includes (1) a set of rules for determining what, when, and the amount that should be recorded for economic events, (2) a framework for facilitating preparation of financial statements, and (3) one or more controls to determine whether errors may have arisen in the recording process. (p. 54)

Financial reporting system A subsystem of accounting that produces financial statements and other reports for external stakeholders. (p. 154)

Financial statements Financial reports that summarize the effects of events on a business. (p. 14)

Financing activities Business activities that involve obtaining funds to begin and operate a business. (p. 10)

Finished goods inventory The cost of finished products on hand that have not been sold. (p. 266)

First-in, first-out (fifo) method A method of inventory costing based on the assumption that the costs of merchandise sold should be charged against revenue in the order in which the costs were incurred. (p. 269)

Fiscal year The annual accounting period adopted by a business. (p. 168)

Fixed asset impairments A condition when the fair value of a fixed asset falls below its book value and is not expected to recover. (p. 538)

Fixed asset turnover ratio The number of dollars of sales that are generated from each dollar of average fixed assets during the year, computed by dividing the net sales by the average net fixed assets. (pp. 418, 645)

Fixed assets Long-lived or relatively permanent tangible assets that are used in the normal business operations; sometimes called plant assets. (pp. 114, 400)

FOB (free on board) destination Freight terms in which the seller pays the transportation costs from the shipping point to the final destination. (p. 226)

FOB (free on board) shipping point Freight terms in which the buyer pays the transportation costs from the shipping point to the final destination. (p. 226)

Free cash flow The amount of operating cash flow remaining after replacing current productive capacity and maintaining current dividends. (p. 597)

Fringe benefits Benefits provided to employees in addition to wages and salaries. (p. 446)

General ledger The group of accounts of a business. (p. 160)

Generally accepted accounting principles (GAAP) Rules for how financial statements should be prepared. (p. 20)

Going concern concept A concept of accounting that assumes a business will continue operating for an indefinite period of time. (p. 22)

Goodwill An intangible asset of a business that is created from such favorable factors as location, product quality, reputation, and managerial skill, as verified from a merger transaction. (p. 414)

Gross pay The total earnings of an employee for a payroll period. (p. 444)

Gross profit Sales minus the cost of merchandise sold. (pp. 26, 212)

Held-to-maturity securities Investments in bonds or other debt securities that management intends to hold to their maturity. (p. 549)

Horizontal analysis A method of analyzing financial performance that computes percentage increases and decreases in related items in comparative financial statements. (pp. 26, 632)

Income from operations (operating income) The excess of gross profit over total operating expenses. (p. 217)

Income statement A summary of the revenue and expenses *for a specific period of time*, such as a month or a year. (p. 14)

Indirect method A method of reporting the cash flows from operating activities as the net income from operations adjusted for all deferrals of past cash receipts and payments and all accruals of expected future cash receipts and payments. (pp. 234, 581)

Intangible assets Long-lived assets that are useful in the operations of a business, are not held for sale, and are without physical qualities; examples are patent or copyright rights. (pp. 12, 114, 412)

Interest The cost of borrowing or lending money. (p. 447)

Interest payable A liability to pay interest on a due date. (p. 11)

Internal controls The policies and procedures used to safeguard assets, ensure accurate business information, and ensure compliance with laws and regulations. (p. 306)

Inventory ledger The subsidiary ledger that shows the amount of each type of inventory. (p. 268)

Inventory shrinkage The amount by which the merchandise for sale, as indicated by the balance of the merchandise inventory account, is larger than the total amount of merchandise counted during the physical inventory. (p. 230)

Inventory turnover The relationship between the volume of goods sold and inventory, computed by dividing the cost of goods sold by the average inventory. (pp. 282, 643)

Investing activities Business activities that involve obtaining the necessary resources to start and operate the business. (p. 12)

Investments The balance sheet caption used to report long-term investments in stocks not intended as a source of cash in the normal operations of the business. (p. 546)

Invoice The bill that the seller sends to the buyer. (p. 223)

Journal The record in which the effects of transactions are recorded in chronological order. (p. 157)

Journal entry The transaction record entered in the journal. (p. 157)

Journalizing The process of recording transactions in the journal. (p. 157)

Last-in, first-out (lifo) method A method of inventory costing based on the assumption that the most recent merchandise inventory costs should be charged against revenue. (p. 269)

Leverage The amount of debt used by the firm to finance its assets; causes the rate earned on stockholders' equity to vary from the rate earned on total assets because the amount earned on assets acquired through the use of funds provided by creditors varies from the interest paid to these creditors. (pp. 465, 638)

Leverage formula A formula that states the rate earned on stockholders' equity as the product of the rate earned on total assets and the ratio of the average total assets divided by average stockholders' equity, or leverage. (p. 638)

Liabilities The rights of creditors that represent a legal obligation to repay an amount borrowed according to terms of the borrowing agreement. (pp. 11, 114)

Lifo conformity rule A financial reporting rule requiring a firm that elects to use lifo inventory valuation for tax purposes to also use lifo for external financial reporting. (p. 278)

Lifo reserve A required disclosure for lifo firms, showing the difference between inventory valued under fifo and inventory valued under lifo. (p. 278)

Limited liability company (LLC) A business form consisting of one or more persons or entities filing an operating agreement with a state to conduct business with limited liability to the owners, yet treated as a partnership for tax purposes. (p. 5)

Liquidity Measures the ability of a business to pay or otherwise satisfy its current liabilities. (p. 464)

Long-term liabilities Liabilities that will not be due for a long time (usually more than one year). (p. 114)

Lower-of-cost-or-market (LCM) method A method of valuing inventory that reports the inventory at the lower of its cost or current market value (replacement cost). (p. 280)

Management Discussion and Analysis (MDA) An annual report disclosure that provides an analysis of the results of operations and financial condition. (p. 653)

Management reporting system A subsystem of accounting that provides internal information to assist managers in making decisions. (p. 153)

Manufacturing A type of business that changes basic inputs into products that are sold to individual customers. (p. 4)

Market rate The rate of return that investors demand for bonds of a specific quality and duration. (p. 451)

Matching concept A concept of accounting in which expenses are matched with the revenue generated during a period by those expenses. (p. 22)

Materials inventory The cost of materials that have not yet entered into the manufacturing process. (p. 266)

Maturity value The amount that is due at the maturity or due date of a note. (p. 366)

Merchandise available for sale The cost of merchandise available for sale to customers. (p. 216)

Merchandise inventory Merchandise on hand and available for sale to customers. (pp. 213, 266)

Merchandising A type of business that purchases products from other businesses and sells them to customers. (p. 4)

Multiple-step income statement A form of income statement that contains several sections, subsections, and subtotals. (p. 214)

Natural business year The fiscal year that ends when a business's activities reach their lowest point in the operating cycle. (p. 169)

Net income The excess of revenues over expenses. (p. 13)

Net loss The excess of expenses over revenues. (p. 13)

Net pay Gross pay less payroll deductions; the amount the employer is obligated to pay the employee. (p. 444)

Net realizable value The amount of cash expected to be realized in the future from a receivable; the estimated selling price of an item of inventory less any direct costs of disposal, such as sales commissions. (pp. 280, 359)

Net sales Revenue received for merchandise sold to customers less any sales returns and allowances and sales discounts. (p. 212)

Normal balance of an account The debit or credit side of an account used to record increases. (p. 156)

Note payable A type of short or long-term financing that requires payment of the amount borrowed plus interest. (p. 11)

Notes receivable Written claims against debtors who promise to pay the amount of the note plus interest at an agreed-upon rate. (pp. 114, 356)

Number of days' sales in inventory The relationship between the volume of sales and inventory, computed by dividing the inventory at the end of the year by the average daily cost of goods sold. (pp. 282, 644)

Number of days' sales in receivables The relationship between sales and accounts receivable, computed by dividing the net accounts receivable at the end of the year by the average daily sales. (pp. 371, 642)

Number of times interest charges are earned A ratio that measures creditor margin of safety for interest payments, calculated as income before interest and taxes divided by interest expense. (pp. 465, 649)

Objectivity concept A concept of accounting that requires accounting records and the data reported in financial statements be based on objective evidence. (p. 22)

Operating activities Business activities that involve using the business's resources to implement its business strategy. (p. 12)

Other comprehensive income Required disclosures that change the stockholders' equity, but are not disclosed as net income or retained earnings. These items include foreign currency items, pension liability adjustments, and unrealized gains and losses on investments. (p. 508)

Other expense Expenses that cannot be traced directly to operations. (p. 217)

Other income Revenue from sources other than the primary operating activity of a business. (p. 217)

Outstanding stock The stock in the hands of stockholders. (p. 496)

Owners' equity The rights of the owners of a company. (p. 17)

Par The monetary amount printed on a stock certificate. (p. 497)

Parent company The corporation owning all or a majority of the voting stock of the other corporation. (p. 549)

Partnership A business owned by two or more individuals. (p. 5)

Patents Exclusive rights to produce and sell goods with one or more unique features. (p. 413)

Payroll The total amount paid to employees for a certain period. (p. 444)

Periodic inventory method The inventory method in which the inventory records do not show the amount available for sale or sold during the period. (p. 216)

Permanent accounts Accounts that are reported on the balance sheet and whose balances carry forward from period to period. (p. 169)

Perpetual inventory method The inventory method in which each purchase and sale of merchandise is recorded in an inventory account. (p. 216)

Petty cash fund A special-purpose cash fund to pay relatively small amounts. (p. 325)

Physical inventory The detailed listing of merchandise on hand. (pp. 230, 268)

Post-closing trial balance The trial balance prepared after the closing entries have been posted to the ledger. (p. 171)

Posting The process of transferring the debits and credits from the journal entries to the accounts in the ledger. (p. 160)

Preferred stock A class of stock with preferential rights over common stock. (p. 498)

Premium The excess of the issue price of a stock over its par value. (pp. 457, 499)

Prepaid expenses Items that are initially recorded as assets but are expected to become expenses over time or through the normal operations of the business; often called deferred expenses. (pp. 12, 101)

Present value The current value of dollars received in the future, after considering the effects of compound interest. (p. 448)

Present value of $1 The present value interest factor for a single sum. This amount is used to convert a single lump sum of money at some point in the future to its value in today's dollars. (p. 448)

Present value of an annuity of $1 The present value interest factor for an annuity. This amount is used to convert an annuity to its value in terms of a single sum in today's dollars. (p. 451)

Price-book ratio The ratio of the market value of a share of common stock to the book value of a share of common stock. (p. 554)

Price-earnings (P/E) ratio The ratio computed by dividing a corporation's stock market price per share at a specific date by the company's annual earnings per share. (pp. 552, 651)

Proceeds The net amount available from discounting a note payable. (p. 443)

Profit margin A measure of the amount earned on each dollar of sales, calculated as the ratio of net income to net sales. (p. 640)

Proprietorship A business owned by one individual. (p. 5)

Purchase return or allowance From the buyer's perspective, returned merchandise or an adjustment for defective merchandise. (p. 215)

Purchases discounts Discounts taken by the buyer for early payment of an invoice. (p. 215)

Quick assets Cash and other current assets that can be quickly converted to cash, such as cash, marketable securities, and receivables. (pp. 464, 648)

Quick ratio A financial ratio that measures the ability to pay current liabilities with quick assets (cash, marketable securities, accounts receivable). (pp. 464, 648)

Quick response A method for optimizing inventory levels in the value chain by electronically sharing common forecast, inventory, sales, and payment information between manufacturers and merchandisers, using the Internet or other electronic means. (p. 281)

Rate earned on stockholders' equity A measure of profitability computed by dividing net income by total stockholders' equity. (p. 636)

Rate earned on total assets A measure of the profitability of assets, without regard to the equity of creditors and stockholders in the assets, calculated as the net income divided by average total assets. (p. 636)

Ratio of fixed assets to long-term liabilities A leverage ratio that measures the margin of safety of long-term creditors, calculated as the net fixed assets divided by the long-term liabilities. (p. 648)

Ratio of liabilities to stockholders' equity A comprehensive leverage ratio that measures the relationship of the claims of creditors to that of owners, calculated as total liabilities divided by total stockholders' equity. (p. 649)

Ratio of total liabilities to total assets The percent of total assets that are funded by total liabilities; a measure of solvency. (p. 466)

Receivables All money claims against other entities, including people, business firms, and other organizations. (p. 356)

Report form The form of balance sheet in which assets, liabilities, and stockholders' equity are reported in a downward sequence. (p. 218)

Residual value The estimated value of a fixed asset at the end of its useful life. (p. 405)

Restructuring charge The cost of accrued employee termination benefits associated with a management-approved employee termination plan. (p. 539)

Retained earnings Net income retained in a corporation. (p. 16)

Retained earnings statement A summary of the changes in the retained earnings in a corporation for *a specific period of time,* such as a month or a year. (p. 15)

Revenue The increase in assets from selling products or services to customers. (p. 12)

Revenue expenditures Costs that benefit only the current period or costs incurred for normal maintenance and repairs of fixed assets. (p. 403)

Rules of debit and credit Standardized rules for recording increases and decreases in accounts. (p. 156)

Sales The total amount charged to customers for merchandise sold, including cash sales and sales on account. (p. 215)

Sales discounts From the seller's perspective, discounts that a seller may offer the buyer for early payment. (p. 215)

Sales return and allowance From the seller's perspective, returned merchandise or an adjustment for defective merchandise. (p. 215)

Sarbanes-Oxley Act of 2002 An act passes by Congress to restore public confidence and trust in the financial statements of companies. (p. 306)

Selling expenses Expenses that are incurred directly in the selling of merchandise. (p. 217)

Serial bonds Bonds whose maturities are spread over several dates. (p. 447)

Service A type of business that provides services rather than products to customers. (p. 5)

Single-step income statement A form of income statement in which the total of all expenses is deducted from the total of all revenues. (p. 217)

Special-purpose fund A cash fund used for a special business need. (p. 326)

Stated value A value, similar to par value, approved by the board of directors of a corporation for no-par stock. (p. 497)

Statement of cash flows A summary of the cash receipts and cash payments *for a specific period of time,* such as a month or a year. (pp. 15, 580)

Statement of stockholders' equity This statement is often prepared in a columnar format, where each column shows the change in each major stockholders' equity classification. (p. 508)

Stock dividend A distribution of shares of stock to stockholders. (p. 507)

Stock option The right to purchase common stock at a fixed price over a limited period of time, often used to provide employee incentives to enhance stock price. (p. 501)

Stock split A reduction in the par or stated value of a common stock and the issuance of a proportionate number of additional shares. (p. 503)

Stockholders Investors who purchase stock in a corporation. (p. 11)

Stockholders' equity The stockholders' rights to the assets of a business. (pp. 17, 115)

Straight-line method A method of depreciation that provides for equal periodic depreciation expense over the estimated life of a fixed asset. (pp. 406, 455)

Subsidiary company The corporation that is controlled by a parent company. (p. 549)

Subsidiary ledger A ledger containing individual accounts with a common characteristic. (p. 221)

Temporary accounts Revenue, expense, and dividend accounts whose balances are transferred to retained earnings at the end of the period. (p. 169)

Temporary investments The balance sheet caption used to report investments in income-yielding securities that can be quickly sold and converted to cash as needed. (p. 544)

Term bonds Bonds of an issue that mature at the same time. (p. 447)

Trademark A name, term, or symbol used to identify a business and its products. (p. 413)

Trading securities Securities that management intends to actively trade for profit. (p. 544)

Transaction An economic event that under generally accepted accounting principles affects an element of the accounting equation and, therefore, must be recorded. (p. 54)

Transaction processing system A subsystem of accounting that records and summarizes the effects of financial transactions on the business. (p. 153)

Treasury stock Stock that a corporation has once issued and then reacquires. (p. 502)

Trial balance A summary listing of the accounts and their balances in the ledger. (p. 161)

Unearned revenues Items that are initially recorded as liabilities but are expected to become revenues over time or through the normal operation of the business; often called deferred revenues. (p. 100)

Unit of measure concept A concept of accounting requiring that economic data be recorded in dollars. (p. 23)

Units-of-production method A method of depreciation that provides for depreciation expense based on the expected productive capacity of a fixed asset. (p. 407)

Unrealized holding gain or loss The difference between the fair market values of the securities and their cost. (p. 545)

Vertical analysis A method of analyzing comparative financial statements in which percentages are computed for each item within a statement to a total within the statement. (pp. 69, 633)

Voucher Any document that serves as proof of authority to pay cash. (p. 318)

Voucher system A set of procedures for authorizing and recording liabilities and cash payments. (p. 318)

Work in process inventory The direct materials costs, the direct labor costs, and the factory overhead costs that have entered into the manufacturing process, but are associated with a product that has not been finished. (p. 266)

Subject Index

Company Index

Pixar
Comparative Balance Sheet
January 3, 2004, and January 1, 2005

(In thousands, except share data)	2004	2005
Assets		
Cash and cash equivalents	$ 48,320	$ 28,661
Investments	473,603	826,123
Trade accounts receivable, net of allowance for doubtful accounts of $186 and $177 as of January 3, 2004 and January 1, 2005, respectively	2,152	5,581
Receivable from Disney, net of reserve for returns and allowance for doubtful accounts of $29,920 and $3,479 as of January 3, 2004 and January 1, 2005, respectively	198,280	68,074
Other receivables	4,465	8,307
Prepaid expenses and other assets	1,047	2,227
Deferred income taxes	51,496	70,424
Property and equipment, net	115,026	125,602
Capitalized film production costs, net	107,667	140,038
Total assets	$1,002,056	$1,275,037
Liabilities and Stockholders' Equity		
Accounts payable	$ 1,803	$ 5,392
Income taxes payable	37,595	14,077
Other accrued liabilities	13,007	26,971
Unearned revenue	9,141	8,502
Total liabilities	$ 61,546	$ 54,942
Commitments and contingencies (Note 7)		
Shareholders' Equity:		
Preferred stock; no par value; 5,000,000 shares authorized, no shares issued and outstanding	—	—
Common stock; no par value; 100,000,000 shares authorized; 55,473,176 and 58,426,252 shares issued and outstanding as of January 3, 2004 and January 1, 2005, respectively	546,999	687,387
Accumulated other comprehensive income (loss)	314	(2,211)
Retained earnings	393,197	534,919
Total shareholders' equity	$ 940,510	$1,220,095
Total liabilities and shareholders' equity	$1,002,056	$1,275,037